20 077 563 82
WITHDRAWN

D1357394

The Handbook of International Migration

The Handbook of International Migration: The American Experience

Charles Hirschman
Philip Kasinitz
Josh DeWind EDITORS

RUSSELL SAGE FOUNDATION
NEW YORK

The Russell Sage Foundation

The Russell Sage Foundation, one of the oldest of America's general purpose foundations, was established in 1907 by Mrs. Margaret Olivia Sage for "the improvement of social and living conditions in the United States." The Foundation seeks to fulfill this mandate by fostering the development and dissemination of knowledge about the country's political, social, and economic problems. While the Foundation endeavors to assure the accuracy and objectivity of each book it publishes, the conclusions and interpretations in Russell Sage Foundation publications are those of the authors and not of the Foundation, its Trustees, or its staff. Publication by Russell Sage, therefore, does not imply Foundation endorsement.

Library of Congress Cataloging-in-Publication Data

The handbook of international migration : the American experience /
Charles Hirschman, Josh DeWind, and Philip Kasinitz, editors.
p. cm.
Includes bibliographical references and index.
ISBN 0-87154-244-7
1. United States—Emigration and immigration. 2. Immigrants—United States.
I. Hirschman, Charles. II. DeWind, Josh. III. Kasinitz, Philip, 1957– .
JV6465.H25 1999 99-32388
304.8′73—dc21 CIP

The paper used in this publication meets the minimum requirements of American National Standard for Information Sciences—Permanence of Paper for Printed Library Materials. ANSI Z39.48–1992.

RUSSELL SAGE FOUNDATION
112 East 64th Street, New York, New York 10021
10 9 8 7 6 5 4 3

To Jo, Dee, and Lisa

Contents

Contributors

CHARLES HIRSCHMAN is professor of sociology at the University of Washington.

PHILIP KASINITZ is professor of sociology at Hunter College and the Graduate Center of the City University of New York.

JOSH DEWIND is program director of the Social Science Research Council and professor of anthropology at Hunter College of the City University of New York.

RICHARD ALBA is professor of sociology and public policy at the State University of New York at Albany.

SUSAN B. CARTER is professor of economics at the University of California, Riverside.

THOMAS J. ESPENSHADE is professor of sociology and faculty associate at the Office of Population Research, Princeton University.

REYNOLDS FARLEY is Dudley Duncan Professor of Sociology at the University of Michigan and research scientist at its Population Studies Center.

WALTER C. FARRELL JR. is professor of social work and associate director of the Urban Investment Strategies Center at the University of North Carolina at Chapel Hill.

NANCY FONER is professor of anthropology at the State University of New York at Purchase.

RACHEL M. FRIEDBERG is assistant professor of economics and core faculty associate of the Population Studies and Training Center at Brown University.

HERBERT J. GANS is Robert S. Lynd professor of sociology at Columbia University.

GARY GERSTLE is associate professor of history at the University of Maryland, College Park.

NINA GLICK SCHILLER is associate professor of anthropology at the University of New Hampshire, Durham and editor of the *Journal of Identities: Global Studies in Culture and Power.*

CHANDRA GUINN is a doctoral candidate in the Department of Sociology at the University of North Carolina at Chapel Hill.

JOHN HIGHAM is John Martin Vincent Professor of History Emeritus at The Johns Hopkins University.

GREGORY A. HUBER is a doctoral candidate in the Politics Department at Princeton University.

JENNIFER HUNT is associate professor of economics at Yale University.

JAMES H. JOHNSON JR. is William Rand Kenan, Jr., Distinguished Professor of Management and director of the Urban Investment Strategies Center at the University of North Carolina at Chapel Hill.

DAVID E. LÓPEZ is associate professor of sociology at the University of California, Los Angeles.

DOUGLAS S. MASSEY is Dorothy Swaine Thomas Professor of Sociology at the University of Pennsylvania.

JOHN HULL MOLLENKOPF is professor of political science and sociology and director of the Center for Urban Research at the Graduate Center of the City University of New York.

VICTOR NEE is Goldwin Smith Professor of Sociology and chair of the Department of Sociology at Cornell University.

JOEL PERLMANN is senior scholar at the Jerome Levy Economics Institute of Bard College and research professor at the college.

PATRICIA R. PESSAR is associate professor in the Anthropology Department and the American Studies Program at Yale University.

DAVID PLOTKE is associate professor of political science at the Graduate Faculty of the New School University.

ALEJANDRO PORTES is professor of sociology, at Princeton University and faculty associate of the Woodrow Wilson School of Public Affairs.

REBECA RAIJMAN is assistant professor of sociolgy at Haifa University in Israel.

NESTOR RODRIGUEZ is associate professor of sociology at the University of Houston.

RUBÉN G. RUMBAUT is professor of sociology at Michigan State University.

GEORGE J. SÁNCHEZ is associate professor in the History Department and the Program in American Studies and Ethnicity at the University of Southern California.

RICHARD SUTCH is Distinguished Professor of Economics at the University of California, Riverside.

MARTA TIENDA is professor of sociology and public affairs at Princeton University. She is also director of the Office of Population Research.

ROGER WALDINGER is professor of sociology and chair of the Department of Sociology at the University of California, Los Angeles.

MIN ZHOU is associate professor of sociology at the University of California, Los Angeles.

ARISTIDE R. ZOLBERG is University in Exile Professor of Political Science at the Graduate Faculty, New School University, and director of the International Center for Migration, Ethnicity, and Citizenship.

Foreword

Reynolds Farley

THIRTY-FIVE YEARS ago no political observer or social scientist predicted that the population of the United States would grow rapidly because of increased immigration, nor that the nation's social and economic structure would change due to the arrival of millions of people from countries around the world. Most demographers agreed that the massive flow of immigrants into this country during the first two decades of this century had ended with the restrictive laws of the 1920s (except for a few groups allowed to enter as a consequence of World War II), but the unforeseen occurred. The United States now receives near record numbers of legal immigrants each year, and the second-generation population—those born in the United States with one or both parents born abroad—is now larger than ever before. Among economically developed nations, only Canada and Australia rival the United States in terms of the contribution immigration makes to population change.

Only economic growth will be more significant than immigration in shaping social and political trends in the United States during the early decades of the twentieth first century. In times of prosperity, employers will successfully lobby for liberal admission policies while in times of labor surplus, efforts to curtail immigration will continue to percolate. At all times, those who celebrate the importance of past immigration and current cultural heterogeneity will disagree with those who see immigrants as a threat to American values and culture. The appeal of the United States as a destination for immigrants–especially from Mexico, Latin America, and Asia–is so firmly established that dramatic changes will be required to reduce immigration significantly below the current level of more than one million people who arrive in this country annually.

The political and scholarly debate about immigration will focus around several issues of major importance, with far-reaching implications for the country. In this volume, Charles Hirschman, Philip Kasinitz, and Josh DeWind have recruited the nation's leading immigration scholars to summarize what is known and what still needs to be investigated about the following questions:

- How does immigration contribute to the nation's economic growth and prosperity? Do immigrants bring necessary skills—and strong backs—to the country, so that their presence leads to higher rates of economic growth and, thereby, to better employment opportunities and larger earnings for most Americans? Or is the contribution of immigration to economic growth a modest one?
- To what extent do immigrants compete with native-born workers for jobs and thus dampen wage increases and raise unemployment rates among the native population? Are some groups of native-born residents, such as those with limited educational attainments, at risk of job loss in times of high immigration?
- How does immigration influence the internal migration of native-born individuals? In other words, does the fact that a high proportion of first generation immigrants settle in just a few ports of entry trigger an out-migration of native-born competitors? Or does the presence of large numbers of immigrants stimulate economic growth so that the native-born remain where they live while immigrants move there? Does a certain density of non-white immigrants or non-English speakers make a place unappealing to native-born persons?
- How do immigrants contribute to the financing of local, state, and federal governments, and what costs do they impose upon taxpayers? How much does the estimate of contributions and costs change when not only first-generation immigrants are considered but also the contributions and costs of the second and even the third generations?
- What is the social and economic trajectory for today's second-generation immigrants? Today's stream of immigrants differs from earlier flows due to the wide range of their educational achievements. Many immigrants, especially those from the Caribbean, Mexico, and Central America, report few years of schooling, but another large fraction, particularly those from Asia and Africa, report much higher levels of education.

Will the children of less-educated immigrants remain toward the bottom of the occupational ladder while children born to highly-educated immigrants prosper? Does this imply that immigration leads to greater economic polarization?

- How will immigration affect the nation's political system and its political parties? Immigrants and their children played a crucial role in developing and shaping the major political parties and provided both the candidates and votes that sustained the New Deal and its successors. What will happen when today's immigrants and their children start to play a much larger role in the political process than they do now?
- What are the implications of immigration for the nation's religions and religious institutions? Traditionally, immigrants have been active participants in religious organizations because they often found them to be welcoming homes, which provided the immigrants with an opportunity to speak their own languages and share traditional customs. Yet in another sense, religious institutions have played a role in hastening the assimilation process. Immigrants also shaped and redirected religions in the United States. What does the future hold for religions as a result of this new flow of immigrants?
- How will race relations be changed by immigration? Three-quarters of immigrants arriving in the 1990s are Latino or Asian. Many of them are seen as non-white, and most are likely to identify themselves as non-white. Will these immigrants and their children be handicapped because of their origins and race? Or will they be the beneficiaries of those far-reaching changes in racial attitudes and policies that occurred after the civil rights movement? Will second-generation immigrants report more favorable social and economic achievements than those of native-born African Americans and Native Americans? From many perspectives, it appears that the children and grandchildren of those eastern and southern European immigrants who came to United States cities between 1880 and 1920 leapfrogged American blacks in educational attainment, occupational achievement, and earnings. Will that social and economic process be repeated with the children of today's Latino and Asian immigrants?
- An extensive literature describes the emergence of ethnic intermarriage and religious intermarriage over the course of the generations, with particularly sharp increases among those who married after the Civil Rights decade. In this new era of civil rights and emphasis upon cultural diversity, will the children of recent immigrants also intermarry with native-born whites and blacks? If so, does this portend the growth of a large multiracial population and, perhaps, a gradual erasing of the nation's traditional color line?
- Will the assimilation process for recent immigrants and their children resemble the process that made most second- and third-generation descendants of Irish, Italian, and Slavic immigrants into unhyphenated Americans? The social and economic scene is now very different and strong civil rights laws prohibit ethnic, religious, and racial discrimination. Does this suggest much more rapid assimilation?
- Will high, sustained rates of immigration to this country gradually or rapidly change the definition and implications of citizenship? In this era of international markets and low-cost foreign travel, will a growing fraction of immigrants prefer to be citizens of both the United States and their country of origin? What are the consequences of having a substantial population of individuals who simultaneously hold citizenship in two nations?

For the first half of this century, immigration was among the topics most frequently studied by American historians and social scientists. The closing of the nation's borders during the middle decades of the century was followed by a great decline in the scholarly investigations of immigration. All of this is about to change. Immigration will soon become one of the leading topics of research for social scientists and policy specialists. Researchers will capitalize upon increasingly diverse arrays of data, from the United States and from other countries, that tell us which groups of immigrants are doing well and why other groups are falling behind. The investigators conducting this new generation of migration studies are sure to borrow extensively from this important volume, since it provides an authoritative summary of the current state of our knowledge about immigration.

Acknowledgments

AT THEIR INITIAL 1994 meeting, the members of the Social Science Research Council (SSRC) Committee on International Migration decided to organize a major conference on the state of theory and research in the field of international migration. The idea was to invite leading scholars and specialists from across the social sciences to assess the stock of knowledge, core theoretical issues, and unresolved empirical questions in international migration and immigration research. The publication of the revised conference essays was intended to be a major landmark—a volume that would be comprehensive in scope and that would provide an orientation for future scholarship and the development of the field.

Five years later, the result of these efforts is finally reaching the hands of readers. At the outset, we underestimated the time, energies, and commitment necessary to organize the conference and to translate the conference presentations into an integrated publication that would measure up to our expectations. We have persevered, not only because of importance of the work, but also because of the unstinting support and unbounded faith of so many good colleagues, supporters, friends, and benefactors. Here we wish to record our gratitude to the many persons whose contributions made it all possible.

The SSRC Committee on International Migration was initially planned and organized by David Featherman, then SSRC president. Alice O'Conner, SSRC program officer, wrote the grant application to the Mellon Foundation and organized the planning meetings that preceded the formation of the committee. Felix V. Matos Rodriquez worked with Alice O'Connor on these activities. Ramon Torrecilha and Eric Hershberg, both SSRC staff officers, also participated in the planning meetings. Kenneth Prewitt, SSRC president during the formative years of the committee, was extremely supportive and gave the introductory address at the conference.

The Andrew W. Mellon Foundation provided the financial support for the SSRC Committee on International Migration. Harriet Zuckerman, Mellon Foundation vice president, was the primary inspiration for the committee and a wise counselor to SSRC presidents and staff. Stephanie Bell-Rose was the Mellon foundation program officer for the SSRC Committee and always provided strong support for the committee's plans and programs.

The conference was held at Sanibel Island, Florida, in January 1996, and even before the event, it became known as the "Sanibel Conference." Planning for the conference, including the scope, themes, participants, and organization, extended over an eighteen month period. Every member of the SSRC Committee on International Migration played multiple roles in the planning and organization of the conference, including chairing sessions and serving as discussants. Robert Bach, John Bodnar, David Card, Douglas Massey, and Deborah Phillips provided critical advice on the planning for the conference. The arranging of the conference, the organization and logistics during the meeting, and the editorial work following the event were only possible with the extraordinary support of Christina Kang, Mary Arnold, Dina Gamboni, Sara Pasko, Christian Fuersich, and Walter Miller who have served as program assistants to the SSRC Committee on International Migration over the last five years.

The Sanibel conference was an exciting intellectual feast with a cast of dozens of paper presenters, session chairs, and discussants. The final wrap-up session consisted of "instant assessments" of the overall conference by Shirley Hune, David Montejano, and Samuel Preston. In addition the authors whose work is contained in this volume, there were many others whose papers, discussion, and active participation at the conference helped to guide and inspire the committee's work and the production of the edited volume. The list of scholars who contributed the conference include: Lawrence Bobo David Card, Lucie Cheng, Bruce Cain, Leo Chavez , Jeff Crisp, Rodolfo de la Garza, ,Hector L. Delgado, Luis Falcon, Todd Gitlin, Bill Ong Hing, Dirk Hoerder, David Howell, Gerald Jaynes, Michel Laguerre, Ivan Light, Terrance McDonald, Edwin Melendez, Elizabeth Mueller, Michael Piore, Lydia Potts, Andres Torres, and Franklin Wilson. Others who participated in the conference include: Frank D. Bean, Peter Benda, Meyer Burstein, Muzaffar Chishti, Donna Gabaccia, Andrés Jiménez, Rose Maria Li, Rebecca Nichols, Alex Stepick, Roberto Suro, and Eric Wanner. Several international scholars were invited to attend the conference and provided valuable advice on future planning for the field, Victor Satzewich, Rainer Bauböck, Stephen Castles, and Malcolm Cross.

In addition to publishing this work, the Russell Sage Foundation (RSF) played an invaluable behind the scenes role in transforming the conference proceedings into a publishable volume. Charles Hirschman spent two weeks during the summer of 1997 at the foundation and was a RSF visiting scholar during the 1998 to 1999 academic year. There are few more pleasant environments on earth for editorial work, or any other scholarly work, than the RSF offices. Eric Wanner, RSF president, communicated his sense of the scope and promise of the volume and then offered just the right amount of encouragement and support to get the job done, including a grant for the publication of a selection of articles in this volume, which appeared in the *International Migration Review.* David Haproff, director of RSF publications, was a model of patience and professionalism whose confidence in our efforts never seemed to waver. Suzanne Nichols, RSF publications production manager, took charge of the project with a sense of purpose and enthusiasm that kept everyone and everything on track. The inspired copyediting by Cindy Buck has improved the clarity of every chapter in the volume. Renolds Farley and Mehdi Bozorgmehr offered constructive suggestions to the authors of every chapter in the volume.

Our final tribute is to the authors of the chapters in the volume. In addition to their intellectual contributions to this volume, their commitment, good cheer, and willingness to revise their chapters, sometimes multiple times, have made our work ever so much easier.

Introduction

International Migration and Immigration Research: The State of the Field

THE LAST DECADES of the twentieth century have witnessed a revival of large-scale immigration to the United States. The rise in the number of immigrants and the dramatic change in their national origins are revealed in a simple comparison between the 1950s and the 1980s. More than two-thirds of the 2.5 million immigrants admitted during the 1950s were from Europe, while more than 80 percent of the 7.3 million immigrants who arrived in the 1980s were from Latin America and Asia (Rumbaut 1996, 25). At century's end, the proportion of persons of foreign birth is inching closer to 10 percent of the total U.S. population (Schmidley and Alvardo 1998). More than 50 million Americans—one-fifth of the total population—are immigrants or the children of immigrants.

As high as these figures may seem to contemporary eyes, a high level of immigration is not an uncommon situation in American history. From the founding days of the republic to present times, international migration has been the defining attribute of American society. The language and political ideals of the early English settlers, as well as their land hunger and frequent disregard for Native American rights, set the stage for later arrivals. The eighteenth-century American economy was built with the labor of free immigrants, indentured servants, and slaves from Europe, Africa, and the Caribbean. During the nineteenth century, immigrants played a disproportionate role in settling the frontier and later contributed much of the labor and consumer demand that fed the industrial revolution. The twentieth century opened with a fierce political and cultural debate that culminated in the closing of the door to free immigration in the 1920s. The low levels of immigration during the following forty years, from the mid-1920s to the mid-1960s, were unusual in American history (Massey 1995). The last third of the twentieth century has seen a return of immigration to center stage in the American drama.

Although the popular version of American history emphasizes continuity from colonial times to the present, the lineage is primarily cultural, not genealogical. The simple fact is that the United States is largely populated by persons whose ancestors lived elsewhere two centuries ago.[1] This country's culture, as well as its politics and economy, has been continually expanded and remolded by successive waves of immigrants. It is hard to imagine any part of American history or popular culture that has not been touched by immigration. The Statue of Liberty is perhaps the most widely understood cultural icon of American society, both at home and abroad. The role of immigrants in American society and their cultural contributions are often celebrated in Hollywood movies. The notion that almost any person from anywhere can "make it in America" has had a powerful impact on the image of America abroad and at home.

As the renewal of immigration has reverberated through American society over the last thirty years—demographically, economically, politically, and culturally—there has been a resurgence of scholarship on immigration in every branch of the social sciences. Taking stock of this fast-moving field is the aim of this volume. In particular, the chapters in this compendium assess the state of theories of international migration, the incorporation of immigrants and their descendants into American society, and the economic, social, and political responses to immigration. Theories are interpretative frameworks that try to make sense of the many "facts," often incomplete and confusing, that emerge from empirical research. Theories also offer conceptual maps that orient scholars to important research questions and modes of inquiry. By addressing the state of theories in the field of immigration research, our objective is to see the big picture—where we have been and where we are going.

In this introduction, we provide a glimpse of some of the significant issues that await the reader. We also explain how this volume came to be and compare the project with another Social Science

Research Council initiative on international migration in the 1920s. We conclude with a discussion of the boundaries of the field of international migration and immigration studies, the links between social science and social policy, and a few thoughts on the future of the field.

Then and Now

It is virtually impossible to understand the present age of renewed immigration to the United States without some historical context. Are the numbers of immigrants too high? Can the United States absorb the newcomers? Has the political response to recent immigrants been hostile or racist? Every scholar who has fresh data on these questions (indeed, every person who has an opinion) is likely to compare the present with the past—or more precisely, with his or her interpretation of the past. How could it be otherwise? History is our template for understanding the present. American history offers an unusually rich panorama of immigrant experiences and national encounters with successive waves of immigrants from many parts of the globe. Sorting and sifting through the past to understand the present is the essential backdrop of most of the chapters in this collection.

There are many pasts to choose from. Indeed, throughout most of the nation's history the profound ambivalence of many Americans about immigration has been expressed in contradictory ways. Although immigration has been a central element of the national fabric throughout American history, and the slogan "nation of immigrants" is used as an emblem of national pride by almost every political and civic leader, there is an undercurrent of xenophobia that seems to be a persistent part of American culture, even among those who are only a generation removed from other lands.

In the late nineteenth century and the early years of the twentieth, as a swelling wave of immigrants from eastern and southern Europe crowded into American cities, many old-stock Americans feared that "their country" was changing for the worse. These fears crystallized in a variety of forms, from sentimental efforts to signal ancestral roots through such organizations as the Daughters of the American Revolution and the Society of the Mayflower Descendants to aggressive efforts of the eugenic and social Darwinist movements to assert the biological inferiority of the newcomers (Baltzell 1964).

Many intellectuals were firmly in the anti-immigrant camp. In 1894 a group of young, Harvard-educated "Boston Brahmins" founded the Immigration Restriction League, a group that had a major influence on pushing Congress toward more restrictive immigration legislation (Bernard 1982, 93). Henry Adams, the nineteenth-century man of letters and descendant of two American presidents, frequently railed against the new immigrants, especially the growing numbers and prominence of Jews in American society (Baltzell 1964, 90–93). The fear of immigrants and hostility toward them during the earlier era of mass immigration were critically analyzed in John Higham's classic book *Strangers in the Land: Patterns of American Nativism, 1865–1925* (1955/1988). In part III of this volume, Professor Higham reflects on the differences between the era about which he wrote and more recent history and considers the possibilities of going beyond an intellectual history of nativism to a social science analysis of the phenomenon.

The United States is once again in an era when opposition to immigration is rising (Espenshade and Huber, this volume). As the numbers of immigrants rose during the 1970s and 1980s, there was a renewal of the intellectual and political debate over immigration to the United States. Some people fear that immigrants will become just like other Americans, while others fear that they will not. Some fear for what the United States is becoming in an age of renewed immigration.

Although the current debate is less inflamed with overt claims about the inherent inferiority of the new immigrants, there are some striking parallels in the discussion over the immigration "problem" between the early and the late decades of this century. Peter Brimelow, a British immigrant, warned the United States that it was admitting an "alien nation" with the new wave of immigration from Asia and Latin America in the 1970s and 1980s (Brimelow 1995). In recent elections, several politicians have played "the immigration card" in hopes of riding into office on the underlying fear of immigrants held by many Americans.

The shifting tides of social and political responses to the new age of immigration are one of the major themes analyzed in part III of this volume (see the chapters by Espenshade and Huber, Mollenkopf, Rodriguez, Sánchez, and by Johnson, Farrell, and Guinn). There is some basis for claims that anti-immigrant sentiments are a persistent undercurrent in American society and rise to the surface whenever immigration rises to a noticeable level. But a comparison with the past indicates that the American reaction to immigration in the late twentieth century is not simply a replay of the early decades of the century. There are significant variations from place to place, and notable changes over time, that defy a simple explanation of continuity. Nor does it appear that anti-immigrant pressures will be able to close the door to continued immigration in the near future.

One of the most important differences between the earlier era and our own time is that the contemporary debate includes more balanced and analytical assessments of the costs and benefits of immigration (see the chapters by Plotke, by Carter and Sutch, and by Friedberg and Hunt). Of course, the political claims of those violently opposed to immigration are generally unrelated to any careful assessment of the costs and benefits of immigration. Nativist appeals are typically framed in terms of moral claims and rights (who belongs and who does not) and of the cultural deficiencies of potential immigrants.[2] These sentiments must contend, however, with a political environment in which 20 percent of the population are first- or second-generation Americans and with a culture that celebrates its immigrant ancestors.

Arguments about the contemporary progress of immigrants can draw on rather different interpretations of the past. When assimilation was thought to be the inevitable outcome for European immigrants, the model could be generalized to all immigrant groups (Gordon 1964). As doubts arose about the assimilation model as an accurate account of the historical immigration experience, the present and possible future scenarios were reinterpreted (Gans 1992a; Glazer and Moynihan 1970). The chapters in part II of this volume evaluate alternative theoretical frameworks with nuanced comparisons of the relative socioeconomic progress of immigrants in the present and the past.

Although the facts about the progress of immigrants and their children during the first half of the twentieth century are not so elastic as to fit any interpretation, there is room for differing emphases. One author may point to the struggles and sufferings of the first generation, while another author chooses to emphasize the socioeconomic mobility of the second generation. Does a narrowing of occupational differences between ethnic groups reveal an open-opportunity structure? Or does the persistence of bigotry in country clubs, college admissions at elite universities, and certain spheres of employment show the true nature of American society? The world is full of contradictions, and selected examples can point to opposite conclusions.

The socioeconomic progress of immigrant communities has been neither immediate nor universal, but the overwhelming weight of evidence is that the children of European immigrants experienced substantial intergenerational socioeconomic mobility. And through residential integration and intermarriage, the social distinctions, and even the ethnic identifications, between European national-origin groups have blurred (see the masterful review in Alba and Nee, this volume). The question that now haunts the field is: What lessons should be drawn for—or predictions made about—the children of the post-1965 immigrants to the United States? The final evidence is not yet in on this question, and it may not be in for several decades; thus, there is a lively debate across the chapters in part II of the volume.

In part I, the authors assess the state of theories of international migration, with a particular focus on explaining why people migrate across international boundaries, and to the United States in particular. For most Americans, the answer is self-evident—if the door is open, then they will come. And if the front door is closed but a back door is open, then they will still come. This perspective, which emphasizes the pulls of the American economy and the centrality of state regulation, is the major theoretical framework in the policy studies wing of the immigration field (Keely 1979; Papademetriou and Hamilton 1995; Teitelbaum and Weiner 1995). It neglects, however, the determinants of international migration in the sending countries and assumes that the potential supply of immigrants is unlimited.

There is a plethora of theories on why people migrate, but relatively little agreement among them on the important causal variables. The problem has been that these theories "belong" to different disciplines or schools of research. Although the standard aim of social science research is to disconfirm theoretical expectations, this is a more difficult task if empirical tests are weak and the field is fragmented into different research communities that espouse independent theories. In such a situation, multiple theories can flourish with few incentives to move toward convergence.

In a very important chapter that could change the character of the field, Douglas Massey reviews and evaluates a number of propositions from different theories of international migration. He reports that the major theories of international migration are not mutually exclusive in their empirical expectations, and indeed there is considerable support from the empirical literature for several of the theories. To our knowledge, this is one of the first efforts to synthesize theories that have been generally thought of as mutually exclusive in the literature (see also Massey et al. 1998).

Other chapters in part I illustrate the challenges of constructing theoretical frameworks and developing interdisciplinary approaches to the study of international migration. Alejandro Portes offers a classic statement on the uses and misuses of theory, citing clear examples from the research literature. Charles Hirschman provides a typology of the development of social theories across the social sciences. Other chapters point to critical gaps in the field, including the significance of gender theory (Pessar); the conceptualization of transmigrants, that is, persons who live and work in multiple societies (Glick Schiller); and the role and development of state regulation of migration (Zolberg).

Immigration Studies and the Social Science Research Council

This book is the product of a conference titled "Becoming American/America Becoming: International Migration to the United States," which met in Sanibel, Florida, on January 18–21, 1996, and was organized by the Committee on International Migration of the Social Science Research Council (SSRC). That committee was created in 1994 with funding from the Andrew W. Mellon Foundation to promote interdisciplinary scholarship and training in the field of immigration studies (for more background, see DeWind and Hirschman 1996).

The formation of the Committee on International Migration reflects both the academic and policy interests of contemporary scholars and the historical role of the Social Science Research Council as a forum for addressing important national issues by bringing together leading scholars from across the social sciences. This context has shaped the committee's assessment of the field, the planning for the Sanibel conference, and this volume.

Policy considerations have had a major influence on the development of the field of international migration and immigration studies over the last two decades. Indeed, academics from almost every discipline have addressed the current policy debates and the significant empirical questions underlying them (Bean, Edmonston, and Passel 1990; Borjas 1990; Hamermesh and Bean 1998a). Questions about problems of measurement of immigration and the consequences of immigration have led to several recent national commissions and National Academy of Science panels (Levine, Hill, and Warren 1985; Smith and Edmonston 1997; U.S. Commission on Immigration Reform 1994; U.S. Select Commission on Immigration and Refugee Policy 1981).

The direction of the Committee on International Migration and the goals of the conference were framed more broadly than the current policy debates and popular controversies. This does not indicate a lack of interest in policy questions, but rather the belief that stepping back from the immediate debate will allow us to understand how and why migration patterns have developed as they have. With this logic, we asked the contributing authors to assess the theoretical status of research on international migration and contemporary immigration to the United States. Such an assessment, we believe, will contribute to better social scientific research, greater public enlightenment, and, in the long run, a more reasoned approach to public policy discussions. Our most fundamental goal is to contribute to the intellectual coherence of international migration studies as an interdisciplinary field within the social sciences. Social science research and theory can provide an understanding that is both a counterweight and a complement to the moral and sentimental voices speaking out in public debates.

Although this is not the only book to present an overview of contemporary immigration, our emphasis on the assessment of social science theories of immigration is probably unique. This priority grew out of the initial discussions among the members of the interdisciplinary SSRC committee. The committee members had to establish first a meaningful dialogue across disciplinary boundaries. Disciplines differ in their vocabularies, their research styles, and even their interpretations of evidence. But underneath the brush, we discovered that all social science disciplines share many of the same theories or explanatory frameworks. By focusing on an assessment of theories of international migration, we hope to enhance interdisciplinary communications and the development of a truly interdisciplinary field of international migration studies.

Although this book aims to provide a comprehensive account of the causes and consequences of international migration, the emphasis is on the

American experience, and in particular on the adaptation of immigrants to living in the United States, the impact of immigrants on this country, and the reactions of Americans to the presence of immigrants. Our initial plan was to address contemporary immigration to the United States from a broadly comparative and historical perspective, but we soon realized that the complexity and scope of such an effort would be too great a challenge. The rapid growth of research on immigration to the United States by scholars from many disciplines suggested that our primary goal should be the integration of this diverse body of scholarship. Putting the contemporary American experience into a broader historical and international context is a high priority for the future activities of the SSRC committee.

The other major goal of the SSRC committee is to strengthen the interdisciplinary field of international migration and immigration studies. The committee has established fellowship programs for predoctoral students and postdoctoral fellows whose research promises to contribute to "theoretical understandings of the origins of immigration and refugee flows to the United States, the processes of migration and settlement, and the outcomes for immigrants, refugees, and native-born Americans" (SSRC 1998). As part of these efforts to encourage a new generation of immigration researchers, the committee has organized workshops to assist students of minority social background to prepare research and funding proposals. We trust that the next assessment of the state of the field will include the work of some of the students whose career beginnings have been encouraged and supported by our committee's initiatives.

This is not the first time that the Social Science Research Council has drawn together scholars to advance research and understanding on international migration. Seventy years ago, from 1924 to 1927, the SSRC first mobilized social scientists to study immigration with the establishment of the Committee on Scientific Aspects of Human Migration. The earlier SSRC committee produced, directly or indirectly, an amazing range of significant books and research articles, including studies of Swedish immigration, Mexican immigration and labor in the United States, statistical compendia of international migrations, and original research on the cityward migration of African Americans (Gamio 1930, 1931; Janson 1931; Kennedy 1930; Kiser 1932; Lewis 1932; Ross and Truxel 1931; Taylor 1930, 1932; Willcox and Ferenczi 1929, 1930).

There are some interesting parallels in the demographic and political contexts behind the founding of the two SSRC committees in 1924 and 1995. Both committees were formed after several decades of mass immigration, an acrimonious public debate on continued immigration, and changes in immigration legislation. The Social Science Research Council had just been created in 1923 with the assistance of private foundations to help bring social scientific knowledge to bear on important national issues. At that time, the social sciences were still trying to establish their scientific credentials, independent of efforts at social reform. The premise was that social science knowledge would have credibility in the public arena only if research conclusions were not seen as politically determined. The fledgling SSRC must have seen the study of immigration and the integration of immigrants into American society as a promising opportunity to demonstrate the importance of social science research as something more than fields of knowledge derived from the natural sciences (Merriam 1926, 187).

The field of international migration may also have been considered an important area by the SSRC because of the prior use, or misuse, of social science research by advocates of immigration restriction. The Dillingham Commission Report of the U.S. Senate, which contained forty-two volumes of papers and statistical analyses, provided a "scientific" base for restrictions on immigration from southern and eastern Europe (U.S. Immigration Commission 1907–1910).[3] The lines between social science analysis and the expression of opinions and prejudices were frequently blurred. Leading American social scientists, including E. A. Ross, a major sociologist, and John R. Commons, a founder of modern economics, wrote books that supported the dominant prejudices of the era, namely, that the new immigrants were unlikely to assimilate into American society (Commons 1907; Ross 1914).

In retrospect, it is clear that the Committee on Scientific Aspects of Human Migration played a critical role in changing the character of social science research on immigration by tilting the field away from advocacy and toward a more scholarly approach. The 1924 SSRC committee, which used the word *Scientific* in its title, was actually an outgrowth of a National Research Council committee on the same subject that had a predominantly natural science orientation (Yerkes 1924). The process of selecting eminent research scholars for committee membership established an important precedent. The other significant aspect of the committee membership was its multidisciplinary composition; included were representatives from anthropology, psychology, economics, political science, and statistics (Abbott 1927, 2–3).

The publications sponsored by the 1924 SSRC committee reveal a remarkable breadth of vision. Several books examined immigration to the United States from the broader context of global migration systems. The inclusion of internal migration, specifically that of African Americans from the South to the North, within the committee's mandated research focus demonstrated the need to reach across traditional areas of academic specialization. In a very fundamental sense, the 1924 committee shared the 1995 committee's strategy of stepping back from the immediate policy debate in order to understand the broader issues. The social scientific publications initiated by the 1924 committee have stood the test of time as reliable analyses—something that we hope will be said about this volume in future decades. The 1924 committee also demonstrated the importance and value of independent social science research even during periods of intense political controversy. Perhaps such times are when an independent social science is needed most of all.

The Organization of This Volume

By all the standard measures of scientific progress, the field of international migration and immigration studies is thriving. In addition to a burgeoning literature of research articles and important monographs (Lieberson 1980; Massey et al. 1987; Portes and Bach 1985), new books for university courses (Daniels 1991; Jacobson 1998; Portes and Rumbaut 1996; Reimers 1992), encyclopedic surveys (Cohen 1995), and proceedings of conferences (IUSSP 1997) have been published in recent years. In spite of this enormous flurry of activity and attention, or perhaps because of it, there appears to be relatively little integration in the field. Scholars from varied disciplines and perspectives bring rather different research questions, assumptions, and analytical frameworks to their inquiries. The explicit goal of this volume is to bring these many strands of work somewhat closer together through the reassessment of theories in the field.

We do not intend to dampen the diversity of a dynamic field under the banner of a new all-encompassing theory. Rather, we set forth three questions—or sets of questions—that can serve to organize theories and research in the field of international migration.

1. What motivates people to migrate across international boundaries, often at great financial and psychological cost?
2. How are immigrants changed after arrival? (Responses to this question address such issues as adaptation, assimilation, pluralism, and return migration.)
3. What impacts do immigrants have on American life and its economic, sociocultural, and political institutions?[4]

The chapters in part I address theories of international migration and some of the foundational concepts in the field. Although these chapters focus primarily on international migration to contemporary American society, the essential questions they raise could be addressed to other times and other countries. Part II focuses on the questions of immigrant adaptation and incorporation into American society. Two generations ago "assimilation" (admittedly defined in different ways) was considered an inevitable outcome for most immigrants, at least those of European origin. In recent years the inevitability and even the desirability of assimilation have been the subject of considerable political controversy and scholarly reassessment. In part III, the authors review how American society has changed and even been transformed with the absorption of immigrants.

The answers to these questions are not straightforward, and this is not simply because the empirical evidence is complicated and sometimes inconclusive. The empirical record can often be murky, but the ways in which questions are posed and embedded in theoretical arguments can matter even more. Theories serve to codify the received wisdom—what issues are important and why—and provide guidance for empirical research. If a theory is to be a useful guide for research, its core must be selective, emphasizing certain aspects of social reality. Assessments of theories, such as the essays in this volume, evaluate not only the empirical evidence associated with a theory but also the assumptions behind the questions.

For each of the three parts of the volume, we have written introductory essays that attempt to provide overviews of the issues, theories, and debates covered in the individual chapters and to assess their contributions to the field of international migration and immigration studies. These introductory essays are not meant to summarize the contents of the individual chapters, but to organize the themes that underpin a field of inquiry and to highlight issues of agreement and disagreement.

Alejandro Portes's pioneering scholarship has identified and explored the core issues in the study of international migration and the adaptation of immigrants to American society (Portes 1996b, 1998; Portes and Bach 1985; Portes and Rumbaut 1996). His essay, a revision of the keynote lecture he gave at the conference, is published as the lead chapter in the volume.

In addition to organizing the development of theory and the interdisciplinary research on international migration, we would also like to try to bring a small amount of conceptual order to the field based on common understandings. Perhaps the place to begin is with a few words on our perception of the scope of the field. Are theories of international migration distinctly different from general theories of migration? Should we distinguish between the fields of international migration studies and immigration studies? On these questions, and on many other conceptual issues, including the relationship between social science theories and research on international migration and the field of immigration policy (including refugee policy), there is no overarching consensus. We offer our own conceptual map on these matters simply to lay out the underlying issues that sometimes cause confusion.

Although international migration can be defined as migration across an international boundary, this does not resolve the question of whether general migration theories subsume international migration. Since well-defined international boundaries and the regulation of movement across them are relatively modern phenomena (and still not in force everywhere), there cannot be a historical division between the two fields. In an ideal theoretical framework of migration, we might wish to distinguish types of migration based on a number of criteria, such as distance, intention of permanence, duration of stay, voluntary or involuntary mobility, and mode of travel. In a framework that used such criteria, crossing an international border would be an important distinction, but hardly one that called for an independent theory.

Nonetheless, the research communities that study international migration and internal migration have taken shape as parallel fields of study rather than as one. In large part, this has happened because of the overriding focus on state policies, the single most important independent variable in studies of international migration, but one that is not meaningful for studies of internal migration. If we were studying internal migration in the former socialist bloc, where internal passports or travel documents were required for domestic migration, this distinction would be of less importance. Another major difference that has certainly influenced the nature of empirical research is the availability of data.

Conventional data sources, such as censuses and national surveys, typically include the universe of persons exposed to the risk of domestic migration. National data sources allow for the comparison of domestic migrants with nonmigrants in comparable places of origin and nonmigrants in the places of destination. There are no comparable data for the study of international migration. By definition, only migrants from other countries are included in censuses and surveys in the country of destination; we know nothing about the numbers and characteristics of nonmigrants in the countries of origin. Administrative data on border crossings are widely used in international migration research, but such data cannot be used to study immigrant selectivity or outcomes in the places of settlement.

International migration studies cover scholarship on the process of movement from one country to another. By definition, the field is comparative, and the units of analysis could be countries, specific international flows, or individuals. Immigration studies, another widely used term, covers generally the same phenomenon, but from the perspective of the receiving society (Jones 1992). Questions about immigrant adaptation and assimilation are central to immigration studies but may be secondary topics in the field of international migration research. One might also consider another subarea with a label of "emigration studies," which would be issues in international migration analyzed from the perspective of the sending county—for example, diaspora studies.

Given that some of these terms are used interchangeably by other authors, we do not try to establish an orthodox vocabulary. In some instances, we refer to the field of "international migration and immigration studies" in order to be as inclusive as possible, although this is an overly long and inelegant phrase. The organization of the parts of this volume—by research questions—represents our vision of how the field should be framed and organized for cumulative empirical research.

Looking Back at the Twentieth Century

The twentieth century has been distinguished by contradictory forces that have both accelerated and retarded long-distance migration. The accelerating forces have included the development of the modern technology of transportation and communication and the integration of a world market. Information about opportunities for land, work, and freedom in distant places spreads more quickly than ever, and the costs of movement have been dramatically reduced.[5] At the same time, the incentives for migration have been spurred by the buildup of population pressure in agricultural regions with only limited capacity for additional labor absorption. The pressures occurred in a historical context in which the traditional feudal or semifeudal economies and the moral order that tied peasants to the land were eroding or collapsing entirely with the spread of the market economy. The net consequence has been a rise in rural-to-urban migration, but it should be noted that the overwhelming share of the movement has been internal rather than international migration.

It is not only proximity that directs the exodus from rural areas to national rather than international destinations. Throughout the twentieth century modern states have created new political bureaucracies to regulate national borders and to monitor those who cross them. These actions cannot be explained by the natural ethnocentrism in any society or the inherent fear of strangers, since these forces have always been present. The rise of modern states over the last century or so has been accompanied by the peculiar ideology that each state should be inhabited primarily by a single "nation" of people who share a common culture, language, and history. Empires rarely cared about the national origins of their inhabitants as long as they paid taxes and did not challenge authority. Many of the new "nation states," however, were created as national homelands for specific populations.

The problem for the United States, and other "settler societies," has been to define who belongs to the nation. The debates over immigration law are part of the larger question of national identity that influences almost every aspect of political, social, and cultural life. In the earlier decades of the twentieth century the forces that wanted American society and culture to be predominantly defined by its eighteenth-century ethnic stock—ignoring the substantial numbers of African Americans and Native Americans—won the political battle with the imposition of the national-origin quotas. From the 1960s through the 1990s, the political winds have been reversed, or at least modified substantially, with a broadening of the ethnic origins of new waves of immigration.

Many of the chapters in this volume report on the controversies and discrepant findings regarding the eventual outcomes of the late-twentieth-century immigration waves. We suspect that many of these debates may be a function of duration of residence or generation in the host country. Indeed, some of the variance in outcomes may be "noise" that results from modest fluctuations over short observation periods. Over the short term it is difficult to measure the net impact of immigration independently of other period effects. There are certain to be short-term problems of adjustment that follow from the initial shocks of arrival; these problems may depend on the characteristics of the migrants, the host community, and unique conditions at the time of arrival. These short-term problems may not, however, be indicative of the long-term impacts of immigration.

An Agenda for the Future

Above and beyond the goals of greater interdisciplinary communications, clearer statements of theory, and more cumulative research, we also have some suggestions for the future research agenda of the field. Most important, we would argue for greater emphasis on the long-term outcomes of international migration on the receiving societies and on immigrants and their descendants. The close links between immigration studies and policy considerations pull the field to the study of short-term outcomes, particularly on issues that might be considered social problems. The initial problems of adjustment are important and should not be neglected, but the impact of international migration may appear to be quite different with a time horizon of fifty years rather than five years. In the balance of this introduction, we develop this argument in the context of a broader assessment of the field of immigration studies, and the social sciences more generally.

As noted earlier, the study of immigration has always been closely tied to considerations of immigration policy. This can be a major stimulus to research, but it can also be a potential liability. The link to policy contributes to considerable public interest in research results and additional sources of support for research and training. Too much attention on policy matters, however, can lead to an exclusive focus on the period immediately after arrival and an assumption that immigration is a "social problem." There is actually a very long list of perceived "immigration problems," including the uprooted migrants who must adapt to strange surroundings and the consequences for the receiving society that must absorb the migrants. This last problem, it is generally assumed, has adverse financial implications and may endanger social integration.

These problems are not entirely imagined. Long-distance migration can be a traumatic experience, and adjustments to new environments are rarely smooth and entirely pleasant (Handlin 1973). The arrival of significant numbers of people from different backgrounds may be profoundly disturbing to those in the receiving society. Immigration probably creates short-term "shocks" to host-community institutions, including labor markets and schools. The sudden increase in population numbers can also add to pressures on the housing market and demand for other scarce community resources. Although these problems are real, the perceptions of policymakers (and perhaps of the broader public) can easily create biases for the research community. In the early decades of the twentieth century these pressures amplified the popular prejudices that marked the writings of social scientists on the dangers of continued immigration (Commons 1907; Ross 1914). At present, these pressures deflect attention from the study of the long-term consequences of immigration.

The study of earlier waves of immigration and the ways in which long-distance migrations have proven to be major pathways of social change are usually consigned to historians and practitioners in other branches of the social sciences (Davis 1989; McNeill and Adams 1978). A subtle bias often emanating from immediate policy perceptions is the assumption that the contemporary situation is unprecedented and that a substantial number of immigrants is a serious problem that requires strong actions by the state.[6] The close study of history is the only guard against such potential biases (Lieberson 1996). Fears were strong at several points in American history that the presence of large numbers of immigrants and continued immigration posed significant problems for the broader society. A few examples might suffice to show that these fears were transitory—lasting less than a generation—and much exaggerated at the time.

At the time of World War I, there were fears that German Americans might have dual loyalties and be somewhat reluctant to join in the war effort against Germany. There was a very substantial German American presence in many midwestern cities, where German culture and institutions, including German-language schools, were a strong presence. With only modest resistance, however, the German American community completely acceded to pressures to "Americanize" during World War I, and almost all signs of an ethnic institutional presence were eliminated (Child 1939; Portes and Rumbaut 1996, 105–7). The same fears and prejudices were aimed at Japanese Americans during World War II, but with a much greater vengeance. In the wake of the attack on Pearl Harbor, all Japanese Americans on the West Coast were rounded up and forced to live in "relocation camps" for several years (Daniels, Taylor, and Kitano 1992).

Contemporary accounts of these events would probably have rationalized these fears and stressed the problems of immigrant absorption. In retrospect, it is clear that the hysteria of potential disloyalty was largely, if not entirely, imagined and that the American government overreacted. Within a fairly short time span the events themselves have disappeared from the national memory, though not necessarily for the peoples whose lives were disrupted. Since there is very little current immigration from either Germany or Japan, these national-origin groups are no longer in the category of newly arrived threat to the social order. Indeed, the contemporary images of German Americans and Japanese Americans are extremely positive. What a difference a generation makes!

Joel Perlmann and Roger Waldinger (this volume) note that many southern and eastern European immigrants, and even the Irish, were not considered "white" by many Americans in the late nineteenth and early twentieth centuries. The fear that the white race would soon be a minority in the United States was a major argument for the national-origin quotas introduced in the 1920s. Although these perceptions seem archaic today, the same fallacy is perpetuated with claims that continuing immigration from Latin America and Asia will lead to white Americans becoming a minority of the U.S. population by the middle of the twenty-first century (Bouvier 1992). With more than 30 percent of Asians and Hispanics marrying outside their community, the current boundaries of the race and ethnic populations are certain to change dramatically in the coming years (Smith and Edmonston 1997, 113–22; Hirschman, forthcoming). Any prediction of the future ethnic composition of the population is certain to be wide of the mark.

Another example of the fallacy of relying on short-term cross-sectional patterns to understand long-term outcomes is revealed with a recent comprehensive assessment of the fiscal impact of immigration (Smith and Edmonston 1997, chs. 6 and 7; see also Smith and Edmonston 1998, chs. 3, 4, and 5). Evaluations of the net cost of immigration to the U.S. fiscal system can be done by comparing the taxes paid by immigrants (or immigrant households) relative to the costs of government benefits received (transfer payments, education, and so on) by the same households. Cross-sectional estimates using this accounting logic, at the state level, show that immigrants are a net economic burden, largely because immigrant families have more children in public schools than do native-born families (Smith and Edmonston 1997, tables 6.2 and 6.3).

An alternative framework is to compute the fiscal impact of immigration that includes the projected taxes and benefits received over the lifetimes of the immigrant and his or her descendants. Cross-sectional estimates are biased because the current costs of educating the children of immigrants are counted, but not the taxes paid from the future earnings of immigrants and their descendants. When longitudinal projections, with a variety of assumptions, are computed for the national fiscal system (including federal, state, and local governments), the net present value of immigration is very positive (Smith and Edmonston 1997, table 7.6). There are social costs of immigrant absorption, but these are magnified in the conventional cross-sectional accounting framework.

The question of the short-term versus long-term impact of international migration on immigrants can be addressed by examining rates of return migration. Assuming that immigrants who eventually leave the United States are acting on some assessment of advantages and disadvantages, return migration offers a crude indicator of dissatisfaction with the migration experience.[7] Although there are no official statistics on emigration from the United States, the best estimates are that about one-third, perhaps more, of immigrants emigrate from the United States (Jasso and Rosenzweig 1990, 124). The rates of return migration from immigrant streams earlier in the century were probably even higher. These figures suggest a moderate degree of "rejection" or short-term dissatisfaction among immigrants, but much less among the children of immigrants, who rarely return to their parental county of origin.

We do not wish to overinterpret the contrast between the rates of emigration of the first- and second-generation immigrants, since there are many plausible reasons for the difference. The point is simply that the pattern is consistent with our argument that measures of the short-term immigrant adaptation or adjustment do not reliably predict long-term (intergenerational) outcomes. Migrants are willing to endure the pains of migration, especially over long distances, only because they are highly motivated. We conjecture that the losses are immediately felt but the gains may be visible only over the span of generations. This means that crosssectional evaluations, especially in the years immediately after migration, may reveal the costs of long-distance migration but not the gains that may result.

These examples suggest that the framing of research questions is critically important. Although the review and development of social science theory are sometimes derided as esoteric exercises, far removed from both the real world and empirical research, we hope that careful readers of this volume will conclude that there is nothing quite so practical and useful as a good theory. A good theory is one that not only poses a plausible causal argument but also suggests the spatial and temporal dimensions to which it applies. Theories that incorporate insights from different disciplines and develop in tandem with empirical research hold the power to illuminate the fundamental character and direction of human societies.

At century's end, the United States is once again making fundamental economic, social, and cultural changes that could scarcely have been imagined only a few decades ago. Immigration appears to be one of the major forces of change and renewal. The authors of the chapters in this volume draw on the accumulated wisdom of history, the best of social science theory and research, and their own creative ideas to explain how immigration has shaped American society over the twentieth century and what it might become in the twenty-first century.

Notes

1. Jeffrey Passel and Barry Edmonston estimate that about one-third of Americans in 1990 were descended from persons who arrived after 1900 and another one-third were descended from nineteenth-century immigrants (Passel and Edmonston 1994, 61). Interestingly, almost 90 percent of blacks were descended from families that had been here for at least four generations before 1900; only about one-third of whites (non-Hispanic) had such deep roots (67–69).
2. These reactions are not unique to American society, and indeed, they may be more moderate in the United States than elsewhere.

3. William P. Dillingham was a senator from Vermont and chair of the Senate committee that produced the report. According to William Bernard (1982, 94), the report "began with the assumption that the new immigrants were racially inferior to the old immigrants from northern and western Europe and manipulated mountains of statistics to provide a 'scientific' rationale for restricting their entry." See also the critique of the Dillingham Commission Report in Handlin (1957).
4. A fourth, perhaps equally important, question is: What impact does international migration have on the sending society? This question is beyond the scope of this volume, but we can note here that although sending countries lose, at least temporarily, the labor and capital of emigrants, in the long term they may receive substantial economic gains through remittances and return migration.
5. These technological and social changes may have led to more rapid increases in temporary movement than in permanent settlement. Just as the cheapening of transportation and the easier flow of information around the globe have allowed greater opportunities for international mobility, they also have allowed people to return to their native countries more easily than was the case for earlier waves of international migrants.
6. Although Stephen Castles and Mark Miller (1998, 4) observe that "international migration has grown in volume and significance since 1945, and most particularly since the mid-1980s," recent research shows that the absolute number of persons living outside their country of birth increased from 1965 to 1990, but the percentage of the world's population classified as international migrants remained at 2.3 percent (Zoltnik 1998).
7. Some immigrants may have come with the intention of making a temporary sojourn to earn money and then to return home. For such individuals, the return home may not be a statement of dissatisfaction with their original migration.

Part I

Theories and Concepts of International Migration

In the opening essay in this section, Alejandro Portes cautions scholars against attempting to formulate a "grand theory" of immigration to the United States. He asserts that a unifying theory, which presumably would seek to explain the origins, processes, and outcomes of international migration, would have to be posed at so general a level of abstraction as to be futile or vacuous. For example, he argues, "the theory that colonial capitalist penetration played a significant role in the initiation of large-scale labor migration from less developed countries says nothing about who among the population of those countries was more likely to migrate, nor can it be tested at the level of individual decisionmaking." Although international migration may result from the connections between individuals deciding to migrate and the broader structural contexts within which they live, Portes argues that micro and macro levels of analysis are not "fungible." Instead, he proposes that theory can be usefully organized around four topics, which encompass the international migration process: the origins, flows, employment, and sociocultural adaptation of immigrants. Although he recognizes that these different aspects of migration are interconnected, he proposes that midlevel theories limited to explaining specified areas of migration or relations between them are preferable to all-encompassing statements.

If formulating a unifying theoretical paradigm is not feasible, then a coherent overall understanding of the origins, processes, and outcomes of international migration to the United States must be based on the collective theoretical efforts of scholars who make the study of immigration a field of the social sciences by combining their diverse disciplinary trainings, research methods, and analytical approaches. The grouping of chapters by some of these scholars within the different parts of this book represents one way of organizing the field into separate and interconnected areas for theoretical analysis. Part I assesses the role of theory in shaping the field of immigration studies in general and more specifically in explaining the origins and processes of international migration and providing conceptual paradigms that link migration to immigrant incorporation. In turn, parts II and III examine theoretical explanations of the outcomes of migration, focusing on immigrant incorporation into American society, its impacts on native-born Americans, and their reactions.

The first and last chapters in part I, by Alejandro Portes and Charles Hirschman, respectively, address the general nature of theory and its relation to research that has and will continue to shape the field of immigration studies. The four chapters in between more specifically address theoretical explanations of immigration to the United States but seek to broaden the explanatory reach of their theoretical approaches in different ways. Douglas Massey and Aristide Zolberg evaluate and synthesize prevailing theories of the origins and process of international migration. Massey focuses on the complementarity of prevailing theories, which tend to emphasize—though not exclusively—the importance of economic factors, while Zolberg brings in an often neglected political perspective regarding the role of the state. Nina Glick Schiller and Patricia Pessar also seek to link different theoretical perspectives, but they do so on the basis of reconceptualizing prevailing understandings of "immigrants" as a basic category of analysis. Identifying immigrants who sustain international ties to their home countries as "transnational migrants," Glick Schiller explores how the transnational activities of migrants and states have influenced one another since the turn of the century. Pessar explores the implications of an "engendered" notion of immigrants for both migration and feminist theory. By showing how various theoretical perspectives can be linked with one another through synthesis and reconceptualization of basic understandings, each of these essays contributes to the intellectual coherence of immigration studies as an interdisciplinary subfield within the social sciences.

Synthesizing Theory

Theories that explain why international migration takes place have often been presented as based in competing and mutually exclusive perspectives and as having distinctive implications for state immigration policies. Assessing the contributions of these theories under the headings of classical economics, new economics, segmented labor market, world systems, social capital, and cumulative causation theories, Douglas Massey concludes in his chapter, "Why Does Immigration Occur?," that, because they "posit causal mechanisms operating at multiple levels of aggregation, the various explanations are not necessarily contradictory." In fact, he adds, the various theories that address different factors as causes of migration—ranging from those considered in individual calculations of advantages to those connected to the transformation of local and regional social, political, and economic structures—are best understood as complementary to one another. Drawing to varying extents on the different insights offered by these distinct theoretical perspectives, Massey provides a synthetic explanation of international migration, its perpetuation, and the cumulative processes that bring migration flows to an end.

Massey's synthesis is based not only on the analytic complementarity between the different theoretical perspectives but also on empirical evidence that supports the validity of each approach. This empirical evaluation, which is not fully described in his chapter, is the result of two projects, the first of which is an exhaustive, five-year review of post-1960 empirical research on population movements in the world's five principal immigrant-receiving areas—North America, Western Europe, the Persian Gulf, Asia and the Pacific, and the Southern Cone of Latin America—undertaken by the Committee on South-North Migration of the International Union for the Scientific Study of Population (Massey et al. 1998). The second tests each theory against a single database of the life histories of immigrants to the United States from thirty-seven-hundred households and twenty-five communities in Mexico (Massey and Espinosa 1997). This empirically grounded approach to testing and synthesizing theory provides something of a model for other efforts at theory building within the field of immigration studies, notably the efforts of Richard Alba and Victor Nee on immigrant assimilation and of others in parts II and III of this book.

Though more inclusive than any other attempt to date to overview migration theory, this synthesis is still somewhat incomplete in relation to the full range of types of international migrants and factors generally considered part of international migration studies. First, the synthesis targets the migration of wage earners, who make up the majority of international migrants. No doubt this synthetic account can also be applied to the migration of salaried professionals and entrepreneurs, but how it might be amended to do so has yet to be specified. Second, this synthesis examines movements that are relatively voluntary compared to the forced migration of refugees and others who flee social or political conflict and human or natural disasters. Finally, as Massey points out, this synthesis neglects the impact of states in controlling migration flows. Raising doubts about just how effectively states are able to regulate immigration, Massey concludes: "They must develop policies that recognize the inevitability of labor flows within a globalized economy."

In his chapter, "Matters of State," Aristide Zolberg takes issue with Massey's view of limited state control over migration and argues for a theoretically grounded account of state agency in shaping emigration and immigration flows. After reviewing the evolution of U.S. immigration legislation and its impact on the rising and falling numbers of immigrants legally admitted to the United States since the late nineteenth century, Zolberg concludes that "international migration theories will be woefully incomplete so long as they fail to take into account the positive and negative roles of states in shaping international population movements." Even illegal immigration to the United States from Mexico, he contends, reflects less a failure of state control than the ambivalence built into U.S. immigration policy and its implementation as a result of the conflicting goals sought by different segments of American society.

Zolberg proposes that a measure of the impact of state immigration policies would be neither total freedom of movement, which would result from open borders, nor zero migration, which could result only from draconian state measures—both of which are politically unrealistic—but rather a ratio between potential emigrants (whose numbers are hard to determine but whose magnitude both Massey and Zolberg agree will grow in the foreseeable future) and those whom states actually permit to immigrate. This view leads Zolberg to describe the immigration policies of most capitalist democracies as being located near the "closed" end of an open-closed continuum.

What theoretical approaches explain the predominantly restrictive immigration policies of advanced industrial states? From an international perspective, Zolberg contends, the restrictive regime is the sine qua non for maintaining not only "the 'Westphalian' international state system"—including "the privileged position of the 'core' states amid highly unequal conditions"—but also states' identities as national communities, which define their independent sovereignty and are necessary for democratic governance. From a domestic perspective, variations in national political processes that formulate immigration policies reflect distinctive class and cultural compromises that determine which immigrants a state will welcome or exclude. As formulated first by other scholars and then critiqued and reformulated by Zolberg, the impact that such external and internal forces have on the creation of immigration policies is mediated by national political processes and structures, ranging from historically derived legal systems to contemporary electoral politics. The national political system shapes and reflects relations between the political elite and the mass public and their perceptions of the impact of immigration on their interests in the context of their nation's shifting international relations, economic fortunes, traditions of immigration and identity, and the cumulative impact of immigration itself.

In this "very preliminary attempt" to synthesize theories of international migration and state policymaking, Zolberg takes the position that, "although much attention has been given to domestic responses . . . policy responses are best understood in the context of major changes in the external situation." But if the twin dynamics of capitalist development and state formation provide the primary motivation for international migration flows, Zolberg concludes, "the international migrations that actually take place are shaped to a considerable extent by the will of the world's states."

Reconceptualizing Theory

Although states may shape the actual flows of international migrants, to what extent should the categories that states use to control migrants also be used as analytical categories by social scientists? For example, should immigrant and refugee flows be conceived as having distinct causes for purposes of explanation in the same way that states separate them into mutually exclusive legal categories for purposes of management? What about the very category of "immigrant"? Does the exit from one nation-state and entry into another, as conceived and controlled by immigration law with categories of temporary and permanent residence or naturalization, reflect the actual social life of international migrants for which scholars ought to seek explanation? States influence not only how migration actually takes place but also how it is analyzed.

In "Transmigrants and Nation-States," Nina Glick Schiller argues for the recognition of a "new paradigm for the study of migration"—an alternative to the conception of immigrant-state relationships underlying Zolberg's and Massey's analyses. In pointing to state agency in shaping international migration flows, Zolberg reminds readers that by definition international migration is "inherently a *political* process" in that "it involves the transfer of a person from the jurisdiction of one state to that of another—in whole or in part—and the eventuality of a change of membership in an inclusive political community." As a result, migration policies regulate not only cross-border movement but also the "acquisition, maintenance, loss, or voluntary relinquishment of 'membership' in all its aspects." Approaching migration and national membership from the perspective of migrant as well as state agency, Glick Schiller argues for the recognition of a different conception of migration, one that she and her colleagues have defined as "transnational." Unlike immigrants, who have been conceived from a state administrative perspective as persons uprooted and transplanted from one nation-state to another, transnational migrants "extend networks of relationship across international borders." "Transmigrants," like immigrants, "invest socially, economically, and politically in their new society," but unlike immigrants, they also "continue to participate in the daily life of the society from which they emigrated but which they did not abandon."

Although Glick Schiller and others have provided examples and case studies of the homeland ties that distinguish transmigrants from immigrants, the transnational paradigm has been formulated so recently that there is much still to be learned about the nature and variety of those ties from empirical research. Researchers have identified these ties with a variety of terms, including "transnational migrant circuits," "transnational communities," and "dense networks across political borders." The limitations of these concepts in capturing the full variety of transnational ties have led Glick Schiller and her associates to adopt the more inclusive term "transnational social field" in order to encompass the full range of social, economic, and political processes in which transnational populations are embedded (Glick Schiller et al. 1992b). Further, in the absence of empirical research that might indicate what proportion of international migrants create or live within transnational social fields, the full extent and impact of transnational migration is difficult to assess.

Glick Schiller addresses two fundamental questions about transnational migration: first, whether it is a new form of human settlement or a new analytical paradigm; and second, what is the relationship between transnational migration and nation-states? Tracing the relationship of migrants and the United States through three stages, Glick Schiller concludes that migrants have been involved in transnational activities at least since the end of the nineteenth century and that these activities have been closely linked with the creation and development of nation-states. In each stage, she finds, transmigrants took different roles in the nation-state-building projects of their home and host countries as they adapted to evolving processes of global capital accumulation. Such ties were sustained even when the "triumph of nation-state ideology" made them "invisible" to social scientists during the post–World War II period.

If transnational migration has been happening for a long time, why is it only now becoming recognized and defined by scholars and political leaders? Glick Schiller suggests that transnational migration was not recognized as such until recent transformations of the relations between states and the global economy made the transnational activities of migrants of interest to both political actors and researchers. Glick Schiller concludes that transnational migrants do not signify a weakening of the authority or significance of states, as claimed by some analysts, but rather "have been and continue to be important to the construction and imagining of states . . . and legitimate nation-state-building processes." Rather than celebrate transnational migration for supposedly eroding state hegemony, she adds, scholars have a responsibility to "think our way out of our entanglement within and our commitment to our national narratives" that today are linked to the construction of transnational and multicultural nation-states and sustain the inequalities of capitalism.

In documenting how transmigrants' social fields have been "shaped and transformed by nation-state-building in both sending and receiving states," Glick Schiller has also sought to explain why migrants decide to establish and maintain lives in two or more countries. Her considerations connect a transnational perspective to discussions of economic, racial, and gendered aspects of immigrant incorporation that are taken up in parts II and III of this volume. "Grim living and working conditions" and the "racialized politics of incorporation," more than patriotism, says Glick Schiller, led turn-of-the-century migrants to "keep a foothold back home" and to participate in transnational political activities. Today, she contends, migrants are motivated to establish transnational ties by economic conditions similar to those of the past and by the racialization of their identities (for example, as Asian, Hispanic, or black), which threatens to place them at the bottom of the U.S. social hierarchy. But, she adds, well-incorporated and prosperous migrants have also built transnational networks when doing so has enabled them to achieve or maintain status back home, though with differential rewards for men and women.

In her chapter "The Role of Gender, Households, and Social Networks in the Migration Process," Patricia Pessar evaluates the contribution that research on households and networks has made to theoretical explanations of international migration. The broader contribution of such "mediating units" of analysis has been to help social scientists analyze the relation between structure and agency on global and local levels. But, she contends, the explanatory power of these theoretical perspectives can be enhanced by their reconception with regard to gender.

In Pessar's view, studies of households and social networks have enabled social scientists to explore the role of "contingent agency" in understanding linkages between the extremes of structural determinism and pure choice. In responding to the macrostructural transformations that are understood to create migration pressures, households and social networks can be seen to guide and constrain the decisions of individuals and determine who actually migrates and who does not.

Research focused on these issues has enabled scholars to analyze how "the local" is in a constant state of resistance and accommodation to "the global." Pessar identifies a number of ways in which this mediating perspective has been incorporated into and contributed to the development and refinement of new economics, network, structural, and transnational theories of international migration.

Pessar explores the contributions that a "gendered perspective" makes not only to advancing understandings of households and networks but also to migration theory. Examining the different and often conflicting experiences of men and women, she argues, has enabled scholars to critique earlier and seemingly idealized notions of immigrant households as being based on egalitarian "moral economies" and as unconstrained in maximizing economic gains in adapting to structural inequities. In fact, continuing research has shown that migrant households are also divided by power hierarchies, disciplined by kinship, gender, and class ideologies, and riven by government legislation and policies. Similarly, recent research demonstrates that, in the context of patriarchal family norms, men and women even in the same families may be permitted unequal access to social networks. Further, migrants once assumed to be benevolently assisting one another have been found to have imposed exploitative relations that resulted in the subordination of women—reflected, for example, in the lower income of women compared to that of men within immigrant enclaves. But engendering migration studies, Pessar recognizes, will require going beyond the earlier focus on the gender-based experiences of women to include those of men and to examine the impact that migration has on relationships between men and women.

After reviewing recent research literature, Pessar concludes that despite high expectations based in early feminist theory that immigration would motivate women to seek greater emancipation, in fact their modest gains have only "nibbled at the margins of patriarchy." These findings have led Pessar to abandon the view of immigrants, based in feminist theory, "that gender hierarchy is the most determinative structure in their lives." Immigrant families, she explains, are buffeted by external forces and injustices linked to class, race, ethnicity, and legal status that make poor immigrant women unwilling "to lose the benefits derived from some patriarchal marital unions" and anxious "to defend and hold together the family while attempting to reform the norms and practices that subordinate them." Faced with similar discrimination, if not threats of economic deprivation, upwardly mobile women hold on to "a more enduring and apparently valued notion of the family and the sexes that features the successful man as the sole breadwinner and the successful woman as the guardian of a unified household." In other words, studies of immigrants reveal that their "unilinear and unproblematic progression from patriarchy to parity is by no means assured."

Although household and network analyses have gained respect in migration studies, Pessar concludes that "the analytic power of these constructs might prove even greater . . . if researchers would recognize that gender organizes both the composition and organization of migrant households and social networks, and that gender also infuses the cultural, social, and political-economic forces acting on both structures." Now that migration scholars have overcome an earlier male bias, she says, "we are moving toward a more fully engendered understanding of the migration process." But in doing so, gender must not be assigned too much weight. "Rather, we must develop theories and analytical frameworks that allow us to capture and compare the simultaneity of the impact of gender, race, ethnicity, nationality, class, and legal status on the lives of different immigrants."

Theory and Research

The contribution of these chapters to the intellectual coherence of the field of international migration studies will come no doubt from the clarity of their critical syntheses and analytical reconceptualizations of immigration theory and the implications of their perspectives with regard to immigrant incorporation. But the persuasiveness of their views will also depend on the guidance they provide to, and the reconfirmation or disconfirmation that they receive from, empirical research.

In his essay, Alejandro Portes describes what he sees as "common pitfalls" regarding the development of theory, characterizes the intellectual building blocks of theoretical propositions, and illustrates what he sees as their proper application in analysis and explanation. Extending this discussion, he then describes a "sampler" of topics for a future research agenda that he believes could advance the field's theoretical development. Portes uses a discussion of "misunderstandings about the ways that we go about developing theory" to provide a clear description of the conceptual building blocks that together constitute theory. These intellectual constituents include delimiting a topic, identifying what aspect of the topic is to be explained, positing explanatory factors, and linking the theory with other similar propositions. To provide illustrative examples of the components of theory, Portes draws on the results of research about immigration to the United States, ranging from descriptive case studies and empirical generalizations to typologies of similarities and differences and predictive statements. Portes reserves the label of theory for "those interrelated sets of propositions that not only 'travel' in the sense of being applicable to different spatial and temporal contexts but also tell a coherent story about certain finite aspects of reality."

In describing the nature and fundamental components of theory, Portes touches on but does not address directly the analytical process by which scholars' understandings progress from basic concepts of empirical reality to more abstract and generalized explanatory understandings. Theory building is integrally tied to research that can contribute to new ideas through inductive generalization leading to new propositions or through deductively designed tests of existing propositions. Yet such intellectual processes are rarely so simple, because the development of ideas that become theories also takes place through the influence and assimilation of positions taken in debates between scholars about one another's research methods, findings, and interpretations. Examples of this complex relationship between research and theory building are provided by the chapters in part I.

The basis of Massey's theoretical synthesis in empirical research provides a model for evaluating and linking theoretical propositions. By employing a common statistical test to correlate empirical research findings with causal factors emphasized in different theories, Massey identified the contributions of each theory as complementary rather than mutually exclusive. This method is based on a debatable epistemological assumption that the analytical concepts constituting different theoretical paradigms, which have been developed in relation to the historical, ethnographic, and survey research methods emphasized differently within each social science discipline, can be translated into factors susceptible to statistical analysis. Massey's synthesis would seem to present a challenge to Portes's contention that micro- and macrolevel theories are not "fungible."

The persuasiveness of Zolberg's argument that "states matter" is based on a theoretical synthesis of structuralist economic and political perspectives that rest on historical examples and international comparisons not easily reduced to factors susceptible to statistical analysis. Could his argument be incorporated into Massey's synthetic approach, or are their theoretical perspectives, as well as their differences regarding the importance of state controls, epistemologically distinct? Zolberg suggests a method of determining the impact of states on international migration by measuring the ratio of potential to actual emigrants. Although such factors may be conceptually consistent with Massey's approach to synthetic analysis, Zolberg points out that these numbers would be difficult, perhaps impossible, to determine through empirical research.

Glick Schiller claims that, within a transnational perspective, "the study of international migration becomes transformed into research into conditions under which migration becomes and is sustained as a transnational process." The extent to which this conception of international migration will actually transform the field depends not only on its analytical contributions, such as the connections that this chapter makes between migrant and state transnational activities, but also on the proportion of international migrants whom research shows to be transmigrants, as opposed to immigrants, in both first and subsequent generations. For example, does the "invisibility" of immigrants' transnational ties in the post–World War II period reflect only the dominance of nation-state ideology, as Glick Schiller argues, or could it also be a result of the severing of homeland ties among a growing proportion of second- and third-generation immigrants as they assimilated into American society? The extent to which scholars reconceive of immigrants as transmigrants will probably be determined by future research findings regarding the breadth and persistence of international migrants' transnational ties.

Pessar's argument that engendering migration and incorporation theory enhances its explanatory power would seem to be a proposition whose payoff will be demonstrated through new research findings and interpretations. To the extent, however, that engendered studies focus on patriarchy and, like feminist perspectives, are oriented by the goal of women's emancipation, such studies, and their explanatory power, may have limited appeal to some male scholars in the field. In this case, the influence of a gendered perspective on the field will probably be affected by the gender of the scholars as well as by findings regarding the migrants whom they study.

Theory and Research in Defining the Field of Immigration Studies

Consistent with his point that topics central to immigration studies require the separate attention of midrange theory, Portes proposes particular topics for future research that have implications for the field as a whole: households and gender, the new second generation, states and state systems, transnational communities, and cross-national comparisons. In the context of describing the importance of research that focuses on units on a higher level of social organization than individuals, such as households, Portes echoes Pessar's call for engendering immigration studies. He describes gender as a "master dimension of social structure," one that can produce novel insights when applied not only to households but also to other immigration phenomena. A similar recasting of research and analysis must take place when researchers shift their focus from first-generation immigrants to their children, who grow up and become a part of American life with backgrounds, interests, and opportunities that may differ from those of their parents.

Portes's discussions of transnational communities and states point to the advantages of placing U.S. immigration in a wider international context. Understanding immigrants' transnational ties can shed light on processes and the extent to which they become incorporated into American economic, social, and political life. Domestic incorporation must be viewed as an international process that extends research and theory beyond the traditionally national borders of immigration studies. Comparing U.S. immigration policies with those of other advanced industrial countries, for example, points to similarities and differences that might otherwise seem idiosyncratic to the United States and of limited theoretical import. (For example, why, in the face of widespread public opposition, are governments in receiving countries unable or unwilling to prevent large-scale immigration? Why does immigration legislation often have consequences that are unintended and contrary to their purpose?) Finally, Portes proposes that placing each of these proposed research topics into an international comparative perspective will contribute to the construction of "concepts and propositions of broader scope" and to understanding "how the specific characteristics of national societies condition the validity of the set of midrange theories that structure the field of immigration."

A comparative perspective focusing on international migration would be broader than the primary focus on U.S. immigration in this volume. That few of the chapters take up international comparisons reflects the decision by members of the Social Science Research Council's Committee on International Migration to take stock of the theoretical coherence of U.S. immigration studies—an undertaking complex and demanding in and of itself—before venturing further afield to develop a wider international or global perspective. There was no doubt that theoretical understandings of U.S. immigration would benefit both from making comparisons between countries and from looking at migrant flows between countries and regions as components of a worldwide migratory system. The assessment of U.S. immigration studies provided in this volume, the committee expected, would provide an intellectual basis for pursuing wider international and global perspectives in the future.

Charles Hirschman's essay on "Theories of International Migration and Immigration," which concludes part I, offers a complementary point of view regarding not only the relationship between theory and research but also the contribution that the essays in this volume make to immigration as a field of study. Reviewing four "ideal types" of theory, he proposes that "understanding the elements of theory construction can, along with substantive knowledge and some inspired thinking, sometimes lead to the greater integration of knowledge and interpretive frameworks that stimulate cumulative empirical research." His discussion of the first type of theory, "social science as ideology," touches on the uneasy relationship between theoretical research and public policy. He describes the separation that immigration scholars have sought to place between social science theory and policy since early in the century, when policymakers used social science research to justify restrictive immigration legislation; this boundary is drawn by focusing on explanations of, rather than prescriptions for, immigration problems. The other three aspects of theory that Hirschman discusses are related to the contributions that research can make to the explanatory goals of the social sciences: going beyond the accumulation of facts to arrive at wider understandings, establishing the superiority of one theory over another by building on "normal science," and developing models that can represent the complexities of society beyond the limitations of midrange theory.

Hirschman's point with regard to ideology is

not that all bias—the personal and social interests that frame research questions and answers—can be eliminated, but rather that distortions from narrow interests can be checked by the social sciences "as a public forum where ideas, evidence, and interpretations are presented for other scientists to review and challenge." Despite a separation of social science explanation from national policy making, one of the most powerful social biases in the study of immigration—one that Hirschman does not particularly pursue—comes from the dominance of a nation-state perspective. The most obvious nation-state influence on understandings of international migration is the categorical separation of immigration from other types of migration, including domestic migration and forced immigration.

Although similarities and direct connections exist between domestic and international migration, U.S. immigration has been studied in isolation from the "Great Migration" of African Americans from the South to the North and the migration of Puerto Ricans to mainland urban centers. U.S. internal migration and immigration studies now constitute "different literatures" and are pursued, for the most part, by different sets of scholars.

State administrative practices, more than the analytic goals of social science, shape the categories of international migrants that are the focus of immigration research. The study of refugees and other forced migrants is generally separated from studies of immigration. Is this not in large measure because nation-states treat the two groups according to different sets of laws, a legal rather than theoretical distinction between "economic" and "political" migrants that reflects the U.S. government's distinct foreign policy toward immigrant- and refugee-sending nations? State categories are similarly embedded in the data on which social scientists depend for their research about U.S. immigration, such as the U.S. census and the reports of the Immigration and Naturalization Service (INS). To what extent does the fact that, for constitutional reasons, neither the U.S. census nor the INS report immigrants' religious affiliations account for the neglect of research about the role that religion plays in the social incorporation of immigrants and the omission of this topic from the essays in this book? Why are the flows not only of refugees but also of nonimmigrant business men and women, foreign students, and tourists omitted from international migration studies if not, in part, because states' interests, more than social science explanations, place them in separate visa categories and distinguish them in legal status from citizens and permanent residents?

The point here is not that the nation-state bias that shapes immigration studies should be eliminated. After all, the crossing of state borders, the sovereign role of states in seeking to control people who do, and differences in political rights and obligations between immigrants, permanent residents, and citizens are essential facts of modern life that in and of themselves demand empirical recognition in the data collected and in theoretical explanation. Nation-states make the distinctions between different forms of migration significant, and recognition of that influence needs to be part of theoretical explanations of immigration. Nevertheless, in drawing boundaries that define immigration studies as a field of the social sciences, the similarities and differences between domestic, international, refugee, transnational, and other forms of migration also need to be defined and recognized, as does the role of the international system of states in shaping them, in order for social scientists to arrive at broader and more powerful theoretical explanations of immigration. The calls by Portes and Hirschman for the field of immigration studies to develop an international comparative perspective and to recognize the ideological biases that frame research challenge social scientists to extend the development of theoretical explanation to include migration both within and beyond national borders—a challenge not taken up by this volume.

In sum, the contribution that the chapters of part I make to the unity and cohesion of the immigration and international migration studies will depend not only on the intellectual syntheses and reconceptualizations that they make of different theoretical propositions but also on the confirmation of their explanatory significance in research. But theory and research will increase field coherence, these chapters suggest, not by leading toward the encompassing uniformity suggested by the notion of a grand theory, but rather by continuing to engage social scientists of diverse disciplines and perspectives in a variety of intellectual relationships that raise new questions, clarify issues, and stimulate new debates. Ultimately it will be the theoretical engagement of scholars, such as that in part I of this volume, that will define and constitute immigration studies as an interdisciplinary subfield of the study of migration within the social sciences.

1 Immigration Theory for a New Century: Some Problems and Opportunities

Alejandro Portes

AT THE TURN OF THE century, many immigrants launched their American careers not only in new cities and new jobs, but with new names. How this happened symbolized the confident and careless way in which the country treated its newcomers then. At Ellis Island, busy immigration inspectors did not have much time to scrutinize papers or to struggle with difficult spellings. When necessary, they just rebaptized the immigrant on the spot. Thus, the German Jew who, flustered by the impatient questioning of the inspector, blurted out in Yiddish, "Schoyn Vergessen" (I forget), was promptly welcomed to America by the inspector as "Sean Ferguson." Poor penmanship plus the similar sound of their native "G" and the English "H" left half of a Ukrainian family named Heskes and the other half Gesker (Kraut 1982, 57).

That sort of symbolic violence reflected well the position of immigrants in the American pecking order and simultaneously gave them a powerful first shove toward assimilation. The country was young then, in the midst of its major period of industrial expansion and poised for world hegemony. The role that newcomers were expected to play in the American labor market was transparent, and the Immigration Office was confidently in control. Out of these foreign masses received so unceremoniously in their American ports of entry grew new urban forms, new institutions, new social problems, and a changed concept of what the nation was about. By World War II the offspring of those eastern Europeans processed and often renamed at Ellis Island were in the trenches. In Norman Mailer's classic war novel *The Naked and the Dead* (1948), most of the platoon led by the Anglo-Saxon lieutenant Hearn are children of immigrants—the Italian Minetta, the Jew Goldstein, the Mexican Martinez.

In the army, as in society, ethnicity was securely established at the core of a man's identity. Women at the time followed a similar, but subordinate, course. It is not necessary for my purposes to inflict on the reader yet another rendition of assimilation theory, the melting pot, and the other concepts that emerged at the time to explain the American immigrant experience. It suffices to make two general points. First, these theories and concepts, arising out of the momentous historical experience of turn-of-the-century immigration, represent our intellectual legacy as we set out to make sense of similar events taking place today. Research on present-day immigration started with the attempt to use assimilation, amalgamation, melting pot, cultural pluralism, and other concepts stemming from that earlier era as interpretive guides.

Second, a good part of that legacy was flawed, in part by stereotypical characterizations of immigrant groups but, more importantly, by a persistent focus on relatively superficial aspects of the process of adaptation. Issues of language, cultural habits, and spatial patterns commonly took precedence over the structural forces driving immigration. Debates took place on whether the widespread adoption of English and Anglicization of immigrant names meant that "Anglo hegemony" was paramount or whether the incorporation of items of Italian, Mexican, and Chinese cuisine into the American menu indicated that a "melting pot" was under way. Those debates ended indecisively because they never addressed the fundamentals of immigration and remained at the level of public perceptions of the process. Those fundamentals were grounded in political economy, and with few exceptions—exemplified by the works of Brinley Thomas (1973), Gerald Rosenblum (1973), and Enrique Santibáñez (1930), among others—the research literature on immigration did not address them systematically.

As we prepare to confront the challenge of advancing immigration theory in the contemporary world, we will do well to reflect on the course traveled so far. It has involved describing the novelty and complexity of contemporary immigration, culling concepts and insights from the classic literature on the subject, and, simultaneously, getting rid of the deadweight of irrelevant debates. Overall, we are well poised to confront the present challenge because the contributions of social scientists from different disciplines have grounded the study of today's immigration firmly on its fundamental realities: the sustained demand for an elastic supply of labor, the pressures and constraints of sending Third World economies, the dislocations wrought by struggles for the creation and control of national states in less developed regions, and the microstructures of support created by migrants themselves across political borders.

Contemporary immigration theory has not only sought to understand the fundamental forces driving the process but has even gone beyond them to explore how social networks, community normative expectations, and household strategies modify and, at times, subvert those structural determinants. This rapid advance suggests that the task of an introductory essay should be to summarize the main theoretical perspectives and research findings and comment on how they relate to one another. This will not do, however, because several quality reviews already exist and because many of the chapters in this volume are also devoted to covering the same terrain. Instead, I will use this opportunity to invite reflection on what may be some of the major pitfalls as we move toward more encompassing and more powerful theoretical models and what are the lines of investigation that offer greatest potential to further this movement.

Immigration Theory for a New Century: Four Common Pitfalls

It seems to me that there are four important misconceptions about the ways that we go about developing theory. Some are misconceptions about what this type of activity entails; others refer to the weight of evidence as it is brought to bear on the products of that activity. Each such problem may be introduced by a somewhat rash statement whose meaning I will then seek to clarify.

Theories Do Not Grow Additively

A first misconception is that the accumulation of evidence leads to theoretical innovation. Generally, this is not the case. Data, whether quantitative or qualitative, may accumulate endlessly without producing any significant conceptual breakthrough. Indeed, much of what we do as part of our everyday work is simply to produce information on one aspect or another of social reality within the intellectual frameworks already in place, without altering them to any significant extent. Ideas, especially those of a broader reach, are few and far between and certainly do not emerge out of masses of data. There is one sense, however, in which the presence of information does lead to conceptual innovation. This happens when puzzles emerge from the accumulated evidence requiring new explanations.

Contradictions may not be self-evident, and indeed it is a theoretical gift to be able to identify them and single them out for analysis. People had seen Chinese and Japanese immigrants engage in small business on the West Coast for decades. Similarly, everyone knew that Jewish and Italian pawnshops, liquor stores, and clothing stores proliferated in urban ghetto areas in the East. Books and articles were even written on the subject, but until Edna Bonacich came along, nobody had asked the obvious questions: Why is small entrepreneurship so widespread among some first-generation immigrants, but not others? And why do they locate their businesses in low-income areas, precisely where the market for most goods and services is poorer? Out of the analysis of this puzzle came the theory of middleman minorities, a keystone to understanding the economic adaptation path followed by a number of immigrant groups and the predecessor of later concepts such as ethnic niches and ethnic enclaves (Bonacich 1973; Bonacich and Modell 1980). When Korean stores were systematically looted during the 1992 riots in Los Angeles, those familiar with the theory had an indispensable tool to understand what was happening and why.

The contemporary literature provides other good examples. We know that immigrants have been coming by the tens of thousands during the last decades and that the destinations of many are the cores of large cities. These are the very areas that have been undergoing a rapid process of deindustrialization, shedding thousands of jobs. Why should job-seeking immigrants want to go there? Why indeed should the flow continue at all in the absence of such opportunities? Saskia Sassen focused on that particular puzzle, and her analysis yielded the concepts of a "degraded manufacturing sector" and increasing service-sector demand in "global cities," concepts that have proven useful for the analysis of immigrant employment and adaptation in recent years (Sassen 1989, 1991).

After the concept of ethnic enclave came along,

a question that emerged was, how could these small ethnic firms retain their labor force? Several authors observed that while entrepreneurs fared well economically, the same was not the case with their employees. Family members and new arrivals provided part of the requisite labor supply, but they did not satisfactorily answer the question of how the more long-term and skilled positions required for the survival of these firms could be staffed. Thomas Bailey and Roger Waldinger (1991a) tackled this particular puzzle, developing the concept of an informal training system, a mechanism that not only replenishes the supply of entrepreneurs in immigrant communities but can offer attractive mobility opportunities for the more experienced and skilled workers. The metaphor of the enclave as a "business engine" rather than as a den of relentless exploitation contributed to our understanding of these structures and of the reasons why apparently exploited workers remain there.

Theoretical breakthroughs do not arise out of additional data, but out of the ability to reconstitute a perceptual field identifying connections not previously seen. Such insights require that we gain some distance from reality in order to identify patterns lost at close range. For purposes of theory, more is not necessarily better, since an avalanche of empirical content can make the task of working out solutions at some level of generalizability more difficult.

Theories Do Not Necessarily Correspond to People's Perceptions

The study of immigration has been, for the most part, data-driven. This is a healthy feature, but it has a significant drawback, namely, the tendency to test theoretical propositions by comparing them with individual self-reports. All theory worthy of the name requires simplification and abstraction. Hence, actors involved in a given process may not be aware of the broader issues at play or may have a different opinion of them. The various stages of the process of acculturation and assimilation, described in Richard Alba and Victor Nee's chapter in this volume, may be at variance with how immigrants themselves view their situations. Thus, a group can be in a rapid process of assimilation according to some external standard, while their members may still consider themselves quite foreign to the receiving society.

People's subjective orientations are certainly important and represent a legitimate field of study, but unless a theory specifically refers to them (such as theories of ethnic identity), it is improper to make them a standard of evaluation. In my hometown of many years, Baltimore, Korean immigrants have developed a vigorous middleman economy in the midst of the African American inner city. Yet when confronted with the concept and its implications, many Korean entrepreneurs would balk and vigorously deny that they are doing this. The usefulness of the theory does not hinge on these reactions, but on how well it can explain and predict these immigrants' patterns of economic adaptation, residential settlement, and relationships with the native minority population.

Once made, the point is obvious, but I believe that it is worth emphasizing since claims to the "higher authority" of the actual participants are a common occurrence. The theory of social capital as it applies to immigrant and ethnic communities provides a case in point. In an article published in 1993, Julia Sensenbrenner and I discussed "bounded solidarity" and "enforceable trust" as sources of social capital in these communities that allow members to gain access to economic resources otherwise unavailable to them and to conduct business transactions flexibly (Portes and Sensenbrenner 1993). The problem comes when investigators try to fit these concepts into everyday perceptions. For some, the theory of social capital suggests that immigrants go about spouting love messages about the solidarity they feel to one another and how trustworthy their fellow ethnics are. Nothing could be further from the truth.

In the heart of Cuban Miami, shopkeepers bicker nonstop with each other, denounce others' unethical business practices, and would be hard put to say a kind word about many of their business associates. Similar tendencies of everyday disagreement and competition are evident in Min Zhou's (1992) description of New York's Chinatown and in the Nees' account of its San Francisco counterpart (Nee and Nee 1992). These are not cozy environments, and, at close range, they appear quite "unsolidaristic." Sources of social capital and their effects are not observable at this level; they manifest themselves instead over time and in aggregates of multiple individual transactions. Bounded solidarity emerges as an aggregate "elective affinity" on the choice of business partners, employees, and customers and in patterns of associational participation. Enforceable trust is reflected in the routine behavior of participants in business transactions, relative to how similar operations are conducted on the outside.

The town of Otavalo in the Ecuadorean Andes

has become justly famous for the economic success of its indigenous population. Based on a dense web of ethnically bounded networks, Otavalans have been able to fan all over the world selling their woolens, native crafts, and even their folk music. In street fairs of large North American and European cities, one can readily spot Otavalans wearing their characteristic pigtails and felt hats. They peddle ponchos, CDs of Andean music, and the crafts of other indigenous tribes sold as their own. However, when David Kyle (1995) visited the town to inquire on the origins of Otavalan entrepreneurship, he found a community riven with factions and, on the surface at least, in conflict with itself. It was only after several layers of public discourse had been peeled off that the patterns of cooperative entrepreneurship and ethnic-bounded business support began to emerge.

There is a second related practice that also does harm to theoretical progress. This may be called the "pseudo-test" and consists of dressing up modest empirical findings as if they were suitable for examining a general hypothesis. The purpose is to exalt the significance of a particular study by linking it up with broader theoretical concerns; in the process, however, invalid inferences are made. There are two variants of the problem. The first occurs when individual instances of marginal importance are held up as contradicting general propositions. Obviously, it is valid to call attention to individual negative findings, but one must have a sense of proportion. A case study of a small group of immigrants cannot, for example, invalidate a general theory supported by large-scale trends. I suspect that this is what Alba and Nee (this volume) have in mind when they complain about how many past critiques of assimilation theory have been grounded on partial evidence. Alba and Nee recognize problems and exceptions to what they call the "canonical statement" by Milton Gordon (1964), but they argue that these difficulties do not entirely eliminate the value of his perspective.

A more serious variant occurs when measurement and sample selection fit the theory awkwardly, but the researcher goes on anyway to draw conclusions about its validity. In the short and eventful life of the concept of ethnic enclave (Wilson and Martin 1982; Portes and Bach 1985), there have been several such instances. In some cases, theoretical predictions derived from the concept have been supported for the wrong reasons; in others, they have been rejected with data that bear little resemblance to the original formulation. In a recent article, the enclave is defined as Hispanic businesses in New York City, and the negative evidence consists of the lower wages and poor working conditions of immigrant women employed by these firms relative to those in nonethnic employment (Gilbertson 1995). To my knowledge, there is no such thing as a "Hispanic" enclave in New York since there is no immigrant nationality that goes by that name. Nor is there anything in the finding of worse employment conditions for a cross-section of immigrant workers in ethnic employment that contradicts the original predictions. The real questions, from the standpoint of that theory, are the viability of these firms, their capacity to spawn new enterprises, and the extent to which workers can become entrepreneurs themselves.

Theoretical insights in the social sciences have the character of a public good. They are not covered by any special form of protection and, once formulated, enter the public domain to be freely used by anyone. This is necessary in order to submit new ideas to logical scrutiny and to the test of empirical evidence, but it has its downside. This consists of theories being invoked rather than seriously examined, either to add luster to modest findings or to serve as a foil for contrary arguments. In recent years social scientists have become increasingly respectful of empirical evidence and leery of doing violence to it. As a result, a methodological literature on issues of measurement, sampling design, and data analysis has grown rapidly. The same respect has not yet been accorded to the basic elements of theory—concepts and propositions—which, as free public goods, have been handled with considerably less concern. As abstracted knowledge, theory is the end product of the scientific enterprise and the necessary guide for its future development. The study of immigration has not had to contend with extremely abstract notions and operates instead at a data-sensitive middle range. For that very reason, concepts that capture and synthesize insights from past research should not be simply invoked but examined with careful attention to their scope and original definitions.

Typologies Are Not Theories

In her analysis of self-identification among second-generation Caribbean youth, Mary Waters (1994) distinguishes between the immigrant-identified, ethnic-identified, and American-identified members of her sample. Studies of the undocumented population commonly distinguish between "visa overstayers" and "entries without inspection" (EWIs). Similarly, research on legal arrivals usually separates refugees and asylees from quota and nonquota immigrants and, more recently, from the amnestied population (U.S. Immigration and Naturalization Service 1996). Along the same lines, Rubén Rumbaut and I developed a typology of manual labor immigrants, professional immigrants, immigrant entrepreneurs, and political refugees as the framework for our description of contemporary U.S.-bound immigration (Portes and Rumbaut 1996).

Typologies such as these are valid intellectual exercises, but they are not theories. This is self-evident in administrative categories, such as those employed by the U.S. Immigration and Naturalization Service. The distinction, for example, between refugees and asylees or between visa overstayers and EWIs does not say anything about the causal origins of each flow or its particular patterns of adaptation. All that these terms reflect is primarily an accident of bureaucratic processing. Typologies such as those of Waters (1994) or Portes and Rumbaut (1996) may become building blocks for theories, but, by themselves, they do not amount to a theoretical statement because they simply assert differences without specifying their origins or anticipating their consequences.

The point is again evident once made, but it is worth emphasizing because the field of immigration encourages and depends on such categorical distinctions, both for research and for administrative purposes. Typologies enter the construction of theory in one of two ways: as interaction effects or as categorical endogenous values. As interaction effects, typologies specify the scope that certain propositions can take or the way that their predictions vary between different categories of people. To take a familiar example from a related field, the typology of labor market segmentation predicts differential effects of human capital variables in the primary and secondary sectors of the labor market. Years of education are expected to have a significant effect on wages in primary-sector employment, but not in the secondary (Edwards, Reich, and Gordon 1975; Gordon 1972). This is an interaction effect. To take a second example, the effects of acculturation are expected to be benign among children of professional immigrants and entrepreneurs, but problematic among the offspring of labor immigrants, especially those living in close proximity to impoverished inner-city areas. This interaction is the core of the concept of segmented assimilation (Fernández-Kelly and Schauffler 1994; Portes and Zhou 1993).

Waters's (1994) typology provides an example of a categorical endogenous variable. The three types of self-identification that she describes can be interpreted as the range of a variable to be explained through various characteristics of immigrant families and the social context that receives them. In turn, these types of identification may be expected to have differential effects on other aspects of immigrant children's social and educational adaptation. An earlier example is Irvin Child's well-known typology of "conformists," "escapists," and "rebels" to describe the stance taken by Italian American youth to the conflict between their parents' efforts at cultural preservation and the pull of the American mainstream (Child 1943). This is also a categorical endogenous variable in need of explanation, and it is expected, in turn, to have some significant consequences on individuals so classified.

To rank as a full-fledged theory, a statement should have four elements: first, a delimitation and description of some patch of reality; second, an identification and definition of a process or characteristic to be explained (the dependent variable); third, one or more explanatory factors and their types of effects, additive or interactive; fourth, a logical link to at least one other similar proposition. By coding as 1 the presence of each of these four elements, it is possible to build a hierarchy of statements used in the course of theory construction as follows:

Description of Specific Instances	*Identification of an Issue or Problem in Need of Explanation*	*Identification of Explanatory Factors*	*Links with Other Predictive Statements*	
1	0	0	0	= Case study
1	1	0	0	= Empirical generalization
1	1	1	0	= Theoretical statement
1	1	1	1	= Theory

Historical accounts of the origins of certain immigrant communities and their present characteristics provide examples of the first type of endeavor. They are descriptive case studies, limited in scope to a certain space and time and focused on a specific sequence of events. Oscar Handlin's (1973) classic study of the Boston Irish, William Thomas and Florian Znaniecki's *The Polish Peasant in Europe and America* (1984), and William Foote Whyte's *Street Corner Society* (1955) are classic examples. Illsoo Kim's (1981) study of Koreans in New York City, Alex Stepick's (1992) account of the Haitian community in South Florida, and Terry Repak's (1995) monograph on Central Americans in Washington, D.C., provide contemporary ones. These studies, which not incidentally are at the core of the immigration literature, are not theory. They provide, instead, the basic materials for the development of theoretical statements and, subsequently, the empirical ground and means to test them.

Along with monographs on particular immigrant groups, we often encounter in the literature statements like: "Mexicans have low levels of entrepreneurship"; "Chinese settle in spatially clustered areas"; "Filipinos have the greatest propensity to acquire U.S. citizenship." These statements, which are sometimes confused with theory, are empirical generalizations. They contain two elements: a referential statement to a certain period, place, or category of people, and a statement of fact about the value or values taken by a certain variable. In each case, there is an assertion that people or events possess specific values or fit into particular profiles, but there is no explanation of how this state of affairs comes about. In contrast to broad descriptive statements, the specific contribution of empirical generalizations is to focus on a limited aspect of reality worthy of attention. As such, they provide a more proximate building block for theory.

A theoretical proposition contains both a universal quantifier specifying its scope of predication and a statement of a relationship between something to be explained and possible factors leading to it. In the best formulations, there is a specification of the character of that relationship (whether additive or interactive) and some clarification of those social contexts in which the prediction is or is not expected to hold. Typologies that specify interaction effects fit here. Because immigration theorizing has generally proceeded at a low level of abstraction, it is perhaps important to note that theoretical statements possess two other characteristics, often missing from those discussed in the literature: first, they are not constrained to a single time and place; second, they can support subjunctive conditionals.

A statement like "among Cuban refugees who arrived between 1960 and 1970 in Miami, social connections in their country of origin led to ready access to business loans" is not a theoretical proposition. Nor is the following, which could be drawn from Robert Smith's excellent monograph on long-distance Mexican migration: "In the village of Ticuaní, Puebla, during the 1980s, the greater the number of migrant families going to New York, the faster the rate of completion of local public works" (Smith 1992). Such statements are accidental universals that specify causal relationships in a particular locality or migrant group, but that lack the requisite level of generality to qualify as theoretical propositions. The latter can "travel"—that is, they are applicable in times and places other than those that gave rise to them in the first place. Thus, a theory of long-distance migration and remittances limited to Mexicans in New York or a theory of entrepreneurship limited to Cubans in Miami would be suspect.

Second, theoretical propositions possess an element of logical necessity that is absent from other statements. This is best seen if one attempts to transform an empirical generalization into a causal proposition. "All immigrants in Salt Lake City are undocumented." This may be true, but it would not support the subjunctive conditional: "For every immigrant, if he or she were in Salt Lake City, he or she would be undocumented." There is nothing about being in Salt Lake City that necessarily brings about the condition "undocumented." Compare this with Douglas Massey's theory of cumulative social networks, which predicts that the greater the number of present or former migrants a person in a sending area knows, the greater the probability that he or she will also migrate (Massey and García España 1987; Massey and Espinosa 1997). This can be transformed into the conditional: "For every person in a sending area, if he or she were to maintain contacts with present or former migrants, he or she would also be more likely to migrate than others with identical characteristics." Migrant networks are not an accident but contain the necessary causal element to produce the predicted outcome.

Philosophers of science such as Ernest Nagel (1961) are content to label isolated theoretical propositions "theories." I would prefer to reserve the label for those interrelated sets of propositions that not only "travel" in the sense of being applicable to different spatial and temporal contexts, but that also tell a coherent story about certain finite aspects of reality. For all its empirical shortcomings, the "canonical" statement of assimilation developed by Gordon (1964) and summarized by Alba and Nee (this volume) exemplifies such a theory. With the help of a few auxiliary assumptions, we can formalize it into a series of logically interrelated causal propositions about the trajectory or trajectories that immigrants are expected to follow after their initial settlement.

Aristide Zolberg's theory of the role of the state system in the origins and control of international migration flows provides a second example. His insight that enforced borders represent the crucial dividing line between the developed world, or "core," and the increasingly subordinate economic periphery can be transformed into a series of propositions about between-country economic inequalities, the role of migration flows in ameliorating them, and the role of political borders in reproducing the global hierarchy (Zolberg, Suhrke, and Aguayo 1986; Zolberg 1989). One of the significant merits of this theory is that it links anew the study of immigration with broader issues of political economy, thus avoiding an exclusive focus on the characteristics and adaptation process of individual migrants.

I have dwelt in such laborious detail over typologies and levels of theory because, in my view, this is the area in the field of immigration that stands in need of greatest attention. While we may rightfully complain about the lack of a parental nationality question in the decennial census or the surprising lack of a national longitudinal survey of immigrants, the fact is that empirical knowledge about contemporary immigration has grown by leaps and bounds in recent years and can be expected to continue doing so. On the other hand, the cumulative character of the enterprise depends on the insertion of the case monographs and typologies developed in the field into some sort of coherent framework that only theory can provide. While abstract speculation may have bedeviled other fields of inquiry, the problem with one so close to the ground as immigration is precisely the opposite. There is some danger that qualitative studies of immigrant communities and quantitative analyses of their economic and political adaptation may pile up without any systematic guide as to what all this information means and how it can be brought to bear, in a focused way, on major policy concerns.

There Is No Overall Encompassing Theory of Immigration

The pitch for theory has its limits too. The final issue is, in a sense, the opposite of that just discussed. There does not seem to be much danger that someone might be attempting a grand theory of immigration anytime soon, but just in case, I would like to argue that this kind of endeavor would be futile. The reason is that the different areas that compose this field are so disparate that they can be unified only at a highly abstract and probably vacuous level. For starters, consider the division between macrostructural issues, such as the role of global capitalist expansion in the onset of migrant flows or the power of the state system to regulate such movements, and microstructural issues, such as the effects of community networks on individual decisions to migrate. Contrary to much conventional wisdom about the need to integrate microstructural and macrostructural theories, I would argue that, in the case of immigration, the two levels are not fungible.

The theory that colonial capitalist penetration plays a significant role in the initiation of large-scale labor migration from less developed countries says nothing about who among the population of those countries is more likely to migrate, nor can it be tested at the level of individual decisionmaking. It requires comparative historical data to establish the existence of such a relationship between overt or covert capitalist penetration and the timing and volume of labor outflows. (For variants of this theory, see Portes and Walton 1981, ch. 3; Sassen 1988.) Similarly, individual-level processes of acculturation and labor market incorporation cannot simply be aggregated into structural effects. One hundred thousand Mexican immigrants trying to learn English and find jobs in Houston, Texas, will have a very different impact there than the same number doing this in Boston, Massachusetts, or Charlotte, North Carolina. Mexican immigrants in Houston are a familiar and expected presence, and their paths of cultural adaptation and labor market participation have been charted by past immigrant generations. Such is not the case in the industrial cities of the Northeast, much less in the emerging metropolitan areas of the South.

Over a decade ago, Robert Bach and I proposed a fourfold categorization of topics around which existing theories of immigration could be organized. Although subject to modification, the classification seems still serviceable. These topics were:

the origins of immigration, the directionality and continuity of migrant flows, the utilization of immigrant labor, and the sociocultural adaptation of immigrants (Portes and Bach 1985, ch. 1).

Each of these topics may be approached theoretically at a close-range level or from a broad structural perspective. For example, the issues of what particular places migrants go to and how long a particular movement lasts may be examined at the level of aggregate labor demand and the past history of labor recruitment in sending areas, as Michael Piore (1979) has done, or at the level of cross-national networks pointing individual immigrants in a particular direction and sustaining the flow over time, as Douglas Massey (Massey et al. 1987) or Sherri Grasmuck and Patricia Pessar (1991) have done. Although obviously interrelated, each of these areas requires separate attention, and hence, midrange theories targeted on one or two of them are preferable to an all-encompassing statement. A general theory of immigration must climb to such a level of abstraction as to render its predictions vacuously true. To assert, for example, that international labor migration and immigrant sociocultural assimilation are both "equilibrium-restoring processes" may be readily accepted without advancing in any way our understanding of either.

In a related vein, the method of analytic induction deserves a final comment. Analytic induction is the attempt to make progressively refined explanations of a particular phenomenon until all exceptions have been taken into account. The method was popular in sociology and anthropology during the fifties and early sixties because it offered the promise of a gradual progression toward explaining the full range of a given phenomenon (Robinson 1951; Turner 1953). That popularity quickly faded when it was discovered that applications of the method ended up redefining the problem until it was coterminous with its explanation. The attempt to account for a social phenomenon in its entirety leads to circular reasoning because it inexorably reduces the conceptual space between the thing to be explained and its alleged causes.

Though no one uses the term "analytic induction" anymore, the logic of the method creeps in all the time in the analysis of social phenomena. To take an example from a related field, the political scientist Robert Putnam redefined the concept of "social capital" from the original statements by James Coleman (1988), who had defined it as an individual or family resource stemming from participation in certain social structures. In Putnam's analysis, social capital became instead a collective feature of communities and even countries, measured by such variables as high levels of voting, high associational participation, and a civic culture. The concept was redefined in this fashion in order to serve as an explanatory factor of differences between cities or countries in democratic governance. Gradually, cause and effect come together until the reasoning becomes circular. Differences between the well-governed cities of northern Italy and the poorly governed ones of the Italian south are thus explained as follows: "'Civic' communities value solidarity, civic participation, and integrity and here democracy works. At the other pole are 'uncivic' regions like Calabria and Sicily, aptly characterized by the French term *incivisme*. The very concept of citizenship is stunted here" (Putnam 1993a, 36). In other words, if your town is "civic," it does civic things; if it is "uncivic," it does not.

Theory building is a delicate enterprise: novel and useful ideas occur rarely, and they are constantly exposed to the risks of misuse and misinterpretation or, alternatively, to the threat of conceptual overreach. We cannot explain everything, but we can explain some things with a reasonable margin of certainty. A set of midrange theories designed to do this by drawing on the wealth of historical and contemporary research on immigration seems the strategy most worth pursuing.

A Sampler of Themes for Immigration Research and Theory

Despite the set of pitfalls just seen, there is reason to be optimistic about theoretical progress in the field of immigration. Part of this optimism is based on what has been accomplished in exploring the structural determinants of contemporary migrant flows and the microstructures that sustain them over time. Also underlying this optimism are the research programs started in recent years that hold the promise not only of adding to our stock of information but also of expanding immigration theory in new directions. To my knowledge, none of these programs began with a clearly delineated theoretical agenda, but their own subject matter dictated the development of new typologies, concepts, and propositions. The list is nonexhaustive and certainly biased toward my own interests and preferences. While other topics of equal merit may be identified, the following ones provide a sampler of research issues with significant theoretical potential.

Transnational Communities

Transnational communities are dense networks across political borders created by immigrants in their quest for economic advancement and social recognition. Through these networks, an increasing number of people are able to lead dual lives. Participants are often bilingual, move easily between different cultures, frequently maintain homes in two countries, and pursue economic, political, and cultural interests that require their presence in both. In a pioneering statement on the topic, Linda Basch and her collaborators (Basch, Glick Schiller, and Blanc-Szanton 1994, 6) describe their initial attitude toward this emergent phenomenon:

> We define "transnationalism" as the process by which immigrants forge and sustain multi-stranded social relations that link together their societies of origin and settlement. We call these processes transnationalism to emphasize that many immigrants today build social fields that cross geographic, cultural, and political borders. . . . An essential element . . . is the multiplicity of involvements that transmigrants sustain in both home and host societies. We are still groping for a language to describe these social locations.

That puzzled attitude toward a novel phenomenon is what makes the study of this topic promising from a theoretical standpoint. In this volume, Glick Schiller argues that similar processes of back-and-forth movement and intensive investments and contacts with sending countries also took place among European immigrants at the turn of the century. I agree, but I would add that the present transnational communities possess a distinct character that justifies coining a new concept to refer to them. This character is defined by three features: the number of people involved, the nearly instantaneous character of communications across space, and the fact that the cumulative character of the process makes participation "normative" within certain immigrant groups.

As studies by Linda Basch, Nina Glick Schiller, and Cristina Blanc-Szanton (1994), Glick Schiller, Basch, and Blanc-Szanton (1992a), Luis Guarnizo (1994), Luin Goldring (1992), and others show, the numbers involved in transnational activities of different sorts—economic, political, and social—can represent a significant proportion of the population of both sending areas and immigrant communities. In this sense, they become a novel path of adaptation quite different from those found among immigrants at the turn of the century. This path is reinforced by technologies that facilitate rapid displacement across long distances and instant communication. The "astronauts"—Chinese entrepreneurs who live in Monterey Park and other California cities but make their living by commuting by air across the Pacific—could not have existed in an earlier era (Fong 1994). Nor could have the immigrant civic committee, described by Smith (1992), who traveled, over the weekend, to the interior of Mexico to inspect public works in their village in order to be back at work in New York City by Monday.

These communication facilities, added to the economic, social, and psychological benefits that transnational enterprise can bring, may turn these activities into the normative adaptation path for certain immigrant groups. Just as in the Mexican towns described by Massey and Goldring (1994) migration north is the "thing to do" during adverse economic times, so involvement in transnational activities may become the thing to do for immigrants otherwise confined to dead-end jobs and an inferior, discriminated status. That path is, of course, at variance with those envisioned by the "canonical" assimilation perspective, with direct implications for immigration theory.

Elsewhere I have argued that the construction of transnational communities by immigrants is a process driven by the very forces promoting economic globalization, as common people are caught in their web and learn to use new technologies (Portes 1996a). Involvement in these emerging activities may represent an effective response of popular groups to the new forces unleashed by globalization and the strategies of large corporate actors. The aphorism "capital is global, labor is local," may still hold in the aggregate, but it is being increasingly subverted by these grassroots initiatives based on long-distance networks and a newly acquired command of communication technologies.

The New Second Generation

A second line of research has to do with the adaptation process of the second generation. The case for the second generation as a "strategic research site" is based on two features.[1] First, the long-term effects of immigration for the host society depend less on the fate of first-generation immigrants than on their descendants. Patterns of adaptation of the first generation set the stage for what is to come, but issues such as the continuing dominance of English, the growth of a welfare-dependent population, the resilience or disappearance of culturally distinct ethnic enclaves, and the decline or growth of ethnic intermarriages will be decided among its children and grandchildren. For example, the much debated issue of the loss of English hegemony in certain American cities heavily affected by immigration will not be settled by immigrants, but by their offspring. Loyalty to the home language among the foreign-born is a time-honored pattern; in the past the key linguistic shift has taken place in the second generation (Lieberson 1981; Lieberson and Hansen 1974; Veltman 1983). Whether this is occurring today represents a major issue for the cities and communities where today's immigrants concentrate.

Second, the experiences of the present second generation cannot be inferred from those of children of earlier European immigrants. The "canonical" statement of assimilation theory may be reread as an abstracted version of the typical course of adaptation among these earlier children of immigrants. With exceptions, that course featured an orderly progression from the poverty and discrimination endured by the first generation to the rapid acculturation of the second generation and its gradual economic advancement. By the third generation, the loss of "ethnic" linguistic and cultural traits, as well as the disappearance of earlier labor market disadvantages, could be virtually complete.

There are reasons to doubt that a similarly benign and straightforward course will be followed by members of today's second generation. First, the proliferation of transnational activities among first-generation immigrants complicates the course of adaptation to be followed by their offspring and renders its outcome uncertain. Second, discrimination against nonwhites and changing requirements of the American labor market create obstacles for economic progress and the fulfillment of rising aspirations among many second-generation youth. Third, and perhaps more insidiously, these difficulties can be readily interpreted within the adversarial framework developed in the inner city among descendants of earlier labor migrants. The blocked mobility experienced by these groups has become translated over time into an oppositional stance toward mainstream society. Socialization into the outlooks and role models provided by this segment of the American population creates yet another hazard in the process of social and economic progress of today's children of immigrants.

The concept of segmented assimilation was coined to call attention to these alternative and not always benign paths and to signal differences with the normative course described by earlier theory. A telling example would be the alternative interpretations given to the speed of acculturation across generations yesterday and today. The fact that children of immigrants often become their "parents' parents" as their knowledge of the new language and culture races ahead has been repeatedly noted, both at the turn of the century and today.

But there is a difference. Whereas the phenomenon of generational role reversal was expected and even celebrated as it took place among children of Europeans, today it compares unfavorably with other acculturation paths and is even regarded as a danger signal. At the time of Irvin Child's (1943) study, Italian American youth who refused to take the step of joining the American cultural mainstream were dubbed "escapists." Today Min Zhou and Carl Bankston (1994) describe how Vietnamese American children who take the same step become prime candidates for downward assimilation. The reason is that rapid acculturation and generational role reversal undercuts parental authority to control youth as they enter an increasingly complex society, marked by the ready availability of countercultural models.

The pattern where the first and second generations learn the ways of American society at different paces may be labeled "dissonant acculturation." The opposite—consonant acculturation—occurs either because parents acculturate at the same speed as their children or because the process is slowed among youth by the influence of the co-ethnic community (Portes and Rumbaut 1996, ch. 7). This last path, dubbed "selective acculturation," has been associated in studies by Mary Waters (1994), Margaret Gibson (1989), Marcelo Suárez-Orozco (1987), Patricia Fernández-Kelly and Richard Schauffler (1994), and others with consistently more favorable adaptation outcomes among second-generation children than those brought about by role reversal. In any case, the typology of dissonant, consonant, and selective acculturation across generations and the different evaluations placed on each type in the research literatures of the 1940s and of the 1990s offer a promising point of departure for theory and for a more sophisticated understanding of the social sequel to large-scale migration.

Households and Gender

For a number of years, the field of immigration studies tended to neglect the role of gender. At present, a new wave of studies is redressing this imbalance. The significance of research on women goes beyond covering a previously neglected segment of the migrant population. Instead, like class and race, gender represents a master dimension of social structure, and a focus on this dimension can yield novel insights into many phenomena. For this to become reality, the analytic focus cannot be exclusively women (or men for that matter), but the socially patterned relationships between the sexes as they influence and, in turn, are influenced by the process of immigration. As Patricia Pessar notes (this volume), "the challenge still remains to branch out from a concentration on female immigrants in order to apply appropriately gender-inflected research questions and methods to both men and women."

There is indeed a variable geometry of relationships between the sexes that is not adequately captured by a single-sex focus or by an unnuanced repetition of the realities of sexual exploitation and subordination. The latter do exist, but they do not exhaust the story. As in the case of class and race, the multiple configurations found in different social contexts are what makes the study of gender relations both interesting and capable of yielding new theoretical insights. A cautionary note must be introduced here about analyses that concentrate exclusively on the individual motivations of household members and the conflict of interests between them. This has often become the center of gender-focused studies.

Undoubtedly, men, women, and children within a household may differ and even struggle for conflicting goals. But an exclusive focus on these internal disagreements makes us lose sight of two other important considerations. First, households can still act as units despite internal differences. Hence, it is possible to theorize at the level of household strategies. An exclusive concentration on individual motivations would do away with the possibility of understanding how these small social units pool resources to organize a process as complex as international migration.

Second, there can be differences between people's perceptions and their actual behavior. On this point, the earlier warning against making respondents' definitions of the situation the ultimate test for theoretical propositions comes in handy. Such definitions are important, but they do not exhaust all there is about a particular social process and may even be at variance with the actual conduct of households when examined in the aggregate. Put differently, theory can exist at different levels of abstraction. Reducing everything to the individual plane would unduly constrain the enterprise by preventing the utilization of more complex units of analysis—families, households, and communities—as the basis for explanation and prediction.

States and State Systems

The analysis of the role of states and state building in the onset of refugee flows, pioneered by Zolberg and his associates, offers an example of a fourth line of investigation with significant theoretical promise (Zolberg, Suhrke, and Aguayo 1986; Zolberg 1989). Detailed accounts of the process leading to major legislation, such as the Immigration Reform and Control Act of 1986, do exist, but they have not been transformed into a systematic theoretical analysis of both the external pressures impinging on the state and the internal dynamics of the legislative and administrative bodies dealing with immigration.

Recent work by James Hollifield (1992) and Gary Freeman (1995a) has begun to move in the direction of a general model of the political forces promoting immigration in the advanced Western democracies. Freeman even provides a typology of countries according to how their particular histories and political systems affect the play of these forces. But as his critic Rogers Brubaker (1995) points out, the model still has to be fleshed out to specify the conditions under which restrictionist and antirestrictionist discourses come into vogue and the adaptation of state agencies to conflicting pressures and demands. There is a need for greater information about the inner workings of state legislative and administrative bureaucracies in order to advance this area of immigration theory beyond the plane of broad generalities.

The research questions that lie at the core of this line of inquiry and hold the potential for theoretical innovation are twofold. How is it that, in the face of widespread public opposition to the continuation of large-scale immigration, governments in the receiving countries have proven unable or unwilling to prevent it? And why is it that recent laws and administrative measures designed to control immigration often end up having consequences that are almost the opposite of those originally intended?

The economic concept of "path dependence" and its sociological equivalent, "cumulative causation," offer suitable points of departure for the analysis of the first question, insofar as they can guide the explanation of recalcitrant immigration flows in the face of widespread public opposition. (For a more detailed discussion of these concepts and related ones in economic sociology, see Portes [1995a].) Yet an inside analysis of how the legislative and administrative branches of the modern state operate to neutralize the manifest public will against mass immigration is only in its early stages.

The outside forces and agents that promote continuation of an open-door policy are easy enough to identify, but the internal dynamics of state agencies, the ways they absorb information and react to conflicting pressures, are not. The recent review of determinants of and constraints on governmental immigration policies in Western Europe by Hollifield (1996) offers a promising point of departure for addressing this question.

Similarly, the Mertonian concept of "unintended consequences" may be used with profit in the analysis of the second question (Merton 1936, 1968). It explains well what happened to certain pieces of recent legislation, most notably the Immigration Reform and Control Act of 1986. The process by which this set of measures, manifestly designed to control immigration, ended up promoting it has been analyzed by a number of authors. Missing still is a broader set of propositions explaining how such a paradoxical outcome could come about and to what extent the same set of forces can explain or predict similar results elsewhere. For instance, French, German, and Scandinavian policies designed to reverse labor migration have generally ended up promoting further immigration and the emergence of permanent ethnic settlements. (For a recent review of the German case, see Kurthen 1995; for the French experience, see Body-Gentrot 1995, and Hollifield 1994; for the Danish case, see Enoch 1994.) The extent to which a common theoretical model is applicable to those experiences and recent American ones remains an open question.

As several political analysts have emphasized, migration control and the perpetuation of social and economic inequalities between advanced countries and the Third World are closely intertwined. The extent to which states succeed in maintaining such controls or are derailed in their enforcement efforts represents a central policy concern as well as a topic of considerable theoretical import.

Cross-National Comparisons

The vigorous resurgence of the sociology of immigration in recent years has been, by and large, a single-country phenomenon. I am less clear about developments in the other social sciences, but what seems certain is that the wave of novel research and theory on immigration in the United States has not been accompanied by a comparative thrust of similar vigor. To be sure, numerous conferences on the topic have been convened that bring together North American, European, and, sometimes, Asian scholars. Comparative reports also have been published that examine how specific policies, such as amnesty programs for illegal aliens, have fared in different advanced countries. Applied research agencies like the Urban Institute and the Rand Corporation have been notably active in these policy comparisons.

These efforts are valuable, but they are not theory. Conferences seldom yield more than a collection of papers that describe how things have evolved in different countries. Applied policy reports do not usually contain general concepts or propositions that help explain present events or anticipate future ones. In the absence of theory, predictions generated by these reports commonly assume an immutable social reality. For example, projections about the ethnic composition of the population of countries receiving mass immigration assume that the racial and ethnic classifications currently in vogue will not be affected by the presence of immigrants and their subsequent patterns of adaptation. Under similar assumptions, projections made in the early twentieth century would have predicted that the American population would become mostly nonwhite fifty years later since the bulk of eastern and southern European immigrants arriving at that time were not considered "white" in the popular and academic racial taxonomy of the time.

Along the same lines, projections made today about the size of the nonwhite population by the mid-twenty-first century do not take into account the effects of the process of segmented assimilation. As it unfolds, it is likely that descendants of immigrants classified today as Asian, as well as some groups coming from Latin America and classified initially as Hispanic, will enter the mainstream, intermarry, and become sociologically "white," redefining the meaning and scope of the term. By the same token, other groups who are phenotypically white or mestizo may become sociologically "black," as this racial term is used today, because of a failed process of second-generation adaptation (see Fernández-Kelly and Schauffler 1994; Waters 1994).

In the absence of theory, what we have today is mostly an amorphous mass of data on immigration to different countries and a series of concepts whose scope seldom exceeds that of a particular nation-state. Needed are explicitly comparative projects that focus on research topics at a higher level of abstraction than those guiding policy concerns and that employ a common cross-national methodology. Each of the four topics outlined—the rise of transnational communities, the adaptation process of the second generation, gender cleavages and household strategies, and the enactment and enforcement of state immigration laws—is amenable to such comparative analysis.

Other subjects that have been dealt with at length in the North American immigration literature lack a comparative dimension. To cite but three examples: the role of social networks and social capital in initiating and sustaining migration flows in different national contexts; the types of immigrant enterprise that exist in different advanced societies and their role in the economic and social adaptation of immigrants; the patterns of racial and ethnic self-identification of first- and second-generation immigrants in countries that promote rapid legal integration while tolerating ethnic differences (the United States), in those that promote legal integration but resist the rise of ethnic subcultures (France), and in those that delay indefinitely legal integration (Germany) (Hollifield 1994; Münz and Ulrich 1995).

Systematic cross-national research is useful for three purposes: first, to examine the extent to which theoretical propositions "travel," that is, are applicable in national contexts different from that which produced them; second, to generate typologies of interaction effects specifying the variable influence of causal factors across different national contexts; third, to produce concepts and propositions themselves of broader scope. In some cases, large-*N* quantitative designs with nation-states as units of analysis are appropriate. In most cases, however, what Adam Przeworski and Henry Teune (1970) call the "small-*N* maximum differences" design or Melvin Kohn (1987) the "nation-as-context" design would be most appropriate. The reason is that these designs are most appropriate to understand how the specific characteristics of national societies condition the validity of the set of midrange theories that structure the field of immigration.

Conclusion

The inventory of theoretical pitfalls and potentially strategic research sites outlined in this essay is meant to be neither exhaustive nor representative of a consensus in our field. It represents a personal vision and hence is subject to well-justified critiques of incompleteness and topical bias. In my defense, I will only adduce that the inventory is based on long experience attempting to tease regularities out of empirical data and that, even if not consensually agreed upon, it may still provide the basis for useful discussion.

Because of rising public interest in immigration, greater priority has been given to the field by the media, foundations, and government agencies. This is both a blessing and a curse, as the new availability of resources has also given rise to a babel of voices seeking access to them. Applied research has its functions, but it can also lead the field astray by focusing on superficial issues and bureaucratically defined problems. The pressure for "policy-relevant" results should not distract us from the painstaking development of concepts and propositions that alone can advance social science knowledge and provide a sound basis for both public understanding of immigration and policies that do not backfire on their original goals.

This chapter is a revised version of the keynote address to the conference "Becoming American/America Becoming: International Migration to the United States," sponsored by the Social Science Research Council, Sanibel Island, Florida (January 18–21, 1996). I thank Robert K. Merton, Aristide Zolberg, and the editors of *IMR* for their comments on the original version. Responsibility for the contents is exclusively mine.

Note

1. The concept of "strategic research site" was coined by Robert K. Merton (1987, 10–11) to refer to an area of research where processes of more general import are manifested with unusual clarity. In his words, "the empirical material exhibits the phenomenon to be explained or interpreted to such advantage and in such accessible form that it enables the fruitful investigation and the discovery of new problems for further inquiry."

2 Why Does Immigration Occur? A Theoretical Synthesis

Douglas S. Massey

THE MODERN HISTORY OF international migration can be divided roughly into four periods. During the *mercantile period,* from 1500 to 1800, world immigration flows were dominated by Europe and stemmed from processes of colonization and economic growth under mercantile capitalism. Over the course of three hundred years, Europeans inhabited large portions of the Americas, Africa, Asia, and Oceania. Although the exact number of colonizing emigrants is unknown, the outflow was sufficient to establish Europe's dominion over large parts of the world. During this period, emigrants generally fell into three classes: a relatively large number of agrarian settlers, a smaller number of administrators and artisans, and an even smaller number of entrepreneurs who founded plantations to produce raw materials for Europe's growing mercantile economies.

Although the number of Europeans involved in plantation production was small, this sector had a profound impact on the size and composition of population in the Americas. Given a preindustrial technology, plantations required large amounts of cheap labor, a demand met partially by indentured workers from East Asia; the most important source of labor, however, came from the forced migration of African slaves. Over three centuries, nearly ten million Africans were imported into the Americas, and together with European colonists, they radically transformed its social and demographic composition.

The second period of emigration, the *industrial period,* began early in the nineteenth century and stemmed from the economic development of Europe and the spread of industrialism to former colonies in the New World. From 1800 to 1925, more than forty-eight-million people left the industrializing countries of Europe in search of new lives in the Americas and Oceania. Of these emigrants, 85 percent went to just five destinations: Argentina, Australia, Canada, New Zealand, and the United States (the last alone receiving 60 percent). Key sending nations were Britain, Italy, Norway, Portugal, Spain, and Sweden, which all exported a large share of their potential population in the course of industrializing. Although international migrants were not exclusively European, the overwhelming majority came from that continent. Of all U.S. immigrants between 1820 and 1920, for example, 88 percent were from Europe, 3 percent were from Asia, and 8 percent came from the Americas.

The period of large-scale European emigration faltered with the outbreak of World War I, which brought European emigration to an abrupt halt and ushered in a four-decade *period of limited migration.* Although emigration revived somewhat during the early 1920s, by then several important receiving countries (most notably the United States) had passed restrictive immigration laws. The onset of the Great Depression stopped virtually all international movement in 1929, and except for a small amount of return migration, there was little movement during the 1930s. During the 1940s international migration was checked by the Second World War. What mobility there was consisted largely of the movements of refugees and displaced persons and was not tied strongly to the rhythms of economic growth and development; this pattern persisted well into the subsequent decade.

The period of *postindustrial migration* emerged during the 1960s and constituted a sharp break with the past. Rather than being dominated by outflows from Europe to a handful of former colonies, immigration became a truly global phenomenon as the number and variety of both sending and receiving countries increased and the global supply of immigrants shifted from Europe to the developing world. Whereas migration during the industrial era brought people from densely settled, rapidly industrializing areas into sparsely settled, rapidly industrializing nations, migration in the postindustrial era brought people from densely settled countries at the earliest stages of industrialization into densely settled, economically mature, postindustrial societies.

Before 1925, 85 percent of all international migrants originated in Europe, but since 1960 Europe has contributed an increasingly small fraction of emigrants to world migration flows as emigration from Africa, Asia, and Latin America has increased dramatically. The number and variety of destination countries have likewise grown. In addition to traditional immigrant-receiving nations such as Canada, the United States, Australia, New Zealand, and Argentina, countries throughout Western Europe now attract significant numbers of immigrants—notably Germany, France, Belgium, Switzerland, Sweden, and the Netherlands. During the late 1970s even longtime sending countries such as Italy, Spain, and Portugal began receiving immigrants from the Middle East and Africa, and after the rapid escalation of oil prices in 1973, several less developed but capital-rich nations in the Gulf region also began to sponsor massive labor migration. By the 1980s international migration had spread into Asia, not just to Japan but also to newly industrialized countries such as Korea, Taiwan, Hong Kong, Singapore, Malaysia, and Thailand.

By 1990, therefore, international migration had become truly a global phenomenon, and reflecting this new salience, social scientists from a variety of disciplines sought to formulate new theories of migration to supplement those developed during the earlier industrial era. Like prior efforts, these theories sought to explain why international immigration began and how it persisted across space and time; but rather than seeking to account for a massive exodus from a rapidly industrializing Europe into rapidly industrializing former colonies, they sought to explicate a more complex migration regime that involved population flows from industrializing to mature economies, a diversity of sources and destinations, vastly reduced costs of transportation, cheaper and more rapid communications, rising governmental intervention, and greater circularity of movements.

Theories of International Migration

Neoclassical Economics

The oldest and best-known theory of international migration has its roots in models developed originally to explain internal labor migration in the process of economic development (Lewis 1954; Ranis and Fei 1961). According to this theory and its extensions, international migration, like its internal counterpart, is caused by geographic differences in the supply of and demand for labor (Todaro and Maruszko 1987). A country with a large endowment of labor relative to capital will have a low equilibrium wage, while a nation with a limited endowment of labor relative to capital will be characterized by a high market wage, as depicted graphically by the familiar interaction of labor supply and demand curves. The resulting differential in wages causes workers from the low-wage or labor-surplus country to move to the high-wage or labor-scarce country. As a result of this movement, the supply of labor decreases and wages eventually rise in the capital-poor country, while the supply of labor increases and wages ultimately fall in the capital-rich country, leading, at equilibrium, to an international wage differential that reflects the costs of international movement, both pecuniary and psychic.

Mirroring the flow of workers from labor-abundant to labor-scarce countries is a flow of investment capital from capital-rich to capital-poor countries. The relative scarcity of capital in poor countries yields a rate of return that is high by international standards, thereby attracting investment. The movement of capital includes the migration of human capital, with highly skilled workers going from capital-rich to capital-poor countries in order to reap high returns on their skills in a human capital–scarce environment, leading to a parallel movement of managers, technicians, and other skilled workers. The international flow of unskilled labor, therefore, must be kept conceptually distinct from the associated international flow of human capital. Even in the most aggregated macrolevel models, the heterogeneity of immigrants along skill lines must be clearly recognized, although the line between skilled and unskilled workers often is not easy to draw.

Associated with this macroeconomic theory is an accompanying microeconomic model of individual choice (Borjas 1989; Todaro 1969, 1976, 1989). In this scheme, individual rational actors decide to migrate because a cost-benefit calculation leads them to expect a positive net return, usually monetary, from movement. International migration is conceptualized as a form of investment in human capital (Sjaastad 1962). People choose to move to where they can be most productive, given their skills, but before they can reap the higher wages associated with greater labor productivity, they must undertake certain investments, which include the material costs of traveling, the costs of maintenance while moving and looking for work, the effort involved in learning a new language and culture, the difficulty experienced in adapting to a new labor market, and the psychological costs of cutting old ties and forging new ones (Todaro and Maruszko 1987).

Potential migrants estimate the costs and benefits of moving to alternative international locations and migrate to where the expected discounted net returns are greatest over some time horizon (Borjas 1989, 1990). Net returns in each future period are estimated by taking the observed earnings corresponding to the individual's skills in the destination country and multiplying these by the probability of obtaining a job there (and for illegal migrants the likelihood of being able to avoid deportation) to obtain "expected destination earnings." These expected earnings are then subtracted from those expected in the community of origin (observed earnings there multiplied by the probability of employment), and the difference is summed over a time horizon from 0 to n, discounted by a factor that reflects the greater utility of money earned in the present than in the future. From this integrated difference, the estimated costs are subtracted to yield the expected net return to migration. In theory, a potential migrant goes to wherever the expected net returns to migration are greatest.

The New Economics of Migration

In recent years a "new economics of labor migration" has arisen to challenge many of the assumptions and conclusions of neoclassical theory (Stark and Bloom 1985). A key insight of this approach is that migration decisions are made not by isolated individual actors but within larger units of interrelated people—typically families or households but sometimes entire communities—in which people act collectively to maximize not only expected income but also minimize risks to income and maximize status within an embedded hierarchy and to overcome a variety of local market failures (Stark 1991; Taylor 1986, 1987).

In most developed countries, risks to household income are managed through institutional mechanisms. Crop insurance programs and futures markets give farmers a way of protecting themselves against natural disasters and price fluctuations, whereas unemployment insurance and government transfers protect workers against the vagaries of the business cycle and structural economic change. Private or government-sponsored retirement programs, meanwhile, protect citizens against the risk of old-age poverty through regular contributions or taxation, in essence spreading a person's income out over time.

Households are in a better position than individuals to control risks to economic well-being by diversifying the allocation of productive resources. Although individuals may use sequential short periods of seasonal migration to diversify the allocation of their labor over time, this strategy is less feasible for international migrants, who face large sunk costs of movement. Households, however, can easily diversify their sources of income by allocating different family workers to different labor markets. Some members may work in the local economy; others may work elsewhere in the same country; and still others may work abroad. As long as economic conditions in the nonlocal labor markets are negatively or weakly associated with those in the home community, households will be able to control risks through geographic diversification. In the event that economic conditions at home deteriorate and productive activities there fail to generate sufficient income, the household can rely on migrant remittances for support.

Markets for credit and capital also tend to be complete and to function well in developed countries, giving most families a means of borrowing to smooth consumption or undertake investment. In the absence of a sound and efficient banking system, however, international migration becomes attractive as a strategy for accumulating funds that can be used in lieu of borrowing. Households simply send one or more workers abroad to accumulate savings or send them home in the form of remittances. Although most migrant savings and remittances go toward consumption, some of the funds are inevitably also channeled into productive investment.

A key proposition of the new economic model is that income is not a homogeneous good, as assumed by neoclassical economics. The source of the income really matters, and households have significant incentives to invest scarce family resources in activities and projects that provide access to new income sources, even if these activities do not increase total income. The new economics of migration also questions the assumption that income has a constant effect on utility across socioeconomic settings—that is, that a $100 real increase in income means the same thing to a person regardless of community conditions and irrespective of his or her position in the local income distribution.

Theorists of the new economics argue that households send workers abroad not only to improve their incomes in absolute terms but also to increase them *relative* to other households, and hence to reduce their *relative* deprivation compared with some reference group (see Stark and Taylor 1989, 1991; Stark 1991). A household's sense of relative deprivation depends on the incomes of which it is deprived in the reference-group income distribution. To illustrate, consider an increase in the income of affluent households. If poor households' incomes are unchanged, then their relative deprivation increases. If household utility is negatively affected by relative deprivation, then even though a poor household's absolute income and expected gains from migration remain unchanged, its incentive to participate in international migration increases if, by sending a family member abroad, it can hope to reap a *relative* income gain in the community. The likelihood of migration thus grows because of the change in *other* households' incomes. Market failures that constrain local income opportunities for poor households may also increase the attractiveness of migration as an avenue for effecting gains in relative income.

Segmented Labor Market Theory

Although neoclassical theory and the new economics of migration lead to divergent conclusions about the origins and nature of international migration, both are essentially microlevel decision models. They differ in the units assumed to make the decision (the individual or the household), the entity being maximized or minimized (income or risk), their assumptions about the economic context of decisionmaking (complete and well-functioning markets versus missing or imperfect markets), and the extent to which the migration decision is socially contextualized (whether income is evaluated in absolute terms or relative to some reference group). Standing distinctly apart from these models of rational choice, however, is segmented labor market theory, which discounts decisions made by individuals and argues that international migration stems from the intrinsic labor demands of modern industrial societies.

Michael Piore (1979) has been the most forceful and eloquent proponent of this theoretical viewpoint, arguing that international migration is caused by a permanent labor demand that is inherent to the economic structure of developed nations. According to Piore, immigration is not caused by push factors in sending countries (low wages or high unemployment), but by pull factors in receiving countries (a chronic and unavoidable need for low-wage workers). The built-in demand for inexpensive and flexible labor stems from four fundamental characteristics of advanced industrial societies and their economies.

The first is structural inflation. Wages not only reflect conditions of supply and demand but confer status and prestige, social qualities that inhere in the jobs to which the wages are attached. In general, people believe that wages should reflect social status, and they have rather rigid notions about the correlation between occupational status and pay. As a result, wages offered by employers are not entirely free to respond to changes in the supply of workers. A variety of informal social expectations and formal institutional mechanisms (such as union contracts, civil service rules, bureaucratic regulations, and company job classifications) ensure that wages correspond to the hierarchies of prestige and status that people perceive and expect.

If employers seek to attract workers for unskilled jobs at the bottom of an occupational hierarchy, they cannot simply raise wages. Raising wages at the bottom of the hierarchy would upset socially defined relationships between status and remuneration. If wages are increased at the bottom, there will be strong pressure to raise wages by corresponding amounts at other levels of the hierarchy. If the wages of busboys are raised in response to a shortage of entry-level workers, for example, they may overlap with those of waitresses, thereby threatening their status and undermining the accepted social hierarchy. Waitresses, in turn, may demand a corresponding wage increase, thus threatening the position of cooks, who will also pressure employers for a raise. Workers may be aided in their efforts by union representatives or contracts.

Thus, the cost to employers of raising wages to attract low-level workers is typically more than the cost of these workers' wages alone; wages must be increased proportionately throughout the job hierarchy in order to keep them in line with social expectations, a problem known as structural inflation. Attracting native workers by raising entry wages during times of labor scarcity is thus expensive and disruptive, providing employers with a strong incentive to seek easier and cheaper solutions, such as the importation of migrant workers who will accept low wages.

The demand for cheap, flexible labor is also augmented by social constraints on motivation embedded within occupational hierarchies. Most people work not only to generate income but also to accumulate social status. Acute motivational problems arise at the bottom of any job hierarchy because there is no status to be maintained and few avenues for upward mobility. The problem is inescapable and structural because the bottom cannot be eliminated from labor markets. Mechanization to eliminate the lowest and least desirable class of jobs will simply create a new bottom tier composed of jobs that used to be just above the bottom rung. Since there always has to be a bottom of any hierarchy, motivational problems are inescapable. What employers need are workers who view bottom-level jobs simply as a means to the end of earning money and for whom employment is reduced solely to income, with no implications for status or prestige.

For a variety of reasons, immigrants satisfy this need, at least at the beginning of their migratory careers. Most migrants begin as target earners, seeking to earn money for a specific goal that will improve their status or well-being at home—building a house, paying for school, buying land, acquiring consumer goods. Moreover, the disjuncture in living standards between developed and developing societies means that even low wages abroad appear to be generous by the standards of the home community; even though a migrant may realize that a foreign job is of low status abroad, he does not view himself as being a part of the receiving society. Rather, he sees himself as a member of his home community, within which foreign labor and hard-currency remittances carry considerable honor and prestige.

The demand for immigrant labor also stems from the inherent duality of labor and capital. Capital is a fixed factor of production that can be idled by lower demand but not laid off; owners of capital must bear the costs of its unemployment. Labor is a variable factor of production that can be released when demand falls, so that workers are forced to bear the costs of their own unemployment. Whenever possible, therefore, capitalists seek out the stable, permanent portion of demand and reserve it for the employment of equipment, whereas the variable portion of demand is met by adding labor. Thus, capital-intensive methods are used to meet basic demand, and labor-intensive methods are reserved for the seasonal, fluctuating component. This dualism creates distinctions among workers, leading to a bifurcation of the labor force.

Workers in the capital-intensive primary sector get stable, skilled jobs working with the best equipment and tools. Employers are forced to invest in these workers by providing specialized training and education. Their jobs are complicated, and because performing them well requires considerable knowledge and experience, firm-specific human capital is accumulated. Primary-sector workers tend to be unionized or highly professionalized, with contracts that require employers to bear a substantial share of the costs of their idling (in the form of severance pay and unemployment benefits). Because of these costs and continuing obligations, workers in the primary sector become expensive to let go; they become more like capital.

In the labor-intensive secondary sector, however, workers hold unstable, unskilled jobs; they may be laid off at any time with little or no cost to the employer. Indeed, the employer will generally lose money by retaining workers during slack periods. The first act of secondary-sector employers during down cycles is to cut their payroll. As a result, employers force workers in this sector to bear the costs of their unemployment. They remain a variable factor of production and are hence expendable.

Thus, the inherent dualism between labor and capital extends to the labor force in the form of a segmented labor market structure. Low wages, unstable conditions, and the lack of reasonable prospects for mobility in the secondary sector make it difficult to attract native workers, who are instead drawn into the primary, capital-intensive sector, where wages are higher, jobs are more secure, and there is a possibility of occupational improvement. To fill the shortfall in demand within the secondary sector, employers turn to immigrants.

In their analysis of the process by which Cuban immigrants were incorporated into the United States, Alejandro Portes and Robert Bach (1985) uncovered evidence of a third employment sector that blends features of primary and secondary labor markets and also yields a structural demand for immigrant labor. Like the secondary sector, ethnic enclaves contain low-status jobs characterized by low pay, chronic instability, and unpleasant working conditions, jobs that are routinely shunned by natives. Unlike the secondary sector, however, the enclave provides immigrants with significant economic returns to education and experience, as well as the very real prospect of upward socioeconomic mobility, thus replicating features of the primary sector.

Not all immigrations produce ethnic enclaves,

however, and studies suggest they are rather hard to create (Logan, Alba, and McNulty 1994). Indeed, the ethnic enclaves identified to this point have formed under rather unusual circumstances of geographic concentration and distinctively timed, class-selective immigration (Portes and Stepick 1993; Wilson and Martin 1982). In general, an enclave economy emerges when an initial wave of elite immigrants possessing significant amounts of financial, human, social, and cultural capital concentrates disproportionately in one urban area and, after becoming established there and founding new business enterprises, employs successive waves of lower-status but aspiring immigrants from the same country.

The existence of a large, concentrated population of co-ethnics creates a demand for specialized cultural products and ethnic services that immigrant entrepreneurs are uniquely qualified to fill. In addition, their privileged access to a growing pool of low-wage immigrant labor gives them an advantage when competing with firms outside the enclave. Immigrants working in the enclave trade low wages and the acceptance of strict discipline on arrival for a greater chance of advancement and independence later on (Portes and Bach 1985). The implicit contract between employers and workers stems from a norm of ethnic solidarity (a form of cultural capital), which suffuses and supports the enclave (Portes and Manning 1986; Portes and Rumbaut 1990). At the same time, social networks and personal linkages to other entrepreneurs (a form of social capital) launch new immigrants on independent careers in small business, and once established, these new entrepreneurs are expected to help and promote other immigrants in return (cultural capital again). The prospects for enclave formation are especially enhanced if the initial immigrants are well educated and possess organizational or business skills (human capital), or if they have access to savings, credit, or government assistance (financial capital).

Although an ethnic enclave may begin with the immigration of entrepreneurs, in order to function effectively over time it requires a steady stream of new workers willing to trade low initial wages for the possibility of later mobility, yielding an independent structural source of labor demand for immigrant workers and complementing that emanating from the secondary sector. As immigrant entrepreneurs arrive, concentrate geographically, and establish new business enterprises that rely on immigrant labor for their survival, immigration can, quite literally, generate its own demand.

The problems of motivation and structural inflation inherent in modern occupational hierarchies, together with the dualism intrinsic to market economies, create a permanent demand for workers who are willing to labor under unpleasant conditions, at low wages, with great instability and little chance for advancement. In the past this demand was met partially by three sets of people with social statuses and characteristics conducive to these sorts of jobs: women, teenagers, and rural-to-urban migrants.

Historically women have tended to participate in the labor force up to the time of the birth of their first child, and to a lesser extent after their children have grown. They have sought to earn supplemental income for themselves or their families. They were not primary breadwinners, and their principal social identity was that of a sister, wife, or mother. They were willing to put up with the low wages and instability because they viewed the work as transient and the earnings as supplemental; the positions they held were not threatening to their main social status, which was grounded in the family.

Likewise, teenagers historically have moved into and out of the labor force with great frequency in order to earn extra money, to gain experience, and to try out different occupational roles. They do not view dead-end jobs as problematic because they expect to get better jobs in the future, after completing school, gaining experience, or settling down. Moreover, teenagers derive their social identities from their parents and families of orientation, not their jobs. They view work instrumentally as a means of earning spending money. The money and the things that it buys enhance their status among their peers (by giving them clothes, cars, music, and so on); the job is just a means to an end.

Finally, rural areas of developed nations for many years provided industrial cities with a steady supply of low-wage workers. Movement from a social and economic backwater to the dynamism and excitement of the city created a sense of upward mobility and personal improvement regardless of the modesty of one's circumstances after migrating, and even menial unskilled jobs in cities provided access to housing, food, and consumer goods that represented a real step up in the world for impoverished migrants from the countryside. As long as large reserves of rural population existed, new industrial nations could look internally to satisfy the emerging demand for unskilled, low-wage labor.

In advanced industrial societies, however, these sources of entry-level workers have shrunk over time because of four fundamental sociodemographic trends: the rise in female labor-force participation, which has transformed women's work into a career pursued for social status as well as income; the rise in divorce rates, which has transformed women's jobs into a source of primary income support; the decline in birth rates and the extension of formal education, which have produced very small cohorts of teenagers entering the labor force; and the urbanization of society, which has eliminated farms and rural communities as potential sources for new migrants to the city. The imbalance between the structural demand for entry-level workers and the limited domestic supply of such workers has generated an underlying, long-run demand for immigrants in developed countries.

Segmented labor market theory neither posits nor denies that actors make rational, self-interested decisions, as predicted by microeconomic models. The negative qualities that people in industrialized countries attach to low-wage jobs, for example, may open up employment opportunities to foreign workers, thereby raising their expected earnings, increasing their ability to overcome risk and credit constraints, and enabling households to achieve relative income gains by sending family members abroad. Recruitment by employers helps to overcome informational and other constraints on international movement, enhancing migration's value as a strategy for family income generation or risk diversification.

World Systems Theory

A social theory approach emerged during the 1950s in response to functionalist theories of social change and development, which held that countries develop economically by progressing through an orderly series of evolutionary stages culminating in modernization and industrialization. In contrast, historical-structural theorists argued that because political power is unequally distributed across nations, the expansion of global capitalism acts to perpetuate inequalities and reinforce a stratified economic order. Rather than experiencing an inexorable progression toward development and modernization, poor countries in reality are trapped by their disadvantaged position within an unequal geopolitical structure, which perpetuates their poverty.

Historical-structural theory reached its peak of influence during the 1960s and 1970s, and it gained particular currency among social scientists in Latin America. Theorists such as Celso Furtado (1965, 1970) and Fernando Cardoso and Enzo Faletto (1969, 1979) observed a deterioration in the terms of trade between wealthy capitalist countries and poor nations in the years after World War II and concluded that developing nations were being forced into dependency by structural conditions dictated to them by powerful capitalist countries. According to Andre Gundre Frank (1969) the forces of global capitalism acted to "develop underdevelopment" within the Third World. This line of historical-structural thinking became known as dependency theory and ultimately embraced a diverse group of scholars who drew inspiration from the work of Paul Baran (1957, 1973) and his conceptualization of the ideas of Marx and Lenin.

A second line of historical-structural theory emerged somewhat later and drew on the work of the dependency theorists, as well as the historiography of the French social historian Fernand Braudel (1981, 1982). Its leading exponent was Immanuel Wallerstein (1974, 1980), who undertook a comprehensive analysis of the global expansion of the capitalist system from the sixteenth century onward. Wallerstein sought to reconstruct the historical processes by which unequal political and economic structures were created and extended throughout the world, and the mechanisms by which noncapitalist and precapitalist regions were incorporated into the global market economy. He classified countries according to their degree of dependency on the dominant capitalist powers, which he termed "core" nations. Those on the "periphery" were the most dependent, whereas those on the "semiperiphery" had slightly more independence in the global marketplace. Nations in the "external arena" remained isolated and largely outside the global capitalist system. Given the scope of this work and its sweeping vision of an expanding global capitalism, this line of thought became known generally as "world systems theory" (Simmons 1989).

At first neither world systems theorists nor dependency theorists had much interest in international migration. During the 1960s and 1970s they focused instead on rural-to-urban migrants and their insertion into the informal urban economy. In contrast to economic theorists such as Michael Todaro (1969, 1976) and sociological theorists such as Everett Lee (1966), who viewed migration as a rational calculation made by individuals to secure material improvement, historical-structural theorists linked migration to the macro-organization of socioeconomic relations, the geographic division of labor, and the political mechanisms of power and domination (see Singer 1971, 1975; Stern 1988).

Only after the economic recessions of the mid-1970s did observers begin to understand that international flows were not just a "temporary" aberration, and that international migration also might be linked to the structural changes that accompanied a nation's insertion into the global marketplace. As the absorption of foreigners emerged as a political issue throughout the developed world, scholars began to apply the precepts of historical-structural theory to analyze the flows of labor they were suddenly observing with new eyes. Like their intellectual forebears, theorists such as Alejandro Portes and John Walton (1981), Elizabeth Petras (1981), Saskia Sassen (1988), and Ewa Morawska (1990) sought to explain international migration not as a product of individual or household decisions but as a structural consequence of the expansion of markets within a global political hierarchy. Although their propositions up to now have not formed a coherent theory so much as a general approach to the study of international migration, historical-structural explanations are generally synthesized under the rubric of "world systems theory."

This theory argues that the penetration of capitalist economic relations into noncapitalist or precapitalist societies creates a mobile population that is prone to migrate. Driven by a desire for higher profits and greater wealth, owners and managers of capitalist firms in core countries enter poorer nations on the periphery of the world economy in search of land, raw materials, labor, and consumer markets. In the past this market penetration was assisted by colonial regimes that administered poor regions for the benefit of economic interests in colonizing societies. Today it is made possible by neocolonial governments and multinational firms that perpetuate the power of national elites who either participate in the world economy as capitalists themselves or offer their nation's resources to global firms on acceptable terms.

World systems theorists posit that international migration emerges in response to the disruptions and dislocations that inevitably occur in the process of capitalist development. As capitalism has expanded outward from its core in Western Europe, North America, Oceania, and Japan, ever larger portions of the globe and growing proportions of the human population have been incorporated into the market economy. To explain how migration flows are generated, some of which have moved abroad, theorists have considered how the influence of global markets is exerted over land, raw materials, and labor within peripheral regions (Massey 1988).

In order to achieve the greatest profit from existing agrarian resources and to compete within global commodity markets, capitalist farmers in peripheral areas seek to consolidate landholding, mechanize production, introduce cash crops, and apply industrially produced inputs such as fertilizer, insecticides, and high-yield seeds. Land consolidation destroys traditional systems of land tenure based on inheritance and common rights of usufruct. Mechanization decreases the need for manual labor and makes many agrarian workers redundant to production. The substitution of cash crops for staples undermines traditional social and economic relations based on subsistence (Chayanov 1966), and because the use of modern inputs produces high crop yields at low unit prices, small, noncapitalist farmers are driven out of local markets. All of these forces contribute to the creation of a mobile labor force displaced from the land with a weakened attachment to local agrarian communities.

The extraction of raw materials for sale on global markets requires industrial methods that rely on paid labor. The offer of wages to former peasants undermines traditional forms of social and economic organization based on norms of reciprocity and fixed role relations and creates incipient labor markets based on new conceptions of individualism, private gain, and social change. These trends likewise promote the geographic mobility of labor in developing regions, often with international spillovers.

Firms from core capitalist countries enter developing countries to establish assembly plants that take advantage of low wage rates, often within special export-processing zones created by sympathetic governments. The demand for factory workers strengthens local labor markets and weakens traditional productive relations. Much of the labor demanded is female, however, and the resulting feminization of the workforce limits opportunities for men; since the new factory work is demanding and poorly paid, however, women tend to work only a few years, after which time they leave to look for new opportunities. The insertion of foreign-owned factories into peripheral regions thus undermines the local economy by producing goods that compete with those made locally; by feminizing the workforce without providing factory-based employment opportunities for men; and by socializing women for industrial work and modern consumption, albeit without providing a lifetime income capable of meeting these needs. The result is the creation of a population that is socially and economically uprooted and prone to migration.

The same capitalist economic processes that create migrants in peripheral regions simultaneously attract them into developed countries. Although some people displaced by the process of market penetration move to cities, leading to the urbanization of developing societies, inevitably many are drawn abroad because globalization creates material, military, and ideological links to the places where capital originates. The foreign investment that drives economic globalization is managed from a small number of global cities, whose structural characteristics create a strong demand for immigrant labor.

In order to ship goods, deliver machinery, extract and export raw materials, coordinate business operations, and manage expatriate assembly plants, capitalists in core nations build and expand transportation and communication links to the peripheral countries where they have invested. These links not only facilitate the movement of goods, products, information, and capital but promote the movement of people by reducing the costs of movement along certain international pathways. Because investment and globalization are inevitably accompanied by the buildup of a transportation and communication infrastructure, the international movement of labor generally follows the international movement of goods and capital in the opposite direction.

The creation and perpetuation of a global trading regime requires an underlying system of international security. Core capitalist nations have both an economic interest in geopolitical order and the military means of preserving it; most of the leading powers maintain relatively large armed forces to deploy as needed to preserve the integrity of the global capitalist system. Threats to the stability of that system are often met by military force projected from one or more of the core nations. After 1945, for example, the threat of Communist expansion in Europe presented such a threat to a weakened capitalism that Britain, France, and the United States stationed large numbers of troops permanently on bases throughout the continent. They also periodically dispatched military forces to various hot spots that cropped up in Africa, the Middle East, Asia, and Latin America over the course of the forty-year cold war with the Soviet Union.

As the leading economic and political power in the postwar capitalist world, the United States has played the most important role in preserving international peace and security in the postwar world, maintaining a uniquely large military establishment and frequently dispatching its armed forces to counter leftist insurgencies, turn back Communist invasions, or quell outbreaks of violence that threaten the capitalist order. In the years since 1945 the United States has intervened covertly or overtly in at least a dozen countries: Iran, Guatemala, Nicaragua, Cuba, the Dominican Republic, Haiti, Grenada, Chile, Somalia, and, of course, Vietnam, Cambodia, and Korea. Most recently it led a multinational force to restore order (and the flow of oil) in Kuwait. In order to retain its capacity to project military power whenever and wherever it is needed, the United States maintains many large military bases in far-flung areas throughout the world.

Each military base and armed intervention, however, creates a range of social and political connections that promote the subsequent movement of immigrants. Soldiers often acquire local spouses who seek to accompany them home when their tour of duty ends, and in the United States (and many other countries) spouses have a privileged claim on entry by virtue of their marriage to a citizen. Spouses, in turn, may seek to sponsor the immigration of their brothers, sisters, mothers, fathers, and minor children. These people have their own claims on entry by virtue of their kinship with a legal resident and, if the spouse ultimately naturalizes, by virtue of their kinship with a citizen.

Large-scale military operations also involve the hiring of numerous support personnel from the local civilian population, creating personal relationships, political debts, and moral obligations that may be invoked to gain access to immigrant visas when the military departs or to obtain refugee status in the event that the client state collapses. If the military presence is long-term, moreover, a host of commercial and service establishments inevitably grow up around the base, further expanding the range of personal interactions and social debts and transmitting new linguistic codes and cultural conventions into the local population. Intensive contact with U.S. troops not only increases the odds of matrimony but also inculcates a knowledge of English and U.S. culture that raises the potential rewards of working in the United States and increases the motivation to do so. For these reasons, therefore, significant military deployments are typically accompanied by sizable return flows of immigrants (Donato 1991; Jasso and Rosenzweig 1990; Schmeidl 1997).

Finally, economic globalization creates ideological and cultural links between core capitalist countries and their peripheries through other means besides military intervention. In many cases, these cultural links are long-standing, reflecting a colonial past when core countries established administrative and educational systems that mirrored their own in order to govern and exploit a peripheral region. Citizens of Senegal, for example, learn French, study at lycées, and use a currency directly tied to the French franc in economic transactions. Likewise, Indians and Pakistanis learn English, take British-style degrees, and join with others in a transnational union known as the British Commonwealth. Even in the absence of a colonial past, the influence of economic penetration can be profound: Mexicans increasingly study at U.S. universities, speak English, and follow American consumer styles closely.

These ideological and cultural connections are reinforced by mass communications and advertising campaigns directed from the core countries. Television programming from the United States, France, Britain, and Germany transmits information about lifestyles and living standards in the developed world, and commercials prepared by foreign advertising agencies inculcate modern consumer tastes within peripheral peoples. The diffusion of core-country languages and cultural patterns and the spread of modern consumption patterns interact with the emergence of a transportation and communication infrastructure to channel international migration to particular core countries.

The world economy is managed from a relatively small number of urban centers where banking, finance, administration, professional services, and high-tech production tend to be concentrated (Castells 1989; Sassen 1991). In the United States global cities include New York, Chicago, Los Angeles, and Miami; in Europe they include London, Paris, Frankfurt, and Milan; and in the Pacific, Tokyo, Osaka, and Sydney qualify. Within these global cities, a great deal of wealth and a highly educated workforce are concentrated, creating a strong demand for the services of unskilled workers (busboys, gardeners, waiters, hotel workers, domestic servants). At the same time, the shifting of heavy industrial production overseas; the growth of high-tech manufacturing in electronics, computers, and telecommunications; and the expansion of service sectors such as health and education create a bifurcated labor market structure with strong demand for workers at both the upper and lower ends but with relatively weak demand in the middle.

Poorly educated natives resist taking low-paying jobs at the bottom of the occupational hierarchy, creating a strong demand for immigrants. Meanwhile, well-educated natives and skilled foreigners dominate the lucrative jobs at the upper tier of the occupational distribution, and the concentration of wealth among them helps to fuel the demand for the type of services immigrants are most willing to provide. Native workers with modest educations cling to jobs in the declining middle, migrate out of global cities, or rely on social insurance programs for support.

Social Capital Theory

The economist Glenn Loury (1977) introduced the concept of social capital to designate a set of intangible resources in families and communities that help to promote social development among young people, but Pierre Bourdieu (1986) pointed out its broader relevance to human society. According to Bourdieu and Loic Wacquant (1992, 119), "social capital is the sum of the resources, actual or virtual, that accrue to an individual or a group by virtue of possessing a durable network of more or less institutionalized relationships of mutual acquaintance and recognition."

The key characteristic of social capital is its convertibility: it may be translated into other forms of capital, notably financial capital—in this case, foreign wages and the remittances they permit (Harker, Mahar, and Wilkes 1990). People gain access to social capital through membership in networks and social institutions and then convert it into other forms of capital to improve or maintain their position in society (Bourdieu 1986; Coleman 1990). Although Alejandro Portes and Julia Sensenbrenner (1993) point out that social capital may have negative as well as positive consequences for the individual, theorists generally have emphasized the positive role it plays in the acquisition and accumulation of other forms of capital (see Coleman 1988, 1990), an emphasis that has been particularly strong in work on migrant networks.

Migrant networks are sets of interpersonal ties that connect migrants, former migrants, and nonmigrants in origin and destination areas through ties of kinship, friendship, and shared community origin. They increase the likelihood of international movement because they lower the costs and risks of movement and increase the expected net returns to migration. Network connections constitute a form of social capital that people can draw on to gain access to various kinds of financial capital: foreign employment, high wages, and the possibility of accumulating savings and sending remittances.

Beginning in the 1920s, sociologists recognized the importance of networks in promoting international movement (see Gamio 1930; Thomas and Znaniecki 1918–20). Drawing on social ties to relatives and friends who have migrated before, nonmigrants gained access to knowledge, assistance, and other resources that facilitated movement (Choldin 1973). Charles Tilly and Charles H. Brown (1967) referred to these ties as the "auspices" of migration; others have labeled them "migration chains" (MacDonald and MacDonald 1974); and Mildred Levy and Walter Wadycki (1973) have called them a "family and friends effect." Edward Taylor (1986, 1987) characterizes them as a form of economic "migration capital." My associates and I (1987, 170) appear to have been the first to identify migrant networks specifically as a form of social capital.

Following Coleman's (1990, 304) dictum that "social capital . . . is created when the relations among persons change in ways that facilitate action," My associates and I (1987) identified migration itself as the catalyst for this change in the nature of social relations. Everyday ties of friendship and kinship provide few advantages, in and of themselves, to people seeking to migrate abroad. Once someone in a personal network has migrated, however, the ties are transformed into a resource that can be used to gain access to foreign employment and all that it brings. Each act of migration creates social capital among people to whom the new migrant is related, thereby raising the odds of their migration (Massey et al. 1987; Massey, Goldring, and Durand 1994).

The first migrants who leave for a new destination have no social ties to draw on, and for them migration is costly, particularly if it involves entering another country without documents. After the first migrants have left, however, the potential costs of migration are substantially lowered for friends and relatives left behind. Because of the nature of kinship and friendship structures, each new migrant creates a set of people with social ties to the destination area. Migrants are inevitably linked to nonmigrants, and the latter draw on the obligations implicit in relationships such as kinship and friendship to gain access to employment and assistance at the point of destination.

Networks make international migration extremely attractive as a strategy for risk diversification or utility maximization. When migrant networks are well developed, they put a destination job within easy reach of most community members and make emigration a reliable and secure source of income. Thus, the growth of networks that occurs through the progressive reduction of costs may also be explained theoretically by the progressive reduction of risks. Every new migrant expands the network and reduces the risks of movement for all those to whom he or she is related, eventually making it virtually risk-free and costless to diversify household labor allocations through emigration.

Once international migration has begun, private institutions and voluntary organizations also tend to arise to satisfy the demand created by a growing imbalance between the large number of people who seek entry into capital-rich countries and the limited number of immigrant visas these countries typically offer. This imbalance, and the barriers that core countries erect to keep people out, create a lucrative economic niche for entrepreneurs and institutions dedicated to promoting international movement for profit, yielding a black market in migration. As this underground market creates conditions conducive to exploitation and victimization, voluntary humanitarian organizations also arise in developed countries to enforce the rights and improve the treatment of legal and undocumented migrants (Hagan and Gonzalez-Baker 1993).

Jon Goss and Bruce Lindquist (1995) point to migrant institutions as a structural complement to migrant networks, arguing that interpersonal ties are not the only means by which international movement is perpetuated. Building on ideas put forth by Anthony Giddens (1990), they argue (1995, 345) that

> international migration is best examined not as a result of individual motivations and structural determinations, although these must play a part in any explanation, but as the articulation of agents with particular interests and playing specific roles within an institutional environment, drawing knowledgeably upon sets of rules in order to increase access to resources.

For-profit organizations and private entrepreneurs provide a range of services to migrants in exchange for fees set on the underground market: surreptitious smuggling across borders; clandestine transport to internal destinations; labor contracting between employers and migrants; counterfeit documents and visas; arranged marriages between migrants and legal residents or citizens of the destination country; and lodging, credit, and other assistance in countries of destination (Prothero 1990). Humanitarian groups help migrants by providing counseling, social services, shelter, legal advice about how to obtain legitimate papers, and even insulation from immigration law enforcement authorities (Christiansen 1996). Over time individuals, firms, and organizations become well known to immigrants and institutionally stable, constituting another form of social capital that migrants can draw on to gain access to foreign labor markets. Recruiting agents can at times be active in creating new flows of migration from areas of labor surplus to areas of labor scarcity.

The recognition of a gradual buildup of institutions, organizations, and entrepreneurs dedicated to arranging immigrant entry, legal or illegal, yields hypotheses that are once again quite distinct from those emanating from microlevel decision models. The theory of social capital accepts the view of international migration as an individual or household decision but argues that acts of migration at one point in time systematically alter the context within which future migration decisions are made, greatly increasing the likelihood that later decisionmakers will choose to migrate.

Cumulative Causation

The theory of cumulative causation argues that over time international migration tends to sustain itself in ways that make additional movement progressively more likely, a process that was first identified by Gunnar Myrdal (1957) and that I later reintroduced to the field (Massey 1990). Causation is cumulative in the sense that each act of migration alters the social context within which subsequent migration decisions are made, typically in ways that make additional movement more likely. So far, social scientists have discussed eight ways that migration is affected in this cumulative fashion: the expansion of networks, the distribution of income, the distribution of land, the organization of agriculture, culture, the regional distribution of human capital, the social meaning of work, and the structure of production. Feedbacks through other variables are also possible but have not been systematically treated.

As just discussed, once the number of network connections in an origin area reaches a critical threshold, migration tends to become self-perpetuating because each act of migration creates the social structure needed to sustain it. Every new migrant reduces the costs and risks of subsequent migration for a set of friends and relatives, and some of these people are thereby induced to migrate, thus further expanding the set of people with ties abroad and, in turn, reducing costs for a new set of people, some of whom are now more likely to decide to migrate, and so on. Over time migratory behavior spreads outward to encompass broader segments of the sending society (Hugo 1981; Massey 1990; Massey, Goldring, and Durand 1994; Taylor 1986).

The new economics of migration argues that as a household's sense of relative deprivation increases, so does the motivation to migrate. After one or two households have begun participating in foreign wage labor, the resulting remittances increase their incomes greatly. Given the costs and risks associated with international movement, moreover, the first households to migrate tend to be located in the middle or upper ranges of the local income hierarchy (Massey, Goldring, and Durand 1994). Seeing some families vastly improve their income through migration makes families lower in the income distribution feel relatively deprived, inducing some of them to migrate; income inequality is thus further exacerbated and the sense of relative deprivation among nonmigrants increases, inducing still more families to migrate, and so on (Stark 1991; Stark and Taylor 1989; Taylor 1992).

An important spending target for many migrants, especially those from rural communities, is the purchase of land. But land is often purchased by migrants abroad typically for its prestige value or as a source of retirement income rather than as a productive investment. International migrants are likely to use their higher earnings to purchase farmland, but they are more likely than nonmigrants to let the land lie fallow since foreign wage labor is more lucrative than local agrarian production. This pattern of land use lowers the demand for local farm labor, thereby increasing the pressures for out-migration. The more out-migration there is, the more people there are with access to the funds necessary to buy land, leading to additional purchases by migrants and more land withdrawn from production, creating land shortages and price inflation and still more pressure for out-migration (Mines 1984; Reichert 1981; Rhoades 1978; Wiest 1984).

When migrant households do farm the land they own, moreover, they are more likely than nonmigrant families to use capital-intensive methods (machinery, herbicides, irrigation, fertilizers, and improved seeds) since they have access to capital to finance these inputs. Thus, migrant households need less labor per unit of output than nonmigrant households, thereby displacing local workers from traditional tasks and again increasing the pressures for out-movement (Massey et al. 1987). The more migration, the greater the capitalization of agriculture and the greater the displacement of agrarian labor, leading to still greater migration.

As migration grows in prevalence within a community or nation, it changes values and cultural perceptions in ways that increase the probability of future migration. Among the migrants themselves, experience in an advanced industrial economy changes tastes and motivations (Piore 1979). Although migrants may begin as target earners seeking to make one trip and earn money for a narrow purpose, after migrating they acquire a concept of social mobility and a taste for consumer goods and styles of life that are difficult to attain through local labor. Once someone has migrated, therefore, he or she is very likely to migrate again, and the odds of taking an additional trip rise with the number of trips already taken (Massey 1986).

At the community level, migration becomes deeply ingrained into the repertoire of people's behaviors, and values associated with migration become part of the community's values. For young men, and in many settings young women as well, migration becomes a rite of passage, and those who do not attempt to elevate their status through international movement are considered lazy, unenterprising, and undesirable (Reichert 1982). Eventually knowledge about foreign locations and jobs becomes widely diffused, and values, sentiments, and behaviors characteristic of the core society spread widely within the sending region (Alarcón 1992; Brettell 1979; Goldring 1996a; Massey et al. 1987; Rouse 1989, 1991).

Migration is a selective process that often tends, initially at least, to draw relatively well-educated, skilled, productive, and highly motivated people away from sending communities, although, as pointed out earlier, migration tends to become less selective over time as the costs and risks fall because of network formation; moreover, this initial selectivity depends critically on the characteristics of migrant labor markets (Taylor 1987). Sustained out-migration thus may lead to the depletion of human capital in sending regions and its accumulation in receiving areas, enhancing the productivity of the latter while lowering that of the former. Over time, therefore, the accumulation of human capital reinforces economic growth in receiving areas while its simultaneous depletion in sending areas exacerbates their stagnation, thereby further enhancing the conditions for migration (Greenwood 1981, 1985; Greenwood, Hunt, and McDowell 1987; Myrdal 1957). Programs of school construction and educational expansion in sending areas reinforce this cumulative migration process because raising educational levels in peripheral rural areas increases the potential returns to migration and gives people a greater incentive to leave for urban destinations at home or abroad.

Within receiving societies, once immigrants have been recruited into particular occupations in significant numbers, those jobs become culturally labeled as "immigrant jobs" and native workers are reluctant to fill them, reinforcing the structural demand for immigrants. Immigration changes the social definition of work, causing a certain class of jobs to be stigmatized and viewed as culturally inappropriate for native workers (Böhning 1972, 1984; Piore 1979). The stigma comes from the presence of immigrants, not from the characteristics of the job. In most European countries, for example, jobs in automobile manufacturing came to be considered immigrant jobs, whereas in the United States they are considered native jobs.

In any bounded population, of course, processes of cumulative causation cannot continue ad infinitum. If migration continues long enough, networks eventually reach a point of numerical saturation within any particular community. More and more community members reside in branch settlements overseas, and virtually all of those at home are connected to someone living abroad or having substantial foreign experience. When networks reach such a high level of elaboration, the costs of migration do not fall as sharply with each new migrant, and migration loses its dynamic momentum for growth. The prevalence of migration in the community approaches an upper limit, and migratory experience becomes so diffused that the stock of potential new migrants becomes very small and is increasingly composed of women, children, and the elderly.

If migration continues long enough, local labor shortages and rising wages in the home community may further dampen the pressures for emigration (Gregory 1986), causing the rate of entry into the international migrant workforce to trail off (Hatton and Williamson 1994a). Observed at the national level, this trend may be difficult to detect because new communities are continuously incorporated into the migratory stream. As the rate of out-migration decelerates in places with longer histories of migration, new areas are drawn into transnational circuits and their rates of migration begin to accelerate. As a result, the total outflow from the nation as a whole may continue to grow as migration spreads from place to place.

Nevertheless, migratory experience eventually becomes widely diffused even across communities, and observers have identified the historical emergence of a characteristic "migration curve" in national populations that have made the transition from emigration to immigration. According to Sune Ackerman (1976), this curve starts at low levels and rises to a peak before declining, yielding what Philip Martin and Edward Taylor (1996) have called a "migration hump" that countries experience in the course of economic development. Timothy Hatton and Jeffrey Williamson (1994b, 9–10) note that "the upswing of the emigration cycle usually coincide[s] with industrialization and rising real wages at home [as] demographic forces, industrialization, and the mounting stock of previous emigrants abroad all serve to drive up the emigration rate. . . . As these forces weakened [historically], the narrowing gap between home and foreign wages began to dominate and emigration receded."

A Synthetic Theoretical Account

Because the above theories posit causal mechanisms operating at multiple levels of aggregation, the various explanations are not necessarily contradictory. It is entirely possible for individuals to engage in cost-benefit calculations; for households to minimize risk and overcome barriers to capital and credit; for both individuals and households to draw on social capital to facilitate international movement; and for the socioeconomic context within which migration decisions are made to be determined by structural forces operating at the national and international levels, often influenced by migration itself. Thus, a synthetic approach to theory construction would seem to be in order.

I recently participated in two major intellectual projects that sought to achieve precisely this kind of synthesis. The first was the Committee on South-North Migration of the International Union for the Scientific Study of Population (IUSSP), which undertook a review of empirical research on population movements into the world's five principal immigrant-receiving areas: North America, Western Europe, the Persian Gulf, Asia and the Pacific, and the Southern Cone of South America. In the course of an exhaustive, five-year, system-by-system analysis, the committee reviewed every available piece of empirical information published since around 1960 to evaluate the efficacy of propositions associated with the various theoretical models, yielding a bibliography that ultimately contained more than nine hundred entries. (For the results of this review, see Massey et al. [1998]; interim findings were published in Massey et al. [1993, 1994] and in Taylor et al. [1996a, 1996b]).

A second project sought to achieve a synthetic understanding of the forces producing and sustaining international migration by analyzing the specific case of Mexico-U.S. migration, the largest sustained flow of immigrants anywhere in the world. This work grows out of an ongoing study that has surveyed documented and undocumented Mexican migrants for more than a decade (see Durand and Massey 1992; Massey et al. 1987; Massey et al. 1994; Massey 1998). With Kristin Espinosa I used these data to test competing theoretical explanations directly against one another within a common statistical framework. We drew on life histories compiled for some thirty-seven-hundred household heads originating in twenty-five separate communities to estimate longitudinal models predicting the likelihood of initial, repeat, and return migration between Mexico and the United States (Massey and Espinosa 1997). So as to broaden the study's inferential base, these communities ranged from rural hamlets to large urban areas and included a variety of economic bases: agrarian villages, commercial agricultural towns, industrial cities, mining towns, fishing villages, tourist cities, as well as a number of diverse metropolitan economies. The resulting data have been shown to be remarkably representative of the entire population of Mexican migrants to the United States (Massey and Zenteno forthcoming).

Together these two efforts provide an unusually firm basis for constructing an empirically grounded, synthetic theory of international migration. Unlike earlier efforts, the IUSSP evaluation is comparative, considering *all* disciplines, *all* contemporary migration systems, and the *entire* world literature on immigration. Likewise, although the Massey and Espinosa (1997) evaluation focuses on just one case, it is comprehensive in the sense that it examines variables operating at multiple levels simultaneously and employs a fully dynamic longitudinal model for statistical analysis. Although, owing to limitations of space, I cannot cite specific studies and statistical estimates to buttress each point, the ensuing synthesis is nonetheless supported by the accumulated record of empirical research and consistent with the best empirical work done to date.

International migration originates in the social, economic, cultural, and political transformations that accompany the penetration of capitalist markets into nonmarket and premarket societies (as hypothesized under world systems theory). In the context of a globalizing economy, the entry of markets and capital-intensive production technologies into peripheral regions disrupts existing social and economic arrangements and brings about a displacement of people from customary livelihoods, creating a mobile population of workers who actively search for new ways of achieving economic sustenance. International migrants tend not to come from poor, isolated places that are disconnected from world markets, but from regions and nations that are undergoing rapid change and development as a result of their incorporation into global trade, information, and production networks. In the short run, therefore, international migration does not stem from a lack of economic development, but from development itself.

One means by which people displaced from traditional livelihoods seek to ensure their economic well-being is by selling their services on emerging national and international labor markets (neoclassical economics). Because wages are generally higher in urban than in rural areas, much of this process of labor commodification is expressed in the form of rural-to-urban migration. This movement occurs even when the probability of obtaining an urban job is low, because when multiplied by high urban wages, even low employment probabilities yield expected incomes above those prevailing in rural areas, where wages and employment are both low. According to the neoclassical model, if the difference between incomes expected in urban and rural sectors exceeds the costs of movement between them, as is typical, people will migrate to cities to reap higher lifetime earnings.

Wages are even higher, of course, in developed countries overseas, and the larger size of these international wage differentials prompts some people displaced in the course of economic development to offer their services on international labor markets by moving abroad for work. International wage differentials are not the only factor motivating people to migrate, however, or even the most important. People displaced in the course of economic growth do not move simply to reap higher lifetime earnings by relocating permanently to a foreign setting (although some do). Rather, households struggling to cope with the jarring transformations of economic development use international migration as a means of overcoming market failures that threaten their material well-being (the new economics of labor migration).

In most developing countries, labor markets—both rural and urban—are volatile and characterized by wide oscillations and structural limitations that render them unable to absorb streams of workers being displaced from precapitalist or noncapitalist sectors. Since national insurance markets are rudimentary and government unemployment insurance programs are limited or nonexistent, households cannot adequately protect themselves from risks to their well-being stemming from under- or unemployment. Thus, the lack of access to unemployment insurance creates an incentive for families to self-insure by sending one or more members overseas for work. By allocating members to different labor markets in multiple geographic regions—rural, urban, and foreign—a household can diversify its labor portfolio and reduce risks to income, as long as conditions in the various labor markets are weakly or negatively correlated (new economics of migration).

Household members who remain behind to participate in the ongoing structural transformation of agriculture, meanwhile, generally lack access to insurance markets for crops and futures. As households shift from subsistence to commercial farming, they are forced to adopt new production methods that make use of untested technologies, unfamiliar crops, and untried inputs. As they plunge into the unknown world of capitalist production, the lack of insurance or futures markets leaves them vulnerable to economic disaster should these new methods fail, providing yet another incentive for families to self-insure against risk through international migration. Should crops fail or commodity prices fall precipitously, households with at least one worker employed overseas will not be left without a means of subsistence (new economics of migration).

Another failure common to developing countries occurs in capital and consumer credit markets. Families seeking to engage in new forms of agriculture or looking to establish new business enterprises need capital to purchase inputs and begin production. The shift to a market economy also creates new consumer demands for expensive items such as housing, automobiles, and appliances. The financing of both production and consumption requires cash, but the weak and poorly developed banking industries characteristic of most developing nations cannot meet the demands for loans and credit, giving households one final motivation for international labor migration. By sending a family member temporarily abroad for work, a household can accumulate savings and overcome failures in capital and consumer credit markets by self-financing production or consumption (new economics of migration).

Whereas the rational actor posited by neoclassical economics takes advantage of geographic disequilibria in labor markets to move abroad *permanently* to achieve higher lifetime earnings, the rational actor assumed by the new economics of labor migration seeks to cope with failures in insurance, futures, capital, and credit markets by moving overseas *temporarily* to repatriate earnings in the form of regular remittances or lump-sum transfers. In this way the household of this rational actor controls risk by diversifying sources of income and self-finances production or consumption by acquiring alternate sources of capital.

Thus, although wage differentials, the favored explanatory factor of neoclassical economics, may account for some of the historical and temporal variation in international migration, failures in capital, credit, futures, and insurance markets, key factors hypothesized by the new economics of labor migration, are also powerful causes. In purely theoretical terms, wage differentials are neither necessary nor sufficient for international migration to occur. Even with equal wages across labor markets, people may have an incentive to migrate if other markets are inefficient or poorly developed.

Although the early phases of economic development in poor nations may create a mobile population seeking to earn more money, self-insure against risk, or self-finance production or consumption, postindustrial patterns of economic growth in wealthy nations yield a bifurcation of labor markets. Jobs in the primary sector provide steady work and high pay for native workers, while those in the secondary sector offer low pay, little stability, and few opportunities for advancement, repelling natives and generating a structural demand for immigrant workers (segmented labor market theory). The process of labor market bifurcation is most acute in global cities, where a concentration of managerial, administrative, and technical expertise leads to a concentration of wealth and a strong ancillary demand for low-wage services (world systems theory). Unable to attract native workers, employers turn to immigrants and often initiate immigrant flows directly through formal recruitment (segmented labor market theory).

Although instrumental in initiating immigration, recruitment becomes less important over time because the same processes of economic globalization that create mobile populations in developing regions and generate a demand for their services in global cities also create links of transportation and communication, as well as politics and culture, to make the international movement of people possible, even likely (world systems theory). Immigration is also promoted by foreign policies and military actions that core capitalist nations undertake to maintain international security, protect foreign investments, and guarantee access to raw materials; these foreign entanglements create links and obligations that generate ancillary flows of refugees, asylees, and military dependents (world systems theory).

Eventually labor recruitment becomes superfluous, for once begun, immigration displays a strong tendency to continue through the growth and elaboration of migrant networks (social capital theory). The concentration of immigrants in certain destination areas creates a "family and friends effect" that channels immigrants to the same places and facilitates their arrival and incorporation. An enclave economy may form if enough migrants arrive under the right conditions, further augmenting the demand for immigrant workers (segmented labor market theory).

The spread of migratory behavior within sending communities sets off ancillary structural changes, shifting distributions of income and land and modifying local cultures in ways that promote additional international movement. Over time the process of network expansion becomes self-perpetuating because each act of migration creates social infrastructure capable of promoting additional movement (the theory of cumulative causation). As receiving countries implement restrictive policies to counter rising tides of immigrants, they create a lucrative niche into which enterprising agents, contractors, and other middlemen move to create migration-supporting institutions that also serve to connect areas of labor supply and demand for purposes of profit, providing migrants with another resource capable of supporting and sustaining international movement (social capital theory).

During the initial phases of emigration from any sending country, the effects of capitalist penetration, market failure, social networks, and cumulative causation dominate in explaining the flows, but as the level of out-migration reaches high levels and the costs and risks of international movement drop, movement is increasingly determined by international wage differentials (neoclassical economics) and labor demand (segmented labor market theory). As economic growth in sending regions occurs, international wage gaps gradually diminish, and well-functioning markets for capital, credit, insurance, and futures arise, progressively lowering the incentives for emigration. If these trends continue, the country ultimately becomes integrated into the international economy as a developed, capitalist nation, whereupon it undergoes a migration transition: net out-migration progressively winds down, and the former sending nation itself becomes an importer of labor.

Migration Theory Reconsidered

All theories thus play some role in accounting for contemporary patterns and processes of international migration, even though different models may be more relevant to explaining particular migration flows, and different explanations carry different weights in different world regions depending on the local circumstances of history, politics, and geography. Generalizing across all theories, I conclude that a satisfactory theoretical account of international migration must contain at least four elements: a treatment of the structural forces that promote emigration from developing countries; a characterization of the structural forces that attract immigrants into developed nations; a consideration of the motivations, goals, and aspirations of the people who respond to these structural forces by becoming international migrants; and a treatment of the social and economic structures that arise to connect areas of out- and in-migration. Any theoretical explanation that embraces just one of these elements will necessarily be incomplete and misleading and will provide a faulty basis for understanding international migration and developing policies to accommodate it.

Each theory specified to date focuses on just one or two of these four elements, so all are necessary to build a comprehensive, integrated understanding of international migration in the late twentieth century. The leading theoretical treatment of the forces that promote emigration from developing countries is world systems theory. Together, world systems theory, segmented labor market theory, and neoclassical macroeconomics offer explanations for why developed countries attract immigrants. Social capital theory and world systems theory explain how structural links emerge to connect areas of origin and destination. Neoclassical economics and the new economics of labor migration deal with the motivations of the people who become international migrants, and the theory of cumulative causation describes how international migration promotes changes in personal motivations and origin, destination, and intervening structures to give immigration a self-perpetuating, dynamic character.

In this seemingly complete theoretical account of the forces that produce and shape international migration, however, one major factor has been sorely neglected: the state. Even though governments may not be able to control fully the powerful forces promoting and sustaining international migration, state policies clearly have an influence in determining the size and composition of the flows. Yet among the theories reviewed here, surprisingly little attention has been devoted to nation-states or their governments as active agents whose behavior shapes, if not controls, international population movements. Segmented labor market theory considers the state relevant only insofar as it acts on behalf of employers to establish labor recruitment programs. World systems theory treats the state primarily as a handmaiden to capitalist interests, projecting military and political power to expand markets, acquire raw materials, and guarantee free trade. Social capital theory mentions the state only insofar as its use of family reunification criteria in immigrant admissions reinforces the operation of migrant networks. The remaining theoretical paradigms—neoclassical economics, the new economics of labor migration, and the theory of cumulative causation—do not deal directly with the state at all.

In general, therefore, contemporary theories of international migration do not consider the state to be a significant independent actor capable of shaping international migration for its own purposes, or for the purposes of the politicians and bureaucrats who administer it. To the extent that the state is discussed at all, moreover, attention has focused primarily on immigrant-receiving nations; little has been said about the interests and behavior of governments or politicians in regions of origin. Thus, the role of the state in initiating and promoting (or stopping and preventing) international migration is remarkably undertheorized and little studied.

Although scholars have surveyed national immigration policies (see Cornelius, Martin, and Hollifield 1994a; Dib 1988; Kubat 1979b; Papademetriou 1996), conducted case studies of specific state agencies (Calavita 1992), and compiled legislative histories of immigration law in specific countries (Hutchinson 1981), with the recent exception of the as yet unpublished work of Eytan Meyers (1995), they have not attempted to theorize the behavior of governments or the actions of politicians themselves. Hypotheses concerning the interests, role, and behavior of the state constitute a missing link in theories of international migration.

The resurgence of massive global migration in the late twentieth century thus offers many formidable challenges to social scientists, policymakers, and the public. For theoreticians, a principal challenge is to model the behavior of nation-states and political actors, filling a void in the general theory of international migration constructed here. Although the field seems to be on the verge of developing a good theoretical model of the structural forces that promote migration from developing to developed nations, as well as a cogent conceptual understanding of the transnational structures that support this movement and of the personal motivations of the migrants who respond to these structural dynamics, what theorists lack at this point is an adequate account of the motivations, interests, and behavior of the political actors who employ state power to influence these processes, and how their interventions affect outcomes at the individual and aggregate levels.

For empirical researchers perhaps the greatest challenge is to design studies that are more closely connected to theory. In considering empirical research from around the world, its most striking feature is the degree to which it is unconnected not just to a particular theory but to any theory at all. If our knowledge of international migration is to advance, researchers must make greater efforts to familiarize themselves with the principal contemporary theories of international migration and to formulate research designs capable of testing their leading propositions. What is especially needed at this juncture are studies that simultaneously test the propositions of several theories, so that the relative efficacy of different explanations can be directly compared and contrasted. Given the current state of knowledge, the "truth" of a theory is less important than how well it compares with others in explaining international migration. Only a handful of studies anywhere test more than two theories at once, let alone examine all the theoretical paradigms reviewed here; at this point in time the research literature is far too restricted geographically to serve as a satisfying basis for generalization. Too many of the rigorous theoretical tests conducted so far have been based on samples of Mexican rural areas, and rural- and urban-origin emigrants may differ in important ways that are not yet well understood, whereas the case of Mexico-U.S. migration is unique by any criterion.

Perhaps the most profound challenge of all will be faced by citizens and policymakers in migrant-sending and -receiving countries. Inhabitants of the latter will have to move beyond the psychological denial that characterizes their approach to immigration policy. They must develop policies that recognize the inevitability of labor flows within a globalized economy, supported by well-established regional networks of trade, production, investment, and communications. Attempts to suppress population flows that are a natural consequence of a nation's participation in these economic networks will not be successful, but they will present grave threats to individual rights, civil liberties, and human dignity.

In sending societies, meanwhile, citizens and policymakers face different but equally vexing issues. Rather than passively acquiescing to emigration and simply waiting for remittances to materialize, developing countries must actively plan to derive benefits from what is potentially an important engine of economic growth. Unless concrete steps are taken to attract migradollars (migrant remittances and savings) and channel them into productive ends, to capture remittances for purposes of foreign exchange, and to forestall the loss of human capital through emigration, development outcomes are likely to be disappointing.

Finally, the globalization of capital and labor markets and the internationalization of production pose strong challenges to the very concept of the nation-state and the idea of national sovereignty, requiring political leaders and citizens in both sending and receiving nations to move beyond nineteenth-century conceptions of territory and citizenship to more expansive notions that embrace the transnational spaces that are currently being formed throughout the world as a result of massive circular migration. These changes are especially daunting because they occur at a time when the forces of globalization are also producing downward pressure on wages and incomes and rising inequality throughout the world.

These are formidable challenges indeed, but they will have to be met, for international migration will surely continue. Barring an international catastrophe of unprecedented proportions, immigration will most likely expand and grow, for none of the causal forces responsible for immigration show any sign of moderating. The market economy is expanding to ever farther reaches of the globe, labor markets in developed countries are growing more rather than less segmented, transnational migration and trade networks are expanding, large stocks of migration-related human and social capital are forming in sending countries everywhere, and the power of the nation-state is faltering in the face of this transnational onslaught. The twenty-first century will be one of globalism, and international migration will no doubt figure prominently within it.

This chapter draws extensively on collaborative research undertaken with Joaquin Arango, Graeme Hugo, Ali Kouaouchi, Adela Pellegrino, and J. Edward Taylor (see Massey et al. 1998).

3 The Role of Gender, Households, and Social Networks in the Migration Process: A Review and Appraisal

Patricia R. Pessar

THIS REVIEW FOCUSES ON the role of gender, households, and social networks in the migration process. The decision to assemble these three structures in one review essay may strike some as quite natural, and others as arbitrary. The three share an epistemological affinity of sorts. Their inclusion in migration scholarship emerged out of a growing consensus regarding the inadequacy of theories and research that privilege either individual migrants (usually conceived of as males or genderless) or global structures and processes, such as the world system and capital accumulation. The inclusion of mediating units, such as gender, households, and social networks, has helped researchers better account for the causes, consequences, and processes of international migration, and they have provided vehicles for a consideration of broader social scientific concerns, such as the dynamic interplay between structure and agency and the relationship between the local and the global. Although I review the many ways in which scholarship on households, social networks, and gender have increased our understanding of migration, I also suggest ways in which these structures might be reconceptualized to enhance their analytical powers.

The difficulty in assembling gender, households, and social networks in one critical review is that they represent different levels of abstraction, with gender being a central organizing feature of social and cultural life—including households, social networks, *and* migration. For this reason, in my discussions of several alternative migration theories and the role of households and social networks in these formulations, I take care to assess whether gender is incorporated adequately into each theory. I also suggest ways in which theory and research might be more fully engendered.[1]

When gender is brought to the foreground in migration studies, a host of significant topics emerge. These include how and why women and men experience migration differently, and how this contrast affects such processes as settlement, return, and transmigration. A gendered perspective demands a scholarly reengagement with those institutions and ideologies that immigrants create and encounter in the "home" and "host" countries in order to determine how patriarchy organizes family life, work, community associations, law and public policy, and so on. It also encourages an examination of the multiple ways in which migration simultaneously reinforces and challenges patriarchy in its multiple forms.

New immigration research is developing a more sophisticated understanding of gender and patriarchy. It avoids the common fallacy of equating gender only with women, and it acknowledges the "transgressive" fact that nonwhite immigrant males may be stripped of patriarchal status and privilege by white men *and* women (Espiritu 1997). Consequently, a new wave of migration scholarship challenges feminists who insist on the primacy of gender, thereby marginalizing racism and other structures of oppression. In place of theories that treat structures like gender and race as mutually exclusive, this recent work urges us to develop theories and design research that capture the simultaneity of gender, class, race, and ethnic exploitation. As this review essay shows, the payoff is explanatory models that account for outcomes that have largely eluded those who employ more unitary frameworks.

A HISTORICAL OVERVIEW

Although gender, households, and social networks are relatively familiar constructs in contemporary writings on migration, this has not always been the case.

The Migrant As Male

Over a decade ago I wrote (Pessar 1986, 273):

> Until recently the term "migrant" suffered from the same gender stereotyping found in the riddles about the big Indian and the little Indian, the surgeon and the son. In each case the term carried a masculine connotation, unless otherwise specified. While this perception makes for amusing riddles, the assumption that the "true" migrant is male has limited the possibility for generalization from empirical research and produced misleading theoretical premises.

To appreciate why women were largely absent from empirical research and writings produced in the 1950s, 1960s, and early 1970s, it is useful to reflect on the theoretical assumptions guiding a great deal of the migration scholarship during that period. Most scholars were influenced by neoclassical theory; according to one popular variant, those individuals with the ability to project themselves into the role of "Western man" headed off to the cities, where the benefits of modern life could be attained (Lewis 1959; Redfield 1955). And indeed, it was males whom scholars alleged were more apt to be risk-takers and achievers, while women, in their portrayal, were guardians of community tradition and stability. Hence, in Everett Lee's (1966, 51) seminal "push-pull" theory of migration, we learn that "children are carried along by their parents, willy-nilly, and wives accompany their husbands though it tears them away from the environment they love."

Migration research of this period also suffered from the more general tendency to disregard women's contributions to economic, political, and social life. As June Nash (1986, 3) writes: "Whether investigators were influenced by neoclassical, Marxist, dependency or developmentalist paradigms, they tended to stop short of an analysis of women's condition in any but the most stereotyped roles in the family and biological reproduction." The same ideological template operated as labor-importing nations, like France, chose to enumerate immigrant women alongside children as dependents rather than workers in official immigration statistics (Morokvasic 1984).

Not surprisingly, researchers of the day designed studies of immigrant populations that included only male subjects. Thus, in the introduction to their 1975 book on migrant workers in Europe, John Berger and Jean Mohr write: "Among the migrant workers in Europe there are probably two million women. Some work in factories, many work in domestic service. To write of their experience adequately would require a book itself. We hope this will be done. Ours is limited to the experience of the male migrant worker" (8). And in 1985 we find Alejandro Portes explaining that the surveys he conducted over the course of the 1970s with Mexicans and Cubans in the United States had to be restricted to male family heads

> because we felt at the time that an exploratory study, directed at comparison of two immigrant groups over time, would become excessively complex were it to encompass all categories of immigrants. In subsequent interviews, however, respondents were also used as informants about major characteristics of other family members, in particular, their wives. (Portes and Bach 1985, 95)

A male bias also existed in the works of many immigration historians of the period who assumed either that only male immigrants' lives were worthy of official documentation and scrutiny (Handlin 1951/1973; Howe 1976) or that the history of male migrants was gender-neutral, thus making it unnecessary to treat women at all except perhaps in a few pages on the family (Bodnar, Weber, and Simon 1982).

Scholarship on Immigrant Women

It was not until the 1970s that feminist theory began to have an impact on migration studies. Once feminist scholarship gained a foothold, it flourished, and today we have a rich and varied corpus exploring women and migration.[2]

This scholarship progressed through a series of stages common to the broader engagement between feminism and the social sciences. Initially researchers attempted to fill in the gaps resulting from decades of research based predominantly on male immigrants.[3]

In their rush to fill this void, the more empirically minded migration scholars tended to treat gender as a mere variable rather than as a central theoretical concept. For example, in Douglas Gurak and Mary Kritz's writings on Dominican and Colombian immigrants in New York City, we learn of high rates of female labor-force participation—far exceeding rates prior to emigration (1982, 1988). Yet these empirical findings are never contextualized in a larger discussion of gender segmentation within the "sending" and "receiving" labor markets (see, for example, Sassen 1984), nor are they extended through an examination of the impact that women's wage labor has had on gender relations within these immigrant families and the wider communities (Pessar 1986, 1988). Although there is now a sizable body of empirical studies on women immigrants aimed at redressing a tradition of male-bias,[4] we are only beginning to take the next step in reformulating migration theory in light of the "anomalous" and unexpected findings revealed in this body of work. This latest scholarship is leading the way to a more engendered approach to international migration—a topic I take up in the latter half of this review.

The Inclusion of Households and Social Networks in Migration Scholarship

Over the last few decades many migration scholars have also included households and social networks in their research designs and analyses. In my view, the decision to include these constructs involved more than the mere promise they held for elucidating the causes and consequences of migration. They have also proven extremely useful in helping social scientists to rethink and reframe larger theoretical concerns that have been, in turn, incorporated into migration theory.

During this period we have witnessed a concerted movement in the social sciences to insert the concept of contingent agency between the extremes of pure choice and structural determinism. For many migration scholars, households and social networks fit the bill. While macrostructural transformations are understood to unleash migration pressures, it is families and social networks, we are told, that respond to these pressures and determine which members of households and communities actually emigrate (Boyd 1989; Grasmuck and Pessar 1991; Wood 1981).

Significant changes in the way Western intellectuals have come to think about imperialism, global capitalism, modernization, assimilation, and acculturation have also spurred renewed interest in migrant households and social networks (Rouse 1989). The many failures associated with transnational capitalism have fueled a growing skepticism about the merits and intentions of Western development. There has been a repudiation of earlier scholarship, which blamed the shortcomings of modernization on the recipients' maladaptive beliefs and institutions. In its place are works that demonstrate a new respect for "traditional" structures, such as peasant households and kin and fictive-kinship networks (Rouse 1989). Thus, social scientists writing in the early 1970s jettisoned the Wirth-Redfieldian model, with its presumption that internal migrants were totally cut off from their rural roots and had become disorganized and atomized in urban settings. The revisionist position held that migrants were "adjusting," "adapting," and "unified" with the help of social networks that facilitated contact with rural, nonmigrant relatives (Brandes 1975; Kemper 1977; Ross and Weisner 1977). And many social scientists described members of peasant households as rationally and collectively devising redressive strategies when faced with nettlesome socioeconomic, political, and environmental constraints. Researchers came to view internal and international migration as adaptive strategies to reduce risk and maximize gains (Dinerman 1978; Stark 1991; Wiest 1973; Wood 1981, 1982).

We see parallels to this loss of confidence in the purported benefits of state intervention and "modernization" on the U.S. domestic front as well. The U.S. civil rights movement brought immigration scholars up short. They were forced to acknowledge that the link between assimilation and social advancement, long touted and well documented in their research on European immigrants and ethnics, had not, and could not, be replicated by African Americans and other people of color owing to a long history of institutionalized racism (Glazer 1993). With the melting pot's fall from grace, long-popular scenarios of "Americanization" leading inevitably to the breakdown of archaic and maladaptive immigrant institutions were abandoned. New studies emerged in their place that documented (and often celebrated) the persistence and adaptive functions of immigrant ties and institutions. In this revisionist context, immigrant and ethnic social networks were depicted as reservoirs of, and conduits for, the investment of social and cultural capital needed for social and economic adjustment (Light 1972; Portes and Rumbaut 1990; Zhou 1992). Immigrant households and families were similarly hailed as loci of economic survival, resistance, and even, occasionally, social advancement (Glenn 1986; Kibria 1993; Pérez 1986).

In the 1970s economic anthropologists and economic historians began to level a critique against the teleological assumptions that animated much of the writings of dependency and world systems theorists. These critics set out to explain how capitalism, rather than necessarily replacing noncapitalist modes of production, could coexist with them and might even strengthen them (Kearney 1986). In the complex economy of migrant households, these researchers found a nexus for the articulation of capitalist and "domestic" modes of production. And, they argued, many migrant households and communities proved successful in resisting total proletarianization by participating in both noncapitalist and capitalist modes of production (de Janvry and Garramon 1977; Griffith 1985; Meillassoux 1981).

Feminist scholarship contributed to this revisionist moment. It critiqued treatments of capitalism and development that privileged male production and male workspaces while disregarding the role women's domestic labor plays in providing surplus value within different capitalist formations (Boserup 1970; Fox 1980; Kuhn and Wolpe 1978). Consequently, by including the household in their studies, several migration scholars were able to offer a more complete analysis of surplus extraction within the migration process (Grasmuck and Pessar 1991; Martin and Beittel 1987) than were available in those accounts that focused exclusively on the migrant worker.

In describing these processes of social and economic articulation at the level of both households and social networks (Uzzell 1979; Whiteford 1981), migration scholars were also contributing to a movement in the social sciences away from the constraints imposed by hermetic and ahistorical community studies. In households and social networks, researchers found more adequate analytical constructs with which to examine the ways in which "the local" is "*always* in flux, in a perpetual historically sensitive state of resistance and accommodation to broader processes of influence that are as much inside as outside the local context" (Marcus and Fischer 1986, 78). Moreover, writings about "transnational households" (Grasmuck and Pessar 1991; Yanagisako 1985), "transnational migration circuits" (Rouse 1989), "articulatory migration networks" (Kearney 1986), "global ethnoscapes" (Appadurai 1990), and "transmigrants" (Basch, Glick Schiller, and Blanc-Szanton 1994; Glick Schiller, Basch, and Blanc-Szanton 1992b) provided new ways of capturing and studying the ways in which people experience and constitute lives in expansive, deterritorialized spaces where social borders do not necessarily conform to national borders. They also offered a vocabulary and framework to move beyond teleological and orientalist binarisms such as "developed" and "underdeveloped" and "First World" and "Third World."

Having observed several ways in which migration scholars' inclusion of households and social networks has facilitated an engagement with broad theoretical concerns, we now turn to a consideration of the manner in which the constructs of the household and social networks have been incorporated into major theories of migration. We also consider the degree to which these theories have proven conducive to studying the role of gender in the migration process.

Households, Social Networks, and Gender in Migration Theories

Neoclassical theory, the first prominent and long-lived theory of migration, actually failed to recognize the importance of either households or social networks (Lewis 1954). According to its proponents, the macroeconomic context for international migration is the wage gap, and actual incidences of out-migration are based on the decisions of individual, rational actors who choose to migrate after a cost-benefit analysis indicates that definitive gains will follow from relocation. Migration is viewed as a self-regulating mechanism to restore equilibrium between "sending" areas, which temporarily possess an excess of labor relative to demand, and "receiving" areas, where capital resources exceed human resources (Spengler and Myers 1977).

When gender is included in such research, it is treated as but one of many determinants in a wage regression analysis. It also assumes that the way in which human capital is translated into wages is the same for women and men (Taylor 1987). This approach begs larger issues, such as the way in which local and external labor markets utilize gender to segment the workforce, thus creating differential incentives for the relocation of men and women. It also overlooks the existence of patriarchal kinship and gender ideologies that may constrain women from migrating regardless of the expected net financial gains from such relocation (Lindstrom 1991).

Over the last few decades advocates of a new approach, termed the "new economics" of migration, have disputed the neoclassicists' assumptions that individuals emigrate only to redress imbalances in international wage rates. Rather, these researchers argue, the true decisionmaking unit is the *household,* not the autonomous individual. This "collective unit" seeks not only to maximize anticipated income but also to minimize risks and to loosen constraints associated with a variety of market failures extending well beyond the labor market (for example, future markets and capital markets) (Taylor 1986).

As Douglas Massey and his collaborators note in

their excellent reviews and appraisals of this and other alternative migration theories (1993, 1994), the new economics perspective can incorporate and account for findings from recent migration research that escape the explanatory power of neoclassical theory. First, there is a growing body of research that shows that households use international migration in a concerted fashion to diversify their labor portfolios (Dinerman 1978; Roberts 1982; Wiest 1973). Second, the new economics, along with other more recent theories of international migration, provides a corrective to the neoclassical assumption that labor-exporting and labor-importing communities and countries are economically autonomous entities. Neoclassicists fail to see how income transfers in the form of remittances and savings contribute to local consumption and production in labor-sending communities; the new economics school factors these inputs into their understanding of the causes, consequences, and processes of migration. They argue, for example, that migrant households routinely increase their levels of consumption and production locally, and that these activities create invidious comparisons on the part of nonmigrant households, whose members may, in turn, come to view out-migration as a solution to their own relative decline in status (Stark, Taylor, and Yitzhaki 1986; Stark and Taylor 1989). This dynamic model also allows for the contingency whereby migrant households' investments of remittances and savings actually promote multiple stints of migration, as members come to rely on out-migration as a mechanism to overcome local capital and risk constraints on investing. In this way, the new economics school helps elucidate the frequent observation that economic development within sending regions need not reduce the pressures for international migration (Massey et al. 1993).

Although the new economics school represents some advancement over neoclassical scholarship, gender again is largely absent from its analysis. For example, researchers limit their analyses to household members' cost-benefit calculations gauged to the market economy and neglect to consider how these calculations may also be informed by what might be called the household political economy. To illustrate, when unmarried Dominican women urge their parents to allow them to emigrate alone, parents weigh the threat to the family's reputation posed by the daughter's sexual freedom and possible promiscuity against the very real economic benefits her emigration will bring. Similarly, in assessing the benefits of return migration, many Dominican immigrant women weigh anticipated personal losses against collective household gains. That is, the women measure the personal gains in gender parity that settlement and blue-collar employment in the United States have brought them against the likelihood of "forced retirement" for the women back on the island in order to mark the family's status gains (Pessar 1995b).

Proponents of *network theory* have also offered a much needed revision of neoclassical theory. They dismiss the neoclassicists' narrow focus on human capital alone and recognize that for many people in developing countries who lack educational and financial resources, network connections provide a valuable form of social capital. Such networks, they argue, are an important component of individual and household economic strategies, including migration. Accordingly, migration scholars have employed network analysis to explain individual intentions to migrate (De Jong et al. 1983), the process of migrant adaptation and settlement (Boyd 1989), and the rates and probabilities of emigration to specific localities (Levy and Wadycki 1973). With rare exceptions (Lindstrom 1991), network theorists have treated migrants as genderless subjects (Taylor 1986).

In contrast to neoclassical, new economics, and network theories, which view international migration as emanating from the rational calculations of individuals or households responding largely to market forces, the *historical-structuralist* perspective features the global penetration of capitalism into peripheral, noncapitalist societies. Theorists who adopt this stance find the origins of contemporary labor migration in the centuries-old processes whereby subsistence economies have become destabilized by agents of merchant and industrial capital, leaving a labor reserve behind in their wake (Burawoy 1976; Portes and Walton 1981). They argue further that the same global circuits that bring capital, technology, and modern forms of transportation, communication, and consumer culture to the periphery from advanced industrial nations also serve as conduits of "surplus" labor from these areas back to select sites (for example, global cities) and labor market sectors (such as the secondary sector and the ethnic enclave) within core nations (Castells 1989; Sassen 1988, 1991). As described in the next section, several theorists have managed to examine the global economy through a gendered optic in order to assess how trends like flexible accumulation have differential impacts on the demand for male and female labor and on incentives for migration (Fernández-Kelly 1983; Lowe 1996; Safa 1995;

Sassen 1996a). There is no doubt that the historical-structuralists have succeeded in directing our attention beyond ahistorical, microlevel structures and processes by incorporating such crucial elements as capital penetration and accumulation, imperialism, the international division of labor, dual labor markets, and global cities into migration theory. However, as Robert Bach and Lisa Schraml observed back in 1982 (324), "perhaps because of these achievements, the historical-structural literature now suffers from excessive repetitions of the functions of labor migration in the development of world capitalism. . . . In a sense we have developed good political-economy but insufficient migration theory."

They, in the company of many other scholars of migration, concluded that intermediary social structures positioned between the individual migrant and macroeconomic structures and processes had to be isolated and studied. In the concepts of the household and social networks, these migration scholars have found appropriate constructs to study individuals' interpretations and responses to broad-based transformations as well as emigration's cumulative impact on communities, regions, and nations (Boyd 1989; Dinerman 1978; Kearney 1986; Massey et al. 1987; Wiest 1973). As will be described shortly, feminist scholars have managed to expand the explanatory power of historical-structural theory by both abandoning earlier notions of socially undifferentiated households and social networks and replacing them with a deep appreciation for gender and generational hierarchies.

Finally, migration scholars have been at the forefront of developing global and transnational theories. In theorizing about deterritorialized identities, cultural productions, and social practices, migration scholars have frequently drawn on the metaphor of a network. Michael Kearney (1986, 558) claims, for example, that "decentered" transnational and global subjects inhabit "reticular social forms . . . which ramify into nations, communities, and many other social bodies and spaces." And Linda Basch, Nina Glick Schiller, and Cristina Blanc-Szanton (1994, 7) define "'transnationalism' as the processes by which immigrants forge and sustain multi-stranded social relations that link together their societies of origin and settlement." Much of the scholarship on transnational migration has concentrated on both the political, economic, and social conditions that promote transnational network formation and the material and social capital that crosses national borders. Less attention has been paid to the production, reception, and character of those cultural items that also cross national borders (Levitt 1999) and may, in turn, encourage out-migration. A notable exception is Arjun Appadurai's (1990) framework for the study of global cultural flows. What is perhaps of most direct relevance to migration scholarship in this theoretically rich framework is Appadurai's proposition that deterritorialized persons (such as tourists, immigrants, and refugees) and deterritorialized ideas, images, and fantasies (transmitted via globalizing forms of media and advertising) encourage persons who are socially embedded in a given locale and habituated to a specific set of identities and practices to imagine a new cartography and to entertain new life possibilities—including migration and exile (see also Clifford 1997). Researchers have also directed our attention to the ways in which global cultural and economic flows may be perceived as threatening to "primordial" identities and loyalties experienced in religious, ethnic, and nationalist terms (Appadurai 1996; Glick Schiller, Basch, and Blanc-Szanton 1995; Sassen 1996b). These perceived threats may, in turn, encourage collective efforts to reassert or reconstitute social boundaries. Subsequent "redressive" actions like ethnic separatism, ethnic conflict, and immigration restriction may have profound impacts on migration.

Households have assumed a place within *transnational migration theory* as well. Researchers stress that household members often develop economic strategies that transcend national labor markets and pursue social reproduction strategies that may similarly stretch across national divides—as, for example, when immigrant women work abroad as nannies and housekeepers while their children remain in their countries of origin (Hondagneu-Sotelo and Avila 1997). Recent work on this phenomenon, termed "transnational mothering," has raised important questions about the meanings, variations, and inequities of motherhood in the late twentieth century. Although gender has been raised as an important point of inquiry by several scholars of transnationalism (Georges 1992; Goldring 1996b; Sutton 1992), it has yet to be adequately incorporated into transnational theory and scholarship.

Shortcomings in the Conceptualization of Households and Social Networks

There is general agreement that the inclusion of the household and social networks in migration theory has helped to elucidate the factors that precipitate and sustain migration, as well as condition its effects. Simultaneously, however, there have been calls to refine the ways in which these analytical constructs have been conceptualized and operationalized.

Rethinking the Household

Criticism has been primarily leveled at formulations of the household. Of the variety of conceptualizations of the household available in social science literature, two perspectives have had a disproportionate impact on migration studies. The first portrays the household as a moral economy, exhibiting social solidarity and income pooling among its members. The second perspective, while not contradictory to the first, emphasizes the role households play in developing strategies for survival—by which is usually meant strategies aimed at maximizing economic gains and adapting to larger structural inequities.

Inspired by feminist scholarship, critics have objected to the moral-economy narrative, which holds that migrant households are organized solely on principles of reciprocity, consensus, and altruism. Although household members' orientations and actions may sometimes be guided by norms of solidarity, these critics have countered, they may equally be informed by hierarchies of power along gender and generational lines; thus, the tension, dissension, and coalition building these hierarchies produce within the migration process also must be examined (Grasmuck and Pessar 1991). A particularly graphic example of a lack of consensus among household members is provided by Pierrette Hondagneu-Sotelo (1994, 43), who describes a young Mexican wife whose fear of abandonment by her migrant husband leads her to pray that he will be apprehended by the border patrol and sent back home to her and her young children. In the sociologist's words: "Once we actually listen to the voices of Mexican immigrants . . . the notion that migration is driven by collective calculations or household-wide strategies becomes increasingly difficult to sustain" (55).

Part of our failure to perceive dissension and contestation may come from researchers' tendencies to assume rather than empirically demonstrate that individual acts of migration emanate from collective household decisionmaking. Another contributing factor, I suspect, is our willingness to take informants' statements at face value rather than interpreting their words dialogically. To advance broader claims to being a family that is both respectable and economically secure, members of rural households may draw on the rhetorical trope of a unitary household, under the undisputed authority of the patriarch, when speaking to "outsiders" about the actions of their own household members (Grasmuck and Pessar 1991; Rouse 1986).

Besides failing to entertain the possibility of conflict and contestation within migrant households, researchers have also tended to view households as essentially passive units whose members are collectively victimized by the larger market economy. We see this vision clearly in the pioneering work of the historical-structuralist Claude Meillassoux (1981). He recognized that the broad range of activities assumed by the migrant wives who remained in rural African communities was essential to the social reproduction of male migrant labor on a seasonal and generational basis. Although he acknowledged that women who engage in noncapitalist activities within the household and migrant community are in a contradictory and exploited relationship vis-à-vis the capitalist economy, Meillassoux did not go on to analyze the equally exploitative social and economic relations *within* migrant households. With such a model of passive and unitary households, we are totally unprepared to account for such "transgressive" practices as the decisions of many Kikuyu women to migrate alone to a nearby city rather than accept the onerous burden of maintaining homes and lands over the duration of their migrant husbands' and fathers' prolonged absences. Nici Nelson describes these exploited women as "voting with their feet" (1978, 89).

Now, almost twenty years after the publication of Meillassoux's work, we continue to compile additional case studies documenting the social reproduction of migrant labor by labor-exporting households (Dandler and Medeiros 1988; Griffith 1985; Soto 1987). What is in far shorter supply, however, are gendered treatments of the strains and limitations on the perpetuation of such labor reserves. For example, we need comparative research on whether and how the "enforced" immobility of migrant wives and sisters is contested by women responding to the increased demand for female labor in both export-oriented industries at "home" and in immigrant-dominated sectors abroad (Grasmuck and Pessar 1991; Mills 1997). There is also a paucity of literature on the limits to the willingness and capacity of grandmothers and other kin to care for the children left behind and to "resocialize" rebellious youth sent home by their distraught migrant parents (Basch et al. 1994; Guarnizo 1997; Matthei and Smith 1998).

By contrast to the passive household acted on by external forces, the second perspective presents us with a household that continuously seeks to adjust itself to the larger socioeconomic and ecological systems. Although this rendering of migrant households holds the promise of addressing the role of structure and agency in the migration process, some have overcompensated by describing "the household" as relatively unconstrained by external conditions. As critics have observed, a "veneer of free choice" is built into the concept of strategies, thus effacing the many external, structural constraints limiting the range of strategies that households can adopt (Grasmuck and Pessar 1991; Pessar 1982; Wood 1982). Moreover, the model of the economically maximizing household fails to specify how strategies develop within the confines of this unit (Bach and Schraml 1982). Failing a specification of the mechanisms of strategy evolution, the implication is that there is no dissension over objectives (Dwyer 1983; Rouse 1986; Schmink 1984).

As an alternative to the "unrestrained household," authors like Charles Wood (1981, 1982) and Kenneth Roberts (1985) have directed our attention to the fact that household sustenance strategies emerge out of an interplay between factors internal to domestic units over which members have some degree of control—such as consumption needs and available labor power—and forces that lie beyond the household unit and are far more resistant to the intervention of migrant household members, for example, job opportunities, inflation, and land concentration. Others have suggested that our formulations of contingent agency within migrant households need not, and should not, be restricted to economic or material constraints. They point, in addition, to cultural constructs such as kinship, gender, and class ideologies. These too shape and discipline household members and, as a consequence, influence how they individually and jointly perceive such abstractions as "consumption needs" and "labor power" and how household members interpret and experience the range of opportunities and constraints external to the domestic unit. Moreover, these symbolic constructs strongly condition the type of strategies that can be imagined and orchestrated both individually and collectively (Fernández-Kelly and García 1990; Grasmuck and Pessar 1991; Kibria 1993; Pessar 1995a; Rouse 1989). Along these lines, we need more research on how images, meanings, and values associated with gender, consumption, modernity, place, and "the family" circulate within the global cultural economy (Appadurai 1990; Featherstone 1990; Lipsitz 1994) and how these "ideoscapes" and "mediascapes" are interpreted and appropriated in varied sites by different household members in ways that either promote or constrain mobility (Mills 1997).

Finally, much of the scholarship that champions the "immigrant family" in the United States as an adaptive social form fails to address first-order historical and political concerns. These writings assume an immigrant household already firmly in place (Pérez 1986). As a consequence, our attention is diverted from the important task of analyzing the interplay of political and economic forces and the subsequent creation of legislation and government policies, which both in the past and in the present effectively block or limit the formation, unification, and material well-being of immigrant families (Espiritu 1997; Garrison and Weiss 1979; Hondagneu-Sotelo 1995; Hondagneu-Sotelo and Avila 1997; Lowe 1996; Mohanty 1991). We also need to turn a critical gaze on the accompanying rhetoric that makes these initiatives "thinkable" and credible. For example, work on the Chinese Exclusion Act points to its racist and sexist precepts; beginning with the 1875 Page Law, all would-be Chinese immigrant women were suspected of being prostitutes who would bring in "especially virulent strains of venereal diseases, introduce opium addiction, and entice young white boys to a life of sin" (Chan 1991, 138). More work needs to be done on the ways in which immigration exclusion and citizenship has depended on what Lisa Lowe calls "a 'technology' of racialization and gendering" (1996, 11).

The failure to problematize the very existence of "adaptive" households obscures a key fact. For immigrants who experience multiple forms of discrimination and exploitation, the ability to maintain a unified household is an accomplishment, not simply a mundane fact of immigrant life. On this score, Pierrette Hondagneu-Sotelo and Ernestine Avila (1997, 565) write:

> Ironically, just at the moment when free trade proponents and pundits celebrate globalization and transnationalism, and when "borderlands" and "border crossings" have become the metaphors of preference for describing a mind-boggling range of conditions, nation-state borders prove to be very real obstacles for many Mexican and Central American women who work in the U.S., and who, given the appropriate circumstances, wish to be

with their children. While demanding the right for women workers to live with their children may provoke critiques of sentimentality, essentialism, and the glorification of motherhood, demanding the right for women workers to choose their own motherhood arrangements would be the beginning of a truly just family and work policies, policies that address not only inequities of gender, but also inequities of race, class, and citizenship status.

Rethinking Social Networks

Researchers sensitive to gender difference have begun to challenge the popular notion that social networks operate in a neutered fashion. We see this misguided assumption clearly represented in those studies of family migration networks that assume that the effects of family networks on individual migration are equivalent for all household members (Taylor 1986). This approach fails to recognize that individuals' access to networks and individual network exchanges are rights and responsibilities informed by gender and kinship norms. Or as David Lindstrom (1991, 26) correctly observes, "Migration networks involve not only the provision of migration assistance, but the reproduction of social roles as well." Thus, in the Mexican rural communities he studied, norms of family honor and beliefs that women are inferior and require surveillance mitigated against the mobilization of family networks for women's migration. Yet with declining household incomes, such patriarchal norms frequently had to be weighed against the much needed earnings that a wife's or daughter's migration might bring. According to Lindstrom, to resolve this contradiction rural households came to depend on a far more limited number of effective network connections mobilized for aiding a female migrant than was the case for her male counterparts. Unlike fathers and sons, responsibility for women's migration and settlement could rarely be delegated to distant kin, friends, or a *coyote*—individuals who could not be confidently charged with the responsibilities of protection and control. In this way, women's mobility was far more restricted than men, since women had to depend almost entirely on the prior existence and willing mobilization of close family migration networks (for example, a migrant father or brother).

Critics also dispute the common assumption that networks are always socially inclusive and maintained by kin, friends, and compatriots who are motivated by obligations and norms of social solidarity. A counternarrative suggests that migrant social networks can be highly contested social resources, not always shared even in the same family. On this score, Hondagneu-Sotelo (1994) found that migrant networks were traditionally available to Mexican males; now that women have developed independent female networks, it is not uncommon for family and household members to use entirely different social networks. This access to alternative networks may be very significant for those women who seek to escape the patriarchal vigilance and control that characterize traditional family networks.

On a related point, there is a paucity of scholarship on the ways in which gender relations within migrant households are differentially affected by alternative patterns of family migration. One study (Hondagneu-Sotelo 1994) revealed that when Mexican men emigrated first and stayed abroad for several years before their spouses joined them ("family stage migration"), the husbands proved more amenable to assisting their wives in the domestic tasks they had mastered in their wives' absence. Conversely, when spouses and children migrated together ("family unit migration"), patriarchal patterns were more likely to be maintained, even when women worked outside the home. We need more research of this kind, especially for those immigrant populations in which the premigration gender structure may be more egalitarian than in the Mexican case.

In addition to avoiding considerations of gender difference and possible contestation, network analysts also tend to overstate altruistic values while missing instances of socioeconomic exploitation (Dinerman 1978; Zhou 1992). Not only does discrimination against U.S. immigrants in both the labor and housing markets promote the development of migrant networks linking newcomers to jobs in the secondary sector and ethnic enclaves and to homes in ethnic neighborhoods, but it also effectively limits the ability of more established immigrants to move beyond these niches. As Sarah Mahler's (1995) research on undocumented immigrants in suburban New York shows, in a context of limited economic alternatives for capital accumulation, newly arrived immigrants may easily become targets for exploitation by their more seasoned co-ethnics. In a clear repudiation of the ethnic solidarity trope, she notes that the drive to produce a surplus monetizes most relationships and teaches many immigrants that to succeed they must recognize and utilize their community's resources—including naive newcomers—for their own benefit. My own research on Latino entrepreneurs in greater Washington, D.C., echoes these observations and urges a more problematized approach to the claims of social solidarity among coethnics—one that delineates those social, cultural, and historical factors that facilitate or impede communalism and mutual support (Pessar 1995c).

Social networks are featured in much of the theorizing and research on ethnic enclaves, since these networks are viewed as key to labor recruitment. They are also seen as conduits for the circulation of the social and cultural capital favorable to the competitive success of immigrant businesses and to the training and social advancement of their workers. For example, the earliest writing on the Cuban enclave in Miami praised it as a mode of economic incorporation that, unlike the secondary sector, provided immigrants with significant returns to education and previous job experience as well as opportunities for training and comparatively higher wages (Portes and Bach 1985). Yet research on the Cuban enclave (Portes and Jensen 1989) and the Chinese enclave in New York City (Zhou 1992; Zhou and Logen 1989), which controls for gender, reveals that women receive few, if any, of the advantages their male counterparts enjoy. In the case of the New York City enclave, Min Zhou (1992, 182) writes, "better-paying jobs in the enclave economy tend to be reserved for men because male supremacy that dominates the Chinese culture (and the Western culture) reinforce gender discrimination in the enclave labor market." And in her study of Dominican and Colombian immigrants employed in Hispanic firms in New York, Greta Gilbertson (1995) also concludes that enclave employment is highly exploitative of women. Indeed, she claims that some of the success of immigrant small-business owners and their male workers comes at the expense of subordinated immigrant women.

Engendering Migration Theory and Research

In her excellent review of the scholarship on immigrant women, Donna Gabaccia (1992) concludes that this body of work has been institutionalized as a subfield in both migration studies as a whole (namely, women and migration) and in the specific bodies of literature on migration within the individual social science disciplines. The challenge remains to branch out from this concentration on female immigrants in order to apply appropriately gender-inflected research questions and methods to both men and women. Only in this way, Gabaccia notes, will we save scholarship on migrant women from ghettoization and produce more comprehensive and truly gendered accounts of migration structures and processes. I have already suggested some ways in which this might be accomplished. The remainder of this essay focuses on the key components needed to attain this end. I note where advances have been made and suggest where future theorizing and research should proceed.

Economic Contexts for Migration

Researchers have only recently begun to explore how changing economic conditions in labor-exporting and labor-importing societies differentially affect men and women, and how this, in turn, may provide them with contrasting incentives and constraints on movement and foreign settlement. Hondagneu-Sotelo (1994), for example, notes that the bracero program provided opportunities for male laborers, who went on to create informal social networks that recruited additional men. It was not until the 1970s that equally effective women-to-women networks were consolidated (Kossoudji and Ranney 1984). In contrast, Irish migration in the nineteenth and early twentieth centuries was female-dominated. As Hasia Diner (1983) and Pauline Jackson (1984) explain, the larger continent-wide transition from an agrarian, feudal mode to an industrial, capitalist one was exacerbated in Ireland by the local norms of single inheritance and single dowry. These changes had a greater impact on women than men, leading increasing numbers of women to conclude that their best chances for employment (overwhelmingly in domestic service) and eventual marriage could be found by emigrating to the United States. It was women who created and maintained the migration chains that linked female kin and friends and produced a pattern of migration that was basically a female mass movements.[5]

Turning to more contemporary times, Saskia Sassen (1984) and María Patricia Fernández-Kelly (1983) argue that export-led production in Third World countries carries different implications for female and male workers, although in both instances it induces migration. The researchers propose that offshore production promotes international migration by creating goods that compete with local commodities; by feminizing the workforce without providing equivalent factory-based employment for the large stock of under- and unemployed males; and by socializing women for industrial work and modern consumption without providing needed job stability over the course of the women's working lives.

For several decades the United States has attracted proportionally more female migrants than other labor-importing countries have, and women constitute the majority among U.S. immigrants from Asia, Central and South America, the Caribbean, and Europe (Donato 1992). This dominance reflects the growth of female-intensive industries in the United States, particularly in service, health care, microelectronics, and apparel manufacturing. According to Yen Le Espiritu (1997, 74), immigrant women, as feminized and racialized labor, are more employable in these labor-intensive industries than their male counterparts owing to "the patriarchal and racist assumptions that women can afford to work for less, do not mind dead-end jobs, and are more suited physiologically to certain kinds of detailed and routine work." She illustrates this assumption with a quote from a white male production manager and hiring supervisor in a California Silicon Valley assembly shop: "Just three things I look for in hiring [entry-level, high-tech manufacturing operatives]: small, foreign, and female. You find those three things and you're pretty much automatically guaranteed the right kind of workforce. These little foreign gals are grateful to be hired—very, very grateful—no matter what" (Hossfeld 1994, 65, as cited in Espiritu 1997).

In a sobering piece on U.S. immigrants' "progress" over the decade of the 1980s, Roger Waldinger and Greta Gilbertson (1994) find that while male immigrants from select countries (for example, India, Iran, Japan) were able to convert their education into higher occupational status rankings than native-born whites of native parentage, *none* of their female counterparts were able to do the same. For example, relatively few females were able to convert high levels of education into prestigious jobs as managers, professionals, or business owners. If the social erasure of immigrant women caused assimilationists to dwell on and celebrate the progress of immigrant *men* alone, Waldinger and Gilbertson's research shows that "making it" in America may, sadly, still be a story about men despite the inclusion of women (440).

Once we examine the way in which labor markets are segmented by gender, as well as by nationality and race, and explore the differential returns immigrant men and women receive for their education and experience, we are well positioned to pose additional questions central to migration studies. In what ways are patriarchal practices in immigrant households and communities reinforced or challenged by the contrasting experiences of men and women in the economic sphere? And how do changes in gender relations influence men's and women's orientations to settlement and return?

Migration and Emancipation

Many scholars have examined the impact of immigrant women's regular wage work on gendered relations. A review of this literature points to the fact that despite gender inequities in the labor market and workplace, immigrant women employed in the United States generally gain greater personal autonomy and independence, while men lose ground (see, for example, Grasmuck and Pessar 1991; Guendelman and Pérez-Itriaga 1987; Hondagneu-Sotelo 1994; Kibria 1993; Lamphere 1987; Pedraza-Bailey 1991). For example, women's regular access to wages and their greater contribution to household sustenance frequently lead to more control over budgeting and other realms of domestic decision making. It also provides them with greater leverage in appeals for male assistance in daily household chores. There is some indication that the smaller the wage gap between partners' earnings, the greater the man's willingness to participate in domestic work (Espiritu 1997; Lamphere et al. 1993; Pessar 1995b). Immigrant women's spatial mobility and their access to valuable social and economic resources beyond the domestic sphere also expand (Hondagneu-Sotelo 1994; Pessar 1995b). We find further evidence that migration and settlement bring changes in traditional patriarchal arrangements in the words of immigrant men and women. In what Nazli Kibria (1993, 108) describes as a tongue-in-cheek description of gender transformations, several Vietnamese immigrant men told her: "In Vietnam the man of the house is king. Below him the children, then the pets of the home, and then the women. Here, the woman is the king and the man holds a position below the pets." Conversely, a Mexican female returnee told her interviewers, "in California my husband was like a *mariposa,* meaning a sensitive, soft, responsive butterfly. Back here in Mexico he acts like a distant *macho*" (Guendelman and Pérez-Itriaga 1987, 268).

The pioneering work on women and migration tended to couch its concerns in stark either-or terms: was migration emancipating or subjugating for women? Most soon concluded that immigrant women did not equally or consistently improve their status in the home, workplace, or community (Morokvasic 1984). For many immigrants, gains have been most pronounced in one domain (the household, for example), while gender subordination continues in other arenas, such as the workplace and ethnic associations (Goldring 1996b; Grasmuck and Pessar 1991). For other immigrant women, gains within a specific sphere, like the household, are frequently accompanied by strains and contradictions. This fact is clearly manifested in Hondagneu-Sotelo and Avila's (1997) research on "transnational mothering." Although many Mexican and Central American immigrant nannies and housekeepers take pride in their paid social reproductive work, especially in caring for other people's children and in stretching the definition of motherhood to encompass breadwinning, there are substantial costs to their achievements. According to the authors, in separating in space and time from their communities of origin, homes, children, and sometimes husbands, these women must "cope with stigma, guilt, and criticism from others" (7). On this score, I think Myra Marx Ferree (1990) is quite right when she observes that many of our feminist models founder because they have sought consistency in working women's lives where no such consistency exists.

Although there is now broad consensus that immigrant women attain some limited, albeit uneven and sometimes contradictory, benefits from migration and settlement, we await the results of the next wave of scholarship. This would consolidate and then deconstruct the available literature to determine those gendered domains in which the greatest and least gains for women have been made. And it would both isolate and interrelate the factors that condition these outcomes. These would include migrants' age, education, employment history (prior and subsequent to emigration), race, ethnicity, sexual preference, social class, and legal status, as well as family structures and gender ideologies (prior to and subsequent to emigration). As we proceed in such a venture, it will be necessary to deconstruct excessively inclusive terms, such as "racial-ethnic" women and "racialized subjects." Promising work lies ahead as we explore the impact of the evolving processes of racialization and social stratification within and between "Asian," "Latino," "Caribbean," and "European" populations (Omi and Winant 1994) on the gendered identities and experiences of specific immigrant populations (Lowe 1996). Finally, in order to assess those factors that facilitate or impede gender parity, it would be wise to reengage systematically those accounts that qualify or dispute the claim that migration improves women's status (Castro 1986; Zhou 1992). For example, we are likely to find less change among immigrant populations like the rural Portuguese whose premigration gender ideologies already assign wives to essential duties in both the domestic and productive spheres (Lamphere 1986).

While not intending to minimize the importance of those factors that may mitigate challenges to patriarchal practices, I want to suggest that differences among researchers regarding the emancipatory nature of migration may originate, at least in part, in the research strategies pursued. In a formal research setting, such as one in which surveys or structured interviews are administered, an immigrant woman's decision to cloak her own and her family's experiences in a discourse of unity, female sacrifice, and women's subordination to the patriarch represents a safe, respectful, and respectable "text." As I look back on my own research, this is the female "voice" that usually emerged from my attempts at survey research. By contrast, my ethnographic collection of discourses revealing family tensions and struggles emerged far more frequently out of encounters when my presence was incidental—that is, not the defining purpose for the ensuing dialogue—or after many months of participant-observation had substantially reduced the initial formality and suspicion (see Pessar 1995a). In light of our increased appreciation for the dialogical nature of the research encounter, I am hardly surprised that the fieldworker who has presented some of the richest and most compelling case material on women's circumvention or contestation of patriarchal authority assumed the role of both "activist" and "researcher" and was no doubt perceived by many of her informants as a transgressive female herself (Hondagneu-Sotelo 1994, xiii). Neither am I surprised that the chronicler of by far the best histories of divergent migration projects spent more than two years studying *a limited number* of immigrant families in both Mexico and northern California and chose to feature in his writings only one family with whom he lived and socialized (Rouse 1986, 1989).

Settlement, Return, and Transnationality

A gendered approach is essential to account for men's and women's orientations to settlement, return, and transmigration. Indeed, gender-free models of migrant settlement and return (see, for example, Piore 1979) are hard to defend in light of informants' statements, like the one cited earlier by the Mexican return migrant who saw her "butterfly" husband turn back into a distant macho, or the joking remark of a Laotian refugee: "When we get on the plane back to Laos, the first thing we will do is beat up the women" (Donnelly 1994, 74). Research shows consistently that gains in gender equity are central to women's desires to settle, more or less permanently, in order to protect their advances (Chavez 1991; Georges 1990; Goldring 1992; Hagan 1994; Hondagneu-Sotelo 1994). By contrast, many men seek to return home rapidly to regain the status and privileges that migration itself has challenged. In my own work I have documented the tendency of many Dominican women to spend large amounts of money on expensive durable goods, such as major appliances and home furnishings, which serve to root the family more securely in the United States and deplete the funds necessary to orchestrate a successful reentry back into Dominican society and economy. Conversely, men often favor a far more frugal and austere pattern of consumption consistent with their claim that "five dollars spent today meant five more years of postponing the return to the Dominican Republic."[6]

Further strides in our understanding of how immigrant women consolidate settlement have been made by Hondagneu-Sotelo (1994), who observes that, as traditional family patriarchy weakens, immigrant women assume more active public and social roles—actions that at once reinforce their improved status in the household and ultimately advance their families' integration in the United States. She identifies three arenas in which this consolidation takes place: the labor market, where women seek permanent, nonseasonal employment; institutions for public and private assistance; and the immigrant or ethnic community. Research shows that women are particularly adept at locating and utilizing the financial and social services available in the new society (Chavira 1988; Kibria 1993) and at using social-networking skills for community building (O'Connor 1990).

As researchers continue to explore community building and community activism among new immigrants, they should bear in mind that women are positioned differently than men with regard to both the broader economy and the state. As women, they are socially assigned responsibility for the daily and generational sustenance of household members, even when, as is the case for many immigrants, family wages are wholly insufficient. Research is badly needed to determine whether and how immigrant women manage to overcome very real concerns about their legal vulnerability when they confront the state over family and community welfare issues (Hondagneu-Sotelo 1995; Sacks 1989; Susser 1982; Zavella 1987).

Recent work on migrants' transnational identities, practices, and institutions alerts us that permanent settlement or permanent return are merely two of the possible outcomes; lives constructed across national boundaries is another. Unfortunately, gender remains largely marginalized within transnational migration theory and research (Hondagneu-Sotelo and Avila 1997; Kearney 1995; Mahler 1996a). We require far more research on the transnational identities and practices of men and women. Based on the few studies that do consider gender, we are left with the impression that men are the major players in transnational social fields (Graham 1997; Ong 1993). Sarah Mahler (1996a) astutely questions the implicit message that women are more passive and argues that when the research focus is shifted from "public" domains, such as international investment and hometown associations, to more "private" ones, like the management of transnational migrant households, a different representation emerges (see also Ho 1993; Hondagneu-Sotelo and Avila 1997; Soto 1987). On this score, Sandhya Shukla (1997) observes that South Asian women have organized across the diaspora and subcontinent around the problem of domestic violence. She notes that through these transnational activities "the South Asian woman" is being constituted as a political subject. As such, some of these women have come to contest the more mainstream, patriarchal narratives of ethnic identity and solidarity emerging in diverse diaspora communities. These mainstream narratives, she claims, are vigorously and romantically nationalist and do not embrace the women's pan-ethnic identity of South Asian. They "are steeped in images of the traditional nuclear family with its specified gender roles as a metaphor for distinctly cultural values in the face of Western change" (270). Shukla's work alerts us to an important dialectic that has received insufficient scholarly attention: the mutually constituting projects of racial and ethnic "othering" of immigrants and ethnics carried out by members of "host" countries and the creation of nationalist, often fundamentalist, counternarratives by these "othered" subjects. What are the roles of men and women in either supporting or challenging these projects? And in what ways are the symbols of nation, diaspora, and belonging imbued with notions of gender and sexuality? Surely much more research is needed to determine how transnational migration identities, practices, and experiences are gendered, and whether patriarchal ideologies and roles are reaffirmed, tempered, or both within transnational social spaces.

We also need to situate gender within the current historical moment—one in which researchers note the contradiction between economic globalization and the renationalizing of politics (Glick Schiller et al. 1995; Harris 1995; Sassen 1996b). One extremely unfortunate by-product of this contradiction is the recent tendency for U.S. policymakers to characterize immigrant women and children as dangerous "others" whose rapacious demands on the public coffers thwart the state's ability to fulfill its social contract with the "authentic" and truly "deserving" members of the nation (Chavez 1998; Hondagneu-Sotelo 1995; Naples 1997).

We would also benefit from building on Lowe's (1996) work on feminized global production and the role of Asian, Asian immigrant, and Asian American women workers. Lowe argues that these women are positioned at the intersection where the contradictions of sexism, racism, and capitalism converge. Their multiply constituted social location complicates unitary emancipatory narratives that privilege gender, race, or class. Not surprisingly, we are beginning to see accounts of community and workplace organizing by such racialized working women who manage to find common cause with a broad coalition of workers despite lines of difference and unequal power that might separate them along axes of gender, race, nationality, and citizenship. We need more theorizing and research on organizations, such as the Garment Workers' Justice Center, the Coalition for Justice in the Maquiladoras, and Justice for Janitors, which draw on immigrant and minority workers to struggle for workers' rights domestically as well as internationally (Lowe 1996).

A Reencounter with Feminist Studies

In my earliest work on Dominican migration, I was quite adamant about the gains I believed Dominican immigrant women had made (Pessar 1986). My enthusiasm originated from several sources: a flush of early feminist optimism (see Pessar 1995a); my observations based on fieldwork in both the Dominican Republic and the United States of changes in gender practices (Grasmuck and Pessar 1991); and a desire to communicate my female informants' pleasure at what they viewed as far more equitable gender relations. Yet, as I have come to both follow the lives of several of these women over the years and critically engage the comparative literature on immigration and patriarchy, I have tempered my enthusiasm. I now conclude that, in general, immigrant women's gains have been modest. In retrospect, I believe many of us anticipated a far greater degree of emancipation for immigrant women because our theoretical guideposts were firmly planted in early feminist theory. To understand why most immigrant women have only nibbled at the margins of patriarchy, we must abandon the notion that gender hierarchy is the most determinative structure in their lives. This leaves us with the far more daunting task of examining the impact on women's and men's lives of multiple and interrelated forms of oppression linked to gender, class, race, ethnicity, and foreign status.

Many American feminists were encouraged by economic trends in the 1970s and 1980s. There was a marked increase in the proportion of dual-wage-earning families, and escalating rates of male unemployment served to underscore the centrality of women's contributions to household budgets. Predictions of profound changes in U.S. gender relations and family structures followed. Heidi Hartmann, for example, disputed the claim that the recent increase in female-headed households was by definition deleterious for women and their families. She wrote (1987, 49): "To the extent that there is a family crisis, it is by and large a healthy one, particularly for women." This was the case, she maintained, because increased economic opportunities for women had, in her words, allowed women "to choose" to head their own households rather than live with men. Along similar lines, Alice Kessler-Harris and Karen Brodkin Sacks observed (1987, 70) that women's improved access to wages allowed them either to resist gender and generational subordination within the family or to "avoid family situations altogether."

A review of the literature on immigrant families unearths scant evidence of a radical revamping of gender ideology and lines of authority or an emancipatory abandonment of conjugal units, despite rates of employment for immigrant women that rival those of native-born Americans. We learn of Vietnamese immigrant women who defend their "traditional" family forms against what they perceive to be individualistic and unregulated American family practices (Kibria 1993), and of

Latina nannies who endorse motherhood as a full-time vocation when financial resources permit (Hondagneu-Sotelo and Avila 1997). We encounter a Dominican woman who describes her divorce as "one of the saddest days in my life. Not only did I lose the respect I once had as a married woman, but my children and I lost the material support [my husband] was able to provide" (Pessar 1995a, 41). Many researchers report that immigrant women view their employment as an extension of their obligations as wives and mothers (Pedraza-Bailey 1991; Segura 1994). With the caveat that they are merely "helping their husbands"—a refrain that immigrant women frequently repeat to researchers (Pessar 1995a; Chavira 1988)—these women manage to keep the fires of patriarchy burning by minimizing long hours in the workplace and their making substantial contributions to the household budget. Why have these immigrant women been less inclined than their white, North American counterparts to level assaults on patriarchal domestic ideologies and practices?

Immigrant Families as Bastions of Resistance

Multiple external forces buffet immigrant families. Legislation informed by racist and sexist discourse has severely challenged the survival and well-being of immigrant families in the past and continues to do so today (Fitzpatrick 1997; Hondagneu-Sotelo 1995; Lowe 1996; Mohanty 1991). Immigrant men are increasingly frustrated and scapegoated; they expect, and are expected, to be the breadwinner. Yet they face structural impediments that block the fulfillment of this role. As Fernández-Kelly and García (1990, 148) remind us: "For poor men and women the issue is not so much the presence of the sexual division of labor or the persistence of patriarchal ideologies but the difficulties of upholding either." Owing to an all too common tendency to conflate male dominance with patriarchy, many social scientists have been slow, or reluctant, to appreciate their informants' unwillingness to lose the benefits derived from some patriarchal marital unions (Nash 1988).[7]

Whether through choice or necessity, large numbers of immigrant women have assumed wage-earning responsibilities. Their pursuit of employment is far more often the result of severe economic need and an expression of vulnerability than an indication of their strength within the home and marketplace (Fernández-Kelly and García 1990). As noted earlier, it is often because they are "small, foreign, and female," and nonwhite, that they enjoy the dubious "advantage" of being the preferred category of labor for the lowest-paid and most insecure segment of the economy. In light of these multiple assaults, it would be patronizing to interpret immigrant women's struggles to maintain intact families as acquiescence to "traditional" patriarchy. In many cases these struggles represent acts of resistance against those forces within the dominant society that threaten the existence of poor, minority families (see Collins 1990; Zinn et al. 1986). This does not mean, as Evelyn Nakano Glenn (1986, 193) reminds us, that immigrant women do not simultaneously experience the family as an instrument of gender subordination. Indeed, their attempts to use wages as leverage for greater gender parity in certain arenas of domestic life attest to this fact. The dilemma confronting many immigrant women, it would seem, is to defend and hold together the family while attempting to reform the norms and practices that subordinate them.

The importance of keeping multiple-wage-earning families intact is underscored by statistics revealing far higher incidents of poverty among female-headed immigrant households than in similar conjugal units (Bean and Tienda 1988; Pessar 1995b; Rosenberg and Gilbertson 1995). Maxine Baca Zinn (1987, 167) provides a more adequate depiction of these female-headed units than that proposed by Hartmann (1987):

> Conditions associated with female-headed families among racial-ethnics are different and should be interpreted differently. Because white families headed by women have much higher average incomes than minority families in the same situation, we must not confuse an overall improvement with what is in fact an improvement for women in certain social categories, while other women are left at the bottom in even worse conditions.

In spite of the many social and material disincentives militating against the disbanding of unions and the formation of female-headed households, there are, nonetheless, several immigrant populations, like Dominicans, with extremely high rates of female-headedness. Research is needed to account for the factors contributing to differing rates of marital instability and female-headedness within and among immigrant populations in the United States (Bean, Berg, and Van Hook 1996). We also require more in-depth investigations to document the survival strategies of poor immigrant families (Menjívar 1995). Several researchers have pointed to the importance of household extension, that is, the incorporation of adults other than the husband and wife into the household. These coresident adults provide additional income to compensate for low earnings or sporadic unemployment and facilitate the labor-force participation of married and single mothers (Angel and Tienda 1982; Kibria 1993; Rosenberg and Gilbertson 1995).

While poor immigrant families may experience difficulties in upholding a patriarchal division of labor and often suffer socially and materially as a consequence of men's unemployment, upwardly mobile couples may confront the opposite challenge. They must confront the "contradiction" that dual wage-earning poses for households that have achieved, by their standards, a middle-class standing. In certain Dominican and Cuban immigrant families, for example, women's "retirement" to the domestic sphere is a favored practice for marking the household's *collective* social advancement (Pessar 1995a; Fernández-Kelly and García 1990). Many of the Dominican women I knew who agreed to leave wage employment clearly viewed their alternatives as being improved social status for the entire family through female retirement, on the one hand, or improved gender relations for the wife through continued wage work, on the other. In leaving the workforce, many of the most conflicted women chose to place immigrant ideology (with its stress on social mobility) and traditional family domestic ideology (with its emphasis on both patriarchy and collective interests) before personal struggle and gains. Such actions, of course, contradict the feminist tenet that women's interests are best served by positioning themselves in both the household and workplace (Ferree 1990). Yet some of my informants saw themselves struggling on another front to challenge the distorted and denigrating cultural stereotypes about Latino immigrants held by many members of the majority culture. As the following quote from one of my female informants illustrates, Dominican women resisted these negative stereotypes by symbolizing the household's respectability and elevated social and economic status in a fashion common to the traditional Dominican middle class: they removed themselves from the visible productive sphere.

> When we had finally purchased our home and our business, Roque insisted that I stop working. He said it would be good for the children and good for all of us. At first I protested, because I never again wanted to be totally dependent upon a man. . . . But then I began to think about how much I have suffered in this country to make something for my family. And I thought, even though we own a home and a business, most Americans think the worst of us. They think we all sell drugs, have too many babies, take away their jobs, or are living off the government (i.e., receiving welfare). I decided, I'm going to show them that I am as good as they are, that my husband is so successful that I don't have to work at all. (Pessar 1995a, 11)

This woman's words echo a broader claim advanced by Espiritu and others: in a hostile environment, "some women of color, in contrast to their white counterparts, view unpaid domestic work—having children and maintaining families—more as a form of resistance to racist oppression than as a form of exploitation by men" (Espiritu 1997, 6).

Other Dominican women accounted for their departure from the workforce in terms similar to those used by the Cuban women interviewed by Fernández-Kelly and García (1990). They had envisioned their employment alongside their husbands as a temporary venture necessary until the family could achieve its goal of social advancement. Once this goal was attained, women's employment apparently contradicted a more enduring and valued notion of the family and the sexes that featured the successful man as the sole breadwinner and the successful woman as the guardian of a unified household. These cases reveal that a unilinear and unproblematic progression from patriarchy to parity is by no means assured. They also point up the need for continuing research on class differences not only between immigrant and native-born women but among immigrant women as well.

Relatively few studies address the question of whether migration promotes or hampers a feminist consciousness (Shukla 1997). Most of these report, not surprisingly, that the majority of the immigrant women studied do not tend to identify as feminists or to participate in feminist organizations (Foner 1986; Hondagneu-Sotelo 1995; Pessar 1984). Immigrant women, we are told, are more likely to base their dissatisfactions and complaints about life in the United States on injustices linked to class, race, ethnicity, and legal-status discrimination than to gender. For example, according to Nancy Foner (1986), her Jamaican female informants experienced racial and class inequalities more acutely than those based on gender, and this sense of injustice gave them a basis for unity with Jamaican men. Moreover, the many domestic workers in their ranks felt no sense of sisterhood with their upper-middle-class white employers, whose "liberation" these immigrant women facilitated by providing inexpensive child care so that their female employers could compete in the male occupational world. Nonetheless, Hondagneu-Sotelo's point is well taken when she concludes (1995, 197) that although none of the Mexican immigrant women she interviewed

> identified "gender subordination" as a primary problem, rearrangements induced by migration do result in the diminution of familial patriarchy, and these transformations may enable immigrant women to better confront problems derived from class, racial/ethnic, and legal-status subordination. Their endeavors may prompt more receptiveness to feminist ideology and organizations in the future.

Clearly, we require more comparative research on both the local and the global processes leading to the development or suppression of feminist consciousness and collective action among immigrants and transmigrants (Sutton 1992).[8]

Conclusion

The challenge to create a respected space for household and network analyses in migration studies has been met. Research focused on households and social networks has enhanced our understanding of how individuals interpret and respond to larger political and economic incentives and constraints; how communities and nations are impacted by the cumulative effects of migration; and how migration can become a self-sustaining process that stimulates further out-migration even after the initial precipitating factors are no longer operational. The analytical power of these constructs might prove even greater, however, if researchers would recognize that gender organizes both the composition and organization of migrant households and social networks, and that gender also infuses the cultural, social, and political-economic forces acting on both structures.

Migration scholars have made great advances in moving beyond an earlier male bias in theory and research. And the days when gender was treated as merely one of several equally significant variables, such as education and marital status, are mostly behind us. We are now moving toward a more fully engendered understanding of the migration process. This essay has noted several key advances and signaled the way to future developments in theory and research. We are starting to accumulate many case studies that document how men and women experience migration differently, and how patriarchy is reaffirmed, reconfigured, or both, as a consequence of international migration. The time is ripe to build on and move beyond these rich individual case studies toward a more inclusive, interpretive framework of migration and patriarchy. In doing so, it will be necessary to discard the notion that gender oppression transcends all divisions among men and women. Rather, we must develop theories and analytical frameworks that allow us to capture and compare the simultaneity of the impact of gender, race, ethnicity, nationality, class, and legal status on the lives of different immigrants. We must also recognize that patriarchy is expressed and manifested not only in the acts of immigrant men and women but in the transactions between immigrants and nationals as well. On this score, important works in cultural studies and ethnic studies (for example, Anzaldúa 1990; Espiritu 1997; Lowe 1996) alert us to the fact that representations of majority white American men and women and those of immigrants and ethnics of color may be mutually constituting. Thus, ideological representations of gender and sexuality are central in the exercise and perpetuation of patriarchal, racial, and class domination, as when representations of Asian men as both hypersexual and asexual and Asian women as both superfeminine and masculine are used to define, maintain, and legitimate white male virility and supremacy (Espiritu 1997; Kim 1990). In sum, an adequate interpretive framework of migration and patriarchy must include a broad array of ideological constructs, social locations, institutions, and social actors which are situated in multiple sites stretched across the transnational social and cultural fields that immigrants inhabit.

This essay benefited greatly from critical readings by Josh DeWind, Pierrette Hondagneu-Sotelo, Sarah Mahler, and several anonymous reviewers. My thanks go to each of them.

Notes

1. In keeping with the volume's focus on U.S. immigration, I restrict myself to a discussion of research on

transnational migration to and between the United States and its labor-exporting partners. Excellent scholarship on gender, households, and social networks also exists for other international migration systems; for example, see Buijs (1993); Morokvasic (1984); Phizacklea (1983); and Simon and Brettell (1986).

2. In addition to the references cited in note 1, see also Brettell and DeBerjeois (1992); Chai (1987); Gabaccia (1992, 1994); Glenn (1990); Pedraza-Bailey (1991); Prieto (1992); Stafford (1984); and Weinberg (1992).
3. In a 1984 article analyzing INS documents, Marion Houstoun, Roger Kramer, and Joan Macklin Barrett show that since 1930 (documented) female newcomers to the United States have annually outnumbered their male counterparts.
4. See notes 1 and 2.
5. For studies of Salvadoran female-led emigration, see Cohen (1977) and Repak (1995).
6. See Matthei and Smith (1998) for a similar discussion of Mexican immigrant couples.
7. I thank June Nash for pointing this out to me.
8. A topic that merits further study would be the national and global initiatives taken by immigrant and refugee women to engender the universalist conception of human rights (see Afkhami 1994; Smith 1994).

4 Matters of State: Theorizing Immigration Policy

Aristide R. Zolberg

"THERE ARE TIMES WHEN, as I look at the regulations of the countries of the world affecting immigrants, I see in my mind's eye the building up of walled-in countries, much like the wall-encircled towns of the medieval period" (Fields 1938, 3). Conjured up two-thirds of a century ago, this metaphoric representation of the outcome of the industrialized world's first immigration crisis is appropriate for our own times as well. Yet considering the pervasiveness of barriers to immigration, mirrored throughout much of the twentieth century by draconian prohibitions on exit that confined hundreds of millions to their countries for many decades, it is remarkable that the role of states in shaping international migration has been largely ignored by immigration theorists. This is acting like the proverbial ostrich, but ignoring the challenge by burying one's head in the sand will not make it go away.

A notable case in point is the recent state-of-the-art assessment published by the Committee on South-North Migration of the International Union for the Scientific Study of Populations (Massey et al. 1993; Massey, Goldring, and Durand 1994).[1] Reviewing a wide range of models purporting to explain why international migration begins and persists, the authors maintain an open-minded stance, allowing that some of these models might be complementary rather than mutually exclusive. Although Massey and his collaborators adopt as their baseline a neoclassical model of migration as the aggregate result of income-maximizing decisions by individuals, they take into account the contributions of heterogeneous approaches, and ultimately suggest (1993, 433) that "it is quite possible . . . that individuals act to maximize income while families minimize risk, and that the context within which both decisions are made is shaped by structural forces operating at the national and international levels."

Although the committee acknowledges that the "context" includes state regulations, its treatment of this factor is itself entirely atheoretical. For example, barriers to entry into another country are included within the equation representing the calculus of potential migrants as the probability of avoiding deportation from the area of destination (1.0 for legal migrants, < 1.0 for undocumented migrants). Nothing is said, however, about how the parameters determining the category "legal immigrants" are established, and thus how "illegal" ones are defined as well; how large the "legal" category is (absolutely and in relation to demand) in specific instances and for the world as a whole; how these categories vary over time and between countries; and especially, since we are in the realm of theory, how such variation might be explained. The authors handle regulations governing access to the labor market in the same manner, as determinants of the probability of employment (1993, 442), but here again, they make no attempt to describe or explain variation between receiving countries or over time, and in particular the contribution of immigration regulation to this variation.

Beyond this, the authors' conceptualization of the individual decisionmaking process does not take into consideration calculations by individuals regarding obstacles to "exit," suggesting an implicit assumption that freedom to leave prevails worldwide. Yet this cannot be taken as a given, since until quite recently a very large proportion of the people who wished to move were not able to do so except at considerable risk. This was the case not only for the many hundreds of millions living in Communist countries but also, throughout the first half of the twentieth century, for colonial populations that were denied access to the documents required for foreign travel—usually even to the home territory of the colonial power, or to other parts of the empire. Recent changes in these parameters have dramatically enlarged the pool of potential international migrants and concomitantly the regulatory load that states of potential immigration face, but even today many who would rationally be inclined to migrate are not free to do so.

In his contribution to this volume, Massey himself acknowledges that, "for theoreticians, a principal challenge is to model the behavior of nation-states and political actors, filling a void in the general theory of international migration we have constructed here." Indeed, this challenge has stood for over a century, ever since Ernst Georg Ravenstein inaugurated the theoretical quest with his two papers on "The Laws of Migration" presented to the Royal Statistical Society, which adumbrate the rational calculus underlying the theory set forth by Massey and his associates today (1885, 198–99; 1889, 286).[2] Four years later he reported further that the propositions generally held true for *internal* migrations in the other European countries for which data were available, as well as in the United States and Canada; he also verified them for *international* migration within Europe.[3] However, in response to critics who questioned his assumptions, Ravenstein conceded that "laws of population, and economic laws generally, have not the rigidity of physical laws, as they are continually being interfered [with] by human agency," and he noted in particular that "currents of migration which would flow naturally in a certain direction traced out for them in the main by geographical features, may thus be diverted, or stopped altogether, by *legislative enactments*" (1889, 241, emphasis added). With respect to exit, he observed that fewer people were leaving Russia than was to be expected in the light of that country's economic conditions because of prohibitive government regulations; with regard to entry, however, his only example pertained to internal movement, notably an enactment in the reign of the first Elizabeth prohibiting new settlement in London—a prohibition, he relates, that in fact was not enforced (1889, 241).

The absence of reference to international restrictions on immigration may be attributable to the fact that earlier in the century England had eliminated all barriers to entry—imposed during the Napoleonic wars for security reasons—as contrary to Manchesterian principles, and that Ravenstein limited his empirical investigation to immigration into European countries, a movement that at this time was generally unfettered as well. However, there were ominous signs of impending change (Zolberg 1978a, 1997). In the very year when Ravenstein's first paper was published, in his native Germany Bismarck massively expelled "undesirable" Poles, including both Jews and non-Jews, and enacted measures to restrict and regulate further immigration from eastern Europe. Even more startlingly, in the brief interval between the first and second papers, rising concern within England itself over the arrival of poor Jews from eastern Europe prompted the founding of the Society for the Suppression of the Immigration of Destitute Aliens and the establishment by the House of Commons of the Select Committee on Immigration to consider whether new legislation was required to deal with the problem (Gainer 1972, 8, 80). The discussion that followed Ravenstein's second presentation affords us a suggestive glimpse of the changing climate: one of the fellows expressed concern over the influx of foreigners into England "as one of the causes of the emigration of Englishmen" (Ravenstein 1889, 304). In the wake of this, in 1905, England enacted what was then the industrial world's most restrictive immigration law, prohibiting the landing of poor aliens of any kind, at the will of port-of-entry officials.

Had Ravenstein addressed himself to trans-oceanic movements, he would undoubtedly have noted that the United States was also moving away from laissez-faire by way of a spate of national measures, including draconian restrictions on the immigration of Chinese women (1875) and Chinese workers (1882); the first comprehensive federal law regulating general immigration (1882); and a prohibition of all immigration involving labor contracts (1885). Also in 1885 one of the new progressive economists, reckoning that massive immigration harmed American workers, proposed subjecting prospective immigrants to a literacy test so as to reduce the flow of unskilled labor; this was passed by both houses of Congress a decade later and became law in 1917.

In retrospect, it can be seen that these initiatives constituted the first stones of a global wall erected by the rich industrial states to protect themselves from "invasion" by the world's poor. Pushed out of rural areas by demographic growth combined with the spreading dynamics of the market and rendered more mobile by a revolution in transportation, the world's poor constituted a much larger and more diverse pool of potential international migrants than ever before. Although construction of the wall was well under way before World War I, the work was then speeded up by security concerns and the onset of the Bolshevik revolution. It is especially noteworthy that most of the wall's national segments were completed *before* the Great Depression set in, so that the overall phenomenon cannot be attributed simply to deteriorating economic conditions in the receiving countries.

In the United States, which then as now constituted one of the largest components of the international migration system, the wall's major elements were put in place in the period from 1896 to 1924 and included the imposition of heavy fees on entering immigrants; a proliferation of prohibited categories based on health, moral, and political criteria; a literacy requirement designed to reduce the flow of unskilled immigrants, especially from eastern and southern Europe; the nearly absolute prohibition of Asian immigration; the reduction of immigration from Europe to about one-fourth its ongoing level; and the allocation of entries on the basis of national origins so as to severely limit arrivals from eastern and southern Europe, with the explicit objective of preserving the character of the United States as a predominantly "Anglo-Saxon," Protestant community (Higham 1994; Hutchinson 1981). Concurrently, the United States elaborated an innovative apparatus of "remote control" that enabled it to deter immigration by regulating embarkation at or near the point of origin (as discussed later in the chapter).

In the decades after World War II, the gates were widened to accommodate political refugees in keeping with cold war imperatives; to facilitate the procurement of temporary labor in the course of the "Bretton Woods boom"; and to allow for family reunion in response to constituency pressures (in the United States), newly institutionalized "family rights" (in most of Europe), and related obligations arising from the recently established international human rights regime. As a number of sociologists have pointed out, over time the flows took on a life of their own by way of the development of networks that lowered the risks and costs of outward movement (Massey et al. 1993, 448–50). The result was a revival of immigration as a significant social phenomenon in most of the traditional "immigration" countries, notably the United States, as well as its appearance de novo in a number of newly affluent countries that had been prominent sources of emigration, such as Italy and Norway.

Reflecting these developments, international migration revived as a social science subject, particularly in sociology and economics. However, focusing on the incoming streams, social scientists paid little or no attention to the fact that the streams were flowing through gates, and that these openings were surrounded by high walls. Since a great deal of international movement was in fact taking place, there was little incentive to surmise about why *more* was *not* taking place. Hence, as the new literature came into being, the "legislative obstacles" to which Ravenstein had alluded did not stimulate the curiosity of social scientists engaged in theory construction.

Of course, the ubiquity of state actions purporting to regulate exit and entry does not necessarily mean that such measures play a significant role in shaping international migrations; they might prove largely ineffective, and in that case, theorists might be justified in ignoring them as a "residual error" that does not warrant explanatory efforts. For example, the IUSSP report's senior author, Douglas Massey, has repeatedly expressed considerable skepticism regarding the effectiveness of U.S. regulations in determining the level and composition of U.S. immigration in the twentieth century, both legal and unauthorized (Donato, Durand, and Massey 1992; Massey and Singer 1995; Massey 1995). In the same vein, the authors of a recent comparative study of immigration policy and policy outcomes in nine industrialized democracies suggest that "the gap between the *goals* of national immigration policy . . . and the actual results of policies in this area . . . is wide and growing wider in all major industrialized democracies" (Cornelius, Martin, and Hollifield 1994b, 3).

In the face of such widespread skepticism, I am compelled by my contention that the neglect of the role of state policies, broadly speaking, constitutes a major flaw in an important theoretical undertaking, to begin by falsifying what amounts to a "null hypothesis," namely, the contention that state regulations regarding exit and entry do not significantly shape international migration. If that hypothesis can be laid to rest—and I believe that a persuasive case can be made to that effect—then surely international migration theory must encompass a theoretically grounded account of state agency. In the second part of this chapter, I review various attempts to come to grips with the subject and incorporate them into a tentative comprehensive framework.

How Effective Are Immigration Controls?

Contrary to many assertions, evidence from historical cases as well as recent developments in immigration policy substantiate Ravenstein's (1889) admonition that "currents of migration which would flow naturally in a certain direction . . . may . . . be diverted, or stopped altogether, by legislative enactments." To begin with, the null hypothesis is easily rejected with regard to emigration, since it is evident that prohibitions on exit can be highly effective. As already noted by Ravenstein a century ago, "Great Russian" emigration was minuscule in relation to the base population and prevailing conditions in the source country.[4] Since there can be no question that today most states that choose to block exit can harness the capacity to do so (Dowty 1987), my discussion will center on the regulation of entry.[5] In the present climate, assessments of the capacity of states to control immigration also have important public policy implications, because widespread perceptions of a catastrophic "loss of control" may precipitate and legitimize the enactment of draconian measures that conflict with other societal objectives and desirable values.

On the immigration side, the null hypothesis is demonstrably false with regard to movement into the United States from noncontiguous countries—movement that today, as in the past, accounts for the largest share of recorded immigration—as well as with regard to immigration to the other English-speaking overseas countries and contemporary immigration to Europe. To what extent regulation is effective with regard to immigration into the United States from Mexico is much less clear, not only because the evidence regarding the effects of the relevant "legislative enactments" is mixed, but especially because American policy objectives are themselves highly ambiguous. Given the focus of this volume, I shall limit the discussion to the United States, focusing on three instances referred to by Massey.

U.S. Quota Period, 1921 to 1965

Boldly questioning common wisdom that the draconian restrictions of the post–World War I period were effective, Massey asserts that "although the national origins quotas, combined with earlier bans on Asian immigration enacted in 1882 and 1917, did play a role in reducing the number of immigrants, I believe their influence has been overstated" (Massey 1995, 635). In support of his contention, he points out that the quotas did not apply to immigrants from the Western Hemisphere, and that after World War I, which induced a sharp drop in immigration, "European immigration began to revive, despite the restrictive quotas" (636). I shall first demonstrate that the second point is not supported by the relevant statistics, and I shall deal with Massey's observation regarding the Western Hemisphere in the next section.

As evidence that U.S. quotas did not reduce immigration significantly, Massey cites statistical evidence to the effect that during the period from 1921 to 1930 some 412,000 immigrants arrived from Germany, 455,000 from Italy, 227,000 from Poland, and 102,000 from Czechoslovakia, supplementing "large numbers" from countries that were not limited by quotas. However, he fails to examine the distribution of these decennial numbers in the years *before* and *after* enactment of the restrictive legislation. When this is done, the evidence clearly contradicts his assertion. The demonstration requires a detailed consideration of the regulations and their consequences.

It is certainly true that World War I induced a sharp drop in immigration—mostly because European belligerents did not allow their populations to leave—and that European immigration rapidly revived afterward, when European men were demobilized and civilian shipping resumed. The most important legislative barrier imposed in the intervening period was a literacy requirement (in the immigrant's own language), enacted in 1917, three decades after it was first advocated as a deterrent. Its ineffectiveness at the time under consideration is hardly surprising, since by World War I the pool of literate males was very large, even among the lower classes of the less developed regions of Europe. Recorded immigration rose from a mere 24,627 in 1919 to 246,295 the following year, and 652,364 in 1921, the last year when it was unrestricted by numerical limits (U.S. Bureau of the Census 1971, 56–59). The escalation suggested that arrivals were well on their way toward the one-million level of the immediate prewar years; given European political and economic upheavals, there was reason to expect that this would soon be exceeded—possibly in keeping with the previous experience of a doubling of incoming numbers in each of the four prewar decades. Interpreted in the light of the pervasive nativism, itself exacerbated by wartime nationalism and reactions to the Russian revolution, these developments and expectations prompted decisionmakers to impose an unprecedented quantitative limit on immigration from Europe (Higham 1994). They further allocated the newly rarefied entries by way of nationality quotas designed to reduce immigration from southern and eastern Europe, an approach first proposed in a congressional report shortly before the war.

Applicable to the independent countries of the

"Eastern Hemisphere" (excluding China, subject to near-absolute exclusion), the 1921 law limited the yearly number of immigrants of each nationality to 3 percent of the number of foreign-born of that nationality enumerated in the United States in 1910, making for a maximum of 356,000 (Hutchinson 1981, 483–87). As a result, European immigration immediately dipped to 216,385, but it then rose again to 307,920 in 1923, and to 364,339 in 1924 (as recent immigrants brought in their spouses and children). The Congress then devised a more draconian law, signed in 1924, which provided for a maximum of 150,000 a year, to be allocated in proportion to the "national origins" of the American population as of 1920. The measure was designed to enlarge the British quota while concomitantly reducing the German, Irish, and Scandinavian allotments, and even more drastically reducing the quotas granted to more recent arrivals, who had not yet produced a large progeny. Since the notion of "national origins" constituted a putative ascendancy, for which there were no official records of any sort, the system required elaborate calculations and was not scheduled to go into effect until 1929; meanwhile, admissions were cut to 2 percent of each of the foreign-born groups as of 1890 (rather than 1910, so as to roll back the southern and eastern tide of the intervening years). The smaller percentage and the change of base year immediately reduced the annual total by more than half, to 165,000. Accordingly, entries from Europe as a whole fell to 148,366 in 1925 and remained below 170,000 a year for the remainder of the decade.

Until 1929 the number of annual entries available to German nationals was quite large; hence, the fact cited by Massey that 412,000 German immigrants arrived in the 1920s is irrelevant. However, when the national-origin system came into effect, the German quota was lowered to 25,957, and this was reflected in an immediate reduction of admissions from 46,751 in 1928 to 26,569 in 1929. As for the other countries he mentions, there can be no doubt as to the acute and immediate effects of restriction. In support of his contention, he points out that the Italian decennial total reached 455,000; however, fully half (222,260) of these came in the single year 1921, *before* the nationality quotas went into effect.[6] A first numerical limitation was then imposed, followed by a more severe one in 1924, as a result of which the average annual level of Italian arrivals for the remainder of the decade (1925 to 1930) fell to 14,969—about 7 percent of 1921 entries.[7] The effect of restriction was even more acute for Poles: of the decennial total, 179,068—79 percent—came in 1921 alone, and the average for the postquota years was 8,111, slightly less than 5 percent of the 1921 level.

Similar demonstrations of the effectiveness of restrictive regulation can be provided for other periods and other groups as well. During the Great Depression decade (1931 to 1940), U.S. immigration from all sources amounted to only 464,275, the lowest level since the 1840s, and immigration from Europe alone numbered 348,289—well below the authorized quota level, which would have amounted to some 1.5 million for the decade. Although this might be interpreted as prima facie validation of the "individual choice" approach as prospective immigrants became aware that the probability of employment was well below 1.0, in reality matters were not that simple. In the face of rising unemployment, Congress attempted to suspend immigration altogether; however, at the request of President Hoover, the State Department determined that it might be reduced well below the ongoing level without new legislation merely by strictly enforcing the clause prohibiting the issuance of visas to persons "likely to become a public charge" (LPC), following the successful use of this approach to reduce Mexican immigration (discussed later). Accordingly, State Department officials instructed European consuls that they were under obligation to consider any applicant dependent on wages as falling automatically into the LPC category (Divine 1957; Hodgdon 1931). This resulted in the immediate turndown of about 80 percent of applicants and the creation of extremely long waiting lists, whose existence indicates quite clearly that the dramatic reduction in European immigration in the early 1930s cannot be attributed in the main to the immigrants' calculations.[8]

The effectiveness of state power is attributable to the elaboration of the unprecedented system of "remote control" referred to earlier. Launched in 1924, this system required all foreign nationals coming from overseas to produce an entry visa prior to boarding a U.S.-bound vessel—a procedure now commonplace in air travel throughout the world. The possibility of developing such a system arose from the fact that, in relation to Europe, the United States was effectively an island. However, for this potential to be actualized, it was necessary to create practically de novo a body of professional consular officials with the authority to exercise gatekeeping functions (Hodgdon 1931) as well as additional regulatory power over U.S. and even foreign shipping companies. Once the system was put in place, prospective immigrants were screened before departure from their home country in accordance with the multiple criteria indicated, including a medical examination administered by U.S. Public Health physicians or local doctors certified by the U.S. government, to the point of making Ellis Island altogether obsolete.

Those familiar with the contemporary scene might surmise that applicants turned down as immigrants might enter as visitors and then remain in the United States as "overstayers." However, the probability of success was low because American consuls were instructed to deny visitor visas to persons judged to be of the "immigrant class."[9] It was still possible to enter surreptitiously by way of Mexico or Canada, but the latter country shortly adopted remote control as well, and Mexico was difficult to reach by direct travel from Europe.[10]

It is notorious that these regulatory mechanisms made it almost impossible for most refugees to gain admission to the United States from 1933 to 1945, a period of mounting political persecution and violence, despite a huge increase in demand (Feingold 1970; Wyman 1968, 1984). The immense visa waiting lists of the period from 1945 to 1965, extending up to fifty years into the future for the least favored nationalities, further suggest that despite various ad hoc laws that raised immigration from certain European countries in the postwar period above the quota level, absent the apparatus of restriction, incoming numbers would have been much higher.

Asian exclusion provides an equally powerful demonstration of the effectiveness of regulation. As analyzed by Bill Ong Hing (1993a), measures of growing severity from 1875 to 1943 reduced decennial Chinese immigration from a high of 123,201 in the 1870s to 14,799 in the 1890s; the level rose slowly to 29,907 in the 1920s and was then reduced to 4,928 in the following decade. American policy not only prevented the expansion of established communities but, thanks to concerted efforts to keep out Chinese women, effected an absolute decline of the population of Chinese ancestry from 118,746 in 1900 to a low of 85,202 in 1920, after which it grew slightly to 106,334 in 1940—still below the 1900 level. This successful containment of an abhorred population group constitutes a unique event in American history.

Overall there can be no better demonstration of state effectiveness than the fact that in the 1920s the United States asserted to the world that it no longer wished to be "a nation of immigrants" and managed to counteract the dynamics of the international population system, including the effect of the networks that had developed in the wake of the immense immigration wave of previous decades. As a result of these efforts, by 1965 the proportion of foreign-born in the population had reached approximately 5 percent, its lowest level since Tocqueville came to America in 1830 and saw it as a nation of settled "Anglo-Americans."

Immigration from Mexico

Against this background of generally effective state action in regulating immigration from overseas, still the major portion of the U.S. intake, the persistence of unregulated movement from Mexico stands out as a deviant case and therefore warrants special theoretical attention.[11] However, it is by no means clear what sort of deviant case it is. Considered in the light of perennial pronouncements by the U.S. government regarding its determination to eliminate illegal immigration, it constitutes an egregious instance of policy failure. However, the odd bundle of legal measures and administrative practices that have accumulated over the decades can also be thought of as amounting to a purposefully weak regulatory system that allows a relatively stable informal "guest worker" program to stay in place, in keeping with the clearly expressed preferences of powerful regional economic entrepreneurs, whose interests have come to be assumed as an obligation by the American state. Assessed in that perspective, on balance the policy must be reckoned a "success."

Mexicans began migrating toward the Texas cotton fields in the later decades of the nineteenth century, when the unprecedented influx of American capital into mining, farming, and transportation transformed Mexico's isolated northern states into "the Border" (Katz 1981, 7). As steadily more draconian measures were deployed to prevent further Asian immigration, Californian fruit and vegetable growers also turned south to find workers to man the rising "factories in the fields" (Coolidge 1909). After 1910 many Mexicans fled northward to escape the upheavals of the Mexican revolution and the ensuing "secret war" waged by the United States against the revolutionaries. Although this was a period of steadily more forceful regulation of overseas immigration, by and large laissez-faire prevailed along the southern border. Following the entry of the United States into World War I, Congress explicitly exempted some seventy thousand Mexicans recruited as agricultural and railroad workers from the array of "qualitative" requirements designed to deter immigration from Europe, notably the LPC clause, the hefty head tax, the prohibition of advance contracts, and the recently enacted literacy test (Rico 1992, 243). After the war the exemption was terminated, but spokesmen for agricultural interests testified before Congress that they objected to any interference with free cross-border recruitment and pointed out that there was no way the requirements could be enforced. They also insisted that Mexicans came to the United States to work but not to live and were endowed with a "homing pigeon instinct" that drove them to return. Thus, Mexican laborers—commonly referred to as "wetbacks" (los mojados)—continued to flow freely throughout the period (Calavita 1992; Craig 1971; Garcia 1980, 142; Garcia y Griego 1988).

Concurrently, formal immigration from Mexico expanded as well, despite the restrictive "qualitative regulations."[12] After the level passed the 50,000 mark in 1920 and reached nearly 90,000 in 1924, the congressional anti-immigration camp urged the adoption of limitative quotas to keep out Mexican "half-breeds," who, as nonwhites, were subject to Jim Crow laws in Texas. However, the State Department argued that this would be interpreted by the Mexican government as an unfriendly act and would interfere with ongoing negotiations to obtain compensation for U.S. properties nationalized by its more revolutionary predecessor. As an alternative, they pledged stricter enforcement of the literacy test and the LPC clause; given widespread poverty and illiteracy, this strategy would prevent ordinary Mexicans from qualifying as legal immigrants (Divine 1957). In keeping with this objective, documented Mexican immigration was reduced to some 40,000 in 1929, 12,703 in 1930, and 3,333 the next year. The average was only 2,232 a year for the 1930s as a whole.

The hybrid regulatory system that emerged along the southern border in the 1920s—an effectively enforced barrier to formal immigration—combined with laissez-faire regarding the movement of labor, makes sense if the objective was to deter, not the physical entry of Mexicans into the United States, but rather their social and political entry into American society. American policy was highly effective in meeting this goal: Mexicans tended to return home when no longer needed, and in any case, their illegal status made it easy for American authorities, whenever they wished, to expel them without complicated legal procedures. Those who stayed on were confined by way of residential segregation and, in sharp contrast with the treatment of immigrants from Europe, were not subject to Americanization efforts. "Success" with Mexican immigrants was indicated by an extremely low rate of naturalization. How much permanent settlement resulted is difficult to estimate because the Bureau of the Census tended to view *all* persons of Mexican origin—including many born in the United States—as only temporary residents (Lorey 1990).

Following the outbreak of World War II, the Mexican government's bargaining power increased because the United States wanted to secure its strategic support. Accordingly, the two states agreed to a labor program based on government-supervised contracts, generally known as the bracero program. However, informal recruitment continued alongside the bracero program because American employers sought to reduce costs by avoiding the regulations and workers sought to avoid exploitation by the Mexican officials who controlled the awarding of the contracts. At the end of the war the United States unilaterally terminated the program under conjoined pressure from employers and organized labor, which had abhorred "contract labor" of any kind ever since the heyday of anti-Chinese agitation. Informal recruitment then resumed, often with the cooperation of U.S. authorities, who legalized "wetbacks" whenever needed by rounding them up on the American side, pushing them over the border, and then readmitting them as temporary workers. Although a commission appointed by President Truman recommended the enactment of sanctions against employers of illegal foreign workers, in accordance with organized labor's wishes this remained a dead letter.

The bracero program was reinstated in 1952 when the outbreak of the Korean War occasioned an acute labor shortage in the United States and concomitantly once again improved Mexico's bargaining position. This time Mexico demanded that the program also provide for employer sanctions, without which there would be no incentive for them to use legal braceros rather than the cheaper and more docile "wetbacks," and it also insisted that Texas be excluded because of its Jim Crow laws. In 1952 the United States duly enacted a law that prohibited aiding, harboring, and concealing illegal immigrants; however, agricultural interests secured the insertion of a clause (popularly known as the "Texas proviso") specifying that the usual and normal practices incident to employment, even the provision of shelter, "shall not be deemed to constitute harboring." The measure thus in effect institutionalized the procurement of illegal immigrants as an informal component of U.S. immigration policy, which continued alongside the bracero system.

In the 1950s the state of California emerged as an actor with distinctive interests in this sphere: the preference of its growers for informal recruitment had occasioned mounting welfare obligations, for which the state had failed to secure additional revenue. Accordingly, the state's Republican governor, Earl Warren, urged his friends in the Eisenhower administration to implement more effective border controls. In response, the administration, from 1954 to 1955, mounted "Operation Wetback," which rounded up and summarily expelled several hundred thousand Mexican workers; the main objective, however, was to persuade U.S. employers to employ braceros rather than "wetbacks." The operation was proclaimed a success when the annual number of contracts soared and apprehensions declined.

In subsequent years the growing mechanization of cotton harvesting, stimulated in part by the higher cost of legal braceros, reduced the demand for temporary labor in Texas, leaving the expanding California fruit and vegetable industries as the main users. However, in 1960, after the CBS documentary *Harvest of Shame* established in the public mind a link between the bracero program and the plight of domestic migrants, the Eisenhower Administration decided to discontinue the program altogether. Its Democratic successors concurred, owing to pressure from labor; following a number of extensions urged by the growers, the bracero program finally expired in 1964. However, in the absence of more effective enforcement, this termination amounted once again to a reinstatement of unregulated procurement, which—according to apprehension reports, widely publicized by the Immigration and Naturalization Service (INS) to increase its budget—began to soar.

Legal immigration again expanded in the postwar period, and by the early 1960s Mexico had emerged as the single largest source country. Arising at a time when the Kennedy administration's immigration reform proposal (discussed in the next section) was wending its way through Congress, this development prompted southern congressional leaders and other defenders of white America to impose an unprecedented ceiling on immigration from the Western Hemisphere as a whole; a decade later, when Mexican immigration stood at around 70,000 a year, the worldwide annual maximum of 20,000 per country (not including nonquota relatives) was imposed as well. This constituted in effect a reinstatement of the hybrid system elaborated in the 1920s.

Amid the stagflation occasioned by the oil crisis in the 1970s, employer sanctions twice passed the House only to be defeated in the more conservative Senate. In the face of increasing outcry over the economic and social consequences of illegal immigration and growing agitation in the more and more politically powerful Sunbelt about expanding Chicano urban communities that were said to resist assimilation, President Carter appointed the Select Commission on Immigration and Refugee Policy (SCIRP) to get around the policy stalemate. In 1981 the commissioners recommended a package deal: the imposition of sanctions on employers of unauthorized foreign workers, and the grant of permanent resident status to illegal aliens who had become de facto permanent residents by entering the United States prior to some specified date (Zolberg 1989). Completed in 1986 after much travail, the Immigration Reform and Control Act (IRCA) offered what was popularly termed an "amnesty" to illegal residents who had entered the United States before 1982. The law also sought to appease the growers by extending a special legalization program to some 1.2 million agricultural workers who had entered later. Although the law made it illegal for any employer to "knowingly" recruit, refer, or hire undocumented workers, it provided only for civil fines and absolved employers from any responsibility for verifying the documents presented to them. Moreover, mechanisms for enforcement remained rudimentary. Altogether, the legalization programs created a pool of some three million permanent residents and prospective citizens, who would eventually stimulate more immigration by way of family reunion.

IRCA also provided considerable support for research on the effects of employer sanctions; it overwhelmingly suggests that after a slight initial deterrent effect, the impact of sanctions on unauthorized entry and employment remains minimal (Kossoudji 1992; Massey and Espinosa 1997; Massey and Singer 1995; Papademetriou, Lowell, and Cobb-Clark 1991). Although some skeptics contend that sanctions cannot possibly work because of the nature of unauthorized immigration, others attribute their ineffectiveness to inadequate enforcement and insist that sanctions would work if properly implemented. However, this would require enlisting employers in the regulatory process by imposing heavier responsibilities on them, as well as enhancing the federal government's police apparatus, notably by instituting some sort of verifiable ID card. Both possibilities have provoked considerable political opposition, from diverse locations on the political spectrum.[13] Employer obligations were raised somewhat in 1996, but it is too early to tell whether this will render the system more effective.

Post-1965 "New" Immigration

Massey (1995, 638) also questions the relevance of regulation with regard to American immigration in the post-1965 period, asserting that the 1965 law, which eliminated the national-origin quota system, "was neither the sole nor the most important cause of the increase in numbers or the shift in origins," and he again suggests that "scholars have generally overstated the role of the 1965 amendments in bringing about the new immigration." It is quite true that the 1965 law was not the *sole* cause of the change in the quantity and characteristics of immigration in the intervening third of a century. This does not demonstrate, however, that immigration *policy* as a whole was irrelevant: the changes in quantity and sources that cannot be attributed to the 1965 law were occasioned mostly by American refugee policy and by the 1986 legalization program discussed previously, both of which were very deliberate policy options.

With regard to composition, the architects of the 1965 law mainly set out to eliminate the national-origin quotas that discriminated against southern and eastern Europeans; in their place, they established an annual maximum of 20,000 immigrants per country worldwide, to be allocated by way of ranked "preferences." The law initially facilitated additional immigration from Italy, Greece, and some other European countries, as intended. Although conservative opponents of the reform warned that the new universalistic approach would also foster an unprecedented growth of immigration from Asia and Africa, its liberal supporters dismissed this prospect as a red herring. In retrospect, it is impossible to establish whether they were being disingenuous or merely lacked an understanding of global migration dynamics. In any case, the change of policy must surely be ranked as a "cause" of the changing composition of immigration, even if some of the consequences it generated were unanticipated.

The quantitative expansion of legal immigration is attributable to the law as well. While it established a worldwide annual quota limit of 290,000 (170,000 for the Eastern Hemisphere, 120,000 for the Western)—raised to 366,000 in 1990—it also provided for new additional nonquota categories, notably the parents of citizens in addition to their spouses and children; these nonquota immigrants account for a very large part of the soaring legal immigration in the post-1965 period.[14] In 1992, for example, they numbered 235,484, an increment of 64 percent above the 366,000 "baseline" annual admissions authorized under the several preferences (Fix and Passel 1994). Although SCIRP considered altering the preference system so as to reduce the "chaining" that accounts for this phenomenon, it was sharply divided on the subject, and perennial congressional efforts in this direction (notably in the course of what emerged as the 1990 law) have so far been unsuccessful, largely because of effective pressures from affected ethnic groups and constituencies. As things stand, there is no doubt that American immigration largely reflects the design of the country's immigration policy, which is highly attuned to family networks by virtue of congressional and presidential responsiveness to organized ethnic constituencies.

Leaving aside the IRCA legalization program discussed earlier, the balance of the post-1965 growth in legal immigration is attributable to U.S. refugee policy. In 1992, for example, refugees and asylees numbered 134,290, an increment of 37 percent above the baseline level of 366,000. Although the 1965 law itself provided for only 10,200 refugees a year (6 percent of the 170,000 admissions allotted to the Eastern Hemisphere), after its enactment the U.S. government repeatedly invoked foreign and security policy imperatives to initiate much larger refugee programs, as it had done ever since the end of World War II (Zolberg 1995).[15] Altogether, between 1945 and 1965, refugee programs increased admissions by about one-third above the level provided for by ordinary immigration regulations.

Similar developments took place in the wake of the 1965 reform. Major episodes include the Cuban "freedom flights," initiated the very year the law was enacted;[16] the resettlement of South Vietnamese associated with the United States at the fall of Saigon in 1975; the intake of Indochinese "boat people" from 1979 on; and the welcoming of Soviet Jews, whose freedom of exit was secured by holding up the threat of trade sanctions. In

1980 Congress enacted a new refugee law, which took refugees out of the quota system altogether and provided instead for the admission of individual asylum seekers in keeping with U.S. obligations under international law, as well as of others whose admission might be "in the national interest," as determined by the president in consultation with Congress. It was estimated that refugees would not exceed 50,000 annually (including some 5,000 qualified asylum seekers); however, by the end of the decade refugees and other humanitarian admissions added between 100,000 and 150,000 a year to the immigration total. It might be noted that after they settle in, asylees and refugees also generate ordinary immigration by way of family reunion.

However one might assess the desirability of these additional flows, there can be no doubt that they are not occasioned by a mere increase in the pool of refugees in the world at large but are entirely the result of deliberate American policy choices. The situation with regard to El Salvador and Haiti is more ambiguous; although American authorities generally turned down individual asylum seekers from those countries and, in the case of Haitians, even resorted to proactive interdiction on the high seas, many of them nevertheless secured an extended de facto haven in the United States thanks to legal actions undertaken by political supporters and a residually permissive societal environment. The 1990 immigration law, which provided temporary protected status for several hundred thousand illegal Salvadorans, in effect converted them into ordinary immigrants.

Evidence from the World at Large

Additional evidence on behalf of the important role of state regulations in shaping immigration can easily be found outside the United States. One of the most dramatic demonstrations is provided by the United Kingdom. Notwithstanding its standing in the first third of the twentieth century as a country with one of the highest per capita incomes in the world and attractive political conditions, as of 1930 it had the lowest proportion of foreign-born of any industrial country on either side of the Atlantic (Kirk 1946), an outcome for which the immigration restrictions it imposed as early as 1905 and reinforced in the 1920s provide the most likely explanation. The growth and composition of immigration to the United Kingdom in the immediate post–World War II years are also attributable to specific policies, notably the decision to initiate and then discontinue the procurement of European "displaced persons" as supplemental workers; the maintenance of an "open-door" policy with regard to Ireland, even after it became fully independent; the largely politically motivated 1948 decision to authorize entry and settlement by "New Commonwealth" citizens; and the recruitment of West Indians into the public sector (notably London Transport) as a way of reducing political tensions in the colonies (Rees 1993). From 1962 on, British immigration policy became increasingly restrictionist, and by the early 1980s legal immigration was reduced to some 50,000 a year—not including the Irish—with a reportedly low level of unauthorized settlement.

Although there is no doubt that this outcome is attributable to British policy, there is some question as to whether it represents a policy success or failure: on the one hand, the annual level of immigration is well below the putative "demand" for entry, and much lower than the actual level of immigration to France or Germany. (The contrast is even greater when population size is taken into consideration.) On the other hand, it remains above the United Kingdom's "zero immigration" objective (Freeman 1994; Layton-Henry 1994). Is the glass half full, or is it half empty? The question is applicable to the regulatory capacity of affluent liberal democracies more generally. Overall, as indicated earlier, the pessimist's perspective has gained the upper hand. This judgment is founded on the notion of a gap between the goals of immigration policy and the actual results achieved, but the preceding discussion suggests that the goals themselves are often ambiguous as well as grossly unrealistic. The significance of the checkered history of U.S. policy regarding its southern border can be elucidated by reflecting on parallels with two other cases of regulation, traffic control and gun control. With regard to the first, the United States has emerged without any apparent contention as a "strong state": it deploys an elaborate system of regulations and subjects every aspiring driver to fairly strict testing and the requirement of a relatively foolproof identification document, which can now be checked in a central location by just about any policeman in the country. Although they are administered by a variety of state and local authorities, these regulations are nevertheless fairly uniform nationwide. Overall, this approach has contributed to the achievement of a remarkably low international ranking in the rate of automobile accidents, a situation that has in fact steadily improved. By contrast, with regard to gun control the United States is a "weak state": it has much more permissive regulations than in comparable societies abroad, generally inadequate enforcement of whatever regulations do exist, and consequently a comparatively high rate of homicide and gunshot wounds. Although a number of factors contribute to this outcome, the determination of a well-organized minority to block the elaboration of an effective regulatory system, while effectively enlisting patriotic sentiment in its cause, is generally acknowledged as a major contributing factor.

Although the prevalence of traffic control indicates that there are no fundamental structural or cultural impediments in American society to the elaboration of a complex system of regulation involving intrusive law enforcement that affects nearly every individual, the case of gun control suggests that the absence of an effective regulatory system is itself a "policy." American immigration policy with regard to incoming overseas movement may be more like traffic control, but its stance regarding movement across its southern border resembles its stance toward gun control. In that light, the high incidence of unauthorized "back-door" migration can hardly be taken as evidence of the ineffectiveness of policy.[17]

The example of traffic control brings up the fundamental importance of selecting realistic objectives in evaluating the effectiveness of policy. No regulatory agency expects to achieve zero speeders or zero accidents; rather, the goals usually consist of a combination of improvement in relation to some established baseline (for example, bringing down the annual rate of accidents in relation to the number of cars on the road, or the number of miles traveled) and the achievement of specific targets, such as the elimination of particularly hazardous spots. Although the INS publishes "apprehensions," this is a "rate" only in relation to time (that is, the number per year), not in relation to actual traffic (attempted crossings).[18] With regard to immigration regulation, the most relevant denominator would be some estimate of "potential immigrants," with actual immigrants—both legal and unauthorized—as the numerator. Although it is impossible to establish such a denominator with quantitative precision, it is not very difficult to set forth a credible order of magnitude.

It is reasonable to surmise that the pool of international migrants aspiring to relocate to the affluent countries of the North has continued to expand under the combined effects of demographic growth in the poorer countries, persistently unequal conditions in the world at large, and widespread information about opportunities elsewhere. Because of the availability of cheap transportation, the nearly total lifting of state-imposed barriers to exit, and the multiplication of networks, potential migrants possess an unprecedented capacity for moving. Yet the combined intake of the affluent countries—including both legal and unauthorized migrants, granting the most generous estimates of the latter—has certainly leveled off since the 1970s, and possibly decreased overall. This is applicable even to the United States, where legal immigration appears to have peaked, and by all reports the rate of unauthorized immigration has reached a plateau as well. In short, international migration theories will remain woefully incomplete so long as they fail to take into account the positive and negative roles of states in shaping international population movements.

International Migration Policies in a Bounded World

A Global Perspective

The starting point for theorizing about migration policies is an understanding that they enter into play not merely as "error factors" in an equation whose parameters are social and economic, but as constitutive elements of international migration as a distinctive social phenomenon. In short, *international* migration is an inherently *political* process, which arises from the organization of the world into a congeries of mutually exclusive sovereign states, commonly referred to as the "Westphalian system" (Zolberg 1978a, 1981a).[19] It involves the transfer of a person from the jurisdiction of one state to that of another—in whole or in part—and the eventuality of a change of membership in an inclusive political community. Accordingly, the relevant policies encompass not only the regulation of outward and inward movement across state borders—including the movement of persons who are not, or declare that they are not, migrants—but also the rules governing the acquisition, maintenance, loss, or voluntary relinquishment of "membership" in all its aspects, political, social, economic, and cultural.

Migration policies vary enormously, both historically and between states in a given period. States have at times prohibited the exit of just about all of their population and used draconian means to implement this policy, such as the imposition of galley slavery in seventeenth-century France to prevent Huguenots from departing for Protestant states, or shoot-to-kill policing in the German Democratic Republic as late as a decade ago. At the same time, they have also acted ruthlessly to push out religious, ethnic, or social groups, and at times laissez-faire has prevailed. All these stances coexisted during the cold war period, suggesting that there is no overall historical trend toward convergence. A similar range of variation can be found on the entry side. States have encouraged and facilitated the importation of slaves, and they have stimulated immigration by providing subsidized travel, lands, security, and easy citizenship or by promising jobs. However, they have also prohibited settlement or, again, adopted a laissez-faire stance. Positive or negative stances with regard to both exit and entry are usually defined in relation to specified categories of persons established on the basis of a wide array of criteria, including objective socioeconomic and cultural attributes (degree of skill, education, wealth; religion, language, nationality, race) as well as putative moral or political disposition (judged likely or unlikely to commit crimes or to support or oppose the regime). As a result, emigration and immigration policies often amount to complex arrays of disparate regulations. States also exhibit considerable variation regarding modes of relinquishing and acquiring membership, including not only formal citizenship but political, social, and cultural rights.

How are we to make theoretical sense of this variation? At the most general level, "whether migration is controlled by those who send, by those who go, or by those who receive, it mirrors the world as it is at the time" (Davis 1974, 96). In terms more consonant with the IUSSP committee's approach, the world can be conceptualized as a "global population system" in relation to which sending and receiving states, much like the migrants themselves, figure as "utility-maximizing" agents that respond to changing world-historical and local conditions by modifying their comportment—in the case of states, their policies regarding exit and entry.

However, two qualifications are called for. As the complexity of contemporary debates on immigration policy in the affluent liberal democracies indicates, "utility" encompasses not only a population's economic value but also its putative value in relation to cultural and political objectives. Moreover, "utility maximizing" cannot be mechanically transposed from individuals to states. As executors of policies, states do not function as autonomous actors (even in the loose sense in which we consider individuals to do so), but rather as instruments manipulated by internal actors who have gained the upper hand in a particular sphere at a given time. Legal and administrative institutions, as well as political traditions, which constitute the legacy of earlier policies, also play a significant role in shaping current responses.

Historically, migration policies have been shaped by the dynamics of world capitalism, on the one hand, and the dynamics of the international state system, on the other, within the context of epochal population dynamics (Zolberg 1981b, 1983a, 1986). Since the global population system and the system of states are both finite, migration policies are extremely interactive: any emigration always entails immediate immigration somewhere else; conversely, the possibility of immigrating affects decisions to emigrate; and the closing or opening of a particular national gate affects the potential flows into other states.[20] However, in contrast with the sphere of international trade, for example, far from being founded on a recognition of this interactivity, state policies regarding emigration and immigration have been notoriously unilateral. As noted by Hannah Arendt (1973, 278), for example, "sovereignty is nowhere more absolute than in matters of emigration, naturalization, nationality, and expulsion." This highlights the theoretical significance of even slight departures from the sovereignty baseline observable today (Soysal 1994).

Exit and entry policies might be arrayed along an axis defined by negative and positive poles. Given the considerable variation in exit policies that can be observed, the impact of these policies on the formation of migration networks, and their interactivity with immigration policies elsewhere, it is evident that a comprehensive theory pertaining to the role of states in regulating international migration must cover the exit side as well. One basic proposition is that the possibility of preventing exit is a requisite for the effective exercise of most types of "predatory rule" (Hirschman 1981; Levi 1988). In the early modern era, under prevailing conditions of demographic scarcity, for the European mercantilist and bellicist state acquisition and retention of human capital for economic production and war was a basic source of power; from this perspective, the most important form of control pertained to *outward* movement. Accordingly, unauthorized emigration was tantamount to treason and punishable by death or enslavement. The continuing significance of this policy stance is highlighted by its resurgence in the twentieth century as the hallmark of totalitarian states with command economies (Dowty 1987; Zolberg 1978b).

The leading patterns of forced exit, including deliberate expulsions as well as escape from persecution or violence, can also be accounted for by the dynamics of state and nation formation within a bounded international system (Zolberg 1983b; Zolberg, Suhrke, and Aguayo 1989). However, given space limitations and this volume's exclusive concern with the United States, in the remainder of this chapter I shall focus on the entry side only. Although considerable attention has been devoted to variation among the contemporary immigration policies of capitalist democracies (Brochmann 1996; Cornelius, Martin, and Hollifield 1994a; Freeman 1995a; Kubat 1979a), the most striking fact about them is that, if one imagines a hypothetical continuum ranging from open to closed borders, they are clustered very narrowly around the closed pole. Notwithstanding the post–World War II modifications noted earlier, which constituted a genuine "liberalization" in relation to the extremely restrictionist regime established by the affluent states in the first quarter of the century, the near-zero baseline remains a constitutive element of the contemporary regime with regard to the supply of entries in relation to the demand for them. As the theorist of international trade Jagdish Bhagwati (1984, 684) noted some time ago, the process of international migration is characterized by "disincentives" rather than "incentives"; this observation led him to hypothesize quite correctly that if the socialist countries were to let people out, "the effective constraint on the numbers migrating would soon become the immigration legislations of the destination countries." Most contemporary European states have in effect adopted a zero-immigration objective but make very limited provisions for asylum seekers and immediate relatives; the traditional immigration countries, including the United States, are similarly determined to keep out the world's population, in general, but make somewhat broader provisions for family reunion and retain an acquisitive element in the form of limited programs for admitting persons who might contribute substantial capital or skills.

Coming to grips with this stark reality is a prerequisite for any meaningful theoretical discussion of the role of states in regulating immigration. Arising from the aggregate policies of the states of the international system, and undertaken in response to domestic considerations as well as interactively in response to each other's policies, the restrictive immigration regime prevails worldwide because it constitutes a sine qua non for maintaining the Westphalian international state system, as well as the privileged position of the core states amid highly unequal conditions (Emmanuel 1972; Nett 1971; Petras 1980; Wallerstein 1974).[21] In less exalted language, economic modeling suggests that the hypothetical elimination of borders would stimulate worldwide economic growth but also result in an equalization of conditions, thus producing a vast redistribution of income to the benefit of the population of poorer countries. In effect, borders prevent labor from commanding the same price everywhere and also prevent people from the poorer countries from gaining access to the bundles of "public goods" dispensed by the more affluent states, which constitute an important part of their populations' income (Hamilton and Whalley 1984).

It is also widely believed that restrictions on access to membership constitute a sine qua non for democratic governance, which requires at least some minimal degree of community. Although there is intense debate over precisely what level of immigration might be allowed for, and what priorities might be established, there is also broad agreement that under present world conditions the level would at best fall far short of the demand for access (Barry and Goodin 1992; Carens 1987; Walzer 1981).

Accordingly, the process of decisionmaking at the level of a given state is driven by two quite distinct types of considerations, each of which relates to a distinct sphere of social interaction. In the perspective of capitalist dynamics, immigrants of any kind—including refugees—are considered primarily as workers. Policies are shaped by the prevailing "class compromise" and by the specific configuration of economic interests in the country in question, in keeping with the imperatives of prevailing technological and economic conditions (Offe 1984; Przeworski and Wallerstein 1985). Immigrants are characteristically welcomed by employers because they reduce the unit cost of labor (that is, they lower wages) and also increase its elasticity; conversely, they are characteristically resented by resident workers as unfair competitors willing to accept lower wages (which constitute an improvement over their income in the country of origin) and below-standard conditions. At worst, they may not only lower wages but altogether displace natives. However, even the most profit-driven capitalists are unlikely to favor a *huge* increase in labor supply that would occasion a major social disruption; hence, in contemporary capitalist democracies, arguments on behalf of open borders appear perennially as the playful musings of free-market ideologues, but almost never in policy debates.

These considerations, usually cast in a Marxian framework, have given rise to a considerable body of work accounting for the tendency of advanced industrial societies to recruit "guest workers" from less developed countries (Burawoy 1976; Castles and Kossack 1985; Petras 1981). An alternative explanation was provided by the theory of labor segmentation, whereby under the conditions of the welfare state the upper strata of the workforce is assimilated into "fixed" capital, leading to the institutionalization of a distinct "flexible" segment—for which, again, guest workers of one sort or another are very convenient (Gordon, Edwards, and Reich 1982; Piore 1979).

Still in the economic sphere, immigrants are also consumers of goods and services, both the ordinary kind that are bought in the marketplace and the public goods that are automatically available to all residents. Immigrants tend to be welcomed by sellers of individual goods and services—for example, by real estate agents in port-of-entry cities—but from the perspective of public goods the situation is more complex. Recent U.S. debates regarding the "balance sheet" of immigration in relation to welfare highlights the difficulty of establishing whether immigrants contribute more in taxes than they consume in public services or whether they are "free riders" (Smith and Edmunson 1997).[22] Because different units of aggregation are used to draw up a balance sheet of the various costs and benefits involved, immigrants may be "good" for the whole economy but "bad" for a particular locality or social group—or vice versa. (For example, they may reinvigorate declining Rust Belt cities.) Incidentally, similar considerations are also applicable to international-level assessments of the economic value of particular human flows by sending and receiving countries as a whole.

However, all types of immigrants—including even temporary workers—also constitute a political and cultural presence, the putative impact of which on the host country's "way of life," "cohesiveness," or, in current discourse, "identity" evokes a distinctive dimension to be considered. Although the process in question is well evoked by classical sociology's concept of "integration," I shall use the term "identity axis." In almost any immigration situation, there are significant groups among the hosts who believe that newcomers in general, or particular groups among them, would jeopardize the established national ways. In the United States alone, just about every cultural attribute imaginable has been found objectionable at one time or another, notably "race"—as constructed in the nineteenth and early twentieth centuries, referring not only to "Asiatics" and blacks but also to "mixed-breed" Mexicans, different European nationalities, and Jews—religion (particularly Roman Catholics from the eighteenth century until quite recently), and language (German speakers in the early twentieth century, Spanish speakers today). Similarly hostile responses have surfaced elsewhere, notably toward Jews from eastern Europe in most of Western Europe yesterday, "Arabs" and Muslims more generally throughout Europe today, and the Sephardic Jews who arrived in Israel in the 1950s, and Ethiopian Jews later on.

Although reactions such as these are attributable in large part to persistent prejudice and xenophobia, which tend to exaggerate the problematic aspects of the situation, it should be recognized that the settlement—or prospective settlement—of any substantial group of people whose culture diverges markedly from the host's own is likely to call the established "cultural compromise" pertaining to religious, linguistic, and racial diversity into question and hence is a legitimate source of concern.[23] The key questions are always: How different can we be? How alike must we be? And how are the answers to these questions to be implemented organizationally and materially? (Zolberg and Long 1999).

As it enters into play with regard to immigration, "identity" centers on nationality.[24] Originating largely in the course of efforts to institutionalize "predatory rule" in late medieval European states, modern nations have come to be perceived by most of their members as familylike bodies, with a common ancestry and a common destiny. Although the formula for identity is usually founded on some objective characteristics of the society, such as the language actually spoken by much of the population and the religion many of them share, the culture of the rulers themselves is always accorded pride of place. However, political culture and ideological orientation may be invoked also, as in the United States and France following their democratic revolutions (Brubaker 1992), or in the confrontation between "the West" and "the East" in the cold war decades.[25]

Much less emphasized by writers on nationality and nationalism is that the formation of national identity always involves a negative aspect as well: we are who we are by virtue of who we are *not*. In this light, nationality involves the delineation of a boundary that denotes simultaneously inclusion and exclusion. Whatever the objective realities may have been in the early modern era, princes and their serving intellectuals emphasized similarities within the national borders and differences between the nation and its neighbors (McNeill 1963). Although the negative "others" are commonly close neighbors with whom perennial wars are fought, and from whom "we" must distinguish ourselves by any means possible, they can also be remote aliens, regarding whom little is known and therefore much can be invented. Groups originally recruited as low-skilled "workers" are especially likely to belong to the "not-us" world and therefore to be considered by many as "unqualified" for membership in the host society; this "wanted but not welcome" syndrome creates especially problematic situations if the workers become permanent settlers (Zolberg 1987).

Differing assessments along these lines precipitate confrontations not only between "natives" and "foreigners" but among the natives themselves—between those who perceive the newcomers as a threat in relation to what is deemed a fragile status quo and others who are more confident in the society's ability to weather change or who welcome the diversity the newcomers would contribute as an enrichment. These alignments are probably related to a more comprehensive cultural cleavage that is emerging as the contemporary equivalent of the older rift between religious and secular camps; it encompasses other "cultural" and "moral" issues such as abortion, feminism, gay rights, and the death penalty. However, the camp of those positively disposed toward immigrants may also include natives who are not particularly open to change but feel an affinity with particular groups of newcomers, notably fellow religionists or ethnics. Sometimes this camp comprises the national community as a whole with respect to populations located in other states who are regarded as "external nationals," on whose behalf the state may devise a "law of return" or some other extremely generous immigration policy.[26]

As noted in the previous section, refugee policy has tended to be driven by strategic considerations arising quite directly from the dynamics of the international political system: providing asylum to the victims of one's enemies was consistent with the imperatives of realpolitik in that it demonstrated the antagonist's evil ways and undermined its legitimacy. Concomitantly, refugees tended to be ranked high on the positive side of the "identity" axis throughout Western countries almost by definition: they were welcomed exclusively on the basis of religious or political affinity with the receivers and therefore were deemed not strangers but brothers and sisters in need. Under these conditions, statecraft and humanitarianism went hand in hand (Zolberg 1983b; Zolberg et al. 1989). By the same token, states were not inclined to help victims who were not "like us": proletarian Communards had almost no place to go after their defeat in 1871, and Jewish victims of Nazism were denied havens as well.

However, in the post–World War II period the international community began moving toward a more universalistic approach, eventually extending refugee status to all those, anywhere in the world, who are outside their country and without government protection as a consequence of "reasonable fear" of persecution. Concurrently, the superpowers expanded the domain of their strategic confrontations to encompass many regions of the Third World, contributing to a vast enlargement of the refugee pool. Although the overwhelming majority remained in their region of origin, some came knocking at the door of the affluent countries, and the fact that an increasing proportion of those who sought asylum were poor people of color—and thereby akin from the perspective of the receivers to immigrant workers—triggered alarm bells and prompted a reconsideration of established policies. This revisionism was facilitated by the end of the cold war, which eliminated at one blow the "realist" foundations of the postwar refugee regime and sharply narrowed the scope of Western states' refugee policies. The United States retained a refugee policy founded almost exclusively on "realist" foreign and security considerations until about 1980; although it then subscribed to the international regime, its actual policy continued to be driven by "realism," with some intrusion of constituency pressures (particularly with regard to Eastern European Jews).

The persistent coexistence of these two very different dimensions of consideration and, concomitantly, of interests—one pertaining to the putative or actual effects of immigration on material conditions, the other having to do with cultural and political conditions—can be represented by cross-cutting axes, each with positive and negative poles, providing for a continuum of alignments from "for" to "against."

Hence, it is possible to adopt a positive position on immigration with respect to one dimension, and a negative position in relation to the other. This accounts for the often remarked upon tendency of immigration politics to straddle the traditional liberal-conservative divide and for the emergence of "strange bedfellow" coalitions for or against particular proposals. Successive attempts to resolve these disparate imperatives in the face of changing conditions shape immigration policy into complex and often inconsistent configurations, such as the segmentation of U.S. policy into a "main gate" dealing with general immigration and a "back door" dealing with the procurement of temporary agricultural workers.

Political Process and Political Institutions

However powerful, the effects of social forces, external or internal, are not automatically translated into policy outcomes but are mediated by established political structures—notably political parties, electoral systems, and the articulation and organization of specialized interests—and political institutions—notably the structure of representation and the allocation of decisionmaking authority and power in the relevant sphere between the executive, the legislative, and the judicial branches of government. These are, of course, the factors on which political scientists have long trained their specialized optical apparatus. The initial emphasis, on the American side, on the role of interest groups yielded important insights into specific cases of immigration policy but fell short of theoretical elaboration (Craig 1971; Divine 1957; Riggs 1950). Recently, however, there have been more self-consciously theoretical efforts.

One valuable contribution is an analysis of the role of distinct modes of interaction between elites and the public in shaping immigration policy (Freeman 1995a). In short, each dimension might foster a distinct mode of interaction between elites and the public, with concomitantly distinct outcomes. On the basis of his own comparative studies of immigration policy in Europe and the United States, Gary Freeman asserts that the political dynamics of immigration policy in liberal democracies "exhibits strong similarities that are, contrary to the scholarly consensus, broadly expansionist and inclusive" (Freeman 1995a, 881). His theoretical starting point is a simple model of politics in which the state actors who make policy are "vote-maximizers" with no special views or interests of their own (except, as we shall see later, for an unexplained commitment to "universalism") but are responsive to pressures from the public, consisting of "utility-maximizers" assumed to have complete information about the consequences of policy alternatives.

Following James Q. Wilson (1980), Freeman (1995a, 894) argues that the public's mode of organization varies as a function of how the costs and benefits resulting from policies are distributed. In the case of immigration, benefits are "concentrated"—notably by providing lower costs for employers in certain economic sectors and gratification for the kin and co-ethnics of incoming groups—whereas costs tend to be diffuse; they include increased competition for jobs among some groups of the resident population and increased demand for certain services. Moreover, the general public's utility-maximizing ability is handicapped by "serious barriers to the acquisition of information" about immigration, and by a "temporal illusion" whereby the short-term benefits of immigration are easily seen but its long-term costs are denied or hidden.

Such a distribution of costs and benefits tends to produce "client" politics: small and well-organized groups intensively interested in a policy develop close working relationships with the officials responsible for it, largely outside of public view and with little outside interference. Consequently, policymakers are more responsive to their immigration-advocating clients than to the more ambivalent or even opposed general public. How and why the public came to hold such views, however, is not specified. As a result, "official policies tend to be more liberal than public opinion and annual intakes larger than is politically optimal" (Freeman 1995a, 897)—where "optimality" is defined as the policies preferred by the median voter.

However, the situation may change as a function of two predictable cycles, the one economic, the other arising from the tendency of migration, through networks, to generate more migration—a proposition that is well established in general international migration theory. Although under those circumstances decisionmakers adopt a less expansive stance, Freeman (1995a) insists that the basic dynamics intervene to mitigate reactions and to prevent abrupt changes of policy.

Distinguishing three groups of receivers, the

English-speaking "settler societies," European "postcolonial" and guest-worker societies, and Europe's "new countries of immigration"—notably Italy, Spain, Portugal, and Greece, to which one might now add some post-Communist countries such as Poland—Freeman (1995a, 892) claims that his "model" accounts for recent developments among all of them. Although all three groups are affected by the conjunction of the two cycles, the cycles' effect on settler countries is mitigated by the persistence of an immigration identity. In the second group, as costs come to be perceived as more concentrated, client politics evolve into interest-group politics and the dynamics of politics are partly reversed, with elites taking the lead in adopting a tightly restrictionist stance.

In commenting on Freeman, Brubaker (1995) has correctly pointed out that the "constrained discourse" regarding ethnicity and race is not a constant feature of liberal democracy and cannot be derived from Freeman's "political economy" model; this is true also of what Freeman (1995a, 892) terms the settler countries' "positive folklore" toward immigration. Both features are historically specific and contingent, and Brubaker suggests more generally that the analysis must make room for a "cultural-political" story that is logically independent of political economy—a suggestion consonant with the framework suggested here (Brubaker 1992, 1995). Indeed, despite his emphasis on economic considerations, Freeman's references to the relinquishment by elites of ethnic and racial categories, as well as to the emergence of the "new Right," reflects his awareness that identity issues do at times play a negative role, and his reference to the pro-immigration stance of kin and co-ethnics suggests that he understands that identity can have a positive value as well.

Freeman's view of elites exclusively as economic actors may also be the source of his erroneous assertion regarding their universalist orientation. As he himself has shown elsewhere—and as he acknowledges in a note in the present work—in Britain racial considerations entered into play from the late 1950s onward (Freeman 1979; 1995a, 891 n. 10). Contemporaneously, in the United States, as noted in the first part of this chapter, while abolishing the national-origin quotas and Asian prohibitions, American political elites imposed unprecedented limits on immigration from the Western Hemisphere with the explicit objective of restricting the immigration of Mexicans and black West Indians. Today as well, on both sides of the Atlantic, elites hardly display a uniformly universalist orientation in immigration politics.

Overall, the situation with regard to identity might be the reverse of what prevails in the economic sphere: the costs of immigration are diffuse, in the sense of a malaise pertaining to "threats to nationality," whereas the benefits are concentrated, in that certain ethnic groups increase their weight and hence their "recognition" and potential political power in the nation. This may account for the reluctance of U.S. elites around the turn of the century to endorse immigration restriction, and for the movement of U.S. elites toward universalism, notably with regard to the elimination of the national-origin quotas directed against Europeans in the 1950s, when these groups became the mainstay of the urban wing of the Democratic Party. Both dimensions make for client politics but involve different sets of clients. The combination of business and of ethnic groups as strange bedfellows in a pro-immigration camp is a characteristic U.S. outcome, and partly a function of the rapid incorporation of immigrants into the body politic (see figure 4.1).

However, the concentrated/diffuse measure should not be applied simplistically. Within the economic sphere alone, for example, since immigration is spatially concentrated, port-of-entry localities may simultaneously reap more benefits than the country at large from the economic stimulation immigration brings about and face a particularly heavy demand for a variety of services; moreover, the perception of costs may be enhanced where local governments have some fiscal autonomy, notably in federal states. Under such conditions, local governments are likely to emerge as important actors in immigration politics, but local circumstances determine whether they will be found on the negative side (for example, New York City in the 1830s or California today) or on the positive side (New York City today).[27] In a similar vein, analysis of the distribution of economic benefits is rendered more difficult by the need to distinguish between "the public" as workers and as consumers: in the United States, for example, not only is the use of unauthorized foreign workers in the produce and garment industries profitable for employers and presumably costly to the workers in those sectors, but it also appreciably lowers the price of these widely used commodities—including for the workers in their role as consumers. The concentrated/diffuse measure thus becomes more heuristic if it is applied to dis-

FIGURE 4.1 The "Strange Bedfellows" of American Immigration Politics

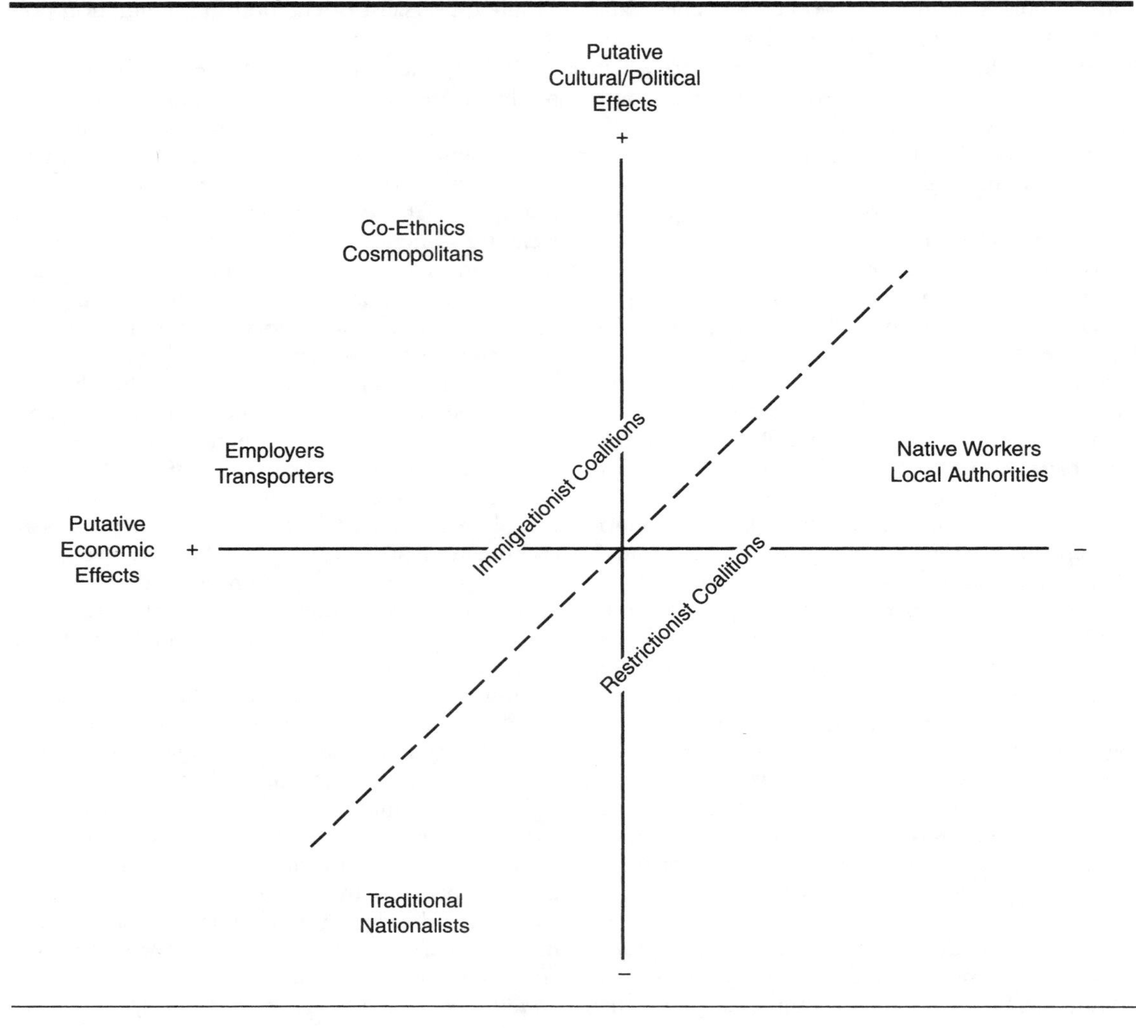

aggregated elements, and when a distinction is made between concentration within economic sectors and concentration in space.[28]

A more serious limitation is that because it emphasizes process exclusively, the model Freeman borrows from Wilson is incapable of providing insight into structure. Although the distribution of costs and benefits of particular policies does shape political dynamics, policy issues do not arise in a political vacuum but rather in a field structured by previous historical experiences, including ongoing policies in the sphere under consideration—about which the model has little or nothing to say. This is evident, first of all, with regard to immigration policy itself. As demonstrated in the preceding section, contemporary policymaking takes place within the context of a prevailing worldwide restrictive immigration regime, which has to be explicitly accounted for. Another matter is that although Freeman speaks of "immigration policy" as of a piece, this ignores an important institutional reality: all states today distinguish between refugees and ordinary immigrants, and in effect also between settlers and workers. Accordingly, rather than a single overall dynamic, we should expect a different process to prevail in each of these policy areas.

Within the sphere of political economy alone, there is a considerable range of variation in how the principal "class" actors are organized, and this in turn makes for major differences in the process and substance of policy: strong or weak labor unions, industrial or craft organization, the presence or absence of "peak associations" among workers and employers, corporatist social compacts or unruly pluralism (Schmitter and Lehmbruch 1979). These structures account not only for variation in political dynamics but also for some variations in policy—such as the organization of formal guest-worker programs in the more corporatist European countries (Germany, the Low Countries, Sweden) as against employer-driven programs, which often involve processes of marginal legality where unions do not participate in the making of industrial policy (as in France and the United States).

This is applicable to the identity dimension as well. For example, the ethnic organizations established by earlier immigrants in the United States have become legitimized as political interlocutors beyond what might be expected on the basis of their electoral weight, forming in the cultural sphere an equivalent of the corporatism that is sometimes found in the political economy sphere (but to a very low degree in the United States); this distinctively shapes the dynamics of immigration politics and also patterns the organizational strategies of more recent immigrants. The standing of these ethnic organizations as clients is thus not merely a function of the concentration of benefits fostered by immigration policy, as demonstrated by the fact that in the absence of this corporatism they do not become clients despite a similar concentration of immigration policy benefits. The Maghrebis in France are a case in point: it is possible to write a detailed account of the politics of French immigration policy in the recent past without any reference to them as organized actors (Weil 1991).

Some of these problems are addressed quite explicitly in a recent study by Keith Fitzgerald (1996, 1), who contends that the application of his "improvisational institutionalism" approach enables him to "solve the most puzzling features" of American immigration policy for the period 1879 to 1965. The work is founded on a disaggregation of immigration policy into three segments dealing with permanent residency ("front-gate immigration"), refugee policy, and "unsanctioned migrant laborers across the U.S. border with Mexico ('back-door immigration')." The core of Fitzgerald's argument is that these segments display distinct policy dynamics, each of which can be accounted for in one of the leading contending theories of policy formation. In his enticingly elegant construction, policy regarding the "front gate" is shaped by the relatively free play of competing societal interests (political science's traditional pluralism), whereas refugee policy is shaped by "realism" (in which the state looms as a major agent pursuing interests of its own) and "back-door" policy comes close to fitting classical class-conflict theories. Inspired by the "structuration" approach of Anthony Giddens (1979), Fitzgerald views the policymaking process as "episodic," with innovation commonly arising from improvised solutions to pressing problems.

Although the disaggregation of immigration policy into discrete components rightly captures an often ignored feature of policy reality—not only in the United States—Fitzgerald is somewhat carried away by the elegance of his theoretical construct. In fact, all three modes of policy formation occur in each of the components indicated. For example, although I fully concur that refugee policy has been driven to a considerable extent by foreign policy considerations, with the policymaking process centering in the foreign- and security-policy sector of the state, pluralist elements have come into play as well, notably by way of ethnic constituency pressures for and against the award of refugee status to particular groups. Conceptualized as distinctive components of any policymaking process, Fitzgerald's three dynamics nicely complement Freeman's concentrated/diffuse measure. However, by itself such a formal approach cannot account for the circumstances under which policymaking in all three spheres arises and changes. For example, it is evident that the weight of realist considerations in the policymaking process is not a constant, but that it rose and fell with the advent of the cold war; hence, there was a turn "from invitation to interdiction" (Zolberg 1995). It is therefore most useful when linked to the sort of historical and externalist framework that is being set forth here.

Conclusion

Reflecting the traditional division of labor among the social sciences, theorists of international migration have tended to ignore or minimize the role of states in shaping their object of study, while theorists of migration policy have tended to approach their subject in a domestic perspective, ignoring the dynamics of the global environment in relation to which regulation of exit and entry occurs, especially its demographic aspect. The framework presented here is a very preliminary attempt to overcome these deficiencies and to use the insights of both sides to construct a more comprehensive theoretical edifice.

The twin global dynamics of capitalist development and of state formation generate powerful thrusts of necessity and force that propel large masses of humanity outside their country of origin, but the international migrations that actually take place are shaped to a considerable extent by the will of the world's states, nearly all of which can muster the capacity to control movement across their borders. If all states were to control emigration with the single-mindedness of the German Democratic Republic, and immigration with the determination of the late-twentieth-century United Kingdom, little or no international migration would take place; conversely, if unattractive states lacked the capacity to control exit and attractive states the capacity to control entry, much more of the world's population would be on the move today than is actually the case. Accordingly, the difference between a hypothetical world of zero migration and an equally hypothetical world of free movement is accounted for by migration policies, broadly defined to encompass all the regulations and controls that states deploy in relation to movement. Although the basic stances of states are shaped by the same twin dynamics, this leaves considerable room for variation in specifics. Many of the policy elements that appear contingent in relation to global dynamics, however, are the product of political structures and institutions that can also be theorized, albeit at another level.

The synthetic approach adumbrated here accounts for the restrictive policy trend observable today among the affluent liberal states. Much attention has been given to domestic responses arising, on the one hand, from the massive economic insecurity precipitated by the resurgence of unemployment and technostructural transformations and, on the other hand, from uncertainty regarding the incorporation challenge posed by a large recent wave of immigration—for many countries of unprecedented proportions. Certainly the most diverse policy responses are best understood, however, in the context of major changes in the external situation—a context that fosters talk of an international "crisis" and prompting strategy specialists to seize on international migration as one of the "new security issues" (Kennedy 1994; Weiner 1995).

There is no gainsaying that the contemporary international configuration is in some ways unprecedented: the expansion of the international migration network to global scale, encompassing quite literally most of the world's population; the further widening of demographic disparities between the more and less developed parts of the world; the lowering of the cost of long-distance travel, rendering it accessible to a very large proportion of the world's population; the lifting of almost all prohibitions on exit; and paradoxically, the liberalization of regulations concerning international travel as the result of concerted action by the very same states that are trying to secure their gates against unwanted immigration. Thanks to the waning of colonialism and the collapse of the Soviet system, for the first time since the modern system of border control and immigration regulation was established in the early decades of the twentieth century most human beings are legally free to leave their countries of origin, so that the burden of regulating international migration falls almost entirely on the countries they wish to enter.

Does this mean an unleashing of masses of international migrants, leading to uncontrolled immigration? This is most unlikely. To begin with, as Ravenstein (1885) suggested a century ago, the first "law" of migration is that people do not move farther than is necessary to make a living; however, it is also the case that the first step is the hardest, so that as more people move locally, the pool of those disposed to travel farther if opportunity beckons increases as well. Moreover, the costs and risks of moving have been steadily reduced by revolutions in long-distance transportation, the proliferation of communications and networks, and the legal and humanitarian constraints that limit the freedom of action of potential receivers. The overwhelming majority of human beings are likely to stay put, but we should expect that the migration pressure from south to north (and now also from east to west)—manifested most dramatically by the willingness of some migrants to take life-threatening risks and pay huge sums of money for a chance at a miserable job in a rich country—will persist in the foreseeable future.

It is evident that changing conditions have fostered a vast increase in the regulatory load that immigration countries must bear, but it is equally evident that in relation to *potential* movement, by and large these countries do manage to exercise a considerable degree of control over their borders. One indicator of the gap between "demand" for entry and "supply" is the lengthening of lines where the opportunity to apply for legal entry is provided. (This encompasses outright immigration in traditional immigration countries as well as asylum everywhere and family reunion in most European countries.) To what extent the unsatisfied demand for entry is met by surreptitious entry or overstaying is obviously hard to say, but the widely reported growth of international traffic in illegal international migrants and the high fees involved—reportedly as much as $30,000 for transportation from mainland China to the United States—suggest that international borders continue to function as a significant deterrent.

The overwhelming proportion of the migration that does occur from south (now including the East) to north takes place either because powerful voices among the hosts want it to take place or because the efforts deployed to deter unauthorized entry or sojourn are minimal. As in other spheres of regulation that involve the policing of comportment by individuals and organizations, there are two questions: What degree of compliance is it realistic to expect in relation to the nature of the process that is being regulated? And what means should be expended to achieve the chosen objective? In addition, who considers the degree of compliance actually achieved insufficient, on what grounds do they reach that judgment, what would be the cost of raising the level—keeping in mind that the law of diminishing returns is likely to kick in at some point and that the means required to achieve greater compliance may clash with other important policy objectives or societal norms—and how would the costs be allocated? In effect, affluent democracies, including the United States, face a narrow range of choices: they must either accept as a fact of life a certain level of unregulated immigration, over and above what they explicitly provide for in their immigration policies, or devise draconian policies that necessarily encroach on their political liberalism.

Notes

1. These publications provide the framework used by Massey in his contribution to this volume.
2. Provoked by a fellow geographer's contention that migration within the United Kingdom appeared to go on without any definite law, Ravenstein (1885, 167) established on the basis of the 1881 census that "the greatest body of our migrants only proceed a short distance," but that long-distance migrants "generally go by preference to one of the great centers of commerce and industry"; he attributed this to "the desire inherent in most men to 'better' themselves in material respects."
3. For unstated reasons, however, Ravenstein did not seek to verify the application of his "laws" to transoceanic migrations.
4. "Great Russian" because czarist prohibitions on exit were softened for minorities, notably Jews (apparently in exchange for hefty payments), Balts, and Ukrainians. The consequences are visible in the prominence of these groups in the overseas receiving states that admitted them (the United States and Canada) but the virtual absence there of a Great Russian diaspora.
5. "Most" because some contemporary states are so extremely weak as to exist only by virtue of international conventions.
6. Italian immigration had reached 265,542 in 1913 and 283,738 in 1914.
7. Although Claudia Goldin (1994, 238, n. 37) has pointed out that the Italian real wage for unskilled workers rose relative to its American equivalent, from a ratio of 0.29 in 1910 to 0.48 in 1925, it is highly unlikely that this would account for a reduction of immigration of the order of twenty to one.
8. These waiting lists warrant serious historical research.
9. The authority of consular officials to deny visitor visas to persons suspected of being immigrants was upheld by the U.S. District Court, District of Vermont, on July 28, 1926 (*American Foreign Service Journal* 4, no. 1 [January 1927]).
10. Nevertheless, there was considerable concern over illegal immigration; although initially the common estimate was 175,000, in 1930 Herbert Hoover's secretary of Labor referred to 400,000 illegal aliens who were taking jobs away from Americans and causing catastrophic unemployment, and the latter number stuck (Davie 1936, 401; Sánchez 1995a, 5).
11. This section is drawn in part from an unpublished report, coauthored with Robert Smith, for presentation at a meeting organized by the U.S. Department of State and the Commission of the European Union (Dublin, December 1996). However, I alone am responsible for the present summary and interpretation (Zolberg and Smith 1996).
12. Mexican immigration, like immigration from other independent countries of the Western Hemisphere such as Canada, Cuba, and Haiti, was not subjected to numerical limitation. Prior to 1965 English Canadians were hardly considered immigrants at all. Although congressional restrictionists objected to French Canadians on grounds of racial inferiority, they provided a supply of cheap and disposable labor for the northeastern lumber industry, and similar practices appear to have prevailed along the Maine-Quebec border as in the Southwest. Indeed, French Canadians were often referred to as "Mexicans of the North" (Divine 1957).
13. Some analysts have suggested that evidence of the ineffectiveness of sanctions of the sort that has been accumulated so far is misleading, because sanctions cannot be expected to be effective immediately; since it entails a major change in the practices of employers nationwide, the new system must be given time to take root. Although the call for patience is drawn in part from the experience of employer sanctions in Western Europe, specialists on the subject are divided in their assessment (Miller 1994, 128–213; Weil 1991).
14. Although under the old system citizens could bring spouses and children outside the quotas, the low level of immigration from 1925 to 1960 ensured that there were new citizens to take advantage of this opportunity.
15. The turning point in refugee policy occurred in 1946,

when, at the request of its occupation officials in Germany, the United States undertook special measures to resettle European "displaced persons" who could not be admitted under the restrictive immigration law in force at the time. This approach was developed further as a weapon in the cold war and in response to constituency pressures (for example, to admit victims of a devastating earthquake in southern Italy).

16. Because Cubans originated within the Western Hemisphere, they were not covered by the 1965 law's refugee provision; instead, they were treated as ordinary immigrants, admitted under the attorney general's "parole" authority to speed the process, but subject to later regularization.
17. It is generally reckoned that approximately half of the estimated three hundred thousand annual illegal aliens are "overstayers" who entered legally, usually on tourist visas. The risk involved was quite low, as the United States did not effectively verify alien departures. Assessed in relation to several million annual nonimmigrant entries, the rate of "failure" is quite low. Although in 1996 the United States enacted legislation designed to deter overstaying by requiring departing aliens to turn in a voucher given them at entry, it is too early to tell whether this will be effective.
18. Rather, it is the other way around: apprehensions are commonly used to estimate the number of crossings, on the basis of an arbitrarily established apprehension ratio, and without specifying whether the crossings are by different individuals.
19. Referring to the 1648 treaty that established the supremacy of individual European sovereigns over their respective territories and the subjects contained therein, and their formal equality under "the law of nations." In recent developments in international relations theory, the concept of "sovereignty" has evolved from a constant into a variable, and there is growing debate over the extent to which sovereignty is being reduced as a concomitant of globalization—and as a result of international migration. However, most states retain a sufficient capacity for controlling inward movement to be considered sovereign for present purposes.
20. Although this is a largely neglected subject, many empirical indications are available. For example, U.S. and British immigration restrictions in the 1920s probably deflected much of the movement from eastern and southern Europe to France (and to a lesser extent the Netherlands and Belgium), whose foreign population, including notably Armenians, Poles, and Italians, approximately doubled in the period from 1921 to 1930. Concurrently, much of Italian emigration was deflected to South America. Another case in point is emigration from the British West Indies in the post–World War II period. From the 1920s on, British West Indians emigrated to the United States, thanks to the availability of entries under the British quota, undersubscribed by emigrants from the British Isles; their numbers are indicated by the fact that among New York City's black population in the 1940 census, some 10 percent were foreign-born. Black immigration proved highly disturbing to American segregationists, who had sought in vain to restrict it formally ever since the 1920s; however, in 1952 they successfully enacted a provision within the Walter-McCarran Act limiting immigration from each colonial dependency to not more than one hundred of the metropolitan country's quota. It is precisely at this time that West Indian emigration to the British Isles, which had been quite minimal, began to soar, and there is little doubt that the American decision contributed to this shift in direction. Conversely, starting in 1962 Britain began to close its door to people of color, whereas in 1965 the United States dropped its invidious restrictions, effective in 1968. Accordingly, West Indian migration was deflected back toward the United States. There were also many indications of interactivity among asylum applicants to various European countries in the 1980s and of the deflection of their efforts toward Canada and the United States when the door was closed.
21. The use of functionalist language here is intentional.
22. It is noteworthy that, in contrast, some European planners in countries with declining populations advocate additional immigration (immigrants tend to be younger than the general population) as a way of securing additional income for near-bankrupt old age insurance funds.
23. The parallel with "class" is more than metaphoric; as with class, "cultural compromises" can be thought of as "peace settlements" in the wake of "culture wars," pertaining to such matters as the degree of recognition of the culture in question and institutional arrangements in the spheres of work, education, and the like. However, contemporary democracies are less well equipped institutionally to deal with cultural matters than with those pertaining to class, perhaps in part because culture has not received the same degree of theoretical elaboration from social scientists dealing with capitalist democracies. Their reluctance to deal with the subject has left a vacuum that is being filled largely by "cultural studies." As with class, there are several questions to be answered: What intellectual tools are most appropriate for tackling the subject? What information should be relied on to assess putative effects? What are appropriate objectives? What measures should be used in the evaluation of strategies to achieve them?
24. My approach owes a great deal to the works of Clifford Geertz (1973), Benedict Anderson (1974), and Fredrik Barth (1969). However, I am putting greater emphasis on "agency" in the form of sustained action by political elites. The notion of a "formula" was suggested by my former colleague Leonard Binder.
25. Whereas Brubaker treats the ethnic and political foundations of nationality as contrasting ideal types, represented by Germany and France, I am inclined to view them as more or less complementary elements that can and do coexist. France is as "ethnic" as it is "republican." This is applicable to the United States as well, notably with regard to the racial and linguistic foundations of nationality in the nineteenth century. Conversely, Germany has long included a comprehensive element in its conception of nationality, as indicated in the 1913 nationality law that still prevails.
26. I am grateful to Long Litt Woon, formerly head of the Norwegian Ministry of Labor's Division of Immigrant Affairs, for pointing out the distinctiveness of "patrials" as a special category of immigrants and for suggesting how they might fit into this framework. The best-known cases are, of course, Israel and Germany; however, nearly all other countries that had an extensive experience of emigration also make such special arrangements, including Italy, Spain, and the United Kingdom, which included the patrial category in the

recasting of its nationality law in 1981. In a similar vein, Canada attributes "points" to applicants who speak one of the country's two "founding" languages, and proposals along these lines have been made in the United States as well with regard to English.

27. In his rejoinder to Brubaker (1995), Freeman (1995b) acknowledges the utility of a spatial approach but does not draw out its implications for the distribution issue.
28. However, the impact can be concentrated on some local communities.

5 Transmigrants and Nation-States: Something Old and Something New in the U.S. Immigrant Experience

Nina Glick Schiller

THE PHONE RINGS, and the news is as she expected. Sitting alone in her basement bedroom in her cousin's home in New York City, Yvette begins to shake. Her older sister in Haiti, a sister she barely knows, is calling to announce the death of Yvette's nephew. Although she has received the call while the body is still warm, Yvette shakes not so much from the loss of the young man, whom she had met only once, as from knowing that it is her obligation immediately to find the money for an elaborate funeral in Haiti complete with cars, band, and imported flowers. The year before, from her salary as a mail clerk in New York, Yvette had buried her niece, whose education and wedding she had also financed; in fact, Yvette has only recently finished paying her debts from that funeral.

Yvette's heavy burden of kinship responsibilities also comes with rewards. In the United States her earnings would make no social mark, even if she were to hoard them or expend them on consumer goods. To her network in Haiti, Yvette is a person of influence. On the few trips she can afford back home, she is treated as a visiting dignitary. Not only do bad economic and political times in Haiti increase the demands on her labor, but what happens in Haiti, both good and bad, affects her sense of who she is and where she belongs. Her fellow workers identify her with Haiti, and her friends at work bring her articles about Haiti. Consequently, the kin work Yvette constantly undertakes in Haiti and her sense of personal accomplishment link her to broader identifications with Haiti as a nation-state. Yvette's continuing home ties, her experience of being identified as Haitian while living and working in the United States, and her daily exposure through Haitian radio and television, which she watches in her kitchen in Queens, all contribute to her understanding that her life is connected to Haiti, even as she and her family strive to become further incorporated into the United States.

Although she is neither a political activist nor part of a Haitian ethnic organization, Yvette's occasionally makes her identification with Haiti clear and public. In June 1997, Yvette sat in a commencement audience in Washington, D.C., with nineteen other kinfolk and family friends, some of whom had flown in from Haiti and Canada, to watch Giselle, her cousin's daughter, graduate from law school. When Giselle was handed her law school diploma, Yvette, who is usually quite proper and somewhat reserved with strangers, jumped up and yelled, "Haiti! Haiti!," surprising even herself. Giselle's victory in obtaining a law school degree from a prestigious university in the United States became Haiti's victory.[1]

In the 1980s a handful of scholars of contemporary migration took note of the transnational networks of immigrants such as Yvette and began to assess the political implications of such processes (Glick Schiller, Basch, and Blanc-Szanton 1992a; Glick Schiller and Fouron 1990; Kearney 1991; Rouse 1989, 1991). To do this, we rejected the prevailing view of immigrants as persons who had uprooted themselves from their old society to settle in a new land. Calling attention to the fact that a significant proportion of the immigrants who settle in and become well incorporated into the United States still maintain home ties, we proposed transnational migration, or transnationalism, as a new paradigm for the study of migration across the borders of nation-states.[2] This new approach makes visible the networks of immigrants that extend across international borders. It posits that even though migrants invest socially, economically, and politically in their new society, they may continue to participate in the daily life of the society from which they emigrated but which they did not abandon. The study of international migration is transformed into an investigation of migration as a transnational process.

In this chapter, I focus on two sets of interrelated questions that have emerged among those building or critiquing this new paradigm of transnational migration. First of all, how new is transnational migration? Are we witnessing a new form of human settlement, or is it only our analytical paradigm that has changed? Second, what is the relationship between transnational migration and nation-states? Does contemporary transnational migration serve as an indicator that the link between state and nation is unraveling and that nation-states are withering or "dithering away"? (Turner 1997, 2)

Often discussed separately, these two sets of questions about transnational migration are nevertheless linked. I explore these linkages through a comparison of the relationships of past and contemporary transnational migrants to the states they left and to the United States. Although I focus on migration to the United States, the paradigm of transnational migration has relevance to the history and contemporary experience of migrants who cross international borders in many locations of the world.[3] For the purpose of historical comparison, I compare contemporary migration to the United States with the migration that occurred between the 1880s and 1920s. As a matter of convenience, I term this period "late-nineteenth-century migration" and the period from the 1970s to the 1990s "late-twentieth-century migration."

My argument is as follows: transnational migration and the transnational political practices of nation-states are not new phenomena. Two things, however, are new. Our paradigm has indeed changed and there also have been significant transformations in the context of transnational migration. These transformations include: the restructuring of the global accumulation and organization of capital; modifications in the relationships between state structures and global economic processes; and altered conceptualizations of nation-states, expressed in the rhetoric of political leaders, the writings of political theorists, and the paradigms of social scientists. By the end of the twentieth century, changing economic and political conditions had facilitated and promoted a reconceptualization of emigrant-sending states as transnational and a new paradigm for the study of migration, that of transnational migration.

The chapter outlines three phases of the relationship between transnational migration and nation-state-building. In the first phase, the late nineteenth century, nation-state building processes in Europe, the United States, Latin America, and Asia took place within the global ascendancy of monopoly capitalism, the growth of finance capital, and a renewed scramble for colonies on the part of competitive European states and the United States (Stavrianos 1981; Sweezy 1942; Wolf 1982). In this phase, a significant proportion of many migrating populations established transnational relationships that contributed to the nation-state-building projects of both their ancestral states and their new homelands. The second phase began after World War II, during an epoch of decolonization. Most European colonies gained their independence, and a vision of the world as a terrain of independent nation-states became triumphant. The global penetration of capital continued, but it was generally discussed under the rubric of development assistance to modernize newly independent nations. Immigrants' transnational networks and political projects were no longer noted by political leaders, scholars, or the immigrants themselves.[4]

The end of the twentieth century is the third phase. The restructuring of the processes of capital accumulation accompanied by the implementation of a neoliberal agenda began to alter the relationship between states and more global economic processes (Gill 1997, 207). In this period, transnational migration and the transnational political activities of immigrants again have become a topic of interest and concern to political actors and researchers alike. Political leaders of emigrant-sending states began to reenvision their states as transnational. At the same time, scholars developed a paradigm of transnational migration. Because the scholarship on international migration began to be read by political actors responsible for changing state policies, the new paradigm has not only reflected but also contributed to the changing relationship between nation-states and immigrants.[5]

The Paradigm of Transnational Migration

To date, systematic efforts to study transnational migration as a particular and differentiated pattern of migration have been weakened by the absence of a clearly defined set of terms that can be utilized in research about past and present migration experiences. The following terminology is proposed. The study of transnational migration is linked to, but in many ways discrete from, the growth of transnational cultural studies (Appadurai 1990; Featherstone 1990; Hannerz 1992) and globalization studies (Robertson 1992).

Transnational cultural studies have focused on the growth of global communications and media, which create images, needs, and desires that transcend borders. Globalization studies have called attention to recent reconfigurations of space, economies and polities and the growth of global cities as part of the process of restructuring capital accumulation (Knight and Gappert 1989; Knox 1994; Sassen 1991). In contrast, those of us who study transnational migration have been concerned with the actual social relationships that immigrants maintain and construct across borders.

In conferences, discussions, and research proposals, the terms "transnational" and "global "are sometimes used interchangeably but are better employed to describe two distinct although related processes. "Global" is best reserved for processes that are not located in a single state but happen throughout the entire globe. Processes such as the development of capitalism are best understood as global because capitalism is a system of production that was developed not in a single state or between states but by various emerging European bourgeois classes utilizing resources, accumulated wealth, and labor throughout the world. On the other hand, I employ the word transnational to discuss political, economic, social, and cultural processes that extend beyond the borders of a particular state, include actors that are not states, but are shaped by the policies and institutional practices of states.[6]

Transnational migration is a pattern of migration in which persons, although they move across international borders and settle and establish social relations in a new state, maintain social connections within the polity from which they originated. In transnational migration, persons literally live their lives across international borders. That is to say, they establish transnational social fields. Persons who migrate and yet maintain or establish familial, economic, religious, political, or social relations in the state from which they moved, even as they also forge such relationships in a new state or states in which they settle, can be defined as "transmigrants" (Glick Schiller, Basch, and Blanc-Szanton 1992b, 1). Transmigrants differ significantly from people with a diasporic tradition. Transmigrants are people who claim and are claimed by two or more nation-states, into which they are incorporated as social actors, one of which is widely acknowledged to be their state of origin. There have been diasporas throughout history. Diasporas are understood most usefully as dispersed populations who attribute their common identity, cultural beliefs and practices, language, or religion to myths of a common ancestry but whose sense of common heritage is not linked to a contemporary state.[7]

The terms "emigrant" and "immigrant" are best utilized for persons who have moved across international borders for the purpose of settlement, whether or not they establish transnational networks.[8] From the point of view of the receiving state, persons are immigrants when they become incorporated into their new country. From the point of view of the sending state, persons are emigrants when they leave home and settle abroad. Persons who move and settle in a new society, whether or not they are transmigrants, can be distinguished from migrants, sojourners, visitors, travelers, or tourists who cross international borders but do not become incorporated into a new polity.

Once the term "transnational migration" became popular, students of migration began to refer to all evidence of movement of people across borders as "transnational." To utilize the concept "transnational migration" as a synonym for movement across international borders is to deprive it of any utility. Nor is it useful to equate transnational migration with the longings that immigrants may feel for home, if these sentiments are not translated into systematic participation in networks that cross borders. On the other hand, there is some indication that transnational migration is more than a first-generation phenomenon, although further research on this subject is needed. The descendants of immigrants may continue to maintain, or may build anew, transnational relationships that reconnect them to the land of their ancestors and establish social relationships that make them participants in more than one state (Glick Schiller and Fouron 1998, 1999; Levitt 1998).

Conceptualizing Transnational Migration

The advantage of the descriptive vocabulary and the methodology I am proposing is that it allows researchers to assess observable social action rather than subjective intentionality. This is particularly important in studies of migration in which there is often a large gap between migrants' subjective descriptions of their intentions in regard to their home country and the actual course of action they pursue. Studies of both past and present immigrants in the United States indicate that most people report that they intend to return home but over time many of these individuals become permanently settled. However, it is also possible for immigrants to see their stay as permanent and yet one day pack up and "go home" (Massey, this volume). Whether their stated intentions are temporary or permanent settlement abroad, immigrants may establish and maintain transnational social relations and organize their lives around a series of "visits" home that sustain these relations.

Research on transnational migration is needed that investigates the range and multiplicity of social networks that immigrants establish.[9] Because there have not been statistical studies of international migration that identify transmigrants, or measure the degree of their multiple incorporation, the number of transmigrants within various past and contemporary populations of immigrants is unknown and the impact of their multiple incorporation has not been assessed.[10] Increasingly, however, scholars of international migration to the United States are reporting that transnational migration is a widespread and cross-class phenomenon. A significant, though unknown, number of political leaders, business, middle-class, and working-class people are living across borders (see, for example, Guarnizo and Smith 1998; Lessinger 1995; Ong 1992, 1993; Pessar 1995; Smith 1998).[11]

To conceptualize the multiplicity of connections that transmigrants maintain in the locality they left behind, many scholars of transnational migration have begun to utilize the concept of "transnational community" (Nagengast and Kearney 1990, 59; see also: Goldring 1996a; Levitt 1998; Rouse 1992; Smith 1994). Michael Kearney has argued that "one of the main challenges to an ethnographic study of transnational migration is the definition of the community of the migrants" (1996, 98). He is correct because there are problems with the term "community" as it is currently used in transnational migration studies. First of all, the term "community" is employed to describe very different units of analysis. Some researchers use the term "transnational community" to refer to a specific locality in which a communal system of leadership and collective action extends across international borders (Boruchoff 1992; Goldring 1996a; Levitt 1998; Smith 1994). Others use the term to refer to people from a specific region such as the Mixteca in Mexico, who develop an ethnic identity such as Mixtec as they engage in transnational migration (Nagengast and Kearney 1990). In a third usage, the size and nature of community is left unspecified. For example, Alejandro Portes (1997, 812) refers to transnational communities as "dense networks across political borders created by immigrants in their quest for economic advancement and social recognition."

In all cases the metaphor of community contains a set of implicit assumptions that impede the analysis of political and economic power. The term reflects and repeats the historic weakness of community studies in anthropology. These stressed affinity, solidarity, cultural homogeneity, and autonomy. They left unmarked the exploitative class relations and divisions of wealth and status that stratify a population, as well as the various links between the state and community elites that enabled the elites to constitute and maintain their exploitative relations within the "community." Similarly, the current usage of the term "transnational community" leaves no conceptual space to address the extent to which more prosperous transmigrants have been able to use the state, as well as transnational activities, to reinforce their positions within their hometowns and cities (DeWind, personal communication, 1998).[12] In addition, by evoking an imagery of transnational community, researchers foster the false impression that immigrants create their own autonomous cultural spaces outside of either sending or receiving states.

To distinguish those localities that maintain their political and social structures across international borders from other more broadly based transnational networks, without equating "locality" with "community," the term "transnational migrant circuit," first suggested by Roger Rouse (1992, 45), proves to be useful. However, "circuits" is a metaphor of closure and as such can also direct research away from the relationship between migrating populations and the political processes of the states within which they are incorporated. To address some of these issues, Linda Basch, Cristina Blanc-Szanton, and I (Basch, Glick Schiller, and Blanc-Szanton 1994) have proposed "transnational social field" as a conceptual and methodological entry point into the broader social, economic, and political processes within which migrating populations are embedded and to which they react.[13] We use "social field," defined as an unbounded terrain of interlocking egocentric networks, as a more encompassing term than "network," which is best applied to chains of social relationships specific to each person (Barnes 1954, 1969; Mitchell 1969; Noble 1973; Turner 1967). Because it focuses our attention on human interaction and situations of personal social relationship, the concept of social field facilitates an analysis of the processes by which immigrants become incorporated into a new state and maintain ongoing social relationships with persons in the sending state. Whether the relationships are egalitarian or exploitative, and whether they are with co-ethnics or others in the new society, are matters of empirical investigation.

The concept of social field directs our attention to the simultaneity of transmigrant connections to two or more states. We have the conceptual space to investigate the ways in which U.S. transmigrants become part of the fabric of daily life in their home state, including its political processes, while simultaneously becoming part of the workforce, contributing to neighborhood activities, serving as members of school and community boards, and entering into U.S. politics. This process of simultaneous incorporation into immigrants' states of origin and settlement has begun to be studied by a growing number of scholars of U.S. migration, many of whom are anthropologists (see Feldman-Bianco 1992; Graham 1997; Guarnizo 1997a; 1998; Lessinger 1995; Mahler 1996b; Pessar 1995b; Smith and Guarnizo 1998).

Past Paradigms and Past Transnational Social Fields

Contemporary observers of late-nineteenth-century migration consistently reported that immigrants in the United States maintained home ties (Foerster 1919; reports of the Immigration Commission of 1911, known as the Dillingham Commission, cited in Wyman 1993, 50). They were aware not only of the high rates of return of southern and eastern European, Turkish, and Mexican migrants, but also of the fact that many of these migrants sent remittances back home regularly while living and working in the United States (Roberts 1912/1990; Warne 1913/1990).[14] However, as U.S. social scientists developed and popularized an assimilationist approach to immigration, the data on the transnational connections of immigrants were interpreted as transitory phenomena, a way station on the road to assimilation. By 1951, in his prizewinning history of U.S. immigration, *The Uprooted,* Oscar Handlin portrayed immigrants as people who permanently leave their home and country behind, and this view was widely accepted both by the general public and by scholars.[15]

Historians of U.S. immigration were the first to critique the concept of immigration popularized by Handlin. Frank Thistlethwaite (1964) argued that immigration between England and the United States was best conceptualized as part of a single Atlantic economy. In the decades that followed, most historians did not follow Thistlethwaite's advice to look beyond discrete national histories. They did show a renewed interest in the high rate of return and circulatory migration of late nineteen century European and Asian immigrants (Bodnar 1985; Hareven 1982; Morawska 1987, 1989, 1997; Vecoli and Sinke 1991; Yans-McLaughlin 1982). An estimated one-quarter to one-third of the people who had left Europe returned home permanently between 1880 and 1930 (Wyman 1993, 6). The data available about "return" actually make it difficult to say what percentage of the migrating population lived transnational lives across borders. However, the difficulties in the data sources have been compounded by a conceptual framework that did not allow for the possibility that significant numbers of people maintained ties to both the society of origin and the society of settlement and moved between them.

Charles Tilly's 1990 review of the historical processes of migration is typical. Tilly stressed the importance of immigrant networks that stretch between immigrants' societies of origin and settlement yet continued to employ a traditional categorization of immigrants into "colonizing, coerced, circular, chain, and career migration" that left no room for the possibility of transnational migration (1990, 88). Actually, the data provided by revisionist historians contain numerous examples of transnational relationships maintained by migrants and their use of these relationships to visit home and return to the United States (Cinel 1991; Hareven 1982; Vecoli and Sinke 1991; Yans-McLaughlin 1982). For example, Mark Wyman (1993), in ***Round Trip to America,*** examines the impact of immigration on both sending and receiving societies by looking at the linkages forged by immigrants through their transnational familial, religious, and political ties. But by conceptualizing his work as a study of "two-way migration," Wyman focuses on the migration rather than the fact of simultaneous incorporation within more than one nation-state.[16]

Meanwhile, researchers of late-twentieth-century immigration to the United States were describing transnational networks but not coming fully to terms with the implications of their descriptions for theories about the nature and locus of immigrant incorporation. In the Caribbean, the importance of these interconnections led to conceptualizing whole states as "remittance societies" (Stinner, de Albuquerque, and Bruce-Laporte 1982; Richardson 1983). Ethnographers and geographers struggled for a vocabulary to describe the migratory paths of the persons with whom they worked. However, each of the terms employed—"sojourner" (Gonzalez 1988), "temporary migrants" (Dandler and Medeiros 1988), "commuters" (Fitzpatrick 1971), immigrants engaged in "circulation" (Conway 1989)—did not capture the patterned interconnections and multiple incorporation of the immigrants. Researchers categorized individuals rather than tracing networks of social relationship.

To adopt transnational migration as the research paradigm is to change the unit of analysis. Persons in the sending and receiving societies become participants in a single social unit. To do this, researchers must boldly sever their concept of society from their concept of national territory. They move outside of the dominant imagery of the nation-state, which contains the expectation that polity, territory, and society coincide. Those of us who began to develop the paradigm of transnational migration stressed the significance of the sustained social interaction that immigrants maintained across borders (Basch, Glick Schiller, and Blanc-Szanton 1994; Glick Schiller, Basch, and Blanc-Szanton 1992b, 1995; Kearney 1991; Nagengast and Kearney 1990; Rouse 1989, 1992).[17]

Unaware of the new historical studies of return migration, many researcher thought they had discovered something brand new.[18] Together with scholars of globalization and transnational public culture, many ethnographers of contemporary migration characterized the breaking down of borders and boundaries as uniquely a late-twentieth-century phenomenon. Most attributed the dramatic changes they observed all around them to technological advances such as electronics and computers (Appadurai 1990, 1993; Hannerz 1992; Smith 1998; Wakeman 1988). We had entered a postmodern and postnational epoch in which "members of transnational communities . . . escape the power of the nation-state to inform their sense of collective identity" (Kearney 1991, 59). "The boundary—the power to impose difference—. . . is being eroded by transnational developments causing the structure of the nation-state to become problematic" (52).

However, available historical research challenges the conclusion that transnational migration is a novel phenomenon contributing to and reflecting the demise of the nation-state. On the contrary, transmigrants helped construct nation-states in many regions of the world in the past and today are active participants in the constitution of transnational nation-states (Glick Schiller 1999b). Many transmigrants were in the past and are in the present "long distance" nationalists (Anderson 1992b). Long distant nationalism is a claim to membership in a political community that stretches beyond the territorial borders of a homeland. That territory, its people, and its government become, through such linkages, a transnational nation-state. Long distance nationalism binds together into a single national body with a shared political project both emigrants and their descendants and persons who have remained in the homeland. As in other versions of nationalism, the concept of a territorial homeland governed by a state that represents the nation remains salient, but national borders are not thought to delimit membership in the nation. Citizens residing within the territorial homeland embrace emigrants and their descendants as part of the nation, whatever legal citizenship the émigrés may have.

To legitimate the connection between the people who can claim membership in the transnational nation-state, long distance nationalism highlights ideas about common descent and shared racialized identities that have long been a part of concepts of national belonging. However, long distance nationalism does not only exist in the domain of the imagination and sentiment. It leads to specific action and these actions linked a dispersed population to a specific homeland and its political system. These actions can include voting, demonstrating, contributing money, artistic creation, giving birth, fighting, killing, and dying when they are done in the name of a transnational nation-state. We can discern three different phases in the relationship between transmigrants and the nation-state.

Phase One: The Role of Transnational Migration in Consolidating Nineteenth-Century Nation-States

In the first phase, transmigrants contributed to the construction and consolidation of territorial nation-states in their homelands. By the nineteenth century the growth of capitalist processes of production and its concomitant cash economy made seasonal and uneven labor demands on rural people in several disparate regions of the world (Chan 1990; Hobsbawm 1975; Krickus 1976). Many workers responded to the uncertainties of early capitalist development by keeping a foothold back home. Seasonal migrants raised cash for taxes, dowries, land purchases, housing purchases and repairs, and the conspicuous consumption that served as markers of elevated social status in their home village. In some regions of Europe this pattern began in the seventeenth century (Moch 1992, 2). In areas such as the central highlands of France, migrants crossed into Spain using commercial networks built on family connections that stretched across borders (85). "Traditional views of static and isolated peasant villages in the preindustrial world simply were inaccurate. . . . Patterns of temporary and permanent migration had characterized Europe and other lands throughout the eighteenth and nineteenth centuries" (Bodnar 1985, 43; see also Thistlewaite 1964, 81). By the nineteenth century family life and the local economy in many localities, including regions of Mexico, China, Russia, and Turkey, were organized around seasonal male migration (Bodnar 1985; Chan 1990; Gutièrrez 1997; Tolopko 1988; Weber 1998; Wong 1982).

By the last decades of the nineteenth century European, Middle Eastern, and Chinese circulatory migrants looked to the Americas for funds to invest at home. The growth of new technologies, including the ocean-going steamship, the telegraph, and regular national postal services (Cinel 1991) made it possible to traverse oceans, maintain home ties, and circulate between two societies. At the time, such innovations were said to have revolutionized communications and made the globe a very small place (Wyman 1993).[19] With the increased distances, migration was often no longer seasonal, although most immigrants of the late-nineteenth and early-twentieth centuries "intended to return" home (Portes and Rumbaut 1996, 102). Migrants settled for relatively longer periods, or even permanently, but many lived within transnational social fields. Between 25 and 60 percent of European immigrants who had settled in the United States made at least one return trip (Bodnar 1985, 53).

Initially most immigrants who maintained transnational ties did so because of allegiance to family and locality rather than because of patriotism or political loyalty to their homeland.[20] Familial ties were maintained by immigrants as part of a broader strategy of migration to purchase land and achieve social security and mobility in the home locality (Krickus 1976; Morawska 1989). Young male immigrant workers in the United States, whether from Italy, Poland, China, or Turkey, organized their living situations so as to maximize the savings they could send or take home. When wives, parents, and cousins joined the migration, the flow of remittances continued, although at lower levels (Alexander 1987). In regions of China, Italy, Sweden, Poland, Ireland, Hungary, Finland, and Italy, remittance money used to purchase land transformed land values and usage (Chan 1990; Cinel 1991; Wyman 1993, 127–36). Transmigrants living in the United States also sponsored improvements in the public facilities of their home locality, including the expansion of hometown ritual life. Chinese immigrants, for example, sent home money to build schools and ancestral temples (Chun 1990, 45). Village priests from southern and eastern Europe visited immigrants settled in the United States bringing news and organizing hometown clubs to contribute money for village projects. Transmigrants often did not challenge the social structures of their homeland because their primary concern was to secure or raise their social position within those structures. The home ties of many immigrants were reinforced by the grim living and working conditions they confronted in what they had thought would be the "golden land." Those who had sought to improve their circumstances by fleeing from economic and political insecurities at home found that in the United States employment was often seasonal or temporary, wages were low, and living expenses were high (Alexander 1987; Bodnar 1985; Wyman 1993). There was no provision for sick, disabled, or elderly workers. Home ties provided some assurance of social support in case of injury or illness.

Because they intended to return, migrants remained concerned with their reputations back home and engaged in an active transnational network of communication that involved both men and women. Ewa Morawska describes "an extended transatlantic system of social control and long-distance management of family and local public affairs" (1989, 262). An Italian scholar in the 1920s who studied a cluster of Sicilian immigrants who had settled two decades earlier on a block of New York City noted: "They receive mail keeping them informed as to the most minute details, and about all the gossip" (reported in Park 1925/1974, 162).

Similar communications and social pressures also can be found in a description of southern Slavic immigrants in 1910: "As long as the definition of crime in the European homeland was clear cut, the immigrant felt that he did not dare commit such an act in this country, for then he would be disgraced in Yugoslavia and would not be received back as a member of his family" (Schermerhorn 1949, 369–70). In other words, the behavior of people living and working in the United States was shaped by transnational social relations because immigrants saw themselves as continuing actors in the society back home. "If the son in Chicago drank heavily, did not save his earnings, or broke other family rules, the village was able to criticize him and exert pressure from afar" (Wyman 1993, 51). Therefore, transmigrants established their own social fields of transnational kinship and hometown solidarities but not their own social worlds. Individuals linked by transnational networks were influenced by the development and dissemination of narratives of national identity in both localities. Their transnational social fields were penetrated, shaped, and transformed by the nation-state-building practices of both sending and receiving states. There were no "third spaces" independent of the regulation, discipline, and hegemonic projects of states.[21] The state practices linked disparate and heterogeneous populations together and forged their loyalty to and identity with a central government apparatus and institutional structure through the construction of a national narrative of belonging. These developments were accompanied by transformations in the ways in which both political leaders and the public thought about the relationship between a state and the population residing within the boundaries of the state. To understand the ways in which transnational migration in the late nineteenth century was linked to the nation-state-building projects in several regions of the world, we must review the economic and political contexts of those migrations.

From the beginning of the expansion of Europe and the development of capitalism, the structures of investment and profit were never based in a single state. Profits were made from raw materials produced in colonial enterprises and distributed in global markets. Increasingly in the nineteenth century, however, governments developed national economic structures that facilitated worldwide capital accumulation, industrial development, and innovation.

As Karl Polanyi (1957 in Gill 1997) noted, the creation of a market society in nineteenth-century Britain was "an unprecedented and revolutionary development insofar as it implied the subordination of all other social and political processes in the creation and maintenance of the capitalist market system. It was also premised in particular upon a strong state able to implement and enforce the measures that created the market society" (quoted in Gill 1997, 207). State-based economic and military power made it possible for European states to consolidate their overseas domains in Africa and Asia and for the United States to expand into the Pacific and the Caribbean. Education, banking and currency, railroads, taxation, postal service, and the military were organized by state-based structures that contributed to the global reach of finance capital and to the rapid movement of labor.

During the same epoch, the dominant classes of an array of states located in Europe, the United States, Latin America, and Asia transformed the ways in which they legitimated their rule (Calhoun 1998; Dikötter 1997; Gellner 1983; Stepan 1991; Takaki 1979/1990). They utilized educational institutions, scholarly theories, print media, public architecture, ceremony, and ritual to unite disparate populations living within a state into a single national community (Anderson 1991; Gellner 1983; Horne 1986). The expansion of technologies of population control, including censuses, emigration and immigration laws and regulations, passports, and citizenship papers, also legitimated the authority of the nation-state by providing concrete manifestations and symbols that those who lived within the territorial borders of a state were a single people.

The state also began to be legitimated through new ideas about the location of sovereignty, which increasingly was said to reside in the nation. In 1789 the French National Assembly declared in its "Declaration of the Rights of Man and of the Citizen" that "the principle of all sovereignty resides essentially in the nation." The concept of nationality was embedded within the rhetoric of the U.S., French, Haitian, and South American revolutions and struggles for independence. However, the ideology, which linked concepts of sovereignty, territory, and nation, developed a mass base only slowly, becoming more widely articulated in Europe during the revolutions in 1848 (Hobsbawm 1975). In much of southern and eastern Europe these ideas did not become part of mass movements until the last third of the nineteenth century (Hobsbawm 1992, 44, 45). The fact that the "people" of a state often did not think of themselves as a single nation was understood by the political leaders of the time. On the occasion of the first meeting of the parliament after the kingdom of Italy had been united in 1861, the Italian leader Massimo d'Azeglio remarked: "We have made Italy; now we have to make Italians" (Hobsbawm 1992, 44, 45).

Consequently, although they came from localities where political classes were engaged in struggling for or consolidating nation-states, late-nineteenth-century immigrants from eastern and southern Europe often arrived in the United States without a clear sense of belonging to a nation-state. Many of them also were unfamiliar with what nationalist leaders were projecting as their national culture. As of 1870, "only 2 to 3 percent of the inhabitants of [Italy] had Italian as their first language. To most Italians, the 'national language was unintelligible and the word Italy was unknown'" (De Mauro 1963, 127, quoted in Cinel (1982, 22). However, as these immigrants to the United States struggled not only to survive but also to prosper and build for themselves lives with meaning and dignity, they entered into the political processes of more than one state. They became not only subjects of states but actors in the nation-state-building processes that structured their life spaces.

At the beginning of the nineteenth century, the dominant classes in many European states encouraged migration. By the end of the century, governments had come to define population as a national resource in the development of industry; they were imposing restrictions on emigration and encouraging those who had left to return (Bodnar 1985, 49, 50). Efforts to reincorporate migrants contributed to the popularization of ideologies of nationalism. Meanwhile, nationalist movements that were fighting to set up independent states contributed to this popularization of nationalism by defining emigrants who had settled elsewhere as part of the national struggle in the homeland for freedom and independence. In both cases nation-state-building politics reached beyond the territorial base of state sovereignty and political leaders encouraged long distance nationalism (Vassady 1982). However, it is important to note, in light of the current debates about transnational migration and deterritorialization, that nineteenth-century nationalist politics that reached beyond territorial borders was still very much about territory. Governments endeavored to reincorporate populations within the territorially based economies they were trying to build. Nationalist movements engaged dispersed populations in the struggle to win national territory.

Italian history provides us with an example of this process. Italian immigrant history is often treated as a special case because many Italian immigrants became nationalists in response to the fascist ideology of Mussolini and the activities his government sponsored in the United States. But Italian government activities on behalf of emigrants predated Mussolini; in the first half of the twentieth century, the policies linking race and nation that became so important to fascist ideology were central to most strains of nationalism.[22] During the years of large-scale Italian emigration to the United States, the Italian census had no category for permanent emigration; it divided the overseas Italian population into only short-term or long-term migrants (Cinel 1982, 66). The Italian government expressed continuing concern for its nationals living abroad. It provided passage for impoverished emigrants who wanted to return through a 1901 law that required steamships serving Italian ports to provide a prescribed amount of free passages. The government denounced the discrimination, mistreatment, and poor working conditions faced by Italian emigrants and provided services for Italians living in the United States. An "Italian Home" in New York City, which provided health, education, and immigration assistance for immigrants, was financed by the Italian government, beginning in 1891. By 1925 Italy was subsidizing fifty-eight Italian organizations based in Italy and twenty-seven based abroad to help immigrants (Wyman 1993, 93, 94).

As the twentieth century progressed, Italian intellectuals and statesmen elaborated their political theory about the relationship between the Italian state and its emigrants. Emigration was defined as a means for Italy as a country without territorial colonies to expand into the world and gain influence and power. Italian emigrant settlements within other nation-states were defined as Italian colonies. Dino Cinel (1982), a historian of Italian emigration, reports that most Italian emigrants who settled in San Francisco made the leap from their home ties based on their personal transnational networks to an identification with Italy in the twentieth century. Much of this identity construction took place after World War I. By the 1930s many Italian immigrant newspapers and organizations in the United States had adopted nationalist rhetoric and referred to Italians settled in the United States as an extension of Italy, an "Italian colony."

Nationalist leaders in Europe, struggling to establish an independent state, also defined their emigrant populations as a continuing part of the struggle for a homeland. The struggle for Poland provides such an example. In the nineteenth century, after all of the territory of the kingdom of Poland had been divided among Russia, Austria-

Hungary, and Prussia, Poland disappeared as a polity. Using the immigrant press in various localities in the United States, Polish leaders struggled to build Polish national identity and to liberate the Polish homeland. In a letter written in 1879 to the Gazeta Polska of Chicago, Agaton Giller, a former member of the Polish national government of the failed insurrection of 1863, made this statement:

> When the mass of Poles in America is morally and nationally raised by the fact of being unified and is economically prosperous . . . it will render great services to Poland, even by the mere fact of representing the Polish name well in America. These services can gradually become very considerable, when the Poles begin to exercise an influence upon the public life in the United States (quoted in Park 1925/1974, 158).

Chinese nationalist leaders adopted a similar stance toward those who had emigrated from China. Their rhetoric built on the theories linking race and nation that they used to delegitimate imperial rule and find a new basis for the popular support of the state (Dikötter 1997). When the Kuomingtang consolidated power in China in 1927, it considered Chinese settled in the United States as its overseas population. In 1928 it set up the Overseas Affairs Bureau, which worked to encourage nationalism toward China (Kwong 1987, 101).

If nationalist movements were transnational, so was the manner in which the European states that were still empires responded to these movements. Hungarian officials in particular aggressively defended the territorial boundaries and legitimacy of their state by claiming authority over its immigrants living in the United States. The prime minister of Hungary told the Hungarian House of Deputies in 1902 that the policies he proposed were designed "to keep the Hungarians in America good Hungarian citizens" (quoted in Wyman 1993, 95).[23] The Hungarian government's intervention in immigrant affairs included "threats, mail seizures, assignment of loyal religious leaders abroad, bribes, and bonuses" to ensure that ethnically differentiated populations such as the Slovaks and Ruthenians were kept friendly. A secret program called "American Action" funded ethnic schools and newspapers and influenced ecclesiastical appointments for both Catholic and Protestant Hungarian churches in the United States (Higham 1982, 74, 75).

The growing tendency to link nation and state and to claim that those who emigrated maintained a sacred responsibility to their homeland resonated in the developing nationalist literatures, some of which specifically were addressed to immigrants in the United States. Typical of this sentiment is a verse by the poet Emil Åbrænyi addressed to "American-Hungarians":

> I know with eager zeal you'd heed,
> The nation's call, and you will cross the seas
> To join our brethren here, to fight, to bleed,
> To die for Magyarland's sweet liberties. (quoted in Wyman 1993, 92)

As illustrated by this poem, much of the nationalist ideology of the day held that immigrants had a responsibility not only to build their ancestral land but also to return home to it. While the Italian government contemplated the possibilities of dual citizenship, the ideological framework of settlements abroad as "colonies" continued to distinguish between the homeland and emigrant settlement (Cinel 1982). Italy made it easy for those who had lost their citizenship when they settled abroad to return to Italy. They could regain their citizenship without cost, but they had to return to live in Italy and renounce all foreign loyalties (Wyman 1993, 94).

Scholars of U.S. immigration have long noted that much of the immigrant national fervor for the home country was "made in America," but they usually have dismissed this as passing sentiments that had no lasting impact on either the United States or the emigrant-sending states (Fuchs 1990; Glazer 1954; Novack 1974; Park 1925/1974). Park (1925/1974, 157–58) put it this way:

> It is an interesting fact that as a first step in Americanization the immigrant does not become in the least American. He simply ceases to become a provincial foreigner. Würtemburgers and Westphalians become in America first of all Germans, Sicilians and Neapolitans become Italians and Jews become Zionists.

In almost the same language, Glazer (1954, 167) reported:

> The newer immigrants . . . became nations in America. The first newspaper in the Lithuanian language was published in this country, not Lithuania . . . and the nation of Czechoslovakia was launched at a meeting in Pittsburgh. . . . [O]ther immigrants were to discover in coming to America that they had left nations behind—nations in which they had had no part at home.[24]

I suggest another interpretation. If Neapolitan emigrants became Italians, Würtemburgers became

German, and Galicians became Polish as they settled in the United States, then we must begin to rethink the terrain on which nation-states develop and national identities are formed (Basch, Glick Schiller, and Blanc-Szanton 1994; Gilroy 1991; Glick Schiller 1999a; Hall 1992). If nineteenth-century immigrants in the United States espoused homeland identities in reaction to their positioning as economically exploited and politically racialized labor, then economic processes and political processes in the United States contributed to the nation-state formation in other regions of the world. Further, at the same time that immigrants, finding themselves economically insecure and socially marginalized in the United States, began to participate in the construction of national identities in their homelands, they shaped the ways in which U.S. national identity was debated and represented.

Additional research needs to be done on the ways in which past transmigrants of different classes participated in nation-state-building projects back home as well as in the redefining of what it meant to be "an American." But we can find evidence of the ways in which immigrant workers began to commit their energies to transnational state building, and their motivations for doing so, in the descriptions of the daily life of immigrant neighborhoods in U.S. factory and mining towns. For example, Louise Lamphere's work (1987) on Central Falls, Rhode Island, provides us with a glimpse of the daily routine of sociability and neighborhood activity through which both male and female Galician immigrants learned a Polish nationalist discourse and engaged in transnational political activities. Galicia, an independent kingdom in the early Middle Ages, became part of Poland in 1382; in 1872 it was annexed by the Austro-Hungarian empire (Vucinich 1959, 2844–55). Although Galician migrants left and returned—and almost half returned home—to a Galicia that was a semiautonomous region of the Austro-Hungarian empire, in the course of their experiences in the United States many came to accept a definition of themselves as Polish.[25] Working in the factories of Central Falls, Galician peasants learned they could find desperately needed social services and recover a sense of self-esteem by participating in Polish nationalist organizations such as the Pulaski Mutual Aid Society and the Society of Polish Knights, a part of the Polish National Alliance. These organizations were established in Galician neighborhoods by priests and middle-class immigrants who identified themselves with the struggle to reestablish an independent Polish state.

A recollection of the Polish Falcons, a paramilitary organization founded in Central Falls in 1908 contains an inventory of the activities of these types of organizations.

> [The Falcons] renewed the life of local Polonia through exercises, singing, marches, celebrations, balls, meetings, lectures, frequent travel contests, frequent theatrical performances, and collection of funds for armed struggle. Thus this organization contributed greatly to the well-being of the Fatherland. (Jubilee Book of the Pulaski Society, quoted in Lamphere 1987, 113)

The Galician peasants were not alone. Immigrants from localities around the world responded to the conditions they found in the United States by developing loyalty to their ancestral homeland and participating in transnational activities to build its state. Their organizations built distant nation-states while contributing to local ethnic pride. Treated as faceless and mindless workers and defined by the press, politicians, and prevailing public opinion as racially different, inferior, and undesirable, large numbers of immigrants responded, as did the Galician peasants, by joining nationalist organizations in their neighborhoods. They sent home sizable sums of money for nationalist causes and sometimes returned to fight for their homelands. In 1912 to 1913 the Pan Hellenic Union sent forty-two thousand Greek Americans to fight for Greece. Serbian Americans left to fight Austria-Hungary and for Serb independence in 1914 (Harrington 1982, 113). It is important to note that this transnational military participation was broadly accepted and reported by the U.S. press (Wyman 1993, 110). The prevailing views about nations as distinctive races legitimated behavior that continued to link southern and eastern European immigrants to their homelands.

After World War I, immigrants in the United States used their ability to lobby and vote to try to influence President Wilson and the political settlement drawn up at the Versailles Conference (Bodnar 1985, 202). Lithuanian immigrant businessmen in the United States funded the Lithuanian delegation to the Congress of Versailles. Immediately after World War I, Lithuanians raised $2 million for an independent Lithuania by selling Lithuanian Freedom Loan Bonds (Harrington 1982, 111.) Meanwhile, the American Hungarian National Federation, a "democratic parliament of

Hungarians," met in Buffalo to organize a campaign to revise the Treaty of Tranon, which had "dismembered Hungary" (Schermerhorn 1949, 337).

When U.S. immigrants acted as transmigrants who sustained homeland nationalism, as well as distant family and village life, they were responding to more than political and economic developments in emigrant-sending countries. They were also reacting to the ways in which the U.S. nation-state-building project had racialized them. Their participation in transnational political activities also can be read as a response to the U.S. racialized politics of immigrant incorporation. Recent scholarship documents the processes through which various immigrant populations in the United States, from the Irish to the Jews, were first racialized and only then "became white," as they defined themselves over and against African Americans. This research contributes to our understanding of the transnational dynamics of "Americanization." (Ignatiev 1995; Roediger 1991; Sacks 1994).

Since the founding of the nation, whiteness and an American nationality have been linked in political rhetoric and in law (Horsman 1981; Lieberson 1980; Page 1997; Saxton 1990). Faced with the need to legitimate the sovereignty of their new and weak national government, and having no monarch or shared historical tradition, the U.S. founding fathers portrayed the United States as a nation unified through its whiteness—in Benjamin Franklin's words, the "lovely white" (Takaki 1979/1990, 14). The republican virtues of self-discipline, self-control, and independence were thought to be concentrated among whites. The Naturalization Law of 1790 allowed only white immigrants to become naturalized citizens. This principle was maintained until 1952 and narrowly interpreted so that even Asian Indians who were acknowledged to be Caucasians were denied the right to become naturalized (López 1996).

Defined by the dominant U.S. society as racially different from U.S. whites, first the Irish and then eastern and southern European immigrants struggled to improve their social status in the United States and to combat the legal and de facto discrimination they faced by distinguishing themselves from blacks. After the annexation of Mexican territory, immigrants from Europe who settled in the Southwest and on the West Coast sought to define their whiteness in opposition to persons of Mexican, Chinese, and Japanese descent. They strengthened their own claims to an American identity by defining these other populations as biologically incapable of culture and civilization (López 1995; Takaki 1979/1990; Winant 1994). In reaction, Mexican, Chinese, and Japanese immigrants also embraced their ancestral national identities, believing that their worth in America would be measured by the strength and prosperity of their homeland.[26]

The dividing line used by various immigrant populations to distinguish themselves from blacks was that immigrants could claim a homeland and be claimed by it. To have a homeland was part of what distinguished white civilizations. Immigrants entered into politics in the United States motivated, at least in part, by the desire to support and strengthen the struggles or national welfare of their home country. Stepping back to analyze the historical process, we can see that as politicized immigrants living in the United States reacted to their racialization by becoming engaged in the transnational political processes of their homelands, they simultaneously reinforced the U.S. discourse of America as a white nation. At the same time, as immigrants sought to raise their status in the United States by embracing their ancestral land through transnational activities, they became active participants in a trajectory of Americanization. Transnational politics became the base area from which racialized immigrants sought to join white America (Ignatiev 1995; Miller 1990; Roediger 1991).

U.S. political officials, the media, and academics in the first decades of the twentieth century contributed to this dynamic through their rhetorical strategies and the type of immigrant organizing they fostered. Although they identified recent immigrants as racially different from the U.S. mainstream, they differentiated them from blacks by identifying immigrant populations as nationalities. Many U.S. political leaders on the municipal, state, and federal levels saw nothing contradictory in incorporating immigrants into the United States by organizing them into separate and distinct nationality groups. Political officials saw such immigrant organizations as a means of combating syndicalism among workers (Cinel 1982, 242–55); they took for granted that immigrants settling in the United States would continue to have separate national identities that linked them to their homeland because national identities were seen as rooted in blood ties and as fundamentally racial.

For example, in 1914 the California Commission on Immigration and Housing, an official body created by the California legislature and whose views were endorsed by the governor of California, recommended that Italian immigrants be organized separately in order to provide for the charitable needs of their own nationality. In 1916, to implement this recommendation, the head of the Associated Charities of San Francisco, a leading charitable organization in that city, brought Italian immigrant leaders together to organize the Italian Welfare Agency (Cinel 1982, 244).

Historians have seen World War I and its aftermath as a turning point that disrupted any continuing identity that past generations of immigrants maintained with their home country. Gary Gerstle (1996a), for example, has argued that after World War I

> a powerful nationalism had settled over America (1915–1925), suffocating the hyphenated or old world identities that had thrived everywhere in the first years of the new century. A new American nationalism had triumphed over multiculturalism. Cultural inventiveness did not end as a result of the rise of jealous and powerful American nationalism, but its character changed. Increasingly the crucial questions shaping inventiveness became not, "How much of an American will I become?" but, "What kind of American will I be?"

It is true that the political loyalties of U.S. immigrants were contested during and after World War I. The National Society of the Daughters of the American Revolution published the *Manual of the United States: For the Information of Immigrants and Foreigners* in English and seventeen other languages and distributed two million copies. "America does not ask you to forget your old home," said the booklet. But when new citizens swore allegiance to the United States, they had to renounce their allegiance to their "former country. . . . You cannot have two countries" (quoted in Fuchs 1990, 64).

However, the historical record provides a wealth of evidence that U.S. government officials, including Presidents Roosevelt, Truman, Johnson, and Nixon, took political actions that reflected and reinforced the belief that immigrants remained connected to their sending nation and to the population back in the national territory. Immigrant populations continued to be called "nationalities" rather than ethnic groups, and the creation or maintenance of these nationality groups became an instrument of U.S. foreign policy. The direction of this policy was set by the U.S. Congress after World War I when it accepted back into the fold those who had sworn allegiance to and fought in foreign armies as long as they had been fighting enemies of the United States (Harrington 1982, 115).[27]

At various periods of U.S. history, nativist leaders have attacked the "foreign" influences and cultures of various immigrant populations, but legal action has been taken against the transnational ties of immigrants only when the immigrants' home countries were declared formal enemies of the United States. When Italy became a U.S. enemy during World War II, Italian schools and institutions supported by the Italian government were restricted. U.S. immigrants' home ties and their right to speak for nation-states abroad were sustained as instruments of foreign policy throughout the history of the adversarial U.S. relationship with the Soviet Union. The organization of "nationality groups" was strengthened after World War II with the admission of refugees from Hungary, Czechoslovakia, Cuba, Vietnam, and Poland under special immigration waivers for refugees from communism.

Most often the relationship between U.S. nationalities and political parties and campaigns has been discussed under the rubric of "the ethnic vote" rather than as immigrant transnational relationships.[28] In many instances, however, U.S. political parties played a significant, if largely forgotten, role in maintaining the national identities and transnational politics of immigrants and their descendants. Both the Democratic and Republican Parties developed nationality divisions built on the assumption that there was a continuing relationship between immigrant populations and their states of origin. Both parties saw these divisions as a critical element in their electoral strategies.

For example, Jack Redding, the party chairman of the Democratic Party at the time, believed that the party's Nationalities Division played a key role in Truman's surprise presidential victory in 1948. The transnational nature of U.S. politics emerges clearly in his memoirs (Redding 1958, 205, 223):

> Although loyal to the United States, many Americans of foreign descent were nevertheless also deeply concerned with the future of the country of their forefathers. Many of them had close relatives still in the old country and they had friends there with whom they corresponded regularly. The welfare of these friends and relatives, still in Europe and Asia, was a matter of great importance. . . . Before the campaign began, concrete evidence of

> the President's interest in the problems of the countries menaced and conquered by Communism had been given over and over. . . . For voters of foreign origin the issues were clearly with the Democratic Party. What remained for us was to carry out an aggressive program of driving those issues home.

In the course of these elections, the Nationalities Division was expanded to become an integral part of the Democratic National Committee. Party strategists continued to believe in its centrality in the decades to come; they renamed the division the "All-American Division" when they moved it to the offices of the Democratic National Committee in 1963, but its functions remained the same (Sendelbach 1967, 23). In the 1970s the Democrats continued to maintain active ties with a range of organizations, from Georgian to Irish, that were still seen as nationality groups. Two years after the Czech uprising, the head of the All-American Division of the National Democratic Party was Czech.

The Republican Party organized its National Republican Heritage Groups during Nixon's 1968 presidential campaign. It was described at the time as "the largest and most aggressive undertaking by any national party in American history" (Weed 1973, 166). Through its Slovak advisors, the Republican National Committee played an active role in helping to organize activities such as the Slovak World Congress that met in Toronto, Canada in 1971 (Weed 1973, 166). Typical of the cold war period was a statement made in a speech to the members of a Hungarian American "Heritage Group" by Ralph Smith, the Republican candidate for an Illinois senatorial seat: "I hope your nation behind the wall of Communism will again see the light of freedom we all love so dearly" (quoted in Weed 1973, 162).

Phase Two: The Global Triumph of Nation-State Ideology and the Unremarked Persistence of Transnational Politics

As indicated in the previous sections, a sector of immigrants and their descendants from the migrations of the 1880s to the 1920s maintained familial ties to their ancestral lands, and these ties often became overlaid with political activities on behalf of these homelands. These ties and the political identities and loyalties on which they were based were a significant aspect of life in twentieth-century America, significant enough to have been credited with the winning of a presidential election in midcentury. However, over the course of the century there were important changes in the political and economic contexts within which these transnational relationships and identities were maintained. As the cold war developed, public opinion about the relationship between individuals and nation-states changed dramatically.

Despite the fact that in the post–World War II period both the United States and the Soviet Union extended their influence throughout the globe, the period was broadly understood as the age of decolonization. Side by side with an acknowledgment of a cold war division of the world into two blocks, political leaders, the media, and citizens of old and newly independent states came to share a vision of a world divided into equal independent nation-states. Each state had its discrete territory, nationality, and national culture. The United Nations, founded in 1945, vigorously propagated nation-state ideology. As former European colonies in Asia, Africa, and the Caribbean achieved formal independence, they contributed to the triumph of the nation-state ideology by establishing schools, museums, and cultural ministries that institutionalized and popularized the links between people, culture, and the territory of the state (LiPuma 1997).

In a world in which nation-states were defined by territorial boundaries, migration between nation-states seemed anomalous. Academic disciplines focused research and scholarly discourse on national histories, and the long history of widespread migration and movement across borders was neglected. For example, Europe, which had experienced centuries of migration, was envisioned as a continent without a history of immigration (Canny 1994). Meanwhile, in the United States Handlin's (1951/1973) vision of immigrants as "uprooted" won broad public acceptance. In the emerging cold war vision of citizenship, a person could be loyal to only one country, and the word *country* was assumed to be synonymous with both nation and state. Beginning in the 1950s, workers were required to take loyalty oaths in order to obtain or retain employment in any public office. Forgotten was the nineteenth-century heritage of political openness to immigrants in which more than half the states had allowed noncitizens the right to vote (DeSipio and de la Garza 1998, 97).[29]

By the 1960s, although a sector of immigrants continued to maintain their home ties, and these identities continued to play a role in both urban and national politics, the term "ethnic group" began to replace the concept of nationality. Social scientists, political leaders, and educators promoted a conception of a culturally plural America, spoke of the "ethnic factor" in U.S. elections, heralded the "white ethnic movement," and celebrated group identities as "ethnic" (Levy and Kramer 1973; Novack 1974; Weed 1973).[30] Although cultural pluralism received more public recognition than in previous decades, these identities increasingly were conceptualized as restricted to the political boundaries of the United States. Roots could be celebrated, but immigrants' home ties and concomitant political identifications were rendered invisible in the new paradigm, even as they continued to play a role in cold war politics.

In the midst of burgeoning celebrations of cultural pluralism and the "white ethnic movement," a new set of immigrants began to enter the United States. Between 1965 and 1996, 20.1 million people arrived as permanent residents (DeSipio and de la Garza 1998, 49). In many ways the economic forces that influenced this migration resembled those at the end of the nineteenth century. As had happened earlier, there was a worldwide change in the organization and deployment of capital. This reorganization brought localities in diverse areas of the world into new relationships to the process of capital accumulation, disrupted local economies, and fostered new migrations to the United States (Sassen 1988). In the last third of the twentieth century, the world had again become a place where new forms of capital penetration were inducing people to leave home to seek opportunities in other countries (UNRISD 1995). Structural adjustment programs guided by neoliberal agendas ended efforts to develop and protect state-based industrial and agricultural development (Schaeffer 1997). By devaluing national currencies, these programs increased the price of the imported manufactured and agricultural goods that replaced national production. In addition, education, health care, and utilities began to be privatized; increasingly services were restricted to only those who could pay. Those with the resources to do so fled from national economies in which the standard of living for the middle class, working class, and rural producers had been devastated in order to service international debts. Their migration was fueled by both personal hopes for a better life abroad and the need to ensure that family members who remained at home had the money to buy imported goods and private services.

U.S. cities, which serve as significant locations in the organization of the new forms of capital, have become important migration destinations (Sassen 1991). However, the same global processes that provide the incentives for continuing migration to the United States make it difficult for immigrants to become fully incorporated into the United States. The restructuring of the global economy has reduced or eliminated in the United States the gains that were won by a sector of industrial workers through decades of union activity and political struggle. In the United States the conditions of employment at the end of the twentieth century resemble those faced by late-nineteenth-century immigrants: a low level of real income, temporary employment, and the absence of public welfare or medical care beyond what may be provided by private charity.[31]

In the face of a reduction in public services and reduced real wages for a large section of the workforce in the 1970s and 1980s, political leaders directed public anger toward immigrants. The governors of Florida and California, for example, blamed undocumented immigrants for the decline in the quality and availability of public services in their states. Meanwhile, the 1986 immigration law, which required that employers verify the legal status of immigrants working for them, made the employment position of these immigrants more insecure. Other legislation made the possibility of immigrant families supporting their young and aged in the United States increasingly difficult. California's Proposition 187 and attacks on bilingual education and federal welfare legislation, rather than deterring the migration of persons who can provide cheap labor, specifically made it difficult for immigrant families to educate their children or care for their sick or aged in the United States (Chavez 1996, 19). The decay of the public education system, particularly in big cities, led immigrants to fear for their children's future and to use wages earned in the United States to educate their children back home (Guarnizo 1997a). These pressures encourage immigrants to maintain or build transnational networks.

As in the past, many of the new immigrants defined themselves as temporary migrants and continued to build ties back home. Unlike the period prior to the 1920s, when the entry of immigrants was not restricted by immigration laws, quotas, and visas, a significant sector of the new immigrants have lacked permanent resident status when they arrive. Their legal insecurity has contributed to their interest in maintaining transnational networks, although they themselves have been unable to move easily across borders.

However, it is often the immigrants who have become well incorporated and prosperous in the United States who are the most active in building transnational networks (Goldring 1998; Lessinger, 1995; Pessar, 1995b). Their motivations closely resemble those of late-nineteenth-century immigrants. In a dynamic that is strikingly similar to past migrations, those who can use their migration experience to achieve or maintain social status back home often are catalysts in setting up transnational networks. Again, the social power within family networks that immigrants obtain by sending a flow of remittances to sustain those left behind exerts a powerful dynamic that connects persons living in different polities. Both men and women participate in the complex dynamic of obligation and prestige that motivates persons to live their lives across borders. However, they obtain differential rewards that are shaped by the gender categories and dynamics of each sending society (Pessar, this volume; Georges 1992).

Although most contemporary immigrants migrate from independent nation-states, many resemble their nineteenth-century predecessors in responding to their experiences in the United States by embracing their homeland identities. As in the past, immigrants from many areas of the world find themselves racialized. They are defined as different from the U.S. mainstream or those with prior claims to belonging in the United States define their membership against the "inferior" newcomers. The racialized categorization of immigrants as Asian, Hispanic, and black erases their specific national identities and contributes to the continuing construction of a "white identity" for the majority of the U.S. population. Immigrants categorized as "black" find this racialization particularly difficult since the categorical denial of their national origins allocates them to the social bottom of the society, the position against which American whiteness is most sharply delineated (Bryce-Laporte 1972, 1980; Charles 1990a, 1990b; 1992; Waters 1990; Williams 1989). Many contemporary immigrants learn to look homeward in response to racial categorization and discrimination. However, until very recently, the home ties and the long distance nationalism of U.S. transmigrants was invisible.

The dominant political rhetoric in the 1970s left no conceptual space for actors in either immigrant-receiving or emigrant-sending countries to take notice of the transnational ties of immigrants. In immigrant-receiving countries such as the United States, Canada, and Australia, political leaders, social scientists, and the general public all assumed that "uprooted" immigrants had abandoned the country of their birth. The immigrants themselves became convinced that they had to choose between the country of their birth and their new land, even though they actually lived their lives across borders. For example, even Haitian immigrants who were deeply embedded in both the United States and Haiti talked about the need to either return home or "forget about Haiti" (Fouron 1983, 1984; Fouron and Glick Schiller 1997). In emigrant-sending countries, political leaders and prevailing public opinion defined persons who had left to settle abroad and their descendants as outsiders. Often the divisions between emigrants and their states of origin were exacerbated by political differences between repressive authoritarian regimes and emigrants who organized political opposition. Emigrants were often construed as culturally inauthentic, politically suspect, or traitorous, even as their remittances made increasingly important contributions to local or even national economies (Feldman-Bianco 1992; Fouron and Glick Schiller 1997; Smith 1998).

Phase Three: The Restructuring of Global Capitalism and Reconstruction of Nation-States

After an initial flurry of discussion about globalization as a process distinctive of the late twentieth century, scholars in a number of disciplines moved to a more nuanced and historical reading of contemporary global processes (Castells 1997; Nonini and Ong 1997; Olds et al. 1999; Mittleman 1997b). An aspect of this developing scholarship of globalization has been a self-reflexive move that notes the way the purview of social science has been constrained by an identification with the nation-state (Turner 1990a). As I have noted, global processes have been central to the development of capitalism. What makes global processes appear novel in the late twentieth century is the context of the period: discrete nation-states with separately structured economies have become accepted as the norm. Rather than witnessing the era of the "postnation" or the "poststate," we find that political leaders and emigrants of a growing number of nation-states are once again reaching beyond the territorial boundaries of the state to reincorporate emigrants and their descendants into projects in their ancestral land. Today's relationship between transmigrants and sending states seems new in the face of the competing ideology that nationals of a state reside within its territory. Consequently, when immigrants construct transnational lives and engage in political activities that build their homelands, and when emigrant-sending states reach out to their populations settled abroad, their actions and political rhetoric seem novel and disruptive of the world order.

Despite the continuities, the past is not being repeated. There are important new aspects of the current wave of transnational nation-state building because this wave is set within a new configuration of capitalism. The current era of globalization is producing new types of relationships between states and processes of commodification, capital accumulation, and investment (Camilleri and Falk 1992; Sassen 1996b; Stallings 1995). Rather than "dithering away," states are experiencing "metamorphosis" (Beck 1997, 139; Turner 1997, 2). "To realize material gain from globalization, the state increasingly facilitates this process, acting as its agent" (Mittleman 1997a, 7). Multinational corporations are finding new ways to use the legal structures of strong states such as the United States, as well as the military and police capacities of states, in their efforts to maintain a structure of law and to compete for greater shares of capital and markets (Panitch 1997; Sassen 1996b) "As states lose control over the national economy, they are forced to enter the fray on behalf of their own multinationals" (Jessop 1994, 262; see also Rosecrance 1996). States that are neither powerful nor the locale of a global city are also affected by current trends: their degree of sovereignty, always tentative, is being further reduced.

In this context, increasing numbers of migrant-sending states are reconstituting their state policies and ideologies to encompass populations living abroad. Mexico, the Dominican Republic, Portugal, and Japan are among a wide range of states that are bent on reclaiming emigrant populations, as well as their descendants (Feldman-Bianco 1992, 1994, 1997; Graham 1997; Reichl 1988; Smith 1997). These states are explicitly redefining themselves as transnational. Within immigrant-receiving countries such as the United States, Canada, and Australia, a range of actors, from government officials to educational institutions, are responding to immigrant populations by proposing a concept of multiculturalism that recognizes immigrant roots but envisions them as "transplanted" within the multicultural terrain of their new country (Bodnar 1985).

At first glance, the policies, practices, and theories of the new transnational nation-states resemble those that developed at the end of the nineteenth century. Again, political leaders of states with high rates of emigration are organizing and claiming to represent populations that are incorporated into the United States. And once again, immigrants in the United States are publicly proclaiming their loyalties to their ancestral lands. However, these developments are taking place in a world different from that of previous migrations and will have different consequences. They are contemporary responses to the ways capital is being deployed, goods and services are being produced, and the inequalities of wealth and power are being organized and legitimated. That is to say, they are reorganizations of states and reconstitutions of ideas of nation, citizenship, and polity in a world where national economies are no longer built by dominant sectors of national capital, although military and vital regulatory power is still based in state structures and is still an aspect of the competition between capitalists (Jessop 1994; Panitch 1997).

Consequently, although there are similarities, contemporary transnational states do differ in their political rhetoric and state practices from those states that implemented transnational policies in earlier eras. Today transmigrants are not expected to come home to fight and die for the motherland or to rebuild the nation, although their visits as tourists are seen as an important aspect of the national economy.[32] Rather, they are expected to stay abroad permanently but to send money home often. And although there is a strong precedent for transmigrants to participate in U.S. politics on behalf of their homeland, homeland governments now advise transmigrants to become U.S. citizens in order to assist their ancestral land.

Some states have changed their constitutions to include emigrant populations as members of their political community. Although these states—among them, Mexico, Colombia, the Dominican Republic, and Portugal—have legally recognized their immigrants as members of their ancestral state, they differ in the degree to which these legal reforms grant emigrants and their descendants rights to political participation in their homeland. Mexican emigrants and their children have been granted dual nationality, not dual citizenship. Nationals cannot vote in Mexican elections. Colombians who live abroad have their own elected representative within the Colombian legislature (Sanchez 1997). Through its Office of Mexicans Living Abroad, the Mexican government organizes and channels the political energies of Mexican emigrants and their descendants settled in the United States. Representatives of this office seek to prevent Mexicans in the United States from emerging as a political opposition to the ruling party in Mexico and to secure a lobby for Mexican interests in the United States (Smith 1997, 1998). Persons of Greek descent are currently able to apply for citizenship in Greece, and the Greek government employs the term spodemoi or "Greeks abroad" for all persons of Greek ancestry (Jusdanis 1991). Ireland is conducting a thriving business in providing Irish passports to persons who are citizens of other states but can prove Irish descent (Tuathail, personal communication, 1998).

A second set of states, such as Haiti, the Philippines, and India, have not allowed dual nationality to their emigrants who have accepted legal membership in other states. However, these states have changed their rhetoric, their policies, and sometimes their tax laws to encourage populations abroad to maintain their home ties. Officials of these states have promoted ideologies that reimagine emigrants and their descendants as part of their ancestral native land and encourage these populations to identify with the politics of the government of the home country, even if they are no longer legally nationals of that state.

Until the 1980s an estimated one million or more persons of Haitian descent living outside of Haitian borders were defined by the Haitian government as traitors to the nation. Meanwhile, political exiles labeled Haitian emigrants "the diaspora," a term they used to define Haitians abroad as exiles obligated to rebuild the homeland. However, in 1991, on the day of his inauguration as president of Haiti, Jean-Bertrand Aristide spoke of the diaspora as "the Tenth Department" (Richman 1992). Haiti is territorially divided into nine administrative departments. In the speech, which was broadcast on WLIB in New York City on January 5, 1991, Aristide began to articulate a nationalist rhetoric that explicitly incorporated the Haitian diaspora within the boundaries of the Haitian nation-state. He spoke of the Haitian immigrants as Haiti's "prodigal children" and welcomed them into the fold of the "Haitian community" under the "aegis and the protection of the political power of the Haitian nation-state." By 1997 the word diaspo (diaspora) had become incorporated into Haitian Kreyol, not as a term for exiles but as a term for persons living abroad who remained Haitian, whatever their formal nationality. Aristide's government, as well as its successors, included many ministers and officials who were transmigrants living within transnational networks. Although the succeeding government abandoned the term "Tenth Department," it preserved the Ministry of Haitians Living Abroad begun by Aristide. Meanwhile, members of the Haitian diaspora organized a campaign to obtain dual nationality through a change in the Haitian constitution.

Contemporary states, as compared to those of the late nineteenth century, are constructing their national discourse in a period of globalization in which it is increasingly difficult to maintain even the semblance of a national economy or to invest in a national infrastructure. In the era of structural adjustment programs and International Monetary Fund (IMF) mandates, states that are not centers of capital are being stripped of the ability to regulate or administer economic activities within the territorial borders of their state (Cox 1997, 26). However, these states continue to play important roles in the construction of categories of identity. Within a globalized economy, transnational narratives may provide political leaders with claims to populations or resources that can bolster the position of their state within global geopolitics.

In one dramatic instance, Portuguese officials reconfigured their nation-state-building project as they struggled to position their state within broad regional and global realignments of economic and political power (Feldman-Bianco 1994, 1997). For centuries voyages of discovery, overseas territories, and emigrant populations have been significant aspects of the Portuguese construction of a nation-state. However, emigrants who settled abroad were defined as traitors to the national project. In contrast, beginning in the 1970s emigrants were called "Portuguese spread around the world" (Feldman-Bianco 1992, 147). By the end of the 1980s Portuguese laws had been changed to grant dual citizenship so that emigrants and their descendants could retain their Portuguese nationality even as they remained citizens of other states. Situated on the periphery of Europe and struggling to enhance its position in both the European Union and the larger world, Portugal is attempting through this reclamation project to bolster its position by claiming leadership of a "global nation." The global nation of Portugal includes populations in states with large markets such as Brazil, in resource-rich states such as Angola, and in powerful states such as the United States. Broad ties of feeling are said to link the members of a "Lusophonic community."[33]

The reemergence of languages of "blood" that equate nation and race is another symptom of the resurgence of long distance nationalism. Political leaders and officials engaged in nation-state-building projects are reinvigorating folk biologies of "blood ties" to legitimate the claims between states and populations abroad. These racialized definitions of nationality allow governments to define immigrants and their descendants as ineligible for citizenship even though they reside within the territory of a state, while claiming as citizens or nationals emigrants and their descendants who have become citizens of other states and live within the borders of that other state. Both states that have instituted or made more salient laws that allow dual nationality and those that try to reincorporate dispersed populations without granting them legal rights to their ancestral homeland confront the challenge of appealing to a dispersed population whose language and daily cultural practices may differ from those in the native land. Given these disparities, many transnational states define the connection between immigrants and their state of origin in terms of shared descent or "common blood."

For example, this linkage between descent and national identity underlies the 1994 changes in the Dominican constitution. Even before these constitutional reforms, persons of Haitian descent born within the borders of the Dominican Republic were defined as black and barred from citizenship, while Dominicans of any skin color were defined as white.[34] Dominican political leaders built cross-class unity by popularizing a nationalism that distinguished between Haitians and Dominicans, not on the basis of culture, language, or location of birth, but on the basis of descent. The 1994 constitutional amendments extend this racialized definition of the Dominican nation to persons living abroad who can claim Dominican descent. The rights of citizenship, including voting, are extended to individuals of Dominican descent who through birth or naturalization are citizens of other countries, creating a new category of dual citizen (Graham 1997).

More research is needed to flesh out the way contemporary long distance nationalism differs from that of the past. Among the significant variables are: the internal political dynamics of states, the placement of states within the restructured global economy, their history of nation-state building, the size and recency of their migrations, and the class positions and power of their emigrant populations (Feldman-Bianco 1992, 1994 1997; Graham 1997; Guarnizo 1997, 1998a; Guarnizo and Diaz 1999; Lessinger 1995; Mahler 1998; Ong 1997; Smith 1997). It is clear that both emigrant-sending and immigrant-receiving states have responded to transmigrants and their political activities. In the United States debates on immigration and national culture are taking place as a block of powerful neoliberal forces work to restructure the apparatus of the state and to build a national consensus that supports that restructuring. These forces seek to maximize their profits within the new contingencies of the global economy by appropriating but streamlining aspects of the government apparatus useful to multinational corporations, such as contract, copyright, and patent law and military force, while public services are reduced or eliminated. In this conjuncture, in which the concept of "public" has been eroded and political leaders preach that government has been an obstacle to individual prosperity, the problem of legitimating the state has reached something of a crisis.

To meet this crisis of legitimacy, U.S. leaders of various educational and philanthropic institutions, as well as politicians, have been looking in disparate directions. Some have continued to popularize the concept of "whiteness" as a source of unity between classes and cultures within the state. Immigrants once again become the outsiders against whom a sense of white solidarity can be built (Rubin 1994). Even as the United States is increasingly dominated by financial institutions, which operate in a global domain and organize globally to protect their interests, U.S. politicians invoke forms of nationalist rhetoric that calls on citizens to defend their borders against alien incursions.

However, a cluster of U.S.-based transnational corporations, U.S. universities, nonprofit organizations, and philanthropic institutions have embraced, alongside the older anti-immigrant rhetoric, the imagery of a "multicultural America." Persons engaged in building this multicultural America sometimes recognize the transnational connections of immigrants while encouraging transmigrants to give their allegiance to the United States. They often conflate the homeland identity and the racial identity of the immigrant in ways that resemble the rhetoric of the political leaders of emerging transnational nation-states. Their use of the term ***multicultural*** to categorize populations that differ widely in their cultural histories but share racialized identities as black, Hispanic, Asian, and Native American, indicates that this new U.S. nation-state-building project is also racialized. In the new U.S. rhetoric of multiculturalism, identity is conceptually separated from political loyalty so that nonwhite persons are thought to maintain their homeland identities but to use them to contribute to the national interests of the United States.

This multiculturalist discourse instills new immigrants with the sense that they are participating in the national destiny shared equally by all citizens of the United States.[35] At the same time, through the rhetoric of multiculturalism, immigrants' transnational ties to home societies serve to connect U.S.-based corporations to other localities within a global economy.[36] Loyalty to the United States continues to be demanded in a context where immigrant transnational connections become instruments of economic and political penetration abroad. Multicultural Americans become useful human capital in competition with Asia-based corporations and provide new entries into Latin American markets. The realignment of the world economy forms the context for refashioning contemporary transnational migrants into U.S. citizens.

The situation in Florida is indicative of a larger trend. On the one hand, political leaders in Florida have targeted illegal aliens as the cause of their shrinking state resources. They called national attention to the issue by suing the federal government for $1.5 billion to recover state expenses for providing services to the undocumented (Borenstein and Gibson, 1994). On the other hand, some of the same political leaders have recognized that immigrants provide Florida with new economic opportunities, exactly because they can provide transnational connections to global markets. In the decade of the 1980s, Miami conducted $26 billion worth of trade with Latin America—not counting tourism. Recognizing the political benefits of immigrants' ties to their home countries or region, Lieutenant Governor of Florida Buddy MacKay declared:

> South Florida will increasingly benefit from its growing presence as the de facto capital of Latin America if it embraces its growing international makeup. Florida's future lies in looking south and outward, and not north and inward. We've got this huge opportunity and we've got to take steps . . . to capitalize on it (Grogan 1994, 9s).

The southern Florida newspaper, the *Sun-Sentinel* highlighted MacKay's views in a story with the headline "U.S. Strategy: End Illegal Tide, Tap New Potential." (Grogan 1994, 9s) The article reported on a symposium of "legislators, academics and immigration officials" who were brought together by the newspaper to advance initiatives for "better managing immigration." The *Sun-Sentinel* went on to say: "The children of immigrants, comfortable in both cultures and benefiting from an American education, will be the key to that opportunity, even if today's immigrants are less inclined than previous generations to blend into the homogenous American landscape." (Grogan 1994, 9s)

A similar recognition of the profitability of multiculturalism is emerging in California and Hawaii, where Asian American transnational ties are recognized and valued as long as they are used for the interests of U.S.-based capital. Aihwa Ong's (1993) interviews with corporate executives is revealing. These executives a multiculturalist perspective in their corporate strategy. The head of the Dole corporation, a company with investments in more than fifty countries, extolled the value of executives of Chinese descent who can operate in China but are U.S. citizens: "This knowledge and ability can help Americans achieve political and business success in the region. . . . [M]uch of their insight and ability can [help] in opening doors for the U.S. to build a new structure for peace in the Pacific" (Ong 1993, 766).

This multicultural logic contains two types of conflation. The interests of the transnational corporation are equated with those of all "Americans." At the same time, persons of Chinese descent are assumed to have knowledge of China because of the way they look rather than because of any specific cultural education they may have. They are constructed as both American and racially and culturally different. Multicultural Americans become useful human capital in competition with Asia-based corporations.

Conclusions and Directions for Future Research and Analysis

In this chapter, I have outlined three different phases of the relationships between transmigrants in the United States and their homelands. In all three phases, immigrants and their descendants have become incorporated into the U.S. body politic by contributing to the nation-state-building projects of their ancestral homelands. Arguing against the authors who see contemporary transnational migration as a product of new technologies and an indicator of a post-nation or post-state epoch, I have demonstrated that late-nineteenth-century communications allowed for trips home and regular news from home. The technologies that have facilitated transnational migration have been part of broader transformations in the processes by which capital is accumulated and organized, processes that have affected the structuring of states and the relationship between government and the population of these states, including transmigrants. Now, as in the past, state-based political processes contribute to the complex dynamic of forces that lead people to live their lives across borders and continue to identify with their homeland.

It is the changing nature of the organization and accumulation of capital and its relationship to state structures and nationalist ideologies that can best account for transformations in transnational migration and transnational nation-state building over time. I noted that this relationship began in the late nineteenth century, in a period when capitalist expansion included the consolidation of state infrastructures such as railroads and post offices and the development of transoceanic travel. In this period significant sectors of the population found it possible and necessary to become transmigrants and in so doing became participants in the nation-state-building projects of both their ancestral states and their new homelands. They contributed to the consolidation of territorial nation-states.

The second phase in the relationship between transnational migration and the state began after World War II. During the second phase changing ideas about the links between national territories and national populations rendered transmigrants invisible. Nonetheless, transnational migration continued and immigrants continued to be engaged in political activities oriented toward their homelands. This was an epoch of decolonization. Most European colonies gained their independence, and a vision of the world as a terrain of independent nation-states became triumphant. The global penetration of capital continued, but it was generally discussed under the rubric of foreign aid for national development and modernization.[37] Transnational networks and the transnational political projects were no longer noted by political leaders, scholars, or the immigrants themselves.

In the third and current phase, transnational migration has become visible again and transmigrants are again contributing to nationalist ideology and political activities in both emigrant-sending countries and in the United States. By the end of the twentieth century, the restructuring of the processes of capital accumulation, accompanied by the implementation of a neoliberal agenda, began to alter the relationship between states and more global economic processes. In this period, transnational migration and the transnational political actions of immigrants became topics of interest and concern to political actors and researchers alike. Political leaders of emigrant-sending states began to reenvision their states as transnational. At the same time, scholars developed a paradigm of transnational migration. Because the scholarship on international migration began to be read by political actors responsible for changing state policies, the new paradigm not only reflected but also contributed to the changing relationship between nation-states and immigrants.

The data on the relationship between late-nineteenth-century transnational migration and nation-state-building projects of that period call into question any notion that transnational migration is an indicator of the contemporary weakening of the significance of nation-states. However, as I have argued, there are significant differences between then and now. At the end of the nineteenth century, a worldwide change in the organization and deployment of capital brought localities in diverse areas of the world into new relationships to the process of capital accumulation, disrupted local economies, and brought new migrations to the United States. The immigrants to the United States helped build and consolidate nation-states back home in a period when the ideology of nation-states tended to define transnational relationships as temporary. In the United States, home ties were seen as only a step in the transition to full assimilation, while to the emigrant-sending countries emigrants were extensions of the mother country. The purpose of emigrant transnational political activities was to strengthen the economy and institutional structure of the home state. Today emigrant-sending states do not want emigrants and their descendants abroad to return home permanently. They do want them to become long distance nationalists who permanently look homeward and support their ancestral land. Multiculturalism has emerged as a variant of U.S. nationalist rhetoric that allows immigrants to continue to identify with their homeland but use this public identification to contribute to the development of U.S.-based corporations. And the further expansion of these corporations is equated with the well-being of the country.

If we recognize salience of contemporary transnational migration, the paradoxical resurgence of nationalist rhetoric and activities in the midst of an intensive era of globalization becomes more comprehensible. However, the new paradigm for the study of migration leaves us with a new and pressing set of questions. Whose interests are advanced by the current revitalization of national narratives? How well are poor immigrants such as Yvette served by this upsurge in nationalism, whether it takes the form of U.S. corporate multiculturalism or the development of Haiti and other emigrant-sending countries as transnational nation-states. I began this chapter with Yvette, who sees herself as part of the Haitian nation which extends into the United States, in order to put the experience of immigrants themselves in the center of the analysis of nation-states and global economic processes. To set directions for future research on the links between transnational migration and the ideologies and practices of the nation-state, it is useful to revisit the persons in Yvette's transnational network and to ask how those people who remained within the territorial boundaries of Haiti experience transnational networks and nation-states.

Even as Yvette's sense of who she is in the world is linked to the lives of those whom she supports in Haiti through her second-shift job in New York City, the people in her network in Haiti build their own sense of worth on the money, used clothes, and electric appliances that Yvette steadily sends to them. The good and money Yvette sends her relatives and friends leads people in her network to understand themselves as part of Haiti that extends into and becomes a part of "America." Sitting in a yard surrounded by persons whose survival depends on the redistribution of Yvette's resources, Marie-Rose Yvette's twenty-year-old niece, told me: "I love Haiti," but also said, "There is no hope for Haiti. It is a beautiful country, but . . . the state is not a responsible state. In the United States the government is good and does things for the people."

Although Marie-Rose is not engaged in any organized political activity and is concerned only about her own future in Haiti, her sense of self is being shaped by her relationship to a distant nation-state that she has never even visited. Although she lives in Haiti, Marie-Rose identifies with the Haitian people but looks to the United States for responsible government. Meanwhile, Yvette, physically located in the United States, perceives the success of the kin in her transnational network as accomplishments of her homeland, Haiti. Intimate, personal, and emotionally charged relationships link transnational networks and the emerging ideologies and practices of transnational nation-states. These connections between the personal and political in the lives of transmigrants continue to legitimate national narratives within restructured global capitalist processes.

We have to ask: Who gains and who loses when Marie-Rose believes that the only hope for Haiti will come from the United States and when Yvette conflates her sense of self with her family living in Haiti and with Haiti itself? Nation-states are imaginings of community backed by concentrations of force, wealth, and an array of both state and civil institutions. Immigrants have been and continue to be important to the construction and imagining of states. Immigrants serve as both racialized others against whom national identities are built and as active actors in the constant constructing of ideologies and practices of nation-states. Past and contemporary transmigrants are active agents in reviving and revitalizing the ideological connections between race and nation. They link folk biology and political theories of nationalism together in a web that legitimates the continuing identification between individuals living in disparate territories (Anderson 1992; Appadurai 1993; Glick Schiller and Fouron 1997). As in past iterations of the nation-state, the benefits of national identities and ideologies of racial difference are differentially distributed

Astute observers have noted the ways in which migration has served as a political safety valve, channeling the aspirations of immigrants toward individual strategies of survival rather than toward collective action, progressive social movements, or radical political solutions (Gonzalez 1976; Guarnizo 1997a). However, such a formulation disarticulates the relationship between the personal transnational networks and the political construction of national identities. Through their personal investment in transnational networks transmigrants are contributing to politicized identities that continue to legitimate nation-state-building projects. Transmigrants such as Yvette and those in her network gain social status through the persons and localities they sustain in their homeland. But the price of these social returns is high. Yvette and the millions of persons might better identify with the mythical Sisyphus than with a transnational nation or with a multicultural America. Like Sisyphus, they are condemned to forever push a heavy burden up a steep hill, only to have it tumble down again and almost crush them with its weight. While nationalist ideologies may be shared, everyone does not obtain equal benefits from their membership in the nation. Both past and contemporary ideologies of the nation-state join people of different class backgrounds, racial constructions, and genders into common political projects in which wealth and power are differentially distributed. Transmigrant leaders are a component of the class forces that gain economic and social capital from these nationalist projects. Transmigrants such as Yvette gain little but the legitimization of their transnational burdens.

For Marie Rose and those who live in the homeland on remittances, ideologies of the transnational nation-state provide them with little but hope that rescue will come from abroad. Yet currently, the personal and political aspirations of many millions of people are being constructed on a foundation of transnational networks and ideologies of transnational nation-states. In an age of global capitalism this revitalized form of nationalism does not serve the interests of the poor. The poor are becoming dramatically poorer, the level of health, education, and nutrition is dropping precipitously for sections of the populations of many states, and in many urban commodity economies all sustenance must be bought, begged, or stolen. Transnational networks of immigrants cannot sustain such burdens (UNRISD 1995). Ideologies of the transnational nation-state cannot by themselves provide people with an understanding of the problems they face or political strategies for their solution.

Scholars of migration have a responsibility not to celebrate transnational migration but to analyze its causes and its consequences for all of our lives. To understand the past and present of nation-states and their relationship to immigrants and to contemplate the future, those of us who study migration need to think our way out of our entanglement with and our commitment to our national narratives. The research task that lies ahead includes exposure of the alliance between the neoliberal agenda, which legitimates disinvestment in state infrastructures and public services, and the construction of the transnational and multicultural nation-states that provide bases for the continuation of the structure of inequality that is capitalism.

As we begin to ask questions about past and present migrations and about immigrants and their descendants, we do more than clarify the historical record and provide an analytical paradigm useful for migration studies. The questions raised by the new interest in transnational migration are fundamentally about whether the world in which we live is qualitatively changing to the detriment of the majority of the world's people, and if so, why. These questions are about those of us who are transmigrants and the states that continue to claim us as their own. But they are equally about how those of us who claim birth rights in states that are now experiencing major settlements of transmigrants understand our pasts, presents, and futures.

This chapter is the result of the support and encouragement of a number of individuals and institutions. Institutional support has been provided by the Rockefeller Foundation through a grant to Instituto de Filosofia e Ciências Humanas, UNICAMP, the Mellon Foundation through a grant to Yale University, the Graduate Dean's Research Fund and the Center for the Humanities of the University of New Hampshire, and the Wenner Gren Foundation. Among the people who have provided encouragement and contributed intellectually to this chapter, and whom I thank, are Linda Basch, Cristina Szanton-Blanc, Carolle Charles, Josh DeWind, Bela Feldman-Bianco, Maud, Georges, and Seendy Fouron, Liana Maris, Pierre Minn, Fanchette and Fabienne Moulin, Patricia Pessar; Lucie Plourde, Rachel Price, Stephen Reyna, Naomi Schiller, and Suzanne Nichols. The chapter builds on a framework about transnational migration and the deterritorialized nation-state developed by Linda Basch, Cristina Szanton-Blanc, and myself between 1986 and 1993.

Notes

1. This description is part of a forthcoming book, *Georgs Woke Up Laughing: Long Distance Nationalism and the Apparent State*, that I am writing together with Georges Fouron. We have changed personal names to protect people's privacy.
2. When my colleagues and I first wrote about transnational migration we called it "transnationalism" (Glick Schiller, Basch, and Blanc-Szanton 1992b, 1). It soon

became clear that the efforts by immigrants to live their lives across borders are just one variant of a range of transnational processes, which include activities by organizations, networks of communications, financial transactions, and the organization of production and distribution. Consequently, it is more appropriate in speaking about migration as a transnational process to speak simply of transnational migration or "transmigration" (Guarnizo 1997a) and reserve the term "transnationalism" for the collective outcome of multiple forms of transnational processes. However one can talk about the transnationalism of immigrants to imply that they are engaged in various processes including migration that cross borders. One further clarification is necessary. A perspective as well as a process can be transnational. A transnational perspective on migration is one that focuses research and theory in migration studies on the multiple ongoing connections that large number of immigrants forge and maintain across the borders of two or more nation-states

3. The relationship between immigrants (Basch, Glick Schiller, and Blanc-Szanton 1994) and nation-states is changing in three types of states: states that primarily receive large numbers of immigrants, such as the United States; states with large emigrations, such as Mexico, the Dominican Republic, the Philippines, and Haiti; and states that have sent or continue to send a significant sector of their own population abroad yet face influxes of immigrants from elsewhere, such as Portugal and India.
4. Scholars did note the growth of transnational corporations during this period, but this discussion remained removed from the study of either the modernization of developing economies or international migration.
5. The political leaders and governmental officials who are aware of the scholarship on transnational migration are generally from countries where there is a closer relationship between the academic and political worlds. In the countries of the Caribbean, Latin America, and certain European states such as Greece and Portugal, academics become political leaders and officials and governmental leaders pay attention to academic writing (Karakasidou 1994). For example, Robert Smith (1997:110) reports discussing Bela Feldman-Bianco's article on Portugal as a global nation with Mexican officials (Feldman-Bianco 1992). Soon after that, I was personally contacted by Mexican officials from the Program for Mexican Communities Abroad who told me that they had read and were using the book I had coedited on transnational migration in which Feldman-Bianco's article appeared (Glick Schiller, Basch, and Blanc-Szanton 1992b). The introduction to that book announces a new paradigm for the study of migration. Feldman-Bianco has worked with Portuguese political leaders to organize conferences in Brazil attended by Portuguese officials, Brazilian officials, and academics to discuss concepts of transnationalism and the transnational nation-state (personal communication, 1997).
6. This distinction has been emphasized by Daniel Mato (1997, 171), who calls for careful research on the contemporary transnational processes through which powerful states, foundations, and corporations interact with members of oppositional movements that have begun to create linkages that span political borders. Mato has defined "transnational" as "relations between two or more social subjects from two or more [nation-states] when at least one of these subjects is not an agent of a government or intergovernmental organization." He also is careful to distinguish the words transnational and global from international, which he defines as "those relations maintained between governments (or their agencies) which invoke the nation-states they are supposed to represent in the mutually supportive so-called international system."
7. I am utilizing a much narrower definition of the word diaspora than is currently used in various forms of diaspora studies (see, for example, Clifford [1994], Cohen [1997] and writings in the journal *Diaspora*) because I believe that while a diasporaic identity can be used to mobilize political support to organize a new state, once an independent state is won, the dispersed population finds that its identity politics is being conducted in an altered political context. Once such a population can claim or be claimed by a state and this is acknowledged by other states, members of a population can relate to each other in institutional ways legitimated by state power. This has happened in the history of the Jews and the Armenians.
8. Those whose emigration from their homeland is not economically motivated but framed in terms of flight from political repression and violence are often designated *refugees*. However, in many situations, "refugee" is a legal status allocated by the receiving state, which may refuse to recognize flights from political violence. Persons who are refugees, whether or not they are allocated this legal status by a receiving state, are a category of immigrant whose ability to set up transnational networks in their homeland usually is limited until the political situation changes in that state.
9. Family and friendship networks often spread across several countries of settlement.
10. It would be possible to develop an index of multiple incorporation based on the degree to which transmigrants had familial, economic, social, religious, and political ties in the country of origin and a country of settlement.
11. The yearly total of remittances is one concrete measure of the ties that transmigrants maintain to their sending society. The economies of most Caribbean countries are dependent on flows of remittances. For example, remittances make up the second-largest source of foreign currency of the Dominican Republic, second only to tourism. A large proportion of the tourist dollars are brought by Dominican transmigrants returning to visit family (Pessar 1995). Countries with much larger economies, such as Mexico or the Philippines, also are coming to see remittances as a critical source of foreign exchange (Noble 1997; Smith 1997).
12. For an eloquent defense of the use of the term "community," see Goldring (1996a) and Smith (1998) For a critique, see Guarnizo (1996). Here Fred Krissman's (1994) research on transnational networks of both mestizo Zacatecans and Mixtexans who have settled in California proves instructive. A stratum of Zacatecan migrants (who come from mestizo "communities") and Mixtecan migrants (who come from Indian "communities") are able to obtain a certain degree of financial prosperity and to become patrons in their hometown by occupying a middleman position between the superexploited farm laborers they bring to the United States from their hometowns and the growers.
13. We built on both Alejandro Portes and Robert Bach's (1985) interest in transnational networks and the ex-

tensive development of network analysis by the Manchester school of social anthropology. J. A. Barnes (1954, 43), one of the first anthropologists to propose the systematic study of networks, conceived of them as a field of social relations based on "ties of friendship and acquaintance which everyone . . . largely builds for himself." He distinguished this field of social relationships from human interaction within groups organized to conduct domestic, agricultural, and administrative activities. The term "social field" also has been used by Pierre Bourdieu in a manner that equates "network" with "social field." According to Richard Jenkins (1992, 84), Bourdieu uses it to focus on the "centrality of social relations for social analysis," defining a field as "a network, or a configuration, of objective relations" (Wacquant 1989, 50, cited in Jenkins 1992, 85).

14. The U.S. Immigration Commission estimated that in 1907 immigrants sent $2.75 million back to Europe (Roberts 1912/1990).
15. Handlin (1957) actually was aware that some immigrants sustained families back home through remittances, and that there was both return migration, and some degree of visiting back and forth. However, he tended to see the people he labeled "returned emigrants" (201–17) as misfits and far removed from the norm.
16. Ewa Morawska (1997) has argued that the concept of "ethnicization" utilized by historians of immigration is similar to that of transnationalism developed by social scientists. The concept first articulated by Victor Greene (1975) and then utilized by Jonathan Sarna (1978) and Morawska does try to look at the role of agency and structure in both the sending and receiving societies. However, the emphasis as reflected in the term itself is on immigrant incorporation into the United States rather than on multiple incorporation into two or more nation-states.
17. Portes and Bach (1985) set the direction when they called for studies of immigrants' transnational networks.
18. Bela Feldman-Bianco's (1992) essay on Portuguese immigration to New Bedford, Massachusetts, is an important exception to this trend. From the beginning her work has demonstrated the changing patterns of Portuguese immigrant transnational migration and its relationship to the state.
19. The enthusiasm of late-nineteenth-century observers for the technological breakthroughs of their day very much resembles the late-twentieth-century assumption that the electronic technology of computers and videos has caused globalization.
20. Exceptions included immigrants who had fled persecution because of their involvement in nationalist or revolutionary movements. An important sector of Portuguese immigrants, who were from a state with a long history of nation-state building, also came with some form of national consciousness (Feldman-Bianco 1994).
21. Homi Bhabha referred to "the Third Space of enunciation" in a discussion of the structure of verbal communication, which introduces "an ambivalence in the act of interpretation" (1994, 36–37). The term is beginning to be used by scholars of transnational processes to refer to a field of social interaction not within the cultural or legal provenance of any state.
22. The link between race and nation was central to the U.S. anti-immigrant sentiment that developed in the first two decades of the twentieth century. Notions of the racial differences between nations were at the core of the 1924 legislation that used national quotas to put severe restrictions on immigration from southern and eastern Europe; these quotas were in force until the 1965 immigration legislation.
23. There were Magyar authorities in Budapest whose rule became consolidated within the Austro-Hungarian empire after 1867 (Wyman 1993, 95). Hungarian authorities in the United States were countered by Slovak leaders who toured the U.S. organizing protests against the Hungarian government's suppression of Slovak nationalism (Alexander 1987, 127–29).
24. Glazer (1954, 161) reports the same trend in the earlier wave of immigrants:

    > The Germans in Europe were a nation before they became a state. Here in America, great numbers of German immigrants came only with the intention of fostering the development of the German nation-state in Europe. . . . The Irish, the second most important element in the earlier immigration, were also a nation before they were a state and, like the Germans, many came here with the intention of assisting the creation of an Irish state in Europe. On one occasion they did not hesitate to organize armies in America to attack Canada.

25. Lamphere (1987, 78) reports that "Galician emigration totaled one million persons between 1871 and 1914. Between 1892 and 1923 more than 17 percent of the entire population left Galicia. . . . Between 1890 and 1910 the net immigration ratio was about 60 percent, meaning that almost half of the immigrants returned." Galicia was divided between Poland and the Soviet Union at the end of World War II. Between 1892 and 1913 more than 17 percent of the population of Galicia left their native land, with the majority emigrating to the United States (Lamphere 1987, 79).
26. Grosfoguel (1997) has argued that the status of contemporary immigrants in the United States and Europe is shaped by whether or not their homelands were colonized and continue to lack political independence.
27. While U.S. laws passed in 1907, 1940, and 1952 stated that U.S. citizenship was forfeited by voting in a foreign election, serving in a foreign army, or holding political offices reserved for nationals, a series of court cases reduced the force of this law so that loss of citizenship came to be defined as limited to situations in which a citizen's actions clearly indicated the intention to relinquish citizenship (Harrington 1982, 109). Even after the court decisions, immigrants continued to be asked at naturalization ceremonies to swear that they abjured all other allegiances. However, passports issued in the 1990s accept as a matter of course the possibility of dual citizenship.
28. For a further development of this argument see Glick Schiller 1999b.
29. In 1926 Arkansas became the last state to strip immigrants who were not citizens of the right to vote (DeSipio and de la Garza 1998, 97).
30. The term "ethnic group" has still not completely replaced "nationality" among second- and third-generation immigrants in New Jersey. In a statewide random sample of people with AIDS in New Jersey that I conducted in 1988, most respondents were unfamiliar with the term ethnic group and referred to their ancestry with the word "nationality."

31. Although by 1997 the official unemployment rate was relatively low, the rate did not reflect the increased number of people who worked part-time, were forced to work two part-time jobs, or were out of the workforce because they were part of the rising prison population or had given up seeking employment (*New York Times,* April 12, 1998).
32. Transmigrants who become involved in political movements for national independence may still join military groups. U.S. newspapers in 1999 carried photographs of Albanian men who lived in the United States signing up for military service in the Kosovo Liberation Army. These photographs resembled that of German men in the United States enlisting to fight for their European homeland at the outbreak of World War I (see Wyman 1993, 111).
33. Beginning in the 1970s with a treaty with Brazil, Portugal took steps to grant some rights to Brazilians to both live and vote in Portugal (Santos 1996). At the very same time, faced with a growing illegal migration from North Africa, Portuguese politicians are trying to develop a definition of citizenship and a sense of a global national community based on descent. They exclude those who are trying to immigrate and cannot claim ties of blood or membership through descent (Feldman-Bianco 1994).
34. In 1991 a number of Dominicans of Haitian ancestry were rounded up and summarily deported to Haiti. The Dominican government claimed that they were surplus Haitian cane workers. Interviews that Georges Fouron and I conducted in a refugee camp in Port-au-Prince indicated that many had been born in the Dominican Republic and spoke only Spanish; the refugees occupied a variety of jobs throughout the Dominican Republic.
35. As in other forms of contemporary nationalist rhetoric, the ideology of multicultural America obscures the multiple ways in which powerful transnational corporations dominate political processes and renders invisible the vast inequalities in wealth and power within the United States.
36. It would also be interesting to explore the degree to which transmigrants that were born or educated in the United States are seen by U.S. political leaders as representatives of U.S. interests when these transmigrants become major players in the ministries of various other nation-states. Often these transmigrants have been educated in U.S. universities and, while living in their home countries, own houses, maintain family networks, and participate in organizational structures in the United States.
37. Scholars did note the growth of transnational corporations during this period.

6 Theories of International Migration and Immigration: A Preliminary Reconnaissance of Ideal Types

Charles Hirschman

NEITHER SCIENTIFIC THEORY nor ideas for empirical research develop out of thin air. Although the image of the solitary researcher working with only her or his imagination persists in the popular imagination, and even in some scholarly circles, research is a profoundly interactive and social process. Most research work invariably originates in a dialogue with the scholarly literature, which serves as the primary means of communication among active researchers. Ideas and hypotheses often arise in response to the published work of other scholars as well as from conversations with colleagues and students. Moreover, the influence of ideas from outside the world of research—from politics, popular thinking, and other fields—can be remarkably influential. These influences from both inside and outside the scholarly world shape the selection of important research questions as well as the methods used to study them.

The development of social science theory is also profoundly affected by the nature of empirical research, especially the constraints on the testing of hypotheses. Since most of the social sciences cannot rely on the classical experimental method, the challenge is to formulate research designs and to collect appropriate data that allow for the post hoc assessment of hypotheses. This is a Herculean task, for without control over all causal variables, it is difficult to rule out all alternative explanations. And since most patterns in the social world are probabilistic and partial, as well as contingent on time and place, the selection of a population or a sample of a population for study may have a critical impact on the nature of the research findings uncovered. In addition to questions of research design, measurement problems loom large in social science. Errors arising from imperfect or unreliable measurement of complex and multidimensional variables are often confounded with "true" empirical patterns. Thus, any assessment of social science knowledge must be devoted to evaluations of research design, the quality of data, and measurement issues as well as the consistency of research findings.

In addition to the verification of hypotheses, social science also faces the challenge of the appropriate scope of theoretical formulations. Although some attempts have been made to posit universal theories that explain the similarities in human behavior and social institutions across all societies, most theoretical frameworks are "middle range," with a limited scope of application, and may be framed in fairly broad and abstract terms. Weak data, problematic empirical tests, and inconsistent research findings leave considerable room for novel interpretations. Given these conditions, there is no one standard path for the development and verification of social science theory.

In this essay, I review some common features of what might be considered "ideal types" of social science theory and illustrate them with references to the literature on international migration and immigration. The ideal types of theory considered here are: social science as ideology, social science as the accumulation of facts, social science as the clash of theories, and social science as the development of models. These types should not be seen as historical stages of social research, because all of them can coexist and indeed even overlap in the same theoretical formulation. An understanding of the elements of theory construction, accompanied by substantive knowledge and some inspired thinking, can sometimes lead to the greater integration of knowledge and to interpretative frameworks that stimulate cumulative empirical research.

SOCIAL SCIENCE AS IDEOLOGY

Social science arose in the nineteenth century as a branch of moral philosophy. There was scarcely any distance in the discourse between what society was and what society ought to be. Over the decades, social science, including its component disciplines, became more institutionalized as "science" as it gained independence from traditional ideologies and self-interest. Nonetheless, the impact of ideology on social science has never disappeared. The Marxian model of linking scientific research to political goals was widely imitated by many groups with quite different political agendas. Some social reformers, eugenicists, and members of social movements saw the development of social science as subservient to their larger social goals.

The social science analyses contained in the forty-one volumes of the Immigration Commission of almost a century ago, popularly known as the Dillingham Report, are classic examples of this genre of research in the field of immigration studies (U.S. Immigration Commission, 1907–10). Conforming to the prevailing intellectual wisdom of the era, these reports showed, with considerable empirical detail, that the "new immigrants" (those coming from eastern and southern Europe) were inferior to the old immigrants (those from northern and western Europe) and less likely to assimilate. These conclusions have been shown to be based largely on a very selective interpretation (and frequent misinterpretation) of data (Handlin 1957; Jones 1992, 152–57). The intellectual climate of early-twentieth-century America generally accepted the social Darwinist ideas of the biological inferiority of nonwhite peoples, and most southern and eastern European immigrants were considered nonwhite (Gould 1996). Given the class, religious, and ethnocentric biases against new immigrants during that era, the influence of ideology on social science is not disguised.

A good share of immigration research continues to be affected, though much less overtly, by ideological pressures. This tendency is illustrated by the almost ubiquitous references to "immigration problems" in popular discussion and much academic writing on the subject. Many researchers begin their studies assuming that immigration causes problems for American society, such as employment dislocation and crowded inner cities and schools by new groups that resist assimilation into the dominant cultural values of the society. The presumption that immigrants cause social problems in the receiving society may lead researchers to conclude that observed temporal and spatial correlations represent causal relationships. There could, of course, be the opposite bias by scholars who assume that immigrants inevitably contribute positively to diversity and other societal goals. Recognizing such biases in the field does not eliminate their influence but may help scholars to be more cautious in their interpretations.

Ideology will always be present in social science since social scientists are human beings whose ideas and motivations (conscious and unconscious) can influence their framing of research problems as well as their interpretations of empirical data. The primary check on the influence of ideology is the open character of science as a public forum where ideas, evidence, and interpretations are presented for other scientists to review and criticize. Over the long run, hypotheses that are confirmed by researchers of varied political and policy persuasions, using different data and methods, will gain ground over tentative findings that are not replicated by other scientific studies. History is not, however, a linear process, and our confidence in the long-run cumulative character of science does not preclude many decades of intellectual stagnation and even decay.

Social Science as the Accumulation of Social Facts

There is a great social (and economic) need for reliable knowledge about the patterns and timing of immigration, the composition of immigrant populations, and the correlates of the geographic and social mobility of immigrants after their arrival. Much of contemporary social science on immigration is focused on the measurement of social facts such as: Where do immigrants settle? Do immigrants receive more governmental social services than they pay in taxes? What has been the trend in economic progress for immigrant groups across generations?

Answers to these questions provide useful information for social service agencies that wish to help immigrants, for businesses that seek to market goods and services to immigrants, and for those who simply want to record the epic lives of immigrants and their families. Social science helps to fill the void for these needs and many more with the collection of reliable data and the basic task of social description. However, as Alejandro Portes (this volume) points out, research findings do not always speak for themselves, nor do they inevitably accumulate to a theory—in the sense of the codification of causal relationships. The reporting of research findings often assumes a theoretical framework that renders the research findings interpretable, but without testing the underlying hypothesis. For example, the reporting of the economic progress of immigrants over time is compatible with a number of theoretical perspectives, both at a societal level (America is a land of opportunity) and at the microlevel (selective emigration of unsuccessful immigrants), but the reporting of the pattern does not explain its occurrence.

Nonetheless, good social description is a valuable contribution of social science. Indeed, with the ubiquity of poor social description (due to nonrepresentative samples, poor measurement, inadequate allowance for random error, and nonintuitive summaries of data), reliable and accurate information is a precious commodity. The immense value of accurate reporting of social facts is illustrated by the economic rewards given for comparable results in other fields—for example, insightful journalism, expert consulting, and influential market research. But the objectives of social science extend beyond the accumulation of descriptive findings.

The goal of social science is explanation—the search for causes that shape societal, community-level, and individual-level variations in outcomes. An example reveals how unexpected findings can generate a new theoretical direction. Consider the question of why some immigrant groups are more successful than other groups or able to move up the economic ladder more quickly than other groups. Knowledge of these differences is the first step in the research process, but specifying the potential explanations and then designing research studies to test derivative hypotheses is the ultimate strategy of science.

A few years ago, there was some tentative evidence that some of the children of the post-1965 wave of immigrants were not engaged in the expected process of upward mobility but were drifting downward to the "underclass." These ideas were first explored in an influential essay by Herbert Gans (1992a), then refined as the "segmented assimilation" hypothesis by Alejandro Portes and Min Zhou (1993). The new hypothesis attempted to move beyond the standard model of intergenerational assimilation and social mobility with the novel interpretation that immigrant families who reinforced traditional values (thus discouraging cultural assimilation into the peer community) were better able to sponsor the socioeconomic mobility of their children. In the space of only a few short years, the segmented assimilation hypothesis has been remarkably influential and has inspired a variety of studies of the "second generation" of the post-1965 immigrants (see the analyses in Portes [1996b] and Oropesa and Landale [1997a]). The development of this hypothesis and the current state of the literature are cogently presented in the chapter by Min Zhou (this volume).

The stream of literature on the second generation reveals the development of social science research on immigrants and their children in American society. There have always been studies reporting significant variations in socioeconomic assimilation across immigrant groups. These findings could be interpreted as mixed evidence for the standard assimilation hypothesis. Was the glass simply half full (assimilation will eventually happen) or half empty (assimilation theory is simply wrong)? Studies that report basic descriptions of trends and patterns have limited value to explain variations across populations. It requires a new hypothesis to suggest how empirical anomalies might be explained. If American society has changed, presenting fewer opportunities for upward mobility and exerting far greater pressures for socialization into oppositional subcultures, then the variations among second-generation advance might be explicable.

Theoretical advance also depends on progress in empirical research. The first step is to document the observed patterns of educational and socioeconomic attainment (Hirschman 1996). More difficult and challenging is the task of collecting data to test theoretical explanations for the variations in the educational and occupational mobility of the second generation. Such research will require data on the relative influence of race and ethnic origins, the socioeconomic status and networks of the families of origin, and the peer community of neighborhoods and schools. Although this model of research is a daunting task, the accumulation of knowledge rests on the development of models and collection of data that go beyond the reporting of social facts.

Social Science as the Clash Between Competing Theories

Theories are the fundamental glue that holds together the knowledge base of science. Theories provide the rationale for the selection of research questions and for the interpretation of research findings. Within the field of international migration studies, there is a plethora of theories, perhaps many more theories than the empirical base would warrant.

Explanations of why people move across international boundaries typically derive from one of several versions of economic theory (Massey, this volume). There are also several structural theories of international migration that posit the importance of international capitalism, international relations, environmental conditions, and the history of prior movements. The study of the adaptation of immigrants has been historically framed as the study of assimilation, but there are many versions of this perspective, as well as a range of theories from the study of race and ethnic relations. The consequences of immigration have not been framed within one general theory but are generally tied to the specific topic of study—economics, politics, intergroup relations, or other aspects of cities or regions. The diversity of theories reflects the multiplicity of disciplines and subdisciplines that are engaged in writing and conducting research on the causes of immigration, the fate of immigrants in receiving societies, and the political, economic, and social impacts of immigration. Is it possible to bring conceptual order to the field? This was the challenge that inspired the conference that led to this volume.

The very richness of theoretical claims, statements, and perspectives makes for very exciting debates and discussions. But in some of these debates research communities may be speaking past each other rather than to each other. This problem is particularly acute when there is an overelaboration of theory unencumbered with empirical research. The considerable scholarly prestige associated with novelty in theoretical directions provides an incentive to develop new theories (or new twists on old theories) that appear to be an advance over the standard models. In many cases, these new theoretical wrinkles are not associated with conventional hypothesis-testing empirical analysis but with illustrative cases or stylized examples.

The other problem with too many vague and imprecise theories is the lack of clear direction for empirical research. A considerable share of empirical research is published as the reporting of social facts—few explicit links are made to hypotheses or theories. Since research findings are often compatible with more than one theory, the significance and meaning of research are usually made clear only when results are elaborated as part of the broader conceptual framework of how the world works. The results of descriptive research can be very valuable (as discussed in the prior section) as the raw materials used by scholars to develop theory or raise questions about theoretical issues. Without such value-added efforts, however, it is difficult for research findings to accumulate into empirical generalizations or to lead to deeper understanding or insight into why things develop as they do.

The norm of theory-driven research is not an automatic process. It is most likely to occur when there is one dominant theory or when there are clear battle lines drawn between contending theories that have well-understood empirical predictions. Most empirical researchers tend to work within schools doing "normal science." Normal science involves refinements in the measurement of important concepts and partial tests of selected hypotheses from the larger theory. Findings that do not conform to the expectations of the broader theory are most likely to be interpreted as due to defects in the data or measurement, or perhaps the influence of unmeasured variables. The ideal model of empirical research as a "critical test" of a central hypothesis of a theory is possible, but unlikely. It typically takes repeated anomalies (nonconfirmation of key hypotheses from a theory) over many years before a theory is weakened (Kuhn 1970). Change in the hegemonic theory in a field is more likely to be the product of incremental support for a rival theory than of the wholesale abandonment of the old theory.

With the assumption that one of the most fundamental tasks of social science is to make explicit the theoretical underpinnings of research, the primary objective of this volume is to assess the state of social science theories of immigration. We asked the authors to reexamine the extant theories in the field and to evaluate their status—both in terms of organizing the research literature and as a guide for continued research. The results of this strategy, we believe, have clarified a number of issues and advanced the field.

In his chapter, Douglas Massey reviews several theories regarding the determinants of international migration and finds that they are not mutually exclusive. Indeed, he has shown convincingly that it is possible to incorporate ideas from different perspectives into empirical research (Massey and Espinosa 1997). This is an important lesson since many researchers work entirely within one theoretical school, primarily for disciplinary or methodological reasons, and assume that adherence to one theory implies the rejection of other theories.

One of the major obstacles to the accumulation of research on the socioeconomic progress of immigrant and ethnic communities has been the presumed inadequacy of the assimilation perspective and the lack of clear alternatives. For many years this has been an area with lots of vague theorizing, on the one hand, and footloose research findings lacking a clear message, on the other hand. Richard Alba and Victor Nee reexamine the empirical support for assimilation theory, and the historical experiences of immigrants from Europe and their children, in particular. Their reassessment shows considerably more support for assimilation as the long-term master trend of immigrant groups in American society than is usually acknowledged in popular thought or academic writings. The thesis of assimilation draws additional support from several other essays in part II, but there are some dissenting views. The segmented assimilation thesis posits that there will be heterogeneity in the process of adaptation and upward mobility for the children of the post-1965 immigrants by national origin, residence, and social class. One of the most valuable contributions of these essays is that the empirical implications of the alternative (nonassimilation) theoretical perspectives are clearly framed. Perhaps there needs to be a better specification of the mechanisms of these contending perspectives, but there should be little doubt as to the major theoretical issues that will guide research on these questions in the coming years.

In the final section of this volume, part III, theoretical perspectives on the consequences of immigration on American society are explored. There is less concentration on the refinement of theoretical issues here, in part because of the wide range of dependent variables examined. How has the presence of immigrants influenced politics, the national economy, and intergroup relations? These are only some of the questions addressed in this section. The vastness of these issues and the diversity of disciplinary traditions involved in their study make it difficult to summarize the contending theoretical frameworks on these questions.

There is, however, one common theme that spans a broad variety of issues concerning the consequences of immigration. The thesis is that immigrants, especially a lot of immigrants, create problems of economic adjustment and social cohesion. There is some logic behind this thesis. The political and economic systems of complex industrial societies are always under strain. The labor market tries to adjust the supply of workers to the demand of jobs, and the influx of outside immigrants is widely assumed to have adverse consequences on the employment prospects and wages of native workers. Governments strive to achieve consensus on national objectives and to provide necessary services within the scope of available fiscal resources. The arrival of immigrants who are not socialized to national norms, who have pressing needs for special services, and whose incomes are insufficient to pay their share of taxes may create significant new problems. If there are race and ethnic divisions and tensions, the addition of more diversity may compound social problems.

The chapters in part III show, however, that this popular thesis is an oversimplification of the complex causal influences of immigration on society. There is, at best, only mixed evidence in support of "immigrants cause problems" hypotheses. Political and economic systems are exceedingly complex, with myriad internal dynamics and contested preferences. Immigrants arrive with varied backgrounds and become incorporated into many different areas and institutions. Just drawing up a checklist of positive and negative impacts is not a straightforward task, let alone specifying causal mechanisms. The testing of whether the number of immigrants actually causes or exacerbates specific problems is an even more complex task. A common practice is to point to an association in time and space between the presence of immigrants and contentious politics, economic downturns, and interethnic violence. This approach can raise the question and suggest a hypothesis, but assertions of cause and effect are typically much less certain.

Social Science as the Development of Models

Social science theories, as discussed earlier, are usually framed in rather abstract terms, such as the direction of an expected change in a dependent variable (assimilation theory) or a global relationship (migration is caused primarily by economic motives). Theoretical ideas such as these are an indispensable resource for the development of scholarly communities. With an organizing principle or a sensitizing concept, it is possible to make empirical generalizations across studies and to design research that focuses on common questions or sets of questions.

Theories pitched at too abstract a level may, however, lead research in a circular rather than a cumulative direction. The problem is exacerbated when a theory is framed in unidimensional terms—pointing to the importance of one major influence in isolation from all other causal factors. The result is often that most derivative hypotheses are phased in simple bivariate relationships—*x* affects *y*. As research progresses, hypotheses are often refined to be contingent to the values of the causal variable or dependent on the value of a third variable. For example, *x* affects *y*, but only up to a certain point or below a certain level (ceiling or threshold impacts), or only in the presence of absence of a third value. The theories that handle these empirical patterns are usually refined in an ad hoc fashion, with explanations that draw on specific cases. Problems often arise in the application of the theory to different populations and in the development of empirical tests.

There is a sharp contrast between a hypothesis framed at the bivariate level and the standard empirical method of multivariate analysis. Is the appropriate empirical test of the bivariate relationship or of the net association after other covariates are "controlled"? Some covariates may simply be confounding variables, and logic may suggest that their influence should be eliminated before "true" causal hypotheses are considered. Other covariates may be intermediate variables that transmit the impact of the causal variable to the outcome. Treating intermediate variables as control variables could lead to mistaken interpretations.

The dilemma is how to move from abstract and unidimensional theories to theoretical models of complex social systems. Models imply more than the impact of one variable on another, but how is that relationship (and others) embedded into a broader system of relationships. The use of complex models is standard in most of the natural and biological sciences, from climatology to human biology. For example, the study of human movement requires understanding of the circulation system, muscles, the nervous system, and other parts of the body as well as their joint interrelationships. The development of models allows researchers to focus on a broad range of questions informed by a systematic framework that includes reciprocal influences. There have been some efforts to develop models of social systems, including the study of international migration, but most efforts have not been influential.

The framework for most classical social science models is "structural-functional" theory. As the name implies, social structures (or institutions) are examined in terms of the societal functions they serve. For example, family structure provides an institutionalized means for the regulation of sexual behavior and for the nurturance and socialization of children. Political institutions exist to resolve disputes and to regulate the use of force in society. Because of some inherent limitations, structural-functionalism has been generally discredited as the principal means to advance sociological theory. First, there was the tendency to equate the particular form of a social structure with the optimal functioning of the broader social system. Moreover, structural-functional theories did not adequately address the question of social change. The claim that institutions change in response to the changing needs of society is very close to a tautology.

In spite of these problems with structural-functionalism, there are few competing alternatives to the logic that the patterns of institutional arrangements across societies are shaped, at least in part, by feedback mechanisms from human capacities, environmental conditions, and the stock of available knowledge. A variety of systematic pressures might arise from collective or individual needs that are likely to influence the forms of social organization and the metabolism of human societies. The task for the development of theoretical models of international migration is to include a broad variety of potential causal variables, including prior history and external conditions.

One of the few examples of the use of models in the migration literature is the classical economic equilibrating model that wages (and other inducements to labor mobility) will vary in response to labor surplus and scarcity. Low wages tend to encourage the out-mobility of labor, and high wages to attract migrants. This model is sometimes referred to as a "push-pull" perspective on migration that is often dismissed because it is too simplistic to be of any potential use for research. It is, of course, the social and economic conditions that give rise to labor surplus and labor scarcity that are the important causal forces, but a close examination of the social system and its mechanisms allows for the development of theory and its refinement. For example, Brinley Thomas (1973) provides a historical analysis of the development of the "Atlantic economy," a model of long swings in capital accumulation, economic growth, and international migration between Great Britain and the United States.

In Thomas's model, migration is not simply an outcome of economic forces, but a pattern that ebbs and flows in magnitude, direction, and composition with other demographic, economic, and social processes. Furthermore, the model is empirically developed and explored in relationship to particular periods in history and world geography. The 35 million Europeans who migrated to the United States (Handlin 1973, 31) were responding to the pressures created by nineteenth-century demographic growth, the collapse of traditional peasant economies, and the opportunities in the New World. Although specific historical circumstances will always be different, the essential elements of the model could be used profitably to explore international migration in other times and places. Comparative and historical studies based on an elaborated theoretical model of long-distance allow for accumulation beyond the reach of isolated studies.

There is not, to our knowledge, a parallel theoretical model of immigrant adaptation or assimilation based on the systemic properties and functioning of modern societies and economies. When discovered, the model may appear as a tautology because it will highlight only the common features of ethnic change, not necessarily all the diversity in outcomes, timing, and process. To be useful, the model must identify the central causal mechanism that links the general functioning of society with the process of ethnic and immigrant change. This is the challenge for scholars in the field of international migration in particular, and for the social sciences more broadly.

Concluding Observations

Theories are essential for making sense of research findings—explaining what is going on. A strong theory can often compensate for poor data. With a well-developed theory of cultural diffusion, archaeologists can often use evidence from a few shards of pottery to postulate the major forms of social structure in ancient societies. Without a well-worked-out theory of social change, policymakers are at sea if they choose to intervene in a society. (Of course, knowledge, or even an awareness of the lack of knowledge, is not a prerequisite for policymaking.) For these reasons, the development of theory must be a high priority for scientific progress, including the several branches of international migration research.

Good theory often begins with empirical generalizations. Observation of systematic patterns or social regularities often leads to an assertion of cause and effect. Key steps include the identification of intervening mechanisms and the recognition of multiple influences. Although more difficult to develop, the ultimate objective is the formulation of a theoretical model that posits feedback mechanisms and the linkages between variables to maintain a system of relationships. Theory that develops in tandem with empirical research can contribute to the cumulative accretion of knowledge about, and explanation of, international migration (and many other topics) in the modern world.

Part II

Immigrant Adaptation, Assimilation, and Incorporation

WHAT HAPPENS TO immigrants and how do they and their children become part of American life? These are the questions that motivate the chapters in part II of this volume. The fundamental concept in the field is assimilation, but it has hardly been a unifying concept. Indeed, the debates over assimilation theory sometimes obscure the many common points of reference for researchers in the field. And as immigration to America has shifted from primarily European roots to more diverse geographical origins, immigration scholarship has increasingly drawn from a broader range of alternative theories and models—from race and ethnic studies in particular. The consequence has been the creation of a more diffuse and eclectic field of immigration studies than was the case during the first half of the twentieth century.

In the earlier era, immigration research not only focused on European immigrants and their children but usually carried the assumption that immigrants could only move up the socioeconomic ladder through acceptance and adoption of Anglo-American middle-class cultural and social standards. In the contemporary research literature, however, there is a greater recognition that American society no longer has a single core culture and that immigrants encounter a much more diverse society. The shift in vocabulary from research on "assimilation" to immigrant adaptation and incorporation reflects these changes in perspective. The key ideas of both the old and new research literatures on immigrant adaptation, assimilation, and incorporation are reviewed and analyzed in the essays in part II.

In their essays, the authors reexamine the core concepts and theories that have shaped the study of immigrants in American society—past and present. Although there is no consensus on a single paradigm or model for the field, there is a remarkable dialogue from one essay to another, especially in comparing the experiences of early-twentieth-century immigrants with the post-1965 immigrant stream. Questions about history are central to contemporary research since almost every researcher, implicitly if not explicitly, frames the present as a contrast with earlier times.

In the first essay in part II, Richard Alba and Victor Nee reassess the state of assimilation theory, beginning with an insightful comparison of Milton Gordon's *Assimilation in American Life* (1964) and Tamotsu Shibutani and Kian Kwan's *Ethnic Stratification* (1965). Alba and Nee laud Gordon's contribution of conceptual clarification but lament the absence of a comprehensive statement of a causal theory in his book. Reading Shibutani and Kwan's work, Alba and Nee point to the possibility of an ecological theory of ethnic change that emphasizes changes in technology, economic institutions, social movements, and new ideas as forces that can change the balance between majority and minority groups. Nevertheless, generating specific and testable hypotheses on ethnic change from these very broad and general institutions and social conditions is sure to be a major challenge.

Alba and Nee assess the state of empirical research and conclude that assimilation has been the master trend among the descendants of European immigrants who arrived during the era of mass immigration (roughly from 1880 to 1924). In support of this conclusion, Alba and Nee note trends in the reduction of socioeconomic inequality and in increasing levels of intermarriage across white ethnic groups over the last half-century. For the post-1965 immigrants and their children, Alba and Nee see many parallels with the past but caution that it is too soon to draw strong conclusions about the eventual fate of the new immigrants to America.

Several of the subsequent chapters also address the uncertainty and debates over comparisons between the descendants of the immigrants from the era of mass European immigration and the experiences of recent immigrants and their children. Herbert Gans notes that many of the classic studies of European immigrant communities were based on the second generation and conducted by "outsiders" who emphasized evidence of strong and rapid acculturation. Much of the research on the contemporary period focuses on the recently arrived first generation and is often conducted by "insiders" from within the ethnic or immigrant community who may be more observant of the social and cultural barriers encountered by immigrants and their children.

The most compelling theoretical account of how and why the new second generation might not follow the path of earlier waves of immigrants is the "segmented assimilation hypothesis." In her chapter, Min Zhou reviews the central elements of this hypothesis and the relevant literature pointing to the increasing socioeconomic diversity within and between new immigrant groups. According to the segmented assimilation hypothesis, there are three potential trajectories of second-generation adaptation. The first trajectory is the traditional path of acculturation and upward mobility by the second generation into middle-class American society and culture. This path is often facilitated by the relative economic success of the immigrant generation. The second trajectory is acculturation into the underclass of American minorities in the inner cities. Second-generation youth in this group adopt "oppositional" attitudes to middle-class society and do not aspire to upward mobility (see also Gans 1992a). The third trajectory is retention by immigrant families of their ethnic culture and identity to protect their children from assimilation into an inner-city culture that may lead to downward mobility. According to the theory, the second generation in this trajectory will aspire to be educationally and economically upwardly mobile but to retain their ethnic culture. This provocative theory has attracted considerable interest, but the empirical evidence is mixed. Most members of the second generation of the post-1965 immigrant wave are still too young to provide a sufficient empirical base for detailed analysis.

Joel Perlmann and Roger Waldinger review the literature on European immigrants and their children during the first half of the twentieth century and conclude that there is probably much more continuity in the experiences of immigrants than might be assumed by some of the pessimistic accounts of the present era. Indeed, they observe that the diversity of socioeconomic outcomes among contemporary immigrants and their children may well be an improvement over the overwhelmingly proletarian lives experienced by most of the immigrant groups of 1890 to 1920. Perlmann and Waldinger also provide the important reminder that many European immigrant groups were often seen as nonwhites in the early twentieth century and that upward mobility was a long and slow process that may have taken two or three generations.

Rubén Rumbaut discusses several anomalies in the study of assimilation. He reports on recent research into several dimensions of immigrant outcomes—including health status and ethnic identity—that shows results opposite to what might be predicted from conventional assimilation theory. On the other hand, he finds, there is considerable evidence for linguistic assimilation: English fluency is all but universal for the second generation, a finding that is confirmed by David López's fine survey of immigrant and ethnic adaptation in southern California.

Marta Tienda and Rebeca Raijman cogently survey the complex array of social forces and conditions, including the political and economic context of reception, that shape the economic outcomes of contemporary immigrants. Their essay highlights several potential avenues for the refinement of assimilation theory. Although "time in the system" may well be correlated with outcomes, including economic advancement, there is a need to specify proximate conditions, historical eras, and the attributes of immigration flows as explanatory variables in the process. One of the most important, and neglected, topics in the study of assimilation and adaptation is the immigrant family. In her chapter, Nancy Foner provides an insightful overview of the cultural and structural dimensions of immigrant family life. Immigrant families often provide the necessary resources to launch the second generation on their path of socioeconomic mobility.

The Ambiguity of Assimilation

There are few words in contemporary academic social science that arouse more negative valence than *assimilation*. It was not always this way. Indeed, assimilation has historically been one of the foundational and far-reaching concepts in American social science. Robert Park and Ernest Burgess, who defined the emerging discipline of sociology with their textbook *Introduction to the Science of Sociology* (1969), first published in 1921, offered a more sophisticated perspective on assimilation than has been evident in many popular and academic discussions—then or now. Assimilation, defined by Park and Burgess (1921/1969, 360) as the sharing of a common historical memory and cultural life by different peoples, was posited to be the likely outcome in the long run, perhaps the very long run. Park and Burgess did not claim that ethnic assimilation was just around the corner. In the short to medium term, the more likely pattern was accommodation, which was an organization of social relations to control conflict and competition (between groups) in order for society to function.

One of the important traditions of the "Chicago School" of sociology, of which Park was a central intellectual leader, was the study of Chicago. Indeed, the city became the social laboratory for much of early American sociological research. In the early decades of the twentieth century, Chicago was a polyglot city with a bewildering diversity of ethnic and immigrant neighborhoods that showed few signs of assimilation. The vision of Park and Burgess was to be able to see beyond the intense degree of intergroup separateness fostered by different languages, churches, ethnic newspapers, and local organizations and to identify the forces that would eventually lead to change. Their primary thesis was that social interaction in primary group settings could erode cultural differences among populations.

> Assimilation naturally takes place most rapidly where contacts are primary, that is, where they are most intimate and intense, as in the area of touch relationship, in the family circle, and in intimate congenial groups. Secondary contacts facilitate accommodations, but do not greatly promote assimilation. The contacts here are external and remote. (1921/1969, 361–62)

It is interesting to note that the Park and Burgess assimilation hypothesis was framed entirely within a scholarly, almost antiseptically scientific, discourse without any reference to the virulent debates over Americanization campaigns and immigration restrictions and the other political and intellectual battles that raged in the early decades of the twentieth century. The analytical insights of Park and Burgess offered a vision of the promise of social science to understand the long-term processes that underpin complex industrial societies—almost the opposite of the frequently heard claim that assimilation theory was part of a societal conspiracy to force immigrants to abandon the cultures and customs of their homelands. Alba and Nee's essay provides a valuable clarification of the early Park and Burgess statements on assimilation.

The ambiguity of the concept of assimilation was simultaneously its major virtue and its central liability. The simple idea that different groups (immigrants and natives) might become more similar over time (across generations) provided a clear direction for empirical research on immigrants and their descendants. The concept provided no clear specification, however, of how the varied dimensions of assimilation (or non-assimilation) were linked to each other, nor was it supported by a fully developed theory of the social conditions that promote (or retard) assimilation of whatever type.

Gordon (1964) provides a cogent statement on the separate dimensions of assimilation with a compelling argument that these dimensions do not always move along the same historical path. Gordon claimed that primary group interaction (structural assimilation) is the linchpin that leads to assimilation in other dimensions. (This is pretty much the essence of the Park and Burgess thesis.) Beyond noting that ethnic prejudice and class divisions were major impediments, Gordon did not provide a general theoretical statement on the conditions that might lead to primary group interactions between the descendants of immigrants and the native population.

In the 1960s and 1970s the assimilation perspective came under attack for empirical and political reasons. The empirical reasons (to be explored later) were based on the persistent subordination of some groups, African Americans in particular. The most visible critique was Nathan Glazer and Daniel Patrick Moynihan's *Beyond the Melting Pot* (1970), which concluded that ethnicity remained an important point of reference for urban politics. Since assimilation research lacked a theory that could account for anomalous findings, the simple evidence of any remaining intergroup differences could be taken as prima facie evidence that the theory was proven incorrect.

Probably more important in the long run was the political attack against assimilation in an era (the 1960s and 1970s) that rebelled against the politics of conformity and celebrated differences. Some scholars and many students assumed that the sociological hypothesis of assimilation was part and parcel of the majority group's disparagement of the unique contributions of minorities and immigrants. In the past there had been a strong dose of nativism in American society, and some leading academics had been allies of the anti-immigrant forces in American intellectual and political life in the early decades of the century. There were, however, few obvious connections between the nativist intellectuals of this earlier era and the academic scholars who conducted research within the general assimilation framework in the post–World War II era.

In retrospect, it seems that provocative ideas without deep theoretical roots, such as assimilation, can be uncritically accepted and used to organize empirical research, but they can also be too easily and uncritically dismissed when intellectual and social fashions shift. Since the concept of assimilation is multidimensional, has many empirical referents, and was not linked to a clearly defined theory, there has been considerable room for ideology and fashion to shape the academic understanding and use of the concept.

Immigrants and Socioeconomic Mobility in the United States

For most of its early history, the United States was a frontier society with more opportunities than people. These conditions attracted, induced, and compelled millions of immigrants, indentured servants, and slaves to make the voyage to North America from the seventeenth through the mid-nineteenth century. The ending of the frontier in the late nineteenth century coincided with the rise of the urban-industrial revolution, which fueled an even greater demand for labor migration. From 1880 to 1920 millions of new immigrants from eastern and southern Europe (and a smaller stream from Asia) changed the ethnic balance in almost every major city (outside of the South) in the United States (Bodnar 1985; Muller 1993).

These geographical and historical conditions that made the United States an immigrant society were not unique in the modern world, but the scale of international migration and the emerging ideology of upward mobility were truly of epic proportions (Handlin 1973; Portes and Rumbaut 1996). The growth of the population of the United States from 4 million in 1790 to 275 million in 2000 has primarily resulted from the influx of more than 62 million immigrants and their descendants (Passel and Edmonston 1994; U.S. Immigration and Naturalization Service 1997, 27). Moreover, immigrants found that the conditions for socioeconomic mobility were particularly favorable in the United States.

Nonetheless, American society has harbored a persistent fear of immigrants and widespread beliefs that they will not adapt to American society, become American citizens, or adopt local ways (Jones 1960). Part of the fear was simply the rhetoric of nativism. The accompanying beliefs reflect a continuity from the antipathy expressed toward Germans and Scotch-Irish early in the eighteenth century (Lieberson 1996) to the fears of "mongrelization" that greeted the southern and eastern European immigrants in the early twentieth century (Higham 1988) and the fears that contemporary immigration from Latin America and Asia will create an "Alien Nation" (Brimelow 1995).

However, immigrants have "made it" in America. (Indeed, it could be claimed that immigrants have made America, but that is another story.) Although some Americans of European heritage may still be sentimentally attached to their ancestral place of origin—"symbolic ethnicity" (Gans 1979), most of them are virtually indistinguishable on most economic and social criteria. This conclusion is based on empirical research showing convergence in socioeconomic status, life chances, residential integration, and intermarriage between the descendants of European immigrants and "old-stock" Americans (Alba and Golden 1986; Duncan and Duncan 1968; Hirschman 1983; Lieberson and Waters 1988; Neidert and Farley 1985; Smith and Edmonston 1997, ch. 8). This conclusion is one of the "established facts" in the research literature and is reported in several of the chapters in this volume.

What is less conclusive is the evidence on the progress of racial minorities, and African Americans in particular. Although there has been a decisive shift away from the "apartheid" structure of state-mandated segregation (or "herrenvolk democracy"; see van den Berghe 1967) that prevailed in the United States prior to the civil rights era, the socioeconomic gains of black Americans have lagged far behind those of white ethnic groups. Although African Americans and most Latinos are not "immigrants" in the conventional sense, the comparison of immigrants and minority groups with native whites has been a common theme of much of the earlier literature of assimilation as well as the newer literature on ethnic diversity in America. In some popular accounts, all "persons of color" are considered disadvantaged because of current or past discrimination, but most studies show that blacks and American Indians encounter greater disadvantages than other groups (Hirschman 1983; Snipp 1989).

Stanley Lieberson's classic *A Piece of the Pie: Black and White Immigrants Since 1880* (1980) showed that the socioeconomic progress of African Africans in northern cities slowed (or stopped entirely) in the 1920s and 1930s as the second generation of southern, eastern, and central European immigrant groups were closing the socioeconomic gap with native-born white Americans. Although there has been some narrowing of the gap from the 1940s to the 1980s, blacks remain profoundly unequal in almost every dimension (Duncan 1969; Farley and Allen 1987; Jaynes and Williams 1989; Massey and Denton 1993; Wilson 1987).

The situations of Asian Americans and Hispanics do not fit neatly into either model: the gradual assimilation of European ethnics or the persistent disadvantage of African Americans. Historically, they were disadvantaged racial minorities, but self-employment and education, especially higher education, has been a greater channel of social and spatial mobility for Hispanic Americans and Asian Americans than for African Americans (Barringer, Gardner, and Levin 1993; Bean and Tienda 1988; Featherman and Hauser 1978, ch. 8; Hirschman and Wong 1984; Light 1984). Mexican Americans face a critical educational deficit, and some recent Asian immigrants are trapped in low-wage sectors of the economy, but for those with higher education, there seem to be much greater opportunities for economic mobility as well as higher rates of intermarriage and residence in integrated neighborhoods (Farley 1996; Frey 1995a; Harrison and Bennett 1995; Massey and Denton 1992).

There is still much uncertainty about the eventual socioeconomic position of the post-1965 immigrants and their children (Chiswick and Sullivan 1995; Hirschman 1996; Massey 1995). Min Zhou reviews the segmented assimilation hypothesis, which suggests the possibility of downward mobility for the second generation of some new immigrant groups. Joel Perlmann and Roger Waldinger, however, are skeptical of this interpretation and see more similarities than differences in the life chances of the contemporary second generation and those of the early-twentieth-century second generation. Tienda and Raijman's finely gauged review points to increasing heterogeneity among recent immigrants: "For Asian, African, and other highly educated groups, the future looks bright; for Central and South American immigrants, and Mexicans in particular, the future looks bleak." Tienda and Raijman also emphasize the importance of U.S. receptivity on the progress of immigrants; the increasing wage differentiation by skills in the U.S. labor market penalizes all lowly educated workers, including a disproportionate number of immigrants.

Integration and Multiculturalism

In most societies with long-standing cultural divisions, there are parallel ethnic societies with cultural divisions reinforced by geography, employment, family and kinship organization, and other institutional networks. Although there may be some institutional spheres in which there is common participation (for example, the market economy), cultural differences usually require separate institutional frameworks if they are to persist across generations. A close look at most multiethnic societies around the globe reveals that regional concentrations and separate economic spheres (sometimes enforced barriers) reinforce historical ethnic divisions in politics, language, and culture (Horowitz 1985).

The United States and a few other settler societies have had a different history, one characterized by ethnic mixing and cultural blending among immigrants from European origins (Dinnerstein and Reimers 1987; Lieberson and Waters 1988). It is not that Americans are more tolerant or open-minded than other peoples, but simply that the frontier, the factory, and labor demand, in general, have pulled migrants from different origins and cultures into common settings and neighborhoods. These common environments create possibilities for interethnic contact and exchange and common socializing experiences. Over the long haul these new settings have broken down some, but not all, of the initial cultural divisions among newcomers, and especially for their descendants in American society.

Although this scenario captures some of the essential aspects of the American immigrant experience, there are some important exceptions and qualifications. Most important, nonwhite immigrant minorities have almost always faced color bars of one sort or another. Second, this is a long-term process: it occurs over the course of two or three generations. In the short to medium term, many immigrants settle in neighborhoods where fellow kinsmen already live, prefer to socialize with persons who share a common language and heritage, and often find employment through ethnic networks. Although some immigrants move easily in the broader society, it is generally the children of immigrants who acquire language fluency and develop new aspirations for economic mobility independent of their ethnic roots (Lieberson 1996).

Many natives see, however, the continuity of ethnic concentrations in certain neighborhoods; the intergenerational dynamics of socioeconomic mobility and cultural absorption are less visible. If immigration continues at moderate levels, ethnic neighborhoods can be maintained almost permanently as the home for the immigrant generation even if most of the children of prior waves of immigrants grow up and leave. Ethnic concentrations can also survive for generations even if only a relatively small minority of each generation remains behind.

There are other conditions that can maintain the primary features of the residential concentration of the immigrant generation and its distinctiveness for longer periods of time. Depressions or long periods of slow economic growth can reduce labor demand in the overall economy and lead to a piling up of the second generation in ethnic enclaves and related sectors of self-employment (Bonacich and Modell 1980). In some settings immigrant groups are incorporated into the political networks of patronage and redistribution if ethnic leaders can deliver voting blocs (Glazer and Moynihan 1970). Other institutions, churches, unions, and voluntary associations concerned with ethnic celebrations can also help to keep alive the vestiges of ethnic distinctiveness. Finally, hostility from the external community, rather than internal pulls of ethnic solidarity, can enforce segregation and other barriers. More than any immigrant group, African Americans have suffered from the last obstacle (Massey and Denton 1993).

These processes are intergenerational and, like the glacier that moves only a few inches every year, may well be largely invisible to contemporary observers. It is only by following the time line of decades or generations, and by following immigrant generations (not the community as a whole), that integrative processes can be observed. In the meantime, it is common for members of the immigrant community and those on the outside to emphasize the cross-sectional differences in culture and inequality.

These long-term dynamics of ethnic change are usually missed in debates over multiculturalism. Those with an investment in ethnic distinctiveness imagine that cultural pluralism is a viable option in a society in which there are neither wide socioeconomic differences by ethnicity nor ethnic barriers to geographic or social mobility (Kallen 1924). On the opposite side are those who fear that open recognition of multiple ethnic cultures in schools or other settings will lead to social fragmentation (Schlesinger 1991). Both sides of this debate assume that current differences in language, civic values, food preferences, music, and other cultural traits can be maintained indefinitely in an open society in which individuals have freedom about where to live, whom to marry, and where to work.

Cultural differences can be transmitted across generations, however, only if ethnic groups live in different neighborhoods, attend separate schools, and have different socioeconomic life chances. Although some religious communities may be exceptional, most white immigrant or ethnic groups in the United States have found that the second and third generations retain little more than symbolic attachments to their ancestral origins (Alba 1990; Waters 1990). For some groups of recent immigrants (and long-resident minorities), however, ethnic identity is not optional because of their race or national origins. Whether these groups will eventually have greater freedom and be able to exercise optional ethnicity is a question of great significance.

The Measurement of Race and Ethnicity and the Politics of Identity

The popular belief in the United States (and in many other societies) is that every person has a racial or ethnic identity that can be defined by descent or origin. In everyday interactions, there are some cues, such as physical appearance, dress, surname, and speech, that may help to identify the ethnic identity of persons who do not already know each other. In many situations, however, these cues may be inadequate or misleading, either because some individuals do not fit the expected ethnic stereotypes or because ethnic identities in general have become blurred beyond the point of social recognition.

Social science research on race and ethnicity faces the same problem of sorting people into categories, but with the advantage of responses to direct questions from each person on their racial or ethnic identity (for an overview, see McKenney and Cresce 1993). In U.S. censuses, two measures have been widely used for this purpose. The first is "race"—a relic of nineteenth-century biological classification, but still one of the core census items. Originally, the race question in the census was used to identify blacks, American Indians, and whites. But over the years a number of additional race categories were added, including a number of Asian national-origin groups such as Chinese, Japanese, Korean, Filipino, and many more. The other census item was the birthplace of the respondent and the birthplace of the respondent's parents. The questions on birthplace allow for the tracking of the first and second generations, but the grandchildren of immigrants were "lost" into the residual category of "native-born of native parentage."

Because of the interest in tracking those ethnic groups not defined by the race question beyond the second generation, and because of the nature of ethnic politics in America, additional questions on Hispanic identity and ancestry have been included in recent censuses (Choldin 1986). The Hispanic question, first added in the 1970 census, is intended to identify persons of Latin American or other Spanish-language origin. In the 1980 census, a new question on ancestry or ethnic origins was added, but the historical questions on the country of birth of the respondent's mother and father were dropped. Although the richness of these new questions might be considered a major stimulus to research on race and ethnicity, it has unexpectedly created a crisis of sorts: the ambiguity and uncertainty of the measurement (and the meaning) of racial and ethnic classifications that were partially disguised with limited data are now painfully evident (Farley 1991).

With a significant and increasing level of intermarriage across racial and ethnic divisions, the assumption of race and ethnicity as ascribed statuses is no longer tenable. The ethnic identity of the offspring of these unions often does not fit neatly into the standard census categories (Xie and Goyette 1997). Comparison of persons along the three dimensions of race, Hispanic origin, and ancestry shows that there are significant numbers of black Hispanics, persons who are white (by race) and American Indian (by ancestry), and other persons of blended and mixed ethnic origins. Although the numbers are not so large as to change the findings based on the conventional ethnic comparisons (del Pinal 1992) and ad hoc rules can be devised to classify inconsistent cases, there is a major crack in the conceptual framework of the mutually exclusive and exhaustive racial and ethnic categories commonly used in research that examines interethnic inequality and change.

A major research issue in the field is whether there has been a narrowing of socioeconomic inequality and cultural differences across immigrant generations and ethnic divisions. If the categories are not consistent over time and persons can change their ethnic identities, or if ethnic identity slips across generations, then the measurement and analysis of ethnic stratification becomes much more complex. The problem is akin to a shift in the boundaries of geographical units or a revision of the occupational classification without a map to translate the old categories into the new system.

The problem is evident in the contentious task of revising "Statistical Directive 15," the Office of Management and Budget set of rules that define racial and ethnic categories for data collection and presentation by government agencies (Edmonston, Goldstein, and Lott 1996; Lott 1998; Office of Management and Budget 1997a, 1997b). Some groups cannot locate the ethnic identity or race that is the major source of their group identity in any of the census questions (for example, some religious groups). A growing number of persons either do not answer the questions or write in that they are "just Americans." Some persons who are of mixed ancestry (and their families) insist on having categories that reflect their multiple identities. With classifications that reflect a variety of criteria (physical appearance, language, treaty status, national or regional ancestry) determined solely by individual subjective choice, it is not too surprising that some persons find the questions difficult to answer and that government agencies have difficulty explaining the logic behind them (Perlmann 1997a).

After deliberate study and efforts to bring representative stakeholders into the process, the Office of Management and Budget has completed the task of revising Statistical Directive 15, which will govern the collection of data in the 2000 census (Office of Management and Budget 1997b). The major change is the designation of five major race categories (American Indian or Alaskan native, Asian, black or African American, native Hawaiian or other Pacific Islander, and white) and two ethnic categories ("Hispanic or Latino" and "not Hispanic or Latino"). In the 2000 census, respondents will be able to check that they are members of one or more racial categories. In the 1980 and 1990 census question on "ancestry," respondents could write in multiple national-origin responses, but opening up the race question to multiple responses is a dramatic new change in government statistical data collection.

The short-run problem for government statisticians and for researchers will be to handle the complexity of multiple responses on race in addition to the other dimensions of Hispanic origin and ancestry. The analysis of trends over time (or across immigrant generations) in socioeconomic inequality between racial and ethnic populations is enormously complicated when there is individual or group mobility across ethnic lines. In the long run, however, these new data may well recast our thinking about race and ethnic change in America. Intermarriage and identity choice may well become more central questions in studies of ethnic stratification. Although these factors have been important factors in the past, our ability to study the phenomenon has been limited to small-scale studies. With these changes in the measurement of race and ethnicity in census data, we may be able to chart patterns in ethnic change as well as changes in socioeconomic change by ethnicity.

Theories of Change in Integration and Ethnic Stratification

Theories of immigrant progress, and of ethnic stratification more generally, require the identification of social mechanisms that lead to change (or retard change). The so-called straight-line assimilation hypothesis, which is typically presented only as a straw-man thesis to be debunked, posits no independent variables beyond the passing of time leading to inevitable assimilation. If assimilation has not yet occurred (or assimilation of a certain type has not reached a certain benchmark), we cannot be sure whether the theory is wrong or not enough time has passed. In this critical sense, the hypothesis cannot be falsified.

Milton Gordon (1964) posited that participation in primary group relationships with persons from other groups ("the area of touch relationship," in the words of Park and Burgess [1921/1969]) is the key causal mechanism that leads to assimilation in other dimensions. But how and why do ethnic groups come into close contact with others? Do some groups want to become more integrated and others to retain their separate niches and institutions? Or is it the preferences and prejudices of the dominant group that determine who is allowed to move into integrated neighborhoods and social circles? And how can the preferences of both insiders and outsiders change or be changed? A useful theory will try to frame these questions in ways that allow testable hypotheses to be generated.

In their chapter, Alba and Nee note the very important contribution of Shibutani and Kwan's (1965) comparative historical theory of race and ethnic change, which posits the reduction of subjective "social distance" between groups as the key dependent variable. The important independent variables in Shibutani and Kwan's ecological framework are changes in the demographic balance, the introduction of new ideas, and technological change. Another classical hypothesis of ethnic change is drawn from the thesis of industrialism, sometimes known as "modernization" theory (Kerr et al. 1964). The central thesis is that competitive economic pressures, and the search for profit in particular, leads employers to try to hire and promote the most-qualified employees. The desire for the most-qualified employees (an indicator of potential productivity) should override traditional hiring practices based on ascriptive criteria such as family, social class of origin, and ethnic origins.

Many critics discount the modernization hypothesis with the obvious empirical observation that many industrial societies with competitive economies have high levels of racial and ethnic discrimination and segregation in employment (Blumer 1965). It is certainly true that competitive capitalism (as well as other comparable institutional frameworks) is not a sufficient condition to eliminate immediately ethnic divisions in society. Indeed, competitive capitalism, with its search for cheaper labor, may have been an important social force maintaining coercive labor systems, including slavery and indentured labor (Bonacich 1972). But the important issue for the development of social theory is to frame the question, not as one of absolutes, but in terms of a relationship between variables that can be tested with longitudinal data. Instead of assuming that modernization is a ubiquitous global force, it might be more useful to posit that tight labor markets (indexed by low levels of unemployment) in a competitive economy with free labor lead to more rapid economic integration of immigrants and their descendants. This is an exceedingly important hypothesis that requires more theoretical elaboration and empirical testing.

Another dimension is political incorporation—the absorption of immigrants (and their children) into political participation and thereby using governmental influence to moderate some of the societal discrimination in contemporary societies. If democracy is widened to allow immigrants to vote and engage in politics more generally, office-seekers will be motivated to win their support. Immigrants and other ethnic groups are not monolithic voting blocs, but they often have some common interests in reducing formal barriers to employment, education, and residential mobility.

One plausible interpretation of twentieth-century American politics is that immigrants and minorities played strategic roles in shifting the electoral balance to Franklin Roosevelt in 1932 and to John Kennedy in 1960. In both cases, the political response was to open political doors even wider to groups that had not been particularly welcome before. This opening also stimulated a backlash. Over the last thirty years, the so-called southern strategy has been to woo whites from the Democratic Party to the Republican Party as blacks and other minorities have become increasingly active in the Democratic Party. Although the backlash strategy has been successful, especially in the South, there has been some moderation in the overt antiminority message as blacks have become an important political constituency in many places, including the South.

Over the long term, how does greater political democracy lead to changes in interethnic relations and integration? As noted earlier, this is a complex question that requires considerable conceptual clarification before appropriate empirical tests can be designed. If politics becomes an arena for competition between ethnic political parties and social movements, then every societal issue will be framed as a "zero-sum" struggle between mobilized ethnic communities. Political leaders who seek interethnic compromises will probably be rejected by their electoral support base as "sellouts." If, on the other hand, members of an ethnic group are courted by political brokers who wish to build electoral coalitions, it may well be that democratic institutions will become an important force for societal integration.

There are other possibilities for developing social theories and hypotheses to organize research on the fate of immigrants and ethnic groups in contemporary societies. The key is to develop propositions that are general enough to identify the central elements of modern institutional change (economic, political, and social) that are likely to affect the internal dynamics of racial and ethnic groups, as well as the nature of the boundaries between them.

American Society as an Experiment in Process

American society has been defined by massive immigration from almost every part of the globe. In addition, the histories of domestic minority populations, including American Indians, African Americans, and Latinos, with native roots have been central to the development of the country. Questions of intergroup relations and ethnic inequality are generally the most salient political issues in American society.

American society is also different from many other societies in that American identity is not defined exclusively in cultural terms. Although the English language and certain political ideals of the early English settlers have special status as the foundations of the society, citizenship and political participation have generally been available to newcomers on relatively egalitarian terms. There are, of course, many raw facts that would challenge this benign interpretation of American society. A short list would include the removal of American Indians from their lands (not once but many times), the enslavement of African Americans until 1863 and the subsequent creation of legalized segregation until the 1960s; the bar against Chinese immigration in 1882; and the national-origin quotas from 1924 to 1965. These historical episodes (and many more could be cited) contradict any claim that American society has treated all racial and ethnic groups equally (Baltzell 1964; Daniels 1991).

Nonetheless, in comparative terms, American society has been more open than many other countries, or at least, it has become more open in terms of immigration laws and citizenship opportunities for those who are allowed to enter. And even if imperfectly practiced, American ideals about individualism, liberty, and equality of justice have become important symbols for immigrant groups and other outsider groups that are trying to make their way into the system and fight discriminatory treatment.

In this sense, American society is an experiment in process. The experience of the massive wave of immigrants from eastern and southern Europe in the early twentieth century and the relatively successful incorporation of their children and grandchildren into the mainstream of American society set the stage of study of contemporary immigration from Asia and Latin America. The chapters that follow wrestle mightily with these issues as they seek to understand whether the course of America's future can be understood through the development of social science theory and the close study of the past.

7 Rethinking Assimilation Theory for a New Era of Immigration

Richard Alba and Victor Nee

ASSIMILATION HAS FALLEN into disrepute. In an essay tellingly entitled "Is Assimilation Dead?" Nathan Glazer (1993, 122) summarizes pithily the contemporary view: "Assimilation today is not a popular term." Glazer writes that he asked some Harvard students what they thought of the term and discovered that "the large majority had a negative reaction to it." The rejection of assimilation is not limited to students. While it was once the unquestioned organizing concept in sociological studies of ethnic relations, in recent decades assimilation has come to be viewed by social scientists as a worn-out theory that imposes ethnocentric and patronizing demands on minority peoples struggling to retain their cultural and ethnic integrity.

Without question, earlier social scientists in this field committed what are now regarded as intellectual sins. For instance, W. Lloyd Warner and Leo Srole (1945, 285ff.), in their classic account of assimilation among ethnic groups in New Haven, describe ethnic groups as "unlearning" their "inferior" cultural traits (inferior, that is, from the standpoint of the host society) in order to "successfully learn the new way of life necessary for full acceptance." Warner and Srole also correlated the potential for assimilation with a hierarchy of racial and cultural acceptability, ranging from English-speaking Protestants at the top to "Negroes and all Negroid mixtures" at the bottom. The depiction of the ethnocentric tendency in classical American assimilation could hardly be clearer.

Yet, whatever the deficiencies of earlier formulations and applications of assimilation, we hold that this social science concept offers the best way to understand and describe the integration into the mainstream experienced across generations by many individuals and ethnic groups, even if it cannot be regarded as a universal outcome of American life. In this essay, we attempt to rehabilitate assimilation in order to render it useful in the study of the new immigration. (We are not alone in this attempt; see, for instance, Barkan 1995; Kazal 1995; Morawska 1994.) Our reformulation of assimilation emphasizes its utility for understanding the social dynamics of ethnicity in American society, as opposed to its past normative or ideological applications. As a state-imposed normative program aimed at eradicating minority cultures, assimilation has been justifiably repudiated. But as a social process that occurs spontaneously and often unintentionally in the course of interaction between majority and minority groups, assimilation remains a key concept for the study of intergroup relations. In what follows, we review the sociological literature on assimilation with an eye to assessing its strengths and weaknesses; assay the validity of arguments for rejecting assimilation in understanding the new immigration; and sift through recent studies for clues concerning assimilation's course among the new immigrant groups.

THE CANONICAL ACCOUNT

Whatever the precise words, conceptions of assimilation have been central to understanding the American experience at least since colonial times. The centrality of assimilation for the scientific understanding of immigration is more recent, traceable to the Chicago School of the early twentieth century and especially to the work of Robert E. Park, W. I. Thomas, and their collaborators and students (McKee 1993). The social science use of assimilation thus emerged at the high point of a previous era of immigration and by means of observations in a city where the first and second generations then constituted the great majority of residents.

Park and E. W. Burgess (1921/1969, 735) provided an early definition of assimilation: "a process of interpenetration and fusion in which persons and groups acquire the memories, sentiments, and attitudes of other persons and groups and, by sharing their experience and history, are incorporated with them in a common cultural life." When read closely, this definition does not appear to require what many critics assume is a necessary condition of assimilation—namely, the erasure of all signs of ethnic origins. Instead, it equates assimilation with the social processes that bring ethnic minorities into the mainstream of American life. The limited extent of the assimilation Park envisioned was made even clearer by another definition he later created for the *Encyclopedia of the Social Sciences* (1930, 281): "social" assimilation was "the name given to the process or processes by which peoples of diverse racial origins and different cultural heritages, occupying a common territory, achieve a cultural solidarity sufficient at least to sustain a national existence."

Park's legacy is closely identified with the notion of assimilation as the end-stage of a "race relations cycle" of "contact, competition, accommodation, and eventual assimilation," a sequence that, in the most famous statement of it, was viewed as "apparently progressive and irreversible" (Park 1950, 138; see Barkan 1995, 39–40; Lal 1990, 41–45). In depicting the race relations cycle, Park was rather deliberately painting with broad brush strokes on a large canvas, for the cycle refers obliquely to the processes in the modern world, including long-distance labor migration, that are bringing once separated peoples into closer contact. Competition is the initial, unstable consequence of contact, as groups struggle to gain advantages over one another, and eventuates in the more stable stage of accommodation, where a social structure of typically unequal relations among groups and a settled understanding of group position have come into being (Shibutani and Kwan 1965; Lal 1990, 41–45). But no matter how stable it is, accommodation will eventually be undermined by the personal relationships that cross group boundaries, according to Park (1950, 150), who wrote that "in our estimates of race relations we have not reckoned with the effects of personal intercourse and the friendships that grow up out of them."

Park has been faulted by many later writers for appearing to portray assimilation as an inevitable outcome in multiethnic societies (see, for example, Lyman 1973; Stone 1985). This is implied in Park's conception of stages. However, recent scholarship, as by Lal (1990), argues that the race relations cycle played but a minor role in Park's sociology and that its fame rests more on his students' writings than on his own (see also McKee 1993, 109–11). Park's students and associates did in fact make seminal contributions to the formulation of assimilation (see, for example, Burgess 1925; Warner and Srole 1945; Wirth 1928/1956).

Assimilation Concepts: Milton Gordon's Framework

The confusion among various formulations of assimilation in the early sociological literature has often been noted (see, for example, Barkan 1995; Gordon 1964; for other general reviews of assimilation concepts, see Abramson 1980; Gleason 1980; Hirschman 1983). This problem was not solved until Milton Gordon's *Assimilation in American Life* (1964) provided a systematic dissection of the concept. His multidimensional formulation has proven attractive in part because it readily lends itself to operationalization and hypothesis formulation suitable for middle-range research. Although Gordon conceived of seven dimensions in all, the critical distinction in his conceptual scheme lay between acculturation and what he termed "structural" assimilation, by which he meant the entry of members of an ethnic minority into primary-group relationships with the majority group. This distinction, and its emphasis in particular on the character of an individual's primary-group affiliations, suggests one of the limitations of Gordon's scheme, namely, that it is oriented to a microsociological account of assimilation not conceptually integrated to larger social processes (for example, the dynamics of ethnic boundaries [Barth 1956]). Nevertheless, Gordon's conceptual scheme proved to be useful to many students of ethnicity and has profoundly influenced scholarship on assimilation and ethnic change.

Acculturation, the minority group's adoption of the "cultural patterns" of the host society, typically comes first and is inevitable to a large degree, Gordon argued. His discussion makes clear that these patterns extend beyond the acquisition of the English language, to dress and outward emotional expression and to personal values (Gordon 1964, 79). He distinguished intrinsic cultural traits, those that are "vital ingredients of the group's cultural heritage," exemplified by religion and musical tastes, from extrinsic traits, which "tend to be products of the historical vicissitudes of the group's adjustment to the local environment" and thus are deemed less central to group identity (79). The distinction would seem to imply that extrinsic traits are readily surrendered by the group in making more or less necessary accommodations to the host society, but its implications are less clear about intrinsic ones. Certainly Gordon had no expectation that fundamental religious identities—such as Catholic or Jewish—are given up as a result of acculturation.

Gordon defined a cultural standard that represented the direction and eventual outcome of acculturation—the "middle-class cultural patterns of, largely, white Protestant, Anglo-Saxon origins," which he also described with Joshua Fishman's term as the "core culture" (Gordon 1964, 72). In his view, acculturation was a largely one-way process: except in the domain of institutional religion, the minority group adopted the core culture, which remained, in Gordon's view, basically unchanged by this absorption. Gordon acknowledged only the possibility of change at the margins—"minor modifications in cuisine, recreational patterns, place names, speech, residential architecture, sources of artistic inspiration, and perhaps few other areas" (100).

In Gordon's account, acculturation could occur without being accompanied by other forms of assimilation, and the stage of only acculturation could last indefinitely. The catalyst for more complete assimilation instead is structural assimilation, which Gordon defined as "entrance of the minority group into the social cliques, clubs, and institutions of the core society at the primary group level." He hypothesized that "*once structural assimilation has occurred, . . . all of the other types of assimilation will naturally follow*" (Gordon 1964, 80–81, emphasis in the original). This means in particular that prejudice and discrimination will decline, if not disappear, intermarriage will be common, and the minority's separate identity will wane.

On closer examination, Gordon's hypothesis is ambiguous as to whether it is meant to apply to individuals or groups. Even though the measurement of assimilation was put at the individual level, the hypothesis has been interpreted as applying literally to groups—a reading that becomes obvious when one recognizes that the hypothesized relationships among the different dimensions of assimilation need not hold in fact at the level of individuals. For example, individuals may be structurally assimilated, but prejudice and discrimination can still be widespread, as Gordon clearly understood. This ambiguity is important because of the desirability of formulating a concept of assimilation in which some independence between the individual and group levels is explicitly preserved (Barkan 1995). We will return to this point later.

Another limitation of Gordon's account was that it conceived of assimilation within a two-group framework of analysis (the "Sylvanians" and "Mundovians") and thus did not take account of the multigroup nature of American society. The language used by Gordon's definition ("social cliques, clubs, and institutions of the core society") implies that structural assimilation is to be equated with minority-group relationships to members of the majority group. The problem has been accentuated as American society has become more heterogeneous and the majority group smaller relative to the number of minority groups. Strictly speaking, Gordon's account does not extend to relationships between members of different ethnic minorities. Yet such situations are increasingly common. A broad rather than narrow two-group conception should be entertained if assimilation is to be faithful to the level of ethnic intermixing in American society (especially evident in terms of intermarriage and embodied in the "triple melting pot" idea of Kennedy [1944]).

Perhaps Gordon's structural-assimilation hypothesis should not be given the causal inflection his language implies. The strength of Gordon's conceptual scheme lies in its lucid articulation of some of the key dimensions of assimilation viewed as a composite concept. This leads to the recognition that, to some extent, the dimensions of assimilation can be arranged in terms of stages (Barkan 1995). When his hypothesis is read in this spirit, the core of the assertion is seen to be that structural assimilation signals the maturity of the assimilation process. Indeed, this has been the main use of the concept in the literature, as indicated by the frequent use of intermarriage data to measure assimilation's progress (see, for example, Alba and Golden 1986; Lieberson and Waters 1988).

Identificational assimilation represents a third dimension of Gordon's schema, one that has taken on importance in contemporary discussion of assimilation with respect to both the descendants of European immigrants and the new immigrant groups. Gordon (1964, 71) defined this as the "development of [a] sense of peoplehood based exclusively on [the] host society." He recognized, too, that ethnic identity was not an undifferentiated concept, and he distinguished between "historical identification"—which derived from a sense of the "interdependence of fate," in Kurt Lewin's phrase, and typically extended to the ethnic group as a whole—and "participational identity," whose locus was the segment of the group most socially similar to the individual (the "ethclass," in Gordon's [1964, 53] terminology). With the benefit of hindsight, Gordon's concept of identificational assimilation appears overly demanding, requiring the extinction of any form of ethnic identity in favor of an exclusively national, American identity. Consequently it would seem to imply even the loss of family memories of extra-American origins, which seems not only an extraordinary expectation but one that flies in the face of the data demonstrating that the overwhelming majority of Americans still acknowledge some non-American ethnic ancestry (Lieberson 1985; Lieberson and Waters 1993). However, the knowledge many individuals possess about their family histories should not be conflated with an ethnic identity that has practical consequences (Alba 1990; Gans 1979; Waters 1990).

An important part of Gordon's legacy is his delineation of alternative conceptions of the process and outcome of assimilation in the United States. Gordon described these as "Anglo-conformity" and the "melting pot." (He also identified a third model, "cultural pluralism," which is less relevant to the canonical account.) These alternative conceptions are appropriately viewed as expressions of popular beliefs or ideologies about the constitution of civil society in America. The model of Anglo-conformity, which corresponds in spirit with the campaign for rapid, "pressure-cooker" Americanization during and after World War 1, equated assimilation with acculturation in the Anglo-American mold and ignored other assimilation dimensions, being therefore indifferent to the occurrence or nonoccurrence of structural assimilation. The model of the melting pot has enjoyed several periods of popularity in American discussions of ethnicity, most recently in the immediate aftermath of World War II. It offered an idealistic vision of American society and identity as arising from the biological and cultural fusion of different peoples, and while its exponents usually emphasized the contributions of Europeans to the mixture, it allowed for a recognition of those of non-European groups as well. In terms of Gordon's scheme, the model operated along the dimensions of cultural and structural assimilation. This latter was invoked by the forecast of widespread intermarriage (Gordon 1964, 125; Herberg 1960; Kennedy 1944, 1952). The cultural assimilation portion of the melting pot idea was rather ambiguous, however. Many early exponents spoke in ways that suggested a truly syncretic American culture blending elements from many different groups, but the assertions of later commentators were more consistent with Gordon's own conception—that acculturation is a mostly one-directional acceptance of Anglo-American patterns (Gordon 1964, 127–28).

Gordon was an adherent of neither model. This may come as a surprise to many who know Gordon's views only in the context of the contemporary discussion of assimilation, for he has often been identified with a school that portrays assimilation as an almost inevitable outcome for immigrant groups. But this is not in fact a fair characterization. Although Gordon left little doubt that, in his view, acculturation was inevitable to a large degree, he did not see structural assimilation as similarly foreordained. His analysis of American society led to the conclusion that structural pluralism rather than cultural pluralism was the more accurate description. He envisioned the United States as constituted from ethnic subsocieties, in whose institutions and social networks most individuals spend the major portion of their social lives, literally from cradle to grave in many cases (Gordon 1964, 159).

Straight-Line Assimilation

Another major piece of the canon is the notion of "straight-line assimilation," a phrase popularized by Gans (1973) and Sandberg (1973) to describe an idea stemming from Warner and Srole (1945). The straight-line notion adds a dynamic dimension to Gordon's somewhat static formulation in that it envisions a process unfolding in a sequence of generational steps: each new generation represents on average a new stage of adjustment to the host society, that is, a further step away from ethnic "ground zero," the community and culture established by the immigrants, and a step closer to more complete assimilation (Lieberson 1973). Implied is the idea that generations are the motor for ethnic change, not just the time frame within which assimilation takes place. Each generation faces a distinctive set of issues in its relationship to the larger society and to the ethnic group, and their resolution brings about a distinctive pattern of accommodation. The idea of the generational inevitability of assimilation has been criticized, however, for assuming that all ethnic content is imported by immigrants and not recognizing that it can be created in response to conditions and out of cultural materials in the host society. Critics of the straight-line notion have argued that instead ethnicity may go through periods of re-creation, if not renaissance (Conzen et al. 1992; Glazer and Moynihan 1963/1970; Greeley 1977; Yancey, Ericksen, and Juliani 1976). In recognition of this criticism, Gans (1992a) has modified his description to the "bumpy-line theory of ethnicity," while still adhering to the core of the original concept—namely, that there is a generational dynamic behind ethnic change and that it moves, perhaps with tangents, in the general direction of assimilation.

The generational time frame assumes a view of ethnic change that is decidedly endogenous and that, perhaps ironically, tends to be ahistorical. By casting assimilation in terms of a dynamic internal to the group, the straight-line notion overlooks the impact of historically specific changes—such as, for example, the shifts in residential patterns resulting from the rapid expansion of suburbs in the post–World War II era. This shift, in combination with the hiatus of mass immigration in the 1920s, led to ethnic changes that corresponded closely with generational status—in, for example, mother-tongue competence (Stevens 1985). Such generational effects may not be as pronounced in the current immigration, in which births in an ethnic group may be scattered across decades. Consequently a common set of historical experiences is not likely to coincide with generational status, as was the case in the earlier mass immigration from Europe (and also Japan).

Extensions of the Conceptual Canon

Assimilation has been criticized over the decades both from the outside, by those who reject it as a valid approach, and by others who, operating within its conceptual frame, point out gaps or identify features that seem idiosyncratic to the experiences of some groups. Our concern in this section is to address criticism internal to the framework, leading us to consider some extensions of Gordon's contribution to the canon.

Gordon's concept of culture has been criticized for being static and overly homogeneous. As already noted, Gordon assumed that acculturation involved change on the part of an ethnic group in the direction of middle-class Anglo-American culture, which itself remained largely unaffected, except possibly for "minor modifications." An obvious problem with Gordon's view is that American culture varies greatly by locale and social class; acculturation hardly takes place in the shadow of a single, middle-class cultural standard. What is lacking in Gordon is a more differentiated and syncretic conception of culture, and a recognition that American culture was and is more mixed, much more an amalgam of diverse influences, and that it continues to evolve. Such a conception we find, for example, in Michael Lind's (1995, 8) description of what he calls the "vernacular" culture:

> The national language is American English, in its various regional and subcultural dialects. The national culture is not the high culture of the art galleries and civics classes, but rather the vernacular culture that has evolved in the United States in the past several centuries, and continues to evolve, from the unsystematic fusion of various regional and racial customs and traditions.

It does not require a radical shift in perspective to recognize that assimilation and its expression in the form of acculturation are, at bottom, no more than the attenuation of an ethnic or racial distinction and the cultural and social differences that are associated with it.[1] Such processes can occur by changes in one group that make it more like another or by changes in two (or more) groups that shrink the differences and distance between them—group convergence, in other words. Moreover, acculturation need not be defined simply as the substitution of one cultural expression for its equivalent, whether the replacement comes from the majority or minority cultures, though such substitution certainly takes place. This narrow conception of acculturation is at the root of the frequently encountered view that one group "adopts" the cultural traits of another. The influence of minority ethnic cultures can occur also by an expansion of the range of what is considered normative behavior within the mainstream; thus, elements of minority cultures are absorbed alongside their Anglo-American equivalents or are fused with mainstream elements to create a hybrid cultural mix.

We suspect that ethnic influences on the mainstream American culture happen continuously—as the recent literature on the invention of ethnic and national traditions (Conzen et al. 1992; Hobsbawm and Ranger 1983; Sollors 1989) suggests—and that their occurrence is not limited to the domains where expansion and hybridization are most apparent, such as food and music. An obvious question is how one can recognize the incorporation into American culture of ethnic influences. The hallmark, we think, is that a cultural trait gradually loses its association with an ethnic group. In part, this happens because nongroup members take it on, so that the empirical correlation between the trait and group membership is weakened. In part, it occurs as the trait is no longer labeled in an ethnic way. Over a longer time frame, the ethnic origins of a new element may be forgotten and it becomes part of the mainstream repertoire, like the currently archetypal American recreational practices, which, as Thomas Sowell (1996) notes, are derived from those brought by German immigrants. Similarly, the more intense family contacts that Andrew Greeley (1977) has documented for some groups, such as Irish and Italians, may have gradually influenced American conceptions of family life.

As noted earlier, Gordon's scheme did not recognize the distinction between individual and group levels of ethnic change. Thereby, it inadvertently sidestepped some of the most important lines of investigation within the assimilation framework—the reciprocal effects between group processes and individual attainment. The insight that a theory of assimilation must take the interaction between micro (individual) and mezzo (group or community) levels into account dates at least as far back as Raymond Breton's (1964) hypothesis that an ethnic community's "institutional completeness" influences its members' propensities to assimilate. In other words, the supply side of ethnicity, the group and community context, may be decisive to the outcome at the individual level (Portes and Rumbaut 1996). If at the community level the opportunities to express ethnicity are meager or socially inappropriate, the intent to maintain ethnicity, assuming it exists, may be thwarted or transformed. The desire to find ethnic modes of behavior and expression, then, is likely to succeed where the supply side of ethnicity is fairly rich in possibility. Where individuals assimilate in large numbers and are not replaced by a continuing immigration stream, a pattern characterizing many European-ancestry groups, the supply side of ethnicity is diminished as a whole as well as narrowed in specific respects. Organizations dwindle in membership or find that their members belong to early generations or those with a more parochial outlook. Neighborhoods fail to retain the socially mobile sons and daughters of their residents, and their class character does not change to match the expanding class distribution of the group.

Some gaps in Gordon's account lend themselves to natural extensions by the addition of further dimensions of assimilation. (Odd though it seems, his multidimensional formulation overlooked important forms of assimilation.) Occupational mobility and economic assimilation, the key dimensions of *socioeconomic assimilation,* are not addressed in his discussion of assimilation. Yet this kind of assimilation is of paramount significance, both in itself, because parity of life chances with natives is a critical indicator of the decline of ethnic boundaries, and because entry into the occupational and economic mainstream has undoubtedly provided many ethnics with a motive for social (that is, structural, in Gordon's sense) assimilation. Furthermore, socioeconomic mobility creates the social conditions conducive to other forms of assimilation, since it probably results in equal-status contact across ethnic lines in workplaces and neighborhoods.

Yet the concept of socioeconomic assimilation is not unambiguous, and two different usages need to be distinguished. In one, by far the more common in the literature on ethnicity and assimilation, socioeconomic assimilation is equated with attainment of average or above-average socioeconomic standing, as measured by indicators such as education, occupation, and income (see, for example, Neidert and Farley 1985), a usage that can be traced to Warner and Srole (1945). Since many immigrant groups have entered the American social structure on its lower rungs, this meaning of socioeconomic assimilation is usually conflated with social mobility, leading to the frequently expressed expectation that assimilation and social mobility are inextricably linked. In the second usage, socioeconomic assimilation can be defined as minority participation in institutions such as the labor market and education on the basis of parity with native groups of similar backgrounds. If the emphasis in the first version falls on equality of attainment or position, the emphasis in the second is on equality of treatment: members of the immigrant minority and similarly situated members of native groups (which could be other minorities) have the same life chances in the pursuit of such scarce values as high-status jobs and higher education. The key question for the second version is: To what extent has an ethnic distinction lost its relevance for processes of socioeconomic attainment, except for initial conditions?

The distinction between the two types of socioeconomic assimilation is important because it pertains to whether the relationship between socioeconomic and other forms of assimilation is historically contingent. The descendants of European immigrants of the nineteenth and early twentieth centuries experienced a close link between social mobility and other forms of assimilation. But this may have reflected the opportunity structure available during a particular era in American history (Gans 1992a; Portes and Zhou 1993). The question of whether the possible narrowing of opportunities in the contemporary United States will limit the prospects for socioeconomic assimilation of new immigrant groups or, instead, lead to a different pattern of assimilation must be kept open for the time being. The second kind of socioeconomic assimilation allows for "segmented" assimilation (Portes and Zhou 1993). According to this view, many labor migrants, with Mexicans as the preeminent example, may end up on the lower rungs of the stratification order, while human capital immigrants, common among Asian groups and Russian Jews in the current mass immigration, experience rapid social mobility.

Another dimension of assimilation that has received attention in recent years is residential or, following Massey (1985), *spatial assimilation.* Massey's formulation is the most systematic and has been used as a standard to assess the residential segregation of major racial and ethnic populations in the United States (Massey and Denton 1987, 1993). Spatial assimilation as a concept is linked to a model of incorporation that continues the Chicago School's ecological tradition and that views the spatial distribution of groups as a reflection of their human capital and the state of their assimilation, broadly construed. The basic tenets of the ecological model are that residential mobility follows from the acculturation and social mobility of individuals, and that residential mobility is an intermediate step on the way to structural assimilation. As members of minority groups acculturate and establish themselves in American labor markets, they attempt to leave behind less successful members of their groups and to convert occupational mobility and economic assimilation into residential gain, by "purchasing" residence in places with greater advantages and amenities. This process entails a tendency toward dispersion of minority-group members, opening the way for increased contact with members of the ethnic majority, and thus desegregation. According to the model, entry into relatively advantaged suburban communities that contain many whites is a key stage in the process (Massey and Denton 1988).

Like socioeconomic assimilation, residential assimilation has been given related but distinguishable interpretations in past discussion. Analogously, one is that the residential distribution of the minority approximates that of the majority—in other words, that the group is found in the same locations and in similar concentrations as the majority. This is the condition of no segregation and is applicable only on the group level. A second meaning is that the residential opportunities of minority-group members are equivalent to those of majority-group members with similar resources. "Opportunities" here should be given a broad interpretation to include not just location (for example, access to desirable suburbs), but also housing (home ownership, quality of dwelling). The question of whether minority-group members can achieve residential situations as desirable as those of others with similar qualifications is one that can be posed at the individual level. A third and final meaning of residential assimilation refers to the existence of ethnic neighborhoods, which are generally viewed as housing social structures and cultural milieus supportive of ethnic distinctiveness (see, for example, Alba, Logan, and Crowder 1997; LaRuffa 1988).

Creating Assimilation Theory: Shibutani and Kwan's Ecological Analysis

Even when extended as above, Gordon's analysis, the touchstone for all subsequent studies of assimilation, remains limited. Most important, it lacks a specification of the causal mechanisms giving rise to assimilation. Despite Gordon's reference to theories of assimilation, he did not formulate a theory in this sense. His contribution was to define a multidimensional framework whose descriptive concepts have proven highly useful, allowing analysts to measure the extent of the assimilation of racial and ethnic groups along various empirical dimensions. His linchpin hypothesis asserts that incorporation into primary groups of the dominant group precedes and stimulates other forms of assimilation. Yet the direction of causality could well be the opposite of what was claimed by the structural-assimilation hypothesis, a question that cannot be resolved within Gordon's framework because there is no causal theory of assimilation.

At least one attempt has been made to formulate a more complete theory of ethnic stratification and assimilation; and although it is not now a part of the assimilation canon, we include it in our discussion to suggest a direction in which the canon might fruitfully be expanded. The attempt we have in mind is that of Tomatsu Shibutani and Kian Kwan in *Ethnic Stratification* (1965). Whereas Gordon focused his study on assimilation in American society, Shibutani and Kwan elaborated a theory that expanded on Park's race relations cycle to focus broadly on explaining the dynamics of ethnic stratification across the globe. Despite this reach, their underlying aim was to gain new insights into the American experience of race relations through comparative historical analysis of systems of ethnic domination in diverse historical and societal settings, ranging widely to include Manchu rule over Han Chinese and ethnic stratification in the Roman empire.

As Chicago School sociologists, Shibutani and Kwan employed George Herbert Mead's symbolic interactionism as a core building block of their theory. Following Mead, they argued that how a person is treated in society depends "not on what he is" but on the "manner in which he is defined." Out of necessity, humans place people into categories, each associated with expected behavior and treatment, in order to deal in a routine and predictable manner with strangers and acquaintances outside of their primary groups. Differences giving rise to social distances are created and sustained symbolically through the practice of classifying and ranking. The social distances that arise thereby are the fundament of the color line that segregates minorities and impedes assimilation.

By social distance, Shibutani and Kwan (1965, 263–71) mean the subjective state of nearness felt to certain individuals, not physical distance between groups. In their account, change in subjective states—reduction of social distance—precedes and stimulates structural assimilation, not the reverse, as implied in Gordon's hypothesis. When social distance is low, there is a feeling of common identity, closeness, and shared experiences. But when social distance is high, people perceive and treat the other as belonging to a different category, and even after long acquaintance there are still feelings of apprehension and reserve. Social distance may be institutionalized; for instance, the color line's stereotypes, customs, social norms, and formal institutional arrangements maintain a system of stratification that employs ethnic markers to determine differential access to opportunity structures (Merton 1968). In Shibutani and Kwan's view of the American experience, social mobility through economic advancement, though not as common as it is perceived to be, allows for upward movement in class standing. But the system of ethnic stratification is more rigid. Ethnic identity for nonwhites is especially resilient to change. Although a member of a racial minority can improve his or her position in the opportunity structure, "ethnic identity, in those areas in which it makes a difference, places a ceiling upon the extent to which he can rise" (Shibutani and Kwan 1965, 33).

Shibutani and Kwan intended their theory as an extension of Park's natural history of the race relations cycle. Through a comparative historical approach, they examined case studies of contact, competition, accommodation, and assimilation stemming from migration. Their analysis uncovered many apparent exceptions to Park's optimistic conception of assimilation, for ethnic stratification orders tend to be long-lasting once established and institutionalized. Domination is initially gained through competitive advantages accruing to the group whose culture is best adapted to exploit the resources of the environment. Competition and natural selection push minorities into the least desirable residential locations and economic niches. A stable system of ethnic stratification is rooted in part in a moral order in which the dominant group is convinced that its advantages derive from natural differences and minorities come to believe in their inferiority and accept their lot at the bottom. But the dominant group also upholds its position and privileges through institutionalized power and outright coercion. Individual minority-group members may achieve social mobility and gain economic parity, but as exceptions to the rule. Such upwardly mobile individuals, often of mixed race, acquire a marginal status that gives them a modicum of privilege and respect, but they are fully accepted neither by the dominant group nor by their own ethnic community. In a stable ethnic stratification order, individual assimilation can occur even while the system maintaining dominance remains intact.

Nevertheless, Shibutani and Kwan agree with Park that even stable ethnic stratification orders ultimately tend to become undone and that assimilation occurs at the final stage of the natural history of the race relations cycle. Their use of ecological theory, which informs their analysis of ethnic stratification, plays a central role here, too, contributing a dynamic, macrosociological dimension that is vital to their theoretical framework. It provides the crucial causal links between the microsociological part of the theory and much larger structures and processes.

The causal mechanisms that bring about the reduction of social distance stem from changes in "life conditions" that occur at the ecological level. In the absence of such changes, ethnic stratification orders tend toward stable equilibrium. In explaining the transformation of such orders, Shibutani and Kwan emphasize particularly the importance of technological innovation, which in turn induces alterations in the mode of production. As an illustration, they cite the invention of the automatic cotton picker, which diminished the demand for cheap labor in the South and sparked the migration of poor blacks and whites to the industrial North, altering the pattern of racial stratification throughout the United States. Changes in the economic system associated with technological shifts often introduce opportunities for minority groups to acquire new competitive advantages that make them indispensable to employers. These in turn lead employers to seek institutional changes favorable to the interests of minority groups, changes that, in a capitalist system, are relatively easy to institute when organizations and individuals pursuing profits find it in their economic interest to do so. As a contemporary example, one could point to the role of employers in supporting the immigration of workers, both skilled and unskilled, legal and undocumented, despite the public clamor for greater limits on legal immigration and a curtailing of illegal immigration. At one end of the economic spectrum, the interest of employers stems from the growing labor-market demand for highly skilled workers (for example, computer programmers) because of the postindustrial transformation of the American economy; at the other end, there is a continuing need for elastic sources of low-wage labor in the agricultural sector, in "degraded" manufacturing sectors such as the garment industry, and in personal service such as nannies (Sassen 1988).

Another ecological source of change stems from shifts in the often unstable demographic balance between majority and minority groups. As the relative size of minority groups increases, shifts in power become likely. For example, the increasing percentage of nonwhites in the United States contributes to the pressure on employers and schools to institute changes, such as policies promoting the value of diversity, to accommodate a more heterogeneous population; similar changes can also be observed in other countries with large immigrant populations, such as Germany, where multiculturalist pressures have also arisen as an accommodative response to growing population diversity (Cohn-Bendit and Schmid 1992). Likewise, increases in population density, mainly in cities, alter ethnic relations by increasing the probability of chance meetings and, eventually, of stable relationships between members of different ethnic groups.

The effects of ecological changes notwithstanding, Shibutani and Kwan assert that the most immediate source of a decline in social distance occurs when other changes stimulate the introduction of new ideas that challenge values and cultural beliefs previously taken for granted—as in the discrediting of white supremacist ideologies in the postcolonial world—and a "transformation of values" ensues. "Systems of ethnic stratification begin to break down when minority peoples develop new self-conceptions and refuse to accept subordinate roles. As they become more aware of their worth in comparison to members of the dominant group, what they had once accepted as natural becomes unbearable" (Shibutani and Kwan 1965, 350). In Shibutani and Kwan's account, the context giving rise to higher rates of assimilation often follows the outbreak of protests and opposition. Social movements are the engine that sparks interest among dominant elites in instituting changes and reforms to alter the relationship between majority and minority in a manner that promotes assimilation.

We intend our brief discussion of Shibutani and Kwan's theory of ethnic stratification to sketch the outline of a missing component in the canon of assimilation, but not necessarily to provide the exact blueprint. Without a dynamic of the sort provided by this theory, Gordon's analysis of assimilation remains static, allowing for individual-level assimilation but not for more wholesale shifts in ethnic and racial boundaries. (As we noted earlier, Gordon remained a structural pluralist in his view of American society.) The link between microsociological changes in social distance, and thus interethnic relations and structural assimilation, and macrosociological shifts points in the direction in which a theory of assimilation must move. Although the causal mechanisms that the Shibutani-Kwan theory posits may be revised in light of new research, clearly any analysis of the potential for assimilation in the United States, or anywhere else for that matter, cannot rely solely on confidence in processes of individual-level assimilation alone but must pay attention to macroscopic processes rooted in population ecology and to how these impinge on prospects for assimilation.

How Relevant Are the Differences Between Past and Present Eras of Immigration?

There is abundant evidence that assimilation has been the master trend among the descendants of the immigrants of the previous era of mass immigration, who mainly came from Europe in the period before 1930. This assimilation can be equated, above all, with long-term processes that have eroded the social foundations for ethnic distinctions and ultimately the distinctions themselves. These processes have brought about a rough parity of opportunities (among groups, not individuals) to obtain the desirable social goods of the society, such as prestigious and remunerative jobs, and loosened the ties between ethnicity and specific economic niches (Greeley 1976a; Lieberson 1980; Lieberson and Waters 1988; Neidert and Farley 1985). Parity here refers to a broad convergence toward the life chances of the "average" white American, which has particularly affected the descendants of immigrants from peasant backgrounds (such as southern Italians) and does not exclude the exceptional achievements of a few small groups, such as eastern European Jews. Assimilation has diminished cultural differences that once served to signal ethnic membership to others and to sustain ethnic solidarity; one result has been an implosion of European mother tongues (Alba 1988; Stevens 1992; Veltman 1983). Assimilation is also associated with a massive shift in residence during the postwar era—away from urban ethnic neighborhoods and toward ethnically intermixed suburbs (Alba, Logan, and Crowder 1997; Gans 1967; Guest 1980)—and with relatively easy social intermixing across ethnic lines, which has resulted in high rates of ethnic intermarriage and ethnically mixed ancestry (Alba 1995; Alba and Golden 1986; Lieberson and Waters 1988). Finally, assimilation finds expression in the ethnic identities of many whites, which are "symbolic" in the sense defined by Herbert Gans and involve few commitments in everyday social life (Alba 1990; Gans 1979; Waters 1990).

Admittedly, the causes of this assimilation of European-ancestry ethnic groups are much less well understood than is the result. But at a minimum, the fact that this assimilation has involved groups with very different characteristics at the time of immigration and varied histories in the United States suggests that the forces promoting it have been, and perhaps still are, deeply embedded in American society. Yet many scholars of contemporary immigration reject assimilation as a likely outcome on a mass scale for contemporary immigrant groups. One of the most compelling arguments they raise is that assimilation, as represented by the canonical account, is specific to a set of historical circumstances that characterized mass immigration from Europe but does not, and will not, apply to contemporary non-European immigrant groups (see, for example, Massey 1994; Portes and Rumbaut 1996). In this section, we look at several of these arguments in detail and consider countervailing perspectives.

The Absence of a Foreseeable Hiatus in the Immigration Stream

The decisive halt in the stream of mass immigration from Europe in the late 1920s, induced by restrictive immigration legislation followed by the Great Depression, is widely thought to have been fateful for ethnic groups. The ensuing, four-decade interruption in steady, large-scale immigration virtually guaranteed that ethnic communities and cultures would be steadily weakened over time. The social mobility of individuals and families drained these communities, especially of native-born ethnics, and undermined the cultures they supported. There were few newcomers available as replacements. Over time the modal generation shifted from the immigrant to the second, and then from the second to the third.

Many students of the post-1965 immigration believe that a similar hiatus in the contemporary immigration stream is unlikely. One reason is the apparent disinclination of the federal government to ratchet down the level of immigration, though this may be changing as the political climate generated by immigration issues heats up (see, for example, Brimelow 1995). The legislation that has set the main parameters for immigration during the 1990s, the Immigration Act of 1990, appears to have raised the level of legal immigration above the nearly record-setting pace of the 1980s (Heer 1996; Reimers 1992, 262). Moreover, recent attempts to control the immigration flow, such as the 1986 Immigration Reform and Control Act (IRCA), have generally had unanticipated and even counterproductive consequences in the end—perhaps, many suggest, because the immigration-generating forces in the United States and in sending societies are so powerful that they thwart or bypass the attempts of the U.S. government to harness them (Donato, Durand, and Massey 1992; Heer 1996).

Movement across national borders appears to be an endemic feature of the contemporary international system, and this adds to the difficulty of substantially limiting contemporary immigration. UN projections of the world population suggest very large population increases in the near future (by 2025), which will occur mostly outside the highly developed nations and thus add to the huge reservoir of people available to move (Heer 1996, 137–45). Needless to say, emigration from less developed countries is not just a product of population pressure but of the curve of economic development, which instills in broad segments of the population consumption tastes that cannot be satisfied by their native economies, and of the historical linkages between less and more developed nations in the international system (Portes and Rumbaut 1996; Sassen 1988). Further, it is more difficult for national governments to control emigration than was the case a century ago. Such forces seem likely to engender large, difficult-to-control population movements far into the future, as exemplified by the large legal and illegal flows from Mexico to the United States.

If immigration to the United States continues indefinitely at its current level, then population projections show that many of the ethnic groups arising from it will be dominated by the first and second generations well into the next century (Edmonston and Passel 1994). This will create a fundamentally different ethnic context from that faced by the descendants of European immigrants, for the new ethnic communities are highly likely to remain large, culturally vibrant, and institutionally rich. Ethnic community life in combination with ethnic economies, according to this scenario, are likely to provide particularistic channels of mobility. In sum, there are likely to be strong incentives to keep ethnic affiliations alive even for the third generation, as long as the distance between the generations does not grow so great as to alienate them from one another.

Yet if there is any proven rule in population projections, it is that the patterns of the present cannot be projected indefinitely into the future, for they will change in unforeseeable ways. The level of immigration could go up, to be sure, but it could also go down—as a result of restrictive legislation backed up by tougher enforcement, a decline in the attractiveness of the United States to one or more of the main sources of current immigration, a weakening of the forces generating emigration from these countries, or some combination of these changes. Despite the current pessimism about efforts to control immigration flows to the United States, especially the undocumented immigration, control is not impossible, as is shown by the example of Germany, which has lengthy land borders with eastern Europe, a potential source of many immigrants, but only a small residential population of undocumented immigrants in comparison with that of the United States.

Moreover, a decline in the attractiveness of the United States to potential immigrants could happen for any of a number of reasons—such as changes in the labor market that eliminate some of the niches exploited by immigrants, declines in the relative quality of life in the metropolitan areas that are the main receiving areas of immigration, or a rise in the relative attractiveness and accessibility of other countries as immigrant destinations. An example from recent immigration history gives empirical force to this point. When the Immigration Act of 1965, frequently taken as the watershed event for contemporary immigration, was under consideration by Congress, a common argument was that it would lead to greatly increased immigration from the countries of southern and eastern Europe, whose applicants would qualify under the family reunification provisions. Italy alone was said to have a backlog of 250,000 visa applications (Reimers 1992, 72). Yet, though there was a temporary, modest rise in immigration from Italy, the anticipated surge did not occur. In the interim, the United States had become less attractive to prospective Italian immigrants because of the emergence of the European Common Market. Why should Italians come to the United States when they could go instead to Germany and Switzerland and be able to return home at frequent intervals?

Raising the prospect of a future decline in the general level of immigration is admittedly speculative. We are on firmer ground, we believe, in predicting that the immigration of some groups will decline and will not live up to the assumption of continued inflow far into the future. The assumption, in other words, will hold selectively, not uniformly. One reason for suspecting such declines is that the level of economic development of some sending nations may approach or even catch up to that of the United States, undermining a principal motive for immigration. This has happened in the case of Japan, which sent many immigrants around the turn of the century but currently is the source for few immigrants, other than managers in Japanese companies who are doing tours of duty at U.S. branches. It could well happen in the cases of Korea and Taiwan. Indeed, there are signs of an incipient decline in Korean immigration: between 1990 and 1994 the number of immigrant visas allocated to Koreans fell by 60 percent while the number returning home surged (Belluck 1995; Min 1996). For groups whose immigration abates, the prediction of ethnic communities continually revitalized by new immigration will prove inaccurate.

Finally, it perhaps should not be assumed that the cessation of mass immigration was essential to opening the way for assimilation for the descendants of late European immigration. We do not know whether and to what extent assimilation would have taken place in any case. It is certainly a plausible hypothesis that assimilation would have proceeded, albeit at a slower pace. Similarly, in the new era of mass immigration, even if immigration continues at present levels, there is no reason to assume that the second and third generations will be locked into the same communal life and economic niches of the first generation. With the possible exception of Mexican immigration, which might be compared to the French Canadian situation, the numbers of immigrants from each of the many immigrant streams are small relative to the overall U.S. population. Far from the closed ethnic boundaries common to situations of stable ethnic stratification often involving only a few ethnic groups, such heterogeneity increases the likelihood of chance meeting and associations across groups. Moreover, as long as ethnic economies are populated by small businesses with limited opportunities for advancement, the direction of job changes over time, even for the first generation, will be to secure jobs with better conditions of employment and returns to human capital in the mainstream economy (Nee, Sanders, and Sernau 1994).

The Racial Distinctiveness of Many New Immigrant Groups

A common argument holds that the descendants of earlier European immigrations, even those composed of peasants from economically backward parts of Europe, could eventually assimilate because their European origins made them culturally and racially similar to American ethnic core groups, those from the British Isles and some northern and western European countries. The option of assimilation will be less available to the second and later generations of most new immigrant groups because their non-European origins mean that they are more distinctive, with their distinctiveness of skin color especially fateful.

While we wish to avoid at all cost a Panglossian optimism about American racism, we find this argument less compelling than many do, because we think that it treats perceptions of racial difference as more rigid than they have proven themselves historically. We grant that American treatment of non-Europeans has generally been characterized by racist discrimination of a more extreme cast than anything experienced by even the most disparaged of the European groups, as the well-known examples of the Chinese Exclusion Act of the late nineteenth century and the internment of Japanese Americans during World War II testify. Nevertheless, the view that the pathway to assimilation was smoothed for the descendants of European immigrants by their racial identification is an anachronism, inappropriately imposing contemporary racial perceptions on the past. There is ample evidence that native-born whites perceived some of the major European immigrant groups, such as the Irish, Jews, and Italians, as racially distinct from themselves and that such perceptions flowered into full-blown racist theorizing during the high-water period of mass immigration in the early decades of this century (Higham 1974). This is not just a matter of a language usage in which "race" was treated as a synonym for "nation" or "ethnic group." Many Americans believed that they could identify the members of some groups by their characteristic appearance (for example, "Jewish" facial features), and nineteenth-century caricatures of the Irish frequently gave them a distinctly simian cast. A curious residue of these racial perceptions has been left behind in a once common epithet for Italians—"guinea." As H. L. Mencken observed in *The American Language* (1963), the term originated in a word for slaves from the African coast. It is, in short, a color word.

Over time, racial perceptions of the most disparaged European groups shifted. The Irish, and perhaps other groups, initially struggled to put some racial and social distance between themselves and African Americans (Ignatiev 1995; Roediger 1991). But as these groups climbed the socioeconomic ladder and mixed residentially with other whites, their perceived distinctiveness from the majority faded. (World War II, a watershed in many ways for ethnic relations among whites, also had a powerful impact on attitudes toward European ethnics.) Intermarriage both marked this shift and accelerated it. We see no a priori reason why a similar shift could not take place for some contemporary immigrant groups and some segments of others. We are thinking here particularly of Asian groups and light-skinned Latinos. In the case of some Asian groups, the relatively high intermarriage rates of their U.S.-born members suggest their acceptability to many whites, the most frequent partners in intermarriage, and the absence of a deep racial divide (Lee and Yamanaka 1990; Qian 1997). James Loewen's (1971) study of Chinese immigrants who migrated from the western states to the South in the 1870s documents a transformation of racial attitudes that parallels that for the Irish. When Chinese laborers first arrived in the Mississippi Delta, they joined free blacks as part of the "colored" agricultural labor force in a race-segregated society. Chinese immigrants and their descendants gradually "crossed over" to gain acceptance in the white community by distancing themselves socially from blacks and acculturating to southern white culture. The post-1965 immigration of Asians to the United States has taken place in the substantially different historical context of the post–civil rights movement and a new era of mass immigration. Although Loewen's case study of the Mississippi Chinese may not be applicable to the current immigration, it nonetheless shows that ethnic identity and boundaries are socially constructed and malleable.

The most intractable racial boundary remains that separating those deemed phenotypically black in the United States from whites. This boundary is likely to exert a powerful influence on the adaptation possibilities of immigrant groups, depending on where they are situated with respect to it. The evidence of this influence is already apparent; it is registered in the research observations about the identificational dilemmas confronted by the children of black Caribbean parentage (Waters 1994; Woldemikael 1989) and recognized in the concept of "segmented assimilation" (Portes and Zhou 1993). But despite such evidence, there is also the countervailing experience of South Asian immigrants. Although South Asians have dark skin color, they are the highest income group in the United States and are predominantly suburban in their residence (Portes and Rumbaut 1996). Their experience suggests that it is not dark skin color per se but the appearance of connection to the African American group that raises the most impassable racist barriers in the United States.

The Impact of Economic Restructuring on Immigrant Opportunity

The assimilation of European-ancestry Americans is linked to opportunities for social mobility that, within a brief historical period, brought about a rough parity of life chances across many ethnic groups (though not within them, as life chances remained structured by social class origins) (Greeley 1976a; Lieberson 1980). These opportunities were in turn linked to historically contingent, broad avenues of intergenerational movement that allowed immigrants of peasant origins with few work skills of relevance in an urban, industrial economy nevertheless to gain a foothold through steady employment, often in manufacturing sectors to start with (Bodnar 1985). According to a common view, similar openings are not to be found with the same frequency in the contemporary economy because of economic restructuring, which has led to the elimination of many manufacturing jobs and the degradation of others and to their replacement in the spectrum of jobs open to immigrant workers with low-level service jobs, which do not offer comparable wages, stability of employment, or mobility ladders (Sassen 1988). This result of economic restructuring is described by Portes and Zhou (1993) as an "hourglass economy," with a narrowed band of middle-level jobs and bulging strata at the bottom and the top. The presumption is that it will be more difficult for the descendants of contemporary immigrants, many of whom enter the labor force at or near the bottom, to make the gradual intergenerational transition upward because footholds in the middle of the occupational structure are relatively scarce (Portes and Zhou 1993). Movement into the top strata requires substantial human capital, particularly higher educational credentials that is not likely to be within reach of all members of the second generation. A conclusion drawn by a number of scholars is that, to a degree not true of European ethnics, the current second generation is at risk of experiencing no, or even downward, mobility unless the American economy becomes more dynamic than it has been since the early 1970s (Gans 1992a).

Without question, economic opportunities are critical to the assimilation prospects of new immigrant groups. But the restructuring of the economy does not have an equally negative impact on the opportunities of all groups because of the enormous variety among groups in the forms of capital—economic, cultural, and social—they bring with them and in the degree of support provided by the community contexts they enter (Light 1984; Portes and Rumbaut 1996; Waldinger 1986–87, 1996a). Some groups, like the Cubans of Miami, have distinguished themselves by the development of ethnic subeconomies that are likely to afford the second generation better-than-average chances to succeed in the educational system and enter professional occupations. Others—several Asian groups spring readily to mind—enjoy, whether because of the professional occupations of their immigrant parents or the cultural capital they possess, high levels of educational attainment in the United States (Gibson 1989; Hirschman and Wong 1986; Light and Bonacich 1988; Model 1988; Nee and Sanders 1985). Moreover, the 1980s economic restructuring has stimulated economic growth in the 1990s, and this has brought about a sharp reduction of unemployment. As a result of tighter labor markets, even low-skilled manual laborers have experienced increases in hourly earnings.

The significance of economic restructuring for the second and subsequent generations would appear to be greatest for those groups described by Portes and Rumbaut (1996) as "labor migrant" groups, like the Mexicans. Even here, we caution that the distinction from the experiences of comparable European groups (such as southern Italians) can be overdrawn, for they, too, did not enter an economy that was continuously generating a generous supply of opportunities for secure employment and upward mobility. A large portion of the second generation of the southern and eastern European groups came of age in the teeth of the Depression. Like the children of some contemporary immigrants, many in the earlier second generation responded to their perceived lack of opportunity and to their rejection at the hands of nativist whites by constructing what are now called "reactive identities," identities premised on value schemes that inverted those of the mainstream in important ways. We know, for instance, that during the 1930s and perhaps afterward the children of southern Italian immigrants were widely perceived as posing problems in the educational system; they had high rates of dropout, truancy, and delinquency (Covello 1972), all signs that they were rejecting the conventions and values of a system that they perceived as rejecting them.

Yet the analyses of Stanley Lieberson (1980) demonstrate that the U.S.-born members of these groups experienced a fairly steady upgrading of educational and occupational attainment, even in the cohorts whose life chances would have been most affected by the Depression. This suggests to us that the emphasis on economic restructuring in the discussion of assimilation chances for contemporary immigrant groups may produce an overly pessimistic reading of their prospects. Our additional remarks can only be suggestive at this point. But since there is as yet no fully satisfactory explanation for the assimilation of the once disparaged southern and eastern European groups, it seems premature to judge the assimilation chances of contemporary immigrant groups as diminished because the socioeconomic structure of the United States has changed in the interim. As Joel Perlmann and Roger Waldinger (this volume) note, to insist that assimilation is likely only if the situation of contemporary groups parallels that of earlier ones in precise ways seems to require that history do something it almost never does: repeat itself exactly. With respect to mobility, such an insistence loses sight of the ability of individuals and groups to adjust their strategies to the economic structures they find. We note in particular that the focus of the economic restructuring argument as applied to immigrants has been almost entirely on the labor market, and it has therefore ignored the educational system. However, not only has the association between social origins and educational attainment weakened over time (Hout, Raftery, and Bell 1993), but postsecondary education is more available in some of the states where immigrants have concentrated (California and New York especially) than elsewhere in the nation. Perhaps the pathways followed by earlier groups have been narrowed over time, but other pathways are likely to have opened up.

Our purpose in this section should not be misunderstood. We are not denying that there are differences, and important ones, between the immigrations of the past and present and in the circumstances facing immigrant groups after arrival, nor are we claiming that the parallels between the situations faced by the descendants of contemporary immigrants and those of earlier ones are so strong that patterns of assimilation among European Americans can be inferred as a likely outcome for new immigrant groups. But the distinctions between these situations are not as clear-cut as they are usually made out to be. None of them is, in our judgment, sufficiently compelling to rule out a priori the possibility of assimilation as a widespread outcome for some, or even most, contemporary immigrant groups. It is therefore imperative to examine with an open mind the cultural, residential, educational, and other patterns established by the new immigrants and their children for clues about the potential importance of assimilation.

Evidence of Assimilation by New Immigrant Groups

The evidence bearing on the assimilation of new immigrant groups remains fragmentary in important respects, but it is nevertheless essential to review it for hints about the trajectory of these groups, especially across generations. It is critical at the outset, however, to emphasize the limited nature of the data available about the second generation and the virtual absence of any about the third or later generations. It is widely accepted that the immigrant generation does experience changes as it accommodates itself to life in a new society, but that these changes are limited for individuals who come mostly as adults and have been socialized in another society, invariably one quite different from the United States. Hence, the changes experienced by the immigrants themselves cannot be decisive for conclusions about assimilation. It is only with the U.S.-born, or at a minimum the foreign-born who immigrate at young ages and are raised mostly in the United States (usefully labeled by Rumbaut [1994b] as the "1.5 generation"), that there is the possibility of assessing the limits of assimilation for new immigrant groups. But even in the case of the second generation, the literature on the assimilation of white ethnics offers reason to be cautious about inferences.

For most European groups, the assimilation of the second generation was partial. Indeed, the well-known studies of this generation depict in general individuals whose lives were profoundly affected by their ethnic origins, who mostly resided in ethnic communities and exhibited in a variety of ways thinking and behavior characteristic of the group as well as some degree of loyalty to it. (For the Italians, for example, there are the studies of Child 1943; Gans 1962/1982; Whyte 1943/1955.) It was only with the third and, in some cases, the fourth generation that the powerful undercurrent of assimilation came unmistakably to the surface. (As Stephen Steinberg [1981] notes, the fourth generation is the first to lack direct contact with the immigrant generation.) But for the new immigrant groups, the second generation is still young (Mexicans being the principal exception), and the studies that focus on it generally can track only its progress in school. The probative value of evidence about the second generation must be carefully examined.

A second critical limitation is the very limited time of exposure to American society for the subjects of many of the studies of new immigrant groups. Half of the Punjabi Sikh high school students on whom Margaret Gibson's (1988) study focuses arrived in the United States within the five years preceding the fieldwork; all of the subjects of Marcelo Suarez-Orozco's (1989) study of Central American refugee schoolchildren had come within the preceding five years; the data-gathering stage of Nazli Kibria's (1993) study of the Vietnamese was carried out in 1983–85, within ten years of the beginning of the large-scale influx of Vietnamese; and so on. Much of the data we possess about new immigrant groups can be characterized as pertinent to the earliest phases of their settlement in the United States, the phase that Park characterized as involving contact and competition. In the past histories of immigration and intergroup relations in the United States, the period of stable accommodation extended beyond the first and second generations. Thus, the observations that assimilation is far from complete and that immigrants and their children do not appear to want to assimilate should not be regarded as definitive for the longer-term changes that will occur to these groups.

In what follows, because we must limit our review of the evidence for reasons of space, we have chosen the two areas that we, as researchers, know best.

Socioeconomic Attainment

As many scholars have noted, a defining feature of the post-1965 immigration is the diversity of the socioeconomic backgrounds of contemporary immigrants. Rather than hailing primarily from rural communities, the new immigrants come from both rural and urban backgrounds, from underdeveloped regions of the Western hemisphere as well as from industrially developed areas of East Asia. Occupationally, the new immigration encompasses the full spectrum of jobs, from those at the bottom occupied by unskilled labor migrants to jobs in the mainstream economy held by skilled professional and technical migrants. Professional immigrants—engineers, mathematicians, computer scientists, natural scientists, teachers, and health workers—come mainly from Asian countries, and nearly one-quarter come from other developing countries (Kanjanapan 1994). Hence, they are predominantly nonwhite. Many human-capital immigrants enter the labor market from professional and graduate schools in the United States. Their transition to jobs in the mainstream economy involves a school-to-job transition not dissimilar from that of the native-born. Most professional immigrants, however, enter the labor force through the occupational and family reunification categories of the 1965 immigration law (Jasso and Rosenzweig 1990). Human-capital immigrants educated abroad, after a period of downward adjustment, appear to shift into mainstream jobs as they acquire local work experience and acquire facility with the English language (Farley 1996), or they go into self-employment (Nee,

Sanders, and Sernau 1994; Sanders and Nee 1996).[2]

The economic assimilation of human-capital immigrants is less well known, however, than are the experiences of immigrant entrepreneurs and workers in the ethnic economy and of traditional labor migrants. These are the groups that clump together into visible ethnic economies and communities. They are also the groups on which researchers have concentrated their attention because of theoretical and empirical differences centering on assimilation theory (Portes and Bach 1985; Wilson and Portes 1980) and because of growing concerns over the declining quality of immigrants (Chiswick 1986; Greenwood 1983) and its consequences for prospects for economic assimilation (Borjas 1990).

The Ethnic Economy The early literature on ethnic economies focused on the experiences of Asian immigrant groups, the Chinese and Japanese (Light 1972; Bonacich and Modell 1980). These studies emphasized the importance of the ethnic economy in providing employment and profit for minorities facing harsh societal hostility. Despite institutional racism that excluded Asian ethnics from opportunities in the mainstream economy, these groups were able to sustain themselves through small-business economies that created alternative sources of opportunities under group control. This pattern gave rise to a stable accommodation that provided the economic basis for rearing and educating a second generation. The salient feature of the Chinese and Japanese ethnic economies was the extensive reliance on ethnic resources and solidarity in the accumulation of start-up capital and in competition with white firms.

In many respects, the ethnic economies of early Chinese and Japanese immigrants served a role in the subsequent assimilation of Asian ethnics similar to the role of such an economy in the Jewish immigrant community. They provided a means for survival and modest economic gain when racial discrimination barred even the college-educated second generation from opportunities in the mainstream economy. The abatement of societal hostility and the assimilation of the American-born generations of Asian ethnics following World War II resulted in a secular decline of Chinatowns, a trend that was not reversed until the start of the post-1965 immigration (Nee and Nee 1973/1992). The Japanese ethnic economy was never fully reconstituted after the internment experience (Bonacich and Modell 1980). But once the color line broke down, the assimilated second generation abandoned parental small businesses to seek jobs in the mainstream. Implied in this choice was a perception of the limited nature of the economic mobility and opportunities provided by the ethnic economy, which was constituted by very small firms with limited capital and bounded markets (Bonacich and Modell 1980; Nee and Nee 1973/1992).

In the case of Chinese immigrant workers, Don Mar (1991) has shown that jobs in the enclave provide even lower earnings than do those in the competitive secondary sector, which has been presumed to be associated with economic disadvantages for immigrants. Analyzing the job transitions of Asian immigrants, Victor Nee, Jimy Sanders, and Scott Sernau (1994) found that enclave workers receive lower net earnings and lower returns to their human capital, but immigrants who previously worked for a co-ethnic employer are more likely to enter into self-employment. In Reynold Farley's (1996, 191) analysis of the 1990 census, Chinese men earned the lowest net wages of male income earners in any immigrant group. Farley attributed this to the enclave economy effect on workers' wages: "More so than other streams of current immigrants, it appears that the uneducated from China are concentrated in or trapped in a low-wage enclave economy, helping to explain why the Chinese are less effective than other immigrants in translating their characteristics into earnings."

One response to the enclave-economy debate has been to question the limits of the central concept (Sanders and Nee 1987). Ivan Light and his colleagues (1994) have argued that a broader concept of an ethnic economy better serves the needs of research. Defined as the self-employed and their co-ethnic employees, the ethnic economy can be readily measured (Bonacich and Modell 1980). By contrast, the enclave-economy concept is empirically unwieldy. Alejandro Portes and Robert Bach (1985) were unable to specify its boundaries with the precision needed for empirical study. Ivan Light and Stavros Karageorgis (1994) also point out that the debate over the enclave hypothesis overlooks a key datum: ethnic enterprises in fact employ very few paid co-ethnic employees. Hence, the main object of study is not the co-ethnic employee in the ethnic economy, but the self-employed. Another limitation of the enclave concept is that relatively few ethnic economies have the spatial concentration and breadth of firms required to qualify as enclave economies (Logan, Alba, and

McNulty 1994). This is not strictly speaking a limitation of the hypothesis, but of its relevance for groups other than Cubans in Miami, Koreans in Los Angeles, Japanese in Honolulu, and a few other cases.

A side effect of the enclave-economy debate therefore was to focus attention on the economic assimilation of immigrant entrepreneurs. Although researchers agree that self-employment constitutes an important aspect of the immigrant experience, they disagree about the relative advantages it confers. George Borjas (1990) argues that the self-employed in the ethnic economy are not better off than immigrant workers with similar human capital. However, according to Alejandro Portes and Min Zhou (1996), the analysis of earnings, when conducted with nominal income values rather than the logged form preferred by economists, reveals the "success stories" in the population of self-employed. In Los Angeles, for example, self-employed Asian immigrants earn six dollars more per hour than other immigrants with comparable characteristics (Nee, Sanders, and Sernau 1994). Yet, as Portes and Zhou concede, if the average return for immigrant entrepreneurship is the main concern, then Borjas is right in arguing that entrepreneurs in the ethnic economy are not particularly successful.

Although the ethnic economy is an important institutional arrangement for immigrants, by no means does it provide the main route for their economic advancement. We agree with Borjas's assessment that "self-employment represents an important component of the immigrant experience in the U.S. labor market" (1986, 505). However, in our view, the literature on the economic incorporation of contemporary immigrants risks overstating its significance (Aldrich and Waldinger 1990; Light and Karageorgis 1994). It is useful to keep in mind that just 14 percent of native-born non-Hispanic whites are self-employed, and only Korean immigrants show a higher concentration (28 percent) in self-employment.[3] Despite the emphasis on immigrant entrepreneurship, in other words, all other immigrant groups report a lower level of involvement in the small-business sector than whites (Farley 1996). The modal labor-market experience of immigrants is in neither the ethnic economy nor small-business ownership, but in the open economy. Immigrant workers may first establish a foothold in the immigrant labor market by working in the ethnic economy, but over time the direction of job changes is generally toward jobs with better remuneration and conditions of work, and these are mostly available in the mainstream labor market. Nee, Sanders, and Sernau (1994) show in their study of Asians in the Los Angeles immigrant labor market that ethnic boundaries and labor-market sectors are much more permeable than they are assumed to be by the segmented labor-market literature.

Immigrants in the Open Labor Market In the analysis of economic assimilation of immigrant workers, labor economists have contributed important findings. Barry Chiswick's (1977, 1978a) pioneering studies of the earnings of immigrants indicated that after an initial period of income decline, which he interpreted as stemming from the "cost of immigration," the earnings of immigrants gradually achieved parity within a ten- to fifteen-year time line and then surpassed the earnings of native-born workers of the same ethnic background. However, this finding was subsequently challenged by Borjas (1985, 1987a) as inconclusive because Chiswick relied on a cross-sectional research design, which conflated aging and immigration-cohort effects. By examining cohort changes, Borjas's analysis suggested that in the past five decades there was a major decline in the skills of immigrants. He pooled the 1970 and 1980 census data and found that the earnings growth of recent cohorts did not exceed the earnings levels of the native-born and were lower than the growth experienced by earlier cohorts of immigrants. He concluded that the Third World origin of many immigrants accounted for the decline in immigrant "quality," or human capital, compared with the earlier immigration from Europe. Like Chiswick's analysis, Borjas's conclusions are vulnerable because he used census cross-sectional data. Even though he pooled data from two decennial censuses to examine cohort effects, he was nonetheless unable to study changes in earnings for the same workers while they acquired work experience and human capital in the United States. (His data were not longitudinal, in other words.) Moreover, the effect of the deep economic recession in the 1980s could not be taken into account in his analysis.

The debate stimulated by Borjas's criticism of Chiswick's optimistic forecast has been largely inconclusive, according to the assessment of Marta Tienda and Zai Liang (1994). To be sure, considerable variation exists in the quality of cohorts by national origin in the post-1965 immigration. The lower average skills of immigrants overall stem from the large relative size of the immigration from Mexico and some less-developed regions of Asia and Latin America. Other contingents of immigrants, such as those from India and Korea, are considerably more highly educated than the average American. Moreover, the effect of lower skills on economic mobility depends on the comparison group, as Robert LaLonde and Robert Topel (1991) have shown. If the comparison group consists of the U.S.-born members of the same ethnic group, then Chiswick's results are confirmed: even recent cohorts of immigrants quickly achieve economic parity. This is not the case when native-born Americans in general make up the comparison group. But immigrants who came to the United States as children do achieve economic parity with the latter group of workers (Borjas and Freeman 1992). This finding is, of course, consistent with assimilation theory. Furthermore, Sherrie Kossoudji (1988, 254) demonstrated empirically that "not being able to speak English imposes a real cost on some immigrant workers, both by reducing observed earnings and by altering occupational opportunities. Generally, immigrants who do not speak English are 'pushed down' the occupational ladder." She concludes from her findings that English language ability not only is a measure of assimilation, but it is also a "specific skill necessary for mobility in the labor market."(225) A different order of problem with respect to economic assimilation is posed, however, by the large-scale migration of poorly educated and illegal aliens (Borjas 1994a). One facet of the problem is that illegal immigrants concentrate in particular geographical locations (such as California) and then in enclaves within these. Spatial concentration of undocumented immigrants probably leads to substantial differences from other immigrants in the extent of economic disadvantage, which in turn is translated into a lower rate of economic assimilation for the children of illegal immigrants. Farley (1996), in examining the low educational background of Hispanic immigrants—legal and illegal—conjectures that the children of Hispanic immigrants in general may continue to suffer the consequences of their parents' low stock of human capital.

Overall, the economic literature on earnings assimilation suggests that post-1965 immigrants are handicapped not so much by race as by a lack of usable human capital (Borjas 1994a). If earnings growth is slow, this is accounted for by the low stocks of human capital of recent cohorts of immigrants from developing economies. Their slower pace of economic assimilation can be attributed to the transformation of the American economy, that is, the general erosion of labor-market demand for unskilled labor and the increasing demand for highly skilled workers (Katz 1994), though this affects natives and immigrants alike. By contrast, the sociological literature has highlighted the adverse labor-market experience of racial minorities, with sociological analysts often conflating the cost of immigration with the cost of race. When the former is controlled for, however, the earnings gap between non-Hispanic whites and native-born children of immigrants narrows, so that Asian ethnics—mostly Chinese and Japanese among the U.S.-born old enough to be in the labor market—achieve substantive parity with whites in earnings growth (Farley 1996; Nee and Sanders 1985).

The relative openness of the American labor market stems from the regulatory environment facing large firms and bureaucracies. In the post–civil rights era, Title VII and other civil rights legislation make it more costly for firms (except possibly small businesses, owing to the difficulty of monitoring and enforcement) to discriminate by gender and race. As a result, the workplace is more regulated today than it was at the time of the earlier immigrant waves to the United States. The principle of equality under the law has been definitively extended to legal immigrants and naturalized citizens. Even illegal immigrants are entitled to due process and have legal rights. As Lance Liebman (1992, 372) observed in a review of key court cases defining immigrant rights, "The net effect . . . would seem to be that aliens are a protected class for purposes of constitutional adjudication, that state rules barring aliens from particular occupations will be scrutinized carefully by courts to see whether it is appropriate that a particular job be restricted to persons . . . even federal restrictions are constitutionally dubious unless enacted by Congress and justified by significant needs."

However, equality under the law does not extend to illegal immigrants, even though they are entitled to due process and possess limited rights of access to public services. This class of immigrants, estimated to be about 2.6 million at the time of the 1990 census (Fix and Passel 1994), is likely to concentrate in the underground, informal ethnic and open labor markets in order to avoid deportation. Undocumented status restricts their labor-market mobility since it effectively closes off opportunities to find jobs in the regulated portion of the urban labor market—that is, in large firms and government bureaucracies, where monitoring and enforcement of immigration laws are routine. The penalty for illegal status to human-capital immigrants is high, which in part explains why there are so few highly educated workers among the undocumented. Most illegal aliens have no more than an elementary school education, and a sizable number have no formal schooling. For instance, two-thirds of immigrants from Mexico and El Salvador have only a few years of formal schooling (Farley 1996). Marta Tienda and Audrey Singer's (1995, 134) analysis shows that the pattern of earnings growth of undocumented immigrants reflects "economywide shifts in the structure of wages as well as changing returns to different levels of schooling." In their view, the fact that "wages of undocumented immigrants increased at all is remarkable" given the general performance of the U.S. economy in the 1980s and the restrictions on labor mobility faced by illegal aliens.

The jobs that immigrants find in U.S. labor markets closely correspond to their level of education (Bean and Tienda 1987; Farley 1996). Human-capital immigrant streams—from India, China, Africa, Western Europe, and Canada—have a higher proportion of professionals and managers than the native-born American population. By contrast, immigrant groups with large numbers of workers who come with little formal education—from Cuba and other Caribbean nations, El Salvador, Mexico, and other Central American countries—are disproportionately represented in low-wage blue-collar and service jobs. Consequently a bimodal attainment pattern is evident in the occupations and earnings of human-capital immigrants and labor migrants, roughly corresponding to the differences between Asian and Hispanic immigrants. Farley (1996) has compared the earnings of immigrants as reported in the 1990 census with the earnings of native-born workers in fourteen immigrant metropolises, including New York, Los Angeles, Miami, Washington, D.C., and Houston. He confirms the pattern, first discovered by Chiswick (1977), that the cost of immigration is most clearly felt in the years immediately following arrival in the United States, but that considerable economic mobility occurs over time. After twenty-five years of residence in the United States, immigrants report earnings that are 93 percent of those of native-born non-Hispanic whites. The earnings gap between immigrants and the native-born was smaller for women than for men.

However, taking the national origins of immigrants into account unveils a mixed picture of economic assimilation for non-European immigrants in the nation as a whole. Hispanic men—foreign and native-born—earn substantially less than Anglos, while Asian men—including the foreign born—earn as much as men of the majority group. For women, the wage gap between Hispanic and Anglo workers is nearly as large as among men, but Asian women report higher wages than do Anglos. When Farley controlled for social and demographic characteristics—place of residence, education, reported English-speaking ability, work disability, and marital status—he found that Hispanic men earn 84 percent and foreign-born Asian men 87 percent as much as their Anglo counterparts. But native-born Asian men have achieved earnings parity with comparable Anglo males, and accordingly their position has improved since the 1980 census. The wage gap is less for women, with both native- and foreign-born Asian women and native-born Hispanic women earning more than comparable Anglo women. In sum, the early analyses of the 1990 census report results that are in line with expectations of assimilation theory. If anything, the economic assimilation of immigrants has progressed more rapidly for many post-1965 immigrants than it did for the earlier waves of immigrants from Europe, owing to the technological transformation of the American economy, which results in increased demand for high-skilled workers.

Spatial Patterns

One of the most noted features of the new immigration is its high degree of geographic concentration (Farley 1996; Portes and Rumbaut 1996; Waldinger 1989). Just a handful of states and metropolitan areas receive a majority of new immigrants and remain the primary areas of residence and work for immigrants and their children. Of the immigrants who came during the late 1980s, more than 80 percent ended up in only six states: California, New York, Florida, Texas, New Jersey, and Illinois, in order of share (Farley 1996, 169; see also Portes and Rumbaut 1996). Concentration within specific metropolitan areas is nearly as extreme: Los Angeles, San Francisco, New York City, Miami, Houston, and Chicago, taken in their broadest sense as what the Census Bureau defines as "Consolidated Metropolitan Statistical Areas," were the places of settlement for more than half of the immigrants of 1985–1990. In total, only fourteen metropolitan areas had above-average concentrations of the foreign-born in their populations as of 1990, but these fourteen, some of them among the largest metropolitan regions of the country, accounted for two-thirds of all immigrants (Farley 1996, 185).

Some degree of geographic concentration is an inevitable by-product of immigration, which is guided by social networks and leads to settlement patterns determined partly by the need of new immigrants, unfamiliar with American society and frequently lacking proficiency in English, for assistance from kin and co-ethnics (Massey 1987). Even so, the impression is that the degree of geographic concentration among new immigrant groups exceeds that of older ones at a comparable stage of immigration (Massey 1994). Only immigrant groups with a heavy professional stratum—Indians, for example—appear to be exceptions to contemporary concentration, since job considerations for professionals typically override the tendency to settle where large numbers of fellow ethnics have already done so. Places of settlement are also initially more dispersed for refugees, whose original destinations in the United States are usually determined by government agencies and private sponsorship, but secondary migration tends to bring about greater ethnic concentration, exemplified by the roles of Miami as a mecca for Cubans and of Orange County, California, for Vietnamese (Gold 1992; Portes and Rumbaut 1996). The high degree of geographic concentration of the new immigrant groups is consistent with the notion that institutionally complete ethnic communities will support ethnicity for the second and subsequent generations and retard assimilation.

But the concentration of immigrant groups in a small number of metropolitan areas and of specific groups in an even smaller number appears incompatible with the rapid growth of ethnic populations that is projected to occur if immigration remains at its current level. The projections of the National Research Council (Smith and Edmonston 1997), for instance, suggest in their middle-of-the-road scenario that by 2020 Latinos and Asians, the two racial and ethnic populations receiving the bulk of the new immigration, will nearly double their combined share of the population, going from 12 percent (in 1990) to 22 percent. It seems self-evident that these groups cannot remain as concentrated in a few states and metropolitan areas as they are today if growth occurs on this scale, although the implications of any dispersal can be debated. One possibility is the emergence of a much larger number of immigrant cultural centers, especially those associated with Spanish speakers, given their size in the immigrant stream (Massey 1994). Other areas of the country might begin to resemble the multicultural concentrations presently epitomized by Los Angeles, Miami, and New York. Yet the hypothesis that movement away from areas of original settlement tends to be associated with a ratcheting forward of assimilation, which seems generally borne out in the experiences of European-descent groups, is also plausible in application to new immigrant groups, in which case new areas of concentration may be more culturally and ethnically diverse than they were before but not as diverse as the original immigrant meccas. Much will depend on whether any dispersal is the result of a movement by native-born generations away from ethnic centers or of a fanning out of the immigration stream itself.

One form of spatial dispersal is less conjectural: within the regions where they reside, new immigrants are on the whole only moderately segregated from the non-Latino white majority. In particular, research into metropolitan levels of residential segregation has established that, by the measure of standard segregation indices such as the index of dissimilarity, Asian and Hispanic segregation from the majority is considerably less than that of African Americans and within a range usually deemed "moderate." Analyzing 1990 census data for all metropolitan areas with substantial black populations ($N = 232$) and at a small unit of aggregation, the census block group, which should raise segregation index values on average, Reynolds Farley and William Frey (1994) found that the average index of dissimilarity between Hispanics and non-Hispanics was .43, virtually unchanged from the 1980 index calculated in an equivalent way. That of Asians and non-Asians was also .43, representing in this case a slight increase from the 1980 value (.41). By contrast, the average 1990 value for blacks was .64 (see also Massey and Denton 1987). Given that the Asian and Hispanic populations are growing rapidly through immigration and that newly arrived immigrants tend to enter communities where their group is already present in sizable numbers, an increase in the level of segregation is not unexpected and tells little about changes in the residential patterns of more long-standing Asian residents. In sum, the metropolitan-wide studies suggest that the segregation of new immigrant populations is not extreme, just as was true of earlier European immigrants. A drawback of this research is that little attention has been paid to the residential patterns of specific groups within the Asian and Hispanic populations; obviously such residential patterns can vary considerably. Also, sufficient attention has not been paid to the segregation of black immigrants, although an analysis of the impact of race on the residential situations of Hispanics strongly suggests that immigrants with black skin are likely to be channeled into black neighborhoods (Denton and Massey 1989; see also Kasinitz 1992).

Metropolitan-wide levels of segregation are aggregates that can disguise great individual variation in residential situation. Individual-level analyses are therefore warranted to determine how residential situation corresponds with personal and household characteristics, such as nativity and income. The model of spatial assimilation leads to the hypothesis that residential exposure to members of the racial and ethnic majority should increase in tandem with socioeconomic standing, acculturation as measured by proficiency in speaking the English language, and generational status. Richard Alba and John Logan have conducted a series of relevant studies for some of the main metropolitan regions of immigrant concentration, and by and large their findings uphold the spatial-assimilation hypothesis (see Alba and Logan 1993; Alba, Logan, and Stults 1998; Logan and Alba 1993; Logan, Alba, and Leung 1996; Logan, Alba, McNulty, and Fisher 1996; see also White, Biddlecom, and Guo 1993). For Asians and Latinos, the most powerful determinant of the racial and ethnic composition of their neighborhoods (census tracts) is their own socioeconomic position: the greater their income and the higher their educational status, the larger the percentage of non-Latino whites in the population of the neighborhood where they reside. The ability to own a home also tends to increase residential exposure to the majority group, as does residence in the suburbs, which reflects socioeconomic status to an important degree. Linguistic acculturation is yet another determinant, but generational status (nativity) has little influence once these other variables are taken into account. The difference associated with linguistic assimilation is especially sizable among Latinos and is most pronounced between those who speak only English at home and those who do not speak English well. Bilinguals, who speak a mother tongue but are also proficient at English, are intermediate in terms of residing with non-Latino whites. The Alba-Logan analyses reveal again the important role played by skin color among Latinos. Light-skinned Latinos—that is, those who describe themselves on census forms as "white" (about half of all Latinos in 1990)—find it easiest to enter neighborhoods with large numbers of non-Latino whites. Latinos who describe themselves racially as other than white or black reside on average in neighborhoods where the percentage of non-Latino whites is modestly lower, while those who self-describe as "black" (a small minority of all Latinos) live, as noted earlier, with far fewer members of the racial and ethnic majority.

The general consistency of these individual-level patterns with those predicted by the spatial-assimilation model suggests that the residential integration of immigrant and second-generation households with the majority population ought to increase over time. But a powerful countervailing trend is produced by the impact of continuing immigration into the metropolitan regions where immigrants and their children are concentrated. The immigration into these regions, combined with the apparent inclination of native groups to move away from them (Frey 1995b), is altering the racial and ethnic composition of their neighborhoods in a way that reduces the availability of majority-group members as neighbors for upwardly mobile immigrant households. This impact is apparent when the Alba-Logan analyses are compared between 1980 and 1990, for the diversity of the neighborhoods where Asians and Latinos live increased noticeably during the 1980s (and presumably continues to increase). Still, even in the areas where the impact from immigration has been heaviest, middle-income, linguistically assimilated Asian and Latino suburbanites tended as of 1990 to live in areas where non-Latino whites predominate. This statement is most in jeopardy in Los Angeles and Miami, the two regions with the highest proportions of foreign-born in their populations and where, therefore, the racial and ethnic shifts spurred by immigration are the most developed (Farley 1996, 170). In other regions of immigrant settlement, such as San Francisco or New York, which have the third- and fourth-highest concentrations of new immigrant groups, the neighborhoods of even modestly affluent Asians and Latinos generally contain quite substantial non-Latino white majorities. Presumably the same would be even more true for most other metropolitan regions, where the concentrations of new immigrant groups are necessarily more modest.

From the standpoint of spatial-assimilation theory, the most intriguing feature of the residential patterns of new immigrants is frequent settlement in suburbs immediately upon, or soon after, arrival in the United States (Alba and Logan 1991; Alba, Logan, Stults, et al. 1999; Waldinger 1989). This hallmark of the new immigration presents a remarkable contrast to the process of spatial assimilation as experienced by earlier, European immigrant groups, whose members generally first established urban enclaves and subsequently migrated as individuals and families to suburbs, typically after spending a generation or more in cities (Alba, Logan, and Crowder 1997; Glazer and Moynihan 1963/1970; Massey 1985). However, according to 1990 census data, 43 percent of immigrants who arrived during the 1980s and were living in metropolitan areas already resided outside of central cities, that is, in areas commonly designated as "suburban." The percentages of suburbanites were particularly high and growing among Asian groups; according to unpublished findings of Nee and Sanders's (1985) study of the residential mobility of Asian immigrants in Los Angeles, within the first decade after their arrival many immigrant families "buy up" into ethnically mixed, suburban neighborhoods. Thus, in 1990, 58 percent of Filipino households in metropolitan areas of the nation were located in suburbs, up from 49 percent in 1980 (these data come from Alba, Logan, Stults, et al. 1999). The comparable 1990 figure for whites is only modestly higher, 67 percent. The lowest suburbanization percentage among Asian groups is found for the Chinese, who have long-standing urban enclaves (Nee and Nee 1973/1992; Zhou 1992), but their 1990 figure, 46 percent, still represents a substantial increase from what it was a decade before (38 percent), despite the heavy immigration of ethnic Chinese during the 1980s. Rates of suburbanization are on average lower for Latino groups, although they are near 50 percent for two of the three largest, Mexicans (46 percent in 1990) and Cubans (51 percent).

The obvious question is whether suburbanization will have the same meaning for new immigrant groups that it held for older ones. There cannot be a definitive answer at this point in the history of the new immigration; the available indicators yield a mixed picture. In any event, one has to recognize that the term "suburbia" now covers such a vast range of residential contexts that a single, unqualified answer is ultimately unlikely. On one side of the ledger is the indisputable existence of extensive suburban ethnic enclaves, such as Monterey Park in Los Angeles (Horton 1995). The huge Los Angeles barrio is also for the most part outside of the central city. While these are but two examples, and relatively extreme ones, evidence of a more general pattern comes from the Alba-Logan analyses of the predictors of suburban residence in the 1980 and 1990 censuses (Alba and Logan 1991; Alba, Logan, Stults, et al. 1999). Specifically for Asian groups, they find that during the 1980s suburban residence became much less selective of the linguistically assimilated. This suggests that barriers to suburban entry have fallen for freshly arrived immigrants, who may not speak English well. They can now reside in suburbia without detriment to their ability to function in daily life (for example, in shopping or recreational activities), presumably because they find sufficient numbers of co-ethnics and an ethnic infrastructure in their vicinity. However, among Latino groups, linguistic assimilation is more consistently a predictor of suburban residence. It should also be noted that, among all immigrant groups, suburban residence is linked to higher socioeconomic position, as the spatial-assimilation model would predict.

On the other side of the ledger is the strong evidence that suburbanization means greater residential integration with non-Latino whites, the racial and ethnic majority. This finding emerges from the Alba-Logan analyses of who lives in which neighborhoods. After socioeconomic standing, residence in a suburb rather than a city is the strongest predictor of the percentage of non-Hispanic white in the neighborhoods where Asians and Latinos live; even in the metropolitan regions most affected by the new immigration—and where, therefore, many new immigrants are potential neighbors—this variable still typically adds about twenty percentage points to the share of the neighborhood constituted by the racial and ethnic majority. Perhaps this has little bearing for the immigrants themselves, who may find enough co-ethnics in their vicinity to maintain a life like the one they would have in a more traditional ethnic enclave, but it is likely to have a considerable impact on their children, who grow up in contexts that bring them in frequent contact with whites and members of other groups in schools and in play groups.

The evidence on residential patterns exhibits a contradictory quality that is probably inevitable at an early stage in the unfolding of the consequences of large-scale immigration. Immigrant groups are rather strongly concentrated in a small number of metropolitan regions, which continue to receive the bulk of the immigration stream. Within these regions, the immigrant groups are not strongly segregated from the majority population, and their exposure to non-Hispanic whites through their neighborhoods increases rather predictably with improvements in English-language proficiency, income and education, and the purchase of a home or movement to the suburbs. While these seem like signs of incipient spatial assimilation, it is too early to draw such a conclusion, and much more research is needed on the impact of residential context. We are not yet able to say with any confidence whether residence in an area with many members of the majority is necessarily associated with greater and more socially intimate contact with the majority. There is also a dearth of data about forms of ethnic affiliation, such as ethnic churches, that might serve as agents of ethnic socialization for the children of suburbanized immigrants. Given the significance of suburbanization for many new immigrant groups, such questions demand more research attention than they have received.

CONCLUSION

Assimilation as a concept and as a theory has been subjected to withering criticism in recent decades. Much of this criticism rejects assimilation out of hand as hopelessly burdened with ethnocentric, ideological biases and as out of touch with contemporary multicultural realities. It has been common in this critique to portray assimilation as reliant on simplistic conceptions of a static homogeneous American culture and to target the normative or ideological expression of assimilation, Anglo-conformity. While we think that this criticism is frequently unfair in that it fails to consider, and properly discount, the intellectual and social context in which the canonical statements of assimilation were written, we recognize that it often enough hits the mark. But there is danger in the view of many critics that they have provided a strong rationale for rejecting assimilation rather than for amending it. We believe that the latter is the appropriate course, for assimilation still can make a powerful contribution to an understanding of the contemporary ethnic scene in the United States. It must, in our view, remain part of the theoretical tool kit of students of ethnicity and race, especially those who are concerned with the new immigration.

One challenge that must be faced is whether the language of assimilation can bear this refashioning. If the terminology of assimilation is so freighted with bias and ambiguity, as many critics believe, then perhaps it must be abandoned and a new vocabulary invented, even if this merely redeploys some of assimilation's conceptual arsenal. We think a change in language would be unwise. Assimilation has had a central place in the American experience, and the issue of the continuity between the experiences of European Americans and those of new immigrant groups lies at the very heart of the doubts about the relevance of assimilation for the contemporary United States. To invent a new vocabulary is, in effect, to foreclose the examination of this issue with a terminological solution, separating contemporary realities from past ones with new words. The question of continuity must be left open.

In the most general terms, assimilation can be defined as the decline, and at its endpoint the disappearance, of an ethnic and racial distinction and the cultural and social differences that express it. This definition does not assume that one of these groups must be the ethnic majority; assimilation can involve minority groups only, in which case the ethnic boundary between the majority and the merged minority groups presumably remains intact. Assimilation of this sort is not a mere theoretical possibility, as the assimilation of many descendants of earlier Caribbean black immigration into the native African American group indicates. Nevertheless, the type of assimilation that is of greatest interest does involve the majority group. The definition given here avoids a pitfall common to conventional definitions, which focus exclusively on the minority ethnic group, assuming implicitly that only it changes. By intent, our definition is agnostic about whether the changes wrought by assimilation are one-sided or more mutual. Indeed, there should be no definitional prescription on this point, for it is likely that the one-sidedness of the changes depends on the minority group, the era, and the aspect of group difference under consideration. Language acculturation in the United States appears to be overwhelmingly one-sided, even if American English contains many borrowings from other tongues, indigenous and immigrant, for we still understand the English of the British and they ours, indicating that our language has not strayed very far from its roots. Acculturation in some other areas—cuisine is the most obvious perhaps—is more mutual.

The above definition of assimilation is formulated at the group level, and the next question is: How is it to be translated to the individual plane?

Here there may be no alternative to defining assimilation in a more one-sided manner. It seems impossible to discuss assimilation at the individual level in any meaningful way as other than changes that make the individuals in one ethnic group more like, and more socially integrated with, the members of another. When assimilation implicates both majority and minority groups, the assimilation of individuals of minority origins involves changes that enable them to function in the mainstream society. From their point of view, acculturation, say, takes place in the direction of the mainstream culture, even if on another plane that culture is itself changing through the ingestion of elements from minority cultures. Over time, then, the cultural and social distance that minority-group individuals traverse while assimilating may narrow.

Though its definition of assimilation requires modification, the canonical account, especially as extended in the direction suggested by Shibutani and Kwan, has much to offer to the analysis of contemporary immigrant groups. Assimilation as a social process is in progress along a variety of indicators, as our review of the evidence indicates. The socioeconomic mobility of the new immigrants shows a distinct bimodal pattern. Human-capital immigrants in particular appear to be experiencing substantial economic and residential mobility. By contrast, labor migrants have made slower progress, a finding that Borjas has attributed to the very low educational attainment of migrants from Central America and other underdeveloped regions of the world. Analyses of spatial assimilation show a mixed pattern of ethnic concentration and residential mobility. Labor migrants appear to concentrate in ethnic communities, while human-capital immigrants show rapid transition to suburban residence and are less likely to congregate into dense settlement patterns. Not only does the early evidence attest to assimilation as a social process being experienced to a greater or lesser extent by new immigrants, but it is difficult even to discuss the new immigration without encountering the need to refer to the very substantial literature on assimilation. Only by contrasting differences and similarities between the old and new immigration will scholars gain a deeper understanding of the meaning of ethnicity in this new era of immigration.

Notes

1. We view "racial" distinctions as a type of "ethnic" distinction, one in which physical characteristics constitute part of the way that a group is socially defined (for a reasoned justification of this usage, see Waldinger and Bozorgmehr 1996a). In our usage, then, the term "racial" is implied in "ethnic." Because this usage is not universal, however, we sometimes use both terms to remind the reader that our discussion includes racial as well as nonracial ethnic groups.
2. Korean immigrants have concentrated in small businesses as a strategy of accommodation (Min 1996). While Korean immigrants have achieved significant economic gains through ethnic enterprise, South Asian immigrants are the ethnic group with the highest median income of any group in the United States (Portes and Rumbaut 1996). South Asian immigrants have not established ethnic enclave economies.
3. English-speaking Filipino and South Asian human-capital immigrants find professional and white-collar jobs in the mainstream economy; consequently they are the least likely of the Asian immigrant groups to establish ethnic enterprises, and they also do better economically than the Korean immigrants (Farley 1996; Min 1984). The exceptionally high self-employment of Koreans has stimulated numerous studies of small-business participation among Korean immigrants. In explaining the rise of the Korean ethnic economy, some scholars point to South Korea's export-driven economy, which provides entrepreneurial opportunities for Korean immigrants (Kim 1981; Light and Bonacich 1988). Others have advanced a disadvantage hypothesis, according to which Korean immigrant entrepreneurship is viewed as a rational response of predominantly college-educated, urban, middle-class immigrants who lack English-language skills to limited opportunities in the mainstream economy (Kim 1985; Min 1984; Yoon 1991, 1996). In their view, Korean entrepreneurship is an emergent phenomenon.

8 Toward a Reconciliation of "Assimilation" and "Pluralism": The Interplay of Acculturation and Ethnic Retention

Herbert J. Gans

FOR MUCH OF THE LAST HALF of the twentieth century, sociologists of ethnicity have been classified into two positions that are usually described as assimilationist or pluralist.[1] The positions have long been widely used, but even so, they suffer from at least three conceptual and other shortcomings.

First, the empirical researchers placed in one or the other position are frequently conflated with the normative thinkers so that the former are then wrongly characterized as favoring that position. Sometimes empirical researchers are even being accused of hiding their norms behind empirical language. (A possible solution, for which it is probably too late, would be to use different concepts for empirical and normative purposes.) In any case, my purpose in writing this essay is strictly empirical.

Second, even among empirical researchers, the discussion about whether the descendants of the now "old" European immigration and the members of today's "new" mainly non-European one are assimilating socially, economically, and culturally or whether they are retaining significant ties to their ethnic heritage has become polar. As a result, what is in reality a range of adaptations is sometimes being turned into a dichotomy, and a moral one, with the alleged assimilationists, and particularly "straight-line theory," becoming the villains in a social scientific morality play.

Third, the labels attached to each position are adding to the polarization, for they are misleading. The so-called assimilationists have actually been emphasizing acculturation (becoming American culturally but not necessarily socially), while pluralism has taken on such a multiplicity of meanings that it is no longer useful as an empirical concept. Consequently, I will call the latter, that is, those who seek to avoid acculturation and to retain ethnic ties, ethnic retentionists, and shall hereafter write about acculturationists and retentionists.

When positions are polarized and start hardening into theoretical ones inured to further data, empirical research—and straight thinking with it—suffer.[2] Before the study of the new immigration is distorted in this fashion, the either-or polarization should be put to rest as soon as possible.

Fortunately, the polarization is almost entirely unnecessary, and this chapter suggests a reconciliation between the two positions.[3] It does so by using two arguments. One argument is that if acculturation is distinguished from assimilation, it is clear that acculturation begins in the immigrant generation, although researchers may qualify it as "partial" or "additive" (Gibson 1989). It is not accompanied by assimilation, however.

Even the third generation, which may have become almost entirely acculturated, still retains a significant number of ethnic social ties, particularly familial ones, and cannot be said to have assimilated. However, this is not at odds with ethnic retention theory, for most of its advocates are concerned mainly with the retention of ethnic social ties and place less emphasis on cultural retention.

The other argument suggests that whatever empirical differences remain between the two empirical positions may be a result of differences both in the research and in the researchers, particularly those collecting their own survey, interview, or ethnographic data. The original students of the European immigration who developed the acculturationist position probably obtained much of their data from second-generation adults, while the data about the new immigration is coming mainly from first-generation adults. Although studies of the second generation are becoming increasingly popular already, these are so far conducted mainly among schoolchildren and teenagers who still live with their parents and are under more retentionist pressures from their parents than they will be later.

Furthermore, the major researchers and theorists of the European immigration were, as Robert K. Merton (1973) put it, outsiders who were neither members of nor had any great personal interest in the groups they studied. Many of their contemporary successors, however, are insiders who often come from the ethnic groups they are studying and may be personally concerned with the survival of these groups. Thus, as a result of who was studied and of the perspectives of the two cohorts of researchers, an overly acculturationist theory of the old immigration has arisen, as well as an overly retentionist theory of the new immigration.

Like Merton, I use insiders and outsiders as empirical concepts, and the observations in this chapter are not intended as criticism of either. The research of both is needed for the full understanding of any set of immigrants or other group.[4]

Acculturation and Assimilation

My distinction between acculturation and assimilation is hardly original, for it was conventional usage at the University of Chicago in the late 1940s. I use it here because I consider it more helpful to understanding immigrants and their descendants than the single concept used by Alba and Nee (1997) or the overly detailed seven-item concept proposed by Milton Gordon (1964). The Chicago distinction, of which both Gordon and Alba and Nee are aware, is based on the difference between culture and society, and accordingly, acculturation refers mainly to the newcomers' adoption of the culture, that is, the behavior patterns or practices, values, rules, symbols, and so forth, of the host society (or rather an overly homogenized and reified conception of it). Assimilation, on the other hand, refers to the newcomers' move out of formal and informal ethnic associations and other social institutions and into the host society's nonethnic ones.[5]

The major virtue of the original Chicago distinction is to underline the generations of empirical research demonstrating that acculturation and assimilation operate at different speeds (Rosenthal 1960). By the third generation, the descendants of the newcomers are culturally almost entirely American and often lack interest in or even knowledge of their ancestors' origins. Still, the opportunity for any but the most formal or superficial assimilation into American primary and secondary groups may not even become available until the third generation.

There are at least two reasons why acculturation is always a faster process than assimilation. That ever-changing mix of old WASP and modern immigrant features that we call American culture is an immensely powerful and attractive force for immigrants—and was already powerful even before they encounted this country's mass media.[6] The media still entices the children of most immigrants, particularly those coming from societies that lack their own commercial popular cultures. Indeed, historically few ethnic cultures have been able to compete with American popular culture, and even religious groups that keep their young people separate from it, like the Amish and Chassidim, must provide some form of substitute. This could change, at least for today's immigrants who come from countries with their own commercial popular cultures, although for the moment most of the world's popular cultures are still young enough to be influenced by, or imitations of, American popular culture.[7]

Second, ethnics can acculturate on their own, but they cannot assimilate unless they are given permission to enter the "American" group or institution.[8] Since discrimination and other factors often lead to the denial of that permission to the immigrant, and even to the second generation, assimilation will always be slower than acculturation.[9]

When the assimilation-acculturation distinction is used in research, researchers immediately notice the virtually inevitable lag of assimilation behind acculturation. If researchers' personal values do not influence data collection, and all other things are equal, empirically inclined retentionists should come up with virtually the same finding as their acculturationist peers: that little assimilation is taking place even as the old country culture erodes. In that case, however, the empirical differences between the acculturationists and retentionists begin to shrink, at least if conceptual differences do not get in the way. Moreover, even the normative dispute should decline, at least among retentionists who place great value on the survival of the ethnic community but are less concerned with the preservation of the immigrant culture.

To be sure, the distinction between the cultural and the social that I have drawn here cannot always be applied empirically, for the retention of the ethnic community also involves the retention of some ethnic cultural practices, particularly those that are intrinsic to ethnic institutions such as the family and other primary groups, practices that therefore cannot be ended without virtually destroying these groups. For example, if members of the second generation remain loyal to the immi-

decade, a movement was popularly, but incorrectly, interpreted as a larger ethnic revival among "white ethnics" (Gans 1979). However, what might today be called identity has long expressed itself on a small scale on factory floors and in other workplaces where minor conflicts of various kinds have often been displaced on ethnic joking (Halle 1984, 181). Overt ethnic conflicts, including violent ones, in which ethnic identity also plays a role have been part of American history for a long time.

It is too early to tell what forms today's major expressions of identity—personal, group, or both—will take among the second generation, since most of its members are still too young for college or the workplace. In addition, identities may change in the passage from adolescence to adulthood. Perhaps some of these expressions will be associated with cultural retention and an effort to resist the temptations of assimilation sometimes even available to nonwhite second-generation college students heading for predominantly white campuses. Moreover, identities can also be reactions to events in the larger society, so that, for example, the resurgence of ethnic identity feelings among California Mexicans could be a response to that state's anti-immigrant politics (Rumbaut 1997a).

Richard Alba (1990) and Mary Waters (1990) had already indicated in their 1990 volumes that ethnic self-naming or self-identification is usually accompanied by continued acculturation and assimilation, including intermarriage. However, even the more intense search for personal identity, either at the level of feelings or action, can be an accompaniment to acculturation and even assimilation, with identity becoming an actual or symbolic substitute for ethnic cultural practices and affiliations. In fact, developing an identity or getting involved in identity groups can sometimes be easier, especially for the second generation, than trying to fight the temptations of acculturation or retaining "boring" ethnic practices. In any case, there need be no inherent contradiction between identity and acculturation, and the two processes can operate independently.

Moreover, the history of the European immigrants suggests that identity is more apt to develop among racial groups and white ethnics living amid whites, and white nonethnics (as on college campuses), in multiracial or ethnic neighborhoods, or in areas fighting external threats such as the arrival of lower-status newcomers. Conversely, people who are embedded in homogeneous white ethnic neighborhoods or organizations and have little to do with nonethnics need not even be aware of their identity. A good example is New York City's socialist movement, which was so heavily Jewish that immigrants and second-generation Jews in it had no reason to pay attention to their ethnic identity.[18]

Ethnic identity is also compatible with assimilation. For example, ethnic group leaders may lead public lives in the ethnic community while devoting part of their private life to assimilatory activities, including those leading to their upward mobility. Furthermore, since part of their ethnic leadership requires them to associate with leaders from the dominant groups in society, they may even be participating in some on-the-job assimilation, voluntary and involuntary, if only in order to be able to work with leaders of dominant groups (see, for example, Kasinitz 1992).

Racial minorities diverge in these respects from ethnic groups because racial identity, or at least racial pride, is almost always required to fuel struggles against the white majority and racial discrimination. Immigrants who are also members of racial minorities may be shedding their old country culture, but whatever their ethnic identity, the racial identity they have had to develop in the United States could have unexpected implications for their ethnic identity (see Rumbaut 1997a).

Since immigrants and the next generation may be involved in future conflicts over multiculturalism, culture wars, and identity politics, if not necessarily today's versions thereof, researchers will have many opportunities to chart the connections between these activities, acculturation, and ethnic retention. They can also observe whether and how seemingly dissimilar reactions can occur concurrently.

Immigration and Ethnic Researchers

A final way of approaching the reconciliation of the acculturationists and retentionists involves the researchers themselves. We, the people who are doing the actual research, too often leave ourselves out of the analysis because the field retains remnants of the asocial positivism once dominant in the social sciences, which ignored the social beings who were doing the research. When researchers understand, however, that they are an intrinsic part of their own research, and when they then compare studies concerned with the earlier European immigrants and today's newcomers, two differences that can affect their findings, and thus also their respective positions, become apparent.[19]

First, the two sets of researchers have studied immigrants at different times; second, they are themselves different in origin and values. With some exceptions, the researchers who studied the European immigrants did not really begin their empirical research until the 1920s, at least forty years after the first eastern and southern Europeans arrived in large numbers. The major empirical study of the Chicago School, Louis Wirth's *The Ghetto,* was published in 1928, and the major ethnic volume of the 1930s "Yankee City" studies of W. Lloyd Warner and his associates, *The Social Systems of American Ethnic Groups* by Warner and Leo Srole, appeared in 1945. The first major sociological study of Italians in America was by Caroline Ware (1935); the second, by Irvin Child, appeared in 1943.[20]

Moreover, only a few of the sociologists of the time came from eastern European backgrounds and thus neither spoke nor were encouraged to learn the immigrant languages. As a result, the researchers probably got most of their data from the second generation, including much of what they learned about the immigrants. Consequently the picture of a homogeneous and holistic immigrant culture was most likely affected by nostalgic recall.

More important, what was most visible to the researchers about the second generation was its public acculturation rather than its more private ethnic retention. In addition, as I pointed out earlier, the researchers could not have met many of the most determined retentionists, since these would have returned to the old country before World War I. However, they also saw no social assimilation, either because it did not exist often enough or because they failed to notice it, or both.[21]

It is no wonder, then, that the early researchers supported the "contact" theory that Robert Park had first developed in the 1910s, although the influence of Park or his colleagues and students on the next generations of ethnic researchers was surely relevant as well.

Furthermore, the European immigrants came to America at a time of rapid and almost continuous economic growth. Although some worked in ethnic enclaves and never had to learn English, many were employed in the larger American economy. Economic growth encouraged yet others to leave their jobs in the ethnic enclaves, however, and that in turn encouraged acculturation. To be sure, the business cycle did not abate when the immigrants came, but no social scientists were around to study how the immigrants fared during the terrible depressions at the end of the nineteenth century, or even during the one that followed just after World War I. Admittedly, the Yankee City studies took place during the Great Depression, and no one has yet figured out how and why the ethnics of Newburyport, Massachusetts, hardly an affluent city even in better times, continued to acculturate and to provide one of the models for straight-line theory.

The researchers who are now studying the new immigration report on a very different set of newcomers. For one thing, they began their research much more quickly than the earlier researchers, and they have obtained their data directly from the first generation. Moreover, that first generation is very different from the one written about by the researchers of the old European immigration. Among other things, many are middle-class and highly educated, especially among the Southeast Asian, South Asian, Middle Eastern, and Caribbean immigrations, and thus they are very different from the almost entirely poor and often illiterate immigrants who came from Europe a century or more ago.

Since today's researchers are studying the immigrants, they naturally see more retention than acculturation (Alba and Nee 1997, 850). Because so many of the immigrants are nonwhite, they will experience even less social assimilation, and because the parts of the economy in which many of them work are growing less slowly or more irregularly than those of a century ago, they will experience less economic assimilation, too.[22] In addition, the researchers are obtaining more accurate pictures of the old country cultures (few of which are as preindustrial as those left behind by the old European immigrants) than the museumlike versions the first ethnic researchers often learned from the second generation they studied.

Because today's researchers are seeing first-generation life up close, they also see its dynamic qualities, the immigrants' need or temptation to change practices and associates in unpredictable ways to respond to the opportunities or exigencies of the moment, and to retreat to the bosom of the ethnic or racial group when dominant group politics turns against them or other disasters strike. Last but not least, as I suggested previously, the second generation they now see still lives largely at home and must obey ethnic and other parental dictates.

No wonder, then, that theories of assimilation may not make sense to many of today's researchers, and that some feel the need to express their doubts about such theories. They see little or no acculturation among the first generation, and even less assimilation. They are gathering evidence of ethnic retention in the second generation, especially among middle-class children (see, for example, Rumbaut 1995), even as they report the acculturation and attempted assimilation of lower-class adolescents, for example, West Indians and Vietnamese, who reject their old country of origin to join (or try to join) native-born neighborhood gangs (Woldemikael 1989; Zhou and Bankston 1994).

All this differs sharply from most of the findings reported about, and the assimilation or straight-line theory applied to, the earlier immigrants. Although the rejection of straight-line theory by today's researchers is understandable, it may also be somewhat premature, and may yet be contradicted when today's second generation reaches the same life cycle position as the second generation studied by the researchers of the old immigration.

The Researchers, Old and New

There is, however, yet another set of reasons why today's ethnic researchers see so much ethnic retention where their predecessors saw acculturation. The first ethnic researchers were largely *outsiders* vis-à-vis the people they studied; today's are more often *insiders,* and that difference further helps to explain their divergent findings.[23]

The distinction between insiders and outsiders is not hard and fast. Accordingly, the terms are also not easily defined. For my purposes here, insiders and outsiders can be defined—overly simply, to be sure—either by their ancestry or by their values, or by both criteria.[24] If the definition emphasizes ancestry, the issue is whether the researchers share the ethnic, racial, or other origins of the people they study. When the researchers cannot be asked directly, last names sometimes offer a clue to ancestry.

If the values criterion is applied, the issue is whether the researchers favor ethnic retention, cultural or social, or whether, whatever their values as outsiders, they are neutral toward and unconcerned with the groups' ethnic futures. This criterion is fairly easy to apply in empirical research if and when retentionists build their values explicitly into their research questions or state them openly. The task becomes more complicated when values have to be inferred from the theoretical and empirical questions researchers ask or the concepts and frames they use.[25]

The studies of researchers remain to be done, and what follows here is a set of hypotheses about the insider-outsider status of the two eras of immigrant researchers, with an emphasis on the sociologists among them who conducted empirical studies.

Most of the researchers who first studied the European immigration were outsiders—and for two good reasons. First, American empirical sociology did not exist when the European immigration began in the 1870s. Indeed, much of the Chicago School immigration research took place in and after the 1920s, when Congress ended the European immigration. Second, the European immigrant groups were too poor to have their own social science researchers.[26] In fact, it took most of them two or three generations—and the help of the GI Bill after World War II—to choose social science research careers.

As a result, the pioneer immigrant researchers, for example, Robert Park, Ernest Burgess, W. I. Thomas, Caroline Ware, and Lloyd Warner, were mostly WASPs, although hardly upper-class ones. Almost all were also assimilationists, but not necessarily deliberate ones. If they favored the Americanization of the immigrants, they unthinkingly reflected both the conventional wisdom and values of their era and their class, particularly in the decades when a kind of retentionist alternative was mainly to be found in anthropology.

Rather, they were researchers who generally considered themselves value-neutral even if they were not. Too many sometimes used the racist vocabulary then still being applied to immigrants and their descendants, and most ignored the nonwhite immigrants who also came to America during the European immigration (DeWind and Kasinitz 1997, 1104).[27]

A few of the first empirical researchers were insiders by background—for example, Louis Wirth and Leo Srole were Jewish—but virtually all were outsiders in terms of their values.[28] After World War II, however, sociologists from a variety of ethnic backgrounds, and predominantly from the second generation, undertook empirical research. A large number applied outsider values, including those who wrote only about their own group and those who moved into comparative ethnic research, for example, Milton Gordon, Tamotsu Shibutani, and, in the next cohort, Richard Alba,

Steven Steinberg, and Mary Waters, among others.[29]

Concurrently, however, other sociologists of ethnic origin from the same post–World War II cohort have written as apparent or actual retentionists. Although they may report evidence of acculturation, they emphasize exceptions or accompany their findings with warnings that the ethnic community—or in the case of Jews, the religious one—must act to stop these trends. In the Jewish community they have sometimes been described as survivalists; they include Stephen Cohen, Nathan Glazer, and Marshall Sklare. Like-minded researchers from other ethnic groups are, for example, Richard Gambino, Andrew Greeley, and Peter Kivisto.[30]

The students of the new immigration seem to be following a speeded-up version of the pattern that developed among their European predecessors. The first researchers, among them Edna Bonacich, Ivan Light, Philip Kasinitz, and Roger Waldinger, were once more outsiders by ancestry. However, the new immigrants of middle-class origin often included some social science researchers, or they sent their young people, a few from the "1.5 generation," into graduate sociology programs. Many have come from Southeast Asian families, among them Won Moo Hurh, Illsoo Kim, Pyong Gap Min, and Min Zhou, although South Asian, Middle Eastern, African, Latino, and Caribbean researchers have also entered the field.

The immigrant, 1.5, or second-generation newcomers are insiders by ancestry, and many study, or begin their careers by studying, their own groups. As early as 1984, 86 percent of the references in a "Selected Bibliography on Korean-Americans" bore Korean or other Asian names (Hurh and Kim 1984, 259–71).[31] My impression, which still requires empirical testing, is that many often follow insider values as well.

This pattern is continuing among new cohorts of young researchers in the 1990s. Thus, a study of 138 researchers applying for grants (most for dissertations) to the Social Science Research Council's Migration Division in 1997 showed that 53 percent were studying their own groups; 18 percent were looking at groups other than their own; and 29 percent were writing on general or comparative topics.[32] However, among the 65 applicants whose racial or ethnic background suggested that they or their parents were newcomers, 80 percent were studying their own group, and 20 percent were writing on general topics.[33] No one was studying groups other than their own.

There are two exceptions to the insider pattern described here. One is disciplinary: only one-fifth of all political scientists applying to SSRC, but 70 percent of sociologists, were studying their own group.[34] Although it is possible that disciplinary career pressures account for this difference, a more likely explanation is self-recruitment. American sociology has always attracted significant numbers of immigrants or their descendants.[35]

The other exception to the insider pattern described here is associated particularly with poor or non-English-speaking immigrant groups that have not yet produced social science researchers. Thus, the earliest student of poor Southeast Asian groups, such as the Hmong, the Laotians, and the Cambodians, has been the Cuban immigrant Rubén Rumbaut, although his comparative study was initially planned to include a sample of Cuban immigrants as well.[36] The first writings about the Russian newcomers have come from native-born American researchers such as Rita Simon, Nancy Foner, and Steven Gold. Some groups have been studied by both insiders and outsiders, for example, Mexicans, Puerto Ricans, West Indians, and South Asians.

Since most of the newcomer studies are about the immigrants, research about them will necessarily yield a predominance of retentionist findings, since few newcomers, at least among the adults, will have had time for much acculturation—or for attaining a position allowing them to assimilate into American groups. That so many of the researchers are insiders only reinforces this pattern, especially if and when the insiders also adhere to retentionist values. Still, even outsiders who study the first generation are likely to find more retention than acculturation, not to mention assimilation.

Various other characteristics of the new immigration research can be explained by the fact that the subjects of study are immigrants. One is the emphasis on so-called entrepreneurial activities, since immigrants with any kind of capital have traditionally turned to storekeeping or petty manufacturing, using their profits to educate their children for higher-status jobs. Most likely, they are also more often retentionists than people who go to seek their fortune in the larger economy—if only for the instrumental reason that their incomes often depend on their fellow immigrants.[37]

However, the second generation, once grown into adulthood, will have some choice between various kinds of retention and acculturation. Those who intermarry, particularly with whites, can even achieve assimilationist goals, thus overturning the old finding derived from the European immigration that intermarriage and related kinds of social assimilation are available only to later generations.

Unless political or economic conditions bring about a sudden halt to further immigration, many of today's immigrant groups are going to be replenished by further sets of newcomers just as the second generation of the post-1965 arrivals enters adulthood in large numbers. Nonetheless, their degree of choice about retention and acculturation should not be affected by the concurrent replenishment process.[38] As a result, the insider or outsider status, in background or values, of the researchers who study this second generation will begin to matter, for the researchers could use their values, theories, and concepts to produce findings that diverge, at least to some extent, from the behavior and values of the people they study.[39] Still, what they could do in theory is no guide to what they will do in practice. After all, it is also possible that the second generation of researchers who will begin to appear in visible numbers some time early in the twenty-first century will not be the same kinds of insiders and outsiders as today's researchers.

Conclusion

The study of the new immigration is only just beginning, and as already indicated, most of the ideas about the second generation so far have been based on data about schoolchildren. "So far" is an important qualifier, however, and as immigration research expands and the second and then the third generations grow to adulthood, studies of the new immigration are apt to come up with findings different from today's. Although we now know how much assimilation depends on economic and political processes that make immigrants and their descendants either attractive or threatening to other Americans, the findings about acculturation may not be very different in the long run from those accumulated about the European immigration.

Those findings cannot be completely similar, however, because the United States and the world have changed drastically since the earlier European immigration. In addition, while the Europeans were also viewed as darker races when they arrived, they were able to become white more easily than is possible for many of today's nonwhite immigrants.

My personal hunch is that in the long run students of the new immigration will report findings similar to many of the past findings of rapid acculturation and slower assimilation. However, as long as researchers are divided into insiders and outsiders, a modified version of the present division between acculturationists, value-neutrals, and retentionists will also continue.

Whatever the disadvantages of that tripartite division and the disagreements it generates, there are also advantages. Despite the wish of some sociologists for less "fragmentation" and for the restoration of a "core," such a core is also apt to be dominated by one paradigm or "school," with a decline of vitality as one result. The reappearance of a core in immigration research seems unlikely, however, and the present diversity of researchers and frames may even increase. The members of this diverse field should therefore know—or learn—how to understand their differences, and to understand also how much they themselves contribute to divergent findings and theories.

Consequently they must transcend the largely dismal record of self-awareness and self-examination encouraged by positivism and scientism and begin instead to study their own research—and themselves—as a regular part of their research. If socially structured, such reflexivity will help make sure that differences of findings or perspectives do not turn into polarization and transform disagreeing researchers into enemies or villains.

In the long run, the danger of polarization should decline as the proportion of insider and outsider researchers is more balanced, and the special contributions each can make are realized. In addition, the continuing diversity of the American population, enhanced no doubt by future sets of newcomers, will not be kind to theoretical and other intellectual polarizations among the researchers.

My thanks to Richard Alba, Margaret Chin, Stephen Cornell, Jennifer Lee, Roger Waldinger, and an anonymous reviewer of this volume for helpful comments on earlier versions of this essay.

Notes

1. The same division has existed among sociologists studying religions associated with ethnic groups, such as Judaism.
2. I should note that such theoretical polarization is more likely if it accords with or accompanies political-ideological polarization, for example, about issues that di-

vide the left and right, or those involving race, nationalism, and other subjects being debated or fought over in the larger society.

3. The observations and hypotheses of this essay were partly inspired by the comprehensive analytic defense of assimilation by Richard Alba and Victor Nee (1997) and its later version (this volume). The inspiration stems from Alba and Nee's choice of a single concept, assimilation, to cover all the various cultural, social, and other processes that it entails. It set me off on a stimulating intellectual path that led to some related and many unrelated ideas.
4. In the long run, more balance between insider and outsider research is desirable. At present such balance is impossible, either because not enough outsiders or insiders are studying particular groups—for example, no insider researchers yet exist—or outsider research cannot even be undertaken because some immigrant groups do not make themselves accessible to interviewing and other face-to-face research by outsiders.
5. Although I was a graduate student at the University of Chicago in the late 1940s, I did not know the origin of the distinction, and some additional research for this essay has not reduced my ignorance. Robert Park had already distinguished between the two terms twenty-five years earlier but saw both as referring to culture, pointing out that "ethnologists" used acculturation for "primitive societies" while sociologists, who studied "historical peoples," used the term "assimilation" (Park and Burgess 1921, 771). They even indicated briefly that "social structure changes more slowly than material culture," but they illustrated their thesis with examples from preindustrial societies. (749–50).

   Perhaps the coteaching by the university's sociologists and cultural anthropologists that began in the mid-1940s, as well as the increasingly visible acculturation of the descendants of the European immigrants and the continued social discrimination against them, produced the distinction that I was taught. However, the earliest publication using it that I could find was Erich Rosenthal (1960), who had also been a teacher of mine in the 1940s.
6. In fact, the mass media many first encountered were the silent movies that were shown in storefronts in New York's Lower East Side and other immigrant neighborhoods beginning early in the twentieth century.
7. As a result, some researchers of the new immigration suggest that the newcomers are already somewhat familiar with American culture before they come. This raises the fascinating question of what, and how much, the American culture transmitted over the mass media, which is mostly entertainment, teaches prospective newcomers about the United States and how to live there. It also supplies a new site and population to study the old question of what effects the mass media have on people's behavior and values. My thinking about these matters has been helped by personal communication with Robert Smith and Roger Waldinger.
8. For an earlier, somewhat similar analysis that distinguishes between the acceptance of newcomers depending on whether they are superordinate or subordinate to the indigenous population, see Lieberson (1961).

When newcomers are denied assimilation for a long ime, ethnic and racial minorities often set up parallel stitutions that are similar to those that have rejected them, for example, country clubs, debutante balls, and other organizations and activities that help to demarcate high status. Researchers need to find out whether this pattern will be repeated among the newcomers—and what variations will occur among the many Asian Americans who are marrying native-born whites.

10. Likewise, Stephen Steinberg (1981) has shown that sometimes the third generation remains loyal to some family practices only until the grandparents die.
11. Won Moo Hurh and Kwang Chung Kim (1984, 27) call attention to other involuntary factors, such as ethnic segregation and economic and ecological conditions in the host society.
12. Here is a good example of where polarization can hurt research, since generally each "side" is likely to ask only questions that reflect its own hypotheses.
13. Strictly speaking, the advocates of reconstruction and invention were at odds with what Alba and Nee (1997) call canonical assimilation theory.
14. The immigrants may share similar national, or homeland, loyalties, but only if and when they come from functioning nations or feel allegiance to a common homeland. Many of the newcomers arrive, just as did many of the European immigrants, with hatred of the nation-state that oppressed or exploited them, or they come from countries where identification with the nation-state was limited to urban residents or members of the dominant "tribes."
15. For a veritable catalog of Jewish American ethnic inventions that Americanize and acculturate Jewish religious and secular practices brought over from Europe, as well as other inventions that Judaize American practices that had found favor with the immigrants and their children as they moved up the American class structure, see Joselit (1994).
16. For useful discussions of the problems of defining and of researching identity, see, for example, Alba and Nee (this volume) and Yinger (1994, 156–57).
17. I would also want to distinguish what people name themselves for outside consumption—for example, if asked while performing a variety of roles in the larger society; and for inside consumption, how they would describe or name their ingroup identity.
18. Admittedly, socialist ideology did not encourage interest in ethnicity and ethnic identity, despite the later amalgamation of socialist and nationalist goals, for example, in Zionism. Also, actual socialist organizations, particularly outside New York City, divided themselves along ethnic group lines.
19. My argument here is based on a sociology of knowledge approach from the work of Karl Mannheim (1936), who emphasized that research theories and findings reflect the researchers' "perspectives," which in turn result in part from where they stand vis-à-vis the people studied—and, I would add, the methods and concepts used to study them.
20. A third, William Foote Whyte's classic *Street Corner Society* (1943), appeared the same year, but while the fieldwork was done among Boston's North End immigrant and second-generation Italians and the book is still widely read half a century later, it is not normally read as an ethnic study.
21. They could, of course, have noticed it among the descendants of the earlier European immigration, from Ireland and northern Europe, but the Chicago School was so concerned with studying the new immigrants

that, for example, Park and Burgess (1921) never mentioned the earlier arrivals at all in their various lengthy discussions of assimilation and Americanization.

22. Some of the retention among Southeast Asians, South Asians, and Caribbeans is deliberate, established to maintain their economic position and social status in an America where nonwhites are often almost automatically assigned to the working or lower classes (see, for example, Gibson 1988; Waters 1996).
23. I am indebted to Merton's classic essay (1973), even though I use somewhat different conceptions of insiders and outsiders.
24. Needless to say, a full definition would require even more criteria, as well as the generational, class, and other factors that qualify their ancestry and impinge on their values.
25. Other conceptions and definitions of the two types of researchers deal with the quality and kinds of insights, theories, and findings each is best able to develop. Merton raised these issues in his 1973 article, but they are beyond the scope of this analysis.
26. For this reason alone, it would be interesting to study the novelists, journalists, and other writers who undertook quasi-sociological research among their own people.
27. Some were opposed to immigration and the European immigrants and believed in the genetic inferiority of the European immigrants and blacks. The immigration researchers were probably less guilty of what we now call racism than some of their fellow social scientists, but retrospectively, it is difficult to establish who simply repeated the conventional wisdom of the WASP intellectual and professional strata of the day and who was guilty of more personal and more extreme racism. It is possible, however, to identify the researchers who were politically active in efforts to restrict immigration or discriminate against blacks.
28. This is particularly true of Wirth, whose 1928 book about Chicago's West Side Jewish ghetto was often openly critical of many of the eastern European Jews he studied. Actually, as a middle-class Jew of German origin, Wirth was an outsider by origin as well, since at that time the class, religious, and ethnic differences, not to mention antagonisms, between Jews from eastern and western Europe were considerable. Perhaps he is best classified as a hostile insider.
29. Some began by studying their own group and then moved on to others or to more comparative research, among them Richard Alba and this author.
30. Many little-known ethnic researchers write in retentionist tones about their own ethnic groups, but their works are often published by ethnic presses that generally do not reach the national research community.
31. Most of the remaining 14 percent of the citations were American or other "Anglo" names (computed by this author).
32. This pattern is only somewhat stronger among the applicants for dissertation grants, presumably the youngest. Of the 88 whose topics I could classify, 58 percent were studying their own groups and 18 percent other groups, with the remaining 24 percent researching general or comparative topics.

    The data on which this analysis is based come from the proposal titles and subtitles, as well as the ethnic or racial self-identifications, of the year's 150 grant applicants, minus the 18 for which I was unable to determine whether they were studying individual groups or not. I am grateful to Josh DeWind, the director of the SSRC International Migration Program, who proposed analyzing the SSRC applicants, provided a first rough count, and then made the data available for my analysis.

    For a subsequent discussion of outsiders and insiders, see Gans (1999a, 1306–09); for a more comprehensive survey of insiders and outsiders, spanning four generations of migration researchers, see Rumbaut (1999a).
33. I selected this group from applicants who identified themselves as Latino, Asian (including South Asian), Caribbean, or African.
34. The remaining 81 percent of the sixteen political scientists were studying general topics. (Even so, three of the eight political scientists whom I identified as newcomers were studying their own groups.)

    Conversely among the thirty-seven sociologists (who are the subjects of this part of the paper), 19 percent were looking at groups other than their own and 11 percent were researching general topics. Among sociologists I classified as newcomers (twenty-four of the thirty-seven), all but one was studying his or her own group.
35. The children of some recent immigrants, for example, Koreans or Vietnamese, interested in American history might have problems finding enough study topics in the short history of their groups in America. In any case, this kind of analysis needs to be undertaken for all the social science disciplines.
36. None of the SSRC applicants indicated they were studying Hmong, Cambodians, Vietnamese, or Laotians, but not all the applicants specified in their subtitles which Asians or Asian Americans they were studying. Even so, judging by last names at least, Korean researchers constituted the largest number of Asian researchers, although not all indicated they were studying Korean populations.
37. Entrepreneurs are also easier to study, being fewer in number, more visible, and more concentrated than immigrants who have gone to work in the larger economy.
38. Here I disagree with some researchers, including Alba and Nee (1997, 843), who believe that the constant replenishment by new immigrants will slow down acculturation. The new immigrants will surely replenish immigrant institutions deserted by earlier arrivals, but they either do not associate with the earlier immigrants, may be rejected by them as "greenhorns" if they try, or are exploited economically if they are employed by them. Thus, they have few opportunities for any replenishment of the earlier immigrants, but in any case, are usually more concerned with becoming as Americanized as they are.
39. By then, disciplinary differences among researchers may also have to be considered, at least if anthropologists studying the United States maintain their current preoccupations with and sympathies for preindustrial or exotic culture and are thus more likely to be retentionist than the sociologists.

9 Assimilation and Its Discontents: Ironies and Paradoxes

Rubén G. Rumbaut

I have endeavoured to guard myself against the enthusiastic prejudice which holds that our civilization is the most precious thing that we possess or could acquire and that its path will necessarily lead to heights of unimagined perfection. . . . One thing only do I know for certain and that is that man's judgments of value follow directly his wishes for happiness—that, accordingly, they are an attempt to support his illusions with arguments.

—Sigmund Freud, *Civilization and Its Discontents* (1930/1961, 110–11)

Material goods have gained an increasing and finally an inexorable power over the lives of men as at no previous period in history. . . . In the field of its highest development, in the United States, the pursuit of wealth, stripped of its religious and ethical meaning, tends to become associated with purely mundane passions, which often actually give it the character of sport. . . . For of the last stage of this cultural development, it might well be truly said: "Specialists without spirit, sensualists without heart; this nullity imagines that it has attained a level of civilization never before achieved."

—Max Weber, *The Protestant Ethic and the Spirit of Capitalism* (1904–5/1958, 182)

Precisely because a particular action is not carried out in a psychological or social vacuum, its effects will ramify into other spheres of value and interest. . . . The empirical observation is incontestable: activities oriented toward certain values release processes which so react as to change the very scale of values that precipitated them. . . . Here is the essential paradox of social action—the "realization" of values may lead to their renunciation.

—Robert K. Merton, "The Unanticipated Consequences of Purposive Social Action" (1936, 902–3)

What it all comes down to is that we are the sum of our efforts to change who we are. Identity is no museum piece sitting stock-still in a display case, but rather the endlessly astonishing synthesis of the contradictions of everyday life.

—Eduardo Galeano, *The Book of Embraces* (1991, 124–25)

Few concepts in the history of American sociology have been as all-encompassing and consequential as "assimilation," or as fraught with irony and paradox. Few have so tapped and touched the pulse of the American experience. That master concept long ago penetrated the public discourse and seeped into the national narrative, offering an elemental explanation for a phenomenal accomplishment—the remarkable capacity of a self-professed nation of immigrants to absorb, like a giant global sponge, tens of millions of newcomers of all classes, cultures, and countries from all over the world.[1] And yet, few concepts have been so misused and misunderstood, or erected on such deep layers of ethnocentric pretensions. Few have so thoroughly conflated the real with the rhetorical, the idea with the ideal and the ideological, mixing descriptions of what is observable with prescriptions of what is desirable. And few have so tellingly entailed and entangled an attempt to support national illusions with arguments.

There is a certain fateful passivity and one-wayness implied in "assimilation." As it is most commonly used—which is to say, unthinkingly—the term connotes a more or less fixed, given, and recognizable target state to which the foreign element is to "Americanize," dissolving into "it," becoming, in that elusive and expansive word, "American." That exosmotic usage recalls the no-nonsense coerciveness of Theodore Roosevelt's plain formulation of a century ago: "There can be no fifty-fifty Americanism in this country . . . there is room here only for 100 per cent Americanism, only for those who are American and nothing else."[2] But it also recalls Ralph Linton's devastating spoof of the "100 Per Cent American,"[3] as well as Henry James's contemporary critique of Roosevelt (1898/1992, 253): "Impaired . . . by the puerility of his simplifications," James wrote bitingly in 1898, "Mr. Roosevelt makes very free with the 'American' name, but it is after all not a symbol revealed once for all in some book of Mormon dug up under a tree. Just as it is not criticism that makes critics, but critics who make criticism, so the national type is the result not of what we take from it, but of what we give to it, not of our impoverishment, but of our enrichment of it."

That critical interactive view was not, to be sure, in vogue in sociological treatments of the subject around midcentury. In *The Social Systems of American Ethnic Groups* (1945), for example, Lloyd Warner and Leo Srole described the straight-line "progressive advance" of eight immigrant groups in the major status hierarchies of "Yankee City" (Newburyport, Massachusetts), explicitly linking upward social mobility to assimilation, which they saw as determined largely by the degree of ethnocultural (religion and language) and above all racial difference from the dominant group. While "racial groups" were subordinated through caste restrictions on residential, occupational, associational, and marital choice, the clash of "ethnic groups" with the dominant institutions of the "host society" was not much of a contest, particularly among the young. The polity, the industrial economy, the public school, the American family system, all undercut and absorbed ethnicity in various ways, so that even when "the ethnic parent tries to orient the child to an ethnic past . . . the child often insists on being more American than Americans" (284). And for the upwardly mobile, with socioeconomic success came intermarriage and the further dilution of ethnicity.[4]

That view of assimilation as linear progress, with sociocultural similarity and socioeconomic success marching in lockstep, was not so much challenged as refined by Milton Gordon in *Assimilation in American Life* (1964), published ironically on the eve of the beginning of the latest era of mass immigration to the United States—and of the denouement of the concept itself in the wake of the 1960s. He broke down the assimilation sequence into seven stages, of which "identificational assimilation"—that is, a self-image as an unhyphenated American—was the end point of a process that began with cultural assimilation, proceeded through structural assimilation and intermarriage, and was accompanied by an absence of prejudice and discrimination in the "core society." Once structural assimilation (extensive primary-level interaction with members of the "core group") had occurred, either in tandem with or subsequent to acculturation, "the remaining types of assimilation have all taken place like a row of tenpins bowled over in rapid succession by a well placed strike" (81). For the children of white European immigrants, in fact, the acculturation process was so "overwhelmingly triumphant" that "the greater risk consisted in alienation from family ties and in role reversals of the generations that could subvert normal parent-child relationships" (107). Still, what it was that one was assimilating to remained largely taken for granted.

Gordon was aware of the ways in which the ideal and the ideological get wrapped up in the idea of assimilation, and he saw "Anglo-conformity" as the most prevalent ideology of assimilation in American history.[5] But he was about to be ambushed by the unexpected: he could not have guessed at the time, not even in a wild flight of fancy, what was in store for both American society and his assimilation paradigm. What had seemed like a bland and straightforward enough description—an observable outcome of adaptation to new environments, a familiar process of "learning the ropes" and "fitting in" through which "they" become like "us," a convergence hypothesis, a sort of regression to the mean[6]—was to become an explosive and contested prescription, value-laden with arrogant presumptions of ethnic superiority and inferiority and fraught with the bitter baggage of the past and the fractious politics of the present. By 1993, after years of academic neglect and disrepute, no longer privileged in intellectual circles as either proverbial or canonical, Nathan Glazer could ask, matter-of-factly, "Is Assimilation Dead?"

Yet no sooner was that funereal question posed than, in what may be yet another of the pendulum swings that have characterized scholarship on American immigration, incorporation, and ethnicity in this century—as well as an effort to rescue the baby from the bathwater—several major essays appeared that provide thoroughgoing reappraisals of the sociology and historiography of assimilation, casting a critical look not only at the concept, theory, and latest evidence but also at the historical contexts that have shaped the ideas and ideals embodied in the notion of assimilation (see especially Alba and Nee 1997; Barkan 1995; Kazal 1995; Morawska 1994). Thus, Kazal (1995) sees the apogee of the concept in the 1950s and early 1960s as reflecting the need generated by World War II for national unity and the postwar tendency to see American history as a narrative of consensus rather than conflict; and the political and social upheavals of the 1960s as shattering the "consensus school" and the rationale for studying assimilation, bringing back instead a focus on the ethnic group and ethnic resilience and more inclusive conceptions of American society. "To know how immigrants came to fit in, one had to understand what it was they were fitting into. . . . When the notion of an Anglo-American core collapsed amid the turmoil of the 1960s, assimilation lost its allure" (1995, 437). The point is well taken, an invitation to a self-reflexive sociology of knowledge that is keenly conscious of the fact that all our theories of reality are socially and historically grounded (see the essays in Kivisto and Blanck 1990).

Still, in the ideological contest, partly through policies and programs of "Americanization" and other intentional efforts, coercive or not, to make a process described by social observers into a practice prescribed by the guardians of the social order; partly by the patronizing ethnocentrism built into assumptions about immigrant adjustment that equated "foreign" with "inferior" and the ways of the "host" or "core" society and culture with "superior"; partly as a product of the linear logic of a positivist narrative within which the tale, and the *telos,* of assimilation is told; indeed, partly as a corollary to the central myth of progress at the heart of the core culture[7]—in these and other ways it became difficult to disentangle the rhetorical from the historical, and the use of the term itself was tarred with the suspicion that an Anglo-conformist demand hid within it, like an ideological Trojan Horse. As a result, as Alba and Nee (1997) argue, "assimilation as a scientific concept has fallen into undeserved disrepute."

It is in these conceptual interstices between theory, rhetoric, and reality that irony and paradox emerge (or at least what may appear paradoxical from the vantage of the prevailing worldview). By focusing on ironies and paradoxes—on evidence that contradicts orthodox expectations and points instead to assimilation's discontents—my aim in this chapter is to test empirically the conception of assimilation as a linear process leading to improvements in immigrant outcomes over time and generations in the United States, to unmask underlying pretheoretical ethnocentric pretensions, and to attempt to identify areas in need of conceptual, analytical, and theoretical refinement. For it is precisely through the examination of ironic and paradoxical cases—in effect, deviant case analyses of "outcomes of events that mock the fitness of things"[8]—that fruitful reformulations can be stimulated, considered, and advanced.

Assimilation and Its Discontents

A few years ago, I heard a Vietnamese physician present data he had collected each year since 1975 on blood cholesterol levels of Vietnamese children in Connecticut. As the only co-ethnic physician in the area, he provided primary health care services for the bulk of Vietnamese families who had been resettled there—including routine annual physical exams and blood tests. The results of those blood tests among the children showed that their cholesterol levels increased without exception for each year of residence in the United States. On reflection, that by-product of assimilation to the American diet should surprise no one, but that is not, needless to say, the sort of assimilative upward mobility that Warner and Srole (1945) had in mind.

Nor does it fit with the view that assimilation is a more or less linear process of progressive improvement in the immigrant's adjustment to American life. That view is premised on an implicit deficit model: to get ahead immigrants need to learn how to "become American," to overcome their deficits with respect to the new language and culture, the new health care and educational systems, the new economy and society. As they shed the old and acquire the new over time, they surmount those obstacles and make their way more successfully—a process more or less completed by the second or third generation. Since today's immigration is overwhelmingly composed of newcomers from developing nations in Asia and Latin America, concerns have been raised about the speed and degree to which they can become assimilated—and hence about the social "costs" of the new immigrants—before they begin to produce net "benefits" to the new society. Recent research findings, however, especially in the areas of immigrant health, risk behavior, educational achievement, and ethnic self-identity, raise significant questions about such assumptions. Indeed, the findings often run precisely in the *opposite* direction of what might be expected from traditional perspectives on assimilation. Some of those findings on the relationship of assimilation, broadly conceived, to various types of outcomes are highlighted below.

Epidemiological Paradoxes: Is Assimilation Hazardous to Infant Health?

It seems only appropriate to begin at the beginning: with babies. Over the last decade a remarkably consistent and compelling body of evidence about the pregnancy outcomes of immigrant and native-born women has been emerging that turns the usual hypotheses about assimilation and socioeconomic status on their head. In particular, the research literature has pointed to an infant health "epidemiological paradox" among new immigrants (Markides and Coreil 1986). It turns out that high-risk groups, particularly low-income immigrants from Mexico and Southeast Asia, show unexpectedly favorable perinatal outcomes. When these findings first came to light, particularly with reference to those classified as Hispanics, there was a tendency to dismiss them as a result of migration selectivity or incomplete data. After all, immigrants of lower socioeconomic status, such as refugees from Vietnam, Cambodia, and Laos and undocumented migrants from Mexico, El Salvador, and Guatemala, generally combine high fertility rates with high poverty rates and face formidable barriers in accessing health care and prenatal care services (Rumbaut et al. 1988). Conventional wisdom would expect these least "Americanized" groups of disadvantaged newcomers to exhibit worse-than-average health outcomes, but the opposite is true. Indeed, it soon enough became clear that these results could not be explained away by special circumstances or bad data.

In one of the first such reports, R. L. Williams, N. J. Binkin, and E. J. Clingman (1986) analyzed data from California's matched birth-death cohort file for four groups: non-Hispanic whites, blacks, U.S.-born Hispanics (mostly of Mexican descent), and Mexican immigrants. In terms of maternal risk factors, the Mexican-born women had less education, more children, shorter birth spacings, and a later start to prenatal care than any of the other three groups. Yet, in terms of perinatal outcomes, the Mexican-born women had the lowest percentage of low-birthweight babies, the lowest postneonatal infant mortality rates, and neonatal and total infant mortality rates that just matched those of the lower-risk white mothers. African Americans had the highest rates in these categories, followed by U.S.-born Hispanics and whites. The authors could not explain why the Mexican immigrants, despite their adverse socioeconomic circumstances and higher risk factors, produced such positive outcomes, but they speculated that it could be "the result of better nutrition, lower rates of smoking and alcohol consumption, or a higher regard for parental roles . . . [or that] migration has selected out healthier individuals among newly arrived Latinos" (1986, 390). An earlier study had found similarly that Chinese Americans had lower fetal, neonatal, and postneonatal mortality rates than whites and other major ethnic and racial groups, and the superior health profile of Chinese infants was observed at every level of maternal education and for all maternal ages (Yu 1982). Again, the available vital statistics lacked data with which to measure possible explanatory factors.

We reported similar evidence in a study of linked live birth and infant death records in San Diego County for the period 1978 to 1985, covering some 270,000 live births (Rumbaut and Weeks 1989). The data showed that the infant mortality rate was lowest for Southeast Asians (6.6 per 1,000), followed by other Asians (7.0), Hispanics (7.3), non-Hispanic whites (8.0), and African Americans (16.3). In fact, among the Southeast Asians, the lowest infant death rates in the county were found for the Vietnamese (5.5) and the Cambodians (5.8). These highly positive outcomes were all the more remarkable because the Indochinese refugee groups (including the Vietnamese) had significantly higher rates of poverty, unemployment, welfare dependency, fertility, prior infant mortality (before arrival in the United States), and late use of prenatal care services than any other racial or ethnic group in the San Diego metropolitan area, and because a high proportion of refugee mothers came from rural backgrounds and had little or no prior education or literacy, proficiency in English, or readily transferable occupational skills. We also found that those results were not unique to San Diego but were reflected statewide. In 1985 the state of California began publishing data on live births and infant deaths for more detailed ethnic groupings, including Vietnamese and Cambodians, using mother's place of birth as the principal criterion for ethnic identification. We compiled these statewide data and confirmed that during the late 1980s the Cambodians and Vietnamese had infant mortality rates of 5.2 and 7.5, compared to 7.7 for Mexican-born women and 8.5 for non-Hispanic whites (Weeks and Rumbaut 1991). These differences were statistically significant. But just what it was that explained these differences could not be determined on the basis of the available vital statistics. The Indochinese and Hispanics had lower infant mortality rates regardless of whether the mother was a teenager or not, and regardless of whether the mother was married or not; the findings also held after controlling for birthweight and onset of prenatal care.

Other regional studies with widely different ethnic populations in different parts of the country have reported similarly unexpected outcomes. In Illinois, J. W. Collins and D. K. Shay (1994) discovered that foreign-born Mexican and Central American mothers residing in very-low-income census tracts had much better pregnancy outcomes than either Puerto Rican or other U.S.-born Hispanics. In Massachusetts a study of low-income black women served by Boston City Hospital found significant differences in health behaviors and birth outcomes between natives and immigrants—the latter mostly from Haiti, Jamaica, and other Caribbean and African countries (Cabral et al. 1990). Compared to the U.S.-born, the foreign-born women had better prepregnancy nutrition; they were far less likely to use cigarettes, marijuana, alcohol, cocaine, or opiates during pregnancy; and they gave birth to babies who were larger in head circumference and significantly less likely to be of low birthweight or premature—health advantages that remained even after controlling for many of the factors suspected to influence fetal growth.

Research with national-level data sets confirms these findings across the board, while their significance grows: by 1995 foreign-born mothers accounted for nearly one-fifth of all U.S. births (18 percent), but over four-fifths (82 percent) of all Asian-origin babies and nearly two-thirds (62 percent) of all Hispanic-origin babies in the United States were born to immigrant women (see Landale, Oropesa, and Gorman 1999). A recent review of the literature (Eberstein 1991) cites research indicating that among blacks and Hispanics nationally, pregnancy outcomes (birthweight, infant mortality) are better for babies born to immigrant than to native mothers. Among Hispanics, an analysis of the 1983 and 1984 national data sets showed that infant mortality and low birthweight rates were lower for babies born to foreign-born versus U.S.-born Mexican and Cuban mothers, and for island-born versus mainland-born Puerto Rican mothers—again, despite a lack of correspondence between the socioeconomic profiles of these Hispanic groups and their health outcomes (Becerra et al. 1991).

More conclusive evidence comes from a new study using the 1989, 1990, and 1991 Linked Birth/Infant Death national data sets (Landale, Orapesa, and Gorman 1999). The study examined the birth outcomes of immigrant versus native-born mothers among ten ethno-racial groups—Chinese, Filipino, Japanese, other Asian, Mexican, Puerto Rican (island-born versus mainland-born), Cuban, Central and South American, non-Hispanic blacks, and non-Hispanic whites. The babies of immigrant mothers had lower rates of prematurity, low birthweight, and infant mortality than those of U.S.-born mothers. For each of the main groups, native-born mothers were also more likely than foreign-born mothers to be young (less than twenty) and single, and to have smoked cigarettes during their pregnancies. In multivariate models the gap in birth outcomes by nativity and ethnicity was attenuated, but the offspring of immigrant mothers retained a health advantage over those of native-born mothers.

We attempted to unravel the reasons for this infant health paradox by examining an in-depth data set drawn from the Comprehensive Perinatal Program (CPP) in San Diego County providing prenatal care services to low-income pregnant women (see Rumbaut and Weeks 1996, 1998). The CPP data set consisted of nearly five hundred independent variables per case (including most of those listed in the research literature as likely biomedical and sociocultural determinants of pregnancy outcomes) for a large sample of both foreign-born (mostly immigrants from Mexico and various Asian countries) and U.S.-born women, matched to infant health outcome measures collected from hospital records for every baby delivered by CPP mothers from 1989 to 1991. The analysis focused on the identification of maternal risk factors that best explained observed ethnic or nativity differences in pregnancy outcomes, such as birthweight, diagnoses at birth, complications, and length of hospitalization of the baby. Our findings suggest that caution should be exercised in jumping too quickly to conclusions based solely on racial classifications, nativity status, education, or length of time in the United States. For instance, it turns out that the best infant health outcomes were observed for certain "Asian" immigrant groups (the Indochinese, who were also the least educated of all), but the worst outcomes for a "white" immigrant group (Arab Muslims from countries in the Middle East, who were also the most educated of all). And while immigrants indeed do better than natives overall, the most assimilated immigrants (white Europeans and Canadians) do worse than U.S.-born Asians, Hispanics, and blacks.

Still, given these caveats, the following general

picture emerges from our data: Asians and Hispanics (mostly foreign-born) clearly had superior outcomes relative to non-Hispanic whites and blacks (mostly U.S.-born); and within racial and ethnic groups, outcomes were better for immigrants than for natives. Specifically, native-born women (who in this sample were mainly non-Hispanic whites) were significantly more likely than immigrant women (who in this sample were mainly Mexicans and Indochinese) to: have higher levels of education, employment, and per capita income; be taller and heavier and to gain more weight during their pregnancies; have had fewer live births and more abortions; have diets lower in fruits and cereals and higher in fats and milk products; report more medical conditions, especially venereal disease and genitourinary problems; smoke, abuse drugs and alcohol, and be at risk for AIDS; have a personal history of significant psychosocial problems, including having been a victim of child abuse and now of spousal abuse, and having currently stressful relationships both with the father of the baby and with their own family and parents; be depressed, considered at risk psychosocially, and referred to a social worker; and have generally poorer pregnancy outcomes—which is why infant health outcomes seem to worsen as the levels of education, English literacy, and general assimilation of the mother increase. In this context, then, part of the assimilation puzzle begins to clear up: that is, relative to the foreign-born in this sample of low-income women, the comparative socioeconomic advantages of the U.S.-born appear to be overwhelmed by biomedical, nutritional, and psychosocial disadvantages.

The Hispanic Health and Nutrition Examination Survey (HHANES) of 1982 to 1984, with a very large regional sample of Mexicans, Puerto Ricans, and Cubans, has also provided a wealth of evidence that contradicts orthodox theoretical expectations. For example, low-birthweight rates were significantly higher for (more acculturated) second-generation U.S.-born women of Mexican descent compared with (less acculturated) first-generation Mexico-born women, despite the fact that the latter had lower socioeconomic status, a higher percentage of mothers over thirty-five years of age, and less adequate prenatal care (Guendelman et al. 1990). The risk of low birthweight was about four times higher for second- than first-generation primiparous women, and double for second- over first-generation multiparous women. Other studies based on the HHANES have also observed this association between greater acculturation and low birthweight (Scribner and Dwyer 1989). In addition, first-generation Mexican women, despite their socioeconomic disadvantages, had a lower risk of eating a poor diet than second-generation Mexican American women, whose nutrient intake resembled that of non-Hispanic white native women (Guendelman and Abrams 1995). For the immigrants, food choices actually deteriorated as income increased—and as the degree of assimilation increased (as indicated in this study by generational status).

Findings from the HHANES have shown a link between increasing acculturation and health risk behaviors (Marks, García, and Solis 1990), cigarette smoking (Haynes et al. 1990), and drug use (Amaro et al. 1990; see also Vega and Amaro 1994). Adverse effects of acculturation have also been reported among Mexican Americans with respect to alcohol consumption patterns (Gilbert 1989) and psychological distress (Kaplan and Marks 1990). Indeed, intriguing questions have been raised by recent research on the mental health of ethnic minorities in the United States, including immigrants and refugees. A review of prevalence rates reported in the most important research studies conducted over the past two decades suggests that rapid acculturation does not necessarily lead to conventionally anticipated outcomes (Vega and Rumbaut 1991). Thus, teenage children of middle-class Filipino immigrants, the most "Americanized" of contemporary Asian-origin newcomer groups and among the most socioeconomically advantaged, exhibit higher rates of suicidal ideation and attempts than most other immigrant groups (Kann et al. 1995; Rumbaut 1994b, 1999; Wolf 1997).

Adolescent Health and Risk Behavior: Patterns of Intra- and Intergenerational Assimilation

Perhaps at no stage of the life course are assimilative processes more intensely experienced, or assimilative outcomes more sharply exhibited, than during the formative years of adolescence. A new source of data—the National Longitudinal Study of Adolescent Health ("Add Health")—provides a unique opportunity to examine intragenerational and intergenerational processes and outcomes of assimilation among a large, nationally representative sample of adolescents. The data come from the first wave of the study, which in 1995 surveyed over twenty thousand adolescents (and their parents) enrolled in grades seven to twelve in eighty high schools drawn from a stratified probability sample of high schools nationwide, and it included an oversample of high-income black youth and several ethnic samples. The sample includes sizable numbers of immigrant children and children of immigrants, and for the former data were collected on age at arrival and length of residence in the United States. An analysis focusing on physical health characteristics and risk behaviors of three generational groups—first (immigrant children), second (native-born children of immigrant parents), and third or higher (native-born of native-born parents) generations—broken down by major national-origin groups, provides a tell-tale test of the linear progress hypothesis (Harris 1999).

First, looking at intergenerational results, for virtually every empirical indicator, second-generation youth have poorer physical health outcomes and are more prone to engage in risk behavior than the foreign-born youth. In particular, Harris (1999) found that second-generation youth were more likely than the first generation to report poor or fair health, to have missed school owing to a health or emotional problem in the previous month, to have learning disabilities, to be obese,[9] to have asthma, to ever have had sex (and at a younger age), and to have engaged in deviant behaviors (delinquency, violence, or substance abuse). Outcomes for the third and later generations vary significantly across race and ethnic groups, but in general native minorities report the poorest health and the highest levels of risk behaviors. The findings, which remain after adjusting for age differences, suggest a strongly linear assimilative pattern—but in the direction of deteriorating rather than improving outcomes.

Second, looking at intragenerational results for the foreign-born youth (that is, by length of residence in the United States), the pattern of assimilation outcomes reinforces the above conclusion: the longer the time in and exposure to the United States, the poorer the physical health outcomes, and the greater the propensity to engage in each of the risk behaviors measured. Furthermore, a breakdown by national or regional origin for the most sizable subsamples—Mexico, Cuba, Puerto Rico (island-born versus mainland-born youth and parents), Central and South America, China, the Philippines, Vietnam, other Asia, Africa and the Afro-Caribbean, Europe, and Canada—generally confirm the intergenerational patterns, with outcomes worsening the further removed from the immigrant generation, most strongly among Mexicans and Filipinos. A main exception—where first-generation youth are more likely to engage in some risk behaviors than the second generation (earlier sexual initiation and more substance abuse)—involves, interestingly enough, youths who were in some respects more Americanized prior to immigration: those from the English-speaking Caribbean and from Europe and Canada.

Despite these positive results among immigrant youth, their families actually had the highest poverty rates in the sample (38 percent), while natives of the third and later generations had the lowest (20 percent). By contrast, third-generation youth were the least likely to live in intact families, and the most likely to live with a single parent, whereas second-generation youth were most likely to live with both natural parents.[10] Controlling in multivariate analyses for socioeconomic status, family structure, degree of parental supervision, and neighborhood contexts actually increased the protective aspects of the immigrant first generation on both physical health and risk behavior outcomes. In fact, on both of these outcome indices the results showed that every first-generation nationality (with the sole exception of island-born Puerto Ricans, who are not immigrants but U.S. citizens) had significantly fewer health problems and engaged in fewer risk behaviors than the referent group of native non-Hispanic whites. These findings vividly parallel those discussed earlier with respect to infant health and mortality and, while still consistent with a linear hypothesis of assimilation to native norms, run directly contrary to the expectation of progressive improvement over time.

The Assimilation of Criminal Propensities? A Look at Young Adult Men

Equally striking and unexpected are the results of a systematic analysis of patterns of incarceration among immigrants and natives in the United States over the past two decades; it suggests that "immigrants may assimilate to the (higher) criminal propensities of natives" (Butcher and Piehl 1997). The study, carried out by two economists, was intended as a contribution to the economic research literature and the public policy debate on the consequences of immigration, focusing on an outcome that had received virtually no scholarly attention despite its clear societal significance: the social costs of crime and punishment. Indeed, during the 1980s, a decade that saw the largest (legal and illegal) flows of immigrants to the United States since the turn of the century, the number of people incarcerated in state or federal prisons skyrocketed, doubling from 138 per 100,000 population in 1980 to 271 per 100,000 in 1989. In addition, since conventional theories of crime and incarceration predict higher rates for young adult males from racial and ethnic minority groups with lower educational attainment—characteristics that describe a much greater proportion of the composition of the immigrant population than of that of the native-born—it followed that immigrants would be expected to have higher incarceration rates than natives. But the results turned these expectations on their head.

The study used data from the 5 Percent Public Use Microdata Samples of the 1980 and 1990 censuses to measure the institutionalization rates of immigrants and natives at both time periods. Since only the 1980 census identifies the type of institutional setting (correctional facility, mental hospital, home for the aged, drug treatment center, or other institution), the analysis focused on men aged eighteen to forty, among whom the vast majority of the institutionalized are in correctional facilities. (For them, with disability status controlled, the data confirm that institutionalization is a good proxy for incarceration.) Among men aged eighteen to forty, immigrants in both 1980 and 1990 had significantly lower educational attainment than natives, with the gap widening over the decade; Mexicans accounted for fully 30 percent of all male immigrants in the United States in that age group. The institutionalization rate for men aged eighteen to forty increased sharply from 1980 to 1990, with the most dramatic increases registered among native-born blacks and Hispanics. But immigrant men had much *lower* institutionalization rates than the native-born in both 1980 and 1990, and the advantage for immigrants held when broken down by race or ethnicity and education; for example, the rates for U.S.-born blacks, whites, Asians, and Hispanics were consistently higher than for foreign-born blacks, whites, Asians, and Hispanics.

Butcher and Piehl (1997) examined the rates for national-origin groups and for refugees versus immigrants, finding that Mexicans and refugees had *lower* institutionalization rates than other immigrants and *much lower* rates than natives in both years; and that Cuban, Colombian, and Afro-Caribbean groups all had lower rates than natives in 1980 but somewhat higher rates in 1990—with the Cubans who came in the controversial 1980 Mariel boatlift having the highest rate of any group in 1990. (Indeed, many of them were placed directly into institutional facilities in the United States on arrival and were still held in 1990.) Still, in models controlling for country of origin and likely determinants of institutionalization, the only immigrant "group" that always had higher rates than native-born men was "country not specified." Further, the authors showed that "if natives had the same institutionalization probabilities as immigrants, our jails and prisons would have one-third fewer inmates"; conversely, "in 1990, if immigrants had the same 'returns' to their characteristics as natives, they would have almost double the institutionalization rates of natives" (1997, 34, 11).

Finally, to examine what happens as immigrants spend more time in the United States, the study focused on the experience and characteristics of different cohorts who had arrived at five-year intervals. Most of these cohorts of immigrants were found to be less likely to be institutionalized than the native-born, and the difference in institutionalization probabilities between natives and these cohorts only became wider as race, ethnicity, and education controls were added. More to the point, in both the 1980 and 1990 samples, the longer immigrants had resided in the United States, the higher were their institutionalization rates. (The sole exception involved those who arrived in the early 1980s, a cohort skewed by the composition of the Mariel entrants.) In other words, immigrants assimilate to the rates of the native born—but again, in this instance, the assimilative pattern is in the direction of worsening outcomes. For reasons that remained unclear, the more recent immigrants were not only less likely to be institutionalized (relative to natives) than earlier arrivals were after a similar length of residence in the United States, but also appeared to assimilate to native norms less quickly than earlier immigrants.

Educational Paradoxes: Is Assimilation Detrimental to Academic Achievement?

What is the relationship of immigrant assimilation to academic achievement? Given the enormous variability in the socioeconomic status of immigrant families in the United States today, their language handicaps, and the relative recency of arrival of so many, how does the school performance of their children stack up with that of natives' children? Relatively few studies, including a handful of ethnographies, have explored these questions systematically, but still, their results are also remarkably consistent and relevant to our concerns in this chapter.

Part of the difficulty in obtaining useful data to

address these issues is that school systems do not collect information on the nativity or immigration status of students or their parents. A rough proxy for immigrant family status may be obtained from the home-language census that is mandated by law in public school systems such as those in California to ascertain the English proficiency of students whose primary home language is not English. Those students are then assessed and classified as LEP (limited English proficient) or FEP (fluent English proficient). One large-scale study in the San Diego Unified School District (the country's eighth-largest, with a sizable and diverse immigrant population) obtained data on educational achievement for the entire high school student cohorts (all sophomores, juniors, and seniors, including all active and inactive students) for two periods: the 1986–87 and 1989–90 school years, covering a combined total of nearly eighty thousand students (see Rumbaut 1995; Portes and Rumbaut 1996). Among Asian and Hispanic students, about one-quarter spoke English only, while three-fourths spoke a language other than English at home (with a larger proportion of FEPs than LEPs overall among them, although varying greatly by national origin: the overwhelming proportion of Filipinos were FEP, while an equally large proportion of Cambodians and Laotians were LEP). Cumulative academic grade point averages (GPAs) earned by the students since the ninth grade were compared for all the ethnic groups by language status. The overall GPA for white non-Hispanic students was 2.24, above the overall district norm of 2.11, but (except for Hispanics) all of the non-English immigrant minorities outperformed their English-only co-ethnics as well as majority white students. This applied in most cases to FEP and LEP students alike, though clearly FEP students did significantly better. The highest GPAs were found for immigrant Chinese, Korean, Japanese, Vietnamese, and Filipino students. More remarkable still, even the Hmong, whose parents were preliterate peasants from the Laotian highlands (and who were at the time referred to derisively by U.S. Senator Alan Simpson as "the most indigestible group in society"),[11] and the more recently arrived Cambodians, who were mostly rural-origin survivors of the Khmer Rouge "killing fields" of the late 1970s, were outperforming all native-born English-only American students; and again this pattern applied for both FEP and LEP students among these refugee groups. This finding held for GPAs in both ESL (English as a Second Language) and mainstream courses; that is, the refugees' GPAs were not an artifact of the curriculum (Rumbaut and Ima 1988; see also Caplan, Choy, and Whitmore 1991).

A more systematic analysis of the educational progress of children of immigrants in San Diego city schools was recently provided by our Children of Immigrants Longitudinal Study (CILS).[12] Survey data (supplemented by academic records from the school system) were collected in 1992 (T1) and again over three years later in 1995–96 (T2). The T1 sample totaled 2,420 Mexican, Filipino, Indochinese (Vietnamese, Cambodian, Lao, and Hmong), and other Asian and Latin American students who were enrolled in the eighth and ninth grades in San Diego city schools (a grade level at which dropout rates are still relatively rare, to avoid the potential bias of differential dropout rates between ethnic groups at the senior high school level). Most of the respondents were fourteen or fifteen years old at T1, and the sample was evenly split by gender, grade, and generation: 45 percent were U.S.-born children of immigrant parents (the "second generation"), and 55 percent were foreign-born youths who immigrated to the United States before age twelve (the "1.5" generation).[13] Only 1.4 percent of the sample in San Diego checked "white" to a structured question on racial self-identification. The respondents were tracked over time, including students who dropped out or transferred from the school district, and over 85 percent (2,063) were successfully reinterviewed by T2. By that time most were about eighteen years old and entering young adulthood.

Academic GPAs for all schools in the San Diego district were compared against the GPAs earned in grades nine through twelve in those schools by the entire original T1 sample of 2,420 children of immigrants from 1992 to 1995. The result showed that at every grade level the children of immigrants outperformed the district norms, although the gap narrowed over time and grade level. For example, only 29 percent of all ninth-graders in the district had GPAs above 3.0, compared to a much higher 44 percent of the ninth-graders from immigrant families, and while 36 percent of ninth-graders districtwide had low GPAs under 2.0, only half as many (18 percent) of the children of immigrants performed as poorly. Those differentials declined over time by grade level, so that the advantage by the twelfth grade was reduced to a few percentage points in favor of the children of immigrants. Part of that narrowing of the GPA seemed to be due to the fact that a greater proportion of students districtwide dropped out of school than did the youth from immigrant families. The multi-year dropout rate for grades nine through twelve in the San Diego schools was 16.2 percent, nearly triple the rate of 5.7 percent for the entire original sample of children of immigrants. That dropout rate was significantly lower than the dropout rates for preponderantly native non-Hispanic white (10.5 percent) and black (17.8 percent) high school students. Among the students from immigrant families, the highest dropout rate (8.8 percent) was that for Mexican-origin students, but even that rate was noticeably lower than the district norm, and slightly lower than the rate for non-Hispanic whites.

These results are remarkable enough in view of the relatively low socioeconomic status of a substantial proportion of the immigrant families. They become all the more remarkable in the context of other school data. At T1 over one-quarter (29 percent) of the sample were classified as LEP, ranging from virtually none of the native-born Filipinos to around two-thirds of the foreign-born Mexican, Cambodian, and Hmong students. That classification is supported by nationally standardized ASAT (Abbreviated Stanford Achievement Test) scores measuring English reading skills: the sample as a whole scored just below the fortieth percentile nationally, and the foreign-born groups with the highest proportion of LEP students scored in the bottom quartile nationally. On the other hand, all groups do better in math computation than on English reading tests. At T1 their ASAT math achievement test scores placed the sample as a whole at the fiftieth percentile nationally, with some students achieving extraordinarily high scores (notably the "first-wave" Vietnamese and Chinese, Japanese, Indian, and Korean students, placing most of them in the top quartile nationally).

One key reason for these students' above-average academic GPAs, despite significant socioeconomic and linguistic handicaps, is elementary: they worked for it. At both T1 and T2 these students reported spending an average of over two hours per day on homework, with the foreign-born students compensating for language and other handicaps by significantly outworking their U.S.-born peers. (By comparison, national data suggest that American high school students average less than an hour daily on homework.) From the end of junior high at T1 to the end of senior high at T2, the level of effort put into schoolwork increased across all nationalities. The sole exception in this regard were the Hmong, who at T1 posted the highest average number of daily homework hours (2.9) but decreased to 2.6 hours at T2 (still above the sample average and well above the national average); not surprisingly, that drop in effort was matched by the drop in their GPAs from 2.92 (at T1) to 2.63 (at T2), the main drop in GPA among all the groups in the sample. Overall, the children of immigrants generally maintained their level of GPA attainment from T1 (2.80) to T2 (2.77).

In multivariate analyses at T1, examining a wide range of likely predictors, the number of daily homework hours emerged as the strongest single predictor of higher GPAs, while the number of hours spent watching television daily was significantly associated with lower GPAs (see Rumbaut 1995, 1997b). By T2 the data show that students who had dedicated more hours to schoolwork in junior high did significantly better in terms of educational achievement three years later. More significant for our purposes here is the *negative* association of length of residence in the United States and second-generation status with both GPA and educational aspirations. What is more, students whose parents were both immigrants outperformed their counterparts with one U.S.-born parent. Those results do not support a conventional linear assimilation hypothesis.

Similar findings on educational achievement, aspirations, and attitudes have been reported by Kao and Tienda (1995) using national-level data from the National Educational Longitudinal Study (NELS) with a 1988 sample of over twenty-five thousand eighth-graders, and by a secondary analysis of the earlier High School and Beyond (HSB) data set, with a sample of over twenty-one thousand tenth- and twelfth-graders followed since 1980 over a six-year period (Vernez and Abrahamse 1996), both finding a deterioration in outcomes over generations in the United States. Essentially the same general intergenerational pattern has also been reported in ethnographic case studies in California of Mexican-origin and Punjabi Sikh students (see Gibson 1989; Matute-Bianchi 1991), and by a comparative cross-generational and cross-national study using projective tests (such as the Thematic Apperception Test [TAT]) of Mexican, Mexican immigrant, Mexican American, and non-Hispanic white students (Suárez-Orozco and Suárez-Orozco 1995). And remarkably consistent results about the erosion of an ethos of achievement and hard work from the immigrant generation to the third generation have also been recently reported from a three-genera-

TABLE 9.1 Language Shifts, Ethnic Self-Identity, and Perceptions of Discrimination Among Children of Immigrants in San Diego, California, by Nativity of the Children and National Origin of Their Parents, 1992 (T1) and 1995 (T2)

Characteristics by National Origin and Nativity	*Time*	*Mexico*		*Philippines*		*Vietnam*		*Cambodia*	*Laos*		*All Others*		*Total*		
		FB	*US*	*FB*	*US*	*FB*	*US*	*(FB)*	*Lao (FB)*	*Hmong (FB)*	*FB*	*US*	*FB*	*US*	*TOTAL*
Language															
Prefers English	T1	32.1%	52.8%	81.4%	95.8%	43.9%	91.5%	67.0%	51.7%	66.0%	55.7%	92.9%	56.1%	78.4%	66.0%
	T2	62.5	78.2	92.6	98.0	69.0	91.5	85.2	74.1	58.0	72.7	99.0	75.8	89.8	82.0
Speaks English	T1	38.5	74.1	75.2	94.3	45.9	95.7	48.9	44.1	22.0	59.8	93.9	52.2	86.2	67.3
"very well"	T2	48.2	77.7	83.3	93.6	47.8	89.4	50.0	49.0	30.0	70.5	93.9	58.5	87.0	71.2
Speaks Non-English	T1	74.0	44.8	23.2	2.0	41.3	10.6	33.3	42.0	50.0	49.4	11.2	43.4	20.3	33.1
language "very well"	T2	78.1	49.9	23.0	3.6	38.7	4.3	33.3	40.6	44.0	50.6	18.2	43.7	25.7	36.3
Ethnic self-identity[a]															
"American"	T1	0.0	2.8	0.3	5.2	2.4	8.5	2.3	0.7	4.0	3.4	18.4	1.3	5.8	3.3
	T2	0.0	2.0	1.0	2.0	0.0	2.1	0.0	0.7	0.0	3.4	9.2	0.6	2.7	1.6
Hyphenated-American	T1	14.7	40.0	50.8	66.2	43.9	70.2	46.6	28.7	26.0	18.2	38.8	35.8	53.0	43.4
	T2	12.1	39.3	21.9	48.4	28.2	51.1	30.7	19.6	12.0	9.1	25.5	20.2	42.4	30.1
National origin	T1	33.5	8.2	41.8	21.5	45.9	19.1	40.9	61.5	62.0	44.3	11.2	44.3	15.7	31.6
	T2	67.9	26.3	72.7	42.5	56.1	36.2	48.9	67.1	48.0	18.2	11.2	60.7	32.3	48.1
Racial/pan-ethnic	T1	51.3	44.9	3.5	1.2	0.4	0.0	1.1	2.1	2.0	22.7	17.3	13.2	19.8	16.1
	T2	18.8	27.7	0.6	2.0	14.5	8.5	20.5	11.2	38.0	58.0	40.8	15.8	16.8	16.2
Mixed ethnicity, other	T1	0.4	3.7	3.5	5.9	7.5	2.1	9.1	7.0	6.0	11.4	14.3	5.4	5.7	5.5
	T2	1.3	4.8	3.9	5.2	1.2	2.1	0.0	1.4	2.0	11.4	13.3	2.7	5.7	4.0
Discrimination[b]															
Has experienced being	T1	62.5	63.8	60.8	66.2	65.5	70.2	61.4	71.3	56.0	64.8	58.2	63.7	64.5	64.0
discriminated against	T2	68.8	64.4	69.1	68.9	71.8	70.2	65.9	74.8	82.0	60.2	63.3	69.9	66.8	68.5
Expects discrimination	T1	33.5	35.6	35.0	41.0	33.3	40.4	38.6	46.2	40.0	29.5	32.7	35.8	37.9	36.7
regardless of merit	T2	39.3	38.4	43.7	44.2	36.9	40.4	39.8	43.4	50.0	42.0	31.6	40.9	40.7	40.8

Source: Children of Immigrants Longitudinal Study (CILS), San Diego sample, N = 2,063.
Notes: FB = Foreign-born; US = U.S.-born. Figures are column percentages.
[a] Responses to the open-ended survey question: "How do you identify, that is, what do you call yourself?" "Hispanic," "Chicano," "Latino," "Black," and "Asian" are classified as racial/pan-ethnic identities; a Hmong ethnic identity is included under "national origin"; "Cuban-Mexican" or "Chinese-Thai" under "mixed" identities.
[b] Responses to (1) an open-ended question on experiences of discrimination, and (2) an item asking to agree or disagree with the statement: "No matter how much education I get, people will still discriminate against me." Data above show percent who agreed.

tional study of a sample of eleven hundred secondary school students in California (Fuligni 1997), and from a survey of more than twenty thousand teenagers from nine high schools in Wisconsin and California (for an overall summary, see Steinberg 1996).

The Arrow and the Boomerang: Linguistic Assimilation and Ethnic Self-Identity

Similarly provocative findings come from our panel study (CILS) of the adaptation of children of immigrants in San Diego, described earlier, focusing for our purposes here on changes in their patterns of English preference and proficiency and in their ethnic self-identities. Indeed, language and identity are presumed to be intimately linked. A "straight-line" hypothesis would predict additional movement over time and generation in the direction of both increasing linguistic assimilation (Anglicization) and increasing identificational assimilation (Milton Gordon's term)—that is, of a primary self-identity as an unhyphenated "American." We can check that with the newly available evidence.

Our findings on language preference, a key index of cultural assimilation, are unequivocal. Over 90 percent of these children of immigrants report speaking a language other than English at home, mostly with their parents. But as seen in table 9.1, at T1 two-thirds of the total sample (66 percent) already preferred to speak English instead of their parents' native tongue, including 56 percent of the foreign-born youth and 78 percent of the U.S.-born. Three years later the proportion had grown significantly to over four-fifths (82 percent), including 76 percent of the foreign-born and 90 percent of the U.S.-born. The most linguistically assimilated in this respect were the Filipinos, among whom 93 percent of those born in the Philippines (where English is an official language) and 98 percent of those born in the United States preferred English by T2. But even among the most mother-tongue-retentive group—the Mexican-origin youth living in a Spanish-named city on the Mexican border with a large Spanish-speaking immigrant population and a wide range of Spanish radio and TV stations—the force of linguistic assimilation was incontrovertible: while at T1 only one-third (32 percent) of the Mexico-born children preferred English, by T2 that preference had doubled to 62 percent; while just over half (53 percent) of the U.S.-born preferred English at T1, that proportion had jumped to four-fifths (78 percent) three years later.

A main reason for this rapid language shift in use and preference has to do with increasing fluency in English (both spoken and written) relative to level of fluency in the mother tongue. Respondents were asked to evaluate their ability to speak, understand, read, and write in both English and the non-English mother tongue; the response format (identical to the item used in the U.S. census) ranged from "not at all" and "not well" to "well" and "very well." Over two-thirds of the total sample reported speaking English "very well" (67 percent at T1, and 71 percent at T2), compared to only about one-third who reported an equivalent level of spoken fluency in the non-English language. Naturally, these differentials are much more pronounced among U.S.-born youth, most of whom (87 percent) spoke English "very well" at T2, while only one-fourth of them could speak the parental language "very well." But even among the foreign-born, those who spoke English very well surpassed by 59 percent to 44 percent those who spoke the foreign language just as well.

And the differences in reading fluency (not shown) are much sharper still: those who could read English "very well" tripled the proportion of those who could read a non-English language very well (68 percent to 23 percent). Only the Mexico-born youth maintained by T2 an edge in their reported knowledge of Spanish over English, and even they nonetheless indicated a preference for English. The ability to maintain a sound level of literacy in a language—particularly in languages with entirely different alphabets and rules of syntax and grammar, such as many of the Asian languages brought by immigrants to California—is nearly impossible in the absence of schools that teach it and a community that values it and in which it can be regularly practiced. As a consequence, the bilingualism of these children of immigrants becomes increasingly uneven and unstable. The data vividly underscore the rapidity with which English triumphs and foreign languages atrophy in the United States—even in a border city like San Diego—as the second generation not only comes to speak, read, and write it fluently but gradually prefers it overwhelmingly over their parents' native tongue. This linear trajectory of rapid linguistic assimilation is constant across nationalities and socioeconomic levels and suggests that, over time and generation, the use of and fluency in the foreign language will inevitably decline—

and at an even faster clip than has been the age-old pattern in American history.

In both surveys, an identical open-ended question was asked to ascertain the respondent's ethnic self-identity. The results (and the wording of the question) are presented in the middle panel of table 9.1. Four main types of ethnic identities became apparent: a plain "American" identity; a hyphenated-American identity; a national-origin identity (such as Mexican, Filipino, Vietnamese); and a panethnic minority identity (for example, Hispanic, Latino, Chicano, Asian, black). The way that adolescents see themselves is significant. Self-identities and ethnic loyalties can often influence patterns of behavior and outlook independently of the status of the families or the types of schools that children attend. Unlike language, which changes in straight-line fashion, like an *arrow,* ethnic self-identities vary significantly over time—yet not in linear fashion but in a reactive, dialectical fashion, like a *boomerang.* The data in table 9.1 illustrate that pattern compellingly.

In 1992 almost one-third (32 percent) of the sample identified by national origin; the largest proportion (43 percent) chose a hyphenated-American identification; a small fraction (3.3 percent) identified as plain "American"; and 16 percent selected a panethnic minority identity. Whether the young person was born in the United States made a great deal of difference in the type of identity selected at T1: the foreign-born were three times more likely to identify by national origin (44 percent) than were the U.S.-born (16 percent); conversely, the U.S.-born were much more likely to identify as American or hyphenated-American than were the foreign-born, and somewhat more likely to identify in panethnic terms. Those findings at T1 seemed suggestive of an assimilative trend from one generation to another. But by the T2 survey—conducted in the months after the passage, with 59 percent of the vote, of Proposition 187 in California in November 1994—the results were quite the opposite from what would have been predicted by a straight-line identificational assimilation perspective.

In 1995 the biggest gainer by far in terms of the self-image of these youths was the foreign nationality identity, increasing from 32 percent of the sample at T1 to nearly half (48 percent). This boomerang effect took place among both the foreign-born and the U.S.-born, most notably among the youth of Mexican and Filipino descent—the two largest immigrant groups in the United States—an apparent backlash during a period (1992 to 1996) of growing anti-immigrant sentiment and at times overt immigrant bashing in the country, above all in California. Overall, panethnic identities remained at 16 percent at T2, but that figure conceals a notable decline among Mexican-origin youth in "Hispanic" and "Chicano" self-identities and an extremely sharp upswing in the proportion of youths who had come to identify panethnically as "Asian" or "Asian American," especially among the smallest groups such as the "other Asians" (Chinese, Korean, Japanese, Thai) and the Hmong. The simultaneous rapid decline of both the plain "American" (cut in half to a minuscule 1.6 percent) and hyphenated-American (dropping from 43 percent to 30 percent) self-identities points to the rapid growth of a reactive ethnic consciousness (see Portes 1984; Rumbaut 1994b). Furthermore, the strongest scores for the salience or importance that the youths gave to their chosen identities were reported for national-origin identities, and the weakest for plain "American" ones, with hyphenates scoring in between in salience.

Thus, change over time in this context has been not toward assimilative mainstream identities (with or without a hyphen), but rather toward a more proudly militant or nationalistic reaffirmation of the immigrant identity for the largest groups, and toward panethnic identities among the smallest groups, as these youths become increasingly aware of the ethnic and racial categories in which they are persistently classified by mainstream society. While the results are based on a limited measure taken at two points in time spanning the period from middle to late adolescence, they nevertheless go against the grain of a linear assimilation perspective. In any case, "becoming American" for these children of immigrants may well turn out to be a lifelong occupation, itself a suggestion of the importance of applying a contextualized life-course perspective to the analysis of social change and individual identity.

This process of growing ethnic awareness is in turn intertwined with these adolescents' experiences and expectations of racial and ethnic discrimination. These are detailed in the bottom panel of table 9.1. Reported experiences of discrimination increased somewhat from 64 percent to 69 percent of the sample in the last survey. Virtually every group reported more such experiences of rejection or unfair treatment against themselves as they grew older, with the Hmong registering the sharpest increase (to 82 percent), but about two-thirds of every other nationality in San Diego uniformly reported such experiences. Among those suffering discrimination, their own race or nationality is overwhelmingly perceived to account for what triggers unfair treatment from others. Such experiences tend to be associated over time with the development of a more pessimistic stance about the chances of being able to reduce discriminatory treatment on meritocratic grounds through higher educational achievement. As table 9.1 shows, in both surveys the students were asked to agree or disagree with the statement "No matter how much education I get, people will still discriminate against me." In 1992, 37 percent of the total sample agreed with that gloomy assessment; by 1995 the proportion agreeing had edged up to 41 percent. Such expectations of external discrimination on ascribed rather than achieved grounds—and thus of perceived danger and threatening circumstances beyond one's control—have also been found, in multivariate analyses of both the T1 and T2 survey data, to be significant predictors of depressive symptoms (see Rumbaut 1994b, 1999b).

Still, it is important to underscore the fact that despite their awareness of the realities of American racism and intolerance, most of these adolescents continued to affirm a sanguine belief in the promise of equal opportunity through educational achievement—including nearly 60 percent in the latest survey who disagreed with the statement that people would discriminate against them regardless of educational merit. Even more tellingly, 63 percent of these youths agreed in the original survey that "there is no better country to live in than the United States," and that endorsement increased to 71 percent three years later. Significantly, those most apt to endorse that view were the children of Vietnamese exiles whose families had found a favorable context of reception in the United States through a historic refugee resettlement program organized by the federal government. The groups least likely to agree with that statement were those who had most felt the sting and the stigma of racial and ethnic discrimination. Milton Gordon's (1964) assimilation sequence, it is well to recall here, ultimately required routine social acceptance and an absence of prejudice and discrimination in the "core society." It takes two to tango, after all—and to assimilate.[14]

Assimilation from What? To What? For What?

As has by now been amply documented, the diversity and dynamics of the "new immigration" to the United States over the past few decades differ in kind, in many respects, from the last period of mass immigration in the first few decades of the century. The immigrants themselves differ greatly in their social class and national origins, and so do the American society, economy, and polity that receive them—raising perennial questions about their modes of incorporation and challenging conventional accounts of assimilation processes that were framed during previous epochs of mass migration. In this respect, the differences in the *historical contexts* of immigration and incorporation themselves need to be taken far more seriously and systematically into account if we are to deepen our understanding of these processes; too often sociological analyses present "structural" and "cultural" explanations in a decontextualized historical vacuum, to their impoverishment. A few thoughts are proposed in what follows to tease out some of the conceptual and analytical questions posed by the new realities that are not taken into account by conventional perspectives on assimilation. But before looking forward to these, it may be useful to glance briefly backward at the original canonical statement, too often misread and trivialized—the seminal work by Park and Burgess—and see what may still be gleaned from it.

Accommodation and Assimilation: A Generational Divide?

In their *Introduction to the Science of Sociology* (1921/1924, 735), arguably the most influential single text in the history of American sociology, Park and Burgess gave the concept of assimilation its classic formulation: "a process of interpenetration and fusion in which persons and groups acquire the memories, sentiments, and attitudes of other persons and groups, and, by sharing their experience and history, are incorporated with them in a common cultural life." They distinguished systematically between "four great types of interaction"—competition, conflict, accommodation, and assimilation—which they related respectively to economic, political, social, and cultural institutions.[15] The distinction they elaborate between accommodation and assimilation is instructive. An *accommodation* (of a conflict, or to a new situation) may take place quickly, and the person or group is typically a highly conscious protagonist of the process of accommodating those circumstances. In *assimilation,* by contrast, the changes are more subtle and gradual, and the process is typically unconscious, so that the person is incorporated into the common life of the group largely unaware of how it happened. Assimilation thus takes place most rapidly and completely in primary—intimate and intense—social contacts, whereas accommodation may be facilitated through secondary contacts, which are too distant and remote to promote assimilation. Since the nature of the social contacts (especially the interpersonal intimacy, "the great moral solvent") is what is decisive, it follows that "a common language is indispensable for the most intimate associations of the members of the group," and its absence is "an insurmountable barrier to assimilation," since it is through communication that gradual and unconscious changes of the attitudes and sentiments of the members of the group are produced.[16]

The psychosocial mechanisms through which assimilation occurs, a key issue but one addressed by Park and Burgess only in passing, are those of "imitation and suggestion." The end result is not "like-mindedness,"[17] but rather "a unity of experience and orientation, out of which may develop a community of purpose and action" (759). Race and place become critical structural determinants of the degree of assimilation precisely insofar as they delimit possible forms of primary social contact; for Park and Burgess, social relations are inevitably embedded and bounded in space, and that is why social distance is typically indexed by physical distance and patterns of residential segregation. In sum, an exegesis of their argument compels the conclusion that *accommodation* is the modal adaptation of first-generation adult immigrants, while *assimilation* can become a modal outcome ultimately only for the malleable young and for the second generation, who are like palimpsests, and then only if and when permitted by structural conditions of inclusion at the primary group level (see Park and Burgess 1921/1924, 735, n. 2).[18]

This formulation underscores the centrality of both the 1.5 and second generations of children of immigrants as strategic research sites (see Merton 1987) for the study of assimilation processes and outcomes. Or perhaps it may be more precise to say that the *family,* albeit an underprivileged social structure in most of our professions, may be *the* strategic research site for understanding the dynamics of immigration and of immigrant adaptation processes, as well as for their long-term consequences. Indeed, immigration to the United States is largely a family affair, and kinship is the basis for long-standing selection criteria built into U.S. immigration law. Immigrant families come in all shapes, haves and have-nots alike, from manual laborers to professionals to entrepreneurs to once well-heeled exiles, and they confront dramatically different contexts of adaptation. To make sense of their diversity—and of the complexity of assimilation processes and outcomes that then ensue, particularly among the 1.5 and second generations—we need to recognize from the outset that it makes no sense to speak of a singular immigrant or immigrant family experience.

Often the most insightful statements of what goes on within such families are found in both fictional and nonfictional autobiographical (yet not filiopietistic) tracts written with a perspicaciously nuanced mastery of the new language by children of immigrants (for a selected list, see Rumbaut 1997b). Why and how? Perhaps because of the emancipatory and innovative energies that marginality—for all, and possibly because of all, its emotional costs—can release in individuals who come of age between colliding cultural worlds, between centripetal and centrifugal force fields, outside of the routinized social comfort zones that ossify reflection, who are less bound to worship the idols of any tribe, and who manage to achieve a creative synthesis of insiderness and outsiderness, proximity and distance, aloofness and involvement; perhaps when such marginal and malleable individuals in their formative years, in whose minds those dissonant worlds and memories conflict and fuse (see Park 1928), become critically self-conscious of the relativity of intergroup boundaries and "imagined communities" and assimilation processes and can make them an object of sustained inquiry, they become not so much "citizens of the world" or of "America" as of their own imaginations. We can learn much from that literature—often much more than from academic texts.

Socioeconomic Assimilation: Origins Shape Destinies

"Socioeconomic assimilation" is characteristically defined as achieving "parity" with the native majority in such indicators as education, employment, and income. A leading economist puts the matter this way:

> When a newly arrived immigrant first enters the U.S. labor market, his wage is much lower than that of natives. Over time, the immigrant becomes proficient in the English language, learns about alternative job opportunities, and acquires skills that are valued by American employers. As immigrants adapt to the U.S. labor market, therefore, they become more and more like natives, and their wages begin to catch up to those of natives. . . . Economic assimilation is defined as the rate at which immigrant earnings catch up with those of natives

as both groups age in the United States. (Borjas 1990, 97, 99)

Put this way, "immigrants" and "natives" are considered as lump sums, as if these were homogeneous aggregates worthy of meaningful comparison, and assimilative processes are reduced to a game of catch-up measured in dollars.

Among the many problems with that formulation, of course, is the fact that a substantial proportion of contemporary immigrants *exceed* such native norms by a wide margin, especially in education, from the start. These more highly educated professional or managerial immigrants are more likely to speak English, to live in the suburbs ("spatially assimilated," relatively dispersed, and "invisibly" at that—that is, they are not publicly perceived as a "problem"), and to accommodate readily to "American ways." Still others immigrate precisely because of the demand for their labor by American employers, who prefer it over that of natives or more "assimilated" workers (see Tienda and Stier 1996; Waldinger 1997). What then does the concept of "socioeconomic assimilation" mean for immigrant groups who arrive in the United States already well above (let alone at "parity" with) the educational and occupational medians of the native majority population—who are relatively affluent and integrated almost from the get-go? Or for those who are valued by employers precisely because they are not?

Available occupational data from the Immigration and Naturalization Service (INS)—the percentage of professionals, executives, and managers at the time of immigrant admission—show that over the past three decades, more than 2 million immigrant engineers, scientists, university professors, physicians, nurses, and other professionals and executives and their immediate families have been admitted into the United States. From the late 1960s to the early 1980s, worldwide about one-third of all legal immigrants to the United States (excluding dependents) were high-status professionals, executives, or managers in their countries of origin. The proportion of these so-called brain-drain immigrants declined somewhat to 26.5 percent in the late 1980s—still a higher percentage than that of the native-born American population—before rebounding again to 34 percent in 1993 and 35 percent in 1995, despite the fact that the overwhelming majority of immigrants had been admitted under family preferences over this period (Rumbaut 1997b).

There are very sharp differences in the class character of contemporary *legal* immigration to the United States. Regionally, the flows from Asia, Africa, and Europe had achieved rough parity with each other by the 1980s, with close to half (44 to 48 percent) of all occupationally active immigrants from these regions in 1993 consisting of professionals and managers (well above the norm for the native-born population), in sharp contrast to the less than 10 percent from Latin America and the Caribbean (well below the U.S. norm). Highly skilled immigrants have dominated the flows of Indians, Koreans, Filipinos, and Chinese (including especially the Taiwanese) since the 1960s, and their proportions increased noticeably after the passage of the Immigration Act of 1990, which nearly tripled the number of such employment-based visas. By contrast, legal immigration from Mexico, El Salvador, the Dominican Republic, and (until recently) Italy has consisted predominantly of manual laborers and low-wage service workers, as has also been the case among refugees from Laos and Cambodia and the more recent waves of Vietnamese, Cubans, and Haitians. In fact, the diversity of contemporary immigration is such that, among all ethnic groups in America today, native and foreign-born, different immigrant nationalities account at once for the *highest* and the *lowest* rates of education, self-employment, home ownership, poverty, welfare dependency, and fertility, as well as the lowest rates of divorce and female-headed single-parent families, and the highest proportions of children under eighteen residing with both natural parents. These differential starting points, especially the internal socioeconomic diversification of particular waves and "vintages" within the same nationalities over time, augur differential modes of incorporation and assimilation outcomes that cannot be extrapolated simply from the experience of earlier immigrant groups of the same nationality, let alone from immigrants as an undifferentiated whole. Origins shape destinies.

Segmented Assimilation or an Irreversible "Race Relations Cycle"?

In addition to those differing starting points, recent scholarship has suggested that the incorporation of today's new immigrants and their children is likely to be segmented and to take different pathways, depending on a variety of factors and contexts—including the changing structure of economic opportunity, the consequences of pervasive racial discrimination, and the segment of American society to which particular immigrant groups are exposed (Fernández-Kelly and Schauffler 1994; Gans 1992a; Portes 1995b; Portes and Rumbaut 1996; Portes and Zhou 1993; Zhou 1997a). Thus, one path may follow the so-called straight-line theory (or bumpy-line theory, as Gans [1992b] suggests may be a more apt term) of assimilation into the middle-class majority; an opposite type of adaptation may lead to downward mobility and assimilation into the inner-city underclass; yet another may combine upward mobility and heightened ethnic awareness within solidaristic immigrant enclaves (see Portes and Zhou 1993). Such divergent modes of incorporation in turn are likely to be accompanied by changes in the character and salience of ethnicity—including "linear" and "reactive" processes of ethnic solidarity and identity formation—and hence by divergent modes of ethnic self-identification (Rumbaut 1994b).

Other paths are possible, to be sure, and in any case, segmented assimilation processes—that is, adaptations that take place within specifiable opportunity structures and through the influence of differential associations, reference groups, experiences and attachments, especially in primary social relationships stratified by race, religion, region, and class—are nothing new in the American experience, nor in descriptions of it. Almost two decades ago, for instance, Harold Abramson (1980) directly posed the question "assimilation to what?" and suggested three possible paths: essentially Anglo-conformity; assimilation into a minority ethnicity (such as the absorption of West Indian blacks into the larger African American community through marriage and acculturation); and ethnogenesis. An even clearer illustration of segmented assimilation was provided by Ruby Jo Reeves Kennedy over five decades ago (1944) in her concept of a "triple melting pot," involving ethnic intermarriage and blending within Protestant, Catholic, and Jewish religious groupings. And Alexis de Tocqueville, writing over sixteen decades ago in *Democracy in America* (1835), described his own notion of triple segmentation in a chapter on "The Present and Probable Future Condition of the Three Races That Inhabit the Territory of the United States," noting that "fortune had brought [the Indians, Negroes, and Europeans] together on the same soil, where although they are mixed, they do not amalgamate, and each race fulfills its destiny apart," with the Europeans fated to homogenize into a dominant Anglo-American mold (quoted in Abramson 1980, 153).[19]

Indeed, Robert Park himself proposed a triptych of trajectories of incorporation—a fact lost entirely alongside the far more familiar but formulaic and misbegotten "straw-man" use to which his concept of a "race relations cycle" has been put (see McKee 1993). As the idea of the cycle became reified and popularized, assimilation was posited as the final stage of a natural, progressive, inevitable, and irreversible four-step process in international and race relations. But in a prolific career, Park wrote about a race relations cycle only twice: first in a sentence near the end of a 1926 article, "Our Racial Frontier in the Pacific," published in the periodical *Survey Graphic*; and then eleven years later (1937) in a brief introduction to a book on interracial marriage in Hawaii written by one of his former students. In the first instance, he was arguing against the likelihood that a "racial barrier"—based on "that somewhat mythical entity that we call race," which the passage of exclusionary laws sought to establish by barring Asian migration to the United States—could be much of a match against the global economic, political, and cultural forces that had brought about "an existing interpenetration of peoples . . . so vast and irresistible that the resulting changes assume the character of a cosmic process. New means of communication enforce new contacts and result in new forms of competition and of conflict. But out of this confusion and ferment, new and more intimate forms of association arise" (1926, 141, 149). And in his 1937 introduction, in any event, he explicitly rebutted any notion of a unilinear assimilative outcome to race conflict and change ("what are popularly referred to as race relations"):

> It is not possible to predict with any certainty the final outcome, except that . . . when stabilization is finally achieved, race relations will assume one of three configurations. They will take the form of a caste system, as in India; they will terminate in complete assimilation, as in China; or the unassimilated race will constitute a permanent racial minority within the limits of a national state, as in the case of the Jews in Europe. . . . All three types of change are involved . . . in what we may describe as the "race relations cycle." (1937, xiii)

Cultural Assimilation: Premigration Americanization and the Role of the Mass Media

A persistent assumption in conventional depictions of "cultural assimilation" or acculturation is that immigrants start at some point near American cultural ground zero and then proceed only post-arrival to "become American" in word, in deed, and ultimately in thought. Along these lines, current restrictionist discourse even makes the point that a "moratorium" in immigration is needed to give folks already here a chance to "assimilate." But in fact many immigrants (and nonimmigrants) these days are already "Americanized" to varying degrees in their countries of origin long before they even set foot in the United States, a reflection of the global reach and widespread diffusion of American consumption patterns, lifestyles, and popular culture—its intangible "soft power."[20] Many immigrants may have visited the United States in the past and established contacts (including family and friends) with whom they keep in regular communication, or they may even have been living in the United States for years before seeking an immigrant visa. This is so above all in the case of countries with whom the United States has close economic, military, political, cultural, and historical ties. Indeed, the ultimate boomerang effect lies in the fact that contemporary immigration to the United States can be seen as a dialectical consequence of the expansion of the nation to its post–World War II (and now post–cold war) position of global hegemony. *Who* is doing the assimilating, and *from what, to what,* and *for what,* are critical questions that need to be placed not only within the appropriate structural contexts but in historical contexts as well.

To varying degrees of closeness, the many millions of immigrants and their children in the United States today are embedded in often intricate webs of family ties, both here and abroad. Such ties form extraordinary transnational linkages and networks that can, by reducing the costs and risks of migration, expand and serve as a conduit to additional and thus potentially self-perpetuating migration. A recent poll in the Dominican Republic yielded a stunning statistic: *half* of the 7.5 million Dominicans have relatives in the United States, and two-thirds would move to the United States if they could. Similarly, by the end of the 1980s national surveys in Mexico had found that about half of adult Mexicans were related to someone living in the United States, and that one-third of all Mexicans had been to the United States at some point in their lives; more recent surveys by Douglas Massey and his colleagues suggest still larger proportions (see Massey and Espinosa 1997). Deep structural linkages and potentially vast social networks of family and friends are implied by those figures; these microsocial structures can shape both future migration and adaptation processes. The proportion of immigrants in the United States in 1990 who hailed from countries in the English-speaking Caribbean, notably from Jamaica, Barbados, Trinidad, Belize, and Guyana, already constituted between 10 and 20 percent of the 1990 populations of their respective countries—a growing double-digit group that now includes El Salvador (Rumbaut 1992). By the same token, despite nearly four decades of hostile relations, at least one-third of Cuba's population of 11 million (and maybe half of Havana's) now have relatives in the United States and Puerto Rico, while (according to the 1997 Cuba poll conducted by Florida International University) over 75 percent of first- and second-generation Cubans in Miami have relatives in Cuba—ironically, a greater degree of structural linkage than ever before in the history of U.S.-Cuba relations. Only Mexico (by far) and the Philippines (a U.S. colony for half a century) have sent more immigrants to the United States than Cuba since 1960. The history of U.S.-Cuba relations is a long and complex one ("bound to us by ties of singular intimacy," is how President William McKinley put it in his State of the Union message in 1899—an intimacy that led to a revolutionary divorce in 1959). Still, Wayne Smith, an informed observer of the historical development of these ties and of the Americanization of the Cuban scene, could write recently that at least in the cities "it is probably fair to say that by 1959, no other country in the world, with the exception of Canada, quite so resembled the United States" (quoted in Rumbaut 1992).

Moreover, the role of the mass media, especially television, has been little studied systematically in the literature on cultural assimilation; curiously, researchers have not explored in any depth the impact of exposure to the media's pervasive dissemination of impersonal messages and cultural propaganda—what might be called the *context of perception*—in shaping the acculturation (pre- and post-arrival) of immigrant groups, and particularly of their children's worldview. (The ethnic-immigrant media is largely an adult first-generation resource.) After all, the so-called post-1965 immigration is also the first immigrant generation to live and grow up in the age of television, when the medium itself has been part of the message. Indeed, the two coincided historically: the critical shift from print to televised media—from the "Age of Exposition" to the "Age of Entertainment" (see Postman 1985)—occurred during the 1960s and has intensified since.

Television is the most widely shared experience in the United States: as of 1990 the Census Bureau reported that 98 percent of all U.S. households had at least one television set (and on average two sets per household), and that the members of an average household watched television over seven hours per day. The only activity American children engage in more than watching television is sleeping. In short, television and other mass media are powerful "assimilative" agencies, and while the jury is still out on the extent of its effects on viewers' attitudes and behavior, available evidence (see Rumbaut 1997b) points to negative consequences for children of immigrants of this mode of cultural assimilation par excellence on such indicators of "successful" outcomes as educational attainment and aspirations.

Linguistic Assimilation: English as a Global Language

After two centuries of Pax Britannica and then American hegemony since World War II, much of the world already speaks English (itself a "glorious mongrel") as a second language or even as an official language[21]—and so do many immigrants to the United States *before* their arrival. Immigrants from India and the Philippines stand out in that regard, and for that matter those from Germany and Iran, as do the substantial majority of immigrants from Africa (over three-fifths of those counted in the 1990 census, with Egypt and Nigeria alone accounting for one-third of all African immigration)—to say nothing, of course, of the Jamaicans and others from the English-speaking Caribbean, the Canadians, the Irish, and the British themselves (who continue to send a substantial number of immigrants to their former colony).

Uncritical discussions of "linguistic assimilation" often presuppose that immigrants start at some point near English-language zero and then proceed to learn to speak, read, and write it, but that is not at all the case across the board. Of the 20 million foreign-born persons counted in the 1990 census, 21 percent spoke English *only,* and another 53 percent spoke it "very well" or "well," even though close to half (44 percent) had just arrived in the United States during the 1980s. The 26 percent who reported that they spoke it "not well" or "not at all" included, disproportionately, the elderly (especially those in dense ethnic enclaves, such as Cubans in Miami), the undocumented, and the least educated among recent arrivals (see Rumbaut 1994a).

One other point concerning the acquisition of the English language by non-English-speaking immigrants: although sociologists are not wont to admit it, there is a biology of language learning that is as powerful a factor as any in the arsenal of the social sciences to explain the patterns of linguistic assimilation—including the fact that of all the dimensions of assimilation, language acquisition is the one most likely to follow a straight-line trajectory, and within one generation at that. Essentially, the capacity to learn and to speak a language like a native is a function of age, and it is especially good between the ages of three and the early teens; immigrants who arrive before the age of twelve or so (whom I have called "1.5ers") are considerably more likely to speak English without an accent, while those who arrive after puberty may learn it, but not without a telltale accent. "After puberty, the ability . . . to adjust to the physiological demands of verbal behavior quickly declines. The brain behaves as if it had become set in its ways and primary basic language skills not acquired by that time, except for articulation, usually remain deficient for life" (Lennenberg 1967, 53; see also Laponce 1987; Bialystok and Hakuta 1994).

Indeed, without strong social structural supports, the chances of sustaining bilingualism seem slim, even among highly motivated individuals and despite the range of benefits it can confer. As Laponce (1987, 15, 21) puts it:

> Bilingualism is costly, in terms of both memory and reaction time. Thus for an individual to become or remain bilingual, the social benefit must outweigh the mental cost; and this mental cost explains why the tendency toward unilingualism never entirely disappears . . . and merely confirms the norm: the mind works more quickly and with less effort in a unilingual semantic system; its natural inclination is toward unilingualism.

Positive bilingualism thus requires the collaboration of parents, teachers, and children:

> These children do not choose to become bilingual; society forces them to do so. If society and parents collaborate in an undertaking perceived by the child to be socially advantageous, success will probably be achieved; but if the child sees no important social advantage in the undertaking, he or she will probably fail in it. The biological and mental obstacles to the acquisition of two languages can be overcome only with a heavy expenditure of social and psychological energy. . . . Within a bilingual society, the

minority group tends to learn the language of the dominant group, rather than vice versa.

For all of these reasons, in any event, linguistic assimilation is the domain of adaptation most likely to proceed exactly as a linear function, and in the direction predicted by assimilation theory.

Political Assimilation, Naturalization, Emigration, and Selectivity

A central dimension of the process of immigrant incorporation involves their political "assimilation," naturalization, and voting patterns (see Portes and Rumbaut 1996, ch. 4). (What Gordon called "civic assimilation" referred to immigrants' "not raising by their demands . . . any issues involving value or power conflict" with the native majority [1964, 70].) While I cannot dwell on this here, it is worth noting in passing that one of the paradoxical and unintended consequences of the passage of Proposition 187 in California by a landslide margin, and its political aftereffects in legislation already passed or pending in the U.S. Congress to eliminate eligibility for medical and social services for legal permanent residents and to deny citizenship to the U.S.-born children of illegal immigrants, was a rush by noncitizen immigrants to apply for naturalization in California, New York, South Florida, and elsewhere, overwhelming the ability of the INS to process them (see Ojito 1998). Another was the response of the Mexican government to consider extending dual nationality to permit persons of Mexican origin in the United States to maintain their right as Mexican citizens to own property in Mexico, while at the same time gaining the political power to vote as U.S. citizens (see Fritz 1998; Verhovek 1998). Ironically, although the British and Canadians have been viewed as the most "assimilated" immigrants in the United States, they share (with Mexicans) about the lowest rates of naturalization among all long-term immigrants in the country. Why this is so is not at all clear—and underscores the need for comparative cross-national studies of citizenship, membership, and modes of political inclusion and exclusion.

Many immigrants do not stay in the United States but leave after a period of time. When we talk of "assimilation" we are, of course, talking primarily about the children (and grandchildren) of those immigrants who came and stayed in the United States; practically no attention is paid, however, comparatively or otherwise, to those who came and went back to their countries of origin or elsewhere, despite the fact that *emigration* was very substantial in the early part of this century and remains so today (even granting that reliable data are absent and that none have been officially collected since 1957—itself a reflection of a mindset that ignores the relevance of knowing more about who the emigrants are, although such study may tell us a great deal more about who the immigrants who remain are).

This is only one dimension of a broader issue of "selectivity" in immigration flows that deserves more analytical attention. Immigrants who stay long enough to be included in accounts of "assimilation" have already gone through multiple layers of selection at the time of entry—from self-selection (relative to those who do not immigrate) to (legal) selection by the criteria of U.S. immigration and refugee policies—to which is added still more selectivity in the decision to stay rather than return. Exactly how such "selection" factors shape adaptation processes and outcomes, and how they may distinguish the motives and frames of reference of first- versus second-generation immigrants in such processes, are matters that remain to be investigated systematically and critically.

Assimilation as an "Endlessly Astonishing Synthesis"

To study the "assimilation" of persons and groups in American life is, among other things, to examine the modes of incorporation of periphery to core, and to reflect on the tumultuous histories and social processes that have made (and are continuing to make) "Americans" out of a remarkable and motley crew. Indeed, as these histories unfold, we might recall, metaphorically, an old dictum—ontogeny recapitulates phylogeny: the biographical process of becoming American today recapitulates the historical process of America becoming fragmented across color lines, classes, creeds, races, and places.

If in this chapter we have considered various ways in which paradox emerges between the rhetoric and the reality of assimilation American-style, it is in part a reflection of the paradoxical character and internal contradictions of American society itself. In his comparative survey *American Exceptionalism: A Double-Edged Sword* (1996, 26–27), Seymour Martin Lipset put the matter this way:

> Exceptionalism is a two-edged phenomenon; it does not mean better. This country is an outlier. It is the most religious, optimistic, patriotic, rights-

oriented, and individualistic . . . it has the highest crime rates . . . the most people locked up in jail . . . the most lawyers per capita of any country in the world. It also has close to the lowest percentage of the eligible electorate voting, but the highest rate of participation in voluntary organizations. The country remains the wealthiest in real income terms, the most productive in worker output, the highest in proportions of people who graduate from or enroll in higher education . . . but the least egalitarian among developed nations with respect to income distribution, at the bottom as a provider of welfare benefits, the lowest in savings, and the least taxed. . . .

The positive and negative are frequently opposite sides of the same coin. . . . The stress on success . . . presses the unsuccessful to violate the rules of the game. Individualism as a value leads not only to self-reliance and a reluctance to be dependent on others, but also to independence in family relationships, including a greater propensity to leave a mate if the marital relationship becomes troubled. America is the most moralistic country in the developed world. . . . Given this background, it is also not surprising that Americans are also very critical of their society's institutions and leaders.

Given this background, indeed, it is not at all surprising that assimilation has its ironies and its paradoxes—and its discontents.

As an analytical tool, the concept of assimilation need not be used unimaginatively as a bland, deterministic, and formulaic depiction of mechanical adjustments (producing as outcome a "tasteless, colorless fluid of uniformity," as Randolph Bourne [1916, 90] put it in his vigorous and provocative essay "Trans-National America," published eight decades ago but still fresher than this morning's newspaper and worth rereading periodically whenever intellectual somnambulance begins to set in)—or worse, pejoratively as a synonym for campaigns of coerced Americanization, on the one hand, and a cover for racism, on the other.[22] More intriguingly, assimilation need not be, or be seen as, a zero-sum game. If it is to be rescued from the intellectual gulch of disrepute into which it fell, it will help to give free rein to the "sociological imagination," à la C. Wright Mills (1961), to grasp the human variety in the intersections of biography and history within social structure.

Assimilation looks to the future, not to the past; it works its alchemy chiefly in the realm of the young, and the malleable next generation, but mostly superficially on those already formed adults who made the fateful decision to come and who bring with them a dual frame of reference. Assimilation is about seduction, and not simply coercion; about discovery, and not only loss and twilight; about profound conflicts of loyalties and a kind of existential red-alertness, and not merely conforming to group pressure (as if the process of assimilation were but a gigantic Asch experiment) and taking the path of least resistance. It is also about creative interminglings and extraordinary hybridities, and not at all simply surrender on the terms of a dominant core.

Assimilating processes involve the inventiveness of human agency, mothered by necessity and the sheer weight of circumstance, and the dialectical ironies of human history, suffused by pervasive processes of change of which the protagonists may be no more conscious than fish are of water—all the more so in a world that seems to be changing faster than are the individuals who seek to adjust to it. Neither assimilator nor assimilatee is a fixed, static thing in any case; both are permanently unfinished creations with vexing degrees of autonomy. The ultimate paradox of assimilation American-style may well be that in the process, what is being assimilated metamorphoses into something quite dissimilar from what any of the protagonists ever imagined or intended, and the core itself is ineluctably transmuted, even as it keeps its continental name: America (named for an Italian adventurer, at that).

For Milton Gordon, in *Assimilation in American Life,* the final stage of the process that began with acculturation and moved through structural assimilation and intermarriage came with the embrace of an identity as an unhyphenated "American." But in a world in perpetual motion, the very notion of a final stage, with its authoritative assurance of inevitability and irreversibility, is little more than a comforting illusion—or a tragic litany. In *The Book of Embraces,* by appropriate contrast, the Uruguayan novelist Eduardo Galeano has a haunting passage—he calls it a "celebration of contradictions" (1991, 124–25)—that expresses vividly the dialectical sense of paradox and poetic justice that I have sought to convey from the opening epigraphs of this essay:

Idiot memory repeats itself as tragic litany. Lively memory, on the other hand, is born every day, springing from the past and set against it. . . . Human history . . . is born as it dies and builds as it destroys. . . . Every loss is a discovery. Courage is born of fear, certainty of doubt. What it all comes down to is that we are the sum of our efforts to change who we are. Identity is no museum piece sitting stock-still in a display case, but rather the endlessly astonishing synthesis of the contradictions of everyday life.

This essay expands the argument presented in "Assimilation and Its Discontents: Between Rhetoric and Reality," *International Migration Review* 31, no. 4 (1997): 923–60, and "Paradoxes (and Orthodoxies) of Assimilation," *Sociological Perspectives* 40, no. 3 (1997): 483–511, both based on the paper presented at the Social Science Research Council Conference on which this book is based. I gratefully acknowledge the support provided by research grants from the Andrew W. Mellon Foundation and the Russell Sage Foundation, to the Children of Immigrants Longitudinal Study (CILS), some results from which are herein reported. I am especially indebted to Robert K. Merton and Nicos N. Mouratides for their insightful comments and close readings of an earlier draft of this essay.

Notes

1. For all the hue and cry about the allegedly inassimilable "new immigration" from pre–World War I Europe, Robert Park could write at the time (1914) that "in America it has become proverbial that a Pole, Lithuanian, or Norwegian cannot be distinguished, in the second generation, from an American born of native parents. . . . As a matter of fact, the ease and rapidity with which aliens, under existing conditions in the United States, have been able to assimilate themselves to the customs and manners of American life have enabled this country to swallow and digest every sort of normal human difference, except the purely external ones, like color of the skin" (quoted in Park and Burgess 1921/1924, 757–58).
2. Park and Burgess would have advised a different approach: "Not by the suppression of old memories, but by their incorporation in his new life is assimilation achieved. . . . Assimilation cannot be promoted directly, but only indirectly, that is, by supplying the conditions that make for participation. There is no process but life itself that can effectually wipe out the immigrant's memory of his past. The inclusion of the immigrant in our common life may perhaps best be reached, therefore, in cooperation that looks not so much to the past as to the future. The second generation of the immigrant may share fully in our memories, but practically all that we can ask of the foreign-born is participation in our ideals, our wishes, and our common enterprises" (1921/1924, 739–40).
3. Lest Linton's witty essay fade from the collective memory, a few sentences will convey the gist of his incontrovertible jab, penned a decade after the end of mass European immigration to the United States (1937, 427–29): "There can be no question about the average American's Americanism or his desire to preserve this precious heritage at all costs. Nevertheless, some insidious foreign ideas have already wormed their way into his civilization without his realizing what was going on. Thus dawn finds the unsuspecting patriot garbed in pajamas, a garment of East Indian origin. . . . On awakening he glances at the clock, a medieval European invention. . . . He then shaves, a masochistic rite first developed by the heathen priests of ancient Egypt and Sumer. . . . He will begin [breakfast] with coffee, an Abyssinian plant first discovered by the Arabs. . . . Meanwhile, he reads the news of the day, imprinted in characters invented by the ancient Semites by a process invented in Germany upon a material invented in China. As he scans the latest editorial pointing out the dire results to our institutions of accepting foreign ideas, he will not fail to thank a Hebrew God in an Indo-European language that he is a one hundred percent (decimal system invented by the Greeks) American (from Americus Vespucci, Italian Geographer)."
4. Oliver Cox criticized Warner and Srole's formulation as a simplistic "birds-of-a-feather hypothesis," pointing to the paradoxical meaning of "assimilation" in the context of racial conflict in the United States, in his contemporary *Caste, Class, and Race* (1948, 545–48, n. 318).
5. Of the other two main ideological tendencies, "cultural pluralism" more often reflected the sentiments of the immigrants themselves, and the "melting pot" metaphor had been dismissed by Park and Burgess as a "'magic crucible' notion of assimilation" through which "the ideal of assimilation was conceived to be that of feeling, thinking, and acting alike" (1921/1924, 735). Much later Nathan Glazer and Daniel Patrick Moynihan would write (1963, xcvii), famously, that "the point about the melting pot . . . is that it did not happen. . . . The American ethos is nowhere better perceived than in the disinclination of the third and fourth generation of newcomers to blend into a standard, uniform national type."
6. An instructive example of assimilative processes among immigrants—that is, literally, of becoming similar to the native population in the place of destination—is found in studies of breast cancer incidence and mortality rates. The rates of breast cancer incidence among immigrant women originating from countries with lower breast cancer risk have been found to increase toward the rates observed in destination countries with populations at higher risk for this disease. In the United States, such cancer risks have been shown to be less for first-generation than for second-generation Americans generally; more specifically, foreign-born Japanese, Chinese, Cuban, and Mexican women were at lesser risk than their U.S.-born co-ethnics, with the risk for the immigrants tending to increase with length of residence in the United States. A recent study of immigrants in Australia and Canada examined the impact of exposure to new environments and lifestyles on breast cancer rates by determining mortality rates for women who had immigrated from both comparatively lower- and higher-risk countries, and then comparing the rates to those found for native-born Australians and Canadians. In Australia the mortality rates for twelve of sixteen (75 percent) immigrant groups from lower-risk countries and ten of fourteen (71 percent) from higher-risk countries shifted toward the rate of native-born

Australians. In Canada the rates for twelve of twenty (60 percent) immigrant groups from lower-risk countries and four of five (80 percent) groups from higher-risk countries also converged to the rate of native-born Canadians. The substantial majority of immigrant groups "assimilated" their breast cancer mortality rates, up or down, from the rate observed in their country of origin toward that of the native-born in the country of destination. This convergence was most evident for immigrants coming from countries with rates that were substantially different from that prevailing in the destination country (Kliewer and Smith 1995).

7. See *Progress: Fact or Illusion?* (Marx and Mazlish 1996) for a superb collection of essays on the subject.
8. A paraphrase of David Matza's definition of irony, quoted in Louis Schneider's thoughtful essay "Ironic Perspective and Sociological Thought" (1975, 325).
9. Results from the 1996 Wave II Add-Health nationally representative sample showed significant increases in adolescent obesity from the foreign-born first generation to the U.S.-born second and third generations among Hispanic and Asian-origin groups (Popkin and Udry 1998). The proportion of American adolescents whose body mass index (BMI) was above the eighty-fifth percentile based on the 1995 World Health Organization (WHO) standard—the measure of obesity used in this analysis—was 26.5 percent. But among Asian-origin groups, the proportion of obese youth more than doubled from the first generation (11.6 percent) to the second (27.2 percent) and third (28 percent) generations, and among Hispanics, obesity levels increased from 24.5 percent among immigrant adolescents to 32 percent in the second and third generations. The process of assimilating to an American lifestyle of lesser physical activity and higher-fat diets was fingered as the likely culprit in these rapid shifts, which in turn portend increases in U.S. obesity over the next several decades, accompanied by the sorts of health problems that are strongly associated with obesity, such as high blood pressure and diabetes.
10. The intergenerational findings on family structure reflect census and other data that indicate lower rates of divorce and single-parent families in the first (immigrant) generation but striking increases in the prevalence of marital disruption over time and generations in the United States, particularly by the third generation. See Jensen and Chitose (1994) and Rumbaut (1997b, 26–28).
11. Quoted in Fadiman (1997). When he made this remark in 1987, Simpson was the ranking minority member of the Senate Subcommittee on Immigration and Refugee Affairs.
12. The CILS study has also followed a sample of over 2,800 youth in South Florida. For details and results of the baseline survey on both coasts, see Rumbaut (1994b), Portes (1995b), and Portes and Rumbaut (1996, ch. 7).
13. I had coined the concept of the "1.5" generation in the 1970s to describe the situation of immigrant children who are socialized and begin their primary schooling abroad but immigrate before puberty (about age twelve) and complete their education in the country of destination. Subsequently I have distinguished among the fundamentally different developmental stages and social contexts of children who immigrate before the age of five (preschool) and between the ages of thirteen and seventeen (adolescence and secondary school), and labeled them "1.75ers" and "1.25ers," respectively. For an empirical test of this typology, see Oropesa and Landale (1997b).
14. In a similar vein, Ari Shavit (1997, 52) points to the irony that as American Jews find acceptance and success, they become "an endangered species": "Curiously, it is precisely America's virtues—its generosity, freedom and tolerance—that are now softly killing the last of the great Diasporas. It is because of its very virtues that America is in danger of becoming the most luxurious burial ground ever of Jewish cultural existence."
15. Of these, "assimilation takes place not so much as a result of changes in the organization as in the content, i.e., the memories, of the personality. The individual units, as a result of intimate association, interpenetrate, so to speak, and come in this way into possession of a common experience and a common tradition. The permanence and solidarity of the group rest finally upon this body of common experience and tradition" (Park and Burgess 1921/1924, 510).
16. Karl Mannheim, in his seminal essay on "The Problem of Generations," made this observation about how a "stratum of habits" is "unconsciously and unwittingly" transmitted (1928/1996, 130–31, 151–52): "What is consciously learned or inculcated belongs to those things which in the course of time have somehow, somewhere, become problematic and therefore invited conscious reflection. This is why that [vital] inventory of experience which is absorbed by infiltration from the environment in early youth often becomes the historically oldest stratum of consciousness which tends to stabilize itself as the natural view of the world." More specifically: "The child or adolescent is always open to new influences if placed in a new milieu. They readily assimilate new unconscious mental attitudes and habits, and change their language or dialect. The adult, transferred to a new environment, consciously transforms certain aspects of his modes of thought and behaviour, but never acclimatizes himself in so radical and thoroughgoing a fashion. . . . It appears that language and accent offer an indirect indication as to how far the foundations of a person's consciousness are laid, his basic view of the world stabilized."
17. Park again: "The extent and importance of the kind of homogeneity and 'like-mindedness' that individuals of the same nationality exhibit has been greatly exaggerated. Like-mindedness . . . contributes little or nothing to national solidarity. Likeness is, after all, a purely formal concept which by itself cannot hold anything together" (1914; quoted in Park and Burgess 1921/1924, 759).
18. This is an analytical frame quite different from that of another classic of the period, William Thomas and Florian Znaniecki's *The Polish Peasant in Europe and America* (1918–20/1958), an immigrant family–centered analysis based partly on a methodology of life-course narratives, but one *not* focused on individual assimilation (as has often but erroneously been asserted in the literature) but on ethnic group formation. Thomas and Znaniecki themselves, writing before the publication of Park and Burgess's seminal text, were quite clear on that point: "The problem of individual assimilation is at present an entirely secondary and unimportant issue. . . . The fundamental process which

has been going on during this period is *the formation of a new Polish-American society* out of those fragments separated from Polish society and embedded in American society" (quoted in Conzen 1996, 18).

19. But even that putative homogenization hinged on one's vantage point: already in the 1850s, as Harold Abramson (1980) reminds us, Orestes Brownson, the coiner of the term "Americanization," a Vermont Yankee by birth, and an assimilationist with an antipathy for the Irish, was asked by those same Irish he was urging to Americanize, what form of Americanism they were to conform to—New England, Virginia, or Kentucky? (see Lasch 1991, 184–97).
20. Joseph Joffe, writing from Germany, argues the point this way: "Are people risking death on the high seas to get to China? How many are willing to go for an M.B.A. at Moscow U.? . . . How many people want to dress and live like the Japanese? . . . Imagine a roomful of 14-year-olds—from Germany, Japan, Israel, Russia and Argentina . . . wearing Levi's and baseball caps. . . . How would they relate to one another? They would communicate in English, though haltingly and with heavy accents . . . about icons and images 'made in the U.S.A.' One has to go back to the Roman Empire for a similar instance of cultural hegemony. Actually there is no comparison. . . . America's writ encircles the globe, penetrating all layers of society. Modern mass culture, for better or worse, is American. . . . China, Russia and Europe are strong in some areas and potentially mighty in others. But their cultures do not 'radiate.' They do not offer a universal allure—values and ways of doing things that appeal to the rest of the world" (1997, 43).
21. Esperanto never had a chance. As Laponce (1987, 200) observed, "Linguistic strength is basically political strength. Lyautey used to say that a language is a dialect that has a navy. Whether with the help of sailors, airmen, or atomic bombs, languages assert themselves by force, even when this force is not actually used. A major state that champions a language is usually particularly intolerant of linguistic diversity; its history is typically one of progressive absorption of peripheral languages and minorities." See Crystal (1997) for a fascinating history and an accurate, sober, and non-triumphalist assessment of the status of English as a global language—made all the more ironically intriguing by the fact that the suggestion for the need for such a book came from U.S. English, the nativist organization pushing to make English de jure the "official" language of the United States even as it has become de facto the world's predominant language.
22. See also Hollinger (1995) for a stimulating perspective on the prospects of a cosmopolitanism in a "post-ethnic America" that, like Bourne's "trans-national America," reaches beyond multiculturalism and identity politics (the ethnocentrism of every conceivable ethnos) as well as beyond the ethnocentrism of Anglo-conformity.

10 Segmented Assimilation: Issues, Controversies, and Recent Research on the New Second Generation

Min Zhou

THE SEGMENTED ASSIMILATION theory offers a theoretical framework for understanding the process by which the new second generation—the children of contemporary immigrants—becomes incorporated into the system of stratification in the host society and the different outcomes of this process. Alejandro Portes and I (Portes and Zhou 1993, 82) have observed three possible patterns of adaptation that are most likely to occur among contemporary immigrants and their offspring: "One of them replicates the time-honored portrayal of growing acculturation and parallel integration into the white middle-class; a second leads straight into the opposite direction to permanent poverty and assimilation into the underclass; still a third associates rapid economic advancement with deliberate preservation of the immigrant community's values and tight solidarity." We refer to the divergent destinies from these distinct patterns of adaptation as "segmented assimilation," posing an important theoretical question of what makes some immigrant groups become susceptible to downward mobility and what allows them to bypass or depart from this undesirable route. This chapter examines the issues and controversies surrounding the development of the segmented assimilation theory and reviews the state of recent empirical research relevant to this theoretical approach.

ASSIMILATION TO WHAT? CONCEPTS, ANOMALIES, AND CONTROVERSIES

Classical Assimilationism Revisited

In the literature on immigrant adaptation, the assimilation perspective has dominated much of the sociological thinking on the subject for the most part of this century. Central to this perspective are the assumptions that there is a natural process by which diverse ethnic groups come to share a common culture and to gain equal access to the opportunity structure of society; that this process consists of gradually deserting old cultural and behavioral patterns in favor of new ones; and that, once set in motion, this process moves inevitably and irreversibly toward assimilation. Classical assimilationists argue that migration leads to the situation of the "marginal man": the immigrant is pulled in the direction of the host culture but drawn back by the culture of his or her origin (Park 1928; Stonequist 1937). This painful bipolar process, as Robert Park sees it, entails a natural race relations cycle of contact, competition, accommodation. Under the influence of biotic forces (impersonal competition) and social forces (communication and cooperation), diverse immigrant groups from underprivileged backgrounds are expected to abandon their old ways of life eventually and to become completely "melted" into the mainstream through residential integration and occupational achievement in a sequence of succeeding generations.

While Park emphasizes the natural process that leads to the reduction of social and cultural heterogeneity and neglects structural constraints, Lloyd Warner and Leo Srole (1945) highlight the potency of such institutional factors as social class, phenotypical ranking, and racial or ethnic subsystems in determining the rate of assimilation (also in terms of residential and occupational mobility). According to Warner and Srole, the assimilation of ethnic minorities is especially problematical because the subordination of minority groups is largely based on ascribed characteristics. They argue that, although differences in social status and economic opportunity based on culture and language will disappear over the course of several generations, the social mobility of readily identifiable minority groups, especially blacks, is likely to be confined within racial-caste boundaries. They thus identify skin color, language of origin, and religion as key factors in determining the level of acceptance of minorities by the dominant group. These factors, they maintain, are combined with socioeconomic status to set the speed of complete assimilation for various groups.

While Warner and Srole make an important contribution to the Parkian tradition by introducing into the framework the interaction effects between internal group characteristics and external institutional factors in explaining the pace of assimilation, Milton Gordon (1964) provides a typology of assimilation to capture the complexity of the process, ranging from cultural, structural, marital, identificational, attitude-receptional, and behavior-receptional to civic assimilation. In Gordon's view, immigrants begin their adaptation to their new country through cultural assimilation, or acculturation. Cultural assimilation is for Gordon a necessary first step and the top priority on the agenda of immigrant adjustment. However, Gordon argues, acculturation does not automatically lead to other forms of assimilation (that is, large-scale entrance into the institutions of the host society or intermarriage), and acculturation may continue indefinitely even when no other type of assimilation occurs. Ethnic groups may remain distinguished from one another because of spatial isolation and lack of contact, and their full assimilation will depend ultimately on the degree to which they gain the acceptance of the dominant population. Structural assimilation, in contrast, is the "keystone of the arch of assimilation" that will inevitably lead to other stages of assimilation (Gordon 1964, 81). Though vague about how groups advance from one stage to another and what causes change, Gordon anticipates nevertheless that most ethnic groups will eventually lose all their distinctive characteristics and cease to exist as ethnic groups as they pass through the stages of assimilation, eventually intermarrying with the majority population and entering its institutions on a primary-group level.

From the classical assimilationist standpoint, distinctive ethnic traits such as old cultural ways, native languages, or ethnic enclaves are sources of disadvantages (Child 1943; Warner and Srole 1945; Wirth 1928/1956). These disadvantages negatively affect assimilation, but the effects are greatly reduced in each of the successive generations, since native-born generations adopt English as the primary means of communication and become more and more similar to the earlier American population in life skills, manner, and outlook. Although complete acculturation to the dominant American culture may not ensure all immigrants full social participation in the host society, immigrants must free themselves from their old cultures in order to begin rising up from marginal positions. Between the 1920s and the 1950s, the United States seemed to have absorbed the great waves of immigrants, who arrived primarily from Europe. Sociological studies have indicated progressive trends of social mobility across generations of immigrants and increasing rates of intermarriage, as determined by educational attainment, job skills, length of stay since immigration, English proficiency, and level of exposure to American culture (Alba 1985a; Chiswick 1977; Greeley 1976b; Lieberson and Waters 1988; Sandberg 1974; Wytrwal 1961).

Anomalies

Beginning in the 1960s, the classical assimilation perspective, as applied to the more recently arrived non-European immigrant groups, has met with challenges. Instead of eventual convergence of these groups into the mainstream core, as predicted by assimilation theories, recent research has witnessed several anomalies. The first anomaly concerns the persistent ethnic differences across generations. Conventional assimilation models of immigrant adaptation predict assimilation as a function of the length of U.S. residence and succeeding generations. But this is not how it always seems to work. Recent studies have revealed an opposite pattern: the longer the U.S. residence, the more maladaptive the outcomes, whether measured in terms of school performance, aspirations, or behavior and regardless of immigrant groups (Kao and Tienda 1995, Rumbaut and Ima 1988; Suárez-Orozco and Suárez-Orozco 1995). Nancy Landale and Sal Oropesa (1995) found that the disadvantages were reproduced, rather than diminished, in poor immigrant families who had lived a longer time in the United States. They found, for example, significant increases of children living in single-parent families across generations of U.S. residence and across many Asian and Latin American nationality groups. By the third generation, in particular, the prevalence of female headship among all nationality groups of Latin American children (ranging from 40 percent of Mexicans and 50 percent of Cubans to 70 percent of Dominicans) and Filipino children (40 percent) constituted a serious disadvantage. This situation implies that even if the parental generation is able to work hard to achieve higher positions and higher incomes, their children's access to these gains may be seriously circumvented by acculturation.

Studies of intergenerational mobility have also revealed divergent rather than convergent outcomes, suggesting that early and insignificant differentials in advantage result in substantial differences in educational and occupational mobility in later years (Becker 1963; Goffman 1963; Perlmann 1988). In their study of the educational attainment of twenty-five religio-ethnic groups in the United States, Charles Hirschman and Luis Falcon (1985) found that neither generation nor length of U.S. residence significantly influenced educational outcomes. Specifically, children of highly educated immigrants consistently fared much better in school than did fourth- or fifth-generation descendants of poorly educated ancestors, regardless of religio-ethnic background. In a study of the Irish, Italian, Jewish, and African Americans in Providence, Rhode Island, Joel Perlmann (1988) showed that, even with family background factors held constant, ethnic differences in levels of schooling and economic attainment persisted in the second and later generations and that schooling was not equally commensurate with occupational advancement for African Americans as it was for other European Americans across generations.

Clearly, adaptation outcomes vary depending on the socioeconomic assets immigrants have brought with them; these assets in turn determine where they settle—in affluent middle-class suburbs or in impoverished inner-city ghettos. Although the emergence of a middle-class population is a distinctive aspect of today's immigration, a disproportionately large number of immigrant children have converged on underprivileged and linguistically distinctive neighborhoods. There the immigrants and their children come into direct daily contact with the poor rather than with the middle-class; they are also apt to encounter members of native minorities and other immigrants rather than members of the dominant majority, creating new obstacles for assimilation.

Another anomaly is what Herbert Gans (1992a) describes as "the second-generation decline." Gans notes three possible scenarios for today's new second generation: education-driven mobility, succession-driven mobility, and niche improvement. He observes that immigrant children from less fortunate socioeconomic backgrounds have a much harder time than other middle-class children in succeeding in school, and that a significant number of the children of poor, especially dark-skinned, immigrants face multiple risks of being trapped in permanent poverty in an era of stagnant economic growth and in the process of Americanization because they "will either not be asked, or will be reluctant, to work at immigrant wages and hours as their parents did but will lack job opportunities, skills and connections to do better" (1992a, 173–74). Gans anticipates a dismal prospect for the children of the less fortunate who must confront high rates of unemployment, crime, alcoholism, drug use, and other pathologies associated with poverty and the frustration of rising expectation. Joel Perlmann and Roger Waldinger (this volume) call this phenomenon "the second-generation revolt." They argue that such revolt is not merely caused by exogenous factors, such as racial discrimination, declining economic opportunities, and exposure to the adversarial outlooks of native-born youths, but also by endogenous factors inherent in the immigration process, including pre-immigration class standing and the size and nature of immigrant inflows.

Still another anomaly is the peculiar outcomes of contemporary immigrant adaptation. In America's fastest-growing knowledge-intensive industries, foreign-born engineers and other highly skilled professionals disproportionately take up various key technical positions, and some even occupy ownership positions. In immigrant enclaves, ethnic commercial banks, corporate-owned restaurants, and chain supermarkets stand side by side with traditional rotating credit associations, coffee or tea houses, and mom-and-pop stores (Zhou 1992). In upscale middle-class suburbs, wealthy immigrants buy up luxurious homes and move right in, jumping several steps ahead and bypassing the traditional bottom-up progression (Horton 1995; Waldinger and Tseng 1992). In urban public schools, neither valedictorians nor delinquents are atypical among immigrant children regardless of timing and racial or socioeconomic backgrounds. For example, in the past fifteen years, 1.5- or second-generation immigrant children have dominated the list of the top ten award winners of the Westinghouse Science Talent Search, one of the country's most prestigious high school academic contests. Many of these immigrant children are recent arrivals and from families of moderate socioeconomic background (Zhou 1997b). Although immigrant children are overrepresented among award winners or on academic fast tracks, many others are extremely vulnerable to multiple high-risk behaviors, school failure, street gangs, and youth crime. Even Asian Americans, the so-called model minority, have seen a steady rise of youth gang membership. Some of the Asian gang members are from suburban middle-class families, attend magnet schools, and are exceptionally good students.

Controversies and Alternative Perspectives

These anomalies lead directly to questions about the applicability of classical straight-line assimilation theory, invoking heated theoretical debate and the development of alternative frameworks. Gans has advanced a bumpy-line approach to defend classical assimilationism (Gans 1992a, 1992b). He argues (1992b, 42) that acculturation or Americanization has continued among immigrants, "be they the descendants of the European immigrants who arrived here between 1880 and 1925, or . . . the latest newcomers to America." However, Gans asserts, these immigrants also construct their own acculturation and assimilation in response to environmental pressures. Schools, American peers, and the media exert powerful influences on immigrant children; the prevailing youth culture and the freedoms (particularly personal choices in dress, dating, and sexual practices) that were unavailable in their old country also overwhelm them. Because of exposure, these children are likely to develop expectations of life in the United States much higher than those of their parents; they will not be willing to accept immigrant parental work norms or to work in "un-American" conditions, as many of their parents do. Thus, some of the children may not even be able to carry out their parents' wishes and expectations of moving up and "making it in America," much less to fulfill their own expectations. Gans looks at these divergent patterns as various bumps (either imposed by the host society or invented by immigrants themselves) on the road to eventual assimilation into "non-ethnic" America. He implies that for the new second generation, especially for the children of dark-skinned, poor, and unskilled immigrants, "delayed acculturation" may be more desirable.

Richard Alba and Victor Nee (this volume) are also enthusiastic defenders of classical assimilationism. They believe that assimilation should work for contemporary immigrants because it worked so well in the past for turn-of-the-century immigrants. They argue that the anomalies noted earlier are adverse effects of contemporary structural changes that classical assimilationism is unable to anticipate. First, the continuously high rate of mass immigration has limited the host society's "breathing space" for absorbing and integrating immigrants and has constantly replenished ethnic communities, setting up a major roadblock to assimilation. Second, the growing "hourglass" economy, with knowledge-intensive, high-paying jobs at one end and labor-intensive, low-paying jobs at the other, has taken away several rungs of the mobility ladder that are crucial for enabling immigrants, especially those with little education and few job skills, to start from the bottom and then climb up. Third, the changing political and ideological structure that increasingly advocates multiculturalism has also slowed down assimilation. Alba and Nee consider the diverse outcomes among contemporary immigrants simply the differences in the speed of assimilation and attribute them to variations in premigration as well as postmigration human-capital characteristics, the spatial distribution of co-ethnic populations, group size, and continual mass migration. Despite intergroup differences, Alba and Nee expect that, over time, contemporary immigrants will look more like other Americans and become assimilated into the American middle class through intermarriage, residential integration, and occupational mobility.

These arguments generally assume that there is a unified core of American society, be it "non-ethnic" America or "middle" America, into which immigrants are expected to assimilate, and that, with enough time, all immigrants and their offspring will eventually assimilate, regardless of national origin, phenotypical characteristics, or socioeconomic background. Other scholars disagree; their criticisms target primarily the assimilationist ideas of a unified core, ethnic-cultural inferiority, and irreversible assimilation. What is being debated, though, is not whether assimilation will happen among contemporary immigrants but whether the assimilation framework is applicable to their American experiences.

Multiculturalists forcefully reject the assimilationist assumption of a unified core. Scholars from this perspective perceive American society as a fluid and heterogeneous collection of ethnic and racial minority groups, as well as the dominant majority group of European Americans (Glazer and Moynihan 1970; Handlin 1973). They believe that immigrants are active shapers of their own lives rather than passive beneficiaries or victims of "ineluctable modernizing and Americanizing forces" (Conzen 1991; Greeley 1976b). Thus, they are concerned with the fundamental question of how different the world may look if the experiences of the excluded are placed at the center of our thinking. From this standpoint, it is not assumed that the premigration cultural attributes inherent to ethnicity are inferior or that they should necessarily be absorbed by the core culture of the host society; rather, these characteristics are constantly reshaped and reinvented by interaction with the host society. Greeley (1976b, 32) contends that "ethnicity is not a way of looking back to the old world . . . [but] rather a way of being American, a way of defining yourself into the pluralist culture which existed before you arrived." Kathleen Conzen and her associates (1992, 4–5) conceptualize ethnicity as "a process of construction or invention which incorporates, adapts, and amplifies preexisting communal solidarities, cultural attributes, and historical memories" grounded in the real-life context and in social experience. According to these scholars, premigration cultural attributes cannot be equated with homeland cultures, because immigrants tend to select carefully not only what to pack in their trunks to bring to the United States but also what to unpack once settled. Also, homeland cultural norms and values may not be entirely inconsistent with American ones. Just as some aspects of immigrant cultural patterns may continue in a state of uneasy coexistence with American requirements as a host country, other aspects of immigrant cultural patterns may "fit" the requirements of life here or may even be prerequisites for "making it in America" (Fukuyama 1993). Still others are modified, changed, adapted, transformed, reformed, and negotiated in the course of immigrant adjustment (Garcia 1996).

The multicultural perspective offers an alternative way of viewing the American host society, treating members of ethnic minority groups as a part of the American population rather than as foreigners or outsiders and presenting ethnic or immigrant cultures as integral segments of American society. However, the questions of "second-generation decline" and "second-generation revolt" remain unanswered within this theoretical framework. While emphasizing how people construct or invent their own ethnicity, it understudies how they also construct their own acculturation and assimilation. Gans points out that the pressures of both formal acculturation (through schooling) and informal acculturation (through American peers and the media) will undoubtedly impinge on the second generation (Gans 1992a).

The elusiveness of ethnic characteristics also creates problems in the use of the multicultural framework as an explanatory tool. Each generation passes cultural patterns, which are often subtle, to the next, but the mechanisms of this process are unclear, and many assumptions and attitudes of ethnic group members are hard to identify and measure (Archdeacon 1983). Also, the constituents of American diversity are not equal; maintaining a distinctive ethnicity can both help and hinder the social mobility of ethnic group members. For example, first-generation members of some immigrant minority groups, such as Mexicans, have been less able to motivate their children to excel in school and move upward in American society, while other groups, such as Chinese and Koreans, have far more often succeeded in pushing younger people to pursue upward social mobility (Perlmann and Waldinger, this volume). After all, how immigrants become incorporated into the American mosaic is never clearly theorized.

Another major theoretical stance is the structural perspective, which offers a framework for understanding the differences in the social adaptation of ethnic minority groups in terms of the advantages and disadvantages inherent to social structures rather than in the process of acculturation or selective Americanization. The structuralists also refute the assimilationist assumption of a "non-ethnic" unified core and present American society as a stratified system of social inequality in which different social categories—whether birth-ascribed or not—have unequal access to wealth, power, and privilege (Barth and Noel 1972; Blau and Duncan 1967). From this perspective, immigrants and ethnic minorities are constrained by the ethnic hierarchy, which systematically limits their access to social resources such as opportunities for jobs, housing, and education, resulting in persistent racial and ethnic disparities in levels of income, educational attainment, and occupational achievement (Zhou and Kamo 1994). Consequently, the benefits of "becoming American" depend largely on what stratum of American society absorbs the new immigrants. Overall, the structural perspective raises skepticism about eventual assimilation and interethnic accommodation, as suggested by the assimilation perspective and implied by the multicultural perspective, because of inherent conflicts between the dominant and subordinate groups in the hierarchy. On the issue of immigrant adaptation, this perspective maintains that the process of becoming American may not lead uniformly to middle-class status but rather to different rungs on the ethnic hierarchy. The structural perspective has considerable plausibility in that it takes into account the effects of structural constraints. However, this theoretical framework is constructed at the "grand" level to predict macroprocesses and general patterns of social mobility; it is thus insufficient to explain the varied and disparate outcomes of a given process or pattern for diverse ethnic groups and for the members of these groups who themselves display diverse socioeconomic characteristics.

Divergent Destinies: New Theoretical Developments and Research

Theoretical controversies surrounding classical assimilationism are generally concerned with how immigrants adapt to American society and with the forces that promote or impede their progress. The assimilationists, multiculturalists, and structuralists have approached similar issues from different standpoints. Assimilationists focus on the changes that a new environment can bring about in cultural patterns and describe how immigrants and their succeeding generations gradually move away from the old country ways. Multiculturalists consider the perpetual reshaping and reinventing of the original immigrant cultural patterns as an indispensable part of American society, and argue that these cultural patterns may never completely disappear. Structuralists emphasize that the extent to which immigrants adopt host-country ways and the benefits of adopting these ways depend on the social and economic structures of the host country. Although each of these perspectives makes a significant contribution to our understanding of the process of immigrant adaptation, the divergent outcomes of this process have been understudied. The segmented assimilation theory has thus emerged to fill the gap, advancing an alternative framework for delving into the complex process of immigrant adaptation in postindustrial America.

Segmented assimilation can be viewed as a middle-range theory that focuses on why different patterns of adaptation emerge among contemporary immigrants and on how these patterns necessarily lead to the destinies of convergence or divergence. Drawing on the existing literature, this theory places the process of becoming American, in terms of both acculturation and economic adaptation, in the context of a society consisting of segregated and unequal segments and considers this process to be characterized by at least three possible multidirectional patterns: the time-honored upward mobility pattern dictating acculturation and economic integration into the normative structures of middle-class America; the downward mobility pattern, in the opposite direction, dictating acculturation and parallel integration into the underclass; and economic integration into middle-class America with lagged acculturation and deliberate preservation of the immigrant community's values and solidarity (Portes and Zhou 1993). The theory attempts to explain what determines the segment of American society into which a particular immigrant group may assimilate.

Possible determinants involve a range of individual-level factors and contextual factors. The most important individual-level factors influencing immigrant adaptation include education and other factors associated with exposure to American society, such as aspiration, English-language ability, place of birth, age on arrival, and length of residence in the United States. Structural factors include racial status, family socioeconomic background, and place of residence. The assimilation models also specify these two sets of variables, suggesting that educational achievement, stronger aspiration and motivation, proficiency in English, native birth or arrival at a young age, longer U.S. residence, lighter skin color, higher family class status, and residence outside ethnic enclaves should contribute to successful adaptation (Alba and Nee, this volume). However, the segmented assimilation theory diverges from the classical framework with regard to the effects of these determinants: it assumes that these two sets of determinants are in themselves of minimum importance and focuses instead on the interaction between the two. The discussion that follows elaborates on the conceptualization of the interaction effects, delineates some of the major concepts and propositions about segmented assimilation, and reviews empirical evidence from recent research that bears on these theoretical ideas.

Structural Constraints: Changes in the Context of Reception

The contemporary American context that greets immigrants and their children has changed drastically from the context that greeted turn-of-the-century European immigrants. Several trends are particularly noteworthy. The most visible trend in the past two decades is seen in the widening gap between rich and poor, which progressively narrowed for most of the twentieth century. The part of the American workforce referred to as "knowledge workers" or "symbolic analysts" has seen its economic advantages steadily increase as information technology and management have become more critical to the economy (Drucker 1993; Reich 1992). At the same time, the situation of most American workers has worsened. Between 1979 and 1989 the incomes of the top 5 percent of American wage-earners increased from $120,253 to $148,438, while the incomes of the bottom 20 percent decreased from $9,990 to $9,431 (U.S. Bureau of the Census 1984, 1994). Over the course of the 1980s, 80 percent of American workers saw their real hourly wages go down by an average of about 5 percent. Not only do blue-collar jobs, the kinds of jobs generally available to newly arrived immigrants, pay less than in previous years, but there are also far fewer of them. Jobs in manufacturing and in unskilled labor have been disappearing at a particularly rapid rate (Mishel and Bernstein 1992). Although the American economy has not yet taken on the shape of an "hourglass," the trend is toward expanding classes of poor and rich and a shrinking middle class. In such an economic structure, even U.S.-born Americans find their chances for economic mobility lessening. The situation for many immigrants is bleaker, except for the unusually fortunate, the highly educated, and the highly skilled (Waldinger 1996b).

Contemporary economic hardships are different from the hardships of the Great Depression and the hardships in many Third World countries. Although there is a growing class of poor Americans, there are relatively few deaths from starvation in the United States. Until the early 1990s, the welfare state had made access to public assistance relatively easy (Rumbaut 1994a; Tienda and Liang 1994). Although opportunities for stable jobs with good incomes were rare for low-income individuals, food stamps and Aid to Families with Dependent Children (AFDC) were readily available. Public assistance did not provide a comfortable way of life, for welfare payments averaged less than half the amount defined as poverty-level income (Sancton 1992); it did, nonetheless, provide a means of existence for the chronically poor and the unemployed or underemployed. Yet members of this expanding class of poor were not being offered chances for socioeconomic improvement; they were, for the most part, being fed, housed, and maintained in social and economic limbo.

These unfortunate circumstances were exacerbated just prior to the 1996 presidential election when President Bill Clinton signed a Republican welfare reform bill. The bill, which limits public assistance to two continuous years and mandates a five-year lifetime maximum, provides neither public jobs nor child care for recipients who exceed the limit, and nothing for their children. The implementation of the bill will change the nature of the welfare state in new and significant ways. It will cut off the lifeline of the poor, especially children, driving them into deeper poverty; it will also exclude legal immigrants from access to most basic forms of assistance, forcing poor immigrant families to sink or swim. The long-term effects of the welfare bill remain to be seen, but it appears that thousands of children will be thrown into poverty and that chances for the truly disadvantaged to get out of poverty will be even more limited.

Another trend is the increasing concentration of poverty in inner cities, where most low-skilled immigrants converge. The poor are not, of course, being housed evenly across the American landscape. Even before new information technologies and the globalization of production began shrinking the American working class, the automobile industry had promoted the suburbanization of the middle class. With the contraction of American manufacturing and the suburbanization first of middle-class populations and later of middle-class jobs, poverty has become concentrated in urban areas (Herbers 1986; Muller 1981). These changes have adversely affected not only individual minority members but also minority communities. In central cities, African Americans, Mexican Americans, Puerto Rican Americans, and other members of immigrant minority groups do not simply predominate in entire neighborhoods but are also the poorest of their respective groups who are left behind by their affluent co-ethnics. Institutional discrimination and segregation have exacerbated the social and economic processes of minority concentration in low-income communities (Massey and Denton 1993; Moore 1989; Moore and Vigil 1993; Wilson 1987).

The creation of concentrated low-income neighborhoods has had social consequences for the people who live in these locales, and particularly for young people, who form their expectations from the world they see around them. Increasing unemployment has resulted in a decrease in the number of marriageable men in these communities and a corresponding increase in female-headed households. Without middle-class models, without roles in economic production, and without roles in families, young men in low-income communities tend to become marginalized and alienated (Darity and Myers 1995; Testa and Krogh 1995; Wilson 1987). Social isolation and deprivation have given rise to an "oppositional culture" among young people who feel excluded from mainstream American society and oppressed by it.

Neighborhoods affect schools, since public school attendance in the United States is based on place of residence. The economic and social influences are also felt in neighborhood schools. Moreover, students in schools shape one another's attitudes and expectations. In a disruptive urban environment caught between rising hopes and shrinking opportunities, younger members of native-born minorities have become increasingly skeptical about school achievement as a viable path to upward mobility and have thus responded to their bleak future with resentment toward adult middle-class society and rejection of mobility goals.

Third, lowered chances for mobility create frustration and pessimism for all American young people, but these emotions are most strongly felt by those at the bottom. When those at the bottom are also members of historically oppressed minority groups, the frustration is compounded by the need to maintain self-esteem, so that rejection of middle-class mores and opposition to authority become important strategies for psychological survival (Fordham 1996). Likewise, although there is a strong anti-intellectual streak in American youth culture at all socioeconomic levels, the rejection of academic pursuits is especially intense in minority schools, where many students tend to identify teachers and school administrators with oppressive authority, see little hope in their future entry into the middle class, and rebel against learning. A sizable proportion of today's second-generation children live in poor urban neighborhoods and thus go to underprivileged schools dominated by other immigrant children or other minority students. These schools provide poor learning environments and are often even dangerous places. Many immigrant children find themselves in classrooms with other immigrant children speaking a language other than English or with other native minority children, who either have trouble keeping up with schoolwork or consciously resist academic achievement. Because students in schools shape one another's attitudes and expectations, such an oppositional culture negatively affects the educational outcomes of immigrant children.

Class and "Color"

Family socioeconomic status shapes the immediate social conditions for adaptation. As noted earlier, class status is the most crucial factor because it determines the type of neighborhood in which children live, the quality of the school they attend, and the group of peers with whom they associate. James Coleman and his associates (1966) report that children do better if they attend schools where classmates are predominantly from higher socioeconomic backgrounds. Children who live in poor inner-city neighborhoods confront social environments drastically different from those of affluent suburban neighborhoods. These children suffer from unequal distribution of educational resources, which seriously curtails their chances in life, trapping them further in isolated ghettos (Davis 1993; Jencks and Mayer 1990). Ghettoization, in turn, produces a political atmosphere and a mentality that preserve class division along racial lines, leading to the greater alienation of inner-city children from American institutions and further diminishing their chances for upward mobility (Fainstein 1995).

Class has a direct impact on the adaptation outcomes of immigrant children. Those from middle-class backgrounds are able to benefit from financially secure families, good schools, safe neighborhoods, and other formal and informal organizations that provide support and ensure better life chances for them. Children with poorly educated and unskilled parents, in contrast, often find themselves growing up in underprivileged neighborhoods subject to poverty, poor schools, violence, drugs, and a generally disruptive social environment.

The "color" status of the majority of contemporary immigrants sets them apart from European Americans. Although many of them may have never experienced prejudice associated with a particular skin color or racial type in their homelands, immigrant children, especially those whose phenotypes resemble African Americans, face a reality in their host society in which their ascribed physical features may become a handicap, creating additional barriers to upward mobility (Portes 1995a; Waters 1994). Recent research has found that the socioeconomic circumstances of today's predominantly non-white second generation vary by skin color. Using the 1990 census data, Oropesa and Landale (1997a) show that poverty rates for immigrant children ranged from 21 percent among non-Latino European Americans to 24 percent for non-Latino African Americans, 27 percent for Asian Americans, and 41 percent for Latino Americans. Among the second generation (U.S.-born with at least one foreign-born parent), there was a substantial drop in poverty rates for all racial groups, but the magnitude of the decline varied by race: while poverty rates between the first (or the 1.5) and second generations dropped more than half among non-Latino European American and Asian American children, they dropped less than one-third among non-Latino African American and Latino American children. The conditions for third-generation children (U.S.-born children with U.S.-born parents) were most disturbing: except for Asian Americans, there was no appreciable socioeconomic improvement between second- and third-generation non-Latino European Americans and Latino Americans, but there was a significant deterioration among third-generation non-Latino African Americans, whose poverty rate jumped up to 40 percent, an increase of twenty-six percentage points from that of their first-generation counterparts. These statistics reveal an obvious effect of race, implying a severe class handicap associated with skin colors.

Racial status influences the social adaptation of immigrant children in ways closely connected to family socioeconomic status. Indeed, William Julius Wilson (1978) has argued that contemporary racial inequality has become largely a matter of social class. Past racism, in his view, essentially delays the entry of racial minority members into full participation in the American economy even before the old blue-collar opportunities have disappeared, leaving nonwhites in jobless neighborhoods. While the Wilsonian approach focuses on the impact of economic restructuring, the segmented assimilation theory places more emphasis on the effect of continuing racial discrimination.

One such effect is residential segregation on the basis of class and race. Douglas Massey and Nancy Denton (1987) provide convincing evidence that the physical and social isolation of many black Americans is produced by ongoing, conscious discriminatory actions and policies, not simply by racism experienced in the past. Consequently the inequalities of class and race that plague American society are carried into the American educational system. Inner-city schools then become "arenas of injustice" that provide unequal opportunities on the basis of race and class (Keniston and the Carnegie Council on Children 1977). Mary Davis (1993) found that poor African American and Latino American families who moved from inner-city neighborhoods did better in school and in labor markets than those left behind. The pattern generally held true for immigrant children who attended suburban schools.

Another effect is the development of an "adversarial subculture" among those trapped in inner-city ghettos (Portes and Zhou 1993, 83). The children and grandchildren of earlier immigrants or native minorities who failed to move up the socioeconomic ladder have concentrated in inner cities, and to a large extent, their unfortunate circumstances are a direct result of racial discrimination coupled with economic restructuring (Wilson 1978). These downtrodden native minorities have thus reacted to racial oppression by constructing resistance both as conformity—"unqualified acceptance of the ideological realm of the larger society"—and, more frequently, as avoidance—"willful rejection of whatever will validate the negative claims of the larger society" (Fordham 1996, 39). Consequently they develop an adversarial outlook that has more to do with the willful refusal of mainstream norms and values than with the failure of assimilation (Fordham 1996; Kohl 1994; Wilson 1996). School achievement is seen as unlikely to lead to upward mobility, and high achievers are seen as sellouts to oppressive authority. This adversarial outlook can exercise a powerful influence on the newcomers and their children in inner cities (Portes 1995a; Portes and Zhou 1993).

The confrontation with the inner city places the second generation in a forced-choice dilemma. If they strive to meet their parents' expectations for academic achievement, they are likely to be ostracized as "uncool," "nerdy," or "acting white" by their American peers in schools. If they submit to peer pressure and attempt to become "American," on the other hand, they are likely to adopt the cultural ways, including the language and behavior, of the inner city. The forced-choice dilemma confronting Chicano and Puerto Rican youth is a case in point. Margaret Gibson (1989) and Philippe Bourgois (1991), in their respective studies, found that Chicano students and Puerto Rican students who did well in school were forcefully excluded by their co-ethnic peers as "turnovers" acting "white." This phenomenon is affected by three structural factors: the immediate

American context in which an adversarial outlook prevails; the internal structure of the immigrant community; and the social ties linking the second generation to this particular context and to the immigrant community (Portes 1995a). In inner cities, the development of, or exposure to, an adversarial outlook can either lead to downward mobility or confine immigrant offspring to the same slots at the bottom level from which they began (De Vos 1975; Hirschman and Falcon 1985; Ogbu 1974; Perlmann and Waldinger, this volume; Portes 1995a; Portes and Zhou 1993; Zhou 1997b). In other words, this type of assimilation can cause immigrant children to be stigmatized and condemned by their own community as well as by the larger society; it can also destroy all of their parents' hopes for them.

The Ethnic Factor: Advantages and Disadvantages

But how can one account for the fact that immigrant children tend to do better than their American peers of similar racial status and socioeconomic background who attend public schools in the same neighborhoods? John Ogbu (1974) attributes different outcomes to a group's social status in the receiving society. He distinguishes between immigrant minorities (arriving in this country voluntarily) and castelike minorities (originally brought to this country by force). In his line of reasoning, the different historical experiences of groups shape their perceptions of the host society and, hence, their strategies of adaptation to that society. Either group members of racial minorities could accept an inferior caste status and a sense of basic inferiority as part of their collective self-definition or they could create a positive view of their heritage on the basis of cultural and racial distinction, thereby establishing a sense of collective dignity (see also De Vos 1975).

Although this is true for both voluntary immigrant minorities and involuntary castelike minorities, the difference lies in the advantageous or disadvantageous aspects of racial or ethnic identity. Ogbu (1989) shows from his research on Chinese American students in Oakland, California, that, in spite of cultural and language differences and relatively low economic status, these students had grade point averages that ranged from 3.0 to 4.0. He attributes their academic success to the integration of these students into the family and the community, which placed a high value on education and held a positive attitude toward public schools.

Race or ethnicity may be related to performance in the school system for cultural reasons as well as for purely socioeconomic reasons. It is possible that cultural values, such as a tradition of respect for teachers, affect how young people respond to the American institution of public education. The experience of immigration, moreover, can reshape cultural values. Ogbu points out that immigrant groups frequently seek upward mobility, so that education often comes to occupy a central place in immigrant aspirations (Ogbu 1974, 1983, 1989, 1991). But the deliberate cultivation of ethnicity may also be a factor. Gibson (1989), for example, found that the outstanding performance of Punjabi children in a relatively poor rural area of northern California was a result of parental pressure on children to stay close to their own immigrant families and to avoid excessive Americanization. Similarly, Nathan Caplan, John Whitmore, and Marcella Choy (1989) found that Southeast Asian refugee children (not including Cambodians and Hmongs) excelled in the American school system despite the disadvantaged location of their schools and their parents' lack of education and facility with English. These researchers, too, attributed Southeast Asian academic achievement to cultural values and practices unique to ethnic families. Even among Southeast Asian refugees, intraethnic effect was significant. Rubén Rumbaut and Kenji Ima (1988) found that Vietnamese high school students did much better in both GPAs and test scores than their Cambodian and Laotian peers, and that overall the strongest predictor of GPA was the measure of ethnic resilience.

Although more recent studies of the educational experiences of Asian American children indicate that parents' socioeconomic status, length of U.S. residence, and homework hours significantly affect academic performance, these studies also show that controls for such factors do not eliminate the effect of ethnicity (Kao and Tienda 1995; Portes and Rumbaut 1996; Rumbaut 1995, 1996b; Rumbaut and Ima 1988). Portes and Rumbaut (1996; see also Rumbaut 1996b) report findings from a large random sample of second-generation high school students in Florida and southern California, showing that parents' socioeconomic status, length of U.S. residence, and homework hours significantly affected academic performance, but that controlling for these factors did not eliminate the effect of ethnicity. Grace Kao and Marta Tienda (1995) found, based on data from the National Education Longitudinal Studies (NELS), that parental nativity and children's birthplace had different effects on children's academic outcomes depending on race and ethnicity. Alejandro Portes and Dag MacLeod (1996), also using NELS, reported that the negative effect of disadvantaged group membership among immigrant children was reinforced rather than reduced in suburban schools, but that the positive effect of advantaged group membership remained significant even in inner-city schools.

In recent research on adolescent development, though originally not intending to focus on ethnic differences, Laurence Steinberg (1996) uncovered the surprisingly prominent and strong role that ethnicity plays in structuring adolescents' lives, both in and outside of school. He found that Asian American students outperformed European American students, who in turn outperformed African American and Latino American students by significantly large margins, and that the ethnic differences remained marked and consistent across the nine different high schools under study and after controlling for social class, family structure, and place of birth of parents. He also found that the ethnic effect persisted in important explanatory variables of school success, such as the belief in the payoff of schooling, attributional styles, and peer groups. Steinberg concludes that ethnicity is just as important a factor as social class and gender in defining and shaping the everyday lives of American children.

However, the advantages attached to ethnicity may be limited for castelike minorities. If a socially defined racial minority group wishes to assimilate but finds that the normal paths of integration are blocked on the basis of race, the group may be forced to pursue alternative survival strategies that enable them to cope psychologically with racial barriers but do not necessarily encourage school success. María Eugenia Matute-Bianchi (1986) found that the relationship between scholastic achievement and ethnicity did not hold for native-born Chicanos and Cholos, who had been uprooted from their Mexican heritage and were trapped in a castelike minority status. They reacted to their exclusion and subordination with resentment, regarded efforts toward academic achievement as "acting white," and constructed an identity in resistance to the dominant majority white society. Marcelo Suárez-Orozco (1991) reached similar conclusions about native-born Mexican Americans, who perceived the effect of the educational system as continued exploitation.

Nonetheless, not all immigrant groups can fit into the category of immigrant or voluntary minority. Patricia Pessar (1987, 124–25) notes that many first-generation Dominican immigrants were able to improve their living standards by pooling resources in their households and that they were mostly satisfied with what they achieved, comparing their lives in the United States to their lives in the Dominican Republic. However, she casts doubt on whether the struggle of first-generation immigrants will steer the second generation toward upholding their parents' aspirations and fulfilling their own expectations of socioeconomic mobility. She speculates that Dominican children are likely to be frustrated and disappointed if they find themselves trapped on the lower rungs of the occupational ladder because of "blatant discrimination" and "lack of access to prestigious social networks" linking them to higher professions. Alejandro Portes and Alex Stepick (1993) and Mary Waters (1994, 1997) have also noted such a trend among Haitian youth in Miami and West Indian youth in New York City toward rapid assimilation into ghetto youth subcultures, at the cost of giving up their immigrant parents' pride of culture and hopes for mobility on the basis of ethnic solidarity. Joel Perlmann and Roger Waldinger (this volume) also point out that the prospect of downward assimilation disproportionately affects children of Mexican immigrants.

Immigrant Cultures Versus Leveling Pressures

If growing up in poor neighborhoods has adverse social consequences for native-born minority children, how then do neighborhood and peer-group settings affect the children of contemporary immigrants? Socioeconomic status and race are not all that counts; just as important is the social capital embedded in the family and the ethnic community. Recent research has shown that immigrant children from intact families (especially with the two natural parents) or from families associated with tight-knit social networks consistently show better psychological conditions, higher levels of academic achievement, and stronger educational aspirations than those in single-parent or socially isolated families (Portes 1995a; Portes and Schauffler 1994; Rumbaut 1994b, 1996b; Suárez-Orozco 1989; Zhou and Bankston 1994).

Since members of racial or ethnic minorities can respond to the disadvantages imposed by the larger society by establishing group solidarity, it is important to consider the extent to which immigrants and their children are able to use a common ethnicity as a basis for cooperation to overcome structural disadvantages. In the segmented assimilation framework, ethnic networks are conceptualized as a form of social capital that influences children's adaptation through support as well as control. The central argument is that individual and macro-structural factors interact with specific immigrant cultural patterns and the group characteristics to shape the fates of immigrants and their offspring. An immigrant culture, which may be referred to as the "original" culture, consists of an entire way of life, including the languages, ideas, beliefs, values, behavioral patterns, and everything else that immigrants bring with them to their new country. This original culture may be seen as hindering the adaptation of members of the ethnic group (the assimilationist perspective) or as promoting this adaptation (the multiculturalist perspective). Seeing immigrant cultures as American microcosms of other nations, however, involves overlooking the historically dynamic nature of all cultures. As discussed previously, cultures may persist while adapting to the pressures of American society, resulting in many similar patterns of cultural orientation among different immigrant groups (Conzen 1991). These newly adapted cultural patterns are often confused with those of the original culture. American ethnic foods offer an example of this cultural reshaping. Each type of ethnic food, Italian, Mexican, or Chinese, is distinctive in itself, but all of them are quite similar in the process of fitting the taste of the general American public. If a particular dish does not appeal to the public taste, it will not be known or accepted as an ethnic dish no matter how authentic it may be.

Similarly, the cultural traits that characterize a group depend not only on how the group selects these traits as its identifying characteristics but also on how the larger society treats them. If the cultural characteristics an immigrant group selects for display in the United States are approved by the mainstream, the group will generally be considered to have an advantageous culture; if not, its culture is deemed deficient. For example, most of the Asian subgroups whose original cultures are dominated by Confucianism, Taoism, or Buddhism—such as Chinese, Korean, Japanese, and Vietnamese—often selectively unpack from their cultural baggage those traits suitable to the new environment, such as two-parent families, a strong work ethic, delayed gratification, and thrift. Also, they either bury at the bottom of their trunks or keep strictly to themselves other traits considered not so fit, such as nonconfrontation, passivity, submissiveness, and excessive family obligations. Since the traits unpacked resemble the ideals of the mainstream (WASP) culture, these "proper" original cultures set a tone of favorable treatment, which may help the group to focus on other difficulties of adjustment and enable group members to capitalize on the ethnic resources.

On the other hand, if a group displays characteristics that are not comparable to the ideals of the mainstream, or that seem similar to the characteristics identified with or projected onto native-born minorities, such as matriarchal families, these traits will be combined with the racial or ethnic factor and be seen as "deficient" cultural characteristics, and thus the group will be stigmatized. The unfavorable treatment received by groups so stigmatized can exacerbate the situation and trap it in a vicious cycle. Therefore, the effect of an immigrant culture varies depending not only on the microsocial structures on which that culture is based but also on the macrosocial structures of the larger society of which the immigrant culture is a part.

However, to maintain a cultural tradition is one thing, and to pass that tradition on to the next generation is quite another, especially when the process occurs in a different cultural environment. The clash between the parents' social world and the children's is the most commonly cited problem of intergenerational relations in immigrant communities. In fact, intergenerational conflicts are not simply a unique immigrant phenomenon (Berrol 1995; Child 1943); they are also an American phenomenon rooted in the American tradition of a "moral rejection of authority" (Gorer 1963, 53). In a recent comparative study of adolescents, Carola Suárez-Orozco and Marcelo Suárez-Orozco (1995) found that intergenerational conflicts were more common among European American adolescents, who were more ambivalent toward authority and schooling and more peer-oriented, than among Latino American adolescents, who were more respectful of authority and more family-oriented. They attribute this gap to the impact of the changing American youth culture, which glorifies contempt for authorities and emphasizes peer recognition; the implication of their analysis is that assimilating into the American youth culture could cause more harm than good for immigrant adolescents.

The frequent difficulties facing the new second generation arise from the struggles of individuals to balance the demands of American culture with those of immigrant cultures (Dublin 1996). Portes and Rumbaut (1996, ch. 7) conceptualize the acculturation gaps between immigrant parents and their children in a typology of "generational consonance versus dissonance." Generational consonance occurs when parents and children both remain unacculturated, or both acculturate at the same rate, or both agree on selective acculturation. Generational dissonance occurs when children neither correspond to levels of parental acculturation nor conform to parental guidance, leading to role reversal and intensified parent-child conflicts. According to Portes and Rumbaut, these acculturation patterns interact with contextual factors—racial discrimination, urban subcultures, and labor-market prospects—to affect the adaptational outcomes of children. When contextual factors are unfavorable—as they are for the majority of today's second generation—consonant acculturation enables immigrant children to lean on the material or moral resources available in the family and the immigrant community; it thus increases the probability of upward assimilation. By contrast, dissonant acculturation severs ties between children and their adult social world, deprives children of family or community resources, and leads them further and further away from parental expectations. In inner cities, immigrant children who rebel against parental values and mobility expectations are likely to identify with the leveling-downward norms of their immediate social environment and to acculturate into an adversarial outlook in response to discrimination and blocked mobility, as exemplified by Haitian children in Miami and West Indian children in New York City (Portes and Stepick 1993; Waters 1994, 1997).

Social Capital: Networks of Support and Control

How is it possible to ensure that immigrants and their offspring maintain their cultural values and work habits and learn the skills for socioeconomic advancement? Or what enables immigrant families and their children to withstand the leveling pressures from the inner city? The key is to examine the networks of social relations—namely, how individual families are related to one another in the ethnic community and how immigrant children are involved in these networks. The networks of social relations involve shared obligations, social supports, and social controls. When, for example, Korean Americans obtain from other Korean Americans low-interest loans requiring little collateral, or Chinese American students receive encouragement and approval in after-school Chinese-language classes for their general academic orientation, these are forms of social support inherent in particular patterns of social relations within the ethnic community. When, on the other hand, a group member experiences disapproval, or even ostracism, from co-ethnics for failing to attain a respected occupation, this is a form of social control.

My colleague Carl Bankston and I (Zhou and Bankston 1998) have proposed a model of ethnic social relations and examined it with a community-based study of Vietnamese adolescents in New Orleans. In the Vietnamese community in New Orleans, we observe that Vietnamese adolescents are constantly reminded of their duty to show respect for their elders, to take care of younger siblings, to work hard, and to make decisions with the approval not only of their parents but of the community where other families practice similar values. In this "watchful and ever-vigilant" community, young Vietnamese find little competition from other desiderata because the social world of their families is restricted to the closed and highly integrated circles of the ethnic group. Since what is considered good or bad is clearly specified and closely monitored by these networks, young people find it hard to "to get away with much." We conclude that the conformity to traditional family values and behavioral standards requires a high level of family integration into a community that reinforces these values and standards. The outcomes of adaptation, therefore, depend on how immigrant children fit in their own ethnic community, or in their local environment if such an ethnic community is absent, and how their ethnic community or the local environment fits in the larger American society. In the case of the Vietnamese, being part of a Vietnamese network appears to offer a better route to upward mobility than being Americanized into the underprivileged local environment—or for that matter, into the native-born mainstream youth subcultures.

Clearly social support and social control may channel individuals into particular forms of behavior, using both material and social-psychological means; however, both stem from relationships based on value orientations brought from the home country and adapted to the circumstances of the host country. Here two sociological concepts—James Coleman's (1988, 1990) concept of social capital and Émile Durkheim's (1897/1951) concept of normative integration—are most relevant. Coleman defines social capital as a system of relationships that promotes advantageous outcomes for participants in the system. More specifically, he explains that social capital in the raising of children comprises the norms, the social networks, and the relationships between adults and children that are of value for the child's growing up. In Coleman's view, social capital exists within the family but also outside the family, in the community.

Norms, social networks, and relationships between adults and children may have absolute value; that is, some types of relationships or norms may be of value to children in any environment. In the contemporary American context, certain general characteristics of immigrant families, such as being intact and promoting respect for elders, may help children advance in any segment of the host society. If, however, these families live in social environments that are not conducive to academic achievement and upward mobility, then these characteristics may take on even greater importance. As Bankston and I (Zhou and Bankston, 1998) have suggested, accepting community-prescribed norms and values and cultivating social relationships are important to the adaptation of immigrant children. In disadvantaged neighborhoods where difficult conditions and disruptive elements dominate, immigrant families may have to preserve traditional values by means of ethnic solidarity to prevent the next generation from acculturating into the underprivileged segments of American society in which their community is located.

Furthermore, the community provides a context in which social capital is formed. The adult society surrounding a family can reinforce familial support and direction, mediating between individual families and the larger social setting. Immigrant children and parents often interact with one another in immigrant communities. If patterns of interaction are contained within a tight-knit ethnic community, these children and parents are likely to share their similar experiences with other children and parents. In this way, the community creates a buffer zone to ease the tension between individual self-fulfillment and family commitment. The community also moderates the original cultural patterns, legitimizes reestablished values and norms, and enforces consistent standards. As Betty Sung (1987, 126) observed of immigrant children in New York's Chinatown or satellite Chinatowns in the mid-1980s:

> [Bicultural] conflicts are moderated to a large degree because there are other Chinese children around to mitigate the dilemmas that they encounter. When they are among their own, the Chinese ways are better known and better accepted. The Chinese customs and traditions are not denigrated to the degree that they would be if the immigrant child were the only one to face the conflict on his or her own.

However, membership in any group is a matter of degree. Individuals may belong to social groups to varying degrees. If norms, values, and social relationships within an ethnic group do influence the adaptation of group members, the influence should logically depend on the extent to which individuals hold the group's norms and values and participate in its social relationships. Hence, participation in social relationships and acceptance of group norms and values are interrelated: the more individuals associate with a particular group, the greater their normative conformity to the behavioral standards and expectations prescribed by the group. However, ethnic communities can also hinder the adaptation of young members of immigrant groups. Richard Rodriguez, in his eloquent memoir *Hunger of Memory* (1983), maintains that his own success has depended on leaving his Spanish-speaking neighborhood behind. Similarly, it is possible that immigrant children must cast off their traditions and language to participate fully in American society. The question is whether the person who succeeds in leaving the poor ethnic community represents an outlier or a trend.

The ethnic context also serves as an important mechanism for social control. For this reason, the concept of social capital can be treated as a version of one of the oldest sociological theories, Durkheim's theory of social integration. Durkheim (1897/1951) maintains that individual behavior should be seen as the product of the degree of integration of individuals in their society. The greater the integration of individuals into a social group, the greater the control of the group over the individual. In the context of immigrant adaptation, children who are more highly integrated into their ethnic group are likely to follow the forms of behavior prescribed by the group and to avoid the forms of behavior proscribed by the group. In considering whether a particular ethnicity should be seen as a source of social capital or as a disadvantage, then, it is necessary to examine how integration into that particular ethnic community affects the adaptation of young people.

Although networks of ethnic social relations are important sources of support and control, recent research has found evidence that family and ethnic ties tend to deteriorate with longer duration of U.S. residence, as in the case of refugees from Central America (Gil and Vega 1996). Researchers have also cautioned that even strong cultural identities and social ties, which may be considered sources of social capital, may sometimes be insufficient because of racial or class disadvantages. In a study of an African American community in the ghetto, Carol Stack (1974) shows that African American families depend on patterns of co-residence, kinship-based exchange networks, for survival. This means of survival, however, demands the sacrifice of upward mobility and geographic movement and discourages marriage because of structural constraints such as the inexorable unemployment of African American women and men. Welfare policies have disrupted the support networks and conspired against the ability of the poor to build up equity. Similarly, María Patricia Fernández-Kelly (1995) found, in a study of teenage pregnancies in a Baltimore ghetto, that kinship networks in ghettos were often graced with strong family and friendship bonds but that these networks lacked connections to other social networks that controlled access to larger sets of opportunities. Moreover, symbols of ethnic pride and cultural identity that developed in reaction to social isolation and racial domination (for example, the sparkling mounds of braided hair of young African American women) became signals that barred access to resources and employment in the larger society. Such truncated networks and reactive ethnicity could severely limit the ability of children to envision alternative paths out of the ghetto and to turn cultural capital into resourceful social capital (see also Fordham 1996; Kohl 1994).

Conclusion

For the new second generation, growing up American can be a matter of smooth acceptance or of traumatic confrontation. The children of today's diverse immigrant groups are generally eager to embrace American culture and to acquire an American identity by becoming indistinguishable from their American peers. Some immigrant children, however, may be perceived as "unassimilated" even when they try hard to abandon their ethnic identity. Others may be accepted as well adjusted precisely because they retain a strong ethnic identity. In the long journey to becoming American, their progress is largely contingent on the human and financial capital that their immigrant parents bring along, the social conditions from which their families exit as well as the context that receives them, and their cultural patterns, including values, family relations, and social ties, reconstructed in the process of adaptation. The host society offers uneven possibilities to different immigrant groups. These unequal possibilities may limit the opportunities of some immigrant groups, but they do not necessarily constitute a complete denial of opportunity.

The segmented assimilation theory recognizes the fact that immigrants are today being absorbed by different segments of American society, ranging from affluent middle-class suburbs to impoverished inner-city ghettos, and that becoming American may not always be an advantage for the immigrants themselves or for their children. When immigrants enter middle-class communities directly, or after a short transition, it may be advantageous for them to acculturate and assimilate. When they enter the bottom of the ethnic hierarchy of drastic social inequality, the forces of assimilation are exerted mainly by the underprivileged segments of this structure, and this pressure is likely to result in distinct disadvantages, viewed as maladjustment by both mainstream society and the ethnic community. Such contextual differences mean that paths to social mobility may lead to upward as well as downward outcomes. For those who start from the very bottom, of course, the outcome is not so much assimilating downward as staying where they are. The question is, what makes some immigrant groups susceptible to the downward path, or to the permanent trap, and what allows others to avoid it?

Major determinants can include factors external to a particular immigrant group, such as racial stratification, economic opportunities, and spatial segregation, and factors intrinsic to the group, such as financial and human capital on arrival, family structure, community organization, and cultural patterns of social relations. These two sets of factors affect the life chances of immigrant children not only additively but also interactively. Particular patterns of social relations in the family or the ethnic community may sometimes counter the trend of negative adaptation even in unfavorable situations. When immigrant children are under pressure to assimilate but are unsure which direction of assimilation is more desirable, the family or the ethnic community can make a difference if it is able to mobilize resources to prevent downward assimilation. Likewise, when the children are received in inner cities, they may benefit from cultivating their ties in their ethnic communities to develop forms of behavior likely to break the cycle of disadvantage and to lead to upward mobility. The focus on the interaction between structural factors and sociocultural factors in recent research has shed new light on our understanding of the complex process of assimilation in the second generation.

The interest in the new second generation has recently been growing. However, there is still a big gap between the strategic importance of the new second generation and current knowledge about its conditions (Portes 1996c). The following questions may stimulate further theoretical inquiry: Will members of a generation born or reared in the United States gradually be pulled away from a heritage vastly different from those of the Europeans who arrived over the course of this century? Will those who rebel against this heritage adjust best socially and economically? Will racial barriers limit the participation of immigrant children in American life? How would being hyphenated Americans influence the ways in which immigrant children become assimilated, and why may some of these ways be more advantageous than others? Will immigrant families and ethnic communities continue to affect the lives of children of the second generation? Will the cultural distinctiveness of hyphenated Americans eventually melt down into a pot of Anglo-American homogeneity? If not, what will ethnic diversity mean for the offspring of today's new second generation?

Each of these questions has theoretical as well as practical implications. Given the unique characteristics of the second generation of new immigrants and our scanty knowledge about the complex ways in which its members are "becoming American," future studies are both urgent and necessary.

11 Social and Linguistic Aspects of Assimilation Today

David E. López

THE MOST FREQUENTLY posed question surrounding the "new immigration" is economic: Will immigrant groups entering near the bottom of American society, as nearly all did in the past, make the same intergenerational climb up the ladder of success, or will they be stuck in the cellar? This question is particularly pressing in California, where poor Latino immigrants and their children constitute a minority on the way to becoming the majority. Evidence is mixed, and ultimately only time will tell. In the meantime, we have the unique opportunity to study the myriad adaptation processes, cultural and social-structural as well as economic, as they occur, both among immigrants and in the emerging second generation. Just imagine the wealth of data we might have had the last time around if the social sciences had been sufficiently developed in 1910! Of course, this is a responsibility as well as an opportunity: we are in the first few pages of this latest chapter in the story of ethnicity in America, and caution and humility in our tentative conclusions are certainly warranted.

In this chapter, I review data on language maintenance and shift in southern California, supplemented by some data on marriage patterns and ethnic identity, to try to make sense of the patterns of cultural and social change that immigrant communities are undergoing. Viewed alone, the language data appear to provide compelling evidence that the "straight-line" assimilation theory that Herbert Gans (1979), Richard Alba (1985b), and others derived from the experience of European American ethnics earlier in this century is equally applicable to the new immigration ethnic communities. But as Milton Gordon (1964) himself emphasized over thirty years ago, acculturation is the norm even among groups that remain highly segregated socially. Consequently I also consider behavioral and attitudinal aspects of ethnic identity, including both "hard" measures of social assimilation like marriage as well as "soft" measures like identity. Finally I examine one of the most intriguing alternatives to complete assimilation, on the one hand, and continued ethnic particularism, on the other: the development of panethnic ties, in which ethnic political solidarity and personal identity shift from national origin to more general levels of ethnicity, such as "Latino" or "Asian American."

THEN AND NOW

As Richard Alba and Victor Nee (1995) have argued, four factors likely to affect social and cultural assimilation distinguish today's immigration from the past. First, there is much greater socioeconomic diversity, both within and between groups, among today's immigrants, a large portion of whom arrive as educated and middle-class professionals. Thus, for many immigrant communities economic questions are secondary and certainly of no serious public policy relevance. Who really cares about the mobility prospects of children whose parents are both doctors? On the other hand, the diversity provides a much greater range of variability to study, leading us away from the unidimensional straight-line assimilation perspective that is the unavoidable heritage of studying European immigration.

Second, we live in an era that is much more tolerant and supportive of multiculturalism, or what used to be known as cultural pluralism. There is no national consensus and conflicts abound, to be sure: witness the rumpus around "ebonics" or the growing opposition to bilingual education. But in comparison to the nativism and outright racism of eighty years ago, we live in a tolerant era, and one in which minority rights are more protected. The current skirmishes surrounding the assertion of ethnic particularism have probably increased sentiments of ethnic solidarity and separateness more than suppressed them.

Third, most immigrants today are "non-white" by current U.S. definitions, and few would argue that white racism is dead in America. To be sure, the situation is complex. Asians and Mexicans have had a rough time for most of the twentieth century in the United States, but they have experienced nothing like the overwhelming discrimination and repression faced by African Americans. In the past Jews and southern Europeans were often stigmatized in quasi-racialized terms, though it would be a mistake to equate this with the attitudes toward and treatment of blacks and Asians in the same era. Racial variation within the Latino population and the lower salience of the racial "lines" separating them and Asians from whites further confound any assessment of the importance of racialization in understanding the assimilation of today's immigrant communities. Clearly race "matters"; it is equally clear that it does not determine.

Finally, whether or not one agrees with Douglas Massey (1994) that today we live in a time of "perpetual immigration," it certainly is continuing, with no signs of abating in the near future. The assimilation of the second and third generations emanating from European immigration took place over decades during which ties to the old countries were weakened because few newcomers were arriving in the United States. Today's second generation and, probably, tomorrow's third will grow up in communities replenished by successive waves of new immigrants, communities with strong transnational ties to their countries. Certainly these social and cultural ties will provide at least the potential for greater cultural maintenance than was possible in the past.

The View from California

Driven largely by immigration since 1965, California is now the most multiethnic state in the country and is well on the way to becoming a distinctive multiethnic "society," with no one majority group (U.S. Bureau of the Census 1993b). Non-Hispanic whites ("Anglos"), long the dominant group demographically, economically, and politically, now constitute only about half the population. African Americans continue to decline as a proportion of the state's population, and Asian Americans, at 12 percent of the total, now outnumber them nearly two to one. Mexican Americans and other Latinos constitute nearly one-third of the state's population, and projections suggest that they will be the single largest group early in the next century. There are wide disparities in the average socioeconomic status of these groups, with whites and most Asian subgroups, immigrant as well as native, at the top, immigrant Latinos at the bottom, and blacks and older native-born Latinos in between.

Much of the data I draw on comes from southern California and was generated from the "Ethnic Los Angeles" project, under the general direction of Roger Waldinger (Waldinger and Bozorgmehr 1996b). Both Los Angeles and, to a lesser extent, California generally are home to more immigrants and new immigrant-origin ethnic communities than any other part of the country, and conversely, immigration has had a greater impact there than anywhere else. The focus on California necessarily emphasizes some groups and processes and neglects others. The principal advantage of this geographical focus is that it looks at processes of immigration adaptation and assimilation precisely where they are most consequential, both for the groups themselves and for the surrounding society. Since the maintenance of ethnic communities and cultural patterns like languages is apt to be stronger in highly ethnic environments, it is logical to assume that the rates of adaptation and assimilation are actually greater in other parts of the country.

Linguistic Assimilation

Los Angeles today is among the most linguistically diverse cities in the world. This diversity is largely the consequence of recent immigrants speaking their mother tongues—not exactly a surprising phenomenon. The interesting question for research and theory, and also for social policy, is the degree to which they pass their language on to their children and their children's children.

Intergenerational language maintenance and shift have been researched in various settings worldwide, but the best-known work is based on the experience of immigrant-origin communities in the United States. Several decades ago, Joshua Fishman (1965, 1972) proposed what has come to be known as the "Fishman model" of language shift: adult immigrants continue to use their mother tongues in most domains, especially the home, thereby transmitting the ethnic mother tongue to the second generation. But these children grow up using the socially dominant language in most public and private domains, sometimes to the point of responding to their parents in the dominant language while understanding what the parents say in the ethnic tongue. The second generation, including those who are ethnically endogamous, tend to shift to the dominant language in all domains by the time they are adults, including the home, generally the last domain of ethnic-language use. This means that the third generation has little opportunity to learn the ethnic mother tongue, which becomes an aspect of symbolic ethnicity, to use Herbert Gans's (1979) term, rather than a used language.

Fishman originally proposed this model for European immigrant tongues. In fact, we have only general knowledge of the dynamics of language maintenance and shift from 1870 to 1940: fluctuating Census Bureau policy with respect to questions about language and ethnicity makes retrospective studies difficult. But we do know the result: few third-generation Americans speak their non-English mother tongue. Coupled with evidence from Canada and Australia, this observation suggests that this commonsense model of language shift accurately describes the experience of most European immigrants into English-speaking countries (Evans 1987; Noro 1990).

Research done in the late 1970s and early 1980s indicated that Asian languages had a fate similar to that of European immigrant languages, and that, despite appearances, intergenerational shift was more the rule than the exception for Spanish as well (López 1978, 1982; Veltman 1983). Spanish appeared to persist in some isolated rural settings without the stimulus of continued immigration. But these isolated cases had become increasingly rare even a decade ago. The Fishman model of substantial language shift by the third generation appeared to apply to Spanish in the West and Southwest as well, though language shift even among urban Latinos was apparently less rapid than for other groups.

Does this model of language shift apply today in Los Angeles? As Stanley Lieberson and Timothy Curry (1971) pointed out long ago, and as recent analysts have reemphasized, the rate of language shift and the potential for stable bilingualism are affected by demographic and contextual factors as well as by individual desires. Two demographic factors have consistently been found to be associated with higher levels of language maintenance: isolation, in sheer numbers, from the dominant population and concentration (Bills 1989; Lieberson and Curry 1971; Sole 1990; Stevens 1992; Veltman 1983, 1988, 1991). Both factors are stronger for Spanish than for Asian languages. Over three million Spanish speakers reside in the Los Angeles area. In several parts of the city, there are large neighborhoods that house predominantly Latinos, and there are smaller pockets of Latino communities throughout the region. A much smaller proportion of Asians reside in ethnic neighborhoods; instead, they are spread throughout middle-class neighborhoods all around the city. There are more Latinos in Chinatown than Chinese; there are more Latinos in Koreatown than Koreans.

Nearly twenty years ago, I concluded a brief piece on language maintenance (among Chicanos, but the conclusion applied to other groups as well) by saying that language shift to English monolingualism may be neither desirable nor necessary, but that in the absence of large-scale continuing immigration, it was exceedingly likely (López 1978). Other researchers (for example, Veltman 1983) came to much the same conclusion. What we should have seen but did not at the time was that large-scale immigration was very much continuing, resulting in a wave that would overwhelm native-born Asian Americans and, to a lesser degree, Latino populations. In Los Angeles today, about half of all Latino adults are immigrants, and an even higher proportion of Latino children are immigrants or the progeny of immigrants. About three-quarters of all Asians are either immigrants or their children.

There is nothing new about these numbers, but the implications for the use of languages other than English are profound, at least in the short run. The most obvious consequence is that Los Angeles is now home to a lot more speakers of these languages, at all age levels. And to the degree that these speakers constitute communities of language users, these communities should facilitate the maintenance of ethnic languages among second- and third-generation individuals who might otherwise shed them. Judging by data from Los Angeles, precisely this is happening among Latinos, who tend to live in comparatively homogeneous neighborhoods throughout the city. Asians, who tend to be much more dispersed and are divided into many different language groups, show little evidence of intergenerational language maintenance.

This combination of contextual, demographic, and political factors gives us reason to believe that ethnic-language maintenance in general may be greater in the Los Angeles area today than it was in the past, especially for Latinos. The preceding discussion leads us to hypothesize that Spanish-language maintenance in the Los Angeles area today should be somewhat higher than it was in the past. This hypothesis follows largely from the changed demographic context of increased concentration and absolute numbers of Spanish speakers. Asian languages, in contrast, have no extraordinary contextual support outside of the ethnic enclaves that house only a small portion of their communities, so there is no reason to expect notable levels of language maintenance. We hypothesize that Asian rates of both intergenerational and (for immigrants) intragenerational language maintenance will be well below Latino rates.[1]

Unfortunately, census data are not ideally suited for pursuing these hypotheses. For a thorough study of language maintenance, one needs independent measures of both upbringing (mother tongue) and current language, as well as the ability to separate the population into at least three generational groups (foreign-born, native of foreign parents, native of native). Ideally each measure would specify the language used in particular domains (at home with parents, with siblings, with friends, in school, at work, and so on). Even better would be mother tongue data that came from an earlier survey, not the respondent's memory. In practice these ideal conditions are never met in large data sets; the last even minimally adequate national data set was collected in 1976, during the early stages of the great rise in immigration. In 1980 the Census Bureau adopted a new two-part language question (repeated in 1990) that asks what language other than English the respondent speaks at home, and if he or she does not speak only English at home, how well he or she speaks English. In fact, these are not quite self-reports, since census questionnaires are typically filled out by one individual (or by interviewing one individual) in each household.

There is also the problem of what the language question means. Does a positive response to "Does this individual speak a language other than English at home?" mean that she or he usually speaks it? Or only occasionally? With whom? The question is not a good indicator of the use of languages other than English outside the home. On the other hand, it is a fair indicator of the language context of the home, the most important setting for passing language on from generation to generation. The self-report of English-speaking ability is even more suspect and subject to a wide range of interpretation by respondents. The meaning of the responses ("very well," "well," "not well," "not at all") is only roughly comparable from person to person and household to household and may vary across language groups and age groups.

With all these potential problems, it is amazing that the pattern of results produced by the language questions appears to be so reasonable. The questions are crude, and at the level of individuals the responses might well be meaningless. But the consistency of results that researchers have found with the 1980 census (Bills 1989; Sole 1990) and now reported for the 1990 census clearly indicates that, at least in a relative sense, the questions "work." The 1980 and 1990 census "language at home" question does produce much higher estimates of non-English-language use than the questions used in earlier surveys about the language an individual spoke most often. The English competence question produces results more comparable to national surveys in the 1970s. Both questions have ambiguous intrinsic meaning, but they are good bases for our purpose here: comparative studies across generations and ethnic groups. The reader needs to keep in mind that both questions probably produce high estimates of the phenomenon in question (speaking a language other than English regularly and ability to speak English).

Table 11.1 does show very large differences in ethnic-language use between U.S.-born and foreign-born groups; it also points to some ethnic differences. About 95 percent of all Latino immigrants and the same percentage of post-1980 Asian immigrants continue to speak their language at home. Asian immigrants who arrived before 1980 have slightly lower rates. The rates for immigrants who are not Asian or Latino are considerably lower, at least at the national level. Ethnic-language use drops markedly for all native-born groups, but here the ethnic differences are sharper: U.S.-born Asians speak their ethnic language at home considerably less than native Latinos. In greater Los Angeles the rates are 41 percent and 63 percent, respectively. Much of the great gap between the Hispanics and Asians, on the one hand, and the much lower rates of using a language other than English for "others" is surely due to the fact that the immigrant origins of most of the latter are further in the past. If the comparisons were with specific white groups with substantial amounts of recent immigration (Iranians, Armenians), the contrasts would probably not be so striking.

The 1980 and 1990 censuses do not distinguish between the second generation (children of immigrants) and the third or later generations. For-

TABLE 11.1 Persons Over Age Five Who Speak a Language Other Than English at Home, by Nativity and Ethnicity, in the United States and Greater Los Angeles, 1990

	Total	*U.S.-Born*	*Immigrants Before 1980*	*Immigrants 1980 to 1990*
United States				
All residents	14%	8%	72%	88%
Asians and Pacific Islanders (API)	73	35	87	95
Hispanics	78	66	95	96
Not API or Hispanic	6	4	50	64
Greater Los Angeles				
All residents	38	17	84	94
Asians and Pacific Islanders	79	41	89	96
Hispanics	81	63	95	96

Source: for the United States: U.S. Department of Commerce, *1990 Census of Population: Persons of Hispanic Origin in the United States,* and *1990 Census of Population: Asians and Pacific Islanders in the United States;* for greater Los Angeles: tabulated from the Public Use Sample of the *1990 Census of Population.*

tunately, the November 1989 Current Population Survey (CPS) does allow for this crucial distinction, and it also contains the same language questions as the 1990 census. The CPS samples are not large enough to allow the analysis of separate Asian ethnic groups. To minimize the possible effects of life-cycle and historical changes, I have limited analysis to those between twenty-five and forty-four. This focus produces generally lower rates of language maintenance than shown in table 11.1, which includes large numbers of minor children in immigrant households and older persons, who also tend to have higher rates of language maintenance. A further refinement is that we have separated the "1.5" generation (those foreign-born individuals who immigrated before the age of ten) from other immigrants, since we know that age at immigration affects language patterns. We have no way of knowing what proportion of the "third" generation is actually that, as opposed to later generations. Even with these limitations, these data provide considerable insight into intergenerational patterns.

Table 11.2 gives the percentage of each group that reports speaking only English at home. For each group, home English monolingualism increases from one generation to the next. Though the sample sizes are smaller, the results for greater Los Angeles are clearer than the national data, which include other Latino subgroups, including the complex Puerto Rican case. For Mexicans, English monolingualism at home rises slightly for the 1.5 generation from 2 percent (first generation) to 6 percent. It then jumps to 28 percent for the true second generation and reaches 57 percent for "native of native" Mexican Americans. But if the pattern of shift is substantial, the actual rate of English home monolingualism reached by the third generation is still only slightly more than 50 percent. The Asian pattern of language shift is more rapid, and the eventual third-generation rate of English monolingualism is substantially higher—92 percent compared to 57 percent for Hispanics. Asians, in the aggregate, more closely approximate the standard pattern of language shift than do Latinos.

BILINGUALISM

Table 11.2 emphasizes complete language shift from generation to generation. The assumption is that most of those who stop using their ethnic language at home have also largely ceased to use it out of the home; certainly they are not passing it on to their children. But there is another interesting and, many would say, more desirable alternative: the intergenerational maintenance of ethnic languages coupled with complete competence in English. Debates have raged for years over the possibility, measurement, and benefits of such intergenerational bilingualism. Language activists in the 1960s enthusiastically interpreted correlations between bilingualism and IQ in some private Canadian schools as evidence of "increased flexibility" among bilinguals. In fact, they were just measuring social class. Since then, bilingualism has become conflated with bilingual education, and enthusiastic but usually poorly trained researchers have tried to prove that bilingualism equals bilingual education and that both are good for individuals and society (Reagan 1984; San Miguel 1984;

TABLE 11.2 Persons Twenty-Five to Forty-Four Who Speak English Only at Home, by Ethnicity and Generation, United States and Greater Los Angeles, 1989

<table>
<tr><th></th><th>All Hispanics</th><th>Mexican</th><th>All Asians</th><th>Chinese</th></tr>
<tr><td>United States</td><td></td><td></td><td></td><td></td></tr>
<tr><td>First generation</td><td>6%</td><td>2%</td><td>11%</td><td>8%</td></tr>
<tr><td>1.5 generation</td><td>11</td><td>4</td><td>29</td><td>22</td></tr>
<tr><td>Second generation</td><td>30</td><td>27</td><td>77</td><td rowspan="2">65</td></tr>
<tr><td>Native of native</td><td>38</td><td>44</td><td>82</td></tr>
<tr><td>Greater Los Angeles</td><td></td><td></td><td></td><td></td></tr>
<tr><td>First generation</td><td>3</td><td>2</td><td>15</td><td>*</td></tr>
<tr><td>1.5 generation</td><td>13</td><td>6</td><td>*</td><td>*</td></tr>
<tr><td>Second generation</td><td>28</td><td>28</td><td>75</td><td>*</td></tr>
<tr><td>Native of native</td><td>57</td><td>57</td><td>92</td><td>*</td></tr>
</table>

Source: Tabulated from the Public Use Sample of the November 1989 Current Population Survey. Note that these figures differ somewhat from the 1990 census results.
*Sample size too small for calculation.

compare, Nielson and Lerner 1986). Serious sociolinguistic research long ago concluded, however, that the only clear advantage of bilingualism is that one can speak two languages—no minor accomplishment, to be sure, but not anything that clearly translates into dollars or points on an IQ test. Research indicating that bilingualism, ceteris paribus, may have some additional long-run advantages has usually been carried out in the context of elite educational contexts or in other ways in which ordinary socioeconomic factors intrude, as Alejandro Portes and Rubén Rumbaut (1990) concede. This may turn out to be true for the latest crop of bilingual boosting (Portes and Schauffler 1994; Zhou and Bankston 1994) as well, but it is too early to tell.

The best indicator of bilingualism in census data is the proportion of individuals who speak their ethnic language at home but report that they also speak English very well. Obviously this operational definition of bilingualism is crude, but it is adequate for comparing groups with each other: high rates among native-born generations suggest substantial intergenerational transmission of bilingualism. Table 11.3 shows that native-born Latinos have substantially higher rates of continuing bilingualism than do Asians. Both nationally and in greater Los Angeles, second- and third-generation Latinos report that they speak Spanish at home but also speak English very well, at rates of 40 percent to over 50 percent. Second-generation Asian rates are less than half the Latino rates; among the third generation, they are less than one-fourth.

Taken together, tables 11.2 and 11.3 show the clear contrasts between Asian and Latino language patterns. Figure 11.1 gives the proportion in each ethnic and generation group who either speak English only or, if they speak another language at home, report that they speak English very well. Immigrants speak their ethnic tongues at home and usually do not attain proficiency in English, though a significant minority of Asian immigrants arrive and continue to function as bilinguals. Among Asians the shift to English monolingualism is nearly universal by the third generation, when only about one in ten Asians is bilingual. Among the Latino third generation, bilingualism is also less common than English monolingualism, but it is about four time more common than among Asians.

I mentioned earlier that it is extremely difficult to draw firm conclusions about a second generation that is still, on average, of school age. Firm conclusions about the language patterns that this generation passes on to its children can be drawn only after its members have formed families. But it is possible to study assimilation processes among second-generation children. Recognizing this, a research team led by Alejandro Portes and Rubén Rumbaut devised a panel study of second-generation youth in San Diego and Miami, the Children of Immigrants Longitudinal Study (CILS). Even the first phase, reported in some detail in *The New Second Generation* (Portes 1996b), provided evidence of very rapid language shift among second-generation middle school children (Portes and Schauffler 1994).

The preliminary results of the second phase in San Diego are now emerging, and they demon-

TABLE 11.3 Persons Twenty-Five to Forty-Four Who Speak Ethnic Language at Home and Speak English Very Well, by Ethnicity and Generation, United States and Greater Los Angeles, 1989

	All Hispanics	*Mexican*	*All Asians*	*Chinese*
United States				
First generation	17%	10%	36%	34%
1.5 generation	48	39	31	38
Second generation	53	54	19	32 (second generation and native of native combined)
Native of native	45	47	11	
Greater Los Angeles				
First generation	15	10	44	*
1.5 generation	31	34	*	*
Second generation	49	48	23	*
Native of native	39	40	8	*

Source: Tabulated from the Public Use Tape of the November 1989 Current Population Survey. These figures vary somewhat from the 1990 census results.
*Sample size too small for calculation.

strate an overwhelming shift to English, with very little likelihood that the second generation will continue to use their ethnic tongues in any but symbolic ways, or to talk with their parents. Rumbaut (1997c) reports that a substantial to overwhelming majority of each national-origin second generation and 1.5 generation group (now in the eleventh and twelfth grades) prefer English to their mother tongues. As in the census and CPS data reviewed earlier, there are definite differences by national origin: 92 to 98 percent of the Asian second-generation groups prefer English, in comparison to 78 percent of the Mexican Americans. Perhaps the most striking ethnic difference is this: only 4 percent of the Vietnamese and Filipino second generations say they can still speak their ethnic language "very well," in contrast to fully 50 percent of the Mexican Americans. Clearly there is still a substantial degree of bilingualism present among the latter, and they are likely to maintain it throughout much of their lives if they continue to live in environments in which they have the opportunity to use Spanish. A declining but still substantial portion will probably pass Spanish on to their children. In contrast, there is no likelihood that the Asian languages will survive into the third generation.

In sum, even in southern California, with its dense immigrant neighborhoods and proximity to Mexico, language shift, and presumably other aspects of acculturation among Latinos, is proceeding along the same lines as in the past. The intergenerational pattern is slower, to be sure, than that of Asian languages, but it is incontrovertible. It is popular today to emphasize that acculturation and assimilation do not necessarily follow the lines of "Anglo-conformity" but, rather, are segmented according to specific local circumstances. Doubtless this is true for some aspects of acculturation, for example, Cambodian youth forming gangs as a way to combat black and Latino gangs in the poor neighborhoods in which they find themselves. But all these gang members will be banging in English.

SOCIAL ASSIMILATION

Nevertheless, we should remember Gordon's (1964) crucial insight: acculturation has long been characteristic of most groups, including those that continue to be excluded from social integration and economic opportunity, such as African Americans, as well as many groups that actively resist social assimilation. From his perspective in the 1960s, Gans (1962) saw that his "urban villagers" were largely acculturated, linguistically and otherwise, to working-class American patterns, even though they remained socially apart for a combination of external and voluntary reasons. Gordon concluded much the same with respect to Jews, African Americans, and European Catholics. Twenty years later, Alba (1985b) and other observers, including Gans himself, saw that Italians and other Catholics, as well as Jews, did indeed move rapidly toward social assimilation by the third generation, but in the second, acculturation without social assimilation was the norm. There is, then, no particular reason to expect that second-generation acculturation today will lead in any quick and

FIGURE 11.1 Proportion Who Speak English Only or Very Well, by Generation and Ethnicity: Los Angeles 1990

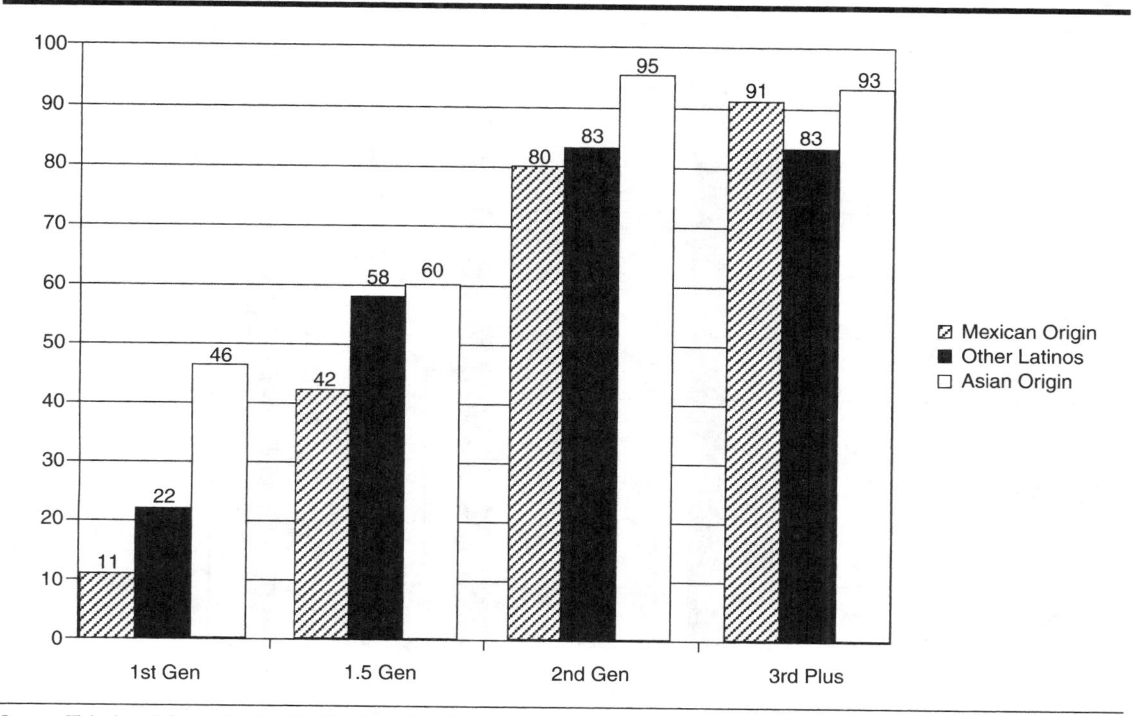

Source: Tabulated from the Public Use Sample of the November 1989 Current Population Survey. Note that these figures differ somewhat from the 1990 census results.

decisive way to social assimilation—or for that matter, to economic success.

What can we say about the pattern of social assimilation among the new second generation? Not a great deal, if we mean the children of recent immigrants currently being studied by Portes, Rumbaut, and others. They are simply too young. If language use is both a good and the most commonly available indicator of cultural maintenance, then intermarriage is the best and most easily available indicator of social assimilation. Ethnic groups with low rates of in-marriage simply cease to be groups. At the other end of the spectrum, groups with continuing high rates of in-marriage are the very archetype of unassimilated minorities. This is true whether the in-marriage is voluntary or imposed, and whether it stems from geographical isolation, group size, religious conviction, or societal rejection. Any conclusions about marriage patterns, and about social assimilation generally, must wait until the children of today's children of immigrants are grown up.

On the other hand, even in the middle of this century there were substantial numbers of native-born Latinos and "older" Asian subgroups like Chinese and Japanese Americans. Recent decennial censuses do not distinguish between second and subsequent generations, but comparing the marriage patterns of older native-born Asians and Latinos with young adults of the same groups does provide a rough comparison between second and third generations. Figure 11.2 does precisely that: it compares the in-marriage rates of two age cohorts of native-born women in greater Los Angeles, by ethnicity: those who were between fifty-five and sixty-four in 1990, and those who were twenty-five to thirty-four. Of course, this generational comparison is also a historical comparison, between marriage patterns today and those of thirty years ago. There is no easy way to distinguish between generational and historical factors, and in fact I presume that at least some of the change reflects the declining salience of racial lines over time. But it is worth recalling that, in the view of Alba (1985b) and others, historical change with respect to ethnic boundaries was very much a part of the "twilight of ethnicity" for European Americans.

FIGURE 11.2 In-Group Marriage Rates for U.S.-Born Women in Los Angeles, 1990

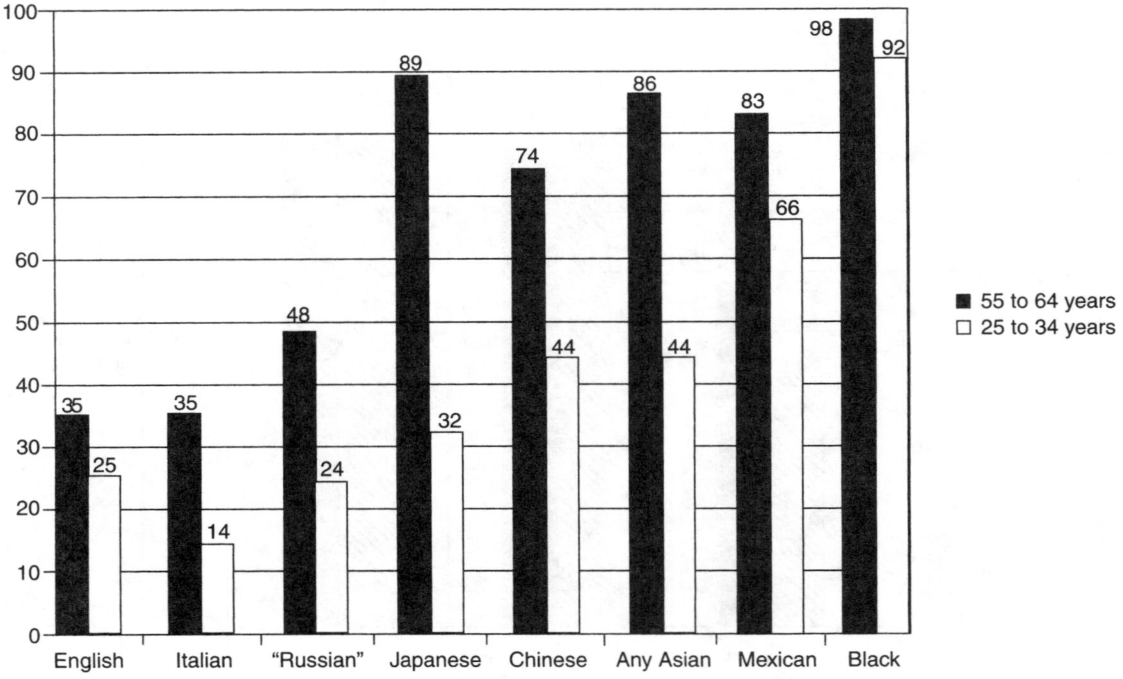

	English	Italian	"Russian"	Japanese	Chinese	Any Asian	Mexican	Black
55 to 64 years	35	35	48	89	74	86	83	98
25 to 34 years	25	14	24	32	44	44	66	92

Source: Tabulated from the U.S. Department of Commerce, 1990 Census of Population, Public Use. Microdata Sample.

Figure 11.2 shows that for all the European- (including the "Russians," a rough proxy for Jews) and Asian-origin groups, the decline in in-marriage has been substantial. The black rate has declined the least and is still the highest; Mexican women are the second most endogamous today, with relatively little change between the two cohorts. Asians, in contrast, have over the past thirty years shifted from among the most endogamous to rates of in-marriage approaching the rates for white women. This is true for the Japanese and Chinese subgroups, and significantly, it is also true when all Asian subgroups are combined into one panethnic Asian category. Let me underline the last point: on the evidence of these data, there is no evidence that Asian Americans are shifting from national-origin to panethnic (among all Asians) marriage patterns, though pan-Asian in-marriage does certainly exist.

Earlier in this chapter, I noted the complexity of assessing the relevance of race for understanding assimilation today. Figure 11.2 provides several intriguing hints in this regard: thirty years ago endogamy was the norm for Asians as well as Mexicans and blacks, but today over half of Asian women marry across racial lines. This suggests both intergenerational change and profound changes in societal attitudes. I am sensitive to reifying what are essentially social categories, but by no stretch of the imagination is the Asian-white divide less "racial" than the Mexican-white or even the black-white lines. Racial variation among Mexicans, both phenotypically and in terms of social classification, is notoriously broad and complex. The phenotype variation among "black" Americans is nearly as great, though of course the social classification is draconian and absolute. Whatever has changed in the meaning of the Asian-white boundary, it seems that it can be conceptualized in much the same terms that Alba (1985b) used to discuss change in the meaning of being Italian: both the salience of the boundary itself and its correlation with socioeconomic characteristics can change over time.

ATTITUDINAL ETHNICITY AND THE QUESTION OF PANETHNICITY

Elsewhere (López and Espiritu 1990), I have argued that we may be moving into a new era in which panethnicity—the extension of ethnic sentiments and solidarity to more general levels, away from subgroup and national origins—might provide a third alternative to continued narrow ethnic identity, on the one hand, and the surrender to assimilation, on the other. My coauthor and I still believe that these processes of panethnicity can be observed, at the levels of both personal identity and political solidarity, but in this era of mass immigration, personal identity continues to be strongly based on national origin. Panethnicity is important politically, especially as a rallying cry for the diverse Asian groups that are otherwise bound together by little more than rough phenotypical similarities and very rough economic similarities. As we argued in 1990, the tendency of others to blur Asian subgroups, and to lump together Latino subgroups as well, could combine with the objective bases of commonality shared by each set of subgroups to strengthen supra-ethnic identities and solidarities. But for the moment the massive new immigration itself works against the generalization of ethnic solidarity as fresh arrivals bring with them a strong sense of their own specific national and regional identities.

The effects of official and societal blurring of subgroups cannot be overestimated: violence against Asians is often directed against "Japs" who are in fact Chinese or Vietnamese. The recent publicity about campaign financing improprieties was generalized to Asian Americans, but in fact it was a specifically transnational Chinese phenomenon. This racial lumping, combined with a very general and variable cultural similarity, is apparently enough to overcome the lack of linguistic or religious bases of solidarity. Latinos, in contrast, do share substantial religious and linguistic (even if symbolic) similarities that facilitate political cooperation between subgroups at the national level and the incorporation of smaller groups into the Mexican American mainline in California. But at least on the evidence of the slight but suggestive data reviewed here, this political solidarity is not translating into genuine panethnicity at the level of identification and the social organization of family life, at least among the second generation.

The data reviewed earlier on marriage patterns provide modest evidence for panethnicity among Asians: pan-Asian marriages do certainly occur, but they have not supplanted marriage based on national and subethnic origins.

For evidence relating to ethnic identity, we turn again to the CILS data on second-generation youth (Rumbaut 1997c). That study asked, "How do you identify, that is, what do you call yourself?" in 1992 and again in 1995. Responses to this open-ended question were divided into hyphenated-American, national-origin, and racial-panethnic[2] responses, as well as two categories that were hardly used at all: "American" and "mixed." Among the two Asian subgroups included, Filipinos and Vietnamese, the 1.5 generation shows a clear preference for national-origin identities, especially in 1995, while the second generation is split between national-origin and nation-specific hyphenated-American labels. Neither opts for a panethnic term in any significant numbers. The data for Mexicans are harder to interpret (see note 2), but there does seem to be a marked increase in preference for nation-specific terms for both the 1.5 and second generations from 1992 to 1995. Certainly there was no growth in the use of panethnic terms, even if "Chicano" is considered to be (incorrectly, in my view) panethnic.

It is difficult to say how these high levels of nation-specific ethnic consciousness will play out in the lives of these children. A clear majority of each group did say that their ethnic identity was "very important" to them. Does that mean that they will marry only within their subgroup? If so, they will be following the pattern of second-generation European Americans, as well as Asian Americans, fifty years ago. Does it mean that their political sentiments and activities will be equally focused? This is much more difficult to foresee. In California, where the Latino population is overwhelmingly Mexican in origin, there is little compelling need for panethnicity, though Central Americans and other Latinos are typically invited to join the Mexican American and Chicano majority. In contrast, Asian subgroups have no choice but to cooperate, whether they like to or not; Asian American politics in California has both strong panethnic and strong subgroup tendencies.

Some Tentative Conclusions and Implications

There is compelling evidence that cultural assimilation ("acculturation," in Gordon's [1964] language) and social assimilation are proceeding at least as rapidly as they did among immigrant communities early in this century, as indicated by language patterns, which are both the best single pattern of cultural change and an early indicator of social assimilation. As in the past, acculturation is proceeding much more rapidly than social assimilation. In southern California linguistic acculturation and marital assimilation are proceeding much more rapidly for Asians than for Latinos.

The patterns of assimilation today are indeed more complex, but the key difference lies in the diversity of the socioeconomic origins of different national-origin groups; since many Asian groups enter the U.S. class structure at or well above the national average, their processes of assimilation are fundamentally different from those of Latino immigrants, who on average are starting out at the bottom, as Italians and Poles did a century ago. This suggests that the experience of earlier immigrants may provide a guide to the future of Latino immigrants, while the phenomenon of middle- and upper-middle-class Asian immigration requires a new conceptualization for understanding patterns of acculturation and assimilation as well as for socioeconomic adaptation.

The evidence reviewed here regarding linguistic patterns, marriage, and ethnic identity preferences provides little reason to think that strong panethnic identities will develop among Latinos or Asians in California. Panethnicity continues to be largely a political phenomenon, not a mass movement from subgroup to panethnic identities and social arrangements.

Notes

1. One other line of explanation has been offered by sociolinguists: Asian languages are simply too distant from English; English-Asian bilingualism is a job for virtuosos, not large natural-speech communities. A related sociolinguistic factor sometimes mentioned is that Asian languages have strong hierarchical social relations built into them, structures of relations that Asian youth reject in the United States. Both these arguments sound good to me, a nonlinguist, but it is worth pointing out that a large and growing proportion of educated Asians in Asia and throughout the diaspora are of necessity bilingual in English and their mother tongue, and often trilingual if circumstances demand.
2. Unfortunately, in the data currently available to me "Chicano" was classified as a panethnic response, even though it is commonly used to mean native-born of Mexican descent, and proud of it.

12 Immigrants, Past and Present: A Reconsideration

Joel Perlmann and Roger Waldinger

THIRTY YEARS AFTER the 1965 Hart-Celler Act brought renewed immigration to the United States, the immigration research agenda is slowly shifting from the newcomers to their children. While the timing is hardly fortuitous—the immigrants' children have only recently become a sizable presence in American schools and are just now moving from the schools into the labor market—the striking feature of this emerging scholarship is pessimism. Recent publications by Herbert Gans, Alejandro Portes, Rubén Rumbaut, and Min Zhou—leading students of American ethnic life—outline, with clarity and acuity, the reasons for concern: coming from everywhere but Europe, today's newcomers are visibly identifiable and enter a mainly white society still not cured of its racist afflictions. Shifts in the structure of the economy aggravate the impact of discrimination: while poorly educated immigrant parents seem to have no trouble getting started at the very bottom, the shift toward knowledge-intensive jobs requires that the next generation do well in school if it wishes to surpass the achievements of the foreign-born. With big-city schools in more trouble than ever before, the outlook for successful passage through the educational system seems dim. Since second-generation expectations are unlikely to remain unchanged, we can count on a mismatch between the aspirations of immigrant children and the requirements of the jobs they seek (Gans 1992a; Portes and Rumbaut 1996; Portes and Zhou 1993; Zhou and Bankston 1998).

There is another factor influencing scholarly views of today's immigrant children, and that has to do with the past. Though the historical comparisons have not been fully articulated, the new scholarship offers a story that reads like this: the descendants of the last great migration started out at the very bottom, but they have now either caught up with, or surpassed, their WASP betters of yore (Lieberson and Waters 1988). While one might find cause for comfort in the success of yesterday's downtrodden, future developments are likely to follow a different, less hopeful path. To begin with, the immigrants of old shared a common European heritage with the then-dominant WASPs, and that blunted discrimination's edge. The old factory-based economy also allowed for a multigenerational move up the totem pole. Immigrant children could do better if they just hung on through the high school years, after which time well-paid manufacturing jobs would be open to them. The third or fourth generation would continue on through college and beyond, completing the move from peddler to plumber to professional. By contrast, the restructuring of the U.S. economy gives the children of today's immigrants no time to play catch-up; strong and extended performance is the requirement for moving ahead.

That the situation of today's immigrant children is in some ways distinctive lies beyond debate. But we argue that the interpretive stance toward the past, and toward certain features of the present situation as well, puts the contemporary situation in an especially unfavorable light. This chapter takes another, albeit still preliminary, look at prospects for the second generation in light of historical experience. We begin with a quick overview of second-generation upward mobility in the past. We then take up what appear to be the crucial similarities and differences between the past and present prospects of the second generation.

SECOND-GENERATION LESSONS

Oscar Handlin's celebrated quip—"Once I thought to write a history of the immigrants in America. Then I discovered that the immigrants were American history" (1951, 3)—does not oblige us to consider all American immigrations. For our purpose, the wave of 1890 to 1920, heavily dominated by immigrants from southern and eastern Europe and the last mass immigration to occur before legislation choked off the European flow, provides the crucial comparison. Compared to their predecessors, the immigrants of the turn of the century were far more likely to converge on the nation's cities and far less likely to move into agriculture—in striking parallel to the situation today. These "new immigrants" of old encountered an economy very different from the postindustrial capitalism of late-twentieth-century America but nonetheless far closer to the contemporary situation than the American economy of 1850 or before. The period from 1890 to 1920 also saw far smaller waves of migration from Mexico, Asia, and the Caribbean, and some will think that the experiences of these populations are relevant to how those of similar regional and racial origin will fare today. We disagree; the issue is whether today's immigrant children are likely to adapt in ways that parallel or diverge from the trajectory followed by their second-generation predecessors, who were overwhelmingly of southern and eastern European origins. The appropriate way to ask the question about race is to ask whether being an Asian, black, or Mexican immigrant is a big handicap for immigrants today, a handicap that distinguishes them from southern and eastern Europeans of the last wave. That Asian, black, or Mexican immigrants faced especially destructive discrimination in 1900 does not address that crucial question; assuming otherwise is to reify racial classifications.

The great majority of the immigrants of 1890 to 1920 entered the American economy and class structure near the bottom, dramatically below the average native-born family's position. True, there were entrepreneurs among the immigrants of old—mainly persons with a background in trade or crafts (as among the Jews) or unskilled laborers who somehow managed to move into entrepreneurial endeavors. Nonetheless, in 1910, as table 12.1 shows, immigrants from all major groups, save the British, were far more likely to work at the least skilled jobs than were native whites of native parentage, and all were less likely to work in white-collar jobs, whether at high or low levels. Low levels of literacy also distinguished these groups from the natives and from late-nineteenth-century immigrants from northwestern Europe—just over half of the "other eastern and southern Europeans" reported that they could read, and just over half of the Italians could not speak English, for example. Though the Jews entered America at occupational and literacy levels above those of their counterparts from southern and eastern Europe, they still began with quite a disadvantage compared to the native-born. The children of immigrants were a good deal less likely than the children of natives to remain in school, and those who remained in school were more likely to have fallen behind in grade attainment.

It is within the context of these generalizations that studies of the economic mobility of European immigrants fall. These studies are of two kinds: a set of historical studies of mobility among European immigrants and their children, and a series of ancestry studies based chiefly on the 1980 and 1990 censuses, which provide novel information on individuals who are later-generation descendants of immigrants—third, fourth, fifth, or later generations. These two strands of research treat populations that do not quite connect, the first group focusing on immigrants and their children, and the second on a set of distant descendants, with the bridging generation(s) often falling from view (as with the Germans, Irish, and English). The research results highlight this gap: the historical studies of social mobility tend to show that ethnic differences in the economic standing of groups remained very important into the second generation; the outcome studies based on ancestry show that eventually these differences disappeared.

The American studies of social mobility were mostly conducted in the 1960s and 1970s, when they were a staple crop among the then-new social historians. Associated most closely with the name of Stephan Thernstrom (1964, 1973), these studies came to a crashing halt in the late 1970s, in part owing to increasing disenchantment with quantification among historians, and in part because the research on social mobility in particular quickly reached a conceptual impasse. These studies had sought to explore the extent to which upward mobility characterized American life. Several conclusions quickly emerged: that social mobility in America had indeed been considerable; that it was not as salient as stated in the most naive versions of the rags-to-riches stories of the Horatio Alger type; that it was more salient than Thernstrom's first, paradigmatic study (of Newburyport, Massachusetts) had suggested; and that the quality of the data then available (and of the quantitative skills of most authors) were too poor to determine whether the extent of American social mobility varied much across time and place or whether American social mobility rates differed much from European social mobility rates. Given this state of affairs, interest declined (for historical studies, see Thernstrom 1973, ch. 9; Bodnar 1985, ch. 6; see also Ferrie 1995).

TABLE 12.1 Immigrants and Ethnics in 1910

	First Generation							
	British	*Irish*	*Scand.*	*German*	*Italian*	*Polish*	*Jews EE*	*Other E&S Eur*
Men ten to sixty-four, occupations (percent of nonfarm)								
percent Mgrl, prof	10	6	6	10	2	2	9	3
percent Technical, sales	15	11	8	14	7	5	29	8
percent Craft	40	22	41	34	23	23	31	25
percent Ops, laborers	28	47	39	34	59	68	28	60
All males ten and over								
percent speaking English	99	100	91	90	49	46	78	51
percent able to read	99	96	98	97	65	73	90	55
Percent fourteen- to eighteen-yr-old in school								
Boys	45	47	48	39	28	28	57	N/A
Girls	47	49	54	37	34	26	55	N/A

	Second Generation				
	British	*Irish*	*Scand.*	*German*	*NWNM*
Men ten to sixty-four, occupations (percent of nonfarm)					
percent Mgrl, prof	12	11	10	11	13
percent Technical, sales	22	21	27	21	24
percent Craft	31	24	25	27	24
percent Ops, laborers	30	35	33	32	32
All males ten and over					
percent speaking English	99	99	99	98	99
percent able to read	98	98	98	98	96
percent fourteen- to eighteen-year-old in school					
Boys	N/A	N/A	N/A	N/A	58
Girls	N/A	N/A	N/A	N/A	60

Source: Watkins, 1994: Tables B1, B2, B3, B4

Notes: First generation = foreign born; second generation = native born with at least a foreign-born mother. NWNM = native born of native mothers. For group definitions, *see* Watkins (1994, 366–71). "Other East and Southern Europeans" includes Greeks, Russians, Magyars, Bohemians and Moravians, Slovaks, Lithuanians and Letts, Slovenians, and Croatians.

The historians were also interested in educational differences among ethnic groups, although historical information on school attainment was rare since the U.S. census had begun asking about grades of school completed only in 1940; the question that had been asked earlier, whether a given child was in school in the census year, was a poor proxy for school performance. The studies that did manage to include information on schooling supported the generalization that was obvious from published surveys of the time: the children of native-born parents were more likely to be in school and in the higher grades than were the children of immigrants. Also, some immigrant groups differed dramatically in the amount of schooling their children received, although much of this difference is easily explained by dramatic differences in the levels of economic well-being of the families. Nonetheless, there do appear to have been some significant differences in years of schooling completed by different ethnic groups, even when all measurable family background factors are taken into account. The classic difference between the Jews and other immigrant groups from southern and eastern Europe, such as the Italians, is a case in point. On the other hand, the other easily observed major line of division is between immigrants from more and less economically developed parts of Europe (as, for example, around 1910 between the Slavs and Italians, on the one hand,

and the British, Germans, and Scandinavians, on the other). The value of schooling for the social progress of these groups—measured as returns to schooling—may have differed somewhat. (Again, contrasts between Jews and others have been made in the literature.) However, the truly glaring ethnic difference in terms of returns to schooling involves the low degree of occupational advancement experienced by relatively better educated blacks in the North compared to various white groups with the same education (see Lieberson 1980; Perlmann 1988).

All this impinges in tantalizing but ill-developed ways on the study of today's second generation. For our purposes, studies of immigrant and second-generation mobility compared to the mobility of natives yield mildly interesting results—establishing, for example, that there were indeed differences in the starting points and in the degree of upward mobility by ethnic origins—but explaining such differences is another matter. The description of the extent of mobility through the second generation sounds rather different if one reads Stephen Thernstrom's summary (1973, 249–52) or John Bodnar's (1985, 169–75)—two major efforts at synthesis. However, the most important observation about this historical literature in the present context is that it focused on the question of the extent of mobility by group much more than on paths to upward mobility; it is precisely the question of paths, however, that lies at the heart of today's debate. The extent to which the second generation was in fact crucially indebted to semiskilled jobs in factories and the extent to which the decline in those jobs today means that route is now blocked are not well-developed themes of this historical mobility literature.

Skipping a generation or two from the immigrants and their children to the "twilight" of European-origin ethnicity, we have the ancestry studies from 1980 to 1990 (Alba 1985a, 1988, 1990; Hirschman and Falcon 1985; Lieberson and Waters 1988; Neidert and Farley 1985; Waters 1990). These show that socioeconomic assimilation has been accomplished largely for the European-origin groups and that the rank ordering of well-being today is generally unrelated to that at the turn of the century, with the experience of Jews notably at variance from this generalization. The matter of pathways once again appears—where the groups stand in the contemporary ethnic division of labor and whether they occupy positions of any distinctiveness are questions that remain largely unasked (see, however, Lieberson and Waters 1988).

We note one curious exception: in contrast to these sociological studies of ancestry that stress convergence, George Borjas (1994b) stresses that a key ordering at the time of immigration, 1910 literacy levels in the immigrants' country of origin, continued to be correlated with the economic position of their descendants for perhaps a century. How well these perspectives can be meshed neither he nor the relevant sociologists (for example, Lieberson and Waters 1988; Neidert and Farley 1985; Alba 1990) have undertaken to show. We suspect that the resolution is a matter of interpretive spin—the "convergence today" need not contradict "differences [that] lasted as long as a century." Also, Borjas tends to focus on third and later generations, while some sociologists have tried to separate the third from the fourth and later generations. Nevertheless, the contrast between Borjas and the sociologists is important. Economists read Borjas, sociologists read their colleagues, and historians do not regularly read the literature produced by either discipline. Since Borjas's writings are also widely read and cited by policy analysts in connection with immigration restriction issues, this divergence of emphasis regarding the "common knowledge" about the long-term character of immigrant absorption should not be ignored.

In any case, our perspective leads us to stress that the "catching up" occurred not in the first or second generation, but in those later generations on whom data are difficult to obtain. By the third generation, the levels of intermarriage among groups of European origin became very high, so that the grandchildren of Slavic immigrants are also the grandchildren of many other ethnic groups. The ancestry question bypasses this problem by throwing it in the lap of the respondent—with whom does he or she identify? Yet if our goal is to understand socioeconomic mobility from the second generation to the present-day generation, we need the sort of data the genealogist wants—the actual ethnic ancestors of individuals, not the subjective identities of the present generation. Much more than the scarcity and complexity of data is involved here. The substantive significance of all this is that the socioeconomic assimilation of the immigrants' descendants occurred at the same time that the meaning of ethnic descent became complex and indistinct, and these two developments are part of one story, a story as yet poorly told because of the available data, as well as its subtlety and complexity.

Second-Generation Starting Points

Given the distinctive economic characteristics of the post-1965 immigrants, one might not have expected the discussions of their children's prospects to have turned pessimistic so quickly. In contrast to the immigrants of 1890 to 1920, concentrated at the bottom of the occupational distribution, socioeconomic diversity is a salient feature of the new immigration. High-skilled immigrants have played a modest but significant role in immigration to the United States ever since the enactment of the Hart-Celler Act in 1965. Notwithstanding charges that America's immigrants are of "declining quality," the 1990 census found that a college degree was as common among all immigrants as among natives (one out of five). Moreover, the highly skilled are often present at levels well above the U.S. average, with the college-graduate share ranging from 27 percent among Russians to 65 percent among Indians. Consequently a good proportion of the recent arrivals begin not at the bottom but in the middle class or above. In contemporary Los Angeles, for example, coveted professional occupations have become immigrant concentrations: more than 35 percent of the pharmacists in the Los Angeles region are foreign-born, as are more than 25 percent of the dentists and more than 20 percent of the engineers, various computer specialists, and physicians.

At the same time, many of today's immigrants do start at the bottom. Thus, in 1990 only 5 percent of all U.S.-born adults, but 18 percent of the foreign-born adults, had received no secondary schooling. We can refine this contemporary native-immigrant comparison in a crucial way: a great share of the immigrants coming in at the bottom are from Mexico, which is also by far the most important sending country numerically—22 percent of the 1990 foreign-born population was from Mexico. The next most prominent source country, the Philippines, accounted for less than 5 percent. If we look at the immigrants from the many other sending countries, we find that the educational achievements of native-born and (non-Mexican) foreign-born adults no longer appear very different. The foreign-born are actually more likely to have reached college than the native-born, although other foreign-born adults are still overrepresented among those with little or no formal schooling. In other words, if we ignore for a moment the Mexican immigration, we observe an immigration that is 80 percent as large as the current one, and at immigrants who, on average, were beginning their progress through the American economy no worse off than Americans who were not immigrants. The usual generalizations about contemporary immigration provide no hint of this reality.

Mexicans loom large among the foreign-born population, but even more so among the children of the foreign-born. Roughly one out of every three immigrant children has at least one Mexican-born parent. Because those parents live under depressed socioeconomic circumstances, the size and characteristics of the Mexican population strongly influence the overall profile of today's second generation, as can be seen in table 12.2, which supplements the usual comparison of the children of immigrants and natives with a further contrast between Mexicans and all other immigrants. The three indicators displayed in table 12.2—percentage of children living in households where the head is on public assistance, a single parent, a college graduate, or employed in an upper white-collar occupation—are recalculated from research done by others (Oropesa and Landale 1995) and are not meant to be determinative. Still, they suggest a pattern more complex and nuanced than one would expect given prevailing notions of the second generation. These three indicators show the children of all immigrants are living in less desirable circumstances than their native-born counterparts. But that disadvantage disappears when the Mexican population is excluded from the analysis, the lead passing to the children of the foreign-born.

A more complete analysis would certainly muddy the waters further; we have no doubt, for example, that the proportion of non-Mexican-origin immigrant children living in households with heads who lack a high school degree or work in blue-collar jobs is higher than the average among natives. At this stage of the game, however, our ambitions are not so great as to require a complete analysis of the most recent U.S. census. The thrust of this chapter concerns the contrast with the children of the wave of 1890 to 1920; from that perspective, one is hard-pressed to argue that today's immigrant children—Mexicans excepted—are starting out from circumstances less favorable than those of the past. And they may indeed be better: to note that 30 percent of today's non-Mexican second generation live in households where the

TABLE 12.2 Characteristics of Immigrant Children, Aged Zero to Seventeen, 1990

	First Generation	*Second Generation*	*First and Second Generations*	*Third-Generation plus*
Head College Graduate				
Total	20	22	21	23
Mexican	3	4	4	8
Non-Mexican	27	30	30	23
Head Single Parents				
Total	25	18	20	25
Mexican	23	19	20	39
Non-Mexican	25	17	19	25
Head Upper White-Collar				
Total	16	22	21	25
Mexican	4	6	6	13
Non-Mexican	21	30	28	25

Source: Oropesa and Landale 1995.
Notes: First Generation = born abroad; Second Generation = born in United States of at least one foreign-born parent.

head has a college degree is no trivial observation in light of the historical experience—especially when the level for all natives is seven percentage points lower.

Regardless of comparisons to immigrants of the past, today's debate asks about the effect of the "new economy." While the new economy may render the children of non-Mexican immigrants vulnerable, it must be having about the same influence on the children of the native-born. In the new economy, children in some of these immigrant families may indeed be confronted with "missing rungs" on the ladder out of the bottom—but no more so on average than the children of native-born families. Only the Mexican immigrant population, therefore, stands distinctively at risk, and only its magnitude makes immigrants as a whole appear distinctively exposed to the winds of economic change. By contrast, at the turn of the century no single group could have altered the generalization that most immigrants were much more likely than natives to start out near the bottom (see table 12.1). Indeed, that generalization applied to every one of the major southern and eastern European groups—the relatively better-skilled Jews included.

SECOND-GENERATION RACE: THEN

The European immigrants of 1890 to 1920, write Alejandro Portes and Min Zhou (1993, 76), were "uniformly white"; consequently "skin color reduced a major barrier to entry into the American mainstream." Using the categories of Milton Gordon (1964), Herbert Gans concurs (1992a, 177): "While dark-skinned immigrants from overseas cultures will also acculturate, racial discrimination will not encourage their assimilation, at least not into white society."

"Race," as the historian Barbara Fields has argued, explains nothing, but is something that has to be explained. So contentions such as these beg the question at hand: Under what conditions do such categorical distinctions among groups gain salience? A look at other societies demonstrates that neither skin color nor any other physical attribute is a necessary condition for the erection of racial divisions. The central complaint of modern European anti-Semitism was precisely the point that the Jews had become indistinguishable from everyone else. And current French attitudes are far less antagonistic to black Africans or Antilleans than to North Africans, yet the latter are frequently blond and of fair complexion.

One can agree that race is a social construction and still retort that by the late nineteenth century, "the social construction of race" in the particular historical context of the United States had led to an association between skin color, on the one hand, and slavery and its legacy, on the other. But this historical legacy, as two streams of American historical writing emphasize, did not fully determine how the European immigrants of the past would be slotted into the American racial classifications. A generation ago, John Higham's *Strangers in the Land* (1955) showed the influence of racial thinking—with its distinctions between the "Nordic," "Alpine," and "Mediterranean" races—in intellectual and political circles and in the framing of the immigration restriction legislation of the 1920s. As applied to the European immigrants, those racial classifications often employed visible physical features, including differences in skin color. In the nineteenth century, for example, the Irish were labeled a "race" and regularly characterized as "savage," "simian," "low-browed," and "bestial" (Roediger 1991). Black Americans were referred to as "smoked Irishmen," suggesting that these two groups were then looked at through a remarkably similar lens (Ignatiev 1995). Later observers stressed the "Saracen blood" of the southern Italians, whose "dark complexion . . . sometimes resembles African more than Caucasian hues" (Rieder 1985, 32).

Over the past half-dozen years, several scholars have taken such evidence seriously and linked it to the very low social-class position of the immigrant arrivals. It is easy to imagine, they point out, that the immigrants could have been defined not as "white," perhaps not as black, but as some distinctive, stigmatized "other." That such an alternative grouping never emerged had much to do with the actions of the immigrant European groups themselves: they engaged in deliberate strategies that distinguished themselves from blacks and, in turn, yielded "whitening." We need not argue that contemporaries distinguished "races" of the "Nordic" and "Mediterranean" kind in quite the same way as they constructed the racial opposition between "Negroes" and "whites," nor even that they would necessarily have excluded "Mediterraneans" from the broader "white" category. It suffices, for today's debate, to note that they saw "racial" divisions among "whites" and that these divisions included looks and even skin "hue"—a meaning for "peoples of color" around 1900 (see Higham 1955; Rieder 1985, 32; Roediger 1991; Ignatiev 1995).

Moreover, these racial divisions faded at a very gradual pace. Social scientists today will make sport of Edward A. Ross, whose book *The Old World in the New* (1914) contains such gems as this remark from a physician: "The Slavs are immune to certain kinds of dirt. They can stand what would kill a white man" (quoted in Lieberson 1980, 25). But it is well to remember that as late as 1945 Lloyd Warner and Leo Srole could distinguish between "light" and "dark" "Caucasoids," the latter "a mixture of Caucasoid and Mongoloid" blood, slated for very gradual assimilation—anywhere from six generations to "a very long time in the future which is not yet discernible" (286–93).

It could not have been more than a few years after 1945 that Warner and Srole's "dark Caucasoids" became "white ethnics." Racial perceptions changed as the Irish, Poles, Italians, and Jews moved ahead; in this sense, for the descendants of the European immigrants, race was an achieved, not an ascribed, status. Yet today we are told that the earlier immigrants were able to move ahead because they were white and that the immigrants of today will have trouble doing so because they are not white. At best, this view drastically needs to be fleshed out with historical detail and with ample shades of gray; at worst, it mistakes cause and effect.

Second-Generation Race: Now

The recent historical treatment of "whiteness" attends to the processes by which the European immigrants distanced themselves from the natives of African descent. As Robert Orsi writes (1992, 318), "Proximity—real and imagined—to the dark-skinned other was pivotal to the emergence" of the hyphenated identities that the European ethnics established in their quest for acceptance in America. The struggle for place in a contested ethnic order provided ample motivations for the newcomers to resolve any ambiguity over how their racial identity was to be defined. The "effort to establish the border against the dark-skinned other required an intimate struggle, a contest against the initial uncertainty over which side of the racial dichotomy the swarthy immigrants were on and against the facts of history and geography that inscribed this ambiguity on the urban landscape" (Orsi, 1992, 318). Labor competition furnished additional incentives, though since the Italians often found themselves pitted against the Irish, and the Irish against the Germans, the conflict over jobs does not suffice to explain why they all became white (see Ignatiev 1995). But they did; and in becoming white, the immigrants and their descendants also became party to strategies of social closure that maintained black exclusion and ensured more stable employment and better wages for others of their own kind.

Can today's immigrants draw on a similar ethnic card? The answer is not yet in, but there is no question that they certainly can try, especially when it comes to differentiating themselves from poorer, less-educated African Americans who fall at the bottom of the racial order. We all know about the tensions that suffuse the relations between African Americans and the new middleman minorities that run businesses in the Harlems and Wattses of today's United States. Whatever their causes, these conflicts yield the consequence of shifting entrepreneurial, but visibly identifiable, immigrants to the advantaged side of America's racial division.

It is not difficult to imagine that professional or entrepreneurial immigrants find rewards for falling on the "right side" of the color divide. We suggest that the same can be said for the labor migrants whose presence so many Americans now seem to dislike. Certainly urban employers in New York, Los Angeles, or Chicago have come to prefer immigrants to native-born, American blacks (Kirschenman and Neckerman 1991; Waldinger 1996a, 1996c).

As in the past, conflict at the racial divide coexists with tensions among workers of diverging national or regional attachments. We have repeatedly heard reports of bad blood between Mexicans and various Central American groups, as well as of intra-ethnic conflict within Central American populations, when interviewing employers in the Los Angeles region.[1] Nevertheless, far more Latino hostility seems to be directed toward blacks.

Today then, as at the turn of the century, the second generation will move into a context in which their parents have been busily at work distancing themselves from native blacks. But there is a rejoinder to the argument just advanced, namely, the contention that the geographic and ethnic origins of the new immigrants leave them in no position to play the "race card." From this perspective, the influence of the past is important in that it defines today's newcomers as "people of color." Consequently immigrants from Latin America, the Caribbean, or Asia will not be able to separate themselves from castelike treatment, unlike the immigrants of the past (see, for example, Okihiro 1994, ch. 2).

One need only look at the present dynamics of white-Asian relations to realize that the argument for this sort of historical continuity falls short. It is not just that all of the legislated racial divisions seem now curiously barbarous and are disowned; in crucial respects, the eradication of the legal barriers is paralleled by changes in social conditions. There are Asians at the bottom of the class structure, but there are Asians throughout the class structure as well, in impressive numbers. Further, the educational achievement of large numbers of Asians ensures that for significant numbers of the second generation the disappearance of the manufacturing jobs on the lower rungs of the economy is about as relevant to their economic advancement as it is for readers of this volume. Moreover, trends in intermarriage between the offspring of new Asian immigrants are far closer to historic trends in immigrant-native intermarriage than to historic trends in black-white intermarriage. In contrast to the pattern that prevailed during the great immigrations of 1830 to 1920, a quantitatively meaningful plurality of "races" is now evident in the United States. At the same time, white, Asian, Hispanic, and Native American groups are engaged in extensive intermingling. The conjunction of these two facts alone may help diminish the significance of the black-white divide in American life. In the same way, the fact that tremendous numbers, and great proportions, of the Latin American arrivals come with an interracial legacy—having "Indian" and black ancestors as well as white ancestors—also creates a novel and quantitatively massive race complexity in America (Perlmann 1997b; Wright 1994). All this may help erode the centrality of the black-white divide.

Acknowledging these tendencies, we think, yields both a pessimistic scenario and an optimistic one. The pessimistic scenario suggests that the crucial line will remain between blacks and all others, with some segmented assimilation leading a fraction of the second generation to integrate into the black population and the rest into some as yet undefined category that may not be "white" in any meaningful sense and may not remain designated as such. All we lack to make this scenario more plausible is a term in the popular culture to replace white—a term that can include Asians and Hispanics easily enough and that essentially means "native-born and not black." If that term emerges, we should note it as an important and worrisome development.

The more optimistic forecast rests on the evolution of black-white relations themselves. It may seem worse than frivolous in a period of so much black-white tension to insist on the prospect for qualitative change in relations across that divide—or, if not frivolous, then hard to take seriously. One need not argue that black-white dynamics are at a happy pass to understand that they have shifted enormously for the better in the past six decades. It is highly significant that black-white intermarriage remains low, but with 10 percent of young black men marrying whites, it is now significantly above zero and rising (Alba 1995, 17). If the social class and educational situation of inner-city blacks is a national disaster, there is nevertheless also a serious growth in the black middle class and in black collegiate enrollment. The point is simply that the black-white divide, while remaining terribly salient, is itself very different from what it was when immigrants and their children defined themselves in the past.

One measure of change even in the most recent years is the fate of the phrase "the browning of America," denoting the expectation that the crucial divide will separate non-Hispanic whites from all others, to be loosely united as "browns." In this sense, the term "browning of America" is as common today as was the term "the greening of America" a generation ago—and about as reliable in predictive value. Another measure, along a different dimension, is the problem that federal agencies have in trying to fit the children of racial intermarriages into their racial classification systems. These problems should be viewed as symptoms of transition to a time when those classifications will seem quaintly passé. The present racial situation is in flux, as *Time* magazine told us in 1997 in connection with Tiger Woods ("Multiracialism: The Melding of America," May 5, 32–39). If we truly believe that race is socially constructed, then we should know that the broader dynamics of American culture and politics, not the skin complexion of the new immigrants, will matter most to their absorption. Race, as David Montejano has written (1987, 4), "represents an arena of struggle and accommodation." For that reason, the new second generation will have some say in America's complex racial and ethnic order.

Second-Generation Advance

Clearly one form of contemporary adaptation "replicates the time-honored portrayal of growing acculturation and parallel integration into the white middle class" (Portes and Zhou 1993, 82). There is little question that many, possibly even most, of today's immigrant children are heading upward, exemplified by the large number of Asian students enrolled in the nation's leading universities—some the children of workers, others the descendants of immigrants who moved right into the middle class. The rapid Asian ascent evokes parallels with the past, most clearly with the first- and second-generation Russian Jews who began appearing at the City College of New York and then at Harvard, Columbia, and other prestigious schools shortly after 1900.

If there is a similarity between the past and present experiences of second-generation movement into the middle class, we are more struck by variation—in particular, the distinctive institutional reactions to the Jewish and Asian inflows, respectively, into higher education. The history of the quotas against Jewish students is reasonably well known. By the second decade of the twentieth century, the number of Jews seeking admission to elite academic institutions was still a relatively small minority of the Jewish age cohort, but the numbers were nonetheless large enough to create a notable presence and to discomfit the then-dominant WASPS. Columbia University, positioned "at the gateway of European immigration," was the first to try turning the situation around: it implemented a new set of admission procedures that successfully reduced the Jewish share of entering students from 40 percent to 17 percent by 1934 (Wechsler 1977, 163–64, 168). By the end of the 1920s, Harvard, Yale, Princeton, Duke, Rutgers, Barnard, Adelphi, Cornell, Johns Hopkins, Northwestern, Penn State, Ohio State, Washington and Lee, and the Universities of Illinois, Kansas, Minnesota, Texas, Virginia, and Washington had all adopted measures that restricted Jewish enrollment (Dinnerstein 1994, 85–86). Professional schools essentially followed the same course.

Less well known are the circumstances under which these policies were reversed. The tide began to change during World War II, when the draft made it harder for colleges, like so many institutions, to pursue discriminatory practices without immediately harming themselves. More decisive, however, was the new legal and social environment that emerged during the war and thereafter. Having just endured a conflict fought to promote democracy—and in which racial equality emerged as a war issue—Jews felt themselves newly emboldened to act: in 1945 the American Jewish Congress challenged Columbia University's tax exemption in court, arguing that New York State tax laws forbade discrimination by tax-exempt institutions on grounds of race or religion (Wechsler 1984). Unsuccessful before the bench, Jewish organizations moved on to the political arena, there to reap greater rewards: in 1946 the New York City Council passed a resolution, clearly aimed at Columbia, that threatened the tax-exempt status of colleges and universities that used racial or religious criteria in selecting students. Anxious to avert any similar threat, Yale acted preemptively, outlawing quotas and giving first priority to students of highest merit (Oren 1985). In 1948 New York State forbade discrimination on grounds of religion or race in higher education and simultaneously established a state university, threatening the hegemony of Columbia and the other privates while also promising greater accessibility to Jews, Catholics, and blacks. Other states shortly followed suit, with antidiscrimination laws even more stringent than New York's.

Other postwar developments hastened the assault on quotas. As John Skrentny (1997) has argued, post–World War II competition with the Soviet Union led the United States to embrace a "new moral model," rendering earlier discriminatory practices illegitimate. Global competition also placed a greater premium on preparation of a labor force suited for a technologically advanced economy, further pushing universities to open, rather than close, doors. Thus, the 1947 report of Truman's Commission on Higher Education linked expansion of educational opportunity with its equalization, blasting the quotas directed against Jews (as well as the confinement of black students to black colleges) (Levine 1986); the American Council on Higher Education weighed in with additional condemnation and documentation of anti-Jewish restriction. And so the era of anti-Jewish discrimination in higher education ended quickly in some places, like medical schools, and not until the mid- to late 1960s in others, like Yale and Princeton (Wechsler 1982).

An echo of this earlier controversy arose in the 1980s, amid charges that prestigious colleges, private and public, had established quotas against Asians, just as they had against Jews several decades before (see Wang 1988, 201–5). By the mid-1980s, something strange was happening at elite educational institutions. Public institutions, even the more selective among them, were rapidly increasing their Asian enrollments and admitting Asians in much the same fashion, and using the same criteria, as for everyone else. But Asian students with records comparable to those of their white counterparts were not doing as well when it came to admission to the most selective, private institutions. Moreover, Asian enrollments, which had been rising quite sharply in the late 1970s and early 1980s, suddenly flattened out at schools like Princeton, Brown, Harvard, and Stanford (Hsia 1988, 90–91).

If the pattern was reminiscent of the earlier experience, and the underlying cause familiar—competition with native whites over scarce and valued resources—the controversy worked itself out in different ways. In contrast to the earlier experience, Asian administrators, faculty, and students were numerous and influential, sufficiently so that their voices could not be ignored. Several of the universities accused of discrimination—Princeton, Harvard, Stanford, and Brown, to name just a few—took a critical look at their own admissions practices and then took steps that led to significant increases in Asian American admissions (United States Civil Rights Commission 1992, 111–12).

The external response also proved distinctive. In contrast to the Jews, who in the 1920s and 1930s were isolated politically and intimidated by a rising tide of anti-Semitism, Asian American organizations were able and willing to use political influence; that in turn galvanized the scrutiny of outside monitors. When admissions policies at the University of California at Berkeley became highly suspect, the state's leading Democratic politicians "held numerous fact-finding hearings, intervened by bringing together university officials and Asian American community leaders, passed special resolutions on admissions, and had the state Auditor General undertake an unprecedented audit of admissions policies" (Nakanishi 1995, 277). In Washington, D.C., both liberals and conservatives kept the spotlight on allegations of discrimination in admissions. Even Harvard was not exempt from review: the Office of Civil Rights undertaking a major investigation that cleared Harvard of charges of discrimination but found that Asians did suffer from the preferences granted to alumni children and athletes.

There are a number of lessons to be drawn from this story of Asian and Jewish efforts to scale the ivy walls. First, note the sequence of changes in second-generation status. East European Jewish acculturation had proceeded rapidly, judged by success in academic achievement. Second-generation Jews did not find that their parents' ethnic economy served "as a platform enabling them to climb into the mainstream economy at high levels" (see Alba and Nee 1997); nor were they able to move up the pecking order by taking over the positions vacated by others who moved even further ahead. Instead, above a certain level of attainment and outside the expanding ethnic niche, Jews encountered exclusion. Scholastic success had moved them into competition with the nation's elite, who found effective means of blocking Jewish ascent. Moreover, the reaction in the academic world reflected broader social patterns, in which the doors of New York's large corporate organizations were generally closed (Broun and Britt 1931, 224). In the strongly nativist, anti-Semitic environment of the 1920s and 1930s, organized efforts to overturn discriminatory practices were of little avail. Hence, the second generation was forced to fall back on the institutions of the ethnic community, which by the 1930s included not just a greatly expanded business sector but also substantial employment in the civil service (Waldinger 1996a).

Changed power relations after World War II upended the exclusionary practices put into place during the interwar years. Once quotas were removed, the Jewish presence on campuses swelled. Contact probabilities shifted, producing greater exposure to Gentiles, which in turn accelerated Jewish "structural assimilation" into the American mainstream, to use the concept made famous by Milton Gordon (1964). But this portrait stands at variance with the belief that "the process of assimilation [of the European-origin groups] largely depended on individual decisions to leave the immigrant culture behind and embrace American ways" (Portes and Zhou 1993, 76). The Asian chapter of our story reveals the same dynamics of exclusion and conflict that followed educational attainment and adequate economic resources to support college enrollment.

The contemporary controversy also arose in a different historical moment. Earlier struggles against discrimination had changed the rules of the game—the struggles over the Jewish quotas themselves, the post–World War II climate, and not least the civil rights movement. It had become far more difficult for dominant groups to engage in strategies of social closure than was the case earlier in the century. Moreover, insider groups operated under greater constraint than before, while outsider groups enjoyed more leverage within the affected institutions and more scope for mobilization outside them. The relatively high class standing of Asian immigrants did not simply carry them to the threshold of membership, as in the Jewish case earlier in the century, but generated the resources needed to quickly overturn barriers. And the advantages derived from the more open society of the late twentieth century should temper generalizations about the determining position of skin pigmentation in the fate of the new second generation.

The Second Generation in the Hourglass Economy

Gans (1992a) and Portes and Zhou (1993) argue that the mismatch between aspiration and opportunity is greater today than before. In their view, the conundrum of the contemporary second generation lies in the continuing transformation of the U.S. economy. The manufacturing economy of old allowed for a three-, possibly four-, generational sequence of modest steps that took the immigrants' descendants far beyond the bottommost positions to which their ancestors had been originally consigned. By contrast, today's occupational segmentation has "reduced the opportunities for incremental upward mobility through well-paid, blue-collar positions" (Portes and Zhou 1993, 85). The declining viability of small business reduces the possibilities for advancement through the expansion of businesses established by the immigrant generation. The general stalling of mobility reduces the chances for ethnic succession: Jews and Italians followed the Irish into the public sector as the latter moved on to more lucrative pursuits; because today's civil servants are unlikely to enjoy the same options, this path of mobility will be closed off to today's second generation (Gans 1992a). Thus emerges the hourglass economy—many good jobs at the top, many bad jobs at the bottom, few decent jobs in between. How, then, will the second generation move up? This formulation of the question, coupled with consideration of the racial origins of the second generation, drives the new second-generation literature to its pessimism.

One restriction on the scope of the hourglass argument is that the crisis will not affect the offspring of the very large fraction of immigrants who arrive with useful skills—for example, with educational attainments comparable to the median among white American workers. These immigrants can and do support an extended education for their second-generation children. The children of immigrants comprise 41 percent of the first-year students enrolled in the City University of New York—a rate that leaves immigrant children overrepresented in the third-largest public system of higher education in the United States by a factor of almost 50 percent (City University of New York 1994, 10). The New York experience is not unique: nationwide 74 percent of all college-age immigrants are enrolled in some form of post-secondary schooling as opposed to 65 percent among the native-born; likewise, in-school rates for immigrant eighteen- to twenty-one-year-olds are above native-born levels (Vernez and Abrahamse 1996, 38).

But what of the rest, the less fortunate segment envisioned by "segmented assimilation"? One restriction of the theory's explanatory power is its poor specification of supply and demand. The theory stresses the changing nature of the U.S. economy, thereby implying that the economy's demand for low-skilled work (especially in manufacturing) is what pulled the relevant steps off the mobility ladder. What about the supply of low-skilled workers, given several decades of high-volume immigration? The increasing supply of low-skilled workers can dramatically change the outlook for such workers just as much as the real or imagined changes in demand for them in the "new economy." What is more, to the extent that supply (or demand, for that matter) drives down their prospects and they are less able to help support their children's schooling, their children may be channeled into similar or only slightly better jobs than their parents. If so, the second generation, too, is hurt by the magnitude of supply over an extended period. A more refined specification of the supply and demand for low-skilled workers, then, is a desideratum for the theory of "missing steps on the ladder of mobility." The pessimists may retort that, strictly speaking, more refined specification would not matter to the claim that the steps on the old ladder are now missing. True, but the specification does matter for a broader understanding of what is happening.

These considerations aside, it does seem reasonable to think that the less educationally successful of today's second generation, especially those from the immigrant families entering near the bottom, will be likely to run into trouble. But do they differ, in this respect, from their counterparts of the past? Questions about the future of yesterday's second generation were commonplace earlier in the century. At the time, contemporaries did not fret over the possibility that a large number of jobs would remain at the bottom of an economy shifting toward an hourglass shape. Nevertheless, they observed that an increasing proportion of decent jobs required extended levels of schooling, and they argued forcefully and often that the children of workers generally, and the children of the immigrant workers in particular, would not obtain those jobs unless they were convinced to stay in school longer than it seemed their wont to do (see Bremner et al. 1974; Douglas 1921; Krug 1969, chs. 8, 10; Lazerson 1971, ch. 5).

It is one thing to remember that contemporary observers were concerned about the prospects of yesterday's immigrant children, and another thing to note that those concerns were founded in a reality of continuing educational disadvantage, and still another thing to argue that because predictions were wrong in the past they are wrong today. Obviously we do not make this last claim. Nevertheless, insofar as the predictions were wrong, they do suggest caution in simply assuming that growing demands for high-skilled labor foreclose the possibility that the children of immigrants can move beyond their parents. Moreover, the historical parallel is instructive insofar as it is in part true: the economy did in fact require more jobs for the educated, but the second generation and their children also found pathways to amelioration, in part by acquiring the additional increments of schooling that the industrial economy of the period 1920 to 1970 demanded. Both the relatively slow pace of economic change and the ability of the ethnics to respond to the changes are relevant.

Other considerations also suggest some optimism. For one thing, as Portes and Zhou (1993) themselves were careful to stress, the shift toward the hourglass-shaped labor force is happening fairly slowly. There are many low-skill jobs in that economy. Second, the U.S. economy is enormous: today's second generation is a relatively small fraction of its workforce. If there is one cliché about ethnicity and the economy, it is that ethnic groups are not randomly distributed but are clustered in various niches, which both provide shelter from competition and yield mechanisms for progress up the ladder. Unless we rule out the emergence of second-generation niches, the observation that manufacturing jobs generally have declined in this economy does not end the task of analysis but begins it; it is not impossible, for example, that despite any decline, the remaining decent, less-skilled jobs are heavily populated by and sufficient for the today's second-generation aspirants.

Finally, remember that most employed persons without college degrees are neither immigrants nor their children nor native-born racial minorities. If the new hourglass economy poses serious problems of upward mobility for the offspring of these workers, it thereby confronts American society and all its working-class families with a very serious and widespread problem. For once it would seem to be true that we really can ignore ethnicity and focus on class.

Second-Generation Revolt?

The immigrants arrive willing to do the jobs that natives won't hold; however low the jobs may fall in the U.S. hierarchy, they still offer wages and compensation superior to the opportunities back home. Having been exposed to different wage and consumption standards from the start, the children want more. This process inheres in the immigration experience, an endogenous source of changing aspirations and outlooks; following Michael Piore (1979), we can call this "second-generation revolt." To say it is inherent in the immigration experience is to imply that it is by no means unique to the current second generation, but rather that it characterized those of the past as well. Both Gans (1992a) and Portes and Zhou (1993) draw on this source of changing attitudes. However, especially in the formulation of Portes and Zhou, other factors, exogenous to this process, are found to be interacting with it. For them, whether second-generation "careers . . . keep pace with their U.S.-acquired aspirations" (85) will be answered in a new historical context. These new exogenous factors include the racial composition of the new immigration and the nature of the hourglass economy already discussed. Also new is a kind of cultural diffusion. The new immigrants converge on central cities, where they live in close contact with earlier established native minorities. Proximity to African and Mexican Americans yields exposure to the "adversarial" norms of "marginalized youth." As immigrant children come into contact with the reactive subculture developed by native minorities, they undergo a process of "socialization" that "can effectively block parental plans for intergenerational mobility" (83).

In the concept of an "oppositional" or "adversarial" culture we see the shadow of the anthropologist John Ogbu (1978). For Ogbu, an oppositional culture is the indigenous response adopted by African Americans and other supposedly like groups to the experience of oppression and exploitation in America. On the one hand, the legacy of discrimination breeds ties of extraordinary, kinlike solidarity; not only does group loyalty take primacy over the quest for individual achievement, but any effort to break out from the pack is seen as a betrayal of the group and appropriately sanctioned. On the other hand, African Americans have pursued a strategy of cultural inversion, as have the other subordinated groups, responding to mainstream society's rejection by rejecting the mainstream and its values (see Gibson 1988; Matute-Bianchi 1986). As Douglas Foley (1991, 66) puts it, "This sort of occupational logic dictates that they must choose between being occupationally successful (white) and culturally successful (black). Quite ironically, the battle to preserve their ethnic culture becomes the very thing that dooms castelike minorities of color to academic failure."

But just as second-generation revolt is not a phenomenon distinctive to African Americans or Ogbu's other castelike minorities, there is good reason to assume that an oppositional culture does not characterize today's second generation alone. As we've emphasized, discrimination and stigmatization were well known to the earlier generations of European immigrants. Whatever the faults of today's multicultural education, it could not possibly be as dismissive of the immigrants' background and culture as were the Americanization programs of the 1910s, 1920s, and 1930s; a common reaction to this curriculum must have been resentment and opposition, especially in those schools where alienation from school values of educational achievement and extended education were prevalent.

Nor should we forget that solidarity has always been among the most cherished of working-class values, with effects besides those one sees on the picket line. Here is Pete Hamill (1994, 110–11, 146), a son of an Irish immigrant, on growing up in Brooklyn during the 1940s:

> In the final three years of grammar school at Holy Name, I always finished at the top of the class in grades, averaging 98 or 99, was placed on the honor roll and granted awards for general excellence. But there was an assumption that if you got good grades you must be soft, a sissy, or an AK—an ass kisser. This was part of the most sickening aspect of Irish-American life in those days: the assumption that if you rose above an acceptable level of mediocrity, you were guilty of the sin of pride. You were to accept your place and stay in it for the rest of your life; the true rewards would be given to you in heaven, after you were dead. There was ferocious pressure to conform, to avoid breaking out of the pack; self-denial was the supreme virtue. . . . It was arrogant, a sin of pride, to conceive of a life beyond the certainties, rhythms, and traditions of the Neighborhood. Sometimes the attitude was expressed directly. . . . More often, it was implied. But the Neighborhood view of the world had fierce power. Who did I think I was? Forget these kid's dreams, I told myself, give 'em up. Do what everybody else does: drop out of high school, go to work, join the army or navy, get married, settle down, have children.

This pressure for leveling in solidarity again implies a we-they division between the neighborhood and the middle-class norms. That the precise cultural content of the division is not that which Ogbu describes does not mean that the we-they division was less oppositional.

Other descriptions of second-generation youth culture in the early twentieth century make the skepticism about the value of schooling and the opposition between ethnic youth and schools explicit. Ewa Morawska (1985, 267–68) provides this summary of the second-generation outlook among the East European immigrants in a Pennsylvania steeltown:

> The sons and the daughters of the immigrants were . . . keenly aware of the gulf between . . . [the] ideals [of the dominant society] and their actual chances in Johnstown. This perception was summarized by Mike T., a second generation Serb, born in 1905: "At school we learned [about how man is master of his fate], but we knew that we had a double strike against us, foreign extraction and poor and uneducated parents." In the perceptions of the second generation, some schooling and some personal advancement were correlated, but education, the basis of individual achievement in the dominant cultural paradigm, "was not the most important [factor] for your future." By and large, success was determined by particularistic considerations: "In 70 percent of the cases, it mattered more who your father was, his nationality and all . . . and whom he knew, and whom you knew."

Caroline Ware's book in 1935, on the Italians of Greenwich Village in the 1920s and the 1930s, sounds the same themes of skepticism toward the value of education, combined with cultural conflicts between school and community. "Among the boys in the district," she wrote, "it had always been very much the code to hate school. Although there is nothing unique in boy's antagonism to school, the intensity with which the local boys hated school was conspicuous" (1935/1965, 337). As Ware tells it, the conflict had various roots: the curriculum and teachings had little in common with what the children learned in the streets; the schools disregarded the cultural background of the children; they also rejected the behavioral norms that the children had acquired at home, which "often set the children vigorously against the school." Writing contemporaneously, Leonard Covello (1943/1972) recounts a similar story about the Italians of East Harlem; there the accent lies on the extraordinary cohesion of the Italian community and on the way in which parental pressures and children's preferences converged to produce high dropout rates by the high school years. Composed twenty-five years later, Gans's (1962, 133) description of the Italians of Boston's West End differs only in degree: the students are poorly motivated; the parents are ambivalent; the schools clash with the attractions of the children's peer groups; the "junior high school principal's main problem [is] truancy, and the parental acquiescence concerning this." The school was "anathema to many" of the teenagers, in large measure for the reasons adduced by Caroline Ware twenty-five years earlier—it sought to train them for a way of life diametrically opposed to the one for which they had been prepared at home (Gans 1962, 68). And a good part of that opposition stemmed from the parents' rejection of middle-class society and its values and their hostility toward individualistic striving. What little we know of more contemporary, ethnic working-class communities suggests that the school-child antagonism has not since been significantly tempered (see, for example, MacLeod 1987).

Moreover, the accommodation to the routine of working-class life was often made grudgingly, and few of the sixteen-year-old boys who dropped out of high school, as did Hamill, made a beeline for the factory. Instead, they spent their time on the street corner, hanging around, drinking liquor, and getting into fights. Hamill describes the "times of the gangs" in pages differing little from those of today's newspapers, only in that the arsenal of violence was not as complete (see Spergel 1964, 38–47). Whether gangs were present or not, the nature of the youth labor market made for an extended "moratorium," as Paul Osterman (1980) termed it, in which youths were excluded from positions of the primary or craft type and bounced from one more or less casual job to another. Unstable employment was compatible with that form of protest against the routines and aims of both school and work described by Gans as "action-orientation": youths "want the material appurtenances of modern life—especially cars and spending money—and they want to be freed from the routine-seeking society which 'bugs'—or imposes on—them" (1962, 68). Since the youth labor market provided plenty of jobs, deficient only because they were boring and badly paid, action-orientation could persist until other commitments forced a reckoning with routinization (see Spergel 1964, 149–52; Wial 1988).

The historical evidence, reviewed earlier, is certainly not definitive. However, it implies that an "oppositional culture" can emerge from the immigrant working-class experience without exposure to a "proximal host" comprising visible, stigmatized, native-born minorities. Our discussion of "second-generation revolt" points to greater continuities in the experiences of immigrants past and present; it reminds us of the difficulties experienced by the earlier groups. It also suggests that the time frame for immigrant accommodation was extended and that we should not expect anything different to happen today.

The comparison also brings class back into current debates. Though the context for the earlier discussion is ethnic, the explanatory factors seem to be of a different nature, having to do with the disarticulation between schools, on the one hand, and the world of manual work to which immigrant children were destined, on the other. That disconnection breeds revolt: working-class children perceive that school has little to do with their chances in life, and they also react against the middle-class culture of the school and its denigration of working-class life and labor. Indeed, Ogbu's concept of an "oppositional culture" recalls Paul Willis's (1977/1981) influential description of rebellious "lads" versus the no less working-class, but bourgeois-minded, "earholes." Yet Willis's account of Birmingham, England, tells a story of working-class, adolescent revolt pure and simple—not a story of "second-generation" revolt at all, much less the second generation of today's immigration of color into the changing American economy. Are there subtle differences between the rebellion of Willis's working-class youth, Piore's second generation, Ogbu's castelike minorities, and the youth passing through Portes and Zhou's lowest path of segmented assimilation? There may be, but we are struck by how much is common among these descriptions, and class-based.

Whether mainly or only partly a class phenomenon, the youthful revolt described here is almost certainly conditioned by the subsequent opportunities that working-class children encounter. School could be flaunted with relative impunity as long as there was a vibrant factory-based economy, to which unsuccessful students had access through the help of relatives and neighborhood friends. The stronger the industrial economy, the greater the value placed on manual work, a priority that in turn sanctioned youth rebellion and gave it a ritualized form. Though the literature is fragmentary, it appears that these same circumstances persist, in attenuated form, in the remaining ethnic working-class enclaves in the Northeast and Midwest. One can certainly hypothesize that similar conditions come into play in Los Angeles, with its massive, thriving factory-based economy and the movement of Mexican immigrants and Mexican Americans into the ranks of the skilled working class. But outcomes are sure to take a different form in a deindustrialized city like New York or in a service-based city like Miami, where school dropouts have few alternatives and the erosion of the industrial economy has severely devalued manual work. Since these are also the conditions that have intensified the "oppositional culture" among native minorities, it may be common experience, and not exposure, that yields self-defeating rebellion among the children of the inner city, whether of foreign-born or native-born roots.

Conclusion: Second-Generation Prospects

The descendants of the last great immigration to the United States have now moved far up the totem pole; from the perspective of the 1990s, it is hard to imagine that their adaptation to America could have turned out differently. But this view of an inexorable climb up the social ladder is certainly not how the children and grandchildren of the European immigrants experienced the process themselves. Their beginnings, as we have noted, were not particularly promising; nor were the established groups of the time ready to accept the newcomers and their descendants. Even the most skilled of the lot, the Jews, found that rapid acculturation and the acquisition of schooling were not sufficient to open the doors. The acquisition of full membership was an uncertain, protracted process to which the immigrants and their descendants contributed—through attempts both to undo obstacles to progress and to place themselves on the white side of America's racial divide.

At a minimum, this portrait of the past suggests that, overall, the children of the post-1965 immigration begin with disadvantages no greater than those encountered by immigrant children before. That generalization is probably too cautious. On the one hand, the immigrants' class composition is far more heavily weighted toward the middle class than was true earlier in the century. On the other hand, American society is more receptive to immigrant incorporation—in large measure owing to the efforts by earlier groups of outsiders (including native-born blacks) to widen access to opportunity. Two themes emerge from this comparison: class and agency.

Class

While America's new immigrant population is extraordinarily diverse, its overwhelmingly largest component—the Mexicans—falls at the very bottom of the skill ladder; the Mexicans are even more heavily represented among the immigrants' children. Absent the Mexicans, today's second generation looks little different from the rest of the American population in socioeconomic characteristics. Those characteristics are not sufficient to guarantee satisfactory adjustment to the economy of the next generation, but the same can be said for young, "third-generation-plus" Americans of any ethnic stripe. The immigrant children most notably at risk are the Mexicans (most notable, surely, in numbers and as notable as any other immigrant group in the low level of economic well-being). It is the presence of a single large group, so far below the others in skills, that distinguishes today's from yesterday's second generation. However, we note that the advent of the new economy means trouble for the children of the native-born members of America's working class, who also find themselves in conflict with the middle-class values and expectations of schools. These are the main reasons why we should worry about the future for the offspring of Mexican immigrants and of other less-skilled newcomers.

Agency

As did their predecessors, the children of today's new immigrants will transform America. The relatively high class background of so many immigrant children makes it more likely that they will do so quickly and on their own terms—witness the contrast between the Jewish and Asian fate in higher education. That higher class standing is also likely to change the import of race, historically fluid except at the black-white divide, and currently under rapid transition even there. One can certainly imagine that some section of African, Latin American, and Asian-origin Americans will find themselves pigeonholed in some new but stigmatized and subordinated "other" category. But other options are clearly visible. The ever growing ethnic diversity of American life—thanks, in large measure, to immigration itself—suggests that those possibilities are more likely. We expect that today's second generation will make itself busy reshaping the meaning of race—an endeavor to be pursued with at least some modicum of success.

The authors are grateful for the support of the Levy Institute and the Spencer Foundation.

NOTE

1. This generalization is based on ongoing research by Roger Waldinger.

13 Immigrants' Socioeconomic Progress Post-1965: Forging Mobility or Survival?

Rebeca Raijman and Marta Tienda

THREE SETS OF circumstances have changed the economic prospects of recent immigrants. First, the composition of immigrants has shifted toward Asia and Latin America, away from their historically (white) European-origin countries, and the education (skill) composition of new arrivals has become more diversified relative to earlier periods. Recent cohorts exhibit a close correspondence between region of origin and completed schooling, with the most educated immigrants arriving from Asian, African, and European countries, and the least educated from Latin America. Trends in the education and national-origin composition of recent arrivals are germane for appreciating immigrants' socioeconomic progress because they define the association between group membership and socioeconomic inequality over time (Borjas 1994a; Chiswick and Sullivan 1995; Portes and Rumbaut 1990; Rumbaut 1996a; Smith and Edmonston 1997; Tienda and Liang 1994).

Second, opportunities for earning a living and for achieving upward mobility have changed dramatically over the past quarter-century. Compared to prior eras of heavy immigration (most notably at the turn of the century), the wages of unskilled workers have eroded appreciably. Also, the returns to education have been rising since 1973, reversing a two-decade trend that had significantly narrowed the wage gap between high school- and college-educated workers in the post-World War II era (Freeman 1993; Karoly 1993; McFate 1994; Murphy, Karoly, and Welch 1993). These changes in economic opportunities are important not only for immigrants, who historically have occupied low-status positions as a way of gaining a foothold in the U.S. economy, but also for unskilled U.S. natives, who have experienced diminished income and employment opportunities precisely at a time when immigration flows have expanded.

Third, U.S. reception factors have changed. The 1980s and 1990s represent a period of national retrenchment in social obligations to U.S. citizens, but even more with respect to immigrants. This is evident in the term limits on welfare benefits included in the Welfare Reform Act of 1996; in the exclusion of legal immigrants from access to means-tested health benefits and income transfers; in the provisions of the antiterrorist legislation authorizing deportation of legal immigrants ever convicted of a felony; and in the spate of referenda to assert the primacy of English (Portes and Schauffler 1996; Tienda and Liang 1994). Restrictionism is also evident at the federal level in the numerous attempts to reduce immigration by lowering admission quotas and to regulate diversity through preference for immigrants from selected countries, such as Ireland. Political scapegoating, which often blames immigrants for the declining fortunes of U.S. citizens, has fueled anti-immigrant hostility. Although there is growing consensus that immigrants are a net, albeit modest, benefit to the U.S. economy (see Smith and Edmonston 1997), such evidence is meaningless when public perceptions and media messages convey the opposite.

Whatever merit there may have been in previous portrayals of immigrants' assimilation and mobility, the social and economic significance of ascribed traits, and of immigrant status in particular, continues to fluctuate in accordance with political and economic moods. Not only do unskilled workers command relatively lower wages than they did in the past, but tolerance for inequality and intolerance for diversity appears to have risen (Tienda 1999). How, then, will recent and future arrivals fare in the U.S. labor market? Has the social and economic significance of birthplace changed, and if so, is this relationship contingent on education, changing opportunities, or intensified competition and discrimination? What guidance do prior theoretical frameworks provide for understanding and predicting the labor market successes and failures of immigrants? Although we do not pretend to provide definitive answers, in this essay we critically review evidence that addresses them and suggest productive avenues for resolving persisting puzzles.[1]

Our general goal in this essay is to discuss the economic progress of immigrants in light of changes in economic opportunities and the changing composition of immigration. To achieve this objective, the next section reviews the dominant theoretical approaches to the study of immigrant socioeconomic assimilation and identifies their main contributions and shortcomings. The following section surveys and evaluates empirical evidence from various analytical approaches about the economic incorporation of immigrants. Our goal is both to identify points of tension and agreement and to suggest promising lines for future research, which we elaborate in the concluding section.

Approaches to Immigrant Integration

Economic integration refers to the process by which immigrants accumulate job experience in the U.S. labor market as their tenure in the host country increases. The dominant approaches to understanding how U.S. immigrants assimilate economically build on mainstream theoretical frameworks, notably the human-capital and status attainment traditions in economics and sociology, respectively, as well as the structuralist reformulation they engendered. Accordingly, we use these approaches to organize our review and assessment of current knowledge about immigrants' socioeconomic assimilation and to identify promising directions for new insights.

Barry Chiswick's (1978b, 1979) pioneering study comparing wages of native and immigrant men based on the 1970 census marks the beginning of modern studies about economic assimilation. Chiswick compared the earnings of native and immigrant workers of different ages at a single point in time and quite optimistically concluded that immigrants' earnings would exceed those of comparably skilled natives within a generation.[2] Because he had access only to a single cross-section of data, Chiswick made powerful, albeit implicit, ceteris paribus assumptions about the continued growth of employment opportunities, the characteristics of the immigrant pool, and the reception factors confronted by successive immigrant cohorts. On the heels of one of the longest periods of sustained wage growth in U.S. history, Chiswick's assumptions about constant employment and wage opportunities were reasonable. This is because the downturn of wages that began after 1973 was not perceptible from intercensus surveys until the late 1970s and early 1980s. Furthermore, the demographic impacts of changes in immigrant admission policies had only begun to unfold at the time Chiswick conducted his analyses. His conclusions, moreover, were consistent with general assessments of immigrant experience throughout the nineteenth and early twentieth centuries (Lieberson 1980). Chiswick's later paper (1979), which claimed to have discovered universal patterns, flagged group-specific variation in rates of economic assimilation (that is, wage growth), yet he underplayed the importance of unequal wage growth profiles for comparably skilled men of Asian, Hispanic, and other origins.

In several highly influential papers, George Borjas (1985, 1987b, 1990, 1994a) challenged Chiswick's conclusions by pointing out that from a single snapshot it is impossible to separate assimilation and cohort effects.[3] Not only did Borjas insist that immigrants do not overtake the wages of natives *within* a generation, but he also questioned whether immigrants could ever reach parity with their native-born counterparts. Borjas correctly pointed out that it is inappropriate to draw inferences about how earnings of different age cohorts *change* over time from a single snapshot of data. Therefore, he used two cross-sections of decennial census data to compare wage differentials between native and foreign-born cohorts and to assess the wage growth of specific age cohorts ten years later. That is, immigrants aged twenty in 1970 were compared with a native cohort aged thirty in 1980 to reflect the fact that both the natives and immigrants had aged. This synthetic cohort approach has the advantage of drawing age-specific comparisons over time to approximate the actual wage growth experienced by a real cohort.

To bolster his position that immigrants cannot reach parity with native workers, Borjas coined the phrase "declining immigrant quality" as shorthand for education differences between natives and successive cohorts of immigrants. While conceding that average education levels of recent cohorts have been rising over time, he correctly notes that the education levels of the native-born population have risen faster, resulting in a larger nativity gap in the completed schooling of workers over time. However, Borjas's conclusions about so-called declining immigrant quality can result from changes in demand, notably the fall in wages of unskilled workers, which he systematically underplays (see, for example, Borjas 1995). Borjas's work also can be criticized for ignoring the dramatic changes in period conditions (see, for example, the criticism in Freeman and Holzer 1991) and for not considering the selective effects of emigration in producing slower rates of earnings growth among more recent immigrant cohorts.[4]

Robert LaLonde and Robert Topel (1990) reconsidered the issue of declining immigrant quality using a synthetic cohort approach to model assimilation. However, unlike Borjas, they considered how changes in labor demand influenced immigrants' wage mobility. Like Chiswick, they show strong wage growth for most (but not all) immigrant groups, and like Borjas, they agree that the average skill composition of immigrants declined relative to natives, but not relative to prior arrivals. Because they did not show declining returns to skill within education levels, their work helps bridge the gap between Chiswick's and Borjas's research findings.[5] Specifically, LaLonde and Topel acknowledge the importance of changes in labor demand (that is, the relative growth of unskilled jobs) and labor supply (the changing volume and educational composition of recent immigrant cohorts) in shaping the economic mobility of both recent and earlier immigrant cohorts. However, in the absence of longitudinal data to trace the *actual* wage growth of *real* cohorts, it is impossible to settle this debate conclusively.

Through the 1980s and early 1990s the spate of empirical studies framed within the human-capital approach portrayed the economic assimilation of immigrants based largely on wages and annual earnings (Borjas 1985, 1987b, 1990, 1994a; Chiswick 1978b, 1979; LaLonde and Topel 1990). Sociologists amplified the early research agenda by considering educational and occupational achievements among immigrants of varying national origins, often, but not always, from a comparative frame of reference (see reviews in Borjas and Tienda 1985; Hirschman 1983; Massey 1981; Tienda 1983b). Individualistic approaches generally ignore the influence of social and cultural contexts on socioeconomic outcomes. These approaches presume that individuals are rational actors who possess full knowledge about job opportunities, wages, and other market conditions and are free to enter the labor market at will. However, these approaches have failed to explain why workers who are endowed with similar levels of human capital but differ in ascribed characteristics experience unequal labor market outcomes.

Although an individualistic orientation dominated the empirical study of immigrants' economic mobility, the resurgence of interest in market segmentation research during the early 1980s influenced the study of immigrant earnings in two ways. First, it sensitized analysts to the need to consider labor market characteristics in explaining dispersion in immigrant earnings (Borjas 1987b; Evans 1989; Tienda and Lii 1987; Tienda and Wilson 1992). Second, it enticed some analysts to frame nativity differentials in earnings within the dual labor market framework (Portes and Bach 1985; Portes and Stepick 1985). Claims that structural factors influence individual outcomes did little to reveal *which* are most relevant for understanding earnings dispersion, nor *how* they operate to constrain or enhance immigrants' economic mobility. This is because adequate theoretical and operational marriages that combined constructs at multiple levels of analysis seldom occurred. Early attempts to model structural influences (for example, labor market conditions and job characteristics) on individual outcomes were essentially reduced-form individual-level analyses with labor market characteristics appended to individual records and with little regard for portraying how particular structures bound economic opportunities. At best, studies in this empirical research genre specified statistical interactions between individual and labor market characteristics (Tienda and Lii 1987); at worst, the influences of job characteristics and labor market conditions on immigrants' earnings were specified as additive or interaction effects in multivariate models (Tienda 1983a; Portes and Stepick 1985).

As one of the preeminent scholars of modern immigration research, Alejandro Portes's substantial contributions to the field stand as a notable exception because he has advanced theoretical development of immigrants' economic fortunes by situating the study of immigrant assimilation as an individual attainment process within a structural frame of reference (Portes 1981). His construct—modes of incorporation—explicitly recognizes that individual attainment processes and outcomes depend crucially on contexts of reception (Portes 1981, 1995a; Portes and Rumbaut 1990). Portes's conception of an immigrant enclave as a vertically and horizontally integrated local economy buttressed by residential concentration and a replenishment of new immigrant laborers transcended the limitations of exclusively individualistic approaches for portraying economic and social achievements (Portes and Bach 1985; Wilson and

Portes 1980).[6] In other words, Portes and his associates emphasized that both individual characteristics (human capital) and structural arrangements (contexts of reception) circumscribe the life chances, the economic opportunities, and ultimately the socioeconomic successes of immigrants. He also called attention to the prevalence of informal employment among unskilled immigrant workers in the United States, as well as in other industrialized economies and industrializing societies (Portes 1995a; Portes and Manning 1986; Portes and Sassen-Koob 1987; Portes and Stepick 1985; Sassen 1987; Stepick 1989).

In an attempt to synthesize insights garnered from studies based on the dual labor market (Piore 1975, 1979), the enclave economy (Portes and Bach 1985; Portes and Manning 1986), and the informal economy (Portes and Sassen-Koob 1987; Portes, Castells, and Benton 1988), Portes and Stepick (1985) proposed a fourfold classification scheme consisting of primary, secondary, enclave, and informal employment. This scheme, which builds on the dual labor market literature that was popular during the early to mid-1980s (Piore 1975, 1979), merely appends informal employment and enclave-sector employment as alternative modes of incorporation with direct or indirect consequences for immigrant earnings. Their fourfold typology is an advance over prior attempts to specify how market segmentation constrains labor market outcomes, but the scheme is highly problematic for several reasons. First, it confuses market segmentation with the nature of worker engagement because informal employment can arise in any sector (primary, secondary, or enclave). Second, although their expanded segmentation scheme increases the number of market sectors through which immigrants can enter the host labor market, it maintains the dualistic conceptualization of market segmentation that was highly criticized for being overly simplistic (see Hodson and Kaufman 1982; Kaufman, Hodson, and Fligstein 1981). Finally, it implies that enclaves are alternative modes of labor market integration without clearly specifying the relationship, if any, to primary, secondary, or informal employment.

Despite the heuristic value of market segmentation approaches, one important lesson from the 1980s debate is that dichotomous classification schemes are inadequate to portray the highly complex dimensions of labor market segmentation (Hodson and Kaufman 1982; Kaufman et al. 1981; Parcel and Mueller 1983). This lesson would appear to be even more important in light of profound changes in the industrial structure of employment and the changing skill and ethnic composition of recent U.S. immigrants. Portes and Stepick's (1985) expanded segmentation scheme presumes that informal employment and enclave employment are alternatives to secondary- or primary-sector employment. This is not necessarily so, because informality can occur in a broad array of economic arrangements for any given individual or family, and because individuals can be simultaneously located in multiple economic sectors and derive income from various jobs (Tienda and Raijman 1997, forthcoming).

To summarize the main implications of human-capital and structural approaches for understanding immigrants' socioeconomic progress, we offer the following observations. Although structuralist scholars have subjected individualistic approaches to important criticisms, it does not follow that education and various types of labor market skills, notably English proficiency, are unimportant in predicting the socioeconomic outcomes of immigrants. Human-capital skills are highly influential in shaping immigrants' economic futures. Structuralist perspectives, while acknowledging the importance of reception contexts and variable labor market opportunities in determining the economic fortunes of immigrants, have failed empirically to capture the complexity implied by Portes's notion of a mode of incorporation. Perhaps the main conclusion about approaches to immigrants' economic integration is that *both* individual and structural approaches yield productive insights, and that the latter remain underdeveloped theoretically, but especially empirically.

MAKING IT IN AMERICA: IMMIGRATION AND INEQUALITY

Guided by the theoretical approaches surveyed in the previous section, we present in this section an overview of the state of empirical research regarding immigrants' labor market experiences and socioeconomic progress. Our review is deliberately brief and serves mainly to identify issues and areas where the research agenda has stagnated and to suggest new hypotheses or reevaluations of old hypotheses. We organize our review of empirical evidence around three questions. First, are recent immigrants making economic progress, and has this changed over time? Second, why are some immigrants more successful than others in the labor market? Third, what new insights about economic assimilation can be gleaned from a consideration of structural factors, including contexts of reception and modes of incorporation?

Are Recent Immigrants Making Economic Progress? Ascription, Skills, and Labor Market Outcomes

Immigrants' changing educational composition is crucial for understanding processes of economic assimilation and socioeconomic mobility. Educational attainment of immigrants cannot be totally divorced from changes in country-of-origin composition (Borjas and Tienda 1993; Chiswick and Sullivan 1995; Mare 1995). Although most immigrant populations have improved their educational attainment over time, substantial nativity differentials in completed schooling persist, and for some groups they have widened (Chiswick and Sullivan 1995; Mare 1995). For example, in 1970 the educational distribution of male immigrant and native workers showed that the average immigrant was slightly more likely to be a high school dropout, but also more likely to be a college graduate. By 1990, 37 percent of immigrants were high school dropouts compared to 14 percent of native-born men (Smith and Edmonston 1997). Thus, male immigrants were more than twice as likely as their native-born counterparts to lack a high school education.

Immigrants from Latin America exhibit the lowest educational levels, on average, while immigrants from Asia are the most highly educated. There are, of course, notable exceptions to these generalizations. Proportions of Laotian, Cambodian, Italian, and Haitian immigrants who completed high school and college degrees fell below the U.S. average, while Peruvian, Cuban, Colombian, and Nicaraguan immigrants attained high school or college graduation rates comparable to the U.S. average. Immigrants from Mexico, who average seven and a half years of graded schooling, exhibit the lowest education levels of all immigrants. Other Latin American immigrants as a group averaged eleven years of graded schooling, compared to thirteen or more for immigrants from Asia, Africa, and Europe (Portes and Rumbaut 1990, table 4; Chiswick and Sullivan 1995, table 5.6).

Thus, educational inequality along national-origin lines is a defining characteristic of the U.S. foreign-born population. Robert Mare's (1995) analysis of 1990 census data shows, for example, that Asian natives and immigrants born after 1945 have *higher* rates of college attendance than their white birth cohorts, and Hispanic immigrants have the lowest rates of college participation and completion. Persistent racial, ethnic, and nativity differences in educational attainment imply lifelong differences in socioeconomic welfare, particularly in labor markets that place an increasingly higher premium on educational credentials beyond high school (Mare 1995). Improvements in the educational attainment of second-generation youth could reduce educational attainment along racial and ethnic lines, but the continued replenishment of the foreign-stock population by new immigrants with low levels of schooling can retard the educational progress of second and higher-order generations and widen educational inequities into the future. This is because parents' education constructs a floor below which offspring are not likely to fall, but it also represents a potential ceiling for the achievements of subsequent generations. The latter constraint is especially relevant for populations with extremely low levels of education, notably immigrants from Central America and Mexico.

That the educational levels of recent U.S. immigrants have been declining *relative* to the native-born bears directly on their long-term prospects for socioeconomic integration. For Asian, African, and other highly educated immigrant groups, the future looks bright; for Central and South American immigrants, and Mexicans in particular, the future looks quite bleak. Trends in educational attainment among immigrants imply widening wage and income inequality in the future because the returns to skill have been rising since 1973 (Freeman 1993; Karoly 1993; Murphy, Karoly, and Welch 1993) and because demand for unskilled workers has fallen (McFate 1994).

Labor-force participation and earnings are the two most commonly used measures for assessing the economic progress of U.S. immigrants. The former indicates immigrants' success in securing jobs, and the latter is a key indicator of economic well-being that derives from labor market activity. Two salient trends describe the experience of immigrants since 1960. One is a trend toward converging employment rates between native and foreign-born workers. Previously, average immigrant employment rates were higher than those of native-born workers, but changes in the demand for unskilled workers have begun to undermine the employment advantages enjoyed by poorly educated foreign-born workers. A notable exception to this generalization concerns recent immigrant cohorts, whose employment rates have been declining relative to those of natives. However, with increasing tenure in the United States, most of the initial employment gap of recent immigrants vis-à-vis natives disappears (Smith and Edmonston 1997, tables 5.15 and 5.16). Second, recent wage trends show a different picture of immigrants' economic assimilation. Owing partly to the increased education gap between immigrants and natives, their wage gap widened substantially in recent years. For example, in 1970 the average wage rate of male immigrants was only 0.7 percent below that of the (average) native-born worker; twenty years later male immigrants earned 16 percent less than their native counterparts. Similarly, the wages of female immigrants were lower than those of native-born women by 11.5 percent in 1970, yet the wage gap between native and immigrant women had grown to 22 percent by 1990 (Smith and Edmonston 1997, table 5.5).

Borjas (1994a) attributes the lower average wage growth of immigrants relative to natives to the changing national-origin mix of immigrant flow over time. He decomposed the skill decline into a portion due to changes in the national-origin mix and into a portion due to the changing skill level of immigrants from specific countries. He concluded that the changing national origin explains over 90 percent of the decline in educational attainment and relative wages across successive immigrant waves between 1960 and 1980 (see Borjas 1994a, 1995; see also Borjas and Tienda 1993). In fact, there is a high degree of variation in wage growth experiences among national groups. Mexican immigrants, who complete the fewest years of school and are by far the largest immigrant group, also earned considerably less than native-born workers did. Moreover, they appeared to experience little if any wage convergence over time. In contrast, immigrants from Europe, China, Korea, and Japan experienced significant wage convergence with native workers over the period from 1970 to 1990 (Smith and Edmonston 1997).

Although numerous studies have documented increased returns to skill during the late 1970s and throughout the 1980s (Danziger and Gottschalk 1993), relatively few of these considered whether the influence of ascribed characteristics in shaping economic fortunes also increased. Mare (1995) claims that the labor market position of Hispanics deteriorated during the 1980s, but he does not consider whether and how much this might be attributed to the increased presence of immigrants. For example, he showed that among men with a high school diploma, Hispanic and black men lost ground relative to whites between 1980 and 1990, but this was not the case for Asian or Indian men.[7] That minority men holding college degrees also lost ground relative to whites raises fundamental questions about why returns to skill differ along race and ethnic lines, and whether being Hispanic *and* immigrant, for instance, will cheapen the value of schooling more than either attribute alone.

Other studies show that minority youth and young adults experience more frequent and protracted spells of unemployment than non-Hispanic whites of comparable skills and experience (Ahituv et al. 1994; Wetzel 1995). These findings are relevant for understanding nativity differentials in income because the higher levels of employment instability that are common among low-wage jobs produce substantial income losses on an annualized basis (Hsueh and Tienda 1995). If immigrants remain disproportionately concentrated in low-wage and marginal jobs, it is conceivable that employment instability will become a crucial mechanism producing future nativity differentials in income. This is a hypothesis worth testing, assuming suitable longitudinal data become available in the future.

A substantial body of evidence (see Smith and Edmonston 1997) shows that the greatest losses in economic well-being during the 1980s were sustained by poorly educated Hispanic immigrants and other low-skill minorities, but it also suggests that factors other than skill are decisive in shaping nativity differentials in economic well-being. When the advantages of more-educated workers are being compounded relative to less-educated workers, it is relevant to ask whether immigrants will lose more than their fair share of the economic pie. Extensive *within*-group heterogeneity in educational and employment outcomes requires new approaches to explain why seemingly comparable schooling continues to render unequal rewards for immigrant and minority populations (Mare 1995; Murphy, Karoly, and Welch 1993). Unfortunately, no study has adequately addressed the question of what share of nativity income differentials reflects changes in the educational composition of successive cohorts, what share results from changing employment and wage returns to education, and what share arises from the changed valuation of immigrant status.[8]

A review of recent empirical work on trends in rising wage and earnings inequality reveals that its racial and ethnic (national-origin) underpinnings have been relatively neglected by the mainstream think tanks and research institutes.[9] Notable exceptions are studies by minority scholars employed at these institutions, such as Ronald Mincy (1990) and Maria Enchautegui (1992). Studies included in the Danziger and Gottschalk (1993) volume provide occasional tabulations for minorities, but virtually all comparisons ignore nativity differentials, treat Hispanics as an undifferentiated group, and neglect Asians altogether. Nativity differentials in wage trends have received the least attention. By not raising fundamental questions about whether and how the exchange value of birthplace may have changed relative to new income and employment opportunities, the default interpretation that income and wage inequality merely reflects group differences in educational attainment is tacitly accepted (Harrison and Bennett 1995; Mare 1995). Moreover, persistent anomalies such as higher employment and wages of unskilled immigrants relative to African Americans with higher levels of education challenge simple human-capital explanations of wage and income inequality (Tienda and Stier 1996; Waldinger and Bozorgmehr 1996b).

Several implications about the future economic prospects of immigrants follow from these trends. One is that the social and economic significance of ascribed traits may have increased as competition for jobs has intensified (Hodge 1973). Specifically, recent immigrants may experience more intense labor market competition with unskilled native workers (especially women, youth, and domestic minorities) than did earlier arrivals. A second implication is that unskilled immigrants admitted after 1973 have experienced limited or no wage mobility since their arrival, and also in comparison to earlier arrivals, because opportunities to earn a family wage have declined. That is, the rate of economic mobility experienced by *all* unskilled immigrants has slowed because of the drop in demand for unskilled workers (McFate 1994; Murphy, Karoly, and Welch 1993). A third possibility is that the increased volume of unskilled new arrivals has slowed the economic fortunes of immigrants. That is, in addition to the lower *demand* for unskilled workers insinuated by the second point, the *supply* of the unskilled may have exceeded the capacity of the economy to absorb them.

These scenarios have testable implications that have not been fully exploited by existing research, owing partly to data limitations but also to the limited success of prior research in portraying changes in reception contexts and in labor demand. With relatively few exceptions, studies of immigrants' economic progress have been based on cross-sectional research designs that are unable to represent actual (as opposed to synthetic) changes in opportunities for earning a living. That those changes have not been addressed satisfactorily partly reflects the inadequacy of existing data sources, but data limitations are not the only reason the research agenda on these topics has stagnated. More novel hypotheses that build on trends in inequality and the persistent race and ethnic differences in earnings among comparably skilled workers are required to advance the research agenda about recent and future trends in immigrants' economic mobility. We have several suggestions along these lines, which are elaborated later in the chapter.

Why Are Some Immigrants More Successful Than Others? Preferential Status and Market Segmentation

Race and ethnic differences in joblessness and wage rates within education levels suggest that simple human-capital arguments are insufficient to account for the observed economic disparities between immigrant and native workers, particularly because of substantial wage dispersion *within* education groups and *among* national-origin groups of comparable education levels. Several studies show that Mexican Americans and Mexican migrants fare better economically and socially than native blacks of comparable or higher education (Tienda and Stier 1996; Trejo 1997). Michael Greenwood and Marta Tienda (1997) report that male Mexican migrants were disadvantaged relative to native blacks in terms of educational attainment and language skills, yet in most states they had higher rates of labor-force participation and usually lower unemployment rates. This suggests that employers may actually *prefer* Mexican immigrants as workers because they allegedly have better work habits and attitudes (Kirschenman and Neckerman 1991; Tienda 1989; Tienda and Stier 1996). A corollary of the preferred worker hypothesis is that immigrant workers accept jobs that native minority workers refuse. This implies that domestic minorities expect better working conditions than immigrants do, and that they therefore require higher wage rates as a condition of accepting a job. Although this hypothesis has never been rigorously tested, studies by Daniel Hamermesh and Frank Bean (1998b) and Marta Tienda and Haya Stier (1996) provide refuting evidence.

Another explanation for the differential success of immigrants in the labor market vis-à-vis domestic minority workers is that, owing to different residential distributions, these groups confront unequal labor market opportunities. Specifically, John Kasarda's (1995) analysis of discrepancies in the spatial distribution of jobs revealed the largest skill mismatch for Hispanics, a finding that is at variance with empirical facts showing that Hispanic immigrants actually have *higher* rates of employment than blacks in most metropolitan areas. This evidence leaves considerable ambiguity about the exchange value of immigrant and minority-group status across labor markets that differ in their foreign-born population shares. That recent immigrants are also highly concentrated in central cities, often adjacent to black ghettos (for example, Chicago and Los Angeles) further undermines the viability of the spatial mismatch hypothesis to explain the anomaly of immigrants' higher employment rates compared to blacks. Kasarda's contention that Hispanics and Asians were less adversely affected than blacks by the decline of blue-collar manufacturing jobs because they were less concentrated in these types of jobs and were able to secure alternative employment in semi- and unskilled service jobs begs the question about why blacks did not enjoy similar advantages. In our judgment, the idea that immigrant workers, and Mexicans in particular, are preferred workers for low-wage jobs remains a viable working hypothesis that merits further investigation.

Mounting empirical evidence that the strongest negative impacts of immigrants on the U.S. labor market accrue to earlier immigrants (see review in Smith and Edmonston 1997; Greenwood and Tienda 1997) suggests gloomy futures for new arrivals. It is conceivable that the glut of potential workers in low-wage markets signals limits to the absorptive capacity of the U.S. economy for unskilled foreign workers. A recent study by Morris Newman (1994) of job applicants in a fast-food establishment showed that the ratio of applicants to minimum-wage job slots was fourteen to one. If Newman's analysis is correct—and it certainly squares with the trend in rising joblessness among unskilled black as well as immigrant workers—then the debate should focus on the criteria used to hire equally unskilled workers for low-wage jobs. Is it color? Is it a random lottery? Is it immigration status? Have market imperfections increased during periods of industrial restructuring (Kasarda 1995)? Or has increased competition for relatively fewer unskilled jobs raised the exchange value of being white *and* U.S.-born?[10]

Unfortunately, too few data sets provide information about employer hiring practices and their impact in determining group differences in labor market outcomes. Qualitative evidence garnered from semistructured interviews with employers has generated various insights suggesting that labor demand is *segmented* not only by skill level but also by qualitative attributes (such as mannerisms, dress, and speech) and by ascribed attributes, such as race and immigrant status (Holzer 1996; Kirschenman and Neckerman 1991). Although market segmentation theory fell into disfavor during the 1980s largely over methodological quibbles, current initiatives to understand what is driving changes in labor demand provide new opportunities to rethink whether and in what ways labor demand has become tied with ascriptive traits. Stated as a semi-rhetorical question, has labor demand become group-specific as well as skill-specific?

Of course, this line of questioning is not new, but its application to understanding immigrants' economic progress is relatively novel. During the 1970s and 1980s sociologists developed elaborate statements about occupational sex-typing and identified both positive and negative labor market consequences of women's concentration in specific jobs. One positive benefit is that typing of jobs by ascriptive traits reserves slots for members of a "preferred" demographic group. The downside is that "group-typed" jobs often command lower wages. The causal mechanisms for this process were never fully unraveled, although numerous researchers documented inverse correlations between wages and the demographic composition of occupations (see Tienda, Smith, and Ortiz 1987). No comparable work exists for the evolution of wages for occupations that experience immigrant succession, but this line of inquiry should prove fruitful in addressing such basic questions as: Do immigrants undercut wages of domestic minority workers? What conditions are conducive to succession of black workers by immigrants in particular jobs, as has occurred in janitorial and domestic service jobs (see Rosenfeld and Tienda 1997)? A better understanding of the mechanisms that produce lower wages in jobs where immigrants have become concentrated should help clarify how the glut of low-skilled workers will be resolved, and especially what "immigrant-typing" of jobs portends for future trends in wage inequality.

Age, nativity, race, and ethnic divisions seem crucial for understanding how low-wage jobs will be rationed among the oversupply of current and future unskilled-job applicants. We make this statement based on impressionistic assessments that fast-food jobs are predominantly a "youth" labor market; that garment assembly remains predominantly an immigrant labor market niche; and that agricultural, lawn care, and gardening jobs are predominantly a Mexican and Central American immigrant labor market niche. The list goes on, but these obvious examples make our point explicit. How, then, are market niches established? Stated differently, how do employer preferences develop and play themselves out to produce a succession of jobs from native-born to foreign-born workers? An answer to this question should clarify what undergirds the association between group membership and labor market position and possibly also shed new light on the demographic underpinnings of rising wages inequality.

Self-Employment and the Ethnic Economy: Beyond the Ethnic Enclave

During the last three decades, nonagricultural self-employment rose in the United States, from 7.4 percent in 1975 to 10.8 percent in 1990 (Aronson 1991; Devine 1992; Fairlie and Meyer 1996; Light and Sanchez 1987; Steinmetz and Wright 1989). In accounting for the increase of self-employment, most studies stress economic factors, such as industrial restructuring, business cycle downturns, and a general decline in wage opportunities for unskilled workers (Balkin 1989; Birch 1987; Piore and Sabel 1984; Steinmetz and Wright 1989). Relatively few studies link the growth of self-employment with international migration (for exception, see Blaschke et al. 1990; Light and Sanchez 1987). Yet sociological research has shown that self-employment is an important avenue for immigrants' labor market assimilation (Bonacich and Modell 1980; Cummings 1980; Light and Bonacich 1988; Portes and Stepick 1985; Portes and Zhou 1992; Waldinger and Aldrich 1990; Yoon 1991; Zhou 1992).

Numerous studies have documented large differentials in rates of self-employment between native- and foreign-born workers (Borjas 1986; Light 1972; Light and Sanchez 1987; Waldinger and Aldrich 1990). Except for very recent arrivals (less than five years of U.S. residence), rates of self-employment are systematically higher among the foreign-born (Borjas 1986). Moreover, several studies have documented large differentials in self-employment rates along national-origin groups (Bates 1987; Borjas 1986; Butler and Herring 1991; Fairlie and Meyer 1996; Kim and Hurh 1985; Yoon 1991), and visible concentrations of immigrants in small businesses in large, metropolitan, immigrant-receiving areas like New York, Los Angeles, Miami, Houston, and Chicago (Kasarda 1995; Portes and Zhou 1992; Yoon 1991). In general, self-employment rates are highest for Asian immigrants (especially Koreans), but for whites the highest self-employment rates are found among Russians, Armenians, and Greeks, and among Hispanics, Cubans exhibit the highest self-employment rates. Among all foreign-born groups, Mexicans exhibit the lowest rates of self-employment.

Studies of self-employment and business ownership complement the body of research about the economic assimilation of foreign-born workers by focusing on a particular form of labor market integration. Several productive lines of inquiry have been pursued to explain the high rates of self-employment among immigrants, as well as the differential representation of national-origin groups. Much less empirical attention has been directed toward the question of whether the proliferation of immigrant-owned and -operated firms is beneficial or detrimental for domestic minority populations, and why this might be so.

One common explanation for high rates of immigrant entrepreneurship, particularly among groups whose educational attainment does not render them disadvantaged relative to the native population, is the "blocked mobility" hypothesis: high-skilled immigrants pursue self-employment in response to anticipated discrimination in the labor market. In other words, owning and operating a business provides an avenue for economic mobility in a "protected" market, that is, a market relatively shielded from competition with native-born workers of comparable skills (Light 1972, 1979, 1980, 1985). This idea is consistent with evidence presented earlier indicating unequal earnings for comparably skilled workers (Mare 1995). However, it warrants further analysis from a comparative frame of reference to ascertain whether "blocked mobility" is unique to highly skilled immigrants, and whether blocked mobility differs from pure discrimination.

Another important consideration for understanding differential patterns of self-employment and entrepreneurship among immigrants is the idea that some groups are more "predisposed" toward entrepreneurship than others (Bonacich and Modell 1980; Light 1972; Light and Bonacich 1988; Zhou 1992). Differential rates of self-employment and business ownership presumably arise because some groups are more willing to take risks that enable them to establish successful businesses.

This hypothesis is implicit in stylized facts about the high representation of Cuban, Korean, and other Asian immigrants in self-employment (Light and Bonacich 1988; Zhou 1992). However, no study to our knowledge has systematically compared the entrepreneurial predispositions of various national-origin groups. In the absence of such information, researchers have generalized about specific groups based on case studies, usually involving a single group or a single location. That this practice has not been challenged reflects the absence of suitable data to develop and test comparative hypotheses.

A recent study of Chicago's Mexican immigrant community (Raijman 1996; Raijman and Tienda forthcoming) challenges the prevailing view that Korean immigrants are unique in their entrepreneurial predispositions (Yoon 1991; Light and Bonacich 1988), and that Mexicans are not entrepreneurial because they have lower representation as owners of formal businesses (Portes and Bach 1985). Although the "Little Village" study (Raijman 1996) was conducted in a predominantly Mexican residential neighborhood, the business community surveyed was ethnically heterogeneous. During the last decade or so, various ethnic groups (Koreans, Arabs, Chinese, Vietnamese, Indian, and Pakistanis) joined the white and Mexican business owners in the area. This rich ethnic diversity permitted an in-depth study of the Hispanic business community as well as comparisons of business formation and maintenance along ethnic lines.

In fact, Raijman (1996; see also Raijman and Tienda forthcoming) documents appreciable ethnic variation in risk-taking dispositions, preference for challenging and difficult goals, and commitment to the business. Based on their risk-taking dispositions, Hispanics ranked as the most entrepreneurial among business owners compared to Koreans, Arabs, South Asians, and non-Hispanic whites (Raijman 1996; Raijman and Tienda forthcoming). Furthermore, when asked about their desire to have a family member assume ownership of their current business, an overwhelming majority of Hispanic immigrant business owners (75 percent) answered affirmatively, compared to only 10 percent of Koreans, 16 percent of non-Hispanic whites, and 26 percent from the Middle East and South Asia. Koreans see business ownership as a way of overcoming blocked mobility, but virtually all want their offspring to acquire "good jobs" (professional or technical) in the open labor market. For Hispanics, business ownership is not solely an instrument for overcoming discrimination in the first generation, but rather a way of creating economic resources to be transmitted to the second generation. Probably anticipating low educational levels for their children, Hispanic immigrants see business ownership as an intergenerational wealth flow, not as a transitional pathway to the mainstream U.S. labor market.

Sociological research conducted by Portes and his associates has advanced the "immigrant enclave economy" notion to explain both the high rates of self-employment among Cubans and their ability to capitalize on and benefit from their residential concentration. Theoretically the enclave sector is a unique mode of incorporation characterized by: locational concentration; vertical and horizontal integration of suppliers and distributors; and extensive reliance on co-ethnic employees (Portes 1981; Portes and Bach 1985; Portes and Manning 1986; Wilson and Portes 1980). Enclaves share many features of primary labor markets because they allegedly provide opportunities for the occupational mobility of employees aspiring to self-employment. Presumably, recent immigrants who enter the U.S. labor market in firms owned and operated by co-ethnics (usually earlier immigrants) are promoted to higher managerial positions when these become available. Under ideal conditions, employees of enclave firms eventually become self-employed with the support of their employers, or they move on to better-paying positions outside the enclave (Portes and Manning 1986; Portes and Stepick 1985). The general implication is that the enclave protects immigrant workers from the competitive forces of the general labor market until they have adjusted to their new environs and, under the best circumstances, affords workers avenues to mobility within ethnic firms or serves as a stepping-stone to other firms.

Because ideas about the necessary and sufficient conditions to define an ethnic enclave were based on a single group in a single location, namely Cubans in Miami, several scholars attempted to verify whether parallel residential arrangements are reproduced among other immigrant groups in different locations. This led to spirited scholarly exchanges about whether immigrant workers do indeed benefit from employment in immigrant enclave firms. Sociological debate on the topic has focused on the consequences of immigrant-owned and -operated enterprises for their workers on two important dimensions: first, opportunities for socioeconomic mobility—specifically the likelihood of acquiring the skills and training necessary for establishing a business—and second, economic returns to human-capital investments within "enclave" firms.

Portes and Bach (1985) were optimistic in claiming that immigrants' employment in enterprises owned and operated by other co-ethnics, even at low wages, promoted economic assimilation by permitting workers to acquire enough knowledge and experience either to establish their own businesses or to compete more effectively in the open labor market (by acquiring knowledge about how U.S. labor markets operate and acquiring language skills). To the extent that this is so, then the time spent by immigrants at low-wage employment can be partly viewed as on-the-job training rather than as exploitation by co-ethnics. Likewise, other scholars have suggested that ethnic firms provide substantial opportunities for skill acquisition in general and entrepreneurial training in particular. So characterized, ethnic firms operate as training arenas that accord their immigrant employees benefits that would not otherwise be available for them in the open market (Bailey and Waldinger 1991a; Waldinger 1985; Zhou 1992). To date, this hypothesis has been mainly evaluated for specific groups in single localities. Unfortunately, attempts to evaluate the generalizability of predictions about how immigrant enclaves work and the consequences of employment in an enclave have been severely hampered by data limitations.

For example, Portes and Bach (1985) collected information about the ethnicity of employers, but they lack data on training practices *within firms.* Although they show that working for a co-ethnic firm at Time 1 is the most important predictor of self-employment at Time 2, this correlation does little to reveal the process (training, resource accumulation, family ties, and so on) that produces the observed outcome. Nor does this finding illuminate the mobility regime that underlies the association between working for an ethnic employer and subsequent business ownership because it ignores immobility, that is, the share of workers who did *not* become self-employed after working in an enclave. Nevertheless, the growth of residentially segregated immigrant communities during the 1970s and 1980s, coupled with high rates of self-employment among foreign-born populations, warrants further investigation to better understand how immigrant enterprises promote or retard the economic progress of immigrants and to spell out more precisely who (which labor groups) are the key beneficiaries and who are the main losers.

Cognizant of the limitations of prior research, including the various surveys conducted by Portes and his associates, we designed the survey of ethnic businesses in Chicago's Mexican immigrant community to overcome the data constraints confronted by other studies, but this study also suffers from a single-city focus (Raijman 1996; Raijman and Tienda forthcoming). Still, Raijman (1996) shows that ethnic-owned firms serve as a steppingstone to business ownership for ethnic compatriots because previous employment in a co-ethnic firm increases the likelihood of acquiring skills relevant for running a business. For example, Hispanics who worked for co-ethnic employers were three times more likely than their counterparts who worked for non-co-ethnic employers to have jobs related to their current line of business, two times more likely to have acquired skills in their previous jobs, and 1.7 times more likely to have held supervisory positions. Hispanic business owners with previous work experience in a co-ethnic firm reported that they were exposed to training opportunities that clearly differed from the experiences of their ethnic counterparts who did not acquire job experience in a co-ethnic firm. One-third of foreign-born Hispanic business owners in Little Village reported that a former employee opened a business (mostly in the same product line) after having worked for them, and over 60 percent of these respondents provided their ex-employees with technical and financial assistance (Raijman 1996; Raijman and Tienda forthcoming). In short, this case study revealed that business opportunities *are* transmitted along ethnic lines, and that immigrant status is a specific form of ethnic currency exchanged in the business world.

The second area of debate about the functions of the ethnic enclave focuses on returns to human-capital investments. This discussion has been relatively unproductive because researchers differ in the data used, the groups compared, and the operationalization of enclave participation (for a synthesis of the "ethnic enclave" debate, see Waldinger 1993). The assertion that enclave employees experienced positive returns on human-capital investments (Portes and Bach 1985) was challenged by other scholars who claimed that immigrant workers were disadvantaged relative to others working in the open economy (Sanders and Nee 1987). Portes's rebuttal that Jimy Sanders and Victor Nee confounded participation in an ethnic enclave with living in an ethnic neighborhood did little to settle the debate because no resolution was reached about whether residence in an ethnically concentrated neighborhood is a necessary or sufficient condition for enclave participation (Evans 1989; Nee and Sanders 1987; Portes and Bach 1985; Portes and Jensen 1987; Wilson and Martin 1982; Wilson and Portes 1980; Zhou and Logan 1989).[11]

To shift the debate in a more fruitful direction, several authors have proposed dropping the "enclave" concept and elaborating the "ethnic economy" idea in a manner that better captures the diversity and complexity of immigrants' economic activities in both salary and wage jobs and in self-employment (Light and Bonacich 1988; Light and Karageorgis 1994; Waldinger 1993). Bonacich and Modell (1980) defined the ethnic economy as including any ethnic or immigrant group's self-employed, employers, and co-ethnic employees. Intended only to distinguish whether work opportunities for a specific group are exclusive or inclusive, the ethnic economy concept is detached from locational clustering of firms, economic interdependence, and co-ethnic employees. From this perspective, an ethnic enclave economy is merely a special case of the ethnic economy (Logan, Alba, and McNulty 1994). However, with the exception of studies about enclaves, relatively few studies have sought to answer questions about what aspects of densely settled immigrant populations are more or less conducive to the emergence of organized ethnic communities. To better understand how unskilled immigrants are able to survive and prosper economically, even in the absence of active support from the U.S. government, it is fruitful to consider the role of organized ethnic communities in generating income opportunities for new arrivals (discussed in the following section).

The big lesson for studies of self-employment and ethnic entrepreneurship is that single-group and single-community studies, while useful in generating ideas and hypotheses about distinct forms of immigrant integration, may not be generalizable to other groups. Worse, they may produce premature conclusions that are subsequently more difficult to rectify. Accordingly, moving on to broader and more encompassing frameworks should improve and expand our knowledge about how immigrants make it in the United States. At a minimum, single-location studies would be more productive if they adopted comparative approaches, but a more comprehensive understanding of the ethnic economies requires multi-site and multi-group comparisons over time. The following section illustrates the fruitful insights that can be garnered from adopting an ethnic economy conceptual framework.

Immigrant Communities and Economic Assimilation: Help or Hindrance?

Since 1970 large flows of immigrants (predominantly from Latin America and Asia) have arrived in U.S. cities precisely at the time when manufacturing and industrial jobs were relocating to nonmetropolitan areas and suburbs or outside the country (Kasarda 1995; Waldinger 1989). Arriving at a time when city neighborhoods were losing their white population, immigrants revitalized neighborhoods that had begun to deteriorate (Morenoff and Tienda 1997). Los Angeles, Miami, New York, and Chicago illustrate how new immigrants have changed the face of declining inner-city neighborhoods (Light and Bonacich 1988; Moore and Pinderhughes 1993; Muller 1993; Padilla 1993; Portes and Stepick 1993; Waldinger 1989; Winnick 1990). Because immigrants are geographically concentrated in a few large cities, residence patterns are highly consequential for understanding socioeconomic mobility. Processes of residential and business succession have created the structural niches in which ethnic business sectors can flourish (Aldrich 1975, 1989; Aldrich et al. 1985; Aldrich and Reiss 1976; Zimmer and Aldrich 1987). Entrepreneurial activity is important for ethnic communities because of potential multiplier effects on economic development (Bates 1989, 1992; U.S. Department of Labor 1989; Gans 1992a; Portes and Zhou 1992; Tienda and Liang 1994).

Why some ethnic groups have been more successful than others converting ethnic residential segregation into successful business communities has not been satisfactorily answered. Several studies have attempted to answer this question by studying Koreans (Light and Bonacich 1988), Japanese (Bonacich and Modell 1980; Light 1972), Chinese (Light 1972; Zhou 1992), Cubans (Portes and Bach 1985), Pakistanis (Werbner 1990), and other ethnic groups (Aldrich et al. 1985; Aldrich and Reiss 1976). Despite the size of the Mexican foreign-born population and its high residential concentration in a few large cities (Greenwood and Tienda 1997), very few studies have analyzed business ownership rates for the largest immigrant group. Mexican immigrants provide a particularly interesting comparison to Cuban and Korean immigrants because they presumably lack the resources and circumstances considered necessary for becoming entrepreneurs (Portes and Bach 1985; Portes and Manning 1986). There are reasons to challenge the idea that business ownership will remain low among densely settled Mexican immigrants.

That ethnic residential concentration may be a necessary condition for the emergence of ethnic economies seems plausible enough, but the institutional arrangements conducive to entrepreneurial success are less clear. The "stepping-stone" hypothesis, which posits that ethnic economies operate as training sectors for prospective business owners, is tenable, but direct empirical evidence remains thin. Viewed from an institutional vantage point, ethnic economies may function as internal labor markets by protecting immigrant workers from the open labor market while providing the training necessary for the future business endeavors of employees in ethnic-owned and -operated firms. Social ties within the ethnic economy enlarge workers' contacts and hence increase the chances that employees will move through a variety of jobs that allow them to acquire skills needed to establish a business (see various chapters in Portes 1995a). As such, informal transmission of know-how can facilitate the proliferation of new firms (Boissevain et al. 1990; Portes and Bach 1985; Portes and Manning 1986; Waldinger 1985, 1993).[12]

Although much of the economic literature assumes that years of schooling directly measure skill and hence worker productivity, the labor market sketch presented earlier revealed that Mexican immigrants complete appreciably lower levels of education than U.S.-born blacks, yet they have higher rates of labor-force participation. We proposed a "preferred worker" hypothesis, namely, that Mexican immigrants are preferred workers to native blacks, particularly in inner-city labor markets where both groups come together and compete for low-wage jobs (Tienda 1989; Tienda and Stier 1996; Wilson 1996). Another reason, advanced by Julian Simon (1989), is that immigrants bring with them ideas about how things are done in other places and, despite limited formal education, may also be predisposed to self-employment because of this practical knowledge. Several students of immigration have argued that immigrants are self-selected for entrepreneurial spirit and work ethic, a fact that is germane for understanding their higher rates of self-employment relative to comparably skilled domestic workers. Finally, unskilled Mexican immigrants often find alternative ways of earning a livelihood, including informal employment and self-employment (Raijman 1996; Rosenfeld and Tienda 1997; Tienda and Raijman forthcoming). The latter option, which appears to be associated with residentially concentrated settlements and may involve economies of scale, has been relatively ignored by students of Mexican immigration (see Rosenfeld and Tienda 1999).

If residential concentration is a necessary, albeit insufficient, condition for economic integration, it follows that Mexican immigrants would have greater possibilities for business ownership in densely settled Mexican communities. Yet despite their relatively high residential concentration, like U.S. blacks, Mexican immigrants have relatively low (official) rates of self-employment and business ownership (Borjas 1986; Portes and Bach 1985), particularly by comparison to migrants from Cuba and Korea. The comparison with Koreans is particularly important because their dispersed settlement patterns and their strong presence in black neighborhoods throw into question the necessity of own-group residential concentration as a condition for immigrant entrepreneurial activity. Surprisingly, few studies have attempted to explain this anomaly. However, the Little Village study in Chicago revealed much higher levels of self-employment among Mexican migrants than revealed by conventional census data (Tienda and Raijman 1997). Much self-employment activity is informal, and self-employment activities are vastly underreported, especially by individuals whose self-employment activity is pursued *in addition* to a job in the formal labor market. Thus, the invisibility of Mexican self-employment based on conventional census data stems from the inability of current reporting categories to capture a variety of informal activities (such as street vending, making house repairs, and providing child care services) that figure prominently in the income-packaging strategies of immigrant families.

Portes and his associates defined the informal economy as a "process of income generation that is unregulated by the institutions of society in a legal and social environment in which similar activities are regulated" (Castells and Portes 1989). According to Portes and Sassen-Koob (1987), informality may refer to the *status of labor* (labor that is undeclared in formal reporting schemes, or labor that lacks access to the social benefits to which it is entitled, including payment equivalent to or in excess of the minimum wage); to the *conditions of work* under which labor is employed (health conditions, safety hazards, or the location of activities that disregard zoning laws); and/or to the *form of management* of firms (including the adoption of fraudulent practices, such as not recording cash transactions).[13] This definition is inconsistent with Portes and Stepick's (1985) treatment of the informal sector as an exclusive alternative to primary, secondary, or enclave labor market sectors because the lack of regulation can occur in many aspects of work arrangements.

This broad definition of informality provides a wide-ranging terrain for hypothesis generation and testing. For example, rates of informal self-employment should be higher among unskilled immigrants than among skilled immigrants, and also among immigrants who are residentially concentrated compared to those who are residentially dispersed (Raijman and Tienda forthcoming; Tienda and Raijman forthcoming). Another testable hypothesis implied by prior studies is that informal self-employment serves as a stepping-stone to formal business ownership (Portes and Sassen-Koob 1987; Portes et al. 1989; Stepick 1989). In Chicago's Little Village, Mexican immigrants use the informal sector as a means of acquiring the skills and capital needed for starting a business in the formal sector (Raijman 1996; Raijman and Tienda forthcoming). However, it is unclear whether this finding, which is based on a single location, also obtains for Mexican immigrants in other communities, or for Mexican immigrants who reside in residentially dispersed communities. Presumably informal economic activities allow enterprising migrants to experiment and to explore the viability of particular types of businesses. By testing the market, possibly accumulating capital or learning about its availability and acquiring rudimentary skills in a particular line of work, informal self-employment can be a conduit to successful business formation (Portes 1995a).

Among established businesses, informality may enhance the likelihood that immigrant enterprises will succeed by permitting income smoothing during slow periods, by lowering transaction costs, or by providing risk insurance (Raijman 1996; Raijman and Tienda forthcoming). Of course, not all businesses lend themselves to informal practices and organizational arrangements, but in residentially concentrated immigrant communities the boundary between formal and informal activities is often blurred. To date, there is little evidence about the share of immigrant business that began informally except through anecdotal accounts that provide neither a clear sense of prevalence nor a sense of differential occurrence among immigrant national-origin groups (for an exception, see Raijman 1996). Notions about how informal employment activities are more or less conducive to the development of formal businesses have been explored with Haitian and Cuban immigrants but seldom with other unskilled immigrants from Latin America or Asia. Evaluating these hypotheses with groups other than those from which the original theoretical ideas were derived would provide a more solid ground for falsification and verification of hypotheses than the single-group comparisons that have dominated the study of economic activity in immigrant communities.

Individuals, Families, and Economic Well-Being

Earlier we discussed the limitations of binary or tripartite segmented labor market schemes for understanding race and ethnic labor market inequality and suggested the need for classification schemes better suited to depicting the complexity of immigrants' modes of incorporation. Our insistence that both employment and self-employment can involve *both* formal and informal labor market arrangements acquires heightened importance for understanding immigrants' socioeconomic progress because family income-packaging strategies usually derive from multiple sources. That is, informal employment need not be an *alternative* to formal employment but rather can occur simultaneously in a broad array of economic arrangements for any given individual or family. Unpacking the multiple income sources of unskilled migrants and their families is highly instructive about how (low-skilled) immigrants forge livelihoods from low-wage markets (see Tienda and Raijman 1997, forthcoming).

In the main, the study of immigrants' socioeconomic progress has been largely driven by analyses of individuals, with little regard to the family contexts in which decisionmaking occurs. This is because the dominant approaches to immigrant socioeconomic assimilation are framed within an individualistic perspective, ignoring the basic idea that individuals organize their consumption and production decisions within family units (Boyd 1989). Although the idea of family labor supply may be difficult to operationalize empirically, the notion of joint decisionmaking within a household context is entirely consistent with neoclassical conceptions of economic behavior. By shifting the unit of analysis from the individual to the family, broadening the definition of labor market status to include multiple job holding, and including income derived from informal economic activities, we raise innumerable possibilities for socioeconomic integration that are not captured by conventional approaches to immigrants' economic progress.

While there is certainly merit to analyzing the economic activities of individuals using census-type data, this provides a limited vision of immigrants' economic integration process. For low-skill workers especially, economic mobility requires labor from various family members. In the short run, innovative income-packaging strategies can facilitate (or even accelerate) immigrants' adaptation to slack labor markets. Urban anthropologists who exploit the case method to illustrate how families forge livelihoods in resource-scarce environments (Lomnitz 1977) have advanced similar ideas. Locating a middle ground between the case method and the statistical survey method holds promise for illustrating how conceptions of immigrants' socioeconomic progress differ when the focus of analysis shifts from the individual to the family, and when multiple income generation activities, including self-employment and informal income generation activities, are considered.

This point is crucial because the multiple-earner family—and within it, multiple job-holding among family members—is a more common income-packaging strategy among immigrant families compared to nonimmigrant families (Tienda and Jensen 1986; Jensen 1988a). Again, the study of Chicago's Mexican immigrant community forcefully illustrates these points and underscores the fact that failure to consider the complexity of immigrant families' income generation strategies underestimates not only labor-force participation and self-employment rates but also measured levels of economic well-being. Specifically, Tienda and Raijman (1997, forthcoming) find that although income from informal self-employment and secondary part-time jobs represents a tiny average share of total family income, for those families involved in such activities (14 percent of all households in the community), the income they produce often makes the difference between being above or below the poverty line. Specifically, Mexican immigrant households in Chicago's Little Village neighborhood that engaged in informal economic activities averaged lower wage and salary incomes than their statistical counterparts who did not pursue informal income activities. For these families, informal employment compensated for income shortfalls from formal but low-wage employment. Almost 19 percent of Mexican immigrants' total family income and 23 percent of labor income was generated by informal self-employment activities. Although it is inappropriate to generalize to all immigrants from the Chicago case study, these insights highlight the promise of considering multiple income activities of individuals and families for better understanding immigrants' socioeconomic progress.

CONCLUSIONS

Changes in the volume and composition of U.S. immigration are fundamental for understanding how changes in the demand for unskilled workers will decide the economic fates of foreign-born workers. In this chapter, we have reviewed three sets of circumstances that influence immigrants' opportunities for earning a living. We have stressed changing labor market conditions because jobs are essential for immigrants to earn a livelihood; because the dramatic decline in the availability of unskilled jobs in the United States has profound implications for recent immigrants, among whom the unskilled predominate; and because there appears to be a growing mismatch between the skills demanded by the U.S. economy and the skills supplied by recent arrivals. These macrostructural trends in the demand for labor and the supply of workers with varying skill levels have direct implications for the short- and long-term economic prospects of immigrant workers.

The growth in the share of unskilled immigrants is all the more significant because it has coincided with *relatively* shrinking demand for unskilled workers. But changes in labor demand are only one explanation for changes in the volume of migrants of varying skill levels, and the sharp fall in demand for unskilled labor does not explain why unskilled immigrants keep coming to the United States and why their labor market prospects appear to be better than those of native blacks. Instead, the probabilities of migration derive from the forces identified by social capital theory (that is, social ties with prior migrants or embeddedness in migrant networks) and the new economics of migration (risk-taking disposition, need for capital, and access to capital) more than from the cost-benefit calculations assumed by neoclassical models (Massey and Espinosa 1997). Furthermore, changes in the demand for unskilled labor have direct and important implications for the integration prospects of recent immigrants because they denote very different opportunities for economic mobility and social integration. This would be so even if the ethnic, racial, and skill composition of the foreign-born population had remained unchanged because the returns to schooling have risen, as have economic inequalities (Danziger and Gottschalk 1993). That the demographic and social characteristics of recent immigrants have changed only complicates the task of diagnosing the relative importance of changing opportunities and changing immigrant characteristics for the economic prospects of new arrivals.

As a tentative conclusion, we propose that the social and economic significance of ascribed traits, and immigrant status in particular, may have increased as competition for relatively fewer low-skill jobs has intensified. And if unskilled immigrants admitted after 1973 have experienced limited or no wage mobility since their arrival, their economic fortunes have been further slowed by the growing volume of unskilled new arrivals. If so—and there is mounting evidence that immigrants compete directly with themselves and less with domestic workers—then the salience of nativity as a stratifying variable has increased and therefore is more highly relevant for understanding socioeconomic attainment now than in the past.[14] To evaluate this hypothesis, nativity should not be construed as a binary category, but rather as a hierarchy defined by both skills and period of arrival.

To better understand whether and how labor market processes undermine socioeconomic attainment, the *actual* forces driving erosion of real wages and contraction of job opportunities are as important as *perceptions* about the terms of competition—whether they are deemed fair or whether some groups are perceived to receive preferential treatment. This suggests another plausible hypothesis worthy of researchers' attention, namely, that public tolerance for ethnic diversity is highly decisive in shaping future incorporation of immigrants (Tienda 1998). In other words, the belief that immigrants are a net, albeit modest, economic benefit for the U.S. economy is less important than the popular perception that the foreign-born (and their children) drain public coffers (mainly school, medical, and welfare budgets) and compete with U.S. workers.[15] Unskilled recent immigrants will confront particularly harsh economic futures if the social climate toward immigrants erodes as their numbers increase, particularly in selected high immigrant-receiving destinations.

Questions about whether immigrants' socioeconomic progress has been undermined by the slowdown in international productivity and rising wage inequality is partly a matter of theoretical perspective, but also a matter of methodological approach. The limits of census data and cross-sectional analysis and inadequate research designs have contributed to many of the debates over findings and theory in the field. As recommended by numerous reports prepared by immigration commissions, a longitudinal survey of immigrants would advance our understanding of assimilation and integration as social processes that transform not only the life chances of immigrants but also the communities in which they settle (for reviews of the recommendations for longitudinal surveys, see Smith and Edmonston 1997; Tienda and Liang 1994).

Several general and specific lessons should be taken from our review of prior studies and suggestions for promising lines of research. We have argued that the failure of most analyses to consider the multiple job holding of individual respondents or the household income-packaging strategies of entire families distorts our understanding of immigrants' socioeconomic progress. Therefore, we recommend going beyond exclusively individualistic approaches to represent immigrants' economic activities. Standard labor market approaches that assume only one job arrangement per worker obscure the role of informality (especially informal self-employment) for earning a livelihood and gaining a foothold in the U.S. economy. This consideration is particularly important for immigrant women, who often supplement family income through informal self-employment. That these activities are not captured through the conventional labor-force status item used by survey instruments implies that immigrant economic activities are underreported in national surveys that rely exclusively on these types of measures.

Because in families involved in informal activities nontrivial shares of total income can be produced outside the formal labor market, the household incomes of a subset of immigrant families may be biased downward in national data sources. Future studies should consider how to capture informal activities and the income they generate when portraying family income-packaging strategies. Furthermore, annualized calculations presume relatively stable employment. But in low-wage markets, nothing could be further from reality. Longitudinal data that adequately depict the labor-force transitions of immigrant workers should help identify how much employment instability contributes to earnings inequality between native and foreign-born populations, and among various nationality groups. Such information can also improve our understanding about the relative weight of marginal workers (unskilled workers in a high-skill economy) and marginal jobs (unstable and low-wage jobs) in sustaining nativity differentials in economic well-being. For example, the Little Village study shows that families participating in the informal economy are slightly more likely to receive means-tested income, and that the average transfer is almost twice that of the total population. Clearly, these families are economically more precarious. Therefore, one might be tempted to entertain the hypothesis that in the absence of income generated by informal activities, rates of participation in means-tested programs might be higher, as would be the aggregate public outlays for these programs. To date, no research has addressed this important and potentially incendiary policy issue.

We also have suggested several benefits and insights from shifting the unit of analysis from the individual to the family in studies of immigrants' economic progress, particularly for those destined to work in low-wage markets. And we recommend that innovative ways be developed to document the pervasiveness of various noneconomic strategies to make ends meet. We fully appreciate that the absence of constructs that lend themselves to the study of family labor supply can retard advances in understanding immigrants' economic progress. However, this is an essential ingredient in answering a basic question such as, "How *do* unskilled immigrants make it in America?"

Our research was supported by a grant from the MacArthur Foundation to the Network on Successful Development Among Youth reared in high-risk settings. We gratefully acknowledge institutional support from the Office of Population Research at Princeton University, and Pamela C. Bye-Erts for technical assistance. Two anonymous reviewers provided extensive comments for which we are grateful. The usual disclaimers apply.

Notes

1. This chapter does not consider the impact of immigrants on native earnings and employment (for example, competition versus complementarity hypotheses). For a detailed review of this debate, see Smith and Edmonston (1997) and Friedberg and Hunt (this volume).
2. Chiswick (1978b) claimed that the annual earnings of recent immigrants in 1970 were 15 percent below those of native-born men, but he estimated that the nativity wage gap would be closed after fourteen years on average. Furthermore, he argued that after thirty years immigrant men's earnings would "overtake" by about 10 percent the earnings of statistically identical native-born men.
3. Cross-sectional analyses draw inferences about how earnings of different cohorts of immigrant workers evolve over time from a single snapshot of the immigrant population. Because the skill composition of recent immigrants has not increased as fast as that of the host-country population, a cross-sectional comparison by age tends to portray an optimistic rate at which immigrants are assimilating in the U.S. labor market. To learn whether immigrants improve their labor market status over time, we must follow immigrants over their careers and compare economic outcomes with those of comparable native workers as their careers progress. This permits differentiating between cohort and assimilation effects (Borjas 1985, 1994a; Smith and Edmonston 1997).
4. A significant fraction of immigrants eventually return to their country of origin. Therefore, the changing composition of immigrant cohorts across censuses suggests that the wage convergence depicted in cross-sectional studies might be biased if the return immigrants differ from those who remain in the United States. If average wages of return migrants are lower than those of migrants who stay, cross-sectional studies probably overestimate wage convergence between migrant and native workers. Conversely, if return migrants are the more successful members of the original immigrant cohort, wage convergence might be underestimated (Borjas 1985; Smith and Edmonston 1997, 15–16).
5. However, it is odd that Chiswick continues to ignore the serious challenge posed by Borjas and others who have adopted the synthetic approaches. The Chiswick-Sullivan chapter for the 1990 census volumes does not cite even a single study by Borjas (see Chiswick and Sullivan 1995).
6. Modes of incorporation encompass three different levels of reception: the government's policy toward different immigrants groups; civic society and public opinion; and the ethnic economy. The combination of the three levels constitutes the overall context of reception confronting a particular immigrant group (Portes 1995a).
7. Mare does provide nativity breakdowns in educational trajectories of race and ethnic groups, but not in wage trajectories.
8. Sheldon Danziger and Peter Gottschalk (1995) conducted a comprehensive decomposition analysis of trends in income inequality, but their focus was not on nativity differentials, which are subsumed under general demographic changes.
9. Racial differences in men's employment and unemployment experiences have been closely monitored for some time (Darity and Schulman 1989; Farley and Allen 1987; Levy 1980; Smith and Welch 1989; Wilson, Tienda, and Wu 1995), but trends in the labor-force activity of Latinos and Asians have been subjected to less empirical scrutiny beyond general descriptions of trends and correlates of outcomes (Bean and Tienda 1987; Cattan 1993; Melendez, Rodriguez, and Figueroa 1991; for an exception on Latinos, see De-Freitas 1991).
10. It is important to stress the relative rather than absolute availability of unskilled jobs because the total number of jobs can increase as the complex U.S. economy expands, but it is relative increases (or decreases) of jobs by skill levels that drive trends in inequality.

11. Because census data do not provide information regarding ethnicity of employers, Sanders and Nee used place of work and place of residence as a proxy. By contrast, Portes's survey collected information about the ethnicity of respondents' employers.
12. Although employment in a co-ethnic firm increases the likelihood of becoming self-employed, co-ethnic employers are not always willing to encourage employees to move into entrepreneurial positions. Employers who fear competition from co-ethnics may be disinclined to disclose too many business secrets to workers who are potential future competitors (Nee, Sanders, and Sernau 1994).
13. Very small enterprises, that is, those that employ less than ten employees, also are classified as informal by Portes and Sassen-Koob (1987), but this decision is neither necessary nor sufficient for conducting business transactions outside of regulation.
14. For an extensive discussion of immigration's effects on jobs and wages, see Smith and Edmonston (1997, chs. 4 and 5); for an explicit focus on Mexican immigrants, see also Greenwood and Tienda (1997). Rosenfeld and Tienda (1997) present evidence that this generalization is not methodology-dependent.
15. The general consensus is that the U.S. economy benefits, on balance, from immigration, even its current composition (Borjas 1995; Smith and Edmonston 1997). Nevertheless, the aggregate national benefit comes at a cost that has significant regional, demographic, and social dimensions. In a nutshell, the benefits from tax revenues largely accrue to the federal government, while state and local governments in jurisdictions where immigrants reside bear a disproportionate share of the costs (especially schooling and health, but also incarceration costs).

14 The Immigrant Family: Cultural Legacies and Cultural Changes

Nancy Foner

IMMIGRANTS LIVE OUT much of their lives in the context of families. A lot has been written about the way family networks stimulate and facilitate the migration process itself; the role of family ties and networks in helping immigrants get jobs when they arrive in the United States; and the role of families in developing strategies for survival and assisting immigrants in the process of adjustment, providing a place where newcomers can find solace and support in a strange land and pool their resources as a way to advance. Along with the increasing interest in gender and generation, there is a growing literature on the position of women and children in immigrant families—and a growing awareness that the family is not just a haven in a heartless world but a place where conflict and negotiation also take place.

In this chapter, I take a different tack. My concern is with the way family and kinship patterns change in the process of immigration, and why. The focus, I want to emphasize, is on first-generation immigrants who come from one world to live in a new one and, in the process, fuse together the old and new to create a new kind of family life. In this account, the family is not simply a site where immigrants create and carry out agendas or strategies; nor are family relations and dynamics reducible to rational economic calculations. Rather, the family is seen as a place where there is a dynamic interplay between structure, culture, and agency—where creative culture-building takes place in the context of external social and economic forces as well as immigrants' premigration cultural frameworks.

Clearly, the host of structural constraints and conditions that immigrants confront in their new environment shapes the kinds of family arrangements, roles, and orientations that emerge among them. So do the norms and values they encounter when they move here. Moreover, immigrants are not passive individuals who are acted upon by external forces. They play an active role in reconstructing and redefining family life. Indeed, members of the family, by virtue of their gender and generation, have differing interests, so that women (and men) and young people (and older people) often try to fashion family patterns in ways that improve their own position and further their aims (see Kibria 1993; Oxfeld 1993).

But something else is at work, too. The cultural understandings, meanings, and symbols that immigrants bring with them from their home society are also critical in understanding immigrant family life. Obviously immigrants do not exactly reproduce their old cultural patterns when they move to a new land, but these patterns continue to have a powerful influence in shaping family values and norms as well as the actual patterns of behavior that develop in the new setting. Indeed, as Nazli Kibria (1993) observes, immigrants may walk a delicate tightrope as they challenge certain aspects of traditional family systems while also trying to retain others.

If we look at the role of immigrants' "cultural roots"[1] in shaping new family patterns, we cannot help but see the ways in which these patterns differ from one group to another, despite the common structural conditions they face and despite common social processes and dynamics of family life. Family patterns among Korean immigrants and Haitians in the United States, to name just two groups, diverge in many ways at least in part because of the cultural background of each group. The very meaning of the term "family" and other basic, taken-for-granted cultural aspects of kinship—who, for instance, is considered a relative—vary among different immigrant populations. Indeed, the particular groups that social scientists study may well influence the models they develop about family life and family change. It is not surprising that scholars who study Asian immigrants, whose family and kinship systems are markedly different from those of Americans, have tended to put more emphasis on the role of cultural continuity with the sending society than have scholars who study Caribbean immigrants, whose family patterns are more like those in this country.

Premigration Cultural Influences

Several studies have pointed out ways in which premigration cultural conceptions and social practices continue to have force in the United States. These conceptions and practices do not continue unchanged, of course. They are restructured, redefined, and renegotiated in the new setting. Yet immigrants continue to draw on premigration family experiences, norms, and cultural frameworks as they carve out new lives for themselves in the United States.

To be sure, the cultures from which immigrants come are themselves always in flux, so that it is misleading to assume a timeless past of family tradition. Indeed, family patterns in the sending society may well have undergone significant transformations in the lifetimes of the immigrants or their parents. In her study of Japanese immigrants who came to the United States in the first decades of this century, Sylvia Yanagisako (1985, 17–18) notes that the Japan in which they grew up in the late nineteenth century was as dynamic as the United States in which their children grew up in the twentieth century. At the end of the nineteenth century, Japan was characterized by great population growth, industrialization, a spreading market economy, and increasing urban migration. At the same time as ideas from the West were finding their way into Japan, the ideology of the ruling warrior class, including ideas about marriage and family practices—such as parentally arranged marriages and standards of primogenitural succession and inheritance—were spreading to the peasantry in a process of "samuraization." To take another example, recent Vietnamese refugees to the United States grew up in Vietnam in the period between the 1950s and 1970s when the upheavals of war and urbanization led to dramatic transformations in traditional kinship structures (Kibria 1993; see also Freeman 1995).

Although there is no such thing as a timeless tradition, immigrants may come to think of life in their home society in these terms. As Yanagisako (1985, 247) puts it, they may construct their own versions of tradition as they reconceptualize the past to make sense of current experience and to speak to current dilemmas and issues. These "invented traditions" can have a life of their own in that immigrants may interpret and act upon the present in light of their models of the past. Monisha Das Gupta (1997, 580) writes of the "museumization of practices" by first-generation Indian immigrants in New York who were engaged in a process of inventing what they understood to be appropriately "Indian" as they sought to distance themselves from what they perceived to be "American." They took pride in being "more Indian than Indians in India" and expected their children to respect and obey their judgments and mandates about desirable behavior.

Among the many factors that help to keep alive (albeit in modified form) cultural patterns from the home country are strong immigrant communities and institutions, dense ethnic networks, and continued, transnational ties to the sending society. Many immigrants are part of what have been called multilocal binational families (Guarnizo 1997b), with parents and children distributed in households across national borders. Whatever their living arrangements, those in the United States are able, through modern transportation, to visit back and forth and, through modern communications, to participate in family events and decisions from a distance (Basch, Glick Schiller, and Blanc-Szanton 1994; Foner 1997; Rouse 1991). This continued, close contact with home communities—or, as Roger Rouse (1991,14) puts it, simultaneous engagement in places with different forms of experience—often strengthens immigrants' attachments to family values and orientations in the home society. Indeed, transnational connections may foster a complex cross-fertilization process as immigrants bring new notions to their home communities at the same time as they continue to be influenced by values and practices there.

This said, consider some of the ways in which the cultural elements immigrants bring with them can have an impact on family life in the United States. In her study of Vietnamese families in Philadelphia, Nazli Kibria (1993) argues that the Vietnamese ideology of family collectivism promoted cooperative, kin-based economic practices that helped families cope and survive in the immigrant setting. The notion that the kin group was of more significance than the individual drew strength from Confucian ideology, including the importance of ancestor worship. In the households she visited, family altars with photographs of deceased relatives were a common sight; the death anniversaries of important departed ancestors were almost always observed with the performance of rites to honor ancestors. Ancestor worship, Kibria (1993,

100) writes, "affirmed the sacredness and essential unity of the kin group as well as its permanence in comparison to the transience of the individual. . . . It also highlighted obligation as a key feature of a member's relationship to the kin group . . . [and] familial obligation was defined by the idea that the needs and desires of the kin group took precedence over personal ones."

Partly because Vietnamese immigrants believe that kinship ties are an effective way to cope with uncertainty and economic scarcity, they engaged in what Kibria calls a process of kin-group reconstruction in the absence of close kin in Philadelphia. They elevated distant kin to the position of closer relatives, placed more importance than they used to on kinship ties forged by marriage, and redefined non-kin with whom they had close "kinship-like ties" as kin, using kinship terms (like the term for brother) to refer to them and their relations. Among recent Hmong refugees in Wausau, Wisconsin, patrilineal clan and lineage ties continue to influence day-to-day relations. Socializing, the anthropologist JoAnn Koltyk (1998) observes, is largely confined to patrilineal kin. Unless they are in the same kin group, Hmong next-door neighbors do not visit each other; indeed, they may not even greet each other.

Another example of the continued impact of premigration cultural beliefs and social practices is arranged marriages among South Asian immigrants. In many South Asian immigrant families, when young people reach marriageable age, an all-points bulletin is broadcast through the networks of family and friends (Lessinger 1995, 121). Sometimes immigrants return to India to find a spouse, or they may rely on friends and relatives there to help in the search.[2] Newspaper advertisements may be used to broaden the pool of candidates. A good number of classified advertisements in Indian immigrant newspapers concern American-born or American-raised people who are looking for spouses. One recent advertisement read: "U.S.-raised Ivy League graduate seeks U.S.-raised girl"; another said: "Match for beautiful progressive U.S.-born medical student. Looking for U.S.-born young man, handsome and professional" (Jaleshgari 1995).

Long Island leaders in predominantly South Asian neighborhoods, according to a recent *New York Times* account, estimate that almost one-half of U.S.-born or U.S.-raised people of South Asian heritage agree to formally arranged marriages (Jaleshgari 1995). Some young people view arranged marriages positively, seeing them as a way to avoid the frightening American dating scene, which may involve premarital sex and rejection. More commonly young people submit, if reluctantly, to having their parents either guide their choices or choose for them (Lessinger 1995, 121). In the close-knit Punjabi Sikh community in rural "Valleyside" California, gossip, shame, and guilt were sanctions that parents used to ensure that children (especially daughters) went along with parental marriage plans. Young people who married without their parents' blessing risked being cut off, although the anthropologist Margaret Gibson (1988, 126–27) notes that Punjabi youths' ties to family and community were so strong that this ultimate sanction was rarely needed.

Elsewhere, despite parental disapproval, many second-generation South Asians exert their will and choose their own partners (see, for example, Das Gupta 1997). New conflicts and tensions have developed around arranged marriages in the United States,[3] and courtship and marriage patterns are changing in many ways. According to Johanna Lessinger (1995, 121), one way the arranged-marriage institution is shifting among Asian Indians in the United States is that caste, language group, and religion have become less important in mate selection if young people are otherwise compatible in terms of education and profession. Another change is that there is greater attention to individual and personal qualities in the framework of arranged marriages—an adaptive response, she suggests, to American life, in which married couples are more isolated from the support of extended kin. Also, as among urban professionals in India, "semi-arranged" marriages are becoming increasingly common in the United States. Parents introduce suitable, prescreened young men and women who are then allowed a courtship period during which to decide whether they like each other well enough to marry. This differs from American-style dating in that the courtship is much shorter, little or no sex is involved, and there is a pragmatic recognition by both parties that the aim is marriage (Lessinger 1995, 121). Still, despite these changes, arranged marriages are alive and well in South Asian immigrant communities and, for better or worse, they are an issue with which the younger generation is often forced to deal.

New Family Patterns

If immigrants bring with them a "memory of things past" that operates as a filter through which they view and experience—and create—new lives in the United States, it is also clear that much changes here. Faced with new circumstances in the United States, many beliefs, values, and cultural symbols, as well as behavior patterns, undergo change. Although some former beliefs and social institutions persist apparently intact, they may change, if only subtly, in form and function in the new environment.

To say that immigrants change, however, does not mean that they become fully assimilated into American culture. Indeed, the classic concept of assimilation glosses over many complexities in the way immigrants and their institutions change in this country. As many scholars have pointed out, the notion of assimilation, as commonly understood, is too simplistic to analyze immigrant change in a complex society like the United States where there is no undifferentiated, monolithic "American" culture. Indeed, the recently developed notion of segmented assimilation is an attempt to refine the assimilation concept. Segmented assimilation refers to the fact that immigrants assimilate to particular sectors of American society: some become integrated into the majority white middle class, and others assimilate into the inner-city underclass (Portes 1995b; Portes and Zhou 1993).

Yet even if we find similar behavior patterns among immigrants and certain Americans, this is not necessarily an indication of assimilation in the sense of internalizing the new ways and values. Rather, these behavior patterns may be independent responses to similar social or economic conditions that immigrants and the American-born face. Moreover, as Yanagisako (1985) argues, immigrants and native-born Americans may have apparently similar norms regarding, for example, conjugal relations, but they may conceptualize these norms in light of different folk histories. These conceptions and models of the past can influence the way people act and thus play a role in further shaping or modifying kinship norms and behavior. Immigrants "interpret their particular cultural histories in ways that generate issues of meaning and symbolic categories that in turn structure their kinship norms" (Yanagisako 1985, 260).

A long line of scholars have recognized that the cultures of immigrant groups differ both from the culture left behind in the sending country and from American mainstream culture. In their study of the Polish peasant in America, William Thomas and Florian Znaniecki (1918–20/1984, 108) wrote of the "creation of a [Polish American] society which in structure and prevalent attitudes is neither Polish nor American but constitutes a specific new product whose raw materials have been partly drawn from Polish traditions, partly from the new conditions in which the immigrants live, and partly from American social values as the immigrant sees and interprets them." Some forty years later Nathan Glazer and Daniel Patrick Moynihan's (1963, 14) critique of the "melting pot" notion tried to elucidate the ways in which New York's immigrant groups had become "something they had not been, but still something distinct and identifiable." And most recently, Margaret Gibson (1989, 25) argues that the end result of assimilation or acculturation among immigrants need not be the rejection of old traits and their replacement; rather, "acculturation may be an additive process or one in which old and new traits are blended."

In my work on Jamaican immigrants, I have found it useful to think of the process by which new cultural and social patterns emerge among them as a kind of creolization process. The term "creolization" has long been used in the Caribbean to describe the social system that developed in Jamaica and other West Indian societies. Neither African nor English, the locally developed system of social relations and cultural forms was something completely new—"creole"—that was created in the context of specific West Indian economic, social, and political circumstances (Mintz and Price 1992; Smith 1967). The population, Raymond Smith (1967, 234) writes, became increasingly "creolized rather than Anglicized, a process which affected Englishmen as well as others."

Thinking in terms of a kind of creolization process occurring among late-twentieth-century immigrants in the United States suggests that we look at the blend of meanings, perceptions, and social patterns that emerges among the immigrants. This blend, needless to say, is different for each immigrant group, reflecting, among other things, its specific cultural, social, and demographic characteristics. At play are the complex processes of change as the customs, values, and attitudes that immigrants bring from home begin to shift in the context of the new hierarchies, cultural conceptions, and social institutions they confront in this country. As I have argued elsewhere (Foner 1977, 1994), Jamaican immigrants do not become exactly like Americans, black or white. Nor do they remain just like Jamaicans in the home society. New meanings, ideologies, and patterns of behavior develop among them in response to the conditions and circumstances they encounter here.

The Vietnamese case cited earlier is a good example of this kind of creolization process. Confucian family ideology lingers on in many ways, but new arrangements also develop as more distant kin, in-laws, and "fictive kin" are drawn into the bosom of the family (Kibria 1993). In my research on Jamaican family life in New York, I also found a mix of old and new. As in Jamaica, the household was primarily women's domain. There seemed to be little change in attitudes toward illegitimacy or common-law unions among most immigrants: these were still widely accepted practices with no stigma attached to them. Much to women's dismay, men continued in New York to have a propensity to wander and to divert resources away from the household. Yet there were also changes. Jamaican women in New York were less tolerant of men's outside sexual exploits and more likely to demand that men help out and spend time at home. There were several reasons for these changes: women had greater financial independence in New York; they were at work and did not have female relatives available to provide assistance; and they were influenced by dominant American values extolling the ideal of marital fidelity and "family togetherness" (Foner 1986, 1994). A number of studies of other groups have shown that though immigrants "bring their own versions of 'traditional' patriarchal codes to the United States" (Pessar, this volume), their households become less patriarchal and more egalitarian here as women gain access to social and economic resources previously beyond their reach and participate more actively in public life (Espiritu 1997; Foner 1998; Grasmuck and Pessar 1991; Hondagneu-Sotelo 1994; Kibria 1993; Pessar 1987).

Sylvia Yanagisako's (1985) detailed analysis of Japanese American kinship provides a good illustration of this kind of culture creation or culture-building process. As Japanese immigrants (and their children) constructed their family lives here, they drew on models of "Japanese" as well as "American" kinship, creating a "Japanese American" synthesis (1985, 22). Japanese American kinship, she writes, is, at all levels of analysis, similar to and different from what has been described as the kinship system of white middle-class Americans. The composition of Japanese American family gatherings and life-cycle celebrations is larger and genealogically more extended than is generally reported for the white middle class. Concerning normative expectations, the filial responsibilities of second-generation (Nisei) sons and daughters appear more sharply defined and more differentiated by gender than the filial responsibilities articulated by middle-class whites. Moreover, the assignment of the role of representative of the sibling group to the elder brother in certain kinship and community affairs such as funerals is not common among other Americans (Yanagisako 1985, 255).

What also holds Japanese kinship together, she argues (Yanagisako 1985, 258), and differentiates it from kinship among other Americans, is

> Japanese Americans' shared model of their cultural history. The model is at the same time a charter for what Japanese American social life should continue to be and how it might change. Other Americans do not share this charter even though they may share many of its provisions, for other Americans do not conceptualize their kinship relations in terms of their connections with an ancestral Japanese past and the experience of Japanese immigrants to America.

The maintenance of extensive transnational connections among certain groups, or certain sectors of groups, adds a further dynamic to the process of change as new family forms develop in the context of transnational communities or migration circuits. For example, in the "multilocal binational families" that are frequently found among Dominicans, one or both parents live in New York City with some or none of their children while other children live on the island in households headed by relatives or nonrelatives (Guarnizo 1997b). Among successful Korean professionals and businessmen, what Pyong Gap Min (1998) calls "international commuter marriages" arise when the husband returns to Korea for a better job while his wife and children remain in the United States to take advantage of the educational opportunities here. They visit several times a year and talk on the phone at least once a week.

Factors Shaping Family Change

Why do family and kinship patterns among immigrants change and develop the way they do? This is obviously an enormously complicated question that would require detailed study of a wide range of groups to determine the combination of factors that produce certain kinds of changes in particular populations. As a way to begin building a framework for studying immigrant family change, I want to suggest some of the factors involved.

I have already discussed the role of premigration family, marriage, and kinship beliefs and practices in shaping family lives here. The demographic composition of the immigrant group also has an impact: sex and age ratios in each group affect marriage and family patterns. For example, a markedly unbalanced sex ratio will encourage marriage outside the group or consign many to remaining single or searching for spouses in the home country. Kibria (1993, 112–21) argues that the scarcity of Vietnamese women in the United States enhanced unmarried women's value in the "marriage market," giving them greater bargaining power in their relationships with men. The women were able to use the threat of leaving a relationship to push partners to meet their demands (see also Goodkind 1997). In other groups, a sizable proportion of old people may ease the child-care burdens of working women (see, for example, Orleck [1987] on Russian Jews). In still other cases, the absence of immigrants' close kin in the new setting creates the need to improvise new arrangements, a reason why "fictive kin" are common in immigrant communities and why men sometimes find themselves filling in as helpmates to their wives in child care and other household tasks.

Quite apart from cultural or sociodemographic features of the immigrant group, external forces in the new environment shape immigrant family lives as they provide new opportunities and constraints as well as new sets of values, beliefs, and standards. There are, for a start, economic conditions and opportunities. The immigration literature is filled with examples of immigrant women gaining authority in the household and increased leverage in relations with their spouses after taking advantage of the greater opportunities for wage employment in the United States and contributing a larger share of the family income. By the same token, declines in men's earning power can reduce their authority (see Kibria 1993, 109–12). Among certain groups, old people have suffered a decline in status in the United States because, among other things, they no longer control valued resources like land (see Chan 1994; Oxfeld 1993).[4] Another scenario has been reported for New York's Korean elderly. Access to government welfare programs in the United States has allowed many to be more independent of their children—economically and residentially—than they would have been in Korea. According to Pyong Gap Min's (1998) account, the Korean elderly welcome these changes, pleased not to have to ask their children for money or to face the restrictions and frequent conflicts that come with living with sons and daughters-in-laws.

Certain kinds of economic arrangements are more likely to support the continued importance of extended kin ties than others. As an example from the period before World II, the predominance of family businesses among the Japanese in Seattle (before the incarceration of the Japanese in internment camps) provided the Issei with an economic base for the stem family system of differentiated filial relations. First sons could be groomed to work in the family business, assume its management, and eventually support elderly parents with the proceeds from an enterprise that they had themselves worked to build. The wives of first sons could be incorporated into the household as useful productive workers as well as reproducers of the next generation. Second sons and daughters could be "married out" of the household to create a ring of affinal ties with other households in the community (Yanagisako 1985, 158).

Immigrants are also inevitably influenced by the dominant American cultural beliefs and values concerning marriage, family, and kinship that are disseminated by the mass media, schools, and other institutions. (The word "influenced" covers a range of immigrant responses, from enthusiastic embrace of certain American beliefs and values to tentative acceptance or even angry rejection of them.) Some family members are more enthusiastic about certain American values and norms than others. Typically women are more eager than men to endorse values that enhance women's position, just as young people generally support new norms that give them greater freedom that their parents may resist.

As I mentioned earlier, I found that Jamaicans were influenced by American notions about the desirability of nuclear family "togetherness" and joint husband-wife activities. Dominican women studied by Sherri Grasmuck and Patricia Pessar (1991) claimed to be patterning their more egalitarian relations with their spouses on what they believed to be the dominant American model. According to Kibria (1993), American notions about the equality of men and women and acceptance of women who smoke, drink beer, and wear "clothes that show their bodies" challenged Vietnamese norms of feminine behavior and gender relations. In general, American ideas about what kinds of dating and premarital sexual behavior are appropriate, as well as about romantic love and free marriage choice, provide ammunition for immigrant children who want to reject arranged marriages and close supervision of their relations with the opposite sex. Indeed, parents may modify their demands in the face of the new American values for fear of alienating their children altogether and creating a legacy of resentment (compare, Yanagisako 1985). Alternatively, serious conflicts may develop when young people (or women), spurred on by changed expectations and expanded economic opportunities, are more assertive in challenging the authority of parents (or husbands) (see, for example, Min 1998; Pessar 1995b). As for divorce, the fact that it is more common among many Asian groups than in the home country is, at least in part, because it is more acceptable in the United States (compare, Donnelly 1994).

Finally, the legal system in the United States provides a further impetus to change, making certain premigration customs and practices illegal or giving legal support to challenges to these practices. One reason wife-beating is less common among Vietnamese immigrants in the United States than in Vietnam is that immigrants are highly conscious that such behavior is "illegal." Kibria tells of cases where women telephoned the police during a physical confrontation with their partners (1993, 121–25). In my research on Jamaicans, I found that children threatened to, and sometimes actually did, call the police to prevent or stop physical abuse from their parents. Parents bitterly resented this new infringement on their authority and ability to discipline their children through physical beatings, but many tempered their behavior as a result.

The U.S. legal system and government agencies can affect family relations by defining family membership and rules, like those pertaining to inheritance, in terms of American cultural assumptions. U.S. immigration laws themselves, based on American notions of the nuclear family, facilitate the immigration of parents, legitimate children, and legal spouses while often separating "illegitimate" children and "common-law" spouses as well as siblings and other close, cooperating kin (see Garrison and Weiss 1987). A study of the Laotian Hmong in California notes that social service agencies affect the Hmong's sense of what constitutes a "family" by using the nuclear (rather than extended) family as the unit of distribution for various kinds of assistance (Chan 1994). And the fact that women are frequently the intermediaries between their households and outside government agencies (including various kinds of public assistance programs) often expands the scope of their activities and plays a role in improving their status in this country (compare, Hondagneu-Sotelo 1994; Kibria 1993).

CONCLUSION

In the wake of the enormous recent immigration to the United States, we are only just beginning to understand the complex ways in which the new arrivals construct—and reconstruct—their family lives here. In this chapter, I have discussed some of the dynamics involved, including the cultural meanings and social practices that immigrants bring with them from their home country as well as structural, economic, and cultural forces in their new environment. As we search for common factors that impinge on and shape immigrants' family lives—or look for evidence of ways in which immigrants are becoming more like "Americans"—we also need to bear in mind that each group puts a unique stamp on family and kinship relations that stems from its special cultural and social background.

Clearly a lot more work needs to be done in this field. We need additional careful cultural—as well as structural—analyses of immigrants' family lives to appreciate the new forms and patterns that develop among them here. Of late, there has been considerable analysis of the way immigrant women's, men's, and younger people's status changes in the United States, but we also need studies that investigate the meanings that immigrants attach to their kinship and family relations. Cultural analysis is important, not because culture constitutes a controlling code and thereby assumes causal priority in the understanding of social action, but because, as the anthropologist Raymond Smith (1988, 27) reminds us, "without adequacy at the level of meaning the other dimensions of the analysis are all too likely to be rooted in the unexamined assumptions of the observer's own culture" (see also Schneider 1968).

The complex interplay between culture, structure, and agency stressed throughout this chapter is involved in other questions that call for further study. This chapter has focused on the first generation, but obviously it is crucial to explore how, and to what extent, present family arrangements, roles, and orientations will leave their mark on the second generation who are born and raised in the United States. Among the immigrants themselves, there is the question of whether some of the changes in family relations I have mentioned here, such as women's increased power in dealings with their spouses, are simply a temporary phase; if circumstances allowed, would premigration forms be reconstituted?[5] Alternatively, shifts in family and kinship relations in the United States may have a lasting effect, altering immigrants' expectations and notions about what is acceptable behavior and "the right thing to do" in the family and among kin. It seems highly likely that changes in actual social relations, however small, will leave a permanent mark and will ultimately impress themselves on normative patterns that guide action. Moreover, there is the intriguing possibility, noted by Richard Alba and Victor Nee (this volume), that family patterns and values among some immigrant groups will affect notions of what is considered "normal" behavior in mainstream America and, over time, become part of the standard repertoire. Whether—and how—such processes will take place in the years ahead is just one of the many questions that pose a challenge for future research.

I would like to thank Josh DeWind, Charles Hirschman, Philip Kasinitz, and Mary Waters for their comments on an earlier version of this article.

NOTES

1. There is no single definition of culture agreed upon by anthropologists. Here I use it to refer to the "taken-for-granted but powerfully influential understandings and codes that are learned and shared by members of a group" (Peacock 1986).
2. A study of Bangladeshis in London found that parents often married their sons to women born and bred in Bangladesh, who they thought would be more willing to live with and be servile to their mothers-in-law than women educated in Britain (Summerfield 1993). According to Lessinger (1995), some young Indian men in the United States like the idea of having a "real Indian wife" who will cater to them as their mothers did. Not surprisingly, young Indian women in this country tend to prefer men who, like themselves, were raised in the United States, because they fear that men from India will demand a kind of service and subservience that they are not prepared to give.
3. The short stories in Chitra Divakaruni's *Arranged Marriages* (1995) show the problems and conflicts for South Asian women in arranged marriages in the United States.
4. In addition to their loss of economic control, Hmong elders found they were no longer consulted as wise men or looked to for advice or to settle quarrels. Unable to speak English, they had to depend on younger people to translate and interpret for them when they visited government offices or hospitals (Chan 1994; on Vietnamese elderly in the United States, see J. Freeman 1995).
5. Pierrette Hondagneu-Sotelo argues that "behavioral changes generated by phases in the migration process that call for a departure from traditional gender arrangements are unlikely simply to disappear when conditions of normalcy return" (quoted in Kibria 1993, 142).

Part III

The American Response to Immigration

AS AMERICA HAS remade the immigrants, immigration has, in every generation, remade America. This is not only because of the large number of immigrants the United States has incorporated, although those numbers are indeed impressive.[1] Nor is it only because of the obvious role that immigrants and their descendants have played in the nation's popular culture, the settlement of the frontier, the creativity of American science and arts, or the extraordinary entrepreneurial and technological innovation that drives the American economy. It is also because of the continuous interaction between immigrants and natives—natives who are, as often as not, the children and grandchildren of previous generations of immigrants. The process of conflict and accommodation has changed both the immigrants and the natives, as well as the nature of American society and culture.

As in the past, the immigration of millions of people since the mid-1960s has irreversibly changed the United States. Given the size of the population flow, it could hardly be otherwise. And perhaps even more than in times past, incorporation is a two-way street. As a more self-consciously pluralist United States incorporates an even more diverse influx of immigrants, the old question "Who shall we welcome?" is once more inextricably tied to the question "Who are *we*, and who will we become?" The chapters in this section examine the question of membership and citizenship in U.S. society, the economic impact of immigration on the society, the fiscal impacts of immigration, the political debates over immigration and their relationship to America's changing but still contentious divisions over race, the possibility of a resurgence of nativism, and the local politics of immigration and ethnic relations in three of the largest immigrant-receiving cities.

AN EVER-CHANGING AMERICA: DEMOGRAPHY, PERCEPTION, AND MEMBERSHIP

In a book devoted to theory and assessments of theory, it is easy to lose sight of the basic facts about immigrants—the trends in numbers, composition, and places of settlement. While a more detailed overview of current immigration trends is presented by Susan Carter and Richard Sutch in this section, a few general reference points will help to set the stage for the discussions that follow.

How much has the newest "new immigration" changed the population of the United States? As important a force as it has been, it is possible to exaggerate the uniqueness of contemporary immigration, both in terms of U.S. history and in terms of international comparisons. The contrast with the long hiatus in immigration from the 1920s to the 1960s at times creates a false image of the present period. In fact, it was the midtwentieth century that was historically unusual in having extremely low levels of immigration (Massey 1995). The 1990 census counted almost 20 million immigrants—about 8 percent of the population—and the figure is predicted to rise to 28 million, or about 9 percent of all Americans, in the year 2000 (Smith and Edmonston 1997, 2–12). Although these figures are up dramatically from 1970 (when only 5 percent of Americans were reported to be foreign-born), current immigration levels are modest in comparison with the first two decades of this century, and almost all of the nineteenth century (Carter and Sutch, this volume).

Although the *absolute number* of immigrants admitted to the United States is now higher than in any other country in world, it is important to note that the proportion of foreign-born persons in the U.S. population is lower than in a number of other countries, including Canada, Australia, and Israel (U.S. Bureau of the Census 1996, 833). At least ten countries now rank ahead of the United States in terms of the ratio of new immigrant arrivals to the resident population (Smith and Edmonston 1997, table 2–11).

The United States population will definitely be larger in the coming decades as a result of immigration than it would have been without it. Assuming the current immigration of about 800,000 net immigrants per year (roughly estimated to be about 800,000 new legal immigrants, plus 300,000 illegal immigrants minus approximately 300,000 emigrants) continues for the foreseeable future (along with medium estimates of other demographic components), the United States would have about 80 million more people in 2050 than it would if immigration were cut to zero immediately (Smith and Edmonston 1997, table 3–3). Numbers alone are, however, less important than the demographic and socioeconomic composition of immigrants and their descendants. Several dimensions of immigration may have a very profound impact on the socioeconomic welfare of the country and the character of American society in the coming decades.

One of the least understood but most important consequences of immigration is its effect on the age structure of the American population. Without future immigration—and with natural increase projected to drop below zero—the age of the U.S. population would shift upward. As a consequence, we would see a much higher ratio of elderly people to the working-age population, a trend that would accelerate in the second decade of the twenty-first century as the baby boom cohorts enter their retirement years (Smith and Edmonston 1997, 99–103). Because the majority of immigrants arrive at the beginning of their work life and a significant share emigrate before reaching retirement (Duleep 1994), continuing immigration helps to keep the population younger, a not inconsequential fact when one considers the problems of financing Social Security and Medicare (see Preston 1996).

Another salient demographic characteristic of contemporary immigration is its geographical concentration. Most immigrants now live in six states and about a dozen major gateway cities (Portes and Rumbaut 1996, 34–49; Smith and Edmonston 1997, 58–62). Indeed, four out of ten recent immigrants live in just two states: California and New York. The drama of immigration is most salient in Los Angeles, New York, Miami, San Francisco, Chicago, Washington, D.C., Houston, San Diego, and a handful of other places (Frey and Liaw 1998). Conversely, most native-born Americans live in areas where immigrants are so few as to be almost invisible. This uneven regional distribution has profound implications for the economic and political consequences of immigration. Although public institutions in the heavily impacted areas, particularly schools and health facilities, are often straining to meet the needs of the newcomers, the local economies of many of these immigrant-receiving regions are also growing rapidly. Although it is perhaps too soon to evaluate the net regional impact of immigration, it is worth noting that poverty among natives is not generally higher and, indeed, in most cases is lower in regions that have received large numbers of immigrants.

Immigration has also made the U.S. population more diverse. Indeed, perhaps the most sensationalized aspect of the contemporary immigration is its "Third World" flavor. Predictions that "nonwhites" will constitute a majority of the national population by the middle of the next century have set off nativist alarms reminiscent of the heyday of immigration from eastern and southern Europe in the early twentieth century (Bouvier 1992; Brimelow 1995). Spokesmen for minority groups and their allies sometimes point to these same projections with a note of inevitable triumph. Yet the assumptions behind these numbers are dubious at best (Hirschman, forthcoming). There are already very high levels of intermarriage between both Asians and Latinos with whites (ranging upward from 30 percent). Even the out-marriage rate for African Americans, while much lower, is beginning to edge upward. Thus, there is a growing fraction of the American population with mixed racial and ethnic ancestry; more than 15 percent of persons who identified themselves as Asian or Hispanic, and 8 percent of persons who identified as black on the 1990 census had one parent of a different racial or ethnic group (Smith and Edmonston 1997, 120–21). This reality often confounds official statistics. Even with the "forced choice" race categories used in prior censuses, there is considerable variation of ethnic identity of persons with mixed ancestry (Xie and Goyette 1997). With the decision of the Office of Management and Budget to allow respondents to check more than one "race" in the 2000 census and other statistical records, the traditional mutually exclusive racial and ethnic divisions are likely to blur even further in the future (Office of Management and Budget 1997b; Perlmann 1997a). Assuming current levels of intermarriage, the mixed-ancestry population is projected to increase from 18 million in 1991 to 81 million in 2050 (Smith and Edmonston 1997, 121).

Whether this new multiplicity of racial identities will undermine America's traditional notions of race is still unclear. The "one-drop rule" of racial definition for African Americans remains deeply rooted in American popular consciousness. Yet if the experiences of southern and eastern European groups in the first half of this century are any guide, the coming decades will see an exponential increase in ethnic intermarriage, shifts in ethnic identity, and perhaps shifts in racial identity as well (Alba 1990; Waters 1990). Thus, population projections that rely on the contemporary definitions of racial and ethnic identity may well be meaningless by the middle of the next century.

Further, the current "official" racial categories—an amalgam of nineteenth-century race thinking, linguistic and nationality groupings, and the politics of ethnicity in contemporary America—have never been particularly coherent. Some of the panethnic census categories, including "Hispanic" (or "Latino") and "Asian and Pacific Islander" have little historical or cultural meaning and may already be on the verge of collapsing under the weight of their own internal diversity. "Hispanic," which until a few decades ago almost always meant Mexican in Los Angeles, Cuban in Miami, and Puerto Rican in New York, now refers to dozens of nationalities that share only a common language—and increasingly not even that: a growing number of Puerto Rican and Mexican American young people are now monolingual English speakers.

The composite "Asian" racial category now includes Chinese, Koreans, Japanese, Filipinos, Vietnamese, Asian Indians, Cambodians, Laotians, Hmong, and many other national, linguistic, and cultural groups (not to mention tens of thousands of international adoptees, most of whom are being raised in white American families!). The idea that in the middle of the next century the descendants of all of these people will continue to form a common "racial" group, either in terms of bureaucratically defined census categories or in terms of daily life experience, seems highly unlikely. Such a scenario would require assumptions of endogamy and cultural continuity that are already implausible. Of course, racial identities and boundaries will continue to be shaped and reshaped in unpredictable ways by historical events, changing demography, and the shifting attitudes of Americans toward each other. The only prediction that can be made with some degree of certainty is that the racial and ethnic divisions of mid-twenty-first-century America will not be the same as today.

It is worth reflecting on how this new diversity came about. The ending of the national-origin quotas and the establishment of the principle of family reunification in 1965 were primarily intended to open the door to southern and eastern Europeans. Indeed, family reunification was accorded central importance in the new policy, in large part to reassure the opponents of renewed immigration that the policies would not substantially change the ethnic composition of the United States. These reforms paved the way, however, for a new influx of immigrants from Asia, the Caribbean, and more recently Africa (Daniels 1991; Massey 1995; Portes and Rumbaut 1996; Reimers 1992). It was immigrants from Taiwan, the Philippines, India, and other Asian countries—who first began to arrive under the criteria for admission of professionals and other skilled workers in the 1960s and 1970s—who would eventually make fullest use of the family reunification provisions.

Latin America was not affected by the Hart-Celler reforms. Yet, while Mexican immigration has much older historical roots in the Southwest, the numbers of Mexican and other Latin American immigrants also expanded enormously after the mid-1960s. At the same time, international events, cold war politics, and the failures of American political and military interventions brought in hundreds of thousands of refugees from Hungary, Cuba, Vietnam, Laos, and Central America from the late 1950s to the 1990s. Once begun, each wave of immigration has spawned another because U.S. immigration law creates preferences for the relatives of immigrants and because informal mechanisms of family solidarity lower the social and financial costs of settlement.

Like other Americans, scholars and policymakers are often in disagreement over whether, on balance, the changes that the new immigration has brought to U.S. society have been positive or negative. Yet there is agreement on one historical fact: they were unintended and largely unanticipated. The Hart-Celler law was never meant to alter the ethnic makeup of the United States. Similarly, the framers of the *bracero* program never intended to foster networks that would link the labor and capital markets of the United States and Mexico; indeed, their intention was quite the opposite! Perhaps, as Douglas Massey (this volume) implies, a different theoretical framework and awareness of different data would have made these results predictable, but no one predicted them at the time. Nor were the cold war policies that led to the welcome of so many Cubans after 1959 meant to transform southern Florida into a center of immigration or to change Miami from a tourist town to a bilingual international center of commerce and finance.

On the other hand, the Hart-Celler law *did* ratify a change in American thinking about the relationship of immigration, ethnicity, and national identity, a change that had gradually coalesced during the preceding decade. This new thinking defined the U.S. national identity as a matter of shared political institutions and civic commitments, not as racial, ethnic, religious, or even cultural identity. This change, perhaps even more than its demographic results, is at the heart of the bill's historical significance. The notion of "civic pluralism" (Fuchs 1990) that the new thinking reflects is now so broadly accepted that it is important to remember that while its roots go back to the beginning of the republic, its acceptance by the majority of Americans is quite new.[2] As recently as the McCarran-Walter Act of 1952 the principle that one of the primary purposes of immigration policy was to shape the nation's ethnic identity was reasserted with broad popular support. Yet only thirteen years later, in the wake of the civil rights movement and the election (and subsequent assassination) of the first Catholic president, a consensus had more or less emerged that deciding who could become an American on the basis of ethnic origin was, in the words of Nathan Glazer, "basically immoral and wrong" (1985, 6). In recent years that consensus seems to have been challenged as more and more Americans voice their discomfort with high levels of immigration. It is noteworthy, however, that with the possible exception of Peter Brimelow (1995), virtually no mainstream critic of immigration today openly advocates selecting immigrants on the basis of race or ethnicity, a practice that had broad popular support only a few decades ago.

What is the impact on American political and civic life of the largely unanticipated diversity? The chapters in this section by Gary Gerstle and David Plotke may serve as a starting point for this discussion. Both take up the question of the meaning of membership and citizenship in multiethnic America, past and present. Gerstle offers a novel and provocative analysis of the images created and used by American historians and intellectuals to describe the ways in which, and the terms on which, previous generations of immigrants became "Americans." He points to the broad acceptance, from the late eighteenth to the early twentieth century, of the "Crèvecoeurian" imagery of Americans being forged as an entirely new people, looking forward to an American future rather than a European past, an idea that he finds echoed in Frederick Jackson Turner's celebration of the frontier and in Israel Zangwill's notion of the melting pot. He notes how this idea was challenged, in different ways, both by Chicago School sociologists and by mid-twentieth-century historians, most notably Oscar Handlin (1957, 1973). Although these writers all accepted the likelihood of eventual assimilation, they saw the shedding of old world ways as deeply conflict-ridden and often more alienating than emancipatory. Gerstle then turns to contemporary scholarship and shows that both those who celebrate American pluralism and those who point to continuing gender and class divisions have reworked these same themes.

Plotke addresses the contemporary relationship between immigration and national self-definition. Examining the politics of incorporation into both formal and informal institutions, and drawing on the growing literature on the nature of citizenship and on civil society, he explores the tensions between ethnic "identity" politics and democratic values in the United States today and asks how an immigration policy can be built on "democratic" principles. In doing so, he sets the stage for the more particular studies of economics and politics that follow.

The Economics of Immigration

In no area of American life has the impact of immigration been more discussed, or more controversial, than in the economy. Native workers naturally fear economic competition with immigrants, who they often see as threatening their hard-won gains. Immigrant workers often arrive "hungry" and are willing to work long hours for lower wages than natives have come to expect. Indeed, during the heyday of American industrialization, employers often deliberately used immigrants (as well as African Americans) as strikebreakers. In some periods the political dynamics created by labor market competition have led to violence and to strange alliances against immigration. Labor unions and other working-class groups were part of the political campaigns against immigration from China and Japan in the 1880s and in the early 1900s. The ethnic and racial divisions of the American working class have often inhibited labor organizing and no doubt partly explain why the United States still lags behind most of the industrialized world in the proportion of its labor force that is unionized.

Yet the role of immigration in the economy is considerably more complex than simple wage competition. In their historical essay, Susan Carter and Richard Sutch argue that the major wave of immigration around the turn of the century was an important element of the economic growth and industrialization of the American economy. Much of the urban proletariat as well as a fair number of the entrepreneurs and industrialists who created the modern American economy were immigrants or the children of immigrants. Would the United States have developed as rapidly or as successfully without an open-door policy of immigration? We cannot know with any certainty, but it does seem clear that the economies of scale produced by immigration played an important role in terms of the size of the domestic market and the available labor force needed for mass production.

Today there are new fears over the economic consequences of continuing immigration to a less industrial United States. The popular assumption that an increase in the supply of labor will drive down wages has been so strong that evidence to the contrary has often been explained away or simply ignored. To be sure, data on the economic impacts of immigration are not always the best, but a consensus is emerging that the economic consequences of immigration for the domestic economy, including the wages of domestic labor, are relatively modest. This research literature on the economic consequences of contemporary immigration is summarized in the chapter by Rachel Friedberg and Jennifer Hunt. Their review of the economic theory and evidence helps shed light on this important, if somewhat counterintuitive finding.

It should be noted, however, that workers do not live or work in the "domestic economy" but rather in given locations and sectors, and often in particular "economic niches." Immigration may have a strong impact on local opportunity structures and levels of ethnic preference and discrimination in ways that tend to "wash out" at the national level. Interestingly, detailed work on particular "enclaves," "networks," and "ethnic niches" within the economy has tended to be the province of sociologists (see in particular the work of Alejandro Portes, Roger Waldinger, and their collaborators) whereas the mathematical models of labor markets of the sort reviewed by Friedberg and Hunt have tended to be the domain of economists. Unfortunately, in this instance, dialogue across disciplinary boundaries has been rare and limited.

There are, of course, many other, sometimes elusive, mechanisms through which immigration may affect the economy. For example, considerable speculation has been devoted to the possibility that contemporary immigrants contribute to increasing productivity by providing specialized skills to rapidly growing industries for which the U.S. educational system has yet to produce sufficient numbers of trained workers (such as computer programmers in Silicon Valley), bringing new technological innovations to the market (through the efforts of the scientists and engineers who are trained in American universities and remain here), and becoming entrepreneurs. Recent immigrants and their children have another potential economic role in acting as brokers to the expanding markets of Asia and Latin America.

Almost as debated as the role of immigration in labor markets and productivity growth has been the growing controversy over the impact of immigrants on the fiscal health of the state. To put it simply, do immigrants and their children contribute more in taxes than they consume in tax-funded services? In addressing this issue, Thomas Espenshade and Gregory Huber report that, on balance, immigrants have made a positive contribution to the U.S. governmental coffers. Yet contrary to the weight of economic evidence, most Americans fear that new immigrants take more from the government in benefits and services than they contribute in taxes. Some of these concerns are no doubt legitimate, at least in the short run and in some places: much of the fiscal benefit of immigration goes to the federal government while the costs are borne disproportionately by the heavily impacted localities. Other such concerns, however, seem to betray deeper anxieties about changes in American life in general and to be only in part about immigrants. Indeed, Espenshade and Huber argue that these popular fears are part of an emerging conservative political mood that seeks to reduce the welfare state in general, as well as to deny benefits to immigrants in particular.

IMMIGRATION, POLITICS, AND RACE

As Espenshade and Huber show, the politics of immigration in American society is complex and closely intertwined with economic perceptions and realities, international relations, and racial and ethnic divisions. This complexity is in part rooted in the deep ambivalence Americans have long felt about immigrants and immigrant incorporation. On the one hand, Americans proudly see their country as a "nation of immigrants." The promise of liberty and opportunity for all is deeply ingrained in the American self-conception. However much actual practice has fallen short of this promise, the fact that it is a central part of the national mythology is significant in itself. And as Alba and Nee argue (this volume), the American record of incorporating diverse peoples is indeed impressive, at least as far as European immigrants are concerned. On the other hand, the nativist fear—and rejection—of the racial and ethnic "other" also runs deep in U.S. history. U.S. nationalism has often been based as much on conflict with outsiders as on a celebration of American distinctiveness. Time and time again the children of yesterday's immigrants have come together as Americans in order to reject today's immigrants, and as one currently fashionable body of historical research reviewed by Gerstle argues, the "whiteness" of the children of immigrants has often been established through conflict with African Americans, Asians, and Latinos.

These two strains, the nativist and the inclusive, have long coexisted in the American political culture. The closing of mass immigration in the 1920s probably represents the high-water mark of the former, while the latter probably reached its zenith in the immigration reforms and civil rights legislation of the mid-1960s. Thus, in his essay, John Higham provides a telling intellectual memoir on why he did not (and could not) write a sequel to his classic treatment of nativism, *Strangers in the Land* (1955). On the other hand, George Sánchez (partially echoing Espenshade and Huber), sees nativism as an increasingly potent political force in contemporary America, particularly to the extent that it has become intertwined with the issue of race.

This relationship, between immigrant incorporation and the politics of race, is clearly one of the defining aspects of the contemporary debate over immigration. At risk of belaboring the obvious, suffice it to say that historically the experience of African Americans and Native Americans contrasts dramatically with that of European immigrants and their descendants. As James Baldwin notes: "The Irish middle passage, for but one example, was as foul as my own, and as dishonorable on the part of those responsible for it. But the Irish became white when they got here and began rising in the world, whereas I became black and began sinking" (Baldwin 1985, xx).

In his essay in this volume, Alejandro Portes makes an insightful reference to Norman Mailer's novel of World War II, *The Naked and the Dead* (1948), in which the children of immigrants "received so unceremoniously" only a generation before—"the Italian Minetta, Jew Goldstein," and yes, even "the Mexican Martinez"—are together in the trenches, unequal perhaps, but Americans without doubt. Yet even at this crucial moment, in which "Americans" are being forged, literally under fire, someone is missing. Blacks, by this time often tenth-generation Americans, were still given the opportunity to die for "their" country only in segregated units.

Distinct as these two histories have been, the language of race and ethnicity has often moved back and forth between the black and the immigrant experiences. Early twentieth-century nativists often used explicitly racial arguments to reject southern and eastern European immigrants, and in recent years African Americans (as the very name implies) have often taken up ethnic language to argue for a culturally based group identity. Further, if African Americans and European immigrants have consistently represented the two poles in thinking about ethnic and racial identity, groups that fit neatly into neither of those categories (Asians, Latinos, black immigrants, and so on), have often occupied an ambivalent position between the two models of minority status in a plural society (see Kasinitz 1992; Vickerman 1999). Prior to the 1960s these groups were small enough, and regionally concentrated enough, that most social scientists and others thinking about race could consign them to the margins of a blacks-versus-immigrants discourse. This is clearly no longer the case: the groups that are neither black nor white are now the fastest-growing in U.S. society. This fact perhaps more than any other separates the current immigration from previous ones, although its full implications are still far from clear.

If racial "otherness" frames the way in which

natives (including black natives) react to today's immigrants, as Sánchez implies, then how does racial status frame the political actions of the immigrants themselves? Immigrants usually arrive with clear economic motives, but often without a great awareness of, or interest in, American politics. (Refugees are the exception; many arrive with a political agenda concerning the politics of their homeland that sometimes has immediate implications for American politics as well.) Yet the realities of American politics, especially at the local level, require that any group with common interests and needs become active in the formal and informal aspects of political life.

Immigrants have a number of common interests, one of which is the continuation of current immigration policy, which allows them to sponsor their relatives for admission. Immigrants also want a modicum of political and economic freedom to pursue their livelihoods without discrimination or bias. Finally, immigrant families are interested in basic social services for their dependent members who need to rely on extra familial assistance. Each of these needs creates political roles as well as potential conflicts for immigrants. Another important interest of immigrants, however, is to be left alone—to be free to pursue their economic aspirations and to promote their children's welfare. Immigrants are often visible because of their color, their language (or accent) and culture, and their lack of insider's knowledge of how the American system is supposed to work. They encounter discrimination in the job and housing markets, and sometimes they practice discrimination against other immigrants and native-born Americans, particularly members of native minorities. Thus, in recent years new arrivals have often been thrust into the heart of the "American dilemma" of race almost before they know the ground rules. Socioeconomic and political dynamics have frequently given rise to interethnic tensions—and sometimes to violence, in Los Angeles, Miami, and other multiethnic urban centers.

All Politics Are Local? Immigration and the Political Life of Large Cities

The final three chapters in part III all deal with local responses to this national issue. Indeed, they give new meaning to the dictum of Congressman Thomas "Tip" O'Neill of Massachusetts that "all politics are local" by serving as a reminder that while the United States makes immigration policy nationally, immigration's impacts and the political responses to those impacts differ profoundly from region to region.

This is in part a reflection of the very real differences in the practical meaning of immigration for various parts of the country. Immigration remains disproportionately a big-city phenomenon, although in recent years it has had a profound impact on some rural areas as well. It also has different impacts on cities *within* the same region: a major impact in New York, but a modest one in Philadelphia; considerable in Washington, D.C., and its suburbs, but far smaller in Baltimore; huge in Miami and significant in Atlanta, but almost imperceptible in Birmingham and Savannah.

The fact that the nation's two largest immigrant-receiving cities are also its two media capitals no doubt helps promote the belief on the part of many Americans that contemporary immigration has a greater impact on their lives than social scientists are able to measure. Former Senator Alan Simpson, when asked why a representative of Wyoming, a state largely unaffected by international migration, should be such a passionate advocate of immigration control, was fond of quoting a constituent who complained that droves of "illegal immigrants" were responsible for the parking problems in Laramie!

Of course, many of the impacts of immigration on the lives of U.S. citizens are real enough, particularly in the heavy immigration-receiving localities. Yet they do not seem to explain the differences in the local politics of immigration between these localities. Consider the unabashedly pro-immigration stand of New York City's Republican Mayor Rudolph Giuliani in comparison with the position taken by most of his fellow Republicans in California! Or compare the shrill anti-immigration rhetoric in California politics in the wake of Proposition 187 (recently toned down a bit as some California Republicans have become concerned about the long-term effects of writing off a generation of Asian and Latino voters) to the much less heated discourse among even very conservative Republicans in Texas.

These differences are no doubt due to local interest-group politics as well as to the differences in local political cultures. In Texas local elites increasingly see that their economic futures are tied to cross-border enterprises and close connections with Mexico. Agribusiness also remains a powerful lobby in Texas, whereas in California its influence, enormous only two decades ago, has slipped as the Republican Party has become increasingly the voice of suburban homeowners. In New York, where "white ethnic" politics remains salient and white ethnic "niches" continue to play a role in the economy, many native whites retain a strong, if increasingly "symbolic" (see Gans 1979) conception of themselves as the children or grandchildren of immigrants. Although this conception by no means guarantees a favorable opinion of current immigrants, it often leads to a guardedly favorable view of immigration in general. The Statue of Liberty and Ellis Island remain among the city's most popular tourist destinations and provide iconographic reference points for local discussions of the issue. Further, in contrast to Texas, California, or Florida, the racial and ethnic diversity of immigration to New York (it has large numbers of black and white as well as Asian and Latino immigrants, and no one sending nation accounts for more than 19 percent of the city's foreign-born population) may discourage a clear racial or ethnic stereotype of "immigrants" in the popular imagination.

The essays by James Johnson, Walter Farrell, and Chandra Guinn, by John Mollenkopf, and by Nestor Rodriguez demonstrate how America's major immigrant-receiving cities differ in terms of the economic, cultural, and institutional infrastructures against which the politics of immigration is played out. The typology of the types of conflict that can arise between immigrants and natives (particularly African American natives) provided by Johnson, Farrell, and Guinn creates a framework for comparison that Rodriguez takes up in his discussion of Houston. Mollenkopf, in comparing New York and Los Angeles, also suggests a hypothesis about the role of the different political structures of the two cities in mediating interethnic conflicts. Read together, the three essays show how local conditions and local history shape the role that immigrants and immigration play: in all three cities, the large number of recent immigrants has reduced the centrality of biracial, white-black politics. In all three, no one racial group has a clear population majority or a monopoly on political power, or will have in the foreseeable future. Yet the three cities have reacted to this new, multiracial reality very differently.

Johnson and his colleagues take as their starting point the underlying interethnic hostilities that they see shaping ethnic relations in Los Angeles. Although some of their types of conflict—for example, Proposition 187–related conflicts—are quite particular to the place and time they are writing about, others, such as conflicts between local merchants and poor communities and those between the police and minority communities, will be familiar to any observer of American cities. Yet one of the most striking aspects of their account is the sense that while the structural factors shaping racial antagonisms today often echo those of the 1960s, we now see new actors in the familiar roles. During the bloody 1992 Los Angeles riot, for example, Korean immigrants played the "part" that Jewish merchants had played during the 1960s, while the members of the inner-city community attacking those merchants turned out to be Central American immigrants as often as African American natives. The new immigration has made the ethnic landscape of American cities infinitely more complicated.

In New York, with its high levels of public employment and extensive public-sector infrastructure, local politics still "counts" in terms of delivering the goods for constituents, and as Mollenkopf notes, the relatively small size of local political districts gives even small and newly arrived groups a meaningful, if limited, political voice. Local government tends to look to ethnic leaders to serve as intermediaries and to broker access to employment and social services. Thus, according to Mollenkopf, one of the reasons "New York works" is that ethnic groups are highly politicized and bargain for their share of a relatively large public-sector pie. Mollenkopf is most specifically concerned with electoral politics, but a similar argument can be made for the civic organizations, neighborhood groups, charitable organizations, voluntary associations, labor unions, and other public and semipublic institutions that Plotke writes about. Over the years New York has developed a dense network of such institutions. This is partly the heritage of earlier immigrations, and although this infrastructure has been under attack in recent years, it is still considerable compared to cities without this historical experience. The City University of New York, for example, has over 210,000 students, over 43 percent of whom are now foreign-born (not the children of immigrants, but immigrants themselves!). There is a huge municipal hospital system that both serves and employs large numbers of immigrants. The public school system, as in most big-city systems, is deeply troubled. Yet unlike most comparable systems, it maintains notable islands of excellence, such as its three exam high schools, two of which are widely regarded as among the nation's best and which largely serve immigrants and the children of immigrants. The large and heavily utilized public library systems and the network of charitable institutions and settlement houses also serve many immigrants. This is particularly true for groups that have ethnic ties to more established groups in New York. For example, the many Jewish immigrants from the former Soviet Union have particularly benefited from the city's powerful network of Jewish social service agencies, which in some cases have also become advocates and service providers for immigrants in general. Similarly, Catholic and Greek Orthodox social service agencies, both a heritage of the early immigrations, are now available for the new arrivals. How important they are, and whether groups tied to such institutions will in the long run do substantially better than ones lacking such networks, has yet to be fully researched. Yet it stands to reason that they should have some impact (for specific examples, see Jones-Correa 1998; Kasinitz 1992; Sanjek 1998).

Los Angeles, by contrast, is a much newer city with far less awareness of an immigrant heritage. The public sector is smaller, employs fewer people, and has far less of a tradition of incorporating immigrants. It is also less centralized: services are divided between the city, the county, the state, the school district, and a host of small municipalities. Sometimes these small municipalities provide immigrants with an opportunity for political control that their numbers would not allow in a larger city (on Monterey Park, for example, see Horton 1995). Yet in general, local politics probably matters less, or at least matters less obviously, in people's lives in Los Angeles. Meaningful countywide electoral districts are enormous, favoring big groups over small ones. This is one reason that politics is often fought out along broad "racial" lines rather than narrowly ethnic ones. The large districts, combined with the automotive infrastructure and the paucity of local public spaces, also serve to increase the importance in local politics of television, which promotes a politics of slogans and symbols rather than service delivery and patronage. Labor unions are generally weaker and less politically connected than in New York, although that fact may make them less beholden to established relationships and allow them to be more aggressive in organizing new industries, including those in which many immigrants work. (Consider the "Justice for Janitors" campaign of the mid-1990s in which the AFL-CIO organized a largely Central American labor force.) Of course, Los Angeles also has a large network of semipublic, private, and religious institutions as well as active ethnic political groups in the immigrant communities. Yet as one might expect in a newer city, the voluntary sector is less well established and has little history of making immigrant incorporation a major goal. Many of the ethnic political groups have more of a social movement character and are more concerned with defending their constituencies' rights than with providing services. Thus, the polarized and racially charged politics that Johnson, Farrell, and Guinn describe exists in an atmosphere of few structural constraints. With fewer mechanisms to arbitrate ethnic conflicts and meet the demands of new groups, conflicts may spin out of control into the sort of mass violence seen in 1992.

Finally, another characteristic of the local political landscape has helped to shape the politics of immigration in Los Angeles. The central role that ballot propositions have come to play in California politics makes it more possible for popular resentments and populist rhetoric to have an impact on government than in systems more mediated by the give-and-take of traditional constituencies and professional politicians. This contrasts not only to the more traditional party-based politics of New York but also to Houston, where the public sector is small and an informal but well-networked probusiness elite works to keep obvious racial and ethnic conflict to a minimum in "free enterprise city" (Feagin 1988). Rodriguez argues that Houston's elite, with both economic ties to Mexico and an interest in the continuing supply of immigrant labor, has effectively kept anti-immigrant sentiment off the political agenda. Even among nonelite groups, community leaders have managed to quietly work together to contain conflicts rather than score political points out of them. Thus, Rodriguez's account of local reactions to conflicts between Asian merchants and Latino and African American customers contrasts markedly with well-known incidents in Los Angeles and New York. Further, Houston's abundant housing stock and lack of controls on growth have generally prevented neighborhood-based conflicts over space of the sort that Johnson, Farrell, and Guinn point to in Los Angeles and that are so clearly central in older, northeastern cities like New York.

Immigration has profoundly reshaped each of these cities. Yet the political, economic, and cultural effects of population change have been different in each, and these differences say at least as much about the history and structure of the cities as they do about the immigrants. Thus, in the coming decades, as the United States comes to grips with its growing diversity, the object of social scientific inquiry may be less *immigration* per se, than the process by which immigrants, and natives, remake American society.

NOTES

1. Consider the demography. In 1790, at the time of the first American census, there were about 3 million Americans. Assuming a relatively robust rate of population growth (1 percent per year) for 210 years, but no immigration, the population of the United States might have been approaching 25 million in the year 2000 instead of the 275 million that will probably be counted in the next census!
2. Some intellectuals, most notably Randolph Bourne, Horace Kallen, and John Dewey, had argued for a broad multiethnic view of American identity since the Progressive era. In the battle over the imposition of the quota system in the 1920s, however, this view lost decisively. The roots of the broad acceptance of a more pluralist view of American identity can probably be traced to the New Deal and the national unifying experience of the World War II, but this view gained acceptance most rapidly in the wake of the civil rights movement.

15 Liberty, Coercion, and the Making of Americans

Gary Gerstle

In 1782 a French immigrant, Hector St. John de Crèvecoeur, published *Letters from an American Farmer*, one of the most influential meditations on what it means to become an American. In his letters, Crèvecoeur portrayed America as a magical place free of the encrusted beliefs, customs, and traditions that had disfigured European society. Here a new race of men had emerged. In a famous passage, Crèvecoeur (1782/1912, 43) wrote:

> What then is the American, this new man? . . . *He* is an American who, leaving behind him all ancient prejudices and manners, receives new ones from the new mode of life he has embraced, the government he obeys, and the new rank he holds. . . . Here individuals of all nations are melted into a new race of men, whose labours and posterity will one day cause great changes in the world.

Crèvecoeur's account of "individuals of all nations" being forged "into a new race of men" has resonated with Americans ever since. John Quincy Adams declared in 1819 (Rischin 1976, 47) that immigrants "must cast off the European skin, never to resume it." Frederick Jackson Turner (Sollors 1986, 5) rhapsodized that "in the crucible of the frontier the immigrants were Americanized, liberated, and fused into a mixed race, English in neither nationality nor characteristics." Israel Zangwill (1909/1923, 33), the Anglo-Jewish author of *The Melting-Pot* (1909), had his protagonist, David, exclaim: "America is God's Crucible, the great Melting-Pot where all the faces of Europe are melting and reforming! . . . Germans and Frenchmen, Irishmen and Englishmen, Jews and Russians—into the Crucible with you all! God is making the American." And Arthur M. Schlesinger, Jr. has recently reprised Zangwill's theme in *The Disuniting of America*, his widely read polemic against multiculturalism. "Those intrepid Europeans," Schlesinger (1991, 13) writes,

> who had torn up their roots to brave the wild Atlantic *wanted* to forget a horrid past and to embrace a hopeful future. They *expected* to become Americans. . . . They saw America as a transforming nation, banishing dismal memories and developing a unique national character based on common political ideals and shared experiences. The point of America was not to preserve old cultures, but to forge a new *American* culture.

Schlesinger and his predecessors said little about what traditions, customs, and habits made up this new American culture.[1] But they all shared a belief that immigrants eagerly became American, making themselves over into a new breed of people—liberty loving, fiercely independent and proud, and increasingly prosperous.

In this essay, I test the Crèvecoeurian myth of Americanization against the rich body of work produced by historians and other students of European immigration in the twentieth century. The myth consists of four distinct claims: first, that European immigrants wanted to shed their old world ways and become American; second, that Americanization was quick and easy because the immigrants found no significant obstacles thrown in their path; third, that Americanization "melted" the immigrants into a single race, culture, or nation, unvarying across space and time; and fourth, that immigrants experienced Americanization as emancipation from servitude, deference, poverty, and other old world constraints.[2]

I focus on literature generated since World War I on European immigration from 1880 to 1920, the era of the so-called new immigrants. Although this was one of two great waves of European immigration since independence, it was numerically the larger and, for scholarship, the more influential. In those years 23 million people came into a society that in 1900 numbered only 76 million. Most came from eastern and southern Europe. The arrival of these immigrants coincided with the emergence of American social science, which is one reason why that wave has preeminently shaped historical and sociological interpretations of the European immigrant experience (Dinnerstein, Nichols, and Reimers 1990; Ross 1991).[3]

The first part of this essay analyzes the long retreat from the Crèvecoeurian myth that began with Robert E. Park and the Chicago sociologists in the 1920s and accelerated during the 1940s and 1950s, when Oscar Handlin dominated the field of immigration history. Park challenged Crèvecoeur's second claim, that Americanization was quick and easy. Handlin undermined the third and fourth claims, arguing that not all immigrants melted into a single pot and that Americanization was an alienating rather than an emancipatory experience. The "new historians of immigration," such as Frank Thistlewaite, Rudolph J. Vecoli, and Herbert G. Gutman, whose writings began to appear in the 1960s and early 1970s, are usually regarded as Handlin's opponents. But I argue that in some ways they were his allies, completing the demolition job on Crèvecoeur that Handlin had done much to advance. They joined Handlin in criticizing Americanization, labeling it exploitative rather than alienating. And they went a step beyond Handlin, challenging Crèvecoeur's first claim that the immigrants wanted to become American. To these new and radical historians, Americanization was a coercive process forced on the newcomers, who preferred maintaining their old cultures to becoming "new," exploited men (see, for example, Park and Burgess 1922; Handlin 1951/1973; Thistlewaite 1991a; Vecoli 1964; Gutman 1976, esp. 3–78).

The second part of this essay analyzes scholars' resurgent interest in questions of Americanization as they sought to explain what the radical perspective of the 1960s could not: that the European immigrants of the century's early years eventually became patriotic Americans. Some scholars, notably Lawrence H. Fuchs (1990) and Werner Sollors (1986), resurrected a key element of the Crèvecoeurian myth by stressing the emancipatory impulse inherent in Americanization. Others remained closer in spirit to the 1960s radicals, emphasizing how class, gender, and race limited or eviscerated the emancipatory potential of Americanism. Both groups found a complexity in Americanization that earlier scholars had rarely discerned. They rejected the Crèvecoeurian notion that all immigrants were being melded into a single race or culture. In their accounts, immigrant individuals and groups voicing varying aspirations and needs were creating many Americanisms; some drew heavily on ethnic roots, others carved out utterly new American identities. Thus, Americanization lost the clean linearity it had possessed in earlier accounts and became a chaotic, pluralistic site of postmodern invention.

The two post-1970s camps differed on the question of volition: Were individuals and groups free to fashion an American identity of their own choosing, or were they constrained by social structures and historical circumstances over which they had little control? The first camp, that of Fuchs and Sollors, argued that the United States was a genuinely plural society where different groups could construct virtually any desired identity. The second camp, which included Roy Rosenzweig (1983), Irving Howe (1976), Lizabeth Cohen (1990), and Gwendolyn Mink (1996), asserted that class and gender constrained the process of invention.

My own work and sympathies lie with the latter group, and I attempt to explain why we have the better argument. I do this by examining not only the writings outlined earlier but also newer scholarship on "whiteness" as a key component of American identity. The work of David R. Roediger (1991), Michael Rogin (1996), and others treats race as more important than class or gender in the making of Americans, but its arguments have reinforced the emphasis of Rosenzweig, Mink, and others on the role of social forces external to the immigrant or ethnic group in determining the direction of Americanization.

Among the critical responses to the newer historiography that are beginning to appear, the most interesting is David A. Hollinger's *Postethnic America* (1995). Hollinger boldly sets forth a "Sollorsian" blueprint for the creation of a heterogeneous society in which individuals of all races will be free to choose whatever identities they wish to claim or create for themselves. Hollinger calls for the revival of a liberal nationalism that, through economic and cultural reform, will create an environment of racial equality in which a "postethnic" society can flourish. I counter that the nation is itself a structure of power that, like class, gender, and race, necessarily limits the array of identities available to Americans seeking diversity. And it is precisely the inattention to this and other structures of power that limits the work of Fuchs, Sollors, Hollinger, and others who, like Crèvecoeur, wish to view Americanization as emancipation. Any analysis of Americanization, past and present, must accord coercion a role in the making of Americans.

The Long Retreat from Crèvecoeur

Robert Park, William Isaac Thomas, Ernest W. Burgess, and others at the University of Chicago were the first scholars to examine systematically the relationship of the immigrant to American society. In works such as *The Polish Peasant in Europe and America* (1918–1920), they created a body of work that shaped historical and sociological studies of immigration for forty years. They disagreed with Crèvecoeur's view that immigrants quickly, enthusiastically, and effortlessly became Americans. Borrowing from the works of the German scholar Ferdinand Tönnies, especially from his seminal theory of *Gemeinschaft* and *Gesellschaft*, the Chicago sociologists sketched out a far more painful and lengthy process of immigrants' disengagement from European roots and assimilation into American society (see Park and Burgess 1922; Park and Miller 1921; Thomas and Znaniecki 1918–1920; on the Chicago School, see Matthews 1977; Persons 1987; Ross 1991).

Industrialization, urbanization, and other modernizing forces, according to the Chicago sociologists, had disrupted the world of the European peasants, stripping their communities and families of resources, self-sufficiency, and stability and forcing them into larger, more complex, and anomic social settings. The journey to America accelerated this modernizing process, as the rural traveler contended with not only cities and industry but also a profusion of ethnic and racial groups. Meeting peoples of other races and cultures made the immigrant conscious of his difference; soon he joined other immigrants who shared his language and culture to compete against other groups for jobs, housing, and political influence. These emergent ethnic groups replaced the shattered families and village institutions that had anchored European peasant communities, and they made possible the immigrants' adjustment to and absorption into American society.

Robert Park (1926/1950, 147–50) believed all immigrants underwent this "race relations cycle . . . of contacts, competition, accommodation, and eventual assimilation." Though the process was slow and difficult, it eventually erased ethnic and racial antagonisms and united all immigrants, minorities, and native-born Americans into a single national community. Park said little about the culture of this new national community, but he clearly regarded its emergence as emancipatory. His language gained uncharacteristic exuberance when he wrote about the melding of diverse peoples in America and elsewhere. A "cosmic process" of global industrialization, he claimed, had generated "a vast unconscious cooperation of races and peoples," making the modern era "the most romantic period in the history of the whole world." Mass communication had brought the peoples of the world closer together, ignited their hopes and dreams, and weakened the most encrusted ethnic and racial antagonisms. In these circumstances, Park declared, the race relations cycle had become "progressive and irreversible."

In describing assimilation in such positive terms and in emphasizing its naturalness, Park unconsciously aligned himself with Crèvecoeur. In Park's view, the melting pot required no special tending by agents of either the state or private regulatory institutions. Just as Crèvecoeur believed, following Jean-Jacques Rousseau, that a natural society (such as the one forming in America) would surpass those deformed by castes, aristocracies, monarchies, and other artificial institutions, so Park argued that society advanced through "natural" social processes and did not respond well to political interventions (Gerstle 1994; on the triumph of naturalism in American social science, see Ross 1991).

In advancing the claims of nature, Park was not simply continuing a line of thought that had been dominant since Crèvecoeur. He was reacting against an extraordinary effort on the part of American intellectuals and reformers to design an interventionist social science. Such social science would give government officials the knowledge and expertise to intercept social processes that had gone awry and to engineer more satisfactory outcomes. This effort is known to us as Progressivism, and from the perspective of immigrant assimilation, it had been a spectacular failure.

Confronting immigrants seemingly walled off in ghettos, who spoke foreign languages, adhered to strange customs, suffered the effects of impoverishment, and appeared indifferent or antagonistic to the United States, Progressive reformers responded with Americanization campaigns on a scale not seen before. In schools, at workplaces, at settlement houses, and in politics, they taught immigrants English, the essentials of American citizenship, skills useful in getting decent employment, and faith in American values and institutions. The Progressives were a confident bunch, sure that their use of government and science would turn immigrants into Americans.[4]

In the emotionally charged atmosphere of

World War I, however, the Progressive plan went off the tracks. War preparedness demanded a unified home front. The government endorsed the one-hundred-percent Americanism campaigns, initiated by private groups to suppress foreign cultural and political traditions that seemed to nurture antiwar or anti-American sentiments. These efforts give rise to an ugly Americanism, intolerant of cultural and political difference and eager to deprive dissenters of their right to free speech. Many Progressives were complicit in these coercive efforts to strip immigrants of their foreign ways. After the war the simmering ethnic and racial antagonisms exploded. The vicious race riots of 1919, Prohibition, the Red Scare, the resurgence of the Ku Klux Klan, Congress's adoption of a racist system of immigration restriction, and the imposition of Jewish quotas at elite private universities all revealed that a nasty and coercive Americanism had triumphed. (On anti-immigrant and antiradical activities, see Higham [1955/1988]; on antiblack sentiment, see Tuttle [1970]).

Liberal social scientists recoiled from this Americanism, shocked that their earlier efforts to engineer assimilation had yielded reaction and intolerance. The confidence they had exhibited in the prewar years drained away, and many abandoned their formal efforts at Americanization and nation building. Too many immigrant cultures, they now believed, were resistant to assimilation; too many native-born Americans were incorrigibly intolerant. No magical fusing of the many ethnic and racial groups in the United States could occur, even with the aid of enlightened government policy and social science. The very word *Americanization* acquired such a bad, nativist odor that many liberal reformers and social scientists stopped using it altogether (Gerstle 1994).

Robert Park tried to evade the wreck of the liberal project by reasserting naturalist principles. No intervention could prevent economic and social processes from advancing assimilation. Many liberals privately shared his hope that the ethnic and racial differences that had produced such hatred and animosity would fade, and that immigrants would become American. But such liberals no longer felt the elation with which a Crèvecoeur or a Zangwill had expressed the vision of immigrants becoming new men. The intellectual retreat from the notion of Americanization as emancipation had begun.

Nowhere was this retreat more evident than in the work of Oscar Handlin, the most important immigrant historian of the mid-twentieth century and the scholar most responsible for establishing the legitimacy of immigration history. Born into a Jewish immigrant family in 1915, Handlin experienced the intolerant 1920s firsthand. At Harvard, where he began his graduate studies in the mid-1930s, he had to contend with the university's ingrained anti-Semitism. Although he triumphed over this adversity by becoming one of the History Department's first Jewish professors and by presiding over the post-1940s transformation of Harvard into a philo-Semitic institution, he did not easily forget the sting of discrimination. This memory may help explain how and why he modified Robert Park's theories of assimilation.[5]

The influence of Park's race relations cycle is apparent everywhere in Handlin's first book, *Boston's Immigrants* (1941). Handlin focused on Irish Catholic immigrants whose old world had been destroyed by the famine of the 1840s and who were utterly unprepared to cope with the competitive, industrializing, Protestant Yankee milieu of antebellum Boston. Yet after a period of severe disorganization characterized by poverty, crime, and family breakdown, the Irish began to adjust. They organized new institutions, seized economic opportunities, and competed successfully against other groups in politics. The Irish had found a niche in Boston society.

Handlin's analysis adhered to the first three stages of Park's race relations cycle (contacts, competition, accommodation). But the final stage of Park's cycle—assimilation—played no part. "Though the Irish acquired a secure place in the community," Handlin wrote, "they remained distinct as a group." The climax of the immigrant experience was not the merging with other groups in a new race of men, but the creation of "group consciousness." The Irish had overcome their disorganization and immiserization by forming a cohesive and proud community able to compete for Boston's prized economic and political goods. This process was a kind of Americanization, for the Irish had adjusted to the American milieu. But it was not assimilation, nor even emancipation, for the Irish remained subordinate in Boston's social system (on Handlin's views about assimilation and Americanization, see Kazal 1995).

By the time Handlin published his classic *The Uprooted* (1951/1973) a decade later, his view of Americanization had become bleaker still. Handlin reprised the key themes of *Boston's Immigrants*: the breakup of the European peasant's world of land, village, and extended family; the difficult journey to America; and the upheaval in personal and group relationships experienced in the cities and factories of industrializing America. As in *Boston's Immigrants,* the immigrants gradually adjusted to their new surroundings, building churches, joining mutual aid organizations, entering politics, and developing group consciousness. But the groups that these immigrants built seemed less sturdy than those constructed by the protagonists of *Boston's Immigrants.*

In *The Uprooted,* Handlin focused on individual immigrants far more than he had in *Boston's Immigrants,* portraying them as ill at ease in the United States, even after their group had successfully adjusted. Handlin admired the immigrants' self-reliance, independence, and resourcefulness; in this sense, they had become true Americans in the Crèvecoeur mold. But these hardy individualists could not escape the loneliness, isolation, and sadness they had felt since their original uprooting. They never found in America the comfort and security they had known in the old world. They remained forever alien and alienated in their new home.

Handlin's tale raised troubling questions about a society that kept its people in a state of perpetual alienation. Handlin regarded the United States as "the land of separated men." Native-born and immigrant Americans alike could count on no established communities, hallowed traditions, or even reflexive habits to give them guidance and instruction. Everything was fluid; every situation required an individual to make a deliberate, rational decision (Handlin 1951/1973, 271–72).

Handlin tried to sustain a belief, reminiscent of Crèvecoeur's fourth claim, that America emancipated its people. The radical individualism demanded of Americans, he suggested, could have liberating, even ennobling, effects. Constant thought and reflection would invigorate the human imagination and, indeed, "all human capacities." Yet writing in the shadow of Nazism and fascism, Handlin worried that ordinary people would find their freedom too hard to manage and would submerge their individuality in groups that promised order, community, and fellow feeling. This flight from freedom had occurred not only in Europe, where totalitarianism had triumphed in the 1930s, but also in the United States, where a growing nativist movement had pressured Congress to curtail immigration in the mid-1920s. That movement, Handlin argued, reflected the weariness of native-born Americans with "constant newness" and their growing desperation for "the security of belonging." Handlin regarded the nativists' triumph as catastrophic, a victory of small-mindedness and conformity over independence and fluidity. Rather than accept the challenge of living as modern men, Americans had retreated into nativist bunkers (Handlin 1951/1973, 272–73).

In making this argument, Handlin had joined an influential discourse on mass society and its deleterious effects on individuality. To David Riesman (1950), William Hollingsworth Whyte (1956), Daniel Bell (1960/1988), and other prominent social critics, it seemed that America had solved the basic problems of production, poverty, and class inequality (see also Pells 1985, 183–261). But the production of abundance demanded a society of huge bureaucratic organizations—corporations, government agencies, and national labor unions—and these, in the critics' eyes, robbed people of their independence and stifled their initiative. Technological advances had aggravated these tendencies by creating the means (radio, movies, television, and national magazines) for private and state organizations to manipulate popular desire. The new mass media threatened to impose a numbing homogeneity and passivity on American society.

To find an antidote to the pressures of mass society, the critics turned to pluralism, a strengthening of civil society by individuals' participation in voluntary organizations. These associations—professional organizations, little leagues, parent-teacher associations (PTAs), bowling leagues, ethnic groups—would occupy the vital middle ground between massive bureaucratic structures and the individual. The stronger, denser, and more varied associational life became, the greater the defense against a bureaucratic order that threatened to conquer civil society. The diversity and energy of pluralism would guard the United States against conformity, mindlessness, and mass tyranny (Gerstle 1993).

Few proponents of pluralism knew much about immigrants or ethnic groups. But those who did, such as Handlin, began to use its precepts to turn Crèvecoeur's theory of America on its head. Rather than the American environment emancipating immigrants from their old ways and making them into a new race of men, immigrants, in fashioning their distinctive group consciousness, would save America from its slide into anomie and conformity. The immigrant, by refusing to assimilate completely, would invigorate the nation's democratic institutions. For a member of a mass society, Handlin wrote in 1949 (416), the ethnic group "is one of the surviving signs of his individuality, [offering] affirmation that he is not simply the anonymous citizen, a serial number on a dog tag or social security card, but the son of parents, with roots in the past, with a meaning larger than his own life." Schlesinger (1949b, 253) affirmed Handlin's perspective by declaring that "a democratic society, based on a genuine cultural pluralism, could go far to supply outlets for the variegated emotions of man, and thus restore meaning to democratic life."

The full radicalism of Handlin's proposition that ethnic groups would reinvigorate American democracy was rarely evident in the 1950s. These were the years of the cold war, and for all their frustration with American society, Handlin and Schlesinger were staunchly anti-Communist and deeply pro-American. They were unwilling to undermine the reputation of the nation and to weaken its resolve. So it remained for another generation of historians, who cast themselves as Handlin's critics and sought to break out of the cold war consensus, to realize the full implications of Handlin's approach.

BEYOND THE MELTING POT, a 1963 study of ethnicity in New York City by Nathan Glazer and Daniel Patrick Moynihan, is often credited with ending the reign of assimilationist paradigms in ethnic history and sociology. But the arguments of Glazer and Moynihan about the persistence and continual re-creation of ethnicity among Irish, Italian, Jewish, Puerto Rican, and black communities in New York largely followed the analytic lines set forth by Handlin. The true break with prevailing interpretations came in a rather obscure article published by Frank Thistlewaite in 1960.

Born, raised, and schooled in England, Thistlewaite was one of the first to bring a European perspective to questions of American immigration. He admired the work of American historians and sociologists on settlement, acculturation, and assimilation, but he criticized their failure to study *emigration*—how Europeans left their homes and began their journey to America. He had been moved by Handlin's epic tale of uprooting, but he did not regard it as serious history. There were no real emigrants in Handlin's story, just mythologized peasants who lived in the same simple, secure circumstances for hundreds of years until cosmic forces expelled them from their Eden. This story bore no relevance to the British emigrants Thistlewaite had studied: Lancashire textile workers, Welsh ironworkers, Yorkshire coal miners, Cornish tin miners, and Staffordshire potters—all skilled workers, veterans of the British industrial revolution who had emigrated to the United States and catalyzed industrialization in that country. Not only did these emigrants retain their occupations in America, they also "preserved the folk customs, speech patterns, the foods and drinks, music, and sports of those Welsh valleys, Lancashire towns, and Cornish mining villages whence they came, to a second and even third generation" (Thistlewaite 1991b, 55).

Thistlewaite's 1960 essay, "Migration from Europe Overseas in the Nineteenth and Twentieth Centuries," was startling in its revelations. He estimated that as many as one-third of the 33 million European immigrants who came to the United States between 1821 and 1924 repatriated. In certain periods, such as the first two decades of the twentieth century, the percentage of return migrants was considerably higher; and among some groups, such as the Balkan peoples, the repatriation rate may have reached an astounding 89 percent (Thistlewaite 1991a, 25).[6]

Thistlewaite also argued that many of the immigrants were skilled industrial workers. The largest such group came from the British Isles, but important streams came from countries such as Italy, which most historians regarded as a prime source of Handlinesque peasants. Numerous Italian emigrants came from the rural areas that Handlin had emphasized, but even they did not fit Handlin's portrait of innocent peasants overwhelmed by the forces of modernization. Many had already participated in capitalist wage labor. Thistlewaite (1991a, 29) referred, for example, to the Peloponnese, an impoverished rural district in Greece, where families often sent "a boy of ten or twelve away to the cities of Greece or Turkey to earn money for his parents, often in brutal conditions, as a bootblack or in a coffeehouse or grocery store." For these Greek peasants, migration to America was not a sharp break from their way of life, but rather a transatlantic version of accustomed journeys within well-established regional labor markets. And just as the boys who went to Greek and Turkish cities saw their trips as efforts to augment their families' incomes, the migrants to America wanted to earn high wages and to help their families back home. Many intended to return to Europe. Some became seasonal migrants, treating the Atlantic as a lake that had to be crossed twice a year on the way to and from work.[7]

Thistlewaite did little new research for his article. Rather, he drew on existing historical work that had been ignored by scholars working in the dominant Handlin school and on migration statistics compiled by demographers and labor statisticians. Thistlewaite raised more questions than he answered. But he threw down the gauntlet to the Handlin school: "Whatever else the experience may have meant, migration often did not mean settlement and acculturation" (Thistlewaite 1991a, 25).

For Rudolph Vecoli, then a graduate student at the University of Wisconsin, reading Thistlewaite's essay was exhilarating. It profoundly shaped his dissertation on Italian laborers in Chicago. His first article, "The *Contadini* of Chicago" (1964), declared war on the Handlinesque concept of uprooting (see Vecoli 1962, 1964, 1991). Other young historians also took up Thistlewaite's challenge to rethink the migration story, and over the next twenty years they changed the face of immigration history. They were influenced not just by Thistlewaite's article but by the radicalization of the academy in the 1960s. They cast themselves as critics of American society—of its capitalist economy, bourgeois individualist culture, and imperialist foreign policy. They rediscovered Karl Marx, sought evidence of conflict rather than adjustment in American history, and loathed the idea of assimilation. (The key works in this school include Bodnar 1982; Gabaccia 1984, 1988; Greene 1968; Gutman 1976, 3–78; Hareven 1982; Hoerder 1983, 1985; Morawska 1985; Ramirez 1991; Vecoli 1964; Yans-McLaughlin 1982. For a magisterial synthesis, see Bodnar 1985.)

Their three major findings have had profound implications for our understanding of immigrants, ethnic culture, and American identity. First, immigrants to the United States frequently considered their journey as travel from one job to another, rather than from one nation to another. They came to make good money in order to help their families or to buy their own farms back home. This instrumental orientation explains the early demographic profiles of most groups of new immigrants (including Italians, Slavs, and Greeks)—men vastly outnumbered women and children. At the outset, this was a migration not of families but of young men in search of work.[8]

Second, immigrants brought their ethnic cultures with them and nourished them in America. Suffering little or none of the disorganization Handlin emphasized, they quickly reestablished cultural institutions dear to them in the old world—churches and synagogues, festivals, socialist and anarchist organizations, nationalist groups, athletic clubs, and musical societies—and developed new ones, such as foreign-language newspapers and mutual benefit societies. They used extended kin and ethnic networks to help each other find work, to challenge capricious employer power, and to assist those in need. They were not lonely individuals overwhelmed by modernity, but members of cohesive groups capable of purposive action.

These immigrants protested developments that threatened the integrity or survival of their ethnic institutions and cultures. The protests took many forms: Italian parents declined to send their children to public schools where they would be exposed to Americanizing influences; French Canadian and Polish Catholics refused to attend mass said by an Irish, Americanizing priest; immigrant groups established schools where the language of their homeland—Polish, Lithuanian, French, Italian, Yiddish—was taught; and Slavic coal miners, Italian laborers, and Jewish garment workers banded together in labor organizations to protest wages and working conditions that threatened the health of their families and ethnic communities.[9]

Third, assimilation and Americanization acted only as negative forces in this new immigrant history. In the eyes of the new historians, most immigrants did not fit the Crèvecoeurian mold. The immigrants did not want to become American; they were sojourners in a harsh capitalist land, hoping to cut the best deal they could and then to leave. Many of those forced to stay still regarded their ethnic cultures as superior to and more humane than the cutthroat, competitive culture they encountered in America. In the premodern collectivism and communal morality upheld by their ethno-religious cultures, they found the means to criticize America's harsh individualism. In a seminal essay, "Work, Culture, and Society in Industrializing America" (1973), Herbert G. Gutman showed how ethnic groups had used cultural practices—"peasant parades and rituals, religious oaths and food riots"—to protest the exploitative practices of American capitalism. He found, for example, this newspaper account of an oath taken by Slavic steelworkers striking in Hammond, Indiana: "The lights of the hall were extinguished. A candle stuck into a bottle was placed on a platform. One by one the men came and kissed the ivory image on the cross, kneeling before it. They swore not to scab" (65–66). (For another example, see Gutman 1976, 62; see also Greene 1968.)

Americanization, to Gutman and others, meant surrender to a capitalist order. This capitulation made sense only for those immigrants who had risen far enough in that order to make capitalism work for them: small businessmen, manufacturers, professionals, journalists, urban bosses, and gangsters. But for the majority of immigrants stuck in the working class, Americanization meant only acquiescence in their oppression. Thus, when these new historians of immigration dealt with Americanization at all, they regarded it in class terms, as a cultural strategy deployed by employers and their ethnic middle-class allies to augment their wealth and power. By enhancing the ethnic elites' access to power, Americanization also increased their influence and control over their own ethnic communities.[10]

In the new immigration histories, then, Americanizing elites were frequently pitted against tradition-minded masses. The elites were intent on becoming Crèvecoeurian "new men"; the masses wanted to remain who they were. The new men embraced bourgeois individualism, while the masses clung to a premodern European collectivism. The European masses' only hope for emancipation was to use their premodern cultures to resist capitalist practices and the false bourgeois consciousness that dominated American culture.

In equating the maintenance of ethnic culture with emancipation, Vecoli, Gutman, and other new immigration historians had arrived at a position similar to Handlin's. Handlin, to be sure, had not made class an important component of his analysis of immigrant communities, nor did he consider that immigrants of one class might have benefited—or suffered—from Americanization more than those of another. Moreover, Handlin had argued that the cultures of ethnic groups had been created in America and were not simple carryovers from Europe. Still, the perception shared by Handlin and Gutman that American society was exploitative and alienating might have generated a stimulating dialogue between the two camps.

This was not to be. By the time Gutman published his 1973 article, Handlin had become a thoroughly alienated man, disgusted by the radicalism of the 1960s and by the grim view of America put forward by the radical historians. He had stopped arguing about the loneliness and isolation of Americans and had started emphasizing the positive features of American society. No fruitful interchanges between the two men or the two camps took place, and the field was the poorer for it.[11]

The influence of the Gutman-Vecoli school was huge. A wholly new picture of American society for the period from 1880 to 1920 emerged. American cities were full of immigrants from eastern and southern Europe, many of whom—perhaps a majority—had no intention of staying in America. They were here to work, to save money, and to return home. They clung tenaciously to their ethnic heritages and never experienced the Handlinesque period of disorganization and isolation. Many were indifferent to the United States, others hostile to a capitalist society that promised much but offered its workers inadequate welfare and safety. An extraordinarily large number displayed their alienation by refusing to naturalize or participate in American politics. As late as 1920, less than one-third of immigrants from Poland, Austria, Hungary, Yugoslavia, Lithuania, Bulgaria, Greece, Italy, and Portugal had become citizens. There were exceptions to this pattern, most notably among Jewish immigrants from Russia. But the pattern remained striking (Thernstrom, Orlov, and Handlin 1980, "Naturalization and Citizenship"). The new historians of immigration had uncovered and celebrated an early multicultural age. The retreat from assimilationist and Crèvecoeurian paradigms was complete.

The Return to Americanization

One of the strengths of the new historians—a single-minded focus on the years of the new immigration—was also a weakness. These scholars had relatively little to say about old immigrant groups, most notably the British, Irish, Germans, and Scandinavians who had arrived in the first wave of immigration, and how they maintained cultural traditions and experienced Americanization across the generations. Nor did they grapple with an inescapable and uncomfortable fact: as indifferent or hostile to America as they may have been prior to 1920, a majority of the new immigrants stayed. They eventually naturalized, voted, and identified themselves as Americans. Some had completed this process by 1930, most by 1940 or 1950. And for many of those immigrants, acquiring an American identity meant more than filling in naturalization forms or casting ballots. It triggered a profound patriotic awakening and an embrace of the idea of America. This emergent patriotism was apparent in the new immigrants' affection for Franklin D. Roosevelt, in their enthusiastic embrace of American ideals during World War II, and in the "America—love it or leave it" attitude with which many of their descendants reacted to student radicals of the 1960s. How did this transformation from immigrant to American occur? Had the new immigrant historians overemphasized the retention of ethnic cultures and the opposition to Americanization before 1920? Or did external social and political forces compel the immigrants to change their attitudes? Historians offered several responses.

One response, forcefully expressed by Lawrence H. Fuchs in *The American Kaleidoscope* (1990), was that the opposition between Americanization and ethnic persistence was false. "Immigrant settlers and their progeny," Fuchs argued, "were free to maintain . . . loyalty to their ancestral religions and cultures while . . . claiming an American identity by embracing the founding myths and participating in the political life of the nation" (15). In Fuchs's telling, if immigrants declared their allegiance to the American political ideals of democracy and individual rights and to the founding documents—the Declaration of Independence, the Constitution, and the Bill of Rights—they became participants in the country's "civic culture." But the civic culture governed only political participation, leaving questions of religion, morals, customs, and traditions to the individual. Many immigrants chose to retain their ethnic culture, creating a system of "voluntary pluralism" that became a defining characteristic of American society. Immigrants, Fuchs argued, were devoted to the United States because it maximized their freedom to be Germans, Slovenes, or Jews. In a sense, Fuchs had rehabilitated the Americanization formula that German immigrants had pioneered in the nineteenth century, by declaring that they would become American in politics while remaining German in culture.[12]

Fuchs did not shrink from pointing out the discriminations visited on newcomers, but he regarded these acts as ephemeral. American history became a saga of the civic culture realizing itself, eventually opening itself even to minority groups—blacks, Indians, Asians, Mexicans—that had long been excluded from democratic participation and voluntary pluralism.

In a work eloquent in argument and encyclopedic in scope, Fuchs married the research findings of the new immigration historians, particularly their emphasis on the survival of ethnic cultures, to a neo-Crèvecoeurian interpretive agenda stressing the emancipatory character of American society. It may seem surprising to place Fuchs in Crèvecoeur's camp. Fuchs had no use for Crèvecoeur's notion that America witnessed the creation of a "new race of men"; indeed, he believed that America gave the "old races" unprecedented opportunities to express their native cultures.[13] Yet his view of America as a land of extraordinary freedom without the constraints of the old world renders him a Crèvecoeurian emancipationist.

Fuchs offered a wonderful solution to the cultural tensions of our own time by declaring, in essence, that we should not worry about them. The long history of intergroup relations in America showed that immigrants who practiced their ethnic traditions were, despite appearances to the contrary, becoming Americans. If only the process had been so easy. Fuchs might have made his case more convincing if he had admitted that some ethnic groups had lost their cultures in America and that the Americanization of European immigrants occasionally entailed coercion rather than emancipation. He might have emphasized the experience of German Americans who, until World War I, easily balanced their dual identities as Americans and Germans. Even as assimilation was eroding this group's Germanness, many individuals within it maintained a vigorous ethnic identity and married it to a deep American patriotism. But the anti-German hysteria and Americanization crusades of World War I made this pluralist experiment impossible to sustain. After that time, Germans could no longer be American in politics and German in culture; they had to be American through and through.[14] Fuchs could still have drawn up a balance sheet, demonstrating that the ethnic groups that benefited from Americanization outnumbered those that did not. Such a strategy would have made his interpretation more compelling and influential.

Fuchs was not alone in his tendency to overlook instances of ethnic loss and patriotic coercion. Much the same message emerged from *Beyond Ethnicity,* published in 1986. Its author, Werner Sollors, a professor of American literature at Harvard University, did not deny the importance of ethnic identity in the American past or present. But he launched an all-out attack on those who stressed its inherited character and who portrayed it as a force invariably opposed to a common "Americanness." Surveying ethnic literature, Sollors uncovered "a grammar of new world imagery and conduct." "Images of exodus and deliverance, newness and rebirth, melting pot and romantic love, jeremiads against establishment figures and lost generations" were the "central codes of Americanness" that, according to Sollors, contributed to "the construction of new forms of symbolic kinship among people who are not blood relatives" (7). Some of the codes of Americanness developed by ethnic writers, such as the melting pot motif, entailed an explicit repudiation of old world traditions and an embrace of the possibilities of the new. But in Sollors's eyes, becoming American could just as easily entail the invention of new ethnic traditions. Among others, he mentioned bebop (a reaction against the appropriation of jazz by whites) and the bat mitzvah (marking the transition of Jewish girls into womanhood). Ethnic groups invented these traditions to maintain their cultural distinctiveness amid pressures toward cultural homogenization. The embrace or creation of an ethnic identity, Sollors argued, allowed Americans to steer a "middle course between ancient narrowness and vulgar monotony. By creating new, not traditionally anchored, group identities and by authenticating them, they could represent individuality and American identity at the same time" (206–7, 241–47). Sollors repudiated the view of ethnicity as a "tradition" opposing modernization. Instead he viewed ethnic identity as the highest expression of modernism (see also Sollors 1989).

Unlike Fuchs, Sollors had little to say about how the American political heritage permitted, even encouraged, such ethnic attachments. For him, America was less a political democracy than a modern mass society, and the celebration of one's ethnicity was less a declaration of equality than an affirmation of individuality in a stultifying, monochromatic world.[15]

Sollors shared with Fuchs the conviction that to declare an ethnic identity was, at bottom, a way of becoming American. He, too, believed the American experience encouraged the creation of ethnic loyalties. With one or two exceptions, Sollors did not dwell on ethnic inventions or notions of Americanness that failed (for the principal exception, see Sollors 1986, 191–95). America was once again, as it had been for Crèvecoeur, the land of possibility.

Sollors, like Fuchs, had repudiated the third aspect of the Crèvecoeurian myth, which claimed that all American immigrants would fuse into one people, alike in their language, customs, and sense of what constituted Americanness. Not only did Sollors's pluralistic America offer immigrants multiple "codes of Americanism" from which to choose, but the choosing and creating of identities had no clear beginning or end. An identity adopted one year could be changed the next; one could select ethnicization over assimilation and still be thoroughly immersed in becoming American. Sollors's America was characterized by a multitude, even cacophony, of voices, each of them "truly American." Crèvecoeur no doubt would have been discomfited by this American Babel. But he might have recognized in Sollors's vision something that infused his own work: enthusiasm for the emancipatory spirit that would let individuals in America toss off their inheritances and embrace the freedom to be something entirely of their own choosing.

Sollors drew on and contributed to the deconstructionist movement then sweeping through literature and American studies departments. He exposed the uncritical and simplistic ways in which the new historians of immigration had sometimes approached questions of tradition and culture. He denied any opposition between ethnic and American culture. Scholars delighted in the mind play of Sollors's account of identities destabilized, inverted, and re-created. Soon Sollors's views on ethnicity began to influence American immigration historians. His book took on added significance because it paralleled work by Eric Hobsbawm, Terence Ranger, Herbert J. Gans, and Mary C. Waters on the "invention of tradition," "symbolic ethnicity," and "ethnic options" (Gans 1979; Hobsbawm and Ranger 1983/1992; Waters 1990).

Sollors's influence among historians was strikingly apparent in a 1992 article by five prominent immigration scholars. Kathleen Neils Conzen, David Gerber, Ewa Morawska, George Pozzetta, and Rudolph Vecoli (1992, 5) made clear their debt to Sollors by asserting that

> ethnic groups in modern settings are constantly recreating themselves, and ethnicity is continuously being reinvented in response to changing realities both within the group and the host society. . . . Ethnic group boundaries . . . must be continuously renegotiated, while expressive symbols of ethnicity (ethnic traditions) must be repeatedly reinterpreted.

The Conzen group established a theoretical distance from Sollors, asserting that ethnicity was more than a "collective fiction," that its destabilization and re-creation assumed "preexisting communal solidarities, cultural attributes, and historical memories" that were "grounded in real life" (1992, 4–5). Moreover, historical context mattered in ways that Sollors had disregarded: "The timing of migrations, the stage of development in country of origin and in country of destination, the incidence of economic and political cycles, . . . generational transitions" (12), and places of settlement—all shaped ethnic invention. But the authors attempted to account for so many variations in ethnicization that they did less to show the influence of historical circumstances and structures than to reproduce Sollors's emphasis on the "continual renegotiation of identities" (6).[16] Still, they showed good instincts in combining emphasis on the inventiveness of ethnic groups with attention to the social structures and historical context that shaped, and sometimes undid, cultural inventions.

HISTORIANS WHO WERE not inspired by Sollors had made progress in achieving the synthesis between agency and structure that had eluded the Conzen group.[17] Most successful were studies of the interaction between mass culture and traditional immigrant cultures. Like Sollors, the authors of those studies were impressed by the cultural ingenuity of the immigrants, but they treated such ingenuity as subject to failure and social constraint.

While these scholars recognized the persistence of ethnic cultures in the new world, they wondered what happened when those ethnic cultures encountered the vaudeville theaters, amusement parks, baseball stadia, movie theaters, and radio culture of the early-twentieth-century United States. That the rise of these mass-cultural institutions constituted a central event in American history was hardly a novel observation. David Riesman (1950), Daniel Bell (1988), Theodor W. Adorno (1945; Adorno and Simpson 1941), and others had made that case in the 1940s and 1950s.[18] Some historians built on that work by arguing that the rise of mass culture had made ordinary citizens passive and susceptible to manipulation and had thus weakened American democracy (see in particular Fox and Lears 1983; Lasch 1984). But such a story line could not easily comprehend the experience of European immigrants and their children.

In the new historical studies of mass culture, immigrants figured as enthusiastic participants in the emerging entertainment industries. At the movies, immigrants could escape the dour supervision of the Protestant Americanizers who controlled recreation on urban playgrounds. In amusement parks and dance halls, young single women could elude the surveillance of prudish immigrant parents and explore their sexuality with young men. As movie theater and dance hall owners, and later as movie moguls, immigrant entrepreneurs discovered opportunities to make money. And immigrant artists invented new kinds of theater, art, and comedy, inspired by the American urban milieux in which they lived. In short, many immigrants viewed the new mass culture as a realm of freedom, opportunity, and invention. But did their participation in these institutions lead to rapid Americanization? (Among other works, see Erenberg 1981; Ewen 1985; Nasaw 1985; Peiss 1986; Rosenzweig 1983; Snyder 1989. On similar patterns after 1945, see Lipsitz 1989, 1990.)

Popular writers, such as Neal Gabler, say yes. A favorite theme of their biographies of entertainers and sports stars is the desire of the immigrant or his child to escape the confines of an ethnic culture and to embrace "America." Involvement in the world of mass entertainment expanded an individual's circle of contacts and immersed him or her in a distinctively American celebrity culture. Moreover, the quest for profits pushed participants to develop movies, radio programs, and games with national appeal. Over the long term, mass culture undoubtedly promoted the Americanization of those ethnics directly involved in the entertainment industries. But in the short term, there were intriguing twists and turns (Gabler 1988; see also Raeburn 1975; Robinson and Spigelgass 1973).[19]

Roy Rosenzweig's (1983, 181–228) study of workers and leisure in Worcester, Massachusetts, for example, shows how early movie theaters—storefront nickelodeons—were extensions of ethnic working-class neighborhoods. Patrons brought into the theaters an ethnic, working-class style of public behavior. Friends engaged in boisterous camaraderie. Customers offered loud, running commentaries on the movies and tolerated the crying babies who had been dragged along by mothers and older siblings determined to catch a show. Lizabeth Cohen (1990, 99–147), in her study of Chicago workers, found that the fusion of movie theater and ethnic neighborhood persisted well into the 1920s. Movie theaters, then, were not simply sites where parochial-minded immigrants were exposed to modern American values; they were also places where ethnic communities constituted themselves and their cultures. Early radio, Cohen discovered, served a similar purpose. Most Chicago stations carried "nationality hours," and as many as four stations were devoted entirely to ethnic programming.

Ethnic radio programming cannot be understood simply as an effort to reproduce old world traditions in the new world. An Italian-language radio hour, for example had to appeal to all Italians in Chicago, and that meant emphasizing, even inventing, aspects of Italian culture and experience that transcended specific villages and regions. These radio programs also had to address the specific concerns of Italians in Chicago. Thus, radio culture was a blend of the old and the new. (On the Mexican encounter with mass culture in Los Angeles, see Sánchez 1993, 171–87.)

Irving Howe (1976, 460–96) offered a wonderful illustration of this phenomenon in his discussion of Yiddish theater. Yiddish theater may appear a simple carryover of traditions from Europe. In fact, Yiddish theater flowered only after Jews had left the shtetls for the urban and secularizing environments of Polish and American cities. The theater that developed in New York drew heavily not only on Jewish folk materials but also on William Shakespeare (among the plays written for the New York Yiddish stage were *The Jewish King Lear* and *Raphael and Shaindele,* a Yiddish version of *Romeo and Juliet*) and Leo Tolstoy, Ivan Turgenev, and other great figures of nineteenth-century Russian literature. In the actors' pursuit of virtuosity and in the passion and unruliness of the enthusiastic audiences, Yiddish theater resembled vaudeville and Italian opera. It was clearly a hybrid institution, possible only after Jews had been released from shtetl life, learned more about other groups' artistic traditions, and gained freedom from both Gentile rulers and local rabbis. But it was unquestionably a Jewish institution, accessible only to those who spoke Yiddish, and it stimulated "vast outpourings of creative energy" that "made the performance of a Yiddish play an occasion for communal pleasure" (493). Yiddish theater helped to create and define Jewish identity in the United States. In this instance, the advent of mass culture had increased the possibilities of ethnic invention and affirmation (see also Levine 1988, 85–104).

The stories of the early days of movies, radio, and ethnic theater seem to fit Sollors's analysis of how immigrants found endless opportunities to invent and reinvent their ethnicities in America.[20] But the stories do not end there. In the movies, the coming of (English) sound and the cultivation by moviemakers and theater owners of middle-class patrons ended the era of the raucous working-class audience. By the 1930s powerful national radio stations had marginalized many of the local, foreign-language stations that flourished in the 1920s. And the Yiddish theater proved too eclectic and unstable an institution to thrive much beyond World War I. Technological change, middle-class power and assertiveness, corporate consolidation in the media industries, Americanization movements, and generational succession within ethnic communities—all contributed to the collapse of cultural inventions. Historical circumstances and social structures undermined experiments in the fashioning of identity.

The double sense of inventiveness and constraint shaped my study (Gerstle 1989, esp. 1–15, 153–95, and 278–309) of how French Canadian workers in Woonsocket, Rhode Island, in the interwar years attempted to bend and twist Americanism to fit their needs and aspirations. Theirs was not a misguided project, I argued, for Americanism was a flexible political language that could accommodate a variety of ideologies and beliefs, including those that promoted working-class emancipation. Like Sollors, I emphasized the multiple "codes of Americanness"; like Crèvecoeur, I showed how "new world imagery" lent itself to visions of personal deliverance and social transformation. The city's trade-union activists portrayed their fight for "industrial democracy" as the latest episode in the American struggle for freedom that had begun with the Pilgrims and the Founding Fathers (see also Barrett 1992; McCartin 1993; Neather 1996).

But the Woonsocket story was not ultimately about freedom. The working-class Americanism that flourished in the 1930s was gone by the late 1940s. Some labor activists had been run out of town, and those who stayed, under the pressure first of war conformity and then of deindustrialization, had relinquished their own Americanism and embraced one that originated in Washington bureaucracies and corporate boardrooms. In Woonsocket state and class power undermined the autonomy and extinguished the inventiveness of one group of Americans-in-the-making. My story became a tale of America as not simply a Crèvecoeurian land of possibility but also a land of constraint. There was much to be lost, as well as gained, through Americanization.

The relatively few studies of gender and American identity also suggest that Americanization involves both inventiveness and constraint. Elizabeth Ewen (1985) has shown how Jewish and Italian working-class women in early-twentieth-century New York forged a "working-class Americanism" of their own, only to see their more acculturated daughters relinquish it in the 1920s and 1930s. Gwendolyn Mink (1996) has explored how Progressive reformers used Americanization campaigns to strip immigrant women of their old world ways—their foods, clothes, housekeeping, and child-rearing habits—and imposed white, middle-class, "American" notions of domesticity. Yet those reformers, Mink acknowledges, believed Americanization would emancipate immigrant women and their children, giving them the behavioral and cognitive tools needed to lift themselves to the "American" level. And Americanization sometimes worked this way, especially for the male children of immigrant mothers, who found in public schools opportunities for education and socioeconomic advancement. Immigrant mothers and their daughters gained few of these benefits, because Americanizers insisted that motherhood and homemaking constituted a woman's only proper roles. For this reason, Mink views Americanization as more coercive than liberatory. Still, she has begun developing a gendered framework that allows her to see Americanization as double-sided, as a source of both freedom and repression. Other scholars should follow Mink's lead, making the home and family life central to the study of Americanization and staying alert to the complexity and contradictory nature of the Americanizing process (see also Boris 1995; McClymer 1991; Sánchez 1993, 98–107).

Race, Nation, and the Making of Americans

For many years immigration historians paid little attention to questions of race. Immigration history was conceived of in Eurocentric terms. The histories of nonwhite, non-European immigrants—Chinese, Japanese, Mexicans, and others—were ignored by most of the major figures in American immigration history and sociology. The relations between European immigrants and blacks received almost no attention. Studies of nonwhite groups were regarded as irrelevant to the main drama of transatlantic migration. It is hardly accidental that the nation's greatest monument to the immigrant—the Statue of Liberty in New York harbor—affirms the Eurocentric tradition and marginalizes the experience of those who came to the United States via the Pacific or across the Rio Grande.

There was a justification for this bias: from 1880 to 1920, the period when the Statue of Liberty was erected, Europeans formed 75 percent of the immigrant population. But that is not the whole story. Three hundred thousand Chinese immigrants arrived in the United States between 1851 and 1882. They might have formed one of the country's largest immigrant groups had Congress not barred them from entering the United States from the 1880s through the early 1940s. The government shut down the immigration of Japanese male laborers in 1907, and of virtually all other Asians in 1917.[21]

Nor were these the first instances of a racialized immigration policy. The First Congress, meeting in 1790, decreed that only free white immigrants were eligible for citizenship. In 1870 Congress amended this law in order to make free African immigrants eligible for citizenship. But the barriers to citizenship for nonwhite Asian immigrants remained in force until the 1950s. Americanization acquired its white, European cast at the country's creation; prejudice against nonwhites shaped citizenship policy for the first 175 years of our republic's history (Gettys 1934; Lopez 1996; Ueda 1994, 18–44).

The privileged position of Europeans appeared in Crèvecoeur's (1782/1912, 43) musings. When he asked his famous question, "What then is the American, this new man?," he did not commence his answer with the words quoted on the first page of this essay. He began: "He is either an European, or the descendant of an European, hence that strange mixture of blood, which you will find in no other country." Crèvecoeur did not acknowledge that Africans and Indians might claim to be American or that they might have contributed to that "strange mixture of blood" that was creating a new race of men. The United States did not just happen to be a nation of European descendants; it wanted to be. And one way European immigrants became Americans was to insist on their cultural and racial superiority to those of darker skins.[22]

Roger Daniels (1962), Ronald T. Takaki (1979), and Alexander Saxton (1971) raised these issues in their pioneering studies of reactions to Asian immigrants in the American West in the nineteenth and twentieth centuries. Building on their work, in 1991 David R. Roediger published a seminal study of how one group of European immigrants, the antebellum Irish, became white (see also Saxton 1990; Horsman 1981).

Roediger was hardly the first to note the deep antagonism between Irish immigrants and blacks in the nineteenth century, but he explored that antagonism with more sophistication and subtlety than his predecessors. He noted the similarities between the Irish immigrants' and free blacks' experiences in northern antebellum cities. Both groups had been shaped by preindustrial cultures where the rhythms of work and play were often at odds with the time and work discipline enforced by America's industrializing order. Both concentrated in the lowliest and most backbreaking occupations; both suffered discrimination at the hands of native-born Protestant whites. A labor historian by training, Roediger wanted to understand why the Irish turned on blacks, a fellow group of wage laborers, instead of making common cause with them.

Roediger began with the low status of wage labor in the new American nation. Wage labor was widely despised not just because it yielded a paltry income but also because it made the worker dependent on his employer, violating the American Revolution's ideal of independent and free citizens. Wage dependency also conjured up images of slavery, the American institution that had sealed the association of servility with dark skin. The Irish feared that they might be seen as black. This was no fantasy. The nativist press of the era frequently depicted the Irish as monkeys, an image also used to infantilize and dehumanize African Americans (Roediger 1991, 65–92).

To remove this black stain on their reputation, the Irish claimed their whiteness conferred on them a security against falling to the level of the African American. Drawing on the words of W. E. B. Du Bois, Roediger argued that whiteness brought the impoverished Irish a "public and psychological wage." Nineteenth-century white workers, Du Bois had written in 1935, "were given public deference . . . because they were white. They were admitted freely, with all classes of white people, to public functions. . . . The police were drawn from their ranks. . . . Their votes selected public officials and while this had small effect upon the economic situation, it had great effect on their personal treatment" (quoted in Roediger 1991, 12). Becoming "white" helped the Irish gain public respect and offered them a psychological escape from their menial status.

But the Irish could not dissociate themselves from black life altogether, for they were profoundly attracted to African American culture. In that culture's alleged simplicity, playfulness, and sensuality, Roediger provocatively argued, the Irish discerned a naturalness and wholesomeness that reminded them of the preindustrial culture that was slipping away from them. The Irish could never directly acknowledge their attraction to black culture, for that would drag them down to the African American level. But they acknowledged it indirectly by "becoming black" through blackface minstrel routines, the most popular entertainment of the urban working class. The more the Irish distanced themselves from "loathsome" blacks in "real life," the safer they felt in exploring on stage their attraction to black culture. (On the psychodynamics of minstrelsy, see Lott 1993b.)

Roediger focused on the same downtrodden Irishmen that Handlin had portrayed fifty years earlier in *Boston's Immigrants* (1941). But the ethnic group's identity was fashioned not by its bruising contact with Boston's Protestant Brahmin elite but by its complex relationship to America's poorest population. While Handlin had emphasized the incompleteness of assimilation, Roediger seemed to suggest that the Irish had fully absorbed the whiteness cherished in American society.

Roediger and other scholars suggest that questions of race figured prominently in the Americanization of new immigrants. In the twentieth century, eastern and southern Europeans found themselves in much the same predicament as the Irish had earlier. Concentrated in the worst industrial jobs, they were often considered racially inferior to "Anglo-Saxon" Americans. Although the courts regarded these European immigrants as white and thus eligible for citizenship, congressmen, scientists, reformers, nativists, and others repeatedly challenged their racial fitness and their ability to function as Americans. Racial considerations justified the drastic limitations on the number of southern and eastern European immigrants allowed to enter the United States under the Immigration Restriction Act of 1924. Thus, the new immigrants and their children had to claw their way into the white race, much as the Irish did a century before them.

That story is only now being told. Matthew Frye Jacobson (1995, 181–216) has argued that America's turn-of-the-century imperial adventures in the Philippines offered eastern European immigrants their first opportunity to join America's great Anglo-Saxon race and to participate vicariously in subduing and uplifting Asia's dark, savage races. Roediger and James Barrett, following Robert Orsi (who followed John Higham), have labeled the new immigrants the "inbetween peoples" to denote their indeterminate racial status—sometimes white, sometimes not—between 1900 and 1940 (Barrett and Roediger 1997; see also Higham 1955/1988, 169; Orsi 1992; Roediger 1994, 181–99). And Richard D. Alba (1990), Arnold R. Hirsch (1983), and I (Gerstle 1995, 1996b) have interpreted the 1940s as the first decade in which the new immigrants and their descendants could lay a secure claim to whiteness (see also Allen 1994; Foley 1997; Frankenberg 1993; Hale 1998; Ignatiev 1995; Jacobson, 1998; Lipsitz 1995a, 1995b; Nelson 1996; Sacks 1994; Sánchez 1995b; Taylor 1995; Williams 1995). Meanwhile, blackface—in vaudeville and in movies of the 1910s and 1920s—permitted immigrants both to explore and to distance themselves from black culture. Michael Rogin (1992a, 1992b, 1994) and Richard Slotkin (1993) have demonstrated how movies promoted ethnic assimilation even while they reinforced the racial division of white from black.

While the accounts differed on how inventive immigrants were in creating American identities, all agreed that race constrained invention. The tension between inventiveness and constraint is particularly acute in Michael Rogin's *Blackface, White Noise* (1996), on moviemaking, race, and immigrant Americanization. Rogin recognized that the cinema gave its ethnic—especially Jewish—producers, directors, and actors opportunities to represent themselves in a variety of roles and masks and thus to negotiate the terms of their entry into American society. Blackface, in his eyes, was a particularly powerful form of cross-dressing, a behavior currently celebrated by postmodernists as a way for subalterns—women, gay men, people of color—to challenge the power of the imperial white, heterosexual man. But Rogin insisted that white men who put on "burnt cork" crossed the racial boundary only to reaffirm it. Even the makers of the progressive race films of the 1940s who were sickened by blackface and embraced racial equality conveyed a belief in the superiority of whites over blacks.

For Roediger, Rogin, and others in their camp, efforts to free American national identity from its affiliation with whiteness have failed. They wish that the nation would turn all its energies toward the "abolition of whiteness," but they doubt this will soon occur. Race, even more than class and gender, still limits the options of those who seek to become American.

Their pessimism, however, has not gone unchallenged. Other scholars and journalists discern an opportunity to reconfigure American identity along nonracialist lines. They point to the diminishing role of black-white relations as the lightning rod of urban politics, to the clamor for a multiracial category on the U.S. census, to the rising rates of racial intermarriage and the resulting hybridization of "American stock."[23] The American studies scholar Shelley Fisher Fishkin (1995, 428) has argued that recent work on "the interrelatedness of blackness and whiteness" will make it increasingly difficult for white racists or black nationalists to deny that Americans of all races have constantly been peering at each other, copying and learning from each other, and thereby creating an "incontestably mulatto" American culture. The historian Gary Nash (1995) has asserted that the racial mixing of whites, Indians, blacks, Mexicans, and Asians has always been central to the American experience.[24] And in his lucid book, *Postethnic America* (1995), David Hollinger has laid out a compelling vision of the United States as a nonracialist, democratic society in which individuals would be free to embrace or to ignore the ethnoracial identities they inherit and to create new ones of their own. Hollinger both affirms diversity as a defining characteristic of the American experience and rejects the essentialist position, embraced by many multiculturalists, that a person must identify with the ethnoracial culture of his or her ancestors.

Hollinger's vision, with its emphasis on the freedom of Americans to choose their identities and to create new races, recalls that of Werner Sollors. This resemblance is hardly accidental: Hollinger praises Sollors's book as the most important work on pluralism and American identity of the last twenty-five years. Hollinger titled his book *Postethnic America* to echo Sollors's *Beyond Ethnicity.* Thus, it is not surprising that Hollinger's work, like that of Sollors, suffers from inattention to social and historical constraints. First, it underestimates the commanding and resilient power of "whiteness." The category has survived by stretching its boundaries to include Americans—the Irish, eastern and southern Europeans—who had been deemed nonwhite. Contemporary evidence suggests that the boundaries are again being stretched as Latinos and Asians pursue whiteness much as the Irish, Italians, and Poles did before them. Asians and Latinos, for example, are marrying "white" Americans at a far greater rate than are African Americans, thus enhancing the ability of their offspring to claim whiteness or "nonblackness." The offspring of black immigrants from the Caribbean, meanwhile, are assimilating into urban African American culture, a racialized process that their parents and their immigrant communities do not control (Edmonston, Lee, and Passel 1994; Hollinger 1995, 187–88; Kalmijn 1993; Lee and

Yamanaka 1990; Root 1992; Spickard 1989; Waters 1994).[25]

Hollinger (1995, 131–72, esp. 148, 157, 165–168) is more sensitive to the influence of class on culture than Sollors. Worried that the class disparity between white and black America might frustrate hopes for a postethnic nation, he calls for a liberal American nationalism that would nurture political movements able to tame capitalist power, promote the interests of the black poor, and bring them into a humane, diverse American community. He boldly—and accurately—asserts that Progressivism, the New Deal, the civil rights movement, and the Great Society were nationalist movements that derived legitimacy from their claim to speak "on behalf of the American nation" (148) as a whole. He argues that resuscitating a humane, civic version of our nationalism, grounded in the ideals of liberty, equality, and democracy, would buoy the prospects for social reform without extinguishing cultural diversity. "The national community's fate," he writes, "can be common without its will being uniform, and the nation can constitute a common project without effacing all of the various projects that its citizens pursue through their voluntary associations" (157).

Hollinger's intriguing analysis downplays the nasty work that building a national community entails. Even where the civic elements of nationalism are exceptionally strong, as in our own society, nationalism demands that boundaries against outsiders be drawn, that a dominant national culture be created or reinvigorated, and that internal and external opponents of the national project be subdued, nationalized, vanquished, and even excluded or expelled. If one argues, as Hollinger does, that the United States made great civic and social-democratic strides during its nationalist heyday from 1930 to 1960, one must also recognize how much the liberty and equality of that era were made possible by the coercion of the 1910s and 1920s. The Progressive nation builders enacted or acquiesced to measures meant to subdue certain groups and to exclude other groups. Woodrow Wilson sanctioned the subordination of blacks by permitting his cabinet members to resegregate their government departments. During World War I, government-endorsed campaigns for "one-hundred-percent Americanism" almost destroyed German Americans as a viable ethnic group and undermined other experiments in cultural pluralism. Campaigns against socialists and syndicalists, who were charged with being un-American and thus beyond the protection of the national community's laws, weakened American radicalism. Congress barred virtually all immigration from East and South Asia; after the war the Supreme Court ruled that a 1790 law made all East and South Asian immigrants ineligible for American citizenship. In 1924 Congress concocted an immigration restriction system to bar Europeans who were deemed racially inferior and politically suspect. America had shrunk its circle of the "we" and had substantially narrowed the range of acceptable cultural and political behavior.[26]

These repressive measures did strengthen the national community after a period of massive immigration and deep cultural diversity. And fortifying the nation, once liberals came to power in the 1930s, did reinvigorate the American commitment to democratic principles and encouraged southern and eastern Europeans and then blacks, Latinos, and Asians to claim their rights to life, liberty, and economic opportunity. But the success of this liberal nationalist project, I would argue, depended on the earlier deployment of the coercive power of the state against Germans, new immigrants, Asians, and political radicals. Liberal progress, in this instance, profited from the earlier period of repression and exclusion.

Today we might consider California's Proposition 187, the new federal law that denies government benefits to noncitizens (the Personal Responsibility and Work Opportunity Reconciliation Act of 1996), the new immigration law stripping illegal aliens of certain rights (the Omnibus Consolidated Appropriations Act of 1997), the "English Only" movement, and attacks on multiculturalism as measures similar to those favored by the Progressive-era nation builders. They aim to exclude certain foreigners and to demand that foreigners already in our midst conform to "American" values and behavior. However much liberal nation builders such as Hollinger may deplore such political developments, they should recognize how important the developments may be to bolstering the nation and thus to creating a political environment in which several nationalisms, including the liberal variety, will flourish.

If Hollinger fails to treat the national community as a structure of power that circumscribes choice and shapes the identities to which individuals and groups can aspire, his work nevertheless points toward a fuller understanding of nationalism's role in shaping Americanization. Historians have yet to take full measure of the powerful nationalism that settled over America in the 1910s and 1920s, suffocating the hyphenated identities that had thrived in the beginning of the century.[27] Historians must examine how the institutions of civil society—corporations, labor unions, universities, the mass media, churches and synagogues, and schools—weakened the pluralist character of pre-1917 America and accelerated national integration. (For a preliminary, though suggestive, study, see Janowitz 1983.) They must also explore the work of nationalism in politics, through Americanization programs, the disciplining of behaviors and peoples deemed un-American, mobilization for war, and patriotic rhetoric promising the poor and downtrodden social and economic equality. Only through such studies will we understand the mixture of opportunity and coercion that transformed eastern and southern European immigrants from reluctant Americans into American patriots and impelled their descendants to reinvent them as archetypal Crèvecoeurian men and women who, in alleged contrast to today's immigrants, quickly tossed off their heritages and became the best and most devoted of Americans.

MOST SCHOLARS REGARD the Crèvecoeurian myth as a poor guide to history. Few would argue that European immigrants quickly became American, that they found no significant obstacles thrown in their path, or that they enthusiastically melded themselves into a single unvarying race or culture. The rich literature produced between 1920 and 1970 has rendered each of these Crèvecoeurian claims untenable. But it would be a mistake to pronounce Crèvecoeur dead, for his last claim, that Americanization was, at bottom, an emancipation from old world constraints, has enjoyed a remarkable renaissance.

The enduring power of the Crèvecoeur myth may lie in its ability to merge with the Enlightenment ideal of freedom central to this country's identity. That ideal blesses the desire to throw off inherited customs and beliefs and to begin anew; a fresh start would put individual and social perfection within human grasp. In the eighteenth century that ideal became associated with revolution and nation building. Both the American and the French revolutionaries saw themselves as breaking sharply with the past and establishing new societies of new men. Hence, Crèvecoeur's vision of immigrants forming a new race meshed with the Founding Fathers' vision of launching a new nation. The two visions are two versions of the Enlightenment call for human emancipation. And at the level of mythology, emancipation—from kings, lords, tyrants, slavery, caste, tribes, superstition, poverty, patriarchy, even heterosexuality—is the very essence of "America."

No account of immigrant Americanization should neglect the drive to be free of the past, to reinvent one's identity, or to reinvigorate old identities. For many immigrants, America has held out the promise of a freedom greater than any they had known before. But as I have tried to show, becoming American cannot be understood in "emancipationist" terms alone, for immigrants invariably encountered structures of class, race, gender, and national power that constrained, and sometimes defeated, their efforts to be free. Coercion, as much as liberty, has been intrinsic to our history and to the process of becoming American.

An earlier version of this chapter was first published in *The Journal of American History* (September 1997): 524–58. Both versions are based on a paper presented at the SSRC Conference on which this volume is based and to the History Department of the University of Virginia. I would like to thank participants at both gatherings—and T. Alexander Aleinikoff, Nelson Lichtenstein, and Eileen Boris in particular—for their valuable feedback. I would also like to thank the following individuals for their careful readings of this essay: David Abraham, Susan Armeny, John Bodnar, Lizabeth Cohen, Sheldon Hackney, Matthew Jacobson, Russell Kazal, Elizabeth Lunbeck, Julie Plaut, Arno Mayer, Maria Mazzenga, Roy Rosenzweig, Robert Rubin, David Thelen, and Leah Williams.

NOTES

1. By culture they usually meant the political culture defined by two American beliefs: that all human beings are created equal and possess inalienable rights to life, liberty, and the pursuit of happiness and that all governments are the creation and servants of the people and derive their legitimacy from the people's consent. Immigrants, in the eyes of Arthur M. Schlesinger Jr. and other purveyors of the Crèvecoeur myth, embraced that political culture and became deeply attached to the American nation that espoused it. By stressing the political, Schlesinger and others implicitly emphasized the British contribution to this new culture, for eighteenth-century America was, in governance and political thought, profoundly British. Adherents of the Crèvecoeur school were not precise about how to reconcile such English roots with the emphasis on hybridity.
2. For insight into Crèvecoeur, himself, see Rischin (1981).
3. This essay focuses on works that have been influential in setting the scholarly agenda, whether general histories of immigration or monographs on particular

groups. The essay does not survey the large, distinguished, and complex literatures devoted to the history of particular groups such as Germans, Jews, Italians, Poles, and Irish. For other recent historiographical efforts to grapple with issues of Americanization and assimilation, see Kazal (1995) Barkan (1995), Morawska (1994); Salvaterra (1994); Zunz (1985). See also the valuable essays by Rudolph J. Vecoli (1979, 1985) surveying the fields of immigration and ethnic history. My own education in these matters has benefited enormously from the work of John Higham and Philip Gleason. See, for example, Higham (1955/1988, 1975; Gleason 1980, 1992). Comprehensive histories of the American immigrant experience include Dinnerstein, Nichols, and Reimers (1990), Archdeacon (1983), and Daniels (1991).

4. Although rightward-leaning Progressives insisted that immigrants conform to existing American values and left-leaning ones welcomed the infusion of immigrant traditions and values into American culture, through 1916 the two groups of Progressives cooperated (Gerstle 1994). On Progressives' efforts at Americanization, see Higham 1955/1988); O'Leary (1999); Lissak (1989); McClymer (1991); Carlson (1975).
5. On anti-Semitism at Harvard University, see Novick (1988, 172–73). For a biographical sketch, see Jones (1969). Marcus Lee Hansen is sometimes cited as a rival to Handlin in terms of influence on the field of immigration history, and his reputation is enjoying something of a revival. But he died in 1938 at the young age of forty-five, and over the following thirty years, his work generated far less interest and attracted far fewer disciples than did Handlin's (Hansen 1940a, 1940b). For an appreciation of Hansen, see Rischin (1979), and Kivisto and Blanck (1990).
6. The records on return migrants were problematic, and they frustrated efforts to develop precise percentages. Nevertheless, historians agree that the number of return migrants far exceeded what Oscar Handlin, Robert E. Park, and others thought possible (see Wyman 1993).
7. Patterns of migration established themselves, not from Greece and Italy to America, but from particular European towns to particular neighborhoods in American cities; Thistlewaite (1991a) used the phrase "chain migration" to describe this phenomenon.
8. The Irish and Jewish migrations were exceptions to this pattern. See Kessner (1977); Miller (1985).
9. The new immigrant historians disagreed over the importance of the immigrant family. To some, such as Virginia Yans-McLaughlin, Tamara K. Hareven, and John Bodnar, it was by far the most important cultural institution. They tended to see churches, musical societies, and newspapers as belonging to small, middle-class ethnic elites or to groups outside the ethnic community. But other historians, such as Herbert G. Gutman and Victor H. Greene, saw the family as only one of the institutions that gave ethnic groups cohesion.
10. For an interpretation of Americanization as a cultural weapon wielded by elites against the immigrant masses, see Bukowczyk (1984); see also Miller (1990); Miller (1985); Korman (1965); and Meyer (1980). The Bukowczyk, Korman, and Meyer articles have been reprinted with others on this theme in Pozzetta (1991).
11. I can testify to this personally. I was a graduate student at Harvard in the late 1970s, excited by Gutman, and intrigued by Handlin, but there could be no conversation with Handlin about Gutman.
12. This Americanization formula had survived the assault on German American ethnicity in World War I largely through the work of the Harvard-trained German Jewish philosopher Horace Kallen and his disciples. The German, or German American, roots of Kallen's pluralism have not, to my knowledge, been explored. On Kallen, see Gerstle (1994); Schmidt (1995); and Walzer, (1992). On the Germans' Americanization formula, see Conzen (1985).
13. Ethnic cultures became stronger in the United States than they had been in their native lands through a process of ethnicization. Fuchs (1990, 70–71) quoted Louis Adamic's claim that America allowed his *Slovenstvo* (love of Slovene transitions) "wider and fuller expression than I could ever have found had I remained at home." Fuchs did not note that the Slovenes of Europe had no state of their own and were denied autonomy in celebrating Slovene traditions.
14. The definitive account of the German American experience has yet to be written. Suggestive works include Luebke (1974); Detjen (1985); Holli (1981); Berquist (1984); and Kazal (1998).
15. In this regard, Sollors rehabilitated a theme that Handlin stressed in *The Uprooted* (1951/1973).
16. This may reflect the perils of joint authorship. Individual works of these authors are more successful in situating ethnic invention in specific historical settings. See particularly Gerber (1989); Conzen (1985).
17. One of the most interesting such efforts is Higham (1990).
18. This case has also been made in the 1920s. See Lippmann (1925); Lynd and Lynd (1929). On the 1950s critique of mass culture, see Pells (1985, 183–261).
19. Celebrity culture itself can be treated as a cultural invention that changed American culture. See Susman (1984).
20. Indeed, Sollors (1986, 247–48) offers a brief commentary on Yiddish theater that touches on some of the same points made by Howe.
21. Of the 300,000 Chinese who immigrated to the United States, approximately 150,000 returned to China. The government limited Japanese immigration through the Gentlemen's Agreement of 1907, in which Theodore Roosevelt prevailed upon the Japanese government to prevent Japanese male laborers from immigrating to the United States; in return, Roosevelt pressured the San Francisco Board of Education to stop excluding Japanese children from the city's public schools. The Immigration Act of 1917 barred immigrants from India, Siam, Arabia, Indo-China, the Malay Peninsula, Afghanistan, New Guinea, Borneo, Java, Ceylon, Sumatra, Celebes, and parts of Russian Turkestan and Siberia (Gulick 1918, 33); Konvitz (1946).
22. Crèvecoeur wrote a good deal about the Indians he encountered in his travels through Nantucket and Martha's Vineyard and the black slaves he observed in South Carolina. The decline of the Indian population and civilization in New England troubled him, and chattel slavery, especially as it was practiced in the southern states, appalled him. But even as he recognized the humanity of Indians and Africans, he could not envision them as Americans (1782/1912, esp. 102–9, 160–73).

23. The metamorphosis of the pop singer Michael Jackson from "black" to "white" and his witty play on racial identity in his music video "Black or White" may come to be seen as a symbol of our age (Begley 1995; Cose 1995; Morgenthau 1995; Sleeper 1993a, 1993b, 1997).
24. The phrase "interrelatedness of blackness and whiteness" is Ralph Ellison's; the phrase "incontestably mulatto" is Albert Murray's. Gary Nash constructs a new pantheon of American heroes, white men—John Rolfe, William Byrd, Patrick Henry, Thomas Jefferson, Sam Houston—who loved or married across the color line. The Founding Fathers must be turning over in their graves.
25. George Sanchez (1993) has borrowed and cleverly adapted an interpretive framework conceived by scholars of European ethnicity; in pulling the Chicano experience closer to that of Europeans, he may also have widened the distance separating it from that of African Americans.
26. As part of my book on American nationalism, I am writing an account of the coercive measures undertaken by the American state from 1910 to 1930, to reconstitute the American nation. For partial accounts, see Carlson (1975); Grantham (1955); Higham (1955/1988); Ichioka (1988); Lopez (1996); Luebke (1974); O'Leary (1999); Peterson and Fite (1957); Weinstein (1967/1984); Weiss (1969). Hollinger (1995, 144) understands that nations work best when they possess enough state apparatus to provide, in the words of Michael Ignatieff (1993, 13), "security and civility for their citizens." But he says little about how such an apparatus endows a nation—or those in charge of the state apparatus—with the power to determine who would be admitted and who would be kept out, which groups would be subjected to cultural or political discipline and which would be allowed to be free.
27. Some new works point us in the right direction, in effect elaborating on the suggestion of John Higham and Oscar Handlin fifty years ago that the early twentieth century, the 1920s in particular, was a pivotal moment when the forces of social control and conformity gained an edge over those of pluralism and individualism. See Bodnar (1992); Handlin (1951/1973); Higham (1981, 1955/1988); Kammen (1993). See also the stimulating essays in Bodnar (1996) and O'Leary (1999).

16 Immigration and Political Incorporation in the Contemporary United States

David Plotke

THE POLITICAL MEANING of the large immigration to the United States in the last two decades has been vigorously debated. In this chapter, I make two main claims about its effects and significance. First, immigration at recent levels does not endanger democratic practices. Second, political incorporation is less difficult for new citizens than it was at the beginning of the twentieth century. To sustain this view, I evaluate contemporary immigration in the context of American political development. I frequently compare immigration today with its features during the last major phase of immigration early in the twentieth century.

My argument moves from an account of political debates and institutions to a normative discussion. This sequence is appropriate to the subject. To make sense of immigration requires attention to normative issues about citizenship and democratic practices. These issues are a large part of the ongoing debate, which links claims about what immigrants do and what institutions require with arguments about how democratic political life ought to be conducted.

I argue that the United States should continue to allow large-scale immigration at current or even higher levels. I also argue that relatively open immigration should be accompanied by policies aimed at political incorporation. This approach should be based on recognizing the democratic value of immigration as well as the crucial role of boundaries.

Public debates about immigration now include arguments about immigration levels, characteristics of immigrants (country, education, skills), citizenship, economic and social change, culture, and national identity. In these debates, critics of immigration hold the initiative, even if policies continue to permit substantial new immigration.[1] As a result, arguments about immigration are largely negative. This dynamic leaves too little room for appreciating the value and benefits of immigration and focuses instead on just how bad the damage from immigration may be.[2]

Immigration brings energetic new participants into American economic and social life. Although its economic effects are uneven, over time there are substantial net benefits. Socially immigration offers an opportunity for Americans to encounter other cultures and languages as significant and durable realities, not as curiosities or vacation experiences.

The political case for immigration is often put defensively. It is framed as an obligation toward those in need, despite the cost. This obligation exists, but it concerns limited if important cases; it does not furnish an adequate general argument in favor of immigration. Today large numbers of immigrants and potential immigrants are leaving circumstances that are difficult but not wholly degraded or life-threatening.

In political terms, liberal democrats should generally favor immigration for three reasons. First, immigration is now one of the activities that together constitute a contemporary practice of free association. If a right to free association entails the freedom of members of a polity to leave it, there must somewhere be a possibility of entry. Otherwise there would be no way to sustain the exit option. More positively, the possibility of immigration is closely connected to several elements of free association. Potential members of a polity may wish to join it. Existing members of a polity may wish to associate with prospective members. These choices do not express unconditional rights, but they have real weight in a scheme of liberal and democratic political relations.

Second, immigration provides a regular means for reflecting on the meaning of American political institutions and commitments, through dialogue with those seeking to become citizens. Clearly immigration is not the only way to provide such reflection, but there are not dozens of other major possibilities, and we should welcome whatever real opportunities exist.

Third, immigration directly and indirectly encourages political innovation. Immigrants may enter politics with new ideas, or at least new perspectives on prevailing practices. Less directly, the entry of new members into a system of democratic political competition will over time cause new issues to arise and challenge conventional alignments. As part of political competition, such challenges can help sustain and develop democratic practices.

Immigration has political as well as social and economic advantages. These are compelling enough to make relatively open immigration policies the basic position for decent contemporary regimes. Yet the view that immigration to the United States now causes great and increasing harm drives much of our immigration debate.

Debates About Immigration

The recent immigration to the United States has been very large. Following the Immigration and Nationality Act of 1965, immigration went from two and a half million in the 1950s to four million, seven million, and nine million in the 1960s, 1970s, and 1980s.[3]

The political actions and views of recent immigrants are diverse, of course, but not too difficult to characterize in broad terms. Recent immigrants who have become citizens generally do not vote at high rates. At some points (and among some groups), their voting rate may exceed the low rate of the general population—this may have been the case in the 1996 presidential election. Taking new citizens as a group, they are centrist and mildly pro-Democratic. But they are not a political group—they are neither united in their political views nor self-defined politically as a coherent entity. New citizens undertake vigorous interest-group activity when they perceive major laws and initiatives as a threat to their own position or, in some cases, as a threat to the future prospects for immigration from their country of origin.[4] In the current American political context, these are not exotic attributes. Why, then, is debate about immigration so heated? And why is there so much anti-immigration talk when most political forces have an apparent interest in seeing whether they can forge ties with at least parts of the population of new citizens?

One reason that debates about immigration can readily become intense is because they usually raise questions about national self-definition. Thus, they are apt to cause latent divisions to become explicit. There are also strategic reasons for the sharpness of these arguments. Because views about immigration cut across conventional positions, the issue appeals to political actors who hope to gain by upsetting these alignments. Some Republicans, for example, hope the ambivalence of many African Americans about immigration will provide a basis for weakening their ties to the Democratic Party.

The disruptive character of immigration as a political issue provides a good starting point for understanding the fierce ongoing arguments. The political left and right are divided about immigration and new citizens.[5] Both contain a republican or neorepublican wing and a libertarian wing.[6] Neorepublicans want less immigration and more active public direction of the process of incorporation; libertarians want more immigration and less regulation.

Proponents of a neorepublican view on the right claim that limiting immigration will help to preserve American political and social values. This position has been expressed by Patrick Buchanan and others, who warn that recent immigration encourages political and cultural disorder. Schools and families are recommended for newcomers as key means of political incorporation. Some proponents of this view also advocate legal measures, such as English-only language restrictions, on grounds that these measures will accelerate incorporation and reduce the costs of immigration.

Right libertarians (whose views dominate in the editorial pages of the *Wall Street Journal*) support expansive if not completely open immigration. They strongly mistrust public guidance of incorporation, especially when it involves special services or programs for immigrants. This is not because they reject the aim of incorporation, but because they view markets as central and even sufficient for shaping new citizens.

Left libertarians also support more rather than less immigration, but they are skeptical of the market's role in political incorporation. This perspective is influential among academic critics of current immigration policies and within nongovernmental organizations committed to aiding immigrants. Proponents of this perspective criticize policies intended to produce more rapid incorporation, on grounds that they disadvantage immigrants while sustaining the political and cultural domination of elites. Instead, they recommend government economic and social policies aimed at improving the condition of newcomers.[7]

Left neorepublicans emphasize shared values

and experiences as the basis for a democratic culture and politics (Lind 1995). They are much more willing to limit immigration than are those on the libertarian side of the left, though they reject the most stringently restrictive proposals. Left neorepublicans envision a large role for public action in shaping incorporation; schools figure prominently, along with parties and civic associations.

In vigorous and unsettled debates, the main dynamic favors moderate versions of the views of the neorepublican right. These views dominate popular and elite debates with their insistence on limiting immigration and affirming values that are depicted as both American and republican. If moderate versions of the position of the neorepublican right do well politically, this is partly due to the weaknesses of the competition. The right libertarian view, which proposes open immigration plus market discipline for immigrants, has had real trouble in finding active mass support. Its proponents seem hostile to politics, to the point of preferring that levels of immigration simply be determined by market forces. Their view often appears insensitive to the immediate difficulties faced by many immigrants. It conflicts with the widespread public support for at least minimal aid to those in serious need.

Proponents of the left or center-left neorepublican views rarely get to the point of discussing seriously how they would limit immigration. Nor are they clear about how their mode of incorporation would differ in practice from that of the neorepublican right. Instead, they are preoccupied with calls to reinvigorate civic and political life.

The left libertarian view proposes open borders, expanded social welfare provision, and multiculturalism. Partisans of this view often seem to reject the very notion of boundaries, either as territorial limits that citizens of a country might enforce or as cultural and social limits to diversity within a polity.[8] Given these features, the left libertarian view is often effective as a critique of unfair practices, but not plausible as a framework for immigration policies.

Actual policies yield considerably more legal immigration than one would predict from the shape of the debate. There is also more immigration than one would predict from the results of public opinion studies; in a 1994 survey, 62 percent of respondents said immigration should be decreased, while only 27 percent said it should remain about the same.[9] In the last two decades, immigration law was reformed several times; the result of these measures is more openness to immigration than in preceding decades (Schuck 1998). Policies aim to regulate but not eliminate immigration and to increase the educational and skill levels of immigrants.[10]

The gap between policy results on the one hand and public opinion and the shape of the public debate on the other results from several factors. First, background themes in American politics celebrate immigration and make it hard to construct a plausible political stance that opposes new immigration in an unqualified way. Such a stance seems narrowly nationalist, not patriotic. As a result, anti-immigration sentiment is often ambivalent and volatile. Second, the opposition to immigration is normally diffuse and difficult to organize, while advocates of immigration can often operate through networks and associations that reduce the costs of political action. Third, debates about immigration and the treatment of recent immigrants occur in a context where courts are a major factor. On balance, the courts are likely to improve the position of new and recent immigrants by defending individual rights.

Although the neorepublican right has played a key role in shaping debates about immigration, there is little chance of its ideas being implemented in a way that would limit immigration to repeat the closure of the 1920s. As immigration continues, so will the gap between public opinion and policies. There is little indication that the debate about immigration will be absorbed into other political alignments. Thus, immigration will remain contentious.

Despite their popularity, even moderate versions of the position of the neorepublican right are too restrictive. These positions rely on dubious nativist and even racialist themes. They articulate a strong cultural and political opposition to new immigrants, sometimes with little understanding of their actual experiences and commitments. Thus, to take an important example, many immigrants from East Asia, Eastern Europe, and Central and South America are likely to regard democratic institutions as valuable in themselves. After the last several decades of political battles, who could say that Mexican, Korean, Russian, or Guatemalan immigrants know or care nothing about democracy?

A fair immigration policy in a democratic framework requires innovation beyond current alternatives. This policy should allow relatively high levels of immigration, within specified and recognized limits. A fair immigration policy should also aim to

FIGURE 16.1 Contemporary Arguments About Immigration

	Less Immigration	*More Immigration*
Less public direction of political incorporation		Right libertarianism Left libertarianism
More public direction of political incorporation	Right neorepublicanism Left neorepublicanism	

encourage political incorporation. Such a policy might best be developed from the southeast quadrant of figure 16.1; this figure illustrates the current debate.

This position is by no means self-evident, and it requires several types of justification. The next section of this chapter presents my main arguments. I claim that immigrants pose little danger to American political life. I also claim that although new citizens often find political incorporation to be difficult, that process is less daunting than it was at the beginning of the twentieth century. To support these arguments, I discuss American understandings of citizenship. The immigration debate intersects two areas of contention: the tension between civic and ethnic elements of American citizenship, and the large gap between activist norms of citizenship and undemanding practical standards.

I then assess the prospects for political incorporation via three historically important institutions: political parties, voting, and civic associations. Although it is important not to romanticize the treatment of immigrants by parties and civic groups earlier in this century, the relative decline of these institutions nonetheless spells trouble for political incorporation.

That discussion leads to an assessment of three means of political incorporation via nonpolitical forms: schools, market relations, and mass media. These forms are more effective today than they were in the early twentieth century. Together they more than compensate for the relative decline of parties and voting in political incorporation. In discussing political incorporation in both its political and nonpolitical forms, I emphasize the shift from local and specific modes of political incorporation to national and general forms.

The final section returns to the ongoing political debate. The debate could be improved, and racialist and nativist themes diminished, if the purely critical stance of the libertarian left gave way to a more programmatic conception. Such a shift would require recognizing the basic and legitimate role of boundaries in democratic politics.

My focus is on political institutions and on debates about the meaning and value of immigration. Thus, I do not attempt any sustained discussion of the economic effects of immigration. Nor do I consider the cultural dimension of immigration seriously, even though its alleged effects in this area are part of the political debate. A reasonable treatment of these issues, beyond a simple assertion of positions, would cause a long chapter to become even longer. Moreover, these matters are addressed by other chapters in this volume.

IS IMMIGRATION DANGEROUS?

To address political questions about immigration in the United States I focus on new citizens who have entered the country as immigrants. I use the terms "immigrant" and "new citizen" as equivalents in this context. I do not focus on how immigrants become citizens. Issues about the naturalization process, including rates of naturalization among immigrants from various countries, are analytically distinct from the question of how new citizens are incorporated into politics.

My approach would be unwarranted if only a small portion of immigrants wanted U.S. citizenship. Then it might make better sense to talk about the political action of all immigrants, whatever their citizenship status. Alternatively, if legal barriers to gaining citizenship were insurmountable—if all immigration today took the form of a large guest-worker or *bracero* program—too much of interest would be missed by focusing on new citizens. Neither is the case. Although the rate of naturalization varies across countries of origin, it is substantial within the first eight to ten years after arrival and larger over time.[11] Given the large proportion of immigrants who want and can gain citizenship, the precise rate of naturalization is not crucial for this discussion. There is much to be said about the political situation of immigrants who will not become citizens, but it is not my topic here.

I address two questions about relations between new citizens and American politics. First, do immigrants pose significant problems for American political institutions? Strong claims about the costs and dangers of large-scale immigration have been made. Yet immigration does not entail major dangers, even at the high level of the last twenty years.

Immigration does not threaten American political life partly because our politics is not very demanding. Today the normal practice of citizenship requires only limited political participation in the United States. Someone is regarded as a legitimate citizen if he or she obeys the law, period. Voting is encouraged but not required; the same goes for interest in public affairs. Immigrants who become citizens can readily reach this low threshold.

The idea that immigrants can meet conventional standards of citizenship without any great dangers arising for American politics is not obvious. Critics of immigration often assert that it directly threatens core features of American politics. In reality, immigration is not a major source of such dangers. But the immigration debate raises important political questions in a relatively direct way. The vivid presence of large numbers of immigrants affords a powerful opportunity for people to highlight their concerns. When someone declares that nonvoting immigrants exemplify our problems, and someone else warns that immigrants will cause trouble by voting as a narrow faction, both are making points about what they regard as defects of American political life.

There are good grounds to worry about politics in the United States. But immigration is not a major or direct source of the problems that most merit concern. Some critics of immigration would dispute this judgment. Others might partly acknowledge it but insist that our problems are so serious that it is acceptable to use almost any device to gain attention for them. A more plausible and interesting response (though it is not common) would depict the pressures arising from immigration as a key source of trouble at the margin. Even if immigration is not the original or primary cause of political trouble, one might contend, it strains institutions and practices already in distress. Immigration may even push a troubled political system toward irremediable deterioration.

My second question is: How do immigrants now fare with political incorporation? By incorporation I mean two related attributes of entry into a political system. A citizen (or group of citizens) is incorporated when legal and political obstacles do not prevent him or her from routinely performing the characteristic main activities of current citizens, and when he or she is recognized as a citizen. The first aspect of this definition signifies a status that is normally sufficient to protect individuals from legal and political assaults; their possession of a practical right to act politically would greatly raise the expected costs of such assaults. But the lack of explicit obstacles to participation defines only a limited notion of citizenship, with little political influence and little interaction with other citizens. To be a citizen in a sustained and effective way usually requires recognition by other citizens.

I use "political incorporation" rather than "inclusion" or "assimilation," two terms often applied to the political experience of new immigrants. Both terms suggest less conflict and disagreement than is common in political entry—to be assimilated or included in a polity seems almost to be absorbed into it. "Incorporation" is a better term because it indicates both inclusion and the formation of the group that is being incorporated. To say that a group has been incorporated into a polity signals the formation of that group as a new and distinctive part of the polity. This implies change in the polity, and the possibility of conflict between the new group and other political agents.

Immigrants today do face barriers to political incorporation. Some of the problems have a significant racial dimension. Yet on balance, the barriers to political incorporation are less daunting than at most points earlier in American history.

The political prospects of immigrants today are relatively good for three reasons. First, contemporary immigrants benefit from the expansion of citizenship produced by the democratic movements of the twentieth century, from female suffrage to the labor movement and the civil rights and Chicano movements.[12] The chances of a purely coercive exclusion of new citizens from politics have greatly declined. Second, the relatively low level of political involvement among most citizens enables new entrants to comply readily with conventional practices. Third, political incorporation is aided by the prevalence of abstract forms of political incorporation that do not rely on arduous efforts to gain local knowledge.

In the early twentieth century, Progressive writers condensed immigration and citizenship issues by asking who should be an American.[13] In addition to concerns about national identity, this question registered the enduring presence of deep political inequalities such that many adults were not full citizens in a contemporary democratic sense. Thus, in 1910 one could be an adult legal subject of the U.S. government without being entitled to vote or gain public office. This was the case for women, most African Americans, many Mexican Americans, and parts of several other smaller groups. In this context, the naturalization process was a matter of great political importance because it defined whether immigrants were to become full democratic citizens as well as legal subjects.

Now the number of exceptions to full political citizenship among adults has diminished greatly.[14] Instead of debating who is an American, we are more likely to consider what an American should do. The answer to the first question is that any adult legal subject of the United States is an American, in the full democratic sense.

In terms of political incorporation, this democratic shift greatly benefits new immigrants. The latter rarely face effective mechanisms for simply excluding them from politics, whether exclusion is official or through nongovernmental coercion. After the civil rights movement and decades of rights-oriented litigation, government policies are open to challenge if they target any group of citizens for exclusion from important areas of political life.[15] Certainly voting requirements and districting are not likely to be shaped so as to favor new immigrants. But that is not the right reference. In historical terms, contemporary barriers to explicit and discriminatory exclusion are notable.

A second reason for new citizens' relatively favorable situation regarding political incorporation concerns the practical standards for legitimate citizenship. Current citizens are not required to do much politics. New citizens can comply without great difficulty. Thus, the modesty of prevailing standards eases the way for new citizens to gain incorporation.

A third major change also favors the political entry of new citizens. There has been a shift toward forms of incorporation that are more abstract and general, notably mass media, education, the market, and national politics centered on presidential elections. Key local modes of political incorporation in prior periods, notably party organizations and communal associations, are less able to bring newcomers into the political system.

Newcomers are not greeted by and soon linked with local forms of political and social activity. They have to make their way into politics through abstract media whose referents are mainly regional or national. Yet this effort does not require a major accumulation of context-dependent local knowledge or a long passage of time. Entrants can utilize knowledge gained elsewhere (about how markets, schools, and mass politics work). It is hard to exclude new citizens from abstract and general forms of incorporation, even when there is considerable public hostility toward them. On balance, the shift to more general and national means of incorporation makes that process less difficult, more rapid, and harder to block.

To claim that political incorporation is now less problematic for new immigrants requires a frame of reference. I compare contemporary American practices regarding incorporation and citizenship with the experience of the first two decades of the twentieth century. Immigration then was a larger phenomenon than today in percentage terms. There was much debate about the political meaning of immigration and widespread fear that immigrants would be a source of dangerous political disorder (see Higham 1994; Mink 1986). Comparing immigration at the beginning and end of the twentieth century locates current debates in the American historical context.

Conflicts About American Citizenship

Concepts of citizenship figure prominently in arguments about immigration and political incorporation. Two groups of issues are contested: relations between citizenship and national identity in the United States, and competing views of citizens' political roles.

In relations between immigration and political institutions, the starting point should not be the dangers posed by new immigrants. Existing means of incorporation are adequate to produce competent citizens, as citizenship is now understood. Yet asserting this view does not fully address the concerns that arise about the political dangers of immigration. The reason is that much of the debate about the political effects of immigration is really an indirect way of taking up troubling questions about citizenship. What should American citizenship mean? What kinds of citizens should newcomers become, and how might that happen? Do newcomers threaten democratic politics? In these questions, two arguments are linked. One is about the political significance of new immigrants; the other is about what it should mean for anyone to be a citizen.

Citizenship and National Identities

What might new immigrants endanger? How could they be a political problem? The answers depend partly on how one views American citizenship. In comparative terms, citizenship in the United States is often described as civic or political, while German citizenship (for example) is called ethnic (Brubaker 1992). To define citizenship as political has two referents. One is to state and territory, taking all residents of a territory as subjects of a state, and thus as (at least potential) citizens. The other reference is to the political process within that state; newcomers can become citizens by showing they understand and agree with the political principles involved.

Ethnic citizenship is different. It means that an individual belongs to a cultural and social entity (a people or a nation) on grounds of heritage, language, religion, or other attributes. When members of this ethnic group form a state, full citizenship derives from ethnic membership. (See Preuss 1993.)

The contrast between political and ethnic citizenship remains useful in distinguishing the United States from countries like Germany in terms of who is recognized as a citizen and on what grounds. But this contrast is misleading if it is taken to mean that ethnic and national elements are absent from American notions of citizenship.

American citizenship has been primarily political in affirming that members of the United States are those who choose to organize their political life on the basis of liberal and democratic political principles.[16] Yet there have been ethnic, cultural, and racial elements in the predominant understandings and practices of American citizenship. These elements were certainly present when inhabitants of newly acquired territories were often excluded from full citizenship in an expanding nation. In the second half of the nineteenth century, it would have been hard to persuade the Spanish-speaking residents of California or Texas and their descendants that American citizenship lacked ethnic elements (see Almaguer 1994; Montejano 1987).

Influential conceptions of Americanism blur the distinction between political and ethnic citizenship. These conceptions depict Americans as not only agreeing with the main principles of the founding documents but also as members of a historically developed community. The founding documents and their political and constitutional elaboration are crucial in defining that community. But over time many citizens of the United States tend to conceive "America" in communal as well as political terms. In this sense, one can refer to American folkways and conventions as well as American constitutional commitments.

When American citizenship is considered in mainly political terms, it is commonly held that American nationality derives from the political elements of the founding and their later reaffirmation. American nationality does not express the political essence of a previously formed ethnic and cultural group. Yet that nationality is often construed as going beyond its political foundation. Thus, citizens are supposed to recognize each other as members of a united American people with democratic commitments.

The interplay of ethnic and political elements is evident in how American history is understood. The main narratives of the American founding, and of national renewal through the Civil War, focus on rebellion against unjust authority. First there is rebellion against Europe and monarchy. Then there is war against the slave power in the South (Foner 1980; Wood 1969).

This story has two sides. The main tendency is toward openness, based on the view that the founding and the Civil War articulate enduring political principles. Anyone who agrees with those principles is a potential citizen. This remains the basic legal requirement for naturalization.[17] The other tendency is toward closure—contemporary Americans conceive the national narrative as an account of how their own distinctive community was formed and sustained. To belong fully to this community requires a connection to the nation's history beyond agreeing to liberal and democratic principles.[18]

Contemporary immigration highlights the tension between more open and more closed notions of membership in the United States. If the national community is historically defined and clearly delimited as both a political and cultural order, there may be no room for the Guatemalans, Haitians, or Vietnamese who are arriving in substantial numbers, given their very different origins and experiences. If the national community is instead considered as an expression of political agreement among free and equal citizens, it is relatively open. Large numbers of people who are willing to affirm basic political principles should then be admitted. It is especially difficult to deny entry to those who might be called politicized immigrants. These are people who may not have directly experienced political repression, but whose lives have been deeply influenced by political turmoil and struggles about democratization, such as immigrants from Central America and Eastern Europe.

While a sharp contrast in comparative terms is more complex when seen up close, political notions of citizenship and relatively open interpretations of American identity together continue to define the United States as a nation of immigration. A political conception of American citizenship implies that large numbers of potential Americans now exist outside the boundaries of the United States, among those willing and often eager to adhere to the main principles that frame American political practices. Given the growing recognition of liberal and democratic principles across nations in recent decades, the number of potential Americans in this sense is on the rise.

The prevailing political notion of citizenship strongly encourages openness to immigration, even if current citizens disagree with pro-immigration policies. Critics of immigration run major political risks (if they aim to build majorities) when they make an explicit and aggressively ethnic case for exclusion. They can be attacked for making judgments based on pure prejudice. Their vulnerability to such charges is due in part to their failure to specify the content of an American community that lies beyond explicit political principles yet contains and even constitutes political agreement. Yet this failure does not make anti-immigration beliefs disappear. Instead, the presence of numerous immigrants whose appearance and experiences mark them off from the majority of current citizens remains as a reminder, painful to some, of the barriers to making a liberal and democratic polity into a taut community.

Three Forms of Citizenship

Even when a political or civic concept of citizenship predominates, the choice to allow substantial immigration requires reflection on what newcomers are supposed to agree with and do. What does citizenship mean? Should a citizen simply obey the law, or should he or she actively strive to participate in and sustain democratic practices?

Today immigration highlights tensions between norms and practices of citizenship. If we understand American citizenship as vigorous and sustained political engagement amid shared cultural understandings, it readily follows that immigrants are a political problem when they differ culturally from present Americans. And this sort of argument is the basis for a good deal of criticism of immigration. However, if it is enough to obey the law and pay occasional attention to national elections in order to be regarded as a decent citizen, then immigrants present no problem so long as they respect the law and are not antagonistic to democratic political procedures.

Immigration (when it often leads to citizenship) requires that we say what is expected of citizens. This means defining the shape and extent of the political commitment required for decent forms of political order. And what is said to immigrants and new citizens is declared to the entire polity. Should citizens actively seek a life of civic engagement? Or is it sufficient for them to respect the law and the procedures that produce and sustain constitutional forms? There are three main conceptions of citizenship in the contemporary United States.

One view centers on the notion of a law-abiding citizen. This citizen obeys the law without showing much interest in politics. He or she may sometimes vote but is not greatly concerned with national or local politics. This view entails a minimal conception of what citizenship entails. Its proponents include conservative liberals who are suspicious of political as against market forms of decisionmaking. Here citizenship norms do not require or even encourage political involvement. Such involvement is a choice that law-abiding citizens should not be compelled to make. This view is widespread among Americans who express distaste for politics and affirm strong commitments to work and family. Political involvement is expected to provide few rewards, especially compared with the main alternatives.

A second conception centers on the figure of the concerned (or active) citizen. Such citizens pay attention to politics. They usually vote and sometimes participate in campaign efforts or civic associations. Their primary concerns are not mainly in the political sphere, but this disinterest is due more to the attraction of other activities than to a basic rejection of politics. These citizens often feel they should be more politically involved. Their sense of civic responsibility provides a standard they often do not meet. In sum, concerned citizens are interested in but not preoccupied with politics.[19]

A third conception of citizenship is neorepublican or participatory. It centers on notions of active self-government and political commitment by individuals and holds that citizens should be highly active in politics. The well-being of the political community should be a central personal aim. And politics is regarded as a crucial part of a decent life, a major source of individual fulfillment and self-respect.[20]

To regard this conception as amounting to a rigorous adherence to the norms affirmed by a concerned citizen is misleading. It fails to grasp the high importance that neorepublican conceptions ascribe to politics in shaping worthy individual lives. Here political involvement is both a strong intrinsic good and a vital means of sustaining the benefits of a worthy regime. Many political and social activists, in parties, interest groups, movements, and civic associations, support this view.

Citizenship Norms And Practices

At the level of norms and in political thought, neorepublican and activist liberal conceptions have much more strength than in terms of practices. Relevant norms are widely expressed in public statements by political leaders, in civics classes, and elsewhere. These norms contain neorepublican and participatory elements within a framework dominated by the model of a concerned and responsible citizen. Practices, however, are mainly divided between activities appropriate to a concerned citizen and those of a law-abiding citizen (actual neorepublicans are rare) (on participation, see Verba, Schlozman, and Brady 1995).

There is a big gap in contemporary American politics. *Widely accepted norms propose much more political engagement than is characteristic of citizenship practices.* Minimal citizenship is what most people actually do, even if it is not often endorsed with enthusiasm. Despite broad support for official norms of concerned citizenship, practical judgments are very tolerant of minimal citizenship. In the contemporary United States few are stigmatized who obey the law, vote occasionally in presidential elections and rarely at other times, pay infrequent attention to national political affairs, and decline to participate in local parties or civic associations.

It is possible to estimate the distribution of individuals among these forms of citizenship. Studies of voting and political and civic participation indicate that the third group of minimal or law-abiding citizens is clearly the largest, including at least two-thirds and probably more of the population. Concerned citizens—who regularly vote in local, state, and national elections and routinely engage in significant further political and civic action—make up at the most one-quarter and more likely one-fifth or less of the population. Neorepublican or participatory citizens are scarce, amounting to no more than 5 percent of the total.[21]

A vivid sign of the gap between norms about citizenship and citizenship practices appears in the large difference between actual voting rates and the public's evaluation of the importance of voting. Voting rates reach 50 percent of those eligible only in presidential elections and fall steeply in state and local elections. Yet when people are asked to assess the importance of voting, over three-quarters respond that voting should be a core obligation for citizens.[22] A good citizen votes regularly and responsibly. The gap between official norms—which opinion surveys are apt to elicit—and practices is clearly very large. Half or more of the population fail to meet political commitments that they recognize.

The resulting tensions make the situation ripe for political conflict. One common response amounts to splitting norms into two groups. Official and widely respected norms still center on the model of a concerned citizen, while citizens develop a set of less demanding norms for which the practices of a minimal, law-abiding citizen are good enough. One does not have to posit sinister or mysterious psychological processes to see how easy it might be to locate some of the resulting concerns in clearly demarcated groups like immigrants.

Given these divergent views and practices, what are new citizens likely to hear about the kind of citizens they should be? Naturalization procedures have often been stringent, as if they were intended to produce concerned citizens who are active in political and civic life and view the public good as a major aim. But new citizens are required to make few actual commitments beyond their assent to the Constitution. They are entitled to a bundle of political rights (a vote) and a bundle of social opportunities (including entry to various markets). The question of whether to engage in politics is left to them, and in the contemporary context there is relatively little expectation that they will do so. This amounts to a minimal conception of citizenship.

New citizens have to be addressed formally and directly by the government and thus by prior citizens.[23] In this context, a real problem arises. If we say that citizenship simply means obeying the law, we acknowledge that the valued model of a concerned and politically active citizen is not to be taken very seriously. But if we say that the model of a concerned citizen really should be implemented and supported through public action and strong norms, what do we make of the routine absence of so many of its recommended practices?

The first route makes it easier for newcomers (and longtime Americans) to feel they are proper citizens. But it means a clear rejection of many commitments that most Americans claim to take seriously regarding the democratic virtues of political participation and civic engagement. Yet the second option is made very problematic by the fact that few Americans are eager to bring their normal practices into compliance with activist (much less neorepublican) political norms.

In sum, immigration raises serious political issues when the need to speak to new immigrants about their political responsibilities and opportunities draws attention to conflicts about citizenship. These conflicts concern the extent to which American citizenship does and should contain ethnic elements, as well as the character of the political practices expected of responsible citizens. As immigration highlights these conflicts, it is understandable that concerns about a decline in the vigor and quality of citizenship practices are expressed in terms of the problems allegedly posed by immigrants. In extreme forms, the claim is that immigrants threaten our present community. More plausibly, the idea is that continued large-scale immigration makes it harder to sustain an already uncertain national political and cultural integration.

In reality, the views and practices that together form a model of minimal citizenship gained broad acceptance over a number of decades. This model was dominant well before the new immigration became a major topic of debate. Recent immigrants did not devise this model. They encountered it when they arrived. In this minimal conception, all citizens have the same basic political rights, irrespective of their views, social position, origins, or capacities. Having these rights entails no obligation beyond the important commitment to obey laws produced through legitimate processes.

If citizenship ought to be minimal in this way, most immigrants can rapidly become good citizens. Moreover, when this model of minimal citizenship prevails, claims about the ethnic character of American citizenship seem to lack any functional basis. It cannot be claimed that strong ethnic ties are needed to constitute minimal citizens. (This might be argued more plausibly regarding a vigorously republican form of citizenship.) Instead, ethnic claims about citizenship seem to be open expressions of prejudice, with little serious political content.

This conclusion is not an endorsement of minimal citizenship. In my view, American political life would be improved if citizenship practices more closely resembled the model of a concerned citizen. (It would take a separate chapter to justify this position.) Here the point is that citizenship models are crucially a matter of political choice. These choices should be made as clearly as possible. Such clarity is harder to gain when longstanding problems are attributed to external sources (immigrants) rather than being located in the prior course of political development in this country. Thus, it is important to distinguish between a politically effective metaphor (the new citizen disengaged from politics) and an actual condition—the large gap between citizenship norms and practices in the United States.

Parties, Voting, and Unions—Problems for Political Incorporation

Amid disagreement about the meaning of citizenship, how should we think about immigrants and political incorporation? In what ways is immigration a problem for American political institutions? When do immigrants face major problems of political entry? I address these questions first by looking at how political institutions operate vis-à-vis immigrants. I start with parties. (On American parties in the nineteenth and early twentieth centuries, see McCormick [1986] and Silbey [1991]; on parties in the last half-century, see Shafer [1991] and Wattenberg [1996].)

Political Parties at the End of the Century

In the early twentieth century, political parties played a major role in political incorporation. This was accomplished locally by urban machines and nationally through party competition (Banfield and Wilson 1963; Erie 1988; Wolfinger 1972). Immigrants were involved in local politics by the leaders of political machines who made it their business to turn out the vote. In exchange, new citizens gained services and material benefits. The machine story is usually told with a combination of approval (for the incorporation that did occur) and a muted acknowledgment of problems.

Yet the political incorporation accomplished by urban party organizations was uneven. Although machines delivered material benefits to immigrant communities, the scale of this distribution is often overstated, while the negative political effects of clientelism and patronage networks get too little attention. If delivering benefits meant a sort of recognition, it did not have to mean more than the thinnest form of representation. The quality and extent of political participation were circumscribed in most cities dominated by machines, and this limited the incorporation of immigrants. In some cases, one can describe this restriction as part of the purpose of the machines, whose leaders sought to defend the main parties against labor-based political challenges (see Ansell and Burns 1997).

Nationally the post-1896 political configuration was not friendly to the political aspirations of recent immigrants from southern and eastern Europe, even though growth and open immigration counted for a great deal (Burnham 1982a). In this Republican-dominated party system, the leading forces favored economic growth, national integration, modernization, and cultural assimilation. The Republican political leadership was opposed by highly factionalized Democratic forces, some of whom were (for sectional and religious reasons) often antagonistic to new immigrants (see Burner 1968; Cohen 1990; Schlesinger 1957–60). Small leftist parties provided important means for new citizens to voice complaints, especially on labor issues, but these parties rarely offered viable ways to escape political marginality (Shannon 1967; Weinstein 1954).

The major political shifts that occurred from 1928 through the next decade transformed the political landscape for turn-of-the-century immigrants and their children. The Republican Party system was dismantled, and new space was opened for working- and lower-middle-class immigrants to have a much greater political role. Via the New Deal and the labor movement, they were linked with an emergent Democratic political order (Plotke 1996). The process of building this new regime diminished the power of state and local political machines.[24] Machines did not disappear, and Roosevelt was often happy to ally with them. But the New Deal moved decisions toward the national level and reduced the role of machines in supplying jobs and positions.

The evolution of the Democratic political order put an expanded national state at the center of American politics. Yet over time the relative decline of the Democratic Party and other nonstate political forms had a surprising result. By the time the Democratic national regime fell apart in the late 1960s and early 1970s, urban machines had often disappeared. Local and state party forms were relatively weaker, and most political structures had become more national.

Today political parties are weak means of political incorporation and education. As local organizations, they often barely exist. As national organizations, they link political entrepreneurs in loose networks. Party competition remains an important device that can stimulate political incorporation. Relatively discrete immigrant communities can be targets for local partisan initiatives. But such concentration is not the rule. Thus, both the diversity and geographic dispersion of contemporary immigrants lessen opportunities for their political incorporation via conventional political organizations.

The majoritarian bias of America political institutions has often been tempered by federalism. National minorities may be local majorities, and there they can gain real power. Yet the forms of new immigration may not be conducive to such efforts. The nationalization of American politics diminishes the rewards of local success for everyone. And because of the great diversity of recent immigration, by class, nationality, and ethnicity, forming local majorities based on particular immigrant groups is harder and less likely, although immigrants are highly concentrated in particular states and metropolitan areas.

The diversity of contemporary immigration is a major reason that opportunities are limited for local political efforts based on immigrant communities. People from the five leading countries of immigration to the United States made up an average of 70 percent of all immigrants in the four decades beginning in 1881. From 1981 to 1990 the cognate figure was only 40 percent. From 1881 to 1920 the average contribution of the three leading countries to all immigration in each decade was 58 percent; the equivalent figure for the 1980s was only 22 percent. From 1881 to 1920 the single leading country contributed an average of over 22 percent of all immigrants; in the 1980s the figure was 14 percent.[25] Beyond the leading countries, the number of countries making a significant contribution to immigration has also increased.

This diversity among immigrants reduces the chance for political entrepreneurs and party organizations to win local office by seeking to represent particular immigrant groups and communities. Even in metropolitan areas where new immigrants are highly concentrated, electoral districts usually contain substantial numbers of several different immigrant groups.

Immigrants who have become citizens will usually be among the large and heterogeneous publics addressed by contemporary parties as these parties search for money and votes. Parties now feature entrepreneurial candidates and media-based forms of publicity and organization. They try to get out the vote during election campaigns. Candidates appeal to voters via direct mail, radio, and television. Many new citizens are reached by these efforts, but they are usually addressed as part of larger publics. Those who are running electoral campaigns seek voters and thereby try to attract new citizens as well as others. But campaigns always operate at the margin, seeking the most effective use of limited resources. In this context, the search for the next likely vote is rarely apt to focus on groups of new immigrants whose political identification is unclear and whose prior voting record may be nonexistent.

In this context, does immigration threaten parties? It is hard to see how this could happen. For the most part, immigrants simply increase the number of constituents to whom parties need to address themselves. If some groups of immigrants remain outside the reach of the parties, problems arise in terms of democratic norms. For the parties themselves, however, low levels of incorporation are not necessarily a problem. Contemporary parties already fail to involve millions of potential supporters (Piven and Cloward 1988; Wolfinger and Rosenstone 1980). This has not destroyed their position, even if it has helped to weaken their authority.

To demonstrate that immigrants really endanger parties would require an argument based on something other than the number of immigrants and the general weakness of parties. It would require showing that we are nearing a hazardous situation, partly owing to nonvoting and limited political participation. It would require showing that immigrants are distinctly uninvolved. Then one might claim that adding many more immigrants could tip a fragile balance and damage political parties in dramatic and serious ways. No one has made a plausible case for this view, and it is hard to imagine one.

Immigrants do not pose much of a problem for contemporary parties. Yet the parties' weakness poses a problem for notions of concerned or neorepublican citizenship. Parties are in principle crucial means for connecting citizens to the electoral process. When parties are not good at incorporating new political forces, this is a problem even if they continue to propose candidates and fill offices. Thus, in democratic terms, it matters a great deal whether the main substitutes for party organizations can incorporate and mobilize citizens. This problem makes it reasonable to be very concerned about interest groups, civic organizations, movements, media networks, and political action committees. But there is no compelling reason to address this concern via arguments about the effects of new immigrants. Reducing immigration would not strengthen parties in any discernible way.

A better question is whether the nationalization and relative decline of parties create serious problems for new immigrants. These changes do limit a classic form of political incorporation for immigrants. But the loss should not be overstated. The old machines were not as effective, and certainly not as democratic, as many have claimed. And not all earlier immigrant groups were happily and smoothly incorporated into politics. There were cases of nondemocratic dependence, and there were instances of exclusion, as when immigrants from one nation were a small minority in a city whose machine was dominated by other ethnic groups. If local parties are less attractive as means of entering politics, they are also less effective as means of blocking entry for those not favored by a dominant local or state coalition.

On balance, new immigrants do suffer from the weakening of local political parties. The damage caused by the shift from machines and local parties to entrepreneurial candidates and national parties is significant; immigrants with fewer economic and social resources are probably hurt most.

The Decline of Voting

From the early twentieth century on, there has been a large decline in voting rates in the United States.[26] The main exceptions to this decline occurred during the political mobilizations of the 1930s and after the elimination of voting restrictions for blacks in the South (Andersen 1979; Davidson and Grofman 1994). The decline has taken place over decades, rather than being condensed in several brief periods. It mainly preceded the expanded immigration of recent decades (see Burnham 1987; Stanley and Niemi 1995). Today voting rates are so low that we cannot really regard voting as required for legitimate citizenship, though it is widely seen as a worthy activity.

How does this change look from the double perspective of political institutions and recent immigrants? Regarding political institutions, immigrants are not a serious problem when they decline to vote. If new citizens vote at a lower-than-average rate, they do not differ from many other groups. Low voting rates make clear that the model of a concerned citizen is not widely practiced. If immigrants are not participating vigorously, they do not jeopardize an actual political community composed of concerned (much less neorepublican) citizens. Again, the claim would have to be made that nonvoting by immigrants will detonate more serious problems. This claim would not be easy to defend: with so many nonvoters, what is the problem with adding even quite a few more?

For immigrants' political incorporation, however, the decline of voting has a negative significance. If regular voting were a stronger practical norm, and most people usually voted, then more political incorporation would result from routine electoral competition. Since voting rates are so low, especially for state and local offices, that mode of political incorporation has diminished for new citizens.

Immigrants who do not vote will not get much attention from the government or parties. This is clearly a problem for democratic principles. But it is not necessarily a serious problem for the major political forces now on the scene. Some analysts warn that the growth of a large population of new citizens who are politically and socially marginal may result in political disorder and even civil violence, as in Los Angeles. But such warnings are not likely to motivate major political forces to place the electoral mobilization of these new citizens at the center of their attention.

Although the low voting rate hinders political incorporation, the extent of the damage is uncertain. If new citizens want to vote at high levels, they face fewer barriers than immigrants met at the beginning of this century. Recent immigrants benefit from the decades of civil rights and voting rights litigation that has undermined barriers to voting. The overall decline in voting even has an ironic side: it may open space for new immigrants by removing an obstacle to their recognition as citizens. If regular voting is not really required for citizenship, immigrants who do not vote cannot be stigmatized as bad citizens.

Civic Associations

A notable literature analyzes and regrets the loss of community in contemporary political and social life in the United States (see Putnam 1993b, 1995). It too often relies on a romantic view of the past, and it takes little account of the expansion of interest groups and movements that has occurred since the 1960s. Nonetheless, this literature plausibly depicts civic and communal groups and networks as weak and diffuse. If critics exaggerate the forces of decline in American civic life, they call attention to a striking gap between civic life in the United States, which still appears robust in comparative terms, and political participation, which does not (Verba et al. 1995, 70–71).

If civic groups and networks are thin, immigrants create additional political strains only insofar as one wants to encourage a more than minimal practice of citizenship. A law-abiding citizen is no more obligated to join an association than to vote. Thus, it is hard to see how new immigrants would strain political institutions via their effects on associational life. It would require an ingenious argument to show that the weakness of associational life makes the political system vulnerable to destabilization by new entrants. The easy rejoinder is that new immigrant groups can create their own associations. Thus, rather than straining political forms, new immigrants might complement and enrich them through their own new civic efforts.

More serious problems arise if one asks whether a weakened civic life greatly hinders immigrants as they seek political incorporation. If civic groups and associations are fewer and weaker, the implication is that such groups are less available as means of political incorporation for newcomers. In democratic terms, it is not sufficient to encourage immigrants to build their own associations. Politically significant groups require time, money, and relations with preexisting associational networks, and all these resources are scarce for most new immigrant groups.

Given the decline of parties and of voting, the thinness of institutions between individuals and the state can create problems of incorporation, especially if the aim is to produce concerned or participatory citizens.

Labor Unions and Political Incorporation

In principle, labor unions might be significant associations for immigrants. Yet relations between trade unions and immigration are not easy. There is labor market competition between immigrants and unionized workers, and between nonunionized working-class citizens and less skilled newcomers (Borjas, Freeman, and Katz 1997).

Unionization might serve as a major means of social and political incorporation for immigrants—and unions have an interest in making this happen. But a broad and sustained surge of unionization among immigrants is not likely. The weakness of unions today makes them cautious about taking major initiatives (see Brody 1980, 173–257; Rogers 1990). Immigrant workers are often located in sectors that pose major economic obstacles to unionization (for example, small labor-intensive firms in highly competitive markets). In a political context that is not friendly to unions, obstacles to organizing illegal immigrants are especially daunting—and effective labor organization in some settings would require joint action by legal and illegal immigrant workers.

The diversity of recent immigrants is also relevant. When immigrants from different countries work in the same firms and industries, obstacles to cooperation can be daunting. The union drives of the 1930s were several decades removed from the massive immigration of the early twentieth century. Not only had the political situation changed radically, but the social and cultural incorporation of the earlier immigrants had helped to produce a new American working class, with milder internal cleavages than at the beginning of the century (see Cohen 1990; Gerstle 1989). The years of greatest union strength—the mid-1930s through the mid-1960s—were also years of limited immigration.

One might still expect bursts of union activity among immigrants, especially when workers from a single country or region are concentrated in an industry. But it is hard to imagine unions playing a large role in the political and social incorporation of immigrants in the United States today. A labor movement that has failed to organize many workers of any kind in the last two decades is not likely to build unions in sectors where working-class immigrants are found. (On labor's decline in the 1980s and 1990s, see Freeman and Medoff 1984; Troy 1990.)

The decline of unions is a problem for American political institutions and for many new immigrants. For institutions this decline means that claims by economic elites about the political requirements of economic growth often go uncontested. For new immigrants, unions' weakness limits political incorporation among the economically most disadvantaged groups. These immigrants also need the protection from unregulated labor markets that unions can provide by increasing low wages, establishing grievance procedures, and providing a voice in labor relations.

Ironically, this may be the only case where immigration is doing real damage to an American civic and political institution. Immigration is in no sense a primary cause of unions' weakness. As table 16.1 shows, the long decline of American unions was under way in the 1960s and 1970s, before the recent immigration. There are several far more important sources of union weakness, including employer hostility and unions' own difficulty in devising strategies for renewed growth. Yet immigration probably made a further negative contribution in the 1980s and 1990s, especially at the low end of the American labor market.

It may be that the condition of labor unions has reached a tipping point, so that even modest negative pressures can have large effects. It is not credible to make this case about most American institutions—adding yet another group to the electorate whose members vote at low rates, for example, is not likely to cause major new decay. But unions have declined so far over the last three decades that further reductions in their strength will cause them to disappear from large parts of the economy. Thus, any additional strains can trigger severely negative consequences.

TABLE 16.1 Union Membership, 1930 to 1995

Year	*Total Union Membership (thousands)*	*Percentage of Labor Force*	*Percentage of Nonagricultural Labor Force*
1930	3,401	6.8	11.6
1935	3,584	6.7	13.2
1940	8,717	15.5	26.9
1945	14,322	21.9	35.5
1950	14,267	22.3	31.5
1955	16,802	24.7	33.2
1960	17,049	23.6	31.4
1965	17,299	22.4	28.4
1970	19,381	22.6	27.3
1975	19,611	20.7	25.5
1980	22,366	20.9	24.7
1985	16,996	18.0	18.2
1990	16,740	16.1	16.3
1995	16,359	14.9	15.1

Source: For figures from 1930 to 1970 I have used U.S. Department of Labor, Bureau of Labor Statistics (1979, table 150). For later years I rely on successive January issues of *Employment and Earnings*, U.S. Department of Labor, Bureau of labor Statistics.

For union leaders and organizers the situation is dreadful. If they urge restrictions on immigration, they are likely to alienate groups with which they need to collaborate. If they wishfully deny that immigration sometimes intensifies labor market competition and hinders unionization, their practical problems are not reduced in the least.

Beyond the distinctively difficult case of unions, immigrants do not have negative effects of any real weight on American political institutions. Parties, voting, and civic associations all have their problems, which in each case were well elaborated prior to the large immigration of the last two decades. The new immigration has not revitalized these institutions, but that is not a reasonable standard. Regarding political institutions, the case against immigration is very weak.

As regard the political incorporation of new citizens, parties, voting, civic associations, and unions have all declined. We have not lost a golden age when immigrants were happily and smoothly welcomed into American politics. Nonetheless, these declines signal real problems of political incorporation.

The Political Contribution of Nonpolitical Institutions

Given the problems posed for new citizens by the decline of several major political institutions, do other resources exist for political incorporation? Have there been compensating shifts elsewhere? Positive changes can be found, primarily in settings outside the party and electoral systems.

Schools for Democracy?

American education has always been implicated in debates about citizenship (Levine 1996; Ravitch 1974, 173–80). Arguments for public education stress its capacity to encourage political incorporation. This point has been made in more or less democratic forms (to produce democratic citizens, or to avoid political challenges). There are signs that schools in the early twentieth century focused more on civic education than they do today. The need for civic education was widely discussed, often in terms of the challenge posed by massive immigration. When I began to investigate this topic, I thought there had been a substantial net decline in schools' contribution to the political incorporation of newcomers. I now think the contribution of schools to political incorporation has become more important.

It is hard to define the right comparison. It would be mistaken to take high school civics classes or college classes about government from the early years of this century and consider them as a central part of the political socialization of immigrants. Most immigrants then received little high school education, either in this country or in their country of origin. The best approach is to compare the overall civic education received by the average (immigrant) student at both points in time. In those terms, the extent of civic education has increased over the course of this century, and the educational system today can play a larger role in political incorporation.

Immigrants who arrive as children and young people today receive much more education in the United States than they did early in the twentieth century. Moreover, the level of education of recent adult immigrants is much higher than in prior major phases of immigration. One study found that in 1988, two-thirds of the foreign-born population over the age of twenty in the United States had graduated from high school. One-fifth had received four or more years of postsecondary education. A critic of contemporary education might respond by saying that more years of bad education in the United States or elsewhere is not necessarily a good thing from the standpoint of American citizenship. Extensive professional training acquired in other countries is not the same as a democratic civic education. The first point confuses current educational problems with the massive expansion and democratization of secondary and postsecondary education. Education was very limited for much of the population in the early twentieth century. The second claim misses the significance of the global spread of democratic commitments in recent decades—computer specialists from India or medical professionals from the Philippines now often arrive with considerable knowledge of democratic practices.

There are fewer obstacles to education serving as a means of political incorporation for immigrants than at earlier points in this country's history. Even linguistic barriers have declined. This claim runs counter to newspaper accounts of schools in Los Angeles where students arrive speaking dozens of different languages. In reality, because of the international dominance of English as the language of commercial and intellectual life and of mass entertainment, a larger part of the immigrant population arrives with some knowledge of English than was previously the case. Spanish speakers make up the largest linguistic group among recent immigrants. Compared with many immigration experiences, the divide between Spanish and English is relatively easy to cross. In the early twentieth century, many immigrants' first language (Polish, Hungarian, and so on) was much further from English than is Spanish. Comparing this country with other major contemporary immigrant destinations, the problems of transition from Spanish to English are less than those of going from Turkish to German or Arabic to French.

Increased levels of education now provide expanded means of political incorporation. This shift illustrates how modes of political incorporation have become more general and abstract. In schools people learn general principles about citizenship, participation, and politics rather than gaining local political knowledge via membership in a party or civic organization.

The Market as a Site of Political Education

The market is not primarily a place to learn about politics, yet such learning does occur. Elements of strategic action that are strongly encouraged in the market can be used in making political choices. And market agents sometimes learn that cooperation is better than pure self-aggrandizement. (On individual learning in the market, see Lane 1991, 237–59; on the social dimensions of market activity, see Streeck 1992.)

The common observation that the economy is not only markets but also institutions and discourses is pertinent for political incorporation. Routine action in market contexts leads many individuals to engage in varied forms of association. When participants in market relations acquire organizational as well as strategic knowledge, they gain skills that are politically relevant.

Compared with the early twentieth century, market participation also entails political learning in more specific ways, because markets are politically regulated. Thus, many market participants need to learn something about labor law, zoning, antidiscrimination law, or environmental regulation (see McCann 1986; Sunstein 1990). This way of learning about politics involves a large part of the population, as long-term participation in the market has become the normal condition for the great majority of people in the United States. Women typically spend large parts of their adult lives in paid employment. For recent immigrants, labor-force participation is certainly presumed (with some variance based on family structures and commitments). Thus, whatever political learning and incorporation is likely to result from participating in market relations will probably occur for most immigrants, even if that learning often occurs in harsh circumstances.

The point is not that the market provides an ideal civic education. A critic of my sketch might reply that it is hard to see how market-based political education could extend much beyond a minimal notion of law-abiding citizenship. Some of what people learn about strategic action amounts to knowing how to be effectively noncooperative. And what people learn about politics from the market varies greatly by income and occupation.

These points express a reasonable skepticism of the contemporary inclination to attribute all virtues to market relations. Yet they understate the degree to which most market activity contains cooperative and associational elements. Participation in highly regulated contemporary markets imparts skills and experiences that are important for learning how to be a citizen.

Market learning about politics tends to be strategic and instrumental. That may or may not be normatively desirable, but in the context of the actual practices of citizenship in the United States, it is not problematic. Market participation is a reasonably good way to learn something about how to combine respect for rules with action on behalf of one's own interests—and these are central elements of a model of minimal citizenship. Given the broad participation of immigrants in market relations, that setting is for many newcomers a crucial way to learn about American social and political life.[27]

Mass Media and Political Learning

New immigrants enter a polity and culture where mass media are central for communication and debate about politics. Television, radio, and newspapers are a major source of political information and education. Compared with the early twentieth century, the amount and even the quality of information available to new immigrants have increased, especially regarding national issues. (For recent studies of media and political campaigns, see Iyengar 1987, 1991.)

Clearly there are problems with learning about politics through television and newspapers. News and entertainment shows are often misleading (see Gitlin 1987; Jamieson 1996; Page 1996). But what is the point of reference? In the early twentieth century, churches, communal networks, and political organizations played a relatively larger educational role. There was often a more vital local press. Yet the information provided by these sources was, on balance, thinner, less reliable, and more thoroughly partisan than what is now available to recent immigrants. Newcomers today are exposed to the vast mass of information and pseudo-information that streams through the media each day. It is not always easy to distinguish the accurate from the distorted, and both from the fantastic, but this is a common cultural problem rather than a special burden for immigrants to bear.

It is also likely that the massive export of American mass media products has significant effects on the political side of immigration to the United States. Through radio, television, and movies, the United States has become much more familiar to people in many parts of the world than it was early in the twentieth century or even two decades ago. To the extent that claims about the Americanization of international culture are right, new immigrants are apt to arrive already knowing something about their new country. This reduces the degree to which new immigrants might strain political institutions. And it reduces obstacles to political incorporation for immigrants, who enter an already half-known country. Electronic media convey large amounts of information about politics and political norms to prospective and actual immigrants to the United States. Thus, they play a major role in political incorporation—again, in an abstract form.

As with the market, this form of political education is best suited to producing minimal citizens. Those who pay attention to the mass media are not compelled to participate in politics in other ways. Even if one hopes that the audience for information about national politics contains many people who will seek to participate further in politics, nothing requires them to do so.

A Balance Sheet

Have political changes over the course of the twentieth century made immigration more or less problematic for American institutions? Have obstacles to the political incorporation of new immigrants been increased or reduced by those changes?

Immigration at or near recent levels does not endanger political institutions. Parties, voting, and civic associations have indeed declined. This has not been due to immigration, which was greatly restricted for much of the century. The large immigration of the last fifteen to twenty years occurred after the main processes of political decline were well under way. Immigration at expanded levels may have helped to sustain that decline, but it has not made a large or decisive contribution.

With regard to the second question, declines in party organization, voting rates, and civic associations have made conventional modes of political incorporation less available to immigrants. Yet the expansion of schooling, the presumption that adults participate in markets, and the growth of mass media all provide expanded means of political incorporation.

How should we sum up these gains and losses? It is hard to know what measure to use: How many points in the national voting rate equal one additional year of education per citizen? For present purposes, these measurement problems need not be resolved. Political incorporation means a practical capacity to do what "normal" citizens do as well as recognition as a citizen. The decline in conventional forms of political incorporation has accompanied a shift in citizenship norms and practices. The prevalent model is now one of minimal, law-abiding citizenship. Given this model, the decline in conventional political modes of incorporation is more than compensated for by the expansion of more general and abstract media of incorporation (schools, the market, media). Means of political incorporation clearly now exist that are sufficient to allow most immigrants to engage in minimal citizenship practices. Contemporary immigrants also benefit considerably from the elimination of secondary categories of citizenship (women) and virtual subjection (African Americans in the South) that played a large role in American politics in 1900 (Rogers Smith 1997, 347–409).

Yet the recognition of (naturalized) immigrants as full citizens often remains contested. Opponents of immigration in general or of specific immigrant groups may charge that immigrants do not appear to be real Americans. Sometimes this is simply ethnic or racial hostility. There are cases, however, when political criticism of recent immigrants focuses on their alleged inability to act as concerned or even participatory citizens. Here the conversation becomes complicated, because analysts are criticizing immigrants for not complying with standards that most Americans do not really uphold.

Such criticism of immigrants might be called displacement, or even hypocrisy. These labels will not clarify or advance the arguments, because critics of immigration are able to make connections with real public anxieties about the decline of citizenship. A more adequate response to critics who charge that immigration has damaged the practice of citizenship would open up the debate about citizenship to encourage a full consideration of why parties and voting have decayed for so long. In this framework, the very modest role of immigration can be properly assessed.

The international pool of potential Americans—people willing and able to be law-abiding citizens in the American constitutional system—is large and expanding. This raises questions about immigration policies. But there is little reason to give priority to questions about possible negative effects of immigrants on American political institutions.

A Democratic Immigration Policy?

Opposition to immigration on grounds that it strains democratic political institutions and practices in the United States is unwarranted. Yet there is certainly a need for debate about contemporary citizenship norms and practices, and their relations. For this debate we should move the focus away from the alleged political inadequacies of immigrants. Whatever the difficulties entailed in the ascension of a model of minimal citizenship, new and recently arrived citizens are not responsible for them. Clear examples are provided by twenty-eight-year-old lower-middle-class native citizens who have never voted or by citizens who vote (when they do) on the basis of only one issue and show little interest in other public matters.

On democratic grounds it might be better if the model of concerned citizenship prevailed. In this model, a large majority of citizens would vote regularly in presidential elections, while majorities or at least strong minorities would vote in other elections. Lesser but substantial minorities would take a serious interest in varied public political issues, and many would participate in political campaigns and civic efforts. Severe restrictions on immigration (or harsh treatment of immigrants) will not make this form of citizenship any more widespread in American politics.

Nonetheless, debate about immigration will continue. To conclude, I consider how this debate might be changed (and improved) by rebuilding one position within it. To do so requires taking up a basic question about immigration: On what grounds, if any, is it legitimate for a democratic polity to have an immigration policy?

I have argued that as regards politics the main arguments against immigration in the United States are overstated or wrong. My account might seem to endorse a pure libertarian view that immigration should simply be open. Commitments to free association and expression do go a long way toward establishing a premise in favor of immigration. But open immigration per se is not a viable or defensible position.

Open borders may be better than unfairly closed borders. Diversity is certainly better than coercive and imposed unity. But the left libertarian position is exhausted in such critiques and has little capacity to reshape the current debate. This position typically rejects arguments made in terms of American national interests and dismisses the economic and social objections made to immigration. These moves allow conservative neorepublicans to speak on behalf of general interests regarding both national and welfare concerns. Moreover, the left libertarian suspicion of efforts at political and cultural integration allows opponents to dominate even the political and cultural arguments. What remains for left libertarians is to fight against legal or policy measures that humiliate and discriminate. In recent years there have been a number of such measures, and the libertarian left performs a valuable service in contesting them. No exit from political marginality results, however, because it is evident that an obligation to treat visitors and noncitizen residents decently does not create an obligation to open borders.

The strategic problems of the libertarian left register theoretical difficulties that have long existed for broad currents of liberal and democratic thought. As many have noted, liberal democrats have trouble with boundaries. Perhaps because their universalistic principles seem to recognize no barriers, actual boundaries are not theorized. They are regarded as facts of political life—in the background yet unavoidable.[28]

Two currents of contemporary political thought tend to reject boundaries. One current is cosmopolitan and liberal. Drawing on critiques of nationalism and ethnic and religious chauvinism, its proponents affirm a common humanity across borders (Carens 1995). They propose a world of universal citizens with equal rights. In principle, those rights should operate everywhere—borders encumber individuals who should be able to go where they want.

Another current rejects boundaries owing to skepticism about nation-states (and institutions in general). Advocates of this view see boundaries as arbitrary means of containing populations and securing domination. In criticizing boundaries, they cite debatable ideas about global economic trends to support the claim that nation-states are decreasingly important. As with many claims of economic determination, the economy is assigned responsibility for producing the political effects that are most difficult for that theory to justify. In this case, the idea is that because globalization is rapidly effacing the role of nation-states, we should question and perhaps even reject national boundaries and national citizenship. (See Glick Schiller, Basch, and Blanc-Szanton 1994; see also Raskin 1993.) By overstating the decline of nation-states, analysts are relieved of having to show why it would be good if national boundaries were to diminish and even disappear regarding citizenship.

Advocates of a cosmopolitan liberal view and postmodern critics of national boundaries are influential. This is partly because their formulations respond to a discomfort with boundaries, especially national boundaries, that is widespread in liberal and democratic theory. For cosmopolitan liberals (and some postmodern theorists), one root of this unease is a misunderstanding of what it means to be committed to the idea that liberal and democratic principles are generally applicable. Because these principles apply very widely, if not everywhere (this reasoning goes), boundaries that divide and separate citizens are without any real justification.

This conception confuses two features of liberal and democratic principles. One is their range: How large is the set of areas to which they can reasonably be applied? The other feature is their form: How can these principles best be applied? These features of liberal and democratic principles are analytically distinct. They refer, on the one hand, to the extent of the political and social space to which liberal and democratic principles apply, and, on the other, to how that space can be organized.

The proper range of liberal and democratic commitments is very broad. It is generally right to be skeptical of those who claim that such principles, while worthy, do not really apply in a particular setting. But this wide range does not answer the question of form. In fact, these principles cannot take shape in a single encompassing structure, as a universal polity.

Boundaries make it possible for liberal and democratic commitments to gain a durable presence. They are not an unfortunate imposition of messy empirical realities onto an ideal world. If particular boundaries are conventional or traditional, the need for boundaries has principled bases. That need would not disappear if adherence to liberal and democratic principles became general and unqualified. In fact, unbounded liberal and democratic entities could not exist.

Liberal democracy is not a sort of default political condition. It has to be built; to do so requires inclusion. Inclusion cannot occur without limits. Otherwise one is included in nothing. Thus to build any specific democratic polity means establishing boundaries. No boundaries means no inclusion and thus no democratic politics.

The basic role of boundaries is linked to two core themes of modern democratic theory: deliberation and decisions. Neither dimension of democratic theory plays a large role in the arguments of those who advocate open borders. These currents affirm a third strand of democratic theory not only as very important but as a commitment that trumps others. This strand centers on minority rights. In cosmopolitan formulations, minority rights are conceived as individual opportunities to exercise liberties and make plans across borders. In postmodern terms, minority rights are construed as means of resistance for dominated or marginal groups.

A conception focused on maximizing one democratic value is not best understood as an ardent and focused way to support democracy, whatever the view of its proponents. Such a conception is problematic because sustaining a democratic polity requires balancing commitments. Core commitments include extensive deliberation, equality in making legitimate decisions, and protecting minority rights. To show the democratic character of boundaries—and to indicate the problems with a conception of democracy centered almost exclusively on minority rights—I consider whether it is legitimate to have an immigration policy.[29]

Can a Democratic Polity Limit Immigration?

If liberal democracy requires boundaries, does that mean a democratic country is entitled to limit immigration? This might seem like a ridiculous question, but it is not. There is a good sign that it is not ridiculous: we do not believe a liberal democratic country has a right to an emigration policy. Individuals' right to leave their country of birth and citizenship is reasonably derived from primary liberal and democratic commitments.

Yet the legitimacy of an immigration policy is often simply presumed rather than argued directly. And many arguments consist only of gestures that affirm the durable reality of a nation-state, implying that by definition, the state (or perhaps the people) can decide who enters its territory.

Most of the arguments to be made in defense of an immigration policy have been weakened by the deep changes that have occurred in the last century in democratic countries regarding the status of outsiders. Historically outsiders were considered in one of two ways: as enemies, or as people who had a claim on mutual aid in dire circumstances but were otherwise not politically or legally relevant. Today outsiders are widely recognized as actors with rights. This does not mean that a universal right to full political citizenship exists anywhere one chooses. Instead, across democratic countries there is a presumed right to a thin civic citizenship, to free expression and association. From at least World War II to the end of the century, international commitments to human rights have greatly enhanced the position of noncitizen residents.

In the United States and a number of other countries, noncitizen residents and even nonresidents can exercise notable civic rights. A noncitizen cannot be prosecuted for engaging in an otherwise permitted form of speech or religious activity. Noncitizens are generally allowed to join whatever organizations will let them do so. Thus, the right of citizens to associate with noncitizens is nearly symmetrical.

In this new context, left libertarian critiques of immigration policies go further to claim that almost any restrictions are coercive. A democratic country really has no more right to control immigration than emigration. Anyone should be able to enter a country if he or she wishes to do so, perhaps conditional on an agreement to comply with the law.

Is this conception valid? Arguments for open borders have considerable resources, especially when they draw on more conventional liberal formulations regarding human rights. These arguments cast serious doubt on most claims about limiting immigration. Here I will look briefly at the limits of arguments in favor of an immigration policy based on national and cultural identity, economic welfare, and rights of free association among current citizens.

Cultural Identity

Immigration policies are often justified in terms of the need to preserve a nation's cultural identity. If this need were deemed legitimate, it might warrant legislation and regulation about the cultural practices of citizens. But it would not warrant the exclusion of sincere applicants—people who seriously promise to be (or soon become) French or Danish. And it certainly could not justify excluding citizens from adjacent or nearby countries with a similar language and culture (Peru and Ecuador, Rwanda and Burundi, Ukraine and Belarus). Many democratic countries, and virtually all of the richer ones, confront a vast supply of sincere outsiders. That is, many potential immigrants would in good faith seek to enter fully into a new culture if given the opportunity, so long as the conditions of entry were not degrading. In this setting, the cultural or national claim in favor of an immigration policy cannot be sustained—what can be justified is a set of filters to remove the least sincere immigrants.

Economic Need

A state socialist country facing severe shortages of all kinds might have a good argument for an immigration policy—scarcity requires exclusion. But the few such countries today have never had a big immigration problem. Perhaps a poor country next to an even poorer country could make a similar argument about the limits imposed by scarcity (for example, the Dominican Republic blocking immigration from Haiti).

Yet countries with regulated market economies, especially prosperous countries, have ample means of handling the social costs of immigration. These can be attached to immigrants as individuals, or to the individuals and groups within the receiving country who benefit most directly from transactions with immigrants. This problem is sure to produce conflict, but not uniquely so; what is involved is reaching a fair and acceptable distribution of costs. Then the level of immigration would be set mainly by the domestic demand for foreign labor and the foreign demand for entry into a country. We might say that the sum of regulatory efforts concerned with these economic activities was an immigration policy, but that would stretch this term well beyond its current meanings.

I do not mean to minimize the regulatory problems that result from immigration. But regulatory problems are rarely cited as grounds for prohibiting transactions altogether. Why should the transactions that constitute a large part of the immigration process be prohibited rather than regulated, while markets exist in such areas as pollution rights? Many economic arguments against immigration are in reality protectionist claims accompanied by nationalist and communitarian appeals.

Immigration as an Admission Policy?

In the context of free association, the argument for an immigration policy usually works by analogy: a polity is like a club in being able to choose its own members. To prohibit the members of a club from having an admissions policy jeopardizes their right to exist as a distinct organization.

People certainly have the right to form clubs, which thereby have a right to exist. But this social argument for an immigration policy founders on the problems with the analogy between a club and a polity.

The problems become clear if one takes the perspective of the applicant for admission to a club. He or she can also claim a right of association, that is, he or she wishes to associate with the people who are in the club. We allow them to exclude him or her in large part because of two background assumptions that are rarely spelled out: there exists something like a market in clubs, so that failure to gain membership in any single club does not lead to full social exclusion; and clubs mainly operate within a distinctive sphere of status and sociability, rather than serving as gatekeepers for opportunities to obtain other major goods. In this situation, there is a conflict between the rights of the members of the existing association to define it as they wish and the desire of an individual to affiliate. But no grave harm results from giving more weight to the right of current members to associate freely. The individual in question has real choices, so that if a club rejects his or her application, he or she may be disappointed but not thereby oppressed.

Where there is only one club, and that club controls economic and political as well as social resources, membership policies are a different matter. When an individual requests admission to a state, he or she is not usually facing a real market in states—do not worry if Canada would not admit you, try Spain. And given the richness of modern citizenship, seeking admission to membership in a polity is a means of gaining access not only to sociability and status but to a wide and crucial range of opportunities.

If the club analogy were followed, we would say that immigration should be open to everyone who meets the standards of membership currently practiced by the state. Anyone can join who is willing to respect the laws and participate appropriately in the process by which they are designed and implemented. The current standing of noncitizens as people who are entitled to thin civic rights would seem sufficient to justify them in choosing to join a state and comply with its laws and procedures, given their own right of association. Why should the criteria for their admission differ from those for continued membership? Thus, the special monopoly form of the state and its privileged gatekeeping status limit the worth of the club analogy as a basis for an immigration policy.

I asked whether a liberal democratic country can develop and enforce an immigration policy? There appear to be strong objections to a policy based on claims about cultural maintenance, economic needs, or the associational rights of current citizens. Perhaps there really is no good basis for an immigration policy.

The Political Bases of Immigration Policies

Yet there are a strong and, in my view, decisive political arguments in favor of an immigration policy. A commitment to open borders fits most easily with the element of democracy centered on minority rights. Minority rights, construed in cosmopolitan or postmodern terms, can be the starting point for arguing that prospective new entrants should be admitted at will. From a cosmopolitan perspective, every individual outside the polity (including noncitizen residents) in a sense constitutes a minority. Each such person can reasonably ask why all legal and political aspects of citizenship should not be made available to another person whose basic rights deserve respect.

In postmodern terms, each minority in a polity would be entitled to enlist as many members of their group from elsewhere to join them as they wished. And others might be entitled to enter on grounds of membership in minority groups whose history significantly intersected that of the receiving country. There is a big problem with these ways of opening borders—it would be very difficult even to designate a minority in a polity truly without boundaries. But it might be possible to reconcile minority rights and open borders for a period.

The libertarian rejection of immigration policy has less plausibility in terms of the deliberative component of democracy. New entrants to a discussion should generally be welcomed. But there would be serious problems regarding time constraints if the discussion could always be reopened and sustained by new entrants. And there would be further problems due to extremely varied levels of understanding of major political issues. Although these issues might be addressed by a proper scheme of representation, it seems doubtful that democratic deliberation and entirely open borders would go well together for long.

A policy of open borders—no immigration policy—has an affinity with the democratic commitment to minority rights, though there are logical problems. Such a policy would be in considerable tension with a commitment to serious deliberation. And it would be in severe conflict with the third democratic commitment I identified earlier: a commitment to making decisions by politically equal citizens. If one wants to sustain this feature of democracy, doing so presents basic and probably insuperable obstacles to a pure politics of open immigration. Without boundaries—that is, barriers to entry and an immigration policy—democratic political continuity is not possible. The forms of calculation and trust required to make decisions among equal citizens in a democratic polity cannot be sustained.

To show why an immigration policy is required to maintain democratic continuity, I will use an example based on a single decision: voters' choices among parties to form a national government.

Imagine that Country A has no immigration policy. Any number of people can come and claim citizenship at any time. Then consider an election in that country, with two parties of roughly equal strength contesting for national power. Party 1 believes it is likely to lose a close election. To avoid defeat, that party goes to Country B and asks a large number of its citizens to become citizens of Country A and to vote for it, offering various inducements. Seeing its victory in danger, Party 2 makes a similar move toward Country C.

In this process, the possibility of making reasonable political calculations would disappear rapidly. Any trust among parties would soon be gone. There would be several roads to the early breakdown of democratic political practices.

First, decisions would be unstable. If the size of the electorate were indeterminate, extreme instability would result. From one election to the next, all major decisions would be open to reversal. At first this might seem only to exaggerate the normal process of political competition. But it would soon become clear that no coherent political course could be established and sustained. Losing actors would simply try to change the membership of the polity. This would result in a rapid and thorough devaluation of deliberation and participation in political life.

Second, results would be illegitimate. Losers of an election would reject it on grounds that the outcome was unfair. It was not based on a coherent democratic process. The results would be purely a function of competing forces' capacity to import supporters. In this context, actors would no longer regard equal citizenship as even an abstract or ideal characterization of the polity. Elections would not be regarded as valid without that basic legitimation, and actors would question whether to obey laws derived from them.

Given such pressures, political life would likely dissolve. Prior to an election, competing parties would anticipate instability. This would reduce the expected value of winning. Actors would also expect the legitimacy of the results to be in question. This illegitimacy would further reduce the value of winning; it would also increase the danger of losing, because one would expect to be subject to an illegitimate and insecure government. Given these bleak prospects, political actors would move to preempt the results of electoral contests, at first through efforts at pacts among competing forces. No such pacts could last, given the lack of trust. Consequently, elections would become tests of extrapolitical strength. Initially the focus would be on money to create new voters, then on coercion to limit an opponent's recruits—and the electoral framework would soon be ruptured.

In sum, an unbounded polity would devalue politics within it. Political actors would not trust that democratic decisions would be sustained. They would not regard the elections as legitimate. And a significant number of political actors would take measures to subvert elections they no longer regarded as having a democratic character. They would question the potential gains and fear the possible losses of elections that became direct tests of resources and force.

One might respond by pointing out that in any polity where less than 100 percent of those eligible vote efforts could be made to mobilize new voters. What is the difference between new voters within and outside the polity? Within the polity, political actors know who the nonvoters are and how to try to reach them, though there are no guarantees of success. These variables are open to democratic modes of calculation whose premise is the need to constitute a majority among equal citizens. Outside the polity, the supply of potential voters is virtually unlimited. From within the polity, an electoral process whose members are in principle unknown appears arbitrary. Perhaps judgments might be made through a calculation based on the willingness of competing parties within the polity to expend resources to import favorable voters. But if such process and calculations based on it were set fully in motion, equal citizenship as a political matter would disappear.

A democratic political process requires a fixed maximum number of participants at any time. Otherwise, routine strategic calculation based on democratic premises is not possible. Political forces cannot make reasonable judgments about what to do to achieve majorities in favor of projects they support. For those who believe this is no great loss because strategic calculation should not be part of democracy, it is necessary to recall that democracy is about making decisions. These decisions are to be made as the result of deliberative processes, with due attention paid to minority rights—but they are nonetheless decisions. They have to be made amid various types of scarcity, and they are backed by legitimate force. In reaching such decisions, strategic calculation is unavoidably part of the story.

An immigration policy defines the number of new entrants available for political projects and thus for competition. So long as the prospective number is known, the rate of increase from one to the next election is open for debate. The rate can be high without jeopardizing the ability of actors to make strategic judgments in a democratic framework. In that respect, the rate of immigration into the United States in the last several decades is acceptable. The key point is that debates about immigration should have an outcome that specifies the size of the new electorate within a definite range. This requirement derives from basic features of democratic politics as a means by which equal citizens can make decisions.

In this context, the limits of a left libertarian view of immigration are apparent. Adherents of this position oppose virtually any immigration policy on grounds that it impedes an actual or prospective minority. But this position cannot serve to reconcile commitments to immigration and to democratic processes. To make a decision fairly requires knowing who is entitled to participate in it.

There are very good grounds for taking relatively open immigration as a starting point. Yet the reluctance of proponents of left libertarian views to acknowledge democratic commitments other than minority rights is analytically unwarrented and politically disabling. It is hard to make a serious critique of the deep hostility to politics of the right libertarian position if one shares its suspicion of democratic decisionmaking. It is also hard to criticize neorepublican views, in their right or left variants, if one simply affirms diversity and heterogeneity and rejects any sort of incorporation.

To develop a reasonable and compelling immigration policy that is consistent with democratic principles, it is important that the left libertarian view be reshaped. The resulting position may be so different that it no longer fits into the northeastern quadrant of figure 16.1. Instead, it might well occupy a zone that is now mainly empty. The southeastern quadrant includes positions that prefer more rather than less immigration, not only on economic or mutual aid grounds but as a desirable attribute of a democratic politics. At the same time, to value immigration involves recognizing the positive importance of borders in constituting democratic politics. This recognition in turn requires specifying the number of immigrants to be accepted. Positions in this quadrant include a strong commitment to public means of incorporation. The aim is not cultural but political, to achieve a common recognition of liberal democratic procedures and a common capacity to participate in them.

Immigration into the contemporary United States is, on balance, a very good thing. Immigration should be relatively open while policies should aim to facilitate political incorporation. I have developed this position via two routes. One route is historical and comparative, based on judgments about the effects of immigration and the experiences of immigrants in the United States in the twentieth century. The second route is normative and focuses on the role of democratic commitments as regards immigration and its limits. These arguments define a framework in which immigration policies might be developed. To do so with full attention to practical complexities is a project that reaches well beyond the present effort.

Thanks to Ann Guthmiller, Shelley Hurt, Damien Jackson, and Mark Redhead for their research assistance and comments.

Notes

1. Perhaps the most widely discussed recent work on immigration is also one of the most negative assessments of its effects; see Brimelow (1995).
2. There is a structural reason why one might expect the debate about the social and economic effects of immigration to have a more negative character than those effects might warrant: the costs of immigration are often concentrated and visible while the benefits are widely diffused.
3. These estimates include all forms of immigration. Legal immigration was 3.2 million in the 1960s, 4.5 million in the 1970s, and 7.3 million in the 1980s, or about three-quarters of the estimated total (U.S. Immigration and Naturalization Service 1992, table 2, "Immigration and Selected Country of Last Residence, Fiscal Years 1820–1991").
4. Claims about the political action of new citizens requires caution because of the small number of studies, problems of small sample size, and uncertainty about the scale of reporting errors; see DeSipio (1996), Jones-Correa (1997), Ong, Bonacich, and Cheng (1994), and Waldinger and Bozorgmehr (1996b).
5. Most of the basic commitments of the contemporary left and right were forged in the 1930s, early in the cold war, and in the conflicts of the 1960s. Immigration was not a central public issue at any of these points. Thus it rarely appears in Nash's (1979) intellectual and organizational history of conservatism in the first decades after World War II or Morone's (1990) assessment of popular politics in the four decades beginning with the Depression.
6. By neorepublican or republican I mean views for which a strong, common public life is a vital and primary good, one sufficiently valuable to trump at least some significant rights claims by individuals. By libertarian I mean positions that oppose most government activity save that required to preserve order and protect individuals' physical security.
7. A key position in the immigration debate, which I call left libertarian, is not often expressed clearly in positive terms. It more often appears as a sharp critique of proposals from the neorepublican right, such as anti-immigration ballot measures. A common formulation of this position in academic writing is to say that one or another proposal by the neorepublican right is unworkable because deep structural forces preclude it. A sophisticated form of this argument underlies Alejandro Portes and Rubén G. Rumbaut's valuable study *Immigrant America* (1990). They say that severely limiting immigration is not feasible because of the deep forces that favor it, many of them initiated from the United States (234). See also Jacobson (1996, 71).
8. Soysal (1994) focuses on Europe rather than the United States. She claims that her analysis is not meant as a normative argument, but it is likely that someone presenting the left libertarian case in a theoretically serious debate would return frequently to her book.
9. Questions about immigration were asked in 1994 as part of the General Social Survey of the National Opinion Research Center (NORC). Respondents were pessimistic about the economic effects of immigration: 62 percent doubted that it would bring economic growth, and 85 percent thought it would increase unemployment. Opposition to immigration was cultural as well as economic: 68 percent of respondents said that immigration would make it harder to keep the country united. NORC figures are cited in Mitchell (1996).
10. Recent changes in social welfare policy reduce the benefits that immigrants can expect, both because the overall scale of benefits has been reduced and because permanent residents were a notable target of benefits reductions. The 1996 Welfare Reform Act (public law 104–193, sects. 401, 403, 431, August 22, 1996) restricted the eligibility of "qualified aliens" (mainly permanent residents and people with refugee status) for federal, state, and local benefits programs, including TANF (the successor to AFDC), SSI, and food stamps.
11. Portes and Rumbaut (1990, 120) focus on naturalization rates in their chapter on politics. They cite data showing that within ten years of immigration 25 percent of the 1970 immigration cohort had been naturalized. In this data the peak year of naturalization was the seventh, though naturalization remained significant in the tenth year; thus, one would expect the figure eventually to reach at least 40 percent for that cohort. That figure is confirmed by a later study (cited in DeSipio and de la Garza 1998, 83), conducted by the INS, which found that, as of 1992, 39.6 percent of immigrants admitted in 1977 had been naturalized.
12. The Chicano movement in the 1960s and 1970s helped limit the prospects of a durable guest-worker program on a large scale. Although the *bracero* program was eliminated in 1964, before the full emergence of the Chicano movement, that movement nonetheless helped to block the construction of new forms of partial citizenship (see Barrera 1979, 113–30; Galarza 1977).
13. Most Progressives wanted to incorporate immigrants and believed government could play a major role. For some commentators, such as Horace Kallen (1924), incorporation entailed cultural pluralism, while others, such as Herbert Croly (1914), favored a more unitary national result (see also Wiebe 1967, 209; Rogers M. Smith 1997, 412–24; Bourne 1977).
14. This change makes the naturalization process less interesting from a political perspective. In principle, that process now has only one outcome—producing a democratic citizen. There are no serious prospects of reestablishing distinct levels of legal citizenship either among present citizens or among newcomers. For a critique of the political status of guest workers in democratic countries, see Walzer (1983, 56–61).
15. The historic events were the passage of the Civil Rights and Voting Rights Acts in 1964 and 1965. The Civil Rights Act (public law 88–352, 288) posits that completion of the sixth grade merits a presumption of literacy. This provision greatly limits serious efforts to restrict the voting of new citizens.
16. The civic view of citizenship is linked with the legal reality of citizenship by birth in the United States by a theory of implied consent. Thus, immigrants who become citizens must explicitly and actively consent to specified political and legal principles, while those born here are presumed to consent. Obviously this understanding raises dificult questions, but I will not consider them here.

17. "No person shall be naturalized as a citizen of the United States upon his or her own application unless that person can demonstrate a knowledge and understanding of the fundamentals of the history, and of the principles and form of government, of the United States" (National Archives and Records Administration 1998, 594–95).
18. Most formulations are neither purely civic nor entirely ethnic. In a mainly civic formulation that links immigration and citizenship, Schlesinger (1991, 121) concludes: "The future of immigration policy depends on the capacity of the assimilation process to continue to do what it has done so well in the past: to lead newcomers to an acceptance of the language, the institutions, and the political ideals that hold the nation together." Civic formulations become quasi-ethnic in Bellah and others (1985).
19. Images similar to what I am calling a concerned citizen play a significant role in the main pluralist studies of American politics in the 1950s and 1960s. Empirical research revealed a large gap between actual practices and republican norms. Images of concerned citizens appeared as a substitute for the highly active citizens who could rarely be found. But even these images were a good deal more participatory and activist than the majority of American citizens appeared to be.
20. In addition to the neorepublican works cited earlier, see Barber (1984) and Sunstein (1988).
21. In 1992, 55 percent of those eligible voted for president. In recent off-year congressional elections, 35 to 40 percent of those eligible have voted; in local elections, the figure usually drops below 30 percent. In recent presidential elections, less than 10 percent of the population reported attending one or more political meetings related to the election, and roughly 5 percent reported doing some work for a party or candidate. The latter figure—5 percent—sets an upper limit for the number of neorepublican or participatory citizens. The proportion of the population voting for congressional candidates certainly sets an upper limit on the number of concerned citizens. The actual size of this group is much smaller, given the number of people who occasionally vote in off-year national elections and have little or no additional involvement in politics. (The figures on participation are from American National Election Studies, various years). In Verba, Schlozman, and Brady's recent study (1995, 51), 8 percent of their respondents reported doing campaign work, but if the degree of overreporting was similar to that regarding voting, the actual figure would have been 5 or 6 percent.
22. In a 1996 survey, 53 percent of respondents considered voting an essential obligation, while another 29 percent considered it a very important obligation. "1996 Survey of American Political Culture," *The Public Perspective* (February–March 1997): 14.
23. The naturalization process includes an examination about American history and politics; the test has to be evaluated and changed over time (National Archives and Records Administration 1998, 594–97; Nauman 1994, 278).
24. This point is made in the main histories of the Roosevelt administration, such as Leuchtenburg (1963). After the 1930s, the low immigration of the midcentury decades may have been a further source of the weakening of the machines, since it reduced the number of prospective clients.
25. The figures are based on INS data summarized in DeSipio and de la Garza (1998, 19–21).
26. Only one moment has been the site of major empirical controversy. Some analysts find a big decline in voting in the late nineteenth and early twentieth centuries, owing partly to Progressive reforms. Others argue that this decline has been overstated because poor records and electoral fraud inflated voting rates in the late nineteenth century (Burnham 1982b; Converse 1972).
27. Extensive market participation also tends to lessen linguistic differences. Much has been made of ethnically based markets in the United States where non-English speakers do business in their own languages. Such niches exist, but the proportion of immigrants who work in such settings is limited. And there have been large historical changes in the other direction. Much of the immigrant population in the nineteenth and early twentieth centuries was economically active in three settings whose importance has greatly diminished: family farms; domestic economies with a male as the primary or exclusive wage earner; and factories whose unskilled workers needed very little English.
28. For example, Robert Dahl (1989, 148, 207) recognizes the difficulty of boundary questions and brackets them in favor of analyzing what goes on within specified boundaries (also see Baubock and Rundell 1998).
29. Obviously attention to minority rights is not problematic as such. The focus on minority rights has encouraged important analyses of topics such as ethnicity, language, and nationality (see Kymlicka 1995).

17 Historical Perspectives on the Economic Consequences of Immigration into the United States

Susan B. Carter and Richard Sutch

TODAY IS NOT the first time that high and rising levels of immigration into the United States have brought the economic consequences of immigration to the forefront of both policy and scholarly debate. Figure 17.1 displays the official figures on the number of immigrants admitted into the United States between 1820 and 1996. In the long view afforded by this table, current flows, high as they are, only now are approaching the record levels reached in the period before World War I.[1] Having been there before, there may be something to gain by reviewing the scholarship on the economic impacts of immigration during this earlier period. Then as now, there was public concern that immigration would lower wages of the resident population, particularly the wages of the least-skilled Americans. Connected to this concern was and is the fear that immigration, or at least too much immigration, fragments society and leads to social and political unrest.

This chapter contrasts the last great episode of immigration to the United States with our current experience. Because of the temporal distance, issues connected with the earlier experience can be examined in a relatively dispassionate way. Moreover, since the implications of the earlier episode have had time to work themselves out, a comparison of the two episodes can assist in placing the current situation within the context of our country's long-run growth and economic development.

As we will show, the consensus of scholarly opinion reached in the 1960s was that the mass immigration into the United States during the three-quarters of a century before World War I had, on the whole, profoundly positive economic and social effects. In this consensus view, immigration enhanced the rate of economic growth, improved the welfare of resident workers, moderated the business cycle, and had no impact on the distribution of income. Those conclusions of the historical scholarship were frequently cited by supporters of immigration liberalization in the 1960s and may have played a role in the abolition of the restrictive quota system in 1965.

By contrast, empirical studies employing data spanning the last twenty-five years have tended to emphasize the negative impacts of immigration and to support restrictionist policies (Borjas 1996; Frey 1995b). Of course, there are many reasons why scholarly views about the impacts of the earlier and the current immigration flows might differ. Here we highlight the distinctive features of the theoretical approach taken by scholars who achieved the earlier consensus. It emphasized the interconnectedness of various sectors within the economy and the far-reaching effects of immigration-induced increases in the size of the labor force. It is an approach that is in very little evidence today.

ECONOMIC GROWTH MODELS AND THE IMPACTS OF IMMIGRATION

Mass immigration into the United States occurred during a period of very rapid economic growth and America's ascendancy to international industrial leadership (Abramovitz 1993; Abramovitz and David 1973, 1996; Paul Romer 1996; Wright 1990). Most of the historians and economic historians who have studied that earlier immigration tried to assess its relationship to these positive economic developments. To do so, they relied explicitly or implicitly on a model of economic growth and of factor mobility. Because some readers may be unfamiliar with this literature, we begin with some key definitions and a simple version of the model.

FIGURE 17.1 Immigrants to the United States, 1820 to 2000

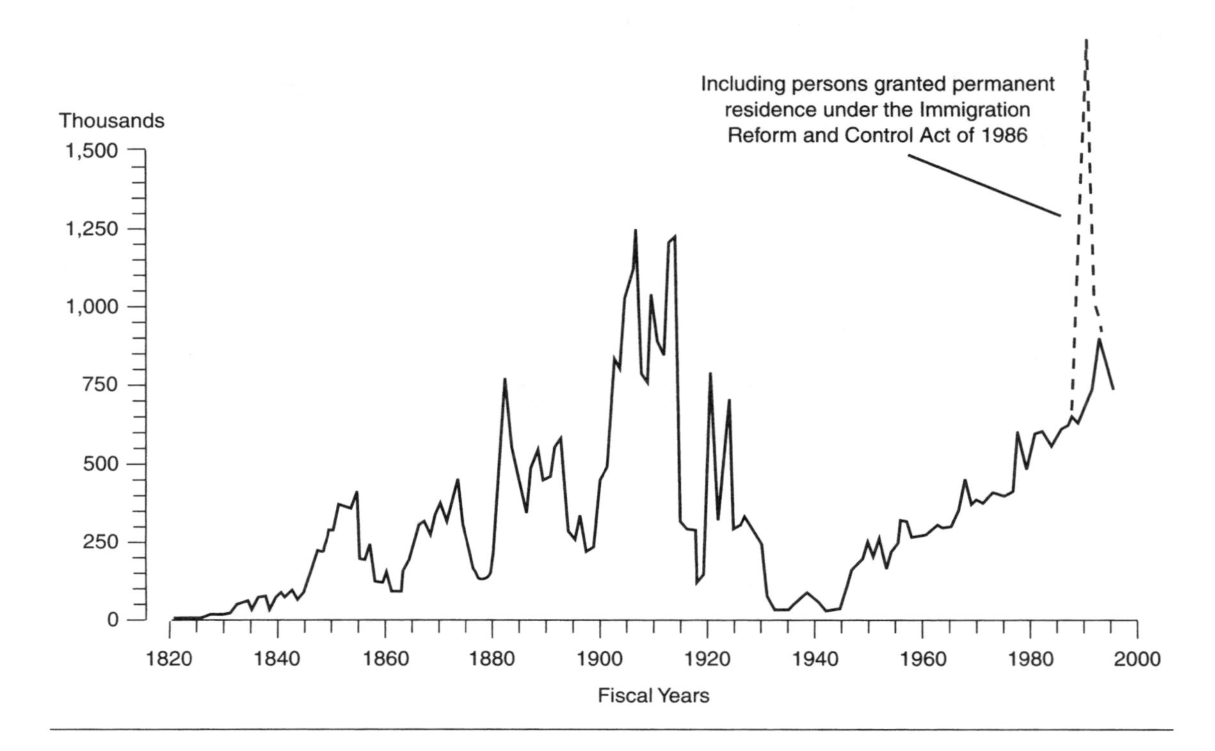

Defining Economic Growth

There is little doubt that immigration caused the American population and the American labor force to grow more rapidly than they would have in its absence. Figure 17.2 shows the contribution of net immigration to American population growth.[2] During the period of mass immigration preceding World War I, immigration accounted for somewhere between one-third and one-half of U.S. population growth.

More people meant more output. Population, after all, is fundamental to production, not only because people supply the required labor, but because the population's demand for goods and services provides an incentive for production. Thus, mass immigration made the late-nineteenth- and early-twentieth-century American economy—measured, say, by real gross domestic product (GDP)—grow more rapidly than it would have without immigration. This is, we think, what the historian Maldwyn Allen Jones had in mind when he wrote in his classic book *American Immigration* (1960, 309–10):

> The realization of America's vast economic potential has . . . been due in significant measure to the efforts of immigrants. They supplied much of the labor and technical skill needed to tap the underdeveloped resources of a virgin continent. This was most obviously true during the colonial period. . . . But immigrants were just as indispensable in the nineteenth century, when they contributed to the rapid settlement of the West and the transformation of the United States into a leading industrial power.

This concept of growth, however, sometimes called "extensive growth," is not what economists usually mean by the phrase "economic growth." Instead, for economists, the growth of labor productivity, the growth of per capita output, or the growth in the average real wage—in other words, what is called "intensive growth"—is the concept of greater interest. Labor productivity for the economy as a whole is measured by dividing GDP by the number of workers. Thus, if productivity is to grow, GDP must grow *faster* than the number of workers. If per capita output is to grow, GDP

FIGURE 17.2 Net Immigration's Contribution to National Population Growth, 1820 to 1995

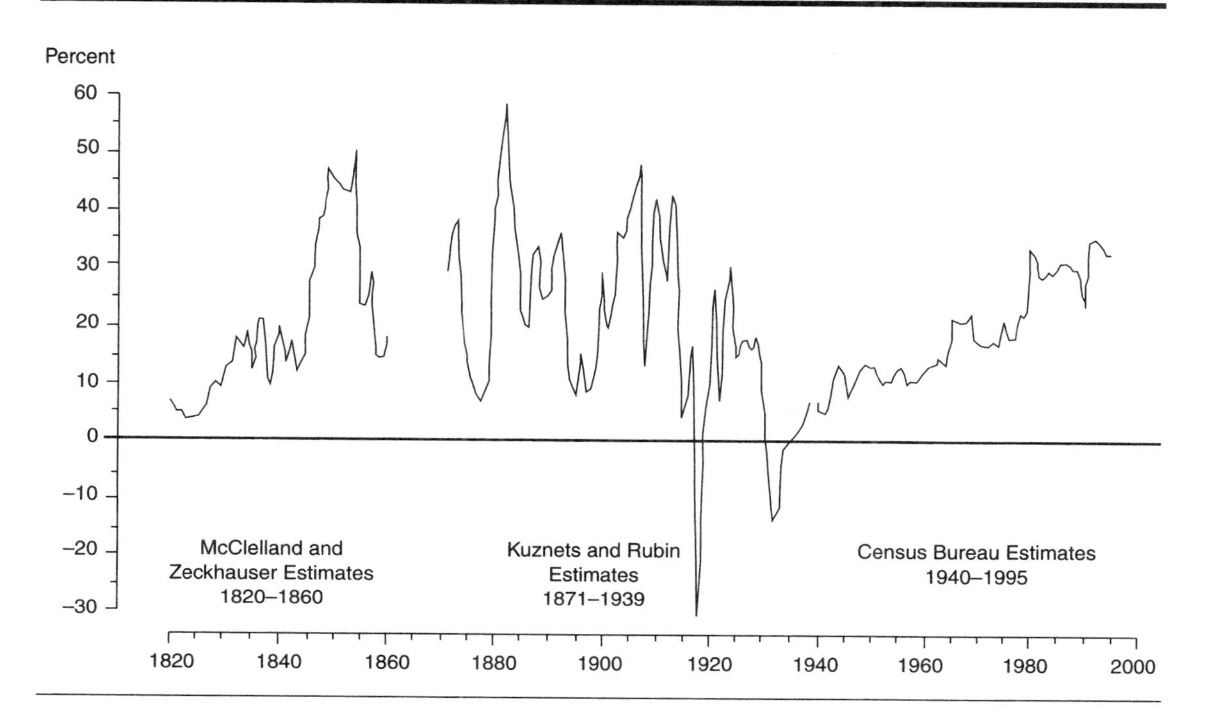

must grow faster than the population. So the question becomes: Does immigration increase or reduce labor productivity? If workers are paid a wage that reflects their productivity, we can ask the same question in a different way: Does immigration increase or reduce the real wage?[3]

The statistical record is clear: intensive economic growth did take place during the era of mass immigration. Per capita GDP grew in real terms (Balke and Gordon 1986). Labor productivity grew as well, and real wages rose (Long 1960; Rees 1960, 1961). Nonetheless, this evidence is not adequate to rule out a harmful role for immigration. During the late nineteenth century, and indeed for most of our history, output per worker was growing.[4] Thus, the real question is: Did immigration retard or accelerate the *rate* of intensive growth?

At first glance, it would appear that there is no clear consensus among economic historians about the impact of turn-of-the-century immigration on the rate of intensive growth. The most careful of the several reviews of the historical literature, that by Jeremy Atack and Peter Passell (1994, 236–37), concluded that immigration had a large, positive, and "profound" effect on the rate of growth measured in per capita terms. Without immigration, the rate of growth would have been slower and the resident population would have been poorer. At the same time, Jeffrey Williamson (1982, 254) asserts, "The issue in American historiography . . . has never been whether immigration tended to suppress the rise in the real wage. . . . Surely, in the absence of mass migrations, the real wage would have risen faster." Timothy Hatton and Jeffrey Williamson tested the proposition that the pace of economic growth was slowed by immigration in their book *The Age of Mass Migration* (1998, ch. 8). They conclude that late-nineteenth- and early-twentieth-century immigration significantly retarded the growth of real wages and living standards economy-wide.

Some of these differences can be reconciled by examining implicit differences in the authors' definitions of the population of interest and in their handling of composition effects. Other differences are rooted in disagreements not about immigration directly but about the workings of the economy.

Defining the Population of Interest

Which is the population for which the effects of immigration are to be measured? Is it the entire population, including the newly arrived immigrants? Is it the population resident in the United States at the time of the immigrants' arrival? Perhaps it is the native-born, or even the native-born of native parentage. Are workers alone to be considered, or the workers and their dependents? Just workers and their families, or capitalists and landowners as well? Any of these populations may be a legitimate focus of attention. The appropriate definition depends on the question being asked. One source of confusion in the literature stems from the fact that scholars have not always been explicit about the definition they have chosen.[5]

Untangling Composition Effects

To measure the impact of immigration on the wages of natives and of past immigrants, one needs to partition the population between the resident population and the new immigrants and consider changes in the welfare of the resident population alone. For the most part, however, long-term historical data on wages, income, and wealth are available only for the population as a whole. Scholars are forced to deduce the impact of immigration on the welfare of the resident population (or the native-born, or the native-born of native parents) from data on the entire population.

Such a project is fraught with hazards. Average wages may fall at the same time that the wages of *both* the resident population and the newly arrived immigrants are rising rapidly. This would occur if, say, there were a rapid influx of new immigrants who earned wages well below those of the resident workers.

Specifying a Model of Economic Growth

Other differences in scholarly opinion arise from differences in modeling strategy. To assess the impact of immigration on intensive economic growth, many economic historians have implicitly or explicitly relied on a theoretical construct known as the aggregate production function. This approach asserts that the aggregate output produced by an economy (its GNP) is determined by the quantities and qualities of its "factors of production"—capital, labor, and land. Technological progress plays a role as well, either because better machines and tools are used ("embodied" technical change) or because existing machines and tools are organized in better ways ("disembodied" technical change).

Capital includes machinery and buildings and other structures—all of the manufactured physical inputs into the production process that contribute to the level of output. Labor includes number of persons involved in the production process, their hours of work per day, their days of work per year, the intensity of their work effort, and their level of skill. Land includes improvements to land, natural resources, and raw materials. A key feature of this theoretical construct is that it focuses attention on the productivity of factors of production and on the possibility of *substitution* among them. Thus, for example, an increase in the supply of farm labor (perhaps from immigration) would supposedly induce farmers to adopt more hand-harvesting of fruits and vegetables. Another feature of this theoretical construct is its emphasis on incentives. Thus, the same influx of farm labor would supposedly raise the productivity of land and thereby create an incentive to expand the number of acres under cultivation.

To assess the impact of immigration using the production function approach requires a comparison between the historical record and an explicit counterfactual—a comparison of "what was" with "what might have been" had immigration flows been absent or reduced. To assess the impacts of immigration the investigator must specify a general equilibrium model of the labor and capital and land markets and of the production and distribution of output.[6]

The counterfactual method has a long history in cliometric work. By now it is clear that the outcomes of such exercises are quite sensitive to the specification of the formal theoretical model that describes the workings of the counterfactual universe (Fogel 1967). The aggregate production function must be specified mathematically and assigned numerical parameters. There are many technical questions. What is the degree of substitutability between the factors of production? That is, is the production function Cobb-Douglas, Constant Elasticity of Substitution (CES), or Leontief? Are there economies of scale? Is the growth of the capital stock constrained by the flow of savings or by available investment opportunities? Is the model static or dynamic? The results also depend on the assumptions built into the model about the distribution of wealth, income, and employment. Are workers paid their marginal product? Are governments redistributive? Do immigrants import or export capital? Do immigrants and native-born have different savings propensities? Is the macroeconomy Keynesian or neoclassical? Since the conclusions reached via counterfactual modeling are sensitive to the model's structure, the persuasiveness of any exercise depends on the plausibility of the model specification.

Given this state of affairs, we feel that the most helpful thing we can do is to describe some of the prominent arguments about relevant aspects of the late-nineteenth- and early-twentieth-century economy that appear in the literature and bear on the debate about the impacts of immigration.

Capital Dilution: The Impact of Immigration on the Capital-Labor Ratio

An influx of immigrants who do not bring capital with them will have the effect of "diluting" the country's capital stock, that is, reducing the economywide capital-labor ratio. If capital and labor are substitutes (and all researchers assume that they are), this reduction in the capital-labor ratio will raise the rate of return to capital and lower the real wage of workers. The worker's wage falls because after the influx of new labor each worker has on average less capital with which to work. With less capital, labor's productivity and hence the wage are reduced. At the same time, each unit of capital has more labor with which to cooperate. Thus, the productivity of capital and the return to capital owners is enhanced. On balance, the impact of the reduction in the capital-labor ratio on the resident population is predicted by theory to be positive. Capital owners gain, resident workers lose, and the gains of capital owners exceed the losses of resident workers. This is because the labor and capital owned by residents can produce more output after the arrival of the immigrants than before. Immigrants increase output by more than they take home in wages.[7]

In his discussion of the probable magnitudes of the redistribution effected by this mechanism in the modern era, George Borjas (1995, 8–9) estimates that native workers lose about 1.9 percent of GDP and that native capital owners gain approximately 2.0 percent of GDP. Borjas suggests that the relatively small net surplus—one-tenth of 1 percent of GDP—compared with the larger transfers from labor to capital, "probably explains why the debate over immigration policy has usually focused on the potentially harmful labor market impacts rather than on the overall increase in native income."

When considering the relevance of this redistribution for the period of rapid immigration in the early part of this century, we note, first, that many of the resident workers were also capital owners.[8] Lebergott (1964, 512–13) estimates that as late as 1900 about one-third of the labor force were at the same time owners of land and capital. They were self-employed farm owners and the owners and operators of small retail shops and manufacturing plants. Others were providers of professional and personal services (Carter and Sutch 1996). Also we note that a substantial fraction of American household heads and workers owned their own homes. Michael Haines and Allen Goodman (1995) put the level at over one-third about the turn of the century. To the degree that the arrival of new immigrants increased the demand for housing, owners of the existing stock of housing would enjoy capital gains.[9]

Second, a substantial fraction of the turn-of-the-century working-class population owned capital assets indirectly through the agency of insurance companies. Roger Ransom and Richard Sutch (1987, 386) estimate that in 1905 there were approximately 9 million Tontine insurance policies outstanding at a time when there were only about 18 million households. These Tontine policies were, in effect, self-financed pension funds invested in assets and equities whose value rose (or fell) with the return to capital.

Because of the widespread ownership of capital by resident workers at the turn of the century, any immigration-initiated redistribution of income among *individuals* was far more muted than the redistribution between labor and capital as *factors of production*. Though we know of no empirical work on this topic, the fact of widespread worker ownership of assets suggests that workers may not have been greatly harmed by capital dilution even if there was a depressing effect on the real wage in the short run.

A third point to note in connection with the capital dilution argument is that, whatever immigration's impact on the returns to capital, asset values, and real wages, the effects are likely to have been transitory (Easterlin 1968, 36–41). Higher returns to capital would, in a dynamic economy, increase the demand for capital; that is, it would shift the demand for investment outward. If the supply of savings is elastic, or if the supply of savings shifted outward as a consequence of immigration, then the capital stock would increase, the capital-labor ratio would rise, real wages would rise, and the return to capital would fall back to normal levels.[10] We will return to these possibilities shortly.

Pressure on the Land: The Impact of Immigration on Natural Resource Utilization

Fear of environmental damage and restricted supplies of natural resources, especially land and nonrenewable resources such as energy, are an important source of anti-immigration sentiments in the United States today. In a 1982 fund-raising letter for Zero Population Growth, Paul Ehrlich (quoted in Simon 1989, 188) warned that population increase generally, and immigration in particular, would make the country "more crowded, more polluted, more ecologically unstable, . . . and far, far more precarious than we can possibly imagine."

The Immigration Reform and Control Act of 1986 (which, before passage, was known as the Simpson-Rodino bill) developed as an effort to regain control of our borders and was justified in terms of its potential in slowing the rate of growth of the U.S. population (Reynolds and McCleery 1988). Julian Simon (1989, 188) attributes to Senator Alan Simpson (R-WY) the following statement in 1981: "The issue is whether we can or should give up benefits which stem from low population density—cleaner air, less traffic congestion, easy access to parks, and reduced anxiety levels."

These concerns are relatively recent ones and were not addressed in the literature assessing the impacts of the pre–World War I migrations. In fact, the concern of contemporaries and of historians who studied the period was the opposite one. Might immigration *slow* the rate of growth of the resident population?[11]

Nonetheless, there is a historical literature on the impacts of population growth and economic development on changes in environmental quality and on the supply of resources, including nonrenewable resources. We offer a brief tour.

Immigration and Environmental Quality

The message of this work is well summarized by David Card (1996, 5), who notes: "Perhaps the most important insight that economic theory offers about the impact of immigration—and a point that noneconomists typically find very confusing—is that population size per se is not necessarily a problem."

From the point of view of economics, environmental problems stem from poorly articulated property rights. Upstream residents will foul rivers unless they are prohibited by law or required to pay damages. Herdsmen will overgraze the commons; fishermen will overfish ponds. In this view, there is no one-to-one correlation between population size or density and environmental quality. Thus, even sparsely settled lands can suffer serious environmental damage (think of the near-extinction of the American bison), while areas with rapidly growing populations can enjoy improvements (think of air quality in Los Angeles following the adoption of air quality controls). In particular, many notable improvements in environmental quality have occurred in rapidly growing urban areas following government-initiated public health, sanitation, and zoning programs.[12]

Immigration and the Supply of Nonrenewable Natural Resources

The historical research conducted by Gavin Wright (1990) suggests that known reserves of nonrenewable resources such as petroleum and metal ores actually *grow along with* population and economic development. This is true in spite of the fact that resources are used up in the development process. The reason for the growth is that economic development provides the economic incentives to discover and extract new sources of supply. Historically, the discovery process has always outpaced utilization. The real prices of nonrenewable resources (oil, iron ore, coal, and so forth) have actually fallen over time.

Wright (1990) and Paul David and Wright (1996) credit America's ascendancy to world industrial leadership about the turn of the century to the unusually rapid growth in the size of the American market. This was the result of an increase in both population and in income per capita. The rapid growth in the size of the American market led to a large potential payoff to the discovery and recovery of natural resources. Entrepreneurs responded to these incentives by making discoveries.

The Impact of the High Labor-Force Participation of Immigrants

If a larger fraction of the population participates in the labor force, that will cause output per capita to rise even if the productivity of labor remains unchanged. Most economic historians place great weight on the fact that immigrants who arrived in the last era of mass migration were far more likely

FIGURE 17.3 Proportion of Immigrants Who Were Male, 1820 to 2000

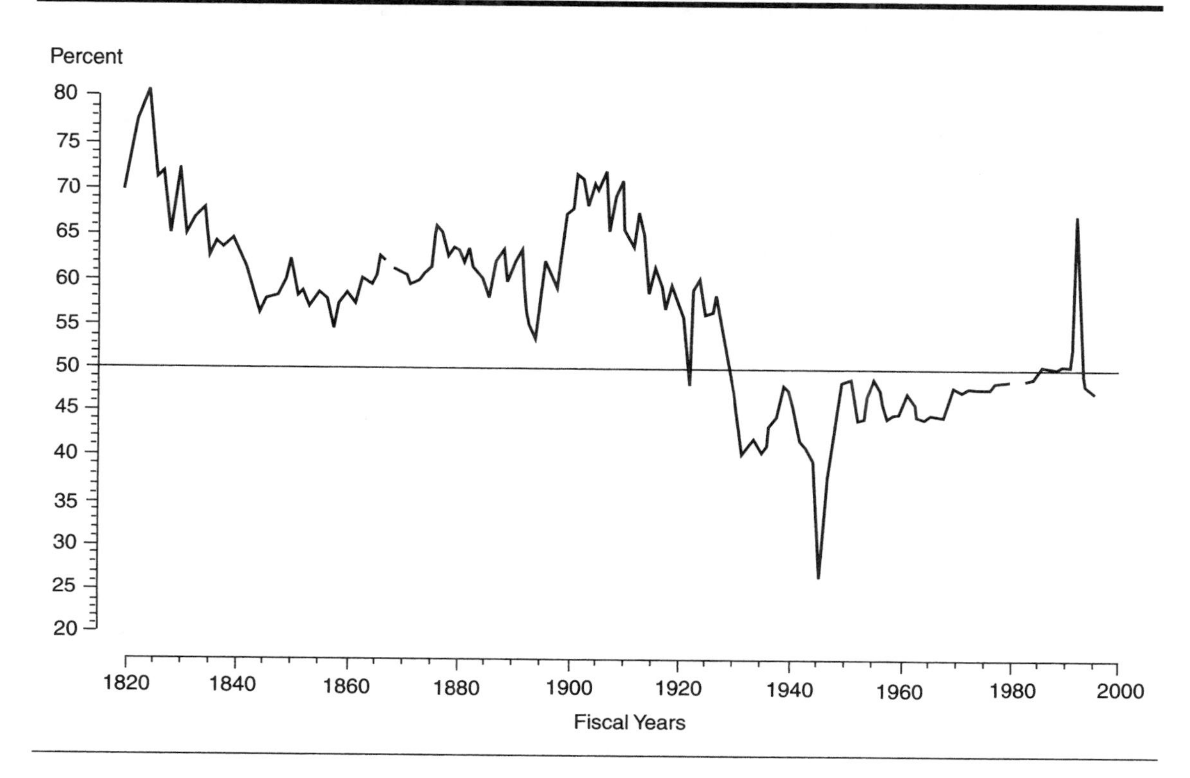

to participate in the labor force than was the average American at the time. This pattern is shown in table 17.1, which displays the share of the native and foreign-born populations engaged in the workforce for the decennial census years 1870 through 1940. The participation rate for the foreign-born is 50 percent or more from 1880 onward, with the rate rising with the rising tide of immigration. The participation rate of the native-born is only about two-thirds of this level. Simon Kuznets (1952/1971, 397) explained the high labor-force participation of immigrants in this way:

> Because the immigrants were predominantly males, because by far the preponderant proportion of them (over 80 percent) were over 14 or 15 and in the prime working ages, and because their participation in the labor force tended to be higher than that of the native population even for the same age and sex classes, the share of foreign born among the gainfully occupied was, throughout the period, markedly greater than their share in total population.

TABLE 17.1 Labor-Force Participation Rate, Native-Born and Foreign-Born, 1870 to 1940

Year	*Native-Born*	*Foreign-Born*
1870	29.7%	48.5%
1880	32.0	52.2
1890	33.1	55.1
1900	35.5	55.5
1910	37.7	57.8
1920	37.8	55.7
1930	38.1	52.2
1940	39.1	50.5

Source: Calculations are based on Kuznets (1952, 196–204).
Note: "Labor-force participation rate" is defined here as the share of the total population of a given nativity that is engaged in the workforce.

The data on the gender and age of immigrants are available beginning in 1820.[13] The long time series on the male share of immigrants is plotted in Figure 17.3. The predominance of males is a phenomenon of the entire period of uncontrolled immigration, but it disappears within a decade following the imposition of limitations in 1921.[14] Figure 17.4 displays data on the gender composition of immigrants by age from the 1907-to-1910 period with the most recent data available on gen-

FIGURE 17.4 Proportion of Immigrants Who Were Male, 1907 to 1910 and 1992 to 1995

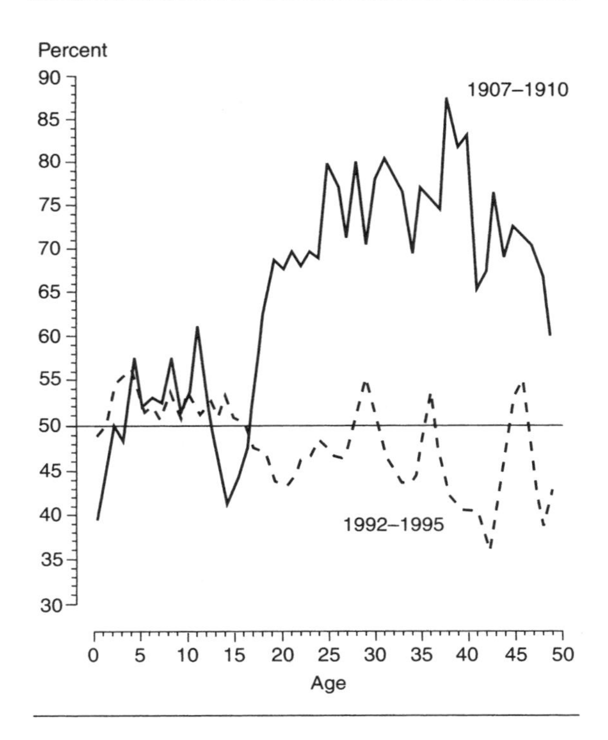

FIGURE 17.5 Age Distribution of Immigrants, 1907 to 1910 and 1992 to 1995

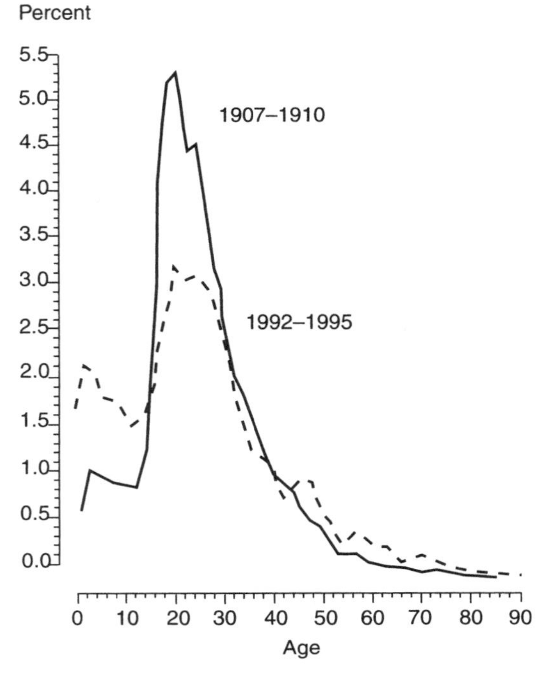

der composition by age. The proportion of male immigrants was well over 70 percent in the age range eighteen to forty from 1907 to 1910. This represents a male-female ratio of more than two to one. For those in their late twenties, the ratio is greater than three to one. The data from the beginning of the century, when the age of independence was younger than today, show a modest imbalance in favor of young women aged twelve through sixteen, undoubtedly produced by the earlier maturation of girls. In marked contrast is the relative gender equality in immigration in the modern data. In the prime migration age cohorts, women actually predominate.

The overwhelming proportion of immigrants are young adults. This was true in the past, and it is so today as well. Figure 17.5 contrasts the age distribution of immigrants from 1907 to 1910 with those for 1992 to 1995. Clearly the propensity to immigrate is strongest from ages eighteen to thirty in both periods. One difference is that the early immigrants were less likely to be accompanied by young children than is true today. This difference reflects the sharp increase in the propensity of women to migrate since the imposition of restrictions. With the striking predominance of males among the young adults who constituted the bulk of all immigrants in the past, there were few children in the early immigrant flows.

If these foreign-born workers were as productive as the native-born, and if their arrival did not depress the capital-labor ratio (that it *did not* is commonly supposed in the historical literature), then immigration would cause per capita income of the resident population to rise more rapidly than it would have in the absence of immigration (Gallman 1977, 30).

The first element of the argument—that per capita incomes tend to rise because of the immigration-induced increase in the labor-force participation rate—is well established. The balance of the argument—that immigration had a positive impact on the economic well-being of the *resident* population—depends on two assumptions that are not as well supported by empirical work. First, are the foreign-born as productive as native-born workers? This issue is discussed later, but the consensus is that any differences in the average productivity of the native- and foreign-born workforce were small. The second key point—the impact of immigration on capital formation—has been left largely to assumption and speculation. Very little empirical work with historical data has been reported in the literature.

The Impact of Immigration on Physical Capital Formation

Simon Kuznets has argued that American economic growth was constrained by an inelastic supply of savings (Kuznets 1961). Moses Abramovitz and Paul David (1973, 1996) and David (1975) prefer a model in which expanding opportunities for investment (in turn driven by the flow of technological innovation) play the chief dynamic role, pushing out along a responsive and elastic supply of funds. The debate has not been settled. What we know is that the capital stock grew fast enough to prevent any decline in the capital-labor ratio. Abramovitz and David (1973) report that the capital-labor ratio grew 0.6 percent annually between 1800 and 1855, 1.5 percent between 1855 and 1890, and 1.34 percent between 1890 and 1927 (Abramovitz 1993, table 1 [223]). What was the mechanism behind this relative increase in the capital stock? What was the likely role played by immigration? Because of the dispute, we consider two cases sequentially.

Case 1: Savings Is the Constraint on Capital Formation

In Case 1, immigration would have to increase the rate of capital formation either by increasing the importation of capital from abroad or by increasing the flow of domestically generated saving. Immigrants may have brought substantial amounts of capital with them when they moved. Although little empirical work has been done on this question, it is generally supposed that the amount of immigrant-supplied capital was trivial and, indeed, that any such inward flows were partially offset by an outward flow of "remittances" from immigrants to friends and relatives in the old country.[15] Alternatively, the foreign-born population may have attracted foreign investment to the American economy by alerting prospective investors in their country of origin of American investment opportunities, by borrowing from friends or relatives abroad, or by acting as intermediaries connecting the foreign investor with an American borrower. Another possibility is that the higher rates of return to capital produced by the capital dilution effect attracted capital from abroad. Brinley Thomas (1954/1973, 1961) incorporated such a mechanism into his model of the Atlantic economy.

There is an extensive literature on international capital flows in this period (Davis and Cull 1994; Edelstein 1982), although we know of no systematic study of immigration-induced investment flows from abroad. We note the fact that much of the flow of British investment abroad was directed to economies with a high proportion of English settlers—the United States, Canada, and Australia (Davis and Gallman 1973, 1991; Edelstein 1974). A. K. Cairncross (1953) noted that England's position as the primary source of international capital flows during the late nineteenth and early twentieth centuries gave the United States an important advantage.

A second mechanism that might link immigration to capital formation in the saving-constrained case is the behavior of the immigrants themselves. They may have been unusually heavy savers and investors in the American economy. Such behavior was hypothesized by Roger Ransom and Richard Sutch (1984, 49–51) in the context of a life-cycle model of saving. They make two points. First, since the bulk of turn-of-the-century immigrants arrived as young adults, they entered the country at a life-cycle stage when saving is typically heavy. Second, upon arrival most immigrants owned very little in the way of marketable, tangible wealth, particularly in relation to their earning power in their new home country. Partly this was because the immigrants had consumed much of their wealth in financing their passage to the United States; partly this was because they were poor by American standards before they left their country of origin. When they began participating in the new, higher American income stream, they found themselves in an "asset-income disequilibrium"—that is, their stock of assets was too low relative to their current and foreseeable income. Under these circumstances, they would attempt to restore the balance by saving heavily.

What evidence is there that immigrants were particularly heavy savers? There has not been much research on the question. One bit of evidence consistent with higher saving rates among the foreign-born is their differentially high rates of self-employment. These nativity-based differentials were just as evident in the past as they are today (Aldrich and Waldinger 1990; Aronson 1991; Borjas 1986; Borjas and Bronars 1989; Carter and Sutch 1992b; Higgs 1976; Light and Bonacich 1988). Since entry into self-employment requires

FIGURE 17.6 Self-Employment Rates for Male, Foreign-Born, Non-Farm Workers, by Age Cohort, 1910

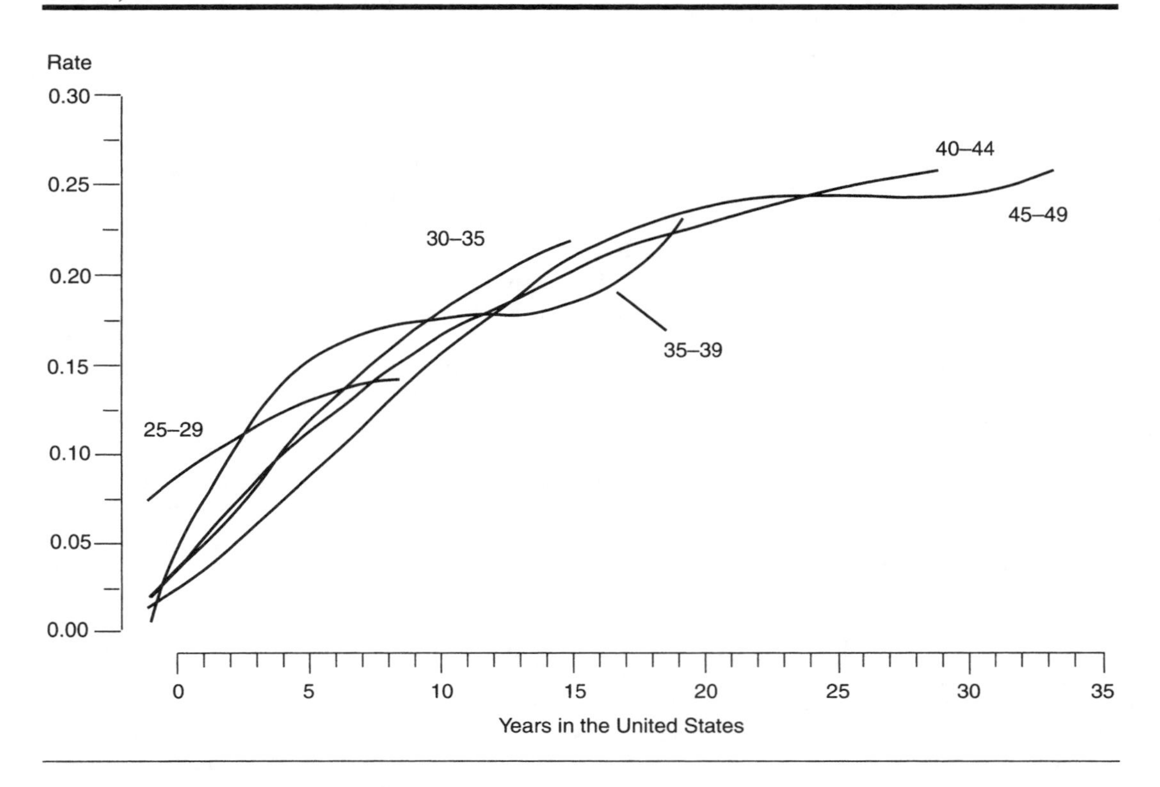

physical and human-capital acquisition, these data suggest differentially high saving rates among the foreign-born. The 1910 Public Use Microdata Sample allows us to give a particularly vivid demonstration of the probable role of financial (and human) capital acquisition on the part of immigrants *after their entry into the United States.* In figure 17.6, we show the fraction of the foreign-born self-employed among cohorts of men in their twenties, thirties, forties, and fifties in 1910, arrayed by the number of years they had been living in the United States. The shorter the line, the younger the cohort in 1910. This diagram suggests that newly arrived immigrants, whatever their age, begin their American employment careers as wage workers and then increasingly move into self-employment eight to twelve years later. The consistency of the upward movement, for men arriving at different ages, suggests heavy saving rates in the years following their arrival into the United States.

The saving rates of immigrants may have been higher than those of the native-born. Figure 17.7 displays self-employment rates by age for both the native- and foreign-born male non-farm workforce in 1910. We restrict the foreign-born population to those who had been resident in the United States for fifteen years or more and were at least thirty-three years of age. This restriction eliminates the sojourners and also those who arrived in the United States as children. Figure 17.7 shows that the self-employment rates at each age of these two groups are quite similar. Both groups show movement at about the same rate into self-employment between the early thirties and midforties. If we imagine that some of the movement of the native- (but not the foreign-) born at these ages was facilitated by the receipt of an inheritance, then the similarity of their rates of movement into self-employment suggests *heavier* saving on the part of immigrants.

A second piece of evidence of differentially high rates of saving among the foreign-born is Michael Haines and Allen Goodman's (1995, table 7.3 [220–21]) finding of higher homeownership for the foreign-born in several samples of household heads from the turn of the century.[16]

Whether the additional "boom in saving" trig-

FIGURE 17.7 Self-Employment Rates for Native-Born and Foreign-Born Male Non-Farm Workers, by Age, 1910

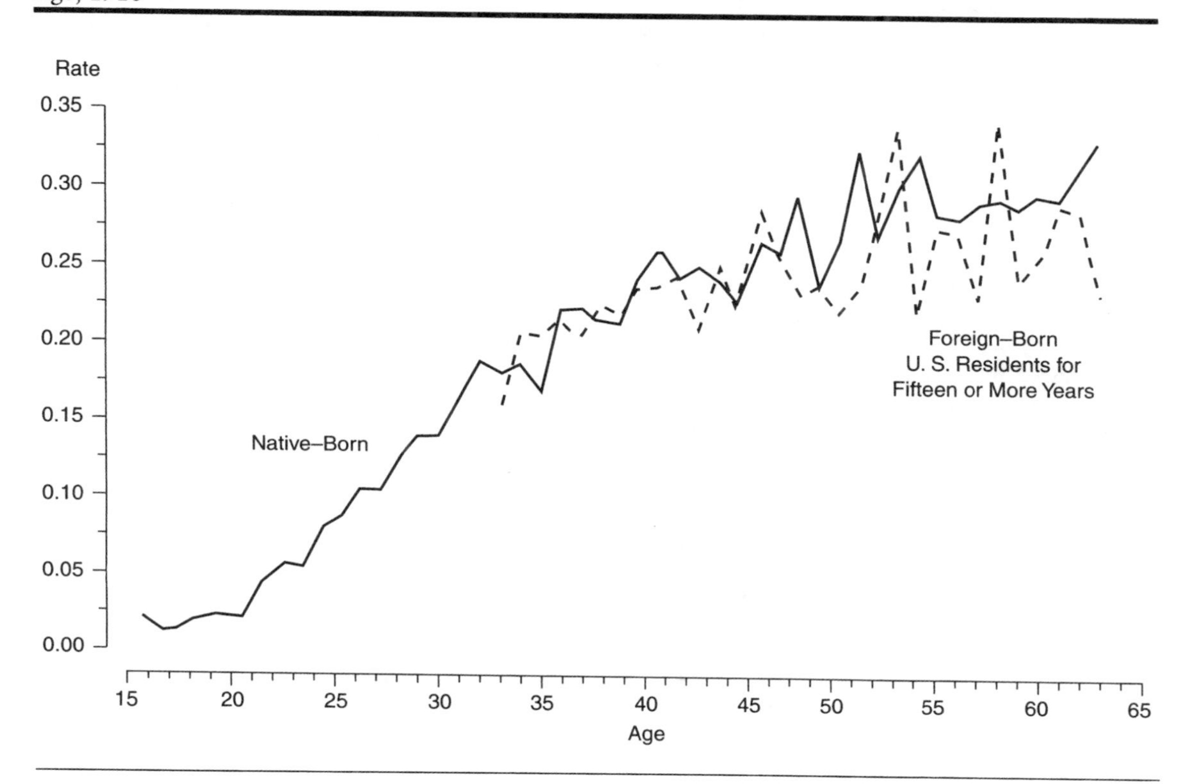

gered, as Ransom and Sutch (1984) hypothesize, by immigration was strong enough by itself to both offset the initial capital dilution and raise the overall capital-labor ratio remains an open question. What is clear is that aggregate American saving rates were very high during this period. Gross saving as a fraction of gross domestic product exceeded 20 percent (Davis and Gallman 1973, 1991; Ransom and Sutch 1984). What is also clear is that the capital-labor ratio did not fall during this period—it rose. How much of that increase can be attributed to the savings of immigrants remains a question for further research and the resolution of the debate concerning the constraints to capital formation.

Case 2: Demand Is the Constraint on Capital Formation

If savings were supplied elastically, then a link between immigration and capital formation would have to lie in an effect of immigration on the demand for capital. But there is a strong argument for such an effect. Kuznets (1958, 34) argued that immigration would shift the demand for capital outward by stimulating the demand for housing, urban infrastructure, and other "population-sensitive capital formation." Kuznets's hypothesis is undoubtedly correct. To complete the argument and say that immigration therefore led to more capital formation requires something more. Either saving would have to be very elastic or the saving rate of immigrants would have to exceed that of residents, as in case 1. If saving were inelastic in supply, and if there had been no immigration-induced shift of the supply of saving, then the increased demand for investment would have simply pushed up the rate of interest rather than increased the capital stock. What we observe is that real interest rates were low and falling during the last half of the nineteenth century, and that they rose only moderately during the period of mass immigration in the early decades of the twentieth century (Temin 1971, 70–74; Williamson 1974b, 97). This evidence suggests that immigration helped stimulate the increase in the capital stock and in the capital-labor ratio by pushing out both the supply of and the demand for capital.

We lean heavily toward the side of the debate that argues that saving was an active constraint on capital formation. Our view rests on our belief in the historical applicability of Franco Modigliani's (1966, 1986) life-cycle model of savings and the implication of that model that the supply of domestic savings is not likely to be interest-elastic. We are impressed with evidence that the flow of capital from abroad in this period was relatively small in magnitude (Davis and Gallman 1973; North 1960; Simon 1960) and not very interest-sensitive (Ransom and Sutch 1984). Finally, we are impressed by a variety of historical studies that seem to support the Kuznets version of the mechanism behind capital formation. Some examples are the work of Jeffrey Williamson (1974b), Paul David and John Scadding (1974), and Roger Ransom and Richard Sutch (1988). If savings were an active constraint on investment, then the high saving rate of immigrants was an important stimulus to American capital formation and economic growth.

The Impact of Immigration on Inventive Activity

The United States became a world leader in many technologies over the late nineteenth and early twentieth centuries (Mokyr 1990, 268; Wright 1990). Rapid immigration may have contributed to this ascendancy by the simple fact that the foreigners enlarged the size of the economy. In a larger economy, more is being produced at any one time. A greater volume of production created more opportunities to discover better ways of doing things (Kelley 1972). Historians of technology have demonstrated the quantitative importance of this "learning by doing" in stimulating technological advance. Small incremental improvements, repeated many times, appear to have contributed more than well-known breakthroughs to advances in design and reductions in the costs of production (David 1975; Rosenberg 1982). By promoting extensive economic growth, immigration gave the country's inventors and tinkerers more to do, thereby offering them more opportunities to learn (Higgs 1971; Kahn and Sokoloff 1993; Sokoloff 1988; Sokoloff and Kahn 1990).

Adam Smith (1776, 11) thought that invention was accelerated by the division of labor, which in turn was limited by the size of the market. Robert Higgs (1971) found a link between patenting activity and urbanization in the United States during the period from 1870 to 1920. Julian Simon and Richard Sullivan (1989) show a connection between population size and the invention of new agricultural techniques. Since the foreign-born enlarge the population, tend to reside in urban areas, and expand the size of the market, there is a scholarly consensus that immigration accelerates inventive activity.

Immigrants may have played a more direct role in this development as well. Some scattered evidence suggests that immigrants accounted for more than their share of the major inventive breakthroughs in this era. A list of names of the "great" American inventors suggests a disproportionate share of immigrants. Why might this be a systematic aspect of the invention process rather than a coincidence or the result of a flawed sampling procedure? A good answer, we think, is that the United States was the leading laboratory for invention in the world at the time, with the most advanced industries and one of the highest rates of capital formation. Thus, it would be a magnet for would-be inventors, scientists, and innovators who would benefit from working conditions, resources, and venture capital not available in their home country.

The Impact of Immigration on Technological Diffusion

Invention has no impact on economic performance unless the new ideas diffuse; are embodied in new machines, organizations, and structures; and are actually used in the production of goods and services. The new, mass-production techniques introduced in the era of mass immigration required new machines and the redesign of the factory itself. Effective use of refrigeration technology required new railroad cars, and use of the electric motor to drive machines required new designs for both the machinery and the layout of the factory. So, too, with continuous flow technology, department store merchandising, and nearly all of the other important innovations of this era. Immigration helped to speed the diffusion of new technologies by enhancing the rate of growth of the population and the gross domestic product of the economy, thereby stimulating a rapid growth in the capital stock. In the process of undertaking the new investment required, the latest and most productive technology was adopted. By providing an incentive for new investment, rapid extensive growth of the economy lowered the average age of capital, bringing more of the advanced techniques into the production process (Nelson 1964). Had the country not welcomed the new immigrants to its shores, aggregate demand would have grown more slowly, there would have been less new investment, and the diffusion of new technologies would have been delayed (Rosenberg 1982, 249).

The Impact of Immigration on the Exploitation of Economies of Scale

To the extent that there were and are large unexploited economies of scale in various industries (external to the firm), then the extensive growth of the economy by itself would expand per capita output. Hollis Chenery (1960), in a study of the productivity of manufacturing workers across sixty-three countries, found that, other things being equal, a doubling of a country's size would increase the productivity of its workers by 20 percent. The models of growth most often invoked by economic historians, however, do not envision such an effect as a possibility. They begin with the view that the various sources of and contributions to economic growth may be separately and independently calculated and then added up without consideration of economywide increasing returns. But if the research begins with such a model, one is certain to come to the conclusion, independent of the data collected and the historical research undertaken, that no single measurable source of growth is by itself very important (Abramovitz 1993). Recently Paul Romer (1986, 1996) has urged a reconsideration of the use of models that explicitly incorporate economies of scale for addressing broad-scope, long-run questions such as the one at hand.

As far as we are aware, no one has explicitly tried to examine turn-of-the-century immigration as a possible accelerator of endogenous growth using the "new growth theory" advocated by Romer. Some evidence has been put forward, however, to lend support to the notion of increasing returns that work at the level of the national economy (Cain and Paterson 1986). Louis Johnston (1990) has attempted to model these effects by suggesting that the productivity-enhancing effect of scale is proportional to the total stock of capital, and he suggests a specific parameterization. Based on his study of increasing returns in the mid-nineteenth century, he suggests that the rate of growth of output might be increased by a factor equal to 5 percent of the increase in the capital stock on account of economies of scale and quite apart from the direct contribution of capital stock growth to economic growth. Bradford De Long (1995) suggests the true factor might be as high as 10 percent.

What would such parameters mean for the impact of immigration? If the flow of new immigrants increased the labor force by 4 to 8 percent over a decade and eventually increased the capital stock by the same proportion, then output would be increased by 0.2 to 0.8 percentage points more than the direct effects of the increase in labor and capital would suggest. This translates to a 5 to 10 percent increase in productivity. This extra supplement to growth, although proportional to the increase in capital, is not entirely captured in an increase in business profits. Instead, the entire economy is made more productive, and both labor and capital share in the "disembodied" increase in efficiency.

So far, empirical modeling with the new growth theory is in its infancy. The profession is far from persuaded that the economies-of-scale effects are or were significant, and the parameterization of such effects is little advanced from educated speculation. Yet in the hands of a skillful economic historian, the notion of economies of scale can be made to sound plausible and in good theoretical company as well. Consider Moses Abramovitz's (1993, 225–26) account:

> In the nineteenth century . . . capital's share [in national income] rose substantially—by 19 percent during the first half and by another 19 percent during the second half, a 41 percent increase overall. It is this result that creates, as I say, at least a presumption that technology was advancing, not in the neutral fashion that the growth accounts assume, but in a capital-using fashion. A series of powerful forces, each manifestly connected with technological progress, worked in this direction. First, the great expansion in the total size of the domestic market and its increasingly unified character encouraged production on a larger scale and heavier investment in the application of steam power and in more specialized capital equipment. This, indeed, is the message of all the great economists of the nineteenth and early twentieth centuries, in a line stemming from Adam Smith, running through Böhm-Bawerk, Sidgwick, and Taussig, and stretching to Allyn

Young. But these men did not see the economies of scale as a source of growth separate from technological progress itself. Rather, they thought of the advances they saw with their own eyes as an emerging technology that was both capital and scale intensive. It was increasingly specialized and roundabout in its organization; required increasing amounts of capital per worker to employ it; and therefore demanded larger-scale operations in its plants and in the aggregate to make the heavier use of capital economical. . . . [Second, the] rise of cities, itself a requirement of scale-intensive production, was another capital-intensive development. It required heavy investment in structures for housing, trade, finance, government, and schools and, especially in its early stages, for streets, water supplies, sewage disposal, and urban transport. . . . [Third, the] westward movement . . . by attracting immigrants, enlarged the effective aggregate scale of the economy.

The Impact of Immigration on the Supply of Human Capital

Simon Kuznets (1952/1971, 397) made an argument for a positive impact of immigration on the native-born that suggests a very large effect coming from the importation of human capital.

> Considering the magnitude and duration of [the immigration flow], it is difficult to exaggerate its importance as a factor in the economic growth of the United States. Since immigration brought in a large labor force, the cost of whose rearing and training was borne elsewhere, it clearly represented an enormous capital investment that dwarfed any capital inflows of the more orthodox type.

Larry Neal and Paul Uselding elaborated on this point (Neal and Uselding 1972; Uselding 1971). They began by noting that most immigrants came to the United States as young adults and entered the labor force, thus producing output, earning wages, and consuming almost immediately upon their arrival. Their income can be thought of as the return to the "human capital" they imported when they moved to this country. Yet that human capital—manifest both in its potential for purely physical labor and in the skills and learned abilities of immigrants—was created in another country. The American economy (and a new American) earned the returns from the human capital that had been transferred from—and without payment to—the economy that spent its resources on raising the individual to young adulthood and endowing him or her with education and other valuable skills. Freed of having to pay for this importation of human capital, the American economy was able to invest the equivalent resources in physical or human capital produced at home. Neal and Uselding calculate the contribution to the U.S. capital stock of these gifts. They suggest that immigration might have contributed as much as 9 percent of the capital stock by 1850, 18 percent by 1880, and 42 percent by 1912 (but see Gallman 1977). With this larger capital stock—the proportions here are larger than the same immigrants' contribution to the labor force—the national capital-labor ratio was higher than it would have been otherwise. Thus, labor productivity was higher than it would have been without immigration.

The Selectivity of Immigration: The Question of "Quality"

The historical literature has given considerable attention to the issue of immigrant "quality." Though the use of the term "quality" is unfortunate, the larger question is interesting. Did the United States attract the more highly skilled, the more entrepreneurial, and the more adventurous from abroad, or did it receive the "tired, . . . poor, your huddled masses," the unlucky, the least educated, and the least able? Presumably "high-quality" immigrants would accelerate economic growth, vitalize and enrich the society, and more quickly assimilate into the American "melting pot." "Low-quality" immigrants would, it has often been charged, be more likely to become a burden on the economy, exacerbate inequality, and prove to be a disruptive social force.

In 1891 Francis Walker, the first president of the American Economic Association and former superintendent of the U.S. Bureau of the Census, expressed his opinion on the matter with little generosity (as quoted in Handlin 1959, 73–74):

> No one can surely be enough of an optimist to contemplate without dread the fast rising flood of immigration now setting in upon our shores. . . . There is no reason why every stagnant pool of European population, representing the utterest failures of civilization, the worst defeats in the struggle for existence, the lowest degradation of human nature, should not be completely drained off into the United States. So long as any difference of economic conditions remains in our favor, so long as

the least reason appears for the miserable, the broken, the corrupt, the abject, to think that they might be better off here than there, if not in the workshop, then in the workhouse, these Huns, and Poles, and Bohemians, and Russian Jews, and South Italians will continue to come, and to come by millions.

The discussion of immigrant "quality" is intimately bound up with the pull-versus-push debate about the motives underlying immigration. If immigrants were pushed out of their home country by increasing immiserization, lack of jobs, or the shortage of land, the presumption is that they would tend to be individuals from the lower tail of the skill and resourcefulness distributions of their country of origin. On the other hand, if immigrants were pulled to the United States by the attractiveness of American opportunities, they would be more likely to come from the upper tail of the home-country distribution.

Whether looked at from the point of view of the attributes of the arrivals or the push-versus-pull controversy, the consensus achieved by economic historians is that, before World War I, the United States attracted immigrants from the upper-tail of the skill distribution in their countries of origin (Dunlevy and Gemery 1978; Easterlin 1971). Even Brinley Thomas (1954/1973, 56–62), one of the few writers who saw a strong role for push factors in motivating immigration, believed that migrants to the United States tended to come from the upper strata of their own societies. And Joel Mokyr (1983, 247–52), in his study of the migration from Ireland during the famine of the 1840s—surely an extreme example of a "push" migration—concluded that immigrants to the United States came from the upper tail of the Irish occupational distribution (See also Baines 1985, 51–52; Erickson 1972, 1981, 1986, 1989, 1990; Van Vugt 1988a, 1988b).

Whether these select workers from Europe's perspective appeared as high-skilled and advantaged competitors in the American labor market is more controversial. It could be true that immigrants selected from the upper tail of their home country's distribution of skills and other endowments nevertheless fell below the median of native-born American workers. Oscar Handlin, in his classic history of immigration to America, *The Uprooted* (1951/1973, 58, 60), emphasized the agricultural background of immigrants and asked, "What could the peasant do here?"

This view also appears in some surveys of American history. The textbook by Gary Nash and others (1996, 604), for example, reports that "most immigrants" after the Civil War "had few skills." Other textbooks assert that the quality of immigrants fell over time. A popular textbook in economic history states: "It is probably true that immigrants after 1880 were less skilled and educated than earlier immigrants" (Walton and Rockoff 1994, 402).[17]

The quantitative evidence on skill differences between native- and foreign-born workers does not support this view. There appear to be no significant skill differences—at least when these are measured by occupational differences—and the relative occupational standing of immigrants does not appear to have fallen over time. The standard reference on this topic is Peter Hill (1975, 59), who examined data from the federal occupational censuses looking for clues about the relative skills of native- and foreign-born workers. He categorized occupations as "skilled," "semiskilled," or "unskilled," using the classification devised by Alba Edwards (1943), and compared the distribution of the native- and foreign-born workforces across these categories.[18] Hill's tabulations are shown in table 17.2. Compared with natives, the

TABLE 17.2 Skill Distribution of the Labor Force by Nativity, as a Percentage of the Total Workforce, 1870 to 1920

	Skilled		*Semiskilled*		*Unskilled*	
Year	*Native-Born*	*Foreign-Born*	*Native-Born*	*Foreign-Born*	*Native-Born*	*Foreign-Born*
1870	43.0	36.6	12.7	23.2	44.3	40.2
1880	43.1	38.6	14.6	25.4	42.2	36.0
1890	49.4	40.5	17.3	25.0	33.3	34.5
1900	45.8	39.5	17.6	26.7	36.6	33.8
1910	[a]	41.9	[a]	23.8	[a]	34.3
1920[b]	56.1	44.6	15.9	23.8	28.0	32.2

Source: Hill (1975), table 6.56.

[a] These estimates are constructed from data in the published censuses. Data for the total native-born population are not available for 1910, although they do exist for the native white population.

[b] Hill's figures for the foreign-born in 1920 do not sum to 100 percent. Hill does not comment on this.

foreign-born were slightly less likely to have been employed in skilled positions, but they were *much more* likely to have held semiskilled jobs. During the period of mass immigration, foreign-born workers tended to cluster in the middle of the American occupational distribution. Proportionately native-born American workers were concentrated both above and below them on the occupational ladder.

Overall, Hill (1975, 58) concluded that there was "very little difference in the quality of the native and foreign born labor forces." Moreover, Hill could find "no definite trend," even though "most writers seem to feel that the later immigrants were of much lower quality than the earlier ones." Hill's conclusions now represent the consensus among economic historians: the mass immigrations before World War I do not appear to have reduced the "quality" of the resident American workforce.

The Impact of Immigration on the Real Wage

We come to a topic on our list of possible economic impacts of immigration that is most often used to suggest a negative impact. Throughout the period of open immigration, contemporary observers, and especially spokesmen for labor, charged that the inflow of immigrants depressed the real wage of labor. The "more the supply of labor the lower must certainly become its price," said Henry Carey, a prominent economist in 1873 (quoted in Lebergott 1964, 161). This, Carey argues, would not be a small and transitory effect like that produced by capital dilution, but a large and permanent reduction in real wages.

Carey's reasoning, as we reconstruct it today, would appear to rest on a simple model of the supply and demand for labor analogous to the familiar supply and demand for a single commodity (say, wheat). If this analysis is meant to apply to all labor, it is, of course, naive. The supply-and-demand analysis of labor markets only makes sense when applied to the market for a specific type of labor (say, slate miners). The macroeconomic view of the labor market is quite different. An increase in the quantity of labor employed would immediately change the demand for labor: the new labor would earn income, spend this income, increase aggregate demand, and thus increase the demand for labor. After adjusting to the shock of capital dilution, real wages would be unchanged.

As far as we are aware, all studies that conclude that immigration depressed the real wage of labor rely on partial-equilibrium microlevel models. For example, Stanley Lebergott (1964, 163; 1984, 34) seems to have had the simple model in mind when he attributed the increase in wages during World War I and the "Roaring Twenties" to reduced immigration. If the restrictions on immigration had been the *only* change in the economy during this period, and there had been no economic responses to the arrival of immigrants, then Lebergott's argument might persuade. As it is, there are many reasons why real wages might have risen during this dynamic period.

Timothy Hatton and Jeffrey Williamson (1998, ch. 8) have a more complex model in mind when they argue that rapid immigration in the two decades between 1890 and 1910 caused wages to be lower in 1910 than they would have been in the absence of immigration. Their calculations are complicated but ultimately depend on an assumption built into their model that an increase in the labor force produces a permanent fall in the real wage arising from capital dilution. Hatton and Williamson's calculations are derived using two technical concepts, the Phillips Curve and the CES production function. The Phillips Curve is an inverse relationship between the rate of wage inflation and the unemployment rate (Phillips 1958). It is derived from a model of the aggregate labor market rather than from a microlevel supply-demand model. The Phillips relationship summarizes the experience of many economies: an increase in the unemployment rate is associated with a slowing in the rate of growth of wages. Hatton and Williamson adopt this notion to predict the impact of an influx of immigrants. They argue that immigration, by increasing the labor supply, raised the unemployment rate and slowed wage rate growth. They make this argument despite the fact that unemployment by any measure was relatively low (4.7 to 4.9 percent) for the period 1900 to 1913 (Lebergott 1964; Christina Romer 1986; Weir 1992). They ignore the strong *negative* relationship between immigration and the unemployment rate in those years; that relationship would suggest exactly the opposite impact of immigration on wages. Hatton and Williamson get around this seeming contradiction by combining the Phillips relationship with an aggregate demand for labor derived from a CES production function (no economies of scale) and then, by substitution, eliminating the unemployment rate from their estimating equation. Their formulation reduces the

FIGURE 17.8 Real Hourly Wages in Manufacturing (1899 Prices)

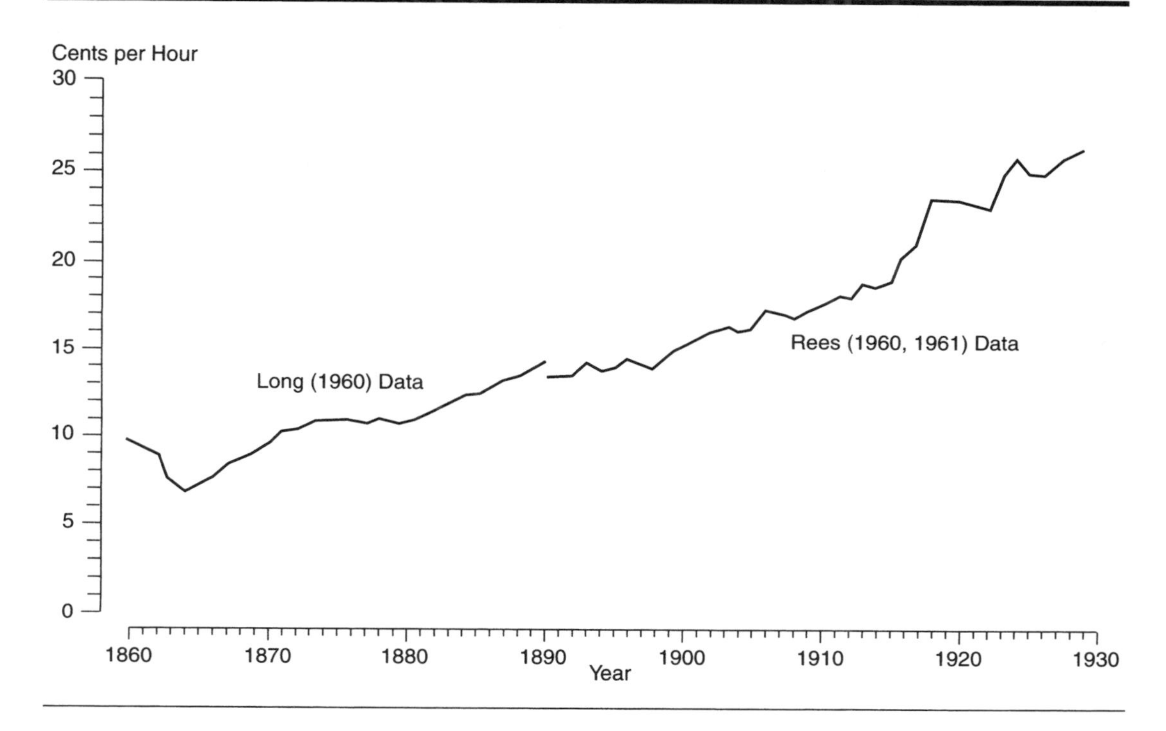

Phillips Curve to a positive relationship between the real wage and output per worker. Hatton and Williamson estimate the change in output per worker by looking at changes in labor supply. For them, "the long run impact of labor force growth on output is simply the labor share [they use 0.6 as a constant in their analysis] times labor force growth" (1998, 172). Hatton and Williamson's calculation, then, is simply an empirical estimation of the transitory capital dilution argument discussed earlier. By assumption, they rule out any impact of immigration on the capital stock. They exclude all of the dynamic effects summarized earlier that are thought to have generated a positive effect of immigration on real wages and the rate of economic growth. The work of other economic historians suggests that dynamic responses to the labor inflows were wide-ranging and quantitatively important.[19]

At this point it is worth pointing out two facts that are not in dispute. The first is that, whatever the effect of immigration, real wages of labor rose throughout the period between the Civil War and World War I. Figure 17.8 displays data on the real wage in manufacturing (Long 1960; Rees 1960, 1961). There is no striking slowdown of real wage growth during the period of most rapid immigration between 1900 and 1914.

The second point is that the waves of immigrants ebbed and flowed in synchronization with the economy. When immigration rates were high, the economy was booming; when immigration rates slowed, the economy was depressed. We are not suggesting that immigration *led to* an improvement in employment. Rather, we agree with Richard Easterlin (1968, 30–33), who interpreted these patterns as evidence that immigration responded to changes in America's demand for labor.

In conclusion, then, there is no evidence that immigrants reduced wages, lowered the living standards of the resident population, or raised unemployment rates.

THE IMPACT OF IMMIGRATION ON WAGE INEQUALITY

Although the proposition that immigration could depress all real wages the way a bumper wheat crop would depress the price of wheat is supported by neither theory nor data, the proposition that immigrants might have an unfavorable effect on

FIGURE 17.9 Williamson-Lindert Index of Wage Inequality: Ratio of Skilled to Unskilled Wages, Urban Workers, 1855 to 1945

Source: Williamson and Lindert (1980, 307).

the wages of some occupations or groups is another matter entirely. If, say, a large influx of slate miners from Wales were to arrive in the slate mines of Michigan, they might well increase the supply of labor relative to the demand for slate and drive down the wages of native-born workers in that industry. Since it is unlikely that the Welsh slate miners would increase by a measurable degree the aggregate demand for slate in the economy, there would be no offsetting effect on demand for slate miners.

If immigrants are disproportionately low-skill, then their arrival might have a negative impact on the wages of other low-skill workers. If immigrants all flock to a single region, then they might soon overwhelm local labor markets. Their geographic concentration would probably harm the native-born workers in these areas, exacerbate regional income inequality, slow cultural and linguistic assimilation, and even retard their own economic advancement. The historical literature has focused on three dimensions of immigrants' impact on wage inequality: wage differentials based on skill, on race, and on geography.

Immigration and the Skill Differential in Wages

Jeffrey Williamson and Peter Lindert (1980, 307) have assembled a variety of measures of the skill differential in wages for a period spanning nearly two centuries. In figure 17.9, we display one of their measures—the relative wages of skilled and unskilled urban workers for the period 1858 to 1939.

This measure does show a pronounced *rise* in the relative earnings of the skilled between 1896 and the beginning of World War I, the period of mass immigration. In the view of Williamson and Lindert (1980, 236), however, immigration was not responsible for this increase in inequality and played only a "minor role in explaining the resurgence of wage rate inequality at the start of this century." Instead, Williamson and Lindert emphasize the importance of the "pattern of technological progress": "Acceleration of productivity in the skill-intensive tertiary sector explains why teachers, mechanics, carpenters, and other skilled groups enjoyed rising wage advantages in the first decade of this century."

Immigration and Racial Wage Differentials

Another large literature focuses on the impact of foreign immigration on the geographic mobility and relative wages of black Americans. For the early period, Brinley Thomas (1954/1973) suggested that the mass immigration from Europe in the decades before World War I kept African Americans "bottled up" in the agricultural South. There is no doubt that their wages in the low-productivity, stagnant, and oppressive South were lower than they would have been in the dynamic and prosperous North in the fifty years between Emancipation and World War I. Their failure to migrate in any significant numbers is one of the mysteries of late-nineteenth-century American economic history. There is no shortage of explanations in the literature, but other than Thomas's speculations, no one emphasizes the role of immigration. Ransom and Sutch (1975, 1977) emphasized the institutional structure of the crop-lien, tenant-farming system of post–Civil War agriculture, in which blacks were "locked in" by a form of "debt peonage." Gavin Wright (1986) discussed the role of the peculiar and controlling labor markets of the South. Robert Margo (1990) stressed the inadequate southern schooling system, which left most blacks ill prepared to compete for urban jobs. Stewart Tolnay and E. M. Beck (1995) explored the role of extralegal coercion. Whether the hypothetical absence of competition from European immigrants in this era would have induced blacks to overcome these oppressive forces and begin their "Great Migration" before the 1920s is an important and unanswered historical question.

Immigration and Regional Wage Differentials

Regional wage differentials have been a persistent feature of American labor markets, at least since 1840 (Easterlin 1960; Rosenbloom 1996; Williamson 1964). One question is whether immigration acted to exacerbate or to ameliorate these differentials.

Immigrants tend to concentrate geographically in a small number of "magnet" destinations.[20] This is true today, and it was also true during the earlier wave of mass immigration preceding World War I. There are two principal hypotheses in the literature regarding the forces that create these magnets. One is that these destinations are regions of high opportunity and high wages that attract inmigration of the foreign-born and residents alike. Another view is that immigrants flock to cities that already have thriving immigrant communities with well-developed ethnic support networks, without reference to their relative economic prosperity.

If the first view is correct, then immigration would serve to accelerate economic growth by removing allocative inefficiencies and relieving bottlenecks. It would also tend to reduce wage inequality by expanding the labor supply in high-wage markets. The second view, by contrast, suggests that immigrants would soon overcrowd local labor markets and the ethnic neighborhoods that originally attracted them.

One recent study that bears on the relative importance of these two hypotheses was conducted by Claudia Goldin (1994), who was interested in the impacts of immigration on inter-city differences in wage rates about the turn of the century. In the cross-section, Goldin finds a strong *positive* relationship between the fraction of a city's population that was foreign-born and the city's average wage. In other words, cities with a large fraction of immigrants had the highest wages. We are persuaded by Goldin's (1994, 247) conjecture that "immigrants sought out labor markets with high wages." Goldin also finds that the arrival of immigrants caused wage rates to rise more slowly than they might have had the immigrants not come. More precisely, "in general, a 1-percentage-point increase in the population share that was foreign born depressed wages by about 1 to 1.5 percent" relative to cities with fewer foreign-born (250). In other words, without the influx of immigrants, wages in high-wage cities would have been higher still. Because of their propensity to move to high-wage cities, immigrants helped to equalize inter-city wage rate differences by alleviating labor shortages. Had there been no immigration, native-born workers would have moved to fill these positions, and the negative wage impact would have still been felt by the native-born residents of boom cities. To blame the immigrants for the adjustment back to equilibrium is simple scapegoatism.[21]

In conclusion, the work of economic historians does not identify any systematic role for immigration in raising wage inequality during the era of mass immigration. This "result" is not surprising. Recall the evidence presented earlier indicating that immigrants fell in about the middle of the American skill distribution. In any case, although the urban skilled-unskilled wage differential did rise, this rise seems to have been the result of forces other than immigration. Blacks remained bottled up in the low-wage South, but this, too, seems to have been due to factors other than im-

FIGURE 17.10 Immigrant Return Rate: Departures as a Percentage of Arrivals, 1870 to 1950

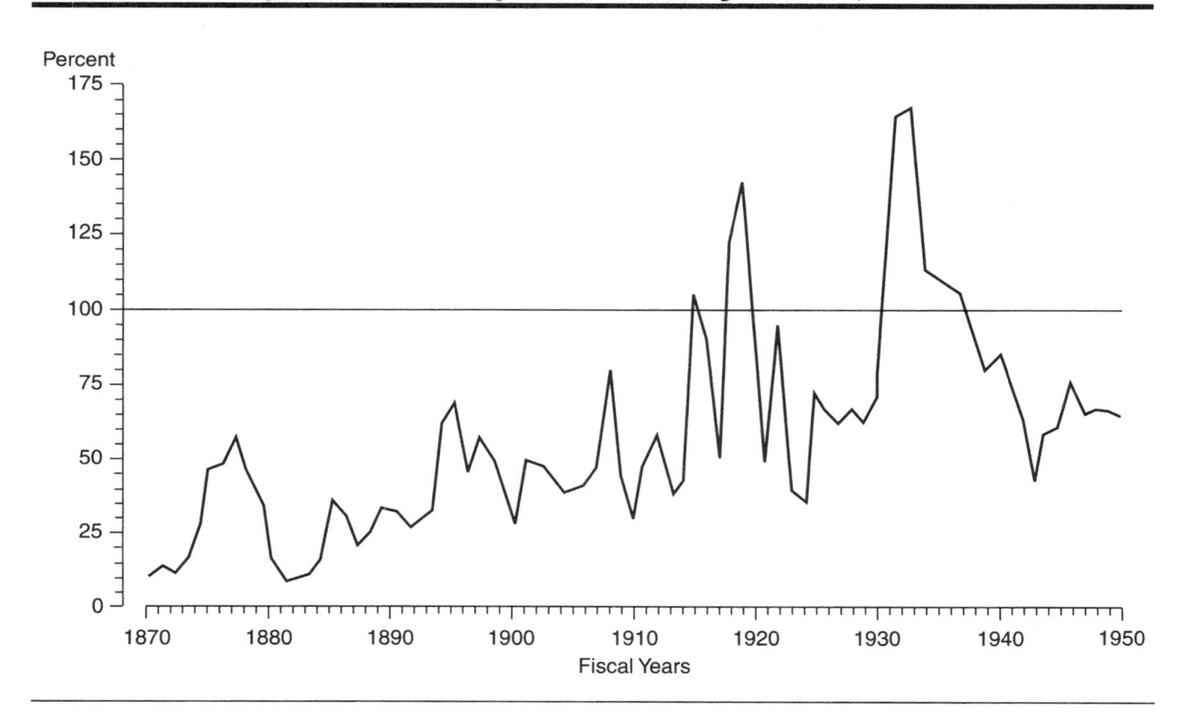

migration. In the meantime, regional wage inequality was reduced by the propensity of immigrants to locate in high-wage cities.

IMMIGRATION AND THE BUSINESS CYCLE

In the period of essentially unrestricted immigration before the 1920s, the annual inflows were extremely sensitive to economic conditions in the United States. Prosperous years attracted far more immigrants than depression years. This cyclical sensitivity is evident in figure 17.10, which displays the number of immigrant arrivals each year beginning in 1820. Between 1891 and 1895, for example, when the unemployment rate almost doubled from 4.5 to 8.5 percent, the number of immigrants fell by more than half, from 560,000 to 259,000. Even more dramatic is the almost 40 percent reduction in the number of immigrants in a single year, from 1.3 million in 1907 to 783,000 in 1908, in response to a sharp jump in the unemployment rate from 3.1 to 7.5 percent between those same years (U.S. Bureau of the Census 1975/1997a, C-89; Weir 1992, 341). Harry Jerome (1926, 208) concluded that the lag between economic activity and immigration in this period was only one to five months.

The strong sensitivity of migration to the U.S. business cycle in the pre-quota era essentially disappeared with the imposition of regulation (although the impact of the Great Depression is evident). As figure 17.8 shows, in the recent period immigration flows have increased in almost every year, with little sensitivity to year-to-year changes in macroeconomic conditions. This is because immigration is today closely regulated, and because there are more people who wish to migrate than visa slots available. Most successful immigrants have been waiting for admission for several years. Today year-to-year changes in the number of immigrants reflect policy changes, not changes in demand for admission.

It was not just the inflow of immigrants that responded to economic conditions in this country; the outflow of emigrants also responded to the rate of unemployment. Kuznets and Rubin (1954, table B-1 [95–96]) estimated return migration for the period 1870 to 1908 based on official reports of passenger departures and several assumptions about the mix of American citizens and returning immigrants in the departure data, the mortality of foreign-born in the United States, and the mortality of Americans when visiting abroad.[22] Figure 17.10 displays these departures as a fraction of all arrivals. The return rate rose from less than 10 percent in 1870 and 1881 to over 70 percent just before World War I. This increasing propensity of the United States to attract sojourners makes sense given the declining cost of transatlantic passage due to the continual technological improvement of the steamship following the introduction of scheduled service on the North Atlantic in the 1860s (Baines 1991; Wyman 1993).

Figure 17.10 shows large increases in the rate of departure during the business downturns after 1873, in 1885, after 1893, and in 1908. Throughout the period preceding World War I, the inward and outward movements of immigrants show a negative correlation. In 1910 and 1913, when arrivals were up, departures were down. In 1912, when arrivals were down, departures were up. The relationship changes with the onset of the war. Both arrivals *and* departures were down during the war years, and up during the immediate postwar period.

Brinley Thomas (1954/1973) has developed an elegant model of the "Atlantic Economy" as an integrated economic unit with flows of immigrants, goods, and capital moving in a rhythm of self-reinforcing and inversely related long-swing Kuznets Cycles.[23] This raises the possibility that immigration acted as a "governor" for the economy, slowing down the booms and cushioning the depressions.

Charles Kindleberger (1967), commenting on the European economy in the post–World War II period, has emphasized the potentially important role that sojourners might play in moderating the business cycle. In the upturns an elastic labor supply from abroad might relieve bottlenecks, moderate wage increases, and thereby extend an expansion. In downturns a reduced labor supply could alleviate the downward pressure on the wage rates earned by the resident population and reduce the drain on public coffers for support of the unemployed.

Recently, Hatton and Williamson (1998, ch. 8) have revived the issue of the role of sojourners in moderating the consequences of economic fluctuations in the United States. They compare the actual course of the business cycle of the 1890s with a "no-guest-worker counterfactual" and conclude that the impact of guest workers on the business cycle was "surprisingly small." Yet this assessment is based on their finding that "free migration muted the rise in unemployment during the biggest pre–World War I depression, 1892 to 1896, by only a quarter" (161). Size is in the eye of the beholder, but some would judge this effect as gratifyingly large.[24] Clearly an important area for further research would be to improve our understanding of the impact of the sojourner on the American economy at the turn of the century, especially in light of the possibility that temporary workers admitted as "nonimmigrants" and illegal migrants might be playing a similar role in the American economy today.

Concluding Observations

In this chapter, we have tried to highlight the distinctive features of the theoretical approach taken by scholars who analyzed the impacts of the mass migration into the United States in the two decades preceding World War I. Broadly speaking, this literature is couched in terms of the aggregate production function. The approach emphasizes advancing technology, productivity change, and changes in "factor proportions," chiefly the capital-labor ratio. Thus, capital accumulation, innovation, and change in the participation rate and skills of the labor force play the most important roles in explaining changes in the standard of living over time. The production-function approach directs attention to the close interrelatedness between the many diverse elements in the economy. Thus, an increase in immigration may, in the first instance, affect only the wages of resident workers who face direct competition. But beyond this immediate impact, immigration may have far-reaching impacts on the entire structure of the economy, including the labor-force participation, skill level, and sectoral distribution of the resident population; the amount and quality of capital; the organization of production; and the composition of output.

A notable difference between the historical studies and the recent literature on the impact of immigration is the propensity of the current literature to concentrate only on the first-round consequences. It is easy to show that these will be harmful to resident workers who face direct competition. Economic historians writing about the earlier period of high immigration went beyond the first-round effects. Taking a long-run perspective, they identified many aspects of the mass immigration that were beneficial from the point of view of the resident population.

One consequence of the neglect of growth and

development effects in the current literature is that attention is focused on the redistributive effects of immigration—redistributive either through the labor market or through the tax and transfer systems of the government. These "zero-sum" redistributions always create some losers. If history is any guide, however, the dynamic impacts of immigration accelerate the rate of growth so substantially that the redistributive effects are swamped. In the past, according to the consensus view, every group gained from immigration. Some gained relatively more than others, no doubt, but it is hard to find evidence that immigration reduced real wages of the resident population, worsened the income distribution, harmed the black population, or exacerbated the unemployment problem.

This is not to say that a broader, more wide-ranging approach to the current immigration will necessarily turn up the same or different but equally positive effects. In its specifics, the American economy is very different today than it was at the turn of the century. Labor markets are more rigid, segregated, and regulated. The government engages in more redistribution. Immigration, too, is different. It is now regulated. Immigrants are more likely to be motivated by considerations of family reunification or escape from persecution or wars than by economic opportunity. What is unlikely to have changed, however, is the intense interrelatedness of the many different elements within the economy.

Our historical overview, with its benign conclusions, is not a substitute for thinking hard about our current situation. It does suggest, however, that scholars might profitably take a longer view and shift at least some of their attention away from the redistributive issues and toward the impact of immigrants on productivity change, growth, and economic development.

This chapter was not presented at the Social Science Research Council Conference on Becoming American/America Becoming: International Migration to the United States, Sanibel Island, Florida (January 18–21). It was originally prepared at the request of the National Academy of Sciences for the U.S. Commission on Immigration Reform and presented to the Panel on Demographic and Economic Impacts of Immigration into the United States in September 1996. We would like to thank Ron Lee, James Smith, and Gavin Wright for their detailed comments and suggestions. Other participants at the meeting were also generous with their comments and perceptive questions. On other occasions we received valuable advice from James Dunlevy, Claudia Goldin, Christopher Hanes, Peter Lindert, and Simone Wegge. The students of the Universidad de San Andres, Buenos Aires, gave us an invaluable international perspective when we presented an early draft of the chapter at their seminar in April 1997. Joseph Ferrie and Jeffrey Williamson made available manuscripts of their forthcoming books on the economic history of immigration. Organizations that provided data used in this chapter include the Historical Labor Statistics Project at the University of California, the Social History Research Laboratory at the University of Minnesota, and the Interuniversity Consortium for Political and Social Research at the University of Michigan. We have also received assistance from Robert Barde, Tiffany Lee, and Chris Meissner. We are grateful to all these individuals and institutions.

Notes

1. These data tend to understate the level of the current flows relative to the earlier waves of immigration since they include only legal immigrants and, after 1907, exclude individuals coming into the country for temporary work. On the pitfalls of inferring long-run trends from the official series on immigrants, see Barde, Carter, and Sutch (1996).
2. Data on net immigration come from McClelland and Zeckhauser (1983) for 1820 to 1860, Kuznets and Rubin (1954) for 1870 to 1940, and U.S. Bureau of the Census (1990b, 1993a) for the recent period.
3. There are other influences on the real wage besides productivity. Of particular importance in this context would be discrimination (presumably against immigrants and in favor of native-born workers) and unionization (presumably weakened by heavy immigration).
4. In the early era of mass immigration between 1901 and 1913 (two business cycle peaks), annual additions to per capita output averaged 1.7 percent per year. (This calculation is based on figures reported in U.S. Bureau of the Census [1975/1997a, series F4]). As a result of this annual rate of growth over the twelve-year period, average per capita income increased nearly 25 percent. Moreover, this calculation understates the improvement in the well-being of the resident populations, since newly arrived immigrants are included in the 1913 population.
5. Thus, it becomes clear only after a careful reading that Stanley Lebergott (1964, 163) is interested in the impact of immigration on the wage rates of the entire population of workers, including the wages of the newly arrived immigrants. Nonetheless, Hatton and Williamson (1998, ch. 8) cite Lebergott in support of their contention that immigration slowed the growth rate of wages of *natives* and of *past immigrants* in the early decades of this century.
6. For an early and influential example of the counterfactual method that uses a computable general equilibrium model to examine the immigration question with

late-nineteenth-century data, see Williamson (1974b). Williamson concludes: "An America without immigrants indeed would have grown very differently from the way she actually did in the late nineteenth century" (387).

7. Edward Denison (1962, 177) suggests that workers will take home only 77.3 percent of the increase (labor's share in national income); the rest goes to the resident owners of capital and land. Other scholars estimate an even lower share for labor—closer to 60 percent (Abramovitz 1993; Taylor and Williamson 1997).
8. This is true today as well. Many workers own shares of pension and mutual funds that give them a direct and substantial owner's share in the nation's capital stock.
9. For evidence on the strong positive impact of immigration on the relative price of housing in New York City during the period 1830 to 1860, see Margo (1996).
10. These dynamic effects take about two to three years to work themselves out. This estimate is based on the typical length of a business cycle recovery in this period (Zarnowitz 1992, 23) and the on discussion by Easterlin (1968) of the adjustment process. See also the extensive literature on the response of construction investment to shortages (Abramovitz 1964, 130; Burns 1935; Derksen 1940). The dynamics of the adjustment process are complex, and quantification of the length of the lags is difficult. One reason is that causation runs in two directions: immigration stimulates investment and, at the same time, investment may stimulate immigration.
11. This is the so-called Walker Hypothesis, put forward by Francis Amasa Walker (1891).
12. For an overview of the literature on the role of the public health movement in improving environmental quality and reducing mortality, see Johansson (1994).
13. U.S. Bureau of the Census (1975/1997a, series C138–39); U.S. Immigration and Naturalization Service (1979, table 10; 1990, table 11; 1997, table 12). Official data on gender are not available for 1868, 1980, or 1981.
14. The spike in 1991 is the result of the Immigration Reform and Control Act of 1986. Individuals whose status was legalized by this act were disproportionately male.
15. For estimates, see North (1960, 612–61) and Simon (1960, 672).
16. An extensive collection of budget studies from the turn of the century surveyed both foreign- and native-born American workers (Carter, Ransom, and Sutch 1991). Often included was a question about the length of time an immigrant had been in the United States. These surveys, if handled carefully, might be used to estimate the differential savings propensities of immigrants and native-born workers. This work has yet to be done.
17. This exact sentence has been passed down to this edition of the textbook from Robertson (1973, 387), through Walton and Robertson (1983, 444). None of the editions offers a citation or evidence.
18. Hill (1975) classified farmers as "skilled," whereas the convention is to classify them as unskilled. Since the native-born were far more likely than the foreign-born to be farmers, Hill's scheme raises the relative measured skill level of the native-born.
19. Hatton and Williamson (1997) also use a computable general equilibrium model to assess the impact of immigration on wages. In their modeling, they rule out any possible dynamic effects of immigration. They also rule out the possibility of economies of scale. Not surprisingly, their analysis with this model suggests that immigration lowered the wage of the resident workforce.
20. For analyses of immigrant settlement patterns in the period prior to World War I, see Dunlevy (1980, 1983); Dunlevy and Gemery (1977a, 1977b, 1978); Dunlevy and Saba (1992); Gallaway and Vedder (1971, 1972); Gallaway, Vedder, and Shukla (1974); Lee (1957).
21. Goldin's (1994) estimates were made to help understand the reasons for a political sentiment to restrict immigration. In a sense, it was the "scapegoat factor" that she was attempting to measure.
22. Before 1908 the official statistics on immigrants counted only arrivals. They did not distinguish between permanent settlers and temporary guest workers, nor was there any comprehensive count of returning immigrants during this period.
23. See Albert Fishlow (1965, 200–203) for a critique of the Thomas model.
24. We have a number of technical reservations about the structure of the Hatton-Williamson counterfactual upon which their judgment is based, and also about their data on unemployment in the 1890s (Carter and Sutch 1992a). We strongly suspect that their procedure has biased the estimated impact downward.

18 Immigration and the Receiving Economy

Rachel M. Friedberg and Jennifer Hunt

THE PUBLIC DEBATE OVER immigration policy in the United States has become quite heated in recent years. The passage of Proposition 187 in California in 1994, making illegal aliens ineligible for public health and education services, and the Personal Responsibility and Work Opportunity Reconciliation Act of 1996, which curtailed immigrants' eligibility for public assistance, may herald the beginning of a new period of tighter restrictions on immigration and immigrant rights in the United States.

In assessing where the U.S. government should stand on issues related to immigration policy, it is important to have a firm grasp of the facts concerning immigration's effect on the U.S. political system, society, and economy and to sort out the facts from the myths. This chapter is about the economic dimension of immigration's impact on the United States.

Those who favor tight restrictions on immigration often argue that immigration has strong detrimental effects on the U.S. economy. They assert that immigrants have an adverse impact on the labor market outcomes of the native-born population, and that through the competition they create in the labor market, the job opportunities of the U.S. population suffer. Groups lobbying against immigration argue that we must guard against these detrimental consequences of immigration in our country. They assert that not only do immigrants take jobs away from American workers, but immigrants also drag down levels of pay, toward the standard of living of the countries from which they come.

Some supporters of relatively liberal entry laws contend that, despite these potential economic costs, it is our moral obligation as a nation to share the political freedom and economic opportunity we enjoy with others who wish to live here. Yet other advocates of more open immigration argue that the opponents of immigration have the economic evidence all wrong. They assert that immigrants do not compete with native-born workers but rather fill occupational slots that native-born workers would not be willing to take. They add that immigrants provide these services at a low cost to American employers and consumers. Moreover, they argue, immigrants revitalize our economy with their initiative and entrepreneurial spirit and contribute to economic growth.

This chapter outlines the major questions addressed in the economics literature concerning the impact of immigration on the receiving economy. The emphasis is on the effects of immigration on the labor market outcomes of the receiving population, including the impact on their wages, employment rates, unemployment rates, income growth, and migration patterns. The following section discusses the theory used in analyzing these questions, while the subsequent section provides a critical overview of the existing empirical evidence. Immigration has been an area of very active research in economics in recent years: most of the studies surveyed here have come out within the last five years.

To preview the conclusion of this chapter, to the extent that the literature in this area can be said to be in consensus, its conclusion is that immigration does not have significant adverse effects on the receiving economy. Immigrants are not found to cause a drop in the employment rates of the U.S. labor force, and although some studies find economically significant negative effects of immigrants on native wages, these magnitudes are very likely overestimates.

ECONOMIC THEORY FOR THE STUDY OF IMMIGRATION

Theory

Economics does not have a body of theory developed specifically for the purpose of studying immigration. Rather, immigration is examined in the context of the field of economics, which studies the particular aspect of immigration under consideration, using the tools and methodology standard to that field. Analyzing the effect of immigration on tax revenue and public assistance expenditures falls under the rubric of public finance; the consequences of immigration for economic growth call for the framework of macroeconomics; and the impact of immigrants on the employment opportunities of the native-born is a question for labor economics. Advances or changes in the approaches taken to studying immigration therefore follow changes in the field more generally. Almost no new theory has been developed specifically for obtaining answers to questions of immigration.

Models

Wages and Employment The fundamental model used to evaluate the labor market impact of immigration is that of supply and demand in the market for labor services. The interaction of sellers (workers) and buyers (employers) leads to a certain volume of transactions (the level of employment) at a certain price (the going wage rate). Labor economics studies the determination of the equilibrium price and quantity transacted in this market.

The values of those two variables depend on supply-and-demand conditions and on their interaction. A large supply of a good tends to depress its price and raise the quantity transacted, while scarcity on the supply side tends to raise the price of the good and lower the quantity transacted. High demand for a good tends to raise its price and raise the quantity traded. Conversely, low demand tends to lower the price and lower the quantity traded.

The most salient way in which immigration fits into this model is that immigration represents an increase in the number of workers interested in working at any given level of the wage rate. The result is an outward shift of the labor supply curve. According to the basic model of supply and demand, if there is no accompanying change in demand, this increase in supply will lead to a fall in the wage and a rise in the total number of people employed. (This is a movement down the labor demand curve, which indicates for any given wage how many workers firms will want to employ.) However, the rise in employment will not be as large as the immigration. Because the wage has fallen, some people will no longer desire to work—these may be immigrants or natives. If some are natives, the native employment rate (the ratio of employed people to population) will fall. From the employers' point of view, the wage has not fallen enough to warrant accommodating the full increase in labor supply. Total output is higher: because inputs have become cheaper, optimal output levels for firms rise. Looked at this way, the increase in employment may be said to be due to a "scale effect."

This analysis may be made richer by consideration of other factors of production—namely, inputs used in the production process such as natural resources, capital, and different types of workers. The analysis so far implicitly assumes that all production takes place with one type of worker, and that workers, both native and immigrant, are identical. If natives and immigrants are identical, they may be called perfect substitutes. There may instead be two types of workers in production, skilled and unskilled, which are imperfect substitutes in production. A firm could produce the same output by reducing the number of one type of worker and increasing the number of the other, but it will not replace one for one, as an additional worker has a different effect on production depending on his or her type.

In many situations, immigrants are unskilled, so we can model immigration as an expansion in the supply of unskilled workers (assuming that unskilled immigrants and unskilled natives are identical, or perfect substitutes). As in the simpler case, this expansion will lead to a fall in the wages of the unskilled, and the desired output level of firms will rise, since inputs have become cheaper (scale effect). This rise in output is likely to increase demand for skilled workers, tending to raise their wage. However, unskilled workers are now a more attractive option in the production process relative to the skilled, since their wages have fallen, and thus firms will shift the mix of workers away from skilled workers and toward unskilled workers (the "substitution effect"). This effect will tend to decrease demand for skilled workers, thus decreasing their wage. Hence, the net effect of unskilled immigration on the wages of skilled natives is ambiguous; it depends on the relative sizes of the scale and substitution effects. In general, immigrants reduce the wages of workers for whom they are perfect substitutes and have an ambiguous effect on the wages of those for whom they are imperfect substitutes.

Immigration increases the return to factors with which immigrants are complements. Two factors are called complements when they must be used together in production—for example, scalpels and surgeons. It is thought, more generally, that capital equipment and skilled workers may be complements: if a firm reduces the amount of capital it uses, it cannot keep output constant by increasing the number of skilled workers. Without capital to work with, skilled workers cannot contribute to production.

Consider the case of immigration of people who are perfect substitutes for skilled natives. Using reasoning similar to that of the previous case, we see that this will cause a fall in the wages of skilled workers. This wage reduction will cause a scale effect, inducing firms to use more of all inputs and tending to raise wages of unskilled workers and the return to capital. As skilled workers become relatively cheaper, firms will substitute skilled workers for unskilled ones, leaving the net effect on the wages of the unskilled ambiguous. However, since capital is complementary to skilled labor, there is no such substitution of skilled labor for capital: rather, the increased use of skilled labor leads to an increase in the use of capital. The return to capital therefore unambiguously rises. In general, immigration raises the return to factors with which it is a complement.

Popular fears of the effects of immigrants on wages often center on the idea that immigrants bid down wages by being prepared to work for less than natives. (Economists express this idea by saying that immigrants may have lower reservation wages than natives.) This is particularly likely in the case of illegal immigrants, whose options are more limited than those of comparable natives. If this is true, it means that immigrants have a steeper labor supply curve than natives: at low wages few natives but more immigrants will want to participate in the labor force, while at high wages most of both groups will want to participate. So when immigrants arrive, they increase labor supply more at the low end, thus decreasing wages further than an inflow of people identical to natives would have done.

The theory outlined so far assumes that the receiving economy does not trade with the rest of the world. The realization that countries trade with one another leads to models that have strong predictions about wages and prices throughout the world: the most simple trade model predicts that wages, prices, and the return to capital will be equalized across the world (so-called factor price equalization). The factor price equalization prediction comes from the following reasoning. With free trade, the relevant market for a good is the world market, and the price will be set in this market. Just as there would be a single price for a good in a closed economy with many firms, with free trade there will be a single world price for a good, determined by world supply and world demand by firms and consumers in many countries. The borders are irrelevant. It is assumed that no one country produces enough of a good to be able to alter the world price through changes in production.

If firms in all countries use the same technology (and this is an important and contentious assumption), labor demand for each firm (how much labor is demanded at any given wage level), which is determined by technology and the price of output, will be the same in all countries producing the same set of goods. This will lead to wages being equal in all countries: if one country has less labor, this would appear in our closed economy analysis to lead to the wage being higher in that country. However, this higher wage will induce firms in that country to increase production of goods using more capital and to reduce production of goods using labor intensively, thus decreasing labor demand and leading to the wage falling to the world level. Thus, a country's endowment of labor and capital will determine which goods it exports and which it imports. This luxury of adjusting the product mix with no change in goods prices was not available to the closed economy.

According to this analysis, immigration has no effect on wages in receiving or sending countries. An influx of labor into a country will cause it to produce more labor-intensive goods and less capital-intensive goods. Through this adjustment, the wage will return to its old level: the adjustment may be thought of as an export of immigrants in the form of higher exports (or lower imports) of labor-intensive goods. A similar analysis may be applied to emigration, and indeed, the whole analysis holds for prices and movements of capital.

Notice that factor price equalization, which predicts that immigration will not affect wages, also implies that there is no (economic) incentive for migration. Adding the real-world feature of tariffs to the model, however, can generate migration from poor to rich countries. Rich countries often impose tariffs on the import of labor-intensive goods (raising their domestic price above the world price). When this tariff induces domestic firms to produce more of the labor-intensive good, labor demand and hence wages both rise. This rise will occur (although it will not be beneficial to the country as a whole) if capital and labor cannot cross borders. If immigration is possible, however, people will seek to move to countries with such tariffs, lowering the wage. (Since the domestic price of the protected good can fall, the analysis in this situation is similar to the closed economy analysis.) Immigration will continue until the wage returns to the world level (by which time labor will be so abundant that the country will specialize in the production of that good).

The predictions of this most simple trade model are thought to be unrealistic, but even more complex versions of the model predict that small numbers of immigrants will have no effect on the wage. The initial analysis relied on the assumption that countries have similar enough factor endowments to produce the same goods. If there is an array of products with technologies requiring different intensities of labor and capital inputs, the mix of products a country produces will be determined by its endowment of factors. Small inflows of immigrants will lead to adjustment in production and trade of the existing goods, and the wage will be unaffected. However, a large enough inflow will lead to a fall in the wage and to a change by the country in its product mix toward more labor-intensive products.

Another assumption of the simple model that appears unrealistic is that all countries produce a given good with the same technology. If some countries have a technological advantage in the production of, say, labor-intensive goods, wages will be higher, inducing immigration to those countries. As in the simple trade model, this immigration will not affect the wage until the mix of products changes to be more labor-intensive. The advantage of this model is in proposing an economic incentive for migration (see Markusen 1983).

If the country receiving immigrants is a large one, the increase in output of labor-intensive goods spurred by immigration will be large enough to reduce the world price of these goods. This may reduce the wage, even under conditions where factor price equalization would hold for a small country.

Theoretical models thus have predictions ranging from a definite fall in the wage and employment rate (the closed economy case) to a wage fall after a certain threshold of immigration is passed, to no fall in wages (open economy models). Empirical work is therefore needed to resolve the question of whether immigration has any effect, and if so, how much.

Unemployment For theoretical purposes, a person is said to be unemployed if he or she would like to work at the wage offered to those with a job but cannot find a job. For empirical or, more simply, measurement purposes, emphasis is placed on the search process: only jobless persons actively searching for a job are unemployed. Others are considered out of the labor force, even if they would accept a job were it offered to them. Studies often measure the impact of immigration on the unemployment rate, which is defined as the ratio of the number of unemployed to the number in the labor force. An unemployed person is considered to be in the labor force, even though he or she does not have a job, so the labor force is the sum of employed and unemployed individuals. The labor-force participation rate, another variable of interest in the immigration context, is thus the ratio of those in the labor force to the population.

Simple economic models of labor supply and demand do not predict the existence of unemployment but rather predict that wages will adjust so that all who want to work at the going wage are able to do so. Many models analyzing the effect of immigration on wages hence have implications about employment, but not about unemployment. The closed economy model predicts that the fall in the wage allows employment to rise, but by less than the amount of the immigration, implying a fall in the labor-force participation rate. The simple open economy model does not incorporate a labor-force participation decision and results in trade adjustments, permitting employment to rise by the amount of the immigration.

The simplest explanation of the existence of unemployment predicts "frictional" unemployment. If an individual does not have a job, and wishes to find one, he or she will not have perfect information about what is available, and furthermore, applications can introduce delays, so that the job search will take some time. Thus, at any time a certain amount of unemployment will exist due to workers taking some time to discover and choose among possibilities and going through selection procedures established by firms. There are several reasons why individuals without a job may be searching for one: one example is entrants to the labor market, either first-time entrants who just finished their studies or people who temporarily left the labor force and now wish to work again. Another important category of unemployed workers are those who might have lost their previous job owing to "sectoral shifts." Over time the fortunes of sectors or industries wax and wane, possibly owing to technological innovation, for example. In recent years, the computer industry has grown and taken on new workers, while the typewriter industry has shrunk and laid off workers. Owing to the changing fortunes of industries, there will always be a certain amount of churning in the labor market. The changing fortunes of firms within an industry will have the same effect.

Both open and closed economy models predict that workers and capital will shift toward labor-intensive sectors in response to immigration, and even that new sectors will be established as the product mix changes. In the short run, this shift is likely to cause some frictional unemployment as workers look for new jobs and capital relocates. The immigrants themselves will, of course, suffer more unemployment than natives in the short run, since all of them wishing to work need to search for jobs, while only some of the natives will need to change sectors.

Economists have other explanations for unemployment, explanations that in turn have implications for the impact of immigration. Theory predicts, for example, that the minimum wage should cause unemployment. Minimum-wage legislation arises in response to a perception that the market wages for some groups are too low and that a higher wage should be legislated. If the minimum wage for a group is set above the market wage, the amount of labor demanded will fall to below what it would have been at the market wage. By contrast, the labor supplied will rise with the wage. Employment will obviously equal labor demanded, and hence a group of people who want to work at the offered wage will not be able to and are thus unemployed. There may be different minimum wages affecting different groups: some states in the United States have one general minimum wage, for example, and a subminimum wage for younger workers. In some countries and in some periods, minimum wages by occupation have been set.

The effect of union bargaining on unemployment is conceptually similar to that of the minimum wage. If unions bargain a wage above the market wage, employment will fall and unemployment will occur. Unions should cause unemployment only if they are active in all sectors of the economy. If there are nonunionized sectors, people displaced from union sectors may seek jobs in these sectors, pushing down the wage there. Some may prefer to keep trying for a better-paying union job, however, causing "wait" unemployment. Unions may negotiate wages by industry or occupation, or they may take age, experience, or tenure into account in setting the wage.

If there is immigration of people who are perfect substitutes for workers facing a wage fixed above the market rate, either a minimum wage or a union contract wage, there can be no downward adjustment of the wage. The amount of labor supplied will increase, and since the wage does not respond, unemployment will increase. It is again likely that in the short run the unemployment will disproportionately affect immigrants.

A more complex set of ideas about unemployment comes under the heading of "efficiency wages." These seek to explain why employers might voluntarily pay a wage above the market wage, a practice that would cause unemployment if practiced by all firms. (If not, workers should move to other firms, as in the union case.) The original motivation came from the development economics literature, which postulated that paying workers more might allow them to feed themselves better and make themselves more productive. In a developed country context, it is surmised that if firms cannot monitor their employees' output perfectly or cheaply, a good strategy may be payment of a higher wage to motivate them to work better (Shapiro and Stiglitz 1984). Then workers have more incentive to work harder: if they lose their job, they will face a wage reduction. Since if all firms do this unemployment arises, an additional motivation is the fear of unemployment if shirking is discovered. A related motivation may be a desire of firms to avoid quits, which they may find costly. Yet another hypothesis, the "fair wage" hypothesis, is that firms choose to pay efficiency wages to their less skilled workers to avoid the possibility of them becoming disgruntled at the wage gaps between the more and less skilled workers in the firm. Finally, firms may choose to pay efficiency wages in order to discourage their workers from trying to form a union, which might be even more costly to firms than efficiency wages.

If immigration occurs in a situation of efficiency wages, the increase in the size of the labor force allows firms to lower the wage and raise employment. However, the lower wage must be accompanied by a rise in the unemployment rate to maintain workers' incentive not to shirk. How the rise in unemployment is distributed across natives and immigrants is an empirical question.

Several unemployment theories thus suggest that immigration will increase unemployment. Efficiency wages may lead to higher long-run unemployment. The minimum wage may also do so if it is indexed to the real wage, as in France; if it has a fixed nominal level, however, as in the United States, it becomes less binding over time. New legislation may take the increase in labor supply into account. Likewise, unions may eventually take the increase in labor supply into account. An increase in frictional unemployment, however, should be only temporary.

Economic Growth The determination of growth in a country's average income per person, including the influence of immigration on that process, has been a subject of interest among macro and international economists rather than labor economists. Income may be thought of as the sum of wages and the return to capital, and income growth is likely to imply higher wages and returns to capital, although in principle it could come from growth in one or the other. The starting point of growth analysis is a model developed in the 1950s by Robert Solow (1956). A typical modified model assumes that production takes place using (physical) capital, labor, and human capital. Human capital refers to the knowledge or skill in which individuals may invest in order to make themselves more productive. It is assumed that individuals (labor) may migrate, bringing their human capital with them, but that physical capital cannot move internationally, and furthermore, that there is no trade between countries.

In this model, immigrants migrate to countries with high ratios of physical capital to labor, and hence high wage rates. The more capital a worker uses, the more productive he or she is, and hence the higher the wage he or she earns; the higher wage naturally attracts immigrants. The higher the ratio of physical to human capital, and hence the return to human capital, the more human capital the immigrants will bring with them. Analogous reasoning applies here: if the available skill in a country is matched with a lot of capital, it will be very productive and small increases in skill will bring significant productivity and hence wage increases. Thus, in this situation it will be particularly worthwhile for individuals with a lot of skill (human capital) to immigrate.

The key issue in the impact of immigration is whether immigrants bring enough human capital to offset their dilution of physical capital in the receiving economy. All else (and human capital in particular) being equal, immigration will reduce the productivity of workers, since the amount of capital per worker will fall and hence wages will fall. However, the increased human capital that might result from immigration is assumed to lead to an increase in the capital stock and makes all workers more productive. If immigrants have little human capital, their impact is akin to that of faster population growth in slowing per capita growth. If immigrant human-capital levels are higher than natives' by a sufficient amount, growth will be speeded up. Models of this type, as well as extensions that show how much people in a country save, have the obvious limitation of ignoring trade and capital mobility, although some steps have been taken to rectify this (see Braun 1992).

A common assumption in economics is that of constant returns to scale: if all inputs to production are changed by some multiple, output will be changed by that multiple. Intriguing outcomes arise if the possibility of increasing returns to scale is considered. With increasing returns to scale, the doubling of all inputs, for example, will lead to more than doubling of output. Thus, immigration to a country will increase output more than proportionately, raising both the wage and the return to capital and causing growth in per capita income (see Brezis and Krugman 1996).

METHODOLOGIES

Most of the recent research activity in the economics of immigration has not focused on improving existing theories of the economy but rather has been directed toward improving our ability to measure empirically the effects of immigration. The major developments in the field have been in the area of methodological approaches to empirical research. Researchers aim to measure the changes in economic variables that can be attributed to immigration. An underlying presumption of the research in economics is that the mechanisms at work are general ones, and that, with certain caveats, the conclusions of these studies can be applied to other labor market settings as well (other countries, time periods, and so on). This section reviews and critiques the empirical approaches used in the recent literature in the field and surveys the findings of that work.

Empirical economics involves the application of econometrics—tools of statistical analysis—to data on the exogenous and endogenous variables of interest, in order to generate predictions about the state of the endogenous variables. The question posed is usually of the form "Holding all other factors constant, what happens to variable Y when there is a change in variable X?" In this case, the questions are: What happens to various measures of economic conditions when there is a change in the level of immigration? The quality of an empirical study clearly depends on the quality of the model, the quality of the data, and the degree to which the assumptions under which the econometric technique yields unbiased results are satisfied.

A fundamental problem faced by social scientists is that, unlike researchers in the hard sciences, they cannot generally perform controlled experiments. The variable of interest is therefore not the only factor changing, so that it is difficult to isolate its effect. In the absence of controlled experiments, the next best alternative is to observe a natural experiment. Later in this section, we review some analyses of natural experiments relevant to the study of immigration. Most empirical economic research, however, has neither artificial nor natural experiments to use and must turn to other methods. In the area of immigration, the following techniques have been applied.

Exploiting the Geographic Dimension

In order to conduct an empirical investigation of the hypothesis that immigrant inflows have an impact on local economic conditions, it is necessary to collect data that display variation in the variables of interest. That variation can take place across any of several dimensions, including time or space. (Other dimensions could include different skill levels in the workforce, different industrial sectors of the economy, and so on.) This section describes the research that is more heavily based on spatial rather than temporal variation.

The Single Cross-sectional Approach Studies of immigration that emphasize geographic variation often use as their unit of observation the region, state, or SMSA (Standard Metropolitan Statistical Area), which encompasses the entire metropolitan area of a city. A cross-sectional data set is one in which observations on the variables of interest are made for many individual or geographic units at the same point in time. An example of such a data set is the Public Use Microdata Sample of the decennial U.S. census of population. Using this data set, in which the unit of observation is individual people, one can construct state or city-level measures of the fraction of the population that is foreign-born, the percentage of the labor force that is unemployed, the average earnings of employed workers, and so on, at a point in time in the census year.

The simplest approach to studying the relationship between immigration and domestic labor market conditions would be to collect cross-sectional data and to look for relationships among the variables of interest, such as a negative correlation between the density of immigrants in a city and that city's wage rate. If cities with more immigrants are found to have lower wages, that finding would be consistent with the hypothesis that immigrants have a depressing effect on the local wage level.

Data from the 1990 census can be used to perform this exercise (U.S. Bureau of the Census 1993b). Taking the unit of observation to be the metropolitan area, and using as the sample the largest thirty metropolitan areas in the United States, one can compute the correlation between the average wage and salary income of households in the metropolitan area and the percentage of that metropolitan area's population that is foreign-born. Contrary to what the hypothesis of an adverse impact of immigration would predict, the correlation between these two variables is actually positive in that data.

Should this result lead us to the conclusion that immigration raises the income levels of the people in the cities to which the immigrants migrate? The answer is no. There are several problems with the most basic approach just outlined.

The first problem with the basic cross-sectional approach is that factors other than immigration that may affect wages are not taken into account. The conceptual basis of this first approach lies in the idea that variation in immigration is random, rather like a drug intervention in a medical study. By giving the drug to some patients and not others, and then comparing the health outcomes of patients who receive more or less of the treatment, the researcher can learn about the drug's effects. But if the people in the control group are systematically different from those in the treatment group (that is, there is nonrandom assignment), the study is invalid. Differences in the ex-post medical condition of the two groups of subjects may be due to their original heterogeneity rather than to any effect of the drug under evaluation.

In the study of immigration, the equivalent condition is that, along dimensions related to the outcomes of interest, cities that receive more immigrants must not be, ex ante, systematically different from those that receive fewer immigrants. Immigrants must be, in essence, "randomly assigned" to cities. There are many factors apart from immigration that determine the level of wages in a city. If immigration is correlated with these factors, the correlation between immigration and wages may just be picking up the correlation between the third factor and wages. If these factors are observable variables on which the researcher has information, this bias can be eliminated by correcting for those factors (by including measures of them in a multivariate regression analysis). If the factors are unobservable, it is more difficult to obtain unbiased estimates. This problem is termed "omitted variable bias."

The second problem with the single cross-sectional approach is that of "endogeneity" (or "simultaneity"): in the relationship between two variables, the causality can run in both directions. If immigrants systematically choose to settle in locations with better labor market conditions, but their arrival causes a deterioration in those conditions, the sign of the resulting correlation between those two variables will be ambiguous. It will represent a combination of both phenomena and will not be amenable to a causal interpretation.

The Multiple Cross-Sectional Approach An improvement on an approach using cross-sectional data from one year is an estimation strategy that involves using two (or more) cross-sections of data. By using two point-in-time observations on the same set of geographic units, it is possible to circumvent some of the problems just pointed out.

Rather than correlating the stock of immigrants with the level of wages in a city, the fundamental idea behind this second approach is to look at the relation between the change in the stock of immigrants (that is, the net inflow) between two points in time and the change in the wage level between two points in time. In other words, it examines the correlation between changes in variables rather than levels of variables. This approach will go some way toward avoiding both the omitted variables bias and the endogeneity problem.

This method will help with the omitted variables bias if the omitted variables do not change over time and are hence subtracted away when the problem is considered in terms of changes in variables rather than in levels of variables. Such omitted variables may be referred to as "fixed effects." An example of something we think affects wages that does not change over time is the weather. Firms in cities with good weather and natural amenities are thought to be able to pay lower wages to their workers than firms in remote or unpleasant locations. Paying workers more to induce them to live in a place with less pleasing amenities is called a compensating differential. Since the weather does not change over time, however, we expect weather to have no effect on changes in wages.

Might the weather factor lead to a spurious cross-sectional finding of immigrants raising wages? If immigrants care less about the weather than natives, there are likely to be more immigrants than natives in regions with bad weather—and hence high wages. This would lead to an apparent finding that immigrants raise wages. However, this correlation would not be due to any true positive impact of the immigrants, but only to the correlation between immigration and a factor that does have a positive impact on wages. In this example, using the naive cross-sectional approach would lead to an underestimate of the negative impact of immigration on wages.

The existence of interindustry wage differentials that are fairly stable over time might also cause wage differences across cities that are hard to control for in the cross-sectional analysis. Economists have long been aware of the fact that workers in some industries are paid more than in others. These differences appear to be for reasons unrelated to worker characteristics that affect productivity; they are more related to the economic rents, or profit levels, present in the industry. The auto industry is an example of a relatively high-paying industry. The city of Detroit has a heavy concentration of jobs in the auto industry for mostly historic and institutional reasons unrelated to current economic conditions or to immigration. Detroit is an example of a city with idiosyncratically high wages (holding constant the characteristics of the workers in that city). If immigrants move to cities with idiosyncratically high wages, the correlation between wage levels and immigration could well turn out to be positive even if the attributes of those cities, such as the educational level of their workforces, are controlled for. This positive correlation would lead researchers to reach the mistaken conclusion that immigration does not have a negative impact on wages.

Looking at changes between two cross-sections may also help solve the causality issue (endogeneity). If immigrants care only about the level of wages in a city, and not about the growth in wages, a correlation between changes in wages and changes in immigrant density will reflect causality running from immigrants to wages and not the reverse. This assumption seems strong, however, so the causality issue may not be fully solved by this technique.

A study that takes the multiple cross-sectional approach is that by Claudia Goldin (1994).

Goldin studies the impact of immigration in the United States around the turn of the century. She uses several cross-sectional data sets from the period 1890 to 1923, including city-level wage surveys and the decennial censuses of population from that period. Goldin studies the effect of a change in the fraction of a city's population that was foreign-born (immigrant density) on the change in that city's wage level over the same period, analyzing different time periods and different occupation and industry groups. The results vary for the different groups and time periods, but the most common result is that a one-percentage-point increase in immigrant density reduces wages by between 1.0 and 1.6 percent.

A new study by George Borjas, Richard Freeman, and Lawrence Katz (1997) uses the same approach to analyze decennial U.S. census data from 1960 to 1990. They find that the measured impact of immigration on wages is highly sensitive to the time period studied, as well as to the level of geographic aggregation chosen. Not only the magnitude but even the direction of the effect varies. These inconsistent results lead them to conclude that studies exploiting geographic variation in immigration are unreliable. Reasons for this will be discussed further later in the chapter.

Another study that takes the approach of examining changes in variables, rather than just their levels, is that by Robert LaLonde and Robert Topel (1991). LaLonde and Topel further improve on the naive single cross-sectional approach by using individual-level data on men. In addition to immigrant density, they include as explanatory variables in the analysis other city-level factors that plausibly affect wages, including any fixed effects. It would not be possible to identify and correct for city fixed effects in a single cross-sectional data set at the city level.

LaLonde and Topel (1991) study both levels and changes in the key variables of interest, using data from the 1970 and 1980 U.S. censuses of population. Their approach is to study the impact of immigrants on the wages of groups for which new immigrants might, ex ante, be expected to be the closest substitutes in the labor market. The largest effect they find is that increasing the density of new immigrants in a local labor market by 10 percent reduces the wages of other new immigrants in that area by 0.3 percent. The effects for young African Americans and Latinos are of the same size but are not statistically significant. The results are the same regardless of whether the authors use as their earnings variable weekly or annual wages. This implies that the factor making these two variables differ—weeks of employment—is not significantly affected by immigration.

These two studies conclude that immigration is not a cause for concern about wages, but a number of imperfections remain in their approach. The Goldin study is affected by what may be called the composition problem. City-level wages are a composite of the wages of immigrants and natives in that location. If immigrants earn less than natives, cities with higher proportions of immigrants will have lower-than-average wages, even if immigrants have no negative impact on the native wage. This problem is well known and usually arises when the data do not allow immigrants and natives to be distinguished, hence precluding an examination of the outcomes for natives alone.

The remaining concern about LaLonde and Topel's paper is one that applies generally to papers relying primarily on cross-sectional variation in immigrant density (including Goldin's) and is related closely to the earlier discussion of trade and factor price equalization. This will be discussed in the next section.

The Issue of Factor Price Equalization When using the geographic approach, even if immigration would have a strong impact on employment and wage levels in a city, such an effect may not be detectable when labor markets are linked. An analogy can be made to a pool of water. If a bucket of water is poured into the pool, the water level at that particular spot will not be higher than the water level in the rest of the pool. Using a geographic, or cross-sectional, approach would lead to the conclusion that pouring water into a pool does not affect the amount of water it contains. This approach would miss the fact that the overall water level of the pool had risen.

Applying this analogy to the labor market, because goods and factors of production can (at least in theory) flow freely across the United States, we might expect that high wages in one geographic area would cause workers to flow in or firms to flow out, bringing the wage level back into line with wages elsewhere. The same would apply to the prices of other factors of production or to the unemployment rate.

As already explained in the previous section, economic theory predicts that, in the face of flows of goods, labor, and capital, prices will tend toward equality across different geographic areas. Although there is no strong evidence of factor price equalization across countries, it is more probable that it holds within countries. If the tendency toward factor price equalization is strong, the geographic approach will miss much of immigration's impact by focusing on differences across areas rather than on the aggregate.

One way of studying whether flows leading to factor price equalization nullify the cross-sectional approach is to look at one example of such a flow, namely, the migration of labor within the country. If immigration to a particular location leads to offsetting migration flows within the country, then, as in the analogy to the pool, the geographic approach will not pick up immigration's full impact.

Studies of internal migration in the United States are mixed in their conclusions about the reaction of internal migration to immigration from abroad. Two papers, by Randall Filer (1992) and by Michael White and Lori Hunter (1993), use data from the 1970s and conclude that internal migration does indeed offset inflows from abroad, tending to equalize population growth across areas. William Frey (1995d) confirms this finding for migration by low-income people, using 1990 census data, as do George Borjas, Richard Freeman, and Lawrence Katz (1997) using data from the 1960 to 1990 censuses. Timothy Hatton and Jeffrey Williamson (1995) also find evidence of this in data from the turn-of-the-century United States. They find that in the period 1880 to 1910 immigrants predominantly arrived in the Northeast, pushing natives to the West. However, other work—by Kristin Butcher and David Card (1991), Michael White and Zai Liang (1994), and Card (1997)—using recent U.S. data, does not find evidence of offsetting migration flows. Two studies of the European experience—Jörn-Steffen Pischke and Johannes Velling (1997) looking at Germany and Jennifer Hunt (1992) studying France—also do not find that internal migrants avoid areas of high immigration.

Other, more direct studies of factor price equalization indicate that, contrary to the example of the pool of water, the process of equalization across the aggregate labor market is quite slow. A recent study by Jörg Decressin and Antonio Fatàs (1995) finds that shocks to labor market conditions across regions in Europe take about four years to dissipate. In the United States, Olivier Blanchard and Lawrence Katz (1992) find that labor market shocks persist for even longer, with the local effects on unemployment and labor-force participation remaining for six years and the effects on wages persisting for as long as a decade. These durations indicate that the problems posed to the geographic approach by factor price equalization are not very serious.

The Instrumental Variables Approach The major problem remaining for cross-sectional studies using data at a level other than the individual level (that is, most studies, which use geographic units of observation) is that of causality. Immigrants' choice of location may be based not only on the level of the wage but also on the growth in the wage, so that differencing will not eliminate the causality problem. In some cases, a statistical solution called instrumental variables estimation may be used to establish causality.

There are many questions in economics in which the empirical identification of a particular causal effect is difficult because the observed relationship between two variables of interest involves more than one direction of causality. If variable X affects the level of variable Y, but variable Y also affects the level of variable X, it is difficult to identify separately the two effects that lead to their correlation. One way to isolate the effect of X on Y is to find a variable that is correlated with variable X but uncorrelated with any factor affecting variable Y. Call this variable Z. Using the instrumental variables estimation technique, the correlation of Z with X can be used to estimate the effect of X on Y. A variable such as Z is called an instrumental variable or "instrument."

In the case of immigration, the identification problem arises from the possibility that two connected phenomena are occurring. First, the more immigration there is to a city, the more its wage level falls. Second, the more the wage in a city falls, the less immigration there is to that city. In order to test the first proposition, it is necessary to find a variable that is correlated with immigration to a city (that is, the change in the immigrant density) but does not itself influence that city's wage level and is not correlated with other omitted factors that do (which would cause a simultaneous feedback to changes in immigration).

Using instrumental variables estimation to correct the endogeneity problem that may exist in other studies has a potential second beneficial effect on the estimation as well. If the instrumental variable, in addition to being uncorrelated with nonimmigration factors affecting wages, is also uncorrelated with the flows of capital, labor, and goods that lead to factor price equalization, the instrumental variables approach will get around the problem of factor price equalization posed by the other approaches as well.

Because so few variables in economics can really be considered exogenous (that is, not determined within the system being studied), it would very often be desirable to use the instrumental variables technique to solve the identification problem in estimation. However, much empirical analysis calls for instrumenting for the same reason that it is difficult to identify an instrumental variable in any given estimation situation: it is hard to find a variable that is correlated with X and yet uncorrelated with Z, except through its correlation with X.

One study that identifies such an instrumental variable is that by Joseph Altonji and David Card (1991). Altonji and Card set out to study the effect of changes in the immigrant density of a city on the change in that city's labor market outcome variables. The instrument needed in this case is one that is correlated with the change in the city's immigrant population but does not itself influence the change in labor market outcomes. The instrument they identify is the density of immigrants in that city in the base year. Ann Bartel (1989) found that in the 1970s immigrants tended to settle in cities where other similar immigrants already lived. Thus, the original immigrant density of a city is a good predictor of future immigration to that city. Assuming that the original ethnic makeup of a city in a base year does not have an effect on changes in the labor market from that base year to a later year, the fraction of a city's population who were foreign-born in the base year can be used to instrument for the change in that density over time. If these assumptions are correct, this study avoids all the problems mentioned.

Altonji and Card (1991) use data from the 1970 and 1980 U.S. censuses. They focus on the groups thought most likely to face competition in the labor market from immigrants: white male high school dropouts, and African American and white females, and African American males with a high school education or less. They study several different labor market outcomes. Their results suggest that immigrants had an unexpected negative effect on unemployment in the census week, the opposite of the expected result. Immigrants also had a negative effect on the fraction of the population who worked in the previous years and on weekly earnings in the previous year. No significant impact was found on the labor-force participation rate, the employment-to-population ratio in the census week, or the number of weeks worked in the previous year. The magnitudes of the coefficients imply that a one-percentage-point increase in the percentage of foreign-born in a city reduces the unemployment rate by 0.23 percentage points; reduces the number who worked in the previous year by 0.25 percentage points; and reduces wages of unskilled natives by 1.2 percent, at most. Put in terms of an elasticity, a 10 percent increase in the foreign share of the population implies a 0.86 percent fall in weekly earnings (wages).

The technique developed by Altonji and Card (1991) is applied to data from West Germany by Pischke and Velling (1997). Their data cover changes over the period from 1985 to 1989. This study finds no significant adverse effect of immigration on employment or unemployment.

A new study by Card (1997) divides workers into ten skill groups and, using the 1990 census, estimates the effect of changes in the relative supplies of different skill groups caused by immigration across cities on employment and wages, finding small effects.

It is sometimes difficult to decide without some point of comparison whether the size of an effect is large or small. For the Altonji and Card (1991) result, an interesting comparison is with the effect of "generational crowding," studied by Finis Welch (1979). Welch sought to estimate how much the earnings of baby boomers were lowered by the large numbers in their age group or cohort. The theoretical basis is that people of different ages are imperfect substitutes in production, and that we can apply the same analysis to the case of an increase in fertility that we did to an increase in the number of unskilled workers, for example. We expect that a shift out in the supply of an age group will lower the wages of that age group. Welch finds that an expansion in the cohort size of 10 percent had an effect on weekly wages of white male high school dropouts very similar to the immigrant effect calculated by Altonji and Card. His finding that the effect on annual wages is considerably larger suggests that an important part of generational crowding comes through less employment, while Altonji and Card found small or positive effects on employment outcomes. Furthermore, the actual increase in cohort size induced by the baby boom is calculated by Welch to have reduced high school dropout wages by 12 percent between 1967 and 1975. To cause the same wage reduction would require a 140 percent (or ten-percentage-point) increase in the immigrant share, using Altonji and Card's estimate.

Using Production Functions The production function is a mathematical formula that expresses the quantity of output as a function of the quantity of the various inputs to the production process (namely, factors of production). Data on inputs and output can be used to estimate empirically the form and parameters of production functions. These parameter estimates reveal the relative contributions of different factors of production as well as on what the marginal contribution of each factor depends. They show the rate at which it is possible to trade off one input for another in production, what is known as the elasticity of substitution among factors. If we make the common assumption that factors are paid according to their marginal contribution to output, the estimated production function parameters can be used to calculate the effect that a change in the quantity of one factor would have on the market price of another factor.

Applied to the case of immigration, immigrants and natives are allowed to represent two distinct inputs to the production process. Empirically estimating a production function with native and foreign-born labor as two of the inputs allows estimation of the effect on the wages of the native-born of an increase in the number of foreign-born. In theory, this wage impact could be positive or negative, depending on the relationship between these two factors of production.

A 1982 paper by Jean Grossman uses this approach to gauging the wage impact of immigration. Grossman estimates the form of the production function using cross-sectional data from 1970 on the inputs and outputs of SMSAs across the United States. Her estimates suggest that a 10 percent rise in the number of immigrants employed in a city lowers the wages of natives in that city between 0.2 and 0.3 percent. In a similar study of Canada for 1980, Ather Akbari and Don DeVoretz (1992) find virtually no effects and conclude that immigrants do not have an impact, except possibly in those industries in which they are most heavily concentrated.

George Borjas (1987b) performs the conceptually closely related exercise of estimating labor demand functions using SMSA-level data from the 1980 census. He finds that a 10 percent rise in the number of immigrants reduces the wages of natives by at most 0.4 percent. (Both Borjas and Grossman find that the wages of earlier immigrants are more strongly affected.) This is about half the size of the Altonji and Card (1991) estimate.

Using the 1980 and 1990 censuses, David Jaeger (1996) estimates the elasticity of substitution between immigrants and native workers for various educational groups and concludes that within educational groups immigrants and natives are nearly perfect substitutes. He then estimates an aggregate production function and finds substantial effects: immigration explains up to one-third of the decline in the wages of high school dropouts during the 1980s.

Exploiting the Time Dimension

Some researchers have used greater—or in some cases total—reliance on time series variation in data to circumvent the thorny issues associated with factor price equalization and endogenous immigrant location choice present in more geography-based analyses. Pure time series data consist of observations at different points in time of a single entity, usually a country. "Panel" data combine cross-sectional and time series variation by following several entities—which may be individuals, firms, or countries—over time. If time series data on the relevant variables, such as wages and immigration, are used at the national level, the estimate of the impact of immigration comes from seeing how changes in immigrant flows over time are correlated with changes in wages over time. The estimate therefore is not influenced by where in the country immigrants settle, nor by the fact that the impact of immigrants may be spread around the country. However, time series estimation has its own endogeneity problem: more immigrants will choose to go to (or will be allowed to enter) a country at times when labor market outcomes are favorable in that country. Thus, time series will also tend to underestimate the impact of immigrants unless the instrumental variables technique is used.

Time Series David Pope and Glenn Withers (1993) use pure time series analysis for Australia over the period from 1861 to 1981 and find no negative effects of immigration on native unemployment or wages. In their study, they use the labor market characteristics of sending countries and transport costs to Australia as instrumental variables for the migration rates. These variables are likely to influence migration rates but are unlikely to influence Australian labor market outcomes in other ways.

Hatton and Williamson (1995) use time series data for the United States between 1890 and 1913 and find that a one-percentage-point increase in the proportion of immigrants in the labor force reduced wages by 0.4 to 0.5 percent. This is close to half the magnitude found by Goldin (1994) (and by Altonji and Card [1991]), although, given the huge immigrant flows of this period, it still translates into substantially lower wages than in the absence of immigration. Because of constraints on the historical data, the results are affected by the composition problem.

Wage Inequality Literature A series of recent papers motivated by rising inequality in the United States has put more weight on time series variation in immigration rates. A very large number of papers have sought to document and explain the rise in U.S. wage inequality, a level of inequity which is high by international standards (for a summary, see Levy and Murnane 1992). The ratio of the wage at the ninetieth percentile of the distribution to the wage at the tenth percentile of the distribution (a simple measure of inequality), for example, rose by almost 30 percent from the late 1960s to 1987 (Katz and Murphy 1992) and was about 28 percent higher than in Britain in 1989 (Katz, Loveman, and Blanchflower 1995). Much attention has been given to the fact that in the 1980s a contribution to the rise in overall inequality was made by an increase in the return to education—that is, by an increase in the wage gaps between people of different educational levels. The absolute wages of high school dropouts fell over this period, while those of college graduates rose considerably. One hypothesis tested is that immigration of largely unskilled workers may have played a role by increasing the supply of high school dropouts. The usual principle of supply and demand applies here: if the number of high school dropouts rises relative to the number of college graduates, the relative wage of high school dropouts would be expected to fall.

The papers testing this hypothesis have estimated elasticities similar to or smaller than the Altonji and Card (1991) and Goldin (1994) estimates, but the context of wage inequality in which the results are set suggests that immigration may have economically important effects. Such studies have used both national-level time series and a panel of cities and use yearly data from the Current Population Survey (CPS).

Because the variable of interest in these studies is a relative rather than an absolute wage, an assumption is necessary to compare these results to the others discussed. We assume that falls in the relative wage of high school dropouts compared to that of college graduates come entirely from a fall in the high school dropout wage. In fact, some comes from a rise in the college graduate wage, and hence these calculations overstate the negative impact of immigration on the absolute wage of the unskilled.

Borjas, Freeman, and Katz (1992, 1997) use time series data for the United States from 1967 to 1987 using the following estimation strategy. The main variable investigated is the ratio of average college graduate wages in a given year in either the United States or a particular region to average high school dropout wages. A regression is run to establish the influence on this ratio of the relative supply of different educational groups—that is, how the number of high school dropouts or high school graduates relative to college graduates influences the ratio. The studies find as expected that increasing the relative supply of high school dropouts reduces their relative wage. A calculation is then made as to the contribution of immigrants to the high school dropout group in the 1980s, and hence as to the contribution of immigrants to the fall in the relative wage of high school dropouts.

Between 1980 and 1988 immigrants as a proportion of the labor force rose from 6.9 percent to 9.3 percent, and the results of Borjas, Freeman, and Katz's first paper (1992) suggest that over the same period immigration accounted for one-quarter of the 10 percent decline in the relative earnings of high school dropouts. Using the figures on change in immigrant density, and making the assumption that the relative wage change came entirely from a fall in the dropout wage, we can convert this number to make it comparable to those in the studies discussed earlier. Thus, a one-percentage-point increase in the proportion of immigrants reduces the absolute wage of dropouts by at most 1.2 percent, the same magnitude as calculated by Altonji and Card (1991). Borjas, Freeman, and Katz's second study (1997) finds that on the order of half of the decline in the wages of high school dropouts from 1980 to 1995 can be attributed to immigration.

George Borjas and Valerie Ramey (1995) look at relative wages of high school dropouts and college graduates in the United States, using a panel of forty-four SMSAs from 1977 to 1991. Their estimates suggest that a one-percentage-point increase in the fraction foreign-born reduces the wage of high school dropouts relative to college graduates by 0.6 percent. This is half as large as the Altonji and Card (1991) estimate.

Although time series analysis avoids the cross-sectional biases due to immigrant location choice and factor price equalization, data constraints cause the papers emphasizing the time series dimension to introduce new biases, leading to an overstatement of the impact of immigration. The problems arise from the fact that immigrants (and hence immigrant density) can be identified in the CPS only in certain years. This means, first, that in the central regression the wages being measured are those of both immigrants and natives, and hence the regression suffers from the composition problem: it does not measure the effect of the size of educational groups on the wages of native high school dropouts relative to native college graduates, but rather of all high school dropouts to all college graduates. The same problem exists with the independent variable used in the regression (in the case of Borjas, Freeman, and Katz [1992, 1997]): using the relative supplies of all high school dropouts and all college graduates constrains the impact of a native high school dropout to be the same as that of an immigrant high school dropout. A similar comment applies to the findings of Hatton and Williamson (1995), who in their regression estimate the impact of the total labor force on wages.

For the papers using recent data, there is good reason to expect the composition effect to be large and the impact of immigrant dropouts on natives to be lower than the impact of native dropouts on natives: immigrant and native dropouts are unlikely to be good substitutes for each other because even among high school dropouts immigrants have much less education. For males in 1989, 30 percent of U.S.-born high school dropouts had eight or fewer years of education, while 75 percent of foreign-born high school dropouts had eight or fewer years (LaLonde and Topel 1994). A calculation can be made as to the bias introduced by the composition effect: if foreign-born high school dropouts earn 20 percent less than native dropouts, the increase in their number from 1980 to 1988 would be expected to reduce the average dropout wage by 1.5 percent because of the composition effect alone, and this magnitude is large compared to the total impact of 2.5 percent ascribed to immigration in Borjas, Freeman, and Katz (1992, 1997).

Borjas and Ramey (1995) attempt to deal with the second problem by including the percentage foreign-born explicitly on the right-hand side of their regression; doing so avoids constraining the impact of natives to be the same as that of immigrants. However, their foreign-born variable is constructed by interpolating between the 1970 and 1980 censuses and the 1989 CPS, and the time series variation is thus to a large extent a trend.

Growth Studies An empirical assessment of the effect of immigration on growth raises a new set of measurement problems. The principal one is simply that while immigration may affect growth, growth surely affects immigration: at least when choosing among countries with similar levels of economic or labor market well-being, an immigrant will prefer a country with strong growth, which promises higher future levels of well-being than a country with slow (or negative) growth. As always with statistical simultaneity problems, if a good instrumental variable can be found, causality may be established. In this case, a variable that influences immigration but does not directly influence growth is required.

An empirical examination of the impact of immigration on growth is provided by Robert Barro and Xavier Sala-i-Martin (1992) for Japan and the United States. The main thrust of this paper is an issue of current interest to macroeconomists seeking to explain relative standards of living in different countries: whether the per capita income of regions or countries tends to converge over time. They use panel data on regions over time to run regressions, including the level of per capita income and net migration rates as predictors of the growth in per capita income. The coefficient on the level of per capita income is a measure of convergence, or regression to the mean: convergence occurs if regions with currently low levels of income grow faster and countries with currently high levels of income grow slower. The authors assess the effect of immigration not only by the coefficient on immigration but also by its effect on the convergence coefficient. For both Japan and the United States, adding migration to the convergence regressions raises the convergence coefficient slightly and yields a positive coefficient on migration. For the United States, this coefficient suggests that a one-percentage-point higher net migration rate is associated with a growth rate increase of 0.1 percent. These results are for a regression without use of instrumental variables.

Barro and Sala-i-Martin (1992) then propose the use of instrumental variables for migration: temperature and population density of the region. Temperature would be expected to influence migration, but not economic growth, directly, while the idea behind population density is that it is a proxy for housing costs, or possibly for congestion, which would discourage migration but may not directly affect economic growth. When the instrumental variables specification is used, the coefficient for migration becomes statistically insignificant for both the United States and Japan (and the convergence coefficient is virtually unchanged). The point estimate suggests that a one-percentage-point rise in the net migration rate raises long-term growth by 0.01 percent for the United States, and by 0.04 percent for Japan, but statistically it cannot be asserted with confidence that these numbers are different from zero. The authors conclude that migration has little effect on growth. However, the results look as though the instruments may not have been suitable: either they may not have been very highly correlated with migration or they influenced growth through a channel other than migration.

A puzzle arises when the work of Barro and Sala-i-Martin (1992) is compared with that of Blanchard and Katz (1992). The latter study uses data on U.S. states to examine how states adjust to economic shocks. If a state experiences a shock to labor demand not necessarily experienced by the whole country—for example, Texas is hit by a fall in the price of oil—one adjustment mechanism would be for the wage to fall, so as to keep everyone who wished to work at the lower wage employed. This would imply a fall in the labor-force participation rate. Another possibility is that the wage might not fall quickly: in this scenario, employment falls by more than in the first case, labor-force participation falls less, owing to the high wage, and unemployment arises. Finally, rather than remaining unemployed, some people may prefer in the short or long term to leave the state.

Blanchard and Katz (1992) estimate a system of equations for employment growth, participation rates, and unemployment rates in states over time. They find that after a shock to a state's employment growth, participation and unemployment rates eventually return to their preshock levels. Employment returns to its old growth rate, but no higher; as a result, employment is permanently lower than it would have been in the absence of a shock. (Since the growth rate was lower for a while, it would have to rise above its old rate to bring the level of employment back to where it would have been.) Since participation and unemployment rates are back at their old levels, the lower employment must be due to emigration from the state. This picture suggesting that migration is a very important equilibrating mechanism for recovery to shocks to a state is at odds with the Barro–Sala-i-Martin results.

Currently we have only international evidence to turn to in order to shed light on this inconsistency. Juan Dolado, Alessandra Goria, and Andrea Ichino (1993) use a panel of countries to study migration among the Organization for Economic Cooperation and Development (OECD) countries. They base their study on the theoretical growth model described in the theory section by performing what is known as structural estimation, which involves entering the variables into the regressions in nonlinear ways determined by the equations of the theoretical model. Structural estimation, while following theory more closely than the usual linear reduced-form alternative, does not obviate the need to use instrumental variables in cases where simultaneity is an issue. These authors use as their instruments for migration lagged values of migration (the value of migration in the previous period), savings rates, schooling rates, and population density. This paper is also primarily concerned with the convergence issue and therefore does not report the coefficient on the net migration variable. However, the finding that adding migration reduces the convergence coefficient is more in accordance with the Blanchard and Katz finding.

As discussed earlier, the results we should expect here are determined by the human-capital level of the migrants compared to the natives. Dolado, Goria, and Ichino (1993) document that immigrants to OECD countries have lower human capital than natives. George Borjas, Stephen Bronars, and Stephen Trejo (1992) investigate empirically what influences the migration of high- and low-skill individuals within the United States. A theoretical model called the Roy model makes predictions about which sorts of people will migrate from one country to another. Clearly people move from lower to higher wage or income regions, but this calculation is affected by the position of the individual in the distribution of the original region and by their likely position in the distribution of the potential destination. A person with high skills who lives in a region with a compressed wage distribution (where wage gaps between high- and low-skilled individuals are low) will have more to gain from leaving than an unskilled person in the same region and will seek out a region with a dispersed wage distribution (as well as one with a high mean wage). An unskilled person may still want to leave a region of compressed wages if the mean wage is low, but such a person, in addition to seeking a region with a high mean wage, will tend to choose one with a compressed wage distribution.

Borjas, Bronars, and Trejo (1992) find empirical evidence that, conditional on the mean wage, regions with compressed wages encourage the skilled to emigrate, while regions with dispersed wages attract the skilled. This theory and empirical evidence show that the quality of immigrants compared to natives will depend on the dispersion of wages in the receiving country. Migrant quality has not been explicitly accounted for thus far in the internal migration and growth literature. It is possible that doing so might help resolve the puzzle of U.S. internal migration and its effects on growth.

Exploiting Natural Experiments

Certain studies have focused on episodes of immigration that the authors hope suffer less from the factors that make statistical analysis, especially the determination of causality, so problematic. These studies focus on an episode of immigration that was politically motivated and hence does not suffer from the time series problem that immigrants arrive at times when the economy and labor market are doing well. In some cases, the choice of location within the receiving country was also determined to a large extent by noneconomic factors, such as proximity to the point of arrival, which in turn was related to the political event that caused the arrival. Another advantage is that the episodes chosen were very sudden and large inflows that occurred within a brief space of time; focusing on such events should make it easier to isolate responses to the arrivals from other factors that change more gradually over time.

One example of such an episode is the arrival in Miami of the Cuban refugees of the Mariel boatlift in May 1980, examined by David Card (1990). Most of the refugees went to Miami because it is close to Cuba; they increased the population of Miami by about 7 percent. Since both timing and location were fairly exogenous, Card simply examines the evolution of variables of interest in the period immediately following the boatlift, comparing the outcomes with those in similar cities and ascribing differences in patterns to the arrival of the Mariels. Card uses yearly data from the Current Population Survey to follow wages, employment rates, and unemployment rates for unskilled whites and African Americans, for non-Cuban Latinos, and for Cubans. Only Cubans appear to have been negatively affected. It is not possible in the data to distinguish Mariel Cubans from earlier Cuban arrivals, however, and thus the observed decline of Cubans could reflect assimilation difficulties (or lower quality) of the Mariel Cubans. Some information on this point is available from a supplement to the Current Population Survey: it shows that the Mariels did indeed earn less and had higher unemployment than other Cubans, by an amount that is consistent with the "composition effect" being the cause of the observed overall decline for Cubans. Earlier Cubans thus seemed to have been unaffected by the Mariel boatlift. Card finds that population growth in Miami slowed, however, and he speculates that other migration to Miami may have been reduced in response to the boatlift. Since Card examines yearly data, any type of factor price equalization must have happened very quickly.

A second example of such a study is that by Jennifer Hunt (1992), which examines the repatriation to France in 1962 of Algerians of European origin. The independence of Algeria from France, agreed upon in March of that year, prompted the emigration within the space of a year of virtually the entire population of European origin, most of whom went to France. This inflow increased the French labor force by 1.6 percent, but the repatriates were very unevenly distributed through the country: a vast majority settled in the south, where the climate was more similar to Algeria's and a small number of people who had left Algeria during the war of independence had settled. Hunt uses this cross-sectional variation in the 1962 and 1968 census data to assess the impact of the repatriates on the labor market outcomes of natives and addresses the usual cross-section biases by instrumenting the fraction of immigrants with the temperature and the density of pre-1962 repatriates. She finds that a one-percentage-point increase in the repatriate share of the labor force reduced the wage of a region by at most 0.8 percent (zero in some specifications) and raised the unemployment rate of natives by 0.2 percentage points. Hunt found that internal migration within France did not respond directly to the location choice of the repatriates (but did respond insofar as the repatriates affected labor market variables), and that in fact foreign (nonrepatriate) immigrants appeared to be attracted to areas with more repatriates.

In a recent paper, Rachel Friedberg (1997) studies the mass migration of Russians to Israel in the early 1990s. This migration was precipitated by the lifting of emigration restrictions in an unstable Soviet Union and by the open immigration policy of Israel toward Soviet Jews, who faced more restrictive entry policies elsewhere. The immigration was therefore largely exogenous to economic conditions in Israel. Using both individual- and occupation-level data, the paper exploits the fact that the occupational distribution of the Russian immigrants was different from that of the native population. There is a negative cross-sectional relationship between native wages and the presence of Russian immigrants in an occupation. There is a weaker negative relationship between native wage growth and the influx of immigrants. This demonstrates that some of the cross-sectional relationship is due to the fact that immigrants entered low-wage occupations, rather than being fully attributable to a depressing effect of immigration on wages. In addition, since the distribution of immigrants across occupations may not have been exogenous to relative wage or employment growth across occupations, the paper instruments for the influx of immigrants into an occupation, using information on the immigrants' previous occupations in the Soviet Union. When the instrumental variables technique is used, the negative impact disappears. Immigrants entered low-wage, low-wage-growth, contracting occupations but did not have an adverse impact on the labor market outcomes of natives.

A final example of the natural experiment literature is a paper by William Carrington and Pedro deLima (1996) that examines the return of Portuguese colonialists from Africa after a Marxist revolution in 1974 led to the sudden independence of the colonies. They use several approaches to the problem: time series analysis, comparisons with Spain, and cross-sectional analysis across the twelve provinces of Portugal. The approaches give quite different answers, making it difficult in this case to reach a firm conclusion. Apart from this paper, the natural experiment literature adds to the evidence suggesting a limited impact of immigrants on natives.

Computable General Equilibrium

A series of studies of immigration use the computable general equilibrium technique. This technique uses a set of equations describing the whole economy and sets their parameters to numerical values obtained from estimation. Data on immigration can be fed into an appropriate computable general equilibrium model, and predictions of the responses of other variables in the economy can be obtained. These studies (see, for example, Hatton and Williamson 1995; O'Rourke, Williamson, and Hatton 1994; Williamson 1974c; Williamson and Lindert 1980) suggest that the large immigrant flows of the nineteenth century had an important negative impact on real wages, leading to convergence with the old world and higher inequality.

Conclusion

Economic theory predicts variously that immigration may be beneficial or detrimental to the receiving country's workers, or indeed that immigration may have no effect on them. Even the sign of this impact must therefore be determined empirically. Given the widespread nature of the popular view that immigration has large adverse effects on the economic outcomes of the native-born population of the United States, there is surprisingly little evidence to support this. There are several difficulties associated with empirical estimation of the impact of immigration, and we have argued that some studies may over- or underestimate it. Nevertheless, it appears to be difficult to detect large immigration-induced deteriorations in labor market outcomes, while the evidence on the link between immigration and economic growth is for the moment less certain. Most research finds that a 10 percent increase in the fraction of immigrants in the population reduces the wages of even the least skilled native-born workers by at most 1 percent. This magnitude would be large enough for immigration to have been responsible for one-quarter of the rise in wage inequality in the United States in the 1980s. We have argued, however, that the true magnitude is likely to be considerably smaller. Evidence of immigrants reducing employment or labor-force participation rates or increasing the unemployment rate is even harder to find.

In evaluating the overall consequences of immigration for the United States, other factors not considered here—both economic and noneconomic—must be taken into account. These include the effect of immigration on government revenue and expenditures, consumer prices, trade, residential patterns, crime, and the demographic composition of the population, to name a few. The social dimensions of immigration may in fact play a more important role than economic factors in shaping public opinion on immigration. A recent, well-publicized report by the National Academy of Sciences (Smith and Edmonston 1997) concludes that the overall economic gains and losses from immigration are both modest: the domestic gain is between $1 billion and $10 billion per year, in the context of an $8 trillion U.S. economy. Future interdisciplinary research could usefully link economic and social considerations and examine the interaction of both with public opinion.

19 Fiscal Impacts of Immigrants and the Shrinking Welfare State

Thomas J. Espenshade and Gregory A. Huber

To understand the budget negotiations now under way between the President and Congress, it is essential to grasp this philosophical distinction: The Republicans who control Congress want to shrink the Federal Government and reduce its presence in the lives of Americans; the President, for the most part, is comfortable with the place of the Government in American life and in some instances would like to expand it.

—David Rosenbaum (1995, B12)

Unless unions and community groups find ways to coalesce behind national challenges to the orthodoxy of balanced-budget conservatism, what the political system has in store for ordinary people is an interminable series of demands to take less.

—Sidney Plotkin and William E. Scheuerman (1994, 5)

ECONOMIC CONSEQUENCES of immigration are usually sorted into two categories. The one that has received the most attention from economists concerns the labor market impacts of immigrants. How do increased supplies of foreign workers in domestic labor markets affect the earnings and employment opportunities of native workers? Despite a widely shared view among the American public that immigrants take jobs away from U.S. workers, increase unemployment, and depress wages (Espenshade and Hempstead 1996; Espenshade and Belanger 1997), most research has failed to provide strong support for these beliefs (Smith and Edmonston 1997). The research literature has been ably summarized by George Borjas (1994a) and by Rachel Friedberg and Jennifer Hunt (1995, this volume). The main conclusion, based largely on cross-sectional data, is that there are only "modest effects of immigrants on natives' labor market outcomes" (Friedberg and Hunt, 1995, 35). A potentially important qualifier has been added by Donald Manson, Thomas Espenshade, and Thomas Muller (1985), Randall Filer (1992), William Frey (1995a), and Michael White and Lori Hunter (1993). It may be that some natives are indeed adversely affected by foreign workers. If these native workers move out of high immigrant-impact areas to labor markets where they perceive better opportunities, then cross-sectional studies may fail to detect negative effects on wages or employment.

A second topic of economic consequence concerns the fiscal impacts of immigrants. How much do immigrants pay in taxes to federal, state, and local governments, how large are the benefits that immigrants receive in return, and how do the two amounts balance out within various jurisdictional levels? These issues are of more recent origin than the labor market impacts of immigrants and have received less attention, especially from economists. They are, for example, mentioned only in passing in Friedberg and Hunt's chapter in this volume. Satisfactory answers to even the most basic questions are hampered by inadequate data (the inability to separate legal and undocumented migrants in census and administrative records), methodological differences (should estimates be calculated from an aggregate, top-down approach or should they be built up from household-level data?), and conceptual inconsistencies (is the individual, the family, or the household the appropriate unit of analysis, and is marginal or average cost the relevant concept?). A general critique of "accounting" approaches to fiscal impact estimates has been offered by John Isbister (1996), who argues for recasting the analysis in an economic framework.

Despite these difficulties, there are numerous studies of fiscal impacts. Using census data, Borjas (1994a) found that immigrants were slightly less likely than natives to receive cash welfare benefits in 1970, but that immigrant households were overrepresented among the welfare population by 1990. (The fraction of immigrant households receiving welfare was 1.7 percentage points higher than the fraction of native households, 9.1 versus 7.4 percent.) Moreover, tracking immigrant cohorts over time revealed that immigrants "assimilate into welfare" the longer they are in the United States. Panel data for 1984 to 1991 from the Survey of Income and Program Participation show little difference between natives and immigrants in the probability of receiving cash welfare benefits, but a larger native-immigrant differential when other programs are included (Borjas and Hilton 1996). The fraction of immigrant households receiving some kind of public assistance is 50 percent larger than the native fraction (21 versus 14 percent).

Growth in the refugee population helps to explain some of the rising proportion of immigrant households receiving welfare. When refugees are excluded, working-age immigrants are less likely than their native-born counterparts to receive support (Fix and Passel 1994). This conclusion is consistent with Borjas's (1994a) finding that households originating in Cambodia or Laos had a 1990 welfare participation rate of nearly 50 percent. However, because older legal immigrants who do not have a lengthy work history in the United States are ineligible for Social Security, immigrant use of Supplemental Security Income (SSI) and food stamp programs for old-age support contributes to proportionately greater overall use by legal immigrants than citizens (Sorensen and Blasberg 1996). The legal status of immigrant households matters in other ways as well. Georges Vernez and Kevin McCarthy (1995) find that there is a monotonic progression in tax payments, rising from contributions to public revenues by current illegal migrants, to former undocumented migrants who received amnesty under the 1986 Immigration Reform and Control Act (IRCA), to legal immigrants, and finally to the native-born. They point out that these differentials reflect differences in average income rather than immigration status per se.

Fewer examinations have been made of the net fiscal costs of migrants. Michael Fix and Jeffrey Passel (1994, 57) assert that, "contrary to the public's perception, when all levels of government are considered together, immigrants generate significantly more in taxes paid than they cost in services received." These effects are not uniformly distributed across all levels of government. Immigrant households appear to be a fiscal asset only for the federal government. Based on limited evidence, revenues and expenditures seem to be more or less offsetting for state governments, and it is typically at the local level where immigrants are the greatest fiscal drain (Rothman and Espenshade 1992). In some states, both immigrant and native households receive more benefits than they pay for with taxes, but immigrant households appear to have the larger negative impact on local governments (Espenshade and King 1994). These findings—a net state and local cost and a federal surplus—are confirmed by a recent National Academy of Sciences study (Smith and Edmonston 1997).

As suggested earlier, many unanswered questions remain in de facto estimates of the fiscal impacts of immigrants. But this is not the place to attempt to break new empirical or methodological ground. Instead, with this brief review as background, we turn our attention to recent changes in immigration and welfare policy that are likely to alter the fiscal impacts of U.S. immigrants. In combination, these changes are likely to have the effect of reducing the public costs of immigration, both by eliminating or restricting immigrants' access to public benefits and by altering the composition of the legal immigrant flow in favor of higher-income immigrants.

It is not by coincidence that immigration and welfare reform policies come at this moment. They rise out of a sense of public frustration and anxiety with growing economic insecurity and are fueled by stagnant wages, corporate downsizing and white-collar layoffs, the threat of additional jobs lost overseas, and a concern over high taxes. Most workers have seen their real wages either stagnate or decline over the past two decades. Between 1989 and 1991 real median household income also fell by 5 percent (Plotkin and Scheuerman 1994). Recently, however, sustained economic growth has begun to translate into increases in real wages, especially for low-wage workers (Hershey 1997). Nonetheless, greater trade and globalization of markets are recognized as limiting the bargaining power of domestic workers and holding down wages (Palley 1994). As more manufacturing, low-wage service and, increasingly, higher-skill computer programming jobs are exported overseas, a growing fraction of the domestic workforce is engaged in part-time employment. Rising income inequality adds to the sense of relative deprivation among lower-and middle-income families, and the press of accumulating federal deficits means that roughly one in every seven federal dollars spent goes to pay interest on the national debt (Plotkin and Scheuerman 1994).

Adding to this economic uncertainty is the demographic disequilibrium caused by rapid changes in the racial and ethnic composition of the U.S. population (Cornelius 1997). Most of these stem from the volume of immigration, which is now the largest in U.S. history when measured in absolute terms (Fix and Passel 1994). As of March 1996, 9.3 percent of the U.S. population, or 24.6 million persons, were foreign-born (U.S. Bureau of the Census 1997b). This proportion is up from 4.8 percent in 1970 and is the highest since 1940, although it is surpassed by levels that approached 15 percent at the beginning of the twentieth century. The tempo of the current migration is suggested by the fact that roughly one-quarter of the U.S. foreign-born population has entered the United States since 1990. Some areas of the country are affected more than others. California is home to one-third of U.S. immigrants, and one-quarter of California's population is foreign-born. Perhaps not surprisingly, because foreign-born individuals include both legal and undocumented migrants, the largest share of the foreign-born population (nearly 30 percent) originates in Mexico. These demographic changes are affecting the "look" of our population, the foods we eat, and the languages we hear spoken, and together are seen by many as having an unsettling effect on the status quo (Teitelbaum and Weiner 1995).

Declining economic prospects and a growing sense of disquieting demographic change have produced in the United States a new form of isolationism, one that has both domestic and international elements. As in the past, this latest period of isolationist tendencies is marked by a turning inward and attempts to protect the nation from unwanted outside influences. On the international front, we argue that neo-isolationism is reflected in reluctance to commit American troops abroad, a push to retreat from U.S. foreign-aid commitments, and a growing anti-immigrant mood. Domestically, neo-isolationism is reflected in concerns about the cultural makeup of society, a retreat from expensive social welfare obligations (both for immigrants and citizens), and mounting fiscal onservatism.

Anti-immigrant sentiment and fiscal conserva-
n intersect in a new "fiscal politics of immigra-
," language inspired by the influential work of
Calavita (1996). Immigrants are viewed as
f the reason for the high cost of social ser-
nd are especially susceptible to attempts to
government welfare expenditures. Con-
extended to legal immigrants restrictions
ceipt of social services that have custom-
ed only to illegal or undocumented migrants. In addition, Congress has placed new limits on the eligibility of less wealthy applicants for immigration. There is also a state-level component of this activity: several states have attempted to seek reimbursement from the federal government for the costs of social, health, and other services that they have provided to illegal aliens and to withhold education and health benefits from undocumented individuals (California's Proposition 187). These efforts have been enhanced by new grants of federal authority that allow states to distinguish between legal and illegal aliens and between legal aliens and citizens. Because resident aliens cannot vote and because they have no strong constituency apart from immigrant rights groups, immigrants represent an attractive and therefore vulnerable fiscal target from the perspective of federal policymakers.

In laying out this argument we first examine the domestic and international dimensions of neo-isolationism. Then we review the 1996 reforms of U.S. immigration and welfare laws. The chapter's concluding section discusses some of the possible rationales for denying or constraining the benefits eligibility of immigrants who nevertheless are still expected to pay taxes, be available for military service, and otherwise obey the laws of the land.

International Dimensions of Neo-Isolationism

Despite the passage of the North American Free Trade Agreement (NAFTA) and the leading role played by the United States at the International Conference on Population and Development in Cairo in September 1994, there are growing signs in this country of an increasingly introverted attitude toward U.S. foreign policy and international relations in general. Indeed, President Clinton's election in 1992 might be interpreted as evidence that the American electorate cared more about "the economy, stupid" than it did about the triumph of U.S. military might in the Persian Gulf.

The House of Representatives in 1995 approved a bill that would cut U.S. payments for United Nations peacekeeping operations by requiring that Washington's annual peacekeeping dues be reduced by the costs the Pentagon incurs in peacekeeping missions approved by the UN Security Council but not directed by the United Nations. This measure could undermine the UN's financing mechanism, because the United States typically pays about one-third of the UN's $3 billion annual peacekeeping budget, whereas in 1994 the Pentagon spent $1.7 billion in American-run military missions such as the one in Haiti. In addition, the bill would lower to 20 percent the U.S. share for all future United Nations missions. Democrats in Congress viewed the measure as "a test case pitting advocates of internationalism against a growing tide of isolationists" (Schmitt 1995b, A8). Richard Armey (R-Tex.) was quoted as saying, "The nation has gone too far in the direction of globalism . . . and we intend to correct that" (Schmitt 1995a, A9). A deal between Senate congressional leaders and the Clinton administration, struck in June 1997, authorizes payment of nearly two-thirds of the $1.3 billion back dues the United Nations claims the United States owes, on the condition that the United Nations continue its personnel cuts and the U.S. share of UN peacekeeping expenses be reduced (Myers 1997).

Jesse Helms (R-N.C.), chairman of the Senate Foreign Relations Committee, has the backing of congressional Republican leaders to consolidate the Agency for International Development (AID) and two other independent foreign policy agencies into the State Department in an effort to cut foreign aid and save taxpayer money (Greenhouse 1995a). AID is the U.S. government's principal agency for distributing $13.7 billion in aid to such purposes as population stabilization, fighting famine and disease, and increasing literacy around the world. In defense of AID's mission, the agency's head responded, "Because of the impression that has been created that our foreign aid program is nothing more than an international welfare program, it has been possible for demagogues, isolationists and populists, all sometimes in the same person, to exploit that and to exploit people's fears" (Greenhouse 1995b, A18).

Public Opinion Toward Immigrants

Neo-isolationism is also reflected in increasingly nativist attitudes that U.S. residents hold about foreigners.[1] Historically, these attitudes have shifted among tolerance, ambivalence, and outright rejection. Indeed, ever since the founding of the new colonies there have been attempts by former immigrants to keep out the latest arrivals. Restrictive immigration policies were introduced first in the late nineteenth century when "new" immigrant groups from southern and eastern Europe began arriving. Qualitative restrictions against Chinese and Japanese immigrants were followed in the 1920s with quantitative limits and national-origin quotas that had the effect of favoring migrants from northern and western Europe.

The American public adopted a somewhat more liberal perspective on international migration following World War II, sparked in part by an expanding economy, national acceptance of the U.S. role as a world superpower that entailed a responsibility to admit more refugees, and reduced religious and racial prejudice (Harwood 1986a). Liberalized attitudes were expressed in numerous ways, the most important of which were the 1965 amendments to the 1952 Immigration and Nationality Act. These amendments effectively eliminated a system of allocating immigrant visas on the basis of country of origin and established new principles based on family reunification.

This liberalization of public opinion lasted for much of the 1950s and 1960s but was gradually replaced in the late 1970s and early 1980s with a wave of neorestrictionist sentiment that has persisted. For example, two out of three respondents to a 1981 survey believed that levels of legal immigration to the United States should be reduced, a proportion twice as large as that detected in 1965 (Harwood 1986a). Several reasons have been offered for this change in public opinion, including: concerns about the condition of the macroeconomy and growing anxieties over economic insecurity (Day 1990; Moehring 1988); perceptions of immigrants' undesirable cultural traits, including problems involving criminal activity, drug use, disease, and an unwillingness to assimilate into the social or economic mainstream (Cornelius 1982; Day 1990); and worries related to an increase in undocumented immigration (Passel 1986; Reimers 1985). However, these "reasons" at best represent untested hypotheses (Espenshade and Hempstead 1996).

Recent trends in immigration attitudes are summarized in figure 19.1. The solid line measures the proportion of survey respondents in nationwide polls who feel that levels of immigration to the United States should be reduced. The line is relatively flat until 1965, when it rises abruptly, indicating that tolerance for immigration has waned in the last two decades (Schuck 1996). These data are consistent with the belief that broader isolationist attitudes are more prevalent today than a generation ago. The annual U.S. unemployment rate is also graphed in figure 19.1. The two series are highly correlated apart from several years near 1960 when public opinion poll data are missing. Similar patterns in Canadian data have been observed by Nancy Tienhara (1974) and Douglas

FIGURE 19.1 Americans Who Want Immigration Decreased, and Trend in U.S. Unemployment Rate

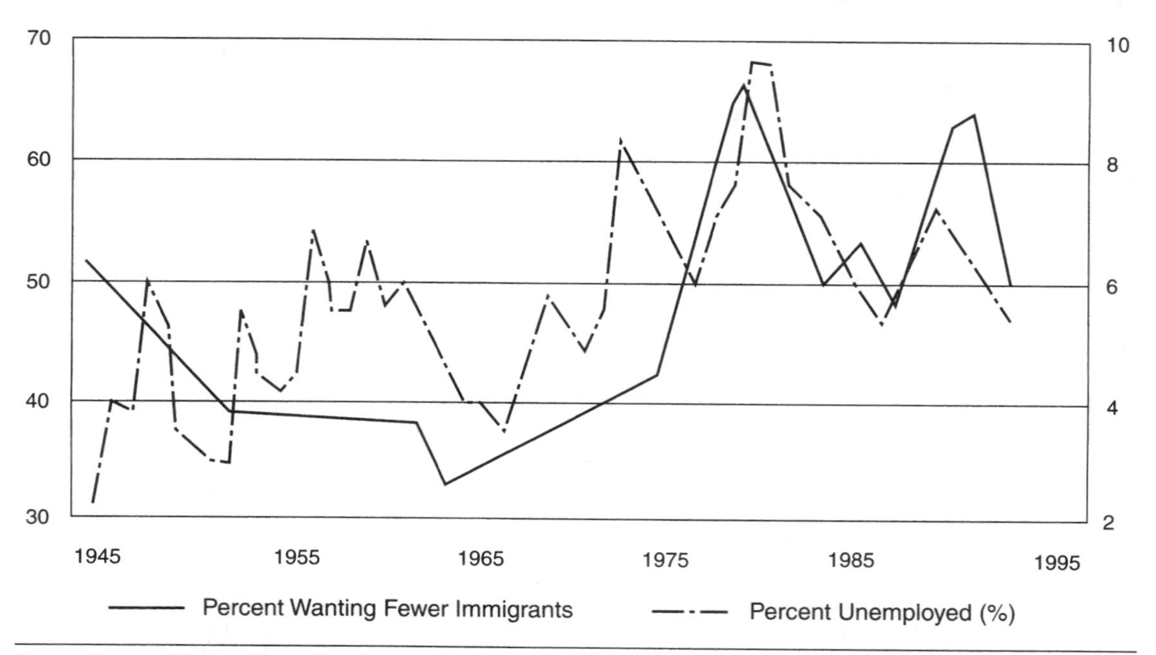

Sources: Percent Wanting Fewer Immigrants: Simon and Alexander (1993), POLL database, Dialog Information Services; Percent Unemployed: U.S. Bureau of the Census (various issues; 1975).

Palmer (1994). Using aggregate U.S. data, Brewton Berry and Henry Tischler (1978) found that feelings toward immigrants are closely linked to the business cycle and suggested that racial prejudice is stimulated by recessions. Palmer (1994), on the other hand, concluded that, whereas opposition to immigration rises and falls with unemployment rates, measures of ethnic intolerance exhibit a secular decline that is relatively uncorrelated with economic conditions.

In June 1993, *CBS News* and the *New York Times* conducted a nationwide public opinion survey among 1,363 adults who were asked a series of questions about the kind of job that President Clinton was doing, the condition of the U.S. economy, and attitudes toward foreigners and U.S. immigrants. An analysis of these microdata provides further information about the correlates of Americans' restrictionist attitudes toward immigrants (Espenshade and Hempstead 1996). Respondents who believe the U.S. economy is deteriorating have significantly more negative opinions about immigration than persons who feel the economy is improving. Moreover, survey participants are more likely to prefer higher levels of immigration if they think the economy is in good condition and that the United States will be an economic superpower in the twenty-first century. Feelings of social and political alienation are also associated with attitudes toward immigration. Those who are most alienated—based on feelings that President Clinton does not care about people like them or that he is out of touch with what ordinary individuals think, or on having a favorable view of Ross Perot (a candidate for disaffected voters) and having voted for Perot—tend to prefer lower levels of U.S. immigration.

One of the most interesting findings in the 1993 poll data is the strong positive correlation between having an isolationist mentality and believing that levels of U.S. immigration should be reduced. Those who think that trading with Japan and other countries is bad for the United States, who oppose NAFTA, and who feel that Japanese and German products are inferior to those produced in the United States generally prefer lower levels of immigration. Furthermore, respondents who have unfriendly feelings toward other countries, who pay little attention to international news, and who feel that the United States has no responsibility to intervene diplomatically, financially, or militarily in the affairs of other countries—even when asked to by its allies or by the United Nations—are more likely also to support lower levels of U.S. immigration.

The paper by Espenshade and Hempstead (1996) is the first to establish an empirical link between immigration attitudes and an isolationist outlook versus a more global perspective. It suggests that people who tend to see the world as an interconnected whole are likely to be more open-minded when it comes to evaluating international flows of goods, capital, and labor. At the same time, their findings are consistent with the view that persons who harbor protectionist sentiments, who feel that the United States has no responsibility for what goes on in other countries, and who insist on an "America First" posture will be the same individuals who are most likely to oppose higher levels of immigration. Based on these findings, it seems reasonable to conclude that neorestrictionist attitudes toward U.S. immigration are one of possibly several important manifestations of emergent neo-isolationist tendencies in the United States.

It may seem paradoxical, but while public opinion was turning negative, U.S. immigration policy and laws protecting the rights of immigrants were being liberalized. As Wayne Cornelius, Philip Martin, and James Hollifield (1994b, 9) have observed, "The gradual extension of rights to ethnic minorities and foreigners over a period of several decades, from the 1960s through the 1980s, is one of the most salient aspects of political development in the advanced industrial democracies." Rooted in the American civil rights movement, this rights-based liberalism is exemplified by the 1982 U.S. Supreme Court case *Plyer v. Doe* (457 U.S. 202), which guaranteed undocumented immigrant children the right to a K-12 public school education; by deportation hearings; by the use of appeal rights for apprehended undocumented immigrants and for political asylum applicants (Harwood 1986b; Noble 1995); and by the availability of interpreters for groups that are non-English-speaking (Harwood 1985). One consequence of expanded rights for immigrants has been an increased difficulty in controlling U.S. immigration (Cornelius, Martin, and Hollifield 1994b; Schuck 1984). Moreover, the Immigration Act of 1990 (public law 101–649) sharply raised the number of immigrant visas available to legal immigrants from 656,000 in fiscal year (FY) 1990 to an annual average of 830,000 in the three years following FY1992, when the new law became fully operational (Papademetriou 1990; U.S. Commission on Immigration Reform 1995). These numbers exclude persons granted permanent residence under IRCA and represent increases in each of the major immigration categories (family-based, employment-based, and diversity programs).

Several factors help explain the failure of restrictionist public opinion to have greater impact on policy or judicial reforms. Americans' attitudes toward immigration are often inconsistent or ambivalent; opinions frequently are not strongly held, even if they are negative; and vocal pro-immigrant interest groups have succeeded in capturing the attention of federal policymakers (Espenshade and Calhoun 1992; Harwood 1986a). Moreover, public opinion changes with the economy, limiting long-term coalition building. Finally, much of the initial opposition to legal immigration observed in survey results may in fact be driven by perceptions of the problem of illegal immigration. Michael Teitelbaum and Myron Weiner (1995) argue, for instance, that survey respondents seem unable to distinguish between questions of legal and illegal immigration.

Domestic Aspects of Neo-Isolationism

Usually the term "isolationism" is reserved for international affairs, but there are also signs along the domestic front that Americans are drawing apart from each other. First, concerns over the cultural and societal makeup of the United States have surfaced, as evidenced by the strict preference expressed by Americans for European immigrants over persons from Asia and Latin America (Espenshade and Belanger 1997). Faced with a growing heterogeneity in immigrants' countries of origin and with a corresponding rise in the diversity of non-English languages used in school and at work, twenty-one states have now passed legislation making English their official state language (State and Local Coalition on Immigration 1995b). Some of these are states with large immigrant populations, including Arizona, California, Florida, and Illinois.

Second, balanced-budget conservatism, as expressed in the Republicans' Contract with America, has become a major force in American politics. This can be traced to the election of Ronald Reagan in 1980, which signaled the public's acceptance of a redefinition of economic problems in the United States. No longer was the issue mainly one of the corporate sector; rather, the problem was that government had become too big. The electorate liked the idea of a balanced budget and less government spending, but it turned out that what they resisted was having fewer government services. Reagan's popular tax cuts were not followed by spending reductions, and the federal deficit ballooned as a result. Between 1981 and 1983 the deficit doubled as a proportion of total government spending (from 12 to 25 percent), and the sight of unprecedented $200 billion annual deficits soon gave rise to what Sidney Plotkin and William Scheuerman (1994, 6) call balanced-budget conservatism, an "omnipresent political focus on deficits, spending cuts, and tax avoidance." Balanced-budget conservatism has gone through several reincarnations, but in the process it has had at least two implications: first, that the size of the deficit, not the health of the macroeconomy, has been the yardstick for measuring congressional budgeting policy; and second, that group has been pitted against group, heightening tensions and leading to a society that is fracturing along race, age, and class lines (Plotkin and Scheuerman 1994). This is perhaps one source of recent attacks on affirmative action: programs to assist disadvantaged groups are seen as resources that could otherwise be used by the majority. In a nationwide poll, in fact, two of every three respondents indicated dissatisfaction with affirmative action (Ayers 1995b).

The Republicans' Contract with America is the latest rebirth of balanced-budget conservatism. Despite Clinton's veto of the omnibus budget reconciliation bill passed by Congress in November 1995 and the subsequent government shutdown, budget negotiations have not focused on whether the budget will be balanced, but how. Indeed, the budget agreement of May 1997 between congressional Republicans and President Clinton reduces both domestic and international spending. The welfare and immigration reforms of 1996 were similar expressions of this trend, with significant cuts in government spending anticipated from both efforts (National Conference of State Legislatures 1996b).

The New Fiscal Politics of Immigration

Two pieces of legislation enacted into law during August and September 1996 are likely to reduce significantly the fiscal burdens of immigration. The first, House Resolution 3734, the Personal Responsibility and Work Opportunity Reconciliation Act of 1996 (Welfare Reform Act) was signed into law by President Clinton on August 22, 1996. The law is a massive overhaul of U.S. welfare policy that reduces federal spending, eliminates the entitlement "right" of support for poor families, and requires able-bodied persons who receive government assistance to work. In particular, the Welfare Reform Act eliminates the Aid to Families with Dependent Children (AFDC) entitlement program, first established in 1935, and replaces it with a state-implemented Temporary Assistance for Needy Families (TANF) program designed to provide short-term cash assistance to poor families (National Conference of State Legislatures 1996a). The second, House Resolution 3610, the 1997 Omnibus Consolidated Appropriations Act (public law 104–208), was signed into law by President Clinton on September 30, 1996. This measure incorporates the Illegal Immigration Reform and Immigrant Responsibility Act of 1996 (Immigration Reform Act), which is an amended version of House Resolution 2202, the Immigration in the National Interest Act of 1995. (House Resolution 2202 died in the autumn of 1996 in the Senate when the Senate refused to close debate on the bill as reported by a House-Senate conference committee.)

Although together these two laws significantly increase efforts to prevent entry of illegal aliens, we are primarily concerned with their effects on the costs of legal immigration. It is important to note, however, that the two laws do not directly reduce legal immigration or the number of refugee or asylee entrants. Nor do they alter the broad criteria for obtaining a permanent resident visa, including the preeminence of the family reunification goals embedded in current immigration law. First we discuss the components of the reforms that affect the flow of legal immigrants and limit their financial liability. Then we examine the outright restrictions on eligibility for social services and the similar state efforts.

First, the Welfare Reform Act reforms the use of affidavits of support. A support affidavit is a contract promise made by a financial sponsor who is a U.S. citizen or permanent resident alien to provide financial assistance to new immigrants to keep them out of poverty.[2] Affidavits are required for all potential immigrants who are unable to demonstrate that they will not become a public charge. They were previously considered unenforceable because several courts had ruled that support affidavits were not legally binding (U.S. General Accounting Office 1995b). Under the Welfare Reform Act, however, affidavits for future immigrants are legally enforceable against the sponsor by either the immigrant or any government that provides a means-tested social service until the immigrant becomes a U.S. citizen or performs ten years of qualifying work. Moreover, the person who petitions for an immigrant to come to the United States must also be the financial sponsor, whereas in the past any citizen or permanent resident could present an affidavit of support. In addition, individuals who sponsor family members under the family reunification segment of current immigration law are now required by the Immigration Reform Act to have an income of at least 125 percent of the federal poverty level. Together, these reforms are likely to make it more difficult for poorer immigrants to find sponsors in the United States and to allow the government to recoup any costs for services provided to sponsored immigrants.

Second, the Welfare Reform Act and the Immigration Reform Act directly reduce the eligibility of legal immigrants (and refugees) for most need-based social services. The programmatic details of these reductions in eligibility are discussed elsewhere (Espenshade, Baraka, and Huber 1997; Fragomen 1997), but the basic pattern is simple: U.S. citizens now have greater access to social services than refugees and legal immigrants, and illegal immigrants remain almost entirely ineligible for federal benefits. For example, legal immigrants (regardless of when they arrived and so long as they have not become naturalized U.S. citizens) are no longer eligible for food stamps, and refugees are eligible for SSI and food stamps only for their first five years in the United States. A further distinction is made between legal immigrants who were present in the country on August 22, 1996, and those who arrived later. For a broad category of federally funded means-tested benefits, legal immigrants present in the United States prior to August 22, 1996, retain their eligibility, whereas all future legal immigrants are not qualified for SSI until they become citizens and are ineligible for other federal benefits for their first five years in the United States. In fact, legal immigrant eligibility for social services is now more similar to that of illegal immigrants than that of citizens.

Writing when these restrictions on benefits were first presented, Michael Fix and Wendy Zimmerman (1995, 2) commented: "Imminent changes in welfare policy would dramatically reorder the relationship of immigrants to the social welfare state. . . . If enacted, they would move the nation closer to an explicit immigrant policy, but it would be a policy of exclusion rather than inclusion." The total cost savings to the federal government from reduced eligibility for immigrants are estimated at $10 billion to $15 billion for the six-year period between 1997 and 2002.[3] This is approximately 30 percent of the projected $43 billion savings from the entire welfare reform bill. Eighty-five percent of these reduced outlays arise from SSI, Medicaid, food stamp, and AFDC programs (Congressional Budget Office 1995; Pear 1997).

State-Led Initiatives

Prior to the federal reforms of 1996, state efforts to recoup or limit the costs imposed by immigrants were sporadic and largely unsuccessful. Individual states expressing concerns about the fiscal impacts of immigrants had looked to the federal government for reimbursement for the costs of benefits and services that they were required to provide, especially to undocumented immigrants (Clark et al. 1994; U.S. General Accounting Office 1994, 1995a). During 1994, six states (Arizona, California, Florida, New Jersey, New York, and Texas) filed separate suits in federal district courts to recover costs they claimed to have sustained because of the federal government's failure to enforce U.S. immigration policy, protect the nation's borders, and provide adequate resources for immigration emergencies (Dunlap and Morse 1995). All lawsuits sought relief for the costs of incarcerating undocumented criminal aliens in state or local correctional facilities, and many included reimbursement for costs of public education, emergency health care, and other social services that states are required by federal mandate to provide to illegal immigrants. The amounts sought ranged from $50.5 million in New Jersey for the FY1993 costs of imprisoning five hundred undocumented criminal felons and for future capital construction expenses to build new prisons to $33.6 billion in the New York case brought by state and local officials for reimbursement for all state and county costs (incarcerations, education, and social services) associated with undocumented immigration between 1988 and 1993 (State and Local Coalition on Immigration 1994b). U.S. district court judges have dismissed all six immigration lawsuits, arguing, among other things, that the suits are not subject to judicial review because the complaints revolve around political and not judicial questions. Some of the states are appealing the decisions.

In separate action, the Justice Department provided relief to key states that house more than 85 percent of all illegal aliens in state prisons. President Clinton's 1994 crime bill earmarked a total of $1.8 billion over six years to help reimburse states for these incarceration costs. The FY1995 appropriation was $130 million, one-third of which was disbursed in October 1994 to the six states filing lawsuits, plus Illinois. California, with more undocumented immigrants than any other state, received nearly 80 percent of the initial disbursement, whereas shares for Arizona, Illinois, and New Jersey totaled less than $1 million (State and Local Coalition on Immigration 1994a). These amounts are less than those requested in state lawsuits. On the other hand, the state-by-state suits fail to recognize that undocumented aliens also pay a variety of state and local taxes that partially offset their use of services (Massey and Espinosa 1997). Moreover, the suits overlook the fact that the 1990 census included a portion of the U.S. undocumented migrant population in the enumerated state totals. Because some federal-to-state government funding formulas take population size into account, states with disproportionate numbers of undocumented aliens have over the years been receiving more federal funding (at the expense of states with few undocumented migrants) than they otherwise would (and perhaps should) have.

However, the 1996 federal reforms have granted the states extensive discretion to limit the eligibility of legal and illegal immigrants for social services. Previously, court rulings that applied the Equal Protection Clause of the Fourteenth Amendment to the U.S. Constitution prevented states from distinguishing between legal immigrants, refugees, and citizens, although illegal immigrants could be denied eligibility for most state programs or for federal programs targeted toward citizens.[4] With certain exceptions, the Welfare Reform Act explicitly grants the states authority to distinguish between citizens, refugees, and legal immigrants in the provision of both federally and state-funded social services. This right to distinguish between citizens and noncitizens is confirmed in the Immigration Reform Act.

These changes have given new force to state efforts to restrict immigrant use of social services. The most important state effort to date is California's Proposition 187. By a margin of three to two in November 1994, voters approved the ballot initiative, which denies public education (including K–12, community colleges, and higher education), health care (except emergency medical services), and social services to undocumented immigrants. The measure requires publicly funded social and health service agencies, school districts, and law enforcement offices to verify the legal status of all applicants and to notify the California attorney general and INS officials of persons determined or suspected of being in the United States illegally. Finally, the proposition creates two new state felony offenses for manufacture or use of false documents to conceal immigration or citizenship status (State and Local Coalition on Immigration 1995a).

Large sections of Proposition 187 were subsequently held unconstitutional in federal court for violations of individual rights and because "the state is powerless to enact its own scheme to regulate immigration" (Ayres 1995a). Specific provisions that were held unconstitutional were those affecting the rights of illegal immigrant children to attend public elementary and secondary school and the reporting requirements whenever someone was known or reasonably suspected to be undocumented. On the other hand, the judge ruled that undocumented immigrants could be denied nonemergency medical aid as well as admission to California state-supported colleges and universities (Lively 1995), but that federal officials (not state or local) first would have to determine the legal status of the applicants and then decide to share that information. Federal courts have since relied on the Welfare Reform Act to lift the injunction against the efforts to deny benefits to illegal immigrants (McDonnell and Ellis 1996). The portions of Proposition 187 denying education to illegal immigrant children and requiring law enforcement officials to detain suspected illegal immigrants remain enjoined.

Whether efforts similar to Proposition 187 will gain attention elsewhere is unclear. More immediately, the direct grants of authority in the Welfare Reform Act require the states to make decisions about the eligibility status for several types of benefits for certain classes of legal immigrants and refugees. This requirement to decide on an explicit policy toward legal immigrants is likely to raise the issue of immigrant assistance versus state cost almost immediately, and quite possibly without the public and vocal fight surrounding Proposition 187. These new state initiatives in many cases are more significant because they move beyond restricting the already limited eligibility of illegal immigrants and instead have the potential to alter the status of many legal immigrants and refugees.

Discussion

The issues that welfare reform poses for the rights of lawful permanent resident aliens and their continued eligibility for public assistance are more philosophical than legal. The Congress was able to deny welfare and other federal benefits to legal immigrants because of its plenary authority over immigration (Pear 1994). Whether it should have is another matter. At their root, welfare reforms raise questions about the meaning of membership in U.S. society. Robert Pear (1994, E5) puts the matter succinctly: "Despite the country's history as a nation of immigrants, popular opinion in the United States has continually vacillated on the question of whom the government is meant to serve: its people or just its citizens."

Opinion over the issue is clearly divided. The U.S. Commission on Immigration Reform (1994, 23) supports a broadly inclusive interpretation of the government's mandate and recommends "against any broad, categorical denial of public benefits to legal immigrants" on the grounds that legal immigrants whom we have affirmatively accepted for permanent residence in the United States should be protected by the social safety net afforded citizens. A similar stance is advocated by Cornelius, Martin, and Hollifield (1994b, 10), who ask, "How can a 'liberal' society tolerate the presence of individuals who are members but not citizens of that society? Should not all individuals who are members (i.e., permanent residents) of a liberal society be accorded the full panoply of rights (social and political as well as civil) enjoyed by those who are citizens?" Stephen Legomsky (1994) raises fairness issues by asking whether it is equitable to remove accustomed rights from legal aliens while insisting that they are still responsible for obeying U.S. laws governing payment of taxes, conscription, and criminal activity.

Supporters of a liberal interpretation of civic inclusion are backed by constitutional principles. Although the federal government has made citizenship a prerequisite for receiving some public assistance, this step contravenes traditions that run deep in America's political culture. The Constitution speaks of "We the People of the United States," not "We the Citizens . . .," and the Bill of Rights is designed to protect the interests of people, not citizens (Pear 1994). Other arguments against eliminating benefits have mentioned the potential adverse effects on the economic well-being of migrants and their children and the additional costs that federal actions may impose on states (Congressional Budget Office 1995).

Nevertheless, a mood swing in Europe and the United States is promoting a far narrower interpretation of the federal government's responsibilities. In an effort to discourage immigration, France tightened citizenship requirements in 1993 by removing automatic citizenship for children born on French soil to foreign parents (Whitney 1996), and similar initiatives are being considered in Congress to reduce illegal immigration (Lewis 1995). In Germany citizenship is defined primarily by blood line, making it almost impossible for a German-born child of a Turkish guest worker to become a German citizen. Despite the forward momentum of rights-based liberalism, recent judicial rulings in the United States and Europe have "whittled away at some of the rights and protections previously accorded to immigrants," and many Western industrialized democracies are grudgingly coming to recognize that "effective control of immigration requires a rollback of civil and human rights for noncitizens" (Cornelius, Martin, and Hollifield 1994b, 10).

On the other hand, specific arguments in support of these tighter restrictions on welfare eligibility for legal immigrants have been advanced. First, legal aliens who choose not to become citizens are demonstrating a questionable commitment to the United States, so it is appropriate to limit their access to the benefits received by citizens. Second, immigrants' sponsors have been shirking their responsibilities to provide financial support. This trend would be reversed if the government did not provide assistance. Third, public assistance becomes a crutch that inhibits immigrants from adapting more quickly to the nation's culture and from seeking productive work. And fourth, public benefits act as a welfare magnet that attracts poor immigrants to the United States who then end up competing with disadvantaged Americans in the labor market (Congressional Budget Office 1995).

This mood swing in the United States is consistent, as we argued earlier, with a rise in a neo-isolationism at home and abroad that has given encouragement to a new fiscal politics of immigration. Growing anti-immigrant sentiment has coalesced with the forces of fiscal conservatism to make immigrants an easy target of budget cuts. The latest round of reforms directed at immigrants seems motivated not so much by a guiding philosophy of what it means to be a member of American society as by a desire to shrink the size of the federal government and to produce a balanced budget. Having little or no voice in the electorate and trapped by the forces of budgetary opportunism and political expediency, legal aliens represent to many policymakers an attractive and altogether vulnerable fiscal target. (See a related interpretation of California's Proposition 187 by Calavita [1996].) Even more than in the past, the consequence of a shrinking welfare state is to metamorphose legal immigrants from public charges to windfall gains for the federal treasury.

The federal reforms also reinforce existing incentives for legal aliens to become U.S. citizens. In addition to guaranteeing the right to vote, citizenship protects immigrants from threatened cuts in eligibility for public assistance and puts them in a privileged position vis-à-vis lawful permanent residents to bring close family members to join them in the United States. Correspondingly, naturalization rates have surged dramatically in the last three years, even prior to the enactment of the congressional reforms (Espenshade, Baraka, and Huber 1997). The U.S. Commission on Immigration Reform (1995) has recommended a renewed emphasis on "Americanization" as part of a total package of legal immigration reforms. Such policies should cultivate a shared commitment to enduring American values of liberty, democracy, and equal opportunity. They should also encourage naturalization as the path to full civic participation. It would have been wholly consistent with the spirit of immigration and welfare reforms if Congress had also eased the path to citizenship by reducing the number of probationary years that legal immigrants must serve. Under current law, in addition to satisfying other eligibility criteria having to do with age, character, English proficiency, and an understanding of U.S. civics, lawful permanent residents must usually reside in the United States continuously for five years before being permitted to apply for naturalization. Shortening this period to, say, two or three years would provide partial relief from the crescendo of reforms that are pressing legal immigrants in the direction of full citizenship. Furthermore, the retroactive restrictions on food stamp benefits to immigrants living in the United States prior to August 22, 1996, are significant for similar reasons, because they affect immigrants who came to the United States with the impression that they would be treated like citizens. The almost immediate and total cutoff in SSI and food stamp benefits to new legal aliens reinforces the impression that reformers sought to save scarce federal dollars rather than increase the subjective perception of the value of citizenship.

This chapter was a revised version of the paper presented at the Social Science Research Council Conference on Becoming American/America Becoming (Sanibel Island, Florida, January 18–21, 1996). Partial support for this research was provided by a grant from the Andrew W. Mellon Foundation. We are grateful to Maryann Belanger and the Office of Population Research Library for bibliographic assistance.

Notes

1. Portions of this section draw on material in Espenshade and Calhoun (1993).
2. Under such a contract, a sponsor must agree to provide support to maintain the sponsored alien at an annual income that is not less than 125 percent of the federal poverty line during the period in which the affidavit is enforceable. The current federal poverty level is $7,740 for a single individual.
3. These savings estimates are probably too large because they assume lower rates of naturalization by legal immigrants than have been observed during the last two years. Because naturalization entitles immigrants to the same benefits as citizens, federal government savings would be reduced if large numbers of legal immigrants naturalized to preserve their benefits (Espenshade, Baraka, and Huber 1997).
4. The Equal Protection Clause states: "No State shall . . . deny to any person within its jurisdiction the equal protection of the laws." In *Graham v. Richardson,* 403 U.S.C. 365 (1971), the Supreme Court ruled that states may not distinguish between legal immigrants, refugees, and citizens in the provision of social services on the grounds that: states are not empowered to make legitimate distinction between these classes of persons; and federal laws preempt state discretion. Discrimination based on refugee and legal immigrant status was deemed a "suspect classification" that cannot be justified without a compelling state interest, which the Supreme Court did not find in a state's desire to reduce spending (National Conference of State Legislatures 1996c).

20 Face the Nation: Race, Immigration, and the Rise of Nativism in Late-Twentieth-Century America

George J. Sánchez

ON APRIL 30, 1992, Americans across the nation sat transfixed by a television event that grew to symbolize the sorry state of race relations in late-twentieth-century urban America. The image of Reginald Denny, a white truck driver, being pulled from his cab at the corner of Florence and Normandie Avenues in South Central Los Angeles, beaten and spat upon by a group of young African American males, quickly became a counterimage of the inhumane beating of the black motorist Rodney King a year earlier. These two episodes of racial conflict, both captured on videotape, dominated representations of the Los Angeles riots in a city haunted by poverty, racism, and police brutality. So aware have all Americans become of a bipolar racial dynamic in this country, usually framed in white-black terms, that we lost an opportunity to dissect one of the most important and complex events of our time. As the perceptive playwright and artist Anna Deveare Smith (1994, xxi) has observed, "We tend to think of race as us and them—us or them being black or white depending on one's own color." Indeed, the Los Angeles riots provide stark, critical evidence of one of the most important social movements of our era: the rise of a racialized nativism directed at recent immigrants and the American-born who racially represent those newcomers.

A closer look at the victims of violence at the corner of Florence and Normandie reveals the way in which the Los Angeles riots were fundamentally an anti-immigrant spectacle at its very beginning. Most people outside of Los Angeles are surprised to hear that Reginald Denny was not the only person injured on that corner. Mesmerized by video images of a single beating of one white man, it is difficult to imagine that at least thirty other individuals were beaten at that same spot, most pulled from their cars, some requiring extensive hospitalization. Most important for my purposes, only one other victim of the violence at that corner besides Denny was white—and he was, like Denny, a truck driver passing through the area. All the others were people of color, including a Mexican couple and their one-year-old child, hit with rocks and bottles; a Japanese American man, stripped, beaten, and kicked after being mistaken for Korean; a Vietnamese manicurist, left stunned and bloodied after being robbed; and a Latino family with five-year-old twin girls, who each suffered shattered glass wounds on the face and upper body. All of these acts of violence occurred before Reginald Denny appeared (see *U.S. News & World Report* 1993).

Indeed, the first victims at Florence and Normandie were Latino residents who lived in the neighborhood. Marisa Bejar was driving her car through the intersection at 5:45 P.M. when a metal-covered phonebook sailed through her car window, opening up a wound that took thirteen stitches to close. Her husband, Francisco Aragon, was hit on the forehead with a piece of wood, while their seven-month-old infant suffered minor scratches when a large metal sign was hurled through the rear window. Minutes later, when Manuel Vaca drove his 1973 Buick into the intersection, Antonine Miller and Damian Williams threw rocks through the windshield, causing Vaca to stop the car. Six men pulled Vaca, his wife, and his brother from their car, then beat and robbed them. As Anthony Brown remembered, he kicked at Vaca "because he was Mexican and everybody else was doin' it." Sylvia Castro, a fourth-generation Mexican American and prominent activist in South Central, was shocked when bricks and bottles shattered her car window. Having worked closely with gang members in the area, she was able to escape with only a bloodied nose by speeding away (*U.S. News & World Report,* 1993).

Later, after Denny's assault was recorded and

broadcast worldwide, several shocked black residents of the area risked their lives to save other victims. James Henry left his porch to pull Raul Aguilar, an immigrant from Belize, to safety after he had been beaten into a coma and a car had run over his legs. Donald Jones, an off-duty fireman, protected Sai-Choi Choi after several men beat and robbed him. Gregory Alan-Williams pulled a badly wounded Takao Hirata from the bloody intersection. Another savior at that corner was the fifty-nine-year-old Reverend Bennie Newton, pastor of the Light of Love Church. He rescued the life of Fidel Lopez, a twenty-year resident of Los Angeles from Guatemala. Lopez, driving to his home one block from the intersection, was pulled from his car and later required twenty-nine stitches in his forehead for a wound resulting from a blow with an auto stereo, seventeen stitches to his ear, which someone had tried to slice off, and twelve stitches under his chin. Lying unconscious in the street from the beating, Lopez had motor oil poured down his throat and his face and genitals spray-painted blue. His life was saved when Newton began praying over his prostrate body with a Bible in the air (McMillan 1992; *U.S. News & World Report,* 1993, 55–57).

Over the four days of the Los Angeles riots, the dynamics of racial and class tensions, rage against the police, and antiforeign sentiment came together in violent, unpredictable fashion. From that corner of Florence and Normandie, the mayhem spread to engulf the city, creating the worst modern race riot in American history. Fifty-two lives were lost and 2,383 people were injured. About $1 billion of damage was done to residences and businesses, and over 14,000 arrests were made. In the first three days of rioting, over 4,000 fires were set and 1,800 people were treated for gunshot wounds. The destruction occurred throughout the Los Angeles basin, and the participants and victims were indeed multiethnic (Oliver, Johnson, and Farrell 1993, 118). But at its core, the Los Angeles riots provide stark evidence of the way in which immigrants provided the perfect scapegoat for American populations frustrated with developments in their society.

The decisions made by angry, young African Americans at that corner as they chose whom to hurt speak volumes to anyone interested in the intertwining of issues of race and immigration in late-twentieth-century America. For some, the decision was not about who was white, but about who was not black. For others, it centered on how Latinos and Asians had "invaded the territory" of South Central, which they claimed as their own turf despite the fact that South Central Los Angeles had a majority Latino population in 1992. Others shouted (as heard on various videotapes) to "let the Mexicans go" but "show the Koreans who rules." Although the violence began as a response to a verdict passed by an almost all-white jury against an almost all-white set of police officers, quickly other people of color—those deemed foreign or foreign-looking—were engaged in the deadly exchange. The meaning of racial and national identities was consistently at issue at the corner of Florence and Normandie, with serious and sometimes bloody outcomes for all participants.

Since May 1992 more clearly visible evidence has appeared that allows most social commentators to identify our current historical moment as one in which we are experiencing a particularly sharp rise in American nativism. Two years after the Los Angeles riots, California voters would resurrect their long-standing history as leaders in anti-immigrant efforts since the days of Chinese exclusion by passing Proposition 187, a state initiative intended to punish illegal immigrants by restricting their access to schools, medical care, and other social services. (For an account of the anti-Chinese sentiment in California that led to the national exclusion act of 1882, see Saxton 1971.) This would be accomplished by deputizing social service providers—teachers, social workers, doctors—as immigration inspectors and forcing them to identify to local law enforcement officials students and clients who had entered the country illegally. Here was legislation that tied issues of crime and immigration together in a tidy package and allowed voters to voice nativist fears in the anonymous sanctity of the voting booth, a populist solution long well known in California. Polls showed that this piece of legislation won widespread approval across a range of ethnic groups, including 67 percent of whites (who formed 80 percent of the total electorate) and 50 percent of both Asian Americans and African Americans, with only 23 percent of Latinos voting in favor (McDonnell 1994a, A3).

One feature of the campaign in favor of Proposition 187 was the prominent role played by California Governor Pete Wilson, a "moderate" Republican who had lost favor with the California electorate when his term coincided with the worst economic performance in the state since the Great Depression. His support of anti-immigrant positions was a centerpiece of his political comeback in

California, where he won reelection from rival Kathleen Brown in November 1994 after coming from as much as twenty percentage points behind. This was not, of course, the first time politicians had found nonvoting immigrants to be the perfect scapegoat for an attempt at political resurrection. Indeed, at the height of the Great Depression in 1930, Herbert Hoover's Labor secretary, William Doak, had promised to rid the country of "four hundred thousand illegal aliens" who he believed were taking jobs away from American citizens, thereby causing the great economic calamity of the period (Hoffman 1974, 36–37).

Indeed, Pete Wilson and Herbert Hoover have more in common than their tortured political paths through economic downturns. Both had previously been ardent supporters of the easing of immigration restrictions before the convenience of immigrant scapegoating in the political process became evident. During World War I, when Hoover had been food administrator for the U.S. government, he had personally encouraged President Woodrow Wilson to exempt Mexican immigrants from the provisions of the 1917 Immigration Act in order to allow them to engage in much-needed agricultural labor and wartime production. In 1985, during the height of the congressional debates over the Immigration Reform and Control Act, then-Senator Pete Wilson was the key player in securing an exemption for California agricultural growers, enabling them to continue using undocumented workers long after more stringent enforcement was already in place in urban areas. Pete Wilson's ill-fated presidential campaign in 1996 cannot obscure the fact that his career remains the epitome of opportunistic politics, taking full advantage of Americans' long-standing fears of immigrants and foreigners when such a strategy could bring success at the polls.

We also have recently witnessed the publication and media hype of a book that can easily be characterized as our era's equivalent to *The Passing of a Great Race,* the 1916 classic by Madison Grant, the man John Higham has called "intellectually the most important nativist in recent American history" (1988, 155). Grant's contemporary counterpart is Peter Brimelow, senior editor at *Forbes* and *National Review.* His *Alien Nation: Common Sense About America's Immigration Disaster* (1995, xv) unabashedly claims that recent immigration is likely "to transform—and ultimately, perhaps, even to destroy . . . the American nation." Within the first ten pages of the book, recent immigrants are blamed for rising crime rates, the health care crisis, lowered overall educational standards, and Americans' alienation from each other. Unlike other nativists, Brimelow wants to be clear that he is offering an overtly racial argument: "Race and ethnicity are destiny in American politics" (xvii) he declares repeatedly, exhorting all Americans to be concerned about restricting the immigration of people who are of a color different from their own.

Signs, therefore, point to a resurgence of a nativism unparalleled in this country since the 1920s. From attacks on immigrants in urban unrest to legislative action attacking immigration policies to academic and media discussions echoing the familiar intellectualized examinations of racialized dissonance of the past, today's nativism is as virulent as any that has gone before. Yet this era's nativism, like this era's immigration, has unique characteristics that differentiate it from that which appeared in the early twentieth century at the height of European immigration to the United States. Traditional hostility toward new immigrants has taken on a new meaning when those immigrants are racially identifiable and fit established racial categories in the American psyche. With the increase of immigration from Asia and Latin America, a new American racism has emerged that has no political boundaries or ethnic categorizations. From the left and right of the political spectrum, and from both white and black individuals, this new racism continually threatens to explode in contemporary American society.

One point worth making is that while nativist discourse is often decidedly linked to racial discourse, they are not one and the same, and they often lead in different directions. Part of the problem in separating racism from nativism is the fact that our collective understanding of what constitutes racism has become murkier since the 1960s. Having long abandoned biological categories of race and definitions of racism that rely fundamentally on individual prejudice, most academic discourse on racism in the social sciences remains unclear and underdeveloped. This lack of clarity has sometimes allowed for the most egregious dismissal of any operative definition of racism. Peter Brimelow (1995, 11), for example, condescendingly defines a racist as "anyone who is winning an argument against a liberal," and then, somewhat more soberly, equates racism with misinformed prejudice or "the sense of committing and stubbornly persisting in error about people, regardless of evidence." This definition, of course, frees him to develop a racially based argument against current immigration patterns on the grounds that he is "not prejudiced" and "also not blind."

One shining exception to the academic murkiness I have been describing is the work of the sociologists Michael Omi and Howard Winant (1994, 71), who define racism as a historically situated project that "creates or reproduces structures of domination based on essentialist categories of race." Not only would this definition allow us convincingly to label Brimelow's project racist, but for the purposes of this exploration, it would allow us to differentiate and complicate our present notions of nativism. To be able to do this is critical because historically there have always been proponents of open immigration who can be characterized as racist. For example, many of the employers of Mexican migrant labor during the 1920s voraciously fought against immigration restriction on the basis that Mexicans were biologically suited for stoop labor. W. H. Knox of the Arizona Cotton Growers' Association belittled nativists' fears of a Mexican takeover of the United States in 1926 by invoking racist constructions of Mexicans to the House of Representatives. (For a fuller explanation of this position, see also Sánchez 1993.)

> Have you ever heard, in the history of the United States, or in the history of the human race, of the white race being overrun by a class of people of the mentality of the Mexicans? I never have. We took this country from Mexico. Mexico did not take it from us. To assume that there is any danger of any likelihood of the Mexican coming in here and colonizing this country and taking it away from us, to my mind, is absurd. (U.S. Congress 1926, 191)

It is not difficult to find other instances, including in the contemporary period, of antirestrictionists espousing racist views of those immigrants they want to entice to come into the country.

Moreover, it should be clearly stated that not all restrictionist positions are fundamentally based on racial assumptions. The late Barbara Jordan, chair of the U.S. Commission on Immigration Reform and former congresswoman from Texas, while presiding over two reports that emphatically favored reduced entry of legal immigrants and the toughening of measures to curb illegal immigration, nevertheless offered a picture of immigration restriction that simultaneously evoked a renewed faith in American diversity. Jordan (1995, A11) wrote:

> Legitimate concern about weaknesses in our immigration policy should not, however, obfuscate what remains the essential point: the United States has been and should continue to be a nation of immigrants. . . . The United States has united immigrants and their descendants around a commitment to democratic ideals and constitutional principles. People from an extraordinary range of ethnic and religious backgrounds have embraced these ideals. . . . We are more than a melting pot; we are a kaleidoscope, where every turn of history refracts new light on the old promise.

Indeed, the active presence of black public figures in contemporary discussions of immigration policy suggests that African Americans will play an increased role in contributing to a more exclusionary definition of American citizenship than has hitherto prevailed. Barbara Jordan was chosen by President Clinton as head of a federal advisory commission charged with proposing new measures to curtail illegal immigration, not just because of her expertise as a former member of the House but also because of her race. Jordan's very presence on such a commission allowed her blackness to deflect potential charges of racism directed at the stringent provisions of the policy recommendations. In this new climate, it is obvious that all Americans can get caught in the white-black paradigm of race relations, a model that relies on opposites, opposites that too often substitute for the complexity and diversity of social and ethnic relations in the United States in the late twentieth century.

To understand the vexing dilemma of these issues, we must remember that two seemingly contradictory directions mark recent scholarship on race in the United States. On the one hand, social scientists throughout the twentieth century have worked hard to challenge the biologistic paradigm that explained racial inferiority as part of a natural order. Despite recent exceptions like Richard Herrnstein and Charles Murray's *The Bell Curve* (1994), most scientific studies reject the notion that race should be equated with particular hereditary characteristics (for example, Omi and Winant 1994, 14–15). Instead, social scientists have increasingly explored how race is a social construction, shaped by particular social conditions and historical moments to reflect notions of difference among human groups. Many academics have subsumed race under other categories deemed more critical to understanding social stratification, such as class or ethnicity. Yet racial theorists increasingly point out that race has its own particular role in modern society that cannot simply be buried as a by-product of other social phenomena (see Almaguer 1994; Fredrickson 1988). Omi and Winant (1994, 55) offer a definition of race that takes into account the instability of a social construction yet does not see race as merely an illusion: "Race is a concept which signifies and symbolizes social conflicts and interests by referring to different types of human bodies."

Indeed, the other major development in academic discussions is that "race matters" in understanding all forms of social conflicts in the modern world, including those that do not, on the surface, appear to be racially inspired (see Hacker 1992; Rogin 1996; West 1993). Indeed, the eruption of ethnic tensions in the wake of the collapse of the Soviet Union has forced non-American scholars to reassess their previous dismissal of these conflicts as holdovers from a premodern age, ones that are likely to disappear in our new postmodern world. In the United States, while this work has shaped a critical reconsideration of the drift toward discounting racial tension as simply a by-product of class antagonism or cultural conflict, it also has largely remained limited to a discussion of the problematic relationship between African Americans and the majority white population. Even when other racial minorities are discussed, a binary relationship with the Anglo majority remains the central focus of these academic studies (see Sánchez 1993, 5–8). The academic discussions of multiculturalism, in other words, have yet to produce a wide array of scholarship that effectively theorizes the fundamental multiracial character of either contemporary or historical U.S. society.

Although many philosophers and theorists have stressed that "race matters" in understanding American society, race in the national imagination has usually been reserved to describe boundaries between whites and blacks (see Cho 1993). (For a recent exploration of "race" in the United States that focuses exclusively on white-black dynamics, see also West 1993.) Indeed, the 1990s has produced many important works by noted social commentators that continue to utilize a strict white-black racial dichotomy. Andrew Hacker (1992, xii), author of *Two Nations: Black and White, Separate, Hostile, Unequal,* justifies his title and emphasis by claiming that Asians and Hispanics "find themselves sitting as spectators, while the two prominent players (Blacks and Whites) try to work out how or whether they can coexist with one another." Although he included voices of Asian Americans and Latinos in his collection of oral histories about "race," Studs Terkel subtitled his 1992 book *How Blacks and Whites Think and Feel About the American Obsession.*

Asian Americans and Latinos, despite their active presence in American society in the mid-nineteenth century, are depicted as only the latest immigrant groups coming to the United States, and they are described as engaging in patterns that more clearly represent early-twentieth-century European immigrant groups than separate racial populations. Hacker (1992, 16), for example, rather than using the actual history of Asian groups or Latinos in the United States, argues that "second and subsequent generations of Hispanics and Asians are merging into the 'white' category, partly through intermarriage and also by personal achievement and adaptation." No more important a figure than the Nobel Prize winner Toni Morrison has made this claim recently in *Time* magazine. In a special issue dedicated to immigration, Morrison (1993, 57) wrote:

> All immigrants fight for jobs and space, and who is there to fight but those who have both? As in the fishing ground struggle between Texas and Vietnamese shrimpers, they displace what and whom they can. Although U.S. history is awash in labor battles, political fights and property wars among all religious and ethnic groups, their struggles are persistently framed as struggles between recent arrivals and blacks. In race talk the move into mainstream America always means buying into the notion of American blacks as the real aliens. Whatever the ethnicity or nationality of the immigrant, his nemesis is understood to be African American.

This perspective, for all its insight into the crucial place of African Americans in American history, ignores the long history of racial discrimination aimed specifically at Asian Americans and Latinos in the United States. National scholars have a responsibility to study the whole nation and its history, but too often East Coast social commentators present a very thin knowledge of U.S. history more than a few miles away from the eastern seaboard. Both "Asians" and "Latinos" have been decidedly constructed as races in American history, long before the decade of the 1960s, and today both these subgroups have become lightning rods for discussions of race, equality, and the meaning of citizenship in contemporary America.

Even more important, a new perspective is needed in order to encourage us to rethink the meaning of multiracial communities in American history. Rather than simply being "communities in transition" to neighborhoods of racial exclusivity, these areas of cultural exchange and conflict can come to represent, at least in the western half of the nation, the norm in American racial and ethnic life, not the exception. Indeed, refocusing on the persistence of these mixed communities allows urban scholars to compare the diversity of ethnic communities in the late twentieth century to the seemingly transitional ethnic communities of the early twentieth century. For Los Angeles and other large metropolitan areas, this perspective is crucial. Watts, for example, in the heart of South Central Los Angeles, had a majority Mexican population until the late 1920s, when African Americans from the American South began to migrate in large numbers to the city. Likewise, Boyle Heights in east Los Angeles was the center of the Los Angeles Jewish community in the 1920s, as well as home to a large Japanese American population stretching east from Little Tokyo and a sizable Mexican American group.

More recently, post–World War II racially restrictive policies of segregation have been replaced by a return to class-based zoning. This change, coupled with extensive post-1965 immigration, has created new communities of racial interaction in most urban centers in the United States. Most of these, however, include few white Americans. Yet multiracial communities as diverse as Uptown and Edgewater in Chicago, Mount Pleasant in Washington, D.C., and Sunset Park and Jackson Heights in New York City have begun to focus attention on this seemingly new phenomenon. This interesting constellation of multicultural enclaves has produced some rather noteworthy, but not altogether new, racial dynamics. Much residential community interaction between blacks, Latinos, and Asian Americans has occurred in urban centers in the American West over the past one hundred years, but never before in such a visible—that is, national—fashion. The histories of these past multiracial communities in the West, therefore, are as important a model for ethnic community as the homogeneous barrio depicted in so many works of Chicano history, or the standard portrait of a completely African American ghetto.

One result of homogeneous depictions of ethnic communities can be seen in the immediate media coverage of "communities" involved in the Los Angeles uprising. The erasure of Latino participation in the Los Angeles riots as both full-fledged victims and victimizers is troubling to those concerned about contemporary discussions of race in American life. In the 1980s Los Angeles County added 1.4 million residents, and nearly 1.3 million—or 93 percent—were Latino (*Los Angeles Times,* 1992, 26). Even though Latinos made up the majority of residents in South Central Los Angeles, and 45 percent of the residential population of Koreatown by 1990, both communities were defined in such a way that Latinos were considered "outsiders" in community politics and media formulations. Latinos were the single largest ethnic group arrested during the period of the riots, not only for curfew violations and undocumented status but also as looters of their local Korean merchants (Kwong 1992; Postrel 1992). Estimates also indicate that between 30 and 40 percent of stores that were lost were Chicano- or Latino-owned (Cho 1993, 205). Moreover, during the three days of rioting, the Immigration and Naturalization Service took advantage of those arrested for curfew violations to deport over two thousand Latino aliens. Yet the wider media and most academic accounts of the events of 1992 in Los Angeles have largely ignored the Latino role because it disturbs strongly held beliefs in notions of community, belonging, and race in this country.[1] It is the constant depiction of Latinos as "newcomers" and "foreigners" that provides insight into the particular form of racialization that surrounds this group in American society.

There are a variety of scholarly works that can help us better understand the unique way in which fear of "foreignness" informs racial discourse in contemporary America. In particular, the intellectual distinction of nativism from racism has been an enduringly helpful legacy of previous work on immigration restriction. John Higham, in his now classic study *Strangers in the Land,* was careful to separate the two. "Nativism," he wrote (1955/1988, 4),

> should be defined as intense opposition to an internal minority on the ground of its foreign (i.e., "un-American") connections. Specific nativistic antagonisms may, and do, vary widely in response to the changing character of minority irritants and the shifting conditions of the day; but through each separate hostility runs the connecting, energizing force of modern nationalism. While drawing on much broader cultural antipathies and ethnocen-

> tric judgments, nativism translates them into a zeal to destroy the enemies of a distinctively American way of life.

Higham was clear about locating modern nationalism at the core of American nativism, particularly a nationalism that was "defensive in spirit" and fearful of the changes in American society that could be wrought by the newcomer. As Higham (1988, 24) reminds us, "unfavorable reactions to the personal and cultural traits" of others were not necessarily nativist, although most were probably racist. "They become so only when integrated with a hostile and fearful nationalism."

Much can be learned from John Higham's own intellectual path in writing *Strangers.* Higham started his study as one of popular attitudes toward immigration restriction but found that he could not contain the study within a focus limited to a legislative program. It grew, therefore, into "a general history of the anti-foreign spirit . . . defined as nativism" (1988, ix). Higham explains that he explores "nativism as a habit of mind" that "illuminates darkly some of the large contours of the American past; it has mirrored our national anxieties and marked out the bounds of our tolerance" (x). Therefore, a comparison of the contours of our own time of intolerance with that of the past is in order.

In chapter 1 of *Strangers,* Higham identifies three major antiforeign traditions that came together to shape American nativism at the end of the nineteenth century. The first was anti-Catholicism, nurtured in Protestant evangelical activism, which deemed Catholics as incapable of the independent thought characterized as critical to American citizenship. The second major tradition was virulent antiradicalism, which depicted the foreigner as prone to political revolution and the overthrow of stable institutions. The third and most important tradition was racial nativism, which was borne out of a confident belief in the Anglo-Saxon origins of the American nation. This form of romantic nationalism would be transformed in the early twentieth century "into a generalized, ideological structure" (Higham 1988, 133), most emphatically emerging from the new scientific racism and the eugenics movement. Indeed, what Higham describes was "the extension to European nationalities of that sense of absolute difference which already divided white Americans from people of other colors" (132).

It is time to consider what factors are at work during our current age that inform and promote our own brand of American nativism. Let me suggest three different antiforeign sentiments that mark the racialized nativism of the end of the twentieth century. The first is an extreme antipathy toward non-English languages and a fear that linguistic difference will undermine the American nation. Despite the fact that English has become the premier international language of commerce and communication, fueled by forces as widespread as multinational corporations, the Internet, popular culture, and returning migrants, Americans themselves consistently worry that immigrants will refuse to learn English and intend to undermine the preeminence of that language within American borders. Captured by statewide "English only" proposals, which began in California but spread quickly across the nation, this fear seems to emanate from Americans' own linguistic shortcomings and their feeling of alienation—created by monolingualism—from the discourse, be it personal, on the job, or on the radio.

A second fear is one directly tied to issues of multiculturalism and affirmative action. Like papist conspiracy theories, this fear involves the uneasy belief that racialized immigrants take advantage of, in the words of Michael Lind (1995, 133), "a country in which racial preference entitlements and multicultural ideology encourage them to retain their distinct racial and ethnic identities." Going beyond the denial of white privilege in contemporary U.S. society, this sentiment directly believes that contrived, misguided, and sometimes secretive government policies have tilted against white people in the 1990s. Though tied to a general antipathy toward people of color, some of these fears are heightened by the place of immigrants and those American-born perceived as racially connected to Latino and Asian immigrants. Even some affirmative action advocates bemoan the extension of programs to nonblacks, in the unexamined belief that U.S. racism has historically been directed against only one racial group incorrectly defined as wholly nonimmigrant. These programs, then, are deemed to be un-American, not only because they contradict America's supposed commitment to equality of opportunity, but also because they are literally favoring "non-Americans" in their results. Lind writes (1995, 135):

> One wonders what James Farmer [the national director of CORE (Congress of Racial Equality) in the early 1960s], the patron saint of quotas, would

have said, if he had been told, in 1960, that by boycotting Northern corporations until they hired fixed numbers of black Americans, he was inspiring a system whose major beneficiaries would ultimately be, not only well-to-do white women, but immigrants and the descendants of immigrants who, at the time of his struggles, were living in Mexico, Cuba, Salvador, Honduras, and Guatemala.

A third antiforeign sentiment has emerged in the 1990s, embodied in California's Proposition 187, which is quite unique and has not been seen since the Great Depression. Current anti-immigrant rhetoric focuses on the drain of public resources by immigrants, both legal and illegal, particularly their utilization of welfare, education, and health care services. Unlike nativist calls that center on immigrants taking jobs from citizens, this sentiment feeds into stereotypes of nonworking loafers; particularly targeted are women who supposedly come to the United States to give birth and sustain their families through the "generous" welfare state. (For an in-depth analysis of this new trend, see Hondagneu-Sotelo 1995.) Even when presented with evidence that immigrants are less likely to seek government assistance than citizens, today's nativists scoff at the data and the researchers. The Proposition 187 proponent Harold Ezell, for example, retorted to one study showing immigrant underutilization of government-sponsored medical programs by saying, "He's obviously never been to any of the emergency rooms in Orange County to see who's using them—it's non-English-speaking young people with babies" (Bailey 1996, B1). (For studies that confirm widespread underutilization of social services by immigrants, see also Blau 1984, 222–39; Jensen 1988b, 51–83; Tienda and Jensen 1986, 372–400.) The notion that immigrants are now coming to the United States to take advantage of welfare, health, and education benefits has led directly to federal legislation that allows states to ban such assistance to even legal immigrants, and this has enabled Governor Wilson to mandate such cutoffs in California.

Although cultural antipathies are often at work in producing fear of newcomers, more often than not economic fears of competition have also played a critical role. Nativism has always cut across political lines, finding adherents on both the right and left. In the 1920s the American Federation of Labor (AFL) played a critical role in encouraging immigration restriction by raising the specter of newcomers' threat to the economic security of the American workingman. AFL President Samuel Gompers, who supported voluntary and relatively unencumbered immigration as late as 1892, had become a virulent nativist by the 1920s (Higham 1974, 49, 71, 321–22). Today's nativists similarly stretch across the political spectrum, from right-wingers like Patrick Buchanan to political "moderates" like Pete Wilson, to self-proclaimed liberals like Michael Lind.

What binds these individuals together is a profound sense of the decline of the American nation. With the rise of nativism since 1965, we are once again witnessing a defensive nationalism in the wake of profound economic restructuring. In place of the period of modernization that pushed the U.S. agricultural economy toward widespread industrial production, we are now witnessing rapid deindustrialization, the rise of a service and high-tech economy, and the worldwide movement of capital, which undercuts the ability of American unions to protect U.S. jobs. This economic transformation, coupled with antagonistic government policies, has certainly undermined central cities in the United States and created fertile ground for nativist sentiments.

Indeed, underlying much of the frustration of the Los Angeles riot participants was the collapse of the inner-city economy, the negative flip side of the new Pacific Rim global economy. Los Angeles had lost 150,000 manufacturing jobs in the previous three years, and it was estimated that each of these jobs took another three associated jobs with it. The new jobs created were disproportionately low-wage and dead-end forms of employment; in fact, 40 percent of all jobs created in Los Angeles from 1979 to 1989 paid less than $15,000 a year. Most of these jobs were taken by recent immigrants to the area, leaving African Americans with few viable options for secure employment. The average earnings of employed black men fell 24 percent from 1973 to 1989, and unemployment swelled to record levels in the inner city. Middle-income Los Angeles was rapidly disappearing, leaving little opportunity for anyone to move up the economic ladder. This inequality was also highly racialized; the median household net worth for Anglos in the city in 1991 was $31,904; it was only $1,353 for non-Anglos.

Clearly one obvious target for the frustration in the inner city were the Korean merchants in South Central; they had replaced the Jews, who left in large numbers after the 1965 Watts riots. In 1990, 145,000 Koreans lived in Los Angeles County, a

142 percent increase over the previous decade and a phenomenal growth from only 9,000 in 1970. Unable to transfer their education and skills to the U.S. labor market, many Korean immigrants had pooled their funds to start small businesses in ethnic communities throughout the city. Koreans now saw their businesses burn to the ground and suffer widespread looting. These small merchants had filled a vacuum created by discrimination against African American entrepreneurs and the abandonment of the inner city by large retail businesses.

Yet much of the damage to Korean businesses occurred in Koreatown itself, where one-third of that community's businesses were located. This community was unique in that it did not represent an area of ethnic succession; well known in the East, such an area is one where one identifiable ethnic group is slowly replaced by another, with the resulting tensions that succession produces. Here two recent immigrant populations met in unequal fashion, both reflecting a culture that had long been part of the Los Angeles racial makeup, but neither with particular historical roots to the area before 1965. Unlike other Asian enclaves in southern California, the residential population of Koreatown was overwhelmingly Latino, and it was this ethnic group that was primarily engaged in the looting of Korean stores (Ong and Hee 1993, 7–8). In fact, 43 percent of those arrested during the riots were Latino, while only 34 percent were African American, contradicting the notion that the Los Angeles riots were a simple black-Korean conflict. Economic frustrations fueled the looting and mayhem of the Los Angeles riots, even though a different racialized nativism set the events of late April 1992 in motion.

It is clear that we are in a period of economic transformation that can and should be compared to the period of industrialization that occurred a century ago; such transformation provides the social context for the rise of nativism in the United States that occurred in both periods. Yet today's economic transformation is intimately tied to an economic globalization propelled by multinational corporations and an age in which capital and information flow relatively freely across national borders. From 1890 to the 1920s the industrial transformation that changed the American economy and fueled international migration led to a breaking down of local community control and toward a national interdependency that propelled Americans to "search for order" in new and varied ways (Wiebe 1967). Not only did bureaucracy and science rise to provide this national order, but immigration restriction and scientific racism emerged as well to provide ideological comfort to Americans in search of a glue to hold together a nation undergoing fundamental social and economic change.

Many Americans have been shielded since World War II from the convulsions of the international economic order by the enormous strength of the U.S. economy, and liberal policies of inclusion have been crafted that assume the continuation of this extraordinary growth. Most important in coming to terms with the complexities of race, immigration, and nativism in the late twentieth century is a perspective that can deal with the multiple meanings of race and equality in American society in an age of liberal political retrenchment and widespread economic restructuring. During the Reagan-Bush administrations and the current era of Republican ascendancy in Congress, hard-fought victories in racial and economic policy were and are continually threatened with extinction. In addition, supposedly "race-neutral" policies, such as tax reform and subsidies to the private sector, have disproportionately and adversely affected racial minorities (Lipsitz 1995a, 371–77).

Yet increasingly we must account for the fact that at least the Reagan-Bush era did not see a reversal of government spending, despite all the rhetoric, but instead witnessed its redirection toward wealthy and corporate interests and away from long-term investment in education, infrastructure, and safety nets for the poor. This "trickle-down" theory of social advancement was the biggest failure of the 1980s and left in its wake a sizable, disgruntled white electorate, one disaffected with politics and clamoring for "change" at every turn. This group helped give the White House to the Democrats in 1992, handed large numbers of votes to Ross Perot, and offered the Republican Party a majority in both houses of Congress for the first time in thirty years in 1994. In this setting, one in which expectations of newfound prosperity grow with every change of political power, a scapegoat must be found amid the citizenry that can be blamed for delaying the promised economic security. For many Americans in our era, the poor, especially the black poor, have served this role of scapegoat; increasingly, however, that role is being transferred to or combined with the blaming of the immigrant.

While the industrial economy was being sent through convulsions over the past thirty years, Americans produced largely cultural explanations for structural social problems. The demonization of black families, for example, served for white Americans as a plausible justification for the economic backwardness of African Americans, despite affirmative action and civil rights. Instead of focusing on the ravages of deindustrialization in both black and white communities, white Americans increasingly revived traditional stereotypes of black laziness. While these racialized beliefs were no longer acceptable public discourse in the post–civil rights era, researchers who take anonymous polls can still ferret out extensive negative race stereotyping in the white community (Lipsitz 1995a, 379–82).

Indeed, it seems to me that cultural beliefs in innate difference have worked together with structural forces of inequality to frame (and hide) discussions of white privilege. The literary scholar Eric Lott (1993a, 474–95) has argued that attitudes toward blackness are shaped by white self-examination and insecurity, rather than by the realities of African American life. Contemporary white perceptions of blacks probably tell us more about the dangers of being "white" in this era than about strongly held beliefs regarding black inferiority. In fact, it is the language of liberal individualism that keeps many whites from seeking structural explanations for racial inequality. However, liberalism has always been a two-edged sword. When economic conditions become tenuous for whites, meritocratic rhetoric about the rewards of hard work and self-reliance also generates individual anxiety and a fear of personal victimization. Whites who are faced with economic failure or insecurity in spite of their racial privilege become a sure breeding ground for the scapegoating of racial others. This classic projection further obscures the need to acknowledge or understand the structural and economic sources of one's own oppression.

Closer analysis of the workings of liberal language deepens our understanding of the relationship between liberal racial attitudes and the structural causes of inequality. For example, liberal individualism, as a dominant value in American society, has an impact on the actions of individuals of all races. Indeed, a look at liberalism's impact on blacks and other racial minorities, including recent immigrants to the United States, would reveal that routine, systematic, and unyielding discrimination does not necessarily lead to collective protest. More often than not, it produces a sense of individual victimization and anger. The Los Angeles riots demonstrated that injustice can provoke African American rage not only against white authority but against "racialized others," most notably Asians and Latinos living among blacks in newly "reintegrated" communities.

Today the United States finds itself increasingly having to compete economically with nations from all over the world, including Third World nations trying to gain a stronger foothold in the international exchange of goods and services. At the same time, American corporations seem to have become internationalized themselves, and more interested in gaining profit than in maintaining an economic nationalism rooted in American hegemony. (For an analysis of this development, see Hollinger 1995.) It is not difficult to understand how immigrants from these developing nations can be seen as both drains on our national economy and symbols of countries that threaten American economic hegemony and the dream of a multicultural future in the post–Cold War era. These conditions have produced increasing calls for a "liberal nationalism" in the United States from the left side of the political spectrum, calls that often have gone hand in hand with calls for severe restrictions on immigration to the United States. In an analysis intended to aid working-class Americans, particularly American blacks, Michael Lind (1995, 319–20) has written: "The most promising way to quickly raise wages at the bottom of the income ladder in the United States is to restrict immigration."[2] Though always claiming that such efforts should not be characterized as nativist, those issuing these renewed calls for nationalism and protectionism on the backs of recent and future immigrants are defensive in a way that points toward the eruption of a "liberal nativism" in American political discourse.

Interestingly, Americans have been better able to identify this new nativism when it emerges in other nations. The resurgence of neo-Nazi hatred toward foreigners in Germany is regularly reported as racial nativism and connected to the German history in the Hitler era. When Japanese officials deride American workers while maintaining stringent restrictions on immigration, Americans are quick to identify this as racial nativism. But in the United States, the history of white-on-black racism blinds Americans to a recognition of any other form of interracial tension. Racism against Asians and Latin Americans is dismissed as either a "natural by-product" of immigrant assimilation or an extension of the white-black dichotomy. Moreover, when African Americans perform acts of racism, they are quickly ignored or recast as simply a threat to a white-dominated society.

As the actions of participants in the violence at the intersection of Florence and Normandie indicate, interracial understanding and an inclusive sense of "community" are not simply formed by living in close proximity to those from other racial or ethnic groups. Rather, what is disturbing about the Los Angeles riots is the insistence that "community" reflects a single racial group. The irony of black protesters stopping construction projects in South Central Los Angeles because no one from the "community" was employed, even when Latino workers were their neighbors, seemed to be lost on everyone concerned. Moreover, these strategies of protest usually encouraged African American entrepreneurs who had left the residential neighborhood to return to invest and to hire (but not to live), with the untested assumption that they would be more likely to hire other blacks.

Indeed, to equate "community" with a particular racialized "identity" seems more to naturalize a recent geography of local communities that can easily forget the multiracial histories of the past. In Los Angeles commentators rarely discuss the longstanding Asian and Latino communities that have been part of the region's history since the city's founding, relying instead on depictions of these racial groups as almost wholly recent immigrants. Ironically, African Americans become the perfect choice to project this historical amnesia and defend the sanctity of national boundaries, since their presence alone deflects any charge that anti-immigrant policies are racist. Since race in this nation has been constructed as a white-black affair, the continuation of this bipolar approach becomes critical to the ideology of an ordered American nation. In the United States no less than in Germany or Japan, the power embedded in certain notions of territory must be critiqued and analyzed for the grounds upon which certain peoples and histories are privileged. Indeed, racialized immigrants have become the step stools for claims of American citizenship in the late twentieth century.

How have the immigrants themselves responded to these recent attacks? One response has been a marked increase in political involvement among all immigrants in U.S. politics, on both the local and national levels (Hondagneu-Sotelo 1996, 101). Within communities of immigrants from various nations in Asia, political involvement has usually emerged within racialized organizations that are increasingly panethnic in orientation (Espiritu 1992). Although immigrants from Latin America have seemed to lag in their commitment to a pan-Latino consciousness, recent anti-immigrant efforts in California may have produced in them a decided turn toward political strategies and identities that go beyond national origins. (For a discussion of the hesitancy of Latino immigrants in New York to give up identities based strictly on national origin, see Oboler 1995; for contrary developments in California, see Rodriguez 1996.) Immigrant citizens and American-born ethnics in these communities have also heightened their political involvement to fight for the rights of immigrants with the acknowledgment that their own racial construction often hangs in the balance. Surprisingly, this acknowledgment of common ties has even stretched beyond party affiliation. In California, Republican Bill Davila, the high-profile spokesperson and former CEO of Vons supermarkets, took out a full-page advertisement in 1994 asking voters to reject Proposition 187, even though he supported Pete Wilson's reelection campaign, calling the measure a "divisive, unproductive, initiative . . . turning neighbor against neighbor" (Rodriguez 1996, 27).

Ironically, one of the most concrete expressions of this new political consciousness is the upsurge in the rates of naturalization among legal immigrants across the nation. The INS office in Los Angeles began receiving as many as two thousand applications a day for naturalization after passage of Proposition 187, and offices around the country experienced similar increases. An all-time high was reached in 1995, with over one million immigrants becoming new American citizens (McDonnell 1995a; Pachon 1995; Ramos 1995). With the legalization of previously undocumented immigrants by the 1986 IRCA law, more long-term immigrant residents of the United States see the protection of citizenship in this time of immigrant-bashing and reduced benefits as a way to protect themselves and their families. At least one leading political scientist who has studied the issue extensively warns of new challenges by the anti-immigrant forces to the very process of naturalization (Pachon 1996). And the historian cannot stop from asking whether we will see a return to deportations of naturalized Americans, as was practiced in the McCarthy era to rid communities of labor leaders and civic activists who were considered threats by virtue of the 1952 McCarran-Walter Immigration Act.

While on the surface these developments of political incorporation seem to reflect patterns of Americanization among earlier European immigrant groups to the United States, this is a decidedly ambivalent Americanism borne of racial tension and antiforeign sentiment. One 1994 statewide poll in California found that 25 percent of immigrants in the state personally feared discrimination and violence directed at them by virtue of looking foreign (Pachon 1995). As the sociologist Rubén Rumbaut has put it: "The moral of the story is we reap what we sow. When you welcome people to a community, you encourage them to feel they matter and that they have a stake here. But if you sow hate, you'll reap the products of hate" (Bailey 1996). It is certainly time for all Americans to ask themselves what sort of future we are sowing when we attack those who look to come to contribute to American society. For Americans who can hardly escape their own racial backgrounds, the legacy of this new nativism is likely to be reflected in American politics and society for quite some time to come.

NOTES

1. One notable exception has been the demographic work of Melvin L. Oliver, James H. Johnson, Jr., and Walter C. Farrell, Jr. (1993), which calls for a recognition of the underlying tension between Latino residents of Koreatown and their Korean employers, landlords, and retailers.
2. While these calls for restricting immigration are rising in volume and quantity, the social science literature on this question is much more split as to the effect of immigration restriction on the wage levels of American citizens.

21 Instead of a Sequel, or, How I Lost My Subject

John Higham

PUBLISHED IN 1955, *Strangers in the Land: Patterns of American Nativism 1865–1925* was my first book. Memories of Senator Joseph McCarthy's infamous career of anti-Communist fear-mongering were still vivid. Southern defiance of a Supreme Court order to integrate the public schools was producing an ideological clash as dangerous as any the country had faced since the Civil War (Klarman 1994). It was a good time to be uncovering and examining critically the nationalist hysterias of the past. I had chosen those of the early twentieth century, directed against immigrants and foreign ideas, for they seemed significantly yet obscurely connected with the hobgoblins of my own day. Aided by the paperback revolution, my book took off on a long and happy life of college classroom assignments.

Amid the approval that my study of nativism seemed to elicit from its many readers, I had to wonder from time to time what had become of my subject. Where indeed were the nativists, that they permitted this unflattering portrait of themselves to go unremarked? Colleagues sometimes urged me to write a sequel. At least until recently, I never felt that I understood what had happened well enough even to try. What, for example, could I say about the McCarthyites who raged against Ivy Leaguers as carriers of alien ideas but showed not a trace of concern about what foreign people might be bringing in?

My story had been a dramatic one, in which a great upheaval in American thought, feeling, and policy had transpired. So I left it to stand—unsatisfactorily—as a study of a distinct period from the 1880s to the 1920s. The decades that followed revealed an America that was becoming far more cosmopolitan and less racially arrogant than it had been earlier. From the 1930s to the 1980s the question of the stranger never assumed any strong shape or clear significance. Yet the underlying issues were surely far from dead. Complacency seemed inappropriate.

Now an acrid odor of the 1920s is again in the air. It rises from vast fortunes accumulating around new technology; from a grasping individualism eroding traditional constraints on the market; from a reckless hedonism in popular culture and a resurgent religious conservatism mobilizing against it; from a profound distrust of the state, a reviving isolationism, a growing demand for immigration restriction, and a deadlock in race relations. Nonetheless, the 1920s have not returned. Much has changed. On issues of race, national identity, and nativism, I am persuaded that changes in American society and culture are far more significant than continuities.

May the same be said of the point of view I bring to these questions? Have I, too, changed? Perhaps not so much. Although *Strangers in the Land* is an artifact of the early 1950s, I believe I am the same kind of historian I was then. Critics will doubtless disagree. For them, I have fallen behind in the feverish pursuit of theory and prescription of relevance. If so, that is surely congruent with my own sense of inner continuity. It is true that I have come gradually to a view of the exclusionary impulses in American life that is more qualified than what I had in my youth. In my own mind, this personal development arises less from new insights than from a desire to correct old ones, by taking account of changes around me.

Since *Strangers in the Land* is the starting point for this belated reconsideration, I need to review the basic concepts that guided me then and to ask what may still be useful for interpreting the experience of recent years. These questions will entail some further reflection on what has become obsolete in the argument that *Strangers* advances, and what has been neither useful nor obsolete but simply overlooked. After clarifying my present relation to the book, I will make some suggestions for recasting the story of ethnic and racial conflict and exclusion.

The original object of my project was simple

enough. Having already published an undergraduate paper on southern nationalism before the Civil War, I was looking for a way to study the dangers of nationalism over a long enough span of time to show what could inflame xenophobia and perhaps also what resisted it. A preliminary probe of newspapers in the mid-1880s shocked me. The virulence of feelings against radical immigrants was almost incredible. I set out therefore to write a narrative history of the rise in the 1880s of a great wave of antiforeign attitudes and ideas, its partial subsidence around the turn of the century, and its surge to new heights during and after World War I.

As perceptive readers have noticed, drawing distinctions was basic to my method. Racism and nativism were different things, though often closely allied. Racism, the older and more categorical of the two, divided the whole of creation into hierarchized types. It was more consistently concerned with horizontal distinctions between civilization and barbarism than it was with boundaries between nation-states. In contrast, nativism always divided insiders, who belonged to the nation, from outsiders, who were in it but not of it. Although always a species of nationalism, nativism could incorporate racism because both were militantly defensive of a cherished heritage. Racism, however, sought not only to exclude alien races but also to enforce indelible differences of status within one's own society, thereby preventing defilement by an allegedly inferior descent group. Nativism signaled danger; racism spelled degradation. Nativism could espouse assimilation. Racism could not. It became a large part of my story of nativism.

But not the whole of that story. In denying that nativism was necessarily racist, I was laying the basis for a further set of distinctions, namely, between varieties of nativism. The interplay between three strands of nativism formed the overall design of the project, and its special feature was the story of how nativism *became* racialized and thus tremendously intensified. The older of the two additional strands, anti-Catholicism, was rooted in the wars of the Reformation. In Protestant countries it inspired fears that priests and their mentally enslaved followers were conspiring to subvert republican institutions. The third strand was antiradical nativism, which identified immigrants as shock troops of class warfare, European style. All three nativisms remained very much alive throughout the period I was studying, but the racist strand came more and more to the fore.

This garland of entwined distinctions sprang from the premium I placed on conceptual clarity. That in turn followed from the fact that I came to the study of race and nationality from intellectual history at a time when everything depended on how you defined your terms. As an undergraduate, I had fallen under the spell of a great philosopher, Arthur O. Lovejoy (1936, 1948), the reigning master of subtle discriminations between "unit ideas." My three nativisms were my unit ideas.

Accordingly, I added two further distinctions that marked the limits of my field of inquiry. Both helped to identify my subject by making clear what it left out. One of these distinctions contrasted nativism with an alternative form of nationalism, which opposed nativism and could fight racism as well. This I called "America's cosmopolitan faith": a concept of nationality that stressed the diversity of the nation's origins, the egalitarian dimension of its self-image, and the universality of its founding principles. More recently, I have described this liberal strain in national consciousness as "American universalism" (Higham 1993). Others, viewing it less favorably than I do, call it "American exceptionalism." Unfortunately, in *Strangers in the Land* I discussed it for only a few pages now and then.

During the period I was writing about, American universalism was generally at a low ebb. It struggled at a disadvantage against the aggressive and dynamic thrust of nativism. Moreover, it had a problem of internal contradiction. It was inspiring, yet also oxymoronic. It defined Americans as a peculiar people while grounding their identity in the rights of man. Despite its weakness during the fin-de-siècle heyday of Western imperialism, this inclusive nationalism bore a message of hope, which I failed to emphasize enough. Although devastatingly defeated in an era of lynchings, scientific racism, and war fevers, American universalism lived on, still looking to the future to reduce disparities between cosmopolitan ideals and parochial realities. Its importance in my argument was simply to demonstrate that nationalism was not always exclusionary and defensive. It had given some Americans, including many newcomers, a means of resisting nativism on staunchly patriotic grounds. Regrettably, I failed to make explicit the further point that American universalism could revive and become once more a precious resource for a liberal politics. It tells us that the dream of a widening interracial community is not just an airy abstraction. The aspiration for such a community has endured because it is rooted in national pride.

A second major decision that shaped the scope and direction of *Strangers in the Land* sprang from a conviction that no single book could tell a coherent story of nativism (or rather, of nativisms) while also doing justice to the far larger subject of ethnocentrism. Obviously nativism was an inflamed and nationalistic type of ethnocentrism. It was therefore related to—and surely influenced by—the myriad ways in which people of all kinds favor their own group and assert its superiority without necessarily being either nativists or racists in a strict sense. Beneath the ebb and flow of the nativism that I was charting I noted in 1955 a vast "cultural subsoil" of habits, preferences, appearances, and capacities that no historian had studied and I certainly knew very little about (Higham 1955/1988, 24).

I dealt with this problem simply by bringing it up every once in a while. To illustrate the abounding variety of ethnocentric stereotypes and predelictions circulating in popular culture was easy enough, but to assess their bearing on a study of ideologies was a different matter altogether. Consequently I was able only sketchily to observe the social contexts in which nativism functioned, and I explicitly excluded the frictions *between* ethnic minorities (Higham 1955/1988, x–xi). This neglect of ethnocentrism in its widest dimensions I have come to regard as the great shortcoming of *Strangers in the Land.*

Just two years after the book was published I confessed to these second thoughts. The confession was made in a paper read at an annual meeting of the Catholic Historical Association, "Another Look at Nativism" (Higham 1958). I pointed out that the very term "nativism"—invented to describe principles advanced by an antiforeign and anti-Catholic political party in the 1850s—directed attention to ideologies, not to actual social processes or conditions. My treatment of nativism, like most earlier accounts, had focused on the rigid systems of ideas that propagandists manipulate to distort reality. Repelled as I was not only by the xenophobias of the past but also by the nationalist delusions of the cold war going on around me, I had highlighted the most inflammatory aspects of ethnic conflict.

I had tried, to be sure, to take account of social conditions, and in some measure I had succeeded. But that was doubly difficult to do in the intellectual climate of the 1950s. One's vivid awareness of the destructive power of irrational belief systems dovetailed with a contemporary fascination in social science with the preconceived distortions of "prejudice." It may not be too much to say that ideology and prejudice were then the twin lodestars of social psychology.

It was time, I told my Catholic audience, to look at the fabric of society—time to look at interactions, not just at attitudes, and so to throw light on the overall structure of a multiethnic social order. That structure would have to encompass much that was being screened out by the concentration of historians on ideologies and prejudices. We were neglecting, for example, frictions between minorities, comparative rates of social and geographical mobility within the United States, tendencies of native-born Americans to side with some minorities against others, and the striking differences in acceptance of particular immigrant groups in one part of the country as opposed to another.

To illustrate these suggestions I drew on my latest research, which the American Jewish Committee was sponsoring, on relative rates of social mobility (and accompanying status rivalries) experienced by Jews, Germans, Irish Catholics, and Norwegians in various parts of the country. I was able to show—at least to my own satisfaction—that organized nativism was not a problem for Jews in the nineteenth century, but social discrimination was. It arose inescapably from competition for social status and material advancement, which touched the daily life of Jews more intimately than all the ancient memories of Christian persecution or the nightmares of Jewish world dominion (Higham 1984, 95–174).[1] My conclusion in 1957 was emphatic. "The nativist theme, as defined and developed to date," I declared, "is imaginatively exhausted" (Higham 1958, 147–8).

And so it proved to be, at least for a long time. No other major book on nativism appeared in the next thirty years (Bennett 1988). My short address of 1957 was published in due course and, for a few years, rather widely reprinted (Higham 1966, 1971). This early attention arose at least partly because my modest attempt to compare historical statistics on the social mobility of different ethnic groups anticipated a major shift of interest among American historians during the 1960s: a shift from intellectual to social history, and from national history to local studies of group behavior (Higham 1989, 235–64). As the shift acquired its own momentum, however, my article sank into oblivion. At the same time, the sales of *Strangers in the Land* skyrocketed. In spite of a growing fascination among historians with the coping strategies of little people, coercive ideologies were what they and their students wanted more and more to read about.

THESE AFTERTHOUGHTS on what *Strangers in the Land* neglected should convey some sense of the awesome amplitude that an ideal history of xenophobia and ethnic conflict might have had. Reflections on what I marginalized in 1955, however, do not go very far in explaining how I lost my subject. Why did I not settle down to the making of a more inclusive history of nativism *and* ethnocentrism? Why did I let go, instead of extending my grasp? I could plead the lack of a suitable temperament or turn of mind for a project so rigorously statistical. Though true enough, that would be insufficient. Unfortunately, there was a worm in my apple, not just a deficiency in my appetite. The causal scheme that *Strangers* rested on had a defect that haunted me. Let us turn from what I neglected to what I concentrated on.

The primacy that *Strangers in the Land* assigned to ideologies demanded a careful examination of why those powerful systems of belief changed. From the outset I observed successive eras of crisis and confidence in public opinion: confidence in the early 1880s, crisis in the 1890s, recovery in the early twentieth century, crisis again from 1915 to the mid-1920s. But this was merely descriptive. At an explanatory level, I pointed to the "social and economic problems of an urban-industrial society" as the root cause of the rise of nativism in the late nineteenth century (1955/1988, 98). Essentially, I advanced an economic explanation. It seemed substantiated by a sharp decline of nativist ferment at the very end of the century. When the long depression of that decade lifted, social anxieties relaxed, and urban renewal flowered, and anti-foreign agitation subsided.

My difficulty was that a major nativist resurgence from about 1906 onward seemed far less dependent on the economic causes that stood out in the 1890s. Nativists now demanded that all foreigners be completely transformed into Americans forthwith and—inconsistently—that the blood of inferior races must stop pouring into American veins. Together, these demands shaped the mood of "100 percent Americanism" that permeated World War I and the early 1920s. Yet, with brief exceptions, this was a time of abounding prosperity.

Even some help from psychological theories of aggression and displacement left my economic interpretation inadequate. Material conditions caused nativist behavior in the first half of the book; ideas caused nativist behavior in the second half. I could not explain why the arrow of causation ran one way in one period and another way in the next.

After publishing my own critique of the book and elaborating it in essays on anti-Semitism, I drifted away to other subjects for a good many years, during which I explored cultural history as a middle ground between the history of ideas and the history of society. I never lost a deep interest in American nationalism. But everything in the intellectual milieu from the 1960s to the 1980s discouraged its scrutiny. The boom in social history fragmented into a multitude of subspecialties, which paid scant attention to one another and less to a national framework. Political history, in spite of a few distinguished books, was largely neglected. Generalizations about national character and national institutions collapsed. Ethnic history flourished, but only as an internalized preoccupation. Young scholars did good work on individual ethnic groups from a perspective located inside the group, which was usually their own. Relations between an ethnic group and the larger American environment that contained it were either ignored or treated as repressive. Comparisons between groups were generally perceived as invidious. Japanese Americans, for example, were taught to repudiate as loathsomely prejudicial a popular post–World War II label: "the model minority." In 1983, well before the term "multiculturalism" gained prominence, I wrote gloomily: "A pluralistic ethos—a celebration of group autonomy and social diversity—[has] supplied an ideological sanction for the disaggregation of American history" (242).

Gradually, however, the inhibitions that constrained the writing of national history and constricted the formulations of ethnic history have seemed to relax. Now that the cold war is over and Marxism, like other solid convictions, has melted into air, there is a reviving need to give more meaning to American history as a whole. Surely it must be possible to join national history with ethnic history without an a priori pitting of one against the other. Perhaps, I thought, this could be done by imagining a new history of American nationalism that would do justice to the universalist strain and (on the basis of recent monographic research) take adequate account of an overall social structure. Such a history would impart to the cosmopolitan faith I left on the margin of my first book a dynamism of its own. But the story would also foreground the social processes that I gestured at in "Another Look at Nativism." Those processes—so vital in structuring the American pattern of ethnic relations—could now be seen throughout the fabric of American nationalism, weaving that fabric in one era and now unraveling it in another. I have not carried these speculations very far. But musing on the distinctive structures of American nationalism and American ethnicity has turned my thoughts back to my early attempt at schematizing ethnic behavior.

Let us suppose that ethnic tensions are best understood within a context of nation building. The entire span from the 1850s to the 1960s was a time when Americans were elaborating a thickening matrix of national institutions and national culture. National consciousness—that is, an awareness of and attachment to an American identity—penetrated ever more deeply and widely through the regions and peoples of the United States. The victory of the Union in the Civil War was one giant step, the building of a national rail network another. The creation of a common, compulsory school system was a third. The unifying experiences of the Great Depression, the New Deal, and World War II were still another. A good overall label for the nation-building impetus, a label widely used in the nineteenth century, is "consolidation" (McClay 1994, 5–6, 21–41, 105–48, 189–90).

Sometimes nation building faltered. That happened during the looming threat of disunion in the 1850s. It happened again in the class crisis of the 1890s and during the deep strains that World War I created in a still highly decentralized society. On such occasions both nativism *and* liberal nationalism could flare up, grappling with one another as rival principles of national unity. The quickening of one ideology could animate the other, each offering a contrastive remedy for the nation-building slowdown. During the Civil War, and immediately afterward in the radical phase of Reconstruction, liberal nationalism prevailed. Nativism virtually disappeared. In the era of World War I, however, nativism won the upper hand (Foner 1988; Kennedy 1980).

After a brief interlude in the late 1920s and early 1930s, nation building resumed in an egalitarian mode. American universalism, fostered initially by a Depression-born sense that all Americans needed to share a common burden, came strongly to the fore. World War II, the most popular of all American wars, further invigorated the myth of a burden-sharing, national community. This in turn prepared the way for a great postwar civil rights movement, which gained its first dazzling success in 1948 when President Truman ordered an end to racial segregation and discrimination throughout the armed forces of the United States (Higham 1997, 3–9; Schlesinger 1949a, 186–209; Sitkoff 1978).

For a generation after World War II, liberal nationalism held the kind of preeminence in public opinion that nativism had exercised in the era of World War I. Because *Strangers in the Land* was so much a vehicle of the transition from one system of thought to the other—from nativism to liberalism—I could not fully comprehend at the time of its publication how far the transition had already gone.

Today we are similarly perplexed to know what has become of the liberal nationalism that reached its finest hour in the civil rights movement of the mid-1960s. Although ethno-racial tensions are widespread and in some ways growing, no revival of a nativist or racist ideology has replaced the fading liberal orthodoxy of the 1950s and 1960s. Are we witnessing an approaching end of nation building itself? Or an erosion of the nation-state as its capacity to maintain national borders and an effective national center weakens? Or is the crucial change largely subjective? Does it flow from a postmodern culture that is abandoning the formulation of problems in terms of beliefs? Are we at last approaching the "end of ideology" that Daniel Bell (1960/1988) anticipated long ago? Either thesis is plausible, one rooted in institutions, the other in habits of thought. Both are compatible with the loosely pluralistic multiplication of social identities that scholars are now encouraged to take into account. Ideology clearly persists, notably in the strong form of multiculturalism that is systematically hostile to an inclusive American identity. But this species of anti-Americanism, like other political creeds, is diminishing. In place of ideologies one senses an increasing indifference to the nation-state.

WHERE DOES this leave students of ethnic conflict and cooperation in our own day? At least for the time being, neither conflict nor cooperation expresses itself any longer, loudly and clearly, in the form of ideology. But ethnic tensions and conjunctions do not and will not go away. We are left, I believe, with the task I identified in the 1950s but failed to pursue: the task of excavating the cultural and social interactions that occur in the structures of everyday life. It seems reasonable to suppose that these often unspoken realities will emerge more clearly in the history of ethnic relations if nativist and racist creeds continue to lose the vivid preeminence that many of us have imparted to them.

To be specific, I want to offer in conclusion two interrelated suggestions concerning fundamental social conditions on which a new history of ethnic relations might be built.

Numbers and Concentration When ethnic conflict erupts, historians routinely mention the numerical proportion between newcomers and the resident population. But this factor is hardly ever given the salience it had for the people who were involved..

Mob attacks on newcomers generally occur when their proportion of a population suddenly increases too rapidly to permit much assimilation. The two great explosions of ethnic turmoil associated with immigration took place at the peak of the greatest waves of immigration in American history, one in the 1850s, when several leading American cities were half foreign-born, the other around World War I, when first- and second-generation immigrants together reached an all-time high in proportion to the older native-born Americans (Carpenter 1927, 25–26; Higham 1984, 13–15).

The disappearance of any such "invasion" during and after the 1930s explains what puzzled me about McCarthyism in the 1950s. Senator McCarthy was a rabid nationalist, exciting fears of hidden Communist influence in the United States. He could have found it among the influential Jews who had been Communists in the 1930s and after. Instead, he chose a Jewish lawyer, Roy Cohn, as chief counsel for his subcommittee. McCarthy and Cohn spared all of the ethnic minorities. Rather, they targeted "Ivy Leaguers" in the State Department (Bennett 1988, 310–15; Schrecker 1986). Jewish immigration to the United States had virtually ended. Assimilation was diffusing a Jewish presence. Absent immigration, anticommunism had lost its nativist edge.

Internal migrations, if they are large and precipitous, destabilize ethnic relations in the same way that foreign immigration can do. Although many blacks view the devastating ghetto riots in northern cities from 1964 to 1968 as historically inevitable, it seems unlikely that they would have occurred if an enormous migration from the rural South—more concentrated than any other internal migration in American history—had not swelled to bursting the segregated black neighborhoods in those cities.

Geographical Mobility Paradoxically, when the movement of peoples is diffuse rather than concentrated, it becomes the great solvent of ethnic discord, and that has been the norm in America. Although immigrants are an unsettling force wherever they appear, in the United States their arrival has often been less stressful than it would be in other countries because here most of the older, supposedly more settled population have themselves been engaged in an endless round of relocations. From east to west, from town to city, from city to suburb, and from one neighborhood to the next—Americans have always been an extraordinarily migratory people (Allen 1977). International migration has invigorated this internal process, yet it has also been absorbed and changed by the same process. Internal mobility has accustomed Americans to living among strangers; to those who feel uncomfortable in the midst of others unlike themselves, mobility can offer a relatively easy exit.

Since the end of slavery, African Americans have participated vigorously in this national habit and, in doing so, have often improved their circumstances. But for blacks a strong association of geographical mobility with freedom came to a devastating halt when they found themselves enclosed in northern cities by the walls of residential segregation. This violation of one of the promises of American life surely heightens the anger that many blacks display toward still poorer minorities, who move more easily, and toward more affluent minorities, who go anywhere they please.

I am touching here on demographic shifts that are far from new. We require no theory of a "new" nativism or a "new" racism to account for the trouble that today's concentrated immigrations from abroad precipitate, especially in urban ghettos like the Watts area in Los Angeles, where a flood of Mexican immigrants is overrunning black neighborhoods.

If ethnic conflict arises so much from immediate social conditions—displacement, on the one hand, and blocked mobility, on the other—what significance attaches to the larger contours of American nationalism? Have scholars been entirely misguided in their attention to beliefs? It would be rash to think so. No nation can be effective without a vision of what it wants to be. If part of our ethnic problem today is the absence of such a vision, surely part of the solution is its recovery. As the bonds of national loyalty loosen, their capacity to unite diminishes along with their capacity to exclude. One must wonder whether the eclipse of liberal nationalism since the 1960s has not deprived all of the nation's minorities of a powerful means of affirming their belonging and their fraternity with one another.

My quick sketch, at the close of this paper, of what a new history of ethnic and race relations might say, is subsequently enlarged in a contribution to a second symposium that met a year later. That longer paper, entitled "Cultural Responses to Immigration," has just been published in *Diversity and Its Discontents: Cultural Conflict and Common Ground in Contemporary American Society,* edited by Neil J. Smelser and Jeffrey C. Alexander. 1999. Princeton: Princeton University Press.

Note

1. For a forceful dissent, see Shapiro (1986). I responded in the same issue (Higham 1986).

22 Immigration Reform and the Browning of America: Tensions, Conflicts, and Community Instability in Metropolitan Los Angeles

James H. Johnson Jr., Walter C. Farrell Jr., and Chandra Guinn

OUR NATION IS IN THE midst of a rather dramatic demographic transformation that is radically changing all aspects of American society, including the racial and ethnic composition of our neighborhoods, schools, workplaces, and social and political institutions. As a consequence of heightened immigration—legal and illegal—and high rates of birth among the newly arrived immigrants, nonwhite ethnic minority groups are projected to surpass non-Hispanic whites to become, collectively, the numerical majority of the U.S. population by the fifth decade of the twenty-first century.

Unfortunately, the nation's emerging multiethnic, demographic realities are not welcomed or embraced by everyone. In fact, the intolerance to immigration-induced population diversity has become so intense that, in some states and cities, police departments are now required to record and maintain statistics on the incidences of racially, ethnically, and religiously motivated violence (Johnson, Oliver, and Roseman 1989). Indeed, it has been argued that one of the root causes of the Los Angeles civil unrest of 1992 was the failure of local elected officials to implement human relations policies to mitigate the widespread intolerance that had accompanied recent changes in the racial and ethnic composition of the Los Angeles population (Johnson and Farrell 1993; Johnson et al. 1992; Luttwak 1992; Postrel 1992).

We believe that the racial and ethnic intolerance underlying the nation's changing demographic realities strongly challenges, and indeed may very well threaten, our ability to establish viable, stable, racially and ethnically diverse communities and institutions (Guthrie and Hutchinson 1995; Johnson et al. 1989; McDaniel 1995; Miller 1994; Rose 1989; Schultz 1993; Stanfield 1994; Teitelbaum and Weiner 1995). To our way of thinking, the nation's growing antagonism toward racial and ethnic diversity, as evidenced by California initiatives like Proposition 187 and Proposition 209 and continuing efforts at the federal level to curtail benefits that currently accrue to tax-paying, legal immigrants (Alarcón 1995; Bowermaster 1995; Hing 1993b; Jost 1995; Lee and Sloan 1994; Valenzuela 1995), is also bad for business and thus threatens the nation's competitiveness in the global marketplace.

Moreover, and perhaps most significant in terms of the future viability of U.S. cities, especially those port-of-entry communities where large numbers of newly arriving immigrants have settled (Roberts 1994), these issues were altogether ignored in President Clinton's National Urban Policy Report *Empowerment: A New Covenant with America's Communities,* released in July 1995 (U.S. Department of Housing and Urban Development 1995). If U.S. cities are to recapture their former premier status in American society, it is imperative, in our view, that we gain a fuller understanding of the nature and basis of this growing intolerance of demographic diversity and then develop strategies to resolve the underlying conflicts (Johnson and Farrell 1993; Johnson and Oliver 1989; Johnson et al. 1989).

Elsewhere we have demonstrated how recent immigration reform policies have contributed to growing income inequality in the United States (Johnson and Farrell 1998). In this chapter, we highlight the root causes of the growing opposition to both immigrants and U.S. immigration policy—the nativist backlash; present a typology of the community-level conflicts that have arisen as a consequence of heightened immigration—legal and illegal—to the United States over the last thirty years; and outline the conditions under which diversity can be brought to the forefront as one of society's strengths.

Background and Context

Over the past thirty years, the origin, size, and composition of the legal immigration stream into the United States has changed dramatically, largely as a consequence of the promulgation of the Hart-Celler Act of 1965 and more recent amendments to it (especially the Immigration Reform and Control Act of 1986 and the Immigration Act of 1990). Between 1920 and 1965 legal immigration to the United States averaged about 206,000 per year, with the major flows originating in northern and western Europe. Since the passage of the Hart-Celler Act, the volume of immigration has increased sharply, averaging over 500,000 per year between the mid-1960s and the mid-1990s, and the origins of the dominant flows have changed—they now originate in the Asian Pacific Triangle region (see figure 22.1). Prior to 1965 immigration from the countries that make up this region was prohibited based on various unfounded theories about the racial and ethnic inferiority and cultural unassimilability of the indigenous population.

The immigrant flow has not been limited to those entering via the hemispheric quota and family or occupation preference provisions established in the Hart-Celler Act and in more recent immigration reforms. The new arrivals, over the last thirty years, have also included a significant number of refugees, parolees, and asylum seekers who were fleeing political persecution in their home countries. According to the Immigration and Naturalization Service (INS), approximately 2.2 million refugees, parolees, and asylees were allowed to settle in the United States between 1961 and 1993 (roughly 65,000 annually).

The flow also has included a substantial number of illegal aliens searching for jobs and an improved quality of life (Zolberg 1995). The number of unauthorized aliens granted amnesty under the IRCA of 1986 is one useful indicator of the impact of illegal immigration on the size and composition of the U.S. resident population. Any illegal immigrant who could demonstrate that he or she had lived in the United States before 1982 was eligible to apply for citizenship under this act. Three million undocumented aliens took advantage of this opportunity to become U.S. citizens (Baker 1997; Lowell and Jing 1994).

The view was that, by granting amnesty to such a large number of people who were residing in the United States illegally, as new legal workers they would saturate domestic labor demand and thereby stem the illegal flow. Research shows, however, that the IRCA of 1986 has been largely ineffective (Andreas 1994). At the completion of the amnesty program in October 1988, there were 2.7 million illegal aliens who remained in the country to take advantage of unskilled and semiskilled jobs in the booming U.S. economy. According to Peter Andreas (1994, 231), "these illegal immigrant workers provided a more permanent base for the social networks that facilitate the arrival of new illegal immigrants." Over the last decade, according to the INS, another 2.4 million immigrants have entered the United States illegally (roughly 275,000 annually). The INS (Center for Immigration Studies 1997b, 1) estimates that "as of October 1996 there were five million illegal aliens living in the United States."

These changes in the origin, size, and composition of the U.S. immigrant population have contributed to what some have characterized as the "browning of America," a rather dramatic change in the racial complexion and cultural orientations of the American population (Chiswick and Sullivan 1995; Hing 1993b; Johnson et al. 1989). These so-called new immigrants—those arriving in the post-1965 period—are phenotypically and culturally distinct from the old immigrants, those arriving in the pre-1965 era, who more closely resembled Anglo-Americans in terms of their physical characteristics and cultural patterns (Johnson and Oliver 1989). Moreover, research shows that the new immigrants are less inclined than the old immigrants to blend fully into American society. Most prefer, instead, to preserve and maintain their own cultural heritages and identities (Johnson et al. 1989).

Largely as a result of high rates of immigration from the Asian Pacific Triangle countries ushered in by these reforms, the nonwhite ethnic minority population (Asians, Hispanics, and blacks) grew more than seven times as fast as the non-Hispanic white "majority" population during the 1980s (Frey 1993). The Asian population doubled from 3.5 million to over 7 million. The Hispanic population increased by more than half—from 14.6 million to 22.3 million. And blacks added 3.5 million to their population, reaching a total count of almost 30 million in 1990. As a result of these increases, the nonwhite ethnic minority population now comprises 60.5 million people—almost one-quarter (24.4 percent) of the total population (Frey 1993).

The impact of these immigration-driven changes

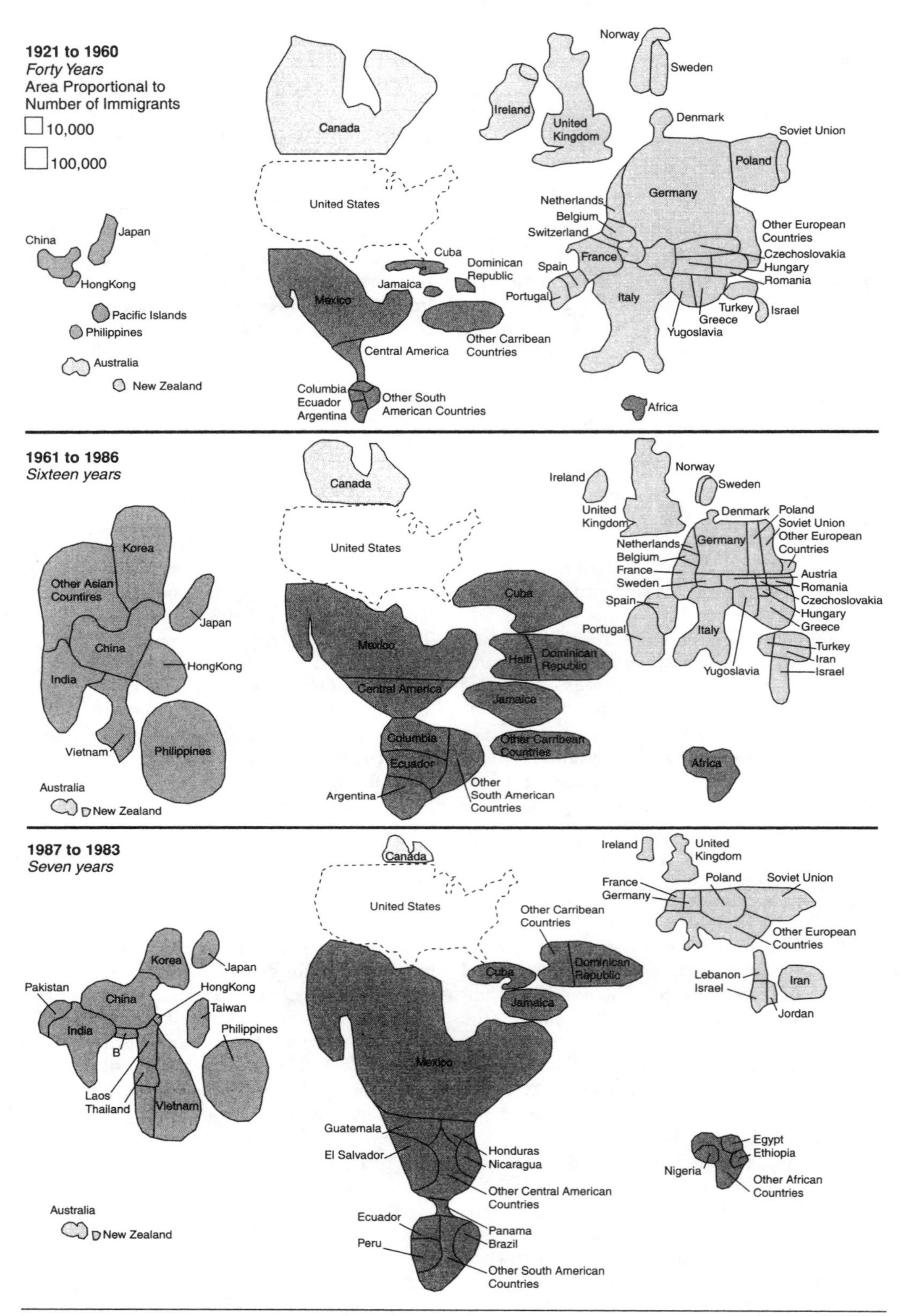

Source: Adapted from Johnson, Oliver, and Roseman (1989).

has not been felt evenly or uniformly in the United States; rather, it has fallen disproportionately on selected states and on selected communities within these states. Seven states—Arizona, Florida, Illinois, New Jersey, New York, Texas, and California—have borne the brunt of this immigration (Brenner 1995; Center for Immigration Studies 1995; Charles 1995), and selected cities within these primary destination states have served as the primary ports of entry for the new immigrants: Seattle, Chicago, El Paso, Houston, Miami, Los Angeles, San Francisco, San Yisdro (California), and San Diego (Johnson and Oliver 1989; Rose 1989).

Notably, Los Angeles stands out among these cities and appears to have replaced New York as the new Ellis Island (Andersen 1983). In large part as a consequence of large-scale immigration from Asia, Mexico, Central America, North Africa, the Middle East, and the Caribbean over the last thirty years, the Los Angeles metropolitan area is now a Third World metropolis (Johnson and Oliver 1989; Oliver and Johnson 1984). According to the most recent census estimates, people of color constitute nearly two-thirds of the population of metropolitan Los Angeles.

Based on the demographic changes taking place during the 1980s, and assuming continued high levels of immigration, the U.S. population is now projected to grow much more rapidly and to become far more diverse in the future than was anticipated by the U.S. Census Bureau as recently as seven years ago. In 1988 the Census Bureau estimated that the U.S. population would continue to grow until 2010, when it would peak at around 300 million, and then remain relatively stable until 2050. But more recent projections indicate that U.S. population growth is not likely to peak in 2010; instead, the nation's population is projected to increase by 50 percent over the next sixty years, reaching 375 million by 2050.

The revised projections are based on the Census Bureau's realization that the U.S. population will not approach zero population growth (ZPG) in the foreseeable future, as assumed in its 1988 projections. Those projections were based, generally, on the assumption that the population growth rates of nonwhite ethnic minority groups would approximate the non-Hispanic white rate by the end of this decade, which currently approaches ZPG (that is, the average white family has about 1.7 children and thus is relatively stable). But more recent analyses based on the 1990 census results and the annual Current Population Survey suggest that this was an unrealistic assumption.

Between now and the year 2050, the black population is projected to increase by 94 percent, the American Indian population by 109 percent, the Hispanic population by 238 percent, and the Asian and Pacific Islander population by 412 percent. By contrast, the non-Hispanic white population is projected to increase by only 29.4 percent over the next sixty years. What this means, of course, is that largely as a consequence of continued high rates of immigration—legal and illegal—and high rates of natural increase among recently arrived immigrants, nonwhite ethnic minority groups will continue to be responsible for the majority of the nation's population growth over the next six decades (Holmes 1995; Martin 1995a, 1995b).

The Nativist Backlash

How has the U.S. citizenry responded to these demographic changes and population projections? Public opinion polls and other data indicate that there is a steadily increasing fear of the so-called browning of America, a growing intolerance of immigrants among native Americans (that is, those who were born in the United States of parents who were also born in America), and growing opposition to what is perceived to be the nation's open-door immigration policy, on the one hand, and its seeming inability to stem the tide of illegal immigration, on the other (Brimelow 1995; Center for Immigration Studies 1997a; Flanigan 1994).

Perceptions of Impacts

At the most general level, U.S. citizens harbor negative views and beliefs about the impact of recent immigration on American society. In a recent *Newsweek* poll, nearly half of those surveyed indicated that "immigrants are a burden on our country because they take jobs, housing and [consume] health care" (Adler and Waldman 1995, 18). Only 40 percent thought that "immigrants strengthen our country because of their hard work and talents." In another *Newsweek* poll, two-thirds of the non-Hispanic whites (66 percent) and nearly half of the blacks (46 percent) surveyed said that the level of immigration to the United States should be decreased (Brownstein 1995).

In California, one of the states that have borne the brunt of immigration, in a 1988 statewide poll, three-fourths of the whites (75 percent) and two-thirds of the blacks (66.9 percent) surveyed said they were worried about the changing makeup of California's population. Underlying their concerns was the belief that the immigration of people of Asian and Hispanic background "will make it hard to maintain American traditions and the American way of life." A majority of both the whites and the blacks surveyed indicated that they thought that the place of English as our common language was being endangered and that the quality of education was being lowered by the recent immigration, especially the influx of Hispanics (Field Institute 1988).

In a recent survey of a multiethnic sample of Los Angeles households (see Johnson, Oliver, and Bobo 1994), several questions were included to gauge the perceived political and economic impacts of continued high rates of immigration on American society. As table 22.1 shows, the black and non-Hispanic white respondents were far more likely than the Hispanic, Korean, Japanese, and Chinese respondents to perceive that continued immigration is likely to have a negative impact on their well-being. Roughly one-half of both the non-Hispanic white and the black survey respondents expressed the belief that they would either have less or a lot less political influence and economic opportunity than they currently have if immigration is allowed to continue at the present rate.

TABLE 22.1 Perceived Impacts of Immigration

Respondent	*Political Influence*[a]	*Economic Opportunity*[b]
Black	52.1	56.8
Hispanic	16.9	33.2
Chinese	2.5	14.7
Korean	4.8	5.9
Japanese	10.9	12.7
White	51.8	46.7

Source: Los Angeles Survey of Urban Inequality.
Note: Reported percentage corresponds to the proportion of survey respondents who expressed the belief that they would either have "less" or "a lot less" political influence and economic opportunity than they currently have if immigration is allowed to continue at the present rate.
[a] If immigration to this country continued at the present rate, how much political influence do you believe people like you (respondent's group—white, black, Asian, Hispanic people) will have (1) much political influence, (2) me, but not a lot more, (3) no more or less than now, (4) t less than now.
immigration to this country continues at the present lo you believe people like you (respondent's group) bably have (1) much more economic opportunity, , but not a lot more, (3) no more or less than now, an now, (5) a lot less opportunity than now?

It is noteworthy that these perceptions are radically different from those of Hispanic, Chinese, Korean, and Japanese survey respondents. No more than one-third of the respondents in any one of these groups shared this view. Given that the latter groups comprised a high percentage of recently arrived immigrants, the difference in their perceptions and those of native-born blacks and non-Hispanic whites regarding the impact of continued high rates of immigration is unsurprising.

Further insights into the nature of the concerns about immigration are evident in tables 22.2 and 22.3, which also were derived from the recent Los Angeles survey. In addition to the rift that our immigration policy has created between the foreign-born and the native-born, it also has prompted considerable antagonism among nonwhite ethnic minority groups. A majority of the blacks surveyed believe that the more influence Asians and Hispanics have in local politics the less influence they will have in local politics. As table 22.2 shows, one-half of the Hispanics surveyed expressed similar concerns about Asians. A majority of the blacks surveyed also agreed with the statement that more good jobs for both Asians and Hispanics would mean fewer good jobs for blacks (table 22.3). In contrast, Hispanics viewed only themselves as being in direct competition with Asians for good jobs.

This high level of opposition to immigration is partially fueled by native Americans' increasing economic insecurity due to massive layoffs and wage stagnation in the U.S. economy. It appears that no one is being spared, not even white males—traditionally the privileged and protected class in the employment arena—as U.S. businesses aggressively reengineer, downsize, or "right-size" their operations in an effort to remain competitive

TABLE 22.2 The More Influence Members (of Target Group) Have in Local Politics, The Less Influence Respondent's Group Will Have in Local Politics (Percent Agreeing)

Respondent	*Asian*	*Black*	*Hispanic*
White	32.6	28.8	35.6
Asian	—	32.0	35.9
Hispanic	50.8	39.9	—
Black	60.5	—	51.4

Source: Los Angeles Survey of Urban Inequality.

TABLE 22.3 More Good Jobs for Members (of Target Group) Means Fewer Jobs for Respondent's Group (Percent Agreeing)

Respondent	*Asian*	*Black*	*Hispanic*
White	32.9	24.0	25.6
Asian	—	24.7	25.0
Hispanic	46.5	35.0	—
Black	68.8	—	61.1

Source: Los Angeles Survey of Urban Inequality.

in the twenty-first-century global marketplace (Grimsley 1995; Lee 1995).

The opposition to immigration also reflects native American opposition to the current push for multiculturalism in all walks of American society (Graham 1994), a movement perceived to be largely motivated by the recent wave of immigrants' unwillingness to assimilate fully—culturally and linguistically—into mainstream American society (Brownstein 1995). And it is partly a response to the role of immigrants in recent, highly publicized events like the World Trade Center bombing, the shootings on the Long Island railroad, and the Los Angeles civil unrest of 1992 (Charles 1995).

Intergroup Attitudes and Stereotypes

The situation is further complicated by the fact that the newly arrived immigrants bring with them from their host societies negative perceptions of and prejudicial attitudes toward native Americans, especially blacks. One author notes, for example, that "Mexican Americans have historically viewed blacks as 'black Anglo-Saxons' in the negative sense of being an inferior imitation of and having an affinity for Anglo culture" (Henry 1980, 224). Another author notes that "Spanish culture traditionally denigrated 'dark skin' and inferiorized its possessors" (Oliver and Johnson 1984, 66).

Chang (1988), a specialist in Asian American studies, argues that Asians, on the other hand, are continuously bombarded with American media exports that contain negative images of blacks. What effect have such exports had on Asians' perceptions of blacks? According to Chang, Asians "have learned and accepted the stereotypes of blacks as criminals, welfare recipients, drug addicts, and/or lazy through American movies, TV shows, and American Forces Korea Network Programs" (10).

Concerns about the enormous burden that the new immigrants, especially those who enter the country illegally, place on city services—hospitals, schools, the welfare system, and the criminal justice system—is one of the sources of public backlash against continued high rates of immigration (Hudson 1995; Jost 1995; Thom 1995; Unz 1994; Valenzuela 1995). In addition, within many communities, newly arriving immigrants settle in formerly all-black residential areas, setting into motion a wide range of interethnic minority conflicts—over jobs, housing, and access to other scarce resources—that are rooted in stereotypes and prejudicial attitudes toward one another (Johnson and Oliver 1989; Oliver and Johnson 1984). Nowhere is this more apparent than in metropolitan Los Angeles (Johnson et al. 1992).

The 1992 Los Angeles County Social Survey (LACSS) (Institute for Social Science Research 1992), which focused on the theme "Ethnic Antagonism in Los Angeles," provides insights into the nature and magnitude of intergroup stereotyping and prejudice in a community in which large numbers of immigrants have settled. The 1992 LACSS was a random digit dial telephone survey of eighteen hundred adults living in Los Angeles metropolitan area households (Bobo et al. 1995a).

In the survey, respondents were asked to rank, on a seven-point scale, members of their own ethnic group and members of each of the other major ethnic categories. The end points of the scales were defined in terms of three key pairs of traits: "intelligent" to "unintelligent," "prefer to live off welfare" to "prefer to be self-supporting," and "hard to get along with" to "easy to get along with." Thus, these data provide insights into the extent to which members of any given group (whites, for instance) rate members of other groups (such as blacks, Asians, or Hispanics) more positively, the same, or more negatively than members of their own groups.

For our purposes here, we focus on the degree to which members of a given group rate members of the other groups more negatively than members of their own group. We shall highlight only the most salient findings (see figure 22.2).

How did non-Hispanic whites, Asians, and Hispanics rate blacks? As panel A of figure 22.2 shows, blacks were viewed negatively with regard to intelligence and welfare dependence, especially by Asians. Nearly two-thirds (63.4 percent) of the Asian respondents viewed blacks as being less intelligent than members of their own group, and over three-fourths (76.8 percent) rated blacks as relatively more likely to prefer to live off welfare. Whites also rated blacks negatively on these two

FIGURE 22.2 Intergroup Stereotypes, Los Angeles County, 1992

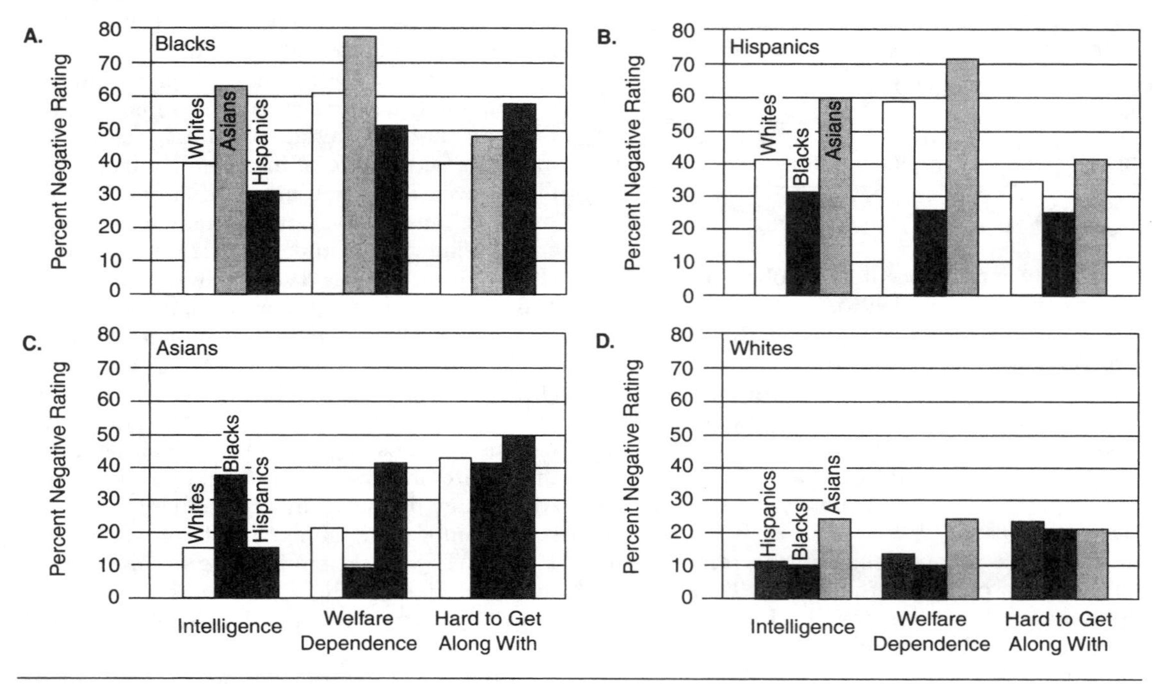

Source: Compiled by authors from the Los Angeles County Social Survey, 1992.

traits, but not nearly as negatively as their Asian counterparts did.

A similar pattern emerged when whites, blacks, and Asians were asked to rank Hispanics (see figure 22.2, panel B). Sixty percent of Asian respondents rated Hispanics as less intelligent than members of their own group, and 71.9 percent rated Hispanics as more likely to prefer to live off welfare. As in the ratings of blacks, whites also had negative ratings of Hispanics on these two traits, but they were not as strongly negative as those of the Asian respondents.

How did whites, blacks, and Hispanics rate Asians? As panel C of figure 22.2 shows, whites, blacks, and Hispanics all view Asians as difficult to get along with. Among the three groups, Hispanics are the strongest in their rating of Asians as difficult to get along with. As we shall discuss later, Hispanics' negative rating of Asians with regard to this trait was one of the touchstones for the burning, looting, and violence that took place in Koreatown, and blacks' negative rating of Koreans was one of the touchstones for the conflagration in South Central Los Angeles, during the 1992 civil disturbance in Los Angeles.

How do Asians, Hispanics, and blacks view non-Hispanic whites? In terms of intelligence and welfare dependence, Asians hold significantly more negative views of non-Hispanic whites than either blacks or Hispanics do (figure 22.2, panel D). Although they rate non-Hispanic whites not nearly so low as they do blacks and Hispanics, roughly one-fourth of Asians rate non-Hispanic whites as less intelligent and more likely to live off welfare than their own group. Asians, blacks, and Hispanics all rate non-Hispanic whites similarly in terms of being difficult to get along with.

Data from the 1992 LACSS also illustrate the extent to which Asians, blacks, Hispanics, and whites oppose or favor social contact of a prolonged or intimate nature with one another (figure 22.3). To elicit feelings of this kind, two questions on social distance were included in the survey. The first asked the survey respondents whether they would favor or oppose living in a neighborhood where half of their neighbors were members of each of the other groups. Responses to this question can be viewed as a test of openness to residential integration. The second question asked respondents whether "they would favor

FIGURE 22.3. Interethnic Attitudes: Toward Inmates or Prolonged Social Contact, Los Angeles County, 1993

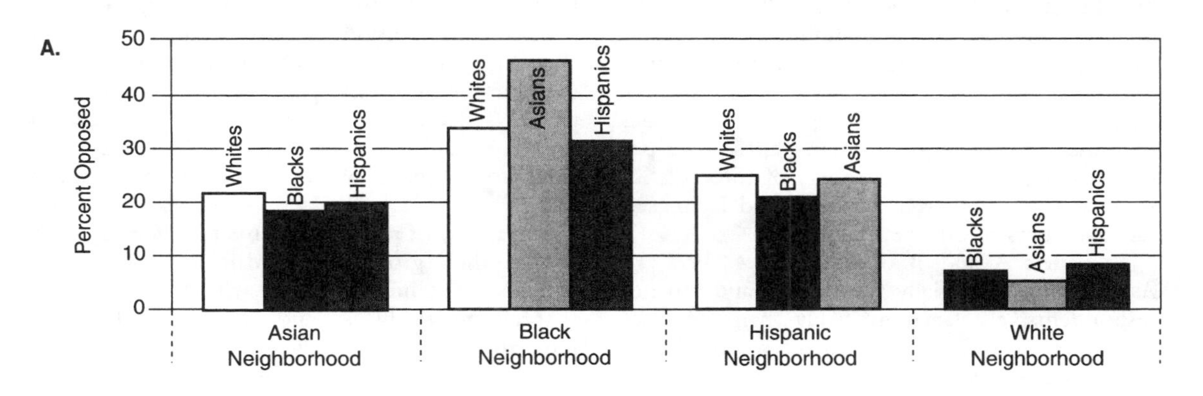

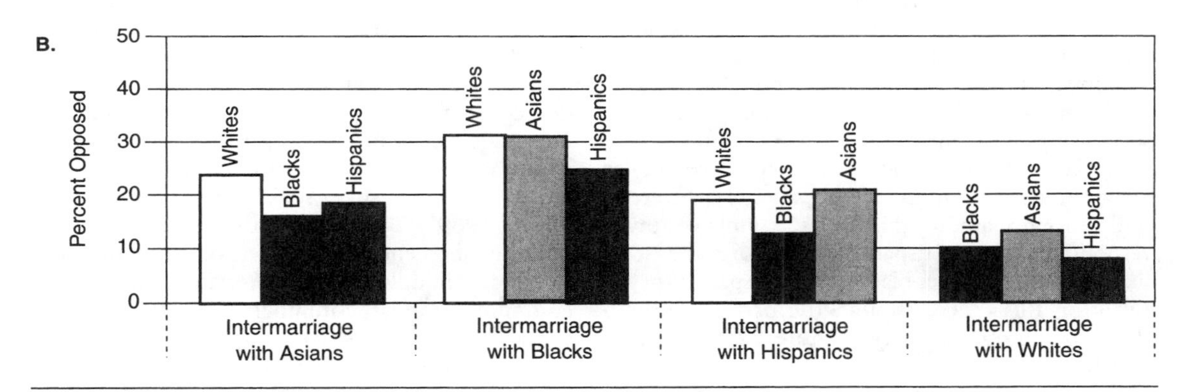

Source: Compiled by authors from the Los Angeles County Social Survey, 1992.

or oppose an interrracial marriage that involved a close relative or family member."

Social distance feelings toward residential integration are depicted in panel A of figure 22.3. The strongest opposition to residential integration emerged when the neighborhood was 50 percent black. Nearly half of the Asian respondents (46.2 percent) and roughly one-third of the Hispanic (32.8 percent) and white (34.3 percent) respondents opposed a residential mixture of this proportion. These and other data in panel A of figure 22.3 are consistent with the results of contemporary studies of racial residential segregation (see Massey and Denton 1992). Among the dominant ethnic groups, blacks are the most highly segregated.

A similar response is evident in panel B of figure 22.3, which depicts the percentage opposed to intermarriage. Again, the strongest opposition is to intermarriage involving blacks. Roughly one-third of the white respondents (32.8 percent) and one-third of the Asian respondents (31.8 percent) opposed an interracial marriage with a black.

In 1994 a much larger sample of Los Angeles County households (4,025) was asked to rate the members of other ethnic minority groups, on a seven-point scale, in terms of a set of traits broader than those included in the 1992 LACSS. The specific traits included in the Los Angeles Survey of Urban Inequality (LASUI) (Institute for Social Science Research 1994) were: "tend to be unintelligent" to "tend to be intelligent," "prefer to be self-supporting" to "prefer to live off welfare," "tend to be hard to get along with" the "tend to be easy to get along with," "tend to speak English well" to "tend to speak English poorly," "tend to be involved in gangs and drugs" to "tend not to be involved in gangs and drugs," and "tend to treat other groups equally" to "tend to discriminate against members of other groups." In addition to the ratings of non-Hispanic white, black, and Hispanic survey respondents, these data provide insights into how members of three distinct Asian groups—Chinese, Koreans, and Japanese—rate members of other ethnic groups.

As panels A and B of figure 22.4 show, the Asian groups, especially the Korean and Japanese respondents, are far more likely than the black, non-Hispanic white, and Hispanic respondents to think that almost all blacks and almost all Hispanics are unintelligent. Roughly half of the Korean and Japanese respondents and one-third of the Chinese respondents expressed this view about blacks and Hispanics.

Similarly, as panels A and B of figure 22.4 show, nearly three-fourths of the Korean respondents and nearly two-thirds of the Chinese and Japanese respondents rated most blacks and Hispanics as preferring to live off welfare rather than being self-supporting. Not unlike their Asian counterparts, a majority of the Hispanic respondents hold similar views of blacks (figure 22.4, panel B). Interestingly enough, among this diverse sample of survey respondents, non-Hispanic whites are the least likely group to rate blacks and Hispanics negatively on this trait, although the percentage who did is not insignificant (see figure 22.4, panels A and B).

The Asian results are reminiscent of the widely publicized negative remarks of two high-ranking Japanese officials several years ago regarding the intellectual abilities of American blacks and Hispanics (*Jet* 1988b). Further, the results also go a long way toward explaining the international marketing by Japanese firms of black dolls with exaggerated physical features (such as black Sambo dolls) and of "darkie" toothpaste during the late 1980s (*Jet* 1988a; *Los Angeles Sentinel*, 1988).

Ratings on the next trait, the extent to which members of each group are perceived to be difficult to get along with, is emblematic of the ethnic tensions arising in Los Angeles and other urban communities that serve as ports of entry for large numbers of Third World immigrants. Nearly half of the black survey respondents rated Asians as difficult to get along with (figure 22.4, panel A), nearly half of the Hispanics (figure 22.4, panel B) and roughly 40 percent of the Asians (figure 22.4, panel C) rate blacks as difficult to get along with, and nearly half of the Korean respondents rated blacks as difficult to get along with (figure 22.4, panel C). In addition to these negative ratings of nonwhite ethnic minorities, nearly 40 percent of the black (figure 22.4, panel A) and Korean (figure 22.4, panel C) respondents and one-third of the Hispanic respondents (figure 22.4, panel B) rated non-Hispanic whites as difficult to get along with.

A majority of the respondents representing each of the ethnic groups captured in the LASUI, except for the Chinese, agreed with the statements that almost all blacks and almost all Hispanics tend to be involved in gangs and drugs (figure 22.4). It is salient, as panels A and B of figure 22.4 show, that this view is not limited to the non-Hispanic white, Korean, and Japanese survey respondents; a majority of the black and Hispanic respondents agreed with these statements about members of their own groups and about the members of each other's group (figure 22.4, panels A and B).

These findings are not surprising given the high degree of media attention devoted to gang warfare, much of which is drug-related, in inner-city communities where newly arrived immigrants and native minorities share social space (Johnson and Oliver 1989). They are also consistent with the findings of recent examinations of why whites and the black middle class are leaving port-of-entry communities in large numbers (Frey 1995c; Johnson and Roseman 1990).

A commonly held view, even among Hispanic survey respondents, is that almost all Hispanics tend to speak English poorly. Two-thirds of black survey respondents (figure 22.4, panel A), roughly half of the Japanese (figure 22.4, panel C) and white (figure 22.4, panel D) survey respondents, and over 40 percent of the Korean (figure 22.4, panel C) and Hispanic (figure 22.4, panel D) respondents shared this view. Also, nearly half of all black survey respondents viewed almost all Asians as tending to speak English poorly (figure 22.4, panel A). None of these ratings are surprising given the enormous schisms between Hispanics and Korean immigrants—who have established, respectively, residences and business enterprises in inner-city ghetto neighborhoods—and native blacks, the long-term residents of these areas. These schisms have been exacerbated in part by language barriers.

Finally, a majority of the black, Hispanic, Korean, and Japanese survey respondents expressed

FIGURE 22.4 Interethnic Stereotypes: Proportion of a Race Negativity Rating Another Race, Los Angeles County, 1994

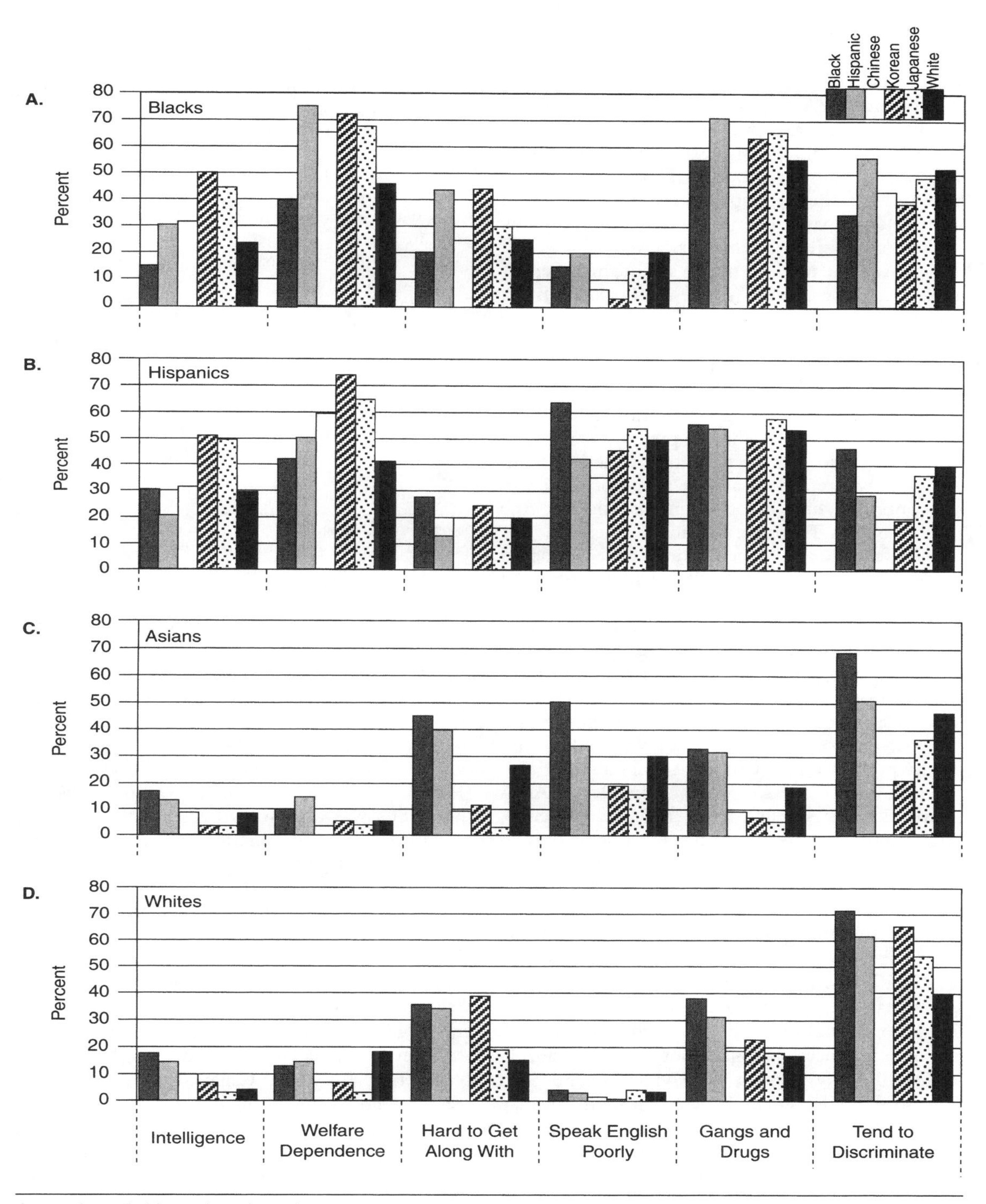

Source: Compiled by authors from the Los Angeles Survey of Urban Inequality.

the view that almost all non-Hispanic whites are prone to discriminate against members of their respective groups (figure 22.4, panels A, B, and C). Only the Chinese respondents were less inclined to express this view. On this trait, black respondents' perception of Asians was almost as strong as their views about non-Hispanic whites (figure 22.4, panel A). Although lower than the ratings of blacks, a significant proportion of the Hispanic and white respondents also expressed the view that almost all Asians are prone to discriminate against members of their groups (figure 22.4, panels B and D). Hispanic, Chinese, and non-Hispanic white survey respondents perceived almost all blacks as prone to discriminate against members of their respective groups (figure 22.4, panels B, C, and D).

Behavioral Responses

These negative perceptions of the impact of immigrants on U.S. society and the prejudicial attitudes and intergroup stereotypes uncovered in recent surveys have generated a wide range of responses to continued high rates of immigration to the United States. Three are highlighted here.

First, these negative perceptions have prompted a high degree of middle-class white flight and middle-class black flight from port-of-entry metropolitan areas (Frey 1995a, 1995c; Johnson and Roseman 1990). As shown in table 22.4, which depicts metropolitan areas with the greatest increases from 1980 to 1990 in total population, non-Hispanic whites, and minorities, nearly half (43 percent) of the national nonwhite ethnic minority population growth was concentrated in five Consolidated Metropolitan Statistical Areas (CMSAs): Los Angeles, New York, San Francisco, Miami, and Houston. Los Angeles alone accounted for 20 percent of the growth (Frey 1993).

Table 22.4 also indicates that there was a high degree of overlap between the areas with the greatest minority population increases and those with the greatest total population increases (Frey 1993, 1995c). Research presented elsewhere suggests that these areas experienced net white out-migration, heightened black out-migration, and, in some instances, net black out-migration during the 1980s (Briggs 1995; Johnson and Grant 1997; Johnson and Roseman 1990). Thus, the overlap illustrates the pivotal role that immigration played in minority population growth in these areas.

TABLE 22.4 Metropolitan Areas With Greatest Increases from 1980 to 1990: Total Population, Non-Hispanic Whites, Minorities

Metropolitan Area	*Increase (thousands)*
Areas with Greatest Total Increase	
Los Angeles CMSA	3,034
Dallas-Fort Worth	955
San Francisco CMSA	885
Atlanta MSA	695
Washington, D.C. MSA	673
Areas with Greatest Non-Hispanic White Increase	
Dallas-Fort Worth CMSA	487
Atlanta MSA	414
Phoenix MSA	412
Tampa-Saint Petersburg MSA	345
Seattle CMSA	324
Areas with Greatest Minority Increase	
Los Angeles CMSA	2,795
New York	1,398[a]
San Francisco CMSA	787
Miami CMSA	635[a]
Houston	484

Source: Frey (1993).

[a] Area experienced gain in minority population and loss in white population.

Non-Hispanic white population growth, as table 22.4 shows, occurred in a geographically distinct set of metropolitan communities during the 1980s: Dallas-Fort Worth, Atlanta, Phoenix, Tampa-Saint Petersburg, and Seattle. Research indicates that these communities were strong economic magnets, while those registering the greatest minority gains were economically distressed areas (Frey 1993). What this means, of course, is that the 1980s was a period of increasing racial and spatial inequality in American society, with black poor and disadvantaged immigrants concentrated in the largest urban centers while middle- and upper-class blacks and whites sought refuge in more hospitable and economically viable residential environments (Frey 1993, 1995a, 1995c).

Second, arguing that immigration in general, and illegal immigration in particular, is a neglected federal problem that will no longer be tolerated at the state level, six states—Arizona, Florida, Illinois, New Jersey, Texas, and California—have filed suits seeking reimbursement for the cost of services rendered to illegal immigrants (Charles 1995). These states are home to 86 percent of all illegal immigrants and 30 percent of all immigrants. The state of California has been most vociferous in this matter and vigilant in its efforts to send a resounding message to Washington about the citizenry's feelings about immigration (Bowermaster 1995).

In addition to the lawsuit filed to recoup funds for services rendered to illegal immigrants, California voters, in the November 1994 elections, endorsed by a margin of 59 to 41 percent the controversial Proposition 187, which was placed on the ballot by the Save Our State Campaign. If affirmed by the Supreme Court, Proposition 187 would deny undocumented illegal aliens access to numerous services and increase the pressure to comply with new and existing laws. Because of legal challenges, Proposition 187 has been tied up in the courts for the last five years. In an effort to accelerate the decision on the faith of the initiative, newly-elected California Governor Gray Davis recently turned the matter over to the U.S. Court of Appeals Mediation Program (Morain 1999). Nevertheless, it has clearly laid the cards of at least one state on the table with respect to the illegal immigration problem. As discussed later, it also has set the stage for substantial conflict among the various racial and ethnic groups in California (Ross 1994; Valenzuela 1995).

Third, at the federal level, pursuant to the Personal Responsibility and Work Opportunity Reconciliation Act of 1996 (the welfare reform legislation), illegal aliens and legal nonimmigrants, such as travelers and students, will be denied most federal benefits. Legal immigrants will generally not be eligible for Supplemental Security Income (SSI) and food stamps until they become citizens or have worked in the United States for at least ten years. Given their ineligibility for federal assistance, the financial status of immigrants' sponsors will be weighed more heavily in decisions regarding who will be allowed to enter the United States (Katz 1996, 2193). Further, as part of President Clinton's omnibus spending package, funding has been authorized to improve border controls and fences, accelerate detention and deportation procedures, create new penalties for alien smuggling, and establish pilot programs aimed at identifying illegal immigrants in the workplace (Carney 1996, 3187).

A Typology of Immigration-Induced Community Conflicts

In describing the kinds of conflicts that have accompanied the changing racial and ethnic composition of the U.S. population as a consequence of heightened immigration over the last thirty years, we draw on case examples from metropolitan Los Angeles. As noted elsewhere, metropolitan Los Angeles is on the leading edge of a dramatic set of economic and demographic changes that are both driven and influenced by the rather large influx of immigrants over the last two decades or so—changes that will ultimately envelop the entire U.S. urban system (Garcia 1985; Johnson et al. 1992). Furthermore, Los Angeles was the site of a major multiethnic rebellion in 1992—the worst civil disturbance in this nation's history—whose root causes stemmed, in large measure, from the tensions and conflicts between native-born and foreign-born populations in the region (Bobo et al. 1995a, 1995b; Johnson and Farrell 1993; Johnson et al. 1992).

In 1960 nearly two-thirds of the metropolitan Los Angeles population was composed of non-Hispanic whites (Oliver and Johnson 1984). By 1990, largely as a consequence of heightened immigration and the substantial exodus of non-Hispanic whites, nonwhite ethnic minority groups (Asians, blacks, and Hispanics) had become, numerically, the majority population of Los Angeles County, accounting for 58 percent of the total (Johnson et al. 1992). Approximately one-third of the metropolitan population was Hispanic. Blacks and Asians each accounted for about 12 percent. Today, according to the most recent census estimates, over two-thirds of the people of Los Angeles are members of nonwhite ethnic minority groups.

Nowhere was this ethnic change more apparent than in the so-called Alameda corridor of South Central Los Angeles, which extends from the downtown area southward along Alameda Boulevard to the San Pedro and Long Beach harbors (Johnson and Oliver 1989; Oliver and Johnson 1984). Two types of transition have occurred in this area.

The first was a black-to-brown population succession in the residential neighborhoods; it began in the 1960s and accelerated in the 1970s and 1980s. In 1970 an estimated 50,000 Hispanics were residing in South Central Los Angeles neighborhoods, representing 10 percent of the area's total population. That number had doubled to 100,000, or 21 percent of the total population, by 1980 (Oliver and Johnson 1984). Today roughly half of the population of South Central Los Angeles is Hispanic.

Concurrent with this black-to-brown residential transition, an ethnic succession also was taking place in the South Central Los Angeles business community. Prior to the Watts rebellion of 1965, most of the businesses in the area were owned and operated by Jewish shopkeepers. In the aftermath of these disturbances, the Jewish business owners fled the area and were replaced not by black entrepreneurs but rather by newly arriving Korean immigrants who opened small retail and service establishments in the area (Freer 1995; Oliver and Johnson 1984).

Paralleling these demographic changes, the Los Angeles economy, driven in large part by government policies designed to create a deregulated business environment to increase the competitiveness of U.S. firms in the global marketplace (Grant and Johnson 1995), has undergone a rather dramatic transformation over the last thirty years (Johnson and Oliver 1992). The restructuring of the Los Angeles economy includes, on the one hand, the decline of traditional, highly unionized, high-wage manufacturing employment and, on the other, the growth of employment in high-technology manufacturing, the craft specialties, and the advanced services sectors of the economy. South Central Los Angeles—the traditional industrial core of the city—bore the brunt of the decline in heavy manufacturing employment, losing 70,000 high-wage, stable jobs between 1978 and 1982, and another 200,000 between 1982 and 1989 (Johnson and Oliver 1992; Johnson et al. 1992).

At the same time that these well-paying stable jobs were disappearing from South Central Los Angeles, local employers were seeking alternative sites for their manufacturing activities. Allen Scott (1986) has shown that, as a consequence of these seemingly routine decisions, new employment growth nodes or "technopoles" emerged in the San Fernando Valley, in the San Gabriel Valley, and in El Segundo near the airport in Los Angeles County, as well as in nearby Orange County.

In addition, a number of Los Angeles–based employers established production facilities in the Mexican border towns of Tijuana, Ensenada, and Tecate. Between 1978 and 1982 over two hundred Los Angeles-based firms, including Hughes Aircraft, Northrop, and Rockwell, as well as a host of smaller firms, participated in this deconcentration process (Soja, Morales, and Wolff 1983). Such capital flight, in conjunction with plant closings, essentially closed off the access of the residents of South Central Los Angeles to what were formerly well-paying, unionized jobs (Johnson and Oliver 1989).

Elsewhere we have shown that, although new industrial spaces were being established elsewhere in Los Angeles County, new employment opportunities were emerging in the Alameda corridor (Johnson et al. 1992). But unlike the manufacturing jobs that disappeared from this area, the new jobs are in competitive sector industries that rely primarily on undocumented immigrant labor and pay, at best, the minimum wage.

Juxtaposing the changes that occurred on the demand side of the Los Angeles labor market and the changes in the composition of the local labor pool, residential communities, schools, and other social and political institutions that have accompanied the massive influx of immigrants into the region, what emerges is a community in which competition and conflict have become the rule rather than the exception (Hing 1993b; Johnson and Oliver 1989; Johnson and Farrell 1993). Here we focus on five types of conflicts: residential transition-induced, entrepreneurially induced, employer-induced, linguistically induced, and Proposition 187–induced.

Residential Transition-Induced Conflict

The growing penetration of the most disadvantaged of the newly arriving immigrants into formerly all-black residential areas of South Central Los Angeles has been a major source of tension and a precipitant of a wide range of interethnic minority conflicts. Nowhere has this type of immigration-induced conflict been more apparent than in the city of Compton, California (Lee and Sloan 1994; McDonnell 1994b).

A suburb of the city of Los Angeles, this formerly all-white community experienced white-to-black population succession, and the new black majority ousted the long-standing white political leadership "in a heated battle that reflected the social tumult of the 1960s" (McDonnell 1994b, 1A). During the 1970s Compton was the most populous community west of the Mississippi where blacks held political sway, and although a significant proportion of the households were poor, it was, in the words of McDonnell (1994b, 1A), "a national symbol of political empowerment despite its persistent poverty." Compton became known as a place where "refugees from the Jim Crow South acquired their piece of the American

Dream, using the ballot box to overcome discrimination" (McDonnell 1994b, 5A).

Over the past two decades, however, Compton has undergone yet another demographic transformation, popularly referred to as black-to-brown population succession. By 1990, according to the U.S. Census Bureau, only 55 percent of Compton's population of 93,500 was black. Hispanics, most of whom were newly arriving immigrants, accounted for the remaining 42 percent. Today, in all likelihood, Hispanics constitute the majority population in Compton.

How have blacks responded to the influx of Hispanic immigrants? They have expressed concerns that the movement of Hispanic immigrants into their residential neighborhoods represents a displacement that is motivated by racism and economic gain (Johnson and Oliver 1989). They claim that the pattern of residential succession is very similar to the kind of block-busting that takes place when blacks move into white neighborhoods. Once a Hispanic family moves into an apartment building, the complex rapidly becomes Hispanic. Owing to the propensity of Hispanics to have multiple wage-earners in the household, blacks contend that landlords are forcing out black tenants and replacing them with Hispanics who pay higher rents (Oliver and Johnson 1984). But the negative sentiments that this process creates are not directed at the economic agents (namely, the real estate agents and the landlords) but rather toward the newly arriving Hispanic immigrants (Johnson and Oliver 1989).

Likewise, the influx of new Hispanic immigrants has created resentment on the part of long-term black residents about the sharing of social services and dominant social institutions (Hernandez and Scott 1980; Bobo et al. 1995b). In particular, blacks express concerns about the high demand placed on existing public services by the new immigrants. Because of the struggles that took place in the 1960s to establish them, blacks feel a sense of exclusive entitlement to some community institutions. They view the Hispanics, particularly undocumented workers, as free-riders gaining all the benefits of public services without having paid the price to get them into the community (Johnson and Oliver 1989; Oliver and Johnson 1984).

During the 1980s nearly three of every four babies born at Martin Luther King Hospital were Hispanic. One Compton resident complained about this: "I don't think it's proper. When we built some of these facilities . . . we didn't find anyone to help us. . . . If they want their share of services they should get active in the community" (Hernandez and Scott 1980, 4). The emotional intensity of such intolerance has only served to polarize the community (McDonnell 1994b).

On the other hand, the newly arriving Hispanics complain about the lack of access to municipal jobs and leadership positions in the local government, about staffing positions in the school system and the content of the curriculum, and about the problem of police brutality in a police department in which the chief and nearly all the officers are black (Lee and Sloan 1994; McDonnell 1994b).

Although Hispanics make up nearly half of Compton's 93,500 residents, "no Hispanic has ever held a seat on the city council and only 14 of the city's 127 member police force are Hispanic" (Lee and Sloan 1994, 57). Moreover, Hispanics are grossly underrepresented in civil service jobs. Hispanic activists accuse blacks of being interested "only in preserving their own jobs in the face of changing demographics" (57). Commenting on the city's black elected officials, one Latino city council candidate said, "They hire people with our tax money. We subsidize our own discrimination" (57). More generally, "some Hispanics in Compton complain that they are worse off today than blacks were in South Africa under apartheid" (McDonnell 1994b, 1A). One Hispanic resident, Compton's only Hispanic elected official, said, "They have been in power too long and they are in denial of the fact that they are no longer the majority" (1A).

In response to the Hispanic charges of oppression, blacks contend that Hispanics are disenfranchising themselves because few vote in local elections. Compton's mayor, who is black, has said: "African Americans fought for the right to vote. . . . Is it [our] responsibility to elect Hispanics?" (Lee and Sloan 1994, 57).

Further, black elected officials in Compton contend that "Hispanics don't grasp that African Americans struggled for years to win power in Compton, or that city jobs are filled through the civil service process." Commenting on the underrepresentation of Hispanics in civil service jobs, Compton's police chief, Hourie Taylor, who is black, observed: "I'd like to see more Hispanics come in at whatever level . . . but you don't just walk up and fire people and replace them with somebody else" (Lee and Sloan 1994, 57).

In response to criticisms of their leadership and

their seeming unwillingness to open up the city to the more recently arriving Hispanic population, black leaders are quick to paint Hispanic activists as "outside agitators" who are mostly U.S.-born, mostly middle-class, and do not live in Compton. By contrast, most of those who live in Compton are noncitizens and thus are unable to vote in elections.

Commenting on the fact that large numbers of Hispanics in Compton are noncitizens, one black leader posed the question: "What does the African American do to empower them [Hispanics] when it's constitutionally illegal [for noncitizens to vote]?" (McDonnell 1994b, 1A). Arguing that the city is caught in what he calls a virtual open-door immigration policy that is beyond local control, he notes, "As they continue to come, schools become crowded [and] dwindling resources in cities such as Compton become more sparse. Animosity and friction [are] the natural product of these things, and that's what we're seeing" (1A).

While black political leaders have resisted Hispanic calls for greater access to municipal jobs and leadership positions in Compton, some black clergymen have called on the politicians to open up the city to Hispanics. Said one minister, "We are today the entrenched group trying to keep out intruders, just as whites were once the entrenched group and we were the intruders" (McDonnell 1994b, 1A). Agreeing with this observation, one Hispanic scholar (cited in McDonnell 1994b, 1A) noted that "some of the things black councilmen say about the Hispanic population sound like the kinds of things southern whites would have said about blacks in the fifties: 'We were here first. We're being pushed out. These are our jobs; how dare you [try to] take them away?'"

Noting the need for cooperation and coalition building, one black leader said (McDonnell 1994b, 1A):

> People need to have a more inclusionary, larger political vision. . . . This is really an issue of poor folks struggling over jobs and opportunities. . . . Unless you have a vision of human relations as quite inclusionary, you end up circling the wagons, and lobbing hand grenades at each other in what is seen as racial or ethnic interest. We all lose in that scenario.

Besides their criticisms of the leadership of city government and the underrepresentation of Hispanics in civil service positions, Hispanic activists have been similarly critical of the Compton public school system and its ability to educate Hispanic children. Paralleling changes in the city's residential communities, the composition of the Compton public schools has changed from predominantly black to predominantly Hispanic. Today 59 percent of the student body is Hispanic, while blacks make up most of the remaining 41 percent. Hispanic activists complain that, while the student body is majority Hispanic, only 5 percent of certified teachers are Hispanic (72 percent are black) and blacks occupy most of the administrative positions in the district. They have been especially critical of the black leadership of the district, which was taken over by the state in 1993 owing to financial difficulties, persistently low test scores, and widespread allegations of mismanagement (McDonnell 1994b, 1A).

Moreover, Hispanic students complain of being ridiculed and beaten by black teachers and security guards, and racially charged fistfights are a constant source of disruption in the school system (Lee and Sloan 1994). Some argue that these altercations are a product of turf wars between black and Hispanic gangs, but others contend that they reflect "the tensions among adults in the community" (McDonnell 1994b, 1A). Commenting on the tensions in the schools, one Hispanic school board member in Compton said: "When you have Hispanics and African Americans telling each other they're going to take over, something's going to give" (Lee and Sloan 1994, 57).

Hispanic parents charge that the black-run school system in Compton discriminates against Hispanic children. Despite the fact that 100 of the last 160 teachers hired have been bilingual, Hispanic parents insist that there is an urgent need for more bilingual teachers. One Hispanic parent said: "I have children in the sixth, seventh, and eighth grades, and they don't know how to read and write" (Lee and Sloan 1994, 57). Another Hispanic immigrant who has two children attending a Compton elementary school stated: "I'm afraid there are children who aren't even learning to read or write because they don't understand English." Most Hispanic parents believe that if more bilingual teachers were hired, their children would learn to read and write.

Many black leaders in Compton (and elsewhere) express opposition to bilingual education, questioning its usefulness as an instructional tool (Headden 1995a, 1995b). Moreover, as we discuss later, public school teachers who are not bilingual see the push for more bilingual instruction as a direct threat to their jobs (Headden 1995a). Finally, Latino students criticize the Compton school system on another front: the curriculum, they claim, is "misguided." Said one student, "I know more about Africa than I do about my own culture, about Mexico" (McDonnell 1994b, 1A).

In an effort to head off trouble during the 1993 to 1994 academic year, city officials and religious leaders sponsored what they termed "Unity Day." Such a proposal itself has been the source of tension: Hispanic activists have characterized the event as a "city-orchestrated effort to divert attention from Hispanic nonrepresentation" (McDonnell 1994b, 1A). In response to the notion of a Unity Day event, one Latino activist said: "They can have all the rallies they want, but it doesn't mean anything until they recognize there's a problem. . . . Blacks are doing the same thing to Hispanics that was done to them" (McDonnell 1994b, 1A).

Interethnic minority tensions in Compton might never have received national attention if a resident had not videotaped a black police officer beating a seventeen-year-old Hispanic youth on July 29, 1994 (McDonnell 1994b). To the chagrin of the police department, Hispanic activists compared the beating to the videotaped beating of Rodney King by the four white police officers in Los Angeles. The event led to "much-publicized allegations of racial prejudice, galvanizing Latinos' demands for power in a city where blacks have a lock on city government, a beleaguered school system, and most municipal jobs" (McDonnell 1994b, 1A). Commenting on the videotaped beating, one outspoken Hispanic advocate said: "This is racism perpetuated by one minority group against another" (1A).

The videotaped beating has forced Compton's black leadership into the ironic position of having to respond to allegations of discrimination. Said Police Chief Taylor, "It's a hard pill to swallow." Other black leaders have responded "angrily to the challenge, dismissing allegations of discrimination while characterizing Latino activists [who issued the challenge] as a self-serving clique of nonresident merchants" (McDonnell 1994b, 1A). And the mayor, who is black, stated: "I see this as a well-constructed attempt to utilize the historical implications of the African American civil rights movement for the benefit of a few people, who in fact probably don't even consider themselves nonwhite. . . . This is really about power and privilege" (1A).

It should be noted here that not all blacks agreed with the mayor and other black leaders who were offended by the accusation of discriminatory behavior on the part of the Compton police department. Many blacks joined the Hispanics in protesting the beating. One said, "It could have just as easily been a black man who was beaten like that" (McDonnell 1994b, A1), indicating a view that heavy-handed tactics by police span ethnic categories.

In response to the foregoing issues, Hispanic activists have issued a set of demands to Compton's black leadership. They have called for the creation of a civilian review board to monitor police behavior, a federal investigation into racial and ethnic conflict in the city, and establishment of an affirmative action and job training program targeted at increasing Hispanic participation. Blacks have not wholeheartedly embraced any of these issues. But the one that has generated the most intense debate centers on the question of whether immigrants who came to this country voluntarily or illegally, and subsequently were awarded legal status, should qualify for affirmative action (Brownstein 1995; Fuchs 1995).

Blacks see this move as being wrong (Brownstein 1995, C2). They acknowledge that "Latinos suffered discrimination often backed by state action until the civil rights movement of the 1960s." However, black leaders are quick to add that "no one has come up with a plausible reason why immigrants (and their children) who have come to America voluntarily in the last two decades should qualify for affirmative action." Obviously this is a political hot potato that is not likely to be easily resolved.

In the midst of all of these contentious issues, some blacks do recognize the need to find ways to accommodate the new Hispanic majority in Compton, even though it might weaken hard-won African American control. Said one black minister, "All of our wishing and all of our praying is not going to make these people [Hispanics] go anyplace else. . . . They are here, they're part of the community, so why not treat them like a part of the community" (McDonnell 1994b, A1). Given the depth of the tensions and contempt that the two groups hold for one another, this goal is likely to be a difficult one to achieve.

McDonnell (1994b, 1A) has aptly summarized the Compton situation:

> The black-brown dispute may provide a glimpse into the potential for future political upheaval in many southern California communities where immigration has drastically altered the demographic mix. Compton is one test case in the politics of the

new Southland, an indication of bumpy times ahead as newcomers' demands clash with established power blocs resistant to change.

Entrepreneurially Induced Conflict

While many of the recently arrived immigrants, especially those from Mexico and other parts of Latin America, have been able to secure employment in the restructured American economy, others are more entrepreneurially oriented, preferring self-employment over working for others (Ablemann and Lie 1995). In Los Angeles, New York, and other port-of-entry communities, Korean immigrants have been especially oriented toward the establishment of small family-owned and -operated businesses, mainly in the black community, and this has been the source of considerable conflict and controversy (MacDonald 1995).

Disadvantaged blacks in these communities see the Korean merchants as "foreigners" who are taking advantage of them by charging high prices, by refusing to invest any of the profits they earn either by employing local black residents or otherwise aiding the community, and by being rude and discourteous in their treatment of black customers. On the other hand, many of the stereotypic views that Koreans have of blacks are confirmed in their daily interaction with some of the most disadvantaged residents of inner-city communities (MacDonald 1995).

In Los Angeles the relationship between members of the black community and the Korean merchants has been and continues to be tense, in large measure because the *Los Angeles Sentinel,* the major black weekly in Los Angeles, has kept a vigilant watch over the situation, reporting both the important and the trivial incidents of Korean-black conflict. Asian storekeepers have been derided consistently for their lack of courteousness to black customers, ranging from refusing to give a cup of water to a paying customer to trying to keep a $200 watch for the nonpayment of a $5 gas bill. Further, the *Los Angeles Sentinel* has consistently questioned how Koreans are able to generate the capital to start or take over a business while willing black entrepreneurs are unable to raise such funds (Aubry 1987; Banks 1985; Cleaver 1983a, 1983b, 1983c, 1983d, 1987). Blacks, in short, see the Korean family enterprises not as an economic accomplishment in the face of strong odds but rather as an unearned opportunity at their expense (Johnson and Oliver 1989).

The Korean-black tensions came to a head during the Los Angeles civil unrest of 1992 (Johnson et al. 1992). Although the verdict in the first Rodney King police brutality trial actually triggered the civil unrest, an earlier controversial verdict in the Latasha Harlins case also played a major role in the conflagration. A videotape revealed that Ms. Harlins—an honors student at a local high school—was fatally shot in the back of the head by a Korean shopkeeper following an altercation over a carton of orange juice. Although the jury found the shopkeeper guilty of felony manslaughter, the judge decided to place her on five years' probation and required her to perform only six months of community service (Johnson et al. 1992).

Partly as a result of this incident, and partly as a function of the sentence handed down in the case, Korean businesses in South Central Los Angeles were strategically targeted in the burning and looting that ensued following the verdict in the Rodney King police brutality trial (Ablemann and Lie 1995; Lee 1995). Nearly half of the buildings either damaged or destroyed were Korean-owned or -operated.

The King verdict also brought to the fore what apparently was a brewing but previously hidden element of entrepreneurial conflict in Los Angeles: antagonisms between Hispanics and Koreans in Koreatown (Johnson and Farrell 1993). Although often viewed as an ethnic enclave demarcated by Korean control of businesses, Koreatown is actually a residentially mixed community with large numbers of Hispanic residents (principally Central American immigrants) and Koreans. It was in this area that Hispanic involvement in the civil unrest was most intense (Johnson and Farrell 1993; Jackson, Johnson, and Farrell 1994). Post-disturbance surveys and focus group research indicate that, by looting and destroying significant number of Korean-owned businesses in Koreatown, Hispanics vented their anger and frustration about the disrespectful treatment and exploitation to which they were routinely subjected as customers and as employees in Korean-owned and -operated establishments (Bobo et al. 1995a; Freer 1995).

In Los Angeles local elected officials have long been aware that tensions between Koreans and blacks are potentially explosive. At both the city and the county levels of government, human relations commissions exist to deal with such problems (Kim 1984). These agencies traditionally have been poorly funded, however, and they have been delegated little or no decisionmaking power or authority to develop policy to resolve the Korean-black conflict. As a consequence, both the city and the county human relations commissions have limited their actions to implementing educational programs that seek to change the stereotypical ways that blacks and Koreans view one another (Jackson, Johnson, and Farrell 1994).

For example, prior to the civil unrest, the City of Los Angeles Human Relations Commission was instrumental in bringing black leaders and Korean entrepreneurs in South Central Los Angeles together for "prayer breakfasts" (Johnson and Oliver 1989). These sessions were supposed to offer an opportunity for the two groups to iron out their differences and promote mutual understanding. Unfortunately, neither this nor any of the other efforts sponsored by the human relations commissions have been very successful. In fact, realizing that little progress had been made in reducing the tensions between the two groups, black and Korean leaders recently agreed to stop holding such meetings (Jackson, Johnson, and Farrell 1994).

Employer-Induced Conflict

Over the past two decades, employers have made organizational changes in the way they do business, especially in the area of labor recruitment, in an effort to remain competitive in the increasingly global economy (Johnson and Oliver 1992; Scott 1986). Research shows that in an effort to keep labor costs down and to maintain a lean but flexible operation, employers, especially in the craft specialty and hospitality industries and increasingly in all sectors of the economy, are either farming out work to subcontractors or meeting the demand for labor with preferential hiring practices (Center for Immigration Studies 1994; Scott 1986; Soja, Morales, and Wolff 1983; Waldinger and Gilbertson 1994). The large-scale influx of immigrants—legal and illegal—into the U.S. labor market has afforded employers this added flexibility in terms of the way they organize and structure their business operations (Johnson and Oliver 1992; Scott 1986).

In Los Angeles and other port-of-entry communities, the large-scale influx of immigrants over the last three decades has created labor surplus environments, that is, labor market conditions in which there are far more job seekers than there are available jobs (Freeman 1991). In the low-wage sectors of the economy, this situation not only tends to depress wages but also affords employers maximum flexibility to pick and choose workers.

Studies by Joleen Kirschenman and Kathryn Neckerman (1991), among others (see also Turner, Fix, and Struyk 1991), indicate that, in such environments, employers display a strong preference for immigrant workers over native workers in general, and over black job seekers in particular. Black workers are perceived to be lazy, inarticulate, untrainable, and, most important, dangerous. Immigrant workers, especially those who are undocumented, are perceived to be more compliant and industrious and thus are highly preferred in the workplace (Johnson et al. 1992; Johnson and Oliver 1989; Lowell and Jing 1994; Oliver and Johnson 1984).

Research shows that employers in such rapidly growing craft specialty industries as garment manufacturing and in hospitality services industries (hotels, motels, restaurants, fast-food outlets, taxi cab companies, and so on) in Los Angeles (Silverstein and Brooks 1994) satisfy their labor demands either by tapping into informal networks of immigrant workers directly or by contracting with firms that have access to such networks (Jackson 1995; Muller and Espenshade 1985; Nomani, Rose, and Ortega 1995; Soja, Morales, and Wolff 1983; U.S. General Accounting Office 1995c).

While there is considerable disagreement in the literature on the actual labor market impacts of immigrants (Borjas 1987b; Chiswick, Chiswick, and Miller 1985; Muller and Espenshade 1985), there is growing evidence that displacement is indeed occurring (Jackson 1995; U.S. General Accounting Office 1995c). In a recent study, for example, Richard Mines (1985) reports that employers in the high-rise office district of Los Angeles contracted with firms that had tapped into networks of recent immigrants to hire janitors. In addition to displacing the black janitors with recently arrived immigrant workers, this practice led to a decline in the wage rate, Mines shows, from $13 per hour to just over the minimum wage.

Other research suggests that similar displacement of veteran workers is occurring in such industries as garment manufacturing, frozen foods, construction and construction cleanup, and hospitality services, all of which were employment sectors that previously had large numbers of black workers. In the garment industry in Los Angeles, for example, an estimated 90 percent of the workforce is foreign-born, most of them undocumented immigrants from Mexico (Andreas 1994).

In a community where recently arrived Hispanic

immigrants and disadvantaged blacks share the same residential neighborhoods, the fact that the former have been able to secure jobs and the latter have not has been a source of enormous tension and conflict (Johnson et al. 1992; Johnson and Farrell 1993). A survey conducted by the *Los Angeles Times* revealed the depth of these concerns. Two-thirds of the black respondents agreed that "undocumented Mexicans . . . take jobs away from American citizens" (Field Institute 1988). Some poor blacks in South Central Los Angeles go so far as to argue that "undocumented workers, particularly Spanish-speaking ones, are principally responsible for the employment crisis among . . . young black men" (Muller and Espenshade 1985, 35; see also Field Institute 1988).

Research shows, however, that these perceptions are misplaced (Bobo et al. 1995b). The black male jobless problem stems from the discriminatory recruitment practices of employers, who openly express disdain for black workers and a preference for undocumented Hispanic workers (Kirschenman and Neckerman 1991; Mueller 1994; Turner, Fix, and Struyk 1991), and from the U.S. government's efforts to create a deregulated business environment to increase the competitiveness of U.S. firms in the global marketplace; this environment has allowed employers to engage in illegal recruitment practices in the first instance (Grant and Johnson 1995).

Employer-induced tensions and conflicts also exist at the upper end of the labor market (Richards 1995; Zachary 1995). Here they are generated by employers' use of the temporary work visa and employment-based provisions of the immigration law to bring in foreign workers for professional-level jobs that might otherwise go to native-born Americans. This is thought to be a common practice in the United States among multinational corporations, universities, and computer and movie companies (Zachary 1995).

Current immigration law permits foreigners with specialized skills to work in the United States for six years. "The law even permits U.S. companies to fire American professionals and replace them with foreigners as a long as the foreigners are paid 'comparable' wages to the departing Americans" (Zachary 1995, A3). However, enforcement is difficult because the federal government acts only when foreigners complain, which is something they rarely do. Thus, it is not known how many companies pay foreigners below market wages (Zachary 1995).

One recent case handled by the U.S. Department of Labor illustrates how employers have used the law to the detriment of American workers (Zachary 1995). A large insurance firm laid off its entire Management Information Services Department staff of 250 programmers and replaced them with foreign programmers brought here from India on H-1B visas. The firm that the insurance company contracted with to provide the computing programming services was accused of paying the forty computer programmers from India below-market wages (Richards 1995).

To settle the case, the contractor was forced to pay $77,000 in back wages to the forty foreign programmers, to hire forty American programmers in the next year, and to spend $1 million to train U.S. workers in the latest software techniques. The company also agreed not to bring any more foreign programmers into this country for ninety days (Zachary 1995).

Complaints about these kinds of practices have led a group of programmers in Austin, Texas, to form a political action committee to protect their jobs (Richards 1995). These and other concerned groups have encouraged members of Congress to press for cuts in the number of such workers allowed entry into the United States under this provision from 65,000 to 30,000 annually. Moreover, there is one bill before the U.S. Congress that is designed to discourage the practice by requiring foreigners to be paid 10 percent more than their American predecessors (Zachary 1995).

Linguistically Induced Conflict

In U.S. communities where large numbers of immigrants have settled, linguistic diversity is now the order of the day (Headden 1995a, 1995b; Keeler 1995). In Los Angeles more than one hundred different languages are spoken in the school system (Lee 1995; Pyle 1995). As a consequence of the large influx of immigrant children into the school system, the demand for bilingual teachers has skyrocketed (Headden 1995b). Nationally there is an estimated shortage of 170,000 bilingual teachers. The situation has created tensions between monolingual teachers and their bilingual counterparts. The former are angry because they are either paid less money or laid off when their linguistic skills do not match those required in the schools. Commenting on the changing ethnic and linguistic composition of the Los Angeles public school system, an elementary school teacher with thirty years of experience said: "There is no way I could get a job in the Los Angeles public schools today" (Headden 1995a, 41).

This reality is an extremely bitter pill to swallow for monolingual English-speaking teachers. Owing to the shortage of bilingual teachers, school officials are recruiting from abroad, a practice that, in many instances, requires that they waive some credential requirements, resulting in the hiring of many teachers who have limited English skills (Headden 1995a, 1995b).

Monolingual public school teachers are not the only group in the U.S. labor market to be disadvantaged by the linguistic diversity that has accompanied recent immigration to the United States. In Miami blacks reportedly are losing tourism jobs to bilingual Cubans, and in Los Angeles, New York, and other port-of-entry communities blacks are also losing jobs in the hospitality industry to immigrants who are bilingual (Jackson 1995; U.S. General Accounting Office 1995c; see also Briggs 1995; Estrada 1995).

Proposition 187–Induced Conflict

That significant numbers of people in the black community voted for Proposition 187 has emerged as a source of black-brown conflict in southern California (Lee and Sloan 1994). Kevin Ross (1994, 5B) suggests that the vote reflects "long-running tensions between the black and Hispanic communities":

> There is fighting in the high schools and prisons, a tenuous gang truce in Venice, a power struggle in Compton. Each of these problems has strained relations between the two groups scrambling for the crumbs. Many black people don't care that Proposition 187 is being financed by racist organizations and that minorities are being pitted against one another. If the initiative creates a McCarthyite police state, the attitude is, "So be it."

Commenting on the more general tensions between blacks and Hispanics, Ross, who is deputy district attorney in Inglewood and political action chairman of the Los Angeles chapter of the National Association for the Advancement of Colored People (NAACP), stated:

> Latino community leaders cannot have it both ways. They cannot expect the African American community to embrace their struggle while they disrespect ours. When studies came out about the lack of Latinos on television and in the news, many of the people interviewed focused more on the number of blacks on the air rather than the bigger problem of who holds the real positions of power. When accusations were made of Latino under-representation in U.S. Postal Service hiring, blacks were the focus of the attention, not the federal government. Attempts to rename Martin Luther King Hospital also was another example where Latinos have pitted themselves against African Americans. Now comes Proposition 187 and blacks are being told that they must join with their minority brothers to fight racism? For many, that is a big pill to swallow.

He states further that:

> The Latino community wants to have their cake and eat it, too, and black people are not having it. Los Angeles County Supervisor Gloria Molina cannot accuse fellow Supervisor Yvonne Brathwaite Burke of being a racist for trying to resolve the problem of day laborers, then ask Burke's constituents to join hands with her and sing "Kumbaya" against Proposition 187. The $15 billion in federal aid this state receives due to the presence of illegal immigrants is still taxpayer money. And for those who insist on comparing African Americans with illegal immigrants, that only serves to further alienate potential allies.

If there is one positive aspect of the controversy surrounding Proposition 187, it is that it forced Hispanics to register and vote. It has been estimated that "about 1,000 new Hispanics voters were registered in Compton before election day." Said one Hispanic activist: "We need to send [Governor Pete] Wilson a 'Thank You' note" for arousing a docile Latino electorate" (Lee and Sloan 1994, 57). What does this portend for black-brown relations? Lee and Sloan (1994, 57) surmise that, "despite all the rhetoric about how Proposition 187 will make life harder for Hispanics, Compton blacks could come to remember it as the issue that pushed them from political power."

Summary and Conclusions

The tensions, conflicts, and community instability associated with heightened immigration—especially of nonwhite immigrant groups—threaten to balkanize America (Frey 1995a; Johnson, Farrell, and Jackson 1994). The yearly influx of immigrants—many of whom are illegal—from Asia, Africa, the Middle East, Latin America, and the Caribbean over the last three decades has resulted in a substantial browning of America. These new immigrants have tended to settle in selected cities on the East and West Coasts, but recent studies indicate that they are also moving into small and medium-sized U.S. cities in all regions of the country (Johnson-Webb and Johnson 1997). Nationally there is growing opposition to the massive influx of immigrants, and in local communities affected by this demographic transformation tensions and conflicts have arisen between native majority citizens and the new arrivals and between native minority citizens and the recent immigrants.

The nativist backlash among native citizens is fueled by the perception that: their culture and traditions are being imperiled; the quality of their education is being lowered; their jobs and housing are being taken; their political influence is being lessened; English is declining as the primary language; and social and health services are being overburdened (see Salin 1997).

Concomitant with the economic downturn in the local and national economies during the late 1980s and early 1990s, all the worst fears and stereotypes of immigrants were manifested. The state of California, which had long been a primary destination point, responded with Proposition 187, a statewide referendum passed in November 1994. It denied educational, health, and social services to illegal immigrants. This initiative, which is being litigated in the courts, has served to exacerbate even further the tensions between native Californians and immigrants across racial lines. Moreover, the hostilities toward immigrants in California have repeatedly been found to exist in a national cross-section of host communities where they have arrived in large numbers.

In addition, large and small businesses, particularly in the garment and hospitality industries, frequently exploit the newly arrived immigrants by paying them minimum and subminimum wages, subjecting them to harsh working conditions, and substituting them for more highly paid native workers. This strategy has specifically been directed toward illegal immigrants who lacked any legal recourse for fear of deportation. The influx of immigrants into many of the nation's urban centers also sparked a major exodus of middle-income native majority and minority citizens as they perceived a decline in their overall quality of life. Furthermore, immigrant succession in the local small-business marketplace (liquor stores, neighborhood corner groceries, and so on) only served to heighten tensions even more. Language and cultural barriers became more pronounced, and local governments were slow or ineffective in their response.

Contemporary conflicts over immigration are not likely to abate as native Americans and immigrants interact with each other through a negative stereotypical prism and in a context of increased social, political, and economic anxiety. Current trends suggest rather strongly that America is on the threshold of escalating racial and ethnic trauma as it attempts to come to grips with the rapidly increasing diversity of its population. The tremors at the local level—California being the foremost example—are harbingers of social turmoil yet to come unless comprehensive proactive programs of human and interpersonal relations are aggressively implemented.

What steps must be taken in order to reduce the tension, conflict, and community instability that have accompanied immigration-induced population diversity? Two steps are highlighted here.

First, future immigration reform policy decisionmaking must not be based on political expediency, the strategy that seems to have characterized recent reforms (see Andreas 1994; Brownstein 1995; Johnson and Farrell 1997; Sun 1995; Tichenor 1994). Rather than trying to appease both the political left and the political right, the federal government must base future reforms on rigorous research and evaluation of the probable social, economic, and environmental impacts of proposals, advanced by both pro- and anti-immigrant enthusiasts, on U.S. communities and native citizens.

The Illegal Immigration Reform and Immigrant Responsibility Act of 1996 (Carney 1996) and the Personal Responsibility and Work Opportunity Reconciliation Act of 1996 (Katz 1996), which reflects in many critical respects the recommendations of the Jordan Commission (Jenks 1995; Krikorian 1995), are the logical places in which to begin this kind of policy analysis and evaluation. Such an approach, we believe, will provide a much stronger basis for immigration reform policymaking—irrespective of whether the goal is to curtail foreign immigration or to maintain a liberal, open-door immigration policy (see National Research Council 1997).

Second, it is imperative to recognize that, even if the federal government were to curtail foreign immigration today, the U.S. population will become far more racially and ethnically diverse over the next twenty years or so through natural population increase alone. In other words, immigration-induced population diversity is here to stay. Thus, it is necessary to develop affirmative steps to ensure that the fruits of a diverse society will materialize in this country, especially in the current climate of economic instability, declining wages, and xenophobia. This will require that strategies be implemented at different levels of society.

At all levels of society, we need stronger enforcement of laws, rules, and regulations that prohibit discrimination and violence based on race, ethnicity, gender, religion, and sexual preference. At the local government level, we must develop and implement human relations policies to mitigate the ethnic antagonisms that accompany demographic change. Human relations commissions have long existed to deal with such problems, but these agencies traditionally have been poorly funded, and they have been delegated little or no decisionmaking power or authority to develop policies to resolve the array of intergroup conflicts that are a part of life in diverse communities. At a minimum, human relations commissions must be adequately funded and given the power and the authority to design and implement educational and intervention programs that seek to change the stereotypical ways in which whites, blacks, Asians, and Hispanics view one another.

At the local community level, especially in racially and ethnically transitional communities like South Central Los Angeles, perhaps the best strategy for overcoming negative stereotypes and resolving interethnic conflicts is to pursue coalition building and agenda setting around issues of common interest and concern. Three such issues come to mind immediately: the poor quality of education that minority children receive in the public school system, drugs and crime, and the lack of good jobs. These are what we term equal opportunity problems; one way or another, they touch the lives of everyone living in our cities. If the diverse groups of people who share these environments are unable to work together on these issues, then the prospects of a diverse America with viable multiethnic communities is indeed bleak.

23 Urban Political Conflicts and Alliances: New York and Los Angeles Compared

John Hull Mollenkopf

ECONOMIC RESTRUCTURING and demographic change have transformed the social geography of New York, just as they have that of Los Angeles, creating new fault lines of intergroup competition and conflict and posing significant new challenges to the local political system. Despite differences between the two cities (Los Angeles has more high-tech industry and Latino residents, while New York specializes in advanced corporate services and has more African Americans), the similarities between the two cities' economies and populations are striking. The nation's largest and second-largest city are key centers of the global culture industry, house large complexes of financial and corporate service firms, and provide comparable images of what the nation's twenty-first-century cities will be like. Both are multiracial cities where no one group constitutes a population majority. Although their white populations have diminished and their ethnic minority communities have grown, neither city is becoming predominantly black; indeed, in both cities middle-class blacks have joined middle-class whites in leaving the city. Los Angeles joined, but did not replace, New York as an Ellis Island: the two cities now house 18 percent of the nation's foreign-born, while their metropolitan areas account for 40 percent. As a result, the two cities have become more ethnically diverse as they have become less white. Hispanics and Asians are the most rapidly growing groups in both cities. Because the same larger forces of change are affecting both cities, and because they are both key nodes in global systems, these similarities are not unexpected. Indeed, both have been strongly affected by other aspects of the postindustrial revolution, such as the feminization of the labor force, changing family organization, and growing income inequality.

These changes have produced broadly similar kinds of tensions in both cities, both in terms of relations between whites and native-born minority groups and between natives and immigrants. If race relations appear to be bad in Los Angeles and growing worse in the wake of the Rodney King trial, the ensuing civil disorders, and the O. J. Simpson trial, matters seem little better in New York. In that city blacks assailed Hasidic Jews in Crown Heights in 1991, Dominicans in Washington Heights rioted on the eve of the 1992 Democratic convention, black nationalists boycotted a Korean merchant in Flatbush, and a black protester shot white and Latino employees and torched a Jewish-owned clothing store in Harlem in December 1995. James Johnson, Walter Farrell, and Chandra Guinn (this volume) report high levels of negative racial stereotyping in Los Angeles, particularly regarding the attitudes of whites and Asians toward blacks and Hispanics, and high levels of perceived racial discrimination. Survey research confirms that similar patterns exist in New York City (Setlow and Cohen 1993).

Yet it can be argued that the two cities have substantially differed in the degree to which these tensions have exploded beyond control and native whites (and blacks) have responded with anti-immigrant sentiment. In Los Angeles the massive rioting after the King trial showed that these tensions would burst social constraints and evoke a widespread reaction against immigrants (and indeed native minorities), as represented in Propositions 187, 209, and 227. New York, by contrast, did not experience a widespread breakdown of civil order, despite the possibility that events in Crown Heights and Washington Heights could reach such proportions. Instead, authorities contained these and other conflicts. Indeed, in contrast to the anti-immigrant sympathies and actions of the voters and many political leaders in California, New York City's residents show more sympathy toward immigrants (an absolute majority of most groups think immigrants add to rather than detract from the city, according to Setlow and Cohen [1993], and even a plurality of Hispanics hold this view) and New York's political elites have adopted a strongly pro-immigrant stance. For example, in contrast to the neutral positions that Los Angeles Mayor Richard Riordan has taken toward anti-immigrant measures, New York's Mayor Rudolph Giuliani, also a relatively conservative Republican, has denounced the termination of immigrants' entitlement to federal benefits and launched a costly effort to promote naturalization among immigrants.

This chapter seeks to compare the sources and trajectories of new forms of intergroup conflict in New York and Los Angeles and to explain why the political systems of the two cities have taken such different approaches to managing these conflicts, mobilizing some dimensions of conflict while dampening others. To anticipate the conclusion, I argue that despite similar intergroup cleavages and comparable levels of group stereotyping, individual-level strife, and low-level collective conflict, New York has managed to avoid the social explosion and native backlash that have characterized Los Angeles for two reasons: first, differences in the political balance among groups in the two cities, and second, differences in the ways in which their political systems create (or lack) incentives for dominant white elites to recognize, incorporate, or co-opt claims from subordinate groups (including new immigrant groups) and for leaders of subordinate groups to accommodate one another. In New York whites must bargain with minorities to form durable electoral majorities, while they need not do so in Los Angeles. In New York all groups, including whites, have a significant immigrant component, whereas nativity pits groups against each other in Los Angeles. Most important, New York's political system provides points of access for all groups, even new immigrants, while the barriers to access in Los Angeles exclude many groups from political representation. All groups must fight it out in one, highly partisan system in New York, while Los Angeles County has eighty-eight separate, nonpartisan jurisdictions. Thus, while New York has put many hazards on the road to political influence, groups have little choice but to travel it. For many, Los Angeles does not make the journey possible.

Intergroup Competition in the Postindustrial City: A Framework for Analysis

As Johnson and his colleagues suggest (this volume), groups challenge one another to enter, establish preferred positions within, and gain closure against other groups, in a number of domains, including: the housing market and the formation of neighborhoods; the labor market and the formation of ethnic employment niches; the consumer market and the formation of ethnic business enclaves; the use of public facilities and the construction of public spaces and cultures; the polity and the system of group representation and incorporation; the management of other organizations that command resources (businesses, the nonprofit sector, trade unions, religious organizations, and so on).

Most important for a group's long-term trajectory are its position in the evolving racial and ethnic division of labor and its relationship to the political process.

It might initially seem that a group's destiny in each of these domains would be governed by its size and growth, perhaps weighted by disposable income. As a group gets larger, it would "naturally" gain influence in each of these areas compared to stable or declining groups. A group might succeed more quickly if it commanded more income, education, and other forms of "cultural capital," but the American ideal of assimilation and pluralism holds that all groups would find a place at the table. We know, however, that things do not work this way.

Once members of a group gain access to relatively favorable positions in the matrix of industries and occupations, the mosaic of residential neighborhoods, and the corridors of power, they seek closure by recruiting kin and co-ethnics to join them, and they use other informal means, sometimes including violence, to keep other groups out. We can generalize to other arenas the model that Roger Waldinger (1996a) elaborated from Stanley Lieberson (1980) to analyze urban labor markets. This model has two parts: the queue of groups striving to enter an arena and the gatekeepers who decide on entry. As Waldinger explains, employers, homeowners, elected officials, and others who formally control decisions about hiring, home sales, or the distribution of public benefits have good reasons to rely on ethnic and immigrant networks, not only because they may be helping their own co-ethnics. Even when they are a different race or ethnicity, these decision-makers will rely on compatible ethnic networks to find reliable workers, bankable home buyers, or loyal political supporters when their own group is shrinking or otherwise cannot fill the need. Once a new group is allowed entry to such a niche, it will seek to routinize its influence over subsequent entry decisions and, once entrenched, use the niche's resources to advance group interests.

Membership in a dominant political coalition typically affords a group crucial leverage in these matters. While changes in the opportunity structure (the economic fate of the industries or neighborhoods colonized), labor or housing supply and demand (the growth or contraction of the group relative to others), and other broad social trends may affect a group's ability to defend its niches, neighborhoods, or political offices, it is the general rule that earlier groups colonize the better niches, enjoy long-term benefits from their position, and use these advantages to springboard into new opportunities. Thus, white Anglo-Saxon Protestants, long a tiny minority in New York City (and even in Los Angeles), continue to hold positions at the pinnacles of the city's economy and society and to have privileged access to the best of the new niches. And the long history of subsequent immigrant and ethnic succession remains imprinted on the lesser occupational niches, neighborhoods, and organizational cultures of the city, long after immigration ceased to feed the Irish American, Italian American, and Jewish populations and long after they became thoroughly assimilated and acculturated. (For the evidence concerning economic niches and neighborhoods in New York City, see Logan 1997a and 1997b.)

However rife with conflict, these processes are time-honored and more or less permanent aspects of life in New York and other large cities (Conzen 1979; Model 1993; Ward 1989, 151–217). Since the 1950s deindustrialization, suburbanization, white flight, and the growth of impoverished minority populations certainly has had a profound and often painful impact on New York City and Los Angeles. The fiscal crisis period of 1975 to 1981 was particularly dismal, leading many elites to question whether New York had a viable future.

Waldinger (1996a) has incisively analyzed the evolution of the city's racial and ethnic division of labor for this period (see also Cordero-Guzman and Grosfoguel 1998; Howell and Mueller 1998; Torres 1995). In 1950 New York was the nation's foremost manufacturing headquarters city; it was also a white, ethnic, blue-collar city characterized by machine-style Democratic Party politics. Turn-of-the-century immigrants from Italy and eastern Europe and their descendants dominated the population, and many still worked in the needle trades, at construction sites, and on the docks. Manufacturing, construction, and wholesale trade accounted for 42.8 percent of the city's 3.47 million jobs. Almost five decades of economic restructuring have dramatically altered this terrain. Advanced corporate services, nonprofit social services, and government now drive the city's economy, while its blue-collar activities, including the headquarters of manufacturing firms, suffered heavy decline. (In 1997 manufacturing, construction, and wholesale accounted for only 15.8 percent of the city's 3.41 million jobs!) The remaining manufacturing employment, such as apparel (which had about 69,000 workers in 1997), survives only because of the influx of Chinese, Dominican, and other immigrant workers. The severe downturn and fiscal crisis of the 1970s, the boom of the 1980s, and the deep recession of 1989 to 1991 accelerated these long-term trends. In short, New York City has become a multiracial, multiethnic, white-collar city with a postindustrial class structure (Mollenkopf and Castells 1991, afterword).

Ethnic political succession mirrored this pattern. Between 1850 and 1950 the Anglo-Saxon Protestant domination of the city's economy was challenged first by Irish and German immigrants, then by Italian and central European Jewish immigrants. Generally speaking, the English and Germans retreated into the private worlds of corporate finance, corporate services, and high culture, to be joined by German Jews; the Irish traversed from public employment and sectors dependent on government contracts into related professions; Italians entered the construction trades and other blue-collar work and rose to lead firms in these sectors, though they remain the least advantaged of the white immigrant groups; and central European Jews started out working in the garment industry and ended up as professionals in education and social services, business services, and corporate finance.

The central place and large size of government in New York City played a critical role in this process of ethnic succession by providing politically ascendant groups with ample "stakes and prizes." Over many generations, Irish cops begat district attorneys, lawyers, public financiers, and cardinals; Italian laborers on public works begat builders and contractors; Jewish teachers and social workers begat lawyers, professors, and investment bankers.

After New York City's black and Puerto Rican populations began to grow rapidly in the 1950s and 1960s, African American New Yorkers began to move out of low-level personal and business service and retail occupations and into an employment niche in government and nonprofit social service agencies, just as they did in most other cities (Stafford 1985; Waldinger 1996a, 106–18). Despite continuing high levels of female-headed households, exclusion from the labor force, and poverty among black families, a substantial black middle class emerged from this niche; some children of hospital workers and social service administrators have become lawyers, professors, and foundation officials (Waldinger 1996a, 206–53; but see Stafford [1984, 1991] on the continuing exclusion of blacks and Hispanics from the best City jobs). A less positive pattern emerged among Puerto Ricans, who remain the poorest group in New York City (Torres 1995). They entered the New York City economy later than blacks, gained access to only its worst occupational locations, and suffered most from the decline of the economic sectors, like the garment industry, that they entered. They, too, sought with some success to create an economic niche in public and social service employment, though they fared less well than blacks. Outside New York City, however, Puerto Ricans have shown strong signs of geographic and economic mobility (Rivera-Batiz and Santiago 1994).

This emergent racial and ethnic division of labor has an important gender dimension. As women have become a larger share of the labor force and the electorate, they have become part of a distinctive geography of household forms. If one examines the distribution of families in which both parents work, one finds concentrations not only in the neighborhoods favored by upper-middle-class professionals, whether white or black, but on the expanding edges of zones of black settlement largely characterized by Caribbean immigrant families and in other immigrant neighborhoods as well. Often these households have one or no children, and the ratio of working parents to children is quite high. In the centers of impoverished neighborhoods, whether those of African Americans, Puerto Ricans, or Dominicans, the percentage of female-headed households can, on the other hand, exceed one-third, and the ratio of working parents to children is low. As the total number of women workers has gradually approached that of men, women have become 60 percent of Democratic registered voters and a majority of the overall vote; according to numerous public opinion polls, they hold consistently more liberal positions on social welfare issues even after controlling for race and ethnicity. Thus, gender has a strong impact on political behavior alongside race, ethnicity, education, and occupation.

As with the earlier groups, politics and government played an important role in determining where blacks and Puerto Ricans have ended up. By the mid-1960s the black and Puerto populations had become sizable enough to provide electoral constituencies on which white Protestant and Jewish reformers drew to create a new, more liberal reform coalition and to displace the Democratic machine supported by ethnic Jewish and white Catholic voters. (As Martin Shefter [1986, 1994] pointed out, regular Democrats and Republicans had worked together at various points to suppress more radical alternatives.) Their success was embodied in the victories of Mayor John V. Lindsay in 1965 and 1969; the Lindsay administration followed a number of policies that advanced black and Puerto Rican interests. Black and Puerto Rican demands for empowerment, the increasing racial and ethnic polarization of New York City politics, and the shifting balance of numbers between whites and minorities, however, tended to push both cosmopolitan and traditional Jews into common political cause with white Catholics. In the past competition between these groups, especially Jewish defection from the Democratic regulars, had been a major source of reform (Gerson 1990). By the end of the 1960s, however, these factors caused the Lindsay coalition to break down and, with the trigger of the fiscal crisis, enabled Mayor Ed Koch to forge an amalgam of white reformers and white regular Democrats on a platform of fiscal austerity, promoting real estate development and rebuffing minority demands (Mollenkopf 1994; Shefter 1985). Though the internal contradictions of the Koch coalition allowed a new, minority-led, reform challenge, the David Dinkins coalition, to dislodge it for one term, its difficulties enabled Republican Mayor Rudolph W. Giuliani to reconstruct the Koch coalition, albeit along narrower and more racially polarized lines (Mollenkopf 1994).

Although blacks only briefly led the formation of an electoral majority, they, and to a lesser extent Puerto Ricans, did become a subordinate part of New York's political establishment. Their employment in the growing number of government programs that serve their communities helped to sustain a black and Puerto Rican middle class; their votes became increasingly important to the Democratic Party in state and national elections; and they held an increasing share of legislative offices as a result of population growth and the creation of minority legislative districts under the mandate of the Voting Rights Act. At the same time, the persistent economic disparities between blacks and Puerto Ricans were accompanied by pervasive, if usually low-key, competition for influence and position in the Democratic Party.

TABLE 23.1 Correlations of Racial Groups Across Election Districts, New York City, 1990 (N = 5,400)

	Non-Hispanic White percent	*Non-Hispanic Black percent*	*Hispanic percent*	*Non-Hispanic Asian percent*	*Non-Hispanic Other percent*
Non-Hispanic White	1.0000	−.7398	−.5961	.0213	−.2056
Non-Hispanic Black	−.7398	1.000	−.0303	−.3163	.0683
Hispanic	−.5961	−.0303	1.0000	−.0484	.1774
Non-Hispanic Asian	.0213	−.3163	−.0484	1.0000	.0156
Non-Hispanic Other	−.2056	.0683	.1774	.0156	1.0000

Source: Center for Urban Research, CUNY Graduate Center, from STF3, 1990 census.

Where does this leave New York City in terms of intergroup relations in the housing market, the labor market, and the political system in the mid-1990s? Tables 23.1 and 23.2 use correlation coefficients to demonstrate the levels of racial and ethnic differentiation across neighborhoods, economic sectors, and political behavior. Table 23.1 shows the likelihood of population groups living near each other across the city's 5,400 election districts. (This method produces results comparable to the traditional index of dissimilarity and, like that index, does not adjust for the relative sizes of different groups.) The table shows that blacks and whites are extremely unlikely to live near each other; that whites and Hispanics are segregated from each other, but at lower levels; and that there is no relationship, positive or negative, between whites and Asians. Blacks are not particularly segregated from, or close to, Hispanics, nor are Asians close to or segregated from Hispanics. Asians, however, do tend to be separated from blacks. In contrast to whites and blacks, Hispanics and Asians do not generally constitute the majority of the populations of the areas where they live. Read spatially, Asians and Hispanics live in the zones of separation and transition between whites and blacks, with Asians on the white side of the divide (for further discussion, see Mollenkopf 1993).

Table 23.2 shows similar, if less pronounced, patterns of separation or similarity across industries, calculated in terms of the percentage of the group working in fifty-one detailed industry classifications. In contrast to the residential patterns, whites are most strongly differentiated from Hispanics but are also fairly strongly differentiated from blacks and Asians. Immigrant Hispanics and Asians both work in industries like apparel and restaurants; native blacks and Hispanics both work in government and social services. Whites, by contrast, concentrate in investment banking, commercial banking, law, and the other corporate services, as well as in education and certain other high-level nonprofit services. (For fuller discussions of the current racial and ethnic division of labor, see Bailey and Waldinger 1991b; Mollenkopf 1988; Waldinger 1996a.)

Finally, table 23.3 presents results from regressions of the racial and ethnic characteristics of the population in each election district on the percentage vote for Mayor David N. Dinkins in the highly polarized 1993 mayoral election and for President Bill Clinton in the more "normal" presidential election of 1992. The first equations regress the non-Hispanic white proportion of the election district population on the electoral outcome. In both the 1992 and 1993 elections, this single variable accounted for a substantial amount of the variance and its coefficient was relatively large and negative with regard to the share of the vote going to the Democratic candidate, although these relationships were twice as strong for the polarized 1993 mayoral race as for the 1992 presidential race. In EDs with *no* white population, both Democratic

TABLE 23.2 Correlations of Racial Groups Across Industries, New York City, 1990 (N = 51 industries)

	Non-Hispanic White percent	*Non-Hispanic Black percent*	*Asian percent*	*Hispanic percent*
Non-Hispanic White	1.0000	−.5033	−.5009	−.7898
Non-Hispanic Black	−.5033	1.0000	−.3433	−.0548
Asian	−.5009	−.3433	1.0000	.5888
Hispanic	−.7898	−.0548	.5888	1.0000

Source: Center for Urban Research, CUNY Graduate Center, from PUMS, 1990 census. Industries weighted by employment.

TABLE 23.3 Regression Analysis of Racial Group Voting, New York City, 1992 to 1993 (N = 5,400 EDs)

	Percent for David Dinkins 1993 Mayoral Election	*Percent for Bill Clinton 1992 Presidential Election*
Equation 1		
Non-Hispanic White percent	−.743	−.315
(Constant)	84.73	83.90
(Adjusted R Square)	.707	.374
Equation 2		
Non-Hispanic Black	.868	.389
Hispanic	.519	.175
Non-Hispanic Asian	−.082	−.118
(Constant)	17.97	56.49
(Adjusted R Square)	.822	.480

Source: Author's tabulations from 1990 census data allocated to election districts and voting results by election district reported by New York City Board of Elections.

candidates were estimated to get 84 or 85 percent of vote. In 100 percent white EDs, Dinkins was estimated to receive just over 10 percent of the vote, while Clinton garnered 52.4 percent of the vote.

The results from the second equation mirror those from the first. In this version, all-white EDs were projected to give Dinkins about 18 percent of the vote and Clinton 56 percent, but those figures rise rapidly with the black and Hispanic population. All-black EDs are estimated to have given virtually all of their votes to Dinkins, while all-Hispanic EDs gave 70 percent. Asian EDs, on the other hand, leaned slightly away from Democrats, subtracting a little from Dinkins's share and slightly more from Clinton's share. This comparison makes it obvious that the 1993 election was highly polarized from a racial and ethnic standpoint, with whites highly opposed, blacks highly in favor, Hispanics largely in favor, and Asians mildly opposed to Mayor Dinkins's reelection. This pattern strongly resembles that of the residential segregation observed in table 23.3. It is also evident, if in a more muted form, in elections that do not pit candidates of different races against each other, such as the 1992 presidential election. (Results for the 1996 presidential election closely resemble those for the 1992 election.)

THE IMPACT OF THE "NEW IMMIGRATION" ON INTERGROUP CONFLICT

Since 1965 immigration has had an enormous impact on the economy and population of New York City. Almost one million of New York's 7.3 million inhabitants told the 1990 census that they had arrived from abroad within the last decade alone. Without their arrival, New York City would surely be a smaller, poorer, and less diverse city. With the arrival of these new immigrants, which continued unabated during the recession of 1989 to 1993, New York joins Los Angeles as the nation's premier magnet for global population flows (Frey and Fielding 1995; Waldinger 1989). And as E. B. White (1949, 42–43) wrote half a century ago, "The collision and the intermingling of these millions of foreign-born people representing so many races and creeds make New York a permanent exhibit of the phenomenon of one world."

Not only is the number of immigrants from Latin America, the Caribbean, and Asia growing relative to all native-born groups, but they are altering the nativity balance within each major racial and ethnic group: immigrants from Russia, Ireland, Italy, and Poland have joined native whites; immigrants from the Caribbean have joined native blacks; immigrants from the Dominican Republic, Cuba, Colombia, Ecuador, Peru, and Mexico have joined (and now outnumber) Puerto Ricans; and immigrants from China, Korea, India, the Philippines, and elsewhere in Asia have generated a new minority group in the city. (For discussions of the overall picture, see Foner 1987; Salvo, Ortiz, and Vardy 1992; Youssef 1992.) The foreign-born and their children now constitute 55.1 percent of all blacks, 58.5 percent of all Hispanics, and 97.5 percent of all Asians in New York City (Mollenkopf, Olson, and Ross 1998, New York table 1). Among younger residents of the city, immigrant and second-generation individuals constitute a substantial majority. Immigration has thus given race and ethnicity new national origins and complicated the patterns of racial and ethnic competition in residential neighborhoods and the labor market. The impact on politics is just beginning but is nonetheless clearly discernible.

The new immigrant groups that arrived without much education or capital sought out employment in the declining blue-collar occupations and industries that whites were leaving, as well as in the growing low-wage service and retail sales industries and occupations that whites would not enter. As Waldinger (1996a) and others have pointed out, employers seeking pliant employees in low-wage settings with high turnover preferred immigrants over native-born minorities. Chinese and Dominican women have thus established large immigrant niches in the apparel industries, while many Chinese men work in restaurants, though Chinese have been more successful at shifting into ownership and the professions (Waldinger 1996a, 122–36). Among the most persistently poor of these groups are Dominicans, who suffer high rates of female-headed households, nonparticipation in the labor force, and poverty. They are less likely than Puerto Ricans to rely on public assistance; instead, many family members contribute low wages to subsistence levels of income. And unlike Chinese, who have intact, multi-earner families and show high rates of intergenerational mobility and educational attainment, long-established Dominican households do not seem to be doing much better than more recent arrivals.

At the same time, New York's new immigrant population is extremely diverse in background and resources. Some groups, like Indians, Koreans, and Filipinos, actually have higher rates of educational attainment than native-born, non-Hispanic whites, and Koreans have high rates of self-employment. Indians have rapidly entered the business professions; though they earn less than whites with comparable education, and thus are experiencing some degree of discrimination, they are doing far better than other immigrants and have higher median family incomes than whites, partly because more family members are working.

New York's Afro-Caribbean population lies between these extremes. Although they come with fewer assets than some Asian groups, they have higher rates of educational attainment and far better English proficiency than Dominican or Chinese immigrants. Because West Indian migration began in the early decades of this century and many became leaders in New York City's emerging black community (Holder 1980), West Indians (and to a lesser extent Haitians) have joined native-born blacks in making inroads in the nonprofit, government-funded social services, especially the health services. (For a comprehensive view of Caribbean New Yorkers, see Kasinitz 1992.)

Much of the intergroup violence that whites have perpetrated against blacks has actually been inflicted on first- or second-generation immigrants. (For a discussion of events up until 1987, see Kornblum and Beshers 1988.) For example, the murder of a West Indian youth, Yousef Hawkins, by white toughs in Canarsie influenced the 1989 mayoral elections, and the 1993 elections were heavily influenced by the accident in which a car in the entourage of the Rebbe of the Lubavitcher Hasidic Jewish sect ran a red light in Crown Heights and careened into Gavin Cato, killing him and setting off three days of black riots against Jews.

The relationships between native-born and foreign-born blacks and Hispanics are deeply ambivalent. On the one hand, these groups are the closest competitors in the labor market. Established black and Puerto Rican politicians often see West Indian and Dominican demands for more offices and appointments as an unwanted challenge to their still unsatisfactory level of political achievement. Emerging immigrant leaders, for their part, see established native minority politicians as an old guard resistant to their legitimate needs. At the same time, native black and Puerto Rican leaders speak in terms of racial or ethnic solidarity and need votes and political support from the immigrant first and second generations, which constitute the demographic future of the city's black and Hispanic populations. Some white political leaders have sought to exploit the cleavages between these groups by favoring Caribbeans and Dominicans, thereby undermining the black and Hispanic challenge to white electoral dominance.

Finally, the rapid growth of the foreign-born population in New York City certainly presents a fundamental challenge for democratic representation. In many parts of the city, one-third to one-half of adults cannot vote, even though they pay taxes. As David Olson (1994) has shown, even eligible voters in such areas are less likely to vote than those who reside in areas with high concentrations of the native-born minority. In general, only a minority of the eligible foreign-born have become naturalized citizens. Many retain attachments to the home country and plan to return. Native-born minority leaders do not seem likely to launch a new wave of the civil rights movement designed to incorporate black and Latino immigrants. It may be that recent anti-immigrant legislation will hasten naturalization, but it is most likely that the full political incorporation of the Caribbean, Dominican, and Chinese populations must await the political maturing of the second generation, just as the full impact of the turn-of-the-century immigration was not felt until their children voted for the New Deal.

The Political Mobilization and Control of Intergroup Conflict

New York City affords a picture of intergroup conflict that clearly diverges from the discussion of Los Angeles by Johnson and his colleagues (this volume), which foresees the potential of a downward spiral of intergroup conflict exacerbated by an increasingly anti-immigrant sentiment among whites. To be sure, racial and ethnic conflicts over jobs, neighborhoods, public space, and political influence beset New York. The mayors of both cities won office largely without minority support, whether native-born or immigrant. Yet New York City does not appear to be on the brink of uncontrolled violence like the 1992 Los Angeles riots, nor does the native white electorate harbor similar anti-immigrant, antiminority sentiments. What differences between Los Angeles and New York account for this outcome? And what do these differences suggest for a broader comparative analysis?

First, consider the greatly different composition of the dominant strata in the two cities. In Los Angeles the white population is predominantly descended from white, midwestern Protestants who are not comfortable with forging biracial alliances (Davis 1990; Oliver 1995; Sonenshein 1993). In New York white Protestants are practically invisible, if still economically and socially powerful. Instead, the city's white population is dominated by first-, second-, and third-generation Catholics and Jews. Far from finding intergroup competition threatening, they are masters of the art. Moreover, less than half of New York's white population is native-born to native parents: 27.4 percent are second-generation and 24.2 percent remain foreign-born (Mollenkopf, Olson, and Ross 1998, New York table 1).

Although whites form roughly one-third of the population in New York City, the city of Los Angeles, and Los Angeles County, they form a distinctly smaller share, as table 23.4 shows, of the active electorate in New York City. In a completely racially and ethnically polarized election, whites could still cast a slim majority of the votes, but it would be far easier for them to sustain their majority position by recruiting some minority support, particularly from Asians or Hispanics. When candidates supported by white voters have run against candidates supported by black voters in racially polarized elections in New York City, they have sought support primarily from Hispanic voters. Asian voters may become a more fertile source of support in the future, but at present they cast too few ballots to swing elections.

In Los Angeles, by contrast, whites are much less likely to have an immigrant background: native-stock individuals account for almost three-quarters of the total, while only 13.7 percent are immigrants (Mollenkopf, Olson, and Ross 1998, Los Angeles table 1; Waldinger 1996a, ch. 14). Whites constitute two-thirds of the active electorate and do not need minority support to win racially or ethnically polarized elections. Indeed, the presence of this kind of polarization guarantees the victory of the white candidate, as the Riordan elections show. In Los Angeles, table 23.4 shows that the ratio between whites' voting and population shares is huge—1.75. In New York the figure is a more modest 1.48. Liberal whites could forge an electoral alliance with blacks in Los Angeles, leading to substantial increases in black representation, without threatening white political dominance. This is not the case in New York.

Differences in the dynamics among native and immigrant minority populations of the two cities also help explain the disparate outcomes. In New York blacks and Hispanics are relatively evenly balanced, and they achieved similar rates of electoral participation in the 1997 mayoral election. Moreover, as has already been said, each contains an immigrant constituency that is challenging native-born leaders for a larger piece of the political pie. This creates a serious potential for political competition between them and offers whites seeking to ensure their position the attractive possibility of playing one group against the other. In Los Angeles, as noted, blacks forged an electoral alliance with whites that produced substantial political representation for them. Indeed, table 23.4 suggests that blacks are overrepresented in the city of Los Angeles and in Los Angeles County. The most formidable challenge to this relationship will come from Mexican Americans and other Hispanics, who form a large majority of the population but are still a tiny fraction of the electorate. They remain strongly underrepresented on the city and county boards of supervisors compared to their

TABLE 23.4 The Political Systems of New York and Los Angeles

	New York City	*City of Los Angeles*	*Los Angeles County*
Population 1997	7,644,371	3,615,498	9,324,811
Non-Hispanic White	35.9%	31.3%	35.4%
Non-Hispanic Black	29.4	10.1	8.2
Non-Hispanic Asian	8.4	8.6	11.5
Hispanic	26.2	49.9	44.7
Habitable land area (square miles)	322	466	1,989
Density (persons/square miles)	23,740	7,759	4,688
Voting age population (VAP) 1997	5,590,119	2,510,985	6,483,004
Foreign-born VAP 1997	2,284,518	1,306,900	2,847,425
Foreign-born percent of VAP	40.9	52.0	43.9
Foreign-born VAP Naturalized 1997	857,731	298,278	780,220
Foreign-born VAP percent Naturalized	37.5	22.8	27.4
Eligible voters 1997	4,163,332	1,502,363	4,415,799
Registered voters (1997)	3,532,348	1,401,336	3,759,498
Registration rate	84.8%	93.3%	85.1%
1996 presidential vote	1,796,533	750,102	2,410,976
1997 mayoral vote	1,319,795	378,965	N.A.
1996 turnout (voting age citizens)	43.2%	49.9%	54.6%
1997 turnout (voting age citizens)	31.7%	25.2%	N.A.
Percent voters Non-Hispanic White	(1997) 53	(1997) 65	(1996) 62
Percent voters Jewish	23	15	14
Percent voters Non-Hispanic Black	21	13	8
Percent voters Non-Hispanic Asian	4	4	3
Percent voters Hispanic	20	15	26
Number of jurisdictions	1	1	88
Size of local legislature	51	15	5
White representation ratio	1.47	2.12	1.69
Black representation ratio	1.00	1.32	2.44
Asian representation ratio	0.00	0.00	0.00
Hispanic representation ratio	0.67	0.40	0.45
Adopted budget 1996–97	$34.946 billion	$4.063 billion	$12.143 billion

Sources: 1997 population figures from the March 1997 current Population Survey; 1997 electorate from *New York Times* and *Los Angeles Times* exit polls; 1996 Voter News Service Exit Poll, Los Angeles County Sample.

population numbers. In contrast to New York, where a candidate supported by whites has a vested interest in allying with Hispanics in a racially polarized contest against a candidate supported by blacks, whites and blacks in Los Angeles may both harbor concerns about the possibly impending political majority of Hispanics.

In New York, moreover, 41.2 percent of the black population is foreign-stock, as is 58.5 percent of the Hispanic population. (Puerto Ricans are, of course, counted as natives.) In Los Angeles only 7.3 percent of the black population is foreign-stock, while 86.8 percent of the Hispanic population is foreign-stock. Nativity is therefore a distinction that cuts through all racial and ethnic groups in New York City, but that pits whites and blacks against Hispanics and Asians in Los Angeles.

A third critical difference between the two cities

concerns the ways in which their political systems shape the expression of group interests and the bargaining (or lack thereof) among them. New York City's political system encourages, indeed requires, groups to make deals with each other and to contain their conflicts. Elected officials from all racial and ethnic groups, whether white, black, or Puerto Rican, have an incentive to seek support from, and adopt at least superficially friendly rhetoric toward, immigrants. By contrast, the depoliticized, fragmented political environment of Los Angeles County leaves few institutional channels for processing and containing intergroup conflict. Los Angeles, the quintessential suburban city, lacks strong, relatively well-defined neighborhoods, which abound in New York City. Members of the boards of supervisors of the city of Los Angeles and of Los Angeles County represent vast, heterogeneous units. Indeed, as table 23.4 shows, a Los Angeles county supervisor represents more than 1.8 million people. New York City has not only fifty-one council seats but fifty-nine community boards with fifty members each and thirty-five community school boards with fifteen members each; this political system provides both a conduit for neighborhood political expression and a supply of entry-level political positions. The counterpart to a Los Angeles county supervisor, a New York City councilperson, represents 150,000 people. The implications for what it takes to run a winning campaign—and therefore the barriers to access—are obvious. The interaction of cohesive neighborhoods represented by relatively small districts fosters the expression of territorially based ethnic interests in New York, while Los Angeles' situation frustrates them. (On this point, see the contrast between Los Angeles and San Antonio offered by Skerry 1993.)

Similarly, New York City has a strongly partisan political system with well-developed Democratic Party clubs in most of the city's assembly districts. It also has large and well-organized public employee unions. The cities in Los Angeles County, by contrast, have weak nonpartisan systems, and the county lacks either a regular or reform Democratic organization. Its public sector is small, and its public employee organizations are correspondingly weak. (If one apportions the Los Angeles County budget to Los Angeles and adds the city budget in table 23.4, it amounts to $8.675 billion for 3.6 million people, or about $2,400 per person; New York's budget is about $4,500 per person.) Although many of New York's political organizations are not what they once were, they do cut across race, ethnicity, and nativity and provide arenas in which to work out intergroup disputes. The Los Angeles political system provides few such opportunities.

Lately, bi- or multiracial coalition formation has suffered in both cities as relatively conservative, white, Republican mayors have replaced more liberal black mayors who relied on votes from whites, blacks, and Hispanics. These mayors won office by mobilizing white voters, who, though a minority of the population, still form a small majority of the electorate. Yet it can be argued that New York's Democratic Party has a more robust history of balancing ethnic interests and managing ethnic competition, if not promoting minority empowerment. It has managed ethnic antagonisms in order to ensure the continuing influence of previously ascendant, now numerically declining, white ethnic groups. But it has achieved this end by providing subordinate groups with a place at the table (and sometimes the trough) and luring them with the prospects of achieving real power.

Jim Sleeper (1993) has argued that Mayors Riordan and Giuliani are creating "Rainbow II" coalitions that appeal not only to native-born whites but to upwardly striving, entrepreneurial Hispanic and Asian immigrants. Certainly Mayor Giuliani and the Republican Party are well advised to foster naturalization campaigns among Asian and Russian immigrants. As the previous discussion should make clear, it will be no simple matter to put bi- or multiracial challenging coalitions together. Many barriers separate white liberals, native-born blacks, Caribbean blacks, Puerto Ricans, and Dominicans; these groups clearly have different social positions and potentially conflicting interests. But they have the common interest of being out of power. If Democrats are to regain the mayoralty, the party's leading candidates will have to find ways to forge working relationships among these disparate groups within the Democratic Party, the public employee unions, and community-based organizations and to develop programs that transcend group boundaries.

As scholars compare the working-out of intergroup tensions across American cities, this comparison of Los Angeles and New York certainly suggests that they must focus on the ways in which local political systems shape the expression and management of such tensions. It may well be that the absence of a meaningful urban politics is what makes Johnson, Farrell, and Guinn's (this volume) depiction of Los Angeles so bleak, while the robust political life of New York City suggests a potential for true progress. To quote E. B. White (1949, 24, 26) once again:

> By rights New York City should have destroyed itself long ago, from panic or fire or rioting or failure of some vital supply line in its circulatory system or from some deep labyrinthine short circuit. . . . But the city makes up for its hazards and its deficiencies with massive doses of a supplementary vitamin—the sense of belonging to something unique, cosmopolitan, mighty, and unparalleled.

The New York experience thus picks up where that of Los Angeles ends: it provides an example of how one system at least fosters the building of alliances between the native-born and immigrants. It does not do so out of altruism or in a search for a more democratic society; nor has it produced the degree of political equality for which we may hope. At the same time, it provides a forum in which groups can and do express their interests, fight it out, and reach an equilibrium. In these respects, the New York system is superior to the lack of representation and the suppression of intergroup bargaining that seems to characterize Los Angeles. Any larger scholarly effort to understand how immigration is affecting intergroup relations across American cities must therefore take into account both the specific dynamic balance among the interests of various native and immigrant racial and ethnic groups and the ways in which the urban political systems mediate the relationships between them.

24 U.S. Immigration and Changing Relations Between African Americans and Latinos

Nestor Rodriguez

INTERNATIONAL MIGRATION is dramatically altering social-demographic landscapes in U.S. urban areas. Since the 1970s large influxes of new immigrants have substantially altered the ethnic and racial populations of large urban centers—for example, New York, Los Angeles, and Houston—with strong ties to the global economy. Large-scale immigration of peoples from Asia, Latin America, and other world regions has contributed to major social change in these settings by establishing new culturally distinct communities (Lamphere 1992). This development of new communities has produced new patterns of inter- and intragroup relation in large U.S. urban centers.

With the expansion and diversification of Asian, Latino, and other ethnic and racial communities, the setting for U.S. urban race relations has been transformed from a mainly binary plane of black-white relations into multidimensional axes of ethnicity, immigrant status, nationality, race, and other social identities (Bach 1993). Especially after the social eruptions in Los Angeles in the spring of 1992, this social recomposition has created concerns among mainstream institutional leaders about the intergroup future of their localities. African Americans and Latinos are prominent players in this future, since collectively they form sizable populations, if not majorities, in many large U.S. cities. Among the five largest central cities in the country, this is true in New York, Los Angeles, Chicago, and Houston (see table 24.1). In the fifth-largest central city, Philadelphia, African Americans and Latinos compose 45.2 percent of the population. In the South, Houston is a critical case of emerging intergroup relations between African Americans and Latinos in the context of high immigration levels. The 1990 census found that Houston has more black residents than any other southern city, and the second-largest Latino population in the South (if not the largest by the mid-1990s). Over 40 percent of Houston's 450,000 Latino residents are first-generation immigrants (U.S. Bureau of the Census 1993c, table 28).

In this chapter, I respond, through two discussions, to James H. Johnson, Walter C. Farrell, and Chandra Guinn's chapter in this volume. In the first discussion, I address the authors' topology of "immigration-induced community conflicts," primarily from the Houston perspective. Using findings from recent intergroup surveys and ongoing ethnographic research in Houston, I argue that tensions, conflict, and community instability are not the only outcome of relations between African Americans and Latinos in contexts of high immigration. Indeed, I attempt to make the case for varied modes of intergroup reactions in such settings, sometimes varying by social identities other than ethnicity or race, and sometimes forming collaborative relations based precisely on identities of minority status.

In the second discussion, I attempt to relate the arena of intergroup relations to larger structural processes related to global change and immigration. These processes are important for relations between African Americans and Latinos because they greatly affect the social geographies and related opportunity structures of intergroup interaction.

VARIED MODES OF INTERGROUP RELATIONS BETWEEN AFRICAN AMERICANS AND LATINOS

To help place specific levels of intergroup relations in Houston into historical perspective, it is necessary to describe the area's dynamic economic growth, its political development, and its attraction for large numbers of immigrants. With the influence of a business elite strongly connected to various levels of government, Houston's economy enjoyed almost nonstop growth in the oil and petrochemical industries between the 1910s and the beginning of the 1980s. So robust was the area's

TABLE 24.1 Racial and Ethnic Population Distributions in the Five Largest U.S. Central Cities, 1990

Central City	*1990 Population (millions)*	*Non-Hispanic White*	*African American*	*Latino*	*Asian American or Pacific Islander*	*American Indian, Eskimo, or Aleutian*
New York	7.32	43.4%	28.8%	23.7%	7.0%	0.3%
Los Angeles	3.49	37.5	13.9	39.3	9.8	0.4
Chicago	2.78	38.2	39.0	19.2	3.7	0.2
Houston	1.63	40.8	28.1	27.2	4.0	0.3
Philadelphia	1.59	52.2	39.9	5.3	2.7	0.2

Source: U.S. Bureau of the Census (1993b), table 171.

economic development, assisted by governmental support, that Houston continued to enjoy substantial business vitality even during the Depression of the 1930s. Until the price of oil collapsed in the early 1980s, Houston enjoyed unparalleled growth as a production and technological center of the world oil economy. This growth depended on an expanding labor force for office and manufacturing jobs and for the many jobs in lower-paying supportive construction and service industries (Shelton et al. 1989).

The Houston area's African American population, which developed in the 1800s from surrounding agricultural communities and a local settlement of freed slaves, provided much labor for the expanding economy, but by as early as the 1910s Mexican immigrant labor had also become a feature of the city's low-paying labor market sector. In the post–World War II era impoverished areas in Mexico became a major labor source for Houston's housing construction and low-paying service industries. Much of the Mexican workforce consisted of undocumented men and women immigrant workers who were afraid to join unions. Even when the area's economy entered a severe recession in the early 1980s, Latino immigration continued unabated as large numbers of Central Americans arrived in the city fleeing social turmoil and political violence in their homelands. By the end of the 1980s Latino workers had become the preferred labor supply in numerous industries that had previously used African American workers. Moreover, the new Mexican and Central American immigrants created new minority communities outside the city's East Side, which was the original settlement area of African Americans and Latinos confined by decades of Jim Crow practices.

Political subordination of Houston African American and Latino populations paralleled the area's economic segmentation by race and ethnicity. The city's government was mainly a white government until the late 1970s. In the nine city council elections between 1961 and 1971, only one African American was elected from the city's racial and ethnic minority populations (Thomas and Murray 1991, 225). One Mexican American was elected as city comptroller in the 1970s, and the first Latino (Mexican American) was elected to city council in 1979, but only after federal pressure led to the changing of electoral district boundaries. The lack of paved streets and the poor quality of street maintenance in minority areas, the very limited supply of public housing, the denial of free lunch programs for low-income school youth, the absence of minority administrators in high-level city offices—all demonstrated the political marginalization of the city's African American and Latino communities for much of the twentieth century (Shelton et al. 1989).

By the 1990s relations between African Americans and Latinos in the Houston area had become characterized by a variety of conditions. Across different institutional settings, these conditions ranged from overt conflict to peaceful coexistence, to collaboration. Although episodes of conflict get the most media attention, quiet behind-the-scenes collaboration may have as much, or more, significance for future relations between African Americans and Latinos, including a large immigrant sector, in the city. Research in the 1990s indicates that perceptions of the predominant aspect of Houston's black-brown relations vary according to what the most recent issue is, whether you ask African Americans or Latinos, and, within each group, whether you ask community leaders or ordinary residents (Romo and Rodriguez 1993).

A survey conducted by the Center for Mexican American Studies (CMAS) at the University of Houston in 1995 attempted to assess the quality of attitudes and relations between African Americans and Latinos in Harris County, which contains most of the city of Houston. The random telephone survey of three hundred adult male and female respondents from each of the area's populations of African Americans, U.S.-born Latinos, and foreign-born Latinos found that African American and Latino residents have seemingly ambivalent views concerning black-brown relations in Houston. In one section of the interview, they responded that relations between the two groups are generally good, while in another section they responded that there is too much conflict between the two groups (Mindiola, Niemann, and Rodriguez 1996). These contrasting views, however, are not necessarily contradictory: the survey respondents may view the occasional political scrimmages between black and brown leaders as "too much" for an otherwise generally more tranquil course of intergroup relations. Overall the survey found that younger and U.S.-born respondents tended to view and accept black-brown relations more favorably.

Residential Transition and Intergroup Relations

The largest numbers of Latino immigrants in Houston in the 1980s settled in Mexican barrios on the city's East Side and in new immigrant settlement zones on the West Side, but some newcomers from Mexico and Central America located rental housing adjacent to, and inside, African American neighborhoods ("wards") near the city's downtown (Rodriguez 1993). Similar to developments in Compton, California, described by Johnson and his colleagues (this volume), this new Latino housing pattern of residing near black neighborhoods represents at least a partial residential transition in the affected ward areas. The impact of the general residential change for African American–Latino relations has been very evident in public schools, as well as in the politics of the Houston Independent School District (HISD).

Not surprisingly, fights between black and Latino youth are occasionally reported in public schools near areas of residential transition. But many African American and Latino youths work together in school activities, maintaining at least a peaceful coexistence, if not a harmonious one. Other African American and Latino youths form integrated black-brown gangs, sometimes united by the common musical culture of gangsta rap. In the teaching workforce of HISD, Latino teachers constitute only 13.4 percent of all teachers (41.2 percent are black), while Latino students represent 50 percent of all students (HISD 1995, 10, 17). Yet Latinos have not mounted a sustained effort to pressure the African American superintendent to bring in greater numbers of Latino teachers. (HISD administrators initiated a program to recruit Latino teachers from abroad but ran into problems validating the credentials of foreign teachers.)

African American–Latino tension and conflict, however, surfaced in the selection of the present African American superintendent of HISD when the school board selected him from among their own. When the HISD school board announced its decision, several Latino leaders objected to the lack of an open, national search, and especially to the absence of any consideration of Hispanic candidates given that Latinos constituted the largest student population in the school district. A group of Latino leaders took the matter to court but lost when the case was dismissed. The Latino interest in the matter eventually died from lack of progress—and the lack of a united Latino front—but not before causing a major cleavage between many African American and Latino leaders in the city. (For a brief description of this and other interethnic incidents in the Houston area, see Inter-Ethnic Forum of Houston 1995, 5–8.) A leading African American figure of the city likened the Latino opposition to the appointment of the African American superintendent to a "political lynching." More recently, the African American and Latino school board members have united to maintain a magnet school in an upper-class neighborhood against the wishes of some of the neighborhood's residents, who want the school for the neighborhood's children.

Intergroup Effects of Asian Entrepreneurship

Similar to the highly publicized cases in California, the Houston area has experienced some cases of tension and conflict between African American residents and Asian store owners. In a handful of cases, African Americans have boycotted Asian-owned stores in their neighborhoods to protest what they perceive to be a lack of concern among Asian business owners for the black communities where they have businesses. In one case similar to the Latasha Harlins case in California, a young Vietnamese clerk in a convenience store owned by his family shot and killed an African American youth who allegedly had become argumentative and left the store with beer without paying. When the store clerk was not convicted for the death,

African Americans boycotted the store and eventually forced the Vietnamese family to sell the business (Inter-Ethnic Forum of Houston 1995).

The population of Vietnamese and other Asian residents in the Houston area grew rapidly in the 1980s, to about 125,000 by the 1990 census (U.S. Bureau of the Census 1993b, table 160). Although all three Asian groups—Chinese, Vietnamese, and Korean— own convenience stores and other small businesses scattered throughout black and Latino neighborhoods, it is the Vietnamese who have developed a large retail and commercial district close to two of Houston's largest African American communities. The Vietnamese district, which contains malls, restaurants, supermarkets, and a variety of legal, medical, and business services, is booming but has little attraction for nearby black residents.

To lessen the intergroup tensions generated by episodes of African American–Asian conflict, leaders from the two communities have met to organize joint community meetings to address their intergroup problems. Of special importance, the meetings involved religious leaders from both communities. Although the intergroup sessions do not reduce class differences between black customers and Asian store owners, they do give both sides an opportunity to address each other in a controlled setting. Perhaps more important, the leaders demonstrate an interest in containing the problem rather than letting it spread. Also, the intergroup meetings create a model for dealing with future confrontations between black residents and Asian store owners.

To be sure, intergroup leadership collaboration in the Houston area appears to be common in most groups. A study conducted by the Tomas Rivera Center (TRC) in 1992 found substantial evidence of this. In the study, a nonprobability mail survey of over five hundred African American, Asian, and Latino community leaders, the respondents reported interacting frequently with leaders from other groups as follows: African Americans 54.8 percent; Anglos 43.9 percent; Asians 38.5 percent; and Latinos 52.5 percent (Romo et al. 1994).

The level of tension described by Johnson and his colleagues (this volume) in Asian-Latino relations in the Los Angeles area is generally not found in the Houston area. For the most part, the two populations live apart. Asian entrepreneurship has become a significant employment source for Latino immigrants in the restaurant businesses. Also, some Asian-Latino partnerships have created popular eating places in Latino immigrant neighborhoods. Indeed, such enterprises appear to be creating a new Asian-Latino business form: customers select dishes from bicultural, Chinese-Mexican menus. The multicultural atmosphere reached a rather intense level in one restaurant near downtown: the Korean owner hired Mexican immigrant cooks to prepare Chinese dishes for mainly African American customers.

A random survey component of the 1992 TRC study also was used to explore intergroup perceptions in the Houston area and found the following regarding relations between African Americans, Asians, and Latinos. Among African American respondents, 41.7 percent viewed relations between blacks and Asians as fair and 13.3 percent viewed those relations as good or very good, while 34.7 percent viewed the relations between the two groups as bad or very bad (Romo et al. 1994). Among Latino respondents, 44.7 percent viewed relations between Latinos and Asians as fair and 17 percent viewed relations as good or very good, while 15.7 percent viewed the relations between the two groups as bad or very bad. The responses clearly indicate an absence of polarization between Asians and the two groups of African Americans and Latinos.

Employment and Intergroup Relations

The rise of immigration in Houston in the last two decades produced an abundant labor supply, particularly for the lower echelons of the area's labor market. In some cases, new Latino immigrant workers became highly visible in jobs previously held by African Americans. These employees included domestic workers, hotel workers, and supermarket maintenance workers.

Indeed, the rise of immigration created a sort of reserved labor market for immigrant labor, that is, employment sectors that contained only immigrant workers and that U.S. workers appeared to shun because of their immigrant labor character (Rodriguez 1995, 219–20).

The reserved immigrant labor markets functioned as quasi-internal labor markets. As such, recruitment and promotion of immigrant workers in specific work settings was only minimally affected by the labor supply outside the immigrant labor force. In many work settings immigrant workers' social networks were a major basis for recruiting new workers, defining the division of labor, and controlling the labor process. A heaven for employers, immigrant-reserved and internal-labor markets thus provided a self-reproducing and self-regulating workforce, at a bargain price.

Reserved immigrant labor markets reduce direct tension and conflict between U.S. and immigrant workers by reducing contact between the two groups of workers. In many workplaces immigrants work in crews consisting of only immigrants (Rodriguez 1987). Encounters with native workers thus occur mainly through interactions with U.S.-born supervisors. In large workplaces immigrants may work among native workers but in separate crews.

Although reserved immigrant labor markets may reduce direct conflict between U.S. and immigrant workers, employment-related tension may develop from the perceptions that immigrants are taking American jobs. The 1995 CMAS survey, however, indicated that blacks in Houston have mixed views about this issue. While a majority (53.7 percent) of the African American respondents agreed somewhat or strongly that immigrants take jobs away from black workers, 39.1 percent disagreed somewhat or strongly that this is true, and 7.2 percent had no opinion (Mindiola et al. 1996). Interestingly, about one-fifth (19.8 percent) of the African American respondents disagreed strongly that immigrants take away jobs from blacks. The unemployment rates among the survey respondents were 7.9 percent for both African American and U.S.-born Latinos, and 5.2 percent for foreign-born Latinos (Mindiola et al. 1996).

Language and Intergroup Relations

Language is one of the most sensitive issues in intergroup relations (Bach 1993, 6). In many areas of the United States Spanish and other non-English languages are used more frequently, and many established residents resent this. They perceive "foreign" languages as a threat not only to English but to American culture in general. In some cases, language differences may even cause tension between groups from the same world region or the same culture. In Houston, for example, some Vietnamese residents dislike the use of Chinese characters on street signs in predominantly Chinese districts, and some U.S.-born Latinos avoid social settings where interaction is carried on mainly in Spanish.

For African Americans, Spanish may represent an additional barrier to employment or job promotion, especially in business and public workplaces increasingly affected by a growing Latino immigrant presence. The results of the 1995 CMAS surrey, however, indicate that African Americans in Houston have mixed views about the use of Spanish language. When asked to respond to the statement "It is okay for people to use Spanish in the workplace," about half (48.6 percent) of the African American respondents agreed somewhat or strongly, almost a similar proportion (45.4 percent) disagreed somewhat or strongly, and 6 percent had no opinion. When asked about the impact of Spanish usage on the country as a whole, 46 percent of the African American respondent said it was somewhat bad or very bad, 42.7 percent said it was somewhat good or very good for the country, and 10.7 percent had no opinion (Mindiola et al. 1996). African Americans in Houston are clearly divided on the issue of Spanish usage.

It is important to understand that the high level of Spanish usage is greatly associated with immigration. In the Houston area, for example, over three-fourths of foreign-born Latinos prefer Spanish for public interaction, but an even larger percentage of U.S.-born Latinos prefer English (Mindiola et al. 1996). Among Latino immigrants, especially the young, the ability to use English increases with length of residence in the United States. A study by the demographer Dowell Myers of immigrants in southern California found that 70 percent of immigrants who had been in the region between the ages of five and fourteen in 1980 had mastered English by 1990 (McDonnell 1995b, A4).

Proposition 187 and Intergroup Relations

According to Johnson and his colleagues (this volume), the black community vote for Proposition 187 has become a source of tension between African Americans and Latinos in southern California. Moreover, as the authors point out, the proposition's passage may prompt Latino immigrants to naturalize and become a voting force that could push blacks from political power. The state of Texas has not attempted to initiate a measure similar to Proposition 187; nevertheless, survey results in the Houston area indicate that black concern about immigration restriction is similar to the larger national sentiment against undocumented immigration. Yet this concern may not necessarily reflect an anti-Latino sentiment.

The TRC and CMAS random surveys demonstrate the African American view of how immigrants affect the Houston area. In the 1992 TRC survey, a majority (53 percent) of African American respondents indicated that the impact of immigrants had been good or very good, while 40.3 percent of them indicated that the impact had been bad or very bad (Romo and Rodriguez 1993, 8–9). The survey, of course, was conducted prior to the anti-immigrant sentiments generated by Governor Pete Wilson's reelection campaign and the promotion of Proposition 187 in California. (As late as the fall of 1993, 58 percent of the respondents in a *Time* magazine poll [Nelan 1993] indicated that immigrants were "basically good, honest people," and only 29 percent of the respondents favored a fence along the U.S.-Mexico border.)

The 1995 CMAS survey indicated that African Americans in Houston had reversed their perceptions of the immigrant impact in the Houston area. The survey found that 36.3 percent of the African American respondents judged the immigrant impact to be good or very good, while a majority (53.6 percent) now viewed the impact to be bad or very bad. Perhaps some of the negative perception stemmed from worries that immigrants were taking advantage of hard-won affirmative action programs; at least one African American elected official in Houston asked for a study on the issue of immigrant employment through affirmative action.

The 1995 CMAS survey indicates that African American support in Houston for immigration restriction is not generally an anti-Latino position. The survey found that a majority (65 percent) of African Americans favor a national identification card to keep undocumented immigrants out of U.S. jobs, but that a majority (58 percent) of Latinos also favor such a proposal (Mindiola et al. 1996). This finding and the finding mentioned earlier that over one-third of African American respondents viewed Houston's immigration to be good or very good suggests that African American concerns about immigration restriction are not particularly prone to induce black-brown conflict. Indeed, in the Houston Independent School District, African American administrators can be found hard at work in multicultural programs supporting Latino immigrant children. In the Harris County Commissioner's Court, an African American commissioner (the only minority member of the all-male court) has questioned proposals to investigate the residency status of county hospital users, an effort directed mainly at undocumented immigrant patients (Inter-Ethnic Forum of Houston 1995).

It is also not clear that the record high levels of naturalization by immigrants will produce a Latino voter backlash against African Americans, especially since many Latinos in California also voted for Proposition 187. From the Houston perspective, equating naturalized Latino citizens with Latino voters is still problematic. The 1995 CMAS survey found that only about 20 percent of the Latino immigrant respondents were U.S. citizens (Mindiola et al. 1996). Although this proportion will increase, previous research has found low to moderate electoral interest in Houston's Latino immigrant communities. Undoubtedly the present Latino immigrant interest in acquiring U.S. citizenship is significantly motivated by concerns about future restrictions against noncitizens, but how this will affect future electoral politics is not clear.

My attempt in this section has been to suggest that relations between African Americans and Latinos in American settings of high immigration can vary considerably across urban areas. I have specifically attempted to demonstrate that the conflictual character of African American–Latino relations in the Los Angeles area, as described by Johnson and his colleagues (this volume), differs significantly from conditions in the large Houston area. Across U.S. urban settings, intergroup histories, institutional conditions, and leadership initiatives may vary sufficiently to produce at least the potential for different intergroup responses to the changes effected by immigration. This is not to say that different localities have completely distinct intergroup trajectories. Major U.S. urban centers may have similar opportunity structures for intergroup relations (but not necessarily identical responses), since these areas are affected by common macrostructural processes—for example, globalization and international migration, which significantly affect the areas' institutional environments.

It is important to understand that opportunities for Latino intragroup relations also vary among U.S. urban areas. For example, some Mexican American political leaders in urban areas along the Texas-Mexico border initially rejected Central American immigrants, while Latinos in other cities of the Southwest participated in the sanctuary movement for these newcomers (Rodriguez and Urrutia-Rojas 1990). Cleavages also developed between Mexican-origin communities as English and Spanish monolingualism and different customs and lifestyles created social distances between the immigrant and U.S.-born generations. Differences of nationality (for example, Mexican versus Central American) exacerbated intragroup divisions in some cases.

Macrostructural Contexts of Immigration and African American–Latino Relations

In the late twentieth century, urban intergroup relations have been substantially affected by underlying structural processes whose reach transcends not only specific urban settings but the very nation-state itself. Three such processes—global economic restructuring, transnational community development, and immigrant incorporation—are as significant for the course of black-brown relations in Los Angeles, Houston, and other major U.S. cities as are social-psychological conditions that may predispose intergroup behavior.

Global Economic Change

A number of works have described processes of global economic restructuring affecting areas in core countries and peripheral regions of the world economy (see, for example, Henderson and Castells 1987). According to Saskia Sassen (1987), this worldwide economic change involves the recomposition of industrial capital, concentrating managerial and specialized services in major urban areas in core countries and relocating manufacturing in peripheral regions. This restructuring stimulates labor migration between peripheral regions as well as to new economic centers in core countries. Immigration becomes a major source of labor for the large array of low-wage service jobs that emerge in the global centers of business management and control in core countries and in a few semiperipheral areas as well.

Global restructuring significantly affects the intergroup prospects of large urban settings in the United States as shifts in capital and labor arrangements repel certain groups and attract others. For example, Sassen (1987) has demonstrated how the restructured economies of New York City, Los Angeles, and San Francisco have attracted immigrant labor from Latin America and Asia as middle-income blue- and white-collar U.S. workers have been laid off. The sociologist Rebecca Morales (1982) has conducted a detailed study of how the social composition of the Los Angeles automobile industry became increasingly immigrant and Mexican as industry owners and managers restructured production to operate with a lower-paid labor force.

Research in Houston has shown that, similar to the recomposition of production, the restructuring of consumption can greatly affect the social landscape and its intergroup relations. According to studies of Houston's vast apartment complex industry, when the world oil economy entered a steep recession in the mid-1980s, apartment real-estate capital on the city's middle-income West Side entered a severe crisis as thousands of office workers left the city after losing their jobs in oil- and petrochemical-related industries and in supportive firms. Facing the loss of billions of dollars invested in thousands of apartment complexes built mainly for young, single, middle-income tenants, apartment owners and managers adopted a temporary strategy of recomposing their shrinking middle-class and mainly Anglo tenant populations with newly arriving immigrants from Mexico and Central America. The city's West Side apartment industry underwent a dramatic restructuring as the names of many apartment complexes were changed from English to Spanish, trilingual rental agents were hired, and rents were reduced by half or more to attract immigrant renters. The strategy attracted large numbers of Latino immigrants, mostly low-income undocumented workers, into the predominantly white West Side districts of the city. As many apartment complexes on the West Side became increasingly identified as new low-cost housing, they also attracted large numbers of African Americans from the wards in the eastern half of the city (Rodriguez 1993).

To the distress of many middle-income established residents on the West Side, the recomposed tenant populations became heartlands of new communities of color as Mexicans, Central Americans, South Americans, Black-Caribs, African Americans, and other groups settled in the apartment complexes. The new apartment communities consisted heavily of working-class families. With the upswing in the area's economy in the late 1980s and 1990s, and with the expected return of middle-income tenants, apartment owners and managers again restructured their apartment complexes to reduce dramatically the presence of black and brown tenants (Rodriguez 1993). Living in fewer affordable apartments, African Americans and Latinos on the West Side nevertheless remain a major source of black-brown intergroup relations in the Houston area.

Transnational Community Development and Intergroup Relations

Macrostructural recomposition may bring different ethnic and racial groups into the same spatial setting, but it does not necessarily produce extensive intergroup relations initially. The Houston case showed that as large numbers of Latino newcomers settled in the city in the 1970s and 1980s, much of their social interaction was maintained with fellow immigrants in their residences and workplaces. Moreover, much of this ingroup interaction was directed to the development of transnational linkages to communities of origin in Mexico, Central America, and other Latin American countries. This led to the creation of transnational communities where family households underwent social reproduction through production and consumption activities in both the United States and the home country (Rodriguez 1995).

In the four large established Mexican barrios in Houston's eastern half, the development of transnational communities in the 1970s and 1980s was actually a historical continuation and dramatic enhancement of processes started by the city's original Mexican immigrants in the 1910s and 1920s (De León 1987). The inward social development of many new immigrants in the barrios initially only reinforced the social and cultural separation between Mexican-origin and African American communities in the city's eastern half. Later, however, as transnational communities prospered and expanded after the city's economic upturn, new Mexican immigrants began to settle in small numbers in the traditional black wards.

Adult African Americans and Latino immigrants mainly avoided interaction in the wards, but their children came together in nearby predominantly black public schools. In one ward setting, fights between black and brown students brought African American and Mexican American community leaders together to intervene.

Across the city, in the West Side apartment complex areas, new Latino immigrants have also constructed transnational structures linking their family households in Houston with their communities of origin back home (Rodriguez 1993). With the exception of casual encounters, Latino immigrants and African Americans usually live socially and culturally apart in the apartment complexes. Sharing a common settlement space, however, the two groups inevitably cross paths in the routine activities of community life. For example, in a large park in the city's southwest area, Latino and African American residents can be found engaged in recreational activities at the same time, but with African American youth on the basketball court and Latinos on the soccer fields. With the exception of a rugby team that uses a playing field a couple of times during the week, the white presence in the park consists mainly of law enforcement officers who occasionally patrol the grounds. Anglo residents in surrounding homes have almost completely stopped using the park, except on days of special community service fairs.

In addition to participating in public school programs that promote intergroup awareness, some African American and Latino residents on the West Side have a chance to learn about each other's cultures and concerns through occasional interethnic festivals organized by churches and other places of worship. In the last couple of years, social service providers in the city's southwest area have also promoted intergroup encounters through monthly luncheon meetings at which they explain their programs and exchange information. One function in the southwest area that draws large numbers of residents and agency representatives is an annual festival in the county park at which Anglos, African Americans, Latinos, and Asians set up booths to represent their organizations and sell different foods to raise funds for a local storefront police station.

The annual fund-raising festival is an exception to the general pattern of separate coexistence among the West Side's African Americans and large Latino immigrant populations. Over time, however, transnational communities are sure to lose some of their inward social tendencies as the U.S.-born children of immigrants look to the United States, not their parents' home countries, for social and cultural standards. First-generation Latino immigrants also will look increasingly toward the United States for future plans and community growth as they acquire greater social incorporation in this country.

Immigrant Incorporation and Intergroup Relations

Working-class immigrant populations have generally achieved initial incorporation into the U.S. social structure through endogenous institutions, including ethnic places of worship, traditional organizations, and culturally familiar neighborhoods. In Houston, as in other urban settings, many new immigrants undergo initial social, cultural, and spatial incorporation in ethnic communities and economic incorporation in mainstream settings (Rodriguez 1993). The latter involves service work in a wide variety of workplaces—restaurants, car washes, supermarkets, office buildings, and so forth—and usually in ethnic crews. Obviously the levels of incorporation (ethnic, mainstream, or interethnic) for the different dimensions (social, cultural, and so on) greatly affect the opportunity for black-brown intergroup interaction.

U.S.-born and immigrant Latinos who undergo social and cultural incorporation primarily through their own ethnic communities will probably have fewer opportunities to develop relations with African Americans, or with any other non-Latino group, outside of their workplaces. Especially for the adults in this socially and spatially concentrated population, the workplace becomes the primary setting of intergroup relations. Indeed, the 1995 CMAS survey found that most respondents identified their workplace as the primary setting of their intergroup relations (Rodriguez 1993). Yet Latino incorporation in ethnic communities does not completely restrict interaction with African Americans at the community level, since some lower-income black residents turn to Latino stores and restaurants in barrios for lower-priced goods and services. Here, class similarity overrides cultural differences.

Similar political perspectives also promote intergroup relations between African Americans and Latino immigrants. African Americans, including the Reverend Jesse Jackson, have participated in Latino immigrant marches and demonstrations against Proposition 187 and other restrictive measures. For example, African American NAACP leaders and unionists joined Latinos in a San Antonio march against Proposition 187 in the spring of 1995. African American women in Houston have traveled to Mexico as election observers and responded to a call for collective action by women after a group of armed men assaulted and raped the official U.S. representative of the Zapatista movement in Mexico (personal communication with Maria Jimenez of the American Friends Service Committee, Houston, November 28, 1995). These examples indicate that at least the civil rights and internationalist sectors in the African American population have supported the political incorporation of Latino immigrants, in the United States and abroad.

The macrostructural context of global restructuring, transnational community development, and immigrant incorporation set part of the stage for emerging intergroup relations, whether cooperative or conflictual, between African Americans and Latinos. Perhaps more than before the macrostructural perspective is important for analyzing the evolving relations between these two groups, since interaction and relations between global regions appear to have reached an unprecedented level in the late twentieth century.

Conclusion

In this chapter, I have compared intergroup relations between African Americans and Latinos in Houston with the description provided by Johnson, Farrell, and Guinn (this volume) for the Los Angeles area. My description of such relations in Houston contrasts with the description provided by Johnson and his colleagues for Los Angeles. I portray Houston as an area more accepting of immigrants and with fewer tensions between African Americans and Latinos. Why do the two cases differ? Part of the answer no doubt lies in the free market philosophy espoused by Houston's business elites and endorsed by many top leaders in the area's minority communities.

As described by the sociologist Joe R. Feagin (1988), a staunchly capitalist philosophy has been the credo of Houston's business elite members, and it includes the image of Houston as the "Free Enterprise City." This is an attitude that welcomes the economic risk-taker, and the immigrant worker seems to be included under this heading. Although individual members of the area's business elite may hold nativistic feelings against newcomers, these sentiments have never been promoted publicly by the private sector. Indeed, when a committee of the Greater Houston Partnership (the area's main growth machine) studied the question of undocumented immigration through invited presentations by government officials and immigration experts, the report of its findings and deliberations was kept from the public eye. In the summer of 1997 the Houston area's main newspaper, the conservative *Houston Chronicle*, endorsed the proposal of pro-immigrant advocates to declare the city a safety zone for immigrants in an attempt to protect undocumented immigrants from being reported to federal agents when seeking public services.

The free-enterprise attitudes of local business

elites reduce the chances for a wholesale scapegoating of immigrants, but there are other factors promoting accommodation between African Americans and Latinos in Houston as well. One factor is the availability of settlement areas. Unlike older industrial cities where newcomers were squeezed into residential areas with established residents, Houston's spacious area and overbuilt housing market offer room for groups to spread out into housing miles away from the city's downtown district, a spread facilitated by the absence of any zoning laws. Although Houston has less than half of Los Angeles' population, according to the 1990 census, it has a larger land area (U.S. Bureau of the Census 1995, table 46). A supply of apartment housing, overbuilt in the late 1970s and early 1980s, provides opportunities for many immigrant groups to settle into separate urban villages.

Also in contrast to the intergroup experiences of older large U.S. cities, incorporation for many of Houston's new Latino immigrants seems to exclude the political arena, reducing the chances for intergroup political conflict. Political machines and patronage played a central role in incorporating European immigrants into mainstream institutions in New York City, Chicago, and other older cities, but the same is not true in Houston. In the mid-1990s the most politically salient issues among Latino immigrants in the Houston area remained focused on political developments in Central America and Mexico. Yet this focus may change within a few years as greater numbers of immigrants become U.S. citizens to avoid losing benefits under federal laws adopted in 1996.

Black-brown intergroup relations in the United States are evolving from a complicated matrix in the late twentieth century that includes global, national, and local levels as well as varying predisposing social-psychological conditions. Yet intergroup relations between African Americans and native and foreign-born Latinos are not totally unpredictable. Black Americans are the most economically stressed group in U.S. society, and therefore it seems logical to hypothesize that the most disadvantaged members of this population, such as the unemployed and the working poor, will react against conditions they perceive to be not in their interests in an already precarious existence. What happened in Los Angeles in April 1992, I believe, is a dramatic example of such a reaction. But as happens in other minority populations, not all African Americans react to change from a racial group perspective; some react from a class or political perspective and form linkages with Latino political actors and social movements. It is difficult to predict black-brown relations, however, with accuracy beyond the contours of possible outcomes because so much about these relations is not structurally predetermined but is the outcome of human agency.

Any attempt to address the course of intergroup relations between African Americans and Latinos in the late twentieth century soon runs into the realization that few theoretical apparatuses are available to help channel the discourse. Race and ethnic relations theories developed in the 1960s and 1970s seem very outdated in explaining black-brown dynamics in today's globalized urban settings, which are dramatically different from two or three decades ago. Anglo-conformity models, for example, are as useless to explain inner-city intraminority relations as they are to explain the present-day appropriation of ethnic cultural content and forms by the white dominant group. Indeed, the very concept of the dominant group has become a variable in urban areas like Miami and the Los Angeles suburb of Monterey Park. Macrostructural perspectives of global capitalist development still lend conceptual power to theorizing about economic relations between groups in advanced Western societies, but they need to be more sensitive to the role of noneconomic identities in the development of intergroup relations in the late twentieth century.

References

Abbott, Edith. 1927. *Report of the Committee on Scientific Aspects of Human Migration, December 18, 1926.* Chicago: Social Science Research Council.

Abelmann, Nancy, and John Lie. 1995. *Blue Dreams: Korean Americans and the Los Angeles Riots.* Cambridge, Mass.: Harvard University Press.

Abramovitz, Moses. 1964. *Evidences of Long Swings in Aggregate Construction Since the Civil War.* New York: Columbia University Press/National Bureau of Economic Research.

———. 1993. "The Search for Sources of Growth: Areas of Ignorance, Old and New." *Journal of Economic History* 53(2): 217–43.

Abramovitz, Moses, and Paul A. David. 1973. "Reinterpreting Economic Growth: Parables and Realities." *American Economic Review* 63(2): 428–39.

———. 1996. "Convergence and Deferred Catch-up: Productivity Leadership and the Waning of American Exceptionalism." In *The Mosaic of Economic Growth,* edited by Ralph Landau, Timothy Taylor, and Gavin Wright. Stanford, Calif.: Stanford University Press.

Abramson, Harold. 1980. "Assimilation and Pluralism." In *Harvard Encyclopedia of American Ethnic Groups,* edited by Stephan Thernstrom, Ann Orlov, and Oscar Handlin (150–60). Cambridge, Mass.: Harvard University Press.

Ackerman, Sune. 1976. "Theories and Methods of Migration Research." In *From Sweden to America,* edited by Harald Runblom and Hans Norman (19–75). Minneapolis: University of Minnesota Press.

Adler, Jerry, and Steven. Waldman. 1995. "What Is an American?: Sweet Land of Liberties." *Newsweek,* July 10, 18.

Adorno, Theodor W. 1945. "A Social Critique of Radio Music." *Kenyon Review* 7(Spring): 208–17.

Adorno, Theodor W., with George Simpson. 1941. "On Popular Music." *Studies in Philosophy and Social Sciences* 9.

Afkhami, Mahnaz. 1994. *Women in Exile.* Charlottesville: University Press of Virginia.

Ahituv, Avner, Marta Tienda, Lixin Xu, and V. Joseph Hotz. 1994. "Initial Labor Market Experiences of Black, Hispanic, and White Men." In *1994 Proceedings of the Industrial Relations Research Association* (17–25). Madison: IRRA.

Akbari, Ather, and Don DeVoretz. 1992. "The Substitutability of Foreign-born Labour in Canadian Production: Circa 1980." *Canadian Journal of Economics* 15(August): 604–14.

Alarcón, Evelina. 1995. "Anti-immigrant Racism and the Fight for Unity." *Political Affairs* 74: 6–11.

Alarcón, Rafael. 1992. "Norteñización: Self-perpetuating Migration from a Mexican Town." In *U.S.-Mexico Relations: Labor Market Interdependence,* edited by Jorge Bustamante, Clark Reynolds, and Raul Hinojosa (302–18). Stanford, Calif.: Stanford University Press.

Alba, Richard D. 1985a. *Italian Americans: Into the Twilight of Ethnicity.* Englewood Cliffs, N.J.: Prentice-Hall.

———. 1985b. "The Twilight of Ethnicity Among Americans of European Ancestry: The Case of Italians." *Ethnic and Racial Studies* 8: 134–58.

———. 1988. "Cohorts and the Dynamics of Ethnic Change." In *Social Structures and Human Lives,* edited by Matilda White Riley, Bettina Huber, and Beth Hess. Newbury Park, Calif.: Sage.

———. 1990. *Ethnic Identity: The Transformation of White America.* New Haven, Conn.: Yale University Press.

———. 1995. "Assimilation's Quiet Tide." *Public Interest* 119(December): 1–18.

Alba, Richard D., and Reid M. Golden. 1986. "Patterns of Ethnic Marriage in the United States." *Social Forces* 65: 202–23.

Alba, Richard, and John Logan. 1991. "Variations on Two Themes: Racial and Ethnic Patterns in the Attainment of Suburban Residence." *Demography* 28: 431–53.

———. 1993. "Minority Proximity to Whites in Suburbs: An Individual-level Analysis of Segregation." *American Journal of Sociology* 98: 1388–1427.

Alba, Richard, John Logan, and Kyle Crowder. 1997. "White Ethnic Neighborhoods and Assimilation: The Greater New York Region, 1980–1990." *Social Forces* 75: 883–912.

Alba, Richard, John Logan, Gilbert Marzan, Brian Stults, and Wenquan Zhang. 1997. "Immigrant Groups and Suburbs: A Test of Spatial Assimilation Theory." State University of New York at Albany. Unpublished paper.

Alba, Richard, John Logan, and Brian Stults. 1997. "Making a Place in the Immigrant Metropolis: The Neighborhoods of Racial and Ethnic Groups, 1990." State University of New York at Albany. Unpublished paper.

Alba, Richard, and Victor Nee. 1995. "The Relevance of Assimilation for Post-1965 Immigrant Groups." Paper prepared for the SSRC Committee on International Migration (September).

———. 1997. "Rethinking Assimilation Theory for a New Era of Immigration." *International Migration Review* 31(4): 826–74.

Aldrich, Howard. 1975. "Ecological Succession in Racially Changing Neighborhoods: A Review of the Literature." *Urban Affairs Quarterly* 10: 327–48.

Aldrich, Howard, John Cater, Trevor Jones, David McEvoy, and Paul Velleman. 1985. "Ethnic Residential Concentration and the Protected Market Hypothesis." *Social Forces* 63: 996–1009.

Aldrich, Howard, and Albert J. Reiss, Jr. 1976. "Continuities in the Study of Ecological Succession: Changes in the Race Composition of Neighborhoods and Their Businesses." *American Journal of Sociology* 81: 846–66.

Aldrich, Howard, and Roger Waldinger. 1990. "Ethnicity and Entrepreneurship." *Annual Review of Sociology* 16: 111–35.

Aldrich, Howard, Catherine Zimmer, and David McEvoy. 1989. "Continuities in the Study of Ecological Succession: Asian Businesses in Three English Cities." *Social Forces* 67: 920–43.

Alexander, June Granatir. 1987. *The Immigrant Church and Community: Pittsburgh's Slovak Catholics and Lutherans, 1880–1915.* Pittsburgh: University of Pittsburgh Press.

Allen, James P. 1977. "Changes in the American Propensity to Migrate." *Annals of the Association of American Geographers* 67(4): 577–87.

Allen, Theodore W. 1994. *The Invention of the White Race,* vol. 1, *Racial Oppression and Social Control.* New York: Verso.

Almaguer, Tomas. 1994. *Racial Fault Lines: The Historical Origins of White Supremacy in California.* Berkeley: University of California Press.

Altonji, Joseph, and David Card. 1991. "The Effects of Immigration on the Labor Market Outcomes of Less-skilled Natives." In *Immigration, Trade and the Labor Market,* edited by John M. Abowd and Richard Freeman (201–34). Chicago: University of Chicago Press.

Amaro, Hortensia, R. Whitaker, J. Coffman, and T. Heeren. 1990. "Acculturation and Marijuana and Cocaine Use: Findings from HHANES 1982–84." *American Journal of Public Health* 80(supplement): 54–60.

Andersen, Kristi. 1979. *The Creation of a Democratic Majority, 1928–1936.* Chicago: University of Chicago Press.

Andersen, Kurt. 1983. "The New Ellis Island." *Time,* June 13, 18–25.

Anderson, Benedict. 1974. *Lineages of the Absolutist State.* London: New Left Books.

———. 1991. *Imagined Communities: Reflections on the Origins and Spread of Nationalism.* Rev. ed. London: Verso.

———. 1992. "The New World Disorder." *New Left Review* 193 (May-June): 2–13.

Anderson, Perry. 1974. *Lineages of the Absolutist State.* London: New Left Books.

Andreas, Peter. 1994. "Border Troubles: Free Trade, Immigration, and Cheap Labour." *The Ecologist* 24: 230–34.

Angel, Ronald, and Marta Tienda. 1982. "Determinants of Extended Household Structure: Cultural Pattern or Economic Need?" *American Journal of Sociology* 87: 1360–83.

Ansell, Christopher K., and Arthur L. Burns. 1997. "Bosses of the City Unite!: Labor Politics and Political Machine Consolidation, 1870–1910." *Studies in American Political Development* 11(1): 1–43.

Anzaldúa, Gloria. 1990. *Making Face, Making Soul/Haciendo Caras: Creative and Critical Perspectives by Women of Color.* San Francisco: Aunt Lute.

Appadurai, Arjun. 1990. "Disjuncture and Difference in the Global Economy." *Public Culture* 2(2): 1–24.

———. 1993. "Patriotism and Its Futures." *Public Culture* 5(3): 411–29.

———. 1996. "Sovereignty Without Territoriality: Notes for a Postnational Geography." In *The Geography of Identity,* edited by Patricia Yaeger (40–58). Ann Arbor: University of Michigan Press.

Archdeacon, Thomas J. 1983. *Becoming American: An Ethnic History.* New York: Free Press.

Arendt, Hannah. 1973. *The Origins of Totalitarianism.* New York: Harcourt Brace Jovanovich.

Aronson, Robert. 1991. *Self-employment: A Labor Market Approach.* Cornell Studies in Industrial and Labor Relations 24. Ithaca, N.Y.: ILR Press.

Atack, Jeremy, and Peter Passell. 1994. *A New Economic View of American History,* 2nd ed. New York: Norton.

Aubry, Larry. 1987. "The State of Los Angeles' Black-Korean Relations." *Los Angeles Sentinel,* March 26, 1.

Ayres, B. Drummond, Jr. 1995a. "California Immigration Law Is Ruled to Be Partly Illegal." *New York Times,* November 21, A10.

———. 1995b. "Conservatives Forge New Strategy to Challenge Affirmative Action." *New York Times,* February 16, A1.

Bach, Robert L. 1993. *Changing Relations: Newcomers and Established Residents in U.S. Communities.* New York: Ford Foundation.

Bach, Robert, and Lisa Schraml. 1982. "Migration, Crisis, and Theoretical Conflict." *International Migration Review* 16(2): 320–41.

Bailey, Eric. 1996. "Services Not Key for Latinas in U.S. Illegally, Study Shows." *Los Angeles Times,* August 25, B1–4.

Bailey, Thomas, and Roger Waldinger. 1991a. "Primary, Secondary, and Enclave Labor Markets: A Training System Approach." *American Sociological Review* 56: 432–45.

Bailey, Thomas, and Roger Waldinger. 1991b. "The Changing Ethnic/Racial Division of Labor." In *Dual City: The Restructuring of New York,* edited by John Mollenkopf and Manuel Castells (43–78). New York: Russell Sage Foundation.

Baines, Dudley. 1985. *Migration in a Mature Economy.* New York: Cambridge University Press.

———. 1991. *Emigration from Europe, 1815–1930.* New York: Cambridge University Press.

Baker, Susan G. 1997. "The 'Amnesty' Aftermath: Current Policy Issues Stemming from the Legislation Progress of the 1986 Immigration Reform and Control Act." *International Migration Review* 30: 5–27.

Baldwin, James. 1985. *The Price of the Ticket*. New York: Basic Books.

Balke, Nathan S., and Robert J. Gordon. 1986. "Historical Data." In *The American Business Cycle: Continuity and Change*, edited by Robert J. Gordon. Chicago: University of Chicago Press/National Bureau of Economic Research.

Balkin, Steve. 1989. *Self-employment for Low-income People*. New York: Praeger.

Baltzell, E. Digby. 1964. *The Protestant Establishment: Aristocracy and Caste in America*. New York: Vintage Books.

Banfield, Edward C., and James Q. Wilson. 1963. *City Politics*. Cambridge, Mass.: Harvard University Press.

Banks, S. 1985. "Korean Merchants, Black Customers—Tensions Grow." *Los Angeles Sentinel*, April 15.

Baran, Paul A. 1957. *The Political Economy of Growth*. Berkeley: University of California Press.

———. 1973. "On the Political Economy of Backwardness." In *The Political Economy of Development and Underdevelopment*, edited by K. Wilber (82–93). New York: Random House.

Barber, Benjamin. 1984. *Strong Democracy*. Berkeley: University of California Press.

Barde, Robert, Susan B. Carter, and Richard Sutch. 1997. "Statistics on International Migrations for the Millennial Edition of *Historical Statistics of the United States*." Paper presented at the Conference on Historical Statistics on Labor, Human Capital, and Labor Markets: A First Look, Stanford, Calif. (1996).

Barkan, Elliot A. 1995. "Race, Religion, and Nationality in American Society: A Model of Ethnicity—from Contact to Assimilation." *Journal of American Ethnic History* 14(2, Winter): 38–101.

Barnes, J. A. 1954. "Class and Committees in the Norwegian Island Parish." *Human Relations* 7: 39–58.

———. 1969. "Networks and Political Process." In *Social Networks in Urban Situations*, edited by J. Clyde Mitchell (51–76). Manchester: Manchester University Press.

Barrera, Mario. 1979. *Race and Class in the Southwest*. Notre Dame, Ind.: University of Notre Dame Press.

Barrett, James R. 1992. "Americanization from the Bottom Up: Immigration and the Remaking of the Working Class in the United States, 1880–1930." *Journal of American History* 79(December): 996–1020.

Barrett, James R., and David Roediger. 1997. "Inbetween Peoples: Race, Nationality, and the 'New Immigrant' Working Class." *Journal of American Ethnic History* 16(Spring): 3–44.

Barringer, Herbert, Robert W. Gardner, and Michael Levin. 1993. *Asians and Pacific Islanders in the United States*. New York: Russell Sage Foundation.

Barro, Robert, and Xavier Sala-i-Martin. 1992. "Regional Growth and Migration: A Japan-United States Comparison." *Journal of the International and Japanese Economies* 6: 312–46.

Barry, Brian, and Robert E. Goodin, eds. 1992. *Free Movement*. University Park: Pennsylvania State University Press.

Bartel, Ann. 1989. "Where Do the New U.S. Immigrants Live?" *Journal of Labor Economics* 7: 371–91.

Barth, Ernest A., and D. L. Noel. 1972. "Conceptual Framework for the Analysis of Race Relations: An Evaluation." *Social Forces* 50: 333–48.

Barth, Frederick. 1956. "Ecologic Relationships of Ethnic Groups in Swat, North Pakistan." *American Anthropologist* 58: 1079–89.

———, ed. 1969. *Ethnic Groups and Boundaries*. Boston: Little, Brown.

Basch, Linda G., Nina Glick Schiller, and Cristina Blanc-Szanton. 1994. *Nations Unbound: Transnational Projects, Postcolonial Predicaments, and Deterritorialized Nation-states*. Langhorne, Penn.: Gordon and Breach.

Bates, Timothy. 1987. "Self-employed Minorities: Traits and Trends." *Social Science Quarterly* 68: 539–51.

———. 1989. "Small-Business Viability in the Urban Ghetto." *Journal of Regional Science* 29: 625–43.

———. 1992. *Banking on Black Enterprise: The Potential of Emerging Firms for Revitalizing Urban Economies*. Washington: Joint Center for Political and Economic Studies.

Baubock, Rainer. 1995. *Transnational Citizenship: Membership and Rights in International Migration*. Brookfield, Vt.: E. Elgar.

Baubock, Rainer, and John Rundell, eds. 1998. *Blurred Boundaries: Migration, Ethnicity, Citizenship*. Aldershot, England: Ashgage Publishing Limited.

Bean, Frank, Ruth Berg, and Jennifer V. W. Van Hook. 1996. "Socioeconomic and Cultural Incorporation Among Mexican Americans." *Social Forces* 75(2): 593–618.

Bean, Frank, Barry Edmonston, and Jeffrey Passel, eds. 1990. *Undocumented Migration to the United States: IRCA and the Experience of the 1980s*. Washington: Urban Institute.

Bean, Frank, and Marta Tienda. 1987. *The Hispanic Population in the United States*. New York: Russell Sage Foundation Monograph Series.

Becerra, J. E., C. Hogue, H. K. Atrash, and N. Pérez. 1991. "Infant Mortality Among Hispanics: A Portrait of Heterogeneity." *Journal of the American Medical Association* 265(2): 217–21.

Beck, Ulrich. 1997. *The Reinvention of Politics: Rethinking Modernity in the Global Social Order*, translated by Mark Ritter. Cambridge: Polity Press.

Becker, Howard S. 1963. *Outsiders: Studies in the Sociology of Deviance*. New York: Free Press.

Begley, Sharon. 1995. "Three Is Not Enough." *Newsweek*, February 13, 67–69.

Bell, Daniel. 1988. *The End of Ideology: On the Exhaustion of Political Ideas in the Fifties*. Cambridge, Mass.: Harvard University Press. (Originally published in 1960)

Bellah, Robert, and others. 1985. *Habits of the Heart:*

Individualism and Commitment in American Life. Berkeley: University of California Press.

Belluck, Pam. 1995. "Healthy Korean Economy Draws Immigrants Home." *New York Times,* August 22, A1, B4.

Bennett, David H. 1988. *The Party of Fear: From Nativist Movements to the New Right in American History.* Chapel Hill: University of North Carolina Press.

Berger, John, and Jean Mohr. 1975. *A Seventh Man: The Story of a Migrant Worker in Europe.* Harmondsworth: Penguin Books.

Bernard, William. 1982. "A History of U.S. Immigration Policies." In Richard A. Easterlin and others, *Immigration: Dimensions of Ethnicity: A Series of Selections from the Harvard Encyclopedia of American Ethnic Groups,* edited by Stephan Thernstrom (75–105). Cambridge, Mass.: Belknap Press of Harvard University Press.

Berquist, James. 1984. "German Communities in American Cities: An Interpretation of the Nineteenth-Century Experience." *Journal of American Ethnic History* 4(Fall): 9–30.

Berrol, Selma C. 1995. *Growing up American: Immigrant Children in America, Then and Now.* New York: Twayne.

Berry, Brewton, and Henry Tischler. 1978. *Race and Ethnic Relations.* Boston: Houghton Mifflin.

Bhabha, Homi. 1994. *The Location of Culture.* London: Routledge.

Bhagwati, Jagdish N. 1984. "Incentives and Disincentives: International Migration." *Weltwirtschaftliches Archiv* 120(4): 678–701.

Bialystok, Ellen, and Kenji Hakuta. 1994. *In Other Words: The Science and Psychology of Second-Language Acquisition.* New York: Basic Books.

Bills, Garland. 1989. "The U.S. Census of 1980 and Spanish in the Southwest." *International Journal of the Sociology of Language* 79: 11–27.

Birch, David L. 1987. *Job Creation in America: How Our Smallest Companies Put Most People to Work.* New York: Free Press.

Blackburn, McKinley L., David E. Bloom, and Richard B. Freeman. 1990. "The Declining Economic Position of Less-skilled American Men." In *A Future of Lousy Jobs?,* edited by Gary Burtless. Washington: Brookings Institution.

Blanchard, Olivier, and Lawrence Katz. 1992. "Regional Evolutions." *Brookings Papers on Economic Activity* 1: 1–61.

Blaschke, Jochen, Jeremy Boissevain, Hanneke Grotenbreg, Isaac Joseph, Mirjana Morokvasic, and Robin Ward. 1990. "European Trends in Ethnic Business." In *Ethnic Entrepreneurs: Immigrant Business in Industrial Societies,* edited by Roger Waldinger, Howard Aldrich, and Robin Ward (79–105). Newbury Park, Calif.: Sage.

Blau, Francine. 1984. "The Use of Transfer Payments by Immigrants." *Industrial and Labor Relations Review* 37: 222–39.

Blau, Peter, and Otis D. Duncan. 1967. *The American Occupational Structure.* New York: Wiley.

Blumer, Herbert. 1965. "Industrialization and Race Relations." In *Industrialization and Race Relations: A Symposium,* edited by Guy Hunter (220–53). London: Oxford University Press.

Bobo, Lawrence D., Camille L. Zubrinksy, James H. Johnson, Jr., and Melvin L. Oliver. 1995a. "Public Opinion Before and After the Spring of Discontent." In *The Los Angeles Riots: Lessons for the Urban Future,* edited by Mark Baldassare (103–33). Boulder, Colo.: Westview.

———. 1995b. "Work Orientation, Job Discrimination, and Ethnicity: A Focus Group Perspective." In *Research in the Sociology of Work,* vol. 5, *The Meaning of Work,* edited by Richard L. Simpson and Ida H. Simpson (45–86). Greenwich, Conn.: JAI Press.

Bodnar, John E. 1982. *Workers' World: Kinship, Community, and Protest in an Industrial Society.* Baltimore.

———. 1985. *The Transplanted: A History of Immigrants in Urban America.* Bloomington: Indiana University Press.

———. 1992. *Remaking America: Public Memory, Commemoration, and Patriotism in the Twentieth Century.* Princeton, N.J.

———, ed. 1996. *Bonds of Affection: Americans Define Their Patriotism.* Princeton, N.J.

Bodnar, John, Michael Weber, and Roger Simon. 1982. *Lives of Their Own: Blacks, Italians, and Poles in Pittsburgh, 1900–1960.* Urbana: University of Illinois Press.

Body-Gentrot, Sophie. 1995. "Models of Immigrant Integration in France and the United States." In *The Bubbling Cauldron: Race, Ethnicity, and the Urban Crisis,* edited by Michael Peter Smith and Joe Feagin (244–62). Minneapolis: University of Minnesota Press.

Böhning, Wolf. R. 1972. *The Migration of Workers in the United Kingdom and the European Community.* Oxford: Oxford University Press.

———. 1984. *Studies in International Labour Migration.* New York: St. Martin's Press.

Boissevain, Jeremy, Jochen Blaschke, Hanneke Grotenbreg, Isaac Joseph, Ivan Light, Marlene Sway, Roger Waldinger, and Pnina Werbner. 1990. "Ethnic Entrepreneurs and Ethnic Strategies." In *Ethnic Entrepreneurs: Immigrant Business in Industrial Societies,* edited by Roger Waldinger, Howard Aldrich, and Robin Ward (131–56). Newbury Park, Calif.: Sage.

Bonacich, Edna. 1972. "A Theory of Ethnic Antagonism: The Split Labor Market." *American Sociological Review* 37(5): 547–59.

———. 1973. "A Theory of Middleman Minorities." *American Sociological Review* 38: 583–94.

Bonacich, Edna, and John Modell. 1980. *The Economic Basis of Ethnic Solidarity: Small Business in the Japanese American Community.* Berkeley: University of California Press.

Boris, Eileen. 1995. "The Racialized Gendered State: Constructions of Citizenship in the United States." *Social Politics* 2(Summer): 160–80.

Borjas, George J. 1983. "The Substitutability of Black, Hispanic, and White Labor." *Economic Inquiry* 21: 93–106.

———. 1984. "The Impact of Immigrants on the Earnings of Native-born." In *Immigration: Issues and Policies,* edited by Vernon M. Briggs, Jr., and Marta Tienda (83–126). Salt Lake City: Olympus.

———. 1985. "Assimilation, Changes in Cohort Quality, and the Earnings of Immigrants." *Journal of Labor Economics* 3: 463–89.

———. 1986. "The Self-employment Experience of Immigrants." *Journal of Human Resources* 21(4): 485–506.

———. 1987a. "Self-selection and the Earnings of Immigrants." *American Economic Review* 77: 531–53.

———. 1987b. "Immigrants, Minorities, and Labor Market Competition." *Industrial and Labor Relations Review* 40(3, April): 382–92.

———. 1989. "Economic Theory and International Migration." *International Migration Review* 23: 457–85.

———. 1990. *Friends or Strangers: The Impact of Immigration on the U.S. Economy.* New York: Basic Books.

———. 1994a. "The Economics of Immigration." *Journal of Economic Literature* 32(4): 1667–1717.

———. 1994b. "Long-run Convergence of Ethnic Skill Differentials: The Children and Grandchildren of the Great Migration." *Industrial and Labor Relations Review* 47(4): 553–73.

———. 1995. "The Economic Benefits of Immigration." *Journal of Economic Perspectives* 9(2): 3–22.

———. 1996. "The New Economics of Immigration: Affluent Americans Gain; Poor Americans Lose." *Atlantic Monthly* 278(5): 72–80.

Borjas, George J., and Stephen G. Bronars. 1989. "Consumer Discrimination and Self-employment." *Journal of Political Economy* 97(3): 581–605.

Borjas, George, Stephen Bronars, and Stephen Trejo. 1992. "Self-selection and Internal Migration in the United States." *Journal of Urban Economics* 32: 159–85.

Borjas, George, and Richard Freeman. 1992. "Introduction and Summary." In *Immigration and the Workforce: Economic Consequences for the United States and Source Areas,* edited by George Borjas and Richard Freeman (1–15). Chicago: University of Chicago Press.

Borjas, George, Richard Freeman, and Lawrence Katz. 1992. "On the Labor Market Effects of Immigration and Trade." In *Immigration and the Workforce: Economic Consequences for the United States and Source Areas,* edited by George Borjas and Richard Freeman (213–44). Chicago: University of Chicago Press.

———. 1997. "How Much Do Immigration and Trade Affect Labor Market Outcomes?" William C. Brainard and George L. Perry, editors. *Brookings Papers on Economic Activity* 1: 1–67.

Borjas, George J., and Lynette Hilton. 1996. "Immigration and the Welfare State: Immigrant Participation in Means-tested Entitlement Programs." *Quarterly Journal of Economics* 111(2, May): 575–604.

Borjas, George, and Valerie Ramey. 1995. "Foreign Competition, Market Power, and Wage Inequality: Theory and Evidence." *Quarterly Journal of Economics* (November): 1075–1111.

Borjas, George J., and Marta Tienda, eds. 1985. *Hispanics in the U.S. Economy.* Orlando, Fla.: Academic Press.

———. 1987. "The Economic Consequences of Immigration." *Science,* February 6, 645–51.

———. 1993. "The Employment and Wages of Legalized Immigrants." *International Migration Review* 27(4): 712–47.

Borenstein, Seth, and William Gibson. 1994. "The State: Florida Helping to Drive Federal Policies. *Son-Sentinel,* October 30, 1994, p. 35.

Boruchoff, Judith. 1992. "Making Sense of Transnational Migration: Theorizing and Experiencing Life in Mexico/Chicago." Paper presented at the ninety-first annual meeting of the American Anthropological Association, Chicago (November 1992).

Boserup, Ester. 1970. *Women's Role in Economic Production.* New York: St. Martin's Press.

Bourdieu, Pierre. 1986. "The Forms of Capital." In *Handbook of Theory and Research for the Sociology of Education,* edited by John G. Richardson (241–58). New York: Greenwood.

Bourdieu, Pierre, and Loic Wacquant. 1992. *An Invitation to Reflexive Sociology.* Chicago: University of Chicago Press.

Bourgois, Philippe. 1991. "In Search of Respect: The New Service Economy and the Crack Alternative in Spanish Harlem." Paper presented at the Conferences on Poverty, Immigration, and Urban Marginality in Advanced Societies, Paris (May 10–11).

Bourne, Randolph S. 1916. "Trans-National America." *Atlantic Monthly* 118: 86–97.

———. 1977. *The Radical Will: Selected Writings, 1911–1918.* New York: Urizen Books.

Bouvier, Leon F. 1992. *Peaceful Invasions: Immigration and Changing America.* Lanham, Md.: University Press of America.

Bowermaster, David. 1995. "Closing the Golden Door: The Immigration Battle." *U.S. News & World Report,* September 25, 42.

Boyd, Monica. 1989. "Family and Personal Networks in International Migration: Recent Developments and New Agendas." *International Migration Review* 23(3): 638–70.

Brandes, Stanley. 1975. *Migration, Kinship, and Community: Tradition and Transition in a Spanish Village.* New York: Academic Press.

Braudel, Fernand. 1981. *The Structures of Everyday Life: Civilization and Capitalism, Fifteenth-Eighteenth Century.* Vol. 1. New York: Harper & Row.

———. 1982. *The Wheels of Commerce: Civilization and Capitalism, Fifteenth-Eighteenth Century.* Vol. 2. New York: Harper & Row.

Braun, Juan. 1992. "Migration and Economic Growth." Working Paper. Harvard University, Department of Economics.

Bremner, Robert H., John Barnard, Tamara K. Haraven, and Robert Mennel, eds. 1974. *Children and Youth in America: A Documentary History.* Cambridge, Mass.: Harvard University Press.

Brenner, Elsa. 1995. "Census Study Sees Ethnic Shifts." *New York Times,* August 6, 1.

Breton, Raymond. 1964. "Institutional Completeness of Ethnic Communities and the Personal Relations of Immigrants." *American Journal of Sociology* 70: 193–205.

Brettell, Caroline. 1979. "Emigrar Para Voltar: A Portuguese Ideology of Return Migration." *Papers in Anthropology* 20: 21–38.

Brettell, Caroline, and Patricia DeBerjeois. 1992. "Anthropology and the Study of Immigrant Women." In *Seeking Common Ground: Multidisciplinary Studies of Immigrant Women in the United States,* edited by Donna Gabaccia (41–63). Westport, Conn.: Greenwood.

Brezis, Elise, and Paul Krugman. 1996. "Immigration, Investment, and Real Wages." *Journal of Population Economics* 9(1, February): 83–93.

Briggs, Vernon. 1995. "Immigration Policy Sends Blacks Back to the South." *The Social Contract* 5: 270–71.

Brimelow, Peter. 1995. *Alien Nation: Common Sense About America's Immigration Disaster.* New York: Random House.

Brochmann, Grete. 1996. *European Integration and Immigration from Third Countries.* Oslo: Scandinavian University Press.

Brody, David. 1980. *Workers in Industrial America: Essays on the Twentieth-Century Struggle.* New York: Oxford University Press.

Broun, Heywood, and George Britt. 1931. *Christians Only: A Study in Prejudice by Heywood Broun.* New York: Vanguard Press.

Brownstein, Ronald. 1995. "Washington Outlook: Affirmative Action, Immigration: Wedge Issues That Need Not Divide." *Los Angeles Times,* February 27, 5A.

Brubaker, Rogers. 1992. *Citizenship and Nationhood in France and Germany.* Cambridge, Mass.: Harvard University Press.

———. 1995. "Comment on 'Modes of Immigration Politics in Liberal Democratic States.'" *International Migration Review* 29(4, Winter): 903–6.

Bryce-Laporte, Roy, ed. 1972. "Black Immigrants: The Experience of Invisibility and Inequality." *Journal of Black Studies* 3: 29–56.

———. 1980. *Sourcebook on the New Immigrants.* New Brunswick, N.J.: Transaction Books.

Buijs, Gina. 1993. *Migrant Women.* Oxford: Berg.

Bukowczyk, John J. 1984. "The Transformation of Working-Class Ethnicity: Corporate Control, Americanization, and the Polish Immigrant Middle Class in Bayonne, New Jersey, 1915–1925." *Labor History* 25(Winter): 53–82.

Burawoy, Michael. 1976. "The Functions and Reproduction of Migrant Labor: Comparative Material from Southern Africa and the United States." *American Journal of Sociology* 81(March): 1050–87.

Burgess, Ernest. 1925. "The Growth of the City: An Introduction to a Research Project." In *The City,* edited by Robert Park, Ernest Burgess, and Roderick McKenzie (47–62). Chicago: University of Chicago Press.

Burner, David. 1968. *The Politics of Provincialism: The Democratic Party in Transition, 1918–1932.* New York: Knopf.

Burnham, Walter Dean, ed. 1982a. *The Current Crisis in American Politics.* New York: Oxford University Press.

———. 1982b. "The Changing Shape of the American Political Universe." In *The Current Crisis in American Politics,* edited by Walter Dean Burnham (25–57). New York: Oxford University Press.

———. 1987. "The Turnout Problem." In *Elections American Style,* edited by A. James Reichley (112–15). Washington: Brookings Institution.

Burns, Arthur F. 1935. "Long Cycles in Residential Building." *Economic Essays in Honor of Wesley Clair Mitchell.* New York: Columbia University Press.

Burtless, Gary. 1990. "Introduction and Summary." In *A Future of Lousy Jobs?,* edited by Gary Burtless (1–30). Washington: Brookings Institution.

Butcher, Kristin F., and David Card. 1991. "Immigration and Wages: Evidence from the 1980s." *American Economic Review* 81: 292–96.

Butcher, Kristin F., and Anne Morrison Piehl. 1997. "Recent Immigrants: Unexpected Implications for Crime and Incarceration." Working Paper 6067. Cambridge, Mass.: National Bureau of Economic Research.

Butler, John, and Cedric Herring. 1991. "Ethnicity and Entrepreneurship in America: Toward an Explanation of Racial and Ethnic Group Variations in Self-employment." *Sociological Perspectives* 34: 79–94.

Cabral, H., L. E. Fried, S. Levenson, Hortensia Amaro, and Barry Zuckerman. 1990. "Foreign-born and U.S.-born Black Women: Differences in Health Behaviors and Birth Outcomes." *American Journal of Public Health* 80(1): 70–72.

Cain, Louis P., and Donald G. Paterson. 1986. "Biased Technical Change, Scale, and Factor Substitution in American Industry." *Journal of Economic History* 46(1): 153–64.

Cairncross, A. K. 1953. *Home and Foreign Investment 1870–1913.* New York: Cambridge University Press.

Calavita, Kitty. 1992. *Inside the State: The Bracero Program, Immigration, and the INS.* New York: Routledge.

———. 1996. "The New Politics of Immigration: 'Balanced Budget Conservatism' and the Symbolism of Prop. 187." *Social Problems* 43(3, August): 284–305.

Calhoun, Craig. 1997. *Nationalism.* Minneapolis: University of Minnesota Press.

Camilleri, Joseph, and Jim Falk. 1992. *The End of Sovereignty?: The Politics of a Shrinking and Fragmented World.* Aldershot: Edward Elgar.

Canny, Nicholas. 1994. *Europeans on the Move: Studies on European Migration, 1500–1800.* Oxford: Clarendon.

Caplan, Nathan, John K. Whitmore, and Marcella H. Choy. 1989. *The Boat People and Achievement in America: A Study of Family Life, Hard Work, and Cultural Values.* Ann Arbor: University of Michigan Press.

———. 1991. *Children of the Boat People: A Study of Educational Success.* Ann Arbor: University of Michigan Press.

Card, David. 1990. "The Impact of the Mariel Boatlift on the Miami Labor Market." *Industrial and Labor Relations Review* 43(2): 245–57.

———. 1996. "Economic Effects of Immigration: Past and Present." In *Immigration, Economy, and Policy in America.* Annandale-on-Hudson, N.Y.: Levy Institute.

———. 1997. "Immigrant Inflows, Native Outflows, and the Local Labor Market Effects of Higher Immigration." Working Paper 5927. Cambridge, Mass.: National Bureau of Economic Research.

Cardoso, Fernando H., and Enzo Faletto. 1969. *Dependencia y desarrollo en América Latina.* México City: Siglo XXI.

———. 1979. *Dependency and Development in Latin America.* Berkeley: University of California Press.

Carens, Joseph H. 1987. "Aliens and Citizens: The Case for Open Borders." *Review of Politics* 49(2, Spring): 251–73.

———. 1995. "Aliens and Citizens: The Case for Open Borders." In *The Rights of Minority Cultures,* edited by Will Kymlicka (331–49). New York: Oxford University Press.

Carlson, Robert A. 1975. *The Quest for Conformity: Americanization Through Education.* New York.

Carney, D. 1996. "Law Restricts Illegal Immigration." *Congressional Quarterly,* November 16, 3287–89.

Carpenter, Niles. 1927. *Immigrants and Their Children, 1920.* Census Monographs, vol. 7. Washington: U.S. Bureau of the Census.

Carrington, William, and Pedro deLima. 1996. "Large-scale Immigration and Labor Markets: An Analysis of the *Retornados* and Their Impact on Portugal." *Industrial and Labor Relations Review* (January): 330–47.

Carter, Susan B., Roger L. Ransom, and Richard Sutch. 1991. "The Historical Labor Statistics Project at the University of California." *Historical Methods* 24(2): 52–65.

Carter, Susan B., and Richard Sutch. 1992a. "The Great Depression of the 1890s: New Suggestive Estimates of the Unemployment Rate, 1890–1905." *Research in Economic History* 14: 347–76.

———. 1992b. "Self-employment in the Age of Big Business: Disguised Unemployment, Hidden Retirement, and the Decline of an American Labor Market Institution." Working Papers on the History of Retirement 7. History of Retirement Project, University of California at Berkeley (June).

———. 1996. "Myth of the Industrial Scrap Heap: A Revisionist View of Turn-of-the-Century American Retirement." *Journal of Economic History* 56(1): 5–38.

Castells, Manuel. 1989. *The Informational City: Information Technology, Economic Restructuring, and the Urban-Regional Process.* Oxford: Basil Blackwell.

———. 1997. *The Information Age: Economy, Society, and Culture.* 3 vols. Cambridge, Mass.: Blackwell.

Castells, Manuel, and Alejandro Portes. 1989. "World Underneath: The Origins, Dynamics, and Effects of the Informal Economy." In *The Informal Economy,* edited by Alejandro Portes, Manuel Castells, and Lauren Benton (11–37). Baltimore: Johns Hopkins University Press.

Castles, Stephen, and Godula Kossack. 1985. *Immigrant Workers and Class Structure in Western Europe.* 2nd ed. London: Oxford University Press.

Castles, Stephen, and Mark J. Miller. 1998. *The Age of Migration.* 2nd ed. New York: Guilford.

Castro, Mary García. 1986. "Work Versus Life: Colombian Women in New York." In *Women and Change in Latin America,* edited by June Nash and Helen Safa (231–55). South Hadley, Mass.: Bergin and Garvey.

Cattan, Peter. 1993. "The Diversity of Hispanics in the U.S. Work Force." *Monthly Labor Review* 116(8): 3–15.

Center for Immigration Studies. 1994. "Immigration and the Labor Market." Paper 9. Washington, D.C.: Center for Immigration Studies (November 1).

———. 1995. "Immigration-Related Statistics: 1995." *Backgrounder* 2–95(July).

———. 1997a. "Immigration Reform and Welfare: The Devil Is in the Details." *Immigration Review* 28: 13.

———. 1997b. "Five Million Illegal Immigrants: An Analysis of New INS Numbers." *Immigration Review* 28: 1–4.

Chai, Alice Yun. 1987. "Freed from the Elders but Locked into Labor: Korean Immigrant Women in Hawaii." *Women's Studies* 13(3): 223–33.

Chan, Sucheng. 1990. "European and Asian Immigration into the United States in Comparative Perspective, 1820s to 1920s." In *Immigration Reconsidered: History, Sociology, and Politics,* edited by Virginia Yans-McLaughlin (37–75). New York: Oxford University Press.

———. 1991. "The Exclusion of Chinese Women." In *Entry Denied: Exclusion and the Chinese Community in America, 1882–1943,* edited by Sucheng Chan. Philadelphia: Temple University Press.

———. 1994. *Hmong Means Free.* Philadelphia: Temple University Press.

Chang, E. T. 1988. "Korean-Black Conflict in Los Angeles: Perceptions and Realities." Paper presented at the Annual Regional Seminar on Koreans, University of California at Berkeley (April 29).

Charles, Carolle. 1990a. "A Transnational Dialectic of Race, Class, and Ethnicity: Patterns of Identity and Forms of Consciousness Among Haitian Migrants in New York City." Ph.D. diss., State University of New York at Binghamton.

———. 1990b. "Distinct Meanings of Blackness: Patterns of Identity Among Haitian Migrants in New York City." *Cimarron* 2(3): 129–38.

———. 1992. "Transnationalism in the Construct of Haitian Migrants' Racial Categories of Identity in New York City." In *Towards a Transnational Perspective on Migration,* edited by Nina Glick Schiller, Linda Basch, and Cristina Blanc-Szanton. New York: New York Academy of Sciences.

Charles, Nick. 1995. "Closing the Door." *Emerge* (July-August): 34–39.

Chavez, Leo. 1991. "Outside the Imagined Community: Undocumented Settlers and Experiences of Incorporation." *American Ethnologist* 18(2): 257–78.

———. "Nativism and Immigration Reform." Paper prepared for American Becoming/Becoming American: International Migration to the United States Conference. Social Science Research Council, Sanibel Island, Florida (January 18–21, 1996).

———. 1998. *Shadowed Lives.* New York: Harcourt Brace.

Chavira, Alicia. 1988. "Tienes que ser valiente: Mexican Migrants in a Midwestern Farm Labor Camp." In *Mexicans at Work in the United States,* edited by Margarita Melville (64–73). Mexican American Studies Monograph 5. Houston: University of Houston Press.

Chayanov, Alexander V. 1966. *Theory of Peasant Economy.* Homewood, Ill.: Richard D. Irwin.

Chenery, Hollis B. 1960. "Patterns of Industrial Growth." *American Economic Review* 50(4): 624–54.

Chicago Tribune. 1996. "Mixed Race Americans Feel Boxed in by Forms." February 14, 8.

Child, Clifton J. 1939. *The German American Presence in Politics 1914–1917.* Madison: University of Wisconsin Press.

Child, Irvin L. 1943. *Italian or American?: The Second Generation in Conflict.* New Haven, Conn.: Yale University Press.

Chiswick, Barry R. 1977. "Sons of Immigrants: Are They at an Earnings Disadvantage?" *American Economic Review* 67(February): 376–80.

———. 1978a. "The Effect of Americanization on the Earnings of Foreign-born Men." *Journal of Political Economy* 86: 897–921.

———. 1978b. "A Longitudinal Analysis of the Occupational Mobility of Immigrants." In *Proceedings of the Thirtieth Annual Winter Meetings, Industrial Relations Research Association,* edited by Barbara Dennis. Madison: IRRA.

———. 1979. "The Economic Progress of Immigrants: Some Apparently Universal Patterns." In *Contemporary Economic Problems,* edited by William Fellner (357–99). Washington: American Enterprise Institute.

———. 1986. "Is the New Immigration Less Skilled Than the Old?" *Journal of Labor Economics* 4: 168–92.

Chiswick, Barry, Carmel Chiswick, and Paul Miller. 1985. "Are Immigrants and Natives Perfect Substitutes in Production?" *International Migration Review* 19(4): 674–85.

Chiswick, Barry, and Teresa Sullivan. 1995. "The New Immigrants." In *State of the Union: America in the 1990s,* edited by Reynolds Farley (vol. 2, 211–70). New York: Russell Sage Foundation.

Cho, Sumi K. 1993. "Korean Americans Versus African Americans: Conflict and Construction." In *Reading Rodney King/Reading Urban Uprising,* edited by Robert Gooding-Williams (196–211). New York: Routledge.

Choldin, Harvey M. 1973. "Kinship Networks in the Migration Process." *International Migration Review* 7: 163–76.

———. 1986. "Statistics and Politics: The 'Hispanic Issue' in the 1980 Census." *Demography* 23: 403–18.

Christiansen, Drew. 1996. "Movement, Asylum, Borders: Christian Perspectives." *International Migration Review* 30: 7–17.

Cinel, Dino. 1982. *From Italy to San Francisco.* Stanford, Calif.: Stanford University Press.

———. 1991. *The National Integration of Italian Return Migration, 1870–1929.* Cambridge: Cambridge University Press.

City University of New York. 1994. *Immigration/Migration and the CUNY Student of the Future.* New York: CUNY.

Clark, Rebecca L., Jeffrey Passel, Wendy Zimmerman, and Michael Fix. 1994. *Fiscal Impacts of Undocumented Aliens: Selected Estimates for Seven States.* Report to the Office of Management and Budget and the Department of Justice. Washington: Urban Institute.

Cleaver, James H. 1983a. "Asian Businesses in Black Community Cause Stir." *Los Angeles Sentinel,* August 18, 1.

———. 1983b. "Asian Attitudes Toward Blacks Cause Raised Eyebrows." *Los Angeles Sentinel,* August 18, 1.

———. 1983c. "Residents Complain About Alleged Asian 'Problem.'" *Los Angeles Sentinel,* August 25, 1.

———. 1983d. "Citizens Air Gripes About Asians." *Los Angeles Sentinel,* September 1, 1.

———. 1987. "One Answer to an Outcry." *Los Angeles Sentinel,* March 19, 1.

Clifford, James. 1994. "Diasporas." *Cultural Anthropology* 9(2): 302–38.

———. 1997. *Routes: Travel and Translation in the Late Twentieth Century.* Cambridge, Mass.: Harvard University Press.

Cohen, Lizabeth. 1990. *Making a New Deal: Industrial Workers in Chicago, 1919–1939.* New York: Cambridge University Press.

Cohen, Lucy. 1977. "The Female Factor in Resettlement." *Society* 14(6): 27–30.

Cohen, Robin, ed. 1995. *The Cambridge Survey of*

World Migration. Cambridge: Cambridge University Press.

———. 1997. *Global Diasporas: An Introduction*. Seattle: University of Washington Press.

Cohn-Bendit, Daniel, and Thomas Schmid. 1992. *Heimat Babylon: Das Wagnis der multikulturellen Demokratie*. Hamburg: Hoffmann und Campe.

Coleman, James S. 1988. "Social Capital in the Creation of Human Capital." *American Journal of Sociology* 94: S95–121.

———. 1990. *Foundations of Social Theory*. Cambridge, Mass.: Belknap Press of Harvard University Press.

Coleman, James S., E. Q. Campbell, C. J. Hobson, J. McPartland, A. M. Mood, F. D. Weinfeld, and R. L. York. 1966. *Equality of Educational Opportunity*. Washington: U.S. Government Printing Office.

Collins, J. W., Jr., and D. K. Shay. 1994. "Prevalence of Low Birthweight Among Hispanic Infants with U.S.-born and Foreign-born Mothers: The Effect of Urban Poverty." *American Journal of Epidemiology* 139(2): 184–92.

Collins, Patricia. 1990. *Black Feminist Thought*. Boston: Hyman.

Commons, John R. 1907. *Races and Immigrants in America*. New York: Macmillan.

Congressional Budget Office. 1995. *Immigration and Welfare Reform*. CBO Papers. Washington: Congressional Budget Office.

Converse, Philip E. 1972. "Change in the American Electorate." In *The Human Meaning of Social Change*, edited by Angus Campbell and Philip E. Converse (263–301). New York: Russell Sage Foundation.

Conway, Dennis. 1989. "Caribbean International Mobility Traditions." *Boletin de Estudios Latinoamericanos y del Caribe* 46(June): 17–45.

Conzen, Kathleen Neils. 1979. "Immigrants, Immigrant Neighborhoods, and Ethnic Identity." *Journal of American History* 66(December): 603–15.

———. 1985. "German Americans and the Invention of Ethnicity." In *America and the Germans: An Assessment of a Three-Hundred-Year History*, edited by Frank Trommler and Joseph McVeigh, 2 vols. (vol. 1, 131–47). Philadelphia: University of Pennsylvania Press.

———. 1991. "Mainstreams and Side Channels: The Localization of Immigrant Cultures." *Journal of American Ethnic History* 10(Fall): 5–20.

———. 1996. "Thomas and Znaniecki and the Historiography of American Immigration." *Journal of American Ethnic History* 16(1): 16–25.

Conzen, Kathleen, David Gerber, Ewa Morawska, George Pozzetta, and Rudolph Vecoli. 1992. "The Invention of Ethnicity: A Perspective from the United States." *Journal of American Ethnic History* 12 (1, Fall): 3–41.

Coolidge, Mary Roberts. 1909. *Chinese Immigration*. New York: Henry Holt.

Cordero-Guzman, Héctor, and Ramon Grosfoguel. 1998. "The Demographic and Socio-Economic Characteristics of Post-1965 Foreign Born Immigrants to New York City." Milano Graduate School, New School University (February). Unpublished paper.

Cornelius, Wayne A. 1982. "America in the Era of Limits: Nativist Reactions to the 'New' Immigration." Working Papers in U.S.-Mexican Studies 3. San Diego: Center for U.S.-Mexican Studies, University of California.

———. 1997. "Appearances and Realities: Controlling Illegal Immigration in the United States." In *Temporary Workers or Future Citizens: Japan and U.S. Migration Policies*, edited by Myron Weiner and Tadashi Hanami (384–427). London: Macmillan.

Cornelius, Wayne A., Philip L. Martin, and James F. Hollifield, eds. 1994a. *Controlling Immigration: A Global Perspective*. Stanford, Calif.: Stanford University Press.

———. 1994b. "Introduction: The Ambivalent Quest for Immigration Control." In *Controlling Immigration: A Global Perspective*, edited by Wayne A. Cornelius, Philip L. Martin, and James F. Hollifield (3–51). Stanford, Calif.: Stanford University Press.

Cose, Ellis. 1995. "One Drop of Bloody History." *Newsweek*, February 13, 70–71.

Covello, Leonard. 1972. *The Social Background of the Italo-American School Child: A Study of Southern Italian Family Mores and Their Effects on the School Situation in Italy and America*. Totowa, N.J.: Rowman & Littlefield. (Originally published in 1943)

Cox, Oliver C. 1948. *Caste, Class, and Race: A Study in Social Dynamics*. New York: Doubleday.

Cox, Robert. 1997. "A Perspective on Globalization." In *Globalization: Critical Reflections*, edited by James Mittleman (21–30). Boulder, Colo.: Lynne Reinner.

Craig, Richard B. 1971. *The Bracero Program*. Austin: University of Texas Press.

Crèvecoeur, Hector St. John de. 1912. *Letters from an American Farmer*. New York. (Originally published in 1782)

Croly, Herbert. 1914. *Progressive Democracy*. New York: Macmillan.

Crotty, William. 1991. "Political Parties: Issues and Trends." In *Political Science: Looking to the Future: American Institutions*, edited by William Crotty (vol. 4, 137–201). Evanston, Ill.: Northwestern University Press.

Crystal, David. 1997. *English as a Global Language*. New York: Cambridge University Press.

Cummings, Scott. 1980. "Collectivism: The Unique Legacy of Immigrant Economic Development." In *Self-help in Urban America: Patterns of Minority Business Enterprise*, edited by Scott Cummings (1–29). Port Washington, N.Y.: Kennikat Press.

Dahl, Robert A. 1961. *Who Governs?: Democracy and Power in an American City*. New Haven, Conn.: Yale University Press.

———. 1989. *Democracy and Its Critics*. New Haven, Conn.: Yale University Press.

Dandler, Jorge, and Carmen Medeiros. 1988. "Temporary Migration from Cochabamba, Bolivia, to Argentina: Patterns and Impact in Sending Areas." In *When Borders Don't Divide: Labor Migration and Refugee*

Movements in the Americas, edited by Patricia Pessar (8–41). Staten Island, N.Y.: Center for Migration Studies.

Daniels, Roger. 1962. *The Politics of Prejudice: The Anti-Japanese Movement in California and the Struggle for Japanese Exclusion.* Berkeley: University of Californai Press.

———. 1991. *Coming to America: A History of Immigration and Ethnicity in American Life.* New York: HarperPerennial.

Daniels, Roger, Sandra C. Taylor, and Harry H. L. Kitano, eds. 1992. *Japanese Americans: From Relocation to Redress.* Seattle: University of Washington Press.

Danzinger, Sheldon, and Peter Gottschalk. 1993. *Uneven Tides: Rising Inequality in America.* New York: Russell Sage Foundation.

———. 1995. *America Unequal.* New York: Russell Sage Foundation.

Darity, William A., Jr., and Samuel L. Myers, Jr. 1995. "Family Structure and the Marginalization of Black Men: Policy Implications." In *The Decline in Marriage Among African Americans,* edited by M. Belinda Tucker and Claudia Mitchell-Kernan (263–308). New York: Russell Sage Foundation.

Darity, William Jr., and Samuel Schulman. 1989. *The Question of Discrimination: Racial Inequality in the U.S. Labor Market.* Middletown, Conn.: Wesleyan University Press.

Das Gupta, Monisha. 1997. "'What Is Indian About You?': A Gendered, Transnational Approach to Ethnicity." *Gender and Society* 11: 572–96.

David, Paul A. 1975. *Technical Choice, Innovation, and Economic Growth.* New York: Cambridge University Press.

David, Paul A., and John L. Scadding. 1974. "Private Savings: Ultrarationality, Aggregation, and 'Denison's Law.'" *Journal of Political Economy* 82(2, pt. 1): 225–50.

David, Paul A., and Gavin Wright. 1996. "Increasing Returns and the Genesis of American Resource Abundance." Publication 472. Center for Economic Policy Research, Stanford University (July).

Davidson, Chandler, and Bernard Grofman, eds. 1994. *Quiet Revolution in the South: The Impact of the Voting Rights Act, 1965–1990.* Princeton, N.J.: Princeton University Press.

Davie, Maurice. 1936. *World Immigration.* New York: Macmillan.

Davis, Kingsley. 1974. "The Migrations of Human Populations." *Scientific American* 231(3): 91–97.

———. 1989. "Social Science Approaches to International Migration." In *Population and Resources in Western Intellectual Traditions,* edited by Michael S. Teitelbaum and Jay M. Winter (245–61). New York: Cambridge University Press.

Davis, Lance E., and Robert J. Cull. 1994. *International Capital Markets and American Economic Growth, 1820–1914.* New York: Cambridge University Press.

Davis, Lance E., and Robert E. Gallman. 1973. "The Share of Savings and Investment in Gross National Product During the Nineteenth Century in the United States." Paper presented at the Fourth International Conference of Economic History, Bloomington, Ind. (1968). *Proceedings*(437–66). Paris: Mouton La Haye.

———. 1991. "Savings, Investment, and Economic Growth: The United States in the Nineteenth Century." Department of Economics, University of North Carolina at Chapel Hill. Unpublished paper.

Davis, Mike. 1990. *Cities of Quartz: Excavating the Future in Los Angeles.* New York: Verso.

Davis, Mary. 1993. "The Gautreaux Assisted Housing Program." In *Housing Markets and Residential Mobility,* edited by G. Thomas Kingsley and Margrey Austin Turner (243–54). Washington: Urban Institute Press.

Day, Christine L. 1990. "Ethnocentrism, Economic Competition, and Attitudes Toward U.S. Immigration Policy." Paper presented at the annual meeting of the Midwest Political Science Association, Chicago (April 5–7).

Decressin, Jörg, and Antonio Fatàs. 1995. "Regional Labor Market Dynamics in Europe." *European Economic Review* 39(9): 1627–56.

DeFreitas, Gregory. 1991. *Inequality at Work: Hispanics in the U.S. Labor Force.* New York: Oxford University Press.

De Janvry, Alain, and Carlos Garramon. 1977. "The Dynamics of Rural Poverty in Latin America." *Journal of Peasant Studies* 4: 206–16.

De Jong, Gordon F., Ricardo Abad, Fred Arnold, Benjamin Carino, James Fawcett, and Robert Gardiner. 1983. "International and Internal Migration Decisionmaking: A Value-based Analytical Framework of Intentions to Move from a Rural Philippine Province." *International Migration Review* 17(3): 470–84.

De León, Arnoldo. 1987. *Mexican Americans in a Sunbelt City.* Houston: Center for Mexican American Studies, University of Houston.

De Long, J. Bradford. 1995. "Late-Nineteenth-Century Tariffs and American Economic Growth." Paper presented at the meetings of the Economic History Association, Chicago (September).

Del Pinal, Jorge H. 1992. "Exploring Alternative Race-Ethnic Comparison Groups in Current Population Surveys." *Current Population Reports,* series P23-182. Washington: U.S. Bureau of the Census.

Denison, Edward F. 1962. *The Sources of Economic Growth in the United States and the Alternatives Before Us.* New York: Committee for Economic Development.

Denton, Nancy, and Douglas Massey. 1989. "Racial Identity Among Caribbean Hispanics: The Effect of Double Minority Status on Residential Segregation." *American Sociological Review* 54: 790–808.

Derksen, J. D. B. 1940. "Long Cycles in Residential Building: An Explanation." *Econometrica* 8(2): 97–116.

DeSipio, Louis. 1996. *Counting the Latino Vote: Latinos as a New Electorate*. Charlottesville: University Press of Virginia.

DeSipio, Louis, and Rodolfo O. de la Garza. 1998. *Making Americans, Remaking America: Immigration and Immigrant Policy*. Boulder, Colo.: Westview.

Detjen, David W. 1985. *The Germans in Missouri, 1900–1918: Prohibition, Neutrality, and Assimilation*. Columbia, Mo.: University of Missouri Press.

Devine, Theresa. 1992. "Inter-industry Variation in the Determinants of Self-employment." University of Chicago. Unpublished paper.

De Vos, George A. 1975. "Ethnic Pluralism: Conflict and Accommodation." In *Ethnic Identity: Cultural Continuities and Change*, edited by G. De Vos and L. Romanucci-Ross (5–41). Palo Alto, Calif.: Mayfield.

DeWind, Josh, and Charles Hirschman. 1996. "Becoming American/America Becoming: A Conference on International Migration to the United States." *Items* 50(2–3): 41–47.

DeWind, Josh, and Philip Kasinitz. 1997. "Everything Old Is New Again." *International Migration Review* 31(4): 1096–1111.

Dib, George. 1988. "Laws Governing Migration in Some Arab Countries." In *International Migration Today*, vol. 1, *Trends and Prospects*, edited by Reginald T. Appleyard (168–79). Perth: University of Western Australia for the United Nations Educational, Scientific, and Cultural Organization.

Dikötter, Frank, ed. 1997. *Racial Discourse in China: Continuities and Permutations in the Construction of Racial Identities in China and Japan*. Honolulu: University of Hawaii Press.

Diner, Hasia. 1983. *Erin's Daughters in America: Irish Immigrant Women in the Nineteenth Century*. Baltimore: Johns Hopkins University Press.

Dinerman, Ina. 1978. "Patterns of Adaptation Among Households of U.S.-bound Migrants from Michoacán, Mexico." *International Migration Review* 12: 485–501.

Dinnerstein, Leonard. 1994. *Anti-Semitism in America*. New York: Oxford University Press.

Dinnerstein, Leonard, Roger L. Nichols, and David M. Reimers. 1990. *Natives and Strangers: Blacks, Indians, and Immigrants in America*. New York.

Dinnerstein, Leonard, and David M. Reimers. 1987. *Ethnic Americans: A History of Immigration*. Cambridge, Mass.: Addison-Wesley Educational Publishers.

Divakaruni, Chitra. 1995. *Arranged Marriage*. New York: Doubleday.

Divine, Robert A. 1957. *American Immigration Policy, 1924–1952*. New Haven, Conn.: Yale University Press.

Dolado, Juan, Alessandra Goria, and Andrea Ichino. 1993. "Immigration Human Capital and Growth in the Host Country." Working Paper. Milan: Fondazione ENI Enrico Mattei.

Donato, Katharine M. 1991. "Understanding U.S. Immigration: Why Some Countries Send Women and Other Countries Send Men." In *Seeking Common Ground: Women Immigrants to the United States*, edited by Donna Gabaccia (159–84). Westport, Conn.: Greenwood.

Donato, Katharine M., Jorge Durand, and Douglas S. Massey. 1992. "Stemming the Tide?: Assessing the Deterrent Effects of the Immigration Reform and Control Act." *Demography* 29: 139–57.

Donnelly, Nancy D. 1994. *Changing Lives of Hmong Refugee Women*. Seattle: University of Washington Press.

Douglas, Paul Howard. 1921. "American Apprenticeship and Industrial Education." *Columbia University Studies in Social Sciences* 95(2).

Dowty, Alan. 1987. *Closed Borders: The Contemporary Assault on Freedom of Movement*. New Haven, Conn.: Yale University Press.

Drucker, Peter F. 1993. *Post-capitalist Society*. New York: HarperCollins.

Dublin, Thomas. 1996. *Becoming American, Becoming Ethnic: College Students Explore Their Roots*. Philadelphia: Temple University Press.

Duleep, Harriet Orcutt. 1994. "Social Security and the Emigration of Immigrants." In International Social Security Association, *Migration: A Worldwide Challenge for Social Security*, Studies and Research 35 (97–128). Geneva: International Social Security Association.

Duncan, Beverly, and Otis Dudley Duncan. 1968. "Minorities and the Process of Stratification." *American Sociological Review* 33(3): 356–64.

Duncan, Otis Dudley. 1969. "Inheritance of Poverty or Inheritance of Race." In *On Understanding Poverty*, edited by Daniel Patrick Moynihan (85–110). New York: Basic Books.

Dunlap, Jonathan C., and Ann Morse. 1995. "States Sue Feds to Recover Immigration Costs." *Legisbrief* 3(1). Washington: National Conference of State Legislatures.

Dunlevy, James. 1980. "Nineteenth-Century European Immigration to the United States: Intended Versus Lifetime Settlement Patterns." *Economic Development and Cultural Change* 29(1): 77–90.

———. 1983. "Regional Preferences and Immigrant Settlement." *Research in Economic History* 8: 217–51.

Dunlevy, James, and Henry A. Gemery. 1977a. "British-Irish Settlement Patterns in the United States: The Role of Family and Friends." *Scottish Journal of Political Economy* 24(3): 257–63.

———. 1977b. "The Role of Migrant Stock and Lagged Migration in the Settlement Patterns of Nineteenth-Century Immigrants." *Review of Economics and Statistics* 59(2): 137–44.

———. 1978. "Economic Opportunity and the Responses of 'Old' and 'New' Migrants to the United States." *Journal of Economic History* 38(4): 901–17.

Dunlevy, James, and Richard P. Saba. 1992. "The Role of Nationality-Specific Characteristics on the Settlement Patterns of Late-Nineteenth-Century European

Immigrants." *Explorations in Economic History* 29(2): 228–49.

Durand, Jorge, and Douglas S. Massey. 1992. "Mexican Migration to the United States: A Critical Review." *Latin American Research Review* 27: 3–42.

Durkheim, Émile. 1951. *Suicide: A Study in Sociology*, translated by J. A. Spaulding and G. Simpson, edited by G. Simpson. New York: Free Press. (Originally published in 1897)

Dwyer, Daisy. 1983. "Women and Income in the Third World: Implications for Policy." International Programs Working Paper 18. New York: Population Council.

Easterlin, Richard A. 1960. "Interregional Differences in Per Capita Income, Population and Total Income, 1840–1950." In *Trends in the American Economy in the Nineteenth Century*. (*Studies in Income and Wealth*, vol. 24). Princeton: Princeton University Press.

———. 1968. *Population, Labor Force, and Long Swings in Economic Growth: The American Experience*. New York: National Bureau of Economic Research.

———. 1971. "Influences in European Emigration Before World War I." In *The Reinterpretation of American Economic History*, edited by Robert Fogel and Stanley Engerman (384–95). New York: Harper & Row.

Eberstein, Isaac W. 1991. "Race/Ethnicity and Infant Mortality." Paper presented at the annual meeting of the American Sociological Association, Cincinnati (August).

Edelstein, Michael. 1974. "The Determinants of U.K. Investment Abroad, 1870–1913: The U.S. Case." *Journal of Economic History* 34(4): 980–1007.

———. 1982. *Overseas Investment in the Age of High Imperialism*. New York: Columbia University Press.

Edmonston, Barry, Joshua Goldstein, and Juanita T. Lott, eds. 1996. *Spotlight on Heterogeneity: The Federal Standards for Racial and Ethnic Classification, Summary of a Workshop*. Washington: National Academy Press.

Edmonston, Barry, Sharon Lee, and Jeffrey Passel. 1994. "U.S. Population Projections for National Group Origins: Taking into Account Ethnicity and Exogamy." In *Proceedings of the American Statistical Association, Social Statistics Section* (100–105). Washington.

Edmonston, Barry, and Jeffrey Passel. 1994. "The Future Immigrant Population of the United States." In *Immigration and Ethnicity: The Integration of America's Newest Arrivals*, edited by Barry Edmonston and Jeffrey Passel (317–53). Washington: Urban Institute Press.

Edwards, Alba M. 1943. *Comparative Occupation Statistics for the United States, 1870 to 1940*. In U.S. Department of Commerce, Bureau of the Census, *Sixteenth Census of the United States: 1940: Population*. Washington: U.S. Government Printing Office.

Edwards, Richard, Michael Reich, and David M. Gordon. 1975. *Labor Market Segmentation*. Lexington, Mass.: Heath.

Emmanuel, Arghiri. 1972. *Unequal Exchange: A Study of the Imperialism of Trade*. New York: Monthly Review Press.

Enchautegui, Maria. 1992. "Work and Wages of Puerto Rican Men During the 1980s." Washington: Urban Institute. Unpublished paper.

Enoch, Helan. 1997. *White Public Space: Routine Practices of Racialized Social Production Workshop: Post-Boasian Studies in Blackness and Whiteness*. New York: New York Academy of Sciences.

Enoch, Yan. 1994. "The Intolerance of a Tolerant People: Ethnic Relations in Denmark." *Ethnic and Racial Studies* 17: 282–300.

Epstein, A. L. 1958. *Politics in an Urban African Community*. Manchester: Manchester University Press.

Erenberg, Lewis A. 1981. *Steppin' Out: New York Nightlife and the Transformation of American Culture, 1890–1930*. Westport, Conn.: Greenwood Press.

Erie, Steven P. 1988. *Rainbow's End: Irish Americans and the Dilemmas of Urban Machine Politics, 1840–1985*. Berkeley: University of California Press.

Erikson, Charlotte J. 1972. "Who Were the English and Scots Emigrants to the United States in the Late Nineteenth Century?" In *Population and Social Change*, edited by David V. Glass and Roger Revelle (347–81). New York: Crane and Russak.

———. 1981. "Emigration from the British Isles to the United States in 1831." *Population Studies* 25(2): 175–97.

———. 1986. "The Uses of Passenger Lists for the Study of British and Irish Emigration." In *Migration Across Time and Nations*, edited by Ira A. Glazier and Luigi De Rosa. New York: Holmes and Meier.

———. 1989. "Emigration from the British Isles to the United States in 1841: Part 1. Emigration from the British Isles." *Population Studies* 43(4): 347–67.

———. 1990. "Emigration from the British Isles to the United States in 1841: Part 2. Who Were the English Emigrants?" *Population Studies* 44(1): 21–40.

Espenshade, Thomas J., Jessica L. Baraka, and Gregory A. Huber. 1997. "Restructuring U.S. Immigration: Implications of the 1996 Welfare and Immigration Reform Acts." Paper presented at the Conference on Migration and Restructuring in the United States, University of Georgia, Athens (May 2–4).

Espenshade, Thomas J., and Maryann Belanger. 1997. "Immigration and Public Opinion." Paper presented at the Conference on Immigration and the Sociocultural Remaking of the North American Space, Harvard University, Cambridge, Mass. (April 10–12).

Espenshade, Thomas J., and Charles A. Calhoun. 1992. "Public Opinion Toward Illegal Immigration and Undocumented Migrants in Southern California." Working Paper 92-2. Princeton, N.J.: Office of Population Research, Princeton University.

———. 1993. "An Analysis of Public Opinion Toward Undocumented Immigration." *Population Research and Policy Review* 12: 189–224.

Espenshade, Thomas J., and Katherine Hempstead.

1996. "Contemporary American Attitudes Toward U.S. Immigration." *International Migration Review* 30(2, Summer): 535–70.

Espenshade, Thomas J., and Vanessa E. King. 1994. "State and Local Fiscal Impacts of U.S. Immigrants: Evidence from New Jersey." *Population Research and Policy Review* 13: 225–56.

Espiritu, Yen Le. 1992. *Asian American Panethnicity: Bridging Institutions and Identities.* Philadelphia: Temple University Press.

———. 1996. "Colonial Oppression, Labor Importation, and Group Formation: Filipinos in the United States." *Ethnic and Racial Studies* 19(1): 29–48.

———. 1997. *Asian American Women and Men: Labor, Laws, and Love.* Thousand Oaks, Calif.: Sage.

Estrada, Richard. 1995. "Immigration Buries Blacks." *The Social Contract* 5: 262–63.

Evans, Mariah D. R. 1987. "Language Skill, Language Usage, and Opportunity: Immigrants in the Australian Labor Market." *Sociology* 21: 253–74.

———. 1989. "Immigrant Entrepreneurship: Effects of Ethnic Market Size and Isolated Labor Pool." *American Sociological Review* 54(6): 950–62.

Ewen, Elizabeth. 1985. *Immigrant Women in the Land of Dollars: Life and Culture on the Lower East Side, 1890–1925.* New York: Monthly Review Press.

Fadiman, Anne. 1997. *The Spirit Catches You and You Fall Down: A Hmong Child, Her American Doctors, and the Collision of Two Cultures.* New York: Farrar, Straus and Giroux.

Fainstein, Norman. 1995. "Race, Segregation, and the State." In *The Bubbling Cauldron: Race, Ethnicity, and the Urban Crisis,* edited by Michael Peter Smith and Joe Feagin. Minneapolis: University of Minnesota Press.

Fairlie, Robert W., and Bruce D. Meyer. 1996. "Ethnic and Racial Self-employment Differences and Possible Explanations." *Journal of Human Resources* 31(4): 757–93.

Farley, Reynolds. 1991. "The New Census Question on Ancestry: What Did It Tell Us?" *Demography* 28: 411–30.

———. 1996. *The New American Reality: Who We Are, How We Got Here, Where We Are Going.* New York: Russell Sage Foundation.

Farley, Reynolds, and Walter R. Allen. 1987. *The Color Line and the Quality of Life in America.* New York: Russell Sage Foundation.

Farley, Reynolds, and William Frey. 1994. "Changes in the Segregation of Whites from Blacks During the 1980s: Small Steps Towards a More Integrated Society." *American Sociological Review* 59: 23–45.

Feagin, Joe R. 1988. *Free Enterprise City: Houston in Political Economical Perspective.* New Brunswick, N.J.: Rutgers University Press.

Featherman, David, and Robert Hauser. 1978. *Opportunity and Change.* New York: Academic Press.

Featherstone, Mike. 1990. *Global Culture: Nationalism, Globalization, and Modernity.* London: Sage.

Feingold, Henry L. 1970. *The Politics of Rescue: The Roosevelt Administration and the Holocaust, 1938–1945.* New Brunswick, N.J.: Rutgers University Press.

Feldman-Bianco, Bela. 1992. "Multiple Layers of Time and Space: The Construction of Class, Race, Ethnicity, and Nationalism Among Portuguese Immigrants." In *Towards a Transnational Perspective on Migration,* edited by Nina Glick Schiller, Linda Basch, and Cristina Blanc-Szanton (145–74). New York: New York Academy of Sciences.

———. 1994. "The State, Saudade, and the Dialectics of Deterritorialization and Reterritorialization." Paper presented at the Wemner Gren Symposium 117, Mijas, Spain (June).

———. 1997. "Immigraçâo, confrontos culturais e (re)construçoes de identidade feminina: O caso das intermediárias culturais." *Horizontes Antropológicos* 3(5): 65–83.

Fernández-Kelly, María Patricia. 1983. *For We Are Sold, I and My People: Women and Industry in Mexico's Frontier.* Albany: State University of New York Press.

———. 1995. "Social and Cultural Capital in the Urban Ghetto: Implications for the Economic Sociology and Immigration." In *The Economic Sociology of Immigration: Essays on Networks, Ethnicity, and Entrepreneurship,* edited by Alejandro Portes (213–47). New York: Russell Sage Foundation.

Fernández-Kelly, María Patricia, and Ana García. 1990. "Power Surrendered, Power Restored: The Politics of Home and Work Among Hispanic Women in Southern California and Southern Florida." In *Women, Politics, and Change,* edited by Louise A. Tilly and Patricia Gurin. New York: Russell Sage Foundation.

Fernández-Kelly, María Patricia, and Richard Schauffler. 1994. "Divided Fates: Immigrant Children in a Restructured U.S. Economy." *International Migration Review* 28(4): 662–89.

Ferree, Myra Marx. 1990. "Between Two Worlds: German Feminist Approaches to Working-class Women and Work." In *Feminist Research Methods: Exemplary Readings in the Social Sciences,* edited by Joyce McCarl Nielsen (174–92). Boulder, Colo.: Westview.

Ferrie, Joseph P. 1995. "Up and Out or Down and Out?: Immigrant Mobility in the Antebellum United States." *Journal of Interdisciplinary History* 26(Summer): 33–55.

Field Institute. 1988. *Statistical Tabulations from the February 1988 Survey of the Field Institute on Ethnic Minorities.* San Francisco: Field Institute.

Fields, Harold. 1938. *The Refugee in the United States.* New York: Oxford University Press.

Filer, Randall. 1992. "The Impact of Immigrant Arrivals on Migratory Patterns of Native Workers." In *Immigration and the Work Force: Economic Consequences for the United States and Source Areas,* edited by George Borjas and Richard Freeman (245–70). Chicago: University of Chicago Press.

Fishkin, Shelley Fisher. 1995. "Interrogating 'Whiteness,' Complicating 'Blackness': Remapping American

Culture." *American Quarterly* 47(September): 428–66.

Fishlow, Albert. 1965. *American Railroads and the Transformation of the Antebellum Economy.* Cambridge, Mass.: Harvard University Press.

Fishman, Joshua. 1965. "The Status and Prospects of Bilingualism in the United States." *Modern Language Journal* 49: 143–55.

———. 1972. *The Sociology of Language.* Rowley, Mass.: Newbury House.

Fitzgerald, K. 1996. *The Face of the Nation: Immigration, the State, and the National Identity.* Stanford, Calif.: Stanford University Press.

Fitzgerald, Patrick. 1996. "A Sentence to Sail: The Transportation of Irish Convicts to Colonial America in the Eighteenth Century." Harvard University, International Seminar on the History of the Atlantic World, 1500–1800. Cambridge (1996).

Fitzpatrick, Joan. 1997. "The Gender Dimension of U.S. Immigration Policy." *Yale Journal of Law and Feminism* 9(1): 23–49.

Fitzpatrick, Joseph P. 1971. *Puerto Rican Americans: The Meaning of Migration to the Mainland.* 2nd ed. Englewood Cliffs, N.J.: Prentice Hall.

Fix, Michael, and Jeffrey S. Passel. 1994. *Immigration and Immigrants: Setting the Record Straight.* Washington: Urban Institute Press.

Fix, Michael, and Wendy Zimmerman. 1995. "Immigrant Families and Public Policy: A Deepening Divide." Immigrant Policy Program. Washington: Urban Institute.

Flanigan, James. 1994. "Keep Immigration on the Side of Common Sense." *Los Angeles Times,* October 30, D1.

Foerster, Robert. 1919. *The Italian Emigration of Our Times.* Cambridge, Mass.: Harvard University Press.

Fogel, Robert W. 1967. "The Specification Problem in Economic History." *Journal of Economic History* 27(3): 283–308.

Foley, Douglas. 1991. "Reconsidering Anthropological Explanations of Ethnic School Failure." *Anthropology and Education Quarterly* 22: 60–86.

Foley, Neil. 1997. *The White Scourge: Mexicans, Blacks, and Poor Whites in Texas Cotton Culture.* Berkeley: University of California Press.

Foner, Eric. 1980. *Politics and Ideology in the Age of the Civil War.* New York: Oxford University Press.

———. 1988. *Reconstruction: America's Unfinished Revolution.* New York: Harper & Row.

Foner, Nancy. 1977. "The Jamaicans: Cultural and Social Change Among Migrants in Britain." In *Between Two Cultures: Migrants and Minorities in Britain,* edited by James. L. Watson (120–50). Oxford: Basil Blackwell.

———. 1986. "Sex Roles and Sensibilities: Jamaican Women in New York and London." In *International Migration: The Female Experience,* edited by Rita James Simon and Caroline B. Brettell (133–51). Totowa, N.J.: Rowman & Allanheld.

———, ed. 1987. *New Immigrants in New York.* New York: Columbia University Press.

———. 1994. "Ideology and Social Practice in the Jamaican Diaspora." Working Paper 65. New York: Russell Sage Foundation.

———. 1997. "What's New About Transnationalism?: New York Immigrants Today and at the Turn of the Century." *Diaspora* 6: 355–76.

———. 1998. "Benefits and Burdens: Immigrant Women and Work in New York City." *Gender Issues* 16: 5–24.

Fong, Timothy P. 1994. *The First Suburban Chinatown: The Remaking of Monterey Park, California.* Philadelphia: Temple University Press.

Fordham, Signithia. 1996. *Blacked Out: Dilemmas of Race, Identity, and Success at Capital High.* Chicago: University of Chicago Press.

Fouron, Georges. 1983. "The Black Immigrant Dilemma in the United States: The Haitian Experience." *Journal of Caribbean Studies* 3(3): 242–65.

———. 1984. "Patterns of Adaptation of Haitian Immigrants of the 1970s in New York City." Ph.D. diss., Teacher's College, Columbia University.

Fouron, Georges, and Nina Glick Schiller. 1997. "Haitian Identities at the Juncture Between Diaspora and Homeland." In *Caribbean Circuits,* edited by Patricia Pessar (127–59). Staten Island, N.Y.: Center for Migration Studies.

Fox, Bonnie. 1980. *Hidden in the Household.* Toronto: Women's Press.

Fox, Richard Wightman, and T. J. Jackson Lears, eds. 1983. *The Culture of Consumption: Critical Essays in American History, 1880–1980.* New York: Pantheon Books.

Fragomen, Austin T., Jr. 1997. "The Illegal Immigration Reform and Immigrant Responsibility Act of 1996: An Overview." *International Migration Review* 31(2): 438–60.

Frank, Andre Gunder. 1969. *Capitalism and Underdevelopment in Latin America.* New York: Monthly Review Press.

Frankenberg, Ruth. 1993. *White Women, Race Matters: The Social Construction of Whiteness.* Minneapolis: University of Minnesota Press.

Fredrickson, George M. 1988. *The Arrogance of Race: Historical Perspectives on Slavery, Racism, and Social Inequality.* Middletown, Conn.: Wesleyan University Press.

Freeman, Gary P. 1979. *Immigrant Labor and Racial Conflict in Industrialized Societies: The French and British Experience, 1945–1975.* Princeton, N.J.: Princeton University Press.

———. 1994. "Can Liberal States Control Unwanted Migration?" *Annals of the American Academy of Political and Social Science* 534(July): 17–30.

———. 1995a. "Modes of Immigration Politics in Liberal Democratic States." *International Migration Review* 29(4): 881–902.

———. 1995b. "Rejoinder." *International Migration Review* 19(4, Winter): 909–13.

Freeman, James. 1995. *Changing Identities: Vietnamese Americans, 1975–1995.* Boston: Allyn and Bacon.

Freeman, Richard B. 1991. "Employment and Earnings of Disadvantaged Young Men in a Labor Shortage Economy." In *The Urban Underclass,* edited by Christopher Jencks and Paul Peterson (103–21). Washington: Brookings Institution.

———. 1993. "How Much Has De-unionization Contributed to the Rise in Male Earnings Inequality?" In *Uneven Tides: Rising Inequality in America,* edited by Sheldon Danzinger and Peter Gottschalk (ch. 4). New York: Russell Sage Foundation.

Freeman, Richard B., and Harry Holzer. 1991. "The Deterioration of Employment and Earnings Opportunities for Less Educated Young Americans: A Review of Evidence." National Bureau of Economic Research. Unpublished paper.

Freeman, Richard B., and James L. Medoff. 1984. *What Do Unions Do?* New York: Basic Books.

Freer, Robin. 1995. "Black-Korean Conflict." In *The Los Angeles Riots: Lessons for the Urban Future,* edited by M. Baldassare (175–204). Boulder, Colo.: Westview.

Freud, Sigmund. 1961. *Civilization and Its Discontents,* translated by James Strachey. New York: Norton. (Originally published in 1930)

Frey, William H. 1993. "The New Urban Revival." *Urban Studies* 30: 741–74.

———. 1995a. "The New Geography of Population Shifts: Trends Toward Balkanization." In *State of the Union: America in the 1990s,* vol. 2, *Social Trends,* edited by Reynolds Farley (271–336). New York: Russell Sage Foundation.

———. 1995b. "Immigration and Internal Migration 'Flight' from U.S. Metropolitan Areas: Toward a Demographic Balkanization." *Urban Studies* 32(4–5): 733–57.

———. 1995c. "Immigration and Internal Migration Flight: A California Case Study." *Population and Environment* 16: 351–75.

———. 1995d. "Immigration Impacts on Internal Migration of the Poor: 1990 Census Evidence for U.S. States." *International Journal of Population Geography* 1: 51–67.

Frey, William H., and Elaine L. Fielding. 1995. "Changing Urban Populations: Regional Restructuring, Racial Polarization, and Poverty Concentration." *Cityscapes* 1(2, June): 1–66.

Frey, William H., and Kao-Lee Liaw. 1998. "The Impact of Recent Immigration on Population Redistribution Within the United States." In *The Immigration Debate: Studies of Economic, Demographic, and Fiscal Effects of Immigration,* edited by James P. Smith and Barry Edmonston (388–448). Washington: National Academy Press.

Friedberg, Rachel. 1997. "The Impact of Mass Migration on the Israeli Labor Market." Working Paper 97–11. Brown University, Population Studies and Training Center.

Friedberg, Rachel, and Jennifer Hunt. 1995. "The Impact of Immigrants on Host Country Wages, Employment, and Growth." *Journal of Economic Perspectives* 9(2, Spring): 23–44.

Fritz, Mark. 1998. "Pledging Multiple Allegiances: A Global Blurring of Boundaries Challenges Notions of Nationality." *Los Angeles Times,* April 6.

Fuchs, Lawrence H. 1990. *The American Kaleidoscope: Race, Ethnicity, and the Civic Culture.* Hanover, N.H.: Wesleyan University Press/University Press of New England.

———. 1995. "What Do Immigrants Deserve?: A Warm Welcome and the Usual Benefits—But Not Affirmative Action." *Washington Post,* January 29, C2.

Fukuyama, Francis. 1993. "Immigrants and Family Values." *Commentary* 95(5): 26–32.

Fuligni, Andrew J. 1997. "The Academic Achievement of Adolescents from Immigrant Families: The Roles of Family Background, Attitudes, and Behavior." *Child Development* 68: 261–73.

Furtado, Celso. 1965. *Development and Underdevelopment.* Berkeley: University of California Press.

———. 1970. *Economic Development of Latin America.* Cambridge: Cambridge University Press.

Gabaccia, Donna R. 1984. *From Sicily to Elizabeth Street: Housing and Social Change Among Italian Immigrants, 1880–1930.* Albany: State University of New York Press.

———. 1988. *Militants and Migrants: Rural Sicilians Become American Workers.* New Brunswick, N.J.: Rutgers University Press.

———. 1989. *Immigrant Women in the United States: A Selectively Annotated Multidisciplinary Bibliography.* Westport, Conn.: Greenwood.

———. 1992. "Introduction." In *Seeking Common Ground: Multidisciplinary Studies of Immigrant Women in the United States,* edited by Donna Gabaccia (xi–xxvi). Westport, Conn.: Greenwood.

———. 1994. *From the Other Side: Women, Gender, and Immigrant Life in the United States, 1820–1990.* Bloomington: Indiana University Press.

Gabler, Neal. 1988. *An Empire of Their Own: How the Jews Invented Hollywood.* New York: Crown Publishers.

Gainer, Bernard. 1972. *The Alien Invasion: The Origins of the Aliens Act of 1905.* London: Heinemann Educational Books.

Galarza, Ernesto. 1977. *Farm Workers and Agribusiness in California, 1947–1960.* Notre Dame, Ind.: University of Notre Dame Press.

Galeano, Eduardo. 1991. *The Book of Embraces.* New York: Norton.

Gallaway, Lowell E., and Richard K. Vedder. 1971. "Mobility of Native Americans." *Journal of Economic History* 31(3): 613–49.

———. 1972. "Geographic Distribution of British and Irish Emigrants to the United States After 1800." *Scottish Journal of Political Economy* 19(1): 19–36.

Gallaway, Lowell E., Richard K. Vedder, and Vishwa Shukla. 1974. "The Distribution of the Immigrant

Population in the United States: An Economic Analysis." *Explorations in Economic History* 11(2): 213–26.

Gallman, Robert E. 1977. "Human Capital in the First Eighty Years of the Republic: How Much Did America Owe the Rest of the World?" *American Economic Review* 67(1): 27–31.

Gamio, Manuel. 1930. *Mexican Immigration to the United States.* Chicago: University of Chicago Press.

———. 1931. *The Mexican Immigrant: His Life Story.* Chicago: University of Chicago Press.

Gans, Herbert J. 1962. *The Urban Villagers: Group and Class in the Life of Italian Americans.* New York: Free Press.

———. 1967. *The Levittowners: Ways of Life and Politics in a New Suburban Community.* New York: Pantheon.

———. 1973. "Introduction." In *Ethnic Identity and Assimilation: The Polish Community,* edited by Neil Sandberg (vii–xii). New York: Praeger.

———. 1979. "Symbolic Ethnicity: The Future of Ethnic Groups and Cultures in America." *Ethnic and Racial Studies* 2 (1): 1–20.

———. 1982. *The Urban Villagers: Group and Class in the Life of Italian Americans.* New York: Free Press. (Originally published in 1962)

———. 1992a. "Second-Generation Decline: Scenarios for the Economic and Ethnic Futures of the Post-1965 American Immigrants." *Ethnic and Racial Studies* 15(2): 173–92.

———. 1992b. "Comment: Ethnic Invention and Acculturation: A Bumpy-Line Approach." *Journal of American Ethnic History* 11(1, Fall): 42–52.

———. 1999a. "Filling in Some Holes: Needed Areas of Immigration Research." *American Behavioral Scientist* 42(9): 1301–12.

———. 1999b. "The Possibility of a New Racial Hierarchy in the Twenty-first Century United States." In *Cultural Territories of Race,* edited by Michelle Lamont (371–90). Chicago and New York: University of Chicago Press/Russell Sage Foundation.

Garcia, Juan Ramon. 1980. *Operation Wetback: The Mass Deportation of Mexican Undocumented Workers in 1954.* Westport, Conn.: Greenwood.

Garcia, M. C. 1996. *Havana USA: Cuban Exiles and Cuban Americans in South Florida, 1959–1994.* Berkeley: University of California Press.

Garcia, Phillip. 1985. "Immigration Issues in Urban Ecology: The Case of Los Angeles." In *Urban Ethnicity in the United States: New Immigrations and Old Minorities,* edited by Lional Maldonado and Joan Moore. Beverly Hills, Calif.: Sage.

Garcia y Griego, Larry Manuel. 1988. "The Bracero Policy Experiment: U.S.-Mexican Responses to Mexican Labor Migration, 1942–1955." Ph.D. diss., Department of History, University of California at Los Angeles.

Garrison, Vivian, and Carol I. Weiss. 1979. "Dominican Family Networks and U.S. Immigration Policy: A Case Study." *International Migration Review* 12(2): 264–83.

———. 1987. "Dominican Family Networks and U.S. Immigration Policy: A Case Study." In *Caribbean Life in New York City,* edited by Elsa Chaney and Constance Sutton (92–116). Staten Island, N.Y.: Center for Migration Studies.

Geertz, Clifford. 1973. *The Interpretation of Cultures.* New York: Basic Books.

Gellner, Ernest. 1983. *Nation and Nationalism.* Oxford: Blackwell.

Georges, Eugenia. 1990. *The Making of a Transnational Community: Migration, Development, and Cultural Change in the Dominican Republic.* New York: Columbia University Press.

———. 1992. "Gender, Class, and Migration in the Dominican Republic: Women's Experiences in a Transnational Community." In *Towards a Transnational Perspective on Migration: Race, Class, Ethnicity, and Nationalism Reconsidered,* edited by Nina Glick Schiller, Linda Basch, and Cristina Blanc-Szanton (81–99). New York: Annals of the New York Academy of Sciences.

Gerber, David. 1989. *The Making of an American Pluralism: Buffalo, New York, 1825–1860.* Urbana: University of Illinois Press.

Gerson, Jeffrey. 1990. "Building the Brooklyn Machine: Irish, Jewish, and Black Succession in Central Brooklyn, 1919–1964." Ph.D. diss., Political Science Program, City University Graduate Center.

Gerstle, Gary. 1989. *Working-class Americanism: The Politics of Labor in a Textile City, 1914–1960.* New York: Cambridge University Press.

———. 1993. "American Liberals and the Quest for Cultural Pluralism, 1915–1970". Unpublished paper.

———. 1994. "The Protean Character of American Liberalism." *American Historical Review* 99(October): 1043–73.

———. 1995. "Race and the Myth of the Liberal Consensus." *Journal of American History* 82(September): 579–86.

———. 1996a. "European Immigrants, Ethnics, and American Identity, 1880–1950." Paper presented at America Becoming/Becoming American Conference. Social Science Research Council, Sanibel Island, Florida (January 18–21, 1996).

———. 1996b. "The Working Class Goes to War." In *The War in American Culture: Society and Consciousness During World War II,* edited by Lewis A. Erenberg and Susan E. Hirsch (105–27). Chicago: University of Chicago Press.

Gettys, Luella. 1934. *The Law of Citizenship in the United States.* Chicago.

Gibson, Margaret A. 1989. *Accommodation Without Assimilation: Sikh Immigrants in an American High School.* Ithaca, N.Y.: Cornell University Press.

Giddens, Anthony. 1979. *Central Problems in Social Theory: Action, Structure, and Contradictions in Social Analysis.* Berkeley: University of California Press.

———. 1990. "Structuration Theory and Sociological Analysis." In *Anthony Giddens: Consensus and Contro-*

versy, edited by John Clark, Celia Modgil, and Sohan Modgil (297–315). New York: Falmer Press.

Gil, A. G. and W. A. Vega. 1996. "Two Different Worlds: Acculturation Stress and Adaptation Among Cuban and Nicaraguan Families." *Journal of Social and Personal Relationships* 13(3): 435–56.

Gilbert, M. 1989. "Alcohol Consumption Patterns in Immigrant and Later-Generation Mexican American Women." *Hispanic Journal of Behavioral Sciences* 9: 299–313.

Gilbertson, Greta A. 1995. "Women's Labor and Enclave Employment: The Case of Colombian and Dominican Women in New York City." *International Migration Review* 29(3): 657–70.

Gill, Stephen. 1997. "Globalization, Democratization, and Indifference." In *Globalization: Critical Reflections,* edited by James Mittleman (205–28). Boulder, Colo.: Lynne Reinner.

Gilroy, Paul. 1991. *There Ain't No Black in the Union Jack: The Cultural Politics of Race and Nation.* Chicago: University of Chicago Press.

Gitlin, Todd, ed. 1987. *Watching Television: a Pantheon Guide to Popular Culture.* New York: Pantheon.

Glazer, Nathan. 1954. "Ethnic Groups in America: From National Culture to Ideology." In *Freedom and Control in Modern Society,* edited by Morroe Berger, Theodore Abel, and Charles H. Page (158–73). New York: Van Nostrand.

———. 1985. *Clamor at the Gates: The New American Immigration.* San Francisco: Institute for Contemporary Studies Press.

———. 1993. "Is Assimilation Dead?" *Annals of the American Academy of Political and Social Science* 530: 122–36.

Glazer, Nathan, and Daniel Patrick Moynihan. 1970. *Beyond the Melting Pot: The Negroes, Puerto Ricans, Jews, Italians, and Irish of New York City.* Cambridge, Mass.: MIT Press. (Originally published in 1963)

Gleason, Philip. 1980. "American Identity and Americanization." In *Harvard Encyclopedia of American Ethnic Groups,* edited by Stephan Thernstrom, Ann Orlov, and Oscar Handlin (31–58). Cambridge, Mass.: Harvard University Press.

———. 1992. *Speaking of Diversity: Language and Ethnicity in Twentieth-Century America.* Baltimore: Johns Hopkin University Press.

Glenn, Evelyn Nakano. 1986. *Issei, Nisei, War Bride: Three Generations of Japanese American Women in Domestic Service.* Philadelphia: Temple University Press.

Glenn, Susan. 1990. *Daughters of the Shtetl.* Ithaca, N.Y.: Cornell University Press.

Glick Schiller, Nina. 1995. "The Implications of Haitian Transnationalism for U.S.-Haiti Relations: Contradictions of the Deterritorialized Nation-state." *Journal of Haitian Studies* 1(1): 111–23.

———. 1999a. "Transnational Nation-States and Their Citizens: The Asian Experience." In *Globalism and the Asia Pacific: Contested Territories,* edited by Peter Dicken, Philip F. Kelly, L. Kong, Kris Olds, H. Wai-chung Yeung (202–18). New York: Routledge.

———. 1999b. "Who Are These Guys?: A Transnational Reading of the U.S. Immigrant Experience." In *Identities on the Move,* edited by Liliana Goldin (15–44). Austin: University of Texas Press.

Glick Schiller, Nina, and Linda Basch. 1995. "The Nation-state Question: Transnational Projects of Immigrants, Ethnographers, and Dominant Classes." Paper presented at the Conference on Caribbean Circuits: Transnational Approaches to Migration, Yale University, New Haven, Conn. (September).

Glick Schiller, Nina, Linda Basch, and Cristina Blanc-Szanton. 1992a. "Towards a Transnationalization of Migration: Race, Class, Ethnicity, and Nationalism Reconsidered." In *Towards a Transnational Perspective on Migration: Race, Class, Ethnicity, and Nationalism Reconsidered,* edited by Nina Glick Schiller, Linda Basch, and Cristina Blanc-Szanton (1–24). New York: New York, Academy of Sciences.

———, eds. 1992b. "Transnational—A New Analytic Framework for Understanding Migration." In *Towards a Transnational Perspective on Migration: Race, Class, Ethnicity, and Nationalism Reconsidered,* edited by Nina Glick Schiller, Linda Basch, and Cristina Blanc-Szanton (1–24). New York: New York, Academy of Sciences.

———. 1995. "From Immigrant to Transmigrant: Theorizing Transnational Migration." *Anthropological Quarterly* 68(1): 48–63.

Glick Schiller, Nina, and Georges Fouron. 1990. "'Everywhere We Go We Are in Danger': Ti Manno and the Emergence of a Haitian Transnational Identity." *American Ethnologist* 17(2): 329–47.

———. 1997. "'Laços de sangue': Os fundamentos do estado-nação transnacional." *Identidades* (special issue of *Revista Crítica de Ciêncians Sociais,* edited by Bela Feldman-Bianco) 48(June): 33–66.

———. 1998. "Transnational Lives and National Identities: The Identity Politics of Haitian Immigrants." In *Transnationalism From Below,* edited by Michael Peter Smith and Luis Guarnizo (130–61). New Brunswick, N.J.: Rutgers University Press.

———. 1999. "Terrains of Blood and Nation: Haitian Transnational Social Fields." *Ethnic and Racial Studies* 22(2): 340–66.

Goffman, Erving. 1963. *Stigma: Notes on the Management of Spoiled Identity.* Englewood Cliffs, N.J.: Prentice-Hall.

Gold, Steven. 1992. *Refugee Communities: A Comparative Field Study.* Newbury Park, Calif.: Sage.

Goldin, Claudia. 1994. "The Political Economy of Immigration Restriction in the United States, 1890 to 1921." In *The Regulated Economy: A Historical Approach to Political Economy,* edited by Claudia Goldin and Gary D. Libecap (223–57). Chicago: University of Chicago Press.

Goldring, Luin. 1992. "La migración México-EUA y la transnacionalización del espacio político y social: Perspectivas desde el México rural." *Estudios Sociológicos* 10(29): 315–40.

———. 1996a. "Blurring Borders: Constructing Transnational Community in the Process of Mexico-U.S.

Migration." *Research in Community Sociology* 6: 69–104.

———. 1996b. "Gendered Memory: Constructions of Rurality Among Mexican Transnational Migrants." In *Creating the Countryside: The Politics of Rural and Environmental Discourse,* edited by D. Melanie DuPuis and Peter Vandergeest (303–29). Philadelphia: Temple University Press.

———. 1998. "The Power of States in Transnational Fields." In *Transnationalism from Below*, edited by Michael Peter Smith and Luis Edwardo Guarnizo (165–95). New Brunswick, N.J.: Rutgers University Press.

Gonzalez, Nancie. 1988. *Sojourners of the Caribbean: Ethnogenesis and Ethnohistory of the Garifuna.* Urbana: University of Illinois Press.

Goodkind, David. 1997. "The Vietnamese Double Marriage Squeeze." *International Migration Review* 31: 108–27.

Gordon, David. 1972. *Theories of Poverty and Unemployment.* Lexington, Mass.: Heath.

Gordon, David, Richard Edwards, and Michael Reich. 1982. *Segmented Work, Divided Workers: The Historical Transformation of Labor in the United States.* Cambridge: Cambridge University Press.

Gordon, Milton. 1964. *Assimilation in American Life: The Role of Race, Religion, and National Origins.* New York: Oxford University Press.

Gorer, Geoffrey. 1963. *The American People: A Study in National Character.* Rev. ed. New York: Norton.

Goss, Jon D., and Bruce Lindquist. 1995. "Conceptualizing International Labor Migration: A Structuration Perspective." *International Migration Review* 29: 317–51.

Gould, Stephen Jay. 1996. *The Mismeasure of Man.* Rev. ed. New York: Norton.

Graham, John L. 1994. "Commentary on Multiculturalism." *Los Angeles Times* (Orange County edition), November 27, 17B.

Graham, Pamela. 1997a. "Nationality and Political Participation in the Transnational Context of Dominican Migration." In *Caribbean Circuits: Transnational Approaches to Migration,* edited by Patricia Pessar (91–126). Staten Island, N.Y.: Center for Migration Studies.

———. 1997b. "Re-imagining the Nation and Defining the District: The Simultaneous Political Incorporation of Dominican Transnational Migrants." Ph.D. diss., University of North Carolina at Chapel Hill.

Grant, David, and James H. Johnson, Jr. 1995. "Conservative Policymaking and Growing Urban Inequality During the 1980s." In *Research in Politics and Society,* vol. 5, *The Politics of Wealth and Inequality,* edited by Richard Ratcliff, Melvin L. Oliver, and Thomas Shapiro (127–60). Greenwich, Conn.: JAI Press.

Grantham, Dewey W., Jr. 1955. "The Progressive Movement and the Negro." *South Atlantic Quarterly* 54(October): 461–77.

Grasmuck, Sherri, and Patricia R. Pessar. 1991. *Between Two Islands: Dominican International Migration.* Berkeley: University of California Press.

Greeley, Andrew. 1976a. *Ethnicity, Denomination, and Inequality.* Beverly Hills, Calif.: Sage.

———. 1976b. "The Ethnic Miracle." *Public Interest* 45: 20–36.

———. 1977. *The American Catholic: A Social Portrait.* New York: Basic Books.

Greene, Victor H. 1968. *Slavic Community on Strike.* South Bend, Ind.: University of Notre Dame Press.

———. 1975. *For God and Country: The Rise of Polish and Lithuanian Consciousness in America.* Madison: State Historical Society of Wisconsin.

Greenhouse, Steven. 1995a. "GOP Backs Merging Foreign Policy Agencies." *New York Times,* February 15, A8.

———. 1995b. "It's a Hard Job Saving Foreign Aid (but the Job Is Still There)." *New York Times,* February 19, A18.

Greenwood, Michael J. 1981. *Migration and Economic Growth in the United States.* New York: Academic Press.

———. 1983. "The Economics of Mass Migration from Poor to Rich Countries: Leading Issues of Fact and Theory." *American Economic Review* 73: 173–77.

———. 1985. "Human Migration: Theory, Models, and Empirical Evidence." *Journal of Regional Science* 25: 521–44.

Greenwood, Michael J., Gary L. Hunt, and John M. McDowell. 1987. "Migration and Employment Change: Empirical Evidence on the Spatial and Temporal Dimensions of the Linkage." *Journal of Regional Science* 26: 223–34.

Greenwood, Michael J., and Marta Tienda. 1997. "U.S. Impacts of Mexican Immigration." In *Binational Study: U.S.-Mexico Migration* (ch. 4). Washington: U.S. Commission on Immigration Reform.

Gregory, Peter. 1986. *The Myth of Market Failure: Employment and the Labor Market in Mexico.* Baltimore: Johns Hopkins University Press.

Griffith, David. 1985. "Women, Remittances, and Reproduction." *American Ethnologist* 12(4): 676–90.

Grimsley, Kirsten D. 1995. "The Downside of Downswing." *Washington Post* (national weekly edition), November 13–19, 16.

Grogan, John. 1994. "U.S. Strategy: End Illegal Tide, Tap the New Potential." *Sun Sentinal,* October 30, 1994, p. 495.

Grosfoguel, Ramón. 1997. "Colonial Caribbean Migrations to France, the Netherlands, Great Britain, and the United States." *Ethnic and Racial Studies* 20(3): 594–612.

Grossman, Jean. 1982. "The Substitutability of Natives and Immigrants in Production." *Review of Economics and Statistics* 64: 596–603.

Guarnizo, Luis Eduardo. 1994. "Los Dominicanyorks: The Making of a Binational Society." *Annuals of the Academy of Political and Social Sciences* 533: 70–86.

———. 1996. "The Rise of Transnation Social Formations: Mexican and Dominican State Responses to Transnational Migration." *Political Power and Social Theory* 12: 45–94.

———. 1997a. "The Emergence of a Transnational Social Formation and the Mirage of Return Migration among Dominican Transmigrants." *Identities: Global Studies in Culture and Power* 4(2): 281–322.

———. 1997b. "'Going Home': Class, Gender, and Household Transformation Among Dominican Return Migrants. "In *Caribbean Circuits: New Directions in the Study of Caribbean Migration,* edited by Patricia Pessar (13–60). Staten Island, N.Y.: Center for Migration Studies.

Guarnizo, Luis Eduardo, and Luz Marian Diaz. 1999. "Transnational Migration." In *Transnationalism from Below,* edited by M.P. Smith and Luis Eduardo Guarnizo (3–34). New Brunswick, N.J.: Rutgers University Press.

Guarnizo, Luis Eduardo, and Michael Peter Smith. 1998. "The Locations of Transnationalism." In *Transnationalism from Below,* edited by Michael Peter Smith and Luis Eduardo Guarnizo. New Brunswick, N.J.: Rutgers University Press.

Guendelman, Sylvia, and B. Abrams. 1995. "Dietary Intake Among Mexican American Women: Generational Differences and a Comparison with White Non-Hispanic Women." *American Journal of Public Health* 85(1): 20–25.

Guendelman, Sylvia, J. Gould, M. Hudes, and B. Eskanazi. 1990. "Generational Differences in Perinatal Health Among the Mexican American Population: Findings from HHANES 1982–84." *American Journal of Public Health* 80(supplement): 61–65.

Guendelman, Sylvia, and Auristela Pérez-Itriaga. 1987. "Double Lives: The Changing Role of Women in Seasonal Migration." *Women's Studies* 13(3): 249–71.

Guest, Avery. 1980. "The Suburbanization of Ethnic Groups." *Sociology and Social Research* 64: 497–513.

Gulick, Sidney L. 1918. *American Democracy and Asiatic Citizenship.* New York: Charles Scribner.

Gurak, Douglas, and Mary Kritz. 1982. "Dominican and Colombian Women in New York City: Household Structure and Employment Patterns." *Migration Today* 10(3–4): 249–71.

———. 1988. "Household Composition and Employment of Dominican and Colombian Women in New York and Dominican Women in the Dominican Republic." Paper presented at the annual meeting of the American Sociological Association, Atlanta (August).

Guthrie, Patricia, and Janis Hutchinson. 1995. "The Impact of Perceptions on Interpersonal Interactions in an African American–Asian American Housing Project." *Journal of Black Studies* 25: 377–95.

Gutièrrez, David. 1997. "Transnationalism and Ethnic Americans: A Case Study in Recent History." Paper presented at the Conference on Immigrants, Civic Culture, and Modes of Political Incorporation: A Contemporary and Historical Comparison. Santa Fe, N.M. (April 24–25).

Gutman, Herbert G. 1976. *Work, Culture, and Society in Industrializing America: Essays in American Working-class and Social History.* New York: Random House.

Hacker, Andrew. 1992. *Two Nations: Black and White, Separate, Hostile, Unequal.* New York: Scribner's.

Hagan, Jacqueline. 1994. *Deciding to Be Legal: A Mayan Community in Houston.* Philadelphia: Temple University Press.

Hagan, Jacqueline M., and Susan Gonzalez-Baker. 1993. "Implementing the U.S. Legalization Program: The Influence of Immigrant Communities and Local Agencies on Immigration Policy Reform." *International Migration Review* 27: 513–36.

Haines, Michael R., and Allen C. Goodman. 1995. "A Home of One's Own: Aging and Homeownership in the United States in the Late Nineteenth and Early Twentieth Centuries." In *Aging in the Past: Demography, Society, and Old Age,* edited by David I. Kertzer and Peter Laslett. Berkeley: University of California Press.

Hale, Grace Elizabeth. 1998. *Making Whiteness: The Culture of Segregation in the South, 1890–1940.* New York: Pantheon Books.

Hall, Catherine. 1992. *White, Male and Middle Class: Explorations in Feminism and History.* New York: Routledge.

Halle, David. 1984. *America's Working Man.* Chicago: University of Chicago Press.

Hamermesh, Daniel S., and Frank D. Bean. 1998a. *Help or Hindrance?: The Economic Implications of Immigration for African Americans.* New York: Russell Sage Foundation.

———. 1998b. "Immigration and the Quality of Jobs." In *Help or Hindrance?: The Economic Implications of Immigration for African Americans,* edited by Dennis S. Hammermesh and Frank D. Bean (75–106). New York: Russell Sage Foundation.

Hamill, Pete. 1994. *A Drinking Life: A Memoir.* Boston: Little, Brown.

Hamilton, Bob, and John Whalley. 1984. "Efficiency and Distributional Implications of Global Restrictions on Labour Mobility: Calculations and Policy Implications." *Journal of Development Economics* 14: 61–75.

Handlin, Oscar. 1941. *Boston's Immigrants: A Study in Acculturation.* Cambridge, Mass.: Harvard University Press.

———. 1949. "Group Life Within the American Pattern: Its Scope and Its Limits." *Commentary* 8(November): 411–17.

———. 1950. *Race and Nationality in American Life.* Garden City: Doubleday.

———. 1957. *Race and Nationality in American Life.* Boston: Little, Brown.

———. 1959. *Immigration as a Factor in American History.* Englewood Cliffs, N.J.: Prentice-Hall.

———. 1973. *The Uprooted: The Epic Story of the Great Migrations That Made the American People.* 2nd ed. Boston: Little, Brown. (Originally published in 1951)

Hannerz, Ulf. 1992. *Cultural Complexity: Studies in the Social Organization of Meaning.* New York: Columbia University Press.

Hansen, Marcus Lee. 1940a. *The Immigrant in Ameri-*

can History, edited by Arthur M. Schlesinger. Cambridge, Mass.: Harvard University Press.

———. 1940b. *The Atlantic Migration, 1607–1860: A History of Continuing Settlement of the United States,* edited by Arthur M. Schlesinger. Cambridge, Mass.

Hareven, Tamara K. 1982. *Family Time and Industrial Time: The Relationship Between the Family and Work in a New England Industrial Community.* Cambridge: Cambridge University Press.

Harker, Richard, Cheleen Mahar, and Chris Wilkes. 1990. *An Introduction to the Work of Pierre Bourdieu: The Practice of Theory.* London: Macmillan.

Harrington, Mona. 1982. "Loyalties: Dual and Divided." In *The Politics of Ethnicity,* edited by Stephan Thernstrom (93–138). Cambridge: Harvard University Press.

Harris, Kathleen Mullan. 1999. "The Health Status and Risk Behavior of Adolescents in Immigrant Families." In *Children of Immigrants: Health, Adjustment, and Public Assistance,* edited by Donald J. Hernández. Washington: National Academy of Sciences Press.

Harris, Nigel. 1995. *The New Untouchables.* New York: Penguin Books.

Harrison, Roderick J., and Claudette E. Bennett. 1995. "Racial and Ethnic Diversity." In *State of the Union: America in the 1990s,* vol. 2, *Social Trends,* edited by Reynolds Farley (141–210). New York: Russell Sage Foundation.

Hartmann, Heidi. 1987. "Changes in Women's Economic and Family Roles in Post–World War II United States." In *Women, Households, and the Economy,* edited by Lourdes Benería and Catherine R. Stimpson (33–64). New Brunswick, N.J.: Rutgers University Press.

Harwood, Edwin. 1985. "How Should We Enforce Immigration Law?" In *Clamor at the Gates: The New American Immigration,* edited by Nathan Glazer (73–91). San Francisco: Institute for Contemporary Studies.

———. 1986a. "American Public Opinion and U.S. Immigration Policy." In *Immigration and American Public Policy,* edited by Rita J. Simon (201–12). *Annals of the American Academy of Political and Social Science,* vol. 487. Beverly Hills, Calif.: Sage.

———. 1986b. *In Liberty's Shadow: Illegal Aliens and Immigration Law Enforcement.* Stanford, Calif.: Hoover Institution Press.

Hatton, Timothy J., and Jeffrey G. Williamson. 1994a. "What Drove the Mass Immigrations from Europe in the Late Nineteenth Century?" *Population and Development Review* 20: 533–60.

———. 1994b. "International Migration 1850–1939: An Economic Survey." In *Migration and the International Labor Market: 1850–1939,* edited by Timothy J. Hatton and Jeffrey G. Williamson (3–32). London: Routledge.

———. 1995. "The Impact of Immigration on American Labor Markets Prior to the Quotas." Harvard University, Department of Economics. Unpublished paper.

———. 1998. *The Age of Mass Migration: Causes and Economic Impact.* Oxford: Oxford University Press.

Haynes, S. G., C. Harvey, H. Montes, H. Nicken, and B. H. Cohen. 1990. "Patterns of Cigarette Smoking Among Hispanics in the United States: Results from the HHANES 1982–84." *American Journal of Public Health* 80(supplement): 47–53.

Headden, Susan. 1995a. "One Nation, One Language?" *U.S. News & World Report,* September 25, 38–42.

———. 1995b. "Tongue-tied in the Schools." *U.S. News & World Report,* September 25, 44–46.

Heer, David. 1996. *Immigration in America's Future: Social Science Findings and the Policy Debate.* Boulder, Colo.: Westview.

Henderson, Jeffrey, and Manuel Castells, eds. 1987. *Global Restructuring and Territorial Development.* Beverly Hills, Calif.: Sage. Henry, Charles P. 1980. "Black–Chicano Coalitions: Possibilities and Problems." *Western Journal of Black Studies* 4: 222–32.

Henry, C.P. 1980. "Black-Chicano Coalitions: Possibilities and Problems." *Western Journal of Black Studies* 4:222–32.

Herberg, Will. 1960. *Protestant-Catholic-Jew.* New York: Anchor.

Herbers, John. 1986. *The New Heartland: America's Flight Beyond the Suburbs and How It Is Changing Our Future.* New York: Times Books.

Hernandez, Marita, and Austin Scott. 1980. "Latino Influx: New Strains Emerge as Watts Evolves." *Los Angeles Times,* August 24, 4.

Herrnstein, Richard J., and Charles Murray. 1994. *The Bell Curve: Intelligence and Class Structure in American Life.* New York: Free Press.

Hershey, Robert D., Jr. 1997. "U.S. Jobless Rate Hits 23-Year Low." *New York Times,* May 3, A1.

Hickman, Bert G. 1973. "What Became of the Building Cycle?" In *Nations and Households in Economic Growth: Essays in Honor of Moses Abramovitz,* edited by Paul David and Melvin Reder. New York: Academic Press.

Higgs, Robert. 1971. "American Inventiveness, 1870–1920." *Journal of Political Economy* 79(3): 661–67.

———. 1976. "Participation of Blacks and Immigrants in the American Merchant Class, 1890–1910: Some Demographic Relations." *Explorations in Economic History* 13(2): 335–50.

Higham, John. 1958. "Another Look at Nativism." *Catholic Historical Review* 44(2): 147–58.

———. 1966. "Another Look at Nativism." In *Pivotal Interpretations of American History,* edited by Carl N. Degler (vol. 2, 139–53). New York: Harper & Row.

———. 1971. "Another Look at Nativism." In *From Roosevelt to Roosevelt: American Politics and Diplomacy, 1901–1941,* edited by Otis L. Graham, Jr. (174–81). New York: Appleton-Century-Crofts.

———. 1974. *Strangers in a Strange Land: Patterns of American Nativism, 1860–1925.* New York: Antheneum. (Originally published in 1955).

———. 1975. *Send These to Me: Jews and Other Immigrants to Urban America.* New York: Atheneum.

———. 1981. "Integrating America: The Problem of Assimilation in the Nineteenth Century." *Journal of American Ethnic History* 1(Fall): 7–25.

———. 1982. "Leadership." In *The Politics of Ethnicity,* edited by Stephan Thernstrom (69–92). Cambridge: Harvard University Press.

———. 1984. *Send These to Me: Immigrants in Urban America.* Baltimore: Johns Hopkins University Press.

———. 1986. "The Strange Career of *Strangers in the Land.*" *American Jewish History* 76(2): 214–26.

———. 1988. *Strangers in the Land: Patterns of American Nativism, 1896–1925.* 2nd ed. New Brunswick, N.J.: Rutgers University Press. (Originally published in 1955)

———. 1989. *History: Professional Scholarship in America.* Baltimore: Johns Hopkins University Press.

———. 1990. "From Process to Structure: Formulations of American Immigration History." In *American Immigrants and Their Generations: Studies and Commentaries on the Hansen Thesis After Fifty Years,* edited by Peter Kivisto and Dag Blanck (11–41). Urbana: University of Illinois Press.

———. 1993. "Multiculturalism and Universalism: A History and Critique." *American Quarterly* 45(2): 195–219.

———. 1994. *Strangers in the Land.* 2nd ed., revised. New Brunswick, N.J.: Rutgers University Press.

———. 1997. *Civil Rights and Social Wrongs: Black-White Relations Since World War II.* University Park: Pennsylvania State University Press.

Hill, Peter J. 1975. "Relative Skill and Income Levels of Native and Foreign-born Workers in the United States." *Explorations in Economic History* 12(1): 47–60.

Hing, Bill Ong. 1993a. *Making and Remaking Asian America Through Immigration Policy, 1850–1990.* Stanford, Calif.: Stanford University Press.

———. 1993b. "Beyond the Rhetoric of Assimilation and Cultural Pluralism: Addressing the Tension of Separatism and Conflict in an Immigration–Driven Multiracial Society." *California Law Review* 81: 863–925.

Hirsch, Arnold R. 1983. *Making the Second Ghetto: Race and Housing in Chicago, 1940–1960.* New York: Cambridge University Press.

Hirschman, Albert O. 1981. "Exit, Voice, and the State." In *Essays in Trespassing: Economics to Politics and Beyond,* edited by Albert O. Hirschman (246–65). Cambridge: Cambridge University Press.

Hirschman, Charles. 1983. "The Melting Pot Reconsidered." *Annual Review of Sociology* 9: 397–423.

———. 1994. "Problems and Prospects of Studying Immigrant Adaptation from the 1990 Population Census: From Generation Comparison to the Process of 'Becoming American.'" *International Migration Review* 28(4): 690–713.

———. 1996. "Studying Immigrant Adaptation from the 1990 Population Census: From Generational Comparisons to the Process of 'Becoming American.'" In *The New Second Generation,* edited by Alejandro Portes (54–81). New York: Russell Sage Foundation.

———. In press. "Race and Ethnic Population Projections: A Critical Evaluation of Their Content and Meaning." In *American Diversity: A Demographic Challenge for the Twenty-first Century,* edited by Nancy A. Denton and Stewart Tolnay. Albany: State University of New York Press.

Hirschman, Charles, and Luis Falcon. 1985. "The Educational Attainment of Religio-Ethnic Groups in the United States." *Research in Sociology of Education and Socialization* 5: 83–120.

Hirschman, Charles, and Morrison G. Wong. 1984. "Socioeconomic Gains of Asian Americans, Blacks, and Hispanics: 1960–1976." *American Journal of Sociology* 90(3): 584–607.

———. 1986. "The Extraordinary Educational Attainment of Asian Americans: A Search for Historical Evidence and Explanations." *Social Forces* 65: 1–27.

Ho, Christine. 1993. "The Internationalization of Kinship and the Feminization of Caribbean Migration: The Case of Afro-Trinidadian Immigrants in Los Angeles." *Human Organization* 52(1): 32–40.

Hobsbawm, Eric. 1975. *The Age of Capital.* New York: Scribner's.

———. 1983. "Introduction." In *Inventing Traditions, and Mass-producing Traditions: Europe in the Invention of Tradition,* edited by Eric Hobsbawm and Terence Ranger. Cambridge: Cambridge University Press.

———. 1992. *Nations and Nationalism Since 1780.* Cambridge: Cambridge University Press.

Hobsbawm, Eric, and Terence Ranger. 1992. *The Invention of Tradition.* Cambridge: Cambridge University Press. (Originally published in 1983)

Hodgdon, A. Dana. 1931. "Extension of Administrative Authority in Immigration Regulation." *American Foreign Service Journal* 8(2, February): 45–49, 84–86.

Hodge, Robert. 1973. "Toward a Theory of Racial Differences in Employment." *Social Forces* 52: 16–31.

Hodson, Randy, and Robert L. Kaufman. 1982. "Economic Dualism: A Critical Review." *American Sociological Review* 47(6): 727–39.

Hoerder, Dirk, ed. 1983. *American Labor and Immigration History, 1877–1920s: Recent European Research.* Urbana: University of Illinois Press.

———, ed. 1985. *Labor Migration in the Atlantic Economies: The European and North American Working Classes During the Period of Industrialization.* Westport, Conn.: Greenwood Press.

Hoffman, Abraham. 1974. *Unwanted Mexican Americans in the Great Depression: Repatriation Pressures, 1929–1939.* Tempe: University of Arizona Press.

Holder, Calvin. 1980. "The Rise of the West Indian Politician in New York City." *AfroAmericans in New York Life and History* 4: 45–59.

Holli, Melvin G. 1981. "The Great War Sinks Chicago's

German *Kultur.*" In *Ethnic Chicago,* edited by Melvin G. Holli and Peter d'A. Jones (460–512). Grand Rapids, Mich.: W. B. Erdman Pubishers.

Hollifield, James F. 1992. *Immigrants, Markets, and States: The Political Economy of Postwar Europe.* Cambridge, Mass.: Harvard University Press.

———. 1994. "Immigration and Republicanism in France." In *Controlling Immigration: A Global Perspective,* edited by Wayne A. Cornelius, Philip L. Martin, and James F. Hollifield (143–75). Stanford, Calif.: Stanford University Press.

———. 1996. "The Migration Crisis in Western Europe: The Search for a National Model." In *Migration, Ethnicity, Conflict,* edited by Klaus Bade (367–402). Osnabrück, Austria: Universitätsverlag Rasch.

Hollinger, David A. 1995. *Postethnic America: Beyond Multiculturalism.* New York: Basic Books.

Holmes, S. A. 1995. "Report of Accelerating U.S. Immigration Will Intensify Debate." *Raleigh News and Observer,* September 3, 30A.

Holzer, Harry J. 1991. "The Spatial Mismatch Hypothesis: What Has the Evidence Shown?" *Urban Studies* 28(1): 105–22.

———. 1996. *What Employers Want.* New York: Russell Sage Foundation.

Hondagneu-Sotelo, Pierrette. 1994. *Gendered Transitions: Mexican Experiences of Immigration.* Berkeley: University of California Press.

———. 1995. "Women and Children First: New Directions in Anti-immigrant Politics." *Socialist Review* 25(1): 169–90.

———. 1996. "Unpacking 187: Targeting Mexicanas." In *Immigration and Ethnic Communities: A Focus on Latinos,* edited by Refugio I. Rochin. Lansing, Mich.: Julian Samora Research Institute.

Hondagneu-Sotelo, Pierrette, and Ernestine Avila. 1997. "'I'm Here, but I'm There': The Meanings of Latina Transnational Motherhood." *Gender and Society* 11(5): 548–69.

Horne, Donald. 1986. *The Triumph of Industrialism.* London: Pluto Press.

Horowitz, Donald. 1985. *Ethnic Groups in Conflict.* Berkeley: University of California Press.

Horsman, Reginald. 1981. *Race and Manifest Destiny: The Origins of American Racial Anglo-Saxonism.* Cambridge, Mass.: Harvard University Press.

Horton, John. 1995. *The Politics of Diversity: Immigration, Resistance, and Change in Monterey Park, California.* Philadelphia: Temple University Press.

Hossfeld, Karen J. 1994. "Hiring Immigrant Women: Silicon Valley's 'Simple Solution.'" In *Women of Color in U.S. Society,* edited by Maxine Baca Zinn and Bonnie Thornton Dill (65–93). Philadelphia: Temple University Press.

Houston Independent School District. 1995. *District and School Profiles 1994–1995.* Houston: Houston Independent School District.

Houstoun, Marion, Roger Kramer, and Joan Macklin Barrett. 1984. "Female Predominance of Immigration to the United States Since 1930: A First Look." *International Migration Review* 18(4): 908–63.

Hout, Michael, Adrian Raftery, and Eleanor Bell. 1993. "Making the Grade: Educational Stratification in the United States, 1925–1989." In *Persistent Inequality: Changing Educational Attainment in Thirteen Countries,* edited by Yossi Shavit and Hans Peter Blossfeld (25–49). Boulder, Colo.: Westview.

Howe, Irving. 1976. *World of Our Fathers: The Journey of the East European Jews to America and the Life They Found and Made.* New York: Simon & Schuster.

Howell, David, and Elizabeth Mueller. 1998. "Immigration and Native-Born Male Earnings: A Jobs-Level Analysis of the New York City Metropolitan Area Labor Market, 1980–1990." Milano Graduate School, New School university (July). Unpublished paper.

Hsia, Jayjia. 1988. *Asian Americans in Higher Education and at Work.* Hillsdale, N.J.: Erlbaum.

Hsueh, Sheri, and Marta Tienda. 1995. "Earnings Consequences of Employment Instability Among Minority Men." *Research in Social Stratification and Mobility* 14: 39–69.

———. 1996. "Gender, Ethnicity, and Labor-Force Instability." *Social Science Research* 25(1): 73–94.

Hudson, Teresa. 1995. "Cutting off Care." *Hospitals and Health Networks* 69: 36.

Hugo, Graeme J. 1981. "Village-Community Ties, Village Norms, and Ethnic and Social Networks: A Review of Evidence from the Third World." In *Migration Decisionmaking: Multidisciplinary Approaches to Microlevel Studies in Developed and Developing Countries,* edited by Gordon F. DeJong and Robert W. Gardner (186–224). New York: Pergamon.

Hunt, Jennifer. 1992. "The Impact of the 1962 Repatriates from Algeria on the French Labor Market." *Industrial and Labor Relations Review* 45: 556–72.

Huntington, Samuel P. 1981. *American Politics: The Promise of Disharmony.* Cambridge, Mass.: Harvard University Press.

Hurh, Won Moo, and Kwang Chung Kim. 1984. *Korean Immigrants in America.* Rutherford, N.J.: Fairleigh Dickinson University Press.

Hutchinson, Edward P. 1981. *Legislative History of American Immigration Policy: 1798–1965.* Philadelphia: University of Pennsylvania Press.

Ichioka, Yuji. 1988. *The Issei: The World of the First-Generation Japanese Immigrants, 1885–1924.* New York: Free Press.

Ignatieff, Michael. 1993. *Blood and Belonging: Journeys into the New Nationalism.* New York: Farrar, Strauss, and Giroux.

Ignatiev, Noel. 1995. *How the Irish Became White.* New York: Routledge.

Institute for Social Science Research. 1992. *Los Angeles County Social Survey.* University of California, Los Angeles: Institute for Social Science Research.

———. 1994. *Los Angeles Survey of Urban Inequality.* University of California, Los Angeles: Institute for Social Science Research.

Inter-Ethnic Forum of Houston, 1995. "The Inter-Ethnic Forum of Houston: Building Bridges Across Diverse Ethnic and Racial Communities: A Proposal." Houston: Inter-Ethnic Forum of Houston (May).

International Union for the Scientific Study of Population, Committee on South-North Migration. 1997. *Proceedings.* Conference on International Migration at Century's End: Trends and Issues. Barcelona, Spain (May 7–10). Liege, Belgium: International Union for the Scientific Study of Population.

Isbister, John. 1996. *The Immigration Debate: Remaking America.* West Hartford, Conn.: Kumarian Press.

Iyengar, Shanto. 1987. *News That Matters: Television and American Opinion.* Chicago: University of Chicago Press.

———. 1991. *Is Anyone Responsible?: How Television Frames Political Issues.* Chicago: University of Chicago Press.

Jackson, Jacqueline J. 1995. "Competition Between Blacks and Immigrants." *The Social Contract* 5: 247–54.

Jackson, Maria R., James H. Johnson, Jr., and Walter C. Farrell, Jr. 1994. "After the Smoke Has Cleared: An Analysis of Selected Responses to the Los Angeles Civil Unrest of 1992." *Contentions: Debates in Society, Culture, and Science* 3: 3–22.

Jackson, Pauline. 1984. "Women in Nineteenth-Century Irish Emigration." *International Migration Review* 18(4): 1004–20.

Jacobson, David. 1996. *Rights Across Borders: Immigration and the Decline of Citizenship.* Baltimore: Johns Hopkins University Press.

———. 1998. *The Immigration Reader: America in a Multidisciplinary Perspective.* Malden, Mass.: Blackwell.

Jacobson, Matthew Frye. 1995. *Special Sorrows: The Diasporic Imagination of Irish, Polish, and Jewish Immigrants in the United States.* Cambridge, Mass.: Harvard University Press.

———. 1998. *Whiteness of a Different Color: European Immigrants and the Alchemy of Race.* Cambridge, Mass.: Harvard University Press.

Jaeger, David. 1996. "Skill Differences and the Effect of Immigrants on the Wages of Natives." Washington: U.S. Bureau of Labor Statistics. Unpublished paper.

Jaleshgari, Ramin. 1995. "Taking Life's Big Step: Marriage (Arranged)." *New York Times* (Long Island weekly edition), August 13.

James, Henry. 1898. "Purely as an American." *Literature* 23(April). Reprinted in *The Faber Book of America,* edited by Christopher Ricks and William L. Vance (252–53). Boston: Faber and Faber, 1992.

Jamieson, Kathleen Hall. 1996. *Packaging the Presidency: A History and Criticism of Presidential Campaign Advertising.* New York: Oxford University Press.

Janowitz, Morris. 1983. *The Reconstruction of Patriotism: Education for Civic Consciousness.* Chicago: University of Chicago Press.

Janson, Florence E. 1931. *The Background of Swedish Immigration, 1840–1930.* Chicago: University of Chicago Press.

Jasso, Guillermina, and Mark R. Rozenzweig. 1990. *The New Chosen People: Immigrants in the United States.* New York: Russell Sage Foundation.

Jaynes, Gerald D., and Robin M. Williams, Jr., eds. 1989. *A Common Destiny: Blacks and American Society.* Washington: National Academy Press.

Jencks, Christopher and Susan Mayer. 1990. "The Social Consequences of Growing up in a Poor Neighborhood." In National Resource Council, *Inner-city Poverty in the United States* (111–86). Washington: National Academy Press.

Jenkins, Richard. 1992. *Pierre Bourdieu.* London: Routledge.

Jenks, R. 1995. "Chances for Immigration Reform Improve." *Immigration Review* 22(Summer): 1–5.

Jensen, Leif. 1988a. "Poverty and Immigration in the United States: 1960–1980." In *Divided Opportunities,* edited by Gary D. Sandefur and Marta Tienda (117–37). New York: Plenum.

———. 1988b. "Patterns of Immigration and Public Assistance Utilization, 1970–1980." *International Migration Review* 22(1): 51–83.

Jensen, Leif, and Yoshimi Chitose. 1994. "Today's Second Generation: Evidence from the 1990 Census." *International Migration Review* 28(4): 714–35.

Jerome, Harry. 1926. *Migration and Business Cycles.* New York: National Bureau of Economic Research.

Jessop, Bob. 1994. "Post-Fordism and the State." *In Post-Fordism: A Reader,* edited by Ash Amin. Oxford: Blackwell.

Jet. 1988a. "Black Stereotypes Used to Market Products in Japan." August 15, 36–37.

———. 1988b. "Japanese Slurs on Blacks Causing Rift Between Them." October 31, 12.

Joffe, Joseph. 1997. "America the Inescapable." *New York Times Magazine,* June 8, 38–43.

Johansson, S. Ryan. 1994. "Food for Thought: Rhetoric and Reality in Modern Mortality History." *Historical Methods* 27(3): 101–25.

Johnson, James H., Jr., and Walter C. Farrell, Jr. 1993. "The Fire This Time: The Genesis of the Los Angeles Rebellion of 1992." *North Carolina Law Review* 71: 1403–20.

———. 1998. "Growing Income Inequality in American Society: A Political Economy Perspective." In *The Growth of Income Disparity,* edited by James Auerbach (133–80). Washington: National Policy Association.

Johnson, James H., Jr., Walter C. Farrell, Jr., and Maria R. Jackson. 1994. "Los Angeles One Year Later: A Prospective Assessment of Responses to the 1992 Civil Unrest." *Economic Development Quarterly* 8: 19–27.

Johnson, James H., Jr., and David Grant. 1997. "Post-1980 Black Population Redistribution Trends in the United States." *Southeastern Geographer* 37: 1–19.

Johnson, James H., Jr., Cloyzell K. Jones, Walter C. Farrell, Jr., and Melvin L. Oliver. 1992. "The Los Angeles Rebellion: A Retrospective View." *Economic Development Quarterly* 6: 356–72.

Johnson, James H., Jr., and Melvin L. Oliver. 1989. "Interethnic Minority Conflict in Urban America: The Effects of Economic and Social Dislocations." *Urban Geography* 10: 449–63.

———. 1992. "Structural Changes in the U.S. Economy and Black Male Joblessness: A Reassessment." In *Urban Labor Markets and Job Opportunity,* edited by George E. Peterson and Wayne Vroman (113–47). Washington: Urban Institute Press.

Johnson, James H., Jr., Melvin L. Oliver, and Lawrence D. Bobo. 1994. "Understanding the Contours of Deepening Urban Inequality: Theoretical Underpinnings and Research Design of Multi-city Study." *Urban Geography* 15: 77–89.

Johnson, James H., Jr., Melvin L. Oliver, and Curtis C. Roseman. 1989. "Ethnic Dilemmas in Comparative Perspective." *Urban Geography* 10: 425–33.

Johnson, James H., Jr., and Curtis C. Roseman. 1990. "Recent Black Out-migration from Los Angeles: The Role of Household Dynamics and Kinship Systems." *Annals of the Association of American Geographers* 80: 205–22.

Johnson-Webb, Karen, and James H. Johnson, Jr. 1997. "North Carolina Communities in Transition: An Overview of Hispanic In-migration." *North Carolina Geographer* 5: 21–39.

Johnston, Louis. 1990. "Endogenous Growth and the American Economy." Ph.D. diss., University of California at Berkeley.

Jones, Maldwyn Allen. 1960. *American Immigration.* 2d ed. Chicago: University of Chicago Press.

———. 1969. "Oscar Handlin." In *Pastmasters: Some Essays on American Historians,* edited by Marcus Cunliffe and Robin W. Winks. New York: Harper & Row.

———. 1992. *American Immigration.* 2nd ed. Chicago: University of Chicago Press. (Originally published in 1960)

Jones-Correa, Michael. 1997. *Between Two Nations: The Political Predicament of Latinos in New York City.* Ithaca, N.Y.: Cornell University Press.

Jordan, Barbara. 1995. "The Americanization Ideal." *New York Times,* September 11, A11.

Joselit, Jenna W. 1994. *The Wonders of America: Reinventing Jewish Culture, 1880–1950.* New York: Hill & Wang.

Jost, Kenneth. 1995. "Cracking Down on Immigration: Should Government Benefits and Service Be Cut Off?" *Congressional Quarterly—Researcher* 5: 99–119.

Jusdanis, Gregory. 1991. "Greek Americans and Diaspora." *Diaspora* 1(2): 209–23.

Kahn, Zorina B., and Kenneth L. Sokoloff. 1993. "'Schemes of Practical Utility': Entrepreneurship and Innovation Among 'Great Inventors' in the United States, 1790–1865." *Journal of Economic History* 52(2): 289–307.

Kallen, Horace. 1924. *Culture and Democracy in the United States.* New York: Boni & Liveright.

Kalmijn, Matthijs. 1993. "Trends in Black-White Intermarriage." *Social Forces* 72(September): 119–46.

Kammen, Michael. 1993. *Mystic Chords of Memory: The Transformation of Tradition in American Culture.* New York: Vintage.

Kanjanapan, Wilawan. 1994. "The Immigration of Asian Professionals to the United States: 1988–1990." *International Migration Review* 29: 7–32.

Kann, Laura, Charles Warren, William Harris, Janet Collins, Kathy Douglas, Mary Elizabeth Collins, Barbara Williams, James Ross, Lloyd Kolbe, and State and Local YRBSS Coordinators. 1995. "Youth Risk Behavior Surveillance: United States, 1993." *Morbidity and Mortality Weekly Report* 44(SS-1): 1–56.

Kao, Grace, and Marta Tienda. 1995. "Optimism and Achievement: The Educational Performance of Immigrant Youth." *Social Science Quarterly* 76(1): 1–19.

Kaplan, M., and G. Marks. 1990. "Adverse Effects of Acculturation: Psychological Distress Among Mexican American Young Adults." *Social Science and Medicine* 31(12): 1313–19.

Karakasidou, Anastasia. 1994. "Sacred Scholars, Profane Advocates: Intellectuals Molding National Consciousness in Greece." *Identities: Global Studies in Cultural Power* 1(1): 35–61.

Karoly, Lynn A. 1993. "The Trend in Inequality Among Families, Individuals, and Workers in the United States: A Twenty-five-year Perspective." In *Uneven Tides: Rising Inequality in America,* edited by Sheldon Danziger and Peter Gottschalk (ch. 2). New York: Russell Sage Foundation.

Kasarda, John D. 1995. "Industrial Restructuring and the Changing Location of Jobs." In *State of the Union,* edited by Reynolds Farley (vol. 1, ch. 5). New York: Russell Sage Foundation.

Kasinitz, Philip. 1992. *Caribbean New York: Black Immigrants and the Politics of Race.* Ithaca, N.Y.: Cornell University Press.

Katz, Friedrich. 1981. *The Secret War in Mexico: Europe, the United States, and the Mexican Revolution.* Chicago: University of Chicago Press.

Katz, Jeffrey L. 1996. "Provisions of the Welfare Bill." *Congressional Quarterly,* August 3, 2192–94.

Katz, Lawrence. 1994. "Labor's Past and Future." *Challenge* 24: 18–25.

Katz, Lawrence, Gary Loveman, and David Blanchflower. 1995. "A Comparison of Changes in the Structure of Wages." In *Differences and Changes in Wage Structures,* edited by Richard Freeman and Lawrence Katz (25–65). Chicago: University of Chicago Press.

Katz, Lawrence, and Kevin Murphy. 1992. "Changes in Relative Wages, 1963–1987: Supply and Demand Factors." *Quarterly Journal of Economics* 107(1): 35–78.

Kaufman, Robert L., Randy Hodson, and Neal Fligstein. 1981. "Defrocking Dualism: A New Approach to Defining Industrial Sectors." *Social Science Research* 10(1): 1–31.

Kazal, Russell. 1995. "Revisiting Assimilation: The Rise,

Fall, and Reappraisal of a Concept in American Ethnic History." *American Historical Review* 100(2, April): 437–72.

———. 1998. "Becoming 'Old Stock": The Waning of German-American Identity in Philadelphia, 1900–1930." Ph.D. dissertation. Philadelphia: University of Pennsylvania.

Kearney, Michael. 1986. "From the Invisible Hand to Visible Feet: Anthropological Studies of Migration and Development." *Annual Review of Anthropology* 15: 331–61.

———. 1991. "Borders and Boundaries of the State and Self at the End of Empire." *Journal of Historical Sociology* 4(1): 52–74.

———. 1995. "The Local and the Global: The Anthropology of Globalization and Transnationalism." *Annual Review of Anthropology* 24: 547–65.

———. 1996. "Post–Melting Pot Realism." *American Anthropologist* 98(4): 867–69.

Keeler, William C. 1995. "Welcoming the Stranger: A Reflection of the Current Immigration Debate." *Migration World* 23: 33.

Keely, Charles B. 1979. *U.S. Immigration: A Policy Analysis.* New York: Population Council.

Kelley, Allen C. 1972. "Scale Economies, Inventive Activity, and the Economics of American Population Growth." *Explorations in Economic History* 10(1): 35–52.

Kemper, Robert. 1977. *Migration and Adaptation: Tzintzuntzan Peasants in Mexico City.* Beverly Hills, Calif.: Sage.

Keniston, K., and the Carnegie Council on Children. 1977. *All Our Children.* New York: Harcourt Brace Jovanovich.

Kennedy, David M. 1980. *Over Here: The First World War and American Society.* New York: Oxford University Press.

Kennedy, Louise V. 1930. *The Negro Peasant Turns Cityward: Effects of Recent Migration to Northern Cities.* New York: Columbia University Press.

Kennedy, Paul. 1994. *Preparing for the Twenty-first Century.* New York: Vintage.

Kennedy, Ruby Jo Reeves. 1944. "Single or Triple Melting Pot?: Intermarriage Trends in New Haven, 1870–1940." *American Journal of Sociology* 49: 331–39.

———. 1952. "Single or Triple Melting Pot?: Intermarriage in New Haven, 1870–1950." *American Journal of Sociology* 58: 56–59.

Kerr, Clark, John T. Dunlop, and Frederick H. Harbison. 1964. *Industrialism and Industrial Man: The Problems of Labor and Management in Economic Growth.* New York: Oxford University Press.

Kessler-Harris, Alice, and Karen Brodkin Sacks. 1987. "The Demise of Domesticity in America." In *Women, Households, and the Economy,* edited by Lourdes Benería and Catherine R. Stimpson (65–84). New Brunswick, N.J.: Rutgers University Press.

Kessner, Thomas. 1977. *The Golden Door: Italian and Jewish Immigrant Mobility in New York City, 1880–1915.* New York: Oxford University Press.

Kibria, Nazli. 1993. *Family Tightrope: The Changing Lives of Vietnamese Americans.* Princeton, N.J.: Princeton University Press.

Kim, Elaine. 1990. "'Such Opposite Creatures': Men and Women in Asian American Literature." *Michigan Quarterly Review* 29(1): 68–93.

Kim, Illsoo. 1981. *New Urban Immigrants: The Korean Community in New York.* Princeton, N.J.: Princeton University Press.

Kim, Kwang Chung. 1985. "Ethnic Resources Utilization of Korean Immigrant Entrepreneurs in the Chicago Minority Area." *International Migration Review* 19: 82–111.

Kim, Kwang Chung, and Won M. Hurh. 1985. "Ethnic Resources Utilization of Korean Immigrant Entrepreneurs in the Chicago Minority Area." *International Migration Review* 19: 82–111.

Kim, Sophia. 1984. "Seeking a Dialogue by Koreans, Blacks." *Los Angeles Times,* June 8, pt. 5, p. 8.

Kindelberger, Charles P. 1967. *Europe's Postwar Growth: The Role of Labor Supply.* Cambridge: Harvard University Press.

King, Miriam, and Steven Ruggles. 1990. "American Immigration, Fertility Differentials, and the Ideology of Race Suicide at the Turn of the Century." *Journal of Interdisciplinary History* 20(3): 347–69.

Kirk, Dudley. 1946. *Europe's Population in the Interwar Years.* Princeton, N.J.: Princeton University Press.

Kirschenman, Joleen, and Kathryn M. Neckerman. 1991. "'We'd Love to Hire Them, But . . .': The Meaning of Race for Employers." In *The Urban Underclass,* edited by Christopher Jencks and Paul E. Peterson (203–24). Washington: Brookings Institution.

Kiser, Clyde V. 1932. *Sea Island to City: A Study of St. Helena Islanders in Harlem and Other Urban Centers.* New York: Columbia University Press.

Kivisto, Peter, and Dag Blanck, eds. 1990. *American Immigrants and Their Generations: Studies and Commentaries on the Hansen Thesis After Fifty Years.* Urbana: University of Illinois Press.

Klarman, Michael J. 1994. "How *Brown* Changed Race Relations: The Backlash Thesis." *Journal of American History* 81(1): 81–118.

Kliewer, Erich V., and Ken R. Smith. 1995. "Breast Cancer Mortality Among Immigrants in Australia and Canada." *Journal of the National Cancer Institute* 87(15, August 2): 1154–61.

Knight, Richard V., and Gary Gappert, eds. 1989. *Cities of Global Society: Urban Affairs Annual Reviews.* Vol. 35: Sage.

Knox, Paul. 1994. "World Cities and Organizations of Global Space." Paper presented at the New Hampshire International Seminar Series, University of New Hampshire. Durham, N.H. (October 7, 1994).

Kohl, Herbert. 1994. *"I Won't Learn from You" and Other Thoughts on Creative Maladjustment.* New York: New Press.

Kohn, Melvin L. 1987. "Cross-national Research as an

Analytic Strategy." *American Sociological Review* 52: 713–31.

Koltyk, JoAnn. 1998. *New Pioneers in the Heartland: Hmong Life in Wisconsin*. Boston: Allyn and Bacon.

Konvitz, Milton R. 1946. *The Alien and the Asiatic in American Law*. Ithaca, N.Y.: Cornell University Press.

Korman, Gerd. 1965. "Americanization at the Factory Gate." *Industrial and Labor Relations Review* 18(April): 396–419.

Kornblum, William, and James Beshers. 1988. "White Ethnicity: Ecological Dimensions." In *Power, Culture, and Place: Essays on New York City*, edited by John Mollenkopf (201–22). New York: Russell Sage Foundation.

Kossoudji, Sherrie. 1988. "English-Language Ability and the Labor Market Opportunities of Hispanic and East Asian Immigrant Men." *Journal of Labor Economics* 6: 205–28.

———. 1992. "Playing Cat and Mouse at the U.S.-Mexican Border." *Demography* (May).

Kossoudji, Sherrie, and Susan Ranney. 1984. "The Labor Market Experience of Female Migrants: The Case of Temporary Mexican Migration to the United States." *International Migration Review* 18(4): 120–43.

Kraut, Alan M. 1982. *The Huddled Masses: The Immigrant in American Society, 1880–1921*. Arlington Heights, Ill.: Harlan Davidson.

Krickus, Richard. 1976. *Pursuing the American Dream*. New York: Anchor Press/Doubleday.

Krikorian, Mark. 1995. "Jordan Commission Issues Interim Recommendations on Legal Immigration." *Immigration Review* 22(Summer): 5–8.

Krissman, Fred. 1994. "The Transnationalization of the North American Agricultural Sector: Mechanization or 'Mexicanization' of Production?" Paper presented at the Eighteenth International Congress of the Latin American Studies Association, Atlanta (March 12).

Krug, Edward A. 1969. *The Shaping of the American High School 1880–1920*. Madison: University of Wisconsin Press.

Kubat, Daniel. 1979a. *The Politics of Migration Policies: The First World in the 1970s*. Staten Island, N.Y.: Center for Migration Studies.

———. 1979b. "Canada." In *The Politics of Migration Policies*, edited by Daniel Kubat (19–36). Staten Island, N.Y.: Center for Migration Studies.

Kuhn, Annette, and Ann Marie Wolpe. 1978. *Materialism and Feminism*. London: Routledge and Kegan Paul.

Kuhn, Thomas S. 1970. *The Structure of Scientific Revolutions*. 2nd ed. Chicago: University of Chicago Press.

Kurthen, H. 1995. "Germany at the Crossroads: National Identity and the Challenge of Immigration." *International Migration Review* 29(4): 914–38.

Kuznets, Simon. 1952. "Long-term Changes in the National Income of the United States of America Since 1870." In *Income and Wealth of the United States: Trends and Structure*. Cambridge: International Association for Research in Income and Wealth. Reprinted as "The Contribution of Immigration to the Growth of the Labor Force" in *The Reinterpretation of American Economic History*, edited by Robert William Fogel and Stanley L. Engerman. New York: Harper & Row, 1971.

———. 1958. "Long Swings in the Growth of Population and in Related Economic Variables." *Proceedings of the American Philosophical Society* 102: 31–36.

———. 1961. *Capital in the American Economy: Its Formation and Financing*. Princeton, N.J.: Princeton University Press/National Bureau of Economic Research.

Kuznets, Simon, and Ernest Rubin. 1954. *Immigration and the Foreign-born*. Occasional Paper 46. New York: National Bureau of Economic Research.

Kwong, Peter. 1987. *The New Chinatown*. New York: Hill and Wang.

———. 1992. "The First Multicultural Riots." In *Inside the Los Angeles Riots: What Really Happened—and Why It Will Happen Again*, edited by Don Hazen (88–93). Los Angeles: Institute for Alternative Journalism.

Kyle, David. 1995. "The Transnational Peasant: The Social Structures of Economic Migration from the Ecuadoran Andes." Ph.D. diss., Department of Sociology, Johns Hopkins University.

Kymlicka, Will, ed. 1995. *Multicultural Citizenship: A Liberal Theory of Minority Rights*. New York: Oxford University Press.

Lal, Barbara Ballis. 1990. *The Romance of Culture in an Urban Civilization: Robert E. Park on Race and Ethnic Relations in Cities*. London: Routledge.

LaLonde, Robert J., and Robert H. Topel. 1990. "The Assimilation of Immigrants in the U.S. Labor Market." Working Paper 3573. Cambridge, Mass.: National Bureau of Economic Research.

———. 1991. "Labor Market Adjustments to Increased Immigration." In *Immigration, Trade, and the Labor Market*, edited by J. Abowd and R. Freeman (167–99). Chicago: University of Chicago Press.

———. 1994. "Economic Impact of International Migration and the Economic Performance of Migrants." Working Paper. University of Chicago.

Lamphere, Louise. 1986. "From Working Daughters to Working Mothers: Production and Reproduction in an Industrial Community." *American Ethnologist* 13(1): 118–30.

———. 1987. *From Working Daughters to Working Mothers: Immigrant Women in a New England Industrial Community*. Ithaca, N.Y.: Cornell University Press.

———, ed. 1992. *Structuring Diversity: Ethnographic Perspectives of the New Immigration*. Chicago: University of Chicago Press.

Lamphere, Louise, Patricia Zavella, and Felipe

Gonzales, with Peter Evans. 1993. *Sunbelt Working Mothers.* Ithaca, N.Y.: Cornell University Press.

Landale, Nancy S., and R. S. Oropesa. 1995. "Immigrant Children and the Children of Immigrants: Inter- and Intra-Group Differences in the United States." Research Paper 95–02. Population Research Group, Michigan State University.

Landale, Nancy S., R. S. Oropesa, and Bridget K. Gorman. 1999. "Immigration and Infant Health: Birth Outcomes of Immigrant and Native Women." In *Children of Immigrants: Health, Adjustment, and Public Assistance,* edited by Donald J. Hernández. Washington: National Academy of Sciences Press.

Lane, Robert E. 1991. *The Market Experience.* New York: Cambridge University Press.

Laponce, J. A. 1987. *Languages and Their Territories,* translated by Anthony Martin-Sperry. Toronto: University of Toronto Press.

LaRuffa, Anthony. 1988. *Monte Carmelo: An Italian American Community in the Bronx.* New York: Gordon and Breach.

Lasch, Christopher. 1984. *The Minimal Self: Psychic Survival in Troubled Times.* New York: Norton.

———. 1991. *The True and Only Heaven: Progress and Its Critics.* New York: Norton.

Layton-Henry, Zig. 1994. "Britain: The Would-be Zero-Immigration Country." In *Controlling Immigration: A Global Perspective,* edited by Wayne A. Cornelius, Philip L. Martin and James F. Hollifield (273–96). Stanford, Calif.: Stanford University Press.

Lazerson, Marvin. 1971. *Origins of the Urban School: Public Education in Massachusetts, 1870–1915.* Cambridge, Mass.: Harvard University Press.

Lebergott, Stanley. 1964. *Manpower in Economic Growth: The American Record Since 1800.* New York: McGraw-Hill.

———. 1984. *The Americans: An Economic Record.* New York: Norton.

———. 1996. *The Opening of the American Mind: Canons, Culture, History.* Boston: Beacon.

Lee, C.S., and L. Sloan. 1994. "Its Our Turn Now—Prop. 187: As California Cracks Down on Illegals, Blacks and Hispanics Fight Deeper Ethnic War." *Newsweek,* November 21, p. 57.

Lee, Everett S. 1957. "Methodological Considerations and Reference Tables." In *Population Redistribution and Economic Growth,* vol. I, edited by Simon Kuznets, Ann Ratner Miller, and Richard A. Easterline. Philadelphia: American Philosophical Society.

———. 1966. "A Theory of Migration." *Demography* 3: 47–57.

Lee, K.W. 1995. "From Dream to Nightmare: The L.A. Riots and the Korean-American Community." *Los Angeles Times,* April 23, Book Review Desk p. 2.

Lee, Sharon, and Keiko Yamanaka. 1990. "Patterns of Asian American Intermarriage and Marital Assimilation." *Journal of Comparative Family Studies* 21(Summer): 287–305.

Legomsky, Stephen. 1994. "Why Citizenship?" *Virginia Journal of International Law* 35: 279–300.

Lenneberg, E. H. 1967. *Biological Foundations of Language.* New York: Wiley.

Lessinger, Johanna. 1995. *From the Ganges to the Hudson: Indian Immigrants in New York City.* Needham Heights, Mass.: Allyn and Bacon.

Leuchtenburg, William E. 1963. *Franklin D. Roosevelt and the New Deal, 1932–1940.* New York: Harper and Row.

Levi, M. 1988. *Of Rules and Revenue.* Berkeley: University of California Press.

Levine, D. O. 1986. *The American College and the Culture of Aspiration.* Ithaca, N.Y.: Cornell University Press.

Levine, Daniel B., Kenneth Hill, and Robert Warren, eds., 1985. Immigration Statistics: A Story of Neglect. Panel on Immigration Statistics, Committee on National Statistics, Commission of Behavioral and Social Sciences and Education, National Research Council. Washington, D.C.: National Academy Press.

Levine, Lawrence W. 1988. *Highbrow/Lowbrow: The Emergence of Cultural Hierarchy in America.* Cambridge.

———. 1996. *The Opening of the American Mind: Canons, Culture, History.* Boston: Beacon Press.

Levitt, Peggy. 1998. "Forms of Transnational Community and Their Impact on the Second Generation: Preliminary Findings." Paper presented at the Conference on Transnationalism and the Second Generation, Harvard University, Cambridge, Mass. (April 3–4).

———. 1999. "Social Remittances: A Local-Level, Migration Driven Form of Cultural Diffusion." *International Migration review* 32(124): 926–49.

Levy, Frank. 1980. "Changes in Employment Prospects for Black Males." *Brookings Papers on Economic Activity* 2: 513–38.

Levy, Frank and Richard Murnane. 1992. "U.S. Earnings Levels and Earnings Inequality: A Review of Recent Trends and Proposed Explanations." *Journal of Economic Literature* 30: 1333–81.

Levy, Mark, and Michael Kramer. 1973. *The Ethnic Factor: How America's Minorities Decide Elections.* New York: Simon & Schuster.

Levy, Mildred B., and Walter J. Wadycki. 1973. "The Influence of Family and Friends on Geographic Labor Mobility: An Intercensal Comparison." *Review of Economics and Statistics* 55: 198–203.

Lewis, Edward E. 1932. "Economic Factors in Negro Migration." *Journal of the American Statistical Association* 27: 45–53.

Lewis, Neil A. 1995. "Bill Seeks to End Automatic Citizenship for All Born in the United States." *New York Times,* December 14, A26.

Lewis, Oscar. 1959. *Five Families: Mexican Case Studies in the Culture of Poverty.* New York: Basic Books.

Lewis, W. Arthur. 1954. "Economic Development with Unlimited Supplies of Labour." *Manchester School of Economic and Social Studies* 22: 139–91.

Lieberson, Stanley. 1961. "A Societal Theory of Race and Ethnic Relations." *American Sociological Review* 21: 902–10.

———. 1973. "Generational Differences Among Blacks in the North." *American Journal of Sociology* 79: 550–65.

———. 1980. *A Piece of the Pie: Black and White Immigrants Since 1880*. Berkeley: University of California Press.

———. 1981. *Language Diversity and Language Contact*. Stanford, Calif.: Stanford University Press.

———. 1985. "Unhyphenated Whites in the United States." *Ethnic and Racial Studies* 8: 159–80.

———. 1996. "Contemporary Immigration Policy: Lessons from the Past." In *Immigrants and Immigration Policy: Individual Skills, Family Ties, and Group Identities,* edited by Harriet Orcutt and Phanindra V. Wunnava (335–51). Greenwich, Conn.: JAI Press.

Lieberson, Stanley, and Timothy J. Curry. 1971. "Language Shift in the United States: Some Demographic Clues." *International Migration Review* 5: 125–37.

Lieberson, Stanley, and Lynn K. Hansen. 1974. "National Development, Mother Tongue Diversity, and the Comparative Study of Nations." *American Sociological Review* 39: 523–41.

Lieberson, Stanley, and Mary Waters. 1988. *From Many Strands: Ethnic and Racial Groups in Contemporary America*. New York: Russell Sage Foundation.

———. 1993. "The Ethnic Responses of Whites: What Causes Their Instability, Simplification, and Inconsistency?" *Social Forces* 72: 421–50.

Liebman, Lance. 1992. "Immigration Status and American Law: The Several Versions of Antidiscrimination Doctrine." In *Immigrants in Two Democracies: French and American Experience,* edited by D. L. Horowitz and G. Noiriel (368–90). New York: New York University Press.

Light, Ivan. 1972. *Ethnic Enterprise in America*. Berkeley: University of California Press.

———. 1979. "Disadvantaged Minorities in Self-employment." *International Journal of Comparative Sociology* 20: 31–45.

———. 1980. "Asian Enterprise in America." In *Self-help in America: Patterns of Minority Economic Development,* edited by Scott Cummings (33–57). Port Washington, N.Y.: Kennikat Press.

———. 1984. "Immigrant and Ethnic Enterprise in North America." *Ethnic and Racial Studies* 7(2): 195–216.

———. 1985. "Immigrant Entrepreneurs in America: Koreans in Los Angeles." In *Clamor at the Gates,* edited by Nathan Glazer (161–78). San Francisco: Institute for Contemporary Studies.

Light, Ivan, and Edna Bonacich. 1988. *Immigrant Entrepreneurs: Koreans in Los Angeles, 1965–1982*. Berkeley: University of California Press.

Light, Ivan, and Stavros Karageorgis. 1994. "The Ethnic Economy." In *Handbook of Economic Sociology,* edited by Neil Smelser and Richard Swedberg (646–71). Princeton, N.J.: Princeton University Press.

Light, Ivan, Georges Sabagh, Mehdi Bozorgmehr, and Claudia Der-Martirosian. 1994. "Beyond the Ethnic Enclave Economy." *Social Problems* 41: 65–79.

Light, Ivan, and Angel A. Sanchez. 1987. "Immigrant Entrepreneurs in 272 SMSAs." *Sociological Perspectives* 30: 373–99.

Lind, Michael. 1995. *The Next American Nation: The New Nationalism and the Fourth American Revolution*. New York: Basic Books.

Lindstrom, David. 1991. "The Differential Role of Family Networks in Individual Migration Decisions." Paper presented at the annual meeting of the Population Association of America, Washington.

Linton, Ralph. 1937. "One Hundred Per Cent American." *American Mercury* 40(160): 427–29.

Lippmann, Walter. 1925. *The Phantom Public*. New York: Harcourt.

Lipset, Seymour Martin. 1996. *American Exceptionalism: A Double-edged Sword*. New York: Norton.

Lipsitz, George. 1989. "Land of a Thousand Dances: Youth, Minorities, and the Rise of Rock and Roll." In *Recasting America: Culture and Politics in the Age of the Cold War,* edited by Lary May (267–84). Chicago: University of Chicago Press.

———. 1990. *Time Passages: Collective Memory and American Popular Culture*. Minneapolis: University of Minnesota Press.

———. 1994. *Dangerous Crossroads*. New York: Verso.

———. 1995a. "The Possessive Investment in Whiteness: Racialized Social Democracy and the 'White' Problem in American Studies." *American Quarterly* 47(3, September): 369–87.

———. 1995b. "Toxic Racism." *American Quarterly* 47(3, September): 416–27.

LiPuma, Edward. 1997. "History, Identity, and Encompassment: Nation Making in the Solomon Islands." *Identities: Global Studies in Culture and Power* 4(2): 213–44.

Lissak, Rivka. 1989. *Pluralism and Progressives: Hull House and the New Immigrants, 1890–1919*. Chicago: University of Chicago Press.

Lively, Kit. 1995. "Judge Says California Ban on Immigrants Is Not Unconstitutional." *Chronicle of Higher Education,* December 1, A40.

Loewen, James. 1971. *The Mississippi Chinese: Between Black and White*. Cambridge, Mass.: Harvard University Press.

Logan, John R. 1997a. "White Ethnics in the New York Economy, 1920–1960." Working Paper. New York: Russell Sage Foundation (April).

———. 1997b. "The Ethnic Neighborhood, 1920–1970." Working Paper. New York: Russell Sage Foundation (May).

Logan, John, and Richard D. Alba. 1993. "Locational Returns to Human Capital: Minority Access to Suburban Community Resources." *Demography* 30: 243–68.

Logan, John R., Richard D. Alba, and Thomas L. McNulty. 1994. "Ethnic Economies in Metropolitan Regions: Miami and Beyond." *Social Forces* 72: 691–724.

Logan, John, Richard Alba, Thomas McNulty, and Brian Fisher. 1996. "Making a Place in the Metropolis: Locational Attainment in City and Suburb." *Demography* 33: 443–53.

Logan, John, Richard Alba, and Shu-Yin Leung. 1996. "Minority Access to White Suburbs: A Multiregion Comparison." *Social Forces* 74: 851–81.

Lomnitz, Larissa Adler. 1977. *Networks and Marginality: Life in a Mexican Shantytown*. Translated by Cinna Lomnitz. New York: Academic Press.

Long, Clarence D. 1960. *Wages and Earnings in the United States, 1860–1890*. Princeton, N.J.: Princeton University Press/National Bureau of Economic Research.

López, David E. 1978. "Chicano Language Loyalty in an Urban Setting." *Sociology and Social Research* 62: 267–78.

———. 1982. *Language Maintenance and Shift in the United States Today: The Basic Patterns and Their Implications*. Los Alamitos, Calif.: National Center for Bilingual Research.

López, David E., and Yen Le Espiritu. 1990. "Panethnicity in the United States: A Theoretical Framework." *Ethnic and Racial Studies* 13: 2.

López, Ian F. Haney. 1995. "The Social Construction of Race." In *Critical Race Theory*, edited by Richard Delgado (191–203). Cambridge, Mass.: Harvard University Press.

———. 1996. *White by Law: The Legal Construction of Race*. New York: New York University Press.

Lorey, David E. 1990. *United States-Mexico Border Statistics Since 1900*. Los Angeles: UCLA Latin American Center.

Los Angeles Sentinel. 1988. "Maker of Racist Toys: Japanese Firm Offers Sensitivity Proposals." October 27, A1, A20.

Los Angeles Times. 1992. *Understanding the Riots: Los Angeles Before and After the Rodney King Case*. Los Angeles: Los Angeles Times.

Lott, Eric. 1993a. "White Like Me: Racial Cross-dressing and the Construction of American Whiteness." In *Cultures of United States Imperialism*, edited by Amy Kaplan and Don E. Pease (474–95). Durham, N.C.: Duke University Press.

———. 1993b. *Love and Theft: Blackface Minstrels and the American Working Class*. New York: Oxford University Press.

Lott, Juanita Tamayo. 1998. *Asian Americans: From Racial Categories to Multiple Identities*. Walnut Creek, Calif.: Altamira Press.

Loury, Glenn C. 1977. "A Dynamic Theory of Racial Income Differences." In *Women, Minorities, and Employment Discrimination*, edited by Phyllis A. Wallace and Anette M. LaMond (153–86). Lexington, Mass.: Heath.

Lovejoy, Arthur O. 1936. *The Great Chain of Being: A Study of the History of an Idea*. Cambridge, Mass.: Harvard University Press.

———. 1948. *Essays in the History of Ideas*. Baltimore: Johns Hopkins University Press.

Lowe, Lisa. 1996. *Immigrant Acts*. Durham, N.C.: Duke University Press.

Lowell, B. Lindsay, and Zhongren Jing. 1994. "Unauthorized Workers and Immigration Reform: What Can We Ascertain from Employers?" *International Migration Review* 28(3): 427–48.

Luebke, Frederick C. 1974. *Bonds of Loyalty: German Americans and World War I*. DeKalb: Northern Illinois University.

Luttwak, Ed. 1992. "The Riots: Underclass Versus Immigrants." *New York Times*, May 15, A29.

Lyman, Stanford. 1973. *The Black American in Sociological Thought: A Failure of Perspective*. New York: Capricorn.

Lynd, Robert S., and Helen Merrell Lynd. 1929. *Middletown: A Study in American Culture*. New York: Harcourt Brace and Company.

Macdonald, Heather. 1995. "The American Nightmare; Why Korean Entrepreneurs Are Fleeing Our Cities." *Washington Post*, May 7, C1.

MacDonald, John S., and Leatrice D. MacDonald. 1974. "Chain Migration, Ethnic Neighborhood Formation, and Social Networks." In *An Urban World*, edited by Charles Tilly (226–36). Boston: Little, Brown.

MacLeod, Jay. 1987. *Ain't No Makin' It: Leveled Aspirations in a Low-income Neighborhood*. Boulder, Colo.: Westview.

Mahler, Sarah. 1995. *American Dreaming: Immigrant Life on the Margins*. Princeton, N.J.: Princeton University Press.

———. 1996a. "Bringing Gender to a Transnational Focus: Theoretical and Empirical Ideas." Florida International University. Unpublished paper.

———. 1996b. *Salvadorans in Suburbia*. New York: Allyn and Bacon.

———. 1998. "Theoretical and Empirical Contributions Toward a Research Agenda for Transnationalism." In *Transnationalism from Below*, edited by M. P. Smith and Luis Eduardo Guarnizo (165–95). New Brunswick, N.J.: Rutgers University Press.

Mailer, Norman. 1948. *The Naked and the Dead*. New York: Holt, Rinehart, and Winston.

Malloy, R., and Mark Kirkorian. 1995. "Three Decades of Mass Immigration: The Legacy of the 1965 Immigration Act." *Immigration Review* 23: 1–4.

Mannheim, Karl. 1936. *Ideology and Utopia*. New York: Harcourt Brace.

———. 1996. "The Problem of Generations." In *Theories of Ethnicity: A Classical Reader*, edited by Werner Sollors (109–55). New York: New York University Press. (Originally published in 1928)

Manson, Donald M., Thomas J. Espenshade, and Thomas Muller. 1985. "Mexican Immigration to Southern California: Issues of Job Competition and

Worker Mobility." *Review of Regional Studies* 15(2, Spring): 21–33.

Mar, Don. 1991. "Another Look at the Enclave Economy Thesis: Chinese Immigrants in the Ethnic Labor Market." *Amerasia* 17: 5–21.

Marcus, George, and Michael Fischer. 1986. *Anthropology as Cultural Critique*. Chicago: University of Chicago Press.

Mare, Robert D. 1995. "Changes in Educational Attainment and School Enrollment." In *State of the Union,* edited by Reynolds Farley (vol. 1, ch. 4). New York: Russell Sage Foundation.

Margo, Robert A. 1990. *Race and Schooling in the South, 1880–1950*. Chicago: University of Chicago Press.

———. 1996. "The Rental Price of Housing in New York City, 1830–1860." *Journal of Economic History* 56(3): 605–25.

Markides, K. S., and J. Coreil. 1986. "The Health of Hispanics in the Southwestern United States: An Epidemiological Paradox." *Public Health Reports* 101: 253–65.

Marks, G., M. García, and J. Solis. 1990. "Health Risk Behaviors in Hispanics in the United States: Findings from HHANES 1982–84." *American Journal of Public Health* 80(supplement): 20–26.

Markusen, James. 1983. "Factor Movements and Commodity Trade as Complements." *Journal of International Economics* 14: 341–56.

Marshall, T. H. 1991. "Citizenship and Social Class." In *Citizenship and Social Class,* edited by T. H. Marshall and Tom Bottomore. London: Pluto.

Martin, David A. 1994. "The Civic Republican Ideal for Citizenship, and for Our Common Life." *Virginia Journal of International Law* 35(1, Fall): 301–19.

Martin, J. 1995a. "The Politics and Demographics of Immigration Reform." *Immigration Review* 23: 4–8.

———. 1995b. "Immigration Contributes over Half of U.S. Population Growth." *Immigration Review* 23: 10–12.

Martin, Philip L., and J. Edward Taylor. 1996. "The Anatomy of a Migration Hump." In *Development Strategy, Employment, and Migration: Insights from Models,* edited by J. Edward Taylor (43–62). Paris: Organization for Economic Cooperation and Development, Development Center.

Martin, William, and Mark Beittel. 1987. "The Hidden Abode of Reproduction: Conceptualizing Households in South Africa." *Development and Change* 28(2): 215–34.

Marx, Leo, and Bruce Mazlish, eds. 1996. *Progress: Fact or Illusion?* Ann Arbor: University of Michigan Press.

Massey, Douglas S. 1981. "Dimensions of the New Immigration to the United States and the Prospects for Assimilation." *Annual Review of Sociology* 7: 57–85.

———. 1985. "Ethnic Residential Segregation: A Theoretical Synthesis and Empirical Review." *Sociology and Social Research* 69: 315–50.

———. 1986. "The Settlement Process Among Mexican Migrants to the United States." *American Sociological Review* 51: 670–85.

———. 1987. "Understanding Mexican Migration to the United States." *American Journal of Sociology* 92: 1372–1403.

———. 1988. "International Migration and Economic Development in Comparative Perspective." *Population and Development Review* 14: 383–414.

———. 1990. "Social Structure, Household Strategies, and the Cumulative Causation of Migration." *Population Index* 56(1): 3–26.

———. 1994. "The New Immigration and the Meaning of Ethnicity in the United States." Paper presented at the Albany Conference on American Diversity.

———. 1995. "The New Immigration and Ethnicity in the United States." *Population and Development Review* 21(3, September): 631–52.

———. 1998. "When Surveys Fail: An Alternative Approach to Studying Illegal Migration." In *The Science of the Self-report: Implications for Research and Practice,* edited by Arthur A. Stone (145–60). New York: Erlbaum.

Massey, Douglas S., Rafael Alarcón, Jorge Durand, and Humberto González. 1987. *Return to Aztlan: The Social Process of International Migration from Western Mexico*. Berkeley: University of California Press.

Massey, Douglas S., Joaquin Arango, Ali Kouaouci, Adela Pelligrino, and J. Edward Taylor. 1993. "Theories of International Migration: Review and Appraisal." *Population and Development Review* 19(3, September): 431–66.

———. 1994. "An Evaluation of International Migration Theory: The North American Case." *Population and Development Review* 20(4): 699–751.

———. 1998. *Worlds in Motion: Understanding International Migration at the End of the Millennium*. International Studies in Demography. New York: Oxford University Press.

Massey, Douglas S., and Nancy A. Denton. 1987. "Trends in Residential Segregation of Black, Hispanics, and Asians: 1970–1980." *American Sociological Review* 52: 802–25.

———. 1988. "Suburbanization and Segregation in U.S. Metropolitan Areas." *American Journal of Sociology* 94: 592–626.

———. 1992. "Residential Segregation of Asian-Origin Groups in U.S. Metropolitan Areas." *Sociology and Social Research* 76: 170–77.

———. 1993. *American Apartheid: Segregation and the Making of the Underclass*. Cambridge, Mass.: Harvard University Press.

Massey, Douglas S., and Kristin E. Espinosa. 1997. "What's Driving Mexico-U.S. Migration?: A Theoretical, Empirical, and Policy Analysis." *American Journal of Sociology* 102(4, January): 939–99.

Massey, Douglas S., and Felipe García España. 1987.

"The Social Process of International Migration." *Science* 237: 733–38.

Massey, Douglas S., and Luin Goldring. 1994. "Continuities in Transnational Migration: An Analysis of Nineteen Mexican Communities." *American Journal of Sociology* 99: 1492–1533.

Massey, Douglas S., Luin P. Goldring, and Jorge Durand. 1994. "Continuities in Transnational Migration: An Analysis of Nineteen Mexican Communities." *American Journal of Sociology* 99: 1492–1533.

Massey, Douglas S., and A. Singer. 1995. "New Estimates of Undocumented Mexican Migration and the Probability of Apprehension." *Demography* 32: 203–31.

Massey, Douglas S., and René Zenteno. Forthcoming. "A Validation of the Ethnosurvey: The Case of Mexico-U.S. Migration." *International Migration Review*.

Mato, Daniel. 1997. "On Global Agents, Transnational Relations, and the Social Making of Transnational Identities and Associated Agendas in Latin America." *Identities: Global Studies in Culture and Power* 4(2): 167–212.

Matthei, Linda Miller, and David A. Smith. 1998. "Belizean 'Boys 'n the Hood'?: Garifuna Labor Migration and Transnational Identity." In *Transnationalism from Below*, edited by Michael Peter Smith and Luis Eduardo Guarnizo (270–90). New Brunswick, N.J.: Transnational Publishers.

Matthews, Fred H. 1977. *Quest for an American Sociology: Robert E. Park and the Chicago School*. Montreal: McGill-Queen's University Press.

Matute-Bianchi, María Eugenia. 1986. "Ethnic Identities and Patterns of School Success and Failure Among Mexican-Descent and Japanese American Students in a California High School: An Ethnographic Analysis." *American Journal of Education* 95(1): 233–55.

———. 1991. "Situational Ethnicity and Patterns of School Performance Among Immigrant and Nonimmigrant Mexican-Descent Students." In *Minority Status and Schooling: A Comparative Study of Immigrant and Involuntary Minorities*, edited by Margaret Gibson and John U. Ogbu (205–47). New York: Garland.

McCann, Michael W. 1986. *Taking Reform Seriously: Perspectives on Public Interest Liberalism*. Ithaca, N.Y.: Cornell University Press.

McCartin, Joseph. 1993. "'An American Feeling': Workers, Managers, and the Struggle over Industrial Democracy in the World War I Era." In *Industrial Democracy: The Ambiguous Promise*, edited by Nelson Lichtenstein and Howell John Harris (67–86). New York: Cambridge University Press.

McClay, Wilfred M. 1994. *The Masterless: Self and Society in Modern America*. Chapel Hill: University of North Carolina Press.

McClelland, Peter, and Richard Zeckhauser. 1983. *Demographic Dimensions of the New Republic: American Interregional Migration, Vital Statistics, and Manumissions, 1800–1860*. New York: Cambridge University Press.

McClymer, John F. 1991. "Gender and the 'American Way of Life': Women in the Americanization Movement." *Journal of American Ethnic History* 10 (Spring): 3–20.

McCormick, Richard L. 1986. *The Party Period and Public Policy*. New York: Oxford University Press.

McDaniel, Antonio. 1995. "The Dynamic Racial Composition of the United States." *Daedalus* 124: 179–98.

McDonnell, Patrick J. 1994a. "Proposition 187 Win Spotlights Voting Disparity." *Los Angeles Times*, November 10, A3.

———. 1994b. "As Change Again Overtakes Compton, So Do Tensions." *Los Angeles Times*, August 21, 1A.

———. 1995a. "Applications for Citizenship Soar in Los Angeles." *Los Angeles Times*, April 10, A1–14.

———. 1995b. "Immigration Study in Southern California Challenges Stereotypes." *Houston Chronicle*, November 3, A4.

McDonnell, Patrick J., and Virginia Ellis. 1996. "Welfare Law Will Allow Wilson to Cut Immigrant Aid." *Los Angeles Times*, November 2, A1.

McFate, Katherine. 1994. "The Future of Work." Washington: Joint Center for Political Studies. Unpublished paper.

McKee, James B. 1993. *Sociology and the Race Problem: The Failure of a Perspective*. Urbana: University of Illinois Press.

McKenney, Nampeo R., and Arthur R. Cresce. 1993. "Measurement of Ethnicity in the United States: Experiences of the U.S. Bureau of the Census." In Statistics Canada and U.S. Bureau of the Census, *Challenges of Measuring an Ethnic World: Science, Politics, and Reality* (173–221). Washington: U.S. Government Printing Office.

McMillan, Penelope. 1992. "Angel in Minister's Collar." *Los Angeles Times*, May 8, B1, 4.

McNeill, William H. 1963. *The Rise of the West: A History of the Human Community*. New York: Mentor Books.

McNeill, William H., and Ruth Adams, eds. 1978. *Human Migration: Patterns and Policies*. Bloomington: Indiana University Press.

Meillassoux, Claude. 1981. *Maidens, Meal, and Money: Capitalism and the Domestic Community*. Cambridge: Cambridge University Press.

Meister, Robert. 1995. "Sojourners and Survivors: Two Logics of Constitutional Protection." *Studies in American Political Development* 9(2): 229–86.

Melendez, Edwin, Clara Rodriguez, and Janis B. Figueroa, eds. 1991. *Hispanics in the Labor Force: Issues and Policies*. New York: Plenum.

Mencken, H. L. 1963. *The American Language*. Abridged ed. New York: Knopf.

Menjívar, Cecilia. 1995. "Kinship Networks Among Immigrants: Lessons from a Qualitative Comparative Approach." *International Journal of Comparative Sociology* 36(3–4): 219–32.

Merriam, Charles. 1926. "Annual Report of the Social Science Research Council." *American Political Science Review* 20: 185–89.

Merton, Robert K. 1936. "The Unanticipated Consequences of Purposive Social Action." *American Sociological Review* 1: 894–904.

———. 1968. *Social Theory and Social Structure*. Enlarged ed. New York: Free Press.

———. 1973. "The Perspectives of Insiders and Outsiders." In *The Sociology of Science: Theoretical and Empirical Investigations,* edited by Norman W. Storer (99–136). Chicago: University of Chicago Press.

———. 1987. "Three Fragments from a Sociologist's Notebook: Establishing the Phenomenon, Specified Ignorance, and Strategic Research Materials." *Annual Review of Sociology* 13: 1–28.

Meyer, Bruce. 1990. "Why Are There So Few Black Entrepreneurs?" Working Paper 3537. Cambridge, Mass.: National Bureau of Economic Research.

Meyer, Stephen. 1980. "Adapting the Immigrant to the Line: Americanization in the Ford Factory, 1914–1921." *Journal of Social History* 14(Fall): 67–82.

Meyers, Eytan. 1995. "The Political Economy of International Immigration Policies." Ph.D. diss., Department of Political Science, University of Chicago.

Miller, John J. 1994. "Immigration, the Press, and the New Racism." *Media Studies Journal* 8: 19–28.

Miller, Kerby A. 1985. *Emigrants and Exiles: Ireland and the Irish Exodus to North America*. New York: Oxford University Press.

———. 1990. "Class, Culture, and Immigrant Group Identity in the United States: The Case of Irish American Ethnicity." In *Immigration Reconsidered: History, Sociology, and Politics,* edited by Virginia Yans-McLaughlin (96–129). New York: Oxford University Press.

Miller, Mark. 1994. "Towards Understanding State Capacity to Prevent Unwanted Migration: Employer Sanctions Enforcement in France, 1975–1990." *West European Politics* 17(2): 184–202.

Mills, C. Wright. 1961. *The Sociological Imagination*. New York: Grove Press.

Mills, Mary Beth. 1997. "Contesting the Margins of Modernity: Women, Migration, and Consumption in Thailand." *American Ethnologist* 24(1): 37–61.

Min, Pyong Gap. 1984. "From White-collar Occupations to Small Business: Korean Immigrants' Occupational Adjustment." *Sociological Quarterly* 25: 333–52.

———. 1996. *Caught in the Middle: Korean Communities in New York and Los Angeles*. Berkeley: University of California Press.

———. 1998. *Changes and Conflicts: Korean Immigrant Families in New York*. Boston: Allyn and Bacon.

Mincy, Ronald. 1990. *Work Force 2000—Silver Bullet or Dud?: Job Structure Changes and Economic Prospects for Black Men in the 1990s.* Washington: Urban Institute.

Mindiola, Tatcho, Yolanda Flores Nieman, and Nestor Rodriguez. 1996. *Findings of Black-Brown Relations in Houston, 1995.* Houston: Center for Mexican American Studies, University of Houston.

Mines, Richard. 1984. "Network Migration and Mexican Rural Development: A Case Study." In *Patterns of Undocumented Migration: Mexico and the United States,* edited by Richard C. Jones (136–58). Totowa, N.J.: Rowman and Allanheld.

———. 1985. "Undocumented Immigrants and California Industries: Reflections and Research." Hearings before the Intergovernmental Relations Committee (November 15).

Mink, Gwendolyn. 1986. *Old Labor and New Immigrants in American Political Development, 1875–1920.* Ithaca, N.Y.: Cornell University Press.

———. 1996. *The Wages of Motherhood: Inequality in the Welfare State, 1917–1942.* Ithaca, N.Y.: Cornell University Press.

Mintz, Sidney, and Richard Price. 1992. *The Birth of African American Culture: An Anthropological Perspective.* Boston: Beacon.

Mishel, Lawrence, and Jared Bernstein. 1992. *The State of Working America: 1992–1993.* Washington: Economic Policy Institute.

Mitchell, J. Clyde. 1969. *Social Networks in Urban Situations.* Manchester: Manchester University Press.

Mitchell, Susan. 1996. *The Official Guide to American Attitudes.* Ithaca, N.Y.: New Strategist.

Mittleman, James. 1997a. "The Dynamics of Globalization." In *Globalization: Critical Reflections,* edited by James Mittleman. Boulder, Colo.: Lynne Reinner.

———. , ed. 1997b. *Globalization: Critical Reflections.* Boulder, Colo.: Lynne Reiner.

Moch, Leslie Page. 1992. *Moving Europeans.* Bloomington: Indiana University Press.

Model, Suzanne. 1988. "The Economic Progress of European and East Asian Americans." *Annual Review of Sociology* 14: 363–80.

———. 1993. "The Ethnic Niche and the Structure of Opportunity: Immigrants and Minorities in New York City." In *The Historical Origins of the Underclass,* edited by Michael Katz (161–93). Princeton, N.J.: Princeton University Press.

Modigliani, Franco. 1966. "The Life-Cycle Hypothesis of Saving, the Demand for Wealth, and the Supply of Capital." *Social Research* 33(3): 160–217.

———. 1986. "Life Cycle, Individual Thrift, and the Wealth of Nations." *American Economic Review* 76(3): 297–313.

Moehring, H. Brian. 1988. "Symbol Versus Substance in Legislative Activity: The Case of Illegal Immigration." *Public Choice* 57: 287–94.

Mohanty, Chandra. 1991. "Cartographies of Struggle: Third World Women and the Politics of Struggle." In *Third World Women and the Politics of Feminism,* edited by Chandra Talpade Mohanty, Ann Russo, and Lourdes Torres (1–47). Bloomington: Indiana University Press.

Mokyr, Joel. 1983. *Why Ireland Starved: A Quantitative and Analytical History of the Irish Economy, 1800–1850.* London: Allen & Unwin.

———. 1990. *The Lever of Riches: Technological Creativity and Economic Progress.* New York: Oxford University Press.

Mollenkopf, John. 1988. "The Postindustrial Transformation of the Political Order in New York City." In *Power, Culture, and Place: Essays on New York City,* edited by John Mollenkopf (273–84). New York: Russell Sage Foundation.

———. 1993. *New York in the 1980s: A Social, Economic, and Political Atlas.* New York: Simon & Schuster Academic Reference Books.

———. 1994. *A Phoenix in the Ashes: The Rise and Fall of the Koch Coalition in New York City Politics.* Princeton, N.J.: Princeton University Press.

Mollenkopf, John, and Manuel Castells, eds. 1991. *Dual City: Restructuring New York.* New York: Russell Sage Foundation.

Mollenkopf, John, Philip Kasinitz, and Mary Waters. 1995. "The Immigrant Second Generation in Metropolitan New York." Unpublished paper.

Mollenkopf, John, David Olson, and Tim Ross. 1998. "Immigrant Political Participation in New York and Los Angeles." Paper presented at the Conference on Governing American Cities: Interethnic Coalitions, Competition, and Conflict, Center for American Political Studies, Harvard University (April).

Montejano, David. 1987. *Anglos and Mexicans in the Making of Texas, 1836–1986.* Austin: University of Texas Press.

Moore, Joan. 1989. "Is There a Hispanic Underclass?" *Social Science Quarterly* 70: 265–83.

Moore, Joan, and Raquel Pinderhughes, eds. 1993. *In the Barrios: Latinos and the Underclass Debate.* New York: Russell Sage Foundation.

Moore, Joan, and James D. Vigil. 1993. "Barrios in Transition." In *In the Barrios: Latinos and the Underclass Debate,* edited by Joan Moore and Raquel Pinderhughes (27–49). New York: Russell Sage Foundation.

Morain, Dan. 1999. "Taxpayer Group Sues Gov. Davis Over Proposition 187." *Los Angeles Times,* June 2, 16A.

Morales, Rebecca. 1982. "Transnational Labor: Undocumented Workers in the Los Angeles Automobile Industry." *International Migration Review* 17(Winter): 570–79.

Morawska, Ewa T. 1985. *For Bread with Butter: The Life-Worlds of East Central Europeans in Johnstown, Pennsylvania, 1890–1940.* New York: Cambridge University Press.

———. 1987. "Sociological Ambivalence: The Case of Eastern European Peasant-Immigrant Workers in America, 1880s–1930s." *Qualitative Sociology* 10(3): 225–50.

———. 1989. "Labor Migrations of Poles in the Atlantic World Economy, 1880–1914." *Comparative Study of Society and History* 31(2): 237–70.

———. 1990. "The Sociology and Historiography of Immigration." In *Immigration Reconsidered: History, Sociology, and Politics,* edited by Virginia Yans-McLaughlin (187–240). New York: Oxford University Press.

———. 1994. "In Defense of the Assimilation Model." *Journal of American Ethnic History* 13(2, Winter): 76–87.

———. 1997. "On New-Old Transmigrations and Transnationalism Qua Ethnicization." Paper presented at the Social Science Research Council Workshop on Immigrants, Civic Culture, and Modes of Political Incorporation: A Contemporary and Historical Comparison, Santa Fe, N.M. (May).

Morenoff, Jeffrey M., and Marta Tienda. 1997. "Underclass Neighborhoods in Temporal and Ecological Perspective: An Illustration from Chicago." *The Annals of the American Academy of Political and Social Science* 551(May): 59–72.

Morgenthau, Tom. 1995. "What Color Is Black?" *Newsweek,* February 13, 63–65.

———. 1984. "Birds of Passage Are Also Women." *International Migration Review* 18(4): 886–907.

Morokvasic, Mirjana. 1984. "Birds of Passage Are Also Women." *International Migration Review* 18(4): 886–907.

Morone, James. 1990. *The Democratic Wish: Popular Participation and the Limits of American Government.* New York: Basic Books.

Morrison, Toni. 1993. "On the Backs of Blacks." In "The New Face of America: How Immigrants Are Shaping the World's First Multicultural Society" (special issue). *Time,* Fall 1993.

Mueller, Elizabeth J. 1994. "Running Hard to Stay in One Place: Low-wage Poverty Among Immigrant Women in Los Angeles." *Economic Development Quarterly* 8: 158–70.

Muller, Peter O. 1981. *Contemporary Suburban America.* Englewood Cliffs, N.J.: Prentice-Hall.

Muller, Thomas. 1993. *Immigrants and the American City.* New York: New York University Press.

Muller, Thomas, and Thomas Espenshade. 1985. *The Fourth Wave.* Washington: Urban Institute Press.

Münz, Rainer, and Rolf Ulrich. 1995. "Changing Patterns of Migration: The Case of Germany, 1945–1994." Paper presented at the German American Migration and Refugee Policy Group, American Academy of Arts and Sciences, Cambridge, Mass. (March 23–26).

Murphy, Kevin M., and Finis Welch. 1993. "Industrial Change and the Rising Importance of Skill." In *Uneven Tides: Rising Inequality in America,* edited by Sheldon Danziger and Peter Gottschalk (101–32). New York: Russell Sage Foundation.

Murrin, John M., Paul E. Johnson, James M. McPherson, Gary Gerstle, Emily S. Rosenberg, and Norman L. Rosenberg. 1996. *Liberty, Equality, Power: A History of the American People.* Fort Worth: Harcourt Brace.

Myers, Steven L. 1997. "United States May Pay Some Arrears to the United Nations." *New York Times,* June 11, A6.

Myrdal, Gunnar. 1957. *Rich Lands and Poor.* New York: Harper & Row.

Nagel, Ernest. 1961. *The Structure of Science.* New York: Harcourt, Brace, and World.

Nagengast, Carol, and Michael Kearney. 1990. "Mixtec Ethnicity: Social Identity, Political Consciousness, and Political Activism." *Latin American Review* 25(2): 61–91.

Nakanishi, Don T. 1995. "A Quota on Excellence?: The Asian American Admissions Debate." In *The Asian American Educational Experience,* edited by Don T. Nakanishi and Tina Y. Nishida. New York: Routledge.

Naples, Nancy. 1997. "The 'New Consensus' on the Gendered 'Social Contract': The 1987–1988 U.S. Congressional Hearings on Welfare Reform." *Signs* 22(4): 907–45.

Nasaw, David. 1985. *Children of the City: At Work and at Play.* New York: Anchor Press/Doubleday.

Nash, Gary. 1995. "The Hidden History of Mestizo America." *Journal of American History* 82(December): 941–64.

Nash, Gary B., Julie Roy Jeffrey, John R. Howe, Peter J. Frederick, Allen F. Davis, and Allan M. Winkler. 1996. *The American People: Creating a Nation and a Society.* New York: Harper & Row.

Nash, George H. 1979. *The Conservative Intellectual Movement in America—Since 1945.* New York: Basic Books.

Nash, June. 1986. "A Decade of Research on Women in Latin America." In *Women and Change in Latin America,* edited by June Nash and Helen Safa (3–21). South Hadley, Mass.: Bergin and Garvey.

———. 1988. "Cultural Parameters of Sexism and Racism in the International Division of Labor." In *Racism, Sexism, and the World-System,* edited by Joan Smith, Jane Collins, Terance Hopkins, and Akbar Muhammad (11–36). Westport, Conn.: Greenwood.

National Archives and Records Administration. 1998. *Code of Federal Regulations 312.2.* Washington: Office of the Federal Register.

National Conference of State Legislatures. 1996a. "Analysis of the Personal Responsibility and Work Opportunity Reconciliation Act of 1996." Washington: NCSL (August 30).

———. 1996b. "Immigrant Provisions in Welfare Reform: Public Law 104–193." Washington: NCSL (September 17.)

———. 1996c. "Welfare Reform Update: Selected Constitutional Issues in Welfare Reform." Washington: NCSL.

National Research Council. 1997. *The New Americans: Economic, Demographic, and Fiscal Effects of Immigration.* Washington: National Academy Press.

Nauman, Gerald L. 1994. "Justifying U.S. Naturalization Policies." *Virginia Journal of International Law* 35(1, Fall).

Neal, Larry, and Paul Uselding. 1972. "Immigration: A Neglected Source of American Economic Growth, 1790 to 1912." *Oxford Economic Papers* 24: 68–88.

Neather, Andrew. 1996. "Labor Republicanism, Race, and Popular Patriotism in the Era of Empire, 1890–1914." In *Bonds of Affection: Americans Define Their Patriotism,* edited by John Bodnar (82–101). Princeton, N.J.: Princeton University Press.

Nee, Victor, and Brett de Bary Nee. 1992. *Longtime Californ': A Documentary Study of an American Chinatown.* New York: Pantheon. (Originally published in 1973)

Nee, Victor, and Jimy Sanders. 1985. "The Road to Parity: Determinants of the Socioeconomic Attainments of Asian Americans." *Ethnic and Racial Studies* 8: 75–93.

———. 1987. "On Testing the 'Enclave Economy' Hypothesis: Reply to Portes and Jensen." *American Sociological Review* 52(6): 745–67.

Nee, Victor, Jimy Sanders, and Scott Sernau. 1994. "Job Transitions in an Immigrant Metropolis: Ethnic Boundaries and the Mixed Economy." *American Sociological Review* 59: 849–72.

Neidert, Lisa J., and Reynolds Farley. 1985. "Assimilation in the United States: An Analysis of Ethnic and Generational Differences in Status and Achievement." *American Sociological Review* 50(6): 840–50.

Nelan, Bruce W. 1993. "Not Quite So Welcomed Anymore." *Time* 143(21, Fall): 10–12.

Nelson, Bruce. 1996. "Class, Race, and Democracy in the CIO: The 'New' Labor History Meets the 'Wages of Whiteness.'" *International Review of Social History* 41(December): 351–74.

Nelson, Nici. 1978. "Female-Centered Families: Changing Patterns of Marriage and Family Among Buzaa Brewers of Mathare Valley." *African Urban Studies* 3: 85–104.

Nelson, Richard R. 1964. "Aggregate Production Functions and Medium-Range Growth Projections." *American Economic Review* 54(4): 575–606.

Nett, Roger. 1971. "The Civil Right We Are Not Ready For: The Right of Free Movement of People on the Face of the Earth." *Ethics* 81(3, April): 212–27.

New York Times. 1998. "Scant Evidence Is Seen of Jobs After Workfare." April 12, 1998, p. 1–20.

Newman, Morris J. 1994. "What Do They Want?: Employers and Employees in the Secondary Labor Market." Paper presented to the Department of Health and Human Services, Office of the Assistant Secretary, Washington, D.C.

Nielsen, François, and Steven J. Lerner. 1986. "Language Skills and School Achievement of Bilingual Hispanics." *Social Science Research* 15: 209–40.

Noble, Constance. 1997. *Maid to Order in Hong Kong: Stories of Filipina Workers.* Ithaca, N.Y.: Cornell University Press.

Noble, Kenneth B. 1995. "In California, Smuggled Refugees of Golden Venture Protest Long Detention." *New York Times,* December 2, A6.

Noble, Mary. 1973. "Social Network: Its Use as a Conceptual Framework in Family Analysis." In *Network*

Analysis: Studies in Human Interaction, edited by Jeremy Boissevain and J. Clyde Mitchell (1–13). The Hague: Mouton.

Nomani, Asraq Z., Frederick Rose, and Bob Ortega. 1995. "Labor Department Asks $5 Million for Alleged Worker Enslavement." *Wall Street Journal*, August 16, B6.

Nonini, Donald, and Aihwa Ong. 1997. "Chinese Transnationalism as an Alternative Modernity." In *Underground Empires: The Cultural Politics of Chinese Transnationalism*, edited by Aihwa Ong and Donald Nonini (331–66). New York: Routledge.

Noro, Hiroko. 1990. "Family and Language Maintenance: An Exploratory Study of Japanese-Language Maintenance Among Children of Postwar Japanese Immigrants in Toronto." *International Journal of the Sociology of Language* 86: 57–68.

North, Douglass C. 1960. "The U.S. Balance of Payments, 1790–1860." In *Trends in the American Economy in the Nineteenth Century*, edited by William N. Parker (573–627). Princeton, N.J.: Princeton University Press/National Bureau of Economic Research.

Novack, Michael. 1974. "The Seventies: Decade of the Ethnics." In *Race and Ethnicity in Modern America*, edited by R. Meister (137–47). Lexington, Ky.: Heath.

Novick, Peter. 1988. *That Noble Dream: The "Objectivity Question" and the American Historical Profession*. New York: Cambridge University Press.

Oboler, Suzanne. 1995. *Ethnic Labels, Latino Lives: Identity and the Politics of (Re)presentation in the United States*. Minneapolis: University of Minnesota Press.

O'Connor, Mary. 1990. "Women's Networks and the Social Needs of Mexican Immigrants." *Urban Anthropology* 19(1): 81–98.

Offe, Claus. 1984. *Contradictions of the Welfare State*, edited by John Keane. Cambridge, Mass.: MIT Press.

Office of Management and Budget. 1997a. "Recommendations from the Interagency Committee for the Review of the Race and Ethnic Standards to the Office of Management and Budget Concerning Changes to the Standards for the Classification of Federal Data on Race and Ethnicity." *Federal Register* 62(131, July 9): 36874–946.

———. 1997b. "Revisions to the Standards for the Classification of Federal Data on Race and Ethnicity." *Federal Register* 62(210, October 30): 58782–90.

Ogbu, John U. 1974. *The Next Generation: An Ethnography of Education in an Urban Neighborhood*. New York: Academic Press.

———. 1978. *Minority Education and Caste: The American System in Cross-cultural Perspective*. New York: Academic Press.

———. 1983. "Schooling the Inner City." *Society* 21(November-December): 75–79.

———. 1989. "Cultural Models and Educational Strategies of Nondominant Peoples." Catherine Molony Memorial Lecture. New York: City College Workshop Center.

———. 1991. "Immigrant and Involuntary Minorities in Comparative Perspective." In *Minority Status and Schooling: A Comparative Study of Immigrant and Involuntary Minorities*, edited by Margaret A. Gibson and John U. Ogbu (3–33). New York: Garland.

Ojito, Mirta. 1998. "A Record Backlog to Get Citizenship Stymies Two Million: The Wait for Naturalization, Six Months in 1996, Is Now Three Times That Long." *New York Times*, April 20.

Okihiro, Gary Y. 1994. *Margins and Mainstreams: Asians in American History and Culture*. Seattle: University of Washington Press.

Olds, Kris Peter Dicken, Philip Kelly, Lily Kong, and Henry Wai-chung, eds. 1999. *Globalism and the Asia-Pacific: Contested Territories. London: Routledge.*

O'Leary, Cecilia Elizabeth. 1999. *To Die For: The Paradox of American Patriotism*. Princeton: Princeton University Press.

Oliver, Melvin. 1995. "Race, Space, and Politics in Los Angeles." Paper presented at the Sociology Colloquium, CUNY Graduate Center (March).

Oliver, Melvin L., and James H. Johnson, Jr. 1984. "Interethnic Conflict in an Urban Ghetto: The Case of Blacks and Latinos in Los Angeles." *Research in Social Movements, Conflict, and Change* 6: 57–84.

Oliver, Melvin L., James H. Johnson, Jr., and Walter C. Farrell, Jr. 1993. "Anatomy of a Rebellion: A Political-Economic Analysis." In *Reading Rodney King/Reading Urban Uprising*, edited by Robert Gooding-Williams (117–41). New York: Routledge.

Olson, David. 1994. "Influences on Voter Turnout in New York City Elections." Paper presented at the 1994 annual meeting of the American Political Science Association, New York (September 1–4).

Omi, Michael, and Howard Winant. 1994. *Racial Formation in the United States from the 1960s to the 1990s*. 2nd ed. New York: Routledge.

Ong, Awiha. 1992. "Limits to Cultural Accumulation: Chinese Capitalists on the Pacific Rim." In *Toward a Transnational Perspective on Migration: Race, Class, Ethnicity and Nationalism Reconsidered*, edited by Nina Glick Schiller, Linda Basch, and Cristina Blanc-Szanton (125–43). New York: New York Academy of Sciences.

———. 1993. "On the Edge of Empires: Flexible Citizenship Among Chinese in Diaspora." *Positions* 1(3): 745–78.

———. 1997. "A Momentary Glow of Fraternity: Narratives of Chinese Nationalism and Capitalism." Identities: Global Studies in Culture and Power 3(3): 331–66.

Ong, Paul, Edna Bonacich, and Lucie Cheng, eds. 1994. *The New Asian Immigration in Los Angeles and Global Restructuring*. Philadelphia: Temple University Press.

Ong, Paul, and Susanne Hee. 1993. *Losses in the Los Angeles Civil Unrest, April 29–May 1, 1992*. Los Angeles: UCLA Center for Pacific Rim Studies.

Oren, Dan A. 1985. *Joining the Club: A History of Jews and Yale*. New Haven: Yale University Press.

Orleck, Annelise. 1987. "The Soviet Jews: Life in

Brighton Beach, Brooklyn." In *New Immigrants in New York,* edited by Nancy Foner (273–304). New York: Columbia University Press.

Oropesa, R. S., and Nancy Landale. 1995. "Immigrant Legacies: The Socioeconomic Circumstances of Children by Ethnicity and Generation in the United States." Working Paper 95-01R. Department of Sociology and Population Research Institute, Pennsylvania State University.

———. 1997a. "Immigrant Legacies: Ethnicity, Generation, and Children's Familial and Economic Lives." *Social Science Quarterly* 78(2): 399–416.

———. 1997b. "In Search of the New Second Generation: Alternative Strategies for Identifying Second-Generation Children and Understanding Their Acquisition of English." *Sociological Perspectives* 40(3): 427–55.

O'Rourke, Kevin, Jeffrey Williamson, and Timothy Hatton. 1994. "Mass Migration, Commodity Market Integration, and Real Wage Convergence." In *Migration and the International Labor Market 1850–1939,* edited by Timothy J. Hatton and Jeffrey G. Williamson (203–20). New York: Routledge.

Orsi, Robert A. 1992. "The Religious Boundaries of an Inbetween People: Street Feste and the Problem of the Dark-skinned 'Other' in Italian Harlem, 1920–1990." *American Quarterly* 44(3, September): 313–47.

Osterman, Paul. 1980. *Getting Started: The Youth Labor Market.* Cambridge, Mass.: MIT Press.

Oxfeld, Ellen. 1993. *Blood, Sweat, and Mahjong: Family and Enterprise in an Overseas Chinese Community.* Ithaca, N.Y.: Cornell University Press.

———. 1995. "Proposition 187 Isn't All That's Propelling Latinos to INS." *Sacramento Bee,* May 22.

Pachon, Harry. 1996. "Attacking Naturalized Americans: The Next Phase of Anti-immigrant Sentiment?" *Los Angeles Times,* June 10.

Padilla, Felix. 1993. "The Quest for Community: Puerto Ricans in Chicago." In *In the Barrios: Latinos and the Underclass Debate,* edited by Joan Moore and Raquel Pinderhughes (129–48). New York: Russell Sage Foundation.

Page, Benjamin I. 1996. *Who Deliberates?: Mass Media in Modern Democracy.* Chicago: University of Chicago Press.

Page, Helen Enoch. 1997. White Public Space: Routine Practices of Racialized Social Production. Paper delivered at Post Bosnian Studies in Blackness and Whiteness, New York Academy of Sciences. New York (March 13–14, 1997).

Palley, Thomas I. 1994. "Capital Mobility and the Threat to American Prosperity." *Challenge* 37(6, November-December): 31–39.

Palmer, Douglas L. 1994. "Anatomy of an Attitude: Origins of the Attitude Toward the Level of Immigration to Canada." Strategic Planning and Research, Immigration Policy, Citizenship, and Immigration Canada (February 3).

Panitch, Leo. 1997. "Rethinking the Role of the State." In *Globalization: Critical Reflections,* edited by James Mittleman (83–113). Boulder, Colo.: Lynne Reinner.

Papademetriou, Demetrios G. 1990. "The Immigration Act of 1990." Washington: U.S. Department of Labor, Bureau of International Labor Affairs.

———. 1996. *Coming Together or Pulling Apart?: The European Union's Struggle with Immigration and Asylum.* Washington: Carnegie Endowment for International Peace.

Papademetriou, Demetrios G., and Kimberly A. Hamilton. 1995. *Managing Uncertainty: Regulating Immigration Flows in Advanced Industrial Countries.* Washington, D.C.: Carnegie Mellon Endowment for International Peace.

Papademetriou, Demetrios, B. Lindsay Lowell, and Deborah Cobb-Clark. 1991. "Employer Sanctions: Expectations and Early Outcomes." In *The Paper Curtain: Employer Sanctions' Implementation, Impact, and Reform,* edited by Michael Fix (145–72). Washington: Urban Institute Press.

Parcel, Toby L., and Charles W. Mueller. 1983. *Ascriptions and Labor Markets: Race and Sex Differences in Earnings.* New York: Academic Press.

Parekh, Bhikhu. 1994. "Discourses on National Identity." *Political Studies* 42: 492–504.

Park, Robert Ezra. 1926. "Our Racial Frontier in the Pacific." *Survey Graphic* 9(May): 192–96. Reprinted in Robert Ezra Park, *Race and Culture* (vol. 1, 138–51). Glencoe, Ill.: Free Press.

———. 1928. "Human Migration and the Marginal Man." *American Journal of Sociology* 33(6): 881–93.

———. 1930. "Assimilation, Social." In *Encyclopedia of the Social Sciences,* edited by Edwin Seligman and Alvin Johnson (281–83). New York: Macmillan.

———. 1937. "Introduction." In *Interracial Marriage in Hawaii* by Romanzo Adams (vii–xiv). New York: Macmillan.

———. 1950. *Race and Culture.* Glencoe, Ill.: Free Press.

———. 1974. "Immigrant Community and Immigrant Press and Its Control." Reprinted in *The Collected Papers of Robert Park,* edited by Everett Hughes, Charles Johnson, Jitsvitchi Masuoka, Robert Redfield, and Louis Wirth (152–64). New York: Arno. (Originally published in 1925)

Park, Robert E., and Ernest W. Burgess. 1921. *Introduction to the Science of Sociology.* Chicago: University of Chicago Press.

———. 1969. *Introduction to the Science of Sociology,* abridged by Morris Janowitz. Student edition. Chicago: University of Chicago Press. (Originally published in 1921)

Park, Robert E., and Herbert A. Miller. 1921. *Old World Traits Transplanted.* New York: Harper.

Passel, Jeffrey S. 1986. "Undocumented Immigration." In *Immigration and American Public Policy,* edited by Rita Simon (181–200). *Annals of the American Academy of Political and Social Science,* vol. 487. Beverly Hills, Calif.: Sage.

Passel, Jeffrey S., and Barry Edmonston. 1994. "Immigration and Race: Recent Trends in Immigration to the United States." In *Immigration and Ethnicity:*

The Integration of America's Newest Arrivals, edited by Barry Edmonston and Jeffrey S. Passel (31–71). Washington: Urban Institute Press.

Peacock, James. 1986. *The Anthropological Lens.* Cambridge: Cambridge University Press.

Pear, Robert. 1997. "Budget Agreement Restores Benefits to Some Legal Immigrants." *New York Times,* May 4, A30.

———. 1994. "Deciding Who Gets What in America." *New York Times,* November 27, E5.

Pedraza-Bailey, Silvia. 1991. "Women and Migration: The Social Consequences of Gender." *Annual Review of Sociology* 17: 303–25.

Peiss, Kathy Lee. 1986. *Cheap Amusements: Working Women and Leisure in Turn-of-the-Century New York.* Philadelphia: Temple University Press.

Pells, Richard H. 1985. *The Liberal Mind in a Conservative Age: American Intellectuals in the 1940s and 1950s.* New York: Harper & Row.

Pérez, Lisandro. 1986. "Immigrant Economic Adjustment and Family Organization: The Cuban Success Story Reexamined." *International Migration Review* 20: 4–20.

Perlmann, Joel. 1988. *Ethnic Differences: Schooling and Social Structure Among the Irish, Italians, Jews, and Blacks in an American City, 1888–1935.* New York: Cambridge University Press.

———. 1997a. *Reflecting the Changing Face of America: Multiracials, Racial Classification, and American Intermarriage.* Public Policy Brief 35. Annandale-on-the-Hudson, N.Y.: Jerome Levy Economics Institute, Bard College.

———. 1997b. "'Multiracials,' Racial Classification, and American Intermarriage: The Public's Interest." Working Paper 195. Annandale-on-the-Hudson, N.Y.: Jerome Levy Economics Institute, Bard College.

Persons, Stow. 1987. *Ethnic Studies at Chicago, 1905–1945.* Urbana: University of Illinois Press.

Pessar, Patricia. 1982. "The Role of Households in International Migration: The Case of U.S.-bound Migrants from the Dominican Republic." *International Migration Review* 16(2): 342–62.

———. 1984. "The Linkage Between the Household and Workplace in the Experience of Dominican Immigrant Women in the United States." *International Migration Review* 18: 1188–1211.

———. 1986. "The Role of Gender in Dominican Settlement in the United States." In *Women and Change in Latin America,* edited by June Nash and Helen Safa (273–94). South Hadley, Mass.: Bergin and Garvey.

———. 1987. "The Dominicans: Women in the Household and the Garment Industry." In *New Immigrants in New York,* edited by Nancy Foner (103–29). New York: Columbia University Press.

———. 1988. "The Constraints on and Release of Female Labor Power: Dominican Migration to the United States." In *A Home Divided: Women and Income in the Third World,* edited by Daisy Dwyer and Judith Bruce (195–215). Stanford, Calif.: Stanford University Press.

———. 1995a. "On the Homefront and in the Workplace: Integrating Immigrant Women into Feminist Discourse." *Anthropological Quarterly* 68(1): 37–47.

———. 1995b. *A Visa for a Dream: Dominicans in the United States.* Boston: Allyn and Bacon.

———. 1995c. "The Elusive Enclave: Ethnicity, Class, and Nationality Among Latino Entrepreneurs in Greater Washington, D.C." *Human Organization* 54(4): 383–92.

Peterson, H. C., and Gilbert C. Fite. 1957. *Opponents of War, 1917–1918.* Madison: University of Wisconsin Press.

Petras, Elizabeth. 1980. "The Role of National Boundaries in a Cross-national Labour Market." *International Journal of Urban and Regional Research* 4(2): 157–95.

———. 1981. "The Global Labor Market in the Modern World Economy." In *Global Trends in Migration: Theory and Research on International Population Movements,* edited by Mary M. Kritz, Charles B. Keely, and Silvano M. Tomasi (44–63). Staten Island, N.Y.: Center for Migration Studies.

Phillips, A. W. 1958. "The Relationship Between Unemployment and the Rate of Change of Money Wage in the United Kingdom, 1861–1957." *Economica* 25(100): 283–99.

Phizacklea, Annie, ed. 1983. *One Way Ticket: Migration and Female Labor.* Boston: Routledge and Kegan Paul.

Piore, Michael. 1975. "Notes for a Theory of Labor Market Stratification." In *Labor Market Segmentation,* edited by Richard C. Edwards, Michael Reich, and David M. Gordon (125–71). Lexington, Mass.: Heath.

———. 1979. *Birds of Passage: Migrant Labor in Industrial Societies.* New York: Cambridge University Press.

Piore, Michael J., and Charles F. Sabel. 1984. *The Second Industrial Divide.* New York: Basic Books.

Pischke, Jörn-Steffen, and Johannes Velling. 1997. "Employment Effects of Immigration to Germany: An Analysis Based on Local Labor Markets." *Review of Economics and Statistics* 79(4, November): 594–604.

Piven, Frances Fox, and Richard Cloward. 1988. *Why Americans Don't Vote.* New York: Pantheon.

Plotke, David. 1996. *Building a Democratic Political Order.* New York: Cambridge University Press.

Plotkin, Sidney, and William E. Scheuerman. 1994. *Private Interest, Public Spending: Balanced-Budget Conservatism and the Fiscal Crisis.* Boston: South End Press.

Pope, David, and Glenn Withers. 1993. "Do Migrants Rob Jobs?: Lessons of Australian History, 1861–1991." *Journal of Economic History* 53: 719–42.

Popkin, Barry M., and J. Richard Udry. 1998. "Adolescent Obesity Increases Significantly in Second- and Third-Generation U.S. Immigrants." *Journal of Nutrition* 128(4, April): 701–6.

Popkin, Samuel L. 1991. *The Reasonable Voter: Communication and Persuasion in Presidential Campaigns.* Chicago: University of Chicago Press.

Portes, Alejandro. 1981. "Modes of Structural Incorporation and Present Theories of Labor Immigration." In *Global Trends in Migration: Theory and Research on International Population Movements,* edited by Mary M. Kritz, Charles B. Keely, and Silvano M. Tomasi (279–97). Staten Island, N.Y.: Center for Migration Studies.

———. 1984. "The Rise of Ethnicity: Determinants of Ethnic Perceptions Among Cuban Exiles in Miami." *American Sociological Review* 49: 383–97.

———. 1995a. "Economic Sociology and the Sociology of Immigration: A Conceptual Overview." In *The Economic Sociology of Immigration: Essays on Networks, Ethnicity, and Entrepreneurship,* edited by Alejandro Portes (1–41). New York: Russell Sage Foundation.

———. 1995b. "Children of Immigrants: Segmented Assimilation and Its Determinants." In *The Economic Sociology of Immigration: Essays on Networks, Ethnicity, and Entrepreneurship,* edited by Alejandro Portes (248–79). New York: Russell Sage Foundation.

———. 1996a. "Transnational Communities: Their Emergence and Significance in the Contemporary World-System." In *Latin America in the World Economy,* edited by Roberto P. Korzeniewidcz and William C. Smith (151–68). Westport, Conn.: Greenwood.

———, ed. 1996b. *The New Second Generation.* New York: Russell Sage Foundation.

———. 1996c. "Introduction: Immigration and Its Aftermath." In *The New Second Generation,* edited by Alejandro Portes (1–7). New York: Russell Sage Foundation.

———. 1997. "Immigration Theory for a New Century: Some Problems and Opportunities." *International Migration Review* 31(4): 799–825.

———, ed. 1998. *The Economic Sociology of Immigration: Essays on Networks, Ethnicity, and Entrepreneurship.* New York: Russell Sage Foundation.

Portes, Alejandro, and Robert L. Bach. 1985. *Latin Journey: Cuban and Mexican Immigrants in the United States.* Berkeley: University of California Press.

Portes, Alejandro, and Jozsef Borocz. 1989. "Contemporary Immigration: Theoretical Perspectives on Its Determinants and Modes of Incorporation." *International Migration Review* 23(Fall): 606–30.

Portes, Alejandro, Manuel Castells, and Lauren A. Benton. 1988. *The Informal Economy: Studies in Advanced and Less Developed Countries.* Baltimore: Johns Hopkins University Press.

Portes, Alejandro, and Leif Jensen. 1987. "What's an Ethnic Enclave?: The Case for Conceptual Clarity—Comment on Sanders and Nee." *American Sociology Review* 52(6): 768–71.

———. 1989. "The Enclave and the Entrants: Patterns of Ethnic Enterprise in Miami Before and After Mariel." *American Sociological Review* 54(6): 929–49.

Portes, Alejandro, and Robert D. Manning. 1986. "The Immigrant Enclave: Theory and Empirical Examples." In *Competitive Ethnic Relations,* edited by Susan Olzak and Joane Nagel (47–68). Orlando, Fla.: Academic Press.

Portes, Alejandro, and Dag MacLeod. 1996. "The Educational Progress of Children of Immigrants: The Roles of Class, Ethnicity, and School Context." *Sociology of Education* 69(4): 255–75.

Portes, Alejandro, and Rubén G. Rumbaut. 1990. *Immigrant America: A Portrait.* Berkeley: University of California Press.

———. 1996. *Immigrant America: A Portrait.* 2nd ed. Berkeley: University of California Press.

Portes, Alejandro, and Saskia Sassen-Koob. 1987. "Making It Underground: Comparative Material on the Informal Sector in Western Market Economies." *American Journal of Sociology* 93(1): 30–61.

Portes, Alejandro, and Richard Schauffler. 1994. "Language and the Second Generation: Bilingualism Yesterday and Today." *International Migration Review* 28(4): 640–61.

———. 1996. "Language Acquisition and Loss Among Children of Immigrants." In *Origins and Destinies: Immigration, Race, and Ethnicity in America,* edited by Silvia Pedraza and Rubén G. Rumbaut (ch. 32). Belmont, Calif.: Wadsworth.

Portes, Alejandro, and Julia Sensenbrenner. 1993. "Embeddedness and Immigration: Notes on the Social Determinants of Economic Action." *American Journal of Sociology* 98: 1320–50.

Portes, Alejandro, and Alex Stepick. 1985. "Unwelcome Immigrants: The Labor Market Experiences of 1980 (Mariel) Cuban and Haitian Refugees in South Florida." *American Sociological Review* 50(4): 493–514.

———. 1993. *City on the Edge: The Transformation of Miami.* Berkeley: University of California Press.

Portes, Alejandro, and John Walton. 1981. *Labor, Class, and the International System.* New York: Academic Press.

Portes, Alejandro, and Min Zhou. 1992. "Gaining the Upper Hand: Economic Mobility Among Immigrant and Domestic Minorities." *Ethnic and Racial Studies* 15: 491–522.

———. 1993. "The New Second Generation: Segmented Assimilation and Its Variants Among Post–1965 Immigrant Youth." *Annals of the American Academy of Political and Social Science* 530(November): 74–96.

———. 1996. "Self-employment and the Earnings of Immigrants." *American Sociological Review* 61: 219–30.

Postman, Neil. 1985. *Amusing Ourselves to Death: Public Discourse in the Age of Show Business.* New York: Penguin.

Postrel, Virginia I. 1992. "The Real Story Goes Beyond Black and White." *Los Angeles Times,* May 8, A11.

Pozzetta, George E., ed. 1991. *Americanization, Social Control, and Philanthropy.* New York: Garland Publishers.

Preston, Samuel. 1996. "A Demographic Perspective on Immigration." Paper presented at the Social Science

Research Council Conference on Becoming American/America Becoming: International Migration to the United States, Sanibel Island, Fla. (January 18–21).

Preuss, Ulrich. 1993. "Constitutional Powermaking for the New Polity: Some Deliberations on the Relations Between Constituent Power and the Constitution." *Cardozo Law Review* 14: 639–60.

Prieto, Yolanda. 1992. "Cuban Women in New Jersey: Gender Relations and Change." In *Seeking Common Ground: Multidisciplinary Studies of Immigrant Women in the United States,* edited by Donna Gabaccia (185–201). Westport, Conn.: Greenwood.

Prothero, R. Mansell. 1990. "Labor Recruiting Organizations in the Developing World: Introduction." *International Migration Review* 24: 221–28.

Przeworski, Adam, and Henry Teune. 1970. *The Logic of Comparative Social Inquiry.* Malabar, Fla.: Robert E. Krieger.

Przeworski, Adam, and Michael Wallerstein. 1985. "Democratic Capitalism at the Crossroads." In *Capitalism and Social Democracy,* edited by Adam Przeworski (205–21). Cambridge: Cambridge University Press.

Putnam, Robert D. 1993a. "The Prosperous Community, Social Capital, and Public Life." *The American Prospect* 9: 35–42.

———. 1993b. *Making Democracy Work: Civic Traditions in Modern Italy.* Princeton, N.J.: Princeton University Press.

———. 1995. "Bowling Alone: America's Declining Social Capital." *Journal of Democracy* 6: 65–78.

Pyle, Amy. 1995. "Bilingual Backlash: A Closer Look at Immigrant Education." *Los Angeles Times,* June 1, 1A.

Qian, Zhenchao. 1997. "Breaking the Racial Barriers: Variations in Interracial Marriages Between 1980 and 1990." *Demography* 34: 263–76.

Raeburn, John. 1975. "Introduction." In *Frank Capra: The Man and His Films,* edited by Richard Glatzer and John Raeburn (vii–xiv). Ann Arbor: University of Michigan Press.

Raijman, Rebeca. 1996. "Pathways to Self-employment and Entrepreneurship in an Immigrant Community in Chicago." Ph.D. diss., Department of Sociology, University of Chicago.

Raijman, Rebeca, and Marta Tienda. Forthcoming. "Immigrants' Pathways to Business Ownership: A Comparative Ethnic Perspective." *International Migration Review.*

Ramirez, Bruno. 1991. *On the Move: French-Canadian and Italian Migrants in the North Atlantic Economy, 1860–1914.* Toronto: McClelland & Stewart.

Ramos, George. 1995. "The Fright Factor as an Incentive to Seek Citizenship." *Los Angeles Times,* April 10, B3.

Ranis, Gustav, and John C. H. Fei. 1961. "A Theory of Economic Development." *American Economic Review* 51: 533–65.

Ransom, Roger L., and Richard Sutch. 1975. "The 'Lockin' Mechanism and Overproduction of Cotton in the Postbellum South." *Agricultural History* 49: 405–25.

———. 1977. *One Kind of Freedom: The Economic Consequences of Emancipation.* New York: Cambridge University Press.

———. 1984. "Domestic Saving as an Active Constraint on Capital Formation in the American Economy, 1839–1928: A Provisional Theory." Working Papers on the History of Saving 1. Berkeley: Institute for Business and Economic Research, University of California at Berkeley (December).

———. 1987. "Tontine Insurance and the Armstrong Commission: A Case of Stifled Innovation in the American Life Insurance Industry." *Journal of Economic History* 47(2): 379–90.

———. 1988. "Capitalists Without Capital: The Burden of Slavery and the Impact of Emancipation." *Agricultural History* 62(3): 133–60.

Raskin, Jamin B. 1993. "Legal Aliens, Local Citizens: The Historical, Constitutional, and Theoretical Meanings of Alien Suffrage." *University of Pennsylvania Law Review* 141: 1391–1470.

Ravenstein, Ernst Georg. 1885. "The Laws of Migration." *Journal of the Royal Statistical Society* 48(78, June): 167–235.

———. 1889. "The Laws of Migration." *Journal of the Royal Statistical Society* 15: 241–305.

Ravitch, Diane. 1974. *The Great School Wars: New York City, 1805–1973: A History of the Public Schools as Battlefield of Social Change.* New York: Basic Books.

Reagan, Timothy. 1984. "Bilingual Education in the United States: Arguments and Evidence." *Education and Society* 2: 65–69.

Redding, Jack. 1958. *Inside the Democratic Party.* Indianapolis: Bobbs-Merrill.

Redfield, Robert. 1955. *The Little Community.* Chicago: University of Chicago Press.

Rees, Albert. 1960. "New Measures of Wage-Earner Compensation in Manufacturing 1914–1957." Occasional Paper 75. New York: National Bureau of Economic Research.

———. 1961. *Real Wages in Manufacturing, 1890–1914.* Princeton, N.J.: Princeton University Press.

Rees, Tom. 1993. "United Kingdom I: Inheriting Empire's People." In *The Politics of Immigration Policies: Settlement and Integration: The First World into the 1990s,* edited by Daniel Kubat (87–107). Staten Island, N.Y.: Center for Migration Studies.

Reich, Robert. 1992. *The Work of Nations: Preparing Ourselves for Twenty-first-Century Capitalism.* New York: Random House.

Reichert, Joshua S. 1981. "The Migrant Syndrome: Seasonal U.S. Wage Labor and Rural Development in Central Mexico." *Human Organization* 40: 56–66.

———. 1982. "Social Stratification in a Mexican Sending Community: The Effect of Migration to the United States." *Social Problems* 29: 422–33.

Reichl, Christopher. 1988. *Japanese Newcomers in Bra-*

zil: A Social Model of Migration. Ann Arbor, Mich.: University Microfilms.

Reimers, David M. 1985. *Still the Golden Door: The Third World Comes to America*. New York: Columbia University Press.

———. 1992. *Still the Golden Door: The Third World Comes to America*. 2nd ed. New York: Columbia University Press. (Originally published in 1985)

Repak, Terry A. 1995. *Waiting on Washington: Central American Workers in the Nation's Capital*. Philadelphia: Temple University Press.

Reynolds, Clark, and Robert K. McCleery. 1988. "The Political Economy of Immigration Law: Impact of Simpson-Rodino on the United States and Mexico." *Journal of Economic Perspectives* 2(3): 117–31.

Rhoades, Robert E. 1978. "Intra-European Return Migration and Rural Development: Lessons from the Spanish Case." *Human Organization* 37: 136–47.

Richards, Larry. 1995. "Middle-class Jobs on the Immigration Chopping Block." *The Social Contract* 5: 291–92.

Richardson, B. 1983. *Caribbean Migrations: Environment and Human Survival on Saint Kitts and Nevis*. Knoxville: University of Tennessee Press.

Richman, Karen. 1992. "*Lavalas* at Home/ A *Lavalas* for Home: Inflections of Transnationalism in the Discourse of Haitian President Aristide." In *Toward a Transnational Perspective of Migration,* edited by Nina Glick Schiller, Linda Basch, and Christina Blanc-Szanton (189–200). New York: New York Academy of Sciences.

Rico, Carlos. 1992. "Migration and U.S.-Mexican Relations, 1966–1986." In *Western Hemisphere Immigration and United States Foreign Policy,* edited by Christopher Mitchell (221–83). University Park: Pennsylvania State University Press.

Rieder, Jonathan 1985. *Canarsie: The Jews and Italians of Brooklyn Against Liberalism*. Cambridge, Mass.: Harvard University Press.

Riesman, David. 1950. *The Lonely Crowd: A Study in the Changing American Character.* New Haven, Conn.: Yale University Press.

Riggs, Fred W. 1950. *Pressures on Congress: A Study of the Repeal of Chinese Exclusion*. New York: King's Crown Press.

Rischin, Moses, ed. 1976. *Immigration and the American Tradition*. Indianapolis: Bobbs-Merrill.

———. 1979. "Marcus Lee Hansen: America's First Transethnic Historian." In *Uprooted Americans: Essays to Honor Oscar Handlin,* edited by Richard L. Bushman, Neil Harris, David Rothman, Barbara Miller Solomon, and Stephan Thernstrom (319–47). Boston: Little, Brown.

———. 1981. "Creating Crèvecoeur's 'New Man.' He Had a Dream." *Journal of American Ethnic History* 1(Fall): 26–42.

Rivera-Batiz, Francisco L., and Carlos Santiago. 1994. *Puerto Ricans in the United States: A Changing Reality*. Washington: National Puerto Rican Coalition.

Roberts, Kenneth. 1982. "Agrarian Structure and Labor Mobility in Rural Mexico." *Population and Development Review* 8: 299–322.

———. 1985. "Household Labour Mobility in a Modern Agrarian Economy: Mexico." In *Labour Circulation and the Labour Process,* edited by Guy Standing (358–81). London: Croom Helm.

Roberts, Peter. 1990. "Restrictions on Immigration Are Unnecessary." In *Immigration: Opposing Viewpoints,* edited by William Dudley (39–46). San Diego: Greenhaven Press. (Originally published in 1912).

Roberts, Sam. 1994. "Hispanic Population Outnumbers Blacks in Four Major Cities as Demographics Shift." *New York Times,* October 9, 34.

Robertson, Roland. 1992. *Globalization, Social Theory and Global Culture*. London: Sage.

Robertson, Ross M. 1973. *History of the American Economy*. 3rd ed. New York: Harcourt Brace Jovanovich.

Robinson, Edward G., with Leonard Spigelgass. 1973. *All My Yesterdays*. New York: Hawthorn Books.

Robinson, W. S. 1951. "The Logical Structure of Analytic Induction." *American Sociological Review* 16: 812–18.

Rodriguez, Gregory. 1996. "Reverse Assimilation: How Proposition 187 Hastened the Latinization of California." *Los Angeles Weekly,* August 9–15, 25–27.

Rodriguez, Nestor P. 1987. "Undocumented Central Americans in Houston: Diverse Populations." *International Migration Review* 21(1, Spring): 4–26.

———. 1993. "Economic Restructuring and Latino Growth in Houston." In *In the Barrios: Latinos and the Underclass Debate,* edited by Joan Moore and Raquel Pinderhughes. New York: Russell Sage Foundation.

———. 1995. "The Real New World Order: The Globalization of Racial and Ethnic Relations in the Late Twentieth Century." In *The Bubbling Cauldron: Race, Ethnicity, and the Urban Crisis,* edited by Michael Peter Smith and Joe R. Feagin (211–25). Minneapolis: University of Minnesota Press.

Rodriguez, Nestor P., and Ximena Urrutia-Rojas. 1990. "Impact of Recent Refugee Migration to Texas: A Comparison of Southeast Asian and Central American Newcomers." In *Mental Health of Immigrants and Refugees,* edited by Wayne Holtzman and Thomas Bornemann (263–78). Austin, Tex.: Hogg Foundation.

Rodriguez, Richard. 1983. *Hunger of Memory: The Education of Richard Rodriguez*. Boston: David R. Godine.

Roediger, David R. 1991. *The Wages of Whiteness: Race and the Making of the American Working Class*. London: Verso.

———. 1994. *Towards the Abolition of Whiteness: Essays on Race, Politics, and Working-class History*. London: Verso.

Rogers, Joel. 1990. "Divide and Conquer: Further 'Reflections on the Distinctive Character of American Labor Laws.'" *Wisconsin Law Review* (1): 1–147.

Rogin, Michael. 1992a. "Blackface, White Noise: The Jewish Jazz Singer Finds His Voice." *Critical Inquiry* 18(Spring): 417–53.

———. 1992b. "Making America Home: Racial Masquerade and Ethnic Assimilation in the Transition to Talking Pictures." *Journal of American History* 79(December): 1050–75.

———. 1994. "'Democracy and Burnt Cork': The End of Blackface, the Beginning of Civil Rights." *Representations* 46(Spring): 1–34.

———. 1996. *Blackface, White Noise: Jewish Immigrants in the Hollywood Melting Pot.* Berkeley: University of California Press.

Romer, Christina. 1986. "Spurious Volatility in Historical Unemployment Data." *Journal of Political Economy* 94(1): 1–37.

Romer, Paul M. 1986. "Increasing Returns and Long-run Growth." *Journal of Political Economy* 94(3): 1002–37.

———. 1996. "Why, Indeed, in America?: Theory, History, and the Origins of Modern Economic Growth." *American Economic Review* 86(2): 202–6.

Romo, Ricardo, and Nestor Rodriguez. 1993. *Houston Evaluation of Community Priorities: Summary Report.* Claremont, Calif.: Tomas Rivera Center.

Romo, Ricardo, and Nestor Rodriguez, with Luis Plascencia and Ximena Urrutia-Rojas. 1994. *The Houston Evaluation of Community Priorities Project: Final Report.* Claremont, Calif.: Tomas Rivera Center (February).

Root, Maria P. P., ed. 1992. *Racially Mixed People in America.* Newbury Park, Calif.: Sage Publications.

Rose, Harold M. 1989. "Blacks and Cubans in Metropolitan Miami's Changing Economy." *Urban Geography* 10: 464–86.

Rosecrance, Richard. 1996. "The Rise of the Virtual State." *Foreign Affairs* 75(4): 45.

Rosenbaum, David E. 1995. "A Budget Debate Not About Dollars, but About Whose Plan Makes Sense." *New York Times,* December 1, B12.

Rosenberg, Emily, and Greta Gilbertson. 1995. "Mothers' Labor-Force Participation in New York City: A Reappraisal of the Influence of Household Extension." *Journal of Marriage and the Family* 57: 243–49.

Rosenberg, Nathan. 1982. *Inside the Black Box: Technology and Economics.* New York: Cambridge University Press.

Rosenbloom, Joshua L. 1996. "Was There a National Labor Market at the End of the Nineteenth Century?: New Evidence on Earnings in Manufacturing." *Journal of Economic History* 56(3): 626–56.

Rosenblum, Gerald. 1973. *Immigrant Workers: Their Impact on American Radicalism.* New York: Basic Books.

Rosenfeld, Michael J., and Marta Tienda. 1997. "Labor Market Implications of Mexican Immigration: Economies of Scale, Innovation, and Entrepreneurship." In *At the Crossroads: Mexico and U.S. Immigration Policy,* edited by Frank D. Bean, Rodolfo de la Garza, Bryan Roberts, and Sidney Weintraub (177–99). New York: Rowman & Littlefield.

———. 1999. "Mexican Immigration, Occupational Niches, and Labor Market Competition: Evidence from Los Angeles, Chicago, and Atlanta, 1970–1990." In *Immigration and Opportunity,* edited by Frank D. Bean and Stephenie Bell-Rose (64–105) New York: Russell Sage Foundation.

Rosenthal, Erich. 1960. "Acculturation Without Assimilation?: The Jewish Community in Chicago." *American Journal of Sociology* 66: 275–88.

Rosenzweig, Roy. 1983. *Eight Hours for What We Will: Workers and Leisure in an Industrial City, 1870–1920.* New York: Cambridge University Press.

Ross, Dorothy. 1991. *The Origins of American Social Science.* New York: Cambridge University Press.

Ross, Edward Alsworth. 1914. *The Old World in the New: The Significance of Past and Present Immigration to the American People.* New York: Century.

Ross, Frank A., and A. A. Truxel. 1931. "Primary and Secondary Aspects of Interstate Migration." *American Journal of Sociology* 37: 435–44.

Ross, Kevin. 1994. "Southern California Voices: A Forum for Community Issues: Proposition 187." *Los Angeles Times,* October 24, 5B.

Ross, Marc Howard, and Thomas Weisner. 1977. "The Rural-Urban Migrant Network in Kenya: Some General Implications." *American Ethnologist* 4(2): 359–75.

Rothman, Eric S., and Thomas J. Espenshade. 1992. "Fiscal Impacts of Immigration to the United States." *Population Index* 58(3, Fall): 381–415.

Rouse, Roger. 1986. "Migration and Family Politics in Family Life: Divergent Projects and Rhetorical Strategies in a Mexican Migrant Community." Paper presented at the annual meeting of the American Anthropological Association, Philadelphia (December).

———. 1989. "Mexican Migration to the United States: Family Relations in the Development of a Transnational Migrant Circuit." Ph.D. diss., Department of Anthropology, Stanford University.

———. 1991. "Mexican Migration and the Social Space of Postmodernism." *Diaspora* 1(Spring): 8–23.

———. 1992. "Making Sense of Settlement: Class Transformation, Cultural Struggle, and Transnationalism Among Mexican Migrants in the United States." In *Towards a Transnational Perspective on Migration: Race, Class, Ethnicity, and Nationalism Reconsidered,* edited by Nina Glick Schiller, Linda Basch, and Cristina Blanc-Szanton (25–52). New York: New York Academy of Sciences.

———. 1994. "Questions of Identity: Personhood and Collectivity in Transnational Migration to the United States." *Critique of Anthropology* 15(4): 351–80.

Rubin, Lillian. 1994. *Families on the Fault Line: America's Working Class Speaks About the Family, the Economy, Race, and Ethnicity.* New York: HarperCollins.

Rumbaut, Rubén G. 1990. "Immigrant Students in California Public Schools: A Summary of Current Knowledge." Report 11. Baltimore: Johns Hopkins University Center for Research on Effective Schooling for Disadvantaged Students.

———. 1992. "The Americans: Latin American and Caribbean Peoples in the United States. In *Americas: New Interpretive Essays,* edited by Alfred Stepan (275–307). New York: Oxford University Press.

———. 1994a. "Origins and Destinies: Immigration to the United States Since World War II." *Sociological Forum* 9(4): 583–621.

———. 1994b. "The Crucible Within: Ethnic Identity, Self-esteem, and Segmented Assimilation Among Children of Immigrants." *International Migration Review* 18: 748–94.

———. 1995. "The New Californians: Comparative Research Findings on the Educational Progress of Immigrant Children." In *California's Immigrant Children: Theory, Research, and Implications for Educational Policy,* edited by Rubén G. Rumbaut and Wayne A. Cornelius (17–69). La Jolla: Center for U.S.-Mexican Studies, University of California at San Diego.

———. 1996. "Origins and Destinies: Immigration, Race, and Ethnicity in Contemporary America." In *Origins and Destinies: Immigration, Race, and Ethnicity in America,* edited by Silvia Pedraza and Rubén G. Rumbaut (21–42). Belmont, Calif.: Wadsworth.

———. 1997a. "Paradoxes (and Orthodoxies) of Assimilation." *Sociological Perspectives* 40(3): 483–551.

———. 1997b. "Ties That Bind: Immigration and Immigrant Families in the United States." In *Immigration and the Family: Research and Policy on U.S. Immigrants,* edited by Alan Booth, Ann C. Crouter, and Nancy S. Landale (3–46). Mahwah, N.J.: Erlbaum.

———. 1997c. "Passages to Adulthood: The Adaptation of Children of Immigrants in Southern California." Report to the Russell Sage Foundation Board of Trustees.

———. 1999a. "Immigration Research in the United States: Social Origins and Future Orienttions." *American Behavioral Scientist* 42(9): 1285–1302.

———. 1999b. "Passages to Adulthood: The Adaptation of Children of Immigrants in Southern California." In *Children of Immigrants: Health, Adjustment, and Public Assistance,* edited by Donald J. Hernández Washington: National Academy of Sciences Press.

Rumbaut, Rubén G., Leo Chávez, Robert Moser, Sheila Pickwell, and Samuel Wishik. 1988. "The Politics of Migrant Health Care: A Comparative Study of Mexican Immigrants and Indochinese Refugees." *Research in the Sociology of Health Care* 7: 148–202.

Rumbaut, Rubén G., and Kenji Ima. 1988. *The Adaptation of Southeast Asian Refugee Youth: A Comparative Study.* Washington: Office of Refugee Resettlement.

Rumbaut, Rubén G., and John R. Weeks. 1989. "Infant Health Among Indochinese Refugees: Patterns of Infant Mortality, Birthweight, and Prenatal Care in Comparative Perspective." *Research in the Sociology of Health Care* 8: 137–96.

———. 1996. "Unraveling a Public Health Enigma: Why Do Immigrants Experience Superior Perinatal Health Outcomes?" *Research in the Sociology of Health Care* 13: 335–88.

———. 1998. "Children of Immigrants: Is 'Americanization' Hazardous to Infant Health?" In *Children of Color: Research, Health, and Public Policy Issues,* edited by Hiram E. Fitzgerald, Barry M. Lester, and Barry Zuckerman (159–83). New York: Garland.

Sacks, Karen Brodkin. 1989. "Toward a Unified Theory of Class, Race, and Gender." *American Ethnologist* 16(3): 534–50.

———. 1994. "How Did Jews Become White Folks?" In *Race,* edited by Stephen Gregory and Roger Sanjek (78–102). New Brunswick, N.J.: Rutgers University Press.

Safa, Helen. 1995. *The Myth of the Male Breadwinner.* Boulder, Colo.: Westview.

Salin, Peter. 1997. *Assimilation, American Style.* New York: Basic Books.

Salvaterra, David L. 1994. "Becoming American: Assimilation, Pluralism, and Ethnic Identity." In *Immigrant America: European Ethnicity in the United States,* edited by Timothy Walch (29–54). New York: Garland.

Salvo, Joseph, Ron Ortiz, and Frank Vardy. 1992. *The Newest New Yorkers: An Analysis of Immigration into New York City During the 1980s.* New York: New York City Department of City Planning.

Sanchez, Arturo Ignacio. 1997. "Transnational Political Agency and Identity Formation Among Colombian Immigrants." Paper presented at the Conference on Transnational Communities and the Political Economy of New York, New School for Social Research, New York (October 19).

Sánchez, George J. 1993. *Becoming Mexican American: Ethnicity, Culture, and Identity in Chicano Los Angeles, 1900–1945.* New York: Oxford University Press.

———. 1995. "Reading Reginald Denny: The Politics of Whiteness in the Late Twentieth Century." *American Quarterly* 47(September): 388–94.

Sancton, Thomas. 1992. "How to Get America off the Dole?" *Time,* May 25, 44–47.

Sandberg, Neil. 1974. *Ethnic Identity and Assimilation: The Polish Community.* New York: Praeger.

Sandel, Michael J. 1996. *Democracy's Discontent: America in Search of a Public Philosophy.* Cambridge, Mass.: Harvard University Press.

Sanders, Jimy, and Victor Nee. 1987. "The Limits of Ethnic Solidarity in the Enclave Economy." *American Sociological Review* 52: 745–73.

Sanders, Jimy, and Victor Nee. "Immigrant Self-Employment: The Family as Social Capital and the Value of Human Capital." *American Sociological Review* 61: 231–49.

Sandrow, Nahma. 1977. *Vagabond Stars: A World History of Yiddish Theater.* New York: Harper & Row.

Sanjek, Roger. 1998. *The Future of Us All*. Ithaca, N.Y.: Cornell University Press.

San Miguel, Guadalupe. 1984. "Conflict and Controversy in the Evolution of Bilingual Education in the United States." *Social Science Quarterly* 65: 505–18.

Santibáñez, Enrique. 1930. *Ensayo acerca de la inmigración mexicana en los Estados Unidos*. San Antonio, Tex.: Clegg.

Santos, Gustavo Adolfo Pedrosa Daltro Santos. 1996. "Saibiá em Portugal: Imigrantes Brasileiros e a Imaginaçâo da Naçâo na Diáspora." B.A. thesis, Department of Anthropology, UNICAMP, Brazil.

Sarna, Jonathan. 1978. "From Immigrants to Ethnics: Toward a New Theory of Ethnicization." *Ethnicity* 5: 73–78.

Sassen, Saskia. 1984. "Notes on the Incorporation of Third World Women into Wage Labor Through Offshore Production." *International Migration Review* 18(4): 1144–67.

———. 1987. "Issues of Core and Periphery: Labor Migration and Global Restructuring." In *Global Restructuring and Territorial Development* (61–73). Beverly Hills, Calif.: Sage.

———. 1988. *The Mobility of Labor and Capital: A Study in International Investment and Labor Flows*. New York: Cambridge University Press.

———. 1989. "New York City's Informal Economy." In *The Informal Economy: Studies in Advanced and Less-Developed Countries,* edited by Alejandro Portes, Manuel Castells, and Lauren A. Benton (60–77). Baltimore: Johns Hopkins University Press.

———. 1991. *The Global City: New York, London, Tokyo*. Princeton, N.J.: Princeton University Press.

———. 1996a. "Toward a Feminist Analytics of the Global Economy." *Indiana Journal of Global Legal Studies* 4(1): 7–41.

———. 1996b. *Losing Control?: Sovereignty in an Age of Globalization*. New York: Columbia University Press.

Saxton, Alexander. 1971. *The Indispensable Enemy: Labor and the Anti-Chinese Movement in California*. Berkeley: University of California Press.

———. 1990. *The Rise and Fall of the White Republic: Class Politics and Mass Culture in Nineteenth-Century America*. London: Verso.

Schaeffer, Robert. 1997. *Understanding Globalization: The Social Consequences of Political, Economic, and Environmental Change*. New York: Rowman & Littlefield.

Schermerhorn, R.A. 1949. *These Our People: Minorities in American Culture*. Boston: D.C. Heath.

Schlesinger, Arthur M., Jr. 1949a. *Paths to the Present*. New York: Macmillan.

———. 1949b. *The Vital Center: The Politics of Freedom*. Boston.

———. 1957–60. *The Crisis of the Old Order,* vol. 1 of *The Age of Roosevelt*. Boston: Houghton Mifflin.

———. 1991. *The Disuniting of America: Reflections on a Multicultural Society*. New York: Norton.

Schmeidl, Susanne. 1997. "Exploring the Causes of Forced Migration: A Pooled Time-Series Analysis, 1971–1990." *Social Science Quarterly* 78: 284–308.

Schmidley, Dianne, and Herman A. Alvarado. 1998. *The Foreign-born Population in the United States: March 1997 (Update). Current Population Reports,* P-20-507. Washington: U.S. Bureau of the Census.

Schmidt, Sarah. 1995. *Horace M. Kallen: Prophet of American Zionism*. Brooklyn: Carlson Publishing.

Schmink, Marianne. 1984. "Household Economic Strategies: Review and Research Agenda." *Latin American Research Review* 19(3): 87–101.

Schmitt, Eric. 1995a. "House Votes Bill to Cut UN Funds for Peacekeeping." *New York Times,* February 17, A1.

———. 1995b. "Stage Set for a Showdown on Foreign Policy." *New York Times,* February 15, A8.

Schmitter, Phillipe C., and Gerhard Lehmbruch, eds. 1979. *Trends Toward Corporatist Intermediation*. Beverly Hills, Calif.: Sage.

Schneider, David. 1968. *American Kinship: A Cultural Account*. Englewood Cliffs, N.J.: Prentice-Hall.

Schneider, Jo Anne. 1994. "Fieval Is an Engineer: Immigrant Ideology and the Absorption of Eastern European Refugees." *Identities: Global Studies in Cultural Power* 1(2–3): 227–48.

Schneider, Louis, 1975. "Ironic Perspectives and Sociological Thought." In *The Idea of Social Structure: Papers in Honor of Robert K. Merton,* edited by Lewis A. Coser (323–37). New York: Harcourt Brace Jovanovich.

Schrecker, Ellen W. 1986. *No Ivory Tower: McCarthyism and the Universities*. New York: Oxford University Press.

Schuck, Peter H. 1984. "The Transformation of Immigration Law." *Columbia Law Review* 84(January): 1–90.

———. 1992. "The Politics of Rapid Legal Change: Immigration Policy in the 1980s." *Studies in American Political Development* 6(1): 37–92.

———. 1996. "Review of *Alien Nation*." *Yale Law Journal* 105(7, May): 1963–2012.

———. 1998. "The Politics of Rapid Legal Change: Immigration Policy, 1980–1990." In *Citizens, Strangers, and In-Betweens: Essays on Immigration and Citizenship*. Boulder, Colo.: Westview Press.

Schultz, Wendy L. 1993. "Culture in Transition: Alternative Futures of Immigration, Ethnic Composition, and Community Conflict Within the United States." *Futures Research Quarterly* 9: 51–72.

Scott, Allen J. 1986. *Metropolis: From Division to Urban Form*. Berkeley: University of California Press.

Scribner, R., and J. Dwyer. 1989. "Acculturation and Low Birthweight Among Latinos in the Hispanic HHANES." *American Journal of Public Health* 79: 1263–67.

Segura, Denise. 1994. "Working at Motherhood: Chicana and Mexican Immigrant Mothers and Employment." In *Mothering: Ideology, Experience, and Agency,* edited by Evelyn Nakano Glenn, Grace Chang, and Linda Rennie Forceyg (211–33). New York: Routledge.

Sendelbach, Sara. 1967. "The All Americans Council: A Study of the Role of the Ethnic Group in Partisan Politics." Washington Semester of the School of Government and Public Administration, American University. Unpublished paper.

Setlow, Carolyn E., and Renae Cohen. 1993. *The 1992 New York City Intergroup Relations Survey.* New York: American Jewish Committee.

Shafer, Byron E., ed. 1991. *The End of Realignment?: Interpreting American Electoral Eras.* Madison: University of Wisconsin Press.

Shannon, David A. 1967. *The Socialist Party of America: A History.* Chicago: Quadrangle Books.

Shapiro, Carl, and Joseph Stiglitz. 1984. "Equilibrium Unemployment as a Discipline Device." *American Economic Review* 74: 433–44.

Shapiro, Edward S. 1986. "John Higham and American Anti-Semitism." *American Jewish History* 76(2): 201–13.

Shavit, Ari. 1997. "Vanishing." *New York Times Magazine,* June 8, p. 52.

Shefter, Martin. 1985. *Political Crisis/Fiscal Crisis: The Collapse and Revival of New York City.* New York: Basic Books.

———. 1986. "Political Incorporation and the Extrusion of the Left: Party Politics and Social Forces in New York City." *Studies in American Political Development* 1: 50–90.

———. 1994. *Political Parties and the State: The American Historical Experience.* Princeton, N.J.: Princeton University Press.

Shelton, Beth Anne, Nestor Rodriguez, Joe R. Feagin, Robert D. Bullard, and Robert D. Thomas. 1989. *Houston: Growth and Decline in a Sunbelt Boomtown.* Philadelphia: Temple University Press.

Shibutani, Tamotsu, and Kian Kwan. 1965. *Ethnic Stratification.* New York: Macmillan.

Shukla, Sandhya. 1997. "Feminisms of the Diaspora Both Local and Global: The Politics of South Asian Women Against Domestic Violence." In *Women Question Politics,* edited by Cathy Cohen, Kathleen Jones, and Joan Tronto (269–83). New York: New York University Press.

Silbey, Joel. 1991. *The American Political Nation, 1838–1893.* Stanford, Calif.: Stanford University Press.

Silverstein, Stuart, and Nancy R. Brooks. 1994. "Proposition 187 Is Affecting Workplace; Immigration: More Companies Have Started Checking Job Candidates' Papers, and Employees Talk of Rising Tensions." *Los Angeles Times,* November 10, D1.

Simmons, Alan B. 1989. "World System-Linkages and International Migration: New Directions in Theory and Method with an Application to Canada." In *International Population Conference, New Delhi 1989* (vol. 2, 159–72). Liège: International Union for the Scientific Study of Population.

Simon, Julian L. 1989. *The Economic Consequences of Immigration.* Oxford, UK: Basil Blackwell.

Simon, Julian L., and Richard J. Sullivan. 1989. "Population Size, Knowledge Stock, and Other Determinants of Agricultural Publication and Patenting: England, 1541–1850." *Explorations in Economic History* 21(1): 21–44.

Simon, Matthew. 1960. "The U.S. Balance of Payments, 1861–1900." In *Trends in the American Economy in the Nineteenth Century,* edited by William N. Parker (628ff.). Princeton, N.J.: Princeton University Press/National Bureau of Economic Research.

Simon, Rita J., and Susan H. Alexander. 1993. *The Ambivalent Welcome: Print Media, Public Opinion, and Immigration.* Westport, Conn.: Praeger.

Simon, Rita, and Caroline Brettell, eds. 1986. *International Migration: The Female Experience.* Totowa, N.J.: Rowman and Allanheld.

Singer, Paul. 1971. "Dinámica de la población y desarrollo." In *El papel del crecimiento demográfico en el desarrollo económico* (21–66). México, D.F.: Editorial Siglo XXI.

———. 1975. *Economía política de la urbanización.* México, D.F.: Editorial Siglo XXI.

Sitkoff, Harvey. 1978. *A New Deal for Blacks: The Emergence of Civil Rights as a National Issue.* New York: Oxford University Press.

Sjaastad, Larry A. 1962. "The Costs and Returns of Human Migration." *Journal of Political Economy* 70: S80–93.

Skerry, Peter. 1993. *Mexican Americans: The Ambivalent Minority.* New York: Free Press.

Skrentny, John David. 1997. *The Ironies of Affirmative Action: Politics, Culture, and Justice in America.* Chicago: University of Chicago Press.

Sleeper, Jim. 1993a. "The End of the Rainbow." *New Republic* (November 1): 20–25.

———. 1993b. "The New Face of America." *Time,* special issue, 142(Fall).

———. 1997. "Toward an End of Blackness: An Argument for the Surrender of Race Consciousness." *Harper's* 291(May): 35–44.

Slotkin, Richard. 1993. *Gunfighter Nation: The Myth of the Frontier in Twentieth-Century America.* New York: Atheneum.

Smith, Adam. 1776. *An Inquiry into the Nature and Causes of the Wealth of Nations.* London: W. Strahan; and T. Cadell, in the Strand.

Smith, Anna Deveare, 1994. *Twilight: Los Angeles, 1992.* New York: Anchor Books/Doubleday.

Smith, James P., and Barry Edmonston, eds. 1997. *The New Americans: Economic, Demographic, and Fiscal Effects of Immigration.* Report from the Panel on the Demographic and Economic Impacts of Immigration. Washington: National Academy Press.

———, eds. 1998. *The New Americans: Studies on the*

Economic, Demographic, and Fiscal Effects of Immigration. Washington: National Academy Press.
Smith, James P., and Finus Welch. 1989. "Black Economic Progress After Myrdal." *Journal of Economic Literature* 27(2): 519–64.
Smith, Michael Peter. 1994. "Can You Imagine?: Transnational Migration and the Globalization of Grassroots Politics." *Social Text* 39(15): 15–33.
Smith, Michael Peter, and Luis Edwardo Guarinzo, ed. 1998. *Transnationalsim From Below.* New Brunswick, N.J.: Rutgers University Press.
Smith, Raymond T. 1967. "Social Stratification, Cultural Pluralism, and Integration in West Indian Societies." In *Caribbean Integration: Papers on Social, Political, and Economic Integration,* edited by Sybil Lewis and T. G. Mathews (226–58). Rio Piedras: Institute of Caribbean Studies, University of Puerto Rico.
———. 1988. *Kinship and Class in the West Indies.* Cambridge: Cambridge University Press.
Smith, Robert C. 1992. "New York in Mixteca: Mixteca in New York." *NACLA Report on the Americas* 26: 1.
———. 1994. "Los Ausentes Siempre Presentes: The Imagining, Making, and Politics of a Transnational Community Between Ticuani, Puebla, Mexico, and New York City." Ph.D. diss., Department of Political Science, Columbia University.
———. 1997. "Transnational Migration, Assimilation, and Political Community." In *The City and the World: New York City's Global Future,* edited by Margaret Crahan and Alberto Vourvoulias Bush. New York: Council on Foreign Relations.
———. 1998. "Transnational Localities: Community, Technology, and the Politics of Membership Within the Context of Mexico-U.S. Migration." In *Transnationalism from Below,* edited by Michael Peter Smith and Luis Guarnizo. New Brunswick, N.J.: Rutgers University Press.
Smith, Robert. 1998. "Transnational Localities: Community, Technology, and the Politicas of Membership Within the Context of Mexico-U.S. Migration." In *Transnationalism from Below,* edited by Michael Peter Smith and Luis Guarnizo (196–238). New Brunswick, N.J.: Rutgers University Press.
Smith, Rogers M. 1997. *Civic Ideals: Conflicting Visions of Citizenship in U.S. History.* Cambridge, Mass.: Harvard University Press.
Snipp, C. Matthew. 1989. *American Indians: The First of This Land.* New York: Russell Sage Foundation.
Snyder, Robert W. 1989. *The Voice of the City: Vaudeville and Popular Culture in New York.* New York: Oxford University Press.
Social Science Research Council. 1996. "Becoming American/America Becoming: A Conference on International Migration to the United States." Unpublished conference outline.
———. 1998. "Fellowships for the Study of International Migration to the United States, 1999–2000." Advertising brochure.
Soja, Ed, Rebecca Morales, and Goetz Wolff. 1983. "Urban Restructuring: An Analysis of Social and Spatial Change in Los Angeles." *Economic Geography* 58: 221–35.
Sokoloff, Kenneth L. 1988. "Inventive Activity in Early Industrial America: Evidence from Patent Records." *Journal of Economic History* 48(4): 813–50.
Sokoloff, Kenneth L., and Zorina B. Kahn. 1990. "The Democratization of Invention During Early Industrialization: Evidence from the United States, 1790–1846." *Journal of Economic History* 50(2): 363–78.
Sole, Yolanda Russinovich. 1990. "Bilingualism: Stable or Transitional?" *International Journal of the Sociology of Language* 84: 35–80.
Sollors, Werner. 1986. *Beyond Ethnicity: Consent and Descent in American Culture.* New York: Oxford University Press.
———. 1989. *The Invention of Ethnicity.* New York: Oxford University Press.
Solow, Robert. 1956. "A Contribution to the Theory of Economic Growth." *Quarterly Journal of Economics* 70: 65–94.
Sonenshein, Raphael J. 1993. *Politics in Black and White: Race and Power in Los Angeles.* Princeton, N.J.: Princeton University Press.
Sorensen, Elaine, and Nikki Blasberg. 1996. "The Use of SSI and Other Welfare Programs by Immigrants." Washington: Urban Institute, Income and Benefits Policy Center.
Soto, Isa María. 1987. "West Indian Child Fostering: Its Role in Migrant Exchanges." In *Caribbean Life in New York City: Sociocultural Dimensions,* edited by Constance R. Sutton and Elsa M. Chaney (131–49). Staten Island, N.Y.: Center for Migration Studies.
Sowell, Thomas. 1996. *Migrations and Cultures: A World View.* New York: Basic Books.
Soysal, Yasemin Nuhoglu. 1994. *Limits of Citizenship: Migrations and Postnational Membership in Europe.* Chicago: University of Chicago Press.
Spengler, Joseph J., and George Myers. 1977. "Migration and Socioeconomic Development: Today and Yesterday." In *Internal Migration: A Comparative Perspective,* edited by Alan Brown and Egon Neuberger (11–35). New York: Academic Press.
Spergel, Irving A. 1964. *Racketville, Slumtown, Haulberg: An Exploratory Study of Delinquent Subcultures.* Chicago: University of Chicago Press.
Spickard, Paul R. 1989. *Mixed Blood: Intermarriage and Ethnic Identity in Twentieth-Century America.* Madison: University of Washington Press.
Stack, Carol B. 1974. *All Our Kin: Strategies for Survival in a Black Community.* New York: Harper Colophon Books.
Stafford, Susan Buchanan. 1984. "Haitian Immigrant Women: A Cultural Perspective." *Anthropologica* 26(2): 171–89.
Stafford, Walter. 1984. *Employment Segmentation in*

New York City Agencies. New York: Community Service Society.

———. 1985. *Closed Labor Markets: Underrepresentation of Blacks, Hispanics, and Women in New York City's Core Industries and Jobs*. New York: Community Service Society.

———. 1991. "Racial, Ethnic, and Gender Employment Segmentation in New York City Agencies." In *Hispanics in the Labor Force*, edited by Edwin Melendez, Clara Rodriguez, and Janis Barry Figueroa (159–80). New York: Plenum.

Stallings, Barbara, ed. 1995. *Global Change, Regional Response: The New International Context of Development*. New York: Cambridge University Press.

Stanfield, Rochelle. 1994. "New Faces of Hate." *National Journal* 26(June 18): 1461–63.

Stanley, Harold W., and Richard G. Niemi. 1995. *Vital Statistics on American Politics*. 5th ed. Washington: Congressional Quarterly Press.

Stark, Oded. 1991. *The Migration of Labor*. Cambridge: Basil Blackwell.

Stark, Oded, and David E. Bloom. 1985. "The New Economics of Labor Migration." *American Economic Review* 75: 173–78.

Stark, Oded, and J. Edward Taylor. 1989. "Relative Deprivation and International Migration." *Demography* 26(1): 1–14.

———. 1991. "Relative Deprivation and Migration: Theory, Evidence, and Policy Implications." In *Determinants of Emigration from Mexico, Central America, and the Caribbean*, edited by Sergio Díaz-Briquets and Sidney Weintraub (121–44). Boulder, Colo.: Westview.

Stark, Oded, J. Edward Taylor, and Shlomo Yitzhaki. 1986. "Remittances and Inequality." *Economic Journal* 101: 1163–78.

State and Local Coalition on Immigration. 1994a. "Justice Department Reimburses States for Imprisoning Illegal Criminal Felons." *Immigrant Policy News: Inside the Beltway* 1(9, November 7).

———. 1994b. "Three More States Sue Feds for Costs of Immigration." *Immigrant Policy News: State-Local Report* 1(2, November 9).

———. 1995a. "California State Ballot Initiative on Undocumented Immigrants (Proposition 187)." Washington: Immigrant Policy Project.

———. 1995b. "Two More States Pass 'Official English' Laws." *Immigrant Policy News: State-Local Report* 2(1, May 12).

Steinberg, Laurence. 1996. *Beyond the Classroom*. New York: Simon & Schuster.

Steinberg, Stephen. 1989. *The Ethnic Myth*. Boston: Beacon.

Steinmetz, George, and Erik O. Wright. 1989. "The Fall and Rise of the Petty Bourgeoisie: Changing Patterns of Self-employment in the Postwar United States." *American Journal of Sociology* 94: 973–1018.

Stepan, Nancy Leys. 1991. *"The House of Eugenics": Race, Gender, and Nation in Latin America*. Ithaca, N.Y.: Cornell University Press.

Stepick, Alex. 1989. "Miami's Two Informal Sectors." In *The Informal Economy*, edited by Alejandro Portes, Manuel Castells, and Lauren Benton (ch. 6). Baltimore: Johns Hopkins University Press.

———. 1992. "The Refugees Nobody Wants: Haitians in Miami." In *Miami Now!*, edited by Guillermo J. Grenier and Alex Stepick (57–82). Gainesville: University of Florida Press.

Stern, Claudio. 1988. "Some Methodological Notes on the Study of Human Migration." In *International Migration Today*, vol. 2, *Emerging Issues*, edited by Charles W. Stahl (28–33). Perth: University of Western Australia for the United Nations Economic, Social, and Cultural Organization.

Stevens, Gillian. 1985. "Nativity, Intermarriage, and Mother-Tongue Shift." *American Sociological Review* 50: 74–83.

———. 1992. "The Social and Demographic Context of Language Use in the United States." *American Sociological Review* 57: 171–85.

———. 1994. "Immigration, Emigration, Language Acquisition, and the English-Language Proficiency of Immigrants in the United States." In *Immigration and Ethnicity*, edited by Barry Edmonston and Jeffrey Passel. Washington: Urban Institute.

Stinner, William, Klaus de Albuquerque, and Roy S. Bruce-Laporte. 1982. *Return Migration and Remittances: Developing a Caribbean Perspective*. Washington: Research Institute on Immigration and Ethnic Studies, Smithsonian Institution.

Stone, John. 1985. *Racial Conflict in Contemporary Society*. London: Fontana Press/Collins.

Stonequist, Everette V. 1937. *The Marginal Man*. New York: Scribner's.

Stravrianos, L. S. 1981. *Global Rift: The Third World Comes of Age*. New York: William Morrow.

Streeck, Wolfgang. 1992. *Social Institutions and Economic Performance: Studies of Industrial Relations in Advanced Capitalist Economies*. Newbury Park, Calif.: Sage.

Suárez-Orozco, Carola, and Marcelo M. Suárez-Orozco. 1995. *Transformations: Migration, Family Life, and Achievement Motivation Among Latino Adolescents*. Stanford, Calif.: Stanford University Press.

Suárez-Orozco, Marcelo M. 1987. "Towards a Psychosocial Understanding of Hispanic Adaptation to American Schooling." In *Success or Failure?: Learning and the Languages of Minority Students*, edited by Henry T. Trueba (156–68). New York: Newbury House.

———. 1989. *Central American Refugees and U.S. High Schools: A Psychological Study of Motivation and Achievement*. Stanford, Calif.: Stanford University Press.

———. 1991. "Immigrant Adaptation to Schooling: A Hispanic Case." In *Minority Status and Schooling: A Comparative Study of Immigrant and Involuntary*

Minorities, edited by Margaret A. Gibson and John U. Ogbu (37–61). New York: Garland.

Suárez-Orozco, Marcelo, and Carola Suárez-Orozco. 1995. "The Cultural Patterning of Achievement Motivation: A Comparison of Mexican, Mexican Immigrant, Mexican American, and Non-Latino White American Students." In *California's Immigrant Children: Theory, Research, and Implications for Educational Policy,* edited by Rubén G. Rumbaut and Wayne A. Cornelius (161–90). La Jolla: Center for U.S.-Mexican Studies, University of California at San Diego.

Summerfield, Hazel. 1993. "Patterns of Adaptation: Somali and Bangladeshi Women in Britain." In *Migrant Women: Crossing Boundaries and Changing Identities,* edited by Gina Buijs. Oxford: Berg.

Sun, Lena H. 1995. "Lumping the Legal with the Illegal." *Washington Post* (national weekly edition), November 20–26, 31.

Sung, Betty L. 1987. *The Adjustment Experience of Chinese Immigrant Children in New York City.* Staten Island, N.Y.: Center for Migration Studies.

Sunstein, Cass R. 1988. "Beyond the Republican Revival." *Yale Law Journal* 97: 1539–90.

———. 1990. *After the Rights Revolution: Reconceiving the Regulatory State.* Cambridge, Mass.: Harvard University Press.

Susman, Walter I. 1984. *Culture as History: The Transformation of American Society in the Twentieth Century.* New York: Pantheon Books.

Susser, Ida. 1982. *Norman Street.* New York: Oxford University Press.

Sutton, Constance. 1992. "Some Thoughts on Gendering and Internationalizing Our Thinking About Transnational Migrations." In *Towards a Transnational Perspective on Migration: Race, Class, Ethnicity, and Nationalism Reconsidered,* edited by Nina Glick Schiller, Linda Basch, and Cristina Blanc-Szanton (241–49). New York: Annals of the New York Academy of Sciences.

Sweezy, Paul. 1942. *The Theory of Capitalist Development.* New York: Monthly Review Press.

Takaki, Ronald. 1990 [1979]. *Iron Cages: Race and Culture in Nineteenth-Century America.* New York: Oxford University Press.

Taylor, Alan M., and Jeffrey G. Williamson. 1997. "Convergence in the Age of Mass Migration." *European Review of Economic History* I: 27–63.

Taylor, Henry Louis, Jr. 1995. "The Hidden Face of Racism." *American Quarterly* 47(September): 395–408.

Taylor, J. Edward. 1986. "Differential Migration, Networks, Information, and Risk." In *Migration Theory, Human Capital, and Development,* edited by Oded Stark (147–71). Greenwich, Conn.: JAI Press.

———. 1987. "Undocumented Mexico-U.S. Migration and the Returns to Households in Rural Mexico." *American Journal of Agricultural Economics* 69: 626–38.

———. 1992. "Remittances and Inequality Reconsidered: Direct, Indirect, and Intertemporal Effects." *Journal of Policy Modeling* 14: 187–208.

Taylor, J. Edward, Joaquin Arango, Ali Kouaouci, Adela Pelligrino, and Douglas S. Massey. 1996a. "International Migration and National Development." *Population Index* 62: 181–212.

———. 1996b. "International Migration and Community Development." *Population Index* 62: 397–418.

Taylor, Paul S. 1930. *Mexican Labor in the United States.* Vol. 1. Berkeley: University of California Press.

———. 1932. *Mexican Labor in the United States.* Vol. 2. Berkeley: University of California Press.

Teitelbaum, Michael S., and Myron Weiner. 1995. *Threatened Peoples, Threatened Borders: World Migration and U.S. Policy.* New York: Norton.

Temin, Peter. 1971. "General Equilibrium Models in Economic History." *Journal of Economic History* 31(1): 58–75.

Terkel, Studs. 1992. *Race: How Blacks and Whites Think and Feel About the American Obsession.* New York: New Press.

Testa, Mark and Marilyn Krogh. 1995. "The Effect of Employment on Marriage Among Black Males in Inner-city Chicago." In *The Decline in Marriage Among African Americans,* edited by M. Belinda Tucker and Claudia Mitchell-Kernan (59–95). New York: Russell Sage Foundation.

Thernstrom, Stephan. 1973. *The Other Bostonians: Poverty and Progress in the American Metropolis, 1880–1970.* Cambridge, Mass.: Harvard University Press.

———. 1964. *Poverty and Progress: Social Mobility in a Nineteenth-Century City.* Cambridge, Mass.: Harvard University Press.

Thernstrom, Stephan, Ann Orlov, and Oscar Handlin, eds. 1980. *Harvard Encyclopedia of American Ethnic Groups.* Cambridge. Mass.: Harvard University Press.

Thistlewaite, Frank. 1964. "Migration from Europe Overseas in the Nineteenth and Twentieth Centuries." In *Populations Movements in Modern European History,* edited by Herbert Moller (73–92). New York: MacMillan.

———. 1991a. Twentieth Centuries." In *A Century of European Migrations, 1830–1930,* edited by Rudolph J. Vecoli and Suzanne M. Sinke (17–49). Urbana: University of Illinois Press.

———. 1991b. "Postscript." In *A Century of European Migrations, 1830–1930,* edited by Rudolph J. Vecoli and Suzanne M. Sinke (55–7). Urbana: University of Illinois Press.

Thom, Linda. 1995. "Babies, Welfare, and Crime." *The Social Contract* 5: 283–90.

———. 1991. "Postscript." In *A Century of European Migrations, 1830–1930,* edited by Rudolph J. Vecoli and Suzanne M. Sinke. Urbana: University of Illinois Press.

Thomas, Brinley. 1972. *Migration and Urban Development: A Reappraisal of British and American Long Cycles.* London: Methuen.

———. 1973. *Migration and Economic Growth: A Study of Great Britain and the Atlantic Economy.* 2nd ed. Cambridge: Cambridge University Press.

Thomas, Robert D., and Richard W. Murray. 1991. *Progrowth Politics: Change and Governance in Houston.* Berkeley, Calif.: IGS Press.

Thomas, William I., and Florian Znaniecki. 1984. *The Polish Peasant in Europe and America,* edited by Eli Zaretsky. 2 vols. Urbana: University of Illinois Press. (Originally published in 1918–1920; reprint, New York: Dover, 1958)

Thompson, Frank V. 1920. *Schooling of the Immigrant.* New York: Harper & Brothers.

Tichenor, Daniel J. 1994. "Immigration and Political Community in the United States," *Responsive Community* 4: 16–28.

Tienda, Marta. 1983a. "Market Characteristics and Hispanic Earnings: A Comparison of Natives and Immigrants." *Social Problems* 31(1): 59–72.

———. 1983b. "Socioeconomic and Labor-Force Characteristics of U.S. Immigrants: Issues and Approaches." In *U.S. Immigration and Refugee Policy: Global and Domestic Issues,* edited by Mary M. Kritz (211–31). Lexington, Mass.: Heath.

———. 1989. "Looking to the 1990s: Mexican Immigration in Sociological Perspective." In *Mexican Migration to the United States: Process, Effects, and Policy Options,* edited by Wayne A. Cornelius and Jorge Bustamante (109–47). La Jolla: Center for U.S. Mexican Studies, University of California at San Diego.

———. 1999. "Immigration, Diversity, and Equality of Opportunity." In *Diversity and Its Discontents,* edited by Jeffrey Alexander and Neil Smelser (129–46). Princeton, N.J.: Princeton University Press.

Tienda, Marta, and Leif I. Jensen. 1986. "Immigration and Public Assistance Participation: Dispelling the Myth of Dependency." *Social Science Research* 15: 372–400.

Tienda, Marta, and Zai Liang. 1994. "Poverty and Immigration in Policy Perspective." In *Confronting Poverty: Prescriptions for Change,* edited by Sheldon H. Danzinger, Gary D. Sandefur, and Daniel H. Weinberg (331–64). New York: Russell Sage Foundation.

Tienda, Marta, and Ding-Tzann Lii. 1987. "Minority Concentration and Earnings Inequality: Blacks, Hispanics, and Asians Compared." *American Journal of Sociology* 93: 141–65.

Tienda, Marta, and Rebeca Raijman. 1997. "Forging Mobility in a Low-wage Environment: Mexican Immigrants in Chicago's Little Village Neighborhood." *Focus* 18(2): 35–40.

———. Forthcoming. "Immigrants' Income Packaging and Invisible Labor Force Activity." *Social Science Quarterly.*

Tienda, Marta, and Audrey Singer. 1995. "Wage Mobility of Undocumented Workers in the United States." *International Migration Review* 29: 112–38.

Tienda, Marta, Shelley A. Smith, and Vilma Ortiz. 1987. "Industrial Restructuring, Gender Segregation, and Sex Differences in Earnings." *American Sociological Review* 52(April): 195–210.

Tienda, Marta, and Haya Stier. 1996. "The Wages of Race: Color and Employment Opportunity in Chicago's Inner City." In *Origins and Destinies: Immigration, Race, and Ethnicity in America,* edited by Silvia Pedraza and Rubén G. Rumbaut (417–31). Belmont, Calif.: Wadsworth.

Tienda, Marta, and Franklin Wilson. 1992. "Migration and the Earnings of Hispanic Men." *American Journal of Sociology* 57: 661–78.

Tienhara, Nancy. 1974. *Canadian Views on Immigration and Population: An Analysis of Postwar Gallup Polls.* Ottawa: Information Canada.

Tilly, Charles. 1990. *Transplanted Networks in Immigration Reconsidered: History, Sociology, and Politics,* edited by Virginia Yans-McLaughlin (79–95). New York: Oxford University Press.

Tilly, Charles, and Charles H. Brown. 1967. "On Uprooting, Kinship, and the Auspices of Migration." *International Journal of Comparative Sociology* 8: 139–64.

Time. 1993. "The New Face of America." *Time* 142(Fall, special issue).

Tocqueville, Alexis de. 1835/19 *Democracy in America.* New York: Basic Books.

Todaro, Michael P. 1969. "A Model of Labor Migration and Urban Unemployment in Less Developed Countries." *American Economic Review* 59: 138–48.

———. 1976. *Internal Migration in Developing Countries.* Geneva: International Labor Office.

———. 1989. *Economic Development in the Third World.* New York: Longman.

Todaro, Michael P., and L. Maruszko. 1987. "Illegal Migration and U.S. Immigration Reform: A Conceptual Framework." *Population and Development Review* 13: 101–14.

Tolnay, Stewart E., and E. M. Beck. 1995. *A Festival of Violence: An Analysis of Southern Lynchings, 1882–1930.* Urbana: University of Illinois Press.

Tolopko, Leon. 1988. *Working Ukrainians in the United States,* book 1, *1890–1924.* New York: Ukrainian-American League.

Torres, Andres. 1995. *Between Melting Pot and Mosaic: African Americans and Puerto Ricans in the New York Political Economy.* Philadelphia: Temple University Press.

Trejo, Steven. 1997. "Why Do Mexican Americans Earn Low Wages?" *Journal of Political Economy* 105(6): 1235(34).

Troy, Leo. 1990. "Is the United States Unique in the Decline of Private-Sector Unionism?" *Journal of Labor Research* 11(2, Spring): 111–43.

Turner, Bryan S. 1990a. "The Two Faces of Sociology." In *Global Culture: Nationalism, Globalization, and Modernity,* edited by Michael Featherstone. London: Sage.

———. 1990b. "Outline of a Theory of Citizenship." *Sociology* 24(2, May): 189–217.

Turner, Marjorie, Michael Fix, and Raymond Struyk. 1991. "Opportunities Diminished, Opportunities Denied: Discrimination in Hiring." Washington: Urban Institute. Unpublished paper.

Turner, Ralph. 1953. "The Quest for Universals in Sociological Research." *American Sociological Review* 18: 604–11.

Turner, Terrance. 1997. "The Dithering Away of the State." Paper presented at the Guggenheim Conference on Globalization, Kona, Hawaii (June 16–18).

Turner, Victor. 1967. "Aspects of Saora Ritual and Shamanism: An Approach to the Data of Ritual." In *The Craft of Social Anthropology,* edited by A. L. Epstein (181–204). London: Tavistock.

Tuttle, William. 1970. *Race Riot: Chicago in the Red Summer of 1919.* New York: Atheneum.

Ueda, Reed. 1994. *Postwar Immigrant America: A Social History.* Boston: Bedford Books of St. Martin's Press.

United Nations Research Institute for Social Development. 1995. *Global Citizens on the Move.* Geneva: UNRISD.

U.S. Bureau of the Census. 1971. *Historical Statistics of the United States, Colonial Times to 1970.* Washington: U.S. Government Printing Office.

———. 1975. *Historical Statistics of the United States: Colonial Times to 1970.* Part 1. Washington: Data Stream Database.

———. 1984. *Census of the Population, 1980: Detailed Characteristics of the Populations: U.S. Summary.* PC80-1D1-A. Washington: U.S. Government Printing Office.

———. 1990. *U.S. Population Estimates, by Age, Sex, Race, and Hispanic Origin: 1980 to 1988,* by Frederick W. Hollmann. *Current Population Reports,* Population Estimates and Projections, series P25, no. 1045. Washington: U.S. Government Printing Office.

———. 1993a. *U.S. Population Estimates, by Age, Sex, Race, and Hispanic Origin: 1980 to 1991,* by Frederick W. Hollmann. *Current Population Reports,* Population Estimates and Projections, series P25, no. 1095. Washington: U.S. Government Printing Office.

———. 1993b. *Census of Population, 1990: General Social and Economic Characteristics.* Washington: U.S. Government Printing Office.

———. 1993c. *1990 Census of Population and Housing: Population and Housing Characteristics for Census Tracts and Block Numbering Areas: Houston-Galveston-Brazoria, TX CMSA; Houston, TX PMSA.* 1990 CPH-3-176C. Washington: U.S. Government Printing Office.

———. 1994. *Statistical Abstract of the United States: 1994.* 114th ed. Washington: U.S. Government Printing Office.

———. 1995. *Statistical Abstract of the United States: 1995.* 115th ed. Washington: U.S. Government Printing Office.

———. 1996. *Statistical Abstract of the United States: 1966.* 116th ed. Washington: U.S. Government Printing Office.

———. 1997a. *Historical Statistics of the United States, Colonial Times to 1970.* Bicentennial edition. Electronic edition (machine-readable data file) edited by Susan B. Carter, Scott S. Gartner, Michael R. Haines, Alan L. Olmstead, Richard Sutch, and Gavin Wright. New York: Cambridge University Press. (Originally published in 1975)

———. 1997b. "The Foreign-born Population: 1996." *Current Population Reports* (March): 20–494.

———. Various issues. *Statistical Abstract of the United States.*

U.S. Civil Rights Commission. 1992. *Civil Rights Issues Facing Asian Americans in the 1990s.* Washington: U.S. Civil Rights Commission.

U.S. Commission on Immigration Reform. 1994. *U.S. Immigration Policy: Restoring Credibility.* Executive Summary. Washington: U.S. Commission on Immigration Reform.

———. 1995. *Legal Immigration: Setting Priorities.* Executive Summary. Washington: U.S. Commission on Immigration Reform.

U.S. Congress, House of Representatives, Committee on Immigration and Naturalization. 1926. *Hearings on Seasonal Agricultural Laborers from Mexico.* 69th Cong., 1st sess.

U.S. Department of Housing and Urban Development. 1995. *Empowerment: A New Covenant with America's Communities: President Clinton's National Urban Policy Report.* Washington: Office of Policy Development and Research.

U.S. Department of Labor, Bureau of International Labor Affairs. 1989. *The Effects of Immigration on the U.S. Economy and Labor Market.* Immigration and Policy Research Report 1. Washington: U.S. Government Printing Office.

U.S. Department of Labor, Bureau of Labor Statistics. 1979. "Union Membership as a Proportion of the Labor Force, 1930–1974." In *Handbook of Labor Statistics 1978.* Bulletin 2000. Washington: U.S. Government Printing Office.

U.S. Department of Labor, Bureau of Labor Statistics. Various years. *Employment and Earnings.*

U.S. General Accounting Office. 1994. *Illegal Aliens: Assessing Estimates of Financial Burden on California.* HEHS-95-22. Washington: General Accounting Office.

———. 1995a. *Illegal Aliens: National Net Cost Estimates Vary Widely.* HEHS-95-133. Washington: General Accounting Office.

———. 1995b. *Welfare Reform: Implications of Proposals on Legal Immigrants' Benefits.* HEHS–95–58. Washington: General Accounting Office.

———. 1995c. "Janitors in the Los Angeles Area." *The Social Contract* 5: 258.

U.S. Immigration Commission. 1907–10. Reports of the Immigration Commission. 41 vols. Washington: U.S. Government Printing Office.

U.S. Immigration Commission. 1911. *Statistical Review of Immigration*. Washington: U.S. Government Printing Office.

U.S. Immigration and Naturalization Service. 1979. *Statistical Yearbook of the Immigration and Naturalization Service, 1979*. Washington: U.S. Government Printing Office.

———. 1990. *Statistical Yearbook of the Immigration and Naturalization Service, 1989*. Washington: U.S. Government Printing Office.

———. 1992. *1991 Statistical Yearbook of the Immigration and Naturalization Service*. Springfield, Va.: National Technical Information Service.

———. 1996. *Statistical Yearbook of the Immigration and Naturalization Service, 1995*. Washington: U.S. Department of Justice.

———. 1997. *Statistical Yearbook of the Immigration and Naturalization Service, 1995*. Washington: U.S. Government Printing Office.

U.S. News & World Report. 1993. "The Untold Story of the Los Angeles Riot." May 31.

U.S. Select Commission on Immigration and Refugee Policy. 1981. *U.S. Immigration Policy and the National Interest: Final Report and Recommendations of the Select Commission on Immigration and Refugee Policy to the Congress and the President of the United States*. Washington: U.S. Government Printing Office.

Unz, Ron K. 1994. "Immigration or the Welfare State: Which Is Our Real Enemy?" *Policy Review* 70(Fall): 33–38.

Uselding, Paul J. 1971. "Conjectural Estimates of Gross Human Capital Inflows to the American Economy: 1790–1860." *Explorations in Economic History* 9(1): 49–61.

Uzzell, Douglas. 1979. "Conceptual Fallacies in the Rural-Urban Dichotomy." *Urban Anthropology* 8: 333–50.

Valenzuela, Abel, Jr. 1995. "California's Melting Pot Boils Over: The Origins of a Cruel Proposition." *Dollars and Sense* (March-April): 28–31.

van den Berghe, Pierre. 1967. *Race and Racism: A Comparative Perspective*. New York: Wiley.

Van Vugt, William E. 1988a. "Prosperity and Industrial Emigration from Britain During the Early 1850s." *Journal of Social History* 5(4): 390–405.

———. 1988b. "Running from Ruin?: The Emigration of British Farmers to the United States in the Wake of the Repeal of the Corn Laws." *Economic History Review* 41(3): 411–28.

Vassady, Bella. 1982. "'The Homeland Cause' as a Stimulant to Ethnic Unity: The Hungarian American Response to Karolyi's 1914 Tour." *Journal of American Ethnic History* 2(1): 39–64.

Vecoli, Rudolph J. 1962. "Chicago's Italians Prior to World War I: A Study of Their Social and Economic Adjustment." Ph.D. diss., University of Wisconsin.

———. 1964. "*Contadini* in Chicago: A Critique of *The Uprooted*." *Journal of American History* 51(December): 404–17.

———. 1979. "The Resurgence of American Immigration History." *American Studies International* 37(Winter): 46–66.

———. 1985. "Return to the Melting Pot: Ethnicity in the Eighties." *Journal of American Ethnic History* 5(Fall): 7–20.

———. 1991. "Introduction." In *A Century of European Migrations, 1830–1930*, edited by Rudolph J. Vecoli and Suzanne M. Sinke (17–49). Urbana: University of Illinois Press.

Vecoli, Rudolph J., and Suzanne M. Sinke. 1991. *A Century of European Migrations, 1830–1930*. Urbana: University of Illinois Press.

Vega, William A., and Hortensia Amaro. 1994. "Latino Outlook: Good Health, Uncertain Prognosis." *Annual Review of Public Health* 15: 39–67.

Vega, William A., and Rubén G. Rumbaut. 1991. "Ethnic Minorities and Mental Health." *Annual Review of Sociology* 17: 351–83.

Veltman, Calvin. 1983. *Language Shift in the United States*. Berlin: Mouton.

———. 1988. "Modeling the Language Shift Process of Hispanic Immigrants." *International Migration Review* 22: 545–62.

———. 1991. "Theory and Method in the Study of Language Shift." In *Language and Ethnicity*, edited by James R. Dow (145–68). Amsterdam: John Benjamin.

Verba, Sidney, Kay Lehman Schlozman, and Henry E. Brady. 1995. *Voice and Equality: Civic Voluntarism in American Politics*. Cambridge, Mass.: Harvard University Press.

Verhovek, Sam Howe. 1998. "Torn Between Nations, Mexican Americans Can Have Both." *New York Times*, April 14.

Vernez, Georges, and Allan Abrahamse. 1996. *How Immigrants Fare in U.S. Education*. Santa Monica, Calif.: Rand Corporation.

Vernez, Georges, and Kevin McCarthy. 1995. *The Fiscal Costs of Immigration: Analytical and Policy Issues*. DRU–958-1-IF. Santa Monica, Calif.: Rand Corporation, Center for Research on Immigration Policy.

Vickerman, Milton. 1999. *Cross Currents: West Indian Immigrants and Race*. New York: Oxford University Press.

Vucinich, Wayne S. 1959. "Galicia." *World Book Encyclopedia* 7: 2844–55.

Wakeman, Fredric, Jr. 1988. "Transnational and Comparative Research." *Items* 42(4): 85–88.

Waldinger, Roger. 1985. "Immigrant Enterprise and the Structure of the Labour Market." In *New Approaches to Economic Life: Economic Restructuring, Unemployment, and the Social Division of Labour*, edited by Bryan Roberts, Ruth Finnegan, and Duncan Gallie (213–28). Manchester: Manchester University Press.

———. 1986–87. "Changing Ladders and Musical Chairs: Ethnicity and Opportunity in Postindustrial New York." *Politics and Society* 15: 369–410.

———. 1989. "Immigration and Urban Change." *Annual Review of Sociology* 15: 211–32.

———. 1993. "The Ethnic Enclave Debate Revisited." *International Journal of Urban and Regional Research* 17: 444–52.

———. 1996a. *Still the Promised City?: African Americans and New Immigrants in Postindustrial New York.* Cambridge, Mass.: Harvard University Press.

———. 1996b. "Ethnicity and Opportunity in the Plural City." In *Ethnic Los Angeles,* edited by Roger Waldinger and Menhdi Bozorgmehr (445–70). New York: Russell Sage Foundation.

———. 1996c. "Who Makes the Beds? Who Washes the Dishes?: Black-Immigrant Competition Reassessed." In *Immigrants and Immigration Policy: Individual Skills, Family Ties, and Group Identities,* edited by Harriet Orcutt Duleep, and Phanindra V. Wunnava (256–88). Greenwich, Conn.: JAI Press.

———. 1997. "Black-Immigrant Competition Reassessed: New Evidence from Los Angeles." *Sociological Perspectives* 40(3): 365–86.

Waldinger, Roger, and Howard Aldrich. 1990. "Trends in Ethnic Businesses in the United States." In *Ethnic Entrepreneurs: Immigrant Business in Industrial Societies,* edited by Roger Waldinger, Howard Aldrich, and Robin Ward (49–78). Newbury Park, Calif.: Sage.

Waldinger, Roger, and Mehdi Bozorgmehr. 1996a. "The Making of a Multicultural Metropolis." In *Ethnic Los Angeles,* edited by Roger Waldinger and Mehdi Bozorgmehr. New York: Russell Sage Foundation.

———, eds. 1996b. *Ethnic Los Angeles.* New York: Russell Sage Foundation.

Waldinger, Roger, and Greta Gilbertson. 1994. "Immigrants' Progress: Ethnic and Gender Differences Among U.S. Immigrants in the 1980s." *Sociological Perspectives* 37(3): 431–44.

Waldinger, Roger, and Yenfen Tseng. 1992. "Divergent Diaspora: The Chinese Communities of New York and Los Angeles Compared." *Revue Européenne des Migrations Internationales* 8(3): 91–111.

Walker, Francis Amasa. 1891. "Immigration and Degradation." *Forum* 11: 634–44.

———. 1896. "Restriction on Immigration." *Atlantic Monthly* 77(464): 822–29.

Wallerstein, Immanuel. 1974. *The Modern World System,* vol. 1, *Capitalist Agriculture and the Origins of the European World Economy in the Sixteenth Century.* New York: Academic Press.

———. 1980. *The Modern World System,* vol. 2, *Mercantilism and the Consolidation of the European World-Economy, 1600–1750.* New York: Academic Press.

Walton, Gary M., and Ross M. Robertson. 1983. *History of the American Economy.* 5th ed. New York: Harcourt Brace Jovanovich.

Walton, Gary M., and Hugh Rockoff. 1994. *History of the American Economy.* 7th ed. Fort Worth: Dryden Press.

Walzer, Michael. 1981. "The Distribution of Membership." In *Boundaries: National Autonomy and Its Limits,* edited by Peter G. Brown and Henry Shue (6–30). Totowa, N.J.: Rowman & Littlefield.

———. 1983. *Spheres of Justice.* New York: Basic Books.

———. 1992. *What It Means to Be an American: Essays on the American Experience.* New York: Marsilio.

———. 1996. "Ethnicity and Immigration." In *Encyclopedia of the United States in the Twentieth Century,* vol. 1, edited by Stanley I. Kutter, Robert Dallek, Thomas K. McGraw, and Judith Kirkwood. New York: Charles Scribner's Sons.

Wang, Ling-Chi. 1988. "Meritocracy and Diversity in Higher Education: Discrimination Against Asians in the Post-Bakke Era." *Urban Review* 20(2): 189–209.

Ward, David. 1989. *Poverty, Ethnicity, and the American City, 1840–1925.* New York: Cambridge University Press.

Ware, Caroline. 1935. *Greenwich Village, 1920–1930: A Comment on American Civilization in the Postwar Years.* New York: Harper.

———. 1965. *Greenwich Village, 1920–1930: A Comment on American Civilization in the Postwar Years.* New York: Harper. (Originally published in 1935)

Warne, Frank Julius. 1990. "Restrictions on Immigration Are Necessary." In *Immigration: Opposing Viewpoints,* edited by William Dudley (31–38). San Diego: Greenhaven Press. (Originally published in 1913)

Warner, Warner Lloyd, and Leo Srole. 1945. *The Social Systems of American Ethnic Groups.* New Haven, Conn.: Yale University Press.

Waters, Mary C. 1990. *Ethnic Options: Choosing Identities in America.* Berkeley: University of California Press.

———. 1994. "Ethnic and Racial Identities of Second-Generation Black Immigrants in New York City." *International Migration Review* 28(4, Winter): 795–820.

———. 1996. "Ethnic and Racial Identities of Second-Generation Black Immigrants in New York City." In *The New Second Generation,* edited by Alejandro Portes (ch. 8). New York: Russell Sage Foundation.

———. 1997. "Immigrant Families at Risk: Factors That Undermine Chances of Success." In *Immigration and the Family: Research and Policy on U.S. Immigrants,* edited by Alan Booth, Ann C. Crouter, and Nancy S. Landale (79–87). Mahwah, N.J.: Erlbaum.

Watkins, Susan Cotts, ed. 1994. *After Ellis Island: Newcomers and Natives in the 1910 Census.* New York: Russell Sage Foundation.

Wattenberg, Martin P. 1996. *The Decline of American Political Parties, 1952–1994.* Cambridge, Mass.: Harvard University Press.

Weber, Devra. 1998. *Historical Perspectives on Mexican Transnationalism: With Notes from Angumacutiro.* Unpublished manuscript. University of Califonia, Los Angeles.

Weber, Max. 1958. *The Protestant Ethic and the Spirit of Capitalism,* translated by Talcott Parsons. New York: Scribner's. (Originally published in 1904–5)

Wechsler, Harold S. 1977. *The Qualified Student: A*

History of Selective College Admission in America. New York: Wiley.

———. 1982. "The Discriminating Ivy League." *History of Education Quarterly* 22: 103–10.

———. 1984. "The Rationale for Restriction." *American Quarterly* 36(Winter): 643–67.

Weed, Perry. 1973. *The White Ethnic Movement and Ethnic Politics*. New York: Praeger.

Weeks, John R., and Rubén G. Rumbaut. 1991. "Infant Mortality Among Ethnic Immigrant Groups." *Social Science and Medicine* 33(3): 327–34.

Weil, Patrick. 1991. *La France et ses étrangers: L'aventure d'une politique de l'immigration de 1938 à nos jours*. Paris: Calmann-Lévy.

Weinberg, Sydney Stahl. 1992. "The Treatment of Women in Immigration History: A Call for Change." In *Seeking Common Ground: Multidisciplinary Studies of Immigrant Women in the United States*, edited by Donna Gabaccia (3–22). Westport, Conn.: Greenwood.

Weiner, Myron. 1995. *The Global Migration Crisis: Challenge to States and to Human Rights*. New York: HarperCollins.

Weinstein, James. 1954. *The Decline of Socialism in America, 1912–1925*. New Brunswick, N.J.: Rutgers University Press.

Weintraub, Daniel M. 1994. "California Closes Its Doors." *State Legislatures* 20: 16–17.

Weir, David R. 1992. "A Century of U.S. Unemployment, 1890–1990: Revised Estimates and Evidence for Stabilization." *Research in Economic History* (14): 301–46.

Weiss, Nancy. 1969. "The Negro and the New Freedom: Fighting Wilsonian Segregation." *Political Science Quarterly* 84(March): 61–79.

Welch, Finis. 1979. "Effects of Cohort Size on Earnings: The Baby Boom Babies' Financial Bust." *Journal of Political Economy* 87: S65–97.

Werbner, Pnina. 1990. *The Migration Process: Capital, Gifts, and Offerings Among British Pakistanis*. Oxford: Berg.

West, Cornel. 1993. *Race Matters*. Boston: Beacon.

Wetzel, James R. 1995. "Labor Force, Unemployment, and Earnings." In *State of the Union*, edited by Reynolds Farley (vol. 1, ch. 2). New York: Russell Sage Foundation.

White, E. B. 1949. *Here Is New York*. New York: Harper & Brothers.

White, Michael, Ann Biddlecom, and Shenyang Guo. 1993. "Immigration, Naturalization, and Residential Assimilation Among Asian Americans." *Social Forces* 72: 93–118.

White, Michael J., and Lori Hunter. 1993. "The Migratory Response of Native-born Workers to the Presence of Immigrants in the Labor Market." Working Paper 93–08. Brown University, Population Studies and Training Center (July).

White, Michael J., and Zai Liang. 1994. "The Effect of Immigration on the Internal Migration of the Native-born Population, 1981–1990." Brown University. Unpublished paper.

Whiteford, Scott. 1981. *Workers from the North: Plantations, Bolivian Labor, and the City in Northwest Argentina*. Austin: University of Texas Press.

Whitney, Craig R. 1996. "Europeans Redefine What Makes a Citizen." *New York Times*, January 7, E6.

Whyte, William Foote. 1955. *Street Corner Society: The Social Structure of an Italian Slum*. Chicago: University of Chicago Press. (Originally published in 1943)

Whyte, William Hollingsworth. 1956. *The Organization Man*. New York.

Wial, Howard. 1988. "The Transition from Secondary to Primary Employment Jobs and Workers in Ethnic Neighborhood Labor Markets." Ph.D. diss., Massachusetts Institute of Technology.

Wiebe, Robert H. 1967. *The Search for Order, 1877–1920*. New York: Hill & Wang.

Wiest, Raymond. 1973. "Wage-Labor Migration and the Household in a Mexican Town." *Journal of Anthropological Research* 29: 180–209.

———. 1984. "External Dependency and the Perpetuation of Temporary Migration to the United States." In *Patterns of Undocumented Migration: Mexico and the United States*, edited by Richard C. Jones (110–35). Totowa, N.J.: Rowman & Allanheld.

Willcox, Walter F., and Imre Ferenczi. 1929. *International Migrations*, vol. 1, *Statistics*. New York: National Bureau of Economic Research.

———. 1930. *International Migrations*, vol. 2, *Interpretations*. New York: National Bureau of Economic Research.

Williams, Brackette. 1989. "A Class Act: Anthropology and the Race to Nation Across Ethnic Terrain." *Annual Review of Anthropology* 18: 401–44.

Williams, R. L., N. J. Binkin, and E. J. Clingman. 1986. "Pregnancy Outcomes Among Spanish-Surname Women in California." *American Journal of Public Health* 76: 387–91.

Williams, Walter E. 1995. "A Tragic Vision of Black Problems." *American Quarterly* 47(September): 409–15.

Williamson, Jeffrey G. 1964. *American Growth and the Balance of Payments, 1820–1913: A Study of the Long Swing*. Chapel Hill: University of North Carolina Press.

———. 1974a. "Migration to the New World: Long-term Influences and Impact." *Explorations in Economic History* 11(4): 357–89.

———. 1974b. "Watersheds and Turning Points: Conjectures on the Long-term Impact of Civil War Financing." *Journal of Economic History* 34(3): 636–61.

———. 1974c. *Late-Nineteenth-Century American Development: A General Equilibrium History*. London: Cambridge University Press.

———. 1982. "Immigrant-Inequality Trade-offs in the Promised Land: Income Distribution and Absorptive Capacity Prior to the Quotas." In *The Gateway: U.S.*

Immigration Issues and Policies, edited by Barry R. Chiswick (251–88). Washington: American Enterprise Institute.

Williamson, Jeffrey G., and Peter H. Lindert. 1980. *American Inequality: A Macroeconomic History.* New York: Academic Press.

Willis, Paul. 1981. *Learning to Labor: How Working-class Kids Get Working-class Jobs.* New York: Columbia University Press. (Originally published in 1977)

Wilson, Franklin D., Marta Tienda, and Lawrence W. Wu. 1995. "Race and Unemployment: Labor Market Experiences of Black and White Men, 1968–1988." *Work and Occupations* 22(3): 245–70.

Wilson, James Q. 1980. *The Politics of Regulation.* New York: Harper & Row.

Wilson, Kenneth, and W. Allen Martin. 1982. "Ethnic Enclaves: A Comparison of the Cuban and Black Economies of Miami." *American Journal of Sociology* 88(1): 135–60.

Wilson, Kenneth, and Alejandro Portes. 1980. "Immigrant Enclaves: An Analysis of the Labor Market Experiences of Cubans in Miami." *American Journal of Sociology* 86(2): 296–319.

Wilson, William Julius. 1978. *The Declining Significance of Race: Blacks and Changing American Institutions.* Chicago: University of Chicago Press.

———. 1987. *The Truly Disadvantaged: The Inner City, the Underclass, and Public Policy.* Chicago: University of Chicago Press.

———. 1996. *When Work Disappears: The World of the New Urban Poor.* New York: Knopf.

Winant, Howard. 1994. *Racial Conditions: Politics, Theory, Comparison.* Minneapolis: University of Minnesota Press.

Winnick, Louis. 1990. *New People in Old Neighborhoods: The Role of New Immigrants in Rejuvenating New York's Communities.* New York: Russell Sage Foundation.

Wirth, Louis. 1956. *The Ghetto.* Chicago: University of Chicago Press. (Originally published in 1928)

Woldemikael, Tekle. 1989. *Becoming Black American: Haitians and American Institutions in Evanston, Illinois.* New York: AMS Press.

Wolf, Diane L. 1997. "Family Secrets: Transnational Struggles Among Children of Filipino Immigrants." *Sociological Perspectives* 40(3): 455–82.

Wolf, Eric. 1982. *Europe and the People Without History.* Berkeley: University of California Press.

Wolfinger, Raymond. 1972. "Why Political Machines Have Not Withered Away and Other Revisionist Thoughts." *Journal of Politics* 34(2, May): 365–98.

Wolfinger, Raymond, and S. Rosenstone. 1980. *Who Votes?* New Haven, Conn.: Yale University Press.

Wong, Bernard. 1982. *Chinatown: Economic Adaptations and Ethnic Identity of the Chinese.* New York: Holt, Rinehart, and Winston.

Wood, Charles. 1981. "Structural Change and Household Strategies: A Conceptual Framework for the Study of Rural Migration." *Human Organization* 40(4): 338–43.

———. 1982. "Equilibrium and Historical-Structural Perspectives on Migration: A Comparative Critique with Implications for Future Research." *International Migration Review* 16(2): 298–319.

Wood, Gordon S. 1969. *The Creation of the American Republic, 1776–1787.* New York: Norton.

Wright, Gavin. 1986. *Old South, New South: Revolutions in the Southern Economy Since the Civil War.* New York: Basic Books.

———. 1990. "The Origins of American Industrial Success, 1879–1940." *American Economic Review* 80(4): 651–68.

Wright, Lawrence. 1994. "One Drop of Blood." *The New Yorker* (July 25): 46–55.

Wyman, David S. 1968. *Paper Walls: America and the Refugee Crisis.* Amherst: University of Massachusetts Press.

———. 1984. *The Abandonment of the Jews: America and the Holocaust 1941–1945.* New York: Pantheon.

Wyman, Mark. 1993. *Round-Trip to America: The Immigrants Return to Europe, 1880–1930.* Ithaca, N.Y.: Cornell University Press.

Wytrwal, Joseph A. 1961. *America's Polish Heritage: A Social History of Poles in America.* Detroit: Endurance Press.

Xie, Yu, and Kim Goyette. 1997. "The Racial Identification of Biracial Children with One Asian Parent: Evidence from the 1990 Census." *Social Forces* 76: 547–70.

Yanagisako, Sylvia. 1985. *Transforming the Past: Tradition and Kinship Among Japanese Americans.* Stanford, Calif.: Stanford University Press.

Yancey, William, Eugene Ericksen, and Richard Juliani. 1976. "Emergent Ethnicity: A Review and a Reformulation." *American Sociological Review* 41(3): 391–403.

Yans-McLaughlin, Virginia. 1982. *Family and Community: Italian Immigrants in Buffalo, 1880–1930.* Ithaca, N.Y.: Cornell University Press.

Yerkes, Robert M. 1924. "The Work of the Committee on Scientific Problems of Human Migration, National Research Council." *Journal of Personnel Research* 3(6): 189–96.

Yinger, Milton J. 1994. *Ethnicity: Source of Strength? Source of Conflict?* Albany: State University of New York Press.

Yoon, In-Jin. 1991. "The Changing Significance of Ethnic and Class Resources in Immigrant Businesses: The Case of Korean Immigrant Businesses in Chicago." *International Migration Review* 25(2): 303–32.

———. 1996. *On My Own: Korean Immigration, Entrepreneurship, and Korean-Black Relations in Chicago and Los Angeles.* Chicago: University of Chicago Press.

Youssef, Nadia H. 1992. *The Demographics of Immigration: A Sociodemographic Profile of the Foreign-born Population in New York State.* Staten Island, N.Y.: Center for Migration Studies.

Yu, Elena. 1982. "The Low Mortality Rates of Chinese Infants: Some Plausible Explanations." *Social Science and Medicine* 16: 253–65.

Zachary, G. Pascal 1995. "U.S. Reaches Pact with Software Firm over Payment of Foreign Professionals." *Wall Street Journal,* August 16, A3.

Zangwill, Israel. 1923. *The Melting-Pot.* New York: Macmillan. (Originally published in 1909)

Zarnowitz, Victor. 1992. *Business Cycles: Theory, History, Indicators, and Forecasting.* Chicago: University of Chicago Press/National Bureau of Economic Research.

Zavella, Patricia. 1987. *Women's Work and Chicano Families.* Ithaca, N.Y.: Cornell University Press.

Zhou, Min. 1992. *Chinatown: The Socioeconomic Potential of an Urban Enclave.* Philadelphia, Temple University Press.

———. 1997a. "Segmented Assimilation: Issues, Controversies, and Recent Research on the New Second Generation." *International Migration Review* 31(4): 975–1008.

———. 1997b. "Growing up American: The Challenge Confronting Immigrant Children and Children of Immigrants." *Annual Review of Sociology* 23: 63–95.

Zhou, Min, and Carl L. Bankston III. 1994. "Social Capital and the Adaptation of the Second Generation: The Case of Vietnamese Youth in New Orleans." *International Migration Review* 28(4): 821–45.

———. 1998. *Growing up American: How Vietnamese Children Adapt to Life in the United States.* New York: Russell Sage Foundation.

Zhou, Min, and Yoshinori Kamo. 1994. "An Analysis of Earnings Patterns for Chinese, Japanese, and Non-Hispanic Whites in the United States." *Sociological Quarterly* 35(4): 581–602.

Zhou, Min, and John Logan. 1989. "Returns on Human Capital in Ethnic Enclaves: New York City's Chinatown." *American Sociological Review* 54(5): 809–20.

Zimmer, Catherine, and Howard Aldrich. 1987. "Resource Mobilization Through Ethnic Networks: Kinship Ties of Shopkeepers in England." *Sociological Perspectives* 30: 422–45.

Zinn, Maxine Baca. 1987. "Structural Transformations and Minority Families." In *Women, Households, and the Economy,* edited by Lourdes Benería and Catherine R. Stimpson (155–72). New Brunswick, N.J.: Rutgers University Press.

Zinn, Maxine Baca, Lynn Weber Cannon, Elizabeth Higginbotham, and Bonnie Thornton Dill. 1986. "The Exclusionary Practices in Women's Studies." *Signs* 11: 290–303.

Zlotnik, Hania. 1998. "International Migration 1965–1996: An Overview." *Population and Development Review* 24: 429–68.

Zolberg, Aristide R. 1978a. "The Patterning of International Migration Policies in a Changing World System." In *Human Migration: Patterns and Policies,* edited by William H. McNeill and Ruth S. Adams (241–86). Bloomington: Indiana University Press.

———. 1978b. "The Patterning of International Migration Policies: A Macro-analytic Framework." Paper presented at the IXX World Congress of Sociology, Uppsala (1978).

———. 1981a. "International Migrations in Political Perspective." In *Global Trends in Migration,* ed. Mary Kritz, Charles Keely and Silvano Tomasi (15–51). Staten Island, N.Y.: Center for Migration Studies.

———. 1981b. "The Origins of the Modern World System: A Missing Link." *World Politics* 33(2): 253–81.

———. 1983a. "'World' and 'System': A Misalliance." In *Contending Approaches to World System Analysis,* edited by William R. Thompson (269–90). Beverly Hills, Calif.: Sage.

———. 1983b. "The Formation of New States as a Refugee-Generating Process." *Annals of the American Academy of Political and Social Science* 467(May): 24–38.

———. 1986. "Strategic Interactions and the Formation of Modern States: France and England." In *The State in Global Perspective,* edited by Ali Kazancigil (72–106). London: Gower/UNESCO.

———. 1987. "Wanted but Not Welcome: Alien Labor in Western Development." In *Population in an Interacting World,* edited by William Alonso (36–74). Cambridge, Mass.: Harvard University Press.

———. 1989. "The Next Waves: Migration Theory for a Changing World." *International Migration Review* 23(3): 403–30.

———. 1991. "Bounded States in a Global Market: The Uses of International Labor Migration." In *Social Theory for a Changing Society,* edited by Pierre Bourdieu and James S. Coleman (301–35). Boulder/New York: Westview/Russell Sage Foundation.

———. 1995. "From Invitation to Interdiction." In *Threatened Peoples, Threatened Borders: World Migration and U.S. Policy,* edited by Michael S. Teitelbaum and Myron Weiner (117–59). New York: Norton.

———. 1997. "Global Movements, Global Walls: Responses to Migration, 1885–1925." In *Global History and Migrations,* edited by Wang Gungwu (279–307). Boulder, Colo.: Westview.

Zolberg, Aristide R., and Long Litt Long. 1999. "Why Islam Is Like Spanish: Cultural Incorporation in Europe and the United States." *Politics and Society* 27 (1, March): 5–38.

Zolberg, Aristide R., and Robert C. Smith. 1996. *Migration Systems in Comparative Perspective: An Analysis of the Inter-American Migration System with Comparative Reference to the Mediterranean-European System.* New York: International Center for Migration, Ethnicity, and Citizenship.

Zolberg, Aristide R., Astri Suhrke, and Sergio Aguayo. 1986. "International Factors in the Formation of Refugee Movements." *International Migration Review* 20(2): 151–69.

———. 1989. *Escape from Violence: Conflict and the Refugee Crisis in the Developing World.* New York: Oxford University Press.

Zunz, Oliver. 1985. "American History and the Changing Meaning of Assimilation." *Journal of American Ethnic History* 4(Winter): 53–72.

Index

Numbers in **boldface** refer to figures and tables.